New American Bible

REVISED EDITION

NEW TESTAMENT
with
PSALMS & PROVERBS

New American Bible

REVISED EDITION

NEW TESTAMENT
with
PSALMS & PROVERBS

*Translated From the Original Languages
With Critical Use of All the Ancient Sources*

Authorized by the Board of Trustees of the
Confraternity of Christian Doctrine
And Approved by the Administrative Committee
of the United States Conference of Catholic Bishops

AMERICAN BIBLE SOCIETY
New York

The New Testament with Psalms & Proverbs from New American Bible - Revised Edition

NEW TESTAMENT

Nihil Obstat   Stephen J. Hartdegen, O.F.M., L.S.S.
                     Censor Deputatus

Imprimatur   + James A. Hickey, S.T.D., J.C.D.
                     Archbishop of Washington
                     August 27, 1986

OLD TESTAMENT

RESCRIPT

In accord with canon 825 §1 of the Code of Canon Law, the United States Conference of Catholic Bishops hereby approves for publication The New American Bible, Revised Old Testament, a translation of the Sacred Scriptures authorized by the Confraternity of Christian Doctrine, Inc.

The translation was approved by the Administrative Committee of the United States Conference of Catholic Bishops in November 2008 and September 2010. It is permitted by the undersigned for private use and study.

Given in the city of Washington, the District of Columbia, on the Feast of Saint Jerome, Priest and Doctor of the Church, the 30th day of September, in the year of our Lord 2010.

Francis Cardinal George, O.M.I.
Archbishop of Chicago
President, USCCB

This edition of the NAB Revised Edition published by
American Bible Society, 1865 Broadway, New York, NY 10023
www.bibles.com

Item 123170
ISBN 978-1-585169-93-1
ABS-10/11-50,000-DP(1)

CONTENTS

Preface to the Revised New American Bible Old Testament...xi
Prefaces to the New American Bible First Edition of the New Testament
    and to the Revised Edition.. xiii

THE GOSPELS Introduction...2
Matthew.. Mt...3
Mark... Mk...56
Luke... Lk...80
John .... Jn.. 121

Acts of the Apostles.. Acts... 152

NEW TESTAMENT LETTERS Introduction 187
Romans... Rom 188
1 Corinthians .... 1 Cor... 207
2 Corinthians .... 2 Cor... 227
Galatians.. Gal 243
Ephesians... Eph 252
Philippians... Phil.. 259
Colossians.. Col 266
1 Thessalonians... 1 Thes 272
2 Thessalonians.. 2 Thes 276
1 Timothy .... 1 Tim 280
2 Timothy.. 2 Tim 286
Titus.. Ti... 290
Philemon .... Phlm 293
Hebrews .... Heb 295

THE CATHOLIC LETTERS Introduction 312
James .... Jas.. 313
1 Peter .... 1 Pt.. 319
2 Peter .... 2 Pt.. 325
1 John .... 1 Jn.. 330
2 John .... 2 Jn.. 335
3 John .... 3 Jn.. 337
Jude... Jude... 339

Revelation.. Rev.. 342

The Book of Psalms... Ps(s) 365
The Book of Proverbs.. Prv 457

Maps 497

COLLABORATORS ON THE OLD TESTAMENT OF THE NEW AMERICAN BIBLE 1970

BISHOPS' COMMITTEE OF THE CONFRATERNITY OF CHRISTIAN DOCTRINE

Most Rev. Charles P. Greco, D.D., Chairman
Most Rev. Joseph T. McGucken, S.T.D.
Most Rev. Vincent S. Waters, D.D.

Most Rev. Romeo Blanchette, D.D.
Most Rev. Christopher J. Weldon, D.D.

EDITORS IN CHIEF

Rev. Louis F. Hartman, C.SS.R., S.S.L., LING.
OR. L., Chairman
Rev. Msgr. Patrick W. Skehan, S.T.D., LL.D.,
Vice-Chairman

Rev. Stephen J. Hartdegen, O.F.M., S.S.L.,
Secretary

ASSOCIATE EDITORS AND TRANSLATORS

Rev. Edward P. Arbez, S.S., S.T.D.
Rev. Msgr. Edward J. Byrne, PH.D., S.T.D.
Rev. Edward A. Cerny, S.S., S.T.D.
Rev. James E. Coleran, S.J., S.T.L., S.S.L.
Rev. John J. Collins, S.J., M.A., S.S.L.
Sr. M. Emmanuel Collins, O.S.F., PH.D.
Prof. Frank M. Cross Jr., PH.D.
Rev. Patrick Cummins, O.S.B., S.T.D.
Rev. Antonine A. DeGuglielmo, O.F.M., S.T.D.,
S.S.L., S.S.LECT. Gen.
Rev. Alexander A. Di Lella, O.F.M., S.T.L.,
S.S.L., PH.D.
Most Rev. John J. Dougherty, S.T.L., S.S.D.
William A. Dowd, S.J., S.T.D., S.S.L.
Prof. David Noel Freedman, PH.D.
Rev. Michael J. Fruenthaner, S.J., S.T.D., S.S.D.
Rev. Msgr. Maurice A. Hofer, S.S.L.
Rev. Justin Krellner, O.S.B., S.T.D.
Rev. Joseph L. Lilly, C.M., S.T.D., S.S.L.
Rev. Roderick F. MacKenzie, S.J., M.A., S.S.D.
Rev. Edward A. Mangan, C.SS.R., S.S.L.

Rev. Daniel W. Martin, C.M., S.T.L., S.S.L.
Rev. William H. McClellan, S.J.
Rev. James McGlinchey, C.M., S.T.D.
Rev. Frederick Moriarty, S.J., S.S.L., S.T.D.
Rev. Richard T. Murphy, O.P., S.T.D., S.S.D.
Rev. Roland E. Murphy, O. Carm., M.A., S.T.D.,
S.S.L.
Rev. Msgr. William R. Newton, M.S., S.S.D.
Rev. Everhard Olinger, O.S.B.
Rev. Charles H. Pickar, O.S.A., S.T.L., S.S.L.
Rev. Christopher Rehwinkel, O.F.M., S.T.D.,
S.S. LECT. GEN.
Rev. Msgr. John R. Rowan, S.T.D., S.S.L.
Prof. J.A. Sanders, PH.D.
Rev. Edward F. Siegman, C.PP.S., S.T.D., S.S.L.
Rev. Msgr. Matthew P. Stapleton, S.T.D., S.S.L.
Rev. Msgr. John E. Steinmueller, S.T.D., S.S.L.
Rev. John Ujlaki, O.S.B., LITT.D.
Rev. Bruce Vawter, C.M., S.T.L., S.S.D.
Rev. John B. Weisengoff, S.T.D., S.S.L.

COLLABORATORS ON THE REVISED NEW TESTAMENT OF THE NEW AMERICAN BIBLE 1986

BISHOPS' AD HOC COMMITTEE

Most Rev. Theodore E. McCarrick, D.D.
Most Rev. Richard J. Sklba, D.D.

Most Rev. J. Francis Stafford, D.D.
Most Rev. John F. Whealon, D.D., Chairman

BOARD OF EDITORS

Rev. Msgr. Myles M. Bourke
Rev. Francis T. Gignac, S.J., Chairman

Rev. Stephen J. Hartdegen, O.F.M., Secretary
Rev. John H. Reumann

REVISERS

Rev. Msgr. Myles M. Bourke
Rev. Frederick W. Danker
Rev. Alexander A. Di Lella, O.F.M.
Rev. Charles H. Giblin, S.J.
Rev. Francis T. Gignac, S.J.
Rev. Stephen J. Hartdegen, O.F.M.
Dr. Maurya P. Horgan

Rev. John R. Keating, S.J.
Rev. John Knox
Dr. Paul J. Kobelski
Dr. J. Rebecca Lyman
Br. Elliott C. Maloney, O.S.B.
Dr. Janet A. Timbie

CONSULTANTS

Rev. Joseph Jensen, O.S.B.
Rev. Aidan Kavanagh, O.S.B.

Dr. Marianne Sawicki

BUSINESS MANAGER

Charles A. Buggé

WORD PROCESSOR

Suzanna Jordan

COLLABORATORS ON THE REVISED PSALMS OF THE NEW AMERICAN BIBLE 1991

BISHOPS' AD HOC COMMITTEE

Most Rev. Enrique San Pedro, S.J.
Most Rev. Richard Sklba, D.D.
Most Rev. Donald W. Trautman, S.T.D., S.S.L.

Most Rev. Emil A. Wcela
Most Rev. John F. Whealon, S.S.L., Chairman

BOARD OF EDITORS

Rev. Richard Clifford, S.J.
Br. Aloysius Fitzgerald, F.S.C.
Rev. Joseph Jensen, O.S.B.

Rev. Roland Murphy, O.Carm.
Sr. Irene Nowell, O.S.B.
Dr. Judith Sanderson

REVISERS

Prof. Gary Anderson
Rev. Michael L. Barré, S.S.
Rev. Christopher T. Begg
Dr. Joseph Blenkinsopp
Rev. Anthony R. Ceresko, O.S.F.S.
Rev. Richard J. Clifford, S.J.
Rev. Aelred Cody, O.S.B.
Prof. Michael D. Coogan
Rev. Alexander A. Di Lella, O.F.M.
Dr. Robert A. Di Vito
Br. Aloysius Fitzgerald, F.S.C.
Rev. Michael D. Guinan, O.F.M.
Rev. William L. Holladay
Rev. William Irwin, C.S.B.
Rev. Joseph Jensen, O.S.B.

Rev. John S. Kselman
Rev. Leo Laberge, O.M.I.
Dr. Conrad E. L'Heureux
Dr. Paul G. Mosca
Rev. Dr. Roland E. Murphy, O.Carm.
Dr. Michael Patrick O'Connor
Rev. Brian J. Peckham, S.J.
Prof. Jimmy J. Roberts
Sr. Eileen M. Schuller, O.S.U.
Dr. Byron E. Shafer
Prof. Mark S. Smith
Prof. Matitiahu Tesvat
Dr. Eugene C. Ulrich
Prof. James C. VanderKam
Rev. Jerome T. Walsh

ENGLISH CONSULTANTS

Dr. Catherine Dunn

Br. Daniel Burke, F.S.C.

BUSINESS MANAGER

Charles A. Buggé

COLLABORATORS ON THE OLD TESTAMENT OF THE NEW AMERICAN BIBLE 2010

BISHOPS' COMMITTEE ON DOCTRINE

SUBCOMMITTEE ON THE TRANSLATION OF SCRIPTURE TEXT

Most Rev. Arthur J. Serratelli, Chairman
Justin Cardinal Rigali
Most Rev. Blase J. Cupich

Most Rev. Richard J. Sklba
Most Rev. Anthony B. Taylor

BOARD OF EDITORS

Dr. Deirdre A. Dempsey
Dr. Robert A. Di Vito
Rev. Francis T. Gignac, S.J.
Rev. Joseph Jensen, O.S.B., Chairman
Rev. Dale Launderville, O.S.B.

Rev. Roland E. Murphy, O.Carm. +
Dr. Kathleen S. Nash
Sr. Irene Nowell, O.S.B.
Rev. James P. M. Walsh, S.J.

REVISERS

Dr. Gary A. Anderson
Reverend Michael L. Barré, S.S.
Reverend Christopher T. Begg
Dr. Joseph Blenkinsopp
Reverend Lawrence Boadt, C.S.P. +
Professor Edward F. Campbell
Professor Anthony Ceresko, OSFS +
Reverend Richard J. Clifford, S.J.
Reverend Aelred Cody, O.S.B.
Dr. John J. Collins
Professor Michael D. Coogan
Reverend T.J. Jeremy Corley
Dr. Toni Craven
Dr. James L. Crenshaw
Reverend Alexander A. Di Lella, O.F.M.
Dr. Robert A. Di Vito
Brother Aloysius Fitzgerald, F.S.C. +
Reverend Joseph A. Fitzmyer, S.J.
Dr. Carole R. Fontaine
Reverend Daniel J. Harrington, S.J.
Dr. Richard S. Hess

Dr. Theodore Hiebert
Dr. William L. Holladay
Dr. Tod Linafelt
Dr. P. Kyle McCarter, Jr.
Dr. Carol Meyers
Dr. Eric Meyers
Dr. Patrick D. Miller, Jr.
Reverend Craig E. Morrison, O. Carm.
Dr. Paul G. Mosca
Dr. Kathleen S. Nash
Professor Robert A. Oden, Jr.
Reverend Gregory J. Polan, O.S.B.
Dr. James J.M. Roberts
Dr. William M. Soll
Dr. Gene M. Tucker
Dr. Eugene C. Ulrich
Reverend Walter A. Vogels, W.F.
Reverend Jerome T. Walsh
Reverend Addison G. Wright, S.S.
Dr. David P. Wright

BUSINESS MANAGERS

Charles Buggé

Mary Elizabeth Sperry

WORD PROCESSORS

Ellen Coughlin

Nancy Hartnagel

COLLABORATORS ON THE BOOK OF PSALMS OF THE NEW AMERICAN BIBLE 2010

REVISED
NEW AMERICAN BIBLE
OLD TESTAMENT

The first step in the genesis of the New American Bible was taken in 1936 when His Excellency, the Most Reverend Edwin V. O'Hara, D.D., chairman of the Episcopal Committee of the Confraternity of Christian Doctrine, invited a group of Catholic Scripture scholars to plan for a revised edition of the Challoner-Rheims New Testament, primarily on the basis of the Vulgate; the plans soon expanded to include the revision of the Old Testament. Archbishop O'Hara's initiative resulted in the formation of the Catholic Biblical Association, whose principal activity in its early years was this work of revision and translation. (For information on the work done on the New Testament, see the "Preface to the New American Bible: First Edition of the New Testament" and "Preface to the Revised Edition.") In 1943 His Holiness Pope Pius XII issued the encyclical *Divino afflante spiritu*, which encouraged Scripture scholars to translate the Scriptures from the original languages. He wrote: "We ought to explain the original text which was written by the inspired author himself and has more authority and greater weight than any, even the very best, translation whether ancient or modern. This can be done all the more easily and fruitfully if to the knowledge of languages be joined a real skill in literary criticism of the same text." Although at this point work on almost twenty of the Old Testament books was completed or near completion, that work was abandoned and the new project of translating from the Hebrew, Greek, and Aramaic was undertaken.

The completed books of the Old Testament were initially published, as they became available, in four volumes: Genesis–Ruth (1952), Job–Sirach (1955), Isaiah–Malachi (1961), and Samuel–Maccabees (1969). Some fifty scholars collaborated on this project; these were mainly Catholics, but, in accord with the suggestion of Vatican II that "with the approval of the church authority, these translations be produced in cooperation with separated brothers" so that "all Christians may be able to use them" (*Dei Verbum*, No. 22), non-Catholics also participated in the work. To this point the translation had been known under the name of the "Confraternity of Christian Doctrine" or CCD for short, but when these parts of the Old Testament were combined with the New Testament in a single volume, it was given the name "New American Bible," in part to reflect its ecumenical character. In producing the new volume certain changes were made from the original four volumes: a retranslation of the Book of Genesis, cross-references, new and expanded exegetical notes.

New translations and revision of existing translations are required from time to time for various reasons. For example, it is important to keep pace with the discovery and publication of new and better ancient manuscripts (e.g., the Dead Sea scrolls) so that the best possible textual tradition will be followed, as required by *Divino afflante spiritu*. There are advances in linguistics of the biblical languages which make possible a better understanding and more accurate translation of the original languages. And there are changes and developments in vocabulary and the cultural background of the receptor language. An obvious example of this is the abandonment in English of the second person singular (use of "thee," "thou," "sayest," "hearest"), which had a major impact on Bible translations. Other changes are less obvious but are nevertheless present. There have been changes in vocabulary; for example, the term "holocaust" is now normally reserved for the sacrilegious attempt to destroy the Jewish people by the Third Reich. Concerns such as these are reflected in what Pope John Paul II spoke of as the "three pillars" of good biblical translation: "A good translation is based on three pillars that must contemporaneously support the entire work. First, there must be a deep knowledge of the language and the cultural world at the point of origin. Next, there must be a good familiarity with the language and cultural context at the point where the work will arrive. Lastly, to crown the work with success, there must be an adequate mastery of the contents and meaning of what one is translating"—and he praised the translation that "utilizes the vocabulary and idioms of everyday speech" ("le parole e le forme della lingua di tutti i giorni"). (From an address to the United Bible Societies, November 26, 2001.)

This new edition is a thorough revision of the already excellent *New American Bible* Old Testament of 1970. Work on most books of the Old Testament, begun in 1994 and completed in 2001, was done by forty revisers and a board of eight editors. The 1991 revision of the Psalter, the work of thirty revisers and six editors, was further revised by seven revisers and two editors between 2009 and 2010. As suggested in the comments above, the revision aimed at making use of the best manuscript traditions available (see below), translating as accurately as possible, and rendering the result in good contemporary English. In many ways it is a more literal translation than the original *NAB* and has attempted to be more consistent in rendering Hebrew (or Greek) words and idioms, especially in technical contexts, such as regulations for sacrifices. In translating the Psalter special effort was made to provide a smooth, rhythmic translation for easy singing or recitation, and to retain the concrete imagery of the Hebrew.

Where the Old Testament translation supposes the received text—Hebrew, Aramaic, or Greek, as the case may be—ordinarily contained in the best-known editions, as the original or the oldest extant form, no additional remarks are necessary. Where the translators have departed from those received texts, e.g., by following the Septuagint rather than the Masoretic text, accepting a reading of what is judged to be a better textual tradition, as from a Qumran manuscript, or by emending a reading apparently corrupted in transmission, such changes are recorded in the revised edition of the *Textual Notes on the New American Bible*. Additional information on the textual tradition for some books may be found in the introduction to the book in the same *Textual Notes*.

In particular, important manuscripts from Cave 4 of Qumran, as well as the most useful recensions of the Septuagint, have been consulted in the preparation of 1 and 2 Samuel. Fragments of the lost Book of Tobit in Aramaic and in Hebrew, recovered from Cave 4 of Qumran, are in substantial agreement with the Sinaiticus Greek recension used for the translation of this book. The lost original Hebrew text of 1 Maccabees is replaced by its oldest extant form in Greek. Judith, 2 Maccabees, and parts of Esther are also translated from the Greek. The translation of The Wisdom of Ben Sira is based on the original Hebrew as far as it is preserved, with corrections from the ancient versions; otherwise, the Greek of the Septuagint is followed. In the Book of Baruch the basic text is the Greek of the Septuagint, with some readings derived from an underlying Hebrew form no longer extant. In the deuterocanonical sections of Daniel (3:24–90; 13:1–14:42), the basic text is the Greek text of so-called Theodotion, occasionally revised according to the Greek text of the Septuagint.

PREFACE TO THE
NEW AMERICAN BIBLE

FIRST EDITION OF THE NEW TESTAMENT

The New Testament translation has been approached with essentially the same fidelity to the thought and individual style of the biblical writers as was applied in the Old Testament. In some cases, however, the problem of marked literary peculiarities had to be met. What by any Western standard are the limited vocabularies and stylistic infelicities of the evangelists cannot be retained in the exact form in which they appear in the originals without displeasing the modern ear. A compromise is here attempted whereby some measure of the poverty of the evangelists' expression is kept and placed at the service of their message in its richness. Similarly, the syntactical shortcomings of Paul, his frequent lapses into anacoluthon, and the like, are rendered as they occur in his epistles rather than "smoothed out." Only thus, the translators suppose, will contemporary readers have some adequate idea of the kind of writing they have before them. When the prose of the original flows more smoothly, as in Luke, Acts, and Hebrews, it is reflected in the translation.

The Gospel according to John comprises a special case. Absolute fidelity to his technique of reiterated phrasing would result in an assault on the English ear, yet the softening of the vocal effect by substitution of other words and phrases would destroy the effectiveness of his poetry. Again, resort is had to compromise. This is not an easy matter when the very repetitiousness which the author deliberately employed is at the same time regarded by those who read and speak English to be a serious stylistic defect. Only those familiar with the Greek originals can know what a relentless tattoo Johannine poetry can produce. A similar observation could be made regarding other New Testament books as well. Matthew and Mark are given to identical phrasing twice and three times in the same sentence. As for the rhetorical overgrowth and mixed figures of speech in the letters of Peter, James, and Jude, the translator must resist a powerful compulsion to tidy them up if only to render these letters intelligibly.

Without seeking refuge in complaints against the inspired authors, however, the translators of *The New American Bible* here state that what they have attempted is a translation rather than a paraphrase. To be sure, all translation can be called paraphrase by definition. Any striving for complete fidelity will shortly end in infidelity. Nonetheless, it must be pointed out that the temptation to improve overladen sentences by the consolidation or elimination of multiplied adjectives, or the simplification of clumsy hendiadys, has been resisted here. For the most part, rhetorically ineffective words and phrases are retained in this translation in some form, even when it is clear that a Western contemporary writer would never have employed them.

The spelling of proper names in *The New American Bible* follows the customary forms found in most English Bibles since the Authorized Version.

Despite the arbitrary character of the divisions into numbered verses (a scheme which in its present form is only four centuries old), the translators have made a constant effort to keep within an English verse the whole verbal content of the Greek verse. At times the effort has not seemed worth the result since it often does violence to the original author's flow of expression, which preceded it by so many centuries. If this translation had been prepared for purposes of public reading only, the editors would have forgone the effort at an early stage. But since they never departed from the threefold objective of preparing a translation suitable for liturgical use, private reading, and the purposes of students, the last-named consideration prevailed. Those familiar with Greek should be able to discover how the translators of the New Testament have rendered any given original verse of scripture, if their exegetical or theological tasks require them to know this. At the same time, the fact should be set down here that the editors did not commit themselves in the synoptic gospels to rendering repeated words or phrases identically.

This leads to a final consideration: the Greek text used for the New Testament. Here, punctuation and verse division are at least as important as variant readings. In general, Nestle-Aland's *Novum Testamentum Graece* (25th edition, 1963) was followed. Additional help was derived from *The Greek New Testament* (Aland, Black, Metzger, Wikgren), produced for the use of translators by the United Bible Societies in 1966. However, the editors did not confine themselves strictly to these texts; at times, they inclined toward readings otherwise attested. The omission of alternative translations does not mean that the translators think them without merit, but only that in every case they had to make a choice.

Poorly attested readings do not occur in this translation. Doubtful readings of some merit appear within brackets; public readers may include such words or phrases, or omit them entirely without any damage to sense. Parentheses are used, as ordinarily in English, as a punctuation device. Material they enclose is in no sense textually doubtful. It is simply thought to be parenthetical in the intention of the biblical author, even though there is no such punctuation mark in Greek. The difficulty in dealing with quotation marks is well known. Since they do not appear in any form in the original text, wherever they occur here they constitute an editorial decision.

PREFACE TO THE REVISED EDITION

The New Testament of *The New American Bible*, a fresh translation from the Greek text, was first published in complete form in 1970, together with the Old Testament translation that had been completed the previous year. Portions of the New Testament had appeared earlier, in somewhat different form, in the provisional Mass lectionary of 1964 and in the *Lectionary for Mass* of 1970.

Since 1970 many different printings of the New Testament have been issued by a number of publishers, both separately and in complete bibles, and the text has become widely known both in the United States and in other English-speaking countries. Most American Catholics have been influenced by it because of its widespread use in the liturgy, and it has received a generally favorable reception from many other Christians as well. It has taken its place among the standard contemporary translations of the New Testament, respected for its fidelity to the original and its attempt to render this into current American English.

Although the scriptures themselves are timeless, translations and explanations of them quickly become dated in an era marked by rapid cultural change to a degree never previously experienced. The explosion of biblical studies that has taken place in our century and the changing nature of our language itself require periodic adjustment both in translations and in the accompanying explanatory materials. The experience of actual use of the New Testament of The New American Bible, especially in oral proclamation, has provided a basis for further improvement. Accordingly, it was decided in 1978 to proceed with a thorough revision of the New Testament to reflect advances in scholarship and to satisfy needs identified through pastoral experience.

For this purpose a steering committee was formed to plan, organize, and direct the work of revision, to engage collaborators, and to serve as an editorial board to coordinate the work of the various revisers and to determine the final form of the text and the explanatory materials. Guidelines were drawn up and collaborators selected in 1978 and early 1979, and November of 1980 was established as the deadline for manuscripts. From December 1980 through September 1986 the editorial board met a total of fifty times and carefully reviewed and revised all the material in order to ensure accuracy and consistency of approach. The editors also worked together with the bishops' ad hoc committee that was appointed by the National Conference of Catholic Bishops in 1982 to oversee the revision.

The threefold purpose of the translation that was expressed in the preface to the first edition has been maintained in the revision: to provide a version suitable for liturgical proclamation, for private reading, and for purposes of study. Special attention has been given to the first of these purposes, since oral proclamation demands special qualities in a translation, and experience had provided insights and suggestions that could lead to improvement in this area. Efforts have also been made, however, to facilitate devotional reading by providing suitable notes and introductory materials, and to assist the student by achieving greater accuracy and consistency in the translation and supplying more abundant information in the introductions and notes.

The primary aim of the revision is to produce a version as accurate and faithful to the meaning of the Greek original as is possible for a translation. The editors have consequently moved in the direction of a formal-equivalence approach to translation, matching the vocabulary, structure, and even word order of the original as closely as possible in the receptor language. Some other contemporary biblical versions have adopted, in varying degrees, a dynamic-equivalence approach, which attempts to respect the individuality of each language by expressing the meaning of the original in a linguistic structure suited to English, even though this may be very different from the corresponding Greek structure. While this approach often results in fresh and brilliant renderings, it has the disadvantages of more or less radically abandoning traditional biblical and liturgical terminology and phraseology, of expanding the text to include what more properly belongs in notes, commentaries, or preaching, and of tending toward paraphrase. A more formal approach seems better suited to the specific purposes intended for this translation.

At the same time, the editors have wished to produce a version in English that reflects contemporary American usage and is readily understandable to ordinary educated people, but one that will be recognized as dignified speech, on the level of formal rather than colloquial usage. These aims are not in fact contradictory, for there are different levels of language in current use: the language of formal situations as not that of colloquial conversation, though people understand both and may pass from one to the other without adverting to the transition. The liturgy is a formal situation that requires a level of discourse more dignified, formal, and hieratic than the world of business, sport, or informal communication. People readily understand this more formal level even though they may not often use it; our passive vocabulary is much larger than our active vocabulary. Hence this revision, while avoiding archaisms, does not shrink from traditional biblical terms that are easily understood even though not in common use in everyday speech. The level of language consciously aimed at is one appropriate for liturgical proclamation; this may also permit the translation to serve the purposes of devotional reading and serious study.

A particular effort has been made to insure consistency of vocabulary. Always to translate a given Greek word by the same English equivalent would lead to ludicrous results and to infidelity to the meaning of the text. But in passages where a particular Greek term retains the same meaning, it has been rendered in the same way insofar as this has been feasible; this is particularly significant in the case of terms that have a specific theological meaning. The synoptic gospels have been carefully translated so as to reveal both the similarities and the differences of the Greek.

An especially sensitive problem today is the question of discrimination in language. In recent years there has been much discussion about allegations of anti-Jewish expressions in the New Testament and of language that discriminates against various minorities. Above all, however, the question of discrimination against women affects the largest number of people and arouses the greatest degree of interest and concern. At present there is little agreement about these problems or about the best way to deal with them. In all these areas the present translation attempts to display a sensitivity appropriate to the present state of the questions under discussion, which are not yet resolved and in regard to which it is impossible to please everyone, since intelligent and sincere participants in the debate hold mutually contradictory views.

The primary concern in this revision is fidelity to what the text says. When the meaning of the Greek is inclusive of both sexes, the translation seeks to reproduce such inclusivity insofar as this is possible in normal English usage, without resort to inelegant circumlocutions or neologisms that would offend against the dignity of the language. Although the generic sense of *man* is traditional in English, many today reject it; its use has therefore generally been avoided, though it is retained in cases where no fully satisfactory equivalent could be found. English does not possess a gender-inclusive third personal pronoun in the singular, and this translation continues to use the masculine resumptive pronoun after *everyone* or *anyone*, in the traditional way, where this cannot be avoided without infidelity to the meaning.

The translation of the Greek word *adelphos*, particularly in the plural form *adelphoi*, poses an especially delicate problem. While the term literally means brothers or other male blood relatives, even in profane Greek the plural can designate two persons, one of either sex, who were born of the same parents. It was adopted by the early Christians to designate, in a figurative sense, the members of the Christian community, who were conscious of a new familial relationship to one another by reason of their adoption as children of God. They are consequently addressed as *adelphoi*. This has traditionally been rendered into English by *brothers* or, more archaically, *brethren*. There has never been any doubt that this designation includes *all* the members of the Christian community, both male and female. Given the absence in English of a corresponding term that explicitly includes both sexes, this translation retains the usage of *brothers*, with the inclusive meaning that has been traditionally attached to it in this biblical context.

Since the New Testament is the product of a particular time and culture, the views expressed in it and the language in which they are expressed reflect a particular cultural conditioning, which sometimes makes them quite different from contemporary ideas and concerns. Discriminatory language should be eliminated insofar as possible whenever it is unfaithful to the meaning of the New Testament, but the text should not be altered in order to adjust it to contemporary concerns. This translation does not introduce any changes, expansions, additions to, or subtractions from the text of scripture. It further retains the traditional biblical ways of speaking about God and about Christ, including the use of masculine nouns and pronouns.

The Greek text followed in this translation is that of the third edition of *The Greek New Testament*, edited by Kurt Aland, Matthew Black, Carlo Martini, Bruce Metzger, and Allen Wikgren, and published by the United Bible Societies in 1975. The same text, with a different critical apparatus and variations in punctuation and typography, was published as the twenty-sixth edition of the Nestle-Aland *Novum Testamentum Graece* in 1979 by the Deutsche Bibelstiftung, Stuttgart. This edition has also been consulted. When variant readings occur, the translation, with few exceptions, follows the reading that was placed in the text of these Greek editions, though the occurrence of the principal variants is pointed out in the notes.

The editors of the Greek text placed square brackets around words or portions of words of which the authenticity is questionable because the evidence of textual witnesses is inconclusive. The same has been done in the translation insofar as it is possible to reproduce this convention in English. It should be possible to read the text either with or without the disputed words, but in English it is not always feasible to provide this alternative, and in some passages the bracketed words must be included to make sense. As in the first edition, parentheses do not indicate textual uncertainty, but are simply a punctuation device to indicate a passage that in the editors' judgment appears parenthetical to the thought of the author.

Citations from the Old Testament are placed within quotation marks; longer citations are set off as block quotations in a separate indented paragraph. The sources of such citations, as well as those of many more or less subtle allusions to the Old Testament, are identified in the biblical cross-reference section at the bottom of each page. Insofar as possible, the translation of such Old Testament citations agrees with that of *The New American Bible* Old Testament whenever the underlying Greek agrees with the Hebrew (or, in some cases, the Aramaic or Greek) text from which the Old Testament translation was made. But citations in the New Testament frequently follow the Septuagint or some other version, or were made from memory, hence, in many cases the translation in the New Testament passage will not agree with what appears in the Old Testament. Some of these cases are explained in the notes.

It is a further aim of the revised edition to supply explanatory materials more abundantly than in the first edition. In most cases the introductions and notes have been entirely rewritten and expanded, and the cross-references checked and revised. It is intended that these materials should reflect the present state of sound biblical scholarship and should be presented in such a form that they can be assimilated by the ordinary intelligent reader without specialized biblical training. While they have been written with the ordinary educated Christian in mind, not all technical vocabulary can be entirely dispensed with in approaching the Bible, any more than in any other field. It is the hope of the editors that these materials, even if they sometimes demand an effort, will help the reader to a fuller and more intelligent understanding of the New Testament and a fruitful appropriation of its meaning for personal spiritual growth.

The New American Bible is a Roman Catholic translation. This revision, however, like the first edition, has been accomplished with the collaboration of scholars from other Christian churches, both among the revisers and on the editorial board, in response to the encouragement of Vatican Council II (*Dei Verbum*, 22). The editorial board expresses gratitude to all who have collaborated in the revision: to all the revisers, consultants, and bishops who contributed to it, to reviewers of the first edition, and to those who voluntarily submitted suggestions. May this translation fulfill its threefold purpose, "so that the word of the Lord may speed forward and be glorified" (2 Thes 3:1).

The Feast of St. Jerome
September 30, 1986

THE
NEW TESTAMENT

THE
GOSPELS

⁓ℰ⁓

The collection of writings that constitutes the New Testament begins with four gospels. Next comes the Acts of the Apostles, followed by twenty-one letters that are attributed to Paul, James, Peter, John, and Jude. Finally, at the end of the early church's scriptures stands the Revelation to John. Virtually all Christians agree that these twenty-seven books constitute the "canon," a term that means "rule" and designates the list of writings that are regarded as authoritative for Christian faith and life.

It is the purpose of this Introduction to describe those features that are common to the four gospels. A similar treatment of the letters of the New Testament is provided in the two Introductions that appear before the Letter to the Romans and before the Letter of James, respectively. The Acts of the Apostles, a work that is both historical and theological, and Revelation, an apocalyptic work, have no counterparts in the New Testament; the special Introductions prefixed to these books treat of the literary characteristics proper to each of them.

While the New Testament contains four writings called "gospels," there is in reality only one gospel running through all of the Christian scriptures, the gospel of and about Jesus Christ. Our English word "gospel" translates the Greek term *euangelion*, meaning "good news." This noun was used in the plural by the Greek translators of the Old Testament to render the Hebrew term for "good news" (2 Sm 4:10; possibly also 2 Sm 18:20, 25). But it is the corresponding verb *euangelizomai*, "to proclaim good news," that was especially significant in preparing for the New Testament idea of "gospel," since this term is used by Deutero-Isaiah of announcing the great victory of God that was to establish his universal kingship and inaugurate the new age (Is 40:9; 52:7; 61:1).

Paul used the word *euangelion* to designate the message that he and the other apostles proclaimed, the "gospel of God" (Rom 1:1; 15:16; 2 Cor 11:7; 1 Thes 2:2, 8–9). He often referred to it simply as "the gospel" (Rom 1:16; 10:16; 11:28; etc) or, because of its content and origin, as "the gospel of Christ" (Rom 15:19; 1 Cor 9:12; 1 Thes 3:2; etc). Because of its personal meaning for him and his own particular manner of telling the story about Jesus Christ and of explaining the significance of his cross and resurrection, Paul also referred to this message as "my gospel" (Rom 2:16; cf. Gal 1:11; 2:2) or "our gospel" (2 Cor 4:3; 1 Thes 1:5; 2 Thes 2:14).

It was Mark, as far as we know, who first applied the term "gospel" to a book telling the story of Jesus; see Mk 1:1 and the note there. This form of presenting Jesus' life, works, teachings, passion, and resurrection was developed further by the other evangelists; see the Introduction to each gospel. The first three of the canonical gospels, Matthew, Mark, and Luke, are so similar at many points when viewed together, particularly when arranged in parallel columns or lines, that they are called "synoptic" gospels, from the Greek word for such a general view. The fourth gospel, John, often differs significantly from the synoptics in outline and approach. This work never uses the word "gospel" or its corresponding verb; nevertheless, its message concerns the same Jesus, and the reader is urged to believe in him as the Messiah, "that through this belief you may have life in his name" (Jn 20:31).

From the second century onward, the practice arose of designating each of these four books as a "gospel," understood as a title, and of adding a phrase with a name that identified the traditional author, e.g., "The Gospel according to Matthew." The arrangement of the canon that was adopted, with the four gospels grouped together at the beginning followed by Acts, provides a massive focus upon Jesus and allows Acts to serve as a framework for the letters of the New Testament. This order, however, conceals the fact that Luke's two volumes, a gospel and Acts, were intended by their author to go together. It further obscures the point that Paul's letters were written before any of our gospels, though the sayings and deeds of Jesus stand behind all the New Testament writings.

THE GOSPEL ACCORDING TO
MATTHEW

The position of the Gospel according to Matthew as the first of the four gospels in the New Testament reflects both the view that it was the first to be written, a view that goes back to the late second century A.D., and the esteem in which it was held by the church; no other was so frequently quoted in the noncanonical literature of earliest Christianity. Although the majority of scholars now reject the opinion about the time of its composition, the high estimation of this work remains. The reason for that becomes clear upon study of the way in which Matthew presents his story of Jesus, the demands of Christian discipleship, and the breaking-in of the new and final age through the ministry but particularly through the death and resurrection of Jesus.

The gospel begins with a narrative prologue (Mt 1:1–2:23), the first part of which is a genealogy of Jesus starting with Abraham, the father of Israel (Mt 1:1–17). Yet at the beginning of that genealogy Jesus is designated as "the son of David, the son of Abraham" (Mt 1:1). The kingly ancestor who lived about a thousand years after Abraham is named first, for this is the genealogy of Jesus Christ, the Messiah, the royal anointed one (Mt 1:16). In the first of the episodes of the infancy narrative that follow the genealogy, the mystery of Jesus' person is declared. He is conceived of a virgin by the power of the Spirit of God (Mt 1:18–25). The first of the gospel's fulfillment citations, whose purpose it is to show that he was the one to whom the prophecies of Israel were pointing, occurs here (Mt 1:23): he shall be named Emmanuel, for in him God is with us.

The announcement of the birth of this newborn king of the Jews greatly troubles not only King Herod but all Jerusalem (Mt 2:1–3), yet the Gentile magi are overjoyed to find him and offer him their homage and their gifts (Mt 2:10–11). Thus his ultimate rejection by the mass of his own people and his acceptance by the Gentile nations is foreshadowed. He must be taken to Egypt to escape the murderous plan of Herod. By his sojourn there and his subsequent return after the king's death he relives the Exodus experience of Israel. The words of the Lord spoken through the prophet Hosea, "Out of Egypt I called my son," are fulfilled in him (Mt 2:15); if Israel was God's son, Jesus is so in a way far surpassing the dignity of that nation, as his marvelous birth and the unfolding of his story show (see Mt 3:17; 4:1–11; 11:27; 14:33; 16:16; 27:54). Back in the land of Israel, he must be taken to Nazareth in Galilee because of the danger to his life in Judea, where Herod's son Archelaus is now ruling (Mt 2:22–23). The sufferings of Jesus in the infancy narrative anticipate those of his passion, and if his life is spared in spite of the dangers, it is because his destiny is finally to give it on the cross as "a ransom for many" (Mt 20:28). Thus the word of the angel will be fulfilled, ". . . he will save his people from their sins" (Mt 1:21; cf. Mt 26:28).

In Mt 4:12 Matthew begins his account of the ministry of Jesus, introducing it by the preparatory preaching of John the Baptist (Mt 3:1–12), the baptism of Jesus that culminates in God's proclaiming him his "beloved Son" (Mt 3:13–17), and the temptation in which he proves his true sonship by his victory over the devil's attempt to deflect him from the way of obedience to the Father (Mt 4:1–11). The central message of Jesus' preaching is the coming of the kingdom of heaven and the need for repentance, a complete change of heart and conduct, on the part of those who are to receive this great gift of God (Mt 4:17). Galilee is the setting for most of his ministry; he leaves there for Judea only in Mt 19:1, and his ministry in Jerusalem, the goal of his journey, is limited to a few days (Mt 21:1–25:46).

In this extensive material there are five great discourses of Jesus, each concluding with the formula "When Jesus finished these words" or one closely similar (Mt 7:28; 11:1; 13:53; 19:1; 26:1). These are an important structure of the gospel. In every case the discourse is preceded by a narrative section, each narrative and discourse together constituting a "book" of the gospel. The discourses are, respectively, the "Sermon on the Mount" (Mt 5:3–7:27), the missionary discourse (Mt 10:5–42), the parable discourse (Mt 13:3–52), the "church order" discourse (Mt 18:3–35), and the eschatological discourse (Mt 24:4–25:46). In large measure the material of these discourses came to Matthew from his tradition, but his work in modifying and adding to what he had received is abundantly evident. No other evangelist gives the teaching of Jesus with such elegance and order as he.

In the "Sermon on the Mount" the theme of righteousness is prominent, and even at this early stage of the ministry the note of opposition is struck between Jesus and the Pharisees, who are designated as "the hypocrites" (Mt 6:2, 5, 16). The righteousness of his disciples must surpass that of the scribes and Pharisees; otherwise, in spite of their alleged following of Jesus, they will not enter into the kingdom of heaven (Mt 5:20). Righteousness means doing the will of the heavenly Father (Mt 7:21), and his will is proclaimed in a manner that is startling to all who have identified it with the law of Moses. The antitheses of the Sermon (Mt 5:21–48) both accept (Mt 5:21–30, 43–48) and reject (Mt 5:31–42) elements of that law, and in the former case the understanding of the law's demands is deepened and extended. The antitheses are the best commentary on the meaning of Jesus' claim that he has come not to abolish but to fulfill the law (Mt 5:17). What is meant by fulfillment of the law is not the demand to keep it exactly as it stood before the coming of Jesus, but rather his bringing the law to be a lasting expression of the will of God, and in that fulfillment there is much that will pass away. Should this appear contradictory to his saying that "until heaven and earth pass away" not even the smallest part of the law will pass (Mt 5:18), that time of fulfillment is not the dissolution of the universe but the coming of the new age, which will occur with Jesus' death and resurrection. While righteousness in the new age will continue to mean conduct that is in accordance with the law, it will be conduct in accordance with the law as expounded and interpreted by Jesus (cf. Mt 28:20, ". . . all that I have commanded you").

Though Jesus speaks harshly about the Pharisees in the Sermon, his judgment is not solely a condemnation of them. The Pharisees are portrayed as a negative example for his disciples, and his condemnation of those who claim to belong to him while disobeying his word is no less severe (Mt 7:21–23, 26–27).

In Mt 4:23 a summary statement of Jesus' activity speaks not only of his teaching and proclaiming the gospel but of his "curing every disease and illness among the people"; this is repeated almost verbatim in Mt 9:35. The narrative section that follows the Sermon on the Mount (Mt 8:1–9:38) is composed principally of accounts of those merciful deeds of Jesus, but it is far from being simply a collection of stories about miraculous cures. The nature of the community that Jesus will establish is shown; it will always be under the protection of him whose power can deal with all dangers (Mt 8:23–27), but it is only for those who are prepared to follow him at whatever cost (Mt 8:16–22), not only believing Israelites but Gentiles who have come to faith in him (Mt 8:10–12). The disciples begin to have some insight, however imperfect, into the mystery of Jesus' person. They wonder about him whom "the winds and the sea obey" (Mt 8:27), and they witness his bold declaration of the forgiveness of the paralytic's sins (Mt 9:2). That episode of the narrative moves on two levels. When the crowd sees the cure that testifies to the authority of Jesus, the Son of Man, to forgive sins (Mt 9:6), they glorify God "who had given such authority to human beings" (Mt 9:8). The forgiveness of sins is now not the prerogative of Jesus alone but of "human beings," that is, of the disciples who constitute the community of Jesus, the church. The ecclesial character of this narrative section could hardly be more plainly indicated.

The end of the section prepares for the discourse on the church's mission (Mt 10:5–42). Jesus is moved to pity at the sight of the crowds who are like sheep without a shepherd (Mt 9:36), and he sends out the twelve disciples to make the proclamation with which his own ministry began, "The kingdom of heaven is at hand" (Mt 10:7; cf. Mt 4:17), and to drive out demons and cure the sick as he has done (Mt 10:1). Their mission is limited to Israel (Mt 10:5–6) as Jesus' own was (Mt 15:24), yet in Mt 15:16 that perspective broadens and the discourse begins to speak of the mission that the disciples will have after the resurrection and of the severe persecution that will attend it (Mt 10:18). Again, the discourse moves on two levels: that of the time of Jesus and that of the time of the church.

The narrative section of the third book (Mt 11:2–12:50) deals with the growing opposition to Jesus. Hostility toward him has already been manifested (Mt 8:10; 9:3, 10–13, 34), but here it becomes more intense. The rejection of Jesus comes, as before, from Pharisees, who take "counsel against him to put him to death" (Mt 12:14) and repeat their earlier accusation that he drives out demons because he is in league with demonic power (Mt 12:22–24). But they are not alone in their rejection. Jesus complains of the lack of faith of "this generation" of Israelites (Mt 11:16–19) and reproaches the towns "where most of his mighty deeds had been done" for not heeding his call to repentance (Mt 11:20–24). This dark picture is relieved by Jesus' praise of the Father who has enabled "the childlike" to accept him (Mt 11:25–27), but on the whole the story is one of opposition to his word and blindness to the meaning of his deeds. The whole section ends with his declaring that not even the most intimate blood relationship with him counts for anything; his only true relatives are those who do the will of his heavenly Father (Mt 12:48–50).

The narrative of rejection leads up to the parable discourse (Mt 13:3–52). The reason given for Jesus' speaking to the crowds in parables is that they have hardened themselves against his clear teaching, unlike the disciples to whom knowledge of "the mysteries of the kingdom has been granted" (Mt 13:10–16). In Mt 13:36 he dismisses the crowds and continues the discourse to his disciples alone, who claim, at the end, to have understood all that he has said (Mt 13:51). But, lest the impression be given that the church of Jesus is made up only of true disciples, the explanation of the parable of the weeds among the wheat (Mt 13:37–43), as well as the parable of the net thrown into the sea "which collects fish of every kind" (Mt 13:47–49), shows that it is composed of both the righteous and the wicked, and that separation between the two will be made only at the time of the final judgment.

In the narrative that constitutes the first part of the fourth book of the gospel (Mt 13:54–17:27), Jesus is shown preparing for the establishment of his church with its teaching authority that will supplant the blind guidance of the Pharisees (Mt 15:13–14), whose teaching, curiously said to be that of the Sadducees also, is repudiated by Jesus as the norm for his disciples (Mt 16:6, 11–12). The church of Jesus will be built on Peter (Mt 16:18), who will be given authority to bind and loose on earth, an authority whose exercise will be confirmed in heaven (Mt 16:19). The metaphor of binding and loosing has a variety of meanings, among them that of giving authoritative teaching. This promise is made to Peter directly after he has confessed Jesus to be the Messiah, the Son of the living God (Mt 16:16), a confession that he has made as the result of revelation given to him by the heavenly Father (Mt 16:17); Matthew's ecclesiology is based on his high christology.

Directly after that confession Jesus begins to instruct his disciples about how he must go the way of suffering and death (Mt 16:21). Peter, who has been praised for his confession, protests against this and receives from Jesus the sharpest of rebukes for attempting to deflect Jesus from his God-appointed destiny. The future rock upon whom the church will be built is still a man of "little faith" (see Mt 14:31). Both he and the other disciples must know not only that Jesus will have to suffer and die but that they too will have to follow him on the way of the cross if they are truly to be his disciples (Mt 16:24–25).

The discourse following this narrative (Mt 18:1–35) is often called the "church order" discourse, although that title is perhaps misleading since the emphasis is not on the structure of the church but on the care that the disciples must have for one another in respect to guarding each other's faith in Jesus (Mt 18:6–7), to seeking out those who have wandered from the fold (Mt 18:10–14), and to repeated forgiving of their fellow disciples who have offended them (Mt 18:21–35). But there is also the obligation to correct the sinful fellow Christian and, should one refuse to be corrected, separation from the community is demanded (Mt 18:15–18).

The narrative of the fifth book (Mt 19:1–23:39) begins with the departure of Jesus and his disciples from Galilee for Jerusalem. In the course of their journey Jesus for the third time predicts the passion that awaits him at Jerusalem and also his resurrection (Mt 20:17–19). At his entrance into the city he is hailed as the Son of David by the crowds accompanying him (Mt 21:9). He cleanses the temple (Mt 21:12–17), and in the few days of his Jerusalem ministry he engages in a series of controversies with the Jewish religious leaders (Mt 21:23–27; 22:15–22, 23–33, 34–40, 41–46), meanwhile speaking parables against them (Mt 21:28–32, 33–46), against all those Israelites who have rejected God's invitation to the messianic banquet (Mt 22:1–10), and against all, Jew and Gentile, who have accepted but have shown themselves unworthy of it (Mt 22:11–14). Once again, the perspective of the evangelist includes not only the time of Jesus' ministry but that of the preaching of the gospel after his resurrection. The narrative culminates in Jesus' denunciation of the scribes and Pharisees, reflecting not only his own opposition to them but that of Matthew's church (Mt 23:1–36), and in Jesus' lament over Jerusalem (Mt 23:37–39).

In the discourse of the fifth book (Mt 24:1–25:46), the last of the great structural discourses of the gospel, Jesus predicts the destruction of the temple and his own final coming. The time of the latter is unknown (Mt 24:36, 44), and the disciples are exhorted in various parables to live in readiness for it, a readiness that entails faithful attention to the duties of the interim period (Mt 24:45–25:30). The coming of Jesus will bring with it the great judgment by which the everlasting destiny of all will be determined (Mt 25:31–46).

The story of Jesus' passion and resurrection (Mt 26:1–28:20), the climax of the gospel, throws light on all that has preceded. In Matthew "righteousness" means both the faithful response to the will of God demanded of all to whom that will is announced and also the saving activity of God for his people (see Mt 3:15; 5:6; 6:33). The passion supremely exemplifies both meanings of that central Matthean word. In Jesus' absolute faithfulness to the Father's will that he drink the cup of suffering (Mt 26:39), the incomparable model for Christian obedience is given; in his death "for the forgiveness of sins" (Mt 26:28), the saving power of God is manifested as never before.

Matthew's portrayal of Jesus in his passion combines both the majestic serenity of the obedient Son who goes his destined way in fulfillment of the scriptures (Mt 26:52–54), confident of his ultimate vindication by God, and the depths of fear and abandonment that he feels in face of death (Mt 26:38–39; 27:46). These two aspects are expressed by an Old Testament theme that occurs often in the narrative, i.e., the portrait of the suffering Righteous One who complains to God in his misery, but is certain of eventual deliverance from his terrible ordeal.

The passion-resurrection of God's Son means nothing less than the turn of the ages, a new stage of history, the coming of the Son of Man in his kingdom (Mt 28:18; cf. Mt 16:28). That is the sense of the apocalyptic signs that accompany Jesus' death (Mt 27:51–53) and resurrection (Mt 28:2). Although the old age continues, as it will until the manifestation of Jesus' triumph at his parousia, the final age has now begun. This is known only to those who have seen the Risen One and to those, both Jews and Gentiles, who have believed in their announcement of Jesus' triumph and have themselves become his disciples (cf. Mt 28:19). To them he is constantly, though invisibly, present (Mt 28:20), verifying the name Emmanuel, "God is with us" (cf. Mt 1:23).

The questions of authorship, sources, and the time of composition of this gospel have received many answers, none of which can claim more than a greater or lesser degree of probability. The one now favored by the majority of scholars is the following.

The ancient tradition that the author was the disciple and apostle of Jesus named Matthew (see Mt 10:3) is untenable because the gospel is based, in large part, on the Gospel according to Mark (almost all the verses of that gospel have been utilized in this), and it is hardly likely that a companion of Jesus would have followed so extensively an account that came from one who admittedly never had such an association rather than rely on his own memories. The attribution of the gospel to the disciple Matthew may have been due to his having been responsible for some of the traditions found in it, but that is far from certain.

The unknown author, whom we shall continue to call Matthew for the sake of convenience, drew not only upon the Gospel according to Mark but upon a large body of material (principally, sayings of Jesus) not found in Mark that corresponds, sometimes exactly, to material found also in the Gospel according to Luke. This material, called "Q" (probably from the first letter of the German word Quelle, meaning "source"), represents traditions, written and oral, used by both Matthew and Luke. Mark and Q are sources common to the two other synoptic gospels; hence the name the "Two-Source Theory" given to this explanation of the relation among the synoptics.

In addition to what Matthew drew from Mark and Q, his gospel contains material that is found only there. This is often designated "M," written or oral tradition that was available to the author. Since Mark was written shortly before or shortly after A.D. 70 (see Introduction to Mark), Matthew was composed certainly after that date, which marks the fall of Jerusalem to the Romans at the time of the First Jewish Revolt (A.D. 66–70), and probably at least a decade later since Matthew's use of

Mark presupposes a wide diffusion of that gospel. The post-A.D. 70 date is confirmed within the text by Mt 22:7, which refers to the destruction of Jerusalem.

As for the place where the gospel was composed, a plausible suggestion is that it was Antioch, the capital of the Roman province of Syria. That large and important city had a mixed population of Greek-speaking Gentiles and Jews. The tensions between Jewish and Gentile Christians there in the time of Paul (see Gal 2:1–14) in respect to Christian obligation to observe Mosaic law are partially similar to tensions that can be seen between the two groups in Matthew's gospel. The church of Matthew, originally strongly Jewish Christian, had become one in which Gentile Christians were predominant. His gospel answers the question how obedience to the will of God is to be expressed by those who live after the "turn of the ages," the death and resurrection of Jesus.

The principal divisions of the Gospel according to Matthew are the following:

    I. The Infancy Narrative (1:1–2:23)
    II. The Proclamation of the Kingdom (3:1–7:29)
    III. Ministry and Mission in Galilee (8:1–11:1)
    IV. Opposition from Israel (11:2–13:53)
    V. Jesus, the Kingdom, and the Church (13:54–18:35)
    VI. Ministry in Judea and Jerusalem (19:1–25:46)
    VII. The Passion and Resurrection (26:1–28:20)

I. THE INFANCY NARRATIVE

CHAPTER 1

The Genealogy of Jesus. [1a]The book of the genealogy of Jesus Christ, the son of David, the son of Abraham.†

*[1:1–2:23] The infancy narrative forms the prologue of the gospel. Consisting of a genealogy and five stories, it presents the coming of Jesus as the climax of Israel's history, and the events of his conception, birth, and early childhood as the fulfillment of Old Testament prophecy. The genealogy is probably traditional material that Matthew inherited. In its first two sections (Mt 1:2–11) it was drawn from Ru 4:18–22; 1 Chr 1–3. Except for Jechoniah, Shealtiel, and Zerubbabel, none of the names in the third section (Mt 1:12–16) is found in any Old Testament genealogy. While the genealogy shows the continuity of God's providential plan from Abraham on, discontinuity is also present. The women Tamar (Mt 1:3), Rahab and Ruth (Mt 1:5), and the wife of Uriah, Bathsheba (Mt 1:6), bore their sons through unions that were in varying degrees strange and unexpected. These "irregularities" culminate in the supreme "irregularity" of the Messiah's birth of a virgin mother; the age of fulfillment is inaugurated by a creative act of God.

Drawing upon both biblical tradition and Jewish stories, Matthew portrays Jesus as reliving the Exodus experience of Israel and the persecutions of Moses. His rejection by his own people and his passion are foreshadowed by the troubled reaction of "all Jerusalem" to the question of the magi who are seeking the "newborn king of the Jews" (Mt 2:2–3), and by Herod's attempt to have him killed. The magi who do him homage prefigure the Gentiles who will accept the preaching of the gospel. The infancy narrative proclaims who Jesus is, the savior of his people from their sins (Mt 1:21), Emmanuel in whom "God is with us" (Mt 1:23), and the Son of God (Mt 2:15).

†[1:1] The Son of David, the son of Abraham: two links of the genealogical chain are singled out. Although the later, David is placed first in order to emphasize that Jesus is the royal Messiah. The mention of Abraham may be due not only to his being the father of the nation Israel but to Matthew's interest in the universal scope of Jesus' mission; cf. Gn 22:18 ". . . in your descendants all the nations of the earth shall find blessing."

a. [1:1] Gn 5:1; 1 Chr 17:11; Gn 22:18.

[2b]Abraham became the father of Isaac, Isaac the father of Jacob, Jacob the father of Judah and his brothers.[c] [3]Judah became the father of Perez and Zerah, whose mother was Tamar.[d] Perez became the father of Hezron, Hezron the father of Ram, [4e]Ram the father of Amminadab. Amminadab became the father of Nahshon, Nahshon the father of Salmon, [5f]Salmon the father of Boaz, whose mother was Rahab. Boaz became the father of Obed, whose mother was Ruth. Obed became the father of Jesse, [6g]Jesse the father of David the king.

David became the father of Solomon, whose mother had been the wife of Uriah. [7‡h]Solomon became the father of Rehoboam, Rehoboam the father of Abijah, Abijah the father of Asaph. [8]Asaph became the father of Jehoshaphat, Jehoshaphat the father of Joram, Joram the father of Uzziah. [9]Uzziah became the father of Jotham, Jotham the father of Ahaz, Ahaz the father of Hezekiah. [10]Hezekiah became the father of Manasseh, Manasseh the father of Amos,[§] Amos the father of Josiah. [11]Josiah

‡[1:7] The successor of Abijah was not Asaph but Asa (see 1 Chr 3:10). Some textual witnesses read the latter name; however, **Asaph** is better attested. Matthew may have deliberately introduced the psalmist Asaph into the genealogy (and in Mt 1:10 the prophet Amos) in order to show that Jesus is the fulfillment not only of the promises made to David (see 2 Sm 7) but of all the Old Testament.

§[1:10] **Amos:** some textual witnesses read **Amon**, who was the actual successor of Manasseh (see 1 Chr 3:14).

b. [1:2–17] Lk 3:23–38. c. [1:2] Gn 21:3; 25:26; 29:35; 1 Chr 2:1. d. [1:3] Gn 38:29–30; Ru 4:18; 1 Chr 2:4–9. e. [1:4] Ru 4:19–20; 1 Chr 2:10–11. f. [1:5] Ru 4:21–22; 1 Chr 2:11–12. g. [1:6] 2 Sm 12:24; 1 Chr 2:15; 3:5. h. [1:7–11] 2 Kgs 25:1–21; 1 Chr 3:10–15.

became the father of Jechoniah and his brothers at the time of the Babylonian exile.

[1:12i]After the Babylonian exile, Jechoniah became the father of Shealtiel, Shealtiel the father of Zerubbabel, [13]Zerubbabel the father of Abiud. Abiud became the father of Eliakim, Eliakim the father of Azor, [14]Azor the father of Zadok. Zadok became the father of Achim, Achim the father of Eliud, [15]Eliud the father of Eleazar. Eleazar became the father of Matthan, Matthan the father of Jacob, [16]Jacob the father of Joseph, the husband of Mary. Of her was born Jesus who is called the Messiah.

[17]Thus the total number of generations from Abraham to David is fourteen generations; from David to the Babylonian exile, fourteen generations; from the Babylonian exile to the Messiah, fourteen generations.*

The Birth of Jesus.† [18]Now this is how the birth of Jesus Christ came about. When his mother Mary was betrothed to Joseph,‡ but before they lived together, she was found with child through the holy Spirit. [19]Joseph her husband, since he was a righteous man,§ yet unwilling to expose her to shame, decided to divorce her quietly. [20j]Such was his intention when, behold, the angel of the Lord§ appeared to him in a dream and said, "Joseph, son of David, do not be afraid to take Mary your wife into your home. For it is through the holy Spirit that this child has been conceived in her. [21]She will bear a son and you are to name him Jesus,** because he will save his people from their sins." [22]All this took place to fulfill what the Lord had said through the prophet:

[23] ††k"Behold, the virgin shall be with child
        and bear a son,
    and they shall name him
        Emmanuel,"

which means "God is with us." [24]When Joseph awoke, he did as the angel of the Lord had commanded him and took his wife into his home. [25]He had no relations with her until she bore a son,‡‡ and he named him Jesus.l

CHAPTER 2

The Visit of the Magi.§§ [1]When Jesus was born in Bethlehem of Judea, in the days of King Herod,¶¶ behold, magi from the east arrived in Jerusalem, [2]saying, "Where is the newborn king of the Jews? We saw his star*** at its rising and have come to do him homage."m [3]When King Herod heard this, he was greatly troubled, and all Jerusalem with him. [4]Assembling all the chief priests and the scribes of the people, he inquired of them where the Messiah was to be born.††† [5n]They said

---

*[1:17] Matthew is concerned with fourteen generations, probably because fourteen is the numerical value of the Hebrew letters forming the name of David. In the second section of the genealogy (Mt 1:6b–11), three kings of Judah, Ahaziah, Joash, and Amaziah, have been omitted (see 1 Chr 3:11–12), so that there are fourteen generations in that section. Yet the third (Mt 1:12–16) apparently has only thirteen. Since Matthew here emphasizes that each section has fourteen, it is unlikely that the thirteen of the last was due to his oversight. Some scholars suggest that **Jesus who is called the Messiah** (Mt 1:16b) doubles the final member of the chain: **Jesus,** born within the family of David, opens up the new age as **Messiah,** so that in fact there are fourteen generations in the third section. This is perhaps too subtle, and the hypothesis of a slip not on the part of Matthew but of a later scribe seems likely. On **Messiah,** see note on Lk 2:11.

†[1:18–25] This first story of the infancy narrative spells out what is summarily indicated in Mt 1:16. The virginal conception of Jesus is the work of the Spirit of God. Joseph's decision to divorce Mary is overcome by the heavenly command that he take her into his home and accept the child as his own. The natural genealogical line is broken but the promises to David are fulfilled; through Joseph's adoption the child belongs to the family of David. Matthew sees the virginal conception as the fulfillment of Is 7:14.

‡[1:18] **Betrothed to Joseph:** betrothal was the first part of the marriage, constituting a man and woman as husband and wife. Subsequent infidelity was considered adultery. The betrothal was followed some months later by the husband's taking his wife into his home, at which time normal married life began.

§[1:19] **A righteous man:** as a devout observer of the Mosaic law, Joseph wished to break his union with someone whom he suspected of gross violation of the law. It is commonly said that the law required him to do so, but the texts usually given in support of that view, e.g., Dt 22:20–21 do not clearly pertain to Joseph's situation. **Unwilling to expose her to shame:** the penalty for proved adultery was death by stoning; cf. Dt 22:21–23.

§[1:20] **The angel of the Lord:** in the Old Testament a common designation of God in communication with a human being. **In a dream:** see Mt 2:13, 19, 22. These dreams may be meant to recall the dreams of Joseph, son of Jacob the patriarch (Gn 37:5–11, 19). A closer parallel is the dream of Amram, father of Moses, related by Josephus (*Antiquities* 2:212, 215–16).

[1:21] **Jesus: in first-century Judaism the Hebrew name Joshua (Greek *Iēsous*) meaning "Yahweh helps" was interpreted as "Yahweh saves."

††[1:23] **God is with us:** God's promise of deliverance to Judah in Isaiah's time is seen by Matthew as fulfilled in the birth of Jesus, in whom God is with his people. The name Emmanuel is alluded to at the end of the gospel where the risen Jesus assures his disciples of his continued presence, ". . . I am with you always, until the end of the age" (Mt 28:20).

‡‡[1:25] **Until she bore a son:** the evangelist is concerned to emphasize that Joseph was not responsible for the conception of Jesus. The Greek word translated "until" does not imply normal marital conduct after Jesus' birth, nor does it exclude it.

§§[2:1–12] The future rejection of Jesus by Israel and his acceptance by the Gentiles are retrojected into this scene of the narrative.

¶¶[2:1] **In the days of King Herod:** Herod reigned from 37 to 4 B.C. **Magi:** originally a designation of the Persian priestly caste, the word became used of those who were regarded as having more than human knowledge. Matthew's magi are astrologers.

***[2:2] **We saw his star:** it was a common ancient belief that a new star appeared at the time of a ruler's birth. Matthew also draws upon the Old Testament story of Balaam, who had prophesied that "A star shall advance from Jacob" (Nm 24:17), though there the star means not an astral phenomenon but the king himself.

†††[2:4] Herod's consultation with the chief priests and scribes has some similarity to a Jewish legend about the child Moses in which the "sacred scribes" warn Pharaoh about the imminent birth of one who will deliver Israel from Egypt and the king makes plans to destroy him.

---

i. [1:12–16] 1 Chr 3:16–19.   j. [1:20] 2:13, 19; Lk 1:35.   k. [1:23] Is 7:14 LXX.   l. [1:25] Lk 2:7.   m. [2:2] Nm 24:17.   n. [2:5–6] Mi 5:1; 2 Sm 5:2.

to him, "In Bethlehem of Judea, for thus it has been written through the prophet:

6 'And you, Bethlehem, land of Judah,
　　are by no means least among the
　　　rulers of Judah;
　since from you shall come a ruler,
　　who is to shepherd my people
　　　Israel.'"

[7]Then Herod called the magi secretly and ascertained from them the time of the star's appearance. [8]He sent them to Bethlehem and said, "Go and search diligently for the child. When you have found him, bring me word, that I too may go and do him homage." [9]After their audience with the king they set out. And behold, the star that they had seen at its rising preceded them, until it came and stopped over the place where the child was. [10]They were overjoyed at seeing the star, [11]°and on entering the house they saw the child with Mary his mother. They prostrated themselves and did him homage. Then they opened their treasures and offered him gifts of gold, frankincense, and myrrh. [12]And having been warned in a dream not to return to Herod, they departed for their country by another way.

The Flight to Egypt. [13†]When they had departed, behold, the angel of the Lord appeared to Joseph in a dream and said, "Rise, take the child and his mother, flee to Egypt,‡ and stay there until I tell you. Herod is going to search for the child to destroy him." [14]Joseph rose and took the child and his mother by night and departed for Egypt. [15§]He stayed there until the death of Herod, that what the Lord had said through the prophet[p] might be fulfilled, "Out of Egypt I called my son." **The Massacre of the Infants.** [16]When Herod realized that he had been deceived by the magi, he became furious. He ordered the massacre of all the boys in Bethlehem and its vicinity two years old and under, in accordance with the time he had ascertained from the magi. [17]Then was fulfilled what had been said through Jeremiah the prophet:

18 [q]"A voice was heard in Ramah,
　　sobbing and loud lamentation;
　Rachel weeping for her children,
　　and she would not be consoled,
　　since they were no more."

The Return from Egypt. [19]When Herod had died, behold, the angel of the Lord appeared in a dream to Joseph in Egypt [20]and said,[r] "Rise, take the child and his mother and go to the land of Israel, for those who sought the child's life are dead."* [21]He rose, took the child and his mother, and went to the land of Israel. [22]But when he heard that Archelaus was ruling over Judea in place of his father Herod,†† he was afraid to go back there. And because he had been warned in a dream, he departed for the region of Galilee. [23‡‡s]He went and dwelt in a town called Nazareth, so that what had been spoken through the prophets might be fulfilled, "He shall be called a Nazorean."

II. THE PROCLAMATION OF THE KINGDOM

CHAPTER 3

The Preaching of John the Baptist.[§§t] [1]In those days John the Baptist appeared, preaching in the desert of Judea[¶] [2][and] saying, "Repent,*** for

---

¶[2:18] Jer 31:15 portrays Rachel, wife of the patriarch Jacob, weeping for her children taken into exile at the time of the Assyrian invasion of the northern kingdom (722–21 B.C.). Bethlehem was traditionally identified with Ephrath, the place near which Rachel was buried (see Gn 35:19; 48:7), and the mourning of Rachel is here applied to her lost children of a later age. **Ramah:** about six miles north of Jerusalem. The lamentation of Rachel is so great as to be heard at a far distance.

[2:20] For those who sought the child's life are dead: Moses, who had fled from Egypt because the Pharaoh sought to kill him (see Ex 2:15), was told to return there, "for all the men who sought your life are dead" (Ex 4:19).

††[2:22] With the agreement of the emperor Augustus, Archelaus received half of his father's kingdom, including Judea, after Herod's death. He had the title "ethnarch" (i.e., "ruler of a nation") and reigned from 4 B.C. to A.D. 6.

‡‡[2:23] **Nazareth . . . he shall be called a Nazorean:** the tradition of Jesus' residence in Nazareth was firmly established, and Matthew sees it as being in accordance with the foreannounced plan of God. The town of Nazareth is not mentioned in the Old Testament, and no such prophecy can be found there. The vague expression "through the prophets" may be due to Matthew's seeing a connection between Nazareth and certain texts in which there are words with a remote similarity to the name of that town. Some such Old Testament texts are Is 11:1 where the Davidic king of the future is called "a bud" (*nēṣer*) that shall blossom from the roots of Jesse, and Jgs 13:5, 7 where Samson, the future deliverer of Israel from the Philistines, is called one who shall be consecrated (a *nāzîr*) to God.

§§[3:1–12] Here Matthew takes up the order of Jesus' ministry found in the gospel of Mark, beginning with the preparatory preaching of John the Baptist.

¶¶[3:1] Unlike Luke, Matthew says nothing of the Baptist's origins and does not make him a relative of Jesus. **The desert of Judea:** the barren region west of the Dead Sea extending up the Jordan valley.

***[3:2] **Repent:** the Baptist calls for a change of heart and conduct, a turning of one's life from rebellion to obedience towards God. **The kingdom of heaven is at hand:** "heaven"

---

*[2:11] Cf. Ps 72:10, 15; Is 60:6. These Old Testament texts led to the interpretation of the magi as kings.

†[2:13–23] Biblical and nonbiblical traditions about Moses are here applied to the child Jesus, though the dominant Old Testament type is not Moses but Israel (Mt 2:15).

‡[2:13] **Flee to Egypt:** Egypt was a traditional place of refuge for those fleeing from danger in Palestine (see 1 Kgs 11:40; Jer 26:21), but the main reason why the child is to be taken to Egypt is that he may relive the Exodus experience of Israel.

§[2:15] The fulfillment citation is taken from Hos 11:1. Israel, God's son, was called out of Egypt at the time of the Exodus; Jesus, the Son of God, will similarly be called out of that land in a new exodus. The father-son relationship between God and the nation is set in a higher key. Here the son is not a group adopted as "son of God," but the child who, as conceived by the holy Spirit, stands in unique relation to God. He is son of David and of Abraham, of Mary and of Joseph, but, above all, of God.

---

o. [2:11] Ps 72:10–11, 15; Is 60:6.　p. [2:15] Hos 11:1.

q. [2:18] Jer 31:15.　r. [2:20] Ex 4:19.　s. [2:23] 13:54; Mk 1:9; Lk 2:39; 4:34; Jn 19:19.　t. [3:1–12] Mk 1:2–8; Lk 3:2–17.

the kingdom of heaven is at hand!"ᵘ ³*It was of him that the prophet Isaiahᵛ had spoken when he said:

"A voice of one crying out in the desert,
  'Prepare the way of the Lord,
    make straight his paths.'"

⁴†ʷJohn wore clothing made of camel's hair and had a leather belt around his waist. His food was locusts and wild honey. ⁵At that time Jerusalem, all Judea, and the whole region around the Jordan were going out to him ⁶and were being baptized by him in the Jordan River as they acknowledged their sins.‡ ⁷When he saw many of the Pharisees and Sadducees§ coming to his baptism, he said to them, "You brood of vipers! Who warned you to flee from the coming wrath?ˣ ⁸Produce good fruit as evidence of your repentance. ⁹And do not presume to say to yourselves, 'We have Abraham as our father.' For I tell you, God can raise up children to Abraham from these stones.ʸ ¹⁰Even now the ax lies at the root of the trees. Therefore every tree that does not bear good fruit will be cut down and thrown into the fire. ¹¹ᶻI am baptizing you with water, for repentance, but the one who is coming after me is mightier than I. I am not worthy to carry his sandals. He will baptize you with the holy Spirit and fire.⁋

¹²**ᵃHis winnowing fan is in his hand. He will clear his threshing floor and gather his wheat into his barn, but the chaff he will burn with unquenchable fire."

The Baptism of Jesus.†† ¹³ᵇThen Jesus came from Galilee to John at the Jordan to be baptized by him. ¹⁴‡‡John tried to prevent him, saying, "I need to be baptized by you, and yet you are coming to me?" ¹⁵Jesus said to him in reply, "Allow it now, for thus it is fitting for us to fulfill all righteousness." Then he allowed him. ¹⁶§§ᶜAfter Jesus was baptized, he came up from the water and behold, the heavens were opened [for him], and he saw the Spirit of God descending like a dove [and] coming upon him. ¹⁷And a voice came from the heavens, saying, "This is my beloved Son,⁋⁋ with whom I am well pleased."ᵈ

CHAPTER 4

The Temptation of Jesus. ¹***ᵉThen Jesus was led by the Spirit into the desert to be tempted by the devil. ²ᶠHe fasted for forty days and forty nights,†††

(lit., "the heavens") is a substitute for the name "God" that was avoided by devout Jews of the time out of reverence. The expression "the kingdom of heaven" occurs only in the gospel of Matthew. It means the effective rule of God over his people. In its fullness it includes not only human obedience to God's word, but the triumph of God over physical evils, supremely over death. In the expectation found in Jewish apocalyptic, the kingdom was to be ushered in by a judgment in which sinners would be condemned and perish, an expectation shared by the Baptist. This was modified in Christian understanding where the kingdom was seen as being established in stages, culminating with the parousia of Jesus.

*[3:3] See note on Jn 1:23.

†[3:4] The clothing of John recalls the austere dress of the prophet Elijah (2 Kgs 1:8). The expectation of the return of Elijah from heaven to prepare Israel for the final manifestation of God's kingdom was widespread, and according to Matthew this expectation was fulfilled in the Baptist's ministry (Mt 11:14; 17:11–13).

‡[3:6] Ritual washing was practiced by various groups in Palestine between 150 B.C. and A.D. 250. John's baptism may have been related to the purificatory washings of the Essenes at Qumran.

§[3:7] **Pharisees and Sadducees**: the former were marked by devotion to the law, written and oral, and the scribes, experts in the law, belonged predominantly to this group. The Sadducees were the priestly aristocratic party, centered in Jerusalem. They accepted as scripture only the first five books of the Old Testament, followed only the letter of the law, rejected the oral legal traditions, and were opposed to teachings not found in the Pentateuch, such as the resurrection of the dead. Matthew links both of these groups together as enemies of Jesus (Mt 16:1, 6, 11, 12; cf. Mk 8:11–13, 15). The threatening words that follow are addressed to them rather than to "the crowds" as in Lk 3:7. **The coming wrath**: the judgment that will bring about the destruction of unrepentant sinners.

⁋[3:11] **Baptize you with the holy Spirit and fire**: the water baptism of John will be followed by an "immersion" of the repentant in the cleansing power of the Spirit of God,

and of the unrepentant in the destroying power of God's judgment. However, some see **the holy Spirit** and **fire** as synonymous, and the effect of this "baptism" as either purification or destruction. See note on Lk 3:16.

[3:12] The discrimination between the good and the bad is compared to the procedure by which a farmer separates wheat and chaff. The **winnowing fan was a forklike shovel with which the threshed wheat was thrown into the air. The kernels fell to the ground; the light chaff, blown off by the wind, was gathered and burned up.

††[3:13–17] The baptism of Jesus is the occasion on which he is equipped for his ministry by the holy Spirit and proclaimed to be the Son of God.

‡‡[3:14–15] This dialogue, peculiar to Matthew, reveals John's awareness of Jesus' superiority to him as the mightier one who is coming and who will baptize with the holy Spirit (Mt 3:11). His reluctance to admit Jesus among the sinners whom he is baptizing with water is overcome by Jesus' response. **To fulfill all righteousness**: in this gospel to **fulfill** usually refers to fulfillment of prophecy, and **righteousness** to moral conduct in conformity with God's will. Here, however, as in Mt 5:6; 6:33, **righteousness** seems to mean the saving activity of God. **To fulfill all righteousness** is to submit to the plan of God for the salvation of the human race. This involves Jesus' identification with sinners; hence the propriety of his accepting John's baptism.

§§[3:16] **The Spirit . . . coming upon him**: cf. Is 42:1.

⁋⁋[3:17] **This is my beloved Son**: the Marcan address to Jesus (Mk 1:11) is changed into a proclamation. The Father's voice speaks in terms that reflect Is 42:1; Ps 2:7; Gn 22:2.

***[4:1–11] Jesus, proclaimed Son of God at his baptism, is subjected to a triple temptation. Obedience to the Father is a characteristic of true sonship, and Jesus is tempted by the devil to rebel against God, overtly in the third case, more subtly in the first two. Each refusal of Jesus is expressed in language taken from the Book of Deuteronomy (Dt 8:3; 6:13, 16). The testings of Jesus resemble those of Israel during the wandering in the desert and later in Canaan, and the victory of Jesus, the true Israel and the true Son, contrasts with the failure of the ancient and disobedient "son," the old Israel. In the temptation account Matthew is almost identical with Luke; both seem to have drawn upon the same source.

†††[4:2] **Forty days and forty nights**: the same time as that during which Moses remained on Sinai (Ex 24:18). The time reference, however, seems primarily intended to recall the

---

u. [3:2] 4:17; 10:7.   v. [3:3] Is 40:3.   w. [3:4] 11:7–8; 2 Kgs 1:8; Zec 13:4.   x. [3:7] 12:34; 23:33; Is 59:5.   y. [3:9] Jn 8:33, 39; Rom 9:7–8; Gal 4:21–31.   z. [3:11] Jn 1:26–27, 33; Acts 1:5.

a. [3:12] 13:30; Is 41:16; Jer 15:7.   b. [3:13–17] Mk 1:9–11; Lk 3:21–22; Jn 1:31–34.   c. [3:16] Is 42:1.   d. [3:17] 12:18; 17:5; Gn 22:2; Ps 2:7; Is 42:1.   e. [4:1–11] Mk 1:12–13; Lk 4:1–13.   f. [4:2] Ex 24:18; Dt 8:2.

and afterwards he was hungry. [3]The tempter approached and said to him, "If you are the Son of God, command that these stones become loaves of bread." [4]He said in reply, "It is written:[g]

> 'One does not live by bread alone,
>   but by every word that comes forth
>   from the mouth of God.'"

[5†]Then the devil took him to the holy city, and made him stand on the parapet of the temple, [6]and said to him, "If you are the Son of God, throw yourself down. For it is written:

> 'He will command his angels concerning
>   you'
> and 'with their hands they will
>   support you,
> lest you dash your foot against a stone.'"[h]

[7]Jesus answered him, "Again it is written, 'You shall not put the Lord, your God, to the test.'"[i] [8]Then the devil took him up to a very high mountain, and showed him all the kingdoms of the world in their magnificence, [9]and he said to him, "All these I shall give to you, if you will prostrate yourself and worship me."[‡] [10]At this, Jesus said to him, "Get away, Satan! It is written:

> 'The Lord, your God, shall you worship
>   and him alone shall you serve.'"[j]

[11]Then the devil left him and, behold, angels came and ministered to him.

The Beginning of the Galilean Ministry.[§] [12k]When he heard that John had been arrested, he withdrew to Galilee. [13]He left Nazareth and went to live in Capernaum by the sea, in the region of Zebulun and Naphtali,[l] [14]that what had been said through Isaiah the prophet might be fulfilled:

> [15] "Land of Zebulun and land of Naphtali,[m]
>   the way to the sea, beyond the
>   Jordan,
>   Galilee of the Gentiles,
> [16] the people who sit in darkness
>   have seen a great light,
> on those dwelling in a land overshadowed
>   by death
>   light has arisen."[n]

[17]¶From that time on, Jesus began to preach and say,[o] "Repent, for the kingdom of heaven is at hand."

The Call of the First Disciples.[**] [18p]As he was walking by the Sea of Galilee, he saw two brothers, Simon who is called Peter, and his brother Andrew, casting a net into the sea; they were fishermen. [19]He said to them, "Come after me, and I will make you fishers of men." [20††]At once they left their nets and followed him. [21]He walked along from there and saw two other brothers, James, the son of Zebedee, and his brother John. They were in a boat, with their father Zebedee, mending their nets. He called them, [22]and immediately they left their boat and their father and followed him.

Ministering to a Great Multitude.[‡‡] [23]He went around all of Galilee, teaching in their synagogues,[§§] proclaiming the gospel of the kingdom, and curing every disease and illness among the people.[q] [24]¶His fame spread to all of Syria, and they brought to him all who were sick with various diseases and racked with pain, those who were possessed, lunatics, and paralytics, and he cured them. [25]And great crowds from Galilee, the Decapolis,[***] Jerusalem, and Judea, and from beyond the Jordan followed him.

---

forty years during which Israel was tempted in the desert (Dt 8:2).

*[4:4] Cf. Dt 8:3. Jesus refuses to use his power for his own benefit and accepts whatever God wills.

†[4:5–7] The devil supports his proposal by an appeal to the scriptures, Ps 91:11a, 12. Unlike Israel (Dt 6:16), Jesus refuses to "test" God by demanding from him an extraordinary show of power.

‡[4:9] The worship of Satan to which Jesus is tempted is probably intended to recall Israel's worship of false gods. His refusal is expressed in the words of Dt 6:13.

§[4:12–17] Isaiah's prophecy of the light rising upon Zebulun and Naphtali (Is 8:22–9:1) is fulfilled in Jesus' residence at Capernaum. The territory of these two tribes was the first to be devastated (733–32 B.C.) at the time of the Assyrian invasion. In order to accommodate Jesus' move to Capernaum to the prophecy, Matthew speaks of that town as being "in the region of Zebulun and Naphtali" (Mt 4:13), whereas it was only in the territory of the latter, and he understands the sea of the prophecy, the Mediterranean, as the sea of Galilee.

¶[4:17] At the beginning of his preaching Jesus takes up the words of John the Baptist (Mt 3:2) although with a different meaning; in his ministry the kingdom of heaven has already begun to be present (Mt 12:28).

**[4:18–22] The call of the first disciples promises them a share in Jesus' work and entails abandonment of family and former way of life. Three of the four, Simon, James, and John, are distinguished among the disciples by a closer relation with Jesus (Mt 17:1; 26:37).

††[4:20] Here and in Mt 4:22, as in Mark (Mk 1:16–20) and unlike the Lucan account (Lk 5:1–11), the disciples' response is motivated only by Jesus' invitation, an element that emphasizes his mysterious power.

‡‡[4:23–25] This summary of Jesus' ministry concludes the narrative part of the first book of Matthew's gospel (Mt 3–4). The activities of his ministry are teaching, proclaiming the gospel, and healing; cf. Mt 9:35.

§§[4:23] **Their synagogues**: Matthew usually designates the Jewish synagogues as **their synagogue(s)** (Mt 9:35; 10:17; 12:9; 13:54) or, in address to Jews, **your synagogues** (Mt 23:34), an indication that he wrote after the break between church and synagogue.

¶¶[4:24] **Syria**: the Roman province to which Palestine belonged.

***[4:25] **The Decapolis**: a federation of Greek cities in Palestine, originally ten in number, all but one east of the Jordan.

---

g. [4:4] Dt 8:3.   h. [4:6] Ps 91:11–12.   i. [4:7] Dt 6:16.   j. [4:10] 16:23; Dt 6:13.   k. [4:12–13] Mk 1:14–15; Lk 4:14, 31.   l. [4:13] Jn 2:12.

m. [4:15–16] Is 8:23 LXX; 9:1.   n. [4:16] Lk 1:79.   o. [4:17] 3:2.   p. [4:18–22] Mk 1:16–20; Lk 5:1–11.   q. [4:23] 9:35; Mk 1:39; Lk 4:15, 44.   r. [4:25] Mk 3:7–8; Lk 6:17–19.

CHAPTER 5

The Sermon on the Mount. [1]*When he saw the crowds,[†] he went up the mountain, and after he had sat down, his disciples came to him. [2]He began to teach them, saying:

The Beatitudes[‡]

[3] "Blessed are the poor in spirit,[§]
   for theirs is the kingdom of heaven.[s]
[4] 'Blessed are they who mourn,[t]
   for they will be comforted.
[5] "Blessed are the meek,[u]
   for they will inherit the land.
[6] Blessed are they who hunger and thirst
      for righteousness,[††]
   for they will be satisfied.
[7] Blessed are the merciful,
   for they will be shown mercy.[v]
[8] ‡‡Blessed are the clean of heart,[w]
   for they will see God.
[9] Blessed are the peacemakers,
   for they will be called children of
      God.

[10] Blessed are they who are persecuted for
      the sake of righteousness,[§§]
   for theirs is the kingdom of heaven.[x]

[11]Blessed are you when they insult you and persecute you and utter every kind of evil against you [falsely] because of me.[y] [12]¶¶Rejoice and be glad, for your reward will be great in heaven.[z] Thus they persecuted the prophets who were before you.

The Similes of Salt and Light.[***] [13a]"You are the salt of the earth. But if salt loses its taste, with what can it be seasoned? It is no longer good for anything but to be thrown out and trampled underfoot.[†††] [14]You are the light of the world. A city set on a mountain cannot be hidden.[b] [15]Nor do they light a lamp and then put it under a bushel basket; it is set on a lampstand, where it gives light to all in the house.[c] [16]Just so,'your light must shine before others, that they may see your good deeds and glorify your heavenly Father.[d]

Teaching About the Law. [17]‡‡‡"Do not think that I have come to abolish the law or the prophets. I have come not to abolish but to fulfill. [18]Amen, I say to you, until heaven and earth pass away, not the smallest letter or the smallest part of a letter will pass from the law, until all things have taken place.[e] [19]Therefore, whoever breaks one of the least of these commandments and teaches others to do so will be called least in the kingdom of heaven. But whoever obeys and teaches these commandments will be called greatest in

---

*[5:1–7:29] The first of the five discourses that are a central part of the structure of this gospel. It is the discourse section of the first book and contains sayings of Jesus derived from Q and from M. The Lucan parallel is in that gospel's "Sermon on the Plain" (Lk 6:20–49), although some of the sayings in Matthew's "Sermon on the Mount" have their parallels in other parts of Luke. The careful topical arrangement of the sermon is probably not due only to Matthew's editing; he seems to have had a structured discourse of Jesus as one of his sources. The form of that source may have been as follows: four beatitudes (Mt 5:3–4, 6, 11–12), a section on the new righteousness with illustrations (Mt 5:17, 20–24, 27–28, 33–48), a section on good works (Mt 6:1–6, 16–18), and three warnings (Mt 7:1–2, 15–21, 24–27).

†[5:1–2] Unlike Luke's sermon, this is addressed not only to the disciples but to the crowds (see Mt 7:28).

‡[5:3–12] The form **Blessed are (is)** occurs frequently in the Old Testament in the Wisdom literature and in the psalms. Although modified by Matthew, the first, second, fourth, and ninth beatitudes have Lucan parallels (Mt 5:3 // Lk 6:20; Mt 5:4 // Lk 6:21b; Mt 5:6 // Lk 6:21a; Mt 5:11–12 // Lk 5:22–23). The others were added by the evangelist and are probably his own composition. A few manuscripts, Western and Alexandrian, and many versions and patristic quotations give the second and third beatitudes in inverted order.

§[5:3] **The poor in spirit**: in the Old Testament, the poor ('anāwîm) are those who are without material possessions and whose confidence is in God (see Is 61:1; Zep 2:3; in the NAB the word is translated lowly and humble, respectively, in those texts). Matthew added **in spirit** in order either to indicate that only the devout poor were meant or to extend the beatitude to all, of whatever social rank, who recognized their complete dependence on God. The same phrase **poor in spirit** is found in the Qumran literature (1QM 14:7).

¶[5:4] Cf. Is 61:2, "(The Lord has sent me) . . . to comfort all who mourn." **They will be comforted**: here the passive is a "theological passive" equivalent to the active "God will comfort them"; so also in Mt 5:6, 7.

**[5:5] Cf. Ps 37:11, ". . . the meek shall possess the land." In the psalm "the land" means the land of Palestine; here it means the kingdom.

††[5:6] **For righteousness**: a Matthean addition. For the meaning of **righteousness** here, see note on Mt 3:14–15.

‡‡[5:8] Cf. Ps 24:4. Only one "whose heart is clean" can take part in the temple worship. To be with God in the temple is described in Ps 42:3 as "beholding his face," but here the promise to **the clean of heart** is that they will **see God** not in the temple but in the coming kingdom.

§§[5:10] **Righteousness** here, as usually in Matthew, means conduct in conformity with God's will.

¶¶[5:12] **The prophets who were before you**: the disciples of Jesus stand in the line of the persecuted prophets of Israel. Some would see the expression as indicating also that Matthew considered all Christian disciples as prophets.

***[5:13–16] By their deeds the disciples are to influence the world for good. They can no more escape notice than **a city set on a mountain**. If they fail in good works, they are as useless as flavorless salt or as a lamp whose light is concealed.

†††[5:13] The unusual supposition of salt losing its flavor has led some to suppose that the saying refers to the salt of the Dead Sea that, because chemically impure, could lose its taste.

‡‡‡[5:17–20] This statement of Jesus' position concerning the Mosaic law is composed of traditional material from Matthew's sermon documentation (see note on Mt 5:1–7:29), other Q material (cf. Mt 18; Lk 16:17), and the evangelist's own editorial touches. **To fulfill** the law appears at first to mean a literal enforcement of the law in the least detail: **until heaven and earth pass away** nothing of the law **will pass** (Mt 5:18). Yet the "passing away" of heaven and earth is not necessarily the end of the world understood, as in much apocalyptic literature, as the dissolution of the existing universe. The "turning of the ages" comes with the apocalyptic event of Jesus' death and resurrection, and those to whom this gospel is addressed are living in the new and final age, prophesied by Isaiah as the time of "new heavens and a new earth" (Is 65:17; 66:22). Meanwhile, during Jesus' ministry when the kingdom is already breaking in, his mission remains within the framework of the law, though with significant anticipation of the age to come, as the following antitheses (Mt 5:21–48) show.

---

s. [5:3–12] Lk 6:20–23.   t. [5:4] Is 61:2–3; Rev 21:4.   u. [5:5] Gn 13:15; Ps 37:11.   v. [5:7] 18:33; Jas 2:13.   w. [5:8] Ps 24:4–5; 73:1.

x. [5:10] 1 Pt 2:20; 3:14; 4:14.   y. [5:11] 10:22; Acts 5:41.   z. [5:12] 2 Chr 36:16; Heb 11:32–38; Jas 5:10.   a. [5:13] Mk 9:50; Lk 14:34–35.   b. [5:14] Jn 8:12.   c. [5:15] Mk 4:21; Lk 8:16; 11:33.   d. [5:16] Jn 3:21.   e. [5:18] Lk 16:17.

MATTHEW 5

13

the kingdom of heaven.* ²⁰I tell you, unless your righteousness surpasses that of the scribes and Pharisees, you will not enter into the kingdom of heaven.

Teaching About Anger.† ²¹"You have heard that it was said to your ancestors,ᶠ 'You shall not kill; and whoever kills will be liable to judgment.'‡ ²²§But I say to you, whoever is angryˢ with his brother will be liable to judgment,ᵍ and whoever says to his brother, 'Raqa,' will be answerable to the Sanhedrin, and whoever says, 'You fool,' will be liable to fiery Gehenna. ²³Therefore, if you bring your gift to the altar, and there recall that your brother has anything against you,ʰ ²⁴leave your gift there at the altar, go first and be reconciled with your brother, and then come and offer your gift. ²⁵Settle with your opponent quickly while on the way to court with him.ⁱ Otherwise your opponent will hand you over to the judge, and the judge will hand you over to the guard, and you will be thrown into prison. ²⁶Amen, I say to you, you will not be released until you have paid the last penny.

Teaching About Adultery. ²⁷"'You have heard that it was said,ʲ 'You shall not commit adultery.' ²⁸But I say to you, everyone who looks at a woman with lust has already committed adultery

with her in his heart. ²⁹††If your right eye causes you to sin, tear it out and throw it away.ᵏ It is better for you to lose one of your members than to have your whole body thrown into Gehenna. ³⁰And if your right hand causes you to sin, cut it off and throw it away. It is better for you to lose one of your members than to have your whole body go into Gehenna.

Teaching About Divorce. ³¹‡‡"It was also said, 'Whoever divorces his wife must give her a bill of divorce.'ˡ ³²But I say to you, whoever divorces his wife (unless the marriage is unlawful) causes her to commit adultery, and whoever marries a divorced woman commits adultery.ᵐ

Teaching About Oaths. ³³§§ⁿ"Again you have heard that it was said to your ancestors, 'Do not take a false oath, but make good to the Lord all that you vow.' ³⁴But I say to you, do not swear at all;¶¶ not by heaven, for it is God's throne; ³⁵nor by the earth, for it is his footstool; nor by Jerusalem, for it is the city of the great King. ³⁶Do not swear by your head, for you cannot make a single hair white or black. ³⁷"'Let your 'Yes' mean 'Yes,' and your 'No' mean 'No.' Anything more is from the evil one.

Teaching About Retaliation. ³⁸†††"You have heard that it was said,ᵖ 'An eye for an eye and a tooth

---

*[5:19] Probably **these commandments** means those of the Mosaic law. But this is an interim ethic "until heaven and earth pass away."

†[5:21–48] Six examples of the conduct demanded of the Christian disciple. Each deals with a commandment of the law, introduced by **You have heard that it was said to your ancestors** or an equivalent formula, followed by Jesus' teaching in respect to that commandment, **But I say to you**; thus their designation as "antitheses." Three of them accept the Mosaic law but extend or deepen it (Mt 5:21–22; 27–28; 43–44); three reject it as a standard of conduct for the disciples (Mt 5:31–32; 33–37; 38–39).

‡[5:21] Cf. Ex 20:13; Dt 5:17. The second part of the verse is not an exact quotation from the Old Testament, but cf. Ex 21:12.

§[5:22–26] Reconciliation with an offended brother is urged in the admonition of Mt 5:23–24 and the parable of Mt 5:25–26 (// Lk 12:58–59). The severity of the judge in the parable is a warning of the fate of unrepentant sinners in the coming judgment by God.

¶[5:22] Anger is the motive behind murder, as the insulting epithets are steps that may lead to it. They, as well as the deed, are all forbidden. **Raqa:** an Aramaic word *rêqā'* or *rêqâ* probably meaning "imbecile," "blockhead," a term of abuse. The ascending order of punishment, **judgment** (by a local council?), trial before the **Sanhedrin**, condemnation to **Gehenna**, points to a higher degree of seriousness in each of the offenses. **Sanhedrin:** the highest judicial body of Judaism. **Gehenna:** in Hebrew *gê-hinnōm*, "Valley of Hinnom," or *gê ben-hinnōm*, "Valley of the son of Hinnom," southwest of Jerusalem, the center of an idolatrous cult during the monarchy in which children were offered in sacrifice (see 2 Kgs 23:10; Jer 7:31). In Jos 18:16 (Septuagint, Codex Vaticanus) the Hebrew is transliterated into Greek as *gaienna*, which appears in the New Testament as *geenna*. The concept of punishment of sinners by fire either after death or after the final judgment is found in Jewish apocalyptic literature (e.g., Enoch 90:26) but the name *geenna* is first given to the place of punishment in the New Testament.

**[5:27] See Ex 20:14; Dt 5:18.

f. [5:21] Ex 20:13; Dt 5:17. g. [5:22] Jas 1:19–20. h. [5:23] Mk 11:25. i. [5:25–26] 18:34–35; Lk 12:58–59. j. [5:27] Ex 20:14; Dt 5:18.

††[5:29–30] No sacrifice is too great to avoid total destruction in **Gehenna**.

‡‡[5:31–32] See Dt 24:1–5. The Old Testament commandment that a bill of divorce be given to the woman assumes the legitimacy of divorce itself. It is this that Jesus denies. (**Unless the marriage is unlawful**): this "exceptive clause," as it is often called, occurs also in Mt 19:9, where the Greek is slightly different. There are other sayings of Jesus about divorce that prohibit it absolutely (see Mk 10:11–12; Lk 16:18; cf. 1 Cor 7:10, 11b), and most scholars agree that they represent the stand of Jesus. Matthew's "exceptive clauses" are understood by some as a modification of the absolute prohibition. It seems, however, that the unlawfulness that Matthew gives as a reason why a marriage must be broken refers to a situation peculiar to his community: the violation of Mosaic law forbidding marriage between persons of certain blood and/or legal relationship (Lv 18:6–18). Marriages of that sort were regarded as incest (*porneia*), but some rabbis allowed Gentile converts to Judaism who had contracted such marriages to remain in them. Matthew's "exceptive clause" is against such permissiveness for Gentile converts to Christianity; cf. the similar prohibition of *porneia* in Acts 15:20, 29. In this interpretation, the clause constitutes no exception to the absolute prohibition of divorce when the marriage is lawful.

§§[5:33] This is not an exact quotation of any Old Testament text, but see Ex 20:7; Dt 5:11; Lv 19:12. The purpose of an oath was to guarantee truthfulness by one's calling on God as witness.

¶¶[5:34–36] The use of these oath formularies that avoid the divine name is in fact equivalent to swearing by it, for all the things sworn by are related to God.

***[5:37] **Let your 'Yes' mean 'Yes,' and your 'No' mean 'No':** literally, "let your speech be 'Yes, yes,' 'No, no.'" Some have understood this as a milder form of oath, permitted by Jesus. In view of Mt 5:34, "Do not swear at all," that is unlikely. **From the evil one:** i.e., from the devil. Oath-taking presupposes a sinful weakness of the human race, namely, the tendency to lie. Jesus demands of his disciples a truthfulness that makes oaths unnecessary.

†††[5:38–42] See Lv 24:20. The Old Testament commandment was meant to moderate vengeance; the punishment

k. [5:29–30] 18:8–9; Mk 9:43–47. l. [5:31] 19:3–9; Dt 24:1. m. [5:32] Lk 16:18; 1 Cor 7:10–11. n. [5:33] Lv 19:12; Nm 30:3. o. [5:34–37] Ps 48:3; Sir 23:9; Is 66:1; Jas 5:12. p. [5:38] Ex 21:24; Lv 24:19–20.

for a tooth.' ³⁹ᵠBut I say to you, offer no resistance to one who is evil. When someone strikes you on [your] right cheek, turn the other one to him as well. ⁴⁰If anyone wants to go to law with you over your tunic, hand him your cloak as well. ⁴¹Should anyone press you into service for one mile,ʳ go with him for two miles.ʳ ⁴²Give to the one who asks of you, and do not turn your back on one who wants to borrow.ˢ

Love of Enemies.† ⁴³"You have heard that it was said, 'You shall love your neighbor and hate your enemy.'ᵘ ⁴⁴But I say to you, love your enemies, and pray for those who persecute you, ⁴⁵that you may be children of your heavenly Father, for he makes his sun rise on the bad and the good, and causes rain to fall on the just and the unjust. ⁴⁶For if you love those who love you, what recompense will you have? Do not the tax collectors‡ do the same? ⁴⁷And if you greet your brothers only, what is unusual about that? Do not the pagans do the same?§ ⁴⁸So be perfect,⁵ just as your heavenly Father is perfect.ᵛ

CHAPTER 6

Teaching About Almsgiving.** ¹"[But] take care not to perform righteous deeds in order that people may see them;ʷ otherwise, you will have no recompense from your heavenly Father. ²When you give alms, do not blow a trumpet

---

should not exceed the injury done. Jesus forbids even this proportionate retaliation. Of the five examples that follow, only the first deals directly with retaliation for evil; the others speak of liberality.

*[5:41] Roman garrisons in Palestine had the right to requisition the property and services of the native population.

†[5:43–48] There is no Old Testament commandment demanding hatred of one's enemy, but the "neighbor" of the love commandment was understood as one's fellow countryman. Both in the Old Testament (Ps 139:19–22) and at Qumran (1QS 9:21) hatred of evil persons is assumed to be right. Jesus extends the love commandment to the enemy and the persecutor. His disciples, as children of God, must imitate the example of their Father, who grants his gifts of sun and rain to both the good and the bad.

‡[5:46] **Tax collectors**: Jews who were engaged in the collection of indirect taxes such as tolls and customs. See note on Mk 2:14.

§[5:47] Jesus' disciples must not be content with merely usual standards of conduct; see Mt 5:20 where the verb "surpass" (Greek *perisseuō*) is cognate with the **unusual** (*perisson*) of this verse.

¶[5:48] **Perfect**: in the gospels this word occurs only in Matthew, here and in Mt 19:21. The Lucan parallel (Lk 6:36) demands that the disciples be **merciful**.

**[6:1–18] The sermon continues with a warning against doing good in order to be seen and gives three examples, almsgiving (Mt 6:2–4), prayer (Mt 6:5–15), and fasting (Mt 6:16–18). In each, the conduct of the hypocrites (Mt 6:2) is contrasted with that demanded of the disciples. The sayings about reward found here and elsewhere (Mt 5:12, 46; 10:41–42) show that this is a genuine element of Christian moral exhortation. Possibly to underline the difference between the Christian idea of reward and that of the hypocrites, the evangelist uses two different Greek verbs to express the rewarding of the disciples and that of the hypocrites; in the latter case it is the verb *apechō*, a commercial term for giving a receipt for what has been paid in full (Mt 6:2, 5, 16).

---

q. [5:39–42] Lk 6:29–30.   r. [5:41] Lam 3:30.   s. [5:42] Dt 15:7–8.   t. [5:43–48] Lk 6:27, 32–36.   u. [5:43] Lv 19:18.   v. [5:48] Lv 11:44; 19:2; Dt 18:13; Jas 1:4; 1 Pt 1:16; 1 Jn 3:3.   w. [6:1] 23:5.

---

before you, as the hypocrites†† do in the synagogues and in the streets to win the praise of others. Amen, I say to you, they have received their reward.ˣ ³But when you give alms, do not let your left hand know what your right is doing, ⁴so that your almsgiving may be secret. And your Father who sees in secret will repay you.

Teaching About Prayer. ⁵"When you pray, do not be like the hypocrites, who love to stand and pray in the synagogues and on street corners so that others may see them. Amen, I say to you, they have received their reward. ⁶But when you pray, go to your inner room, close the door, and pray to your Father in secret. And your Father who sees in secret will repay you. ⁷‡‡In praying, do not babble like the pagans, who think that they will be heard because of their many words.§§ ⁸Do not be like them. Your Father knows what you need before you ask him.

The Lord's Prayer. ⁹¶¶"This is how you are to pray:ʸ

Our Father in heaven,***
    hallowed be your name,
10   your kingdom come,†††
    your will be done,
        on earth as in heaven.ᶻ
11   ‡‡‡ᵃGive us today our daily bread;

---

††[6:2] **The hypocrites**: the scribes and Pharisees, see Mt 23:13, 15, 23, 25, 27, 29. The designation reflects an attitude resulting not only from the controversies at the time of Jesus' ministry but from the opposition between Pharisaic Judaism and the church of Matthew. **They have received their reward**: they desire praise and have received what they were looking for.

‡‡[6:7–15] Matthew inserts into his basic traditional material an expansion of the material on prayer that includes the model prayer, the "Our Father." That prayer is found in Lk 11:2–4 in a different context and in a different form.

§§[6:7] The example of what Christian prayer should be like contrasts it now not with the prayer of the hypocrites but with that of **the pagans**. Their babbling probably means their reciting a long list of divine names, hoping that one of them will force a response from the deity.

¶¶[6:9–13] Matthew's form of the "Our Father" follows the liturgical tradition of his church. Luke's less developed form also represents the liturgical tradition known to him, but it is probably closer than Matthew's to the original words of Jesus.

***[6:9] **Our Father in heaven**: this invocation is found in many rabbinic prayers of the post-New Testament period. **Hallowed be your name**: though the "hallowing" of the divine name could be understood as reverence done to God by human praise and by obedience to his will, this is more probably a petition that God hallow his own name, i.e., that he manifest his glory by an act of power (cf. Ez 36:23), in this case, by the establishment of his kingdom in its fullness.

†††[6:10] **Your kingdom come**: this petition sets the tone of the prayer, and inclines the balance toward divine rather than human action in the petitions that immediately precede and follow it. **Your will be done, on earth as in heaven**: a petition that the divine purpose to establish the kingdom, a purpose present now **in heaven**, be executed **on earth**.

‡‡‡[6:11] **Give us today our daily bread**: the rare Greek word *epiousios*, here **daily**, occurs in the New Testament only here and in Lk 11:3. A single occurrence of the word outside of these texts and of literature dependent on them has been claimed, but the claim is highly doubtful. The word may mean **daily** or "future" (other meanings have also been proposed). The latter would conform better to the eschatological tone of the whole prayer. So understood, the petition would be for a speedy coming of the kingdom (**today**), which is often

---

x. [6:2] Jn 12:43.   y. [6:9–13] Lk 11:2–4.   z. [6:10] 26:42.   a. [6:11] Prv 30:8–9.

12   and forgive us our debts,*
          as we forgive our debtors;[b]
13   and do not subject us to the final test,[†]
          but deliver us from the evil one.[c]

[14‡]If you forgive others their transgressions, your heavenly Father will forgive you.[d] [15]But if you do not forgive others, neither will your Father forgive your transgressions.[e]

Teaching About Fasting. [16]"When you fast,[§] do not look gloomy like the hypocrites. They neglect their appearance, so that they may appear to others to be fasting. Amen, I say to you, they have received their reward. [17]But when you fast, anoint your head and wash your face, [18]so that you may not appear to others to be fasting, except to your Father who is hidden. And your Father who sees what is hidden will repay you.

Treasure in Heaven. [19]¶"Do not store up for yourselves treasures on earth, where moth and decay destroy, and thieves break in and steal.[f] [20]But store up treasures in heaven, where neither moth nor decay destroys, nor thieves break in and steal. [21]For where your treasure is, there also will your heart be.[g]

The Light of the Body.** [22]"The lamp of the body is the eye. If your eye is sound, your whole body will be filled with light; [23]but if your eye is bad, your whole body will be in darkness. And if the light in you is darkness, how great will the darkness be.[h]

God and Money. [24††]"No one can serve two masters.[i] He will either hate one and love the other, or be devoted to one and despise the other. You cannot serve God and mammon.

Dependence on God.‡‡ [25i]"Therefore I tell you, do not worry about your life, what you will eat

[or drink], or about your body, what you will wear. Is not life more than food and the body more than clothing? [26]Look at the birds in the sky; they do not sow or reap, they gather nothing into barns, yet your heavenly Father feeds them. Are not you more important than they?[k] [27]Can any of you by worrying add a single moment to your life-span?[§§] [28]Why are you anxious about clothes? Learn from the way the wild flowers grow. They do not work or spin. [29]But I tell you that not even Solomon in all his splendor was clothed like one of them. [30]¶¶If God so clothes the grass of the field, which grows today and is thrown into the oven tomorrow, will he not much more provide for you, O you of little faith? [31]So do not worry and say, 'What are we to eat?' or 'What are we to drink?' or 'What are we to wear?' [32]All these things the pagans seek. Your heavenly Father knows that you need them all. [33]But seek first the kingdom [of God] and his righteousness,*** and all these things will be given you besides. [34]Do not worry about tomorrow; tomorrow will take care of itself. Sufficient for a day is its own evil.

CHAPTER 7

Judging Others. [1††††]"Stop judging,‡‡‡ that you may not be judged.[m] [2]For as you judge, so will you be judged, and the measure with which you measure will be measured out to you.[n] [3]Why do you notice the splinter in your brother's eye, but do not perceive the wooden beam in your own eye? [4]How can you say to your brother, 'Let me remove that splinter from your eye,' while the wooden beam is in your eye? [5]You hypocrite,§§§ remove the wooden beam from your eye first; then you will see clearly to remove the splinter from your brother's eye.

Pearls Before Swine. [6]"Do not give what is holy to dogs,¶¶¶ or throw your pearls before swine, lest

---

portrayed in both the Old Testament and the New under the image of a feast (Is 25:6; Mt 8:11; 22:1–10; Lk 13:29; 14:15–24).
*[6:12] **Forgive us our debts:** the word **debts** is used metaphorically of sins, "debts" owed to God (see Lk 11:4). The request is probably for forgiveness at the final judgment.
†[6:13] Jewish apocalyptic writings speak of a period of severe trial before the end of the age, sometimes called the "messianic woes." This petition asks that the disciples be spared that **final test**.
‡[6:14–15] These verses reflect a set pattern called "Principles of Holy Law." Human action now will be met by a corresponding action of God at the final judgment.
§[6:16] The only fast prescribed in the Mosaic law was that of the Day of Atonement (Lv 16:31), but the practice of regular fasting was common in later Judaism; cf. *Didache* 9:1.
¶[6:19–34] The remaining material of this chapter is taken almost entirely from Q. It deals principally with worldly possessions, and the controlling thought is summed up in Mt 6:24: the disciple can serve only one master and must choose between God and wealth (**mammon**). See further the note on Lk 16:9.
**[6:22–23] In this context the parable probably points to the need for the disciple to be enlightened by Jesus' teaching on the transitory nature of earthly riches.
††[6:24] **Mammon:** an Aramaic word meaning wealth or property.
‡‡[6:25–34] Jesus does not deny the reality of human needs (Mt 6:32), but forbids making them the object of anxious care and, in effect, becoming their slave.

§§[6:27] **Life-span:** the Greek word can also mean "stature." If it is taken in that sense, the word here translated **moment** (literally, "cubit") must be translated literally as a unit not of time but of spatial measure. The cubit is about eighteen inches.
¶¶[6:30] **Of little faith:** except for the parallel in Lk 12:28, the word translated **of little faith** is found in the New Testament only in Matthew. It is used by him of those who are disciples of Jesus but whose faith in him is not as deep as it should be (see Mt 8:26; 14:31; 16:8 and the cognate noun in Mt 17:20).
***[6:33] **Righteousness:** see note on Mt 3:14–15.
†††[7:1–12] In Mt 7:1 Matthew returns to the basic traditional material of the sermon (Lk 6:37–38, 41–42). The governing thought is the correspondence between conduct toward one's fellows and God's conduct toward the one so acting.
‡‡‡[7:1] This is not a prohibition against recognizing the faults of others, which would be hardly compatible with Mt 7:5, 6 but against passing judgment in a spirit of arrogance, forgetful of one's own faults.
§§§[7:5] **Hypocrite:** the designation previously given to the scribes and Pharisees is here given to the Christian disciple who is concerned with the faults of another and ignores his own more serious offenses.
¶¶¶[7:6] **Dogs** and **swine** were Jewish terms of contempt for Gentiles. This saying may originally have derived from a Jewish Christian community opposed to preaching the gospel

b. [6:12] 18:21–22; Sir 28:2.   c. [6:13] Jn 17:15; 2 Thes 3:3.   d. [6:14] 18:35; Sir 28:1–5; Mk 11:25.   e. [6:15] Jas 2:13.   f. [6:19] Jas 5:2–3.   g. [6:20–21] Lk 12:33–34.   h. [6:22–23] Lk 11:34–36.   i. [6:24] Lk 16:13.   j. [6:25–33] Lk 12:22–31.

k. [6:26] Ps 145:15–16; 147:9.   l. [7:1–5] Lk 6:37–38, 41–42.   m. [7:1] Rom 2:1–2; 1 Cor 4:5.   n. [7:2] Wis 12:22; Mk 4:24.

they trample them underfoot, and turn and tear you to pieces.°

The Answer to Prayers. [7p]"Ask and it will be given to you; seek and you will find; knock and the door will be opened to you.[q] [8]For everyone who asks, receives; and the one who seeks, finds; and to the one who knocks, the door will be opened.[r] [9]Which one of you would hand his son a stone when he asks for a loaf of bread,* [10]or a snake when he asks for a fish? [11]If you then, who are wicked, know how to give good gifts to your children, how much more will your heavenly Father give good things to those who ask him.[s]

The Golden Rule. [12†]"Do to others whatever you would have them do to you.[t] This is the law and the prophets.

The Narrow Gate. [13‡]"Enter through the narrow gate;[s] for the gate is wide and the road broad that leads to destruction, and those who enter through it are many.[u] [14]How narrow the gate and constricted the road that leads to life. And those who find it are few.

False Prophets.[s] [15]"Beware of false prophets, who come to you in sheep's clothing, but underneath are ravenous wolves.[v] [16w]By their fruits you will know them. Do people pick grapes from thornbushes, or figs from thistles? [17]Just so, every good tree bears good fruit, and a rotten tree bears bad fruit. [18]A good tree cannot bear bad fruit, nor can a rotten tree bear good fruit. [19]Every tree that does not bear good fruit will be cut down and thrown into the fire. [20]So by their fruits you will know them.[x]

The True Disciple. [21]"Not everyone who says to me, 'Lord, Lord,' will enter the kingdom of heaven,** but only the one who does the will of my Father in heaven.[y] [22]Many will say to me on that day,[z] 'Lord, Lord, did we not prophesy in your name? Did we not drive out demons in your name? Did we not do mighty deeds in your name?'[a] [23]Then I will declare to them solemnly, 'I never knew you.[††] Depart from me, you evildoers.'[b]

The Two Foundations. [24‡‡]"Everyone who listens to these words of mine and acts on them will be like a wise man who built his house on rock.[c] [25]The rain fell, the floods came, and the winds blew and buffeted the house.[d] But it did not collapse; it had been set solidly on rock. [26]And everyone who listens to these words of mine but does not act on them will be like a fool who built his house on sand. [27]The rain fell, the floods came, and the winds blew and buffeted the house. And it collapsed and was completely ruined."

[28§§]When Jesus finished these words, the crowds were astonished at his teaching, [29§§c]for he taught them as one having authority, and not as their scribes.

III. MINISTRY AND MISSION IN GALILEE***

CHAPTER 8

The Cleansing of a Leper. [1f]When Jesus came down from the mountain, great crowds followed

---

(what is holy, pearls) to Gentiles. In the light of Mt 28:19 that can hardly be Matthew's meaning. He may have taken the saying as applying to a Christian dealing with an obstinately impenitent fellow Christian (Mt 18:17).

*[7:9–10] There is a resemblance between a stone and a round loaf of bread and between a serpent and the scaleless fish called *barbut*.

†[7:12] See Lk 6:31. This saying, known since the eighteenth century as the "Golden Rule," is found in both positive and negative form in pagan and Jewish sources, both earlier and later than the gospel. This is the law and the prophets is an addition probably due to the evangelist.

‡[7:13–28] The final section of the discourse is composed of a series of antitheses, contrasting two kinds of life within the Christian community, that of those who obey the words of Jesus and that of those who do not. Most of the sayings are from Q and are found also in Luke.

§[7:13–14] The metaphor of the "two ways" was common in pagan philosophy and in the Old Testament. In Christian literature it is found also in the *Didache* (1–6) and the *Epistle of Barnabas* (18–20).

¶[7:15–20] Christian disciples who claimed to speak in the name of God are called **prophets** (Mt 7:15) in Mt 10:41; Mt 23:34. They were presumably an important group within the church of Matthew. As in the case of the Old Testament prophets, there were both true and false ones, and for Matthew the difference could be recognized by the quality of their deeds, the **fruits** (Mt 7:16). The mention of **fruits** leads to the comparison with trees, some producing good fruit, others bad.

[7:21–23] The attack on the false prophets is continued, but is broadened to include those disciples who perform works of healing and exorcism in the name of Jesus (Lord**) but live evil lives. Entrance into the kingdom is only for those who do the will of the Father. On the day of judgment (**on that day**) the morally corrupt prophets and miracle workers will be rejected by Jesus.

††[7:23] **I never knew you**: cf. Mt 10:33. **Depart from me, you evildoers**: cf. Ps 6:9.

‡‡[7:24–27] The conclusion of the discourse (cf. Lk 6:47–49). Here the relation is not between saying and doing as in Mt 7:15–23 but between hearing and doing, and the words of Jesus are applied to every Christian (**everyone who listens**).

§§[7:28–29] **When Jesus finished these words**: this or a similar formula is used by Matthew to conclude each of the five great discourses of Jesus (cf. Mt 11:1; 13:53; 19:1; 26:1).

¶¶[7:29] **Not as their scribes**: scribal instruction was a faithful handing down of the traditions of earlier teachers; Jesus' teaching is based on his own authority. **Their scribes**: for the implications of **their**, see note on Mt 4:23.

***[8:1–9:38] This narrative section of the second book of the gospel is composed of nine miracle stories, most of which are found in Mark, although Matthew does not follow the Marcan order and abbreviates the stories radically. The stories are arranged in three groups of three, each group followed by a section composed principally of sayings of Jesus about discipleship. Mt 9:35 is an almost verbatim repetition of Mt 4:23. Each speaks of Jesus' teaching, preaching, and healing. The teaching and preaching form the content of Mt 5–7; the healing, that of Mt 8–9. Some scholars speak of a portrayal of Jesus as "Messiah of the Word" in Mt 5–7 and "Messiah of the Deed" in Mt 8–9. That is accurate so far as it goes, but there is also a strong emphasis on discipleship in Mt 8–9; these chapters have not only christological but ecclesiological import.

---

o. [7:6] Prv 23:9.   p. [7:7–11] Mk 11:24; Lk 11:9–13.   q. [7:7] 18:19.
r. [7:8] Lk 18:1–8; Jn 14:13.   s. [7:11] 1 Jn 5:14–15.   t. [7:12] Lk 6:31.   u. [7:13] Lk 13:24.   v. [7:15] 2 Pt 2:1.   w. [7:16–17] 12:33; Lk 6:43–44.   x. [7:20] 3:10.

y. [7:21] Is 29:13; Lk 6:46.   z. [7:22–23] Lk 13:26–27.   a. [7:22] 25:11–12.   b. [7:23] Ps 5:5; 6:9.   c. [7:24–27] Lk 6:47–49.   d. [7:25–26] Prv 10:25.   e. [7:26] Mk 1:22; Lk 4:32.   f. [8:1–4] Mk 1:40–44; Lk 5:12–14.

him. [2]And then a leper* approached, did him homage, and said, "Lord, if you wish, you can make me clean." [3]He stretched out his hand, touched him, and said, "I will do it. Be made clean." His leprosy was cleansed immediately. [4†]Then Jesus said to him, "See that you tell no one, but go show yourself to the priest, and offer the gift that Moses prescribed;[g] that will be proof for them."

The Healing of a Centurion's Servant.[‡] [5h]When he entered Capernaum,[§] a centurion approached him and appealed to him, [6]saying, "Lord, my servant is lying at home paralyzed, suffering dreadfully." [7]He said to him, "I will come and cure him." [8]The centurion said in reply,[¶] "Lord, I am not worthy to have you enter under my roof; only say the word and my servant will be healed. [9]For I too am a person subject to authority, with soldiers subject to me. And I say to one, 'Go,' and he goes; and to another, 'Come here,' and he comes; and to my slave, 'Do this,' and he does it." [10]When Jesus heard this, he was amazed and said to those following him, "Amen, I say to you, in no one in Israel** have I found such faith. [11i]I say to you,[††] many will come from the east and the west, and will recline with Abraham, Isaac, and Jacob at the banquet in the kingdom of heaven, [12]but the children of the kingdom will be driven out into the outer darkness, where there will be wailing and grinding of teeth." [13]And Jesus said to the centurion, "You may go; as you have believed, let it be done for you." And at that very hour [his] servant was healed.

The Cure of Peter's Mother-in-Law.[‡‡] [14j]Jesus entered the house of Peter, and saw his mother-in-law lying in bed with a fever. [15]He touched her hand, the fever left her, and she rose and waited on him.[k]

Other Healings. [16]When it was evening, they brought him many who were possessed by demons, and he drove out the spirits by a word[§§] and cured all the sick, [17]to fulfill what had been said by Isaiah the prophet:[¶¶l]

"He took away our infirmities
and bore our diseases."

The Would-be Followers of Jesus.[***] [18m]When Jesus saw a crowd around him, he gave orders to cross to the other side.[†††] [19n]A scribe approached and said to him, "Teacher,[‡‡‡] I will follow you wherever you go." [20]Jesus answered him, "Foxes have dens and birds of the sky have nests, but the Son of Man[§§§] has nowhere to rest his head." [21]Another of [his] disciples said to him, "Lord, let me go first and bury my father." [22¶¶¶]But Jesus answered him, "Follow me, and let the dead bury their dead."

The Calming of the Storm at Sea. [23****o]He got into a boat and his disciples followed him. [24]Suddenly a violent storm[††††] came up on the sea, so that the boat was being swamped by waves;

---

*[8:2] **A leper**: see note on Mk 1:40.

†[8:4] Cf. Lv 14:2–9. **That will be proof for them**: the Greek can also mean "that will be proof against them." It is not clear whether **them** refers to the priests or the people.

‡[8:5–13] This story comes from Q (see Lk 7:1–10) and is also reflected in Jn 4:46–54. The similarity between the Q story and the Johannine is due to a common oral tradition, not to a common literary source. As in the later story of the daughter of the Canaanite woman (Mt 15:21–28) Jesus here breaks with his usual procedure of ministering only to Israelites and anticipates the mission to the Gentiles.

§[8:5] **A centurion**: a military officer commanding a hundred men. He was probably in the service of Herod Antipas, tetrarch of Galilee; see note on Mt 14:1.

¶[8:8–9] Acquainted by his position with the force of a command, the centurion expresses faith in the power of Jesus' mere word.

[8:10] **In no one in Israel: there is good textual attestation (e.g., Codex Sinaiticus) for a reading identical with that of Lk 7:9, "not even in Israel." But that seems to be due to a harmonization of Matthew with Luke.

††[8:11–12] Matthew inserts into the story a Q saying (see Lk 13:28–29) about the entrance of Gentiles into the kingdom and the exclusion of those Israelites who, though descended from the patriarchs and members of the chosen nation (**the children of the kingdom**), refused to believe in Jesus. **There will be wailing and grinding of teeth**: the first occurrence of a phrase used frequently in this gospel to describe final condemnation (Mt 13:42, 50; 22:13; 24:51; 25:30). It is found elsewhere in the New Testament only in Lk 13:28.

‡‡[8:14–15] Cf. Mk 1:29–31. Unlike Mark, Matthew has no implied request by others for the woman's cure. Jesus acts on

his own initiative, and the cured woman rises and waits not on "them" (Mk 1:31) but on **him**.

§§[8:16] **By a word**: a Matthean addition to Mk 1:34; cf. 8:8.

¶¶[8:17] This fulfillment citation from Is 53:4 follows the MT, not the LXX. The prophet speaks of the Servant of the Lord who suffers vicariously for the sins ("infirmities") of others; Matthew takes the **infirmities** as physical afflictions.

***[8:18–22] This passage between the first and second series of miracles about following Jesus is taken from Q (see Lk 9:57–62). The third of the three sayings found in the source is absent from Matthew.

†††[8:18] **The other side**: i.e., of the Sea of Galilee.

‡‡‡[8:19] **Teacher**: for Matthew, this designation of Jesus is true, for he has Jesus using it of himself (Mt 10:24, 25; 23:8; 26:18), yet when it is used of him by others they are either his opponents (Mt 9:11; 12:38; 17:24; 22:16, 24, 36) or, as here and in Mt 19:16, well-disposed persons who cannot see more deeply. Thus it reveals an inadequate recognition of who Jesus is.

§§§[8:20] **Son of Man**: see note on Mk 8:31. This is the first occurrence in Matthew of a term that appears in the New Testament only in sayings of Jesus, except for Acts 7:56 and possibly Mt 9:6 (// Mk 2:10; Lk 5:24). In Matthew it refers to Jesus in his ministry (seven times, as here), in his passion and resurrection (nine times, e.g., Mt 17:22), and in his glorious coming at the end of the age (thirteen times, e.g., Mt 24:30).

¶¶¶[8:22] **Let the dead bury their dead**: the demand of Jesus overrides what both the Jewish and the Hellenistic world regarded as a filial obligation of the highest importance. See note on Lk 9:60.

****[8:23] **His disciples followed him**: the first miracle in the second group (Mt 8:23–9:8) is introduced by a verse that links it with the preceding sayings by the catchword "follow." In Mark the initiative in entering the boat is taken by the disciples (Mk 4:35–41); here, Jesus enters first and the disciples follow.

††††[8:24] **Storm**: literally, "earthquake," a word commonly used in apocalyptic literature for the shaking of the old world when God brings in his kingdom. All the synoptics use it in depicting the events preceding the parousia of the Son of Man (Mt 24:7; Mk 13:8; Lk 21:11). Matthew has introduced it here and in his account of the death and resurrection of Jesus (Mt 27:51–54; 28:2).

---

g. [8:4] Lv 14:2–32; Lk 17:14.   h. [8:5–13] Lk 7:1–10; Jn 4:46–53.   i. [8:11–12] 13:42, 50; 22:13; 24:51; 25:30; Lk 13:28–29.   j. [8:14–16] Mk 1:29–34; Lk 4:38–41.

k. [8:15] 9:25.   l. [8:17] Is 53:4.   m. [8:18] Mk 4:35.   n. [8:19–22] Lk 9:57–60.   o. [8:23–27] Mk 4:35–40; Lk 8:22–25.

but he was asleep. ²⁵ᵖThey came and woke him, saying, "Lord, save us!" We are perishing!" ²⁶He said to them, "Why are you terrified, O you of little faith?"† Then he got up, rebuked the winds and the sea, and there was great calm. ²⁷The men were amazed and said, "What sort of man is this, whom even the winds and the sea obey?"

The Healing of the Gadarene Demoniacs. ²⁸qWhen he came to the other side, to the territory of the Gadarenes,‡ two demoniacs who were coming from the tombs met him. They were so savage that no one could travel by that road. ²⁹They cried out, "What have you to do with us,§ Son of God? Have you come here to torment us before the appointed time?" ³⁰Some distance away a herd of many swine was feeding.¶ ³¹The demons pleaded with him, "If you drive us out, send us into the herd of swine."ʳ ³²And he said to them, "Go then!" They came out and entered the swine, and the whole herd rushed down the steep bank into the sea where they drowned. ³³The swineherds ran away, and when they came to the town they reported everything, including what had happened to the demoniacs. ³⁴Thereupon the whole town came out to meet Jesus, and when they saw him they begged him to leave their district.

CHAPTER 9
The Healing of a Paralytic. ¹**ˢHe entered a boat, made the crossing, and came into his own town. ²And there people brought to him a paralytic lying on a stretcher. When Jesus saw their faith, he said to the paralytic, "Courage, child, your sins are forgiven."ᵗ ³At that, some of the scribes††

said to themselves, "This man is blaspheming." ⁴Jesus knew what they were thinking, and said, "Why do you harbor evil thoughts? ⁵Which is easier, to say, 'Your sins are forgiven,' or to say, 'Rise and walk'? ⁶‡‡But that you may know that the Son of Man has authority on earth to forgive sins"—he then said to the paralytic, "Rise, pick up your stretcher, and go home."ᵘ ⁷He rose and went home. ⁸§§When the crowds saw this they were struck with awe and glorified God who had given such authority to human beings.

The Call of Matthew.¶¶ ⁹As Jesus passed on from there,ᵛ he saw a man named Matthew*** sitting at the customs post. He said to him, "Follow me." And he got up and followed him. ¹⁰While he was at table in his house,††† many tax collectors and sinners came and sat with Jesus and his disciples.ʷ ¹¹The Pharisees saw this and said to his disciples, "Why does your teacher‡‡‡ eat with tax collectors and sinners?" ¹²He heard this and said, "Those who are well do not need a physician, but the sick do.§§§ ¹³Go and learn the meaning of the words,ˣ 'I desire mercy, not sacrifice.'¶¶¶ I did not come to call the righteous but sinners."

The Question About Fasting. ¹⁴ʸThen the disciples of John approached him and said, "Why do we and the Pharisees fast [much], but your disciples do not fast?" ¹⁵Jesus answered them, "Can the wedding guests mourn as long as the bridegroom is with them? The days will come when the bridegroom is taken away from them,

---

‡‡[9:6] It is not clear whether **But that you may know . . . to forgive sins** is intended to be a continuation of the words of Jesus or a parenthetical comment of the evangelist to those who would hear or read this gospel. In any case, Matthew here follows the Marcan text.

§§[9:8] **Who had given such authority to human beings:** a significant difference from Mk 2:12 ("They . . . glorified God, saying, 'We have never seen anything like this'"). Matthew's extension to **human beings** of the authority to forgive sins points to the belief that such authority was being claimed by Matthew's church.

¶¶[9:9–17] In this section the order is the same as that of Mk 2:13–22.

***[9:9] **A man named Matthew:** Mark names this tax collector Levi (Mk 2:14). No such name appears in the four lists of the twelve who were the closest companions of Jesus (Mt 10:2–4; Mk 3:16–19; Lk 6:14–16; Acts 1:13 [eleven, because of the defection of Judas Iscariot]), whereas all four list a Matthew, designated in Mt 10:3 as "the tax collector." The evangelist may have changed the "Levi" of his source to **Matthew** so that this man, whose call is given special notice, like that of the first four disciples (Mt 4:18–22), might be included among the twelve. Another reason for the change may be that the disciple Matthew was the source of traditions peculiar to the church for which the evangelist was writing.

†††[9:10] **His house:** it is not clear whether **his** refers to Jesus or Matthew. **Tax collectors:** see note on Mt 5:46. Table association with such persons would cause ritual impurity.

‡‡‡[9:11] **Teacher:** see note on Mt 8:19.

§§§[9:12] See note on Mk 2:17.

¶¶¶[9:13] **Go and learn . . . not sacrifice:** Matthew adds the prophetic statement of Hos 6:6 to the Marcan account (see also Mt 12:7). If mercy is superior to the temple sacrifices, how much more to the laws of ritual impurity.

---

*[8:25] The reverent plea of the disciples contrasts sharply with their reproach of Jesus in Mk 4:38.

†[8:26] **You of little faith:** see note on Mt 6:30. **Great calm:** Jesus' calming the sea may be meant to recall the Old Testament theme of God's control over the chaotic waters (Ps 65:8; 89:10; 93:3–4; 107:29).

‡[8:28] **Gadarenes:** this is the reading of Codex Vaticanus, supported by other important textual witnesses. The original reading of Codex Sinaiticus was Gazarenes, later changed to Gergesenes, and a few versions have Gerasenes. Each of these readings points to a different territory connected, respectively, with the cities Gadara, Gergesa, and Gerasa (modern Jerash). There is the same confusion of readings in the parallel texts, Mk 5:1 and Lk 8:26; there the best reading seems to be "Gerasenes," whereas "Gadarenes" is probably the original reading in Matthew. The town of Gadara was about five miles southeast of the Sea of Galilee, and Josephus (*Life* 9:42) refers to it as possessing territory that lay on that sea. **Two demoniacs:** Mark (5:1–20) has one.

§[8:29] **What have you to do with us?:** see note on Jn 2:4. **Before the appointed time:** the notion that evil spirits were allowed by God to afflict human beings until the time of the final judgment is found in Enoch 16:1 and Jubilees 10:7–10.

¶[8:30] The tending of pigs, animals considered unclean by Mosaic law (Lv 11:6–7), indicates that the population was Gentile.

[9:1] **His own town: Capernaum; see Mt 4:13.

††[9:3] **Scribes:** see note on Mk 2:6. Matthew omits the reason given in the Marcan story for the charge of blasphemy: "Who but God alone can forgive sins?" (Mk 2:7).

---

p. [8:25–26] Ps 107:28–29.   q. [8:28–34] Mk 5:1–17; Lk 8:26–37.
r. [8:31] Lk 4:34, 41.   s. [9:1–8] Mk 2:3–12; Lk 5:18–26.   t. [9:2] Lk 7:48.

u. [9:6] Jn 5:27.   v. [9:9–13] Mk 2:14–17; Lk 5:27–32.   w. [9:10] 11:19; Lk 15:1–2.   x. [9:13] 12:7; Hos 6:6.   y. [9:14–17] Mk 2:18–22; Lk 5:33–39.

and then they will fast.* [16]No one patches an old cloak with a piece of unshrunken cloth,† for its fullness pulls away from the cloak and the tear gets worse. [17]People do not put new wine into old wineskins. Otherwise the skins burst, the wine spills out, and the skins are ruined. Rather, they pour new wine into fresh wineskins, and both are preserved."

The Official's Daughter and the Woman with a Hemorrhage. [18‡]While he was saying these things to them,[z] an official[§] came forward, knelt down before him, and said, "My daughter has just died. But come, lay your hand on her, and she will live." [19]Jesus rose and followed him, and so did his disciples. [20]A woman suffering hemorrhages for twelve years came up behind him and touched the tassel[¶] on his cloak. [21]She said to herself, "If only I can touch his cloak, I shall be cured."[a] [22]Jesus turned around and saw her, and said, "Courage, daughter! Your faith has saved you." And from that hour the woman was cured.

[23]When Jesus arrived at the official's house and saw the flute players and the crowd who were making a commotion, [24]he said, "Go away! The girl is not dead but sleeping."** And they ridiculed him. [25]When the crowd was put out, he came and took her by the hand, and the little girl arose. [26]And news of this spread throughout all that land.

The Healing of Two Blind Men.†† [27b]And as Jesus passed on from there, two blind men followed [him], crying out, "Son of David,‡‡ have pity on us!"[c] [28]When he entered the house, the blind men approached him and Jesus said to them, "Do you believe that I can do this?" "Yes, Lord," they said to him. [29]Then he touched their eyes and said, "Let it be done for you according to your faith." [30]And their eyes were opened. Jesus warned them sternly, "See that no one knows about this." [31]But they went out and spread word of him through all that land.

The Healing of a Mute Person. [32d]As they were going out,[§§] a demoniac who could not speak was brought to him, [33]and when the demon was driven out the mute person spoke. The crowds were amazed and said, "Nothing like this has ever been seen in Israel."[e] [34¶¶]But the Pharisees said,[f] "He drives out demons by the prince of demons."

The Compassion of Jesus. [35***g]Jesus went around to all the towns and villages, teaching in their synagogues, proclaiming the gospel of the kingdom, and curing every disease and illness. [36h]At the sight of the crowds, his heart was moved with pity for them because they were troubled and abandoned,††† like sheep without a shepherd. [37‡‡‡i]Then he said to his disciples, "The harvest is abundant but the laborers are few; [38]so ask the master of the harvest to send out laborers for his harvest."

CHAPTER 10

The Mission of the Twelve. [1§§§]Then he summoned his twelve disciples¶¶¶ and gave them

---

*[9:15] Fasting is a sign of mourning and would be as inappropriate at this time of joy, when Jesus is proclaiming the kingdom, as it would be at a marriage feast. Yet the saying looks forward to the time when Jesus will no longer be with the disciples visibly, the time of Matthew's church. **Then they will fast:** see *Didache* 8:1.

†[9:16–17] Each of these parables speaks of the unsuitability of attempting to combine the old and the new. Jesus' teaching is not a patching up of Judaism, nor can the gospel be contained within the limits of Mosaic law.

‡[9:18–34] In this third group of miracles, the first (Mt 9:18–26) is clearly dependent on Mark (Mk 5:21–43). Though it tells of two miracles, the cure of the woman had already been included within the story of the raising of the official's daughter, so that the two were probably regarded as a single unit. The other miracles seem to have been derived from Mark and Q, respectively, though here Matthew's own editing is much more evident.

§[9:18] **Official:** literally, "ruler." Mark calls him "one of the synagogue officials" (Mk 5:22). **My daughter has just died:** Matthew heightens the Marcan "my daughter is at the point of death" (Mk 5:23).

¶[9:20] **Tassel:** possibly "fringe." The Mosaic law prescribed that tassels be worn on the corners of one's garment as a reminder to keep the commandments (see Nm 15:37–39; Dt 22:12).

[9:24] **Sleeping: sleep is a biblical metaphor for death (see Ps 87:6 LXX; Dn 12:2; 1 Thes 5:10). Jesus' statement is not a denial of the child's real death, but an assurance that she will be roused from her sleep of death.

††[9:27–31] This story was probably composed by Matthew out of Mark's story of the healing of a blind man named Bartimaeus (Mk 10:46–52). Mark places the event late in Jesus' ministry, just before his entrance into Jerusalem, and Matthew has followed his Marcan source at that point in his gospel also (see Mt 20:29–34). In each of the Matthean stories the single blind man of Mark becomes two. The reason why

Matthew would have given a double version of the Marcan story and placed the earlier one here may be that he wished to add a story of Jesus' curing the blind at this point in order to prepare for Jesus' answer to the emissaries of the Baptist (Mt 11:4–6) in which Jesus, recounting his works, begins with his giving sight to the blind.

‡‡[9:27] **Son of David:** this messianic title is connected once with the healing power of Jesus in Mark (Mk 10:47–48) and Luke (Lk 18:38–39) but more frequently in Matthew (see also Mt 12:23; 15:22; 20:30–31).

§§[9:32–34] The source of this story seems to be Q (see Lk 11:14–15). As in the preceding healing of the blind, Matthew has two versions of this healing, the later in Mt 12:22–24 and the earlier here.

¶¶[9:34] This spiteful accusation foreshadows the growing opposition to Jesus in Mt 11 and 12.

***[9:35] See notes on Mt 4:23–25; Mt 8:1–9:38.

†††[9:36] See Mk 6:34; Nm 27:17; 1 Kgs 22:17.

‡‡‡[9:37–38] This Q saying (see Lk 10:2) is only imperfectly related to this context. It presupposes that only God (**the master of the harvest**) can take the initiative in sending out preachers of the gospel, whereas in Matthew's setting it leads into Mt 10 where Jesus does so.

§§§[10:1–11:1] After an introductory narrative (Mt 10:1–4), the second of the discourses of the gospel. It deals with the mission now to be undertaken by the disciples (Mt 10:5–15), but the perspective broadens and includes the missionary activity of the church between the time of the resurrection and the parousia.

¶¶¶[10:1] **His twelve disciples:** although, unlike Mark (Mk 3:13–14) and Luke (Lk 6:12–16), Matthew has no story of Jesus' choosing the Twelve, he assumes that the group is known

---

z. [9:18–26] Mk 5:22–43; Lk 8:41–56. a. [9:21] 14:36; Nm 15:37. b. [9:27–31] 20:29–34.

c. [9:27] 15:22. d. [9:32–34] 12:22–24; Lk 11:14–15. e. [9:33] Mk 2:12; 7:37. f. [9:34] 10:25; Mk 3:22. g. [9:35] 4:23; Lk 8:1. h. [9:36] Nm 27:17; 1 Kgs 22:17; Jer 50:6; Ez 34:5; Mk 6:34. i. [9:37–38] Lk 10:2; Jn 4:35.

authority over unclean spirits to drive them out and to cure every disease and every illness.ʲ ²The names of the twelve apostles˙ are these: first, Simon called Peter, and his brother Andrew; James, the son of Zebedee, and his brother John; ³Philip and Bartholomew, Thomas and Matthew the tax collector; James, the son of Alphaeus, and Thaddeus; ⁴Simon the Cananean, and Judas Iscariot who betrayed him.

The Commissioning of the Twelve. ⁵ᵏJesus sent out these twelve† after instructing them thus, "Do not go into pagan territory or enter a Samaritan town. ⁶ᶫGo rather to the lost sheep of the house of Israel. ⁷As you go, make this proclamation: 'The kingdom of heaven is at hand.'ᵐ ⁸‡Cure ·the sick, raise the dead, cleanse lepers, drive out demons. Without cost you have received; without cost you are to give. ⁹ⁿDo not take gold or silver or copper for your belts; ¹⁰ᵒno sack for the journey, or a second tunic, or sandals, or walking stick. The laborer deserves his keep. ¹¹ᵖWhatever town or village you enter, look for a worthy person in it, and stay there until you leave. ¹²As you enter a house, wish it peace. ¹³If the house is worthy, let your peace come upon it; if not, let your peace return to you.§ ¹⁴§ᑫWhoever will not receive you or listen

to your words—go outside that house or town and shake the dust from your feet. ¹⁵Amen, I say to you, it will be more tolerable for the land of Sodom and Gomorrah on the day of judgment than for that town.ʳ

Coming Persecutions. ¹⁶ˢ"Behold, I am sending you like sheep in the midst of wolves; so be shrewd as serpents and simple as doves. ¹⁷**"But beware of people,ᵗ for they will hand you over to courts and scourge you in their synagogues,ᵘ ¹⁸and you will be led before governors and kings for my sake as a witness before them and the pagans. ¹⁹When they hand you over, do not worry about how you are to speak or what you are to say. You will be given at that moment what you are to say.ᵛ ²⁰For it will not be you who speak but the Spirit of your Father speaking through you. ²¹††Brother will hand over brother to death, and the father his child; children will rise up against parents and have them put to death. ²²You will be hated by all because of my name, but whoever endures to the end‡‡ will be saved. ²³When they persecute you in one town, flee to another. Amen, I say to you, you will not finish the towns of Israel before the Son of Man comes.§§ ²⁴ˣNo disciple is above his teacher, no slave above his master. ²⁵It is enough for the disciple that he become like his teacher, for the slave that he become like his master. If they have called the master of the house Beelzebul,§§ how much more those of his household!

Courage Under Persecution. ²⁶ʸ"Therefore do not be afraid of them. Nothing is concealed that will not be revealed, nor secret that will not be known.***ᶻ ²⁷What I say to you in the darkness, speak in the light; what you hear whispered,

---

to the reader. The earliest New Testament text to speak of it is 1 Cor 15:5. The number probably is meant to recall the twelve tribes of Israel and implies Jesus' authority to call all Israel into the kingdom. While Luke (Lk 6:13) and probably Mark (Mk 4:10, 34) distinguish between the Twelve and a larger group also termed disciples, Matthew tends to identify the disciples and the Twelve. **Authority . . . every illness**: activities the same as those of Jesus; see Mt 4:23; Mt 9:35; 10:8. The Twelve also share in his proclamation of the kingdom (Mt 10:7). But although he teaches (Mt 4:23; 7:28; 9:35), they do not. Their commission to teach comes only after Jesus' resurrection, after they have been fully instructed by him (Mt 28:20).

*[10:2–4] Here, for the only time in Matthew, the Twelve are designated **apostles**. The word "apostle" means "one who is sent," and therefore fits the situation here described. In the Pauline letters, the place where the term occurs most frequently in the New Testament, it means primarily one who has seen the risen Lord and has been commissioned to proclaim the resurrection. With slight variants in Luke and Acts, the names of those who belong to this group are the same in the four lists given in the New Testament (see note on Mt 9:9). **Cananean**: this represents an Aramaic word meaning "zealot." The meaning of that designation is unclear (see note on Lk 6:15).

†[10:5–6] Like Jesus (Mt 15:24), the Twelve are sent only to Israel. This saying may reflect an original Jewish Christian refusal of the mission to the Gentiles, but for Matthew it expresses rather the limitation that Jesus himself observed during his ministry.

‡[10:8–11] The Twelve have received their own call and mission through God's gift, and the benefits they confer are likewise to be given freely. They are not to take with them money, provisions, or unnecessary clothing; their lodging and food will be provided by those who receive them.

§[10:13] The greeting of peace is conceived of not merely as a salutation but as an effective word. If it finds no worthy recipient, it will return to the speaker.

§[10:14] **Shake the dust from your feet**: this gesture indicates a complete disassociation from such unbelievers.

**[10:17] The persecutions attendant upon the post-resurrection mission now begin to be spoken of. Here Matthew brings into the discourse sayings found in Mk 13 which deals with events preceding the parousia.

††[10:21] See Mi 7:6 which is cited in Mt 10:35, 36.

‡‡[10:22] **To the end**: the original meaning was probably "until the parousia." But it is not likely that Matthew expected no missionary disciples to suffer death before then, since he envisages the martyrdom of other Christians (Mt 10:21). For him, **the end** is probably that of the individual's life (see Mt 10:28).

§§[10:23] **Before the Son of Man comes**: since the coming of the Son of Man at the end of the age had not taken place when this gospel was written, much less during the mission of the Twelve during Jesus' ministry, Matthew cannot have meant the coming to refer to the parousia. It is difficult to know what he understood it to be: perhaps the "proleptic parousia" of Mt 28:16–20, or the destruction of the temple in A.D. 70, viewed as a coming of Jesus in judgment on unbelieving Israel.

§§[10:25] **Beelzebul**: see Mt 9:34 for the charge linking Jesus with "the prince of demons," who is named **Beelzebul** in Mt 12:24. The meaning of the name is uncertain; possibly, "lord of the house."

***[10:26] The **concealed** and **secret** coming of the kingdom is to be proclaimed by them, and no fear must be allowed to deter them from that proclamation.

---

j. [10:1–4] Mk 3:14–19; Lk 6:13–16; Acts 1:13.   k. [10:5–15] Mk 6:7–13; Lk 9:1–6.   l. [10:6] 15:24.   m. [10:7] 3:2; 4:17.   n. [10:9–10] Mk 6:8–9; Lk 9:3; 10:4.   o. [10:10] Lk 10:7; 1 Cor 9:14; 1 Tm 5:18.   p. [10:11–15] Mk 6:10–11; Lk 9:4–5; 10:5–12.   q. [10:14] Acts 13:51; 18:6.

r. [10:15] 11:24; Gn 19:1–29; Jude 7.   s. [10:16] Lk 10:3.   t. [10:17–22] Mk 13:9–13; Lk 21:12–19.   u. [10:17] Acts 5:40.   v. [10:19] Ex 4:11–12; Jer 1:6–10; Lk 12:11–12.   w. [10:21–22] 24:9,13.   x. [10:24–25] Lk 6:40; Jn 13:16; 15:20.   y. [10:26–33] Lk 12:2–9.   z. [10:26] Mk 4:22; Lk 8:17; 1 Tm 5:25.

proclaim on the housetops. [28]And do not be afraid of those who kill the body but cannot kill the soul; rather, be afraid of the one who can destroy both soul and body in Gehenna.[a] [29]Are not two sparrows sold for a small coin? Yet not one of them falls to the ground without your Father's knowledge. [30]Even all the hairs of your head are counted. [31]So do not be afraid; you are worth more than many sparrows. [32]*Everyone who acknowledges me before others I will acknowledge before my heavenly Father. [33]But whoever denies me before others, I will deny before my heavenly Father.[b]

Jesus: A Cause of Division. [34c]"Do not think that I have come to bring peace upon the earth. I have come to bring not peace but the sword. [35]For I have come to set

a man 'against his father,
        a daughter against her mother,
    and a daughter-in-law against her
            mother-in-law;
[36]   and one's enemies will be those of
            his household.'

The Conditions of Discipleship. [37d]"Whoever loves father or mother more than me is not worthy of me, and whoever loves son or daughter more than me is not worthy of me; [38]and whoever does not take up his cross[†] and follow after me is not worthy of me. [39†e]Whoever finds his life will lose it, and whoever loses his life for my sake will find it.

Rewards. [40]"Whoever receives you receives me,[§] and whoever receives me receives the one who sent me.[f] [41§]Whoever receives a prophet because he is a prophet will receive a prophet's reward, and whoever receives a righteous man because he is righteous will receive a righteous man's reward. [42]And whoever gives only a cup of cold water to one of these little ones to drink because he is a disciple—amen, I say to you, he will surely not lose his reward."[g]

CHAPTER 11

[1]When Jesus finished giving these commands to his twelve disciples,** he went away from that place to teach and to preach in their towns.

IV. OPPOSITION FROM ISRAEL

The Messengers from John the Baptist. [2††h]When John heard in prison[‡‡] of the works of the Messiah, he sent his disciples to him [3§§]with this question, "Are you the one who is to come, or should we look for another?" [4]Jesus said to them in reply, "Go and tell John what you hear and see: [5¶¶]the blind regain their sight, the lame walk, lepers are cleansed, the deaf hear, the dead are raised, and the poor have the good news proclaimed to them.[i] [6]And blessed is the one who takes no offense at me."

Jesus' Testimony to John.[***] [7]As they were going off, Jesus began to speak to the crowds about John, "What did you go out to the desert to see? A reed swayed by the wind?[j] [8]Then what did you go out to see? Someone dressed in fine clothing? Those who wear fine clothing are in royal palaces. [9]Then why did you go out? To see a prophet?[†††] Yes, I tell you, and more than a prophet. [10]This is the one about whom it is written:

'Behold, I am sending my messenger
        ahead of you;
    he will prepare your way before you.'[k]

---

*[10:32–33] In the Q parallel (Lk 12:8–9), the Son of Man will acknowledge those who have acknowledged Jesus, and those who deny him will be denied (by the Son of Man) before the angels of God at the judgment. Here Jesus and the Son of Man are identified, and the acknowledgment or denial will be before his heavenly Father.

†[10:38] The first mention of the cross in Matthew, explicitly that of the disciple, but implicitly that of Jesus (**and follow after me**). Crucifixion was a form of capital punishment used by the Romans for offenders who were not Roman citizens.

‡[10:39] One who denies Jesus in order to save one's earthly life will be condemned to everlasting destruction; loss of earthly life for Jesus' sake will be rewarded by everlasting life in the kingdom.

§[10:40–42] All who receive the disciples of Jesus receive him, and God who sent him, and will be rewarded accordingly.

¶[10:41] **A prophet**: one who speaks in the name of God; here, the Christian prophets who proclaim the gospel. **Righteous man**: since righteousness is demanded of all the disciples, it is difficult to take the **righteous man** of this verse and **one of these little ones** (Mt 10:42) as indicating different groups within the followers of Jesus. Probably all three designations are used here of Christian missionaries as such.

**[11:1] The closing formula of the discourse refers back to the original addressees, the Twelve.

††[11:2–12:50] The narrative section of the third book deals with the growing opposition to Jesus. It is largely devoted to disputes and attacks relating to faith and discipleship and thus contains much sayings-material, drawn in large part from Q.

‡‡[11:2] **In prison**: see Mt 4:12; 14:1–12. **The works of the Messiah**: the deeds of Mt 8–9.

§§[11:3] The question probably expresses a doubt of the Baptist that Jesus is **the one who is to come** (cf. Mal 3:1) because his mission has not been one of fiery judgment as John had expected (Mt 3:2).

¶¶[11:5–6] Jesus' response is taken from passages of Isaiah (Is 26:19; 29:18–19; 35:5–6; 61:1) that picture the time of salvation as marked by deeds such as those that Jesus is doing. The beatitude is a warning to the Baptist not to disbelieve because his expectations have not been met.

***[11:7–19] Jesus' rebuke of John is counterbalanced by a reminder of the greatness of the Baptist's function (Mt 11:7–15) that is followed by a complaint about those who have heeded neither John nor Jesus (Mt 11:16–19).

†††[11:9–10] In common Jewish belief there had been no prophecy in Israel since the last of the Old Testament prophets, Malachi. The coming of a new prophet was eagerly awaited, and Jesus agrees that John was such. Yet he was **more than a prophet**, for he was the precursor of the one who would bring in the new and final age. The Old Testament quotation is a combination of Mal 3:1; Ex 23:20 with the significant change that the **before me** of Malachi becomes **before you**. The messenger now precedes not God, as in the original, but Jesus.

---

a. [10:28] Jas 4:12.   b. [10:33] Mk 8:38; Lk 9:26; 2 Tm 2:12; Rev 3:5.   c. [10:34–35] Lk 12:51–53.   d. [10:37–39] 16:24–25; Lk 14:26–27.   e. [10:39] Mk 8:35; Lk 9:24; Jn 12:25.   f. [10:40] Lk 10:16; Jn 12:44; 13:20.

g. [10:42] 25:40; Mk 9:41.   h. [11:2–11] Lk 7:18–28.   i. [11:5] Is 26:19; 29:18–19; 35:5–6; 61:1.   j. [11:7] 3:3, 5.   k. [11:10] Ex 23:20; Mal 3:1; Mk 1:2; Lk 1:76.

¹¹Amen, I say to you, among those born of women there has been none greater than John the Baptist; yet the least in the kingdom of heaven is greater than he.* ¹²From the days of John the Baptist until now, the kingdom of heaven suffers violence,† and the violent are taking it by force.¹ ¹³All the prophets and the law‡ prophesied up to the time of John. ¹⁴And if you are willing to accept it, he is Elijah, the one who is to come.ᵐ ¹⁵Whoever has ears ought to hear.

¹⁶ⁿ"To what shall I compare this generation?§ It is like children who sit in marketplaces and call to one another, ¹⁷'We played the flute for you, but you did not dance, we sang a dirge but you did not mourn.' ¹⁸For John came neither eating nor drinking, and they said, 'He is possessed by a demon.'ᵒ ¹⁹The Son of Man came eating and drinking and they said, 'Look, he is a glutton and a drunkard, a friend of tax collectors and sinners.' But wisdom is vindicated by her works."ᵖ

Reproaches to Unrepentant Towns. ²⁰𝑞Then he began to reproach the towns where most of his mighty deeds had been done, since they had not repented. ²¹"Woe to you, Chorazin! Woe to you, Bethsaida! For if the mighty deeds done in your midst had been done in Tyre and Sidon,⁵ they would long ago have repented in sackcloth and ashes.ʳ ²²But I tell you, it will be more tolerable for Tyre and Sidon on the day of judgment than for you. ²³**And as for you, Capernaum:

'Will you be exalted to heaven?ˢ
You will go down to the
netherworld.'

For if the mighty deeds done in your midst had been done in Sodom, it would have remained until this day. ²⁴But I tell you, it will be more tolerable for the land of Sodom on the day of judgment than for you."ᵗ

The Praise of the Father. ²⁵ᵘAt that time Jesus said in reply,†† "I give praise to you, Father, Lord of heaven and earth, for although you have hidden these things from the wise and the learned you have revealed them to the childlike. ²⁶Yes, Father, such has been your gracious will. ²⁷All things have been handed over to me by my Father. No one knows the Son except the Father, and no one knows the Father except the Son and anyone to whom the Son wishes to reveal him.ᵛ

The Gentle Mastery of Christ. ²⁸‡‡"Come to me, all you who labor and are burdened,§§ and I will give you rest. ²⁹¶¶Take my yoke upon you and learn from me, for I am meek and humble of heart; and you will find rest for yourselves. ³⁰For my yoke is easy, and my burden light."

CHAPTER 12

Picking Grain on the Sabbath. ¹***At that time Jesus was going through a field of grain on the sabbath.ˣ His disciples were hungry and began to pick the heads†††of grain and eat them.ʸ ²When the Pharisees saw this, they said to him, "See, your disciples are doing what is unlawful to do on the sabbath." ³He said to them,‡‡‡ "Have

---

*[11:11] John's preeminent greatness lies in his function of announcing the imminence of the kingdom (Mt 3:1). But to be in the kingdom is so great a privilege that the least who has it is greater than the Baptist.

†[11:12] The meaning of this difficult saying is probably that the opponents of Jesus are trying to prevent people from accepting the kingdom and to snatch it away from those who have received it.

‡[11:13] **All the prophets and the law**: Matthew inverts the usual order, "law and prophets," and says that both have **prophesied.** This emphasis on the prophetic character of the law points to its fulfillment in the teaching of Jesus and to the transitory nature of some of its commandments (see note on Mt 5:17–20).

§[11:16–19] See Lk 7:31–35. The meaning of the parable (Mt 11:16–17) and its explanation (Mt 11:18–19b) is much disputed. A plausible view is that the **children** of the parable are two groups, one of which proposes different entertainments to the other that will not agree with either proposal. The first represents John, Jesus, and their disciples; the second those who reject John for his asceticism and Jesus for his table association with those despised by the religiously observant. Mt 11:19c (**her works**) forms an inclusion with Mt 11:2 ("the works of the Messiah"). The original form of the saying is better preserved in Lk 7:35 ". . . wisdom is vindicated by all her children." There John and Jesus are the children of Wisdom; here the works of Jesus the Messiah are those of divine Wisdom, of which he is the embodiment. Some important textual witnesses, however, have essentially the same reading as in Luke.

¶[11:21] Tyre and Sidon were pagan cities denounced for their wickedness in the Old Testament; cf. Jl 4:4–7.

**[11:23] Capernaum's pride and punishment are described in language taken from the taunt song against the king of Babylon (Is 14:13–15).

††[11:25–27] This Q saying, identical with Lk 10:21–22 except for minor variations, introduces a joyous note into this section, so dominated by the theme of unbelief. **While the wise and the learned**, the scribes and Pharisees, have rejected Jesus' preaching and the significance of his mighty deeds, **the childlike** have accepted them. Acceptance depends upon the Father's revelation, but this is granted to those who are open to receive it and refused to the arrogant. Jesus can speak of all mysteries because he is **the Son** and there is perfect reciprocity of knowledge between him and the Father; what has been **handed over** to him is revealed only to those whom he wishes.

‡‡[11:28–29] These verses are peculiar to Matthew and are similar to Ben Sirach's invitation to learn wisdom and submit to her yoke (Sir 51:23, 26).

§§[11:28] **Who labor and are burdened**: burdened by the law as expounded by the scribes and Pharisees (Mt 23:4).

¶¶[11:29] In place of the yoke of the law, complicated by scribal interpretation, Jesus invites the burdened to take the yoke of obedience to his word, under which they **will find rest;** cf. Jer 6:16.

***[12:1–14] Matthew here returns to the Marcan order that he left in Mt 9:18. The two stories depend on Mk 2:23–28; 3:1–6, respectively, and are the only places in either gospel that deal explicitly with Jesus' attitude toward sabbath observance.

†††[12:1–2] The picking of the heads of grain is here equated with reaping, which was forbidden on the sabbath (Ex 34:21).

‡‡‡[12:3–4] See 1 Sm 21:2–7. In the Marcan parallel (Mk 2:25–26) the high priest is called Abiathar, although in 1 Samuel this action is attributed to Ahimelech. The Old Testament story is not about a violation of the sabbath rest; its pertinence

---

l. [11:12] Lk 16:16. m. [11:14] 17:10–13; Mal 3:23; Lk 1:17.
n. [11:16–19] Lk 7:31–35. o. [11:18] Lk 1:15. p. [11:19] 9:10–11.
q. [11:20–24] Lk 10:12–15. r. [11:21] Jl 4:4–7.

s. [11:23] Is 14:13–15. t. [11:24] 10:15. u. [11:25–27] Lk 10:21–22.
v. [11:27] Jn 3:35; 6:46; 7:28; 10:15. w. [11:29] Sir 51:26; Jer 6:16.
x. [12:1–8] Mk 2:23–28; Lk 6:1–5. y. [12:1] Dt 23:26.

you not read what David[z] did when he and his companions were hungry, [4]how he went into the house of God and ate the bread of offering,[a] which neither he nor his companions but only the priests could lawfully eat? [5]*Or have you not read in the law that on the sabbath the priests serving in the temple violate the sabbath and are innocent?[b] [6]I say to you, something greater than the temple is here. [7]†If you knew what this meant, 'I desire mercy, not sacrifice,'[c] you would not have condemned these innocent men. [8]‡dFor the Son of Man is Lord of the sabbath."

The Man with a Withered Hand. [9]eMoving on from there, he went into their synagogue. [10]And behold, there was a man there who had a withered hand. They questioned him, "Is it lawful to cure on the sabbath?"§ so that they might accuse him. [11]*He said to them, "Which one of you who has a sheep that falls into a pit on the sabbath will not take hold of it and lift it out? [12]How much more valuable a person is than a sheep. So it is lawful to do good on the sabbath." [13]Then he said to the man, "Stretch out your hand." He stretched it out, and it was restored as sound as the other. [14]But the Pharisees** went out and took counsel against him to put him to death.[f]

The Chosen Servant. †† [15]When Jesus realized this, he withdrew from that place. Many [people] followed him, and he cured them all,‡‡ [16]but

he warned them not to make him known. [17]This was to fulfill what had been spoken through Isaiah the prophet:

[18] "Behold, my servant whom I have chosen,[g]
        my beloved in whom I delight;
    I shall place my spirit upon him,
        and he will proclaim justice to the
            Gentiles.
[19] He will not contend§§ or cry out,
        nor will anyone hear his voice in the
            streets.
[20] A bruised reed he will not break,
        a smoldering wick he will not
            quench,
    until he brings justice to victory.
[21]   And in his name the Gentiles will
            hope."¶¶

Jesus and Beelzebul. *** [22]hThen they brought to him a demoniac who was blind and mute. He cured the mute person so that he could speak and see. [23]††††All the crowd was astounded, and said, "Could this perhaps be the Son of David?" [24]‡‡‡But when the Pharisees heard this, they said, "This man drives out demons only by the power of Beelzebul, the prince of demons." [25]kBut he knew what they were thinking and said to them,§§§ "Every kingdom divided against itself will be laid waste, and no town or house divided against itself will stand. [26]And if Satan drives out Satan, he is divided against himself; how, then, will his kingdom stand? [27]And if I drive out demons by Beelzebul, by whom do your own people¶¶¶ drive them out? Therefore they will be your judges. [28]****lBut if it is by the Spirit of God that I drive out demons, then the kingdom of God has come upon you. [29]††††How can anyone

---

to this dispute is that a violation of the law was permissible because of David's men being without food.

*[12:5–6] This and the following argument (Mt 12:7) are peculiar to Matthew. The temple service seems to be the changing of the showbread on the sabbath (Lv 24:8) and the doubling on the sabbath of the usual daily holocausts (Nm 28:9–10). The argument is that the law itself requires work that breaks the sabbath rest, because of the higher duty of temple service. If temple duties outweigh the sabbath law, how much more does the presence of Jesus, with his proclamation of the kingdom (**something greater than the temple**), justify the conduct of his disciples.

†[12:7] See note on Mt 9:13.

‡[12:8] The ultimate justification for the disciples' violation of the sabbath rest is that Jesus, the Son of Man, has supreme authority over the law.

§[12:10] Rabbinic tradition later than the gospels allowed relief to be given to a sufferer on the sabbath if life was in danger. This may also have been the view of Jesus' Pharisaic contemporaries. But the case here is not about one in danger of death.

¶[12:11] Matthew omits the question posed by Jesus in Mk 3:4 and substitutes one about rescuing a sheep on the sabbath, similar to that in Lk 14:5.

**[12:14] See Mk 3:6. Here the plan to bring about Jesus' death is attributed to the Pharisees only. This is probably due to the situation of Matthew's church, when the sole opponents were the Pharisees.

††[12:15–21] Matthew follows Mk 3:7–12 but summarizes his source in two verses (Mt 12:15, 16) that pick up the withdrawal, the healings, and the command for silence. To this he adds a fulfillment citation from the first Servant Song (Is 42:1–4) that does not correspond exactly to either the Hebrew or the LXX of that passage. It is the longest Old Testament citation in this gospel, emphasizing the meekness of Jesus, the Servant of the Lord, and foretelling the extension of his mission to the Gentiles.

‡‡[12:15] Jesus' knowledge of the Pharisees' plot and his healing all are peculiar to Matthew.

§§[12:19] The servant's not contending is seen as fulfilled in Jesus' withdrawal from the disputes narrated in Mt 12:1–14.

¶¶[12:21] Except for a minor detail, Matthew here follows the LXX, although the meaning of the Hebrew ("the coastlands will wait for his teaching") is similar.

***[12:22–32] For the exorcism, see note on Mt 9:32–34. The long discussion combines Marcan and Q material (Mk 3:22–30; Lk 11·19–20, 23; 12:10). Mk 3:20–21 is omitted, with a consequent lessening of the sharpness of Mt 12:48.

†††[12:23] See note on Mt 9:27.

‡‡‡[12:24] See note on Mt 10:25.

§§§[12:25–26] Jesus' first response to the Pharisees' charge is that if it were true, Satan would be destroying his own kingdom.

¶¶¶[12:27] Besides pointing out the absurdity of the charge, Jesus asks how the work of Jewish exorcists (**your own people**) is to be interpreted. Are they, too, to be charged with collusion with Beelzebul? For an example of Jewish exorcism see Josephus, *Antiquities* 8:42–49.

****[12:28] The Q parallel (Lk 11:20) speaks of the "finger" rather than of the "spirit" of God. While the difference is probably due to Matthew's editing, he retains **the kingdom of God** rather than changing it to his usual "kingdom of heaven." **Has come upon you**: see Mt 4:17.

††††[12:29] A short parable illustrates what Jesus is doing. The **strong man** is Satan, whom Jesus has tied up and whose **house** he is plundering. Jewish expectation was that Satan

---

z. [12:3–4] 1 Sm 21:2–7.   a. [12:4] Lv 24:5–9.   b. [12:5] Lv 24:8; Nm 28:9–10.   c. [12:7] Hos 6:6.   d. [12:8] Jn 5:16–17.   e. [12:9–15] Mk 3:1–6; Lk 6:6–11.   f. [12:14] Jn 5:18.

g. [12:18–21] Is 42:1–4.   h. [12:22–24] 9:32–34; Lk 11:14–15.   i. [12:23] 9:27.   j. [12:24] 10:25; Mk 3:22.   k. [12:25–29] Mk 3:23–27; Lk 11:17–22.   l. [12:28] Lk 11:20.

enter a strong man's house and steal his property, unless he first ties up the strong man? Then he can plunder his house. [30*][m]Whoever is not with me is against me, and whoever does not gather with me scatters. [31][n]Therefore, I say to you, every sin and blasphemy will be forgiven people, but blasphemy against the Spirit[†] will not be forgiven. [32]And whoever speaks a word against the Son of Man will be forgiven; but whoever speaks against the holy Spirit will not be forgiven, either in this age or in the age to come.

A Tree and Its Fruits. [33][o]"Either declare[‡] the tree good and its fruit is good, or declare the tree rotten and its fruit is rotten, for a tree is known by its fruit. [34][§p]You brood of vipers, how can you say good things when you are evil? For from the fullness of the heart the mouth speaks. [35]A good person brings forth good out of a store of goodness, but an evil person brings forth evil out of a store of evil. [36][¶q]I tell you, on the day of judgment people will render an account for every careless word they speak. [37]By your words you will be acquitted, and by your words you will be condemned."

The Demand for a Sign. [38]Then some of the scribes and Pharisees said to him, "Teacher,[††] we wish to see a sign from you."[r] [39]He said to them in reply, "An evil and unfaithful[‡‡] generation seeks a sign, but no sign will be given it except

the sign of Jonah the prophet. [40]Just as Jonah was in the belly of the whale three days and three nights,[§§] so will the Son of Man be in the heart of the earth three days and three nights. [41][¶¶]At the judgment, the men of Nineveh will arise with this generation and condemn it, because they repented at the preaching of Jonah; and there is something greater than Jonah here. [42]At the judgment the queen of the south will arise with this generation and condemn it, because she came from the ends of the earth to hear the wisdom of Solomon; and there is something greater than Solomon here.[s]

The Return of the Unclean Spirit. [43][¶]"When an unclean spirit goes out of a person it roams through arid regions searching for rest but finds none. [44]Then it says, 'I will return to my home from which I came.' But upon returning, it finds it empty, swept clean, and put in order. [45]Then it goes and brings back with itself seven other spirits more evil than itself, and they move in and dwell there; and the last condition of that person is worse than the first. Thus it will be with this evil generation."

The True Family of Jesus.[†††] [46][u]While he was still speaking to the crowds, his mother and his brothers appeared outside, wishing to speak with him. [47][Someone told him, "Your mother and your brothers are standing outside, asking to speak with you."][‡‡‡] [48]But he said in reply to the one who told him, "Who is my mother? Who are my brothers?" [49]And stretching out his hand toward his disciples, he said, "Here are my mother and my brothers. [50]For whoever does the will of my heavenly Father is my brother, and sister, and mother."

CHAPTER 13

The Parable of the Sower. [1][§§§]On that day, Jesus went out of the house and sat down by the sea.[v]

---

would be chained up in the last days (Rev 20:2); Jesus' exorcisms indicate that those days have begun.

*[12:30] This saying, already attached to the preceding verses in Q (see Lk 11:23), warns that there can be no neutrality where Jesus is concerned. Its pertinence in a context where Jesus is addressing not the neutral but the bitterly opposed is not clear. The accusation of scattering, however, does fit the situation. Jesus is the shepherd of God's people (Mt 2:6), his mission is to the lost sheep of Israel (Mt 15:24); the Pharisees, who oppose him, are guilty of scattering the sheep.

†[12:31] **Blasphemy against the Spirit**: the sin of attributing to Satan (Mt 12:24) what is the work of the Spirit of God (Mt 12:28).

‡[12:33] **Declare**: literally, "make." The meaning of this verse is obscure. Possibly it is a challenge to the Pharisees either to declare Jesus and his exorcisms good or both of them bad. A tree is known by its fruit; if the fruit is good, so must the tree be. If the driving out of demons is good, so must its source be.

§[12:34] The admission of Jesus' goodness cannot be made by the Pharisees, for they are evil, and the words that proceed from their evil hearts cannot be good.

¶[12:36–37] If on the day of judgment people will be held accountable for even their **careless** words, the vicious accusations of the Pharisees will surely lead to their condemnation.

**[12:38–42] This section is mainly from Q (see Lk 11:29–32). Mk 8:11–12, which Matthew has followed in Mt 16:1–4, has a similar demand for a sign. The scribes and Pharisees refuse to accept the exorcisms of Jesus as authentication of his claims and demand a sign that will end all possibility of doubt. Jesus' response is that no such sign will be given. Because his opponents are evil and see him as an agent of Satan, nothing will convince them.

††[12:38] **Teacher**: see note on Mt 8:19. In Mt 16:1 the request is for a sign "from heaven" (Mk 8:11).

‡‡[12:39] **Unfaithful**: literally, "adulterous." The covenant between God and Israel was portrayed as a marriage bond, and unfaithfulness to the covenant as adultery; cf. Hos 2:4–14; Jer 3:6–10.

m. [12:30] Lk 11:23. n. [12:31–32] Mk 3:28–30; Lk 12:10. o. [12:33–35] Lk 6:43–45. p. [12:34] 3:7; 23:33; 15:11–12; Lk 3:7. q. [12:36–37] Jas 3:1–2. r. [12:38–42] 16:1–4; Jon 2:1; 3:1–10; Mk 8:11–12; Lk 11:29–32.

§§[12:40] See Jon 2:1. While in Q the sign was simply Jonah's preaching to the Ninevites (Lk 11:30, 32), Matthew here adds Jonah's sojourn **in the belly of the whale** for **three days and three nights**, a prefigurement of Jesus' sojourn in the abode of the dead and, implicitly, of his resurrection.

¶¶[12:41–42] The Ninevites who **repented** (see Jon 3:1–10) and **the queen of the south** (i.e., of Sheba; see 1 Kgs 10:1–13) were pagans who responded to lesser opportunities than have been offered to Israel in the ministry of Jesus, **something greater than Jonah** or **Solomon**. At the final judgment they will condemn the faithless **generation** that has rejected him.

***[12:43–45] Another Q passage; cf. Mt 11:24–26. Jesus' ministry has broken Satan's hold over Israel, but the refusal of **this evil generation** to accept him will lead to a worse situation than what preceded his coming.

†††[12:46–50] See Mk 3:31–35. Matthew has omitted Mk 3:20–21 which is taken up in Mk 3:31 (see note on Mt 12:22–32), yet the point of the story is the same in both gospels: natural kinship with Jesus counts for nothing; only one who **does the will of his heavenly Father** belongs to his true family.

‡‡‡[12:47] This verse is omitted in some important textual witnesses, including Codex Sinaiticus (original reading) and Codex Vaticanus.

§§§[13:1–53] The discourse in parables is the third great discourse of Jesus in Matthew and constitutes the second part of

s. [12:42] 1 Kgs 10:1–10. t. [12:43–45] Lk 11:24–26. u. [12:46–50] Mk 3:31–35; Lk 8:19–21. v. [13:1–15] Mk 4:1–12; Lk 8:4–10.

²Such large crowds gathered around him that he got into a boat and sat down, and the whole crowd stood along the shore. ³*And he spoke to them at length in parables,† saying: "A sower went out to sow. ⁴And as he sowed, some seed fell on the path, and birds came and ate it up. ⁵Some fell on rocky ground, where it had little soil. It sprang up at once because the soil was not deep, ⁶and when the sun rose it was scorched, and it withered for lack of roots. ⁷Some seed fell among thorns, and the thorns grew up and choked it. ⁸But some seed fell on rich soil, and produced fruit, a hundred or sixty or thirtyfold. ⁹Whoever has ears ought to hear."

The Purpose of Parables. ¹⁰The disciples approached him and said, "Why do you speak to them in parables?" ¹¹‡He said to them in reply, "Because knowledge of the mysteries of the kingdom of heaven has been granted to you, but to them it has not been granted. ¹²ʷTo anyone who has, more will be given§ and he will grow rich;

the third book of the gospel. Matthew follows the Marcan outline (Mk 4:1–35) but has only two of Mark's parables, the five others being from Q and M. In addition to the seven parables, the discourse gives the reason why Jesus uses this type of speech (Mt 13:10–15), declares the blessedness of those who understand his teaching (Mt 13:16–17), explains the parable of the sower (Mt 13:18–23) and of the weeds (Mt 13:36–43), and ends with a concluding statement to the disciples (Mt 13:51–52).

*[13:3] In parables: the word "parable" (Greek *parabolē*) is used in the LXX to translate the Hebrew *māshāl*, a designation covering a wide variety of literary forms such as axioms, proverbs, similitudes, and allegories. In the New Testament the same breadth of meaning of the word is found, but there it primarily designates stories that are illustrative comparisons between Christian truths and events of everyday life. Sometimes the event has a strange element that is quite different from usual experience (e.g., in Mt 13:33 the enormous amount of dough in the parable of the yeast); this is meant to sharpen the curiosity of the hearer. If each detail of such a story is given a figurative meaning, the story is an allegory. Those who maintain a sharp distinction between parable and allegory and insist that a parable has only one point of comparison, and that while parables were characteristic of Jesus' teaching, to see allegorical details in them is to introduce meanings that go beyond their original intention and even falsify it. However, to exclude any allegorical elements from a parable is an excessively rigid mode of interpretation, now abandoned by many scholars.

†[13:3–8] Since in Palestine sowing often preceded plowing, much of the seed is scattered on ground that is unsuitable. Yet while much is wasted, the seed that falls on good ground bears fruit in extraordinarily large measure. The point of the parable is that, in spite of some failure because of opposition and indifference, the message of Jesus about the coming of the kingdom will have enormous success.

‡[13:11] Since a parable is figurative speech that demands reflection for understanding, only those who are prepared to explore its meaning can come to know it. To understand is a gift of God, granted to the disciples but not to the crowds. In Semitic fashion, both the disciples' understanding and the crowd's obtuseness are attributed to God. The question of human responsibility for the obtuseness is not dealt with, although it is asserted in Mt 13:13. The mysteries: as in Lk 8:10; Mk 4:11 has "the mystery." The word is used in Dn 2:18, 19, 27 and in the Qumran literature (1QpHab 7:8; 1QS 3:23; 1QM 3:9) to designate a divine plan or decree affecting the course of history that can be known only when revealed. Knowledge of the mysteries of the kingdom of heaven means recognition that the kingdom has become present in the ministry of Jesus.

§[13:12] In the New Testament use of this axiom of practical "wisdom" (see Mt 25:29; Mk 4:25; Lk 8:18; 19:26), the reference

w. [13:12] 25:29; Mk 4:25; Lk 8:18; 19:26.

from anyone who has not, even what he has will be taken away. ¹³ˣThis is why I speak to them in parables, because 'they look but do not see and hear but do not listen or understand.' ¹⁴ʸIsaiah's prophecy is fulfilled in them, which says:

'You shall indeed hear but not understand,
        you shall indeed look but never see.
¹⁵ Gross is the heart of this people,
        they will hardly hear with their ears,
        they have closed their eyes,
        lest they see with their eyes
        and hear with their ears
    and understand with their heart and be
            converted,
        and I heal them.'

The Privilege of Discipleship. ¹⁶ᶻ"But blessed are your eyes, because they see, and your ears, because they hear. ¹⁷Amen, I say to you, many prophets and righteous people longed to see what you see but did not see it, and to hear what you hear but did not hear it.

The Explanation of the Parable of the Sower.†† ¹⁸ᵃ"Hear then the parable of the sower. ¹⁹The seed sown on the path is the one who hears the word of the kingdom without understanding it, and the evil one comes and steals away what was sown in his heart. ²⁰The seed sown on rocky ground is the one who hears the word and receives it at once with joy. ²¹But he has no root and lasts only for a time. When some tribulation or persecution comes because of the word, he immediately falls away. ²²The seed sown among thorns is the one who hears the word, but then worldly anxiety and the lure of riches choke the

transcends the original level. God gives further understanding to one who accepts the revealed mystery; from the one who does not, he will take it away (note the "theological passive," more will be given, what he has will be taken away).

¶[13:13] Because 'they look . . . or understand': Matthew softens his Marcan source, which states that Jesus speaks in parables so that the crowds may not understand (Mk 4:12), and makes such speaking a punishment given because they have not accepted his previous clear teaching. However, his citation of Is 6:9–10 in Mt 13:14 supports the harsher Marcan view.

⁰⁴[13:16–17] Unlike the unbelieving crowds, the disciples have seen that which the prophets and the righteous of the Old Testament longed to see without having their longing fulfilled.

††[13:18–23] See Mk 4:14–20; Lk 8:11–15. In this explanation of the parable the emphasis is on the various types of soil on which the seed falls, i.e., on the dispositions with which the preaching of Jesus is received. The second and third types particularly are explained in such a way as to support the view held by many scholars that the explanation derives not from Jesus but from early Christian reflection upon apostasy from the faith that was the consequence of persecution and worldliness, respectively. Others, however, hold that the explanation may come basically from Jesus even though it was developed in the light of later Christian experience. The four types of persons envisaged are (1) those who never accept the word of the kingdom (Mt 13:19); (2) those who believe for a while but fall away because of persecution (Mt 13:20–21); (3) those who believe, but in whom the word is choked by worldly anxiety and the seduction of riches (Mt 13:22); (4) those who respond to the word and produce fruit abundantly (Mt 13:23).

x. [13:13] Jn 9:39.   y. [13:14–15] Is 6:9–10; Jn 12:40; Acts 28:26–27; Rom 11:8.   z. [13:16–17] Lk 10:23–24; 1 Pt 1:10–12.   a. [13:18–23] Mk 4:13–20; Lk 8:11–15.

word and it bears no fruit. [23]But the seed sown on rich soil is the one who hears the word and understands it, who indeed bears fruit and yields a hundred or sixty or thirtyfold."

The Parable of the Weeds Among the Wheat. [24]He proposed another parable to them.* "The kingdom of heaven may be likened to a man who sowed good seed in his field. [25]While everyone was asleep his enemy came and sowed weeds[†] all through the wheat, and then went off. [26]When the crop grew and bore fruit, the weeds appeared as well. [27]The slaves of the householder came to him and said, 'Master, did you not sow good seed in your field? Where have the weeds come from?' [28]He answered, 'An enemy has done this.' His slaves said to him, 'Do you want us to go and pull them up?' [29]He replied, 'No, if you pull up the weeds you might uproot the wheat along with them. [30]Let them grow together until harvest;[‡] then at harvest time I will say to the harvesters, "First collect the weeds and tie them in bundles for burning; but gather the wheat into my barn."'"[b]

The Parable of the Mustard Seed.[§] [31c]He proposed another parable to them. "The kingdom of heaven is like a mustard seed that a person took and sowed in a field. [32d]It is the smallest of all the seeds, yet when full-grown it is the largest of plants. It becomes a large bush, and the 'birds of the sky come and dwell in its branches.'"

The Parable of the Yeast. [33]He spoke to them another parable. "The kingdom of heaven is like yeast** that a woman took and mixed with three measures of wheat flour until the whole batch was leavened."[e]

The Use of Parables. [34††]All these things Jesus spoke to the crowds in parables. He spoke to them only in parables, [35]to fulfill what had been said through the prophet:[‡‡]

"I will open my mouth in parables,
    I will announce what has lain
        hidden from the foundation
        [of the world]."[g]

The Explanation of the Parable of the Weeds. [36]Then, dismissing the crowds,[§§] he went into the house. His disciples approached him and said, "Explain to us the parable of the weeds in the field." [37¶¶]He said in reply, "He who sows good seed is the Son of Man, [38]the field is the world,*** the good seed the children of the kingdom. The weeds are the children of the evil one, [39]and the enemy who sows them is the devil. The harvest is the end of the age,[†††] and the harvesters are angels. [40]Just as weeds are collected and burned [up] with fire, so will it be at the end of the age. [41]The Son of Man will send his angels, and they will collect out of his kingdom[‡‡‡] all who cause others to sin and all evildoers. [42h]They will throw them into the fiery furnace, where there will be wailing and grinding of teeth. [43§§§i]Then the righteous will shine like the sun in the kingdom of their Father. Whoever has ears ought to hear.

More Parables.[¶¶¶] [44j]"The kingdom of heaven is like a treasure buried in a field,**** which a person

---

*[13:24–30] This parable is peculiar to Matthew. The comparison in Mt 13:24 does not mean that **the kingdom of heaven may be likened** simply to the person in question but to the situation narrated in the whole story. The refusal of the **householder** to allow his **slaves** to separate **the wheat** from **the weeds** while they are still growing is a warning to the disciples not to attempt to anticipate the final judgment of God by a definitive exclusion of sinners from the kingdom. In its present stage it is composed of the good and the bad. The judgment of God alone will eliminate the sinful. Until then there must be patience and the preaching of repentance.

†[13:25] **Weeds**: darnel, a poisonous weed that in its first stage of growth resembles wheat.

‡[13:30] **Harvest**: a common biblical metaphor for the time of God's judgment; cf. Jer 51:33; Jl 4:13; Hos 6:11.

§[13:31–33] See Mk 4:30–32; Lk 13:18–21. The parables of the mustard seed and the yeast illustrate the same point: the amazing contrast between the small beginnings of the kingdom and its marvelous expansion.

¶[13:32] See Dn 4:7–9, 17–19 where the birds nesting in the tree represent the people of Nebuchadnezzar's kingdom. See also Ez 17:23; 31:6.

[13:33] Except in this Q parable and in Mt 16:12, **yeast (or "leaven") is, in New Testament usage, a symbol of corruption (see Mt 16:6, 11–12; Mk 8:15; Lk 12:1; 1 Cor 5:6–8; Gal 5:9). **Three measures**: an enormous amount, enough to feed a hundred people. The exaggeration of this element of the parable points to the greatness of the kingdom's effect.

††[13:34] **Only in parables**: see Mt 13:10–15.

b. [13:30] 3:12.   c. [13:31–32] Mk 4:30–32; Lk 13:18–19.   d. [13:32] Ez 17:23; 31:6; Dn 4:7–9, 17–19.   e. [13:33] Lk 13:20–21.   f. [13:34–35] Mk 4:33–34.

‡‡[13:35] **The prophet**: some textual witnesses read "Isaiah the prophet." The quotation is actually from Ps 78:2; the first line corresponds to the LXX text of the psalm. The psalm's title ascribes it to Asaph, the founder of one of the guilds of temple musicians. He is called "the prophet" (NAB "the seer") in 2 Chr 29:30, but it is doubtful that Matthew averted to that; for him, any Old Testament text that could be seen as fulfilled in Jesus was prophetic.

§§[13:36] **Dismissing the crowds**: the return of Jesus to the house marks a break with the crowds, who represent unbelieving Israel. From now on his attention is directed more and more to his disciples and to their instruction. The rest of the discourse is addressed to them alone.

¶¶[13:37–43] In the explanation of the parable of the weeds emphasis lies on the fearful end of the wicked, whereas the parable itself concentrates on patience with them until judgment time.

***[13:38] **The field is the world**: this presupposes the resurrection of Jesus and the granting to him of "all power in heaven and on earth" (Mt 28:18).

†††[13:39] **The end of the age**: this phrase is found only in Matthew (Mt 13:40, 49; 24:3; 28:20).

‡‡‡[13:41] **His kingdom**: the **kingdom** of the **Son of Man** is distinguished from that of the Father (Mt 13:43); see 1 Cor 15:24–25. The church is the place where Jesus' kingdom is manifested, but his royal authority embraces the entire world; see note on Mt 13:38.

§§§[13:43] See Dn 12:3.

¶¶¶[13:44–50] The first two of the last three parables of the discourse have the same point. The **person** who **finds** a buried **treasure** and the **merchant** who finds a **pearl of great price** sell **all** that they have to acquire these finds; similarly, the one who understands the supreme value of the kingdom gives up whatever he must to obtain it. The **joy** with which this is done is made explicit in the first parable, but it may be presumed in the second also. The concluding parable of the fishnet resembles the explanation of the parable of the weeds with its stress upon the final exclusion of evil persons from the kingdom.

****[13:44] In the unsettled conditions of Palestine in Jesus' time, it was not unusual to guard valuables by burying them in the ground.

g. [13:35] Ps 78:2.   h. [13:42] 8:12; Rev 21:8.   i. [13:43] Dn 12:3. j. [13:44–45] Prv 2:4; 4:7.

finds and hides again, and out of joy goes and sells all that he has and buys that field. ⁴⁵Again, the kingdom of heaven is like a merchant searching for fine pearls. ⁴⁶When he finds a pearl of great price, he goes and sells all that he has and buys it. ⁴⁷Again, the kingdom of heaven is like a net thrown into the sea, which collects fish of every kind. ⁴⁸When it is full they haul it ashore and sit down to put what is good into buckets. What is bad they throw away. ⁴⁹Thus it will be at the end of the age. The angels will go out and separate the wicked from the righteous ⁵⁰and throw them into the fiery furnace, where there will be wailing and grinding of teeth.

Treasures New and Old. ⁵¹"Do you understand all these things?" They answered, "Yes." ⁵²†And he replied, "Then every scribe who has been instructed in the kingdom of heaven is like the head of a household who brings from his storeroom both the new and the old." ⁵³When Jesus finished these parables, he went away from there.

V. JESUS, THE KINGDOM, AND THE CHURCH

The Rejection at Nazareth. ⁵⁴‡He came to his native place and taught the people in their synagogue.ᵏ They were astonished§ and said, "Where did this man get such wisdom and mighty deeds?ˡ ⁵⁵Is he not the carpenter's son? Is not his mother named Mary and his brothers James, Joseph, Simon, and Judas?ᵐ ⁵⁶Are not his sisters all with us? Where did this man get all this?" ⁵⁷And they took offense at him. But Jesus said to them, "A prophet is not without honor except in his native place and in his own house."ⁿ

---

*[13:51] Matthew typically speaks of the understanding of the disciples.

†[13:52] Since Matthew tends to identify the disciples and the Twelve (see note on Mt 10:1), this saying about the Christian **scribe** cannot be taken as applicable to all who accept the message of Jesus. While the Twelve are in many ways representative of all who believe in him, they are also distinguished from them in certain respects. The church of Matthew has leaders among whom are a group designated as "scribes" (Mt 23:34). Like the scribes of Israel, they are teachers. It is the Twelve and these their later counterparts to whom this verse applies. The scribe . . . instructed in the kingdom of heaven knows both the teaching of Jesus (**the new**) and the law and prophets (**the old**) and provides in his own teaching **both the new and the old** as interpreted and fulfilled by **the new**. On the translation **head of a household** (for the same Greek word translated **householder** in Mt 13:27), see note on Mt 24:45–51.

‡[13:54–17:27] This section is the narrative part of the fourth book of the gospel.

§[13:54–58] After the Sermon on the Mount the crowds are in admiring astonishment at Jesus' teaching (Mt 7:28); here the astonishment is of those who take **offense at him**. Familiarity with his background and family leads them to regard him as pretentious. Matthew modifies his Marcan source (Mt 6:1–6). Jesus is not the carpenter but **the carpenter's son** (Mt 13:55), "and among his own kin" is omitted (Mt 13:57), **he did not work many mighty deeds** in face of such unbelief (Mt 13:58) rather than the Marcan ". . . he was not able to perform any mighty deed there" (Mt 6:5), and there is no mention of his amazement at his townspeople's lack of faith.

k. [13:54–58] Mk 6:1–6; Lk 4:16–30. l. [13:54] 2:23; Jn 1:46; 7:15.
m. [13:55] 12:46; 27:56; Jn 6:42. n. [13:57] Jn 4:44.

---

⁵⁸And he did not work many mighty deeds there because of their lack of faith.

CHAPTER 14

Herod's Opinion of Jesus. ¹ᵒAt that time Herod the tetrarch**ᵖ heard of the reputation of Jesus�q ²and said to his servants, "This man is John the Baptist. He has been raised from the dead; that is why mighty powers are at work in him."

The Death of John the Baptist. ³ʳNow Herod had arrested John, bound [him], and put him in prison on account of Herodias,†† the wife of his brother Philip, ⁴ˢfor John had said to him, "It is not lawful for you to have her." ⁵†Although he wanted to kill him, he feared the people, for they regarded him as a prophet. ⁶But at a birthday celebration for Herod, the daughter of Herodias performed a dance before the guests and delighted Herod ⁷so much that he swore to give her whatever she might ask for. ⁸Prompted by her mother, she said, "Give me here on a platter the head of John the Baptist." ⁹The king was distressed, but because of his oaths and the guests who were present, he ordered that it be given, ¹⁰and he had John beheaded in the prison. ¹¹His head was brought in on a platter and given to the girl, who took it to her mother. ¹²His disciples came and took away the corpse and buried him; and they went and told Jesus.

The Return of the Twelve and the Feeding of the Five Thousand. ‡‡ ¹³ᵘWhen Jesus heard of it, he withdrew in a boat to a deserted place by himself. The crowds heard of this and followed him on foot from their towns. ¹⁴When he

---

¶[14:1–12] The murder of the Baptist by Herod Antipas prefigures the death of Jesus (see Mt 17:12). The Marcan source (Mk 6:14–29) is much reduced and in some points changed. In Mark Herod reveres John as a holy man and the desire to kill him is attributed to Herodias (Mk 6:19, 20), whereas here that desire is Herod's from the beginning (Mt 14:5).

[14:1] **Herod the tetrarch: Herod Antipas, son of Herod the Great. When the latter died, his territory was divided among three of his surviving sons, Archelaus who received half of it (Mt 2:23), Herod Antipas who became ruler of Galilee and Perea, and Philip who became ruler of northern Transjordan. Since he received a quarter of his father's domain, Antipas is accurately designated **tetrarch** ("ruler of a fourth [part]"), although in Mt 14:9 Matthew repeats the "king" of his Marcan source (Mk 6:26).

††[14:3] Herodias was not the wife of Herod's half-brother Philip but of another half-brother, Herod Boethus. The union was prohibited by Lv 18:16; 20:21. According to Josephus (*Antiquities* 18:116–19), Herod imprisoned and then executed John because he feared that the Baptist's influence over the people might enable him to lead a rebellion.

‡‡[14:13–21] The feeding of the five thousand is the only miracle of Jesus that is recounted in all four gospels. The principal reason for that may be that it was seen as anticipating the Eucharist and the final banquet in the kingdom (Mt 8:11; 26:29), but it looks not only forward but backward, to the feeding of Israel with manna in the desert at the time of the Exodus (Ex 16), a miracle that in some contemporary Jewish expectation would be repeated in the messianic age (2 Bar 29:8). It may also be meant to recall Elisha's feeding a hundred men with small provisions (2 Kgs 4:42–44).

o. [14:1–12] Mk 6:14–29. p. [14:1–2] Lk 9:7–9. q. [14:1] Lk 3:1.
r. [14:3–4] Lk 3:19–20. s. [14:4] Lv 18:16; 20:21. t. [14:5] 21:26.
u. [14:13–21] 15:32–38; Mk 6:32–44; Lk 9:10–17; Jn 6:1–13.

disembarked and saw the vast crowd, his heart was moved with pity for them, and he cured their sick. ¹⁵When it was evening, the disciples approached him and said, "This is a deserted place and it is already late; dismiss the crowds so that they can go to the villages and buy food for themselves." ¹⁶[Jesus] said to them, "There is no need for them to go away; give them some food yourselves." ¹⁷But they said to him, "Five loaves and two fish are all we have here." ¹⁸Then he said, "Bring them here to me," ¹⁹and he ordered the crowds to sit down on the grass. Taking* the five loaves and the two fish, and looking up to heaven, he said the blessing, broke the loaves, and gave them to the disciples, who in turn gave them to the crowds. ²⁰They all ate and were satisfied, and they picked up the fragments left over†—twelve wicker baskets full. ²¹Those who ate were about five thousand men, not counting women and children.

The Walking on the Water.‡ ²²ᵛThen he made the disciples get into the boat and precede him to the other side, while he dismissed the crowds. ²³ᵂAfter doing so, he went up on the mountain by himself to pray. When it was evening he was there alone. ²⁴Meanwhile the boat, already a few miles offshore, was being tossed about by the waves, for the wind was against it. ²⁵During the fourth watch of the night,§ he came toward them, walking on the sea. ²⁶When the disciples saw him walking on the sea they were terrified. "It is a ghost," they said, and they cried out in fear. ²⁷At once [Jesus] spoke to them, "Take courage, it is I;⁵ do not be afraid." ²⁸Peter said to him in reply, "Lord, if it is you, command me to come to you on the water." ²⁹He said, "Come." Peter got out of the boat and began to walk on the water toward Jesus. ³⁰ˣBut when he saw how [strong] the wind was he became frightened; and, beginning to sink, he cried out, "Lord, save me!" ³¹Immediately Jesus stretched out his hand and caught him, and said to him, "O you of little

faith," why did you doubt?" ³²After they got into the boat, the wind died down. ³³††ʸThose who were in the boat did him homage, saying, "Truly, you are the Son of God."
The Healings at Gennesaret. ³⁴ᶻAfter making the crossing, they came to land at Gennesaret. ³⁵When the men of that place recognized him, they sent word to all the surrounding country. People brought to him all those who were sick ³⁶ᵃand begged him that they might touch only the tassel on his cloak, and as many as touched it were healed.

CHAPTER 15

The Tradition of the Elders.‡‡ ¹ᵇThen Pharisees and scribes came to Jesus from Jerusalem and said, ²ᶜ"Why do your disciples break the tradition of the elders?§§ They do not wash [their] hands when they eat a meal." ³He said to them in reply, "And why do you break the commandment of God⁵⁵ for the sake of your tradition? ⁴ᵈFor God said, 'Honor your father and your mother,' and 'Whoever curses father or mother shall die.' ⁵"But you say, 'Whoever says to father or mother, "Any support you might have had from me is dedicated to God," ⁶need not honor his father.' You have nullified the word of God for the sake of your tradition. ⁷Hypocrites, well did Isaiah prophesy about you when he said:

[14:31] You of little faith: see note on Mt 6:30. **Why did you doubt?:** the verb is peculiar to Matthew and occurs elsewhere only in Mt 28:17.

††[14:33] This confession is in striking contrast to the Marcan parallel (Mk 6:51) where the disciples are "completely astounded."

‡‡[15:1–20] This dispute begins with the question of the Pharisees and scribes why Jesus' disciples are breaking **the tradition of the elders** about washing one's hands before eating (Mt 15:2). Jesus' counterquestion accuses his opponents of breaking **the commandment of God for the sake of** their tradition (Mt 15:3) and illustrates this by their interpretation of the commandment of the Decalogue concerning parents (Mt 15:4–6). Denouncing them as hypocrites, he applies to them a derogatory prophecy of Isaiah (Mt 15:7–8). Then with a wider audience (**the crowd**, Mt 15:10) he goes beyond the violation of tradition with which the dispute has started. The parable (Mt 15:11) is an attack on the Mosaic law concerning clean and unclean foods, similar to those antitheses that abrogate the law (Mt 5:31–32, 33–34, 38–39). After a warning to his disciples not to follow the moral guidance of the Pharisees (Mt 15:13–14), he explains the **parable** (Mt 15:15) to them, saying that defilement comes not from what **enters the mouth** (Mt 15:17) but from the evil thoughts and deeds that rise from within, **from the heart** (Mt 15:18–20). The last verse returns to the starting point of the dispute (eating with **unwashed hands**). Because of Matthew's omission of Mk 7:19b, some scholars think that Matthew has weakened the Marcan repudiation of the Mosaic food laws. But that half verse is ambiguous in the Greek, which may be the reason for its omission here.

§§[15:2] **The tradition of the elders:** see note on Mk 7:5. The purpose of the handwashing was to remove defilement caused by contact with what was ritually unclean.

⁵⁵[15:3–4] For the commandment see Ex 20:12 (// Dt 5:16); 21:17. The honoring of one's parents had to do with supporting them in their needs.

***[15:5] See note on Mk 7:11.

---

*[14:19] The **taking**, saying the blessing, breaking, and giving to the disciples correspond to the actions of Jesus over the bread at the Last Supper (Mt 26:26). Since they were usual at any Jewish meal, that correspondence does not necessarily indicate a eucharistic reference here. Matthew's silence about Jesus' dividing the fish among the people (Mk 6:41) is perhaps more significant in that regard.

†[14:20] **The fragments left over:** as in Elisha's miracle, food was **left over** after all had been fed. The word **fragments** (Greek *klasmata*) is used, in the singular, of the broken bread of the Eucharist in *Didache* 9:3–4.

‡[14:22–33] The disciples, laboring against the turbulent sea, are saved by Jesus. For his power over the waters, see note on Mt 8:26. Here that power is expressed also by his **walking on the sea** (Mt 14:25; cf. Ps 77:20; Jb 9:8). Matthew has inserted into the Marcan story (Mk 6:45–52) material that belongs to his special traditions on Peter (Mt 14:28–31).

§[14:25] **The fourth watch of the night:** between 3 a.m. and 6 a.m. The Romans divided the twelve hours between 6 p.m. and 6 a.m. into four equal parts called "watches."

⁵[14:27] **It is I:** see note on Mk 6:50.

---

v. [14:22–33] Mk 6:45–52; Jn 6:16–21.   w. [14:23] Mk 1:35; Lk 5:16; 6:12.   x. [14:30–31] 8:25–26.

y. [14:33] 16:16.   z. [14:34–36] Mk 6:53–56.   a. [14:36] 9:20–22. b. [15:1–20] Mk 7:1–23.   c. [15:2] Lk 11:38.   d. [15:4] Ex 20:12; 21:17; Lv 20:9; Dt 5:16; Prv 20:20.

8 e"This people honors me with their lips,·
      but their hearts are far from me;
9 /in vain do they worship me,
      teaching as doctrines human
      precepts.'"

10gHe summoned the crowd and said to them, "Hear and understand. 11It is not what enters one's mouth that defiles that person; but what comes out of the mouth is what defiles one." 12Then his disciples approached and said to him, "Do you know that the Pharisees took offense when they heard what you said?" 13He said in reply,† "Every plant that my heavenly Father has not planted will be uprooted. 14hLet them alone; they are blind guides [of the blind]. If a blind person leads a blind person, both will fall into a pit." 15Then Peter‡ said to him in reply, "Explain [this] parable to us." 16He said to them, "Are even you still without understanding? 17Do you not realize that everything that enters the mouth passes into the stomach and is expelled into the latrine? 18iBut the things that come out of the mouth come from the heart, and they defile. 19jFor from the heart come evil thoughts, murder, adultery, unchastity, theft, false witness, blasphemy. 20These are what defile a person, but to eat with unwashed hands does not defile."

The Canaanite Woman's Faith.¶ 21jThen Jesus went from that place and withdrew to the region of Tyre and Sidon. 22And behold, a Canaanite woman of that district came and called out, "Have pity on me, Lord, Son of David! My daughter is tormented by a demon." 23But he did not say a word in answer to her. His disciples came and asked him, "Send her away, for she keeps calling out after us." 24"*He said in reply, "I was sent only to the lost sheep of the house of Israel." 25kBut the woman came and did him homage, saying, "Lord, help me." 26He said in reply, "It is not right to take the food of the children†† and throw it to the dogs." 27She said, "Please, Lord, for even the dogs eat the scraps that fall from the table of their masters." 28lThen

Jesus said to her in reply, "O woman, great is your faith!‡‡ Let it be done for you as you wish." And her daughter was healed from that hour.

The Healing of Many People. 29Moving on from there Jesus walked by the Sea of Galilee, went up on the mountain, and sat down there. 30mGreat crowds came to him, having with them the lame, the blind, the deformed, the mute, and many others. They placed them at his feet, and he cured them. 31The crowds were amazed when they saw the mute speaking, the deformed made whole, the lame walking, and the blind able to see, and they glorified the God of Israel.

The Feeding of the Four Thousand.§§ 32nJesus summoned his disciples and said, "My heart is moved with pity for the crowd, for they have been with me now for three days and have nothing to eat. I do not want to send them away hungry, for fear they may collapse on the way." 33The disciples said to him, "Where could we ever get enough bread in this deserted place to satisfy such a crowd?" 34Jesus said to them, "How many loaves do you have?" "Seven," they replied, "and a few fish." 35He ordered the crowd to sit down on the ground. 36Then he took the seven loaves and the fish, gave thanks,¶¶ broke the loaves, and gave them to the disciples, who in turn gave them to the crowds. 37oThey all ate and were satisfied. They picked up the fragments left over—seven baskets full. 38Those who ate were four thousand men, not counting women and children. 39And when he had dismissed the crowds, he got into the boat and came to the district of Magadan.

CHAPTER 16

The Demand for a Sign. 1***pThe Pharisees and Sadducees came and, to test him, asked him to show them a sign from heaven. 2†††He said to them in reply, "[In the evening you say, 'Tomorrow will be fair, for the sky is red'; 3qand, in the morning, 'Today will be stormy, for the sky is

---

*[15:8] The text of Is 29:13 is quoted approximately according to the Septuagint.

†[15:13–14] Jesus leads his disciples away from the teaching authority of the Pharisees.

‡[15:15] Matthew specifies **Peter** as the questioner, unlike Mk 7:17. Given his tendency to present the disciples as more understanding than in his Marcan source, it is noteworthy that here he retains the Marcan rebuke, although in a slightly milder form. This may be due to his wish to correct the Jewish Christians within his church who still held to the food laws and thus separated themselves from Gentile Christians who did not observe them.

§[15:19] The Marcan list of thirteen things that defile (Mk 7:21–22) is here reduced to seven that partially cover the content of the Decalogue.

¶[15:21–28] See note on Mt 8:5–13.

**[15:24] See note on Mt 10:5–6.

††[15:26] **The children:** the people of Israel. **Dogs:** see note on Mt 7:6.

‡‡[15:28] As in the case of the cure of the centurion's servant (Mt 8:10), Matthew ascribes Jesus' granting the request to the woman's **great faith**, a point not made equally explicit in the Marcan parallel (Mk 7:24–30).

§§[15:32–39] Most probably this story is a doublet of that of the feeding of the five thousand (Mt 14:13–21). It differs from it notably only in that Jesus takes the initiative, not the disciples (Mt 15:32), and in the numbers: the crowd has been with Jesus **three days** (Mt 15:32), **seven loaves** are multiplied (Mt 15:36), **seven baskets** of **fragments** remain after the feeding (Mt 15:37), and **four thousand** men are fed (Mt 15:38).

¶¶[15:36] **Gave thanks:** see Mt 14:19, "said the blessing." There is no difference in meaning. The thanksgiving was a blessing of God for his benefits.

***[16:1] **A sign from heaven:** see note on Mt 12:38–42.

†††[16:2–3] The answer of Jesus in these verses is omitted in many important textual witnesses, and it is very uncertain that it is an original part of this gospel. It resembles Lk 12:54–56 and may have been inserted from there. It rebukes the Pharisees and Sadducees who are able to read indications of coming weather but not the indications of the coming kingdom in the signs that Jesus does offer, his mighty deeds and teaching.

e. [15:8] Is 29:13 LXX. f. [15:9] Col 2:23. g. [15:10] Mk 7:14. h. [15:14] 23:16, 19, 24; Lk 6:39; Jn 9:40. i. [15:18] 12:34. j. [15:21–28] Mk 7:24–30. k. [15:25] 10:6. l. [15:28] 8:10.

m. [15:30] Is 35:5–6. n. [15:32–39] Mk 8:1–10. o. [15:37] 16:10. p. [16:1–10] Mk 8:11–21. q. [16:3] Lk 12:54–56.

red and threatening.' You know how to judge the appearance of the sky, but you cannot judge the signs of the times.] ⁴ʳAn evil and unfaithful generation seeks a sign, but no sign will be given it except the sign of Jonah."* Then he left them and went away.

The Leaven of the Pharisees and Sadducees. ⁵ˢIn coming to the other side of the sea,† the disciples had forgotten to bring bread. ⁶ᵗJesus said to them, "Look out, and beware of the leaven‡ of the Pharisees and Sadducees." ⁷ᵘThey concluded among themselves, saying, "It is because we have brought no bread." ⁸When Jesus became aware of this he said, "You of little faith, why do you conclude among yourselves that it is because you have no bread? ⁹ᵘDo you not yet understand, and do you not remember the five loaves for the five thousand, and how many wicker baskets you took up? ¹⁰ᵛOr the seven loaves for the four thousand, and how many baskets you took up? ¹¹How do you not comprehend that I was not speaking to you about bread? Beware of the leaven of the Pharisees and Sadducees." ¹²Then they understood' that he was not telling them to beware of the leaven of bread, but of the teaching of the Pharisees and Sadducees.

Peter's Confession About Jesus. ** ¹³ʷWhen Jesus went into the region of Caesarea Philippi†† he

asked his disciples, "Who do people say that the Son of Man is?" ¹⁴ˣThey replied, "Some say John the Baptist,‡‡ others Elijah, still others Jeremiah or one of the prophets." ¹⁵He said to them, "But who do you say that I am?" ¹⁶§§ySimon Peter said in reply, "You are the Messiah, the Son of the living God." ¹⁷Jesus said to him in reply, "Blessed are you, Simon son of Jonah. For flesh and blood¶¶ has not revealed this to you, but my heavenly Father. ¹⁸ᶻAnd so I say to you, you are Peter, and upon this rock I will build my church,*** and the gates of the netherworld shall not prevail against it. ¹⁹ªI will give you the keys to the kingdom of heaven.††† Whatever you bind

A.D. 34 (see note on Mt 14:1). He rebuilt the town of Paneas, naming it **Caesarea** in honor of the emperor, and **Philippi** ("of Philip") to distinguish it from the seaport in Samaria that was also called Caesarea. **Who do people say that the Son of Man is?**: although the question differs from the Marcan parallel (Mk 8:27: "Who . . . that I am?"), the meaning is the same, for Jesus here refers to himself as the **Son of Man** (cf. Mt 16:15).

‡‡[16:14] **John the Baptist**: see Mt 14:2. **Elijah**: cf. Mal 3:23–24; Sir 48:10; and see note on Mt 3:4. **Jeremiah**: an addition of Matthew to the Marcan source.

§§[16:16] **The Son of the living God**: see Mt 2:15; 3:17. The addition of this exalted title to the Marcan confession eliminates whatever ambiguity was attached to the title Messiah. This, among other things, supports the view proposed by many scholars that Matthew has here combined his source's confession with a post-resurrectional confession of faith in Jesus as **Son of the living God** that belonged to the appearance of the risen Jesus to Peter; cf. 1 Cor 15:5; Lk 24:34.

¶¶[16:17] **Flesh and blood**: a Semitic expression for human beings, especially in their weakness. **Has not revealed this . . . but my heavenly Father**: that Peter's faith is spoken of as coming not through human means but through a revelation from God is similar to Paul's description of his recognition of who Jesus was; see Gal 1:15–16, ". . . when he [God] . . . was pleased to reveal his Son to me . . . ."

***[16:18] **You are Peter, and upon this rock I will build my church**: the Aramaic word *kēpā'* meaning **rock** and transliterated into Greek as *Kēphas* is the name by which Peter is called in the Pauline letters (1 Cor 1:12; 3:22; 9:5; 15:4; Gal 1:18; 2:9, 11, 14) except in Gal 2:7–8 ("Peter"). It is translated as *Petros* ("Peter") in Jn 1:42. The presumed original Aramaic of Jesus' statement would have been, in English, "You are the Rock (*Kēpā'*) and upon this rock (*kēpā'*) I will build my church." The Greek text probably means the same, for the difference in gender between the masculine noun *petros*, the disciple's new name, and the feminine noun *petra* (rock) may be due simply to the unsuitability of using a feminine noun as the proper name of a male. Although the two words were generally used with slightly different nuances, they were also used interchangeably with the same meaning, "rock." **Church**: this word (Greek *ekklēsia*) occurs in the gospels only here and in Mt 18:17 (twice). There are several possibilities for an Aramaic original. Jesus' **church** means the community that he **will** gather and that, like a building, will have Peter as its solid foundation. That function of Peter consists in his being witness to Jesus as **the Messiah, the Son of the living God**. **The gates of the netherworld shall not prevail against it**: the netherworld (Greek *Hadēs*, the abode of the dead) is conceived of as a walled city whose **gates** will not close in upon the church of Jesus, i.e., it will not be overcome by the power of death.

†††[16:19] **The keys to the kingdom of heaven**: the image of the keys is probably drawn from Is 22:15–25 where Eliakim, who succeeds Shebna as master of the palace, is given "the key of the House of David," which he authoritatively "opens" and "shuts" (Is 22:22). **Whatever you bind . . . loosed in heaven**: there are many instances in rabbinic literature of the binding-loosing imagery. Of the several meanings given there to the metaphor, two are of special importance here: the giving of

*[16:4] See notes on Mt 12:39, 40.

†[16:5–12] Jesus' warning his disciples against the **teaching of the Pharisees and Sadducees** comes immediately before his promise to confer on Peter the authority to bind and to loose on earth (Mt 16:19), an authority that will be confirmed in heaven. Such authority most probably has to do, at least in part, with teaching. The rejection of the teaching authority of the Pharisees (see also Mt 12:12–14) prepares for a new one derived from Jesus.

‡[16:6] **Leaven**: see note on Mt 13:33. **Sadducees**: Matthew's Marcan source speaks rather of "the leaven of Herod" (Mk 8:15).

§[16:7–11] The disciples, men **of little faith**, misunderstand Jesus' metaphorical use of **leaven**, forgetting that, as the feeding of the crowds shows, he is not at a loss to provide them with bread.

¶[16:12] After his rebuke, the disciples understand that by **leaven** he meant the corrupting influence of **the teaching of the Pharisees and Sadducees**. The evangelist probably understands this **teaching** as common to both groups. Since at the time of Jesus' ministry the two differed widely on points of teaching, e.g., the resurrection of the dead, and at the time of the evangelist the Sadducee party was no longer a force in Judaism, the supposed common teaching fits neither period. The disciples' eventual understanding of Jesus' warning contrasts with their continuing obtuseness in the Marcan parallel (Mk 8:14–21).

[16:13–20] The Marcan confession of Jesus as Messiah, made by Peter as spokesman for the other disciples (Mk 8:27–29; cf. also Lk 9:18–20), is modified significantly here. The confession is of Jesus both as **Messiah and as **Son of the living God** (Mt 16:16). Jesus' response, drawn principally from material peculiar to Matthew, attributes the confession to a divine revelation granted to Peter alone (Mt 16:17) and makes him the **rock** on which Jesus **will build** his **church** (Mt 16:18) and the disciple whose authority in the church **on earth** will be confirmed in **heaven**, i.e., by God (Mt 16:19).

††[16:13] **Caesarea Philippi**: situated about twenty miles north of the Sea of Galilee in the territory ruled by Philip, a son of Herod the Great, tetrarch from 4 B.C. until his death in

r. [16:4] 12:39; Jon 2:1.   s. [16:5–12] Mk 8:14–21.   t. [16:6] Lk 12:1.   u. [16:9] 14:17–21; Jn 6:9.   v. [16:10] 15:34–38.   w. [16:13–16] Mk 8:27–29; Lk 9:18–20.

x. [16:14] 14:2.   y. [16:16] Jn 6:69.   z. [16:18] Jn 1:42.   a, [16:19] Is 22:22; Rev 3:7.

on earth shall be bound in heaven; and whatever you loose on earth shall be loosed in heaven." [20]*b*Then he strictly ordered his disciples to tell no one that he was the Messiah.

The First Prediction of the Passion.† [21]*c*From that time on, Jesus began to show his disciples that he‡ must go to Jerusalem and suffer greatly from the elders, the chief priests, and the scribes, and be killed and on the third day be raised.*d* [22]§Then Peter took him aside and began to rebuke him, "God forbid, Lord! No such thing shall ever happen to you." [23]*e*He turned and said to Peter, "Get behind me, Satan! You are an obstacle to me. You are thinking not as God does, but as human beings do."

The Conditions of Discipleship.⁵ [24]*f*Then Jesus said to his disciples, "Whoever wishes to come after me must deny himself,** take up his cross, and follow me. [25]*g*For whoever wishes to save his life will lose it, but whoever loses his life for my sake will find it.†† [26]What profit would there be for one to gain the whole world and forfeit his life? Or what can one give in exchange for his life? [27]‡‡hFor the Son of Man will come with his angels in his Father's glory, and then he will repay everyone according to his conduct. [28]§§Amen, I say to you, there are some standing here who will not taste death until they see the Son of Man coming in his kingdom."

CHAPTER 17

The Transfiguration of Jesus.⁵⁵ [1]*i*After six days Jesus took Peter, James, and John his brother, and led them up a high mountain by themselves.*** [2]†††jAnd he was transfigured before them; his face shone like the sun and his clothes became white as light. [3]‡‡‡And behold, Moses and Elijah appeared to them, conversing with him. [4]Then Peter said to Jesus in reply, "Lord, it is good that we are here. If you wish, I will make three tents§§§ here, one for you, one for Moses, and one for Elijah." [5]*k*While he was still speaking, behold, a bright cloud cast a shadow over

---

authoritative teaching, and the lifting or imposing of the ban of excommunication. It is disputed whether the image of **the keys** and that of binding and loosing are different metaphors meaning the same thing. In any case, the promise of the keys is given to Peter alone. In Mt 18:18 all the disciples are given the power of binding and loosing, but the context of that verse suggests that there the power of excommunication alone is intended. That **the keys** are those to the **kingdom of heaven** and that Peter's exercise of authority in the church **on earth** will be confirmed **in heaven** show an intimate connection between, but not an identification of, the church and **the kingdom of heaven.**

*[16:20] Cf. Mk 8:30. Matthew makes explicit that the prohibition has to do with speaking of Jesus as **the Messiah**; see note on Mk 8:27–30.

†[16:21–23] This first prediction of the passion follows Mk 8:31–33 in the main and serves as a corrective to an understanding of Jesus' messiahship as solely one of glory and triumph. By his addition of **from that time on** (Mt 16:21) Matthew has emphasized that Jesus' revelation of his coming suffering and death marks a new phase of the gospel. Neither this nor the two later passion predictions (Mt 17:22–23; 20:17–19) can be taken as sayings that, as they stand, go back to Jesus himself. However, it is probable that he foresaw that his mission would entail suffering and perhaps death, but was confident that he would ultimately be vindicated by God (see Mt 26:29).

‡[16:21] **He**: the Marcan parallel (Mk 8:31) has "the Son of Man." Since Matthew has already designated Jesus by that title (Mt 15:13), its omission here is not significant. The Matthean prediction is equally about the sufferings of the Son of Man. **Must**: this necessity is part of the tradition of all the synoptics; cf. Mk 8:31; Lk 9:21. **The elders, the chief priests, and the scribes**: see note on Mk 8:31. **On the third day**: so also Lk 9:22, against the Marcan "after three days" (Mk 8:31). Matthew's formulation is, in the Greek, almost identical with the pre-Pauline fragment of the kerygma in 1 Cor 15:4 and also with Hos 6:2, which many take to be the Old Testament background to the confession that Jesus was raised **on the third day**. Josephus uses "after three days" and "on the third day" interchangeably (*Antiquities* 7:280–81; 8:214, 218) and there is probably no difference in meaning between the two phrases.

§[16:22–23] Peter's refusal to accept Jesus' predicted suffering and death is seen as a satanic attempt to deflect Jesus from his God-appointed course, and the disciple is addressed in terms that recall Jesus' dismissal of the devil in the temptation account (Mt 4:10: "Get away, Satan!"). Peter's satanic purpose is emphasized by Matthew's addition to the Marcan source of the words **You are an obstacle to me.**

⁵[16:24–28] A readiness to follow Jesus even to giving up one's life for him is the condition for true discipleship; this will be repaid by him at the final judgment.

[16:24] **Deny himself: to deny someone is to disown him (see Mt 10:33; 26:34–35) and to deny oneself is to disown oneself as the center of one's existence.

††[16:25] See notes on Mt 10:38, 39.

‡‡[16:27] The parousia and final judgment are described in Mt 25:31 in terms almost identical with these.

§§[16:28] **Coming in his kingdom**: since the **kingdom of the Son of Man** has been described as "the world" and Jesus' sovereignty precedes his final coming in glory (Mt 13:38, 41), the coming in this verse is not the parousia as in the preceding but the manifestation of Jesus' rule after his resurrection; see notes on Mt 13:38, 41.

⁵⁵[17:1–8] The account of the transfiguration confirms that Jesus is the **Son** of God (Mt 17:5) and points to fulfillment of the prediction that he will come in his Father's glory at the end of the age (Mt 16:27). It has been explained by some as a resurrection appearance retrojected into the time of Jesus' ministry, but that is not probable since the account lacks many of the usual elements of the resurrection-appearance narratives. It draws upon motifs from the Old Testament and noncanonical Jewish apocalyptic literature that express the presence of the heavenly and the divine, e.g., brilliant light, white garments, and the overshadowing cloud.

***[17:1] These three disciples are also taken apart from the others by Jesus in Gethsemane (Mt 26;37). **A high mountain**: this has been identified with Tabor or Hermon, but probably no specific mountain was intended by the evangelist or by his Marcan source (Mk 9:2). Its meaning is theological rather than geographical, possibly recalling the revelation to Moses on Mount Sinai (Ex 24:12–18) and to Elijah at the same place (1 Kgs 19:8–18; Horeb = Sinai).

†††[17:2] **His face shone like the sun**: this is a Matthean addition; cf. Dn 10:6. **His clothes became white as light**: cf. Dn 9:3, where the clothing of God appears "snow bright." For the white garments of other heavenly beings, see Rev 4:4; 7:9; 19:14.

‡‡‡[17:3] See note on Mk 9:5.

§§§[17:4] **Three tents**: the booths in which the Israelites lived during the feast of Tabernacles (cf. Jn 7:2) were meant to recall their ancestors' dwelling in booths during the journey from Egypt to the promised land (Lv 23:39–42). The same Greek word, *skēnē*, here translated **tents**, is used in the LXX for the booths of that feast, and some scholars have suggested that there is an allusion here to that liturgical custom.

---

g. [16:25] Lk 17:33; Jn 12:25. h. [16:27] 25:31–33; Jb 34:11; Ps 62:13; Jer 17:10; 2 Thes 1:7–8. i. [17:1–8] Mk 9:2–8; Lk 9:28–36. j. [17:2] 28:3; Dn 7:9; 10:6; Rev 4:4; 7:9; 19:14. k. [17:5] 3:17; Dt 18:15; 2 Pt 1:17.

b. [16:20] Mk 8:30; Lk 9:21. c. [16:21–28] Mk 8:31–9:1; Lk 9:22–27. d. [16:21] 17:22–23; 20:17–19. e. [16:23] 4:10. f. [16:24] Lk 14:27.

them,* then from the cloud came a voice that said, "This is my beloved Son, with whom I am well pleased; listen to him." [6†]When the disciples heard this, they fell prostrate and were very much afraid. [7]But Jesus came and touched them, saying, "Rise, and do not be afraid." [8]And when the disciples raised their eyes, they saw no one else but Jesus alone.

The Coming of Elijah.[‡] [9l]As they were coming down from the mountain, Jesus charged them, "Do not tell the vision[§] to anyone until the Son of Man has been raised from the dead." [10ʂm]Then the disciples asked him, "Why do the scribes say that Elijah must come first?" [11n]He said in reply," "Elijah will indeed come and restore all things; [12o]but I tell you that Elijah has already come, and they did not recognize him but did to him whatever they pleased. So also will the Son of Man suffer at their hands." [13††]Then the disciples understood that he was speaking to them of John the Baptist.

The Healing of a Boy with a Demon.[‡‡] [14p]When they came to the crowd a man approached, knelt down before him, [15]and said, "Lord, have pity on my son, for he is a lunatic[§§] and suffers severely; often he falls into fire, and often into water. [16]I brought him to your disciples, but they could not cure him." [17q]Jesus said in reply, "O faithless and perverse[§§] generation, how long will I be with you? How long will I endure you? Bring him here to me." [18]Jesus rebuked him and the demon came out of him,*** and from that hour the boy was cured. [19]Then the disciples approached Jesus in private and said, "Why could we not drive it out?" [20†††]He said to them, "Because of your little faith. Amen, I say to you, if you have faith the size of a mustard seed, you will say to this mountain, 'Move from here to there,' and it will move. Nothing will be impossible for you." [21][‡‡‡]

The Second Prediction of the Passion.[§§§] [22s]As they were gathering in Galilee, Jesus said to them, "The Son of Man is to be handed over to men, [23]and they will kill him, and he will be raised on the third day." And they were overwhelmed with grief.

Payment of the Temple Tax.[¶¶¶] [24r]When they came to Capernaum, the collectors of the temple tax**** approached Peter and said, "Doesn't your

---

translated **perverse** is the same as that in Dt 32:5 LXX, where Moses speaks to his people. There is a problem in knowing to whom the reproach is addressed. Since the Matthean Jesus normally chides his disciples for their **little faith** (as in Mt 17:20), it would appear that the charge of lack of faith could not be made against them and that the reproach is addressed to unbelievers among the Jews. However in Mt 17:20b (**if you have faith the size of a mustard seed**), which is certainly addressed to the disciples, they appear to have not even the smallest faith; if they had, they would have been able to cure the boy. In the light of Mt 17:20b the reproach of Mt 17:17 could have applied to the disciples. There seems to be an inconsistency between the charge of **little faith** in Mt 17:20a and that of not even a little in Mt 17:20b.

***[17:18] **The demon came out of him:** not until this verse does Matthew indicate that the boy's illness is a case of demoniacal possession.

†††[17:20] The entire verse is an addition of Matthew who (according to the better attested text) omits the reason given for the disciples' inability in Mk 9:29. **Little faith:** see note on Mt 6:30. **Faith the size of a mustard seed . . . and it will move:** a combination of a Q saying (cf. Lk 17:6) with a Marcan saying (cf. Mk 11:23).

‡‡‡[17:21] Some manuscripts add, "But this kind does not come out except by prayer and fasting"; this is a variant of the better reading of Mk 9:29.

§§§[17:22–23] The second passion prediction (cf. Mt 16:21–23) is the least detailed of the three and may be the earliest. In the Marcan parallel the disciples do not understand (Mk 9:32); here they understand and are **overwhelmed with grief** at the prospect of Jesus' death (Mt 17:23).

¶¶¶[17:24–27] Like Mt 14:28–31 and Mt 16:16b–19, this episode comes from Matthew's special material on Peter. Although the question of **the collectors** concerns Jesus' payment of **the temple tax**, it is put to **Peter.** It is he who receives instruction from Jesus about freedom from the obligation of payment and yet why it should be made. The means of doing so is provided miraculously. The pericope deals with a problem of Matthew's church, whether its members should pay the temple tax, and the answer is given through a word of Jesus conveyed to Peter. Some scholars see here an example of the teaching authority of Peter exercised in the name of Jesus (see Mt 16:19). The specific problem was a Jewish Christian one and may have arisen when the Matthean church was composed largely of that group.

****[17:24] **The temple tax:** before the destruction of the Jerusalem temple in A.D. 70 every male Jew above nineteen years of age was obliged to make an annual contribution to its upkeep (cf. Ex 30:11–16; Neh 10:33). After the destruction the Romans imposed upon Jews the obligation of paying that tax for the temple of Jupiter Capitolinus. There is disagreement about which period the story deals with.

---

*[17:5] **Cloud cast a shadow over them:** see note on Mk 9:7. **This is my beloved Son . . . listen to him:** cf. Mt 3:17. The voice repeats the baptismal proclamation about Jesus, with the addition of the command **listen to him.** The latter is a reference to Dt 18:15 in which the Israelites are commanded to **listen to** the prophet like Moses whom God will raise up for them. The command to listen to Jesus is general, but in this context it probably applies particularly to the preceding predictions of his passion and resurrection (Mt 16:21) and of his coming (Mt 16:27, 28).

†[17:6–7] A Matthean addition; cf. Dn 10:9–10, 18–19.

‡[17:9–13] In response to the disciples' question about the expected return of Elijah, Jesus interprets the mission of the Baptist as the fulfillment of that expectation. But that was not suspected by those who opposed and finally killed him, and Jesus predicts a similar fate for himself.

§[17:9] **The vision:** Matthew alone uses this word to describe the transfiguration. **Until the Son of Man has been raised from the dead:** only in the light of Jesus' resurrection can the meaning of his life and mission be truly understood; until then no testimony to **the vision** will lead people to faith.

¶[17:10] See notes on Mt 3:4; 16:14.

**[17:11–12] The preceding question and this answer may reflect later controversy with Jews who objected to the Christian claims for Jesus that Elijah had not yet come.

††[17:13] See Mt 11:14.

‡‡[17:14–20] Matthew has greatly shortened the Marcan story (Mk 9:14–29). Leaving aside several details of the boy's illness, he concentrates on the need for faith, not so much on the part of the boy's father (as does Mark, for Matthew omits Mk 9:22b–24) but on that of his own disciples whose inability to drive out the demon is ascribed to their **little faith** (Mt 17:20).

§§[17:15] **A lunatic:** this description of the boy is peculiar to Matthew. The word occurs in the New Testament only here and in Mt 4:24 and means one affected or struck by the moon. The symptoms of the boy's illness point to epilepsy, and attacks of this were thought to be caused by phases of the moon.

¶¶[17:17] **Faithless and perverse:** so Matthew and Luke (Lk 9:41) against Mark's **faithless** (Mk 9:19). The Greek word here

---

l. [17:9–13] Mk 9:9–13. m. [17:10] Mal 3:23–24. n. [17:11] Lk 1:17. o. [17:12–13] 11:14. p. [17:14–21] Mk 9:14–29; Lk 9:37–43. q. [17:17] Dt 32:5 LXX.

r. [17:20] 21:21; Lk 17:6; 1 Cor 13:2. s. [17:22–23] 16:21; 20:18–19. t. [17:24] Ex 30:11–16; Neh 10:33.

teacher pay the temple tax?" [25]"Yes," he said.[*]
When he came into the house, before he had
time to speak, Jesus asked him, "What is your
opinion, Simon? From whom do the kings of
the earth take tolls or census tax? From their
subjects or from foreigners?" [26†]When he said,
"From foreigners," Jesus said to him, "Then
the subjects are exempt. [27]But that we may not
offend them,[‡] go to the sea, drop in a hook, and
take the first fish that comes up. Open its mouth
and you will find a coin worth twice the temple
tax. Give that to them for me and for you."

CHAPTER 18[§]
The Greatest in the Kingdom. [1u]At that time
the disciples[¶] approached Jesus and said, "Who
is the greatest in the kingdom of heaven?" [2]He
called a child over, placed it in their midst, [3v]and
said, "Amen, I say to you, unless you turn and
become like children,[**] you will not enter the
kingdom of heaven. [4w]Whoever humbles himself like this child is the greatest in the kingdom
of heaven. [5††]And whoever receives one child
such as this in my name receives me.

---

[*][17:25] **From their subjects or from foreigners?:** the
Greek word here translated **subjects** literally means "sons."
[†][17:26] **Then the subjects are exempt:** just as **subjects**
are not bound by laws applying to **foreigners**, neither are
Jesus and his disciples, who belong to the kingdom of heaven,
bound by the duty of paying the temple tax imposed on those
who are not of the kingdom. If the Greek is translated "sons,"
the freedom of Jesus, the Son of God, and of his disciples, children ("sons") of the kingdom (cf. Mt 13:38), is even more clear.
[‡][17:27] **That we may not offend them:** though they are
exempt (Mt 17:26), Jesus and his disciples are to avoid giving
offense; therefore the tax is to be paid. **A coin worth twice the
temple tax:** literally, "a stater," a Greek coin worth two double
drachmas. Two double drachmas were equal to the Jewish
shekel and the tax was a half-shekel. **For me and for you:** not
only Jesus but Peter pays the tax, and this example serves as a
standard for the conduct of all the disciples.
[§][18:1–35] This discourse of the fourth book of the gospel
is often called the "church order" discourse, but it lacks most
of the considerations usually connected with church order,
such as various offices in the church and the duties of each, and
deals principally with the relations that must obtain among
the members of the church. Beginning with the warning that
greatness in **the kingdom of heaven** is measured not by rank
or power but by childlikeness (Mt 18:1–5), it deals with the care
that the disciples must take not to cause the **little ones to sin**
or to neglect them if they stray from the community (Mt 18:6–
14), the correction of members who sin (Mt 18:15–18), the
efficacy of the prayer of the disciples because of the presence of
Jesus (Mt 18:19–20), and the forgiveness that must be repeatedly extended to sinful members who repent (Mt 18:21–35).
[¶][18:1] The initiative is taken not by Jesus as in the Marcan parallel (Mk 9:33–34) but by the disciples. **Kingdom of
heaven:** this may mean **the kingdom** in its fullness, i.e., after
the parousia and the final judgment. But what follows about
causes of sin, church discipline, and forgiveness, all dealing
with the present age, suggests that the question has to do with
rank also in the church, where the kingdom is manifested
here and now, although only partially and by anticipation; see
notes on Mt 3:2; 4:17.
[**][18:3] **Become like children:** the child is held up as a
model for the disciples not because of any supposed innocence of children but because of their complete dependence
on, and trust in, their parents. So must the disciples be, in
respect to God.
[††][18:5] Cf. Mt 10:40.

Temptations to Sin. [6x]"Whoever causes one
of these little ones[‡‡] who believe in me to sin, it
would be better for him to have a great millstone
hung around his neck and to be drowned in the
depths of the sea. [7§§]Woe to the world because of
things that cause sin! Such things must come,
but woe to the one through whom they come!
[8y]If your hand or foot causes you to sin,[¶¶] cut
it off and throw it away. It is better for you to
enter into life maimed or crippled than with two
hands or two feet to be thrown into eternal fire.
[9]And if your eye causes you to sin, tear it out and
throw it away. It is better for you to enter into life
with one eye than with two eyes to be thrown
into fiery Gehenna.
The Parable of the Lost Sheep.[***] [10z]"See that
you do not despise one of these little ones,[†††] for
I say to you that their angels in heaven always
look upon the face of my heavenly Father. [[11]][‡‡‡a]

[‡‡][18:6] **One of these little ones:** the thought passes from
the child of Mt 18:2–4 to the disciples, **little ones** because of
their becoming **like children**. It is difficult to know whether
this is a designation of all who are disciples or of those who
are insignificant in contrast to others, e.g., the leaders of the
community. Since apart from this chapter the designation
little ones occurs in Matthew only in Mt 10:42 where it means
disciples as such, that is its more likely meaning here. **Who
believe in me:** since discipleship is impossible without at least
some degree of faith, this further specification seems superfluous. However, it serves to indicate that the warning against
causing a **little one** to sin is principally directed against whatever would lead such a one to a weakening or loss of faith.
The Greek verb *skandalizein*, here translated **causes . . . to
sin**, means literally "causes to stumble"; what the stumbling
is depends on the context. It is used of falling away from faith
in Mt 13:21. According to the better reading of Mk 9:42, **in
me** is a Matthean addition to the Marcan source. **It would be
better . . . depths of the sea:** cf. Mk 9:42.
[§§][18:7] This is a Q saying; cf. Lk 17:1. The inevitability of
things that cause sin (literally, "scandals") does not take away
the responsibility of **the one through whom they come.**
[¶¶][18:8–9] These verses are a doublet of Mt 5:29–30. In that
context they have to do with causes of sexual sin. As in the
Marcan source from which they have been drawn (Mk 9:42–
48), they differ from the first warning about scandal, which
deals with causing another person to sin, for they concern
what **causes** oneself **to sin** and they do not seem to be related
to another's loss of faith, as the first warning is. It is difficult
to know how Matthew understood the logical connection
between these verses and Mt 18:6–7.
[***][18:10–14] The first and last verses are peculiar to Matthew. The parable itself comes from Q; see Lk 15:3–7. In Luke
it serves as justification for Jesus' table-companionship with
sinners; here, it is an exhortation for the disciples to seek out
fellow disciples who have gone **astray**. Not only must no one
cause a fellow disciple to sin, but those who have strayed must
be sought out and, if possible, brought back to the community. The joy of the shepherd on finding the sheep, though
not absent in Mt 18:13 is more emphasized in Luke. By his
addition of Mt 18:10, 14 Matthew has drawn out explicitly the
application of the parable to the care of the **little ones.**
[†††][18:10] **Their angels in heaven . . . my heavenly Father:**
for the Jewish belief in angels as guardians of nations and individuals, see Dn 10:13, 20–21; Tb 5:4–7; 1QH 5:20–22; as inter-
cessors who present the prayers of human beings to God, see
Tb 13:12, 15. The high worth of the **little ones** is indicated by
their being represented before God by these heavenly beings.
[‡‡‡][18:11] Some manuscripts add, "For the Son of Man has
come to save what was lost"; cf. Mt 9:13. This is practically
identical with Lk 19:10 and is probably a copyist's addition
from that source.

---

u. [18:1–5] Mk 9:36–37; Lk 9:46–48.   v. [18:3] 19:14; Mk 10:15; Lk
18:17.   w. [18:4] 23:12.

x. [18:6–7] Mk 9:42; Lk 17:1–2.   y. [18:8–9] 5:29–30; Mk 9:43–
47.   z. [18:10–14] Ez 34:1–3, 16; Lk 15:3–7.   a. [18:11] Lk 19:10.

¹²What is your opinion? If a man has a hundred sheep and one of them goes astray, will he not leave the ninety-nine in the hills and go in search of the stray? ¹³And if he finds it, amen, I say to you, he rejoices more over it than over the ninety-nine that did not stray. ¹⁴In just the same way, it is not the will of your heavenly Father that one of these little ones be lost.

A Brother Who Sins.[*] ¹⁵ᵇ"If your brother[†] sins [against you], go and tell him his fault between you and him alone. If he listens to you, you have won over your brother. ¹⁶[‡]cIf he does not listen, take one or two others along with you, so that 'every fact may be established on the testimony of two or three witnesses.' ¹⁷dIf he refuses to listen to them, tell the church.[§] If he refuses to listen even to the church, then treat him as you would a Gentile or a tax collector. ¹⁸[¶]eAmen, I say to you, whatever you bind on earth shall be bound in heaven, and whatever you loose on earth shall be loosed in heaven. ¹⁹[**]fAgain, [amen,] I say to you, if two of you agree on earth about anything for which they are to pray, it shall be granted to them by my heavenly Father. ²⁰[††]gFor where two or three are gathered together in my name, there am I in the midst of them."

The Parable of the Unforgiving Servant.[‡‡] ²¹hThen Peter approaching asked him, "Lord, if my brother sins against me, how often must I forgive him? As many as seven times?" ²²[§§]Jesus answered, "I say to you, not seven times but seventy-seven times. ²³ʲThat is why the kingdom of heaven may be likened to a king who decided to settle accounts with his servants. ²⁴[¶¶]When he began the accounting, a debtor was brought before him who owed him a huge amount. ²⁵Since he had no way of paying it back, his master ordered him to be sold, along with his wife, his children, and all his property, in payment of the debt. ²⁶[***]At that, the servant fell down, did him homage, and said, 'Be patient with me, and I will pay you back in full.' ²⁷Moved with compassion the master of that servant let him go and forgave him the loan. ²⁸When that servant had left, he found one of his fellow servants who owed him a much smaller amount.[†††] He seized him and started to choke him, demanding, 'Pay back what you owe.' ²⁹Falling to his knees, his fellow servant begged him, 'Be patient with me, and I will pay you back.' ³⁰But he refused.

*[18:15–20] Passing from the duty of Christian disciples toward those who have strayed from their number, the discourse now turns to how they are to deal with one who sins and yet remains within the community. First there is to be private correction (Mt 18:15); if this is unsuccessful, further correction before **two or three witnesses** (Mt 18:16); if this fails, the matter is to be brought before the assembled community (the church), and if the sinner refuses to attend to the correction of **the church**, he is to be expelled (Mt 18:17). The church's judgment will be ratified **in heaven**, i.e., by God (Mt 18:18). This three-step process of correction corresponds, though not exactly, to the procedure of the Qumran community; see 1QS 5:25–6:1; 6:24–7:25; CD 9:2–8. The section ends with a saying about the favorable response of God to prayer, even to that of a very small number, for Jesus is in the midst of any gathering of his disciples, however small (Mt 18:19–20). Whether this prayer has anything to do with the preceding judgment is uncertain.

†[18:15] **Your brother**: a fellow disciple; see Mt 23:8. The bracketed words, **against you**, are widely attested but they are not in the important codices Sinaiticus and Vaticanus or in some other textual witnesses. Their omission broadens the type of sin in question. **Won over**: literally, "gained."

‡[18:16] Cf. Dt 19:15.

§[18:17] **The church**: the second of the only two instances of this word in the gospels; see note on Mt 16:18. Here it refers not to the entire **church** of Jesus, as in Mt 16:18, but to the local congregation. **Treat him . . . a Gentile or a tax collector**: just as the observant Jew avoided the company of Gentiles and tax collectors, so must the congregation of Christian disciples separate itself from the arrogantly sinful member who refuses to repent even when convicted of his sin by the whole **church**. Such a one is to be set outside the fellowship of the community. The harsh language about **Gentile** and **tax collector** probably reflects a stage of the Matthean **church** when it was principally composed of Jewish Christians. That time had long since passed, but the principle of exclusion for such a sinner remained. Paul makes a similar demand for excommunication in 1 Cor 5:1–13.

¶[18:18] Except for the plural of the verbs **bind** and **loose**, this verse is practically identical with Mt 16:19b and many scholars understand it as granting to all the disciples what was previously given to Peter alone. For a different view, based on the different contexts of the two verses, see note on Mt 16:19.

[18:19–20] Some take these verses as applying to prayer on the occasion of the church's gathering to deal with the sinner of Mt 18:17. Unless an *a fortiori* argument is supposed, this seems unlikely. God's answer to the prayer of **two or three envisages a different situation from one that involves the entire congregation. In addition, the object of this prayer is expressed in most general terms as **anything for which they are to pray**.

††[18:20] **For where two or three . . . midst of them**: the presence of Jesus guarantees the efficacy of the prayer. This saying is similar to one attributed to a rabbi executed in A.D. 135 at the time of the second Jewish revolt: ". . . When two sit and there are between them the words of the Torah, the divine presence (*Shekinah*) rests upon them" (*Pirqê 'Abôt* 3,3).

‡‡[18:21–35] The final section of the discourse deals with the forgiveness that the disciples are to give to their fellow disciples who sin against them. To the question of Peter how often forgiveness is to be granted (Mt 18:21), Jesus answers that it is to be given without limit (Mt 18:22) and illustrates this with the parable of the unmerciful servant (Mt 18:23–34), warning that his **heavenly Father** will give those who do not forgive the same treatment as that given to the unmerciful servant (Mt 18:35). Mt 18:21–22 correspond to Lk 17:4; the parable and the final warning are peculiar to Matthew. That the parable did not originally belong to this context is suggested by the fact that it really does not deal with repeated forgiveness, which is the point of Peter's question and Jesus' reply.

§§[18:22] **Seventy-seven times**: the Greek corresponds exactly to the LXX of Gn 4:24. There is probably an allusion, by contrast, to the limitless vengeance of Lamech in the Genesis text. In any case, what is demanded of the disciples is limitless forgiveness.

¶¶[18:24] **A huge amount**: literally, "ten thousand talents." The talent was a unit of coinage of high but varying value depending on its metal (gold, silver, copper) and its place of origin. It is mentioned in the New Testament only here and in Mt 25:14–30.

***[18:26] **Pay you back in full**: an empty promise, given the size of the debt.

†††[18:28] **A much smaller amount**: literally, "a hundred denarii." A denarius was the normal daily wage of a laborer. The difference between the two debts is enormous and brings out the absurdity of the conduct of the Christian who has received the great forgiveness of God and yet refuses to forgive the relatively minor offenses done to him.

b. [18:15] Lv 19:17; Sir 19:13; Gal 6:1.   c. [18:16] Dt 19:15; Jn 8:17; 1 Tm 5:19.   d. [18:17] 1 Cor 5:1–13.   e. [18:18] 16:19; Jn 20:23.   f. [18:19] 7:7–8; Jn 15:7.

g. [18:20] 1 Cor 5:4.   h. [18:21–22] 6:12; Lk 17:4.   i. [18:23] 25:19.

Instead, he had him put in prison until he paid back the debt. [31]Now when his fellow servants saw what had happened, they were deeply disturbed, and went to their master and reported the whole affair. [32]His master summoned him and said to him, 'You wicked servant! I forgave you your entire debt because you begged me to. [33]Should you not have had pity on your fellow servant, as I had pity on you?' [34]Then in anger his master handed him over to the torturers until he should pay back the whole debt.* [35]†kSo will my heavenly Father do to you, unless each of you forgives his brother from his heart."

VI. MINISTRY IN JUDEA AND JERUSALEM

CHAPTER 19

Marriage and Divorce. [1]‡When Jesus§ finished these words,⁋ he left Galilee and went to the district of Judea across the Jordan. [2]Great crowds followed him, and he cured them there. [3]lSome Pharisees approached him, and tested him,** saying, "Is it lawful for a man to divorce his wife for any cause whatever?" [4]††mHe said in reply, "Have you not read that from the beginning the Creator 'made them male and female' [5]nand said, 'For this reason a man shall leave his father and mother and be joined to his wife, and the two shall become one flesh'? [6]So they are no longer two, but one flesh. Therefore, what God has joined together, no human being must separate." [7]‡‡oThey said to him, "Then why did Moses command that the man give the woman a bill of divorce and dismiss [her]?" [8]He said to them, "Because of the hardness of your hearts Moses allowed you to divorce your wives, but from the beginning it was not so. [9]pI say to you,§§ whoever divorces his wife (unless the marriage is unlawful) and marries another commits adultery." [10][His] disciples said to him, "If that is the case of a man with his wife, it is better not to marry." [11]He answered, "Not all can accept [this] word,⁋⁋ but only those to whom that is granted. [12]Some are incapable of marriage because they were born so; some, because they were made so by others; some, because they have renounced marriage*** for the sake of the kingdom of heaven. Whoever can accept this ought to accept it."

---

*[18:34] Since the debt is so great as to be unpayable, the punishment will be endless.

†[18:35] The Father's forgiveness, already given, will be withdrawn at the final judgment for those who have not imitated his forgiveness by their own.

‡[19:1–23:39] The narrative section of the fifth book of the gospel. The first part (Mt 19:1–20:34) has for its setting the journey of Jesus from Galilee to Jerusalem; the second (Mt 21:1–23:39) deals with Jesus' ministry in Jerusalem up to the final great discourse of the gospel (Mt 24–25). Matthew follows the Marcan sequence of events, though adding material both special to this gospel and drawn from Q. The second part ends with the denunciation of the scribes and Pharisees (Mt 23:1–36) followed by Jesus' lament over Jerusalem (Mt 23:37–39). This long and important speech raises a problem for the view that Matthew is structured around five other discourses of Jesus (see Introduction) and that this one has no such function in the gospel. However, it is to be noted that this speech lacks the customary concluding formula that follows the five discourses (see note on Mt 7:28), and that those discourses are all addressed either exclusively (Mt 10; 18; 24; 25) or primarily (Mt 5–7; 13) to the disciples, whereas this is addressed primarily to the scribes and Pharisees (Mt 23:13–36). Consequently, it seems plausible to maintain that the evangelist did not intend to give it the structural importance of the five other discourses, and that, in spite of its being composed of sayings-material, it belongs to the narrative section of this book. In that regard, it is similar to the sayings-material of Mt 11:7–30. Some have proposed that Matthew wished to regard it as part of the final discourse of Mt 24–25, but the intervening material (Mt 24:1–4) and the change in matter and style of those chapters do not support that view.

§[19:1] In giving Jesus' teaching on divorce (Mt 19:3–9), Matthew here follows his Marcan source (Mk 10:2–12) as he does Q in Mt 5:31–32 (cf. Lk 16:18). Mt 19:10–12 are peculiar to Matthew.

⁋[19:1] **When Jesus finished these words**: see note on Mt 7:28–29. **The district of Judea across the Jordan**: an inexact designation of the territory. Judea did not extend **across the Jordan**; the territory east of the river was Perea. The route to Jerusalem by way of Perea avoided passage through Samaria.

[19:3] **Tested him: the verb is used of attempts of Jesus' opponents to embarrass him by challenging him to do something they think impossible (Mt 16:1; Mk 8:11; Lk 11:16) or by having him say something that they can use against him

(Mt 22:18, 35; Mk 10:2; 12:15). **For any cause whatever**: this is peculiar to Matthew and has been interpreted by some as meaning that Jesus was being asked to take sides in the dispute between the schools of Hillel and Shammai on the reasons for divorce, the latter holding a stricter position than the former. It is unlikely, however, that to ask Jesus' opinion about the differing views of two Jewish schools, both highly respected, could be described as "testing" him, for the reason indicated above.

††[19:4–6] Matthew recasts his Marcan source, omitting Jesus' question about Moses' command (Mk 10:3) and having him recall at once two Genesis texts that show the will and purpose of **the Creator** in making human beings **male and female** (Gn 1:27), namely, that a **man** may **be joined to his wife** in marriage in the intimacy of **one flesh** (Gn 2:24). **What God has** thus **joined** must not be separated by any human being. (The NAB translation of the Hebrew bāśār of Gn 2:24 as "body" rather than "flesh" obscures the reference of Matthew to that text.)

‡‡[19:7] See Dt 24:1–4.

§§[19:9] Moses' concession to human sinfulness (**the hardness of your hearts**, Mt 19:8) is repudiated by Jesus, and the original will of the Creator is reaffirmed against that concession. (**Unless the marriage is unlawful**): see note on Mt 5:31–32. There is some evidence suggesting that Jesus' absolute prohibition of divorce was paralleled in the Qumran community (see 11QTemple 57:17–19; CD 4:12b–5:14). Matthew removes Mark's setting of this verse as spoken to the disciples alone "in the house" (Mk 10:10) and also his extension of the divorce prohibition to the case of a woman's divorcing her husband (Mk 10:12), probably because in Palestine, unlike the places where Roman and Greek law prevailed, the woman was not allowed to initiate the divorce.

⁋⁋[19:11] [**This**] **word**: probably the disciples' "**it is better not to marry**" (Mt 19:10). Jesus agrees but says that celibacy is not for all but only for those **to whom that is granted** by God.

***[19:12] **Incapable of marriage**: literally, "eunuchs." Three classes are mentioned, eunuchs from birth, eunuchs by castration, and those who have voluntarily **renounced marriage** (literally, "have made themselves eunuchs") **for the sake of the kingdom**, i.e., to devote themselves entirely to its service. Some scholars take the last class to be those who have been divorced by their spouses and have refused to enter another marriage. But it is more likely that it is rather those who have chosen never to marry, since that suits better the optional nature of the decision: **whoever can . . . ought to accept it**.

m. [19:4] Gn 1:27.   n. [19:5] Gn 2:24; 1 Cor 6:16; Eph 5:31.   o. [19:7] Dt 24:1–4.   p. [19:9] 5:32; Lk 16:18; 1 Cor 7:10–11.

j. [18:33] Sir 28:4.   k. [18:35] 6:15; Jas 2:13.   l. [19:3–9] Mk 10:2–12.

Blessing of the Children. 13*Then children were brought to him that he might lay his hands on them and pray. The disciples rebuked them, 14*but Jesus said, "Let the children come to me, and do not prevent them; for the kingdom of heaven belongs to such as these." 15After he placed his hands on them, he went away.

The Rich Young Man.† 16*Now someone approached him and said, "Teacher, what good must I do to gain eternal life?"‡ 17He answered him, "Why do you ask me about the good? There is only One who is good.§ If you wish to enter into life, keep the commandments." 18*He asked him, "Which ones?" And Jesus replied, "'You shall not kill; you shall not commit adultery; you shall not steal; you shall not bear false witness; 19honor your father and your mother'; and 'you shall love your neighbor as yourself.'" 20*The young man said to him, "All of these I have observed. What do I still lack?" 21*Jesus said to him, "If you wish to be perfect,†† go, sell what you have and give to [the] poor, and you will have treasure in heaven. Then come, follow me."

22When the young man heard this statement, he went away sad, for he had many possessions. 23‡‡Then Jesus said to his disciples, "Amen, I say to you, it will be hard for one who is rich to enter the kingdom of heaven. 24vAgain I say to you, it is easier for a camel to pass through the eye of a needle than for one who is rich to enter the kingdom of God." 25§§When the disciples heard this, they were greatly astonished and said, "Who then can be saved?" 26wJesus looked at them and said, "For human beings this is impossible, but for God all things are possible." 27xThen Peter said to him in reply, "We have given up everything and followed you. What will there be for us?" 28¶¶yJesus said to them, "Amen, I say to you that you who have followed me, in the new age, when the Son of Man is seated on his throne of glory, will yourselves sit on twelve thrones, judging the twelve tribes of Israel. 29And everyone who has given up houses or brothers or sisters or father or mother or children or lands for the sake of my name will receive a hundred times more, and will inherit eternal life. 30***zBut many who are first will be last, and the last will be first.

CHAPTER 20

The Workers in the Vineyard.††† 1"The kingdom of heaven is like a landowner who went out at dawn to hire laborers for his vineyard. 2After

*[19:13–15] This account is understood by some as intended to justify the practice of infant baptism. That interpretation is based principally on the command not to **prevent** the children from coming, since that word sometimes has a baptismal connotation in the New Testament; see Acts 8:36.

†[19:16–30] Cf. Mk 10:17–31. This story does not set up a "two-tier" morality, that of those who seek (only) **eternal life** (Mt 19:16) and that of those who **wish to be perfect** (Mt 19:21). It speaks rather of the obstacle that riches constitute for the following of Jesus and of the impossibility, humanly speaking, for one who has **many possessions** (Mt 19:22) **to enter the kingdom** (Mt 19:24). Actual renunciation of riches is not demanded of all; Matthew counts the rich Joseph of Arimathea as a disciple of Jesus (Mt 27:57). But only the poor in spirit (Mt 5:3) can **enter the kingdom** and, as here, such poverty may entail the sacrifice of one's **possessions**. The Twelve, who **have given up everything** (Mt 19:27) to follow Jesus, will have as their reward a share in Jesus' (the Son of Man's) **judging the twelve tribes of Israel** (Mt 19:28), and all who have similarly sacrificed family or property for his sake **will inherit eternal life** (Mt 19:29).

‡[19:16] **Gain eternal life:** this is equivalent to "entering into life" (Mt 19:17) and "being saved" (Mt 19:25); the **life** is that of the new age after the final judgment (see Mt 25:46). It probably is also equivalent here to "entering the kingdom of heaven" (Mt 19:23) or "the kingdom of God" (Mt 19:24), but see notes on Mt 3:2; 4:17; 18:1 for the wider reference of the **kingdom** in Matthew.

§[19:17] By Matthew's reformulation of the Marcan question and reply (Mk 10:17–18) Jesus' repudiation of the term "good" for himself has been softened. Yet the Marcan assertion that "no one is good but God alone" stands, with only unimportant verbal modification.

¶[19:18–19] The first five commandments cited are from the Decalogue (see Ex 20:12–16; Dt 5:16–20). Matthew omits Mark's "you shall not defraud" (Mk 10:19; see Dt 24:14) and adds Lv 19:18. This combination of commandments of the Decalogue with Lv 19:18 is partially the same as Paul's enumeration of the demands of Christian morality in Rom 13:9.

[19:20] **Young man: in Matthew alone of the synoptics the questioner is said to be a **young man**; thus the Marcan "from my youth" (Mk 10:20) is omitted.

††[19:21] **If you wish to be perfect: to be perfect** is demanded of all Christians; see Mt 5:48. In the case of this man, it involves selling his possessions and giving to the poor; only so can he **follow** Jesus.

‡‡[19:23–24] Riches are an obstacle to entering the **kingdom** that cannot be overcome by human power. The comparison with the impossibility of a camel's passing **through the eye of a needle** should not be mitigated by such suppositions as that **the eye of a needle** means a low or narrow gate. The **kingdom of God**: as in Mt 12:28; 21:31, 43 instead of Matthew's usual **kingdom of heaven.**

§§[19:25–26] See note on Mk 10:23–27.

¶¶[19:28] This saying, directed to the Twelve, is from Q; see Lk 22:29–30. **The new age:** the Greek word here translated "new age" occurs in the New Testament only here and in Ti 3:5. Literally, it means "rebirth" or "regeneration," and is used in Titus of spiritual rebirth through baptism. Here it means the "rebirth" effected by the coming of the kingdom. Since that coming has various stages (see notes on Mt 3:2; 4:17), **the new age** could be taken as referring to the time after the resurrection when the Twelve will govern the true Israel, i.e., the church of Jesus. (For "judge" in the sense of "govern," cf. Jgs 12:8, 9, 11; 15:20; 16:31; Ps 2:10). But since it is connected here with the time when the **Son of Man** is **seated on his throne of glory**, language that Matthew uses in Mt 25:31 for the time of final judgment, it is more likely that what the Twelve are promised is that they will be joined with Jesus then in judging the people of Israel.

***[19:30] Different interpretations have been given to this saying, which comes from Mk 10:31. In view of Matthew's associating it with the following parable (Mt 20:1–15) and substantially repeating it (in reverse order) at the end of that parable (Mt 20:16), it may be that its meaning is that all who respond to the call of Jesus, at whatever time (**first** or **last**), will be the same in respect to inheriting the benefits of the kingdom, which is the gift of God.

†††[20:1–16] This parable is peculiar to Matthew. It is difficult to know whether the evangelist composed it or received it as part of his traditional material and, if the latter is the case, what its original reference was. In its present context its close association with Mt 19:30 suggests that its teaching

q. [19:13–15] Mk 10:13–16; Lk 18:15–17. r. [19:14] 18:3; Acts 8:36. s. [19:16–30] Mk 10:17–31; Lk 18:18–30. t. [19:18–19] Ex 20:12–16; Dt 5:16–20 / Lv 19:18; Rom 13:9. u. [19:21] 5:48; 6:20.

v. [19:24] 7:14. w. [19:26] Gn 18:14; Jb 42:2; Lk 1:37. x. [19:27] 4:20, 22. y. [19:28] 25:31; Dn 7:9, 22; Lk 22:30; Rev 3:21; 20:4. z. [19:30] 20:16.

agreeing with them for the usual daily wage, he sent them into his vineyard. ³Going out about nine o'clock, he saw others standing idle in the marketplace, ⁴ᵃand he said to them, 'You too go into my vineyard, and I will give you what is just.' ⁵So they went off. [And] he went out again around noon, and around three o'clock, and did likewise. ⁶Going out about five o'clock, he found others standing around, and said to them, 'Why do you stand here idle all day?' ⁷They answered, 'Because no one has hired us.' He said to them, 'You too go into my vineyard.' ⁸ᵗᵃWhen it was evening the owner of the vineyard said to his foreman, 'Summon the laborers and give them their pay, beginning with the last and ending with the first.' ⁹When those who had started about five o'clock came, each received the usual daily wage. ¹⁰So when the first came, they thought that they would receive more, but each of them also got the usual wage. ¹¹And on receiving it they grumbled against the landowner, ¹²saying, 'These last ones worked only one hour, and you have made them equal to us, who bore the day's burden and the heat.' ¹³He said to one of them in reply, 'My friend, I am not cheating you.‡ Did you not agree with me for the usual daily wage? ¹⁴⁸Take what is yours and go. What if I wish to give this last one the same as you? ¹⁵[Or] am I not free to do as I wish with my own money? Are you envious because I am generous?' ¹⁶⁵Thus, the last will be first, and the first will be last."

The Third Prediction of the Passion.** ¹⁷ᵇAs Jesus was going up to Jerusalem, he took the twelve [disciples] aside by themselves, and said to them on the way, ¹⁸ᶜᶜBehold, we are going up to Jerusalem, and the Son of Man will be handed over to the chief priests and the scribes, and they will condemn him to death, ¹⁹and hand him over to the Gentiles to be mocked and scourged and crucified, and he will be raised on the third day."

is the equality of all the disciples in the reward of inheriting eternal life.

*[20:4] **What is just**: although the wage is not stipulated as in the case of those first hired, it will be fair.

†[20:8] **Beginning with the last . . . the first**: this element of the parable has no other purpose than to show how **the first** knew what **the last** were given (Mt 20:12).

‡[20:13] **I am not cheating you**: literally, "I am not treating you unjustly."

§[20:14–15] The owner's conduct involves no violation of justice (Mt 20:4, 13), and that all the workers receive the same wage is due only to his generosity to the latest arrivals; the resentment of the first comes from envy.

¶[20:16] See note on Mt 19:30.

[20:17–19] Cf. Mk 10:32–34. This is the third and the most detailed of the passion predictions (Mt 16:21–23; 17:22–23). It speaks of Jesus' being **handed over to the Gentiles (Mt 27:2), his being **mocked** (Mt 27:27–30), **scourged** (Mt 27:26), and **crucified** (Mt 27:31, 35). In all but the last of these points Matthew agrees with his Marcan source, but whereas Mark speaks of Jesus' being killed (Mk 10:34), Matthew has the specific **to be . . . crucified**.

a. [20:8] Lv 19:13; Dt 24:15.   b. [20:17–19] 16:21; 17:22–23; Mk 10:32–34; Lk 18:31–33.

The Request of James and John.†† ²⁰ᶜThen the mother‡‡ of the sons of Zebedee approached him with her sons and did him homage, wishing to ask him for something. ²¹He said to her, "What do you wish?" She answered him, "Command that these two sons of mine sit, one at your right and the other at your left, in your kingdom." ²²Jesus said in reply, "You do not know what you are asking.§§ Can you drink the cup that I am going to drink?" They said to him, "We can." ²³He replied, "My cup you will indeed drink, but to sit at my right and at my left [, this] is not mine to give but is for those for whom it has been prepared by my Father." ²⁴ᵈWhen the ten heard this, they became indignant at the two brothers. ²⁵But Jesus summoned them and said, "You know that the rulers of the Gentiles lord it over them, and the great ones make their authority over them felt. ²⁶But it shall not be so among you. Rather, whoever wishes to be great among you shall be your servant; ²⁷ᵉwhoever wishes to be first among you shall be your slave. ²⁸ᶠJust so, the Son of Man did not come to be served but to serve and to give his life as a ransom⁵⁵ for many."

The Healing of Two Blind Men.*** ²⁹ᵍAs they left Jericho, a great crowd followed him. ³⁰ʰTwo blind men were sitting by the roadside, and

††[20:20–28] Cf. Mk 10:35–45. The request of the sons of Zebedee, made through their mother, for the highest places of honor in the **kingdom**, and the indignation of **the** other **ten** disciples at this request, show that neither **the two brothers** nor the others have understood that what makes for greatness in the kingdom is not lordly power but humble service. Jesus gives the example, and his ministry of service will reach its highest point when he gives his life for the deliverance of the human race from sin.

‡‡[20:20–21] The reason for Matthew's making **the mother** the petitioner (cf. Mk 10:35) is not clear. Possibly he intends an allusion to Bathsheba's seeking the kingdom for Solomon; see 1 Kgs 1:11–21. **Your kingdom**: see note on Mt 16:28.

§§[20:22] **You do not know what you are asking**: the Greek verbs are plural and, with the rest of the verse, indicate that the answer is addressed not to the woman but to her sons. **Drink the cup**: see note on Mk 10:38–40. Matthew omits the Marcan "or be baptized with the baptism with which I am baptized" (Mk 10:38).

¶¶[20:28] **Ransom**: this noun, which occurs in the New Testament only here and in the Marcan parallel (Mk 10:45), does not necessarily express the idea of liberation by payment of some price. The cognate verb is used frequently in the LXX for God's liberating Israel from Egypt or from Babylonia after the Exile; see Ex 6:6; 15:13; Ps 77:16 (76 LXX); Is 43:1; 44:22. The liberation brought by Jesus' death will be **for many**; cf. Is 53:12. **Many** does not mean that some are excluded, but is a Semitism designating the collectivity who benefit from the service of the one, and is equivalent to "all." While there are few verbal contacts between this saying and the fourth Servant Song (Is 52:13–53:12), the ideas of that passage are reflected here.

***[20:29–34] The cure of the blind men is probably symbolic of what will happen to the disciples, now blind to the meaning of Jesus' passion and to the necessity of their sharing his suffering. As the men are given sight, so, after the resurrection, will the disciples come to see that to which they are now blind. Matthew has abbreviated his Marcan source (Mk 10:46–52) and has made Mark's one man two. Such doubling is characteristic of this gospel; see Mt 8:28–34 (// Mk 5:1–20) and the note on Mt 9:27–31.

c. [20:20–28] Mk 10:35–45.   d. [20:24–27] Lk 22:25–27.   e. [20:27] Mk 9:35.   f. [20:28] 26:28; Is 53:12; Rom 5:6; 1 Tm 2:6.   g. [20:29–34] Mk 10:46–52; Lk 18:35–43.   h. [20:30] 9:27.

when they heard that Jesus was passing by, they cried out, "[Lord,]* Son of David, have pity on us!" 31The crowd warned them to be silent, but they called out all the more, "Lord, Son of David, have pity on us!" 32Jesus stopped and called them and said, "What do you want me to do for you?" 33They answered him, "Lord, let our eyes be opened." 34Moved with pity, Jesus touched their eyes. Immediately they received their sight, and followed him:

CHAPTER 21

The Entry into Jerusalem.† 1iWhen they drew near Jerusalem and came to Bethphage‡ on the Mount of Olives, Jesus sent two disciples, 2saying to them, "Go into the village opposite you, and immediately you will find an ass tethered, and a colt with her.§ Untie them and bring them here to me. 3And if anyone should say anything to you, reply, 'The master has need of them.' Then he will send them at once." 4This happened so that what had been spoken through the prophet might be fulfilled:

5 j"Say to daughter Zion,
    'Behold, your king comes to you,
        meek and riding on an ass,
            and on a colt, the foal of a beast
                of burden.'"

6The disciples went and did as Jesus had ordered them. 7"They brought the ass and the colt and laid their cloaks over them, and he sat upon them. 8††kThe very large crowd spread their cloaks on the road, while others cut branches from the trees and strewed them on the road. 9lThe crowds preceding him and those following kept crying out and saying:

"Hosanna‡‡ to the Son of David;
    blessed is he who comes in the name
        of the Lord;
    hosanna in the highest."

10And when he entered Jerusalem the whole city was shaken§§ and asked, "Who is this?" 11And the crowds replied, "This is Jesus the prophet,¶¶ from Nazareth in Galilee."

The Cleansing of the Temple.*** 12mJesus entered the temple area and drove out all those engaged in selling and buying there. He overturned the tables of the money changers and the seats of those who were selling doves.†††n 13oAnd he said to them, "It is written:

'My house shall be a house of prayer,'‡‡‡
    but you are making it a den of thieves."

---

*[20:30] **[Lord,]:** some important textual witnesses omit this, but that may be because copyists assimilated this verse to Mt 9:27. **Son of David:** see note on Mt 9:27.

†[21:1–11] Jesus' coming to Jerusalem is in accordance with the divine will that he must go there (cf. Mt 16:21) to suffer, die, and be raised. He prepares for his entry into the city in such a way as to make it a fulfillment of the prophecy of Zec 9:9 (Mt 21:2) that emphasizes the humility of the **king who comes** (Mt 21:5). That prophecy, absent from the Marcan parallel account (Mk 11:1–11) although found also in the Johannine account of the entry (Jn 12:15), is the center of the Matthean story. During the procession from Bethphage to Jerusalem, Jesus is acclaimed as the Davidic messianic king by the crowds who accompany him (Mt 21:9). On his arrival **the whole city was shaken**, and to the inquiry of the amazed populace about Jesus' identity the crowds with him reply that he is **the prophet, from Nazareth in Galilee** (Mt 21:10, 11).

‡[21:1] **Bethphage:** a village that can no longer be certainly identified. Mark mentions it before Bethany (Mk 11:1), which suggests that it lay to the east of the latter. **The Mount of Olives:** the hill east of Jerusalem that is spoken of in Zec 14:4 as the place where the Lord will come to rescue Jerusalem from the enemy nations.

§[21:2] **An ass tethered, and a colt with her:** instead of the one animal of Mk 11:2, Matthew has two, as demanded by his understanding of Zec 9:9.

¶[21:4–5] **The prophet:** this fulfillment citation is actually composed of two distinct Old Testament texts, Is 62:11 (**Say to daughter Zion**) and Zec 9:9. The **ass** and the **colt** are the same animal in the prophecy, mentioned twice in different ways, the common Hebrew literary device of poetic parallelism. That Matthew takes them as two is one of the reasons why some scholars think that he was a Gentile rather than a Jewish Christian who would presumably not make that mistake (see Introduction).

[21:7] **Upon them: upon the two animals; an awkward picture resulting from Matthew's misunderstanding of the prophecy.

††[21:8] **Spread . . . on the road:** cf. 2 Kgs 9:13. There is a similarity between the cutting and strewing of the **branches** and the festivities of Tabernacles (Lv 23:39–40); see also 2 Mc 10:5–8 where the celebration of the rededication of the temple is compared to that of Tabernacles.

‡‡[21:9] **Hosanna:** the Hebrew means "(O LORD) grant salvation"; see Ps 118:25, but that invocation had become an acclamation of jubilation and welcome. **Blessed is he . . . in the name of the Lord:** see Ps 118:26 and the note on Jn 12:13. **In the highest:** probably only an intensification of the acclamation, although **Hosanna in the highest** could be taken as a prayer, "May God save (him)."

§§[21:10] **Was shaken:** in the gospels this verb is peculiar to Matthew where it is used also of the earthquake at the time of the crucifixion (Mt 27:51) and of the terror of the guards at Jesus' tomb at the appearance of the angel (Mt 28:4). For Matthew's use of the cognate noun, see note on Mt 8:24.

¶¶[21:11] **The prophet:** see Mt 16:14 ("one of the prophets") and 21:46.

***[21:12–17] Matthew changes the order of (Mk 11:11, 12, 15) and places the cleansing of the temple on the same day as the entry into Jerusalem, immediately after it. The activities going on in **the temple area** were not secular but connected with the temple worship. Thus Jesus' attack on those so engaged and his charge that they were **making** God's **house of prayer a den of thieves** (Mt 21:12–13) constituted a claim to authority over the religious practices of Israel and were a challenge to the priestly authorities. Mt 21:14–17 are peculiar to Matthew. Jesus' healings and his countenancing the children's cries of praise rouse the indignation of **the chief priests and the scribes** (Mt 21:15). These two groups appear in the infancy narrative (Mt 2:4) and have been mentioned in the first and third passion predictions (Mt 16:21; 20:18). Now, as the passion approaches, they come on the scene again, exhibiting their hostility to Jesus.

†††[21:12] These activities were carried on in the court of the Gentiles, the outermost court of **the temple area**. Animals for sacrifice were sold; the **doves** were for those who could not afford a more expensive offering; see Lv 5:7. **Tables of the money changers:** only the coinage of Tyre could be used for the purchases; other money had to be exchanged for that.

‡‡‡[21:13] '**My house . . . prayer':** cf. Is 56:7. Matthew omits the final words of the quotation, "for all peoples" ("all nations"), possibly because for him the worship of the God of Israel by all nations belongs to the time after the resurrection; see Mt 28:19. **A den of thieves:** the phrase is taken from Jer 7:11.

i. [21:1–11] Mk 11:1–11; Lk 19:28–38; Jn 12:12–15.   j. [21:5] Is 62:11; Zec 9:9.

k. [21:8] 2 Kgs 9:13.   l. [21:9] Ps 118:25–26.   m. [21:12–17] Mk 11:15–19; Lk 19:45–46; Jn 2:14–22.   n. [21:12] Lv 5:7.   o. [21:13] Is 56:7; Jer 7:11.

14p The blind and the lame* approached him in the temple area, and he cured them. 15When the chief priests and the scribes saw the wondrous things† he was doing, and the children crying out in the temple area, "Hosanna to the Son of David," they were indignant 16‡qand said to him, "Do you hear what they are saying?" Jesus said to them, "Yes; and have you never read the text, 'Out of the mouths of infants and nurslings you have brought forth praise'?" 17And leaving them, he went out of the city to Bethany, and there he spent the night.

The Cursing of the Fig Tree.§ 18rWhen he was going back to the city in the morning, he was hungry. 19sSeeing a fig tree by the road, he went over to it, but found nothing on it except leaves. And he said to it, "May no fruit ever come from you again." And immediately the fig tree withered. 20When the disciples saw this, they were amazed and said, "How was it that the fig tree withered immediately?" 21tJesus said to them in reply, "Amen, I say to you, if you have faith and do not waver, not only will you do what has been done to the fig tree, but even if you say to this mountain, 'Be lifted up and thrown into the sea,' it will be done. 22uWhatever you ask for in prayer with faith, you will receive."

The Authority of Jesus Questioned.** 23vWhen he had come into the temple area, the chief priests and the elders of the people approached him as he was teaching and said, "By what authority are you doing these things?†† And who gave you this authority?"w 24Jesus said to them in reply, "I shall ask you one question,‡‡ and if you answer it for me, then I shall tell you by what authority I do these things. 25Where was John's

baptism from? Was it of heavenly or of human origin?" They discussed this among themselves and said, "If we say 'Of heavenly origin,' he will say to us, 'Then why did you not believe him?' 26§§xBut if we say, 'Of human origin,' we fear the crowd, for they all regard John as a prophet." 27So they said to Jesus in reply, "We do not know." He himself said to them, "Neither shall I tell you by what authority I do these things.¶¶

The Parable of the Two Sons.** 28"What is your opinion? A man had two sons. He came to the first and said, 'Son, go out and work in the vineyard today.' 29He said in reply, 'I will not,' but afterwards he changed his mind and went. 30The man came to the other son and gave the same order. He said in reply, 'Yes, sir,' but did not go. 31†††Which of the two did his father's will?" They answered, "The first." Jesus said to them, "Amen, I say to you, tax collectors and prostitutes are entering the kingdom of God before you. 32‡‡‡yWhen John came to you in the way of righteousness, you did not believe him; but tax collectors and prostitutes did. Yet even when you saw that, you did not later change your minds and believe him.

The Parable of the Tenants.§§§ 33z"Hear another parable. There was a landowner who planted a

---

§§[21:26] **We fear . . . as a prophet:** cf. Mt 14:5.

¶¶[21:27] Since through embarrassment on the one hand and fear on the other the religious authorities claim ignorance of the origin of John's baptism, they show themselves incapable of speaking with authority; hence Jesus refuses to discuss with them the grounds of his authority.

***[21:28–32] The series of controversies is interrupted by three parables on the judgment of Israel (Mt 21:28–22:14) of which this, peculiar to Matthew, is the first. The second (Mt 21:33–46) from Mark (12:1–12), and the third (Mt 22:1–14) from Q; see Lk 14:15–24. This interruption of the controversies is similar to that in Mark, although Mark has only one parable between the first and second controversy. As regards Matthew's first parable, Mt 21:28–30 if taken by themselves could point simply to the difference between saying and doing, a theme of much importance in this gospel (cf. Mt 7:21; 12:50); that may have been the parable's original reference. However, it is given a more specific application by the addition of Mt 21:31–32. The two sons represent, respectively, the religious leaders and the religious outcasts who followed John's call to repentance. By the answer they give to Jesus' question (Mt 21:31) the leaders condemn themselves. There is much confusion in the textual tradition of the parable. Of the three different forms of the text given by important textual witnesses, one has the leaders answer that the son who agreed to go but did not was the one who did the father's will. Although some scholars accept that as the original reading, their arguments in favor of it seem unconvincing. The choice probably lies only between a reading that puts the son who agrees and then disobeys before the son who at first refuses and then obeys, and the reading followed in the present translation. The witnesses to the latter reading are slightly better than those that support the other.

†††[21:31] **Entering . . . before you:** this probably means "they enter; you do not."

‡‡‡[21:32] Cf. Lk 7:29–30. Although the thought is similar to that of the Lucan text, the formulation is so different that it is improbable that the saying comes from Q. **Came to you . . . way of righteousness:** several meanings are possible: that John himself was righteous, that he taught righteousness to others, or that he had an important place in God's plan of salvation. For the last, see note on Mt 3:14–15.

§§§[21:33–46] Cf. Mk 12:1–12. In this parable there is a close correspondence between most of the details of the story and the

---

*[21:14] **The blind and the lame:** according to 2 Sm 5:8 LXX **the blind and the lame** were forbidden to enter "the house of the Lord," the temple. These are the last of Jesus' healings in Matthew.

†[21:15] **The wondrous things:** the healings.

‡[21:16] **'Out of the mouths . . . praise':** cf. Ps 8:3 LXX.

§[21:18–22] In Mark the effect of Jesus' cursing the fig tree is not immediate; see Mk 11:14, 20. By making it so, Matthew has heightened the miracle. Jesus' act seems arbitrary and ill-tempered, but it is a prophetic action similar to those of Old Testament prophets that vividly symbolize some part of their preaching; see, e.g., Ez 12:1–20: It is a sign of the judgment that is to come upon the Israel that with all its apparent piety lacks the fruit of good deeds (Mt 3:10) and will soon bear the punishment of its fruitlessness (Mt 21:43). Some scholars propose that this story is the development in tradition of a parable of Jesus about the destiny of a fruitless tree, such as Lk 13:6–9. Jesus' answer to the question of the amazed disciples (Mt 21:20) makes the miracle an example of the power of prayer made with unwavering **faith** (Mt 21:21–22).

¶[21:21] See Mt 17:20.

**[21:23–27] Cf. Mk 11:27–33. This is the first of five controversies between Jesus and the religious authorities of Judaism in Mt 21:23–22:46, presented in the form of questions and answers.

††[21:23] **These things:** probably his entry into the city, his cleansing of the temple, and his healings there.

‡‡[21:24] To reply by counterquestion was common in rabbinical debate.

---

p. [21:14] 2 Sm 5:8 LXX. q. [21:16] Ps 8:2 LXX; Wis 10:21. r. [21:18–22] Mk 11:12–14, 20–24. s. [21:19] Jer 8:13; Lk 13:6–9. t. [21:21] 17:20; Lk 17:6. u. [21:22] 7:7; 1 Jn 3:22. v. [21:23–27] Mk 11:27–33; Lk 20:1–8. w. [21:23] Jn 2:18.

x. [21:26] 14:5. y. [21:32] Lk 7:29–30. z. [21:33–46] Mk 12:1–12; Lk 20:9–19.

vineyard,* put a hedge around it, dug a wine press in it, and built a tower. Then he leased it to tenants and went on a journey.ᵃ ³⁴When vintage time drew near, he sent his servants† to the tenants to obtain his produce. ³⁵But the tenants seized the servants and one they beat, another they killed, and a third they stoned. ³⁶Again he sent other servants, more numerous than the first ones, but they treated them in the same way. ³⁷Finally, he sent his son to them, thinking, 'They will respect my son.' ³⁸ᵇBut when the tenants saw the son, they said to one another, 'This is the heir. Come, let us kill him and acquire his inheritance.' ³⁹ᵇThey seized him, threw him out of the vineyard, and killed him. ⁴⁰What will the owner of the vineyard do to those tenants when he comes?" ⁴¹They answeredᶠ him, "He will put those wretched men to a wretched death and lease his vineyard to other tenants who will give him the produce at the proper times." ⁴²**ᶜJesus said to them, "Did you never read in the scriptures:

'The stone that the builders rejected
    has become the cornerstone;
by the Lord has this been done,
    and it is wonderful in our eyes'?

⁴³††Therefore, I say to you, the kingdom of God will be taken away from you and given to a people that will produce its fruit. ⁴⁴[‡‡ The one who falls on this stone will be dashed to pieces; and it will crush anyone on whom it falls.]" ⁴⁵When the chief priests and the Pharisees§§ heard his parables, they knew that he was speaking about them. ⁴⁶And although they were attempting to arrest him, they feared the crowds, for they regarded him as a prophet.

CHAPTER 22
The Parable of the Wedding Feast.¶¶ ¹ᵈJesus again in reply spoke to them in parables, saying, ²"The kingdom of heaven may be likened to a king who gave a wedding feast* for his son. ³†††He dispatched his servants to summon the invited guests to the feast, but they refused to come. ⁴A second time he sent other servants, saying, 'Tell those invited: "Behold, I have prepared my banquet, my calves and fattened cattle are killed, and everything is ready; come to the feast."' ⁵Some ignored the invitation and went away, one to his farm, another to his business. ⁶ᵉThe rest laid hold of his servants, mistreated them, and killed them. ⁷‡‡‡The king was enraged and sent his troops, destroyed those murderers, and burned their city. ⁸Then he said to his servants, 'The feast is ready, but those who were invited were not worthy to come. ⁹Go out, therefore, into the main roads and invite to the feast whomever you find.' ¹⁰The servants went out into the streets and gathered all they found, bad and good alike,§§§ and the hall was filled with guests. ¹¹¶¶¶But

situation that it illustrates, the dealings of God with his people. Because of that heavy allegorizing, some scholars think that it does not in any way go back to Jesus, but represents the theology of the later church. That judgment applies to the Marcan parallel as well, although the allegorizing has gone farther in Matthew. There are others who believe that while many of the allegorical elements are due to church sources, they have been added to a basic parable spoken by Jesus. This view is now supported by the Gospel of Thomas 65, where a less allegorized and probably more primitive form of the parable is found.
  *[21:33] **Planted a vineyard . . . a tower:** cf. Is 5:1–2. The **vineyard** is defined in Is 5:7 as "the house of Israel."
  †[21:34–35] **His servants:** Matthew has two sendings of **servants** as against Mark's three sendings of a single servant (Mk 11:2–5a) followed by a statement about the sending of "many others" (Mk 11:2, 5b). That these servants stand for the prophets sent by God to Israel is clearly implied but not made explicit here, but see Mt 23:37. **His produce:** cf. Mk 12:2 "some of the produce." The **produce** is the good works demanded by God, and his claim to them is total.
  ‡[21:38] **Acquire his inheritance:** if a Jewish proselyte died without heir, the tenants of his land would have final claim on it.
  §[21:39] **Threw him out . . . and killed him:** the change in the Marcan order where the son is killed and his corpse then thrown out (Mk 12:8) was probably made because of the tradition that Jesus died outside the city of Jerusalem; see Jn 19:17; Heb 13:12.
  ¶[21:41] **They answered:** in Mk 12:9 the question is answered by Jesus himself; here the leaders answer and so condemn themselves; cf. Mt 21:31. Matthew adds that the new **tenants** to whom the vineyard will be transferred **will give** the owner **the produce at the proper times.**
  **[21:42] Cf. Ps 118:22–23. The psalm was used in the early church as a prophecy of Jesus' resurrection; see Acts 4:11; 1 Pt 2:7. If, as some think, the original parable ended at Mt 21:39 it was thought necessary to complete it by a reference to Jesus' vindication by God.
  ††[21:43] Peculiar to Matthew. **Kingdom of God:** see note on Mt 19:23–24. Its presence here instead of Matthew's usual

"kingdom of heaven" may indicate that the saying came from Matthew's own traditional material. **A people that will produce its fruit:** believing Israelites and Gentiles, the church of Jesus.
  ‡‡[21:44] The majority of textual witnesses omit this verse. It is probably an early addition to Matthew from Lk 20:18 with which it is practically identical.
  §§[21:45] **The Pharisees:** Matthew inserts into the group of Jewish leaders (Mt 21:23) those who represented the Judaism of his own time.
  ¶¶[22:1–14] This parable is from Q; see Lk 14:15–24. It has been given many allegorical traits by Matthew, e.g., the burning of the **city** of the guests who refused the invitation (Mt 22:7), which corresponds to the destruction of Jerusalem by the Romans in A.D. 70. It has similarities with the preceding parable of the tenants: the sending of two groups of **servants** (Mt 22:3, 4), the murder of the **servants** (Mt 22:6), the punishment of the **murderers** (Mt 22:7), and the entrance of a new group into a privileged situation of which the others had proved themselves unworthy (Mt 22:8–10). The parable ends with a section that is peculiar to Matthew (Mt 22:11–14), which some take as a distinct parable. Matthew presents the **kingdom** in its double aspect, already present and something that can be entered here and now (Mt 22:1–10), and something that will be possessed only by those present members who can stand the scrutiny of the final judgment (Mt 22:11–14). The parable is not only a statement of God's judgment on Israel but a warning to Matthew's church.
  ***[22:2] **Wedding feast:** the Old Testament's portrayal of final salvation under the image of a banquet (Is 25:6) is taken up also in Mt 8:11; cf. Lk 13:15.
  †††[22:3–4] **Servants . . . other servants:** probably Christian missionaries in both instances; cf. Mt 23:34.
  ‡‡‡[22:7] See note on Mt 22:1–14.
  §§§[22:10] **Bad and good alike:** cf. Mt 13:47.
  ¶¶¶[22:11] **A wedding garment:** the repentance, change of heart and mind, that is the condition for entrance into the

a. [21:33] Is 5:1–2, 7.   b. [21:39] Heb 13:12.   c. [21:42] Ps 118:22–23; Is 28:16; Acts 4:11; 1 Pt 2:7.

d. [22:1–14] Lk 14:15–24.   e. [22:6] 21:35.

when the king came in to meet the guests he saw a man there not dressed in a wedding garment. [12]He said to him, 'My friend, how is it that you came in here without a wedding garment?' But he was reduced to silence. [13]*[f]Then the king said to his attendants, 'Bind his hands and feet, and cast him into the darkness outside, where there will be wailing and grinding'of teeth.' [14]Many are invited, but few are chosen."

Paying Taxes to the Emperor.[†] [15g]Then the Pharisees[‡] went off and plotted how they might entrap him in speech. [16]They sent their disciples to him, with the Herodians,[§] saying, "Teacher, we know that you are a truthful man and that you teach the way of God in accordance with the truth. And you are not concerned with anyone's opinion, for you do not regard a person's status. [17¶]Tell us, then, what is your opinion: Is it lawful to pay the census tax to Caesar or not?" [18]Knowing their malice, Jesus said, "Why are you testing me, you hypocrites? [19]**Show me the coin that pays the census tax." Then they handed him the Roman coin. [20]He said to them, "Whose image is this and whose inscription?" [21h]They replied, "Caesar's."[††] At that he said to them, "Then repay 'to Caesar what belongs to Caesar and to God what belongs to God." [22]When they heard this they were amazed, and leaving him they went away.

The Question About the Resurrection.[‡‡] [23i]On that day Sadducees approached him, saying that

there is no resurrection.[§§] They put this question to him, [24j]saying, "Teacher, Moses said, 'If a man dies[¶¶] without children, his brother shall marry his wife and raise up descendants for his brother.' [25]Now there were seven brothers among us. The first married and died and, having no descendants, left his wife to his brother. [26]The same happened with the second and the third, through all seven. [27]Finally the woman died. [28]Now at the resurrection, of the seven, whose wife will she be? For they all had been married to her." [29]***Jesus said to them in reply, "You are misled because you do not know the scriptures or the power of God. [30]At the resurrection they neither marry nor are given in marriage but are like the angels in heaven. [31]And concerning the resurrection of the dead, have you not read what was said to you[†††] by God, [32k]'I am the God of Abraham, the God of Isaac, and the God of Jacob'? He is not the God of the dead but of the living." [33]When the crowds heard this, they were astonished at his teaching.

The Greatest Commandment.[‡‡‡] [34l]When the Pharisees heard that he had silenced the Sadducees, they gathered together, [35]and one of them

kingdom (Mt 3:2; 4:17) must be continued in a life of good deeds (Mt 7:21–23).

*[22:13] **Wailing and grinding of teeth**: the Christian who lacks the wedding garment of good deeds will suffer the same fate as those Jews who have rejected Jesus; see note on Mt 8:11–12.

†[22:15–22] The series of controversies between Jesus and the representatives of Judaism (see note on Mt 21:23–27) is resumed. As in the first (Mt 21:23–27), here and in the following disputes Matthew follows his Marcan source with few modifications.

‡[22:15] **The Pharisees**: while Matthew retains the Marcan union of Pharisees and Herodians in this account, he clearly emphasizes the Pharisees' part. They alone are mentioned here, and the Herodians are joined with them only in a prepositional phrase of Mt 22:16. **Entrap him in speech**: the question that they will pose is intended to force Jesus to take either a position contrary to that held by the majority of the people or one that will bring him into conflict with the Roman authorities.

§[22:16] **Herodians**. see note on Mk 3:6. They would favor payment of the tax; the Pharisees did not.

¶[22:17] **Is it lawful**: the law to which they refer is the law of God.

[22:19] **They handed him the Roman coin: their readiness in producing the money implies their use of it and their acceptance of the financial advantages of the Roman administration in Palestine.

††[22:21] **Caesar's**: the emperor Tiberius (A.D. 14–37). **Repay to Caesar what belongs to Caesar**: those who willingly use the coin that is Caesar's should **repay** him in kind. The answer avoids taking sides in the question of the lawfulness of the tax. **To God what belongs to God**: Jesus raises the debate to a new level. Those who have hypocritically asked about tax in respect to its relation to the law of **God** should be concerned rather with repaying God with the good deeds that are his due; cf. Mt 21:41, 43.

‡‡[22:23–33] Here Jesus' opponents are the **Sadducees**, members of the powerful priestly party of his time; see note

on Mt 3:7. Denying the resurrection of the dead, a teaching of relatively late origin in Judaism (cf. Dn 12:2), they appeal to a law of the Pentateuch (Dt 25:5–10) and present a case based on it that would make resurrection from the dead ridiculous (Mt 22:24–28). Jesus chides them for knowing neither **the scriptures** nor **the power of God** (Mt 22:29). His argument in respect to God's power contradicts the notion, held even by many proponents as well as by opponents of the teaching, that the life of those raised from the dead would be essentially a continuation of the type of life they had had before death (Mt 22:30). His argument based on the scriptures (Mt 22:31–32) is of a sort that was accepted as valid among Jews of the time.

§§[22:23] **Saying that there is no resurrection**: in the Marcan parallel (Mk 22:12, 18) the Sadducees are correctly defined as those "who say there is no resurrection"; see also Lk 20:27. Matthew's rewording of Mark can mean that these particular Sadducees deny the resurrection, which would imply that he was not aware that the denial was characteristic of the party. For some scholars this is an indication of his being a Gentile Christian; see note on Mt 21:4–5.

¶¶[22:24] **'If a man dies . . . his brother'**: this is known as the "law of the levirate," from the Latin *levir*, "brother-in-law." Its purpose was to continue the family line of the deceased brother (Dt 25:6).

***[22:29] The sexual relationships of this world will be transcended; the risen body will be the work of the creative **power of God**.

†††[22:31–32] Cf. Ex 3:6. In the Pentateuch, which the Sadducees accepted as normative for Jewish belief and practice, God speaks even now (**to you**) of himself as the God of the patriarchs who died centuries ago. He identifies himself in relation to them, and because of their relation to him, the living God, they too are alive. This might appear no argument for the resurrection, but simply for life after death as conceived in Wis 3:1–3. But the general thought of early first-century Judaism was not influenced by that conception; for it human immortality was connected with the existence of the body.

‡‡‡[22:34–40] The Marcan parallel (Mk 12:28–34) is an exchange between Jesus and a scribe who is impressed by the way in which Jesus has conducted himself in the previous controversy (Mk 12:28), who compliments him for the answer he gives him (Mk 12:32), and who is said by Jesus to be "not far from the kingdom of God" (Mk 12:34). Matthew has sharpened that scene. The questioner, as the representative of other Pharisees, tests Jesus by his question (Mt 22:34–35), and both

f. [22:13] 8:12; 25:30.   g. [22:15–22] Mk 12:13–17; Lk 20:20–26.   h. [22:21] Rom 13:7.   i. [22:23–33] Mk 12:18–27; Lk 20:27–40.

j. [22:24] Gn 38:8; Dt 25:5–6.   k. [22:32] Ex 3:6.   l. [22:34–40] Mk 12:28–34; Lk 10:25–28.

[a scholar of the law]* tested him by asking, [36]"Teacher,[†] which commandment in the law is the greatest?" [37m]He said to him,[‡] "You shall love the Lord, your God, with all your heart, with all your soul, and with all your mind. [38]This is the greatest and the first commandment. [39n]The second is like it:[§] You shall love your neighbor as yourself. [40§o]The whole law and the prophets depend on these two commandments."

The Question About David's Son.** [41p]While the Pharisees were gathered together, Jesus questioned them,[††] [42‡‡]saying, "What is your opinion about the Messiah? Whose son is he?" They replied, "David's." [43]He said to them, "How, then, does David, inspired by the Spirit, call him 'lord,' saying:

[44] [q]"The Lord said to my lord,
        "Sit at my right hand
            until I place your enemies under
                your feet"'?

[45§§]If David calls him 'lord,' how can he be his son?" [46r]No one was able to answer him a word,

---

his reaction to Jesus' reply and Jesus' commendation of him are lacking.

*[22:35] [A scholar of the law]: meaning "scribe." Although this reading is supported by the vast majority of textual witnesses, it is the only time that the Greek word so translated occurs in Matthew. It is relatively frequent in Luke, and there is reason to think that it may have been added here by a copyist since it occurs in the Lucan parallel (Lk 10:25–28). **Tested**: see note on Mt 19:3.

†[22:36] For the devout Jew all the commandments were to be kept with equal care, but there is evidence of preoccupation in Jewish sources with the question put to Jesus.

‡[22:37–38] Cf. Dt 6:5. Matthew omits the first part of Mark's fuller quotation (Mk 12:29; Dt 6:4–5), probably because he considered its monotheistic emphasis needless for his church. The love of God must engage the total person (**heart, soul, mind**).

§[22:39] Jesus goes beyond the extent of the question put to him and joins **to the greatest and the first commandment** a second, that of love of neighbor, Lv 19:18; see note on Mt 19:18–19. This combination of the two commandments may already have been made in Judaism.

¶[22:40] The double commandment is the source from which **the whole law and the prophets** are derived.

[22:41–46] Having answered the questions of his opponents in the preceding three controversies, Jesus now puts a question to them about the sonship of the Messiah. Their easy response (Mt 22:43a) is countered by his quoting a verse of Ps 110 that raises a problem for their response (43b–45). They are unable to solve it and **from that day on their questioning of him is ended.

††[22:41] **The Pharisees . . . questioned them**: Mark is not specific about who are questioned (Mk 12:35).

‡‡[22:42–44] **David's**: this view of the Pharisees was based on such Old Testament texts as Is 11:1–9; Jer 23:5; and Ez 34:23; see also the extrabiblical Psalms of Solomon 17:21. **How, then . . . saying**: Jesus cites Ps 110:1, accepting the Davidic authorship of the psalm, a common view of his time. The psalm was probably composed for the enthronement of a Davidic king of Judah. Matthew assumes that the Pharisees interpret it as referring to the Messiah, although there is no clear evidence that it was so interpreted in the Judaism of Jesus' time. It was widely used in the early church as referring to the exaltation of the risen Jesus. **My lord**: understood as the Messiah.

§§[22:45] Since Matthew presents Jesus both as Messiah (Mt 16:16) and as Son of David (Mt 1:1; see also note on Mt 9:27),

---

m. [22:37] Dt 6:5.   n. [22:39] Lv 19:18; Jas 2:8.   o. [22:40] Rom 13:8–10; Gal 5:14.   p. [22:41–46] Mk 12:35–37; Lk 20:41–44.   q. [22:44] Ps 110:1; Acts 2:35; Heb 1:13.   r. [22:46] Lk 20:40.

---

nor from that day on did anyone dare to ask him any more questions.

CHAPTER 23[¶¶]
Denunciation of the Scribes and Pharisees. [1s]Then Jesus spoke to the crowds and to his disciples, [2***]saying, "The scribes and the Pharisees have taken their seat on the chair of Moses. [3]Therefore, do and observe all things whatsoever they tell you, but do not follow their example. For they preach but they do not practice. [4]They tie up heavy burdens[†††] [hard to carry] and lay them on people's shoulders, but they will not lift a finger to move them. [5‡‡‡u]All their works

---

the question is not meant to imply Jesus' denial of Davidic sonship. It probably means that although he is the Son of David, he is someone greater, Son of Man and Son of God, and recognized as greater by David who calls him my '**lord**.'

¶¶[23:1–39] The final section of the narrative part of the fifth book of the gospel is a denunciation by Jesus of the scribes and the Pharisees (see note on Mt 3:7). It depends in part on Mark and Q (cf. Mk 12:38–39; Lk 11:37–52; 13:34–35), but in the main it is peculiar to Matthew. (For the reasons against considering this extensive body of sayings-material either as one of the structural discourses of this gospel or as part of the one that follows in Mt 24–25, see note on Mt 19:1–23:39.) While the tradition of a deep opposition between Jesus and the Pharisees is well founded, this speech reflects an opposition that goes beyond that of Jesus' ministry and must be seen as expressing the bitter conflict between Pharisaic Judaism and the church of Matthew at the time when the gospel was composed. The complaint often made that the speech ignores the positive qualities of Pharisaism and of its better representatives is true, but the complaint overlooks the circumstances that gave rise to the invective. Nor is the speech purely anti-Pharisaic. The evangelist discerns in his church many of the same faults that he finds in its opponents and warns his fellow Christians to look to their own conduct and attitudes.

***[23:2–3] **Have taken their seat . . . Moses**: it is uncertain whether this is simply a metaphor for Mosaic teaching authority or refers to an actual **chair** on which the teacher sat. It has been proved that there was a seat so designated in synagogues of a later period than that of this gospel. **Do and observe . . . they tell you**: since the Matthean Jesus abrogates Mosaic law (Mt 5:31–42), warns his disciples against the teaching of the Pharisees (Mt 14:1–12), and, in this speech, denounces the Pharisees as blind guides in respect to their teaching on oaths (Mt 23:16–22), this commandment **to observe all things whatsoever they** (the scribes and Pharisees) **tell you** cannot be taken as the evangelist's understanding of the proper standard of conduct for his church. The saying may reflect a period when the Matthean community was largely Jewish Christian and was still seeking to avoid a complete break with the synagogue. Matthew has incorporated this traditional material into the speech in accordance with his view of the course of salvation history, in which he portrays the time of Jesus' ministry as marked by the fidelity to the law, although with significant pointers to the new situation that would exist after his death and resurrection (see note on Mt 5:17–20). The crowds and the disciples (Mt 23:1) are exhorted not to **follow** the **example** of the Jewish leaders, whose deeds do not conform to their teaching (Mt 23:3).

†††[23:4] **Tie up heavy burdens**: see note on Mt 11:28.

‡‡‡[23:5] To the charge of preaching but not practicing (Mt 23:3), Jesus adds that of acting in order to earn praise. The disciples have already been warned against this same fault (see note on Mt 6:1–18). **Phylacteries**: the Mosaic law required that during prayer small boxes containing parchments on which verses of scripture were written be worn on the left forearm and the forehead (see Ex 13:9, 16; Dt 6:8; 11:18). **Tassels**: see note on Mt 9:20. The widening of **phylacteries** and the lengthening of **tassels** were for the purpose of making these evidences of piety more noticeable.

---

s. [23:1–39] Mk 12:38–39; Lk 11:37–52; 13:34–35.   t. [23:4] Lk 11:46.   u. [23:5] 6:1–6; Ex 13:9, 16; Nm 15:38–39; Dt 6:8; 11:18.

are performed to be seen. They widen their phylacteries and lengthen their tassels. [6*v]They love places of honor at banquets, seats of honor in synagogues, [7]greetings in marketplaces, and the salutation 'Rabbi.' [8†]As for you, do not be called 'Rabbi.' You have but one teacher, and you are all brothers. [9]Call no one on earth your father; you have but one Father in heaven. [10]Do not be called 'Master'; you have but one master, the Messiah. [11w]The greatest among you must be your servant. [12x]Whoever exalts himself will be humbled; but whoever humbles himself will be exalted.

[13†y]"Woe to you, scribes and Pharisees, you hypocrites. You lock the kingdom of heaven[s] before human beings. You do not enter yourselves, nor do you allow entrance to those trying to enter. [[14]][¶]

[15***]"Woe to you, scribes and Pharisees, you hypocrites. You traverse sea and land to make one convert, and when that happens you make him a child of Gehenna twice as much as yourselves.

[16††z]"Woe to you, blind guides, who say, 'If one swears by the temple, it means nothing, but if one swears by the gold of the temple, one is obligated.' [17]Blind fools, which is greater, the gold, or the temple that made the gold sacred? [18]And you say, 'If one swears by the altar, it means nothing, but if one swears by the gift on the altar, one is obligated.' [19]You blind ones, which is greater, the gift, or the altar that makes the gift sacred? [20a]One who swears by the altar swears by it and all that is upon it; [21]one who swears by the temple swears by it and by him who dwells in it; [22]one who swears by heaven swears by the throne of God and by him who is seated on it.

[23b]"Woe to you, scribes and Pharisees, you hypocrites. You pay tithes[‡‡] of mint and dill and cummin, and have neglected the weightier things of the law: judgment and mercy and fidelity. [But] these you should have done, without neglecting the others. [24§§c]Blind guides, who strain out the gnat and swallow the camel!

[25¶¶d]"Woe to you, scribes and Pharisees, you hypocrites. You cleanse the outside of cup and dish, but inside they are full of plunder and self-indulgence. [26]Blind Pharisee, cleanse first the inside of the cup, so that the outside also may be clean.

[27***]"Woe to you, scribes and Pharisees, you hypocrites. You are like whitewashed tombs, which appear beautiful on the outside, but inside are full of dead men's bones and every kind of filth. [28e]Even so, on the outside you appear righteous, but inside you are filled with hypocrisy and evildoing.

---

*[23:6–7] Cf. Mk 12:38–39. 'Rabbi': literally, "my great one," a title of respect for teachers and leaders.

†[23:8–12] These verses, warning against the use of various titles, are addressed to the disciples alone. While only the title 'Rabbi' has been said to be used in addressing the scribes and Pharisees (Mt 23:7), the implication is that **Father** and **'Master'** also were. The prohibition of these titles to the disciples suggests that their use was present in Matthew's church. The Matthean Jesus forbids not only the titles but the spirit of superiority and pride that is shown by their acceptance. **Whoever exalts . . . will be exalted:** cf. Lk 14:11.

‡[23:13–36] This series of seven "woes," directed against the **scribes and Pharisees** and addressed to them, is the heart of the speech. The phrase **woe** to occurs often in the prophetic and apocalyptic literature, expressing horror of a sin and punishment for those who commit it. **Hypocrites:** see note on Mt 6:2. The hypocrisy of the **scribes and Pharisees** consists in the difference between their speech and action (Mt 23:3) and in demonstrations of piety that have no other purpose than to enhance their reputation as religious persons (Mt 23:5).

§[23:13] **You lock the kingdom of heaven:** cf. Mt 16:19 where Jesus tells Peter that he will give him the keys to **the kingdom of heaven.** The purpose of the authority expressed by that metaphor is to give entrance into the kingdom (the kingdom is closed only to those who reject the authority); here the charge is made that the authority of the **scribes and Pharisees** is exercised in such a way as to be an obstacle to entrance. Cf. Lk 11:52 where the accusation against the "scholars of the law" (Matthew's **scribes**) is that they "have taken away the key of knowledge."

¶[23:14] Some manuscripts add a verse here or after Mt 23:12, "Woe to you, scribes and Pharisees, you hypocrites. You devour the houses of widows and, as a pretext, recite lengthy prayers. Because of this, you will receive a very severe condemnation." Cf. Mk 12:40; Lk 20:47. This "woe" is almost identical with Mk 12:40 and seems to be an interpolation derived from that text.

[23:15] In the first century A.D. until the First Jewish Revolt against Rome (A.D. 66–70), many Pharisees conducted a vigorous missionary campaign among Gentiles. **Convert: literally, "proselyte," a Gentile who accepted Judaism fully by submitting to circumcision and all other requirements of Mosaic law. **Child of Gehenna:** worthy of everlasting punishment; for **Gehenna,** see note on Mt 5:22. **Twice as much as yourselves:** possibly this refers simply to the zeal of the **convert,** surpassing that of the one who converted him.

††[23:16–22] An attack on the casuistry that declared some oaths binding (**one is obligated**) and others not (**it means nothing**) and held the binding oath to be the one made by

something of lesser value (**the gold; the gift on the altar**). Such teaching, which inverts the order of values, reveals the teachers to be **blind guides;** cf. Mt 15:14. Since the Matthean Jesus forbids all oaths to his disciples (Mt 5:33–37), this woe does not set up a standard for Christian moral conduct, but ridicules the Pharisees on their own terms.

‡‡[23:23] The Mosaic law ordered tithing of the produce of the land (Lv 27:30; Dt 14:22–23), and the scribal tradition is said here to have extended this law to even the smallest herbs. The practice is criticized not in itself but because it shows the Pharisees' preoccupation with matters of less importance while they neglect **the weightier things of the law.**

§§[23:24] Cf. Lv 11:41–45 that forbids the eating of any "swarming creature." The Pharisees' scrupulosity about minor matters and neglect of greater ones (Mt 23:23) is further brought out by this contrast between straining liquids that might contain a tiny "swarming creature" and yet swallowing **the camel.** The latter was one of the unclean animals forbidden by the law (Lv 11:4), but it is hardly possible that the scribes and Pharisees are being denounced as guilty of so gross a violation of the food laws. To **swallow the camel** is only a hyperbolic way of speaking of their neglect of what is important.

¶¶[23:25–26] The ritual washing of utensils for dining (cf. Mk 7:4) is turned into a metaphor illustrating a concern for appearances while inner purity is ignored. The **scribes and Pharisees** are compared to cups carefully washed on the outside but filthy within. **Self-indulgence:** the Greek word here translated means lack of self-control, whether in drinking or in sexual conduct.

***[23:27–28] The sixth **woe,** like the preceding one, deals with concern for externals and neglect of what is **inside.** Since contact with dead bodies, even when one was unaware of it, caused ritual impurity (Nm 19:11–22), tombs were whitewashed so that no one would contract such impurity inadvertently.

a. [23:20–22] 5:34–35. b. [23:23] Lv 27:30; Dt 14:22; Lk 11:42. c. [23:24] Lv 11:41–45. d. [23:25–26] Mk 7:4; Lk 11:39. e. [23:28] Lk 16:15; 18:9.

v. [23:6–7] Mk 12:38–39; Lk 11:43; 20:46. w. [23:11] 20:26. x. [23:12] Lk 14:11; 18:14. y. [23:13] Lk 11:52. z. [23:16] 15:14.

²⁹*"Woe to you, scribes and Pharisees,† you hypocrites. You build the tombs of the prophets and adorn the memorials of the righteous, ³⁰ᶠand you say, 'If we had lived in the days of our ancestors, we would not have joined them in shedding the prophets' blood.' ³¹ᵍThus you bear witness against yourselves that you are the children of those who murdered the prophets; ³²now fill up what your ancestors measured out! ³³ʰYou serpents, you brood of vipers, how can you flee from the judgment of Gehenna? ³⁴‡ⁱTherefore, behold, I send to you prophets and wise men and scribes; some of them you will kill and crucify, some of them you will scourge in your synagogues and pursue from town to town, ³⁵so that there may come upon you all the righteous blood shed upon earth, from the righteous blood of Abel to the blood of Zechariah, the son of Barachiah, whom you murdered between the sanctuary and the altar. ³⁶Amen, I say to you, all these things will come upon this generation.

The Lament over Jerusalem.§ ³⁷ʲ"Jerusalem, Jerusalem, you who kill the prophets and stone those sent to you, how many times I yearned to gather your children together, as a hen gathers her young under her wings, but you were unwilling!ᵏ ³⁸ᶫBehold, your house will be abandoned, desolate. ³⁹ᵐI tell you, you will not see me again until you say, 'Blessed is he who comes in the name of the Lord.'"

CHAPTER 24

The Destruction of the Temple Foretold. ¹ⁿJesus left the temple area and was going away, when his disciples approached him to point out the temple buildings. ²"He said to them in reply, "You see all these things, do you not? Amen, I say to you, there will not be left here a stone upon another stone that will not be thrown down."

The Beginning of Calamities. ³As he was sitting on the Mount of Olives,†† the disciples approached him privately and said, "Tell us, when will this happen, and what sign will there be of your coming, and of the end of the age?" ⁴‡Jesus said to

---

*[23:29–36] The final woe is the most serious indictment of all. It portrays the **scribes and Pharisees** as standing in the same line as their **ancestors** who murdered **the prophets** and **the righteous**.

†[23:29–32] In spite of honoring the slain dead by building their **tombs** and adorning their **memorials**, and claiming that they would not have joined in their ancestors' crimes if they **had lived in** their **days**, the **scribes and Pharisees** are true children of their ancestors and are defiantly ordered by Jesus to **fill up** what those **ancestors measured out**. This order reflects the Jewish notion that there was an allotted measure of suffering that had to be completed before God's final judgment would take place.

‡[23:34–36] There are important differences between the Matthean and the Lucan form of this Q material; cf. Lk 11:49–51. In Luke the one who sends the emissaries is the "wisdom of God." If, as many scholars think, that is the original wording of Q, Matthew, by making Jesus the sender, has presented him as the personified divine wisdom. In Luke, wisdom's emissaries are the Old Testament "prophets" and the Christian "apostles." Matthew's **prophets and wise men and scribes** are probably Christian disciples alone; cf. Mt 10:41 and see note on Mt 13:52. **You will kill**: see Mt 24:9. **Scourge in your synagogues . . . town to town**: see Mt 10:17, 23 and the note on Mt 10:17. **All the righteous blood shed upon the earth**: the slaying of the disciples is in continuity with all the shedding of righteous blood beginning with that of **Abel**. The persecution of Jesus' disciples by **this generation** involves the persecutors in the guilt of their murderous ancestors. The **blood of Zechariah**: see note on Lk 11:51. By identifying him as **the son of Barachiah** Matthew understands him to be Zechariah the Old Testament minor prophet; see Zec 1:1.

§[23:37–39] Cf. Lk 13:34–35. The denunciation of Pharisaic Judaism ends with this lament over **Jerusalem**, which has repeatedly rejected and murdered those whom God has **sent** to her. **How many times**: this may refer to various visits of Jesus to the city, an aspect of his ministry found in John but otherwise not in the synoptics. **As a hen . . . under her wings**: for imagery similar to this, see Ps 17:8; 91:4. **Your house . . . desolate**: probably an allusion to the destruction of the temple in A.D. 70. **You will not see me . . . in the name of the Lord**: Israel will not see Jesus again until he comes in glory for the final judgment. The acclamation has been interpreted in contrasting ways, as an indication that Israel will at last accept Jesus at that time, and as its troubled recognition of him as its dreaded judge who will pronounce its condemnation; in support of the latter view see Mt 24:30.

¶[24:1–25:46] The discourse of the fifth book, the last of the five around which the gospel is structured. It is called the "eschatological" discourse since it deals with the coming of the new age (the *eschaton*) in its fullness, with events that will precede it, and with how the disciples are to conduct themselves while awaiting an event that is as certain as its exact time is unknown to all but the Father (Mt 24:36). The discourse may be divided into two parts, Mt 24:1–44 and Mt 24:45–25:46. In the first, Matthew follows his Marcan source (Mk 13:1–37) closely. The second is drawn from Q and from the evangelist's own traditional material. Both parts show Matthew's editing of his sources by deletions, additions, and modifications. The vigilant waiting that is emphasized in the second part does not mean a cessation of ordinary activity and concentration only on what is to come, but a faithful accomplishment of duties at hand, with awareness that the end, for which the disciples must always be ready, will entail the great judgment by which the everlasting destiny of all will be determined.

**[24:2] As in Mark, Jesus predicts the destruction of the temple. By omitting the Marcan story of the widow's contribution (Mk 12:41–44) that immediately precedes the prediction in that gospel, Matthew has established a close connection between it and Mt 23:38, ". . . your house will be abandoned desolate."

††[24:3] The **Mount of Olives**: see note on Mt 21:1. The **disciples**: cf. Mk 13:3–4 where only Peter, James, John, and Andrew put the question that is answered by the discourse. In both gospels, however, the question is put **privately**: the ensuing discourse is only for those who are **disciples** of Jesus. **When will this happen . . . end of the age?**: Matthew distinguishes carefully between the destruction of the temple (**this**) and the **coming** of Jesus that will bring **the end of the age**. In Mark the two events are more closely connected, a fact that may be explained by Mark's believing that the one would immediately succeed the other. **Coming**: this translates the Greek word *parousia*, which is used in the gospels only here and in Mt 24:27, 37, 39. It designated the official visit of a ruler to a city or the manifestation of a saving deity, and it was used by Christians to refer to the final coming of Jesus in glory, a term first found in the New Testament with that meaning in 1 Thes 2:19. **The end of the age**: see note on Mt 13:39.

‡‡[24:4–14] This section of the discourse deals with calamities in the world (Mt 24:6–7) and in the church (Mt 24:9–12). The former **must happen** before **the end** comes (Mt 24:6), but they are only **the beginning of the labor pains** (Mt 24:8). (It may be noted that the Greek word translated **the end** in Mt 24:6 and in Mt 24:13–14 is not the same as the phrase "the end of the age" in Mt 24:3, although the meaning is the same.) The latter are sufferings of the church, both from within and without, that will last until **the gospel is preached . . . to all**

---

f. [23:30] Lk 11:47.   g. [23:31] Acts 7:52.   h. [23:33] 3:7; 12:34. i. [23:34–36] 5:12; Gn 4:8; 2 Chr 24:20–22; Zec 1:1; Lk 11:49–51; Rev 18:24.   j. [23:37–39] Lk 13:34–35; 19:41–44.

k. [23:37] 21:35.   l. [23:38] Jer 12:7.   m. [23:39] Ps 118:26.   n. [24:1–44] Mk 13:1–37; Lk 21:5–36.

them in reply, "See that no one deceives you. ⁵For many will come in my name, saying, 'I am the Messiah,' and they will deceive many. ⁶ºYou will hear of wars* and reports of wars; see that you are not alarmed, for these things must happen, but it will not yet be the end. ⁷ᵖNation will rise against nation, and kingdom against kingdom; there will be famines and earthquakes from place to place. ⁸ᵗAll these are the beginning of the labor pains. ⁹ᵗᵈThen they will hand you over to persecution, and they will kill you. You will be hated by all nations because of my name. ¹⁰And then many will be led into sin; they will betray and hate one another. ¹¹Many false prophets will arise and deceive many; ¹²and because of the increase of evildoing, the love of many will grow cold. ¹³ʳBut the one who perseveres to the end will be saved. ¹⁴ˢAnd this gospel of the kingdom will be preached throughout the world as a witness to all nations,§ and then the end will come.

The Great Tribulation.⁵ ¹⁵ᵗ"When you see the desolating abomination** spoken of through

Daniel the prophet standing in the holy place (let the reader understand), ¹⁶then those in Judea must flee†† to the mountains, ¹⁷‡‡ᵘa person on the housetop must not go down to get things out of his house, ¹⁸a person in the field must not return to get his cloak. ¹⁹Woe to pregnant women and nursing mothers in those days. ²⁰§§Pray that your flight not be in winter or on the sabbath, ²¹¶¶ᵛfor at that time there will be great tribulation, such as has not been since the beginning of the world until now, nor ever will be. ²²And if those days had not been shortened, no one would be saved; but for the sake of the elect they will be shortened. ²³ʷIf anyone says to you then, 'Look, here is the Messiah!' or, 'There he is!' do not believe it. ²⁴False messiahs and false prophets will arise, and they will perform signs and wonders so great as to deceive, if that were possible, even the elect. ²⁵Behold, I have told it to you beforehand. ²⁶So if they say to you, 'He is in the desert,' do not go out there; if they say, 'He is in the inner rooms,' do not believe it."** ²⁷ˣFor just as lightning comes from the east and is seen as far as the west, so will the coming of the Son of Man be. ²⁸Wherever the corpse is, there the vultures will gather.

The Coming of the Son of Man. ²⁹†††ʸ"Immediately after the tribulation of those days,

---

nations. **Then the end will come** and those who have endured the sufferings with fidelity **will be saved** (Mt 24:13–14).

*[24:6–7] The disturbances mentioned here are a commonplace of apocalyptic language, as is the assurance that they **must happen** (see Dn 2:28 LXX), for that is the plan of God. **Kingdom against kingdom:** see Is 19:2.

†[24:8] **The labor pains:** the tribulations leading up to the end of the age are compared to the pains of a woman about to give birth. There is much attestation for rabbinic use of the phrase "the woes (or birth pains) of the Messiah" after the New Testament period, but in at least one instance it is attributed to a rabbi who lived in the late first century A.D. In this Jewish usage it meant the distress of the time preceding the coming of the Messiah; here, the **labor pains** precede the coming of the Son of Man in glory.

‡[24:9–12] Matthew has used Mk 13:9–12 in his missionary discourse (Mt 10:17–21) and omits it here. Besides the sufferings, including death, and the hatred of **all nations** that the disciples will have to endure, there will be worse affliction within the church itself. This is described in Mt 24:10–12, which are peculiar to Matthew. **Will be led into sin:** literally, "will be scandalized," probably meaning that they will become apostates; see Mt 13:21 where "fall away" translates the same Greek word as here. **Betray:** in the Greek this is the same word as the **hand over** of Mt 24:9. The handing over to persecution and hatred from outside will have their counterpart within the church. **False prophets:** these are Christians; see note on Mt 7:15–20. **Evildoing:** see Mt 7:23. Because of the apocalyptic nature of much of this discourse, the literal meaning of this description of the church should not be pressed too hard. However, there is reason to think that Matthew's addition of these verses reflects in some measure the condition of his community.

§[24:14] Except for the last part (**and then the end will come**), this verse substantially repeats Mk 13:10. The Matthean addition raises a problem since what follows in Mt 24:15–23 refers to the horrors of the First Jewish Revolt including the destruction of the temple, and Matthew, writing after that time, knew that the parousia of Jesus was still in the future. A solution may be that the evangelist saw the events of those verses as foreshadowing the cosmic disturbances that he associates with the parousia (Mt 24:29) so that the period in which the former took place could be understood as belonging to **the end.**

¶[24:15–28] Cf. Mk 13:14–23; Lk 17:23–24, 37. A further stage in the tribulations that will precede the coming of the Son of Man, and an answer to the question of Mt 24:3a, "when will this (the destruction of the temple) happen?"

[24:15] **The desolating abomination: in 167 B.C. the Syrian king Antiochus IV Epiphanes desecrated the temple by

setting up in it a statue of Zeus Olympios (see 1 Mc 1:54). That event is referred to in Dn 12:11 LXX as the "desolating abomination" (NAB "horrible abomination") and the same Greek term is used here; cf. also Dn 9:27; 11:31. Although the desecration had taken place before Daniel was written, it is presented there as a future event, and Matthew sees that "prophecy" fulfilled in the desecration of the temple by the Romans. **In the holy place:** the temple; more precise than Mark's **where he should not** (Mk 13:14). **Let the reader understand:** this parenthetical remark, taken from Mk 13:14 invites **the reader** to realize the meaning of Daniel's "prophecy."

††[24:16] The tradition that the Christians of Jerusalem fled from that city to Pella, a city of Transjordan, at the time of the First Jewish Revolt is found in Eusebius (*Ecclesiastical History* 3.5.3), who attributes the flight to "a certain oracle given by revelation before the war." The tradition is not improbable but the Matthean command, derived from its Marcan source, is vague in respect to the place of flight (**to the mountains**), although some scholars see it as applicable to the flight to Pella.

‡‡[24:17–19] Haste is essential, and the journey will be particularly difficult for women who are burdened with unborn or infant children.

§§[24:20] **On the sabbath:** this addition to **in winter** (cf. Mk 13:18) has been understood as an indication that Matthew was addressed to a church still observing the Mosaic law of sabbath rest and the scribal limitations upon the length of journeys that might lawfully be made on that day. That interpretation conflicts with Matthew's view on sabbath observance (cf. Mt 12:1–14). The meaning of the addition may be that those undertaking on the sabbath a journey such as the one here ordered would be offending the sensibilities of law-observant Jews and would incur their hostility.

¶¶[24:21] For the unparalleled distress of that time, see Dn 12:1.

***[24:26–28] Claims that the Messiah is to be found in some distant or secret place must be ignored. **The coming of the Son of Man** will be as clear as **lightning** is to all and as **the corpse** of an animal is to **vultures**; cf. Lk 17:24, 37. Here there is clear identification of **the Son of Man** and the Messiah; cf. Mt 24:23.

†††[24:29] The answer to the question of Mt 24:3b, "What sign will there be of your coming?" **Immediately after . . .**

---

o. [24:6] Dn 2:28 LXX.　p. [24:7] Is 19:2.　q. [24:9] 10:17.　r. [24:13] 10:22.　s. [24:14] 28:19; Rom 10:18.　t. [24:15] Dn 9:27; 11:31; 12:11; Mk 13:14.

u. [24:17] Lk 17:31.　v. [24:21] Dn 12:1.　w. [24:23] Lk 17:23. x. [24:27–28] Lk 17:24, 37.　y. [24:29] Is 13:10, 13; Ez 32:7; Am 8:9.

the sun will be darkened,
　　and the moon will not give its light,
and the stars will fall from the sky,
　　and the powers of the heavens will
　　　　be shaken.

[30z]And then the sign of the Son of Man* will appear in heaven, and all the tribes of the earth will mourn, and they will see the Son of Man coming upon the clouds of heaven with power and great glory. [31a]And he will send out his angels[†] with a trumpet blast, and they will gather his elect from the four winds, from one end of the heavens to the other.

The Lesson of the Fig Tree.[‡] [32]"Learn a lesson from the fig tree. When its branch becomes tender and sprouts leaves, you know that summer is near. [33]In the same way, when you see all these things, know that he is near, at the gates. [34]Amen, I say to you, this generation[§] will not pass away until all these things have taken place. [35b]Heaven and earth will pass away, but my words will not pass away.

The Unknown Day and Hour.[¶] [36c]"But of that day and hour no one knows, neither the angels of heaven, nor the Son,** but the Father alone. [37††d]For as it was in the days of Noah, so it will be at the coming of the Son of Man. [38]In [those] days before the flood, they were eating and drinking, marrying and giving in marriage, up to the day that Noah entered the ark. [39]They did not know until the flood came and carried them all away. So will it be [also] at the coming of the Son of Man. [40‡‡e]Two men will be out in the field; one will be taken, and one will be left. [41]Two women will be grinding at the mill; one will be taken, and one will be left. [42§§f]Therefore, stay awake! For you do not know on which day your Lord will come. [43g]Be sure of this: if the master of the house had known the hour of night when the thief was coming, he would have stayed awake and not let his house be broken into. [44]So too, you also must be prepared, for at an hour you do not expect, the Son of Man will come.

The Faithful or the Unfaithful Servant.[¶¶] [45h]"Who, then, is the faithful and prudent servant, whom the master has put in charge of his household to distribute to them their food at the proper time?*** [46]Blessed is that servant whom his master on his arrival finds doing so. [47]Amen, I say to you, he will put him in charge of all his property. [48†††]But if that wicked servant says to himself, 'My master is long delayed,' [49]and begins to beat his fellow servants, and eat and drink with drunkards, [50]the servant's master will come on an unexpected day and at an unknown hour [51i]and will punish him severely[‡‡‡] and assign him a place with the hypocrites, where there will be wailing and grinding of teeth.

CHAPTER 25
The Parable of the Ten Virgins.[§§§] [1]"Then[¶¶¶] the kingdom of heaven will be like ten virgins

---

those days: the shortening of time between the preceding **tribulation** and the parousia has been explained as Matthew's use of a supposed device of Old Testament prophecy whereby certainty that a predicted event will occur is expressed by depicting it as imminent. While it is questionable that that is an acceptable understanding of the Old Testament predictions, it may be applicable here, for Matthew knew that the parousia had not come **immediately after** the fall of Jerusalem, and it is unlikely that he is attributing a mistaken calculation of time to Jesus. **The sun . . . be shaken**: cf. Is 13:10, 13.
  *[24:30] **The sign of the Son of Man**: perhaps this means **the sign** that is the glorious appearance **of the Son of Man**; cf. Mt 12:39–40 where "the sign of Jonah" is Jonah's being in the "belly of the whale." **Tribes of the earth will mourn**: peculiar to Matthew; cf. Zec 12:12–14. **Coming upon the clouds . . . glory**: cf. Dn 7:13, although there the "one like a son of man" comes to God to receive kingship; here **the Son of Man** comes from heaven for judgment.
  †[24:31] **Send out his angels**: cf. Mt 13:41 where they are sent out to collect the wicked for punishment. **Trumpet blast**: cf. Is 27:13; 1 Thes 4:16.
  ‡[24:32–35] Cf. Mk 13:28–31.
  §[24:34] The difficulty raised by this verse cannot be satisfactorily removed by the supposition that **this generation** means the Jewish people throughout the course of their history, much less the entire human race. Perhaps for Matthew it means the **generation** to which he and his community belonged.
  ¶[24:36–44] The statement of Mt 24:34 is now counterbalanced by one that declares that the exact time of the parousia is known only to the **Father** (Mt 24:36), and the disciples are warned to be always ready for it. This section is drawn from Mark and Q (cf. Lk 17:26–27, 34–35; 12:39–40).
  [24:36] Many textual witnesses omit **nor the Son, which follows Mk 13:32. Since its omission can be explained by reluctance to attribute this ignorance to **the Son**, the reading that includes it is probably original.
  ††[24:37–39] Cf. Lk 17:26–27. **In the days of Noah**: the Old Testament account of the flood lays no emphasis upon what is central for Matthew, i.e., the unexpected coming of the flood upon those who were unprepared for it.

  ‡‡[24:40–41] Cf. Lk 17:34–35. **Taken . . . left**: the former probably means **taken** into the kingdom; the latter, **left** for destruction. People in the same situation will be dealt with in opposite ways. In this context, the discrimination between them will be based on their readiness for the coming of the Son of Man.
  §§[24:42–44] Cf. Lk 12:39–40. The theme of vigilance and readiness is continued with the bold comparison of the Son of Man to a thief who comes to break into a house.
  ¶¶[24:45–51] The second part of the discourse (see note on Mt 24:1–25:46) begins with this parable of **the faithful** or unfaithful **servant**; cf. Lk 12:41–46. It is addressed to the leaders of Matthew's church; **the servant has** been **put in charge** of his master's **household** (Mt 24:45) even though that household is composed of those who are his **fellow servants** (Mt 24:49).
  ***[24:45] **To distribute . . . proper time**: readiness for the master's return means a vigilance that is accompanied by faithful performance of the duty assigned.
  †††[24:48] **My master . . . delayed**: the note of delay is found also in the other parables of this section; cf. Mt 25:5, 19.
  ‡‡‡[24:51] **Punish him severely**: the Greek verb, found in the New Testament only here and in the Lucan parallel (Lk 12:46), means, literally, "cut in two." **With the hypocrites**: see note on Mt 6:2. Matthew classes the unfaithful Christian leader with the unbelieving leaders of Judaism. **Wailing and grinding of teeth**: see note on Mt 8:11–12.
  §§§[25:1–13] Peculiar to Matthew.
  ¶¶¶[25:1] **Then**: at the time of the parousia. **Kingdom . . . will be like**: see note on Mt 13:24–30.

---

z. [24:30] Dn 7:13; Zec 12:12–14; Rev 1:7.　a. [24:31] Is 27:13; 1 Cor 15:52; 1 Thes 4:16.　b. [24:35] Is 40:8.　c. [24:36] Acts 1:7.　d. [24:37–39] Gn 6:5–7:23; Lk 17:26–27; 2 Pt 3:6.　e. [24:40–41] Lk 17:34–35.　f. [24:42–44] 25:13; Lk 12:39–40.　g. [24:43] 1 Thes 5:2.　h. [24:45–51] Lk 12:41–46.　i. [24:51] 13:42; 25:30.

who took their lamps and went out to meet the bridegroom. [2]Five of them were foolish and five were wise. [3]The foolish ones, when taking their lamps, brought no oil with them, [4]but the wise brought flasks of oil with their lamps. [5]Since the bridegroom was long delayed, they all became drowsy and fell asleep. [6]At midnight, there was a cry, 'Behold, the bridegroom! Come out to meet him!' [7]Then all those virgins got up and trimmed their lamps. [8]The foolish ones said to the wise, 'Give us some of your oil, for our lamps are going out.' [9]But the wise ones replied, 'No, for there may not be enough for us and you. Go instead to the merchants and buy some for yourselves.' [10]While they went off to buy it, the bridegroom came and those who were ready went into the wedding feast with him. Then the door was locked. [11]†Afterwards the other virgins came and said, 'Lord, Lord, open the door for us!' [12]But he said in reply, 'Amen, I say to you, I do not know you.' [13]kTherefore, stay awake,‡ for you know neither the day nor the hour.

The Parable of the Talents.§ [14]l"It will be as when a man who was going on a journey¶ called in his servants and entrusted his possessions to them. [15]To one he gave five talents;** to another, two; to a third, one—to each according to his ability. Then he went away. Immediately [16]the one who received five talents went and traded with them, and made another five. [17]Likewise, the one who received two made another two. [18]††But the man who received one went off and dug a hole in the ground and buried his master's money. [19]After a long time the master of those servants came back and settled accounts with them. [20]The one who had received five talents came forward bringing the additional five.‡‡ He said, 'Master, you gave me five talents. See, I have made five more.' [21]mHis master said to him, 'Well done,

my good and faithful servant. Since you were faithful in small matters, I will give you great responsibilities. Come, share your master's joy.' [22][Then] the one who had received two talents also came forward and said, 'Master, you gave me two talents. See, I have made two more.' [23]His master said to him, 'Well done, my good and faithful servant. Since you were faithful in small matters, I will give you great responsibilities. Come, share your master's joy.' [24]Then the one who had received the one talent came forward and said, 'Master, I knew you were a demanding person, harvesting where you did not plant and gathering where you did not scatter; [25]so out of fear I went off and buried your talent in the ground. Here it is back.' [26]His master said to him in reply, 'You wicked, lazy servant!§§ So you knew that I harvest where I did not plant and gather where I did not scatter? [27]Should you not then have put my money in the bank so that I could have got it back with interest on my return? [28]Now then! Take the talent from him and give it to the one with ten. [29]¶¶nFor to everyone who has, more will be given and he will grow rich; but from the one who has not, even what he has will be taken away. [30]***And throw this useless servant into the darkness outside, where there will be wailing and grinding of teeth.'

The Judgment of the Nations.††† [31]o"When the Son of Man comes in his glory, and all the angels with him, he will sit upon his glorious throne, [32]pand all the nations‡‡‡ will be assembled

---

*[25:2–4] **Foolish . . . wise:** cf. the contrasted "wise man" and "fool" of Mt 7:24, 26, where the two are distinguished by good deeds and lack of them, and such deeds may be signified by the **oil** of this parable.

†[25:11–12] **Lord, Lord:** cf. Mt 7:21. **I do not know you:** cf. Mt 7:23 where the Greek verb is different but synonymous.

‡[25:13] **Stay awake:** some scholars see this command as an addition to the original parable of Matthew's traditional material, since in Mt 25:5 all the virgins, wise and foolish, fall asleep. But the wise virgins are adequately equipped for their task, and stay awake may mean no more than to be prepared; cf. Mt 24:42, 44.

§[25:14–30] Cf. Lk 19:12–27.

¶[25:14] **It will be as when . . . journey:** literally, "For just as a man who was going on a journey." Although the comparison is not completed, the sense is clear; the kingdom of heaven is like the situation here described. Faithful use of one's gifts will lead to participation in the fullness of the kingdom, lazy inactivity to exclusion from it.

[25:15] **Talents: see note on Mt 18:24.

††[25:18] **Buried his master's money:** see note on Mt 13:44.

‡‡[25:20–23] Although the first two servants have received and doubled large sums, their faithful trading is regarded by the master as fidelity **in small matters** only, compared with the **great responsibilities** now to be given to them. The latter are unspecified. **Share your master's joy:** probably the joy of the banquet of the kingdom; cf. Mt 8:11.

§§[25:26–28] **Wicked, lazy servant:** this man's inactivity is not negligible but seriously culpable. As punishment, he loses the gift he had received, that is now given to the first servant, whose possessions are already great.

¶¶[25:29] See note on Mt 13:12 where there is a similar application of this maxim.

***[25:30] See note on Mt 8:11–12.

†††[25:31–46] The conclusion of the discourse, which is peculiar to Matthew, portrays the final judgment that will accompany the parousia. Although often called a "parable," it is not really such, for the only parabolic elements are the depiction of the **Son of Man** as a **shepherd** and of the **righteous** and the wicked as **sheep** and **goats,** respectively (Mt 25:32–33). The criterion of judgment will be the deeds of mercy that have been done for the **least** of Jesus' **brothers** (Mt 25:40). A difficult and important question is the identification of these **least brothers.** Are they all people who have suffered hunger, thirst, etc. (Mt 25:35, 36) or a particular group of such sufferers? Scholars are divided in their response and arguments can be made for either side. But leaving aside the problem of what the traditional material that Matthew edited may have meant, it seems that a stronger case can be made for the view that in the evangelist's sense the sufferers are Christians, probably Christian missionaries whose sufferings were brought upon them by their preaching of the gospel. The criterion of judgment for **all the nations** is their treatment of those who have borne to the world the message of Jesus, and this means ultimately their acceptance or rejection of Jesus himself; cf. Mt 10:40, "Whoever receives you, receives me." See note on Mt 16:27.

‡‡‡[25:32] **All the nations:** before the end the gospel will have been preached throughout the world (Mt 24:14); thus the Gentiles will be judged on their response to it. But the phrase **all the nations** includes the Jews also, for at the judgment "the Son of Man . . . will repay everyone according to his conduct" (Mt 16:27).

---

j. [25:11–12] 7:21, 23; Lk 13:25–27. k. [25:13] 24:42; Mk 13:33. l. [25:14–30] Lk 19:12–27. m. [25:21] Lk 16:10.

n. [25:29] 13:12; Mk 4:25; Lk 8:18; 19:26. o. [25:31] 16:27; Dt 33:2 LXX. p. [25:32] Ez 34:17.

before him. And he will separate them one from another, as a shepherd separates the sheep from the goats. ³³He will place the sheep on his right and the goats on his left. ³⁴Then the king will say to those on his right, 'Come, you who are blessed by my Father. Inherit the kingdom prepared for you from the foundation of the world. ³⁵ᵠFor I was hungry and you gave me food, I was thirsty and you gave me drink, a stranger and you welcomed me, ³⁶naked and you clothed me, ill and you cared for me, in prison and you visited me.' ³⁷Then the righteous* will answer him and say, 'Lord, when did we see you hungry and feed you, or thirsty and give you drink? ³⁸When did we see you a stranger and welcome you, or naked and clothe you? ³⁹When did we see you ill or in prison, and visit you?' ⁴⁰ʳAnd the king will say to them in reply, 'Amen, I say to you, whatever you did for one of these least brothers of mine, you did for me.' ⁴¹†ᵗThen he will say to those on his left, 'Depart from me, you accursed, into the eternal fire prepared for the devil and his angels. ⁴²ᵗFor I was hungry and you gave me no food, I was thirsty and you gave me no drink, ⁴³a stranger and you gave me no welcome, naked and you gave me no clothing, ill and in prison, and you did not care for me.' ⁴⁴†Then they will answer and say, 'Lord, when did we see you hungry or thirsty or a stranger or naked or ill or in prison, and not minister to your needs?' ⁴⁵He will answer them, 'Amen, I say to you, what you did not do for one of these least ones, you did not do for me.' ⁴⁶ᵘAnd these will go off to eternal punishment, but the righteous to eternal life."

VII. THE PASSION AND RESURRECTION

CHAPTER 26

The Conspiracy Against Jesus. ¹§When Jesus finished all these words,⁵ he said to his disciples,

²ᵛ"You know that in two days' time it will be Passover, and the Son of Man will be handed over to be crucified." ³"Then the chief priests and the elders of the people assembled in the palace of the high priest, who was called Caiaphas, ⁴ʷand they consulted together to arrest Jesus by treachery and put him to death. ⁵But they said, "Not during the festival,†† that there may not be a riot among the people."

The Anointing at Bethany.‡‡ ⁶ˣNow when Jesus was in Bethany in the house of Simon the leper, ⁷a woman came up to him with an alabaster jar of costly perfumed oil, and poured it on his head while he was reclining at table. ⁸When the disciples saw this, they were indignant and said, "Why this waste? ⁹It could have been sold for much, and the money given to the poor." ¹⁰Since Jesus knew this, he said to them, "Why do you make trouble for the woman? She has done a good thing for me. ¹¹ʸThe poor you will always have with you; but you will not always have me. ¹²§§In pouring this perfumed oil upon my body, she did it to prepare me for burial. ¹³Amen, I say to you, wherever this gospel is proclaimed in the whole world, what she has done will be spoken of, in memory of her."

The Betrayal by Judas. ¹⁴ᶻThen one of the Twelve, who was called Judas Iscariot,⁵⁵ went to the chief priests ¹⁵***ᵃand said, "What are you willing to give me if I hand him over to you?" They paid him thirty pieces of silver, ¹⁶and from that time on he looked for an opportunity to hand him over.

Preparations for the Passover. ¹⁷ᵇOn the first day of the Feast of Unleavened Bread,††† the disciples approached Jesus and said, "Where do you

---

*[25:37–40] **The righteous** will be astonished that in caring for the needs of the sufferers they were ministering to the **Lord** himself. **One of these least brothers of mine:** cf. Mt 10:42.

†[25:41] **Fire prepared . . . his angels:** cf. 1 Enoch 10:13 where it is said of the evil angels and Semyaza, their leader, "In those days they will lead them into the bottom of the fire—and in torment—in the prison (where) they will be locked up forever."

‡[25:44–45] The **accursed** (Mt 25:41) will be likewise astonished that their neglect of the sufferers was neglect of the **Lord** and will receive from him a similar answer.

§[26:1–28:20] The five books with alternating narrative and discourse (Mt 3:1–25:46) that give this gospel its distinctive structure lead up to the climactic events that are the center of Christian belief and the origin of the Christian church, the passion and resurrection of Jesus. In his passion narrative (Mt 26 and 27) Matthew follows his Marcan source closely but with omissions (e.g., Mk 14:51–52) and additions (e.g., Mt 27:3–10, 19). Some of the additions indicate that he utilized traditions that he had received from elsewhere; others are due to his own theological insight (e.g., Mt 26:28, ". . . for the forgiveness of sins"; Mt 27:52). In his editing Matthew also altered Mark in some minor details. But there is no need to suppose that he knew any passion narrative other than Mark's.

⁵[26:1–2] **When Jesus finished all these words:** see note on Mt 7:28–29. **"You know . . . crucified":** Matthew turns

Mark's statement of the time (Mk 14:1) into Jesus' final prediction of his passion. **Passover:** see note on Mk 14:1.

[26:3] **Caiaphas was high priest from A.D. 18 to 36.

††[26:5] **Not during the festival:** the plan to delay Jesus' arrest and execution until after the festival was not carried out, for according to the synoptics he was arrested on the night of Nisan 14 and put to death the following day. No reason is given why the plan was changed.

‡‡[26:6–13] See notes on Mk 14:3–9 and Jn 12:1–8.

§§[26:12] **To prepare me for burial:** cf. Mk 14:8. In accordance with the interpretation of this act as Jesus' burial anointing, Matthew, more consistent than Mark, changes the purpose of the visit of the women to Jesus' tomb; they do not go to anoint him (Mk 16:1) but "to see the tomb" (Mt 28:1).

⁵⁵[26:14] **Iscariot:** see note on Lk 6:16.

***[26:15] The motive of avarice is introduced by Judas's question about the price for betrayal, which is absent in the Marcan source (Mk 14:10–11). **Hand him over:** the same Greek verb is used to express the saving purpose of God by which Jesus is handed over to death (cf. Mt 17:22; 20:18; 26:2) and the human malice that hands him over. **Thirty pieces of silver:** the price of the betrayal is found only in Matthew. It is derived from Zec 11:12 where it is the wages paid to the rejected shepherd, a cheap price (Zec 11:13). That amount is also the compensation paid to one whose slave has been gored by an ox (Ex 21:32).

†††[26:17] **The first day of the Feast of Unleavened Bread:** see note on Mk 14:1. Matthew omits Mark's "when they sacrificed the Passover lamb."

---

q. [25:35–36] Is 58:7; Ez 18:7.   r. [25:40] 10:40, 42.   s. [25:41] 7:23; Lk 13:27.   t. [25:42–43] Jb 22:7; Jas 2:15–16.   u. [25:46] Dn 12:2.

v. [26:2–5] Mk 14:1–2; Lk 22:1–2.   w. [26:4] Jn 11:47–53.   x. [26:6–13] Mk 14:3–9; Jn 12:1–8.   y. [26:11] Dt 15:11.   z. [26:14–16] Mk 14:10–11; Lk 22:3–6.   a. [26:15] Zec 11:12.   b. [26:17–25] Mk 14:12–21; Lk 22:7–23.

want us to prepare for you to eat the Passover?"[c] [18]He said, "Go into the city to a certain man and tell him, 'The teacher says, "My appointed time draws near; in your house I shall celebrate the Passover with my disciples."'" [19]The disciples then did as Jesus had ordered, and prepared the Passover.

The Betrayer. [20]When it was evening, he reclined at table with the Twelve. [21]And while they were eating, he said, "Amen, I say to you, one of you will betray me."[†] [22]Deeply distressed at this, they began to say to him one after another, "Surely it is not I, Lord?" [23]He said in reply, "He who has dipped his hand into the dish with me is the one who will betray me. [24‡d]The Son of Man indeed goes, as it is written of him, but woe to that man by whom the Son of Man is betrayed. It would be better for that man if he had never been born." [25§]Then Judas, his betrayer, said in reply, "Surely it is not I, Rabbi?" He answered, "You have said so."

The Lord's Supper. [26¶e]While they were eating, Jesus took bread, said the blessing, broke it, and giving it to his disciples said, "Take and eat; this is my body."**[f] [27]Then he took a cup, gave thanks,[††]

---

*[26:18] By omitting much of Mk 14:13–15, adding **My appointed time draws near**, and turning the question into a statement, **in your house I shall celebrate the Passover**, Matthew has given this passage a solemnity and majesty greater than that of his source.

†[26:21] Given Matthew's interest in the fulfillment of the Old Testament, it is curious that he omits the Marcan designation of Jesus' betrayer as "one who is eating with me" (Mk 14:18), since that is probably an allusion to Ps 41:10. However, the shocking fact that the betrayer is one who shares table fellowship with Jesus is emphasized in Mt 26:23.

‡[26:24] **It would be better . . . born**: the enormity of the deed is such that it would be better not to exist than to do it.

§[26:25] Peculiar to Matthew. **You have said so**: cf. Mt 26:64; 27:11. This is a half-affirmative. Emphasis is laid on the pronoun and the answer implies that the statement would not have been made if the question had not been asked.

¶[26:26–29] See note on Mk 14:22–24. The Marcan-Matthean is one of the two major New Testament traditions of the words of Jesus when instituting the Eucharist. The other (and earlier) is the Pauline-Lucan (1 Cor 11:23–25; Lk 22:19–20). Each shows the influence of Christian liturgical usage, but the Marcan-Matthean is more developed in that regard than the Pauline-Lucan. The words over the bread and cup succeed each other without the intervening meal mentioned in 1 Cor 11:25; Lk 22:20; and there is parallelism between the consecratory words (**this is my body . . . this is my blood**). Matthew follows Mark closely but with some changes.

[26:26] See note on Mt 14:19. **Said the blessing: a prayer blessing God. **Take and eat**: literally, Take, eat. **Eat** is an addition to Mark's "take it" (literally, "take"; Mk 14:22). **This is my body**: the bread is identified with Jesus himself.

††[26:27–28] **Gave thanks**: see note on Mt 15:36. **Gave it to them . . . all of you**: cf. Mk 14:23–24. In the Marcan sequence the disciples drink and then Jesus says the interpretative words. Matthew has changed this into a command to **drink** followed by those words. **My blood**: see Lv 17:11 for the concept that the **blood** is "the seat of life" and that when placed on the altar it "makes atonement." **Which will be shed**: the present participle, "being shed" or "going to be shed," is future in relation to the Last Supper. **On behalf of**: Greek *peri*; see note on Mk 14:24. **Many**: see note on Mt 20:28. **For the forgiveness of sins**: a Matthean addition. The same phrase occurs in Mk 1:4 in connection with John's baptism but Matthew avoids it there (Mt 3:11). He places it here probably because he wishes

---

and gave it to them, saying, "Drink from it, all of you, [28g]for this is my blood of the covenant, which will be shed on behalf of many for the forgiveness of sins. [29‡‡]I tell you, from now on I shall not drink this fruit of the vine until the day when I drink it with you new in the kingdom of my Father." [30§§]Then, after singing a hymn, they went out to the Mount of Olives.

Peter's Denial Foretold. [31h]Then Jesus said to them, "This night all of you will have your faith in me shaken,¶¶ for it is written:[i]

'I will strike the shepherd,
        and the sheep of the flock will be
                dispersed';

[32]but after I have been raised up, I shall go before you to Galilee." [33]Peter said to him in reply, "Though all may have their faith in you shaken, mine will never be." [34***j]Jesus said to him, "Amen, I say to you, this very night before the cock crows, you will deny me three times."[k] [35]Peter said to him, "Even though I should have to die with you, I will not deny you." And all the disciples spoke likewise.

The Agony in the Garden. [36††††]Then Jesus came with them to a place called Gethsemane,‡‡‡ and he said to his disciples, "Sit here while I go over there and pray."[m] [37n]He took along Peter and the

---

to emphasize that it is the sacrificial death of Jesus that brings **forgiveness of sins**.

‡‡[26:29] Although his death will interrupt the table fellowship he has had with the disciples, Jesus confidently predicts his vindication by God and a new table fellowship with them at the banquet of the kingdom.

§§[26:30] See note on Mk 14:26.

¶¶[26:31] **Will have . . . shaken**: literally, "will be scandalized in me"; see note on Mt 24:9–12. **I will strike . . . dispersed**: cf. Zec 13:7.

***[26:34] **Before the cock crows**: see note on Mt 14:25. The third watch of the night was called "cockcrow." **Deny me**: see note on Mt 16:24.

†††[26:36–56] Cf. Mk 14:32–52. The account of Jesus in Gethsemane is divided between that of his agony (Mt 26:36–46) and that of his betrayal and arrest (Mt 26:47–56). Jesus' **sorrow and distress** (Mt 26:37) in face of death is unrelieved by the presence of his three disciples who, though urged to **watch with** him (Mt 26:38, 41), fall asleep (Mt 26:40, 43). He prays that **if . . . possible** his death may be avoided (Mt 26:39) but that his Father's will be done (Mt 26:39, 42, 44). Knowing then that his death must take place, he announces to his companions that **the hour** for his being **handed over** has come (Mt 26:45). Judas arrives with an armed band provided by the Sanhedrin and greets Jesus with a kiss, the prearranged sign for his identification (Mt 26:47–49). After his arrest, he rebukes a disciple who has attacked the **high priest's servant** with a **sword** (Mt 26:51–54), and chides those who have come out to seize him with **swords and clubs** as if he were a **robber** (Mt 26:55–56). In both rebukes Jesus declares that the treatment he is how receiving is the fulfillment of the scriptures (Mt 26:55, 56). The subsequent flight of **all the disciples** is itself the fulfillment of his own prediction (cf. 31). In this episode, Matthew follows Mark with a few alterations.

‡‡‡[26:36] **Gethsemane**: the Hebrew name means "oil press" and designates an olive orchard on the western slope of the Mount of Olives; see note on Mt 21:1. The name appears only in Matthew and Mark. The place is called a "garden" in Jn 18:1.

---

c. [26:17] Ex 12:14–20.   d. [26:24] Is 53:8–10.   e. [26:26–30] Mk 14:22–26; Lk 22:14–23; 1 Cor 11:23–25.   f. [26:26–27] 1 Cor 10:16.

g. [26:28] Ex 24:8; Is 53:12.   h. [26:31–35] Mk 14:7–31.   i. [26:31] Zec 13:7; Jn 16:32.   j. [26:34–35] Lk 22:33–34; Jn 13:37–38.   k. [26:34] 26:69–75.   l. [26:36–46] Mk 14:32–42; Lk 22:39–46.   m. [26:36] Jn 18:1.   n. [26:37–39] Heb 5:7.

two sons of Zebedee,* and began to feel sorrow and distress. ³⁸ᵒThen he said to them, "My soul is sorrowful even to death.† Remain here and keep watch with me." ³⁹ᵖHe advanced a little and fell prostrate in prayer, saying, "My Father,‡ if it is possible, let this cup pass from me; yet, not as I will, but as you will." ⁴⁰When he returned to his disciples he found them asleep. He said to Peter, "So you could not keep watch with me for one hour? ⁴¹Watch and pray that you may not undergo the test.§ The spirit is willing, but the flesh is weak." ⁴²ᵠWithdrawing a second time, he prayed again, "My Father, if it is not possible that this cup pass without my drinking it, your will be done!" ⁴³Then he returned once more and found them asleep, for they could not keep their eyes open. ⁴⁴He left them and withdrew again and prayed a third time, saying the same thing again. ⁴⁵ʳThen he returned to his disciples and said to them, "Are you still sleeping and taking your rest? Behold, the hour is at hand when the Son of Man is to be handed over to sinners. ⁴⁶Get up, let us go. Look, my betrayer is at hand."

The Betrayal and Arrest of Jesus. ⁴⁷ˢWhile he was still speaking, Judas, one of the Twelve, arrived, accompanied by a large crowd, with swords and clubs, who had come from the chief priests and the elders of the people. ⁴⁸His betrayer had arranged a sign with them, saying, "The man I shall kiss is the one; arrest him." ⁴⁹Immediately he went over to Jesus and said, "Hail, Rabbi!"** and he kissed him. ⁵⁰Jesus answered him, "Friend, do what you have come for." Then stepping forward they laid hands on Jesus and arrested him. ⁵¹And behold, one of those who accompanied Jesus put his hand to his sword, drew it, and struck the high priest's servant, cutting off his ear. ⁵²Then Jesus said to him, "Put your sword back into its sheath, for

all who take the sword will perish by the sword. ⁵³Do you think that I cannot call upon my Father and he will not provide me at this moment with more than twelve legions of angels? ⁵⁴But then how would the scriptures be fulfilled which say that it must come to pass in this way?" ⁵⁵††At that hour Jesus said to the crowds, "Have you come out as against a robber, with swords and clubs to seize me? Day after day I sat teaching in the temple area, yet you did not arrest me. ⁵⁶ᵗBut all this has come to pass that the writings of the prophets may be fulfilled." Then all the disciples left him and fled.

Jesus Before the Sanhedrin. ‡‡ ⁵⁷ᵘThose who had arrested Jesus led him away to Caiaphas§§ the high priest, where the scribes and the elders were assembled. ⁵⁸Peter was following him at a distance as far as the high priest's courtyard, and going inside he sat down with the servants to see the outcome. ⁵⁹The chief priests and the entire Sanhedrin¶¶ kept trying to obtain false testimony against Jesus in order to put him to death, ⁶⁰ᵛbut they found none, though many false witnesses came forward. Finally two*** came forward ⁶¹who stated, "This man said, 'I can destroy the temple

---

††[26:55] **Day after day . . . arrest me:** cf. Mk 14:49. This suggests that Jesus had taught for a relatively long period in Jerusalem, whereas Mt 21:1–11 puts his coming to the city for the first time only a few days before.

‡‡[26:57–68] Following Mk 14:53–65 Matthew presents the nighttime appearance of Jesus before the **Sanhedrin** as a real trial. After **many false witnesses** bring charges against him that do not suffice for the death sentence (Mt 26:60), **two came forward** who charge him with claiming to be able to **destroy the temple . . . and within three days** to **rebuild it** (Mt 26:60–61). Jesus makes no answer even when challenged to do so by **the high priest**, who then orders him to declare **under oath . . . whether** he is the **Messiah, the Son of God** (Mt 26:62–63). Matthew changes Mark's clear affirmative response (Mk 14:62) to the same one as that given to Judas (Mt 26:25), but follows Mark almost verbatim in Jesus' predicting that his judges will see him (**the Son of Man**) seated at the right hand of God **and coming on the clouds of heaven** (Mt 26:64). **The high priest** then charges him with blasphemy (Mt 26:65), a charge with which the other members of **the Sanhedrin** agree by declaring that **he deserves to die** (Mt 26:66). They then attack him (Mt 26:67) and mockingly demand that he **prophesy** (Mt 26:68). This account contains elements that are contrary to the judicial procedures prescribed in the Mishnah, the Jewish code of law that dates in written form from ca. A.D. 200, e.g., trial on a feast day, a night session of the court, pronouncement of a verdict of condemnation at the same session at which testimony was received. Consequently, some scholars regard the account entirely as a creation of the early Christians without historical value. However, it is disputable whether the norms found in the Mishnah were in force at the time of Jesus. More to the point is the question whether the Matthean-Marcan night trial derives from a combination of two separate incidents, a nighttime preliminary investigation (cf. Jn 18:13, 19–24) and a formal trial on the following morning (cf. Lk 22:66–71).

§§[26:57] **Caiaphas:** see note on Mt 26:3.

¶¶[26:59] **Sanhedrin:** see note on Lk 22:66.

***[26:60–61] **Two:** cf. Dt 19:15. **I can destroy . . . rebuild it:** there are significant differences from the Marcan parallel (Mk 14:58). Matthew omits "made with hands" and "not made with hands" and changes Mark's "will destroy" and "will build another" to **can destroy** and (can) **rebuild.** The charge is probably based on Jesus' prediction of the temple's destruction; see notes on Mt 23:37–39; 24:2; and Jn 2:19. A similar

---

*[26:37] **Peter and the two sons of Zebedee:** cf. Mt 17:1.

†[26:38] Cf. Ps 42:6, 12. In the Septuagint (Ps 41:5, 12) the same Greek word for **sorrowful** is used as here. **To death:** i.e., "enough to die"; cf. Jon 4:9.

‡[26:39] **My Father:** see note on Mk 14:36. Matthew omits the Aramaic *'abba'* and adds the qualifier **my. This cup:** see note on Mk 10:38–40.

§[26:41] **Undergo the test:** see note on Mt 6:13. In that verse "the final test" translates the same Greek word as is here translated **the test,** and these are the only instances of the use of that word in Matthew. It is possible that the passion of Jesus is seen here as an anticipation of the great tribulation that will precede the parousia (see notes on Mt 24:8; 24:21) to which Mt 6:13 refers, and that just as Jesus prays to be delivered from death (Mt 26:39), so he exhorts the disciples to pray that they will not have to **undergo** the great **test** that his passion would be for them. Some scholars, however, understand **not undergo** (literally, "not enter") **the test** as meaning not that the disciples may be spared **the test** but that they may not yield to the temptation of falling away from Jesus because of his passion even though they will have to endure it.

¶[26:42] **Your will be done:** cf. Mt 6:10.

[26:49] **Rabbi: see note on Mt 23:6–7. Jesus is so addressed twice in Matthew (Mt 26:25), both times by Judas. For the significance of the closely related address "teacher" in Matthew, see note on Mt 8:19.

---

o. [26:38] Ps 42:6, 12; Jon 4:9.   p. [26:39] Jn 4:34; 6:38; Phil 2:8.
q. [26:42] 6:10; Heb 10:9.   r. [26:45] Jn 12:23; 13:1; 17:1.   s. [26:47–56] Mk 14:43–50; Lk 22:47–53; Jn 18:3–11.

t. [26:56] 26:31.   u. [26:57–68] Mk 14:53–65; Lk 22:54–55, 63–71; Jn 18:12–14, 19–24.   v. [26:60–61] Dt 19:15; Jn 2:19; Acts 6:14.

of God and within three days rebuild it.'" [62]The high priest rose and addressed him, "Have you no answer? What are these men testifying against you?" [63"]But Jesus was silent.* Then the high priest said to him, "I order you to tell us under oath before the living God whether you are the Messiah, the Son of God." [64x]Jesus said to him in reply, "You have said so.† But I tell you:

> From now on you will see 'the Son of Man seated at the right hand of the Power' and 'coming on the clouds of heaven.'"

[65]Then the high priest tore his robes and said, "He has blasphemed!‡ What further need have we of witnesses? You have now heard the blasphemy; [66]what is your opinion?" They said in reply, "He deserves to die!" [67§y]Then they spat in his face and struck him, while some slapped him, [68]saying, "Prophesy for us, Messiah: who is it that struck you?"

Peter's Denial of Jesus. [69z]Now Peter was sitting outside in the courtyard. One of the maids came over to him and said, "You too were with Jesus the Galilean." [70¶]But he denied it in front of everyone, saying, "I do not know what you are talking about!" [71]As he went out to the gate, another girl saw him and said to those who were there, "This man was with Jesus the Nazorean." [72]Again he denied it with an oath, "I do not know the man!" [73**]A little later the bystanders came over and said to Peter, "Surely you too are one of them; even your speech gives you away." [74]At that he began to curse and to swear, "I do not know the man." And immediately a cock crowed. [75a]Then Peter remembered the word

that Jesus had spoken: "Before the cock crows you will deny me three times." He went out and began to weep bitterly.

CHAPTER 27

Jesus Before Pilate. [1††]When it was morning,[b] all the chief priests and the elders of the people took counsel‡‡ against Jesus to put him to death. [2]They bound him, led him away, and handed him over to Pilate, the governor.

The Death of Judas. [3c]Then Judas, his betrayer, seeing that Jesus had been condemned, deeply regretted what he had done. He returned the thirty pieces of silver§§ to the chief priests and elders,[d] [4]saying, "I have sinned in betraying innocent blood." They said, "What is that to us? Look to it yourself." [5¶¶]Flinging the money into the temple, he departed and went off and hanged himself. [6]The chief priests gathered up the money, but said, "It is not lawful to deposit this in the temple treasury, for it is the price of blood." [7]After consultation, they used it to buy the potter's field as a burial place for foreigners. [8]That is why that field even today is called the Field of Blood. [9]Then was fulfilled what had been said through Jeremiah the prophet,*** "And they took the thirty pieces of silver, the value

---

prediction by Jeremiah was considered as deserving death; cf. Jer 7:1–15; 26:1–8.
*[26:63] **Silent:** possibly an allusion to Is 53:7. **I order you . . . living God:** peculiar to Matthew; cf. Mk 14:61.
†[26:64] **You have said so:** see note on Mt 26:25. **From now on . . . heaven:** the Son of Man who is to be crucified (cf. Mt 20:19) will be seen in glorious majesty (cf. Ps 110:1) and **coming on the clouds of heaven** (cf. Dn 7:13). **The Power:** see note on Mk 14:61–62.
‡[26:65] **Blasphemed:** the punishment for blasphemy was death by stoning (see Lv 24:10–16). According to the Mishnah, to be guilty of blasphemy one had to pronounce "the Name itself," i.e., Yahweh; cf. *Sanhedrin* 7:4, 5. Those who judge the gospel accounts of Jesus' trial by the later Mishnah standards point out that Jesus uses the surrogate "the Power," and hence no Jewish court would have regarded him as guilty of blasphemy; others hold that the Mishnah's narrow understanding of blasphemy was a later development.
§[26:67–68] The physical abuse, apparently done to Jesus by the members of the Sanhedrin themselves, recalls the sufferings of the Isaian Servant of the Lord; cf. Is 50:6. The mocking challenge to prophesy is probably motivated by Jesus' prediction of his future glory (Mt 26:64).
¶[26:70] **Denied it in front of everyone:** see Mt 10:33. Peter's repentance (Mt 26:75) saves him from the fearful destiny of which Jesus speaks there.
[26:73] **Your speech . . . away: Matthew explicates Mark's "you too are a Galilean" (Mk 14:70).

††[27:1–31] Cf. Mk 15:1–20. Matthew's account of the Roman trial before **Pilate** is introduced by a consultation of the Sanhedrin after which Jesus is **handed over to . . . the governor** (Mt 27:1–2). Matthew follows his Marcan source closely but adds some material that is peculiar to him, the death of **Judas** (Mt 27:3–10), possibly the name **Jesus** as the name of **Barabbas** also (Mt 27:16–17), the intervention of Pilate's **wife** (Mt 27:19), Pilate's washing **his hands** in token of his disclaiming responsibility for Jesus' death (Mt 27:24), and the assuming of that responsibility by **the whole people** (Mt 27:25).
‡‡[27:1] There is scholarly disagreement about the meaning of the Sanhedrin's taking **counsel** (*symboulion elabon*; cf. Mt 12:14; 22:15; 27:7; 28:12); see note on Mk 15:1. Some understand it as a discussion about the strategy for putting their death sentence against **Jesus** into effect since they lacked the right to do so themselves. Others see it as the occasion for their passing that sentence, holding that Matthew, unlike Mark (Mk 14:64), does not consider that it had been passed in the night session (Mt 26:66). Even in the latter interpretation, their handing **him over to Pilate** is best explained on the hypothesis that they did not have competence to put their sentence into effect, as is stated in Jn 18:31.
§§[27:3] **The thirty pieces of silver:** see Mt 26:15.
¶¶[27:5–8] For another tradition about the death of Judas, cf. Acts 1:18–19. The two traditions agree only in the purchase of a field with **the money** paid to Judas for his betrayal of Jesus and the name given to the field, **the Field of Blood.** In Acts Judas himself buys the field and its name comes from his own blood shed in his fatal accident on it. **The potter's field:** this designation of the field is based on the fulfillment citation in Mt 27:10.
***[27:9–10] Cf. Mt 26:15. Matthew's attributing this text to Jeremiah is puzzling, for there is no such text in that book, and **the thirty pieces of silver** thrown by Judas "into the temple" (Mt 27:5) recall rather Zec 11:12–13. It is usually said that the attribution of the text to Jeremiah is due to Matthew's combining the Zechariah text with texts from Jeremiah that speak of a **potter** (Jer 18:2–3), the buying of a **field** (Jer 32:6–9), or the breaking of a potter's flask at Topheth in the valley of Ben-Hinnom with the prediction that it will become a burial place (Jer 19:1–13).

---

w. [26:63] Is 53:7.   x. [26:64] Ps 110:1; Dn 7:13.   y. [26:67] Wis 2:19; Is 50:6.   z. [26:69–75] Mk 14:66–72; Lk 22:56–62; Jn 18:17–18, 25–27.   a. [26:75] Mt 26:34.

b. [27:1–2] Mk 15:1; Lk 23:1; Jn 18:28.   c. [27:3–10] Acts 1:18–19.   d. [27:3] 26:15.

of a man with a price on his head, a price set by some of the Israelites, [10e]and they paid it out for the potter's field just as the Lord had commanded me."

Jesus Questioned by Pilate. [11f]Now Jesus stood before the governor, and he questioned him, "Are you the king of the Jews?"* Jesus said, "You say so.". [12g]And when he was accused by the chief priests and elders,† he made no answer. [13]Then Pilate said to him, "Do you not hear how many things they are testifying against you?" [14]But he did not answer him one word, so that the governor was greatly amazed.

The Sentence of Death. [15‡h]Now on the occasion of the feast the governor was accustomed to release to the crowd one prisoner whom they wished. [16§]And at that time they had a notorious prisoner called [Jesus] Barabbas. [17]So when they had assembled, Pilate said to them, "Which one do you want me to release to you, [Jesus] Barabbas, or Jesus called Messiah?" [18¶]For he knew that it was out of envy that they had handed him over. [19**]While he was still seated on the bench, his wife sent him a message, "Have nothing to do with that righteous man. I suffered much in a dream today because of him." [20i]The chief priests and the elders persuaded the crowds to ask for Barabbas but to destroy Jesus. [21]The governor said to them in reply, "Which of the two do you want me to release to you?" They answered, "Barabbas!" [22††]Pilate said to them, "Then what shall I do with Jesus called Messiah?" They all said, "Let him be crucified!" [23]But he said, "Why? What evil has he done?" They only shouted the louder, "Let him be crucified!" [24‡‡j]When Pilate saw that he was not succeeding at all, but that a riot was breaking out instead, he took water and washed his hands in the sight of the crowd, saying, "I am innocent of this man's blood. Look to it yourselves." [25]And the whole people said in reply, "His blood be upon us and upon our children." [26§§]Then he released Barabbas to them, but after he had Jesus scourged,§§ he handed him over to be crucified.

Mockery by the Soldiers. [27k]Then the soldiers of the governor took Jesus inside the praetorium¶¶ and gathered the whole cohort around him. [28]They stripped off his clothes and threw a scarlet military cloak*** about him. [29]Weaving a crown out of thorns,††† they placed it on his head, and a reed in his right hand. And kneeling before him, they mocked him, saying, "Hail, King of the Jews!" [30m]They spat upon him‡‡‡ and took the reed and kept striking him on the head. [31]And when they had mocked him, they stripped him of the cloak, dressed him in his own clothes, and led him off to crucify him.

---

*[27:11] **King of the Jews**: this title is used of Jesus only by pagans. The Matthean instances are, besides this verse, Mt 2:2; 27:29, 37. Matthew equates it with "Messiah"; cf. Mt 2:2, 4 and Mt 27:17, 22 where he has changed "the king of the Jews" of his Marcan source (Mk 15:9, 12) to "(Jesus) called Messiah." The normal political connotation of both titles would be of concern to the Roman **governor. You say so**: see note on Mt 26:25. An unqualified affirmative response is not made because Jesus' kingship is not what Pilate would understand it to be.

†[27:12–14] Cf. Mt 26:62–63. As in the trial before the Sanhedrin, Jesus' silence may be meant to recall Is 53:7. **Greatly amazed**: possibly an allusion to Is 52:14–15.

‡[27:15–26] The choice that Pilate offers **the crowd** between **Barabbas** and **Jesus** is said to be in accordance with a custom of releasing at the Passover feast **one prisoner** chosen by **the crowd** (Mt 27:15). This custom is mentioned also in Mk 15:6 and Jn 18:39 but not in Luke; see note on Lk 23:17. Outside of the gospels there is no direct attestation of it, and scholars are divided in their judgment of the historical reliability of the claim that there was such a practice.

§[27:16–17] **[Jesus] Barabbas**: it is possible that the double name is the original reading; **Jesus** was a common Jewish name; see note on Mt 1:21. This reading is found in only a few textual witnesses, although its absence in the majority can be explained as an omission of **Jesus** made for reverential reasons. That name is bracketed because of its uncertain textual attestation. The Aramaic name **Barabbas** means "son of the father"; the irony of the choice offered between him and Jesus, the true son of the Father, would be evident to those addressees of Matthew who knew that.

¶[27:18] Cf. Mk 14:10. This is an example of the tendency, found in varying degree in all the gospels, to present Pilate in a relatively favorable light and emphasize the hostility of the Jewish authorities and eventually of the people.

[27:19] Jesus' innocence is declared by a Gentile woman. **In a dream: in Matthew's infancy narrative, dreams are the means of divine communication; cf. Mt 1:20; 2:12, 13, 19, 22.

††[27:22] **Let him be crucified**: incited by the chief priests and elders (Mt 27:20), the crowds demand that Jesus be executed by crucifixion, a peculiarly horrible form of Roman capital punishment. The Marcan parallel, "Crucify him" (Mk 15:3), addressed to Pilate, is changed by Matthew to the passive, probably to emphasize the responsibility of the crowds.

‡‡[27:24–25] Peculiar to Matthew. **Took water . . . blood**: cf. Dt 21:1–8, the handwashing prescribed in the case of a murder when the killer is unknown. The elders of the city nearest to where the corpse is found must wash their hands, declaring, "Our hands did not shed this blood." **Look to it yourselves**: cf. Mt 27:4. **The whole people**: Matthew sees in those who speak these words **the entire people** (Greek *laos*) of Israel. **His blood . . . and upon our children**: cf. Jer 26:15. The responsibility for Jesus' death is accepted by the nation that was God's special possession (Ex 19:5), his own **people** (Hos 2:25), and they thereby lose that high privilege; see Mt 21:43 and the note on that verse. The controversy between Matthew's church and Pharisaic Judaism about which was the true people of God is reflected here. As the Second Vatican Council has pointed out, guilt for Jesus' death is not attributable to all the Jews of his time or to any Jews of later times.

§§[27:26] **He had Jesus scourged**: the usual preliminary to crucifixion.

¶¶[27:27] **The praetorium**: the residence of the Roman governor. His usual place of residence was at Caesarea Maritima on the Mediterranean coast, but he went to Jerusalem during the great feasts, when the influx of pilgrims posed the danger of a nationalistic riot. It is disputed whether **the praetorium** in Jerusalem was the old palace of Herod in the west of the city or the fortress of Antonia northwest of the temple area. **The whole cohort**: normally six hundred soldiers.

***[27:28] **Scarlet military cloak**: so Matthew as against the royal purple of Mk 15:17 and Jn 19:2.

†††[27:29] **Crown out of thorns**: probably of long **thorns** that stood upright so that it resembled the "radiant" **crown**, a diadem with spikes worn by Hellenistic kings. The soldiers' purpose was mockery, not torture. **A reed**: peculiar to Matthew; a mock scepter.

‡‡‡[27:30] **Spat upon him**: cf. Mt 26:67 where there also is a possible allusion to Is 50:6.

---

e. [27:10] Zec 11:12–13.   f. [27:11–14] Mk 15:2–5; Lk 23:2–3; Jn 18:29–38.   g. [27:12] Is 53:7.   h. [27:15–26] Mk 15:6–15; Lk 23:17–25; Jn 18:39–19:16.   i. [27:20] Acts 3:14.

j. [27:24] Dt 21:1–8.   k. [27:27–31] Mk 15:16–20; Jn 19:2–3.   l. [27:29] Zec 11:7.   m. [27:30] Is 50:6.

The Way of the Cross.[*] [32n]As they were going out, they met a Cyrenian named Simon; this man they pressed into service to carry his cross. **The Crucifixion.** [33o]And when they came to a place called Golgotha (which means Place of the Skull), [34p]they gave Jesus wine to drink mixed with gall.[†] But when he had tasted it, he refused to drink. [35q]After they had crucified him, they divided his garments[‡] by casting lots; [36]then they sat down and kept watch over him there. [37]And they placed over his head the written charge[§] against him: This is Jesus, the King of the Jews. [38]Two revolutionaries[¶] were crucified with him, one on his right and the other on his left. [39**r]Those passing by reviled him, shaking their heads [40s]and saying, "You who would destroy the temple and rebuild it in three days, save yourself, if you are the Son of God, [and] come down from the cross!" [41]Likewise the chief priests with the scribes and elders mocked him and said, [42]"He saved others; he cannot save himself. So he is the king of Israel![††] Let him come down from the cross now, and we will believe in him. [43‡‡]He trusted in God; let him deliver him now if he wants him. For he said, 'I am the Son of God.'" [44]The revolutionaries who were crucified with him also kept abusing him in the same way. **The Death of Jesus.** [45§§u]From noon onward,[v] darkness came over the whole land until three in the afternoon. [46w]And about three o'clock Jesus cried out in a loud voice, "*Eli, Eli, lema sabachthani?*"[¶¶] which means, "My God, my God, why have you forsaken me?" [47***]Some of the bystanders who heard it said, "This one is calling for Elijah." [48x]Immediately one of them ran to get a sponge; he soaked it in wine, and putting it on a reed, gave it to him to drink. [49]But the rest said, "Wait, let us see if Elijah comes to save him." [50†††]But Jesus cried out again in a loud voice, and gave up his spirit. [51y]And behold, the veil of the sanctuary was torn in two from top to bottom.[‡‡‡] The earth quaked, rocks were split, [52z]tombs were opened, and the bodies of many saints who had fallen asleep were raised. [53]And coming forth from their tombs after his resurrection, they entered the holy city and appeared to many. [54§§§]The centurion and the men with him who were keeping watch over Jesus feared greatly when they saw the earthquake and all that was happening, and they said, "Truly, this was the Son of God!" [55]There were many women

¶¶ [27:46] *Eli, Eli, lema sabachthani?*: Jesus cries out in the words of Ps 22:2a, a psalm of lament that is the Old Testament passage most frequently drawn upon in this narrative. In Mark the verse is cited entirely in Aramaic, which Matthew partially retains but changes the invocation of God to the Hebrew *Eli*, possibly because that is more easily related to the statement of the following verse about Jesus' calling for Elijah.

*** [27:47] **Elijah**: see note on Mt 3:4. This prophet, taken up into heaven (2 Kgs 2:11), was believed to come to the help of those in distress, but the evidences of that belief are all later than the gospels.

††† [27:50] **Gave up his spirit**: cf. the Marcan parallel (Mk 15:37), "breathed his last." Matthew's alteration expresses both Jesus' control over his destiny and his obedient giving up of his life to God.

‡‡‡ [27:51–53] **Veil of the sanctuary . . . bottom**: cf. Mk 15:38; Lk 23:45. Luke puts this event immediately before the death of Jesus. There were two veils in the Mosaic tabernacle on the model of which the temple was constructed, the outer one before the entrance of the Holy Place and the inner one before the Holy of Holies (see Ex 26:31–36). Only the high priest could pass through the latter and that only on the Day of Atonement (see Lv 16:1–18). Probably the torn veil of the gospels is the inner one. The meaning of the scene may be that now, because of Jesus' death, all people have access to the presence of God, or that the temple, its holiest part standing exposed, is now profaned and will soon be destroyed. **The earth quaked . . . appeared to many**: peculiar to Matthew. The earthquake, the splitting of the rocks, and especially the resurrection of the dead **saints** indicate the coming of the final age. In the Old Testament the coming of God is frequently portrayed with the imagery of an earthquake (see Ps 68:9; 77:19), and Jesus speaks of the earthquakes that will accompany the "labor pains" that signify the beginning of the dissolution of the old world (Mt 24:7–8). For the expectation of the resurrection of the dead at the coming of the new and final age, see Dn 12:1–3. Matthew knows that the end of the old age has not yet come (Mt 28:20), but the new age has broken in with the death (and resurrection; cf. the earthquake in Mt 28:2) of Jesus; see note on Mt 16:28. **After his resurrection**: this qualification seems to be due to Matthew's wish to assert the primacy of Jesus' **resurrection** even though he has placed the resurrection of the dead **saints** immediately after Jesus' death.

§§§ [27:54] Cf. Mk 15:39. The Christian confession of faith is made by Gentiles, not only the **centurion**, as in Mark, but the other soldiers **who were keeping watch over Jesus** (cf. Mt 27:36).

---

* [27:32] See note on Mk 15:21. **Cyrenian named Simon**: Cyrenaica was a Roman province on the north coast of Africa and Cyrene was its capital city. The city had a large population of Greek-speaking Jews. **Simon** may have been living in Palestine or have come there for the Passover as a pilgrim. **Pressed into service**: see note on Mt 5:41.

† [27:34] **Wine . . . mixed with gall**: cf. Mk 15:23 where the drink is "wine drugged with myrrh," a narcotic. Matthew's text is probably an inexact allusion to Ps 69:22. That psalm belongs to the class called the individual lament, in which a persecuted just man prays for deliverance in the midst of great suffering and also expresses confidence that his prayer will be heard. That theme of the suffering Just One is frequently applied to the sufferings of Jesus in the passion narratives.

‡ [27:35] The clothing of an executed criminal went to his executioner(s), but the description of that procedure in the case of Jesus, found in all the gospels, is plainly inspired by Ps 22:19. However, that psalm verse is quoted only in Jn 19:24.

§ [27:37] The offense of a person condemned to death by crucifixion was written on a tablet that was displayed on his cross. The **charge** against Jesus was that he had claimed to be the **King of the Jews** (cf. Mt 27:11), i.e., the Messiah (cf. Mt 27:17, 22).

¶ [27:38] **Revolutionaries**: see note on Jn 18:40 where the same Greek word as that found here is used for Barabbas.

** [27:39–40] **Reviled him . . . heads**: cf. Ps 22:8. **You who would destroy . . . three days**: cf. Mt 26:61. **If you are the Son of God**: the same words as those of the devil in the temptation of Jesus; cf. Mt 4:3, 6.

†† [27:42] **King of Israel**: in their mocking of Jesus the members of the Sanhedrin call themselves and their people not "the Jews" but **Israel**.

‡‡ [27:43] Peculiar to Matthew. **He trusted in God . . . wants him**: cf. Ps 22:9. **He said . . . of God**: probably an allusion to Wis 2:12–20 where the theme of the suffering Just One appears.

§§ [27:45] Cf. Am 8:9 where on the day of the Lord "the sun will set at midday."

---

n. [27:32] Mk 15:21; Lk 23:26.　o. [27:33–44] Mk 15:22–32; Lk 23:32–38; Jn 19:17–19, 23–24.　p. [27:34] Ps 69:21.　q. [27:35] Ps 22:19.　r. [27:39] Ps 22:8.　s. [27:40] 4:3, 6; 26:61.　t. [27:43] Ps 22:9; Wis 2:12–20.　u. [27:45–46] Mk 15:33–41; Lk 23:44–49; Jn 19:28–30.　v. [27:45] Am 8:9.

w. [27:46] Ps 22:2.　x. [27:48] Ps 69:21.　y. [27:51] Ex 26:31–36; Ps 68:9; 77:19.　z. [27:52] Dn 12:1–3.

there, looking on from a distance,* who had followed Jesus from Galilee, ministering to him. [56a]Among them were Mary Magdalene and Mary the mother of James and Joseph, and the mother of the sons of Zebedee.

The Burial of Jesus.[†] [57b]When it was evening, there came a rich man from Arimathea named Joseph, who was himself a disciple of Jesus.[c] [58]He went to Pilate and asked for the body of Jesus; then Pilate ordered it to be handed over. [59]Taking the body, Joseph wrapped it [in] clean linen [60]and laid it in his new tomb that he had hewn in the rock. Then he rolled a huge stone across the entrance to the tomb and departed. [61]But Mary Magdalene and the other Mary remained sitting there, facing the tomb.

The Guard at the Tomb.[‡] [62]The next day, the one following the day of preparation,[§] the chief priests and the Pharisees gathered before Pilate [63d]and said, "Sir, we remember that this impostor while still alive said, 'After three days I will be raised up.' [64]Give orders, then, that the grave be secured until the third day, lest his disciples come and steal him and say to the people, 'He has been raised from the dead.' This last imposture would be worse than the first."[¶] [65]Pilate said to them, "The guard is yours;** go secure it as best you can." [66]So they went and secured the tomb by fixing a seal to the stone and setting the guard.

---

*[27:55–56] **Looking on from a distance:** cf. Ps 38:12. **Mary Magdalene . . . Joseph:** these two women are mentioned again in Mt 27:61 and Mt 28:1 and are important as witnesses of the reality of the empty tomb. A **James** and **Joseph** are referred to in Mt 13:55 as brothers of Jesus.

†[27:57–61] Cf. Mk 15:42–47. Matthew drops Mark's designation of **Joseph** of **Arimathea** as "a distinguished member of the council" (the Sanhedrin), and makes him **a rich man** and a **disciple of Jesus.** The former may be an allusion to Is 53:9 (the Hebrew reading of that text is disputed and the one followed in the NAB OT has nothing about the rich, but they are mentioned in the LXX version). That the tomb was the **new tomb** of **a rich man** and that it was seen by the women are indications of an apologetic intent of Matthew; there could be no question about the identity of Jesus' burial place. **The other Mary:** the mother of James and Joseph (Mt 27:56).

‡[27:62–66] Peculiar to Matthew. The story prepares for Mt 28:11–15 and the Jewish charge that the tomb was empty because the disciples had stolen the body of Jesus (Mt 28:13, 15).

§[27:62] **The next day . . . preparation:** the sabbath. According to the synoptic chronology, in that year **the day of preparation** (for the sabbath) was the Passover; cf. Mk 15:42. **The Pharisees:** the principal opponents of Jesus during his ministry and, in Matthew's time, of the Christian church, join with **the chief priests** to guarantee against a possible attempt of Jesus' **disciples** to steal his body.

¶[27:64] **This last imposture . . . the first:** the claim that Jesus **has been raised from the dead** is clearly the **last imposture; the first** may be either his claim that he would **be raised up** (Mt 27:63) or his claim that he was the one with whose ministry the kingdom of God had come (see Mt 12:28).

[27:65] **The guard is yours: literally, "have a guard" or "you have a guard." Either the imperative or the indicative could mean that Pilate granted the petitioners some Roman soldiers as guards, which is the sense of the present translation. However, if the verb is taken as an indicative it could also mean that Pilate told them to use their own Jewish guards.

---

a. [27:56] 13:55. b. [27:57–61] Mk 15:42–47; Lk 23:50–56; Jn 19:38–42. c. [27:57] Is 53:9. d. [27:63] 12:40; 16:21; 17:23; 20:19.

CHAPTER 28[††]

The Resurrection of Jesus. [1e]After the sabbath, as the first day of the week was dawning,[‡‡] Mary Magdalene and the other Mary came to see the tomb. [2§§f]And behold, there was a great earthquake; for an angel of the Lord descended from heaven, approached, rolled back the stone, and sat upon it. [3g]His appearance was like lightning and his clothing was white as snow. [4]The guards were shaken with fear of him and became like dead men. [5]Then the angel said to the women in reply, "Do not be afraid! I know that you are seeking Jesus the crucified. [6¶¶]He is not here, for he has been raised just as he said. Come and see the place where he lay. [7h]Then go quickly and tell his disciples, 'He has been raised from the dead, and he is going before you to Galilee; there you

---

††[28:1–20] Except for Mt 28:1–8 based on Mk 16:1–8, the material of this final chapter is peculiar to Matthew. Even where he follows Mark, Matthew has altered his source so greatly that a very different impression is given from that of the Marcan account. The two points that are common to the resurrection testimony of all the gospels are that the tomb of Jesus had been found empty and that the risen Jesus had appeared to certain persons, or, in the original form of Mark, that such an appearance was promised as soon to take place (see Mk 16:7). On this central and all-important basis, Matthew has constructed an account that interprets the resurrection as the turning of the ages (Mt 28:2–4), shows the Jewish opposition to Jesus as continuing **to the present** in the claim that the resurrection is a deception perpetrated by the **disciples** who stole his body from the tomb (Mt 28:11–15), and marks a new stage in the mission of **the disciples** once limited to Israel (Mt 10:5–6); now they are to **make disciples of all nations.** In this work they will be strengthened by the presence of the exalted Son of Man, who will be with them **until** the kingdom comes in fullness at **the end of the age** (Mt 28:16–20).

‡‡[28:1] **After the sabbath . . . dawning:** since the sabbath ended at sunset, this could mean in the early evening, for **dawning** can refer to the appearance of the evening star; cf. Lk 23:54. However, it is probable that Matthew means the morning dawn of the day after the sabbath, as in the similar though slightly different text of Mark, "when the sun had risen" (Mk 16:2). **Mary Magdalene and the other Mary:** see notes on Mt 27:55–56; 57–61. **To see the tomb:** cf. Mk 16:1–2 where the purpose of the women's visit is to anoint Jesus' body.

§§[28:2–4] Peculiar to Matthew. **A great earthquake:** see note on Mt 27:51–53. **Descended from heaven:** this trait is peculiar to Matthew, although his interpretation of the "young man" of his Marcan source (Mk 16:5) as an **angel** is probably true to Mark's intention; cf. Lk 24:23 where the "two men" of Mt 24:4 are said to be "angels." **Rolled back the stone . . . upon it:** not to allow the risen Jesus to leave the tomb but to make evident that the tomb is empty (see Mt 24:6). Unlike the apocryphal Gospel of Peter (9:35—11:44), the New Testament does not describe the resurrection of Jesus, nor is there anyone who sees it. **His appearance was like lightning . . . snow:** see note on Mt 17:2.

¶¶[28:6–7] Cf. Mk 16:6–7. **Just as he said:** a Matthean addition referring to Jesus' predictions of his resurrection, e.g., Mt 16:21; 17:23; 20:19. **Tell his disciples:** like the angel of the Lord of the infancy narrative, the angel interprets a fact and gives a commandment about what is to be done; cf. Mt 1:20–21. Matthew omits Mark's "and Peter" (Mk 16:7); considering his interest in Peter, this omission is curious. Perhaps the reason is that the Marcan text may allude to a first appearance of Jesus to Peter alone (cf. 1 Cor 15:5; Lk 24:34) which Matthew has already incorporated into his account of Peter's confession at Caesarea Philippi; see note on Mt 16:16. **He is going . . . Galilee:** like Mk 16:7, a reference to Jesus' prediction at the Last Supper (Mt 26:32; Mk 14:28). Matthew changes Mark's "as he told you" to a declaration of the angel.

---

e. [28:1–10] Mk 16:1–8; Lk 24:1–12; Jn 20:1–10. f. [28:2] 25:51. g. [28:3] 17:2. h. [28:7] 26:32.

will see him.' Behold, I have told you." [8]Then they went away quickly from the tomb, fearful yet overjoyed, and ran to announce* this to his disciples. [9†i]And behold, Jesus met them on their way and greeted them. They approached, embraced his feet, and did him homage. [10]Then Jesus said to them, "Do not be afraid. Go tell my brothers to go to Galilee, and there they will see me."

The Report of the Guard.[‡] [11]While they were going, some of the guard went into the city and told the chief priests all that had happened. [12]They assembled with the elders and took counsel; then they gave a large sum of money to the soldiers, [13]telling them, "You are to say, 'His disciples came by night and stole him while we were asleep.' [14]And if this gets to the ears of the governor, we will satisfy [him] and keep you out of trouble." [15]The soldiers took the money and did as they were instructed. And this story has circulated among the Jews to the present [day].

The Commissioning of the Disciples.[§] [16]The eleven[¶] disciples went to Galilee, to the mountain to which Jesus had ordered them. [17**]When they saw him, they worshiped, but they doubted. [18††k]Then Jesus approached and said to them, "All power in heaven and on earth has been given to me. [19l]Go, therefore,[‡‡] and make disciples of all nations, baptizing them in the name of the Father, and of the Son, and of the holy Spirit, [20m]teaching them to observe all that I have commanded you.[§§] And behold, I am with you always, until the end of the age."

---

since the message to the **disciples** was simply that they were to go to Galilee (Mt 28:10), some think that **the mountain** comes from a tradition of the message known to Matthew and alluded to here. For the significance of **the mountain**, see note on Mt 17:1.

[28:17] But they doubted: the Greek can also be translated, "but some doubted." The verb occurs elsewhere in the New Testament only in Mt 14:31 where it is associated with Peter's being of "little faith." For the meaning of that designation, see note on Mt 6:30.

††[28:18] **All power . . . me:** the Greek word here translated **power** is the same as that found in the LXX translation of Dn 7:13–14 where one "like a son of man" is given **power** and an everlasting kingdom by God. The risen Jesus here claims universal power, i.e., **in heaven and on earth.**

‡‡[28:19] **Therefore:** since universal power belongs to the risen Jesus (Mt 28:18), he gives the eleven a mission that is universal. They are to **make disciples of all nations.** While **all nations** is understood by some scholars as referring only to all Gentiles, it is probable that it included the Jews as well. **Baptizing them:** baptism is the means of entrance into the community of the risen one, the Church. **In the name of the Father . . . holy Spirit:** this is perhaps the clearest expression in the New Testament of trinitarian belief. It may have been the baptismal formula of Matthew's church, but primarily it designates the effect of baptism, the union of the one baptized with the Father, Son, and holy Spirit.

§§[28:20] **All that I have commanded you:** the moral teaching found in this gospel, preeminently that of the Sermon on the Mount (Mt 5–7). The commandments of Jesus are the standard of Christian conduct, not the Mosaic law as such, even though some of the Mosaic commandments have now been invested with the authority of Jesus. **Behold, I am with you always:** the promise of Jesus' real though invisible presence echoes the name Emmanuel given to him in the infancy narrative; see note on Mt 1:23. **End of the age:** see notes on Mt 13:39 and Mt 24:3.

---

*[28:8] Contrast Mk 16:8 where the women in their fear "said nothing to anyone."

†[28:9–10] Although these verses are peculiar to Matthew, there are similarities between them and John's account of the appearance of Jesus to Mary Magdalene (Jn 20:17). In both there is a touching of Jesus' body, and a command of Jesus to bear a message to his disciples, designated as his **brothers.** Matthew may have drawn upon a tradition that appears in a different form in John. Jesus' words to the women are mainly a repetition of those of the angel (Mt 28:5a, 7b).

‡[28:11–15] This account indicates that the dispute between Christians and Jews about the empty tomb was not whether the tomb was empty but why.

§[28:16–20] This climactic scene has been called a "proleptic parousia," for it gives a foretaste of the final glorious coming of the Son of Man (Mt 26:64). Then his triumph will be manifest to all; now it is revealed only to **the disciples,** who are commissioned to announce it to **all nations** and bring them to belief in Jesus and obedience to his commandments.

¶[28:16] **The eleven:** the number recalls the tragic defection of Judas Iscariot. **To the mountain . . . ordered them:**

---

i. [28:9–10] Jn 20:17.   j. [28:16–20] Mk 16:14–16; Lk 24:36–49; Jn 20:19–23.

k. [28:18] Dn 7:14 LXX.   l. [28:19] Acts 1:8.   m. [28:20] 1:23; 13:39; 24:3.

THE GOSPEL ACCORDING TO
MARK

This shortest of all New Testament gospels is likely the first to have been written, yet it often tells of Jesus' ministry in more detail than either Matthew or Luke (for example, the miracle stories at Mk 5:1–20 or Mk 9:14–29). It recounts what Jesus did in a vivid style, where one incident follows directly upon another. In this almost breathless narrative, Mark stresses Jesus' message about the kingdom of God now breaking into human life as good news (Mk 1:14–15) and Jesus himself as the gospel of God (Mk 1:1; 8:35; 10:29). Jesus is the Son whom God has sent to rescue humanity by serving and by sacrificing his life (Mk 10:45).

The opening verse about good news in Mark (Mk 1:1) serves as a title for the entire book. The action begins with the appearance of John the Baptist, a messenger of God attested by scripture. But John points to a mightier one, Jesus, at whose baptism God speaks from heaven, declaring Jesus his Son. The Spirit descends upon Jesus, who eventually, it is promised, will baptize "with the holy Spirit." This presentation of who Jesus really is (Mk 1:1–13) is rounded out with a brief reference to the temptation of Jesus and how Satan's attack fails. Jesus as Son of God will be victorious, a point to be remembered as one reads of Jesus' death and the enigmatic ending to Mark's Gospel.

The key verses at Mk 1:14–15, which are programmatic, summarize what Jesus proclaims as gospel: fulfillment, the nearness of the kingdom, and therefore the need for repentance and for faith. After the call of the first four disciples, all fishermen (Mk 1:16–20), we see Jesus engaged in teaching (Mk 1:21, 22, 27), preaching (Mk 1:38, 39), and healing (Mk 1:29–31, 34, 40–45), and exorcising demons (Mk 1:22–27, 34–39). The content of Jesus' teaching is only rarely stated, and then chiefly in parables (Mk 4) about the kingdom. His cures, especially on the sabbath (Mk 3:1–5); his claim, like God, to forgive sins (Mk 2:3–12); his table fellowship with tax collectors and sinners (Mk 2:14–17); and the statement that his followers need not now fast but should rejoice while Jesus is present (Mk 2:18–22), all stir up opposition that will lead to Jesus' death (Mk 3:6).

In Mark, Jesus is portrayed as immensely popular with the people in Galilee during his ministry (Mk 2:2; 3:7; 4:1). He appoints twelve disciples to help preach and drive out demons, just as he does (Mk 3:13–19). He continues to work many miracles; the blocks Mk 4:35–6:44 and Mk 6:45–7:10 are cycles of stories about healings, miracles at the Sea of Galilee, and marvelous feedings of the crowds. Jesus' teaching in Mk 7 exalts the word of God over "the tradition of the elders" and sees defilement as a matter of the heart, not of unclean foods. Yet opposition mounts. Scribes charge that Jesus is possessed by Beelzebul (Mk 3:22). His relatives think him "out of his mind" (Mk 3:21). Jesus' kinship is with those who do the will of God, in a new eschatological family, not even with mother, brothers, or sisters by blood ties (Mk 3:31–35; cf. Mk 6:1–6). But all too often his own disciples do not understand Jesus (Mk 4:13, 40; 6:52; 8:17–21). The fate of John the Baptist (Mk 6:17–29) hints ominously at Jesus' own passion (Mk 9:13; cf. Mk 8:31).

A breakthrough seemingly comes with Peter's confession that Jesus is the Christ (Messiah; Mk 8:27–30). But Jesus himself emphasizes his passion (Mk 8:31; 9:31; 10:33–34), not glory in the kingdom (Mk 10:35–45). Momentarily he is glimpsed in his true identity when he is transfigured before three of the disciples (Mk 9:2–8), but by and large Jesus is depicted in Mark as moving obediently along the way to his cross in Jerusalem. Occasionally there are miracles (Mk 9:17–27; 10:46–52; 11:12–14, 20–21, the only such account in Jerusalem), sometimes teachings (Mk 10:2–11, 23–31), but the greatest concern is with discipleship (Mk 8:34–9:1; 9:33–50). For the disciples do not grasp the mystery being revealed (Mk 9:32; 10:32, 38). One of them will betray him, Judas (Mk 14:10–11, 43–45); one will deny him, Peter (Mk 14:27, 31, 54, 66–72); all eleven men will desert Jesus (Mk 14:27, 50).

The passion account, with its condemnation of Jesus by the Sanhedrin (Mk 14:53, 55–65; 15:1a) and sentencing by Pilate (Mk 15:1b–15), is prefaced with the entry into Jerusalem (Mk 11:1–11), ministry and controversies there (Mk 11:15–12:44), Jesus' Last Supper with the disciples (Mk 14:1–26), and his arrest at Gethsemane (Mk 14:32–52). A chapter of apocalyptic tone about the destruction of the temple (Mk 13:1–2, 14–23) and the coming of the Son of Man (Mk 13:24–27), a discourse filled with promises (Mk 13:11, 31) and admonitions to be watchful (Mk 13:2, 23, 37), is significant for Mark's Gospel, for it helps one see that God, in Jesus, will be victorious after the cross and at the end of history.

The Gospel of Mark ends in the most ancient manuscripts with an abrupt scene at Jesus' tomb, which the women find empty (Mk 16:1–8). His own prophecy of Mk 14:28 is reiterated, that Jesus goes before the disciples into Galilee; "there you will see him." These words may imply resurrection appearances there, or Jesus' parousia there, or the start of Christian mission, or a return to the roots depicted in Mk 1:9, 14–15 in Galilee. Other hands have attached additional endings after Mk 16:8; see note on Mk 16:9–20.

The framework of Mark's Gospel is partly geographical: Galilee (Mk 1:14–9:49), through the area "across the Jordan" (Mk 10:1) and through Jericho (Mk 10:46–52), to Jerusalem (Mk 11:1–16:8). Only rarely does Jesus go into Gentile territory (Mk 5:1–20; 7:24–37), but those who acknowledge him there and the centurion who confesses Jesus at the cross (Mk 15:39) presage the gospel's expansion into the world beyond Palestine.

Mark's Gospel is even more oriented to christology. Jesus is the Son of God (Mk 1:11; 9:7; 15:39; cf. Mk 1:1; 14:61). He is the Messiah, the anointed king of Davidic descent (Mk 12:35; 15:32), the Greek for which, *Christos*, has, by the time Mark wrote, become in effect a proper name (Mk 1:1; 9:41). Jesus is also seen as Son of Man, a term used in Mark not simply as a substitute for "I" or for humanity in general (cf. Mk 2:10, 27–28; 14:21) or with reference to a mighty figure who is to come (Mk 13:26; 14:62), but also in connection with Jesus' predestined, necessary path of suffering and vindication (Mk 8:31; 10:45).

The unfolding of Mark's story about Jesus is sometimes viewed by interpreters as centered around the term "mystery." The word is employed just once, at Mk 4:11, in the singular, and its content there is the kingdom, the open secret that God's reign is now breaking into human life with its reversal of human values. There is a related sense in which Jesus' real identity remained a secret during his lifetime, according to Mark, although demons and demoniacs knew it (Mk 1:24; 3:11; 5:7); Jesus warned against telling of his mighty deeds and revealing his identity (Mk 1:44; 3:12; 5:43; 7:36; 8:26, 30), an injunction sometimes broken (Mk 1:45; cf. Mk 5:19–20). Further, Jesus teaches by parables, according to Mark, in such a way that those "outside" the kingdom do not understand, but only those to whom the mystery has been granted by God.

Mark thus shares with Paul, as well as with other parts of the New Testament, an emphasis on election (Mk 13:20, 22) and upon the gospel as Christ and his cross (cf. 1 Cor 1:23). Yet in Mark the person of Jesus is also depicted with an unaffected naturalness. He reacts to events with authentic human emotion: pity (Mk 1:44), anger (Mk 3:5), triumph (Mk 4:40), sympathy (Mk 5:36; 6:34), surprise (Mk 6:9), admiration (Mk 7:29; 10:21), sadness (Mk 14:33–34), and indignation (Mk 14:48–49).

Although the book is anonymous, apart from the ancient heading "According to Mark" in manuscripts, it has traditionally been assigned to John Mark, in whose mother's house (at Jerusalem) Christians assembled (Acts 12:12). This Mark was a cousin of Barnabas (Col 4:10) and accompanied Barnabas and Paul on a missionary journey (Acts 12:25; 13:3; 15:36–39). He appears in Pauline letters (2 Tm 4:11; Phlm 24) and with Peter (1 Pt 5:13). Papias (ca. A.D. 135) described Mark as Peter's "interpreter," a view found in other patristic writers. Petrine influence should not, however, be exaggerated. The evangelist has put together various oral and possibly written sources—miracle stories, parables, sayings, stories of controversies, and the passion—so as to speak of the crucified Messiah for Mark's own day.

Traditionally, the gospel is said to have been written shortly before A.D. 70 in Rome, at a time of impending persecution and when destruction loomed over Jerusalem. Its audience seems to have been Gentile, unfamiliar with Jewish customs (hence Mk 7:3–4, 11). The book aimed to equip such

Christians to stand faithful in the face of persecution (Mk 13:9–13), while going on with the proclamation of the gospel begun in Galilee (Mk 13:10; 14:9). Modern research often proposes as the author an unknown Hellenistic Jewish Christian, possibly in Syria, and perhaps shortly after the year 70.

The principal divisions of the Gospel according to Mark are the following:

I.   The Preparation for the Public Ministry of Jesus (1:1–13)
II. The Mystery of Jesus (1:14–8:26)
III. The Mystery Begins to Be Revealed (8:27–9:32)
IV. The Full Revelation of the Mystery (9:33–16:8)
         The Longer Ending (16:9–20)
         The Shorter Ending
         The Freer Logion (in the note on 16:9–20)

I. THE PREPARATION FOR THE PUBLIC MINISTRY OF JESUS*

CHAPTER 1

¹The beginning of the gospel of Jesus Christ [the Son of God].†

The Preaching of John the Baptist. ²ᵃAs it is written in Isaiah the prophet:‡ᵇ

"Behold, I am sending my messenger
          ahead of you;
    he will prepare your way.
³   ᶜA voice of one crying out in the desert:
    'Prepare the way of the Lord,
          make straight his paths.'"

⁴John [the] Baptist appeared in the desert proclaiming a baptism of repentance for the forgiveness of sins. ⁵People of the whole Judean countryside and all the inhabitants of Jerusalem were going out to him and were being baptized by him in the Jordan River as they acknowledged their sins. ⁶John was clothed in camel's hair, with a leather belt around his waist.§ He fed on locusts and wild honey. ⁷And this is what he proclaimed: "One mightier than I is coming after me. I am not worthy to stoop and loosen the thongs of his sandals. ⁸ᵈI have baptized you with water; he will baptize you with the holy Spirit."

The Baptism of Jesus. ⁹ᵉIt happened in those days that Jesus came from Nazareth of Galilee and was baptized in the Jordan by John. ¹⁰On coming up out of the water he saw the heavens being torn open and the Spirit, like a dove, descending upon him.** ¹¹ᶠAnd a voice came from the heavens, "You are my beloved Son; with you I am well pleased."

The Temptation of Jesus.†† ¹²At once the Spirit drove him out into the desert,ᵍ ¹³and he remained in the desert for forty days, tempted

as Elijah who has already come (Mk 9:11–13; Mt 17:10–12; cf. Mal 3:23–24; Lk 1:17).

¶[1:8–9] Through the life-giving baptism with the holy Spirit (Mk 1:8), Jesus will create a new people of God. But first he identifies himself with the people of Israel in submitting to John's baptism of repentance and in bearing on their behalf the burden of God's decisive judgment (Mk 1:9; cf. Mk 1:4). As in the desert of Sinai, so here in the wilderness of Judea, Israel's sonship with God is to be renewed.

[1:10–11] He saw the heavens . . . and the Spirit . . . upon him: indicating divine intervention in fulfillment of promise. Here the descent of the Spirit on Jesus is meant, anointing him for his ministry; cf. Is 11:2; 42:1; 61:1; 63:9. **A voice . . . with you I am well pleased**: God's acknowledgment of Jesus as his unique Son, the object of his love. His approval of Jesus is the assurance that Jesus will fulfill his messianic mission of salvation.

††[1:12–13] The same Spirit who descended on Jesus in his baptism now drives him into the desert for forty days. The result is radical confrontation and temptation by Satan who attempts to frustrate the work of God. The presence of wild beasts may indicate the horror and danger of the desert regarded as the abode of demons or may reflect the paradise motif of harmony among all creatures; cf. Is 11:6–9. The presence of ministering angels to sustain Jesus recalls the angel who guided the Israelites in the desert in the first Exodus (Ex 14:19; 23:20) and the angel who supplied nourishment to Elijah in the wilderness (1 Kgs 19:5–7). The combined forces of good and evil were present to Jesus in the desert. His sustained obedience brings forth the new Israel of God there where Israel's rebellion had brought death and alienation.

*[1:1–13] The prologue of the Gospel according to Mark begins with the title (Mk 1:1) followed by three events preparatory to Jesus' preaching: (1) the appearance in the Judean wilderness of John, baptizer, preacher of repentance, and precursor of Jesus (Mk 1:2–8); (2) the baptism of Jesus, at which a voice from heaven acknowledges Jesus to be God's Son, and the holy Spirit descends on him (Mk 1:9–11); (3) the temptation of Jesus by Satan (Mk 1:12–13).

†[1:1] **The gospel of Jesus Christ [the Son of God]**: the "good news" of salvation in and through Jesus, crucified and risen, acknowledged by the Christian community as Messiah (Mk 8:29; 14:61–62) and Son of God (Mk 1:11; 9:7; 15:39), although some important manuscripts here omit **the Son of God**.

‡[1:2–3] Although Mark attributes the prophecy to Isaiah, the text is a combination of Mal 3:1; Is 40:3; Ex 23:20; cf. Mt 11:10; Lk 7:27. John's ministry is seen as God's prelude to the saving mission of his Son. **The way of the Lord**: this prophecy of Deutero-Isaiah concerning the end of the Babylonian exile is here applied to the coming of Jesus; John the Baptist is to prepare the way for him.

§[1:6] **Clothed in camel's hair . . . waist**: the Baptist's garb recalls that of Elijah in 2 Kgs 1:8. Jesus speaks of the Baptist

a. [1:2–8] Mt 3:1–11; Lk 3:2–16.   b. [1:2] Mal 3:1.   c. [1:3] Is 40:3; Jn 1:23.

d. [1:8] Jn 1:27; Acts 1:5; 11:16.   e. [1:9–11] Mt 3:13–17; Lk 3:21–23; Jn 1:32–33.   f. [1:11] Ps 2:7.   g. [1:12–13] Mt 4:1–11; Lk 4:1–13.

by Satan. He was among wild beasts, and the angels ministered to him.

II. THE MYSTERY OF JESUS

The Beginning of the Galilean Ministry. [14h]After John had been arrested,· Jesus came to Galilee proclaiming the gospel of God: [15i]"This is the time of fulfillment. The kingdom of God is at hand. Repent, and believe in the gospel."

The Call of the First Disciples.[†] [16j]As he passed by the Sea of Galilee, he saw Simon and his brother Andrew casting their nets into the sea; they were fishermen. [17]Jesus said to them, "Come after me, and I will make you fishers of men." [18]Then they abandoned their nets and followed him. [19]He walked along a little farther and saw James, the son of Zebedee, and his brother John. They too were in a boat mending their nets. [20]Then he called them. So they left their father Zebedee in the boat along with the hired men and followed him.

The Cure of a Demoniac. [21k]Then they came to Capernaum, and on the sabbath he entered the synagogue and taught. [22l]The people were astonished at his teaching, for he taught them as one having authority and not as the scribes. [23§]In their synagogue was a man with an unclean spirit; [24¶]he cried out, "What have you to do with us,** Jesus of Nazareth? Have you come to destroy us? I know who you are—the Holy One of God!" [25]Jesus rebuked him and said, "Quiet! Come out of him!" [26]The unclean spirit convulsed him and with a loud cry came out of him. [27]All were amazed and asked one another, "What is this? A new teaching with authority. He commands even the unclean spirits and they obey him." [28]His fame spread everywhere throughout the whole region of Galilee.

The Cure of Simon's Mother-in-Law. [29m]On leaving the synagogue he entered the house of Simon and Andrew with James and John. [30]Simon's mother-in-law lay sick with a fever. They immediately told him about her. [31]He approached, grasped her hand, and helped her up. Then the fever left her and she waited on them.

Other Healings. [32]When it was evening, after sunset, they brought to him all who were ill or possessed by demons. [33]The whole town was gathered at the door. [34]He cured many who were sick with various diseases, and he drove out many demons, not permitting them to speak because they knew him.

Jesus Leaves Capernaum. [35n]Rising very early before dawn, he left and went off to a deserted place, where he prayed. [36]Simon and those who were with him pursued him [37]and on finding him said, "Everyone is looking for you." [38]He told them, "Let us go on to the nearby villages that I may preach there also. For this purpose have I come." [39]So he went into their synagogues, preaching and driving out demons throughout the whole of Galilee.

The Cleansing of a Leper. [40o]A leper[††] came to him [and kneeling down] begged him and said, "If you wish, you can make me clean." [41]Moved with pity, he stretched out his hand, touched him, and said to him, "I do will it. Be made clean."[p] [42]The leprosy left him immediately, and he was made clean.[q] [43]Then, warning him sternly, he dismissed him at once. [44]Then he said to him, "See that you tell no one anything, but go, show yourself to the priest and offer for your cleansing what Moses prescribed; that will be proof for them."[r] [45]The man went away and began to publicize the whole matter. He spread the report abroad so that it was impossible for Jesus to enter a town openly. He remained outside in deserted places, and people kept coming to him from everywhere.

CHAPTER 2

The Healing of a Paralytic. [1‡‡]When Jesus returned to Capernaum[s] after some days, it

---

*[1:14–15] **After John had been arrested**: in the plan of God, Jesus was not to proclaim the good news of salvation prior to the termination of the Baptist's active mission. **Galilee**: in the Marcan account, scene of the major part of Jesus' public ministry before his arrest and condemnation. **The gospel of God**: not only the good news from God but about God at work in Jesus Christ. **This is the time of fulfillment**: i.e., of God's promises. **The kingdom of God . . . Repent**: see note on Mt 3:2.

†[1:16–20] These verses narrate the call of the first Disciples. See notes on Mt 4:18–22 and Mt 4:20.

‡[1:21–45] The account of a single day's ministry of Jesus on a sabbath in and outside the synagogue of Capernaum (Mk 1:21–31) combines teaching and miracles of exorcism and healing. Mention is not made of the content of the teaching but of the effect of astonishment and alarm on the people. Jesus' teaching with authority, making an absolute claim on the hearer, was in the best tradition of the ancient prophets, not of the scribes. The narrative continues with events that evening (Mk 1:32–34; see notes on Mt 8:14–17) and the next day (Mk 1:35–39). The cleansing in Mk 1:40–45 stands as an isolated story.

§[1:23] **An unclean spirit**: so called because of the spirit's resistance to the holiness of God. The spirit knows and fears the power of Jesus to destroy his influence; cf. Mk 1:32, 34; 3:11; 6:13.

¶[1:24–25] **The Holy One of God**: not a confession but an attempt to ward off Jesus' power, reflecting the notion that use of the precise name of an opposing spirit would guarantee mastery over him. Jesus silenced the cry of the unclean spirit and drove him out of the man.

[1:24] **What have you to do with us?: see note on Jn 2:4.

††[1:40] **A leper**: for the various forms of skin disease, see Lv 13:1–50 and the note on Lv 13:2–4. There are only two instances in the Old Testament in which God is shown to have cured a leper (Nm 12:10–15; 2 Kgs 5:1–14). The law of Moses provided for the ritual purification of a leper. In curing the leper, Jesus assumes that the priests will reinstate the cured man into the religious community. See also note on Lk 5:14.

‡‡[2:1–3:6] This section relates a series of conflicts between Jesus and the scribes and Pharisees in which the growing opposition of the latter leads to their plot to put Jesus to death (Mk 3:6).

---

h. [1:14–15] Mt 4:12–17; Lk 4:14–15.   i. [1:15] Mt 3:2.   j. [1:16–20] Mt 4:18–22; Lk 5:2–11.   k. [1:21–28] Lk 4:31–37.   l. [1:22] Mt 7:28–29.

m. [1:29–34] Mt 8:14–16; Lk 4:38–41.   n. [1:35–39] Lk 4:42–44.   o. [1:40–44] Mt 8:2–4; Lk 5:12–14.   p. [1:41] 5:30.   q. [1:42] Lk 17:14.   r. [1:44] Lv 14:2–32.   s. [2:1–12] Mt 9:2–8; Lk 5:18–26.

became known that he was at home.` ²Many gathered together so that there was no longer room for them, not even around the door, and he preached the word to them. ³They came bringing to him a paralytic carried by four men. ⁴Unable to get near Jesus because of the crowd, they opened up the roof above him. After they had broken through, they let down the mat on which the paralytic was lying. ⁵†When Jesus saw their faith, he said to the paralytic, "Child, your sins are forgiven." ⁶†Now some of the scribes were sitting there asking themselves, ⁷"Why does this man speak that way?§ He is blaspheming. Who but God alone can forgive sins?"ᶠ ⁸Jesus immediately knew in his mind what they were thinking to themselves, so he said, "Why are you thinking such things in your hearts? ⁹Which is easier, to say to the paralytic, 'Your sins are forgiven,' or to say, 'Rise, pick up your mat and walk'? ¹⁰§But that you may know that the Son of Man has authority to forgive sins on earth"— ¹¹he said to the paralytic, "I say to you, rise, pick up your mat, and go home." ¹²He rose, picked up his mat at once, and went away in the sight of everyone. They were all astounded and glorified God, saying, "We have never seen anything like this."

The Call of Levi. ¹³**⁎ᵘ**"Once again he went out along the sea. All the crowd came to him and he taught them. ¹⁴ᵛAs he passed by,†† he saw Levi, son of Alphaeus, sitting at the customs post. He said to him, "Follow me." And he got up and followed

him. ¹⁵While he was at table in his house,‡‡ many tax collectors and sinners sat with Jesus and his disciples; for there were many who followed him. ¹⁶§§Some scribes who were Pharisees saw that he was eating with sinners and tax collectors and said to his disciples, "Why does he eat with tax collectors and sinners?" ¹⁷Jesus heard this and said to them [that], "Those who are well do not need a physician,¶¶ but the sick do. I did not come to call the righteous but sinners."

The Question About Fasting.⁎⁎⁎ ¹⁸The disciples of John and of the Pharisees were accustomed to fast.ʷ People came to him and objected, "Why do the disciples of John and the disciples of the Pharisees fast, but your disciples do not fast?" ¹⁹Jesus answered them, "Can the wedding guests fast†††️ while the bridegroom is with them? As long as they have the bridegroom with them they cannot fast. ²⁰But the days will come when the bridegroom is taken away from them, and then they will fast on that day. ²¹No one sews a piece of unshrunken cloth on an old cloak. If he does, its fullness pulls away, the new from the old, and the tear gets worse. ²²Likewise, no one pours new wine into old wineskins. Otherwise, the wine will burst the skins, and both the wine and the skins are ruined. Rather, new wine is poured into fresh wineskins."

The Disciples and the Sabbath.‡‡‡️ ²³As he was passing through a field of grain on the sabbath, his disciples began to make a path while picking the heads of grain.ˣ ²⁴At this the Pharisees said to him, "Look, why are they doing what is unlawful on the sabbath?"ʸ ²⁵He said to them, "Have you never read what David did§§§ when he was in need and he and his companions were hungry? ²⁶How

⁎[2:1–2] **He was at home:** to the crowds that gathered in and outside the house Jesus **preached the word,** i.e., the gospel concerning the nearness of the kingdom and the necessity of repentance and faith (Mk 1:14).

†[2:5] It was the faith of the paralytic and those who carried him that moved Jesus to heal the sick man. Accounts of other miracles of Jesus reveal more and more his emphasis on faith as the requisite for exercising his healing powers (Mk 5:34; 9:23–24; 10:52).

‡[2:6] **Scribes:** trained in oral interpretation of the written law; in Mark's gospel, adversaries of Jesus, with one exception (Mk 12:28, 34).

§[2:7] **He is blaspheming:** an accusation made here and repeated during the trial of Jesus (Mk 14:60–64).

¶[2:10] **But that you may know that the Son of Man . . . on earth:** although Mk 2:8–9 are addressed to the scribes, the sudden interruption of thought and structure in Mk 2:10 seems not addressed to them nor to the paralytic. Moreover, the early public use of the designation "Son of Man" to unbelieving scribes is most unlikely. The most probable explanation is that Mark's insertion of Mk 2:10 is a commentary addressed to Christians for whom he recalls this miracle and who already accept in faith that Jesus is Messiah and Son of God.

⁎⁎[2:13] **He taught them:** see note on Mk 1:21–45.

††[2:14] **As he passed by:** see note on Lk 1:16–20. **Levi, son of Alphaeus:** see note on Mt 9:9. **Customs post:** such tax collectors paid a fixed sum for the right to collect customs duties within their districts. Since whatever they could collect above this amount constituted their profit, the abuse of extortion was widespread among them. Hence, Jewish customs officials were regarded as sinners (Mk 2:16), outcasts of society, and disgraced along with their families. **He got up and followed him:** i.e., became a disciple of Jesus.

‡‡[2:15] **In his house:** cf. Mk 2:1; Mt 9:10. Lk 5:29 clearly calls it Levi's house.

§§[2:16–17] This and the following conflict stories reflect a similar pattern: a statement of fact, a question of protest, and a reply by Jesus.

¶¶[2:17] **Do not need a physician:** this maxim of Jesus with its implied irony was uttered to silence his adversaries who objected that he ate with **tax collectors and sinners** (Mk 2:16). Because the scribes and Pharisees were self-righteous, they were not capable of responding to Jesus' call to repentance and faith in the gospel.

⁎⁎⁎[2:18–22] This conflict over the question of fasting has the same pattern as Mk 2:16–17; see notes on Mt 9:15; 9:16–17.

†††[2:19] **Can the wedding guests fast?:** the bridal metaphor expresses a new relationship of love between God and his people in the person and mission of Jesus to his disciples. It is the inauguration of the new and joyful messianic time of fulfillment and the passing of the old. Any attempt at assimilating the Pharisaic practice of fasting, or of extending the preparatory discipline of John's disciples beyond the arrival of the bridegroom, would be as futile as sewing **a piece of unshrunken cloth on an old cloak** or pouring **new wine into old wineskins** with the resulting destruction of both cloth and wine (Mk 2:21–22). Fasting is rendered superfluous during the earthly ministry of Jesus; cf. Mk 2:20.

‡‡‡[2:23–28] This conflict regarding the sabbath follows the same pattern as in Mk 2:18–22.

§§§[2:25–26] **Have you never read what David did?:** Jesus defends the action of his disciples on the basis of 1 Sm 21:2–7 in which an exception is made to the regulation of Lv 24:9 because of the extreme hunger of David and his men. According to

t. [2:7] Is 43:25. u. [2:13] 4:1. v. [2:14–17] Mt 9:9–13; Lk 5:27–32.

w. [2:18–22] Mt 9:14–17; Lk 5:33–39. x. [2:23–28] Mt 12:1–8; Lk 6:1–5. y. [2:24] Dt 23:25.

he went into the house of God when Abiathar was high priest and ate the bread of offering that only the priests could lawfully eat, and shared it with his companions?"[z] [27]Then he said to them, "The sabbath was made for man,* not man for the sabbath.[a] [28†]That is why the Son of Man is lord even of the sabbath."

CHAPTER 3

A Man with a Withered Hand. [1‡]Again he entered the synagogue.[b] There was a man there who had a withered hand. [2]They watched him closely to see if he would cure him on the sabbath so that they might accuse him. [3]He said to the man with the withered hand, "Come up here before us." [4]Then he said to them, "Is it lawful to do good on the sabbath rather than to do evil, to save life rather than to destroy it?" But they remained silent. [5]Looking around at them with anger and grieved at their hardness of heart, he said to the man, "Stretch out your hand." He stretched it out and his hand was restored.[c] [6§]The Pharisees went out and immediately took counsel with the Herodians against him to put him to death.

The Mercy of Jesus. [7¶]Jesus withdrew toward the sea with his disciples.[d] A large number of people [followed] from Galilee and from Judea. [8]Hearing what he was doing, a large number of people came to him also from Jerusalem, from Idumea, from beyond the Jordan, and from the neighborhood of Tyre and Sidon. [9]He told his disciples to have a boat ready for him because of the crowd, so that they would not crush him. [10]He had cured many and, as a result, those who had diseases were pressing upon him to touch him.[e] [11**]And whenever unclean spirits saw him they would fall down before him and shout, "You are the Son of God."[f] [12]He warned them sternly not to make him known.

The Mission of the Twelve. [13g]He went up the mountain[††] and summoned those whom he wanted and they came to him. [14h]He appointed twelve [whom he also named apostles] that they might be with him[‡‡] and he might send them forth to preach [15]and to have authority to drive out demons: [16§§][he appointed the twelve:] Simon, whom he named Peter; [17]James, son of Zebedee, and John the brother of James, whom he named Boanerges, that is, sons of thunder;[i] [18]Andrew, Philip, Bartholomew, Matthew, Thomas, James the son of Alphaeus; Thaddeus, Simon the Cananean, [19]and Judas Iscariot who betrayed him.

Blasphemy of the Scribes. [20¶¶]He came home.*** Again [the] crowd gathered, making it impossible for them even to eat.[j] [21]When his relatives heard of this they set out to seize him, for they said, "He is out of his mind."[k] [22]The scribes who had come from Jerusalem said, "He is possessed by Beelzebul,"[†††] and "By the prince of demons he drives out demons."[l]

Jesus and Beelzebul. [23]Summoning them, he began to speak to them in parables, "How can Satan drive out Satan? [24]If a kingdom is divided against itself, that kingdom cannot stand. [25]And if a house is divided against itself, that house will not be able to stand. [26]And if Satan has risen up against himself and is divided, he cannot stand;

---

1 Samuel, the priest who gave the bread to David was Ahimelech, father of Abiathar.

*[2:27] **The sabbath was made for man**: a reaffirmation of the divine intent of the sabbath to benefit Israel as contrasted with the restrictive Pharisaic tradition added to the law.

†[2:28] **The Son of Man is lord even of the sabbath**: Mark's comment on the theological meaning of the incident is to benefit his Christian readers; see note on Mk 2:10.

‡[3:1–5] Here Jesus is again depicted in conflict with his adversaries over the question of sabbath-day observance. His opponents were already ill disposed toward him because they regarded Jesus as a violator of the sabbath. Jesus' question **Is it lawful to do good on the sabbath rather than to do evil?** places the matter in the broader theological context outside the casuistry of the scribes. The answer is obvious. Jesus heals the man with the withered hand in the sight of all and reduces his opponents to silence; cf. Jn 5:17–18.

§[3:6] In reporting the plot of the Pharisees and Herodians to put Jesus to death after this series of conflicts in Galilee, Mark uses a pattern that recurs in his account of later controversies in Jerusalem (Mk 11:17–18; 12:13–17). The help of the Herodians, supporters of Herod Antipas, tetrarch of Galilee and Perea, is needed to take action against Jesus. Both series of conflicts point to their gravity and to the impending passion of Jesus.

¶[3:7–19] This overview of the Galilean ministry manifests the power of Jesus to draw people to himself through his teaching and deeds of power. The crowds of Jews from many regions surround Jesus (Mk 3:7–12). This phenomenon prepares the way for creating a new people of Israel. The choice and mission of the Twelve is the prelude (Mk 3:13–19).

**[3:11–12] See note on Mk 1:24–25.

††[3:13] **He went up the mountain**: here and elsewhere the mountain is associated with solemn moments and acts in the mission and self-revelation of Jesus (Mk 6:46; 9:2–8; 13:3). Jesus acts with authority as he **summoned those whom he wanted and they came to him**.

‡‡[3:14–15] **He appointed twelve [whom he also named apostles] that they might be with him**: literally "he made," i.e., instituted them as apostles to extend his messianic mission through them (Mk 6:7–13). See notes on Mt 10:1 and 10:2–4.

§§[3:16] **Simon, whom he named Peter**: Mark indicates that Simon's name was changed on this occasion. Peter is first in all lists of the apostles (Mt 10:2; Lk 6:14; Acts 1:13; cf. 1 Cor 15:5–8).

¶¶[3:20–35] Within the narrative of the coming of Jesus' relatives (Mk 3:20–21) is inserted the account of the unbelieving scribes from Jerusalem who attributed Jesus' power over demons to Beelzebul (Mk 3:22–30); see note on Mk 5:21–43. There were those even among the relatives of Jesus who disbelieved and regarded Jesus as **out of his mind** (Mk 3:21). Against this background, Jesus is informed of the arrival of his mother and brothers [and sisters] (Mk 3:32). He responds by showing that not family ties but doing God's will (Mk 3:35) is decisive in the kingdom; cf. note on Mt 12:46–50.

***[3:20] **He came home**: cf. Mk 2:1–2 and see note on Mk 2:15.

†††[3:22] **By Beelzebul**: see note on Mt 10:25. Two accusations are leveled against Jesus: (1) that **he is possessed** by an unclean spirit and (2) **by the prince of demons he drives out demons**. Jesus answers the second charge by a parable (Mk 3:24–27) and responds to the first charge in Mk 3:28–29.

---

z. [2:26] 1 Sm 21:2–7; Lv 24:5–9.   a. [2:27] 2 Mc 5:19.   b. [3:1–6] Mt 12:9–14; Lk 6:6–11.   c. [3:5] Lk 14:4.   d. [3:7–12] Mt 4:23–25; 12:15; Lk 6:17–19.

e. [3:10] 5:30.   f. [3:11] 1:34; Lk 4:41.   g. [3:13–19] Mt 10:1–4; Lk 6:12–16.   h. [3:14] 6:7.   i. [3:17] Mt 16:18; Jn 1:42.   j. [3:20] 2:2.   k. [3:21] Jn 10:20.   l. [3:22–30] Mt 12:24–32; Lk 11:15–22; 12:10.

that is the end of him. [27]But no one can enter a strong man's house to plunder his property unless he first ties up the strong man. Then he can plunder his house. [28]Amen, I say to you, all sins and all blasphemies that people utter will be forgiven them.[m] [29]But whoever blasphemes against the holy Spirit[*] will never have forgiveness, but is guilty of an everlasting sin." [30]For they had said, "He has an unclean spirit."

Jesus and His Family. [31n]His mother and his brothers arrived. Standing outside they sent word to him and called him. [32]A crowd seated around him told him, "Your mother and your brothers[†] [and your sisters] are outside asking for you." [33]But he said to them in reply, "Who are my mother and [my] brothers?" [34]And looking around at those seated in the circle he said, "Here are my mother and my brothers. [35][For] whoever does the will of God is my brother and sister and mother."

CHAPTER 4

The Parable of the Sower. [1‡]On another occasion[o] he began to teach by the sea.[§] A very large crowd gathered around him so that he got into a boat on the sea and sat down. And the whole crowd was beside the sea on land.[p] [2]And he taught them at length in parables, and in the course of his instruction he said to them, [3§]"Hear this! A sower went out to sow. [4]And as he sowed, some seed fell on the path, and the birds came and ate it up. [5]Other seed fell on rocky ground where it had little soil. It sprang up at once because the soil was not deep. [6]And when the sun rose, it was scorched and it withered for lack of roots. [7]Some seed fell among thorns, and the thorns grew up and choked it and it produced no grain. [8]And some seed fell on rich soil and produced fruit. It came up and grew and yielded

thirty, sixty, and a hundredfold." [9]He added, "Whoever has ears to hear ought to hear."

The Purpose of the Parables. [10]And when he was alone, those present along with the Twelve questioned him about the parables. [11**]He answered them, "The mystery of the kingdom of God has been granted to you. But to those outside everything comes in parables, [12]so that

'they may look and see but not perceive,
    and hear and listen but not
      understand,
in order that they may not be converted
      and be forgiven.'"[q]

[13††]Jesus said to them, "Do you not understand this parable?[r] Then how will you understand any of the parables? [14]The sower sows the word. [15]These are the ones on the path where the word is sown. As soon as they hear, Satan comes at once and takes away the word sown in them. [16]And these are the ones sown on rocky ground who, when they hear the word, receive it at once with joy. [17]But they have no root; they last only for a time. Then when tribulation or persecution comes because of the word, they quickly fall away. [18]Those sown among thorns are another sort. They are the people who hear the word, [19]but worldly anxiety, the lure of riches, and the craving for other things intrude and choke the word, and it bears no fruit. [20]But those sown on rich soil are the ones who hear the word and accept it and bear fruit thirty and sixty and a hundredfold."

Parable of the Lamp. [21s]He said to them, "Is a lamp brought in to be placed under a bushel basket or under a bed, and not to be placed on a lampstand?[t] [22]For there is nothing hidden except to be made visible; nothing is secret except to come to light.[u] [23]Anyone who has ears to hear ought to hear." [24]He also told them, "Take care what you hear. The measure with which you measure will be measured out to you, and still more will be given to you.[v] [25]To the one who has, more will be given; from the one who has not, even what he has will be taken away."[w]

Seed Grows of Itself. [26]He said, "This is how it is with the kingdom of God;[‡‡] it is as if a man

---

*[3:29] **Whoever blasphemes against the holy Spirit**: this sin is called **an everlasting sin** because it attributes to Satan, who is the power of evil, what is actually the work of the holy Spirit, namely, victory over the demons.

†[3:32] **Your brothers**: see note on Mk 6:3.

‡[4:1–34] **In parables** (Mk 4:2): see note on Mt 13:3. The use of parables is typical of Jesus' enigmatic method of teaching the crowds (Mk 4:2–9, 12) as compared with the interpretation of the parables he gives to his disciples (Mk 4:10–25, 33–34) to each group according to its capacity to understand (Mk 4:9–11). The key feature of the parable at hand is the sowing of the seed (Mk 4:3), representing the breakthrough of the kingdom of God into the world. The various types of soil refer to the diversity of response accorded the word of God (Mk 4:4–7). The climax of the parable is the harvest of thirty, sixty, and a hundredfold, indicating the consummation of the kingdom (Mk 4:8). Thus both the present and the future action of God, from the initiation to the fulfillment of the kingdom, is presented through this and other parables (Mk 4:26–29, 30–32).

§[4:1] **By the sea**: the shore of the Sea of Galilee or a boat near the shore (Mk 2:13; 3:7–8) is the place where Mark depicts Jesus teaching the crowds. By contrast the mountain is the scene of Jesus at prayer (Mk 6:46) or in the process of forming his disciples (Mk 3:13; 9:2).

§[4:3–8] See note on Mt 13:3–8.

**[4:11–12] These verses are to be viewed against their background in Mk 3:6, 22 concerning the unbelief and opposition Jesus encountered in his ministry. It is against this background that the distinction in Jesus' method becomes clear of presenting the kingdom to the disbelieving crowd in one manner and to the disciples in another. To the former it is presented in parables and the truth remains hidden; for the latter the parable is interpreted and the mystery is partially revealed because of their faith; see notes on Mt 13:11 and Mt 13:13.

††[4:13–20] See note on Mt 13:18–23.

‡‡[4:26–29] Only Mark records the parable of the seed's growth. Sower and harvester are the same. The emphasis is on the power of the seed to grow of itself without human

m. [3:28] Lk 12:10.   n. [3:31–35] Mt 12;46–50; Lk 8:19–21.   o. [4:1–12] Mt 13:1–13; Lk 8:4–10.   p. [4:1] 2:13; Lk 5:1.

q. [4:12] Is 6:9; Jn 12:40; Acts 28:26; Rom 11:8.   r. [4:13–20] Mt 13:18–23; Lk 8:11–15.   s. [4:21–25] Lk 8:16–18.   t. [4:21] Mt 5:15; Lk 11:33.   u. [4:22] Mt 10:26; Lk 12:2.   v. [4:24] Mt 7:2; Lk 6:38.   w. [4:25] Mt 13:12; Lk 19:26.

were to scatter seed[x] on the land [27]and would sleep and rise night and day and the seed would sprout and grow, he knows not how. [28]Of its own accord the land yields fruit, first the blade, then the ear, then the full grain in the ear. [29]And when the grain is ripe, he wields the sickle at once, for the harvest has come."

The Mustard Seed. [30y]He said, "To what shall we compare the kingdom of God, or what parable can we use for it? [31]It is like a mustard seed that, when it is sown in the ground, is the smallest of all the seeds on the earth. [32*]But once it is sown, it springs up and becomes the largest of plants and puts forth large branches, so that the birds of the sky can dwell in its shade." [33]With many such parables[z] he spoke the word to them as they were able to understand it. [34]Without parables he did not speak to them, but to his own disciples he explained everything in private.

The Calming of a Storm at Sea. [35†]On that day, as evening drew on, he said to them, "Let us cross to the other side."[a] [36]Leaving the crowd, they took him with them in the boat just as he was. And other boats were with him. [37]A violent squall came up and waves were breaking over the boat, so that it was already filling up. [38]Jesus was in the stern, asleep on a cushion. They woke him and said to him, "Teacher, do you not care that we are perishing?" [39]He woke up, rebuked the wind, and said to the sea, "Quiet! Be still!"[‡] The wind ceased and there was great calm. [40]Then he asked them, "Why are you terrified? Do you not yet have faith?" [41§b]They were filled with great awe and said to one another, "Who then is this whom even wind and sea obey?"

CHAPTER 5
The Healing of the Gerasene Demoniac.
[1¶]They came to the other side of the sea, to the territory of the Gerasenes. [2]When he got out of the boat, at once a man[**] from the tombs who had an unclean spirit met him. [3]The man had been dwelling among the tombs, and no one could restrain him any longer, even with a chain. [4]In fact, he had frequently been bound with shackles and chains, but the chains had been pulled apart by him and the shackles smashed, and no one was strong enough to subdue him. [5]Night and day among the tombs and on the hillsides he was always crying out and bruising himself with stones. [6]Catching sight of Jesus from a distance, he ran up and prostrated himself before him, [7]crying out in a loud voice, "What have you to do with me,[††] Jesus, Son of the Most High God? I adjure you by God, do not torment me!" [8](He had been saying to him, "Unclean spirit, come out of the man!") [9‡‡]He asked him, "What is your name?" He replied, "Legion is my name. There are many of us."[d] [10]And he pleaded earnestly with him not to drive them away from that territory.

[11]Now a large herd of swine[§§] was feeding there on the hillside. [12]And they pleaded with him, "Send us into the swine. Let us enter them." [13]And he let them, and the unclean spirits came out and entered the swine. The herd of about two thousand rushed down a steep bank into the sea, where they were drowned. [14]The swineherds ran away and reported the incident in the town and throughout the countryside. And people came out to see what had happened. [15]As they approached Jesus, they caught sight of the man who had been possessed by Legion, sitting there clothed and in his right mind. And they were seized with fear. [16]Those who witnessed the incident explained to them what had happened to the possessed man and to the swine. [17]Then they began to beg him to leave their district. [18]As he was getting into the boat, the man who had been possessed pleaded to remain with him. [19]But he would not permit him but told him instead, "Go home[¶¶] to your family and announce to them all that the Lord in his pity has done for you." [20]Then the man went off and began to proclaim in the Decapolis what Jesus had done for him; and all were amazed.

Jairus's Daughter and the Woman with a Hemorrhage.[***] [21]When Jesus had crossed again

---

intervention (Mk 4:27). Mysteriously it produces **blade** and **ear** and **full grain** (Mk 4:28). Thus the kingdom of God initiated by Jesus in proclaiming the word develops quietly yet powerfully until it is fully established by him at the final judgment (Mk 4:29); cf. Rev 14:15.

*[4:32] The universality of the kingdom of God is indicated here; cf. Ez 17:23; 31:6; Dn 4:17–19.

†[4:35–5:43] After the chapter on parables, Mark narrates four miracle stories: Mk 4:35–41; 5:1–20; and two joined together in Mk 5:21–43. See also notes on Mt 8:23–34 and 9:8–26.

‡[4:39] **Quiet! Be still!**: as in the case of silencing a demon (Mk 1:25), Jesus rebukes the wind and subdues the turbulence of the sea by a mere word; see note on Mt 8:26.

§[4:41] Jesus is here depicted as exercising power over wind and sea. In the Christian community this event was seen as a sign of Jesus' saving presence amid persecutions that threatened its existence.

¶[5:1] **The territory of the Gerasenes**: the reference is to pagan territory; cf. Is 65:1. Another reading is "Gadarenes"; see note on Mt 8:28.

**[5:2–6] The man was an outcast from society, dominated by unclean spirits (Mk 5:8, 13), living among the tombs. The prostration before Jesus (Mk 5:6) indicates Jesus' power over evil spirits.

††[5:7] **What have you to do with me?**: cf. Mk 1:24 and see note on Jn 2:4.

‡‡[5:9] **Legion is my name**: the demons were numerous and the condition of the possessed man was extremely serious; cf. Mt 12:45.

§§[5:11] **Herd of swine**: see note on Mt 8:30.

¶¶[5:19] **Go home**: Jesus did not accept the man's request to **remain with him** as a disciple (Mk 5:18), yet invited him to announce to his own people what the Lord had done for him, i.e., proclaim the gospel message to his pagan family; cf. Mk 1:14, 39; 3:14; 13:10.

***[5:21–43] The story of the raising to life of Jairus's daughter is divided into two parts: Mk 5:21–24; 5:35–43.

---

x. [4:26–29] Jas 5:7. y. [4:30–32] Mt 13:31–32; Lk 13:18–19. z. [4:33–34] Mt 13:34. a. [4:35–40] Mt 8:18, 23–37; Lk 8:22–25. b. [4:41] 1:27. c. [5:1–20] Mt 8:28–34; Lk 8:26–39.

d. [5:9] Mt 12:45; Lk 8:2; 11:26.

[in the boat] to the other side, a large crowd gathered around him, and he stayed close to the sea.ᵉ ²²One of the synagogue officials, named Jairus, came forward.ᶠ Seeing him he fell at his feet ²³and pleaded earnestly with him, saying, "My daughter is at the point of death. Please, come lay your hands on her* that she may get well and live." ²⁴He went off with him, and a large crowd followed him and pressed upon him.

²⁵There was a woman afflicted with hemorrhages for twelve years. ²⁶She had suffered greatly at the hands of many doctors and had spent all that she had. Yet she was not helped but only grew worse. ²⁷She had heard about Jesus and came up behind him in the crowd and touched his cloak. ²⁸†She said, "If I but touch his clothes, I shall be cured." ²⁹Immediately her flow of blood dried up. She felt in her body that she was healed of her affliction. ³⁰Jesus, aware at once that power had gone out from him, turned around in the crowd and asked, "Who has touched my clothes?" ³¹But his disciples said to him, "You see how the crowd is pressing upon you, and yet you ask, 'Who touched me?'" ³²And he looked around to see who had done it. ³³The woman, realizing what had happened to her, approached in fear and trembling. She fell down before Jesus and told him the whole truth. ³⁴He said to her, "Daughter, your faith has saved you. Go in peace and be cured of your affliction."ᵍ

³⁵‡While he was still speaking, people from the synagogue official's house arrived and said, "Your daughter has died; why trouble the teacher any longer?" ³⁶Disregarding the message that was reported, Jesus said to the synagogue official, "Do not be afraid; just have faith." ³⁷He did not allow anyone to accompany him inside except Peter, James, and John, the brother of James. ³⁸When they arrived at the house of the synagogue official, he caught sight of a commotion, people weeping and wailing loudly. ³⁹§ʰSo he went in and said to them, "Why this commotion and weeping? The child is not dead but asleep." ⁴⁰And they ridiculed him. Then he put

them all out. He took along the child's father and mother and those who were with him and entered the room where the child was. ⁴¹¶He took the child by the hand and said to her, "*Talitha koum*," which means, "Little girl, I say to you, arise!" ⁴²The girl, a child of twelve, arose immediately and walked around. [At that] they were utterly astounded. ⁴³He gave strict orders that no one should know this and said that she should be given something to eat.

CHAPTER 6

The Rejection at Nazareth. ¹ⁱHe departed from there and came to his native place,** accompanied by his disciples. ²††When the sabbath came he began to teach in the synagogue, and many who heard him were astonished. They said, "Where did this man get all this? What kind of wisdom has been given him? What mighty deeds are wrought by his hands! ³Is he not the carpenter,‡‡ the son of Mary, and the brother of James and Joses and Judas and Simon? And are not his sisters here with us?" And they took offense at him. ⁴§§ᵏJesus said to them, "A prophet is not without honor except in his native place and among his own kin and in his own house." ⁵So he was not able to perform any mighty deed there,¶¶ apart from curing a few sick people by

---

Between these two separated parts the account of the cure of the hemorrhage victim (Mk 5:25–34) is interposed. This technique of intercalating or sandwiching one story within another occurs several times in Mk 3:19b–21; 3:22–30; 3:31–35; 6:6b–13; 6:14–29; 6:30; 11:12–14; 11:15–19; 11:20–25; 14:53; 14:54; 14:55–65; 14:66–73.

*[5:23] **Lay your hands on her:** this act for the purpose of healing is frequent in Mk 6:5; 7:32–35; 8:23–25; 16:18 and is also found in Mt 9:18; Lk 4:40; 13:13; Acts 9:17; 28:8.

†[5:28] Both in the case of Jairus and his daughter (Mk 5:23) and in the case of the hemorrhage victim, the inner conviction that physical contact (Mk 5:30) accompanied by faith in Jesus' saving power could effect a cure was rewarded.

‡[5:35] The faith of Jairus was put to a twofold test: (1) that his daughter might be cured and, now that she had died, (2) that she might be restored to life. His faith contrasts with the lack of faith of the crowd.

§[5:39] **Not dead but asleep:** the New Testament often refers to death as sleep (Mt 27:52; Jn 11:11; 1 Cor 15:6; 1 Thes 4:13–15); see note on Mk 9:24.

¶[5:41] **Arise:** the Greek verb *egeirein* is the verb generally used to express resurrection from death (Mk 6:14, 16; Mt 11:5; Lk 7:14) and Jesus' own resurrection (Mk 16:6; Mt 28:6; Lk 24:6).

[6:1] **His native place: the Greek word *patris* here refers to Nazareth (cf. Mk 1:9; Lk 4:16, 23–24) though it can also mean native land.

††[6:2–6] See note on Mt 13:54–58.

‡‡[6:3] **Is he not the carpenter?:** no other gospel calls Jesus a carpenter. Some witnesses have "the carpenter's son," as in Mt 13:55. **Son of Mary:** contrary to Jewish custom, which calls a man the son of his father, this expression may reflect Mark's own faith that God is the Father of Jesus (Mk 1:1, 11; 8:38; 13:32; 14:36). **The brother of James . . . Simon:** in Semitic usage, the terms "brother," "sister" are applied not only to children of the same parents, but to nephews, nieces, cousins, half-brothers, and half-sisters; cf. Gn 14:16; 29:15; Lv 10:4. While one cannot suppose that the meaning of a Greek word should be sought in the first place from Semitic usage, the Septuagint often translates the Hebrew *āh* by the Greek word *adelphos*, "brother," as in the cited passages, a fact that may argue for a similar breadth of meaning in some New Testament passages. For instance, there is no doubt that in v 17, "brother" is used of Philip, who was actually the half-brother of Herod Antipas. On the other hand, Mark may have understood the terms literally; see also Mk 3:31–32; Mt 12:46; 13:55–56; Lk 8:19; Jn 7:3, 5. The question of meaning here would not have arisen but for the faith of the church in Mary's perpetual virginity.

§§[6:4] **A prophet is not without honor except . . . in his own house:** a saying that finds parallels in other literatures, especially Jewish and Greek, but without reference to a prophet. Comparing himself to previous Hebrew prophets whom the people rejected, Jesus intimates his own eventual rejection by the nation especially in view of the dishonor his own relatives had shown him (Mk 3:21) and now his townspeople as well.

¶¶[6:5] **He was not able to perform any mighty deed there:** according to Mark, Jesus' power could not take effect because of a person's lack of faith.

---

e. [5:21] 2:13.   f. [5:22–43] Mt 9:18–26; Lk 8:41–56.   g. [5:34] Lk 7:30.   h. [5:39–40] Acts 9:40.

i. [6:1–6] Mt 13:54–58; Lk 4:16–30.   j. [6:3] 15:40; Mt 12:46; Jn 6:42.   k. [6:4] Jn 4:44.

laying his hands on them. [6]He was amazed at their lack of faith.

The Mission of the Twelve. He went around to the villages in the vicinity teaching. [7]He summoned the Twelve* and began to send them out two by two and gave them authority over unclean spirits. [8]He instructed them to take nothing for the journey but a walking stick—no food, no sack, no money in their belts. [9]They were, however, to wear sandals but not a second tunic. [10]He said to them, "Wherever you enter a house, stay there until you leave from there. [11]Whatever place does not welcome you or listen to you, leave there and shake the dust off your feet in testimony against them." [12]So they went off and preached repentance. [13]They drove out many demons, and they anointed with oil many who were sick[m] and cured them.

Herod's Opinion of Jesus.¶ [14]King Herod** heard about it, for his fame had become widespread, and people were saying,[n] "John the Baptist has been raised from the dead; that is why mighty powers are at work in him."[o] [15]Others were saying, "He is Elijah"; still others, "He is a prophet like any of the prophets."[p] [16]But when Herod learned of it, he said, "It is John whom I beheaded. He has been raised up."

The Death of John the Baptist.†† [17]Herod was the one who had John arrested and bound in prison on account of Herodias, the wife of his brother

Philip, whom he had married.[q] [18]John had said to Herod, "It is not lawful for you to have your brother's wife."[r] [19]Herodias‡‡ harbored a grudge against him and wanted to kill him but was unable to do so. [20]Herod feared John, knowing him to be a righteous and holy man, and kept him in custody. When he heard him speak he was very much perplexed, yet he liked to listen to him. [21]She had an opportunity one day when Herod, on his birthday, gave a banquet for his courtiers, his military officers, and the leading men of Galilee. [22]Herodias's own daughter came in and performed a dance that delighted Herod and his guests. The king said to the girl, "Ask of me whatever you wish and I will grant it to you." [23]He even swore [many things] to her, "I will grant you whatever you ask of me, even to half of my kingdom."[s] [24]She went out and said to her mother, "What shall I ask for?" She replied, "The head of John the Baptist." [25]The girl hurried back to the king's presence and made her request, "I want you to give me at once on a platter the head of John the Baptist." [26]The king was deeply distressed, but because of his oaths and the guests he did not wish to break his word to her. [27]So he promptly dispatched an executioner with orders to bring back his head. He went off and beheaded him in the prison. [28]He brought in the head on a platter and gave it to the girl. The girl in turn gave it to her mother. [29]When his disciples heard about it, they came and took his body and laid it in a tomb.

The Return of the Twelve. [30]The apostles§§ gathered together with Jesus and reported all they had done and taught.[u] [31]¶¶He said to them, "Come away by yourselves to a deserted place and rest a while." People were coming and going in great numbers, and they had no opportunity even to eat.[v] [32]So they went off in the boat by themselves to a deserted place.[w] [33]People saw them leaving and many came to know about it. They hastened there on foot from all the towns and arrived at the place before them.

The Feeding of the Five Thousand. [34]When he disembarked and saw the vast crowd, his heart was moved with pity for them, for they were like sheep without a shepherd; and he began to teach them many things. [35]***By now it was already

* [6:7–13] The preparation for the mission of the Twelve is seen in the call (1) of the first disciples to be fishers of men (Mk 1:16–20), (2) then of the Twelve set apart to be with Jesus and to receive authority to preach and expel demons (Mk 3:13–19). Now they are given the specific mission to exercise that authority in word and power as representatives of Jesus during the time of their formation.

† [6:8–9] In Mark the use of a **walking stick** (Mk 6:8) and **sandals** (Mk 6:9) is permitted, but not in Mt 10:10 nor in Lk 10:4. Mark does not mention any prohibition to visit pagan territory and to enter Samaritan towns. These differences indicate a certain adaptation to conditions in and outside of Palestine and suggest in Mark's account a later activity in the church. For the rest, Jesus required of his apostles a total dependence on God for food and shelter; cf. Mk 6:35–44; 8:1–9.

‡ [6:10–11] Remaining in the same house as a guest (Mk 6:10) rather than moving to another offering greater comfort avoided any impression of seeking advantage for oneself and prevented dishonor to one's host. Shaking the dust off one's feet served as testimony against those who rejected the call to repentance.

§ [6:13] **Anointed with oil . . . cured them:** a common medicinal remedy, but seen here as a vehicle of divine power for healing.

¶ [6:14–16] The various opinions about Jesus anticipate the theme of his identity that reaches its climax in Mk 8:27–30.

** [6:14] **King Herod:** see note on Mt 14:1.

†† [6:17–29] Similarities are to be noted between Mark's account of the imprisonment and death of John the Baptist in this pericope, and that of the passion of Jesus (Mk 15:1–47). Herod and Pilate, each in turn, acknowledges the holiness of life of one over whom he unjustly exercises the power of condemnation and death (Mk 6:26–27; 15:9–10, 14–15). The hatred of Herodias toward John parallels that of the Jewish leaders toward Jesus. After the deaths of John and of Jesus, well-disposed persons request the bodies of the victims of Herod and of Pilate in turn to give them respectful burial (Mk 6:29; 15:45–46).

‡‡ [6:19] **Herodias:** see note on Mt 14:3.

§§ [6:30] **Apostles:** here, and in some manuscripts at Mk 3:14, Mark calls apostles (i.e., those sent forth) the Twelve whom Jesus sends as his emissaries, empowering them to preach, to expel demons, and to cure the sick (Mk 6:13). Only after Pentecost is the title used in the technical sense.

¶¶ [6:31–34] The withdrawal of Jesus with his disciples to a desert place to rest attracts a great number of people to follow them. Toward this people of the new exodus Jesus is moved with pity; he satisfies their spiritual hunger by teaching them many things, thus gradually showing himself the faithful shepherd of a new Israel; cf. Nm 27:17; Ez 34:15.

*** [6:35–44] See note on Mt 14:13–21. Compare this section with Mk 8:1–9. The various accounts of the multiplication

l. [6:7–11] Mt 10:1, 9–14; Lk 9:15; 10:4–11.   m. [6:13] Jas 5:14.   n. [6:14–29] Mt 14:1–12.   o. [6:14–16] Lk 9:7–8.   p. [6:15] Mt 16:14.

q. [6:17] Lk 3:19–20.   r. [6:18] Lv 18:16.   s. [6:23] Est 5:3.   t. [6:27–28] Lk 9:9.   u. [6:30] Lk 9:10.   v. [6:31] 3:20; Mt 14:13; Lk 9:10.   w. [6:32–44] Mt 14:13–21; Lk 9:10–17; Jn 6:1–13.

late and his disciples approached him and said, "This is a deserted place and it is already very late. [36]Dismiss them so that they can go to the surrounding farms and villages and buy themselves something to eat." [37]He said to them in reply, "Give them some food yourselves." But they said to him, "Are we to buy two hundred days' wages worth of food and give it to them to eat?" [38]He asked them, "How many loaves do you have? Go and see." And when they had found out they said, "Five loaves and two fish." [39]So he gave orders to have them sit down in groups on the green grass. [40]*The people took their places in rows by hundreds and by fifties. [41]Then, taking the five loaves and the two fish and looking up to heaven, he said the blessing, broke the loaves, and gave them to [his] disciples to set before the people; he also divided the two fish among them all.[†] [42]They all ate and were satisfied. [43]And they picked up twelve wicker baskets full of fragments and what was left of the fish. [44]Those who ate [of the loaves] were five thousand men.

The Walking on the Water.[‡] [45]Then he made his disciples get into the boat[x] and precede him to the other side toward Bethsaida,[§] while he dismissed the crowd. [46]¶And when he had taken leave of them, he went off to the mountain to pray. [47]When it was evening, the boat was far out on the sea and he was alone on shore. [48]Then he saw that they were tossed about while rowing, for the wind was against them. About the fourth watch of the night, he came toward them walking on the sea.** He meant to pass by them. [49]But when they saw him walking on the sea, they thought it was a ghost and cried out. [50]††They had all seen him and were terrified. But at once he spoke with them, "Take courage, it is I, do not be afraid!" [51]He got into the boat with them and the wind died down. They were [completely]

astounded. [52]They had not understood the incident of the loaves.[‡‡] On the contrary, their hearts were hardened.[y]

The Healings at Gennesaret. [53]zAfter making the crossing, they came to land at Gennesaret and tied up there. [54]As they were leaving the boat, people immediately recognized him. [55]They scurried about the surrounding country and began to bring in the sick on mats to wherever they heard he was. [56]Whatever villages or towns or countryside he entered, they laid the sick in the marketplaces and begged him that they might touch only the tassel on his cloak; and as many as touched it were healed.[a]

CHAPTER 7

The Tradition of the Elders.[§§] [1]Now when the Pharisees with some scribes who had come from Jerusalem gathered around him,[b] [2]they observed that some of his disciples ate their meals with unclean, that is, unwashed, hands. [3](For the Pharisees and, in fact, all Jews, do not eat without carefully washing their hands,[¶¶] keeping the tradition of the elders. [4]And on coming from the marketplace they do not eat without purifying themselves. And there are many other things that they have traditionally observed, the purification of cups and jugs and kettles [and beds].) [5]So the Pharisees and scribes questioned him, "Why do your disciples not follow the tradition of the elders[***] but instead eat a meal with unclean hands?" [6]He responded, "Well did Isaiah prophesy about you hypocrites, as it is written:[c]

'This people honors me with their lips,
    but their hearts are far from me;
[7] In vain do they worship me,
    teaching as doctrines human
        precepts.'

---

of loaves and fishes, two each in Mark and in Matthew and one each in Luke and in John, indicate the wide interest of the early church in their eucharistic gatherings; see, e.g., Mk 6:41; 8:6; 14:22; and recall also the sign of bread in Ex 16; Dt 8:3–16; Ps 78:24–25; 105:40; Wis 16:20–21.

*[6:40] **The people . . . in rows by hundreds and by fifties:** reminiscent of the groupings of Israelites encamped in the desert (Ex 18:21–25) and of the wilderness tradition of the prophets depicting the transformation of the wasteland into pastures where the true shepherd feeds his flock (Ez 34:25–26) and makes his people beneficiaries of messianic grace.

†[6:41] On the language of this verse as eucharistic (cf. Mk 14:22), see notes on Mt 14:19, 20. Jesus observed the Jewish table ritual of blessing God before partaking of food.

‡[6:45–52] See note on Mt 14:22–33.

§[6:45] **To the other side toward Bethsaida:** a village at the northeastern shore of the Sea of Galilee.

¶[6:46] **He went off to the mountain to pray:** see Mk 1:35–38. In Jn 6:15 Jesus withdrew to evade any involvement in the false messianic hopes of the multitude.

[6:48] **Walking on the sea: see notes on Mt 14:22–33 and on Jn 6:19.

††[6:50] **It is I, do not be afraid!:** literally, "I am." This may reflect the divine revelatory formula of Ex 3:14; Is 41:4, 10, 14; 43:1–3, 10, 13. Mark implies the hidden identity of Jesus as Son of God.

‡‡[6:52] **They had not understood . . . the loaves:** the revelatory character of this sign and that of the walking on the sea completely escaped the disciples. **Their hearts were hardened:** in Mk 3:5–6 hardness of heart was attributed to those who did not accept Jesus and plotted his death. Here the same disposition prevents the disciples from comprehending Jesus' self-revelation through signs; cf. Mk 8:17.

§§[7:1–23] See note on Mt 15:1–20. Against the Pharisees' narrow, legalistic, and external practices of piety in matters of purification (Mk 7:2–5), external worship (Mk 7:6–7), and observance of commandments, Jesus sets in opposition the true moral intent of the divine law (Mk 7:8–13). But he goes beyond contrasting the law and Pharisaic interpretation of it. The parable of Mk 7:14–15 in effect sets aside the law itself in respect to clean and unclean food. He thereby opens the way for unity between Jew and Gentile in the kingdom of God, intimated by Jesus' departure for pagan territory beyond Galilee. For similar contrast see Mk 2:1–3:6; 3:20–35; 6:1–6.

¶¶[7:3] **Carefully washing their hands:** refers to ritual purification.

***[7:5] **Tradition of the elders:** the body of detailed, unwritten, human laws regarded by the scribes and Pharisees to have the same binding force as that of the Mosaic law; cf. Gal 1:14.

---

x. [6:45–51] Mt 14:22–32; Jn 6:15–21.

y. [6:52] 4:13.   z. [6:53–56] Mt 14:34–36.   a. [6:56] 5:27–28; Acts 5:15.   b. [7:1–23] Mt 15:1–20.   c. [7:6] Is 29:13.

⁸You disregard God's commandment but cling to human tradition." ⁹He went on to say, "How well you have set aside the commandment of God in order to uphold your tradition! ¹⁰For Moses said, 'Honor your father and your mother,' and 'Whoever curses father or mother shall die.'ᵈ ¹¹Yet you say, 'If a person says to father or mother, "Any support you might have had from me is *qorban*"ᵉ (meaning, dedicated to God), ¹²you allow him to do nothing more for his father or mother. ¹³You nullify the word of God in favor of your tradition that you have handed on. And you do many such things." ¹⁴eHe summoned the crowd again and said to them, "Hear me, all of you, and understand. ¹⁵Nothing that enters one from outside can defile that person; but the things that come out from within are what defile." [¹⁶]†

¹⁷‡ᶠWhen he got home away from the crowd his disciples questioned him about the parable. ¹⁸He said to them, "Are even you likewise without understanding? Do you not realize that everything that goes into a person from outside cannot defile, ¹⁹§gsince it enters not the heart but the stomach and passes out into the latrine?" (Thus he declared all foods clean.) ²⁰"But what comes out of a person, that is what defiles. ²¹ʰFrom within people, from their hearts, come evil thoughts, unchastity, theft, murder, ²²adultery, greed, malice, deceit, licentiousness, envy, blasphemy, arrogance, folly. ²³All these evils come from within and they defile."

The Syrophoenician Woman's Faith. ²⁴ⁱFrom that place he went off to the district of Tyre.ˢ He entered a house and wanted no one to know about it, but he could not escape notice. ²⁵Soon a woman whose daughter had an unclean spirit heard about him. She came and fell at his feet. ²⁶The woman was a Greek, a Syrophoenician by birth, and she begged him to drive the demon out of her daughter.ʲ ²⁷He said to her, "Let the

children be fed first." For it is not right to take the food of the children and throw it to the dogs." ²⁸She replied and said to him, "Lord, even the dogs under the table eat the children's scraps." ²⁹Then he said to her, "For saying this, you may go. The demon has gone out of your daughter." ³⁰When the woman went home, she found the child lying in bed and the demon gone.

The Healing of a Deaf Man. ³¹kAgain he left the district of Tyre and went by way of Sidon to the Sea of Galilee, into the district of the Decapolis. ³²And people brought to him a deaf man who had a speech impediment and begged him to lay his hand on him. ³³He took him off by himself away from the crowd. He put his finger into the man's ears and, spitting, touched his tongue; ³⁴then he looked up to heaven and groaned, and said to him, "*Ephphatha!*" (that is, "Be opened!") ³⁵And [immediately] the man's ears were opened, his speech impediment was removed, and he spoke plainly. ³⁶††He ordered them not to tell anyone. But the more he ordered them not to, the more they proclaimed it. ³⁷They were exceedingly astonished and they said, "He has done all things well. He makes the deaf hear and [the] mute speak."ˡ

CHAPTER 8

The Feeding of the Four Thousand.‡‡ ¹In those days when there again was a great crowd without anything to eat,ᵐ he summoned the disciples and said, ²"My heart is moved with pity for the crowd, because they have been with me now for three days and have nothing to eat. ³If I send them away hungry to their homes, they will collapse on the way, and some of them have come a great distance." ⁴His disciples answered him, "Where can anyone get enough bread to satisfy them here in this deserted place?" ⁵Still he asked them, "How many loaves do you have?" "Seven," they replied. ⁶§§He ordered the crowd to sit down on the ground. Then, taking the seven loaves

---

*[7:11] **Qorban**: a formula for a gift to God, dedicating the offering to the temple, so that the giver might continue to use it for himself but not give it to others, even needy parents.

†[7:16] Mk 7:16, "Anyone who has ears to hear ought to hear," is omitted because it is lacking in some of the best Greek manuscripts and was probably transferred here by scribes from Mk 4:9, 23.

‡[7:17] **Away from the crowd . . . the parable**: in this context of privacy the term *parable* refers to something hidden, about to be revealed to the disciples; cf. Mk 4:10–11, 34. Jesus sets the Mosaic food laws in the context of the kingdom of God where they are abrogated, and he declares moral defilement the only cause of uncleanness.

§[7:19] (**Thus he declared all foods clean**): if this bold declaration goes back to Jesus, its force was not realized among Jewish Christians in the early church; cf. Acts 10:1–11:18.

¶[7:24–37] The withdrawal of Jesus to the district of Tyre may have been for a respite (Mk 7:24), but he soon moved onward to Sidon and, by way of the Sea of Galilee, to the Decapolis. These districts provided a Gentile setting for the extension of his ministry of healing because the people there acknowledged his power (Mk 7:29, 37). The actions attributed to Jesus (Mk 7:33–35) were also used by healers of the time.

**[7:27–28] The figure of a household in which children at table are fed first and then their leftover food is given to the dogs under the table is used effectively to acknowledge the prior claim of the Jews to the ministry of Jesus; however, Jesus accedes to the Gentile woman's plea for the cure of her afflicted daughter because of her faith.

††[7:36] **The more they proclaimed it**: the same verb *proclaim* attributed here to the crowd in relation to the miracles of Jesus is elsewhere used in Mark for the preaching of the gospel on the part of Jesus, of his disciples, and of the Christian community (Mk 1:14; 13:10; 14:9). Implied in the action of the crowd is a recognition of the salvific mission of Jesus; see note on Mt 11:5–6.

‡‡[8:1–10] The two accounts of the multiplication of loaves and fishes (Mk 8:1–10; 6:31–44) have eucharistic significance. Their similarity of structure and themes but dissimilarity of detail are considered by many to refer to a single event that, however, developed in two distinct traditions, one Jewish Christian and the other Gentile Christian, since Jesus in Mark's presentation (Mk 7:24–37) has extended his saving mission to the Gentiles.

§§[8:6] See note on Mk 6:41.

---

d. [7:10] Ex 21:17; Lv 20:9; Dt 5:16; Eph 6:2. e. [7:14–23] Mt 15:10–20. f. [7:17] 4:10, 13. g. [7:19] Acts 10:15. h. [7:21] Jer 17:9. i. [7:24–30] Mt 15:21–28. j. [7:26] Mt 8:29.

k. [7:31–37] Mt 15:29–31. l. [7:37] Mt 15:31. m. [8:1–10] 6:34–44; Mt 15:32–39.

he gave thanks, broke them, and gave them to his disciples to distribute, and they distributed them to the crowd. [7]They also had a few fish. He said the blessing over them and ordered them distributed also. [8]They ate and were satisfied. They picked up the fragments left over—seven baskets. [9]There were about four thousand people.

He dismissed them [10]and got into the boat with his disciples and came to the region of Dalmanutha.

The Demand for a Sign. [11]*The Pharisees came forward and began to argue with him,[n] seeking from him a sign from heaven to test him.[o] [12]He sighed from the depth of his spirit and said, "Why does this generation seek a sign? Amen, I say to you, no sign will be given to this generation." [13]Then he left them, got into the boat again, and went off to the other shore.

The Leaven of the Pharisees. [14p]They had forgotten to bring bread, and they had only one loaf with them in the boat. [15†]He enjoined them, "Watch out, guard against the leaven of the Pharisees and the leaven of Herod." [16]They concluded among themselves that it was because they had no bread. [17]When he became aware of this he said to them, "Why do you conclude that it is because you have no bread? Do you not yet understand or comprehend? Are your hearts hardened?[q] [18]Do you have eyes and not see, ears and not hear? And do you not remember,[r] [19]when I broke the five loaves for the five thousand, how many wicker baskets full of fragments you picked up?" They answered him, "Twelve." [20]"When I broke the seven loaves for the four thousand, how many full baskets of fragments did you pick up?" They answered [him], "Seven." [21]He said to them, "Do you still not understand?"

The Blind Man of Bethsaida. [‡] [22]When they arrived at Bethsaida, they brought to him a blind man and begged him to touch him. [23]He took the blind man by the hand and led him outside the village. Putting spittle on his eyes he laid his hands on him and asked, "Do you see anything?"[s] [24]Looking up he replied, "I see people looking like trees and walking." [25]Then he

laid hands on his eyes a second time and he saw clearly; his sight was restored and he could see everything distinctly. [26]Then he sent him home and said, "Do not even go into the village."

III. THE MYSTERY BEGINS TO BE REVEALED

Peter's Confession About Jesus.[§] [27]Now Jesus and his disciples set out for the villages of Caesarea Philippi.[t] Along the way he asked his disciples, "Who do people say that I am?" [28]They said in reply, "John the Baptist, others Elijah, still others one of the prophets." [29]And he asked them, "But who do you say that I am?" Peter said to him in reply, "You are the Messiah." [30]Then he warned them not to tell anyone about him.

The First Prediction of the Passion. [31]*He began to teach them that the Son of Man[u] must suffer greatly and be rejected by the elders, the chief priests, and the scribes, and be killed, and rise after three days. [32]He spoke this openly. Then Peter took him aside and began to rebuke him. [33]At this he turned around and, looking at his disciples, rebuked Peter and said, "Get behind me, Satan. You are thinking not as God does, but as human beings do."

The Conditions of Discipleship. [34]He summoned the crowd with his disciples and said[**] to them, "Whoever wishes to come after me must

---

§[8:27–30] This episode is the turning point in Mark's account of Jesus in his public ministry. Popular opinions concur in regarding him as a prophet. The disciples by contrast believe him to be the Messiah. Jesus acknowledges this identification but prohibits them from making his messianic office known to avoid confusing it with ambiguous contemporary ideas on the nature of that office. See further the notes on Mt 16:13–20.

¶[8:31] Son of Man: an enigmatic title. It is used in Dn 7:13–14 has a symbol of "the saints of the Most High," the faithful Israelites who receive the everlasting kingdom from the Ancient One (God). They are represented by a human figure that contrasts with the various beasts who represent the previous kingdoms of the earth. In the Jewish apocryphal books of 1 Enoch and 4 Ezra the "Son of Man" is not, as in Daniel, a group, but a unique figure of extraordinary spiritual endowments, who will be revealed as the one through whom the everlasting kingdom decreed by God will be established. It is possible though doubtful that this individualization of the Son of Man figure had been made in Jesus' time, and therefore his use of the title in that sense is questionable. Of itself, this expression means simply a human being, or, indefinitely, someone, and there are evidences of this use in pre-Christian times. Its use in the New Testament is probably due to Jesus' speaking of himself in that way, "a human being," and the later church's taking this in the sense of the Jewish apocrypha and applying it to him with that meaning. **Rejected by the elders, the chief priests, and the scribes**: the supreme council called the Sanhedrin was made up of seventy-one members of these three groups and presided over by the high priest. It exercised authority over the Jews in religious matters. See note on Mt 8:20.

[8:34–35] This utterance of Jesus challenges all believers to authentic discipleship and total commitment to himself through self-renunciation and acceptance of the cross of suffering, even to the sacrifice of life itself. **Whoever wishes to save his life will lose it . . . will save it: an expression of the ambivalence of life and its contrasting destiny. Life seen as mere self-centered earthly existence and lived in denial of Christ ends in destruction, but when lived in loyalty to Christ, despite earthly death, it arrives at fullness of life.

---

*[8:11–12] The objection of the Pharisees that Jesus' miracles are unsatisfactory for proving the arrival of God's kingdom is comparable to the request of the crowd for a sign in Jn 6:30–31. Jesus' response shows that a sign originating in human demand will not be provided; cf. Nm 14:11, 22.

†[8:15] The leaven of the Pharisees . . . of Herod: the corruptive action of leaven (1 Cor 5:6–8; Gal 5:9) was an apt symbol of the evil dispositions both of the Pharisees (Mk 8:11–13; 7:5–13) and of Herod (Mk 6:14–29) toward Jesus. The disciples of Jesus are warned against sharing such rebellious attitudes toward Jesus; cf. Mk 8:17, 21.

‡[8:22–26] Jesus' actions and the gradual cure of the blind man probably have the same purpose as in the case of the deaf man (Mk 7:31–37). Some commentators regard the cure as an intended symbol of the gradual enlightenment of the disciples concerning Jesus' messiahship.

---

n. [8:11–13] Mt 12:38–39; 16:1–4.   o. [8:11] Lk 11:16.   p. [8:14–21] Mt 16:5–12; Lk 12:1.   q. [8:17] 4:13.   r. [8:18] Jer 5:21; Ez 12:2.   s. [8:23] 7:33; Jn 9:6.

t. [8:27–30] Mt 16:13–20; Lk 9:18–21.   u. [8:31–38] Mt 16:21–27; Lk 9:22–26.

deny himself, take up his cross, and follow me.ᵛ ³⁵For whoever wishes to save his life will lose it, but whoever loses his life for my sake and that of the gospel* will save it.ʷ ³⁶What profit is there for one to gain the whole world and forfeit his life? ³⁷What could one give in exchange for his life? ³⁸Whoever is ashamed of me and of my words in this faithless and sinful generation, the Son of Man will be ashamed of when he comes in his Father's glory with the holy angels."ˣ

CHAPTER 9

¹ᵗʸHe also said to them, "Amen, I say to you, there are some standing here who will not taste death until they see that the kingdom of God has come in power."

The Transfiguration of Jesus.‡ ²After six days Jesus took Peter, James, and John and led them up a high mountain apart by themselves.ᶻ And he was transfigured before them, ³and his clothes became dazzling white, such as no fuller on earth could bleach them. ⁴Then Elijah appeared to them along with Moses, and they were conversing with Jesus. ⁵⁹Then Peter said to Jesus in reply, "Rabbi, it is good that we are here! Let us make three tents: one for you, one for Moses, and one for Elijah." ⁶He hardly knew what to say, they were so terrified. ⁷Then a cloud came, casting a shadow over them;⁵ then from the cloud came a voice, "This is my beloved Son. Listen to him." ⁸Suddenly, looking around, they no longer saw anyone but Jesus alone with them.

The Coming of Elijah. ⁹As they were coming down from the mountain, he charged them not

to relate what they had seen to anyone, except when the Son of Man had risen from the dead.ᵃ ¹⁰So they kept the matter to themselves, questioning what rising from the dead meant. ¹¹ᵇThen they asked him, "Why do the scribes say that Elijah must come first?" ¹²He told them, "Elijah will indeed come first and restore all things, yet how is it written regarding the Son of Man that he must suffer greatly and be treated with contempt? ¹³But I tell you that Elijah has come and they did to him whatever they pleased, as it is written of him."ᶜ

The Healing of a Boy with a Demon.†† ¹⁴When they came to the disciples,ᵈ they saw a large crowd around them and scribes arguing with them. ¹⁵Immediately on seeing him, the whole crowd was utterly amazed. They ran up to him and greeted him. ¹⁶He asked them, "What are you arguing about with them?" ¹⁷Someone from the crowd answered him, "Teacher, I have brought to you my son possessed by a mute spirit. ¹⁸Wherever it seizes him, it throws him down; he foams at the mouth, grinds his teeth, and becomes rigid. I asked your disciples to drive it out, but they were unable to do so." ¹⁹He said to them in reply, "O faithless generation, how long will I be with you? How long will I endure you? Bring him to me." ²⁰They brought the boy to him. And when he saw him, the spirit immediately threw the boy into convulsions. As he fell to the ground, he began to roll around and foam at the mouth. ²¹Then he questioned his father, "How long has this been happening to him?" He replied, "Since childhood. ²²It has often thrown him into fire and into water to kill him. But if you can do anything, have compassion on us and help us." ²³Jesus said to him, "'If you can!' Everything is possible to one who has faith." ²⁴Then the boy's father cried out, "I do believe, help my unbelief!" ²⁵Jesus, on seeing a crowd rapidly gathering, rebuked the unclean spirit and said to it, "Mute and deaf spirit, I command you: come out of him and never enter him again!" ²⁶Shouting and throwing the boy into convulsions, it came out. He became like a corpse, which caused many to say, "He is dead!" ²⁷But Jesus took him by the hand, raised him, and he stood up. ²⁸When he entered the house, his disciples asked him in private, "Why could

---

*[8:35] **For my sake and that of the gospel**: Mark here, as at Mk 10:29 equates Jesus with the gospel.

†[9:1] **There are some standing . . . come in power**: understood by some to refer to the establishment by God's power of his kingdom on earth in and through the church; more likely, as understood by others, a reference to the imminent parousia.

‡[9:2–8] Mark and Mt 17:1 place the transfiguration of Jesus six days after the first prediction of his passion and death and his instruction to the disciples on the doctrine of the cross; Lk 9:28 has "about eight days." Thus the transfiguration counterbalances the prediction of the passion by affording certain of the disciples insight into the divine glory that Jesus possessed. His glory will overcome his death and that of his disciples; cf. 2 Cor 3:18; 2 Pt 1:16–19. The heavenly voice (Mk 9:7) prepares the disciples to understand that in the divine plan Jesus must die ignominiously before his messianic glory is made manifest; cf. Lk 24:25–27. See further the note on Mt 17:1–8.

§[9:5] Moses and Elijah represent, respectively, law and prophecy in the Old Testament and are linked to Mount Sinai; cf. Ex 19:16–20:17; 1 Kgs 19:2, 8–14. They now appear with Jesus as witnesses to the fulfillment of the law and the prophets taking place in the person of Jesus as he appears in glory.

⁵[9:7] **A cloud came, casting a shadow over them**: even the disciples enter into the mystery of his glorification. In the Old Testament the cloud covered the meeting tent, indicating the Lord's presence in the midst of his people (Ex 40:34–35) and came to rest upon the temple in Jerusalem at the time of its dedication (1 Kgs 8:10).

**[9:9–13] At the transfiguration of Jesus his disciples had seen Elijah. They were perplexed because, according to the rabbinical interpretation of Mal 3:23–24, Elijah was to come

first. Jesus' response shows that Elijah has come, in the person of John the Baptist, to prepare for the day of the Lord. Jesus **must suffer greatly and be treated with contempt** (Mk 9:12) like the Baptist (Mk 9:13); cf. Mk 6:17–29.

††[9:14–29] The disciples' failure to effect a cure seems to reflect unfavorably on Jesus (Mk 9:14–18, 22). In response Jesus exposes their lack of trust in God (Mk 9:19) and scores their lack of prayer (Mk 9:29), i.e., of conscious reliance on God's power when acting in Jesus' name. For Matthew, see note on Mt 17:14–20. Lk 9:37–43 centers attention on Jesus' sovereign power.

---

v. [8:34] Mt 10:38–39; 16:24–27; Lk 14:26–27.   w. [8:35] Jn 12:25.
x. [8:38] Mt 10:33; Lk 12:8.   y. [9:1] Mt 16:28; Lk 9:27.   z. [9:2–13] Mt 17:1–13; Lk 9:28–36.

a. [9:9] 8:31.   b. [9:11–12] Is 53:3; Mal 3:23.   c. [9:13] 1 Kgs 19:2–10.   d. [9:14–29] Mt 17:14–21; Lk 9:37–43.

we not drive it out?" [29]*He said to them, "This kind can only come out through prayer." **The Second Prediction of the Passion.** [30]e*They left from there and began a journey through Galilee, but he did not wish anyone to know about it.[f] [31]He was teaching his disciples and telling them, "The Son of Man is to be handed over to men and they will kill him, and three days after his death he will rise." [32]But they did not understand the saying, and they were afraid to question him.

IV. THE FULL REVELATION OF THE MYSTERY

The Greatest in the Kingdom.[†] [33]They came to Capernaum and, once inside the house, he began to ask them, "What were you arguing about on the way?"[g] [34]But they remained silent. They had been discussing among themselves on the way who was the greatest. [35]Then he sat down, called the Twelve, and said to them, "If anyone wishes to be first, he shall be the last of all and the servant of all."[h] [36]Taking a child he placed it in their midst, and putting his arms around it he said to them, [37]"Whoever receives one child such as this in my name, receives me; and whoever receives me, receives not me but the One who sent me."[i]

Another Exorcist.[‡] [38]John said to him,[j] "Teacher, we saw someone driving out demons in your name, and we tried to prevent him because he does not follow us." [39]Jesus replied, "Do not prevent him. There is no one who performs a mighty deed in my name who can at the same time speak ill of me. [40]For whoever is not against us is for us.[k] [41]Anyone who gives you a cup of water to drink because you belong to Christ, amen, I say to you, will surely not lose his reward.[l]

Temptations to Sin. [42]m*"Whoever causes one of these little ones who believe [in me] to sin, it would be better for him if a great millstone were put around his neck and he were thrown into the sea. [43]If your hand causes you to sin, cut it off. It is better for you to enter into life maimed than with two hands to go into Gehenna,[§] into

the unquenchable fire. [[44]][¶] [45]And if your foot causes you to sin, cut it off. It is better for you to enter into life crippled than with two feet to be thrown into Gehenna. [[46]] [47]And if your eye causes you to sin, pluck it out. Better for you to enter into the kingdom of God with one eye than with two eyes to be thrown into Gehenna, [48]where 'their worm does not die, and the fire is not quenched.'[n]

The Simile of Salt. [49]**"Everyone will be salted with fire. [50]Salt is good, but if salt becomes insipid, with what will you restore its flavor? Keep salt in yourselves and you will have peace with one another."[o]

CHAPTER 10

Marriage and Divorce. [1]He set out from there and went into the district of Judea [and] across the Jordan. Again crowds gathered around him and, as was his custom, he again taught them. [2]††The Pharisees approached and asked, "Is it lawful for a husband to divorce his wife?" They were testing him.[p] [3]He said to them in reply, "What did Moses command you?" [4]They replied, "Moses permitted him to write a bill of divorce and dismiss her."[q] [5]But Jesus told them, "Because of the hardness of your hearts he wrote you this commandment. [6]But from the beginning of creation, 'God made them male and female.[r] [7]For this reason a man shall leave his father and mother [and be joined to his wife],[s] [8]and the two shall become one flesh.' So they are no longer two but one flesh. [9]Therefore what God has joined together, no human being must separate." [10]In the house the disciples again questioned him about this. [11]He said to them, "Whoever divorces his wife and marries another commits adultery against her; [12]and if she divorces her husband and marries another, she commits adultery."

Blessing of the Children. [13]u*And people were bringing children to him that he might touch them, but the disciples rebuked them.[v] [14]When Jesus saw this he became indignant and said

---

¶[9:44, 46] These verses, lacking in some important early manuscripts, are here omitted as scribal additions. They simply repeat Mk 9:48 itself a modified citation of Is 66:24.

[9:49] **Everyone will be salted with fire: so the better manuscripts. Some add "every sacrifice will be salted with salt." The purifying and preservative use of salt in food (Lv 2:13) and the refinement effected through fire refer here to comparable effects in the spiritual life of the disciples of Jesus.

††[10:2–9] In the dialogue between Jesus and the Pharisees on the subject of divorce, Jesus declares that the law of Moses permitted divorce (Dt 24:1) only **because of the hardness of your hearts** (Mk 10:4–5). In citing Gn 1:27 and 2:24 Jesus proclaims permanence to be the divine intent from the beginning concerning human marriage (Mk 10:6–8). He reaffirms this with the declaration that **what God has joined together, no human being must separate** (Mk 10:9). See further the notes on Mt 5:31–32; 19:3–9.

---

*[9:29] **This kind can only come out through prayer:** a variant reading adds "and through fasting."

†[9:33–37] Mark probably intends this incident and the sayings that follow as commentary on the disciples' lack of understanding (Mk 9:32). Their role in Jesus' work is one of service, especially to the poor and lowly. Children were the symbol Jesus used for the *anawim*, the poor in spirit, the lowly in the Christian community.

‡[9:38–41] Jesus warns against jealousy and intolerance toward others, such as exorcists who do **not follow us.** The saying in Mk 9:40 is a broad principle of the divine tolerance. Even the smallest courtesies shown to those who teach in Jesus' name do not go unrewarded.

§[9:43, 45, 47] **Gehenna:** see note on Mt 5:22.

---

e. [9:30–32] 8:31; Mt 17:22–23; Lk 9:43–45.   f. [9:30] Jn 7:1.   g. [9:33–37] Mt 18:1–5; Lk 9:46–48.   h. [9:35] Mt 20:27.   i. [9:37] Mt 10:40; 18:5; Jn 13:20.   j. [9:38–41] Nm 11:28; Lk 9:49–50; 1 Cor 12:3.   k. [9:40] Mt 12:30.   l. [9:41] Mt 10:42; 1 Cor 3:23.   m. [9:42–47] Mt 5:29–30; 18:6–9; Lk 17:1–2.

n. [9:48] Is 66:24.   o. [9:50] Lv 2:13; Mt 5:13; Lk 14:34–35; Col 4:6.   p. [10:2–12] Mt 19:3–9.   q. [10:4] Dt 24:1–4.   r. [10:6] Gn 1:27.   s. [10:7–8] Gn 2:24; 1 Cor 6:16; Eph 5:31.   t. [10:11–12] Mt 5:32; Lk 16:18; 1 Cor 7:10–11.   u. [10:13–16] Mt 19:13–15; Lk 18:15–17.   v. [10:13] Lk 9:47.

to them, "Let the children come to me; do not prevent them, for the kingdom of God belongs to such as these. ¹⁵Amen, I say to you, whoever does not accept the kingdom of God like a child* will not enter it."ʷ ¹⁶Then he embraced them and blessed them, placing his hands on them.

The Rich Man. ¹⁷ˣAs he was setting out on a journey, a man ran up, knelt down before him, and asked him, "Good teacher, what must I do to inherit eternal life?" ¹⁸Jesus answered him, "Why do you call me good?† No one is good but God alone. ¹⁹You know the commandments: 'You shall not kill; you shall not commit adultery; you shall not steal; you shall not bear false witness; you shall not defraud; honor your father and your mother.'ʸ ²⁰He replied and said to him, "Teacher, all of these I have observed from my youth." ²¹Jesus, looking at him, loved him and said to him, "You are lacking in one thing. Go, sell what you have, and give to [the] poor and you will have treasure in heaven; then come, follow me." ²²At that statement his face fell, and he went away sad, for he had many possessions.

²³‡Jesus looked around and said to his disciples, "How hard it is for those who have wealth to enter the kingdom of God!"ᶻ ²⁴The disciples were amazed at his words. So Jesus again said to them in reply, "Children, how hard it is to enter the kingdom of God! ²⁵It is easier for a camel to pass through [the] eye of [a] needle than for one who is rich to enter the kingdom of God." ²⁶They were exceedingly astonished and said among themselves, "Then who can be saved?" ²⁷Jesus looked at them and said, "For human beings it is impossible, but not for God. All things are possible for God." ²⁸Peter began to say to him, "We have given up everything and followed you." ²⁹Jesus said, "Amen, I say to you, there is no one who has given up house or brothers or sisters or mother or father or children or lands for my sake and for the sake of the gospel ³⁰who will not receive a hundred times more now in this present age: houses and brothers and sisters and mothers and children and lands, with persecutions, and eternal life in the age to come. ³¹But many that are first will be last, and [the] last will be first."ᵃ

The Third Prediction of the Passion. ³²ᵇThey were on the way, going up to Jerusalem, and Jesus went ahead of them. They were amazed, and those who followed were afraid. Taking the Twelve aside again, he began to tell them what was going to happen to him. ³³"Behold, we are going up to Jerusalem, and the Son of Man will be handed over to the chief priests and the scribes, and they will condemn him to death and hand him over to the Gentiles ³⁴who will mock him, spit upon him, scourge him, and put him to death, but after three days he will rise."

Ambition of James and John. ³⁵ᶜThen James and John, the sons of Zebedee, came to him and said to him, "Teacher, we want you to do for us whatever we ask of you." ³⁶He replied, "What do you wish [me] to do for you?" ³⁷They answered him, "Grant that in your glory we may sit one at your right and the other at your left." ³⁸ˢᵈJesus said to them, "You do not know what you are asking. Can you drink the cup that I drink or be baptized with the baptism with which I am baptized?" ³⁹They said to him, "We can." Jesus said to them, "The cup that I drink, you will drink, and with the baptism with which I am baptized, you will be baptized; ⁴⁰but to sit at my right or at my left is not mine to give but is for those for whom it has been prepared." ⁴¹When the ten heard this, they became indignant at James and John. ⁴²Jesus summoned them and said to them,ᵉ "You know that those who are recognized as rulers over the Gentiles lord it over them, and their great ones make their authority over them felt. ⁴³But it shall not be so among you. Rather, whoever wishes to be great among you will be your servant; ⁴⁴whoever wishes to be first among you will be the slave of all. ⁴⁵For the Son of Man did not come to be served but to serve and to give his life as a ransom for many."

The Blind Bartimaeus.⁎⁎ ⁴⁶They came to Jericho.ᶠ And as he was leaving Jericho with his disciples and a sizable crowd, Bartimaeus, a blind man, the son of Timaeus, sat by the roadside begging. ⁴⁷On hearing that it was Jesus of Nazareth, he

---

*[10:15] **Whoever does not accept the kingdom of God like a child:** i.e., in total dependence upon and obedience to the gospel; cf. Mt 18:3–4.

†[10:18] **Why do you call me good?:** Jesus repudiates the term "good" for himself and directs it to God, the source of all goodness who alone can grant the gift of eternal life; cf. Mt 19:16–17.

‡[10:23–27] In the Old Testament wealth and material goods are considered a sign of God's favor (Jb 1:10; Ps 128:1–2; Is 3:10). The words of Jesus in Mk 10:23–25 provoke astonishment among the disciples because of their apparent contradiction of the Old Testament concept (Mk 10:24, 26). Since wealth, power, and merit generate false security, Jesus rejects them utterly as a claim to enter the kingdom. Achievement of salvation is beyond human capability and depends solely on the goodness of God who offers it as a gift (Mk 10:27).

§[10:38–40] **Can you drink the cup . . . I am baptized?:** the metaphor of drinking the cup is used in the Old Testament to refer to acceptance of the destiny assigned by God; see note on Psalm 11:6. In Jesus' case, this involves divine judgment on sin that Jesus the innocent one is to expiate on behalf of the guilty (Mk 14:24; Is 53:5). His baptism is to be his crucifixion and death for the salvation of the human race; cf. Lk 12:50. The request of James and John for a share in the glory (Mk 10:35–37) must of necessity involve a share in Jesus' sufferings, the endurance of tribulation and suffering for the gospel (Mk 10:39). The authority of assigning places of honor in the kingdom is reserved to God (Mk 10:40).

¶[10:42–45] Whatever authority is to be exercised by the disciples must, like that of Jesus, be rendered as service to others (Mk 10:45) rather than for personal aggrandizement (Mk 10:42–44). The service of Jesus is his passion and death for the sins of the human race (Mk 10:45); cf. Mk 14:24; Is 53:11–12; Mt 26:28; Lk 22:19–20.

⁎⁎[10:46–52] See notes on Mt 9:27–31 and 20:29–34.

---

w. [10:15] Mt 18:3.   x. [10:17–31] Mt 19:16–30; Lk 18:18–30. y. [10:19] Ex 20:12–16; Dt 5:16–21. z. [10:23] Prv 11:28. a. [10:31] Mt 19:30; Lk 13:30.

b. [10:32–34] 8:31; Mt 20:17–19; Lk 18:31–33. c. [10:35–45] Mt 20:20–28. d. [10:38] Lk 12:50. e. [10:42–45] Lk 22:25–27. f. [10:46–52] Mt 20:29–34; Lk 18:35–43.

began to cry out and say, "Jesus, son of David, have pity on me." [48]And many rebuked him, telling him to be silent. But he kept calling out all the more, "Son of David, have pity on me." [49]Jesus stopped and said, "Call him." So they called the blind man, saying to him, "Take courage; get up, he is calling you." [50]He threw aside his cloak, sprang up, and came to Jesus. [51]Jesus said to him in reply, "What do you want me to do for you?" The blind man replied to him, "Master, I want to see." [52]Jesus told him, "Go your way; your faith has saved you." Immediately he received his sight and followed him on the way.

CHAPTER 11 ·

The Entry into Jerusalem.[*] [1]When they drew near to Jerusalem,[g] to Bethphage and Bethany at the Mount of Olives, he sent two of his disciples [2]and said to them, "Go into the village opposite you, and immediately on entering it, you will find a colt tethered on which no one has ever sat. Untie it and bring it here. [3]If anyone should say to you, 'Why are you doing this?' reply, 'The Master has need of it and will send it back here at once.'" [4]So they went off and found a colt tethered at a gate outside on the street, and they untied it. [5]Some of the bystanders said to them, "What are you doing, untying the colt?" [6]They answered them just as Jesus had told them to, and they permitted them to do it. [7]So they brought the colt to Jesus and put their cloaks over it. And he sat on it. [8]Many people spread their cloaks on the road, and others spread leafy branches that they had cut from the fields. [9]Those preceding him as well as those following kept crying out:[h]

"Hosanna!
    Blessed is he who comes in the
      name of the Lord!
[10]   Blessed is the kingdom of our father
      David that is to come!
Hosanna in the highest!"

[11]He entered Jerusalem and went into the temple area. He looked around at everything and, since it was already late, went out to Bethany with the Twelve.[i]

Jesus Curses a Fig Tree.[†] [12]The next day as they were leaving Bethany he was hungry.[j] [13]Seeing from a distance a fig tree in leaf, he went over to see if he could find anything on it. When he reached it he found nothing but leaves; it was not the time for figs. [14]And he said to it in reply, "May no one ever eat of your fruit again!" And his disciples heard it.

Cleansing of the Temple.[‡] [15]They came to Jerusalem,[k] and on entering the temple area he began to drive out those selling and buying there. He overturned the tables of the money changers and the seats of those who were selling doves. [16]He did not permit anyone to carry anything through the temple area. [17]Then he taught them saying, "Is it not written:

'My house shall be called a house of
    prayer for all peoples'?
But you have made it a den of
    thieves."[l]

[18]The chief priests and the scribes came to hear of it and were seeking a way to put him to death, yet they feared him because the whole crowd was astonished at his teaching. [19]When evening came, they went out of the city.[m]

The Withered Fig Tree. [20n]Early in the morning, as they were walking along, they saw the fig tree withered to its roots. [21]Peter remembered and said to him, "Rabbi, look! The fig tree that you cursed has withered." [22]Jesus said to them in reply, "Have faith in God. [23]Amen, I say to you, whoever says to this mountain, 'Be lifted up and thrown into the sea,' and does not doubt in his heart but believes that what he says will happen, it shall be done for him.[o] [24]Therefore I tell you, all that you ask for in prayer, believe that you will receive it and it shall be yours.[p] [25]When you stand to pray, forgive anyone against whom you have a grievance, so that your heavenly Father may in turn forgive you your transgressions."[q] [26][§]

The Authority of Jesus Questioned.[¶] [27]They returned once more to Jerusalem.[r] As he was walking in the temple area, the chief priests, the scribes, and the elders approached him [28]and said to him, "By what authority are you doing

in action representing Jesus' judgment (Mk 11:20) on barren Israel and the fate of Jerusalem for failing to receive his teaching; cf. Is 34:4; Hos 2:14; Lk 13:6–9.

‡[11:15–19] See note on Mt 21:12–17.

§[11:26] This verse, which reads, "But if you do not forgive, neither will your heavenly Father forgive your transgressions," is omitted in the best manuscripts. It was probably added by copyists under the influence of Mt 6:15.

¶[11:27–33] The mounting hostility toward Jesus came from the chief priests, the scribes, and the elders (Mk 11:27); the Herodians and the Pharisees (Mk 12:13); and the Sadducees (Mk 12:18). By their rejection of God's messengers, John the Baptist and Jesus, they incurred the divine judgment implied in Mk 11:27–33 and confirmed in the parable of the vineyard tenants (Mk 12:1–12).

*[11:1–11] In Mark's account Jesus takes the initiative in ordering the preparation for his entry into Jerusalem (Mk 11:1–6) even as he later orders the preparation of his last Passover supper (Mk 14:12–16). In Mk 10:9–10 the greeting Jesus receives stops short of proclaiming him Messiah. He is greeted rather as the prophet of the coming messianic kingdom. Contrast Mt 21:9.

†[11:12–14] Jesus' search for fruit on the fig tree recalls the prophets' earlier use of this image to designate Israel; cf. Jer 8:13; 29:17; Jl 1:7; Hos 9:10, 16. Cursing the fig tree is a parable

g. [11:1–10] Mt 21:1–9; Lk 19:29–38; Jn 12:12–15. h. [11:9–10] 2 Sm 7:16; Ps 118:26. i. [11:11] Mt 21:10, 17. j. [11:12–14] Mt 21:18–20; Lk 13:6–9.

k. [11:15–18] Mt 21:12–13; Lk 19:45–46; Jn 2:14–16. l. [11:17] Is 56:7; Jer 7:11. m. [11:19] Lk 21:37. n. [11:20–24] Mt 21:20–22. o. [11:23] Mt 17:20–21; Lk 17:6. p. [11:24] Mt 7:7; Jn 11:22; 14:13. q. [11:25] Mt 6:14; 18:35. r. [11:27–33] Mt 21:23–27; Lk 20:1–8.

these things? Or who gave you this authority to do them?" [29]Jesus said to them, "I shall ask you one question. Answer me, and I will tell you by what authority I do these things. [30]Was John's baptism of heavenly or of human origin? Answer me." [31]They discussed this among themselves and said, "If we say, 'Of heavenly origin,' he will say, '[Then] why did you not believe him?' [32]But shall we say, 'Of human origin'?"—they feared the crowd, for they all thought John really was a prophet. [33]So they said to Jesus in reply, "We do not know." Then Jesus said to them, "Neither shall I tell you by what authority I do these things."

CHAPTER 12

Parable of the Tenants.[*] [1]He began to speak to them in parables.[s] "A man planted a vineyard, put a hedge around it, dug a wine press, and built a tower. Then he leased it to tenant farmers and left on a journey.[t] [2]At the proper time he sent a servant to the tenants to obtain from them some of the produce of the vineyard. [3]But they seized him, beat him, and sent him away empty-handed. [4]Again he sent them another servant. And that one they beat over the head and treated shamefully. [5]He sent yet another whom they killed. So, too, many others; some they beat, others they killed. [6]He had one other to send, a beloved son. He sent him to them last of all, thinking, 'They will respect my son.' [7]But those tenants said to one another, 'This is the heir. Come, let us kill him, and the inheritance will be ours.' [8]So they seized him and killed him, and threw him out of the vineyard. [9]What [then] will the owner of the vineyard do? He will come, put the tenants to death, and give the vineyard to others. [10]Have you not read this scripture passage:[u]

'The stone that the builders rejected
　　has become the cornerstone;
[11] by the Lord has this been done,
　　and it is wonderful in our eyes'?"

[12]They were seeking to arrest him, but they feared the crowd, for they realized that he had addressed the parable to them. So they left him and went away.

Paying Taxes to the Emperor. [13†]They sent some Pharisees[v] and Herodians to him to ensnare

him[w] in his speech.[‡] [14]They came and said to him, "Teacher, we know that you are a truthful man and that you are not concerned with anyone's opinion. You do not regard a person's status but teach the way of God in accordance with the truth. Is it lawful to pay the census tax to Caesar or not? Should we pay or should we not pay?" [15]Knowing their hypocrisy he said to them, "Why are you testing me? Bring me a denarius to look at." [16]They brought one to him and he said to them, "Whose image and inscription is this?" They replied to him, "Caesar's." [17]So Jesus said to them, "Repay to Caesar what belongs to Caesar and to God what belongs to God." They were utterly amazed at him.[x]

The Question About the Resurrection.[§] [18]Some Sadducees, who say there is no resurrection, came to him and put this question to him, [19]saying, "Teacher, Moses wrote for us, 'If someone's brother dies, leaving a wife but no child, his brother must take the wife and raise up descendants for his brother.'[y] [20]Now there were seven brothers. The first married a woman and died, leaving no descendants. [21]So the second married her and died, leaving no descendants, and the third likewise. [22]And the seven left no descendants. Last of all the woman also died. [23]At the resurrection [when they arise] whose wife will she be? For all seven had been married to her." [24]Jesus said to them, "Are you not misled because you do not know the scriptures or the power of God? [25]When they rise from the dead, they neither marry nor are given in marriage, but they are like the angels in heaven. [26]As for the dead being raised, have you not read in the Book of Moses, in the passage about the bush, how God told him, 'I am the God of Abraham, [the] God of Isaac, and [the] God of Jacob'?[z] [27]He is not God of the dead but of the living. You are greatly misled."

The Greatest Commandment.[¶] [28]One of the scribes,[a] when he came forward and heard them disputing and saw how well he had answered them, asked him, "Which is the first of all the commandments?" [29]Jesus replied, "The first is this: 'Hear, O Israel! The Lord our God is Lord alone! [30]You shall love the Lord your God with all your heart, with all your soul, with all your mind, and with all your strength.'[b] [31]The second is this: 'You shall love your neighbor as yourself.' There is no other commandment greater than these."[c] [32]The scribe said to him, "Well said, teacher. You are right in saying, 'He is One and there is no other than he.' [33]And 'to love him with all your heart, with all your understanding, with all your strength, and to love your neighbor as

---

*[12:1–12] The vineyard denotes Israel (Is 5:1–7). The tenant farmers are the religious leaders of Israel. God is the owner of the vineyard. His servants are his messengers, the prophets. The beloved son is Jesus (Mk 1:11; 9:7; Mt 3:17; 17:5; Lk 3:22; 9:35). The punishment of the tenants refers to the religious leaders, and the transfer of the vineyard to others refers to the people of the new Israel.

†[12:13–34] In the ensuing conflicts (cf. also Mk 2:1–3:6) Jesus vanquishes his adversaries by his responses to their questions and reduces them to silence (Mk 12:34).

‡[12:13–17] See note on Mt 22:15–22.
§[12:18–27] See note on Mt 22:23–33.
¶[12:28–34] See note on Mt 22:34–40.

s. [12:1–12] Mt 21:33–46; Lk 20:9–19.　t. [12:1] Is 5:1–7; Jer 2:21.　u. [12:10–11] Ps 118:22–23; Is 28:16.　v. [12:13–27] Mt 22:15–33; Lk 20:20–39.

w. [12:13] 3:6.　x. [12:17] Rom 13:7.　y. [12:19] Dt 25:5.　z. [12:26] Ex 3:6.　a. [12:28–34] Mt 22:34–40; Lk 10:25–28.　b. [12:30] Dt 6:4–5.　c. [12:31] Lv 19:18; Rom 13:9; Gal 5:14; Jas 2:8.

yourself' is worth more than all burnt offerings and sacrifices."[d] [34]And when Jesus saw that [he] answered with understanding, he said to him, "You are not far from the kingdom of God." And no one dared to ask him any more questions.[e]

The Question About David's Son.* [35]As Jesus was teaching in the temple area he said,[f] "How do the scribes claim that the Messiah is the son of David? [36]David himself, inspired by the holy Spirit, said:

'The Lord said to my lord,
"Sit at my right hand
until I place your enemies under
your feet."'[g]

[37]David himself calls him 'lord'; so how is he his son?" [The] great crowd heard this with delight.

Denunciation of the Scribes.† [38]In the course of his teaching he said,[h] "Beware of the scribes, who like to go around in long robes and accept greetings in the marketplaces, [39]seats of honor in synagogues, and places of honor at banquets. [40]They devour the houses of widows and, as a pretext, recite lengthy prayers. They will receive a very severe condemnation."

The Poor Widow's Contribution.‡ [41]He sat down opposite the treasury and observed how the crowd put money into the treasury.[i] Many rich people put in large sums. [42]A poor widow also came and put in two small coins worth a few cents. [43]Calling his disciples to himself, he said to them, "Amen, I say to you, this poor widow put in more than all the other contributors to the treasury. [44]For they have all contributed from their surplus wealth, but she, from her poverty, has contributed all she had, her whole livelihood."

CHAPTER 13

The Destruction of the Temple Foretold.§ [1]As he was making his way out of the temple area one of his disciples said to him, "Look, teacher, what stones and what buildings!"[j] [2]Jesus said to him, "Do you see these great buildings? There will not be one stone left upon another that will not be thrown down."

The Signs of the End. [3*]As he was sitting on the Mount of Olives opposite the temple area, Peter, James, John, and Andrew asked him privately,[k] [4]"Tell us, when will this happen, and what sign will there be when all these things are about to come to an end?" [5]Jesus began to say to them, "See that no one deceives you.[l] [6]Many will come in my name saying, 'I am he,' and they will deceive many. [7]When you hear of wars and reports of wars do not be alarmed; such things must happen, but it will not yet be the end. [8]Nation will rise against nation and kingdom against kingdom. There will be earthquakes from place to place and there will be famines. These are the beginnings of the labor pains.

The Coming Persecution. [9m]"Watch out for yourselves. They will hand you over to the courts. You will be beaten in synagogues. You will be arraigned before governors and kings because of me, as a witness before them. [10]But the gospel must first be preached to all nations.** [11]When they lead you away and hand you over, do not worry beforehand about what you are to say.[n] But say whatever will be given to you at that hour. For it will not be you who are speaking but the holy Spirit. [12]Brother will hand over brother to death, and the father his child; children will rise up against parents and have them put to death. [13]You will be hated by all because of my name. But the one who perseveres to the end will be saved.

The Great Tribulation. [14o]"When you see the desolating abomination standing†† where he should not (let the reader understand), then those in Judea must flee to the mountains,[p] [15][and] a person on a housetop must not go down or enter to get anything out of his house,[q] [16]and a person in a field must not return to get his cloak. [17]Woe to pregnant women and nursing mothers in those days. [18]Pray that this does not happen in winter. [19]For those times will have tribulation such as has not been since the

---

§ [13:3–37] Jesus' prediction of the destruction of the temple (Mk 13:2) provoked questions that the four named disciples put to him in private regarding the time and the sign when all **these things are about to come to an end** (Mk 13:3–4). The response to their questions was Jesus' eschatological discourse prior to his imminent death. It contained instruction and consolation exhorting the disciples and the church to faith and obedience through the trials that would confront them (Mk 13:5–13). The sign is the presence of **the desolating abomination** (Mk 13:14; see Dn 9:27), i.e., of the Roman power profaning the temple. Flight from Jerusalem is urged rather than defense of the city through misguided messianic hope (Mk 13:14–23). Intervention will occur only after destruction (Mk 13:24–27), which will happen before the end of the first Christian generation (Mk 13:28–31). No one but the Father knows the precise time, or that of the parousia (Mk 13:32); hence the necessity of constant vigilance (Mk 13:33–37). Luke sets the parousia at a later date, after "the time of the Gentiles" (Lk 21:24). See also notes on Mt 24:1–25:46.

**** [13:10] **The gospel . . . to all nations:** the period of the Christian mission.

†† [13:14] The participle **standing** is masculine, in contrast to the neuter at Mt 24:15.

---

*[12:35–37] Jesus questions the claim of the scribes about the Davidic descent of the Messiah, not to deny it (Mt 1:1; Acts 2:20, 34; Rom 1:3; 2 Tm 2:8) but to imply that he is more than this. His superiority derives from his transcendent origin, to which David himself attested when he spoke of the Messiah with the name "Lord" (Ps 110:1). See also note on Mt 22:41–46.

†[12:38–40] See notes on Mk 7:1–23 and Mt 23:1–39.

‡[12:41–44] See note on Lk 21:1–4.

§[13:1–2] The reconstructed temple with its precincts, begun under Herod the Great ca. 20 B.C., was completed only some seven years before it was destroyed by fire in A.D. 70 at the hands of the Romans; cf. Jer 26:18; Mt 24:1–2. For the dating of the reconstruction of the temple, see further the note on Jn 2:20.

d. [12:33] Dt 6:4; Ps 40:7–9. e. [12:34] Mt 22:46; Lk 20:40. f. [12:35–37] Mt 22:41–45; Lk 20:41–44. g. [12:36] Ps 110:1. h. [12:38–40] Mt 23:1–7; Lk 11:43; 20:45–47. i. [12:41–44] Lk 21:1–4. j. [13:1–2] Mt 24:1–2; Lk 21:5–6.

k. [13:3–8] Mt 24:3–8; Lk 21:7–11. l. [13:5] Eph 5:6; 2 Thes 2:3. m. [13:9–13] Mt 24:9–14; Lk 21:12–19. n. [13:11–12] Mt 10:19–22; Lk 12:11–12. o. [13:14–23] Mt 24:15–22; Lk 21:20–24. p. [13:14] Dn 9:27; Mt 24:15. q. [13:15] Lk 17:31.

beginning of God's creation until now, nor ever will be.[r] [20]If the Lord had not shortened those days, no one would be saved; but for the sake of the elect whom he chose, he did shorten the days. [21]If anyone says to you then, 'Look, here is the Messiah! Look, there he is!' do not believe it. [22]False messiahs and false prophets will arise and will perform signs and wonders in order to mislead, if that were possible, the elect. [23]Be watchful! I have told it all to you beforehand.

The Coming of the Son of Man. [24]"But in those days after that tribulation

the sun will be darkened,
and the moon will not give its light,[t]
[25] and the stars will be falling from the sky,
and the powers in the heavens will
be shaken.

[26*][u]And then they will see 'the Son of Man coming in the clouds' with great power and glory, [27]and then he will send out the angels and gather [his] elect from the four winds, from the end of the earth to the end of the sky.

The Lesson of the Fig Tree. [28v]"Learn a lesson from the fig tree. When its branch becomes tender and sprouts leaves, you know that summer is near. [29]In the same way, when you see these things happening, know that he is near, at the gates. [30]Amen, I say to you, this generation will not pass away until all these things have taken place. [31]Heaven and earth will pass away, but my words will not pass away.

Need for Watchfulness. [32]"But of that day or hour, no one knows, neither the angels in heaven, nor the Son, but only the Father. [33w]Be watchful! Be alert! You do not know when the time will come. [34]It is like a man traveling abroad. He leaves home and places his servants in charge, each with his work, and orders the gatekeeper to be on the watch.[x] [35]Watch, therefore; you do not know when the lord of the house is coming, whether in the evening, or at midnight, or at cockcrow, or in the morning. [36]May he not come suddenly and find you sleeping. [37]What I say to you, I say to all: 'Watch!'"

CHAPTER 14

The Conspiracy Against Jesus. [1†]The Passover and the Feast of Unleavened Bread[‡] were to take

place in two days' time.[y] So the chief priests and the scribes were seeking a way to arrest him by treachery and put him to death. [2]They said, "Not during the festival, for fear that there may be a riot among the people."

The Anointing at Bethany.[§] [3]When he was in Bethany reclining at table in the house of Simon the leper,[z] a woman came with an alabaster jar of perfumed oil, costly genuine spikenard. She broke the alabaster jar and poured it on his head. [4]There were some who were indignant. "Why has there been this waste of perfumed oil? [5]It could have been sold for more than three hundred days' wages and the money given to the poor." They were infuriated with her. [6]Jesus said, "Let her alone. Why do you make trouble for her? She has done a good thing for me. [7]The poor you will always have with you, and whenever you wish you can do good to them, but you will not always have me. [8]She has done what she could. She has anticipated anointing my body for burial. [9]Amen, I say to you, wherever the gospel is proclaimed to the whole world, what she has done will be told in memory of her."

The Betrayal by Judas. [10a]Then Judas Iscariot, one of the Twelve, went off to the chief priests to hand him over to them. [11]When they heard him they were pleased and promised to pay him money. Then he looked for an opportunity to hand him over.

Preparations for the Passover. [12b]On the first day of the Feast of Unleavened Bread, when they sacrificed the Passover lamb,[¶] his disciples said to him, "Where do you want us to go and prepare for you to eat the Passover?" [13]He sent two of his disciples and said to them, "Go into the city and a man will meet you, carrying a jar

12:3–20; 34:18; Lv 23:4–8; Nm 9:2–14; 28:16–17; Dt 16:1–8. The Passover commemorated the redemption from slavery and the departure of the Israelites from Egypt by night. It began at sundown after the Passover lamb was sacrificed in the temple in the afternoon of the fourteenth day of the month of Nisan. With the Passover supper on the same evening was associated the eating of unleavened bread. The latter was continued through Nisan 21, a reminder of the affliction of the Israelites and of the haste surrounding their departure. Praise and thanks to God for his goodness in the past were combined at this dual festival with the hope of future salvation. **The chief priests . . . to death**: the intent to put Jesus to death was plotted for a long time but delayed for fear of the crowd (Mk 3:6; 11:18; 12:12).

§[14:3] At Bethany on the Mount of Olives, a few miles from Jerusalem, in **the house of Simon the leper**, Jesus defends a woman's loving action of anointing his head with perfumed oil in view of his impending death and burial as a criminal, in which case his body would not be anointed. See further the note on Jn 12:7. He assures the woman of the remembrance of her deed in the worldwide preaching of the good news.

¶[14:12] **The first day of the Feast of Unleavened Bread . . . the Passover lamb**: a less precise designation of the day for sacrificing the Passover lamb as evidenced by some rabbinical literature. For a more exact designation, see note on Mk 14:1. It was actually Nisan 14.

*[13:26] **Son of Man . . . with great power and glory**: Jesus cites this text from Dn 7:13 in his response to the high priest, **Are you the Messiah?** (Mk 14:61). In Ex 34:5; Lv 16:2; and Nm 11:25 the clouds indicate the presence of the divinity. Thus in his role of Son of Man, Jesus is a heavenly being who will come in power and glory.

†[14:1–16:8] In the movement of Mark's gospel the cross is depicted as Jesus' way to glory in accordance with the divine will. Thus the passion narrative is seen as the climax of Jesus' ministry.

‡[14:1] **The Passover and the Feast of Unleavened Bread**: the connection between the two festivals is reflected in Ex

r. [13:19] Dn 12:1.   s. [13:24–27] Mt 24:29–31; Lk 21:25–27.
t. [13:24] Is 13:10; Ez 32:7; Jl 2:10.   u. [13:26] 14:62; Dn 7:13–14.
v. [13:28–32] Mt 24:32–36; Lk 21:29–33.   w. [13:33–37] Mt 24:42; 25:13–15.   x. [13:34] Mt 25:14–30; Lk 19:12–27.

y. [14:1–2] Mt 26:2–5; Lk 22:1–2; Jn 11:45–53.   z. [14:3–9] Mt 26:6–13; Jn 12:1–8.   a. [14:10–11] Mt 26:14–16; Lk 22:3–6.
b. [14:12–16] Mt 26:17–19; Lk 22:7–13.

of water.* Follow him. ¹⁴Wherever he enters, say to the master of the house, 'The Teacher says, "Where is my guest room where I may eat the Passover with my disciples?"' ¹⁵Then he will show you a large upper room furnished and ready. Make the preparations for us there." ¹⁶The disciples then went off, entered the city, and found it just as he had told them; and they prepared the Passover.

The Betrayer. ¹⁷ᶜWhen it was evening, he came with the Twelve. ¹⁸†And as they reclined at table and were eating, Jesus said, "Amen, I say to you, one of you will betray me, one who is eating with me." ¹⁹They began to be distressed and to say to him, one by one, "Surely it is not I?" ²⁰He said to them, "One of the Twelve, the one who dips with me into the dish. ²¹For the Son of Man indeed goes, as it is written of him,‡ but woe to that man by whom the Son of Man is betrayed. It would be better for that man if he had never been born."

The Lord's Supper. ²²§While they were eating,ᵈ he took bread, said the blessing, broke it, and gave it to them, and said, "Take it; this is my body." ²³Then he took a cup, gave thanks, and gave it to them, and they all drank from it. ²⁴He said to them, "This is my blood of the covenant, which will be shed⁵ for many. ²⁵Amen, I say to you, I shall not drink again the fruit of the vine until the day when I drink it new in the kingdom of God." ²⁶Then, after singing a hymn,** they went out to the Mount of Olives.ᵉ

Peter's Denial Foretold.†† ²⁷Then Jesus said to them, "All of you will have your faith shaken, for it is written:

'I will strike the shepherd,
    and the sheep will be dispersed.'ᶠ

²⁸But after I have been raised up, I shall go before you to Galilee." ²⁹Peter said to him, "Even though all should have their faith shaken, mine will not be." ³⁰Then Jesus said to him, "Amen, I say to you, this very night before the cock crows twice you will deny me three times." ³¹But he vehemently replied, "Even though I should have to die with you, I will not deny you." And they all spoke similarly.

The Agony in the Garden. ³²‡‡Then they came to a place named Gethsemane,ᵍ and he said to his disciples, "Sit here while I pray."ʰ ³³He took with him Peter, James, and John, and began to be troubled and distressed. ³⁴Then he said to them, "My soul is sorrowful even to death. Remain here and keep watch." ³⁵He advanced a little and fell to the ground and prayed that if it were possible the hour might pass by him; ³⁶he said, "Abba, Father,§§ all things are possible to you. Take this cup away from me, but not what I will but what you will." ³⁷When he returned he found them asleep. He said to Peter, "Simon, are you asleep? Could you not keep watch for one hour? ³⁸⁵⁵Watch and pray that you may not undergo the test.ⁱ The spirit is willing but the flesh is weak." ³⁹Withdrawing again, he prayed, saying the same thing. ⁴⁰Then he returned once more and found them asleep, for they could not keep their eyes open and did not know what to answer him. ⁴¹He returned a third time and said to them, "Are you still sleeping and taking your rest? It is enough. The hour has come. Behold, the Son of Man is to be handed over to sinners. ⁴²Get up, let us go. See, my betrayer is at hand."

The Betrayal and Arrest of Jesus. ⁴³ʲThen, while he was still speaking, Judas, one of the Twelve, arrived, accompanied by a crowd with swords and clubs who had come from the chief priests, the scribes, and the elders. ⁴⁴His betrayer had arranged a signal with them, saying, "The man

---

*[14:13] **A man . . . carrying a jar of water**: perhaps a prearranged signal, for only women ordinarily carried water in jars. The Greek word used here, however, implies simply a person and not necessarily a male.

†[14:18] **One of you will betray me, one who is eating with me**: contrasts the intimacy of table fellowship at the Passover meal with the treachery of the traitor; cf. Ps 41:10.

‡[14:21] **The Son of Man indeed goes, as it is written of him**: a reference to Ps 41:10 cited by Jesus concerning Judas at the Last Supper; cf. Jn 13:18–19.

§[14:22–24] The actions and words of Jesus express within the framework of the Passover meal and the transition to a new covenant the sacrifice of himself through the offering of his body and blood in anticipation of his passion and death. His **blood of the covenant** both alludes to the ancient rite of Ex 24:4–8 and indicates the new community that the sacrifice of Jesus will bring into being (Mt 26:26–28; Lk 22:19–20; 1 Cor 11:23–25).

⁵[14:24] **Which will be shed**: see note on Mt 26:27–28. For many: the Greek preposition *hyper* is a different one from that at Mt 26:28 but the same as that found at Lk 22:19, 20 and 1 Cor 11:24. The sense of both words is vicarious, and it is difficult in Hellenistic Greek to distinguish between them. For **many** in the sense of "all," see note on Mt 20:28.

[14:26] **After singing a hymn: Ps 114–118, thanksgiving songs concluding the Passover meal.

††[14:27–31] Jesus predicted that the Twelve would waver in their faith, even abandon him, despite their protestations to the contrary. Yet he reassured them that after his resurrection he would regather them in Galilee (Mk 16:7; cf. Mt 26:32;

28:7, 10, 16; Jn 21), where he first summoned them to be his followers as he began to preach the good news (Mk 1:14–20).

‡‡[14:32–34] The disciples who had witnessed the raising to life of the daughter of Jairus (Mk 5:37) and the transfiguration of their Master (Mk 9:2) were now invited to witness his degradation and agony and to watch and pray with him.

§§[14:36] **Abba, Father**: an Aramaic term, here also translated by Mark, Jesus' special way of addressing God with filial intimacy. The word *abba* seems not to have been used in earlier or contemporaneous Jewish sources to address God without some qualifier. Cf. Rom 8:15; Gal 4:6 for other occurrences of the Aramaic word in the Greek New Testament. **Not what I will but what you will**: note the complete obedient surrender of the human will of Jesus to the divine will of the Father; cf. Jn 4:34; 8:29; Rom 5:19; Phil 2:8; Heb 5:8.

⁵⁵[14:38] **The spirit is willing but the flesh is weak**: the spirit is drawn to what is good yet found in conflict with the flesh, inclined to sin; cf. Ps 51:7, 12. Everyone is faced with this struggle, the full force of which Jesus accepted on our behalf and, through his bitter passion and death, achieved the victory.

c. [14:17–21] Mt 26:20–24; Lk 22:21–23; Jn 13:21–26.   d. [14:22–25] Mt 26:26–30; Lk 22:19–20; 1 Cor 11:23–25.   e. [14:26–31] Mt 26:30–35; Lk 22:34, 39; Jn 13:36–38.

f. [14:27] Zec 13:7; Jn 16:32.   g. [14:32–42] Mt 26:36–46; Lk 22:40–46.   h. [14:32] Jn 18:1.   i. [14:38] Rom 7:5.   j. [14:43–50] Mt 26:47–56; Lk 22:47–53; Jn 18:3–11.

I shall kiss is the one; arrest him and lead him away securely." ⁴⁵He came and immediately went over to him and said, "Rabbi." And he kissed him. ⁴⁶At this they laid hands on him and arrested him. ⁴⁷One of the bystanders drew his sword, struck the high priest's servant, and cut off his ear. ⁴⁸Jesus said to them in reply, "Have you come out as against a robber, with swords and clubs, to seize me? ⁴⁹Day after day I was with you teaching in the temple area, yet you did not arrest me; but that the scriptures may be fulfilled." ⁵⁰And they all left him and fled. ⁵¹Now a young man followed him wearing nothing but a linen cloth about his body. They seized him, ⁵²but he left the cloth behind and ran off naked.

Jesus Before the Sanhedrin. ⁵³*ᵏThey led Jesus away to the high priest, and all the chief priests and the elders and the scribes came together. ⁵⁴Peter followed him at a distance into the high priest's courtyard and was seated with the guards, warming himself at the fire. ⁵⁵The chief priests and the entire Sanhedrin kept trying to obtain testimony against Jesus in order to put him to death, but they found none. ⁵⁶Many gave false witness against him, but their testimony did not agree. ⁵⁷†Some took the stand and testified falsely against him, alleging, ⁵⁸"We heard him say, 'I will destroy this temple made with hands and within three days I will build another not made with hands.'"ˡ ⁵⁹Even so their testimony did not agree. ⁶⁰The high priest rose before the assembly and questioned Jesus, saying, "Have you no answer? What are these men testifying against you?" ⁶¹‡But he was silent and answered nothing. Again the high priest asked him and said to him, "Are you the Messiah, the son of the Blessed One?" ⁶²Then Jesus answered, "I am;

and 'you will see the Son of Man
        seated at the right hand of the Power
        and coming with the clouds of
        heaven.'"ᵐ

⁶³At that the high priest tore his garments and said, "What further need have we of witnesses?

⁶⁴You have heard the blasphemy. What do you think?" They all condemned him as deserving to die. ⁶⁵Some began to spit on him. They blindfolded him and struck him and said to him, "Prophesy!" And the guards greeted him with blows.ⁿ

Peter's Denial of Jesus. ⁶⁶ᵒWhile Peter was below in the courtyard, one of the high priest's maids came along. ⁶⁷Seeing Peter warming himself, she looked intently at him and said, "You too were with the Nazarene, Jesus." ⁶⁸ˢBut he denied it saying, "I neither know nor understand what you are talking about." So he went out into the outer court. [Then the cock crowed.] ⁶⁹The maid saw him and began again to say to the bystanders, "This man is one of them." ⁷⁰Once again he denied it. A little later the bystanders said to Peter once more, "Surely you are one of them; for you too are a Galilean." ⁷¹He began to curse and to swear, "I do not know this man about whom you are talking." ⁷²And immediately a cock crowed a second time. Then Peter remembered the word that Jesus had said to him, "Before the cock crows twice you will deny me three times." He broke down and wept.ᵖ

CHAPTER 15

Jesus Before Pilate. ¹ᑫAs soon as morning came,ʳ the chief priests with the elders and the scribes, that is, the whole Sanhedrin, held a council.ˢ They bound Jesus, led him away, and handed him over to Pilate. ²Pilate questioned him, "Are you the king of the Jews?"** He said to him in reply, "You say so." ³The chief priests accused him of many things. ⁴Again Pilate questioned him, "Have you no answer? See how many things they accuse you of." ⁵Jesus gave him no further answer, so that Pilate was amazed.

The Sentence of Death.†† ⁶Now on the occasion of the feast he used to release to them one prisoner whom they requested.ˢ ⁷A man called Barabbas‡‡ was then in prison along with the rebels who had committed murder in a rebellion.

---

*[14:53] **They led Jesus away . . . came together**: Mark presents a formal assembly of the whole Sanhedrin (chief priests, elders, and scribes) at night, leading to the condemnation of Jesus (Mk 14:64), in contrast to Lk 22:66, 71 where Jesus is condemned in a daytime meeting of the council; see also Jn 18:13, 19–24.

†[14:57–58] See notes on Mt 26:60–61 and Jn 2:19.

‡[14:61–62] **The Blessed One**: a surrogate for the divine name, which Jews did not pronounce. **I am**: indicates Jesus' acknowledgment that he is the Messiah and Son of God; cf. Mk 1:1. Contrast Mt 26:64 and Lk 22:67–70, in which Jesus leaves his interrogators to answer their own question. **You will see the Son of Man . . . with the clouds of heaven**: an allusion to Dn 7:13 and Ps 110:1 portending the enthronement of Jesus as judge in the transcendent glory of God's kingdom. **The Power**: another surrogate for the name of God.

§[14:68] [**Then the cock crowed**]: found in most manuscripts, perhaps in view of Mk 14:30, 72 but omitted in others.

¶[15:1] **Held a council**: the verb here, *poieō*, can mean either "convene a council" or "take counsel." This reading is preferred to a variant "reached a decision" (cf. Mk 3:6), which Mk 14:64 describes as having happened at the night trial; see note on Mt 27:1–2. **Handed him over to Pilate**: lacking authority to execute their sentence of condemnation (Mk 14:64), the Sanhedrin had recourse to Pilate to have Jesus tried and put to death (Mk 15:15); cf. Jn 18:31.

[15:2] **The king of the Jews: in the accounts of the evangelists a certain irony surrounds the use of this title as an accusation against Jesus (see note on Mk 15:26). While Pilate uses this term (Mk 15:2, 9, 12), he is aware of the evil motivation of the chief priests who handed Jesus over for trial and condemnation (Mk 15:10; Lk 23:14–16, 20; Mt 27:18, 24; Jn 18:38; 19:4, 6, 12).

††[15:6–15] See note on Mt 27:15–26.

‡‡[15:7] **Barabbas**: see note on Mt 27:16–17.

---

k. [14:53–65] Mt 26:57–68; Lk 22:54–55, 63–65, 67–71; Jn 18:12–13. l. [14:58] 15:29; 2 Cor 5:1. m. [14:62] 13:26; Ps 110:1; Dn 7:13; Mt 24:30.

n. [14:65] Lk 22:63–65. o. [14:66–72] Mt 26:69–75; Lk 22:56–62; Jn 18:16–18, 25–27. p. [14:72] Jn 13:38. q. [15:1–5] Mt 27:1–2, 11–14; Lk 23:1–3. r. [15:1] Jn 18:28. s. [15:6–15] Mt 27:15–26; Lk 23:17–25; Jn 18:39–40.

⁸The crowd came forward and began to ask him to do for them as he was accustomed. ⁹Pilate answered, "Do you want me to release to you the king of the Jews?" ¹⁰For he knew that it was out of envy that the chief priests had handed him over. ¹¹But the chief priests stirred up the crowd to have him release Barabbas for them instead. ¹²Pilate again said to them in reply, "Then what [do you want] me to do with [the man you call] the king of the Jews?" ¹³*They shouted again, "Crucify him." ¹⁴Pilate said to them, "Why? What evil has he done?" They only shouted the louder, "Crucify him." ¹⁵†So Pilate, wishing to satisfy the crowd, released Barabbas to them and, after he had Jesus scourged, handed him over to be crucified.

Mockery by the Soldiers. ¹⁶‡ᵗThe soldiers led him away inside the palace, that is, the praetorium, and assembled the whole cohort. ¹⁷They clothed him in purple and, weaving a crown of thorns, placed it on him. ¹⁸They began to salute him with, "Hail, King of the Jews!" ¹⁹and kept striking his head with a reed and spitting upon him. They knelt before him in homage. ²⁰And when they had mocked him, they stripped him of the purple cloak, dressed him in his own clothes, and led him out to crucify him.

The Way of the Cross. ²¹They pressed into service a passer-by, Simon, a Cyrenian,§ who was coming in from the country, the father of Alexander and Rufus, to carry his cross.ᵘ

The Crucifixion. ²²ᵛThey brought him to the place of Golgotha (which is translated Place of the Skull). ²³They gave him wine drugged with myrrh, but he did not take it. ²⁴§ʷThen they crucified him and divided his garments by casting lots for them to see what each should take. ²⁵It was nine o'clock in the morning** when they crucified him. ²⁶††The inscription of the charge against him read, "The King of the Jews." ²⁷With him they crucified two revolutionaries, one

on his right and one on his left.ˣ [²⁸]‡‡ ²⁹§§Those passing by reviled him, shaking their heads and saying,ʸ "Aha! You who would destroy the temple and rebuild it in three days, ³⁰save yourself by coming down from the cross." ³¹Likewise the chief priests, with the scribes, mocked him among themselves and said, "He saved others; he cannot save himself." ³²Let the Messiah, the King of Israel, come down now from the cross that we may see and believe." Those who were crucified with him also kept abusing him.ᶻ

The Death of Jesus. ³³At noon darkness came over the whole land until three in the afternoon. ³⁴And at three o'clock Jesus cried out in a loud voice, "*Eloi, Eloi, lema sabachthani?*"¶¶ which is translated, "My God, my God, why have you forsaken me?"ᵃ ³⁵***Some of the bystanders who heard it said, "Look, he is calling Elijah." ³⁶One of them ran, soaked a sponge with wine, put it on a reed, and gave it to him to drink, saying, "Wait, let us see if Elijah comes to take him down." ³⁷Jesus gave a loud cry and breathed his last. ³⁸†††The veil of the sanctuary was torn in two from top to bottom. ³⁹‡‡‡ᵇWhen the centurion who stood facing him saw how he breathed his last he said, "Truly this man was the Son of God!" ⁴⁰§§§There were also women looking on from a distance.ᶜ Among them were Mary Magdalene, Mary the mother of the younger James and of Joses, and Salome. ⁴¹These women had followed him when he was in Galilee and ministered to him. There were also many other women who had come up with him to Jerusalem.

The Burial of Jesus. ⁴²ᵈWhen it was already evening, since it was the day of preparation, the day before the sabbath, ⁴³Joseph of Arimathea,¶¶¶ a distinguished member of the council, who himself awaiting the kingdom of God, came and courageously went to Pilate and asked for the body of Jesus. ⁴⁴Pilate was amazed that he was already dead. He summoned the centurion and asked him if Jesus had already died. ⁴⁵And when he learned of it from the centurion, he gave the body to Joseph. ⁴⁶Having bought a linen cloth, he took him down, wrapped him in the linen

---

*[15:13] **Crucify him**: see note on Mt 27:22.

†[15:15] See note on Mt 27:26.

‡[15:16] **Praetorium**: see note on Mt 27:27.

§[15:21] **They pressed into service . . . Simon, a Cyrenian**: a condemned person was constrained to bear his own instrument of torture, at least the crossbeam. The precise naming of Simon and his sons is probably due to their being known among early Christian believers to whom Mark addressed his gospel. See also notes on Mt 27:32; Lk 23:26–32.

¶[15:24] See notes on Mt 27:35 and Jn 19:23–25a.

[15:25] **It was nine o'clock in the morning: literally, "the third hour," thus between 9 a.m. and 12 noon. Cf. Mk 15:33, 34, 42 for Mark's chronological sequence, which may reflect liturgical or catechetical considerations rather than the precise historical sequence of events; contrast the different chronologies in the other gospels, especially Jn 19:14.

††[15:26] **The inscription . . . the King of the Jews**: the political reason for the death penalty falsely charged by the enemies of Jesus. See further the notes on Mt 27:37 and Jn 19:19.

‡‡[15:28] This verse, "And the scripture was fulfilled that says, 'And he was counted among the wicked,'" is omitted in the earliest and best manuscripts. It contains a citation from Is 53:12 and was probably introduced from Lk 22:37.

§§[15:29] See note on Mt 27:39–40.

¶¶[15:34] An Aramaic rendering of Ps 22:2. See also note on Mt 27:46.

***[15:35] **Elijah**: a verbal link with Eloi (Mk 15:34). See note on Mk 9:9–13; cf. Mal 3:23–24. See also note on Mt 27:47.

†††[15:38] See note on Mt 27:51–53.

‡‡‡[15:39] The closing portion of Mark's gospel returns to the theme of its beginning in the Gentile centurion's climactic declaration of belief that Jesus **was the Son of God**. It indicates the fulfillment of the good news announced in the prologue (Mk 1:1) and may be regarded as the firstfruit of the passion and death of Jesus.

§§§[15:40–41] See note on Mt 27:55–56.

¶¶¶[15:43] **Joseph of Arimathea**: see note on Mt 27:57–61.

t. [15:16–20] Mt 27:27–31; Jn 19:2–3.   u. [15:21] Mt 27:32; Lk 23:26. v. [15:22–38] Mt 27:33–51; Lk 23:32–46; Jn 19:17–30.   w. [15:24] Ps 22:18.

x. [15:27] Lk 23:33.   y. [15:29] Jn 2:19.   z. [15:32] Lk 23:39.   a. [15:34] Ps 22:2.   b. [15:39–41] Mt 27:54–56; Lk 23:47–49.   c. [15:40] 6:3; Lk 8:2–3.   d. [15:42–47] Mt 27:57–61; Lk 23:50–56; Jn 19:38–42.

cloth and laid him in a tomb that had been hewn out of the rock. Then he rolled a stone against the entrance to the tomb. [47]Mary Magdalene and Mary the mother of Joses watched where he was laid.

CHAPTER 16
The Resurrection of Jesus.* [1]When the sabbath was over,[e] Mary Magdalene, Mary, the mother of James, and Salome bought spices so that they might go and anoint him.[f] [2]Very early when the sun had risen, on the first day of the week, they came to the tomb. [3]They were saying to one another, "Who will roll back the stone for us from the entrance to the tomb?" [4]When they looked up, they saw that the stone had been rolled back; it was very large. [5]On entering the tomb they saw a young man sitting on the right side, clothed in a white robe, and they were utterly amazed.[g] [6]He said to them, "Do not be amazed! You seek Jesus of Nazareth, the crucified. He has been raised; he is not here. Behold, the place where they laid him. [7]But go and tell his disciples and Peter, 'He is going before you to Galilee; there you will see him, as he told you.'"[h] [8]Then they went out and fled from the tomb, seized with trembling and bewilderment. They said nothing to anyone, for they were afraid.

The Longer Ending[†]

The Appearance to Mary Magdalene. [[9i]When he had risen, early on the first day of the week, he appeared first to Mary Magdalene, out of whom he had driven seven demons. [10j]She went and told his companions who were mourning and weeping. [11]When they heard that he was alive and had been seen by her, they did not believe.
The Appearance to Two Disciples. [12k]After this he appeared in another form to two of them walking along on their way to the country.

[13]They returned and told the others; but they did not believe them either.
The Commissioning of the Eleven. [14][But] later, as the eleven were at table, he appeared to them and rebuked them for their unbelief and hardness of heart because they had not believed those who saw him after he had been raised. [15m]He said to them, "Go into the whole world and proclaim the gospel to every creature. [16]Whoever believes and is baptized will be saved; whoever does not believe will be condemned. [17]These signs will accompany those who believe: in my name they will drive out demons, they will speak new languages. [18]They will pick up serpents [with their hands], and if they drink any deadly thing, it will not harm them. They will lay hands on the sick, and they will recover."[n]
The Ascension of Jesus. [19]So then the Lord Jesus, after he spoke to them, was taken up into heaven and took his seat at the right hand of God.[o] [20]But they went forth and preached everywhere, while the Lord worked with them and confirmed the word through accompanying signs.][p]

The Shorter Ending
[And they reported all the instructions briefly to Peter's companions. Afterwards Jesus himself, through them, sent forth from east to west the sacred and imperishable proclamation of eternal salvation. Amen.]

---

*[16:1–8] The purpose of this narrative is to show that the tomb is empty and that Jesus **has been raised** (Mk 16:6) and is **going before you to Galilee** (Mk 16:7) in fulfillment of Mk 14:28. The women find the tomb empty, and an angel stationed there announces to them what has happened. They are told to proclaim the news to Peter and the disciples in order to prepare them for a reunion with him. Mark's composition of the gospel ends at Mk 16:8 with the women telling no one, because they were afraid. This abrupt termination causes some to believe that the original ending of this gospel may have been lost. See the following note.
†[16:9–20] This passage, termed the Longer Ending to the Marcan gospel by comparison with a much briefer conclusion

found in some less important manuscripts, has traditionally been accepted as a canonical part of the gospel and was defined as such by the Council of Trent. Early citations of it by the Fathers indicate that it was composed by the second century, although vocabulary and style indicate that it was written by someone other than Mark. It is a general resume of the material concerning the appearances of the risen Jesus, reflecting, in particular, traditions found in Lk 24 and Jn 20.
     The Shorter Ending: Found after Mk 16:8 before the Longer Ending in four seventh-to-ninth-century Greek manuscripts as well as in one Old Latin version, where it appears alone without the Longer Ending.
     The Freer Logion: Found after Mk 16:14 in a fourth-fifth century manuscript preserved in the Freer Gallery of Art, Washington, DC, this ending was known to Jerome in the fourth century. It reads: "And they excused themselves, saying, 'This age of lawlessness and unbelief is under Satan, who does not allow the truth and power of God to prevail over the unclean things dominated by the spirits [or, does not allow the unclean things dominated by the spirits to grasp the truth and power of God]. Therefore reveal your righteousness now.' They spoke to Christ. And Christ responded to them, 'The limit of the years of Satan's power is completed, but other terrible things draw near. And for those who sinned I was handed over to death, that they might return to the truth and no longer sin, in order that they might inherit the spiritual and incorruptible heavenly glory of righteousness. But . . . .'"

e. [16:1–8] Mt 28:1–8; Lk 24:1–10; Jn 20:1–10.   f. [16:1–2] Mt 28:1; Lk23:56.   g. [16:5]Jn20:12.   h. [16:7]14:28.   i. [16:9–20]Mt28:1–10; Jn 20:11–18.   j. [16:10–11] Lk 24:10–11; Jn 20:18.   k. [16:12–14] Lk 24:13–35.

l. [16:14] Lk 24:36–49; 1 Cor 15:5.   m. [16:15–16] 13:10; Mt 28:18–20; Lk 24:47; Jn 20:21.   n. [16:18] Mt 10:1; Lk 10:19; Acts 28:3–6.   o. [16:19] Lk 24:50–53.   p. [16:20] 1 Tm 3:16.

THE GOSPEL ACCORDING

LUKE

The Gospel according to Luke is the first part of a two-volume work that continues the biblical history of God's dealings with humanity found in the Old Testament, showing how God's promises to Israel have been fulfilled in Jesus and how the salvation promised to Israel and accomplished by Jesus has been extended to the Gentiles. The stated purpose of the two volumes is to provide Theophilus and others like him with certainty—assurance—about earlier instruction they have received (Lk 1:4). To accomplish his purpose, Luke shows that the preaching and teaching of the representatives of the early church are grounded in the preaching and teaching of Jesus, who during his historical ministry (Acts 1:21–22) prepared his specially chosen followers and commissioned them to be witnesses to his resurrection and to all else that he did (Acts 10:37–42). This continuity between the historical ministry of Jesus and the ministry of the apostles is Luke's way of guaranteeing the fidelity of the Church's teaching to the teaching of Jesus.

Luke's story of Jesus and the church is dominated by a historical perspective. This history is first of all salvation history. God's divine plan for human salvation was accomplished during the period of Jesus, who through the events of his life (Lk 22:22) fulfilled the Old Testament prophecies (Lk 4:21; 18:31; 22:37; 24:26–27, 44), and this salvation is now extended to all humanity in the period of the church (Acts 4:12). This salvation history, moreover, is a part of human history. Luke relates the story of Jesus and the church to events in contemporary Palestinian (Lk 1:5; 3:1–2; Acts 4:6) and Roman (Lk 2:1–2; 3:1; Acts 11:28; 18:2, 12) history for, as Paul says in Acts 26:26, "this was not done in a corner." Finally, Luke relates the story of Jesus and the church to contemporaneous church history. Luke is concerned with presenting Christianity as a legitimate form of worship in the Roman world, a religion that is capable of meeting the spiritual needs of a world empire like that of Rome. To this end, Luke depicts the Roman governor Pilate declaring Jesus innocent of any wrongdoing three times (Lk 23:4, 14, 22). At the same time Luke argues in Acts that Christianity is the logical development and proper fulfillment of Judaism and is therefore deserving of the same toleration and freedom traditionally accorded Judaism by Rome (Acts 13:16–41; 23:6–9; 24:10–21; 26:2–23).

The prominence given to the period of the church in the story has important consequences for Luke's interpretation of the teachings of Jesus. By presenting the time of the church as a distinct phase of salvation history, Luke accordingly shifts the early Christian emphasis away from the expectation of an imminent parousia to the day-to-day concerns of the Christian community in the world. He does this in the gospel by regularly emphasizing the words "each day" (Lk 9:23; cf. Mk 8:34; Lk 11:3; 16:19; 19:47) in the sayings of Jesus. Although Luke still believes the parousia to be a reality that will come unexpectedly (Lk 12:38, 45–46), he is more concerned with presenting the words and deeds of Jesus as guides for the conduct of Christian disciples in the interim period between the ascension and the parousia and with presenting Jesus himself as the model of Christian life and piety.

Throughout the gospel, Luke calls upon the Christian disciple to identify with the master Jesus, who is caring and tender toward the poor and lowly, the outcast, the sinner, and the afflicted, toward all those who recognize their dependence on God (Lk 4:18; 6:20–23; 7:36–50; 14:12–14; 15:1–32; 16:19–31; 18:9–14; 19:1–10; 21:1–4), but who is severe toward the proud and self-righteous, and particularly toward those who place their material wealth before the service of God and his people (Lk 6:24–26; 12:13–21; 16:13–15, 19–31; 18:9–14, 15–25; cf. Lk 1:50–53). No gospel writer is more concerned than Luke with the mercy and compassion of Jesus (Lk 7:41–43; 10:29–37; 13:6–9; 15:11–32). No gospel writer is more concerned with the role of the Spirit in the life of Jesus and the Christian disciple (Lk 1:35, 41; 2:25–27; 4:1, 14, 18; 10:21; 11:13; 24:49), with the importance of prayer (Lk 3:21; 5:16; 6:12; 9:28; 11:1–13; 18:1–8), or with Jesus' concern for women (Lk 7:11–17,

36–50; 8:2–3; 10:38–42). While Jesus calls all humanity to repent (Lk 5:32; 10:13; 11:32; 13:1–5; 15:7–10; 16:30; 17:3–4; 24:47), he is particularly demanding of those who would be his disciples. Of them he demands absolute and total detachment from family and material possessions (Lk 9:57–62; 12:32–34; 14:25–35). To all who respond in faith and repentance to the word Jesus preaches, he brings salvation (Lk 2:30–32; 3:6; 7:50; 8:48, 50; 17:19; 19:9) and peace (Lk 2:14; 7:50; 8:48; 19:38, 42) and life (Lk 10:25–28; 18:26–30).

Early Christian tradition, from the late second century on, identifies the author of this gospel and of the Acts of the Apostles as Luke, a Syrian from Antioch, who is mentioned in the New Testament in Col 4:14, Phlm 24 and 2 Tm 4:11. The prologue of the gospel makes it clear that Luke is not part of the first generation of Christian disciples but is himself dependent upon the traditions he received from those who were eyewitnesses and ministers of the word (Lk 1:2). His two-volume work marks him as someone who was highly literate both in the Old Testament traditions according to the Greek versions and in Hellenistic Greek writings.

Among the likely sources for the composition of this gospel (Lk 1:3) were the Gospel of Mark, a written collection of sayings of Jesus known also to the author of the Gospel of Matthew (Q; see Introduction to Matthew), and other special traditions that were used by Luke alone among the gospel writers. Some hold that Luke used Mark only as a complementary source for rounding out the material he took from other traditions. Because of its dependence on the Gospel of Mark and because details in Luke's Gospel (Lk 13:35a; 19:43–44; 21:20; 23:28–31) imply that the author was acquainted with the destruction of the city of Jerusalem by the Romans in A.D. 70, the Gospel of Luke is dated by most scholars after that date; many propose A.D. 80–90 as the time of composition.

Luke's consistent substitution of Greek names for the Aramaic or Hebrew names occurring in his sources (e.g., Lk 23:33; Mk 15:22; Lk 18:41; Mk 10:51), his omission from the gospel of specifically Jewish Christian concerns found in his sources (e.g., Mk 7:1–23), his interest in Gentile Christians (Lk 2:30–32; 3:6, 38; 4:16–30; 13:28–30; 14:15–24; 17:11–19; 24:47–48), and his incomplete knowledge of Palestinian geography, customs, and practices are among the characteristics of this gospel that suggest that Luke was a non-Palestinian writing to a non-Palestinian audience that was largely made up of Gentile Christians.

The principal divisions of the Gospel according to Luke are the following:

I. The Prologue (1:1–4)
II. The Infancy Narrative (1:5–2:52)
III. The Preparation for the Public Ministry (3:1–4:13)
IV. The Ministry in Galilee (4:14–9:50)
V. The Journey to Jerusalem: Luke's Travel Narrative (9:51–19:27)
VI. The Teaching Ministry in Jerusalem (19:28–21:38)
VII. The Passion Narrative (22:1–23:56)
VIII. The Resurrection Narrative (24:1–53)

I. THE PROLOGUE*

CHAPTER 1

¹Since many have undertaken to compile a narrative of the events that have been fulfilled among us,[a] ²just as those who were eyewitnesses from the beginning and ministers of the word have handed them down to us,[b] ³I too have decided, after investigating everything accurately anew, to write it down in an orderly sequence for you, most excellent Theophilus, ⁴so that you may realize the certainty of the teachings you have received.

*[1:1–4] The Gospel according to Luke is the only one of the synoptic gospels to begin with a literary prologue. Making use of a formal, literary construction and vocabulary, the author writes the prologue in imitation of Hellenistic Greek writers and, in so doing, relates his story about Jesus to contemporaneous Greek and Roman literature. Luke is not only interested in the words and deeds of Jesus, but also in the larger context of the birth, ministry, death, and resurrection

of Jesus as the fulfillment of the promises of God in the Old Testament. As a second- or third-generation Christian, Luke acknowledges his debt to earlier **eyewitnesses** and **ministers of the word**, but claims that his contribution to this developing tradition is a complete and accurate account, told in an orderly manner, and intended to provide **Theophilus** ("friend of God," literally) and other readers with certainty about earlier teachings they have received.

a. [1:1–4] Acts 1:1; 1 Cor 15:3.

b. [1:2] 24:48; Jn 15:27; Acts 1:21–22.

II. THE INFANCY NARRATIVE*

Announcement of the Birth of John. [5]In the days of Herod, King of Judea,[†] there was a priest named Zechariah of the priestly division of Abijah; his wife was from the daughters of Aaron, and her name was Elizabeth.[c] [6]Both were righteous in the eyes of God, observing all the commandments and ordinances of the Lord blamelessly. [7]But they had no child,[‡] because Elizabeth was barren and both were advanced in years.[d] [8]Once when he was serving as priest in his division's turn before God, [9]according to the practice of the priestly service, he was chosen by lot to enter the sanctuary of the Lord to burn incense.[e] [10]Then, when the whole assembly of the people was praying outside at the hour of the incense offering, [11]the angel of the Lord appeared to him, standing at the right of the altar of incense. [12]Zechariah was troubled by what he saw, and fear came upon him. [13]But the angel said to him, "Do not be afraid,[§] Zechariah, because your prayer has been heard. Your wife Elizabeth will bear you a son, and you shall name him John.[f] [14]And you will have joy and gladness, and many will rejoice at his birth, [15]for he will be great in the sight of [the] Lord. He will drink neither wine nor strong drink.[¶] He will be filled with the holy Spirit even from his mother's womb,[g] [16]and he will turn many of the children of Israel to the Lord their God. [17]He will go before him in the spirit and power of Elijah** to turn the hearts of fathers toward children and the disobedient to the understanding of the righteous, to prepare a people fit for the Lord."[h] [18]Then Zechariah said to the angel, "How shall I know this? For I am an old man, and my wife is advanced in years." [19]And the angel said to him in reply, "I am Gabriel,[††] who stand before God. I was sent to speak to you and to announce to you this good news.[i] [20]But now you will be speechless and unable to talk[‡‡] until the day these things take place, because you did not believe my words, which will be fulfilled at their proper time."[j]

[21]Meanwhile the people were waiting for Zechariah and were amazed that he stayed so long in the sanctuary. [22]But when he came out, he was unable to speak to them, and they realized that he had seen a vision in the sanctuary. He was gesturing to them but remained mute. [23]Then, when his days of ministry were completed, he went home. [24]After this time his wife Elizabeth conceived, and she went into seclusion for five months, saying, [25]"So has the Lord done for me at a time when he has seen fit to take away my disgrace before others."[k]

Announcement of the Birth of Jesus.[§§] [26]In the sixth month, the angel Gabriel was sent from

---

*[1:5–2:52] Like the Gospel according to Matthew, this gospel opens with an infancy narrative, a collection of stories about the birth and childhood of Jesus. The narrative uses early Christian traditions about the birth of Jesus, traditions about the birth and circumcision of John the Baptist, and canticles such as the Magnificat (Lk 1:46–55) and Benedictus (Lk 1:67–79), composed of phrases drawn from the Greek Old Testament. It is largely, however, the composition of Luke who writes in imitation of Old Testament birth stories, combining historical and legendary details, literary ornamentation and interpretation of scripture, to answer in advance the question, "Who is Jesus Christ?" The focus of the narrative, therefore, is primarily christological. In this section Luke announces many of the themes that will become prominent in the rest of the gospel: the centrality of Jerusalem and the temple, the journey motif, the universality of salvation, joy and peace, concern for the lowly, the importance of women, the presentation of Jesus as savior, Spirit-guided revelation and prophecy, and the fulfillment of Old Testament promises. The account presents parallel scenes (diptychs) of angelic announcements of the birth of John the Baptist and of Jesus, and of the birth, circumcision, and presentation of John and Jesus. In this parallelism, the ascendency of Jesus over John is stressed: John is prophet of the Most High (Lk 1:76); Jesus is Son of the Most High (Lk 1:32). John is great in the sight of the Lord (Lk 1:15); Jesus will be Great (a LXX attribute, used absolutely, of God) (Lk 1:32). John will go before the Lord (Lk 1:16–17); Jesus will be Lord (Lk 1:43; 2:11).

†[1:5] **In the days of Herod, King of Judea:** Luke relates the story of salvation history to events in contemporary world history. Here and in Lk 3:1–2 he connects his narrative with events in Palestinian history; in Lk 2:1–2 and Lk 3:1 he casts the Jesus story in the light of events of Roman history. Herod the Great, the son of the Idumean Antipater, was declared "King of Judea" by the Roman Senate in 40 B.C., but became the undisputed ruler of Palestine only in 37 B.C. He continued as king until his death in 4 B.C. **Priestly division of Abijah:** a reference to the eighth of the twenty-four divisions of priests who, for a week at a time, twice a year, served in the Jerusalem temple.

‡[1:7] **They had no child:** though childlessness was looked upon in contemporaneous Judaism as a curse or punishment for sin, it is intended here to present Elizabeth in a situation similar to that of some of the great mothers of important Old Testament figures: Sarah (Gn 15:3; 16:1); Rebekah (Gn 25:21); Rachel (Gn 29:31; 30:1); the mother of Samson and wife of Manoah (Jgs 13:2–3); Hannah (1 Sm 1:2).

§[1:13] **Do not be afraid:** a stereotyped Old Testament phrase spoken to reassure the recipient of a heavenly vision

(Gn 15:1; Jos 1:9; Dn 10:12, 19 and elsewhere in Lk 1:30; 2:10). **You shall name him John:** the name means "Yahweh has shown favor," an indication of John's role in salvation history.

¶[1:15] **He will drink neither wine nor strong drink:** like Samson (Jgs 13:4–5) and Samuel (1 Sm 1:11 LXX and 4QSamᵃ), John is to be consecrated by Nazirite vow and set apart for the Lord's service.

[1:17] **He will go before him in the spirit and power of Elijah: John is to be the messenger sent before Yahweh, as described in Mal 3:1–2. He is cast, moreover, in the role of the Old Testament fiery reformer, the prophet Elijah, who according to Mal 3:23 (4:5) is sent before "the great and terrible day of the Lord comes."

††[1:19] **I am Gabriel:** "the angel of the Lord" is identified as Gabriel, the angel who in Dn 9:20–25 announces the seventy weeks of years and the coming of an anointed one, a prince. By alluding to Old Testament themes in Lk 1:17, 19 such as the coming of the day of the Lord and the dawning of the messianic era, Luke is presenting his interpretation of the significance of the births of John and Jesus.

‡‡[1:20] **You will be speechless and unable to talk:** Zechariah's becoming mute is the sign given in response to his question in v 18. When Mary asks a similar question in Lk 1:34, unlike Zechariah who was punished for his doubt, she, in spite of her doubt, is praised and reassured (Lk 1:35–37).

§§[1:26–38] The announcement to Mary of the birth of Jesus is parallel to the announcement to Zechariah of the birth of John. In both the angel Gabriel appears to the parent who is troubled by the vision (Lk 1:11–12, 26–29) and then told by

---

c. [1:5] 1 Chr 24:10.   d. [1:7] Gn 18:11; Jgs 13:2–5; 1 Sm 1:5–6.   e. [1:9] Ex 30:7.

f. [1:13] 1:57, 60, 63; Mt 1:20–21.   g. [1:15] 7:33; Nm 6:1–21; Jgs 13:4; 1 Sm 1:11 LXX.   h. [1:17] Sir 48:10; Mal 3:1; 3:23–24; Mt 11:14; 17:11–13.   i. [1:19] Dn 8:16; 9:21.   j. [1:20] 1:45.   k. [1:25] Gn 30:23.

God to a town of Galilee called Nazareth, [27]to a virgin betrothed to a man named Joseph, of the house of David, and the virgin's name was Mary.[l] [28]And coming to her, he said, "Hail, favored one! The Lord is with you."[m] [29]But she was greatly troubled at what was said and pondered what sort of greeting this might be. [30]Then the angel said to her, "Do not be afraid, Mary, for you have found favor with God. [31n]Behold, you will conceive in your womb and bear a son, and you shall name him Jesus. [32o]He will be great and will be called Son of the Most High, and the Lord God will give him the throne of David his father, [33]and he will rule over the house of Jacob forever, and of his kingdom there will be no end."[p] [34]But Mary said to the angel, "How can this be, since I have no relations with a man?"[†] [35]And the angel said to her in reply, "The holy Spirit will come upon you, and the power of the Most High will overshadow you. Therefore the child to be born will be called holy, the Son of God.[q] [36]And behold, Elizabeth, your relative, has also conceived[‡] a son in her old age, and this is the sixth month for her who was called barren; [37]for nothing will be impossible for God."[r] [38]Mary said, "Behold, I am the handmaid of the Lord. May it be done to me according to your word." Then the angel departed from her.

Mary Visits Elizabeth. [39]During those days Mary set out and traveled to the hill country in haste to a town of Judah, [40]where she entered the house of Zechariah and greeted Elizabeth. [41]When Elizabeth heard Mary's greeting, the infant leaped in her womb, and Elizabeth, filled with the holy Spirit,[s] [42]cried out in a loud voice and said, "Most blessed are you among women, and blessed is the fruit of your womb.[t] [43]And how does this happen to me, that the mother of my Lord[§] should come to me? [44]For at the

moment the sound of your greeting reached my ears, the infant in my womb leaped for joy. [45]Blessed are you who believed[¶] that what was spoken to you by the Lord would be fulfilled."[u]

The Canticle of Mary. [46v]And Mary said:[**]

"My soul proclaims the greatness of the
        Lord;[w]
[47]   my spirit rejoices in God my savior.[x]
[48] For he has looked upon his handmaid's
        lowliness;
        behold, from now on will all ages
                call me blessed.[y]
[49] The Mighty One has done great things for
        me,
        and holy is his name.[z]
[50] His mercy is from age to age
        to those who fear him.[a]
[51] He has shown might with his arm,
        dispersed the arrogant of mind and
                heart.[b]
[52] He has thrown down the rulers from their
        thrones
        but lifted up the lowly.[c]
[53] The hungry he has filled with good things;
        the rich he has sent away empty.[d]
[54] He has helped Israel his servant,
        remembering his mercy,[e]
[55] according to his promise to our fathers,
        to Abraham and to his descendants
                forever."[f]

[56]Mary remained with her about three months and then returned to her home.

The Birth of John.[††] [57]When the time arrived for Elizabeth to have her child she gave birth to a

---

the angel not to fear (Lk 1:13, 30). After the announcement is made (Lk 1:14–17, 31–33) the parent objects (Lk 1:18, 34) and a sign is given to confirm the announcement (Lk 1:20, 36). The particular focus of the announcement of the birth of Jesus is on his identity as Son of David (Lk 1:32–33) and Son of God (Lk 1:32, 35).

*[1:32] **Son of the Most High**: cf. Lk 1:76 where John is described as "prophet of the Most High." "Most High" is a title for God commonly used by Luke (Lk 1:35, 76; 6:35; 8:28; Acts 7:48; 16:17).

†[1:34] Mary's questioning response is a denial of sexual relations and is used by Luke to lead to the angel's declaration about the Spirit's role in the conception of this child (Lk 1:35). According to Luke, the virginal conception of Jesus takes place through the holy Spirit, the power of God, and therefore Jesus has a unique relationship with Yahweh: he is Son of God.

‡[1:36–37] The sign given to Mary in confirmation of the angel's announcement to her is the pregnancy of her aged relative Elizabeth. If a woman past the childbearing age could become pregnant, why, the angel implies, should there be doubt about Mary's pregnancy, for **nothing will be impossible for God.**

§[1:43] Even before his birth, Jesus is identified in Luke as the Lord.

¶[1:45] **Blessed are you who believed**: Luke portrays Mary as a believer whose faith stands in contrast to the disbelief of Zechariah (Lk 1:20). Mary's role as believer in the infancy narrative should be seen in connection with the explicit mention of her presence among "those who believed" after the resurrection at the beginning of the Acts of the Apostles (Acts 1:14).

**[1:46–55] Although Mary is praised for being the mother of the Lord and because of her belief, she reacts as the servant in a psalm of praise, the Magnificat. Because there is no specific connection of the canticle to the context of Mary's pregnancy and her visit to Elizabeth, the Magnificat (with the possible exception of v 48) may have been a Jewish Christian hymn that Luke found appropriate at this point in his story. Even if not composed by Luke, it fits in well with themes found elsewhere in Luke: joy and exultation in the Lord; the lowly being singled out for God's favor; the reversal of human fortunes; the fulfillment of Old Testament promises. The loose connection between the hymn and the context is further seen in the fact that a few Old Latin manuscripts identify the speaker of the hymn as Elizabeth, even though the overwhelming textual evidence makes Mary the speaker.

††[1:57–66] The birth and circumcision of John above all emphasize John's incorporation into the people of Israel by the

---

l. [1:27] 2:5; Mt 1:16, 18.   m. [1:28] Jgs 6:12; Ru 2:4; Jdt 13:18.
n. [1:31] Gn 16:11; Jgs 13:3; Is 7:14; Mt 1:21–23.   o. [1:32–33]
2 Sm 7:12, 13, 16; Is 9:7.   p. [1:33] Dn 2:44; 7:14; Mi 4:7; Mt 28:18.
q. [1:35] Mt 1:20.   r. [1:37] Gn 18:14; Jer 32:27; Mt 19:26.   s. [1:41]
1:15; Gn 25:22 LXX.   t. [1:42] 11:27–28; Jgs 5:24; Jdt 13:18; Dt 28:4.

u. [1:45] 1:20.   v. [1:46–55] 1 Sm 2:1–10.   w. [1:46] Ps 35:9; Is
61:10; Heb 3:18.   x. [1:47] Ti 3:4; Jude 25.   y. [1:48] 11:27; 1 Sm
1:11; 2 Sm 16:12; 2 Kgs 14:26; Ps 113:7.   z. [1:49] Dt 10:21; Ps 71:19;
111:9; 126:2–3.   a. [1:50] Ps 89:2; 103:13, 17.   b. [1:51] Ps 89:10;
118:15; Jer 32:17 (39:17 LXX).   c. [1:52] 1 Sm 2:7; 2 Sm 22:28; Jb
5:11; 12:19; Ps 147:6; Sir 10:14; Jas 4:6; 1 Pt 5:5.   d. [1:53] 1 Sm 2:5;
Ps 107:9.   e. [1:54] Ps 98:3; Is 41:8–9.   f. [1:55] Gn 13:15; 17:7;
18:18; 22:17–18; Mi 7:20.

son. [58]Her neighbors and relatives heard that the Lord had shown his great mercy toward her, and they rejoiced with her.[g] [59]When they came on the eighth day to circumcise[h] the child, they were going to call him Zechariah after his father, [60]but his mother said in reply, "No. He will be called John."[i] [61]But they answered her, "There is no one among your relatives who has this name." [62]So they made signs, asking his father what he wished him to be called. [63]He asked for a tablet and wrote, "John is his name," and all were amazed. [64]Immediately his mouth was opened, his tongue freed, and he spoke blessing God.[j] [65]Then fear came upon all their neighbors, and all these matters were discussed throughout the hill country of Judea. [66]All who heard these things took them to heart, saying, "What, then, will this child be?" For surely the hand of the Lord was with him.

The Canticle of Zechariah. [67]Then Zechariah his father, filled with the holy Spirit, prophesied, saying:

[68] †"Blessed be the Lord, the God of Israel,
    for he has visited and brought
        redemption to his people.[k]
[69] ‡He has raised up a horn for our salvation
    within the house of David his
        servant,[l]
[70] even as he promised through the mouth
    of his holy prophets from of old:
[71] salvation from our enemies and
    from the hand of all who hate
        us,[m]

[72] to show mercy to our fathers[n]
    and to be mindful of his holy
        covenant[o]
[73] and of the oath he swore to Abraham our
    father,[p]
    and to grant us that, [74]rescued from
        the hand of enemies,
    without fear we might worship him [75]in
        holiness and righteousness
        before him all our days.[q]
[76] And you, child, will be called prophet of
    the Most High,
    for you will go before the Lord[§] to
        prepare his ways,[r]
[77] to give his people knowledge of salvation
    through the forgiveness of their sins,
[78] because of the tender mercy of our God[s]
    by which the daybreak from on
        high[¶] will visit us[t]
[79] to shine on those who sit in darkness and
    death's shadow,
    to guide our feet into the path of
        peace."

[80]The child grew and became strong in spirit, and he was in the desert until the day of his manifestation to Israel.[u]

CHAPTER 2

The Birth of Jesus. [1]In those days a decree went out from Caesar Augustus[††] that the whole

---

sign of the covenant (Gn 17:1–12). The narrative of John's circumcision also prepares the way for the subsequent description of the circumcision of Jesus in Lk 2:21. At the beginning of his two-volume work Luke shows those who play crucial roles in the inauguration of Christianity to be wholly a part of the people of Israel. At the end of the Acts of the Apostles (Acts 21:20; 22:3; 23:6–9; 24:14–16; 26:2–8, 22–23) he will argue that Christianity is the direct descendant of Pharisaic Judaism.

*[1:59] The practice of Palestinian Judaism at this time was to name the child at birth; moreover, though naming a male child after the father is not completely unknown, the usual practice was to name the child after the grandfather (see Lk 1:61). The naming of the child John and Zechariah's recovery from his loss of speech should be understood as fulfilling the angel's announcement to Zechariah in Lk 1:13, 20.

†[1:68–79] Like the canticle of Mary (Lk 1:46–55) the canticle of Zechariah is only loosely connected with its context. Apart from Lk 1:76–77, the hymn in speaking of **a horn for our salvation** (Lk 1:69) and **the daybreak from on high** (Lk 1:78) applies more closely to Jesus and his work than to John. Again like Mary's canticle, it is largely composed of phrases taken from the Greek Old Testament and may have been a Jewish Christian hymn of praise that Luke adapted to fit the present context by inserting Lk 1:76–77 to give Zechariah's reply to the question asked in Lk 1:66.

‡[1:69] **A horn for our salvation:** the horn is a common Old Testament figure for strength (Ps 18:3; 75:5–6; 89:18; 112:9; 148:14). This description is applied to God in Ps 18:2 and is here transferred to Jesus. The connection of the phrase with **the house of David** gives the title messianic overtones and may indicate an allusion to a phrase in Hannah's song of praise (1 Sm 2:10), "the horn of his anointed."

§[1:76] **You will go before the Lord:** here **the Lord** is most likely a reference to Jesus (contrast Lk 1:15–17 where Yahweh is meant) and John is presented as the precursor of Jesus.

¶[1:78] **The daybreak from on high:** three times in the LXX (Jer 23:5; Zec 3:8; 6:12), the Greek word used here for **daybreak** translates the Hebrew word for "scion, branch," an Old Testament messianic title.

[2:1–2] Although universal registrations of Roman citizens are attested in 28 B.C., 8 B.C., and A.D. 14 and enrollments in individual provinces of those who are not Roman citizens are also attested, such a universal census of the Roman world under Caesar Augustus is unknown outside the New Testament. Moreover, there are notorious historical problems connected with Luke's dating the census **when Quirinius was governor of Syria, and the various attempts to resolve the difficulties have proved unsuccessful. P. Sulpicius Quirinius became legate of the province of Syria in A.D. 6–7 when Judea was annexed to the province of Syria. At that time, a provincial census of Judea was taken up. If Quirinius had been legate of Syria previously, it would have to have been before 10 B.C. because the various legates of Syria from 10 B.C. to 4 B.C. (the death of Herod) are known, and such a dating for an earlier census under Quirinius would create additional problems for dating the beginning of Jesus' ministry (Lk 3:1, 23). A previous legateship after 4 B.C. (and before A.D. 6) would not fit with the dating of Jesus' birth in the days of Herod (Lk 1:5; Mt 2:1). Luke may simply be combining Jesus' birth in Bethlehem with his vague recollection of a census under Quirinius (see also Acts 5:37) to underline the significance of this birth for the whole Roman world: through this child born in Bethlehem peace and salvation come to the empire.

††[2:1] **Caesar Augustus:** the reign of the Roman emperor Caesar Augustus is usually dated from 27 B.C. to his death in A.D. 14. According to Greek inscriptions, Augustus was

---

g. [1:58] 1:14.   h. [1:59] 2:21; Gn 17:10, 12; Lv 12:3.   i. [1:60] 1:13. j. [1:64] 1:20.   k. [1:68] 7:16; Ps 41:13; 72:18; 106:48; 111:9. l. [1:69] Ps 18:3.   m. [1:71] Ps 106:10.

n. [1:72–73] Gn 17:7; Lv 26:42; Ps 105:8–9; Mi 7:20.   o. [1:72] Ps 106:45–46.   p. [1:73–74] Gn 22:16–17.   q. [1:75] Ti 2:12.   r. [1:76] Is 40:3; Mal 3:1; Mt 3:3; 11:10.   s. [1:78–79] Is 60:1–2.   t. [1:78] Mal 3:20.   u. [1:80] 2:40; Mt 3:1.

world should be enrolled. [2]This was the first enrollment, when Quirinius was governor of Syria. [3]So all went to be enrolled, each to his own town. [4]And Joseph too went up from Galilee from the town of Nazareth to Judea, to the city of David that is called Bethlehem, because he was of the house and family of David,[v] [5]to be enrolled with Mary, his betrothed, who was with child.[w] [6]While they were there, the time came for her to have her child, [7]and she gave birth to her firstborn son.[*] She wrapped him in swaddling clothes and laid him in a manger, because there was no room for them in the inn.[x]

[8†]Now there were shepherds in that region living in the fields and keeping the night watch over their flock. [9]The angel of the Lord appeared to them and the glory of the Lord shone around them, and they were struck with great fear.[y] [10]The angel said to them, "Do not be afraid; for behold, I proclaim to you good news of great joy that will be for all the people. [11‡]For today in the city of David a savior has been born for you who is Messiah and Lord. [12]And this will be a sign for you: you will find an infant wrapped in swaddling clothes and lying in a manger." [13]And suddenly there was a multitude of the heavenly host with the angel, praising God and saying:

[14] [s]"Glory to God in the highest[a]
     and on earth peace to those on
        whom his favor rests."

The Visit of the Shepherds. [15]When the angels went away from them to heaven, the shepherds said to one another, "Let us go, then, to Bethlehem to see this thing that has taken place, which the Lord has made known to us." [16]So they went in haste and found Mary and Joseph, and the infant lying in the manger. [17]When they saw this, they made known the message that had been told them about this child. [18]All who heard it were amazed by what had been told them by the shepherds. [19]And Mary kept all these things, reflecting on them in her heart. [20]Then the shepherds returned, glorifying and praising God for all they had heard and seen, just as it had been told to them.

The Circumcision and Naming of Jesus. [21]When eight days were completed for his circumcision,[s] he was named Jesus, the name given him by the angel before he was conceived in the womb.[b]

The Presentation in the Temple. [22†]When the days were completed for their purification[††]

---

regarded in the Roman Empire as "savior" and "god," and he was credited with establishing a time of peace, the *pax Augusta*, throughout the Roman world during his long reign. It is not by chance that Luke relates the birth of Jesus to the time of Caesar Augustus: the real savior (Lk 2:11) and peacebearer (Lk 2:14; see also Lk 19:38) is the child born in Bethlehem. The great emperor is simply God's agent (like the Persian king Cyrus in Is 44:28–45:1) who provides the occasion for God's purposes to be accomplished. **The whole world**: that is, the whole Roman world: Rome, Italy, and the Roman provinces.

*[2:7] **Firstborn son**: the description of Jesus as **firstborn** son does not necessarily mean that Mary had other sons. It is a legal description indicating that Jesus possessed the rights and privileges of the firstborn son (Gn 27; Ex 13:2; Nm 3:12–13; 18:15–16; Dt 21:15–17). See notes on Mt 1:25; Mk 6:3. **Wrapped him in swaddling clothes**: there may be an allusion here to the birth of another descendant of David, his son Solomon, who though a great king was wrapped in swaddling clothes like any other infant (Wis 7:4–6). **Laid him in a manger**: a feeding trough for animals. A possible allusion to Is 1:3 LXX.

†[2:8–20] The announcement of Jesus' birth to the shepherds is in keeping with Luke's theme that the lowly are singled out as the recipients of God's favors and blessings (see also Lk 1:48, 52).

‡[2:11] The basic message of the infancy narrative is contained in the angel's announcement: this child is **savior**, **Messiah**, and **Lord**. Luke is the only synoptic gospel writer to use the title **savior** for Jesus (Lk 2:11; Acts 5:31; 13:23; see also Lk 1:69; 19:9; Acts 4:12). As savior, Jesus is looked upon by Luke as the one who rescues humanity from sin and delivers humanity from the condition of alienation from God. The title *christos*, "Christ," is the Greek equivalent of the Hebrew *māšîaḥ*, "Messiah," "anointed one." Among certain groups in first-century Palestinian Judaism, the title was applied to an expected royal leader from the line of David who would restore the kingdom to Israel (see Acts 1:6). The political overtones of the title are played down in Luke and instead the Messiah of the Lord (Lk 2:26) or the Lord's anointed is the one who now brings salvation to all humanity, Jew and Gentile (Lk 2:29–32). Lord is the most frequently used title for Jesus in Luke and Acts. In the New Testament it is also applied to Yahweh, as it is in the Old Testament. When used of Jesus it points to his transcendence and dominion over humanity.

§[2:14] **On earth peace to those on whom his favor rests**: the peace that results from the Christ event is for those whom God has favored with his grace. This reading is found in the oldest representatives of the Western and Alexandrian text traditions, on the other hand, is the preferred one; the Byzantine text tradition, on the other hand, reads: "on earth peace, good will toward men." The peace of which Luke's gospel speaks (Lk 2:14; 7:50; 8:48; 10:5–6; 19:38, 42; 24:36) is more than the absence of war of the *pax Augusta*; it also includes the security and well-being characteristic of peace in the Old Testament.

¶[2:21] Just as John before him had been incorporated into the people of Israel through his circumcision, so too this child (see note on Lk 1:57–66).

**[2:22–40] The presentation of Jesus in the temple depicts the parents of Jesus as devout Jews, faithful observers of the law of the Lord (Lk 2:23–24, 39), i.e., the law of Moses. In this respect, they are described in a fashion similar to the parents of John (Lk 1:6) and Simeon (Lk 2:25) and Anna (Lk 2:36–37).

††[2:22] **Their purification**: syntactically, **their** must refer to Mary and Joseph, even though the Mosaic law never mentions the purification of the husband. Recognizing the problem, some Western scribes have altered the text to read "his purification," understanding the presentation of Jesus in the temple as a form of purification; the Vulgate version has a Latin form that could be either "his" or "her." According to the Mosaic law (Lv 12:2–8), the woman who gives birth to a boy is unable for forty days to touch anything sacred or to enter the temple area by reason of her legal impurity. At the end of this period she is required to offer a year-old lamb as a burnt offering and a turtledove or young pigeon as an expiation of sin. The woman who could not afford a lamb offered instead two turtledoves or two young pigeons, as Mary does here. **They took him up to Jerusalem to present him to the Lord**: as the firstborn son (Lk 2:7) Jesus was consecrated to the Lord as the law required (Ex 13:2, 12), but there was no requirement that this be done at the temple. The concept of a presentation at the temple is probably derived from 1 Sm 1:24–28, where Hannah offers the child Samuel for sanctuary services. The law further stipulated (Nm 3:47–48) that the firstborn son

---

v. [2:4] Mi 5:2; Mt 2:6.   w. [2:5] 1:27; Mt 1:18.   x. [2:7] Mt 1:25.   y. [2:9] 1:11, 26.   z. [2:11] Mt 1:21; 16:16; Jn 4:42; Acts 2:36; 5:31; Phil 2:11.

a. [2:14] 19:38.   b. [2:21] 1:31; Gn 17:12; Mt 1:21.

according to the law of Moses, they took him up to Jerusalem to present him to the Lord,[c] [23]just as it is written in the law of the Lord, "Every male that opens the womb shall be consecrated to the Lord,"[d] [24]and to offer the sacrifice of "a pair of turtledoves or two young pigeons," in accordance with the dictate in the law of the Lord.

[25]Now there was a man in Jerusalem whose name was Simeon. This man was righteous and devout, awaiting the consolation of Israel,[*] and the holy Spirit was upon him. [26]It had been revealed to him by the holy Spirit that he should not see death before he had seen the Messiah of the Lord. [27]He came in the Spirit into the temple; and when the parents brought in the child Jesus to perform the custom of the law in regard to him, [28]he took him into his arms and blessed God, saying:

[29] "Now, Master, you may let your servant
            go
        in peace, according to your word,
[30] for my eyes have seen your salvation,[e]
[31]   which you prepared in sight of all
            the peoples,
[32]   a light for revelation to the Gentiles,
        and glory for your people Israel."[f]

[33]The child's father and mother were amazed at what was said about him; [34]and Simeon blessed them and said to Mary his mother, "Behold, this child is destined for the fall and rise of many in Israel, and to be a sign that will be contradicted[g] [35](and you yourself a sword will pierce)[†] so that the thoughts of many hearts may be revealed." [36]There was also a prophetess, Anna, the daughter of Phanuel, of the tribe of Asher. She was advanced in years, having lived seven years with her husband after her marriage, [37]and then as a widow until she was eighty-four. She never left the temple, but worshiped night and day with fasting and prayer. [38]And coming forward at that very time, she gave thanks to God and spoke about the child to all who were awaiting the redemption of Jerusalem.[h]

The Return to Nazareth. [39]When they had fulfilled all the prescriptions of the law of the Lord, they returned to Galilee, to their own town of Nazareth.[i] [40]The child grew and became strong, filled with wisdom; and the favor of God was upon him.[j]

The Boy Jesus in the Temple.[‡] [41]Each year his parents went to Jerusalem for the feast of Passover,[k] [42]and when he was twelve years old, they went up according to festival custom. [43]After they had completed its days, as they were returning, the boy Jesus remained behind in Jerusalem, but his parents did not know it. [44]Thinking that he was in the caravan, they journeyed for a day and looked for him among their relatives and acquaintances, [45]but not finding him, they returned to Jerusalem to look for him. [46]After three days they found him in the temple, sitting in the midst of the teachers, listening to them and asking them questions, [47]and all who heard him were astounded at his understanding and his answers. [48]When his parents saw him, they were astonished, and his mother said to him, "Son, why have you done this to us? Your father and I have been looking for you with great anxiety." [49]And he said to them, "Why were you looking for me? Did you not know that I must be in my Father's house?"[§] [50]But they did not understand what he said to them. [51]He went down with them and came to Nazareth, and was obedient to them; and his mother kept all these things in her heart.[l] [52]And Jesus advanced [in] wisdom and age and favor before God and man.[m]

III. THE PREPARATION FOR
THE PUBLIC MINISTRY

CHAPTER 3
The Preaching of John the Baptist.[¶] [1]In the

---

should be redeemed by the parents through their payment of five shekels to a member of a priestly family. About this legal requirement Luke is silent.
[*][2:25] **Awaiting the consolation of Israel:** Simeon here and later Anna who speak about the child to all who were awaiting the redemption of Jerusalem represent the hopes and expectations of faithful and devout Jews who at this time were looking forward to the restoration of God's rule in Israel. The birth of Jesus brings these hopes to fulfillment.
[†][2:35] **(And you yourself a sword will pierce):** Mary herself will not be untouched by the various reactions to the role of Jesus (Lk 2:34). Her blessedness as mother of the Lord will be challenged by her son who describes true blessedness as "hearing the word of God and observing it" (Lk 11:27–28 and Lk 8:20–21).

c. [2:22–24] Lv 12:2–8.   d. [2:23] Ex 13:2, 12.   e. [2:30–31] 3:6; Is 40:5 LXX; 52:10.   f. [2:32] Is 42:6; 46:13; 49:6; Acts 13:47; 26:23.   g. [2:34] 12:51; Is 8:14; Jn 9:39; Rom 9:33; 1 Cor 1:23; 1 Pt 2:7–8.   h. [2:38] Is 52:9.

[‡][2:41–52] This story's concern with an incident from Jesus' youth is unique in the canonical gospel tradition. It presents Jesus in the role of the faithful Jewish boy, raised in the traditions of Israel, and fulfilling all that the law requires. With this episode, the infancy narrative ends just as it began, in the setting of the Jerusalem temple.
[§][2:49] **I must be in my Father's house:** this phrase can also be translated, "I must be about my Father's work." In either translation, Jesus refers to God as his Father. His divine sonship, and his obedience to his heavenly Father's will, take precedence over his ties to his family.
[¶][3:1–20] Although Luke is indebted in this section to his sources, the Gospel of Mark and a collection of sayings of John the Baptist, he has clearly marked this introduction to the ministry of Jesus with his own individual style. Just as the gospel began with a long periodic sentence (Lk 1:1–4), so too this section (Lk 3:1–2). He casts the call of John the Baptist in the form of an Old Testament prophetic call (Lk 3:2) and extends the quotation from Isaiah found in Mk 1:3 (Is 40:3) by the addition of Is 40:4–5 in Lk 3:5–6. In doing so, he presents his theme of the universality of salvation, which he has announced earlier in the words of Simeon (Lk 2:30–32). Moreover, in describing the expectation of the people (Lk 3:15), Luke is characterizing the time of John's preaching in the same way as he had earlier described the situation of other

i. [2:39] Mt 2:23.   j. [2:40] 1:80; 2:52.   k. [2:41] Ex 12:24–27; 23:15; Dt 16:1–8.   l. [2:51] 2:19.   m. [2:52] 1:80; 2:40; 1 Sm 2:26.

fifteenth year of the reign of Tiberius Caesar,* when Pontius Pilate was governor of Judea,[n] and Herod was tetrarch of Galilee, and his brother Philip tetrarch of the region of Ituraea and Trachonitis, and Lysanias was tetrarch of Abilene, [2]during the high priesthood of Annas and Caiaphas,[†] the word of God came to John[o] the son of Zechariah in the desert. [3‡]He went throughout [the] whole region of the Jordan, proclaiming a baptism of repentance for the forgiveness of sins,[p] [4§]as it is written in the book of the words of the prophet Isaiah:[q]

"A voice of one crying out in the desert:
    'Prepare the way of the Lord,[r]
        make straight his paths.
[5] Every valley shall be filled
        and every mountain and hill shall be made low.
    The winding roads shall be made straight,
        and the rough ways made smooth,
[6] and all flesh shall see the salvation of God.'"[s]

[7]He said to the crowds who came out to be baptized by him, "You brood of vipers! Who warned you to flee from the coming wrath?[t] [8]Produce good fruits as evidence of your repentance; and do not begin to say to yourselves, 'We have Abraham as our father,' for I tell you, God can raise up children to Abraham from these stones.[u] [9]Even now the ax lies at the root of the trees. Therefore every tree that does not produce good fruit will be cut down and thrown into the fire."[v]

[10]And the crowds asked him, "What then should we do?" [11]He said to them in reply, "Whoever has two tunics should share with the person who has none. And whoever has food should do likewise." [12]Even tax collectors came to be baptized and they said to him, "Teacher, what should we do?"[w] [13]He answered them, "Stop collecting more than what is prescribed." [14]Soldiers also asked him, "And what is it that we should do?" He told them, "Do not practice extortion, do not falsely accuse anyone, and be satisfied with your wages."

[15x]Now the people were filled with expectation, and all were asking in their hearts whether John might be the Messiah. [16x]John answered them all, saying,[y] "I am baptizing you with water, but one mightier than I is coming. I am not worthy to loosen the thongs of his sandals. He will baptize you with the holy Spirit and fire. [17]His winnowing fan** is in his hand to clear his threshing floor and to gather the wheat into his barn, but the chaff he will burn with unquenchable fire."[z] [18]Exhorting them in many other ways, he preached good news to the people. [19††]Now Herod the tetrarch,[a] who had been censured by him because of Herodias, his brother's wife, and because of all the evil deeds Herod had committed, [20]added still another to these by [also] putting John in prison.

The Baptism of Jesus.[‡‡] [21b]After all the people had been baptized and Jesus also had been

---

devout Israelites in the infancy narrative (Lk 2:25–26, 37–38). In Lk 3:7–18 Luke presents the preaching of John the Baptist who urges the crowds to reform in view of **the coming wrath** (Lk 3:7, 9: eschatological preaching), and who offers the crowds certain standards for reforming social conduct (Lk 3:10–14: ethical preaching), and who announces to the crowds the coming of **one mightier than** he (Lk 3:15–18: messianic preaching).

*[3:1] **Tiberius Caesar:** Tiberius succeeded Augustus as emperor in A.D. 14 and reigned until A.D. 37. The fifteenth year of his reign, depending on the method of calculating his first regnal year, would have fallen between A.D. 27 and 29. **Pontius Pilate:** prefect of Judea from A.D. 26 to 36. The Jewish historian Josephus describes him as a greedy and ruthless prefect who had little regard for the local Jewish population and their religious practices (see note on Lk 1:5). **Herod:** i.e., Herod Antipas, the son of Herod the Great. He ruled over Galilee and Perea from 4 B.C. to A.D. 39. His official title **tetrarch** means literally, "ruler of a quarter," but came to designate any subordinate prince. **Philip:** also a son of Herod the Great, tetrarch of the territory to the north and east of the Sea of Galilee from 4 B.C. to A.D. 34. Only two small areas of this territory are mentioned by Luke. **Lysanias:** nothing is known about this Lysanias who is said here to have been tetrarch of Abilene, a territory northwest of Damascus.

†[3:2] **During the high priesthood of Annas and Caiaphas:** after situating the call of John the Baptist in terms of the civil rulers of the period, Luke now mentions the religious leadership of Palestine (see note on Lk 1:5). Annas had been high priest A.D. 6–15. After being deposed by the Romans in A.D. 15 he was succeeded by various members of his family and eventually by his son-in-law, Caiaphas, who was high priest A.D. 18–36. Luke refers to Annas as high priest at this time (but see Jn 18:13, 19), possibly because of the continuing influence of Annas or because the title continued to be used for the ex-high priest. **The word of God came to John:** Luke is alone among the New Testament writers in associating the preaching of John with a call from God. Luke is thereby identifying John with the prophets whose ministries began with similar calls. In Lk 7:26 John will be described as "more than a prophet"; he is also the precursor of Jesus (Lk 7:27), a transitional figure inaugurating the period of the fulfillment of prophecy and promise.

‡[3:3] See note on Mt 3:2.

§[3:4] The Essenes from Qumran used the same passage to explain why their community was in the desert studying and observing the law and the prophets (1QS 8:12–15).

¶[3:16] **He will baptize you with the holy Spirit and fire:** in contrast to John's baptism with water, Jesus is said to baptize with the holy Spirit and with fire. From the point of view of the early Christian community, the Spirit and fire must have been understood in the light of the fire symbolism of the pouring out of the Spirit at Pentecost (Acts 2:1–4); but as part of John's preaching, the Spirit and fire should be related to their purifying and refining characteristics (Ez 36:25–27; Mal 3:2–3). See note on Mt 3:11.

[3:17] **Winnowing fan: see note on Mt 3:12.

††[3:19–20] Luke separates the ministry of John the Baptist from that of Jesus by reporting the imprisonment of John before the baptism of Jesus (Lk 3:21–22). Luke uses this literary device to serve his understanding of the periods of salvation history. With John the Baptist, the time of promise, the period of Israel, comes to an end; with the baptism of Jesus and the descent of the Spirit upon him, the time of fulfillment, the period of Jesus, begins. In his second volume, the Acts of the Apostles, Luke will introduce the third epoch in salvation history, the period of the church.

‡‡[3:21–22] This episode in Luke focuses on the heavenly message identifying Jesus as Son and, through the allusion to

---

n. [3:1–20] Mt 3:1–12; Mk 1:1–8; Jn 1:19–28.   o. [3:2] 1:80.   p. [3:3] Acts 13:24; 19:4.   q. [3:4–6] Is 40:3–5.   r. [3:4] Jn 1:23.   s. [3:6] 2:30–31.

t. [3:7] Mt 12:34.   u. [3:8] Jn 8:39.   v. [3:9] Mt 7:19; Jn 15:6. w. [3:12] 7:29.   x. [3:15–16] Acts 13:25.   y. [3:16] 7:19–20; Jn 1:27; Acts 1:5; 11:16.   z. [3:17] Mt 3:12.   a. [3:19–20] Mt 14:3–4; Mk 6:17–18.   b. [3:21–22] Mt 3:13–17; Mk 1:9–11.

baptized and was praying,* heaven was opened ²²ᵗᶜand the holy Spirit descended upon him in bodily form like a dove. And a voice came from heaven, "You are my beloved Son; with you I am well pleased."

The Genealogy of Jesus.‡ ²³ᵈWhen Jesus began his ministry he was about thirty years of age. He was the son, as was thought, of Joseph, the son of Heli,ᵉ ²⁴the son of Matthat, the son of Levi, the son of Melchi, the son of Jannai, the son of Joseph, ²⁵the son of Mattathias, the son of Amos, the son of Nahum, the son of Esli, the son of Naggai, ²⁶the son of Maath, the son of Mattathias, the son of Semein, the son of Josech, the son of Joda, ²⁷the son of Joanan, the son of Rhesa, the son of Zerubbabel, the son of Shealtiel, the son of Neri,ᶠ ²⁸the son of Melchi, the son of Addi, the son of Cosam, the son of Elmadam, the son of Er, ²⁹the son of Joshua, the son of Eliezer, the son of Jorim, the son of Matthat, the son of Levi, ³⁰the son of Simeon, the son of Judah, the son of Joseph, the son of Jonam, the son of Eliakim, ³¹ᵍthe son of Melea, the son of Menna, the son of Mattatha, the son of Nathan, the son of David,§ ³²the son of Jesse,ʰ the son of Obed, the son of Boaz, the son of Sala, the son of Nahshon, ³³the son of Amminadab, the son of Admin, the son of Arni, the son of Hezron, the son of Perez,ⁱ the son of Judah,ʲ ³⁴the son of Jacob, the son of Isaac, the son of Abraham,ᵏ the son of Terah, the son of Nahor, ³⁵the son of Serug, the son of Reu, the son of Peleg, the son of Eber, the son of Shelah, ³⁶the son of Cainan, the son of Arphaxad, the son of Shem,ˡ the son of Noah, the son of Lamech, ³⁷the son of Methuselah, the son of Enoch, the son of Jared, the son of Mahalaleel,

---

Is 42:1, as Servant of Yahweh. The relationship of Jesus to the Father has already been announced in the infancy narrative (Lk 1:32, 35; 2:49); it occurs here at the beginning of Jesus' Galilean ministry and will reappear in Lk 9:35 before another major section of Luke's gospel, the travel narrative (Lk 9:51–19:27). Elsewhere in Luke's writings (Lk 4:18; Acts 10:38), this incident will be interpreted as a type of anointing of Jesus.

*[3:21] **Was praying:** Luke regularly presents Jesus at prayer at important points in his ministry: here at his baptism; at the choice of the Twelve (Lk 6:12); before Peter's confession (Lk 9:18); at the transfiguration (Lk 9:28); when he teaches his disciples to pray (Lk 11:1); at the Last Supper (Lk 22:32); on the Mount of Olives (Lk 22:41); on the cross (Lk 23:46).

†[3:22] **You are my beloved Son; with you I am well pleased:** this is the best attested reading in the Greek manuscripts. The Western reading, "You are my Son, this day I have begotten you," is derived from Ps 2:7.

‡[3:23–38] Whereas Mt 1:2 begins the genealogy of Jesus with Abraham to emphasize Jesus' bonds with the people of Israel, Luke's universalism leads him to trace the descent of Jesus beyond Israel to Adam and beyond that to God (Lk 3:38) to stress again Jesus' divine sonship.

§[3:31] **The son of Nathan, the son of David:** in keeping with Jesus' prophetic role in Luke and Acts (e.g., Lk 7:16, 39; 9:8; 13:33; 24:19; Acts 3:22–23; 7:37) Luke traces Jesus' Davidic ancestry through the prophet Nathan (see 2 Sm 7:2) rather than through King Solomon, as Mt 1:6–7.

---

c. [3:22] 9:35; Ps 2:7; Is 42:1; Mt 12:18; 17:5; Mk 9:7; Jn 1:32; 2 Pt 1:17.　d. [3:23–38] Mt 1:1–17.　e. [3:23] 4:22; Jn 6:42.　f. [3:27] 1 Chr 3:17; Ez 3:2.　g. [3:31] 2 Sm 5:14.　h. [3:31–32] 1 Sm 16:1, 18.　i. [3:31–33] Ru 4:17–22; 1 Chr 2:1–15.　j. [3:33] Gn 29:35; 38:29.　k. [3:34] Gn 21:3; 25:26; 1 Chr 1:34; 28:34.　l. [3:34–36] Gn 11:10–26; 1 Chr 1:24–27.

---

the son of Cainan, ³⁸the son of Enos, the son of Seth, the son of Adam,ᵐ the son of God.

CHAPTER 4
The Temptation of Jesus.¶ ¹ⁿFilled with the holy Spirit,** Jesus returned from the Jordan and was led by the Spirit into the desert ²for forty days,†† to be tempted by the devil. He ate nothing during those days, and when they were over he was hungry.ᵒ ³The devil said to him, "If you are the Son of God, command this stone to become bread." ⁴Jesus answered him, "It is written, 'One does not live by bread alone.'"ᵖ ⁵Then he took him up and showed him all the kingdoms of the world in a single instant. ⁶The devil said to him, "I shall give to you all this power and their glory; for it has been handed over to me, and I may give it to whomever I wish.�q ⁷All this will be yours, if you worship me." ⁸Jesus said to him in reply, "It is written:

'You shall worship the Lord, your God,
　　and him alone shall you serve.'"ʳ

⁹‡‡Then he led him to Jerusalem, made him stand on the parapet of the temple, and said to him, "If you are the Son of God, throw yourself down from here, ¹⁰for it is written:

'He will command his angels concerning
　　　　　　　you,
　　to guard you,'ˢ

¹¹and:

'With their hands they will support you,
　　lest you dash your foot against a
　　　　stone.'"ᵗ

¹²Jesus said to him in reply, "It also says, 'You shall not put the Lord, your God, to the test.'"ᵘ ¹³§§When the devil had finished every temptation,ᵛ he departed from him for a time.

¶[4:1–13] See note on Mt 4:1–11.

[4:1] **Filled with the holy Spirit: as a result of the descent of the Spirit upon him at his baptism (Lk 3:21–22), Jesus is now equipped to overcome the devil. Just as the Spirit is prominent at this early stage of Jesus' ministry (Lk 4:1, 14, 18), so too it will be at the beginning of the period of the church in Acts (Acts 1:4; 2:4, 17).

††[4:2] **For forty days:** the mention of forty days recalls the forty years of the wilderness wanderings of the Israelites during the Exodus (Dt 8:2).

‡‡[4:9] **To Jerusalem:** the Lucan order of the temptations concludes on the parapet of the temple in Jerusalem, the city of destiny in Luke-Acts. It is in Jerusalem that Jesus will ultimately face his destiny (Lk 9:51; 13:33).

§§[4:13] **For a time:** the devil's opportune time will occur before the passion and death of Jesus (Lk 22:3, 31–32, 53).

---

m. [3:36–38] Gn 4:25–5:32; 1 Chr 1:1–4.　n. [4:1–13] Mt 4:1–11; Mk 1:12–13.　o. [4:2] Heb 4:15.　p. [4:4] Dt 8:3.　q. [4:6] Jer 27:5; Mt 28:18.　r. [4:8] Dt 6:13.　s. [4:10] Ps 91:11.　t. [4:11] Ps 91:12.　u. [4:12] Dt 6:16; 1 Cor 10:9.　v. [4:13] 22:3; Jn 13:2, 27; Heb 4:15.

IV. THE MINISTRY IN GALILEE

The Beginning of the Galilean Ministry.
[14w]Jesus returned to Galilee in the power of the Spirit, and news of him spread* throughout the whole region.[x] [15]He taught in their synagogues and was praised by all.

The Rejection at Nazareth.[ty] [16]He came to Nazareth, where he had grown up, and went according to his custom‡ into the synagogue on the sabbath day. He stood up to read [17]and was handed a scroll of the prophet Isaiah. He unrolled the scroll and found the passage where it was written:

[18] "The Spirit of the Lord is upon me,§
        because he has anointed me
           to bring glad tidings to the poor.[z]
    He has sent me to proclaim liberty to
           captives
        and recovery of sight to the blind,
           to let the oppressed go free,
[19]   and to proclaim a year acceptable to the
           Lord."

[20]Rolling up the scroll, he handed it back to the attendant and sat down, and the eyes of all in the synagogue looked intently at him. [21]He said to them, "Today this scripture passage is fulfilled in your hearing."¶ [22]And all spoke highly of him and were amazed at the gracious words that came from his mouth. They also asked, "Isn't this the son of Joseph?"[a] [23]He said to them, "Surely you will quote me this proverb, 'Physician, cure yourself,' and say, 'Do here in your native place the things that we heard were done in Capernaum.'"** [24]And he said, "Amen, I say to you, no prophet is accepted in his own native place. [25††]Indeed, I tell you, there were many widows in Israel in the days of Elijah when the sky was closed for three and a half years and a severe famine spread over the entire land.[b] [26‡‡]It was to none of these that Elijah was sent, but only to a widow in Zarephath[c] in the land of Sidon. [27]Again, there were many lepers in Israel during the time of Elisha the prophet; yet not one of them was cleansed, but only Naaman the Syrian."[d] [28]When the people in the synagogue heard this, they were all filled with fury. [29]They rose up, drove him out of the town, and led him to the brow of the hill on which their town had been built, to hurl him down headlong. [30]But he passed through the midst of them and went away.

The Cure of a Demoniac. [31§§]Jesus then went down to Capernaum,[e] a town of Galilee.[f] He taught them on the sabbath, [32]and they were astonished at his teaching because he spoke with authority.[g] [33]In the synagogue there was a man with the spirit of an unclean demon,[h] and he cried out in a loud voice, [34]"Ha! What have you to do with us, Jesus of Nazareth? Have you come to destroy us?¶¶ I know who you are—the Holy One of God!"[i] [35]Jesus rebuked him and said, "Be quiet! Come out of him!" Then the demon threw the man down in front of them and came out of him without doing him any harm. [36]They were all amazed and said to one another, "What is there about his word? For with authority and power he commands the unclean spirits, and they come out." [37]And news of him spread everywhere in the surrounding region.

---

*[4:14] **News of him spread**: a Lucan theme; see Lk 4:37; 5:15; 7:17.

†[4:16–30] Luke has transposed to the beginning of Jesus' ministry an incident from his Marcan source, which situated it near the end of the Galilean ministry (Mk 6:1–6a). In doing so, Luke turns the initial admiration (Lk 4:22) and subsequent rejection of Jesus (Lk 4:28–29) into a foreshadowing of the whole future ministry of Jesus. Moreover, the rejection of Jesus in his own hometown hints at the greater rejection of him by Israel (Acts 13:46).

‡[4:16] **According to his custom**: Jesus' practice of regularly attending synagogue is carried on by the early Christians' practice of meeting in the temple (Acts 2:46; 3:1; 5:12).

§[4:18] **The Spirit of the Lord is upon me, because he has anointed me**: see note on Lk 3:21–22. As this incident develops, Jesus is portrayed as a prophet whose ministry is compared to that of the prophets Elijah and Elisha. Prophetic anointings are known in first-century Palestinian Judaism from the Qumran literature that speaks of prophets as God's anointed ones. **To bring glad tidings to the poor**: more than any other gospel writer Luke is concerned with Jesus' attitude toward the economically and socially poor (see Lk 6:20, 24; 12:16–21; 14:12–14; 16:19–26; 19:8). At times, the poor in Luke's gospel are associated with the downtrodden, the oppressed and afflicted, the forgotten and the neglected (Lk 4:18; 6:20–22; 7:22; 14:12–14), and it is they who accept Jesus' message of salvation.

¶[4:21] **Today this scripture passage is fulfilled in your hearing**: this sermon inaugurates the time of fulfillment of Old Testament prophecy. Luke presents the ministry of Jesus as fulfilling Old Testament hopes and expectations (Lk 7:22); for Luke, even Jesus' suffering, death, and resurrection are done in fulfillment of the scriptures (Lk 24:25–27, 44–46; Acts 3:18).

[4:23] **The things that we heard were done in Capernaum: Luke's source for this incident reveals an awareness of an earlier ministry of Jesus in Capernaum that Luke has not yet made use of because of his transposition of this Nazareth episode to the beginning of Jesus' Galilean ministry. It is possible that by use of the future tense **you will quote me . . .** , Jesus is being portrayed as a prophet.

††[4:25–26] The references to Elijah and Elisha serve several purposes in this episode: they emphasize Luke's portrait of Jesus as a prophet like Elijah and Elisha; they help to explain why the initial admiration of the people turns to rejection; and they provide the scriptural justification for the future Christian mission to the Gentiles.

‡‡[4:26] **A widow in Zarephath in the land of Sidon**: like Naaman the Syrian in Lk 4:27, a non-Israelite becomes the object of the prophet's ministry.

§§[4:31–44] The next several incidents in Jesus' ministry take place in Capernaum and are based on Luke's source, Mk 1:21–39. To the previous portrait of Jesus as prophet (Lk 4:16–30) they now add a presentation of him as teacher (Lk 4:31–32), exorcist (Lk 4:32–37, 41), healer (Lk 4:38–40), and proclaimer of God's kingdom (Lk 4:43).

¶¶[4:34] **What have you to do with us?**: see note on Jn 2:4. **Have you come to destroy us?**: the question reflects the current belief that before the day of the Lord control over humanity would be wrested from the evil spirits, evil destroyed, and God's authority over humanity reestablished. The synoptic gospel tradition presents Jesus carrying out this task.

---

w. [4:14–15] Mt 4:12–17; Mk 1:14–15.   x. [4:14] 5:15; Mt 3:16.   y. [4:16–30] Mt 13:53–58; Mk 6:1–6.   z. [4:18–19] Is 61:1–2; 58:6.   a. [4:22] 3:23; Jn 6:42.

b. [4:25] 1 Kgs 17:1–7; 18:1; Jas 5:17.   c. [4:26] 1 Kgs 17:9.   d. [4:27] 2 Kgs 5:1–14.   e. [4:31–37] Mk 1:21–28.   f. [4:31] Mt 4:13; Jn 2:12.   g. [4:32] Mt 7:28–29.   h. [4:33–34] 8:28; Mt 8:29; Mk 1:23–24; 5:7.   i. [4:34] 4:41; Jn 6:69.

The Cure of Simon's Mother-in-Law. [38]jAfter he left the synagogue, he entered the house of Simon.* Simon's mother-in-law was afflicted with a severe fever, and they interceded with him about her. [39]He stood over her, rebuked the fever, and it left her. She got up immediately and waited on them.

Other Healings.k [40]At sunset, all who had people sick with various diseases brought them to him. He laid his hands on each of them and cured them. [41]†And demons also came out from many, shouting, "You are the Son of God."l But he rebuked them and did not allow them to speak because they knew that he was the Messiah.

Jesus Leaves Capernaum.m [42]‡At daybreak, Jesus left and went to a deserted place. The crowds went looking for him, and when they came to him, they tried to prevent him from leaving them. [43]But he said to them, "To the other towns also I must proclaim the good news of the kingdom of God, because for this purpose I have been sent."n [44]And he was preaching in the synagogues of Judea.§

CHAPTER 5

The Call of Simon the Fisherman.¶o [1]pWhile the crowd was pressing in on Jesus and listening to the word of God, he was standing by the Lake of Gennesaret. [2]He saw two boats there alongside the lake; the fishermen had disembarked and were washing their nets. [3]Getting into one of the boats, the one belonging to Simon, he asked him to put out a short distance from the shore. Then he sat down and taught the crowds from the boat. [4]qAfter he had finished speaking, he said to Simon, "Put out into deep water and lower your nets for a catch." [5]Simon said in reply, "Master, we have worked hard all night and have caught nothing, but at your command I will lower the nets." [6]When they had done this, they caught a great number of fish and their nets were tearing. [7]They signaled to their partners in the other boat to come to help them. They came and filled both boats so that they were in danger of sinking. [8]When Simon Peter saw this, he fell at the knees of Jesus and said, "Depart from me, Lord, for I am a sinful man." [9]For astonishment at the catch of fish they had made seized him and all those with him, [10]and likewise James and John, the sons of Zebedee, who were partners of Simon. Jesus said to Simon, "Do not be afraid; from now on you will be catching men."r [11]When they brought their boats to the shore, they left everything** and followed him.s

The Cleansing of a Leper.t [12]Now there was a man full of leprosy†† in one of the towns where he was; and when he saw Jesus, he fell prostrate, pleaded with him, and said, "Lord, if you wish, you can make me clean." [13]Jesus stretched out his hand, touched him, and said, "I do will it. Be made clean." And the leprosy left him immediately. [14]Then he ordered him not to tell anyone, but "Go, show yourself to the priest and offer for your cleansing what Moses prescribed;‡‡ that will be proof for them."u [15]The report about him spread all the more, and great crowds assembled to listen to him and to be cured of their ailments, [16]but he would withdraw to deserted places to pray.v

The Healing of a Paralytic.w [17]§§One day as Jesus was teaching, Pharisees¶¶ and teachers of the law

---

*[4:38] **The house of Simon**: because of Luke's arrangement of material, the reader has not yet been introduced to Simon (cf. Mk 1:16–18, 29–31). Situated as it is before the call of Simon (Lk 5:1–11), it helps the reader to understand Simon's eagerness to do what Jesus says (Lk 5:5) and to follow him (Lk 5:11).

†[4:41] **They knew that he was the Messiah**: that is, the Christ (see note on Lk 2:11).

‡[4:42] **They tried to prevent him from leaving them**: the reaction of these strangers in Capernaum is presented in contrast to the reactions of those in his hometown who rejected him (Lk 4:28–30).

§[4:44] **In the synagogues of Judea**: instead of **Judea**, which is the best reading of the manuscript tradition, the Byzantine text tradition and other manuscripts read "Galilee," a reading that harmonizes Luke with Mt 4:23 and Mk 1:39. Up to this point Luke has spoken only of a ministry of Jesus in Galilee. Luke may be using **Judea** to refer to the land of Israel, the territory of the Jews, and not to a specific portion of it.

¶[5:1–11] This incident has been transposed from his source, Mk 1:16–20, which places it immediately after Jesus makes his appearance in Galilee. By this transposition Luke uses this example of Simon's acceptance of Jesus to counter the earlier rejection of him by his hometown people, and since several incidents dealing with Jesus' power and authority have already been narrated, Luke creates a plausible context for the acceptance of Jesus by Simon and his partners. Many commentators have noted the similarity between the wondrous catch of fish reported here (Lk 4:4–9) and the post-resurrectional appearance of Jesus in Jn 21:1–11. There are traces in Luke's story that the post-resurrectional context is the original one: in Lk 4:8 Simon addresses Jesus as **Lord** (a post-resurrectional title for Jesus—see Lk 24:34; Acts 2:36—that has been read back into the historical ministry of Jesus) and recognizes himself as a sinner (an appropriate recognition for one who has denied knowing Jesus—Lk 22:54–62). As used by Luke, the incident looks forward to Peter's leadership in Luke-Acts (Lk 6:14; 9:20; 22:31–32; 24:34; Acts 1:15; 2:14–40; 10:11–18; 15:7–12) and symbolizes the future success of Peter as fisherman (Acts 2:41).

[5:11] **They left everything: in Mk 1:16–20 and Mt 4:18–22 the fishermen who follow Jesus leave their nets and their father; in Luke, they leave **everything** (see also Lk 5:28; 12:33; 14:33; 18:22), an indication of Luke's theme of complete detachment from material possessions.

††[5:12] **Full of leprosy**: see note on Mk 1:40.

‡‡[5:14] **Show yourself to the priest . . . what Moses prescribed**: this is a reference to Lv 14:2–9 that gives detailed instructions for the purification of one who had been a victim of leprosy and thereby excluded from contact with others (see Lv 13:45–46, 49; Nm 5:2–3). **That will be proof for them**: see note on Mt 8:4.

§§[5:17–6:11] From his Marcan source, Luke now introduces a series of controversies with Pharisees: controversy over Jesus' power to forgive sins (Lk 5:17–26); controversy over his eating and drinking with tax collectors and sinners (Lk 5:27–32); controversy over not fasting (Lk 5:33–36); and finally two episodes narrating controversies over observance of the sabbath (Lk 5:1–11).

¶¶[5:17] **Pharisees**: see note on Mt 3:7.

---

j. [4:38–39] Mt 8:14–15; Mk 1:29–31. k. [4:40–41] Mt 8:16; Mk 1:32–34. l. [4:41] 4:34; Mt 8:29; Mk 3:11–12. m. [4:42–44] Mk 1:35–39. n. [4:43] 8:1; Mk 1:14–15. o. [5:1–11] Mt 4:18–22; Mk 1:16–20. p. [5:1–3] Mt 13:1–2; Mk 2:13; 3:9–10; 4:1–2.

q. [5:4–9] Jn 21:1–11. r. [5:10] Jer 16:16. s. [5:11] Mt 19:27. t. [5:12–16] Mt 8:2–4; Mk 1:40–45. u. [5:14] 8:56; Lv 14:2–32; Mk 7:36. v. [5:16] Mk 1:35. w. [5:17–26] Mt 9:1–8; Mk 2:1–12.

were sitting there who had come from every village of Galilee and Judea and Jerusalem, and the power of the Lord was with him for healing. ¹⁸And some men brought on a stretcher a man who was paralyzed; they were trying to bring him in and set [him] in his presence. ¹⁹But not finding a way to bring him in because of the crowd, they went up on the roof and lowered him on the stretcher through the tiles* into the middle in front of Jesus. ²⁰When he saw their faith, he said, "As for you, your sins are forgiven."† ²¹Then the scribes‡ and Pharisees began to ask themselves, "Who is this who speaks blasphemies? Who but God alone can forgive sins?"ˣ ²²Jesus knew their thoughts and said to them in reply, "What are you thinking in your hearts?ʸ ²³Which is easier, to say, 'Your sins are forgiven,' or to say, 'Rise and walk'? ²⁴§ᶻBut that you may know that the Son of Man has authority on earth to forgive sins"—he said to the man who was paralyzed, "I say to you, rise, pick up your stretcher, and go home." ²⁵He stood up immediately before them, picked up what he had been lying on, and went home, glorifying God. ²⁶Then astonishment seized them all and they glorified God, and, struck with awe, they said, "We have seen incredible things today."

The Call of Levi.ᵃ ²⁷After this he went out and saw a tax collector named Levi sitting at the customs post. He said to him, "Follow me." ²⁸And leaving everything behind,⁵ he got up and followed him. ²⁹ᵇThen Levi gave a great banquet for him in his house, and a large crowd of tax collectors and others were at table with them. ³⁰The Pharisees and their scribes complained to his disciples, saying, "Why do you eat and drink with tax collectors and sinners?" ³¹Jesus said to them in reply, "Those who are healthy do not need a physician, but the sick do. ³²I have not come to call the righteous but sinners to repentance."

The Question About Fasting.ᶜ ³³And they said to him, "The disciples of John fast often and offer prayers, and the disciples of the Pharisees do the same; but yours eat and drink." ³⁴**Jesus answered them, "Can you make the wedding

guests†† fast while the bridegroom is with them? ³⁵But the days will come, and when the bridegroom is taken away from them, then they will fast in those days." ³⁶‡‡And he also told them a parable. "No one tears a piece from a new cloak to patch an old one. Otherwise, he will tear the new and the piece from it will not match the old cloak. ³⁷Likewise, no one pours new wine into old wineskins. Otherwise, the new wine will burst the skins, and it will be spilled, and the skins will be ruined. ³⁸Rather, new wine must be poured into fresh wineskins. ³⁹[And] no one who has been drinking old wine desires new, for he says, 'The old is good.'"§§

CHAPTER 6

Debates About the Sabbath.¶¶ ¹ᵈWhile he was going through a field of grain on a sabbath, his disciples were picking the heads of grain, rubbing them in their hands, and eating them.ᵉ ²Some Pharisees said, "Why are you doing what is unlawful on the sabbath?" ³ᶠJesus said to them in reply, "Have you not read what David did when he and those [who were] with him were hungry? ⁴[How] he went into the house of God, took the bread of offering,*** which only the priests could lawfully eat, ate of it, and shared it with his companions."ᵍ ⁵Then he said to them, "The Son of Man is lord of the sabbath."

⁶ʰOn another sabbath he went into the synagogue and taught, and there was a man there whose right hand was withered. ⁷The scribes and the Pharisees watched him closely to see if he would cure on the sabbath so that they might discover a reason to accuse him.ⁱ ⁸But he realized their intentions and said to the man with the withered hand, "Come up and stand before us." And he rose and stood there.ʲ ⁹Then Jesus said to them, "I ask you, is it lawful to do good on the sabbath rather than to do evil, to save life rather than to destroy it?" ¹⁰Looking around at them all, he then said to him, "Stretch out your hand." He did so and his hand was restored. ¹¹But they became enraged and discussed together what they might do to Jesus.

---

*[5:19] **Through the tiles:** Luke has adapted the story found in Mark to his non-Palestinian audience by changing "opened up the roof" (Mk 2:4, a reference to Palestinian straw and clay roofs) to **through the tiles,** a detail that reflects the Hellenistic Greco-Roman house with tiled roof.

†[5:20] **As for you, your sins are forgiven:** literally, "O man, your sins are forgiven you." The connection between the forgiveness of sins and the cure of the paralytic reflects the belief of first-century Palestine (based on the Old Testament: Ex 20:5; Dt 5:9) that sickness and infirmity are the result of sin, one's own or that of one's ancestors (see also Lk 13:2; Jn 5:14; 9:2).

‡[5:21] **The scribes:** see note on Mk 2:6.

§[5:24] See notes on Mt 9:6 and Mk 2:10.

¶[5:28] **Leaving everything behind:** see note on Lk 5:11.

**[5:34–35] See notes on Mt 9:15 and Mk 2:19.

††[5:34] **Wedding guests:** literally, "sons of the bridal chamber."

‡‡[5:36–39] See notes on Mt 9:16–17 and Mk 2:19.

§§[5:39] **The old is good:** this saying is meant to be ironic and offers an explanation for the rejection by some of the new wine that Jesus offers: satisfaction with old forms will prevent one from sampling the new.

¶¶[6:1–11] The two episodes recounted here deal with gathering grain and healing, both of which were forbidden on the sabbath. In his defense of his disciples' conduct and his own charitable deed, Jesus argues that satisfying human needs such as hunger and performing works of mercy take precedence even over the sacred sabbath rest. See also notes on Mt 12:1–14 and Mk 2:25–26.

***[6:4] **The bread of offering:** see note on Mt 12:5–6.

---

x. [5:21] 7:49; Is 43:25.   y. [5:22] 6:8; 9:47.   z. [5:24–25] Jn 5:8–9, 27.   a. [5:27–32] Mt 9:9–13; Mk 2:13–17.   b. [5:29–30] 15:1–2.   c. [5:33–39] Mt 9:14–17; Mk 2:18–22.

d. [6:1–5] Mt 12:1–8; Mk 2:23–28.   e. [6:1] Dt 23:26.   f. [6:3–4] 1 Sm 21:1–6.   g. [6:4] Lv 24:5–9.   h. [6:6–11] Mt 12:9–14; Mk 3:1–6.   i. [6:7] 14:1.   j. [6:8] 5:22; 9:47.

The Mission of the Twelve.[*] [12k]In those days he departed to the mountain to pray, and he spent the night in prayer[†] to God. [13]When day came, he called his disciples to himself, and from them he chose Twelve,[‡] whom he also named apostles: [14]Simon, whom he named Peter,[§] and his brother Andrew, James, John, Philip, Bartholomew, [15]Matthew, Thomas, James the son of Alphaeus, Simon who was called a Zealot,[¶] [16]and Judas the son of James, and Judas Iscariot,[**] who became a traitor.

Ministering to a Great Multitude.[m] [17††]And he came down with them and stood on a stretch of level ground. A great crowd of his disciples and a large number of the people from all Judea and Jerusalem and the coastal region of Tyre and Sidon [18]came to hear him and to be healed of their diseases; and even those who were tormented by unclean spirits were cured. [19]Everyone in the crowd sought to touch him because power came forth from him and healed them all.

Sermon on the Plain.[n] [20‡‡]And raising his eyes toward his disciples he said:

"Blessed are you who are poor,[§§]
for the kingdom of God is yours.
[21] Blessed are you who are now hungry,
for you will be satisfied.
Blessed are you who are now weeping,
for you will laugh.[o]
[22] Blessed are you when people hate you,
and when they exclude and insult you,
and denounce your name as evil
on account of the Son of Man.[p]

[23]Rejoice and leap for joy on that day! Behold, your reward will be great in heaven. For their ancestors treated the prophets in the same way.[q]

[24] But woe to you who are rich,
for you have received your
consolation.[r]
[25] But woe to you who are filled now,
for you will be hungry.
Woe to you who laugh now,
for you will grieve and weep.[s]
[26] Woe to you when all speak well of you,
for their ancestors treated the false
prophets in this way.[t]

Love of Enemies.[¶¶] [27u]"But to you who hear I say, love your enemies, do good to those who hate you,[v] [28]bless those who curse you, pray for those who mistreat you.[w] [29]To the person who strikes you on one cheek, offer the other one as well, and from the person who takes your cloak, do not withhold even your tunic. [30]Give to everyone who asks of you, and from the one who takes what is yours do not demand it back. [31]Do to others as you would have them do to you.[x] [32]For if you love those who love you, what

---

*[6:12–16] See notes on Mt 10:1–11:1 and Mk 3:14–15.

†[6:12] **Spent the night in prayer**: see note on Lk 3:21.

‡[6:13] **He chose Twelve**: the identification of this group as the **Twelve** is a part of early Christian tradition (see 1 Cor 15:5), and in Matthew and Luke, the **Twelve** are associated with the twelve tribes of Israel (Lk 22:29–30; Mt 19:28). After the fall of Judas from his position among the Twelve, the need is felt on the part of the early community to reconstitute this group before the Christian mission begins at Pentecost (Acts 1:15–26). From Luke's perspective, they are an important group who because of their association with Jesus from the time of his baptism to his ascension (Acts 1:21–22) provide the continuity between the historical Jesus and the church of Luke's day and who as the original eyewitnesses guarantee the fidelity of the church's beliefs and practices to the teachings of Jesus (Lk 1:1–4). **Whom he also named apostles**: only Luke among the gospel writers attributes to Jesus the bestowal of the name **apostles** upon the Twelve. See note on Mt 10:2–4. "Apostle" becomes a technical term in early Christianity for a missionary sent out to preach the word of God. Although Luke seems to want to restrict the title to the Twelve (only in Acts 4:4, 14 are Paul and Barnabas termed apostles), other places in the New Testament show an awareness that the term was more widely applied (1 Cor 15:5–7; Gal 1:19; 1 Cor 1:1; 9:1; Rom 16:7).

§[6:14] **Simon, whom he named Peter**: see note on Mk 3:16.

¶[6:15] **Simon who was called a Zealot**: the Zealots were the instigators of the First Revolt of Palestinian Jews against Rome in A.D. 66–70. Because the existence of the Zealots as a distinct group during the lifetime of Jesus is the subject of debate, the meaning of the identification of Simon as a Zealot is unclear.

[6:16] **Judas Iscariot: the name **Iscariot** may mean "man from Kerioth."

††[6:17] **The coastal region of Tyre and Sidon**: not only Jews from Judea and Jerusalem, but even Gentiles from outside Palestine come to hear Jesus (see Lk 2:31–32; 3:6; 4:24–27).

‡‡[6:20–49] Luke's "Sermon on the Plain" is the counterpart to Matthew's "Sermon on the Mount" (Mt 5:1–7:27). It is addressed to the disciples of Jesus, and, like the sermon in Matthew, it begins with beatitudes (Lk 6:20–22) and ends with the parable of the two houses (Lk 6:46–49). Almost all the words of Jesus reported by Luke are found in Matthew's version, but because Matthew includes sayings that were related to specifically Jewish Christian problems (e.g., Mt 5:17–20; 6:1–8, 16–18) that Luke did not find appropriate for his predominantly Gentile Christian audience, the "Sermon on the Mount" is considerably longer. Luke's sermon may be outlined as follows: an introduction consisting of blessings and woes (Lk 6:20–26); the love of one's enemies (Lk 6:27–36); the demands of loving one's neighbor (Lk 6:37–42); good deeds as proof of one's goodness (Lk 6:43–45); a parable illustrating the result of listening to and acting on the words of Jesus (Lk 6:46–49). At the core of the sermon is Jesus' teaching on the love of one's enemies (Lk 6:27–36) that has as its source of motivation God's graciousness and compassion for all humanity (Lk 6:35–36) and Jesus' teaching on the love of one's neighbor (Lk 6:37–42) that is characterized by forgiveness and generosity.

§§[6:20–26] The introductory portion of the sermon consists of blessings and woes that address the real economic and social conditions of humanity (the poor—the rich; the hungry—the satisfied; those grieving—those laughing; the outcast—the socially acceptable). By contrast, Matthew emphasizes the religious and spiritual values of disciples in the kingdom inaugurated by Jesus ("poor in spirit," Mt 5:3; "hunger and thirst for righteousness," Mt 5:6). In the sermon, **blessed** extols the fortunate condition of persons who are favored with the blessings of God; the woes, addressed as they are to the disciples of Jesus, threaten God's profound displeasure on those so blinded by their present fortunate situation that they do not recognize and appreciate the real values of God's kingdom. In all the blessings and woes, the present condition of the persons addressed will be reversed in the future.

¶¶[6:27–36] See notes on Mt 5:43–48 and Mt 5:48.

---

k. [6:12–16] Mt 10:1–4; Mk 3:13–19. l. [6:14–16] Acts 1:13. m. [6:17–19] Mt 4:23–25; Mk 3:7–10. n. [6:20–26] Mt 5:1–12.

o. [6:21] Ps 126:5–6; Is 61:3; Jer 31:25; Rev 7:16–17. p. [6:22] Jn 15:19; 16:2; 1 Pt 4:14. q. [6:23] 11:47–48; 2 Chr 36:16; Mt 23:30–31. r. [6:24] Jas 5:1. s. [6:25] Is 65:13–14. t. [6:26] Jas 4:4. u. [6:27–36] Mt 5:38–48. v. [6:27] Prv 25:21; Rom 12:20–21. w. [6:28] Rom 12:14; 1 Pt 3:9. x. [6:31] Mt 7:12.

credit is that to you? Even sinners love those who love them. ³³And if you do good to those who do good to you, what credit is that to you? Even sinners do the same. ³⁴If you lend money to those from whom you expect repayment, what credit [is] that to you? Even sinners lend to sinners, and get back the same amount.ʸ ³⁵But rather, love your enemies and do good to them, and lend expecting nothing back; then your reward will be great and you will be children of the Most High, for he himself is kind to the ungrateful and the wicked.ᶻ ³⁶Be merciful, just as [also] your Father is merciful.

Judging Others. ³⁷ᵃ"Stop judging and you will not be judged. Stop condemning and you will not be condemned. Forgive and you will be forgiven.ᵇ ³⁸Give and gifts will be given to you; a good measure, packed together, shaken down, and overflowing, will be poured into your lap. For the measure with which you measure will in return be measured out to you."ᶜ ³⁹And he told them a parable, "Can a blind person guide a blind person? Will not both fall into a pit?ᵈ ⁴⁰No disciple is superior to the teacher; but when fully trained, every disciple will be like his teacher.ᵉ ⁴¹Why do you notice the splinter in your brother's eye, but do not perceive the wooden beam in your own? ⁴²How can you say to your brother, 'Brother, let me remove that splinter in your eye,' when you do not even notice the wooden beam in your own eye? You hypocrite! Remove the wooden beam from your eye first; then you will see clearly to remove the splinter in your brother's eye.

A Tree Known by Its Fruit.ᶠ ⁴³†"A good tree does not bear rotten fruit, nor does a rotten tree bear good fruit. ⁴⁴For every tree is known by its own fruit. For people do not pick figs from thornbushes, nor do they gather grapes from brambles. ⁴⁵A good person out of the store of goodness in his heart produces good, but an evil person out of a store of evil produces evil; for from the fullness of the heart the mouth speaks. **The Two Foundations.** ⁴⁶ᵍ"Why do you call me, 'Lord, Lord,' but not do what I command? ⁴⁷‡I will show you what someone is like who comes to me, listens to my words, and acts on them.ʰ ⁴⁸That one is like a person building a house, who dug deeply and laid the foundation on rock; when the flood came, the river burst against that house but could not shake it because it had been well built. ⁴⁹But the one who listens and does not act is like a person who built a house on the ground without a foundation. When the river

burst against it, it collapsed at once and was completely destroyed."

CHAPTER 7

The Healing of a Centurion's Slave.ⁱ ¹*When he had finished all his words to the people, he entered Capernaum.⁵ ²A centurion** there had a slave who was ill and about to die, and he was valuable to him. ³When he heard about Jesus, he sent elders of the Jews to him, asking him to come and save the life of his slave. ⁴They approached Jesus and strongly urged him to come, saying, "He deserves to have you do this for him, ⁵for he loves our nation and he built the synagogue for us." ⁶And Jesus went with them, but when he was only a short distance from the house, the centurion sent friends to tell him, "Lord, do not trouble yourself, for I am not worthy to have you enter under my roof.†† ⁷Therefore, I did not consider myself worthy to come to you; but say the word and let my servant be healed. ⁸For I too am a person subject to authority, with soldiers subject to me. And I say to one, 'Go,' and he goes; and to another, 'Come here,' and he comes; and to my slave, 'Do this,' and he does it." ⁹When Jesus heard this he was amazed at him and, turning, said to the crowd following him, "I tell you, not even in Israel have I found such faith." ¹⁰When the messengers returned to the house, they found the slave in good health. **Raising of the Widow's Son.**‡‡ ¹¹ʲSoon afterward he journeyed to a city called Nain, and his disciples and a large crowd accompanied him. ¹²As he drew near to the gate of the city, a man who had died was being carried out, the only son of his mother, and she was a widow. A large crowd from the city was with her.ᵏ ¹³When the Lord

---

§[7:1–8:3] The episodes in this section present a series of reactions to the Galilean ministry of Jesus and reflect some of Luke's particular interests: the faith of a Gentile (Lk 7:1–10); the prophet Jesus' concern for a widowed mother (Lk 7:11–17); the ministry of Jesus directed to the afflicted and unfortunate of Is 61:1 (Lk 7:18–23); the relation between John and Jesus and their role in God's plan for salvation (Lk 7:24–35); a forgiven sinner's manifestation of love (Lk 7:36–50); the association of women with the ministry of Jesus (Lk 8:1–3).

¶[7:1–10] This story about the faith of the centurion, a Gentile who cherishes the Jewish nation (Lk 7:5), prepares for the story in Acts of the conversion by Peter of the Roman centurion Cornelius who is similarly described as one who is generous to the Jewish nation (Acts 10:2). See also Acts 10:34–35 in the speech of Peter: "God shows no partiality . . . whoever fears him and acts righteously is acceptable to him." See also notes on Mt 8:5–13 and Jn 4:43–54.

[7:2] A centurion: see note on Mt 8:5.

††[7:6] **I am not worthy to have you enter under my roof:** to enter the house of a Gentile was considered unclean for a Jew; cf. Acts 10:28.

‡‡[7:11–17] In the previous incident Jesus' power was displayed for a Gentile whose servant was dying; in this episode it is displayed toward a widowed mother whose only son has already died. Jesus' power over death prepares for his reply to John's disciples in Lk 7:22: "the dead are raised." This resuscitation in alluding to the prophet Elijah's resurrection of the only son of a widow of Zarephath (1 Kgs 7:8–24) leads to the reaction of the crowd: "A great prophet has arisen in our midst" (Lk 7:16).

---

*[6:37–42] See notes on Mt 7:1–12; 7:1; 7:5.
†[6:43–46] See notes on Mt 7:15–20 and 12:33.
‡[6:47–49] See note on Mt 7:24–27.

y. [6:34] Dt 15:7–8.   z. [6:35] Lv 25:35–36.   a. [6:37–42] Mt 7:1–5. b. [6:37] Mt 6:14; Jas 2:13.   c. [6:38] Mk 4:24.   d. [6:39] Mt 15:14; 23:16–17, 24.   e. [6:40] Mt 10:24–25; Jn 13:16; 15:20.   f. [6:43–45] Mt 7:16–20; 12:33, 35.   g. [6:46] Mt 7:21; Rom 2:13; Jas 1:22.   h. [6:47–49] Mt 7:24–27.

i. [7:1–10] Mt 8:5–13; Jn 4:43–54.   j. [7:11–17] 4:25–26; 1 Kgs 17:8–24.   k. [7:12] 8:42; 1 Kgs 17:17.

saw her, he was moved with pity for her and said to her, "Do not weep." [14]He stepped forward and touched the coffin; at this the bearers halted, and he said, "Young man, I tell you, arise!" [15]The dead man sat up and began to speak, and Jesus gave him to his mother.[l] [16]Fear seized them all, and they glorified God, exclaiming, "A great prophet has arisen in our midst," and "God has visited his people."[m] [17]This report about him spread through the whole of Judea and in all the surrounding region.

The Messengers from John the Baptist.[*] [18n]The disciples of John told him about all these things. John summoned two of his disciples [19]and sent them to the Lord to ask, "Are you the one who is to come, or should we look for another?"[o] [20]When the men came to him, they said, "John the Baptist has sent us to you to ask, 'Are you the one who is to come, or should we look for another?'" [21]At that time he cured many of their diseases, sufferings, and evil spirits; he also granted sight to many who were blind. [22]And he said to them in reply, "Go and tell John what you have seen and heard: the blind regain their sight, the lame walk, lepers are cleansed, the deaf hear, the dead are raised, the poor have the good news proclaimed to them.[p] [23]And blessed is the one who takes no offense at me."[†]

Jesus' Testimony to John. [24‡]When the messengers of John had left, Jesus began to speak to the crowds about John.[q] "What did you go out to the desert to see—a reed swayed by the wind? [25]Then what did you go out to see? Someone dressed in fine garments? Those who dress luxuriously and live sumptuously are found in royal palaces. [26]Then what did you go out to see? A prophet? Yes, I tell you, and more than a prophet.[r] [27]This is the one about whom scripture says:

'Behold, I am sending my messenger
　　ahead of you,
he will prepare your way before
　　you.'[s]

[28]I tell you, among those born of women, no one is greater than John; yet the least in the kingdom of God is greater than he." [29t](All the people who listened, including the tax collectors, and who were baptized with the baptism of John, acknowledged the righteousness of God; [30]but the Pharisees and scholars of the law, who were not baptized by him, rejected the plan of God for themselves.)

[31s]"Then to what shall I compare the people of this generation? What are they like?[u] [32]They are like children who sit in the marketplace and call to one another,

'We played the flute for you, but you did
　　not dance.
We sang a dirge, but you did not
　　weep.'

[33]For John the Baptist came neither eating food nor drinking wine, and you said, 'He is possessed by a demon.' [34]The Son of Man came eating and drinking and you said, 'Look, he is a glutton and a drunkard, a friend of tax collectors and sinners.'[v] [35]But wisdom is vindicated by all her children."

The Pardon of the Sinful Woman.[¶] [36w]A Pharisee invited him to dine with him, and he entered the Pharisee's house and reclined at table.[**] [37]Now there was a sinful woman in the city who learned that he was at table in the house of the Pharisee.[x] Bringing an alabaster flask of ointment,[y] [38]she stood behind him at his feet weeping and began to bathe his feet with her tears. Then she wiped them with her hair, kissed them, and anointed them with the ointment. [39]When the Pharisee who had invited him saw this he said to himself, "If this man were a prophet, he would know who and what sort of woman this is who is touching him, that she is a sinner." [40]Jesus said to him in reply, "Simon, I have something to say to you." "Tell me, teacher," he said. [41]"Two people were in debt to a certain creditor; one owed five hundred days' wages[††] and the other owed fifty.

---

*[7:18–23] In answer to John's question, **Are you the one who is to come?**—a probable reference to the return of the fiery prophet of reform, Elijah, "before the day of the Lord comes, the great and terrible day" (Mal 3:23)—Jesus responds that his role is rather to bring the blessings spoken of in Is 61:1 to the oppressed and neglected of society (Lk 7:22; cf. Lk 4:18).

†[7:23] **Blessed is the one who takes no offense at me:** this beatitude is pronounced on the person who recognizes Jesus' true identity in spite of previous expectations of what "the one who is to come" would be like.

‡[7:24–30] In his testimony to John, Jesus reveals his understanding of the relationship between them: John is the precursor of Jesus (Lk 7:27); John is the messenger spoken of in Mal 3:1 who in Mal 3:19 is identified as Elijah. Taken with the previous episode, it can be seen that Jesus identifies John as precisely the person John envisioned Jesus to be: the Elijah who prepares the way for the coming of the day of the Lord.

§[7:31–35] See note on Mt 11:16–19.

¶[7:36–50] In this story of the pardoning of the sinful woman Luke presents two different reactions to the ministry of Jesus. A Pharisee, suspecting Jesus to be a prophet, invites Jesus to a festive banquet in his house, but the Pharisee's self-righteousness leads to little forgiveness by God and consequently little love shown toward Jesus. The sinful woman, on the other hand, manifests a faith in God (Lk 7:50) that has led her to seek forgiveness for her sins, and because so much was forgiven, she now overwhelms Jesus with her display of love; cf. the similar contrast in attitudes in Lk 18:9–14. The whole episode is a powerful lesson on the relation between forgiveness and love.

[7:36] **Reclined at table: the normal posture of guests at a banquet. Other oriental banquet customs alluded to in this story include the reception by the host with a kiss (Lk 7:45), washing the feet of the guests (Lk 7:44), and the anointing of the guests' heads (Lk 7:46).

††[7:41] **Days' wages:** one denarius is the normal daily wage of a laborer.

---

l. [7:15] 1 Kgs 17:23; 2 Kgs 4:36. m. [7:16] 1:68; 19:44. n. [7:18–23] Mt 11:2–6. o. [7:19] Mal 3:1; Rev 1:4, 8; 4:8. p. [7:22] 4:18; Is 35:5–6; 61:1. q. [7:24–30] Mt 11:7–15. r. [7:26] 1:76. s. [7:27] Mal 3:1 / Is 40:3.

t. [7:29–30] 3:7, 12; Mt 21:32. u. [7:31–35] Mt 11:16–19. v. [7:34] 15:2. w. [7:36] 11:37; 14:1. x. [7:37] Mt 26:7; Mk 14:3. y. [7:37–38] Jn 12:3.

⁴²Since they were unable to repay the debt, he forgave it for both. Which of them will love him more?" ⁴³Simon said in reply, "The one, I suppose, whose larger debt was forgiven." He said to him, "You have judged rightly." ⁴⁴Then he turned to the woman and said to Simon, "Do you see this woman? When I entered your house, you did not give me water for my feet, but she has bathed them with her tears and wiped them with her hair. ⁴⁵You did not give me a kiss, but she has not ceased kissing my feet since the time I entered. ⁴⁶You did not anoint my head with oil, but she anointed my feet with ointment. ⁴⁷So I tell you, her many sins have been forgiven; hence, she has shown great love.* But the one to whom little is forgiven, loves little." ⁴⁸He said to her, "Your sins are forgiven."ᶻ ⁴⁹The others at table said to themselves, "Who is this who even forgives sins?"ᵃ ⁵⁰But he said to the woman, "Your faith has saved you; go in peace."

CHAPTER 8

Galilean Women Follow Jesus.† ¹Afterward he journeyed from one town and village to another, preaching and proclaiming the good news of the kingdom of God.ᵇ Accompanying him were the Twelve ²ᶜand some women who had been cured of evil spirits and infirmities, Mary, called Magdalene, from whom seven demons had gone out, ³Joanna, the wife of Herod's steward Chuza, Susanna, and many others who provided for them out of their resources.

The Parable of the Sower.ᵈ ⁴ᵉWhen a large crowd gathered, with people from one town after another journeying to him, he spoke in a parable.§ ⁵"A sower went out to sow his seed. And as he sowed, some seed fell on the path and was trampled, and the birds of the sky ate it up. ⁶Some seed fell on rocky ground, and when it

grew, it withered for lack of moisture. ⁷Some seed fell among thorns, and the thorns grew with it and choked it. ⁸And some seed fell on good soil, and when it grew, it produced fruit a hundredfold." After saying this, he called out, "Whoever has ears to hear ought to hear."ᵉ

The Purpose of the Parables.ᶠ ⁹Then his disciples asked him what the meaning of this parable might be. ¹⁰He answered, "Knowledge of the mysteries of the kingdom of God has been granted to you; but to the rest, they are made known through parables so that 'they may look but not see, and hear but not understand.'ᵍ

The Parable of the Sower Explained.§ ¹¹ʰ"This is the meaning of the parable. The seed is the word of God.ⁱ ¹²Those on the path are the ones who have heard, but the devil comes and takes away the word from their hearts that they may not believe and be saved. ¹³Those on rocky ground are the ones who, when they hear, receive the word with joy, but they have no root; they believe only for a time and fall away in time of trial. ¹⁴As for the seed that fell among thorns, they are the ones who have heard, but as they go along, they are choked by the anxieties and riches and pleasures of life, and they fail to produce mature fruit. ¹⁵But as for the seed that fell on rich soil, they are the ones who, when they have heard the word, embrace it with a generous and good heart, and bear fruit through perseverance.

The Parable of the Lamp.⁑ ¹⁶"No one who lights a lamp conceals it with a vessel or sets it under a bed; rather, he places it on a lampstand so that those who enter may see the light.ᵏ ¹⁷For there is nothing hidden that will not become visible, and nothing secret that will not be known and come to light.ˡ ¹⁸Take care, then, how you hear. To anyone who has, more will be given, and from the one who has not, even what he seems to have will be taken away."ᵐ

Jesus and His Family.ⁿ ¹⁹Then his mother and his brothers†† came to him but were unable to join him because of the crowd. ²⁰ᵒHe was told, "Your mother and your brothers are standing outside and they wish to see you." ²¹He said to them in reply, "My mother and my brothers are those who hear the word of God and act on it."‡‡

---

*[7:47] **Her many sins have been forgiven; hence, she has shown great love:** literally, "her many sins have been forgiven, seeing that she has loved much." That the woman's sins have been forgiven is attested by the great love she shows toward Jesus. Her love is the consequence of her forgiveness. This is also the meaning demanded by the parable in Lk 7:41–43.

†[8:1-3] Luke presents Jesus as an itinerant preacher traveling in the company of the Twelve and the Galilean women who are sustaining them out of their means. These Galilean women will later accompany Jesus on his journey to Jerusalem and become witnesses to his death (Lk 23:49) and resurrection (Lk 24:9–11, where Mary Magdalene and Joanna are specifically mentioned; cf. also Acts 1:14). The association of women with the ministry of Jesus is most unusual in the light of the attitude of first-century Palestinian Judaism toward women. The more common attitude is expressed in Jn 4:27, and early rabbinic documents caution against speaking with women in public.

‡[8:4–21] The focus in this section is on how one should hear the word of God and act on it. It includes the parable of the sower and its explanation (Lk 8:4–15), a collection of sayings on how one should act on the word that is heard (Lk 8:16–18), and the identification of the mother and brothers of Jesus as the ones who hear the word and act on it (Lk 8:19–21). See also notes on Mt 13:1–53 and Mk 4:1–34.

§[8:4–8] See note on Mt 13:3–8.

¶[8:11–15] On the interpretation of the parable of the sower, see note on Mt 13:18–23.

**[8:16–18] These sayings continue the theme of responding to the word of God. Those who hear the word must become a light to others (Lk 8:16); even the mysteries of the kingdom that have been made known to the disciples (Lk 8:9–10) must come to light (Lk 8:17); a generous and persevering response to the word of God leads to a still more perfect response to the word.

††[8:19] **His brothers:** see note on Mk 6:3.

‡‡[8:21] The family of Jesus is not constituted by physical relationship with him but by obedience to the word of God.

---

z. [7:48] 5:20; Mt 9:20; Mk 2:5.   a. [7:49] 5:21.   b. [8:1] 4:43.   c. [8:2–3] 23:49; 24:10; Mt 27:55–56; Mk 15:40–41; Jn 19:5.   d. [8:4–8] Mt 13:1–9; Mk 4:1–9.

e. [8:8] 14:35; Mt 11:15; 13:43; Mk 4:23.   f. [8:9–10] Mt 13:10–13; Mk 4:10–12.   g. [8:10] Is 6:9.   h. [8:11–15] Mt 13:18–23; Mk 4:13–20.   i. [8:11] 1 Pt 1:23.   j. [8:16–18] Mk 4:21–25.   k. [8:16] 11:33; Mt 5:15.   l. [8:17] 12:2; Mt 10:26.   m. [8:18] 19:26; Mt 13:12; 25:29.   n. [8:19–21] Mt 12:46–50; Mk 3:31–35.   o. [8:20–21] 11:27–28.

The Calming of a Storm at Sea.ᵖ

²²One day he got into a boat with his disciples and said to them, "Let us cross to the other side of the lake." So they set sail, ²³and while they were sailing he fell asleep. A squall blew over the lake, and they were taking in water and were in danger. ²⁴They came and woke him saying, "Master, master, we are perishing!" He awakened, rebuked the wind and the waves, and they subsided and there was a calm. ²⁵Then he asked them, "Where is your faith?" But they were filled with awe and amazed and said to one another, "Who then is this, who commands even the winds and the sea, and they obey him?"

The Healing of the Gerasene Demoniac.�q

²⁶Then they sailed to the territory of the Gerasenes,† which is opposite Galilee. ²⁷When he came ashore a man from the town who was possessed by demons met him. For a long time he had not worn clothes; he did not live in a house, but lived among the tombs. ²⁸ʳWhen he saw Jesus, he cried out and fell down before him; in a loud voice he shouted, "What have you to do with me, Jesus, son of the Most High God? I beg you, do not torment me!" ²⁹For he had ordered the unclean spirit to come out of the man. (It had taken hold of him many times, and he used to be bound with chains and shackles as a restraint, but he would break his bonds and be driven by the demon into deserted places.) ³⁰Then Jesus asked him, "What is your name?"ˢ He replied, "Legion," because many demons had entered him. ³¹And they pleaded with him not to order them to depart to the abyss.§

³²A herd of many swine was feeding there on the hillside, and they pleaded with him to allow them to enter those swine; and he let them. ³³The demons came out of the man and entered the swine, and the herd rushed down the steep bank into the lake and was drowned. ³⁴When the swineherds saw what had happened, they ran away and reported the incident in the town and throughout the countryside. ³⁵People came out to see what had happened and, when they approached Jesus, they discovered the man from whom the demons had come out sitting at his feet.⁵ He was clothed and in his right mind, and they were seized with fear. ³⁶Those who witnessed it told them how the possessed man had been saved. ³⁷The entire population of the region of the Gerasenes asked Jesus to leave them because they were seized with great fear. So he got into a boat and returned. ³⁸The man from whom the demons had come out begged to remain with him, but he sent him away, saying, ³⁹"Return home and recount what God has done for you." The man went off and proclaimed throughout the whole town what Jesus had done for him.

Jairus's Daughter and the Woman with a Hemorrhage.**

⁴⁰ˢWhen Jesus returned, the crowd welcomed him, for they were all waiting for him. ⁴¹And a man named Jairus, an official of the synagogue, came forward. He fell at the feet of Jesus and begged him to come to his house, ⁴²because he had an only daughter,†† about twelve years old, and she was dying. As he went, the crowds almost crushed him. ⁴³And a woman afflicted with hemorrhages for twelve years,‡‡ who [had spent her whole livelihood on doctors and] was unable to be cured by anyone, ⁴⁴came up behind him and touched the tassel on his cloak. Immediately her bleeding stopped. ⁴⁵Jesus then asked, "Who touched me?" While all were denying it, Peter said, "Master, the crowds are pushing and pressing in upon you." ⁴⁶But Jesus said, "Someone has touched me; for I know that power has gone out from me."ᵗ ⁴⁷When the woman realized that she had not escaped notice, she came forward trembling. Falling down before him, she explained in the presence of all the people why she had touched him and how she had been healed immediately. ⁴⁸He said to her, "Daughter, your faith has saved you; go in peace."ᵘ

⁴⁹While he was still speaking, someone from the synagogue official's house arrived and said, "Your daughter is dead; do not trouble the

---

In this, Luke agrees with the Marcan parallel (Mk 3:31–35), although by omitting Mk 3:33 and especially Mk 3:20–21 Luke has softened the Marcan picture of Jesus' natural family. Probably he did this because Mary has already been presented in Lk 1:38 as the obedient handmaid of the Lord who fulfills the requirement for belonging to the eschatological family of Jesus; cf. also Lk 11:27–28.

*[8:22–56] This section records four miracles of Jesus that manifest his power and authority: (1) the calming of a storm on the lake (Lk 8:22–25); (2) the exorcism of a demoniac (Lk 8:26–39); (3) the cure of a hemorrhaging woman (Lk 8:40–48); (4) the raising of Jairus's daughter to life (Lk 8:49–56). They parallel the same sequence of stories at Mk 4:35–5:43.

†[8:26] **Gerasenes:** other manuscripts read Gadarenes or Gergesenes. See also note on Mt 8:28. **Opposite Galilee:** probably Gentile territory (note the presence in the area of pigs—unclean animals to Jews) and an indication that the person who receives salvation (Lk 8:36) is a Gentile.

‡[8:30] **What is your name?:** the question reflects the popular belief that knowledge of the spirit's name brought control over the spirit. **Legion:** to Jesus' question the demon replies with a Latin word transliterated into Greek. The Roman legion at this period consisted of 5,000 to 6,000 foot soldiers; hence the name implies a very large number of demons.

§[8:31] **Abyss:** the place of the dead (Rom 10:7) or the prison of Satan (Rev 20:3) or the subterranean "watery deep" that symbolizes the chaos before the order imposed by creation (Gn 1:2).

¶[8:35] **Sitting at his feet:** the former demoniac takes the position of a disciple before the master (Lk 10:39; Acts 22:3).

**[8:40–56] Two interwoven miracle stories, one a healing and the other a resuscitation, present Jesus as master over sickness and death. In the Lucan account, faith in Jesus is responsible for the cure (Lk 8:48) and for the raising to life (Lk 8:50).

††[8:42] **An only daughter:** cf. the son of the widow of Nain whom Luke describes as an "only" son (Lk 7:12; see also Lk 9:38).

‡‡[8:43] **Afflicted with hemorrhages for twelve years:** according to the Mosaic law (Lv 15:25–30) this condition would render the woman unclean and unfit for contact with other people.

---

p. [8:22–25] Mt 8:18, 23–27; Mk 4:35–41.   q. [8:26–39] Mt 8:28–34; Mk 5:1–20.   r. [8:28–29] 4:33–35; Mt 8:29; Mk 1:23–24.

s. [8:40–56] Mt 9:18–26; Mk 5:21–43.   t. [8:46] 6:19.   u. [8:48] 7:50; 17:19; 18:42.

teacher any longer." [50]On hearing this, Jesus answered him, "Do not be afraid; just have faith and she will be saved." [51]When he arrived at the house he allowed no one to enter with him except Peter and John and James, and the child's father and mother. [52v]All were weeping and mourning for her, when he said, "Do not weep any longer, for she is not dead, but sleeping." [53]And they ridiculed him, because they knew that she was dead. [54]But he took her by the hand and called to her, "Child, arise!" [55]Her breath returned and she immediately arose. He then directed that she should be given something to eat. [56]Her parents were astounded, and he instructed them to tell no one what had happened.

CHAPTER 9

The Mission of the Twelve.[†] [1w]He summoned the Twelve and gave them power and authority over all demons and to cure diseases, [2]and he sent them to proclaim the kingdom of God and to heal [the sick]. [3]He said to them, "Take nothing for the journey,[‡] neither walking stick, nor sack, nor food, nor money, and let no one take a second tunic. [4]Whatever house you enter, stay there and leave from there.[x] [5]And as for those who do not welcome you, when you leave that town, shake the dust from your feet[§] in testimony against them."[y] [6]Then they set out and went from village to village proclaiming the good news and curing diseases everywhere.

Herod's Opinion of Jesus.[z] [7¶]Herod the tetrarch[**] heard about all that was happening, and he was greatly perplexed because some were saying, "John has been raised from the dead";[a] [8]others were saying, "Elijah has appeared"; still others, "One of the ancient prophets has arisen." [9††b]But

Herod said, "John I beheaded. Who then is this about whom I hear such things?" And he kept trying to see him.

The Return of the Twelve and the Feeding of the Five Thousand.[c] [10]When the apostles returned, they explained to him what they had done. He took them and withdrew in private to a town called Bethsaida. [11]The crowds, meanwhile, learned of this and followed him. He received them and spoke to them about the kingdom of God, and he healed those who needed to be cured. [12]As the day was drawing to a close, the Twelve approached him and said, "Dismiss the crowd so that they can go to the surrounding villages and farms and find lodging and provisions; for we are in a deserted place here." [13d]He said to them, "Give them some food yourselves." They replied, "Five loaves and two fish are all we have, unless we ourselves go and buy food for all these people." [14]Now the men there numbered about five thousand. Then he said to his disciples, "Have them sit down in groups of [about] fifty." [15]They did so and made them all sit down. [16]Then taking[‡‡] the five loaves and the two fish, and looking up to heaven, he said the blessing over them, broke them, and gave them to the disciples to set before the crowd.[e] [17]They all ate and were satisfied. And when the leftover fragments were picked up, they filled twelve wicker baskets.

Peter's Confession About Jesus.[§§] [18f]Once when Jesus was praying in solitude,[¶¶] and the disciples were with him, he asked them, "Who do the crowds say that I am?" [19]They said in reply, "John the Baptist; others, Elijah; still others, 'One of the ancient prophets has arisen.'"[g] [20]Then he said to them, "But who do you say that I am?" Peter said in reply, "The Messiah of God."[***] [21]He rebuked them and directed them not to tell this to anyone.

The First Prediction of the Passion. [22]He said, "The Son of Man must suffer greatly and be rejected by the elders, the chief priests, and the scribes, and be killed and on the third day be raised."[h]

---

*[8:52] **Sleeping**: her death is a temporary condition; cf. Jn 11:11–14.

†[9:1–6] Armed with the power and authority that Jesus himself has been displaying in the previous episodes, the Twelve are now sent out to continue the work that Jesus has been performing throughout his Galilean ministry: (1) proclaiming the kingdom (Lk 4:43; 8:1); (2) exorcising demons (Lk 4:33–37, 41; 8:26–39) and (3) healing the sick (Lk 4:38–40; 5:12–16, 17–26; 6:6–10; 7:1–10, 17, 22; 8:40 56).

‡[9:3] **Take nothing for the journey**: the absolute detachment required of the disciple (Lk 14:33) leads to complete reliance on God (Lk 12:22–31).

§[9:5] **Shake the dust from your feet**: see note on Mt 10:14.

¶[9:7–56] This section in which Luke gathers together incidents that focus on the identity of Jesus is introduced by a question that Herod is made to ask in this gospel: "Who then is this about whom I hear such things?" (Lk 9:9) In subsequent episodes, Luke reveals to the reader various answers to Herod's question: Jesus is one in whom God's power is present and who provides for the needs of God's people (Lk 9:10–17); Peter declares Jesus to be "the Messiah of God" (Lk 9:18–21); Jesus says he is the suffering Son of Man (Lk 9:22, 43–45); Jesus is the Master to be followed, even to death (Lk 9:23–27); Jesus is God's son, his Chosen One (Lk 9:28–36).

[9:7] **Herod the tetrarch: see note on Lk 3:1.

††[9:9] **And he kept trying to see him**: this indication of Herod's interest in Jesus prepares for Lk 13:31–33 and for Lk

23:8–12 where Herod's curiosity about Jesus' power to perform miracles remains unsatisfied.

‡‡[9:16] **Then taking . . .** : the actions of Jesus recall the institution of the Eucharist in Lk 22:19; see also note on Mt 14:19.

§§[9:18–22] This incident is based on Mk 8:27–33, but Luke has eliminated Peter's refusal to accept Jesus as suffering Son of Man (Mk 8:32) and the rebuke of Peter by Jesus (Mk 8:33). Elsewhere in the gospel, Luke softens the harsh portrait of Peter and the other apostles found in his Marcan source (cf. Lk 22:39–46, which similarly lacks a rebuke of Peter that occurs in the source, Mk 14:37–38).

¶¶[9:18] **When Jesus was praying in solitude**: see note on Lk 3:21.

***[9:20] **The Messiah of God**: on the meaning of this title in first-century Palestinian Judaism, see notes on Lk 2:11 and on Mt 16:13–20 and Mk 8:27–30.

---

v. [8:52] 7:13.   w. [9:1–6] Mt 10:1, 5–15; Mk 6:7–13.   x. [9:4] 10:5–7.   y. [9:5] 10:10–11; Acts 13:51.   z. [9:7–9] Mt 14:1–12; Mk 6:14–29.   a. [9:7–8] 9:19; Mt 16:14; Mk 8:28.   b. [9:9] 23:8.

c. [9:10–17] Mt 14:13–21; Mk 6:30–44; Jn 6:1–14.   d. [9:13–17] 2 Kgs 4:42–44.   e. [9:16] 22:19; 24:30–31; Acts 2:42; 20:11; 27:35.   f. [9:18–21] Mt 16:13–20; Mk 8:27–30.   g. [9:19] 9:7–8.   h. [9:22] 24:7, 26; Mt 16:21; 20:18–19; Mk 8:31; 10:33–34.

The Conditions of Discipleship.[i] [23]Then he said to all, "If anyone wishes to come after me, he must deny himself and take up his cross daily* and follow me.[j] [24]For whoever wishes to save his life will lose it, but whoever loses his life for my sake will save it.[k] [25]What profit is there for one to gain the whole world yet lose or forfeit himself? [26]Whoever is ashamed of me and of my words, the Son of Man will be ashamed of when he comes in his glory and in the glory of the Father and of the holy angels.[l] [27]Truly I say to you, there are some standing here who will not taste death until they see the kingdom of God."

The Transfiguration of Jesus.[†] [28m]About eight days after he said this, he took Peter, John, and James and went up the mountain to pray.[‡] [29]While he was praying his face changed in appearance and his clothing became dazzling white. [30]And behold, two men were conversing with him, Moses and Elijah,[§] [31¶]who appeared in glory and spoke of his exodus that he was going to accomplish in Jerusalem. [32]Peter and his companions had been overcome by sleep, but becoming fully awake, they saw his glory** and the two men standing with him.[o] [33]As they were about to part from him, Peter said to Jesus, "Master, it is good that we are here; let us make three tents,[††] one for you, one for Moses, and one for Elijah." But he did not know what he was saying. [34‡‡]While he was still speaking, a cloud came and cast a shadow over them, and they became frightened when they entered the cloud. [35§§p]Then from the cloud came a voice that said, "This is my chosen Son; listen to him." [36]After the voice had spoken, Jesus was found alone. They fell silent and did not at that time¶¶ tell anyone what they had seen.

The Healing of a Boy with a Demon.*** [37q]On the next day, when they came down from the mountain, a large crowd met him. [38]There was a man in the crowd who cried out, "Teacher, I beg you, look at my son; he is my only child. [39]For a spirit seizes him and he suddenly screams and it convulses him until he foams at the mouth; it releases him only with difficulty, wearing him out. [40]I begged your disciples to cast it out but they could not." [41]Jesus said in reply, "O faithless and perverse generation, how long will I be with you and endure you? Bring your son here." [42]As he was coming forward, the demon threw him to the ground in a convulsion; but Jesus rebuked the unclean spirit, healed the boy, and returned him to his father. [43]And all were astonished by the majesty of God.

The Second Prediction of the Passion.[r] While they were all amazed at his every deed, he said to his disciples, [44]"Pay attention to what I am telling you. The Son of Man is to be handed over to men." [45]But they did not understand this saying; its meaning was hidden from them so that they should not understand it, and they were afraid to ask him about this saying.

The Greatest in the Kingdom.[s] [46†††]An argument arose among the disciples about which of them was the greatest.[t] [47]Jesus realized the intention of their hearts and took a child and placed it by his side [48]and said to them, "Whoever receives this child in my name receives me, and whoever receives me receives the one who sent me. For the one who is least among all of you is the one who is the greatest."[u]

Another Exorcist.[v] [49]Then John said in reply, "Master, we saw someone casting out demons in your name and we tried to prevent him because he does not follow in our company." [50]Jesus said to him, "Do not prevent him, for whoever is not against you is for you."

*[9:23] **Daily**: this is a Lucan addition to a saying of Jesus, removing the saying from a context that envisioned the imminent suffering and death of the disciple of Jesus (as does the saying in Mk 8:34–35) to one that focuses on the demands of daily Christian existence.

†[9:28–36] Situated shortly after the first announcement of the passion, death, and resurrection, this scene of Jesus' transfiguration provides the heavenly confirmation to Jesus' declaration that his suffering will end in glory (Lk 9:32); see also notes on Mt 17:1–8 and Mk 9:2–8.

‡[9:28] **Up the mountain to pray**: the "mountain" is the regular place of prayer in Luke (see Lk 6:12; 22:39–41).

§[9:30] **Moses and Elijah**: the two figures represent the Old Testament law and the prophets. At the end of this episode, the heavenly voice will identify Jesus as the one to be listened to now (Lk 9:35). See also note on Mk 9:5.

¶[9:31] **His exodus that he was going to accomplish in Jerusalem**: Luke identifies the subject of the conversation as the **exodus** of Jesus, a reference to the death, resurrection, and ascension of Jesus that will take place in Jerusalem, the city of destiny (see Lk 9:51). The mention of exodus, however, also calls to mind the Israelite Exodus from Egypt to the promised land.

[9:32] **They saw his glory: the **glory** that is proper to God is here attributed to Jesus (see Lk 24:26).

††[9:33] **Let us make three tents**: in a possible allusion to the feast of Tabernacles, Peter may be likening his joy on the occasion of the transfiguration to the joyful celebration of this harvest festival.

‡‡[9:34] **Over them**: it is not clear whether **them** refers to Jesus, Moses, and Elijah, or to the disciples. For the cloud casting its shadow, see note on Mk 9:7.

§§[9:35] Like the heavenly voice that identified Jesus at his baptism prior to his undertaking the Galilean ministry (Lk 3:22), so too here before the journey to the city of destiny is begun (Lk 9:51) the heavenly voice again identifies Jesus as Son. **Listen to him**: the two representatives of Israel of old depart (Lk 9:33) and Jesus is left alone (Lk 9:36) as the teacher whose words must be heeded (see also Acts 3:22).

¶¶[9:36] **At that time**: i.e., before the resurrection.

***[9:37–43a] See note on Mk 9:14–29.

†††[9:46–50] These two incidents focus on attitudes that are opposed to Christian discipleship: rivalry and intolerance of outsiders.

i. [9:23–27] Mt 16:24–28; Mk 8:34–9:1. j. [9:23] 14:27; Mt 10:38. k. [9:24] 17:33; Mt 10:39; Jn 12:25. l. [9:26] 12:9; Mt 10:33; 2 Tm 2:12. m. [9:28–36] Mt 17:1–8; Mk 9:2–8. n. [9:31] 9:22; 13:33. o. [9:32] Jn 1:14; 2 Pt 1:16.

p. [9:35] 3:22; Dt 18:15; Ps 2:7; Is 42:1; Mt 3:17; 12:18; Mk 1:11; 2 Pt 1:17–18. q. [9:37–43] Mt 17:14–18; Mk 9:14–27. r. [9:43–45] 18:32–34; Mt 17:22–23; Mk 9:30–32. s. [9:46–48] Mt 18:1–5; Mk 9:33–37. t. [9:46] 22:24. u. [9:48] 10:16; Mt 10:40; Jn 13:20. v. [9:49–50] Mk 9:38–40.

V. THE JOURNEY TO JERUSALEM: LUKE'S TRAVEL NARRATIVE*

Departure for Jerusalem; Samaritan Inhospitality. [51†]When the days for his being taken up[‡] were fulfilled, he resolutely determined to journey to Jerusalem,[w] [52§]and he sent messengers ahead of him.[x] On the way they entered a Samaritan village to prepare for his reception there, [53]but they would not welcome him because the destination of his journey was Jerusalem. [54]When the disciples James and John saw this they asked, "Lord, do you want us to call down fire from heaven to consume them?"[y] [55]Jesus turned and rebuked them, [56]and they journeyed to another village.

The Would-be Followers of Jesus.[¶] [57z]As they were proceeding on their journey someone said to him, "I will follow you wherever you go." [58]Jesus answered him, "Foxes have dens and birds of the sky have nests, but the Son of Man has nowhere to rest his head." [59]And to another he said, "Follow me." But he replied, "[Lord,] let me go first and bury my father." [60]But he answered him, "Let the dead bury their dead." But you, go and proclaim the kingdom of God."

[61a]And another said, "I will follow you, Lord, but first let me say farewell to my family at home." [62][To him] Jesus said, "No one who sets a hand to the plow and looks to what was left behind is fit for the kingdom of God."

CHAPTER 10

The Mission of the Seventy-two.[††] [1]After this the Lord appointed seventy[-two][‡‡] others whom he sent ahead of him in pairs to every town and place he intended to visit.[b] [2]He said to them, "The harvest is abundant but the laborers are few; so ask the master of the harvest to send out laborers for his harvest.[c] [3]Go on your way; behold, I am sending you like lambs among wolves.[d] [4§§]Carry no money bag,[e] no sack, no sandals;[f] and greet no one along the way. [5]Into whatever house you enter, first say, 'Peace to this household.'[¶¶] [6]If a peaceful person*** lives there, your peace will rest on him; but if not, it will return to you. [7]Stay in the same house and eat and drink what is offered to you, for the laborer deserves his payment. Do not move about from one house to another.[g] [8]Whatever town you enter and they welcome you, eat what is set before you,[h] [9]cure the sick in it and say to them, 'The kingdom of God is at hand for you.'[i] [10]Whatever town you enter and they do not receive you, go out into the streets and say,[j] [11]'The dust of your town that clings to our feet, even that we shake off against you.' Yet know this: the kingdom of God is at hand.[k] [12]I tell you, it will be more tolerable for Sodom on that day than for that town.[l]

Reproaches to Unrepentant Towns.[†††] [13m]"Woe to you, Chorazin! Woe to you, Bethsaida![n] For if

---

*[9:51–18:14] The Galilean ministry of Jesus finishes with the previous episode and a new section of Luke's gospel begins, the journey to Jerusalem. This journey is based on Mk 10:1–52 but Luke uses his Marcan source only in Lk 18:15–19:27. Before that point he has inserted into his gospel a distinctive collection of sayings of Jesus and stories about him that he has drawn from Q, a collection of sayings of Jesus used also by Matthew, and from his own special traditions. All of the material collected in this section is loosely organized within the framework of a journey of Jesus to Jerusalem, the city of destiny, where his exodus (suffering, death, resurrection, ascension) is to take place (Lk 9:31), where salvation is accomplished, and from where the proclamation of God's saving word is to go forth (Lk 24:47; Acts 1:8). Much of the material in the Lucan travel narrative is teaching for the disciples. During the course of this journey Jesus is preparing his chosen Galilean witnesses for the role they will play after his exodus (Lk 9:31): they are to be his witnesses to the people (Acts 10:39; 13:31) and thereby provide certainty to the readers of Luke's gospel that the teachings they have received are rooted in the teachings of Jesus (Lk 1:1–4).

†[9:51–55] Just as the Galilean ministry began with a rejection of Jesus in his hometown, so too the travel narrative begins with the rejection of him by Samaritans. In this episode Jesus disassociates himself from the attitude expressed by his disciples that those who reject him are to be punished severely. The story alludes to 2 Kgs 1:10, 12 where the prophet Elijah takes the course of action Jesus rejects, and Jesus thereby rejects the identification of himself with Elijah.

‡[9:51] Days for his being taken up: like the reference to his exodus in Lk 9:31 this is probably a reference to all the events (suffering, death, resurrection, ascension) of his last days in Jerusalem. He resolutely determined: literally, "he set his face."

§[9:52] Samaritan: Samaria was the territory between Judea and Galilee west of the Jordan river. For ethnic and religious reasons, the Samaritans and the Jews were bitterly opposed to one another (see Jn 4:9).

¶[9:57–62] In these sayings Jesus speaks of the severity and the unconditional nature of Christian discipleship. Even family ties and filial obligations, such as burying one's parents, cannot distract one no matter how briefly from proclaiming the kingdom of God. The first two sayings are paralleled in Mt 8:19–22; see also notes there.

**[9:60] Let the dead bury their dead: i.e., let the spiritually dead (those who do not follow) bury their physically dead. See also note on Mt 8:22.

††[10:1–12] Only the Gospel of Luke contains two episodes in which Jesus sends out his followers on a mission: the first (Lk 10:1–6) is based on the mission in Mk 6:6b–13 and recounts the sending out of the Twelve; here in Lk 10:1–12 a similar report based on Q becomes the sending out of seventy-two in this gospel. The episode continues the theme of Jesus preparing witnesses to himself and his ministry. These witnesses include not only the Twelve but also the seventy-two who may represent the Christian mission in Luke's own day. Note that the instructions given to the Twelve and to the seventy-two are similar and that what is said to the seventy-two in Lk 10:4 is directed to the Twelve in Lk 22:35.

‡‡[10:1] Seventy[-two]: important representatives of the Alexandrian and Caesarean text types read "seventy," while other important Alexandrian texts and Western readings have "seventy-two."

§§[10:4] Carry no money bag . . . greet no one along the way: because of the urgency of the mission and the single-mindedness required of missionaries, even customary possessions should be avoided and even customary greetings should not distract from the fulfillment of the task.

¶¶[10:5] First say, 'Peace to this household': see notes on Lk 2:14 and Mt 10:13.

***[10:6] A peaceful person: literally, "a son of peace."

†††[10:13–16] The call to repentance that is a part of the proclamation of the kingdom brings with it a severe judgment for those who hear it and reject it.

---

w. [9:51] 9:53; 13:22, 33; 17:11; 18:31; 19:28; 24:51; Acts 1:2, 9–11, 22. x. [9:52] Mal 3:1. y. [9:54] 2 Kgs 1:10, 12. z. [9:57–60] Mt 8:19–22.

a. [9:61–62] 1 Kgs 19:20. b. [10:1] Mk 6:7. c. [10:2] Mt 9:37–38; Jn 4:35. d. [10:3] Mt 10:16. e. [10:4–11] Mt 10:7–14. f. [10:4] 9:3; 2 Kgs 4:29. g. [10:7] 9:4; Mt 10:10; 1 Cor 9:6–14; 1 Tm 5:18. h. [10:8] 1 Cor 10:27. i. [10:9] Mt 3:2; 4:17; Mk 1:15. j. [10:10–11] 9:5. k. [10:11] Acts 13:51; 18:6. l. [10:12] Mt 10:15; 11:24. m. [10:13–15] Mt 11:20–24. n. [10:13–14] Is 23; Ez 26–28; Jl 3:4–8; Am 1:1–10; Zec 9:2–4.

the mighty deeds done in your midst had been done in Tyre and Sidon, they would long ago have repented, sitting in sackcloth and ashes. [14]But it will be more tolerable for Tyre and Sidon at the judgment than for you. [15]*°And as for you, Capernaum, 'Will you be exalted to heaven? You will go down to the netherworld.'" [16]Whoever listens to you listens to me. Whoever rejects you rejects me. And whoever rejects me rejects the one who sent me."*p*

Return of the Seventy-two. [17]The seventy[-two] returned rejoicing, and said, "Lord, even the demons are subject to us because of your name." [18]Jesus said, "I have observed Satan fall like lightning[†] from the sky.*q* [19]Behold, I have given you the power 'to tread upon serpents' and scorpions and upon the full force of the enemy and nothing will harm you.*r* [20]Nevertheless, do not rejoice because the spirits are subject to you, but rejoice because your names are written in heaven."*s*

Praise of the Father.*t* [21]At that very moment he rejoiced [in] the holy Spirit and said, "I give you praise, Father, Lord of heaven and earth, for although you have hidden these things from the wise and the learned you have revealed them to the childlike.[‡] Yes, Father, such has been your gracious will.*u* [22]All things have been handed over to me by my Father. No one knows who the Son is except the Father, and who the Father is except the Son and anyone to whom the Son wishes to reveal him."*v*

The Privileges of Discipleship.*w* [23]Turning to the disciples in private he said, "Blessed are the eyes that see what you see. [24]For I say to you, many prophets and kings desired to see what you see, but did not see it, and to hear what you hear, but did not hear it."

The Greatest Commandment.*x* [25]§There was a scholar of the law[¶] who stood up to test him and said, "Teacher, what must I do to inherit eternal life?"*y* [26]Jesus said to him, "What is written in the law? How do you read it?" [27]He said in reply, "You shall love the Lord, your God, with all your heart, with all your being, with all your strength, and with all your mind, and your neighbor as yourself."*z* [28]He replied to him, "You have answered correctly; do this and you will live."*a*

The Parable of the Good Samaritan. [29]But because he wished to justify himself, he said to Jesus, "And who is my neighbor?" [30]Jesus replied, "A man fell victim to robbers as he went down from Jerusalem to Jericho. They stripped and beat him and went off leaving him half-dead. [31]**A priest happened to be going down that road, but when he saw him, he passed by on the opposite side. [32]Likewise a Levite came to the place, and when he saw him, he passed by on the opposite side. [33]But a Samaritan traveler who came upon him was moved with compassion at the sight. [34]He approached the victim, poured oil and wine over his wounds and bandaged them. Then he lifted him up on his own animal, took him to an inn and cared for him. [35]The next day he took out two silver coins and gave them to the innkeeper with the instruction, 'Take care of him. If you spend more than what I have given you, I shall repay you on my way back.' [36]Which of these three, in your opinion, was neighbor to the robbers' victim?" [37]He answered, "The one who treated him with mercy." Jesus said to him, "Go and do likewise."

Martha and Mary.[††] [38]*b*As they continued their journey he entered a village where a woman whose name was Martha welcomed him. [39]‡‡She had a sister named Mary [who] sat beside the Lord at his feet listening to him speak. [40]Martha, burdened with much serving, came to him and said, "Lord, do you not care that my sister has left me by myself to do the serving? Tell her to help me." [41]The Lord said to her in reply, "Martha, Martha, you are anxious and worried about many things. [42]§§There is need of only one thing. Mary has chosen the better part and it will not be taken from her."

[10:15] **The netherworld: the underworld, the place of the dead (Acts 2:27, 31) here contrasted with heaven; see also note on Mt 11:23.*

*†[10:18] **I have observed Satan fall like lightning**: the effect of the mission of the seventy-two is characterized by the Lucan Jesus as a symbolic fall of Satan. As the kingdom of God is gradually being established, evil in all its forms is being defeated; the dominion of Satan over humanity is at an end.*

*‡[10:21] **Revealed them to the childlike**: a restatement of the theme announced in Lk 8:10: the mysteries of the kingdom are revealed to the disciples. See also note on Mt 11:25–27.*

§[10:25–37] In response to a question from a Jewish legal expert about inheriting eternal life, Jesus illustrates the superiority of love over legalism through the story of the good Samaritan. The law of love proclaimed in the "Sermon on the Plain" (Lk 6:27–36) is exemplified by one whom the legal expert would have considered ritually impure (see Jn 4:9). Moreover, the identity of the "neighbor" requested by the legal expert (Lk 10:29) turns out to be a Samaritan, the enemy of the Jew (see note on Lk 9:52).

*¶[10:25] **Scholar of the law**: an expert in the Mosaic law, and probably a member of the group elsewhere identified as the scribes (Lk 5:21).*

***[10:31–32] **Priest . . . Levite**: those religious representatives of Judaism who would have been expected to be models of "neighbor" to the victim pass him by.*

††[10:38–42] The story of Martha and Mary further illustrates the importance of hearing the words of the teacher and the concern with women in Luke.

*‡‡[10:39] **Sat beside the Lord at his feet**: it is remarkable for first-century Palestinian Judaism that a woman would assume the posture of a disciple at the master's feet (see also Lk 8:35; Acts 22:3), and it reveals a characteristic attitude of Jesus toward women in this gospel (see Lk 8:2–3).*

*§§[10:42] **There is need of only one thing**: some ancient versions read, "there is need of few things"; another important, although probably inferior, reading found in some manuscripts is, "there is need of few things, or of one."*

---

o. [10:15] Is 14:13–15.   p. [10:16] Mt 10:40; Jn 5:23; 13:20; 15:23.   q. [10:18] Is 14:12; Jn 12:31; Rev 12:7–12.   r. [10:19] Ps 91:13; Mk 16:18.   s. [10:20] Ex 32:32; Dn 12:1; Mt 7:22; Phil 4:3; Heb 12:23; Rev 3:5; 21:27.   t. [10:21–22] Mt 11:25–27.   u. [10:21] 1 Cor 1:26–28.   v. [10:22] Jn 3:35; 10:15.   w. [10:23–24] Mt 13:16–17.   x. [10:25–28] Mt 22:34–40; Mk 12:28–34.

y. [10:25] Dt 18:18; Mt 19:16; Mk 10:17.   z. [10:27] Lv 19:18; Dt 6:5; 10:12; Jos 22:5; Mt 19:19; 22:37–39; Rom 13:9; Gal 5:14; Jas 2:8.   a. [10:28] Lv 18:5; Prv 19:16; Rom 10:5; Gal 3:12.   b. [10:38–39] Jn 11:1; 12:2–3.

CHAPTER 11

The Lord's Prayer.[c] [1]*He was praying in a certain place, and when he had finished, one of his disciples said to him, "Lord, teach us to pray just as John taught his disciples."[†] [2‡]He said to them, "When you pray, say:

Father, hallowed be your name,
    your kingdom come.
[3]   Give us each day our daily bread[§]
[4]   and forgive us our sins
    for we ourselves forgive everyone in
        debt to us,
    and do not subject us to the final
        test."

Further Teachings on Prayer.[d] [5]And he said to them, "Suppose one of you has a friend to whom he goes at midnight and says, 'Friend, lend me three loaves of bread, [6]for a friend of mine has arrived at my house from a journey and I have nothing to offer him,' [7]and he says in reply from within, 'Do not bother me; the door has already been locked and my children and I are already in bed. I cannot get up to give you anything.' [8]I tell you, if he does not get up to give him the loaves because of their friendship, he will get up to give him whatever he needs because of his persistence.
The Answer to Prayer.[e] [9]"And I tell you, ask and you will receive; seek and you will find; knock and the door will be opened to you.[f] [10]For everyone who asks, receives; and the one who seeks, finds; and to the one who knocks, the door will be opened. [11]What father among you would hand his son a snake when he asks for a fish? [12]Or hand him a scorpion when he asks for an egg? [13]If you then, who are wicked, know how to give good gifts to your children, how much more will the Father in heaven give the holy Spirit[¶] to those who ask him?"

Jesus and Beelzebul.[g] [14]He was driving out a demon [that was] mute, and when the demon had gone out, the mute person spoke and the crowds were amazed. [15]Some of them said, "By the power of Beelzebul, the prince of demons, he drives out demons."[h] [16]Others, to test him, asked him for a sign from heaven.[i] [17]But he knew their thoughts and said to them, "Every kingdom divided against itself will be laid waste and house will fall against house. [18]And if Satan is divided against himself, how will his kingdom stand? For you say that it is by Beelzebul that I drive out demons. [19]If I, then, drive out demons by Beelzebul, by whom do your own people** drive them out? Therefore they will be your judges. [20]But if it is by the finger of God that [I] drive out demons, then the kingdom of God has come upon you.[j] [21]When a strong man fully armed guards his palace, his possessions are safe. [22]But when one stronger[††] than he attacks and overcomes him, he takes away the armor on which he relied and distributes the spoils. [23]Whoever is not with me is against me, and whoever does not gather with me scatters.[k]
The Return of the Unclean Spirit.[l] [24]"When an unclean spirit goes out of someone, it roams through arid regions searching for rest but, finding none, it says, 'I shall return to my home from which I came.' [25]But upon returning, it finds it swept clean and put in order. [26]Then it goes and brings back seven other spirits more wicked than itself who move in and dwell there, and the last condition of that person is worse than the first."[m]
True Blessedness.[‡‡] [27]While he was speaking, a woman from the crowd called out and said to him, "Blessed is the womb that carried you and the breasts at which you nursed."[n] [28]He replied, "Rather, blessed are those who hear the word of God and observe it."
The Demand for a Sign.[§§] [29]While still more people gathered in the crowd, he said to them,[o] "This generation is an evil generation; it seeks a sign, but no sign will be given it, except the sign of Jonah.[p] [30]Just as Jonah became a sign to the Ninevites, so will the Son of Man be to this

---

*[11:1–13] Luke presents three episodes concerned with prayer. The first (Lk 11:1–4) recounts Jesus teaching his disciples the Christian communal prayer, the "Our Father"; the second (Lk 11:5–8), the importance of persistence in prayer; the third (Lk 11:9–13), the effectiveness of prayer.

†[11:1–4] The Matthean form of the "Our Father" occurs in the "Sermon on the Mount" (Mt 6:9–15); the shorter Lucan version is presented while Jesus is at prayer (see note on Lk 3:21) and his disciples ask him to teach them to pray just as John taught his disciples to pray. In answer to their question, Jesus presents them with an example of a Christian communal prayer that stresses the fatherhood of God and acknowledges him as the one to whom the Christian disciple owes daily sustenance (Lk 11:3), forgiveness (Lk 11:4), and deliverance from the final trial (Lk 11:4). See also notes on Mt 6:9–13.

‡[11:2] **Your kingdom come**: in place of this petition, some early church Fathers record: "May your holy Spirit come upon us and cleanse us," a petition that may reflect the use of the "Our Father" in a baptismal liturgy.

§[11:3–4] **Daily bread**: see note on Mt 6:11. **The final test**: see note on Mt 6:13.

¶[11:13] **The holy Spirit**: this is a Lucan editorial alteration of a traditional saying of Jesus (see Mt 7:11). Luke presents

the gift of the holy Spirit as the response of the Father to the prayer of the Christian disciple.

[11:19] **Your own people: the Greek reads "your sons." Other Jewish exorcists (see Acts 19:13–20), who recognize that the power of God is active in the exorcism, would themselves convict the accusers of Jesus. See also note on Mt 12:27.

††[11:22] **One stronger**: i.e., Jesus. Cf. Lk 3:16 where John the Baptist identifies Jesus as "mightier than I."

‡‡[11:27–28] The beatitude in Lk 11:28 should not be interpreted as a rebuke of the mother of Jesus; see note on Lk 8:21. Rather, it emphasizes (like Lk 2:35) that attentiveness to God's word is more important than biological relationship to Jesus.

§§[11:29–32] The "sign of Jonah" in Luke is the preaching of the need for repentance by a prophet who comes from afar. Cf. Mt 12:38–42 (and see notes there) where the "sign of Jonah" is interpreted by Jesus as his death and resurrection.

---

c. [11:1–4] Mt 6:9–15. d. [11:5–8] 18:1–5. e. [11:9–13] Mt 7:7–11. f. [11:9] Mt 21:22; Mk 11:24; Jn 14:13; 15:7; 1 Jn 5:14–15.

g. [11:14–23] Mt 12:22–30; Mk 3:20–27. h. [11:15] Mt 9:34. i. [11:16] Mt 12:38; 16:1; Mk 8:11; 1 Cor 1:22. j. [11:20] Ex 8:19. k. [11:23] 9:50; Mk 9:40. l. [11:24–26] Mt 12:43–45. m. [11:26] Jn 5:14. n. [11:27] 1:28, 42, 48. o. [11:29–32] Mt 12:38–42; Mk 8:12. p. [11:29] Mt 16:1, 4; Jn 6:30; 1 Cor 1:22.

generation. ³¹At the judgment the queen of the south will rise with the men of this generation and she will condemn them, because she came from the ends of the earth to hear the wisdom of Solomon, and there is something greater than Solomon here.�q ³²At the judgment the men of Nineveh will arise with this generation and condemn it, because at the preaching of Jonah they repented, and there is something greater than Jonah here.ʳ

The Simile of Light. ³³"No one who lights a lamp hides it away or places it [under a bushel basket], but on a lampstand so that those who enter might see the light.ˢ ³⁴The lamp of the body is your eye.ᵗ When your eye is sound, then your whole body is filled with light, but when it is bad, then your body is in darkness. ³⁵Take care, then, that the light in you not become darkness. ³⁶If your whole body is full of light, and no part of it is in darkness, then it will be as full of light as a lamp illuminating you with its brightness."

Denunciation of the Pharisees and Scholars of the Law.* ³⁷ᵘAfter he had spoken, a Pharisee invited him to dine at his home. He entered and reclined at table to eat.ᵛ ³⁸The Pharisee was amazed to see that he did not observe the prescribed washing before the meal.ʷ ³⁹The Lord said to him, "Oh you Pharisees!ˣ Although you cleanse the outside of the cup and the dish, inside you are filled with plunder and evil. ⁴⁰You fools! Did not the maker of the outside also make the inside? ⁴¹But as to what is within, give alms, and behold, everything will be clean for you. ⁴²Woe to you Pharisees! You pay tithes of mint and of rue and of every garden herb, but you pay no attention to judgment and to love for God. These you should have done, without overlooking the others.ʸ ⁴³Woe to you Pharisees! You love the seat of honor in synagogues and greetings in marketplaces.ᶻ ⁴⁴Woe to you! You are like unseen graves† over which people unknowingly walk."ᵃ

⁴⁵Then one of the scholars of the law‡ said to him in reply, "Teacher, by saying this you are insulting us too."ᵇ ⁴⁶And he said, "Woe also to you scholars of the law! You impose on people burdens hard to carry, but you yourselves do not lift one finger to touch them. ⁴⁷ᶜWoe to you! You build the memorials of the prophets whom your ancestors killed. ⁴⁸Consequently, you bear witness and give consent to the deeds of your ancestors, for they killed them and you do the building. ⁴⁹ᵈTherefore, the wisdom of God said, 'I will send to them prophets and apostles;§ some of them they will kill and persecute' ⁵⁰in order that this generation might be charged with the blood of all the prophets shed since the foundation of the world, ⁵¹from the blood of Abel to the blood of Zechariah¶ who died between the altar and the temple building. Yes, I tell you, this generation will be charged with their blood!ᵉ ⁵²Woe to you, scholars of the law! You have taken away the key of knowledge. You yourselves did not enter and you stopped those trying to enter."ᶠ ⁵³When he left, the scribes and Pharisees began to act with hostility toward him and to interrogate him about many things,ᵍ ⁵⁴for they were plotting to catch him at something he might say.ʰ

CHAPTER 12

The Leaven of the Pharisees.** ¹Meanwhile, so many people were crowding together that they were trampling one another underfoot.ⁱ He began to speak, first to his disciples, "Beware of the leaven—that is, the hypocrisy—of the Pharisees.

Courage Under Persecution.†† ²ʲ"There is nothing concealed that will not be revealed, nor secret that will not be known.ᵏ ³Therefore whatever you have said in the darkness will be heard in the light, and what you have whispered behind closed doors will be proclaimed on the housetops. ⁴I tell you, my friends, do not be afraid of those who kill the body but after that can do no more. ⁵I shall show you whom to fear. Be afraid of the one who after killing has the power to cast into Gehenna;‡‡ yes, I tell you, be afraid of that one. ⁶Are not five sparrows sold for two small coins?§§ Yet not one of them has escaped the notice of God. ⁷Even the hairs of your head

---

*[11:37–54] This denunciation of the Pharisees (Lk 11:39–44) and the scholars of the law (Lk 11:45–52) is set by Luke in the context of Jesus' dining at the home of a Pharisee. Controversies with or reprimands of Pharisees are regularly set by Luke within the context of Jesus' eating with Pharisees (see Lk 5:29–39; 7:36–50; 14:1–24). A different compilation of similar sayings is found in Mt 23 (see also notes there).

†[11:44] **Unseen graves:** contact with the dead or with human bones or graves (see Nm 19:16) brought ritual impurity. Jesus presents the Pharisees as those who insidiously lead others astray through their seeming attention to the law.

‡[11:45] **Scholars of the law:** see note on Lk 10:25.

§[11:49] **I will send to them prophets and apostles:** Jesus connects the mission of the church (apostles) with the mission of the Old Testament prophets who often suffered the rebuke of their contemporaries.

¶[11:51] **From the blood of Abel to the blood of Zechariah:** the murder of Abel is the first murder recounted in the Old Testament (Gn 4:8). The Zechariah mentioned here may be the Zechariah whose murder is recounted in 2 Chr 24:20–22, the last murder presented in the Hebrew canon of the Old Testament.

**[12:1] See notes on Mk 8:15 and Mt 16:5–12.

††[12:2–9] Luke presents a collection of sayings of Jesus exhorting his followers to acknowledge him and his mission fearlessly and assuring them of God's protection even in times of persecution. They are paralleled in Mt 10:26–33.

‡‡[12:5] **Gehenna:** see note on Mt 5:22.

§§[12:6] **Two small coins:** the Roman copper coin, the assarion (Latin *as*), was worth about one-sixteenth of a denarius (see note on Lk 7:41).

---

q. [11:31] 1 Kgs 10:1–10; 2 Chr 9:1–12. r. [11:32] Jon 3:8, 10. s. [11:33] 8:16; Mt 5:15; Mk 4:21. t. [11:34–36] Mt 6:22–23. u. [11:37–54] 20:45–47; Mt 23:1–36; Mk 12:38–40. v. [11:37] 7:36; 14:1. w. [11:38] Mt 15:2; Mk 7:2–5. x. [11:39–41] Mt 23:25–26. y. [11:42] Lv 27:30; Mt 23:23. z. [11:43] 20:46; Mt 23:6; Mk 12:38–39. a. [11:44] Mt 23:27. b. [11:45] Mt 23:4.

c. [11:47–48] Mt 23:29–32. d. [11:49–51] Mt 23:34–36. e. [11:51] Gn 4:8; 2 Chr 24:20–22. f. [11:52] Mt 23:13. g. [11:53] 6:11; Mt 22:15–22. h. [11:54] 20:20. i. [12:1] Mt 16:6; Mk 8:15. j. [12:2–9] Mt 10:26–33. k. [12:2] 8:17; Mk 4:22.

have all been counted. Do not be afraid. You are worth more than many sparrows.[l] [8]I tell you, everyone who acknowledges me before others the Son of Man will acknowledge before the angels of God. [9]But whoever denies me before others will be denied before the angels of God.[m]

Sayings About the Holy Spirit.[*] [10]"Everyone who speaks a word against the Son of Man will be forgiven, but the one who blasphemes against the holy Spirit will not be forgiven.[n] [11]When they take you before synagogues and before rulers and authorities,[o] do not worry about how or what your defense will be or about what you are to say. [12]For the holy Spirit will teach you at that moment what you should say."

Saying Against Greed. [13†]Someone in the crowd said to him, "Teacher, tell my brother to share the inheritance with me." [14]He replied to him, "Friend, who appointed me as your judge and arbitrator?"[p] [15]Then he said to the crowd, "Take care to guard against all greed, for though one may be rich, one's life does not consist of possessions."[q]

Parable of the Rich Fool. [16]Then he told them a parable. "There was a rich man whose land produced a bountiful harvest. [17]He asked himself, 'What shall I do, for I do not have space to store my harvest?' [18]And he said, 'This is what I shall do: I shall tear down my barns and build larger ones. There I shall store all my grain and other goods [19]and I shall say to myself, "Now as for you, you have so many good things stored up for many years, rest, eat, drink, be merry!"'[s] [20]But God said to him, 'You fool, this night your life will be demanded of you; and the things you have prepared, to whom will they belong?' [21]Thus will it be for the one who stores up treasure for himself but is not rich in what matters to God."[‡]

Dependence on God. [22†]He said to [his] disciples, "Therefore I tell you, do not worry about your life and what you will eat, or about your body and what you will wear. [23]For life is more than food and the body more than clothing. [24]Notice the ravens: they do not sow or reap; they have neither storehouse nor barn, yet God feeds them. How much more important are you

than birds![u] [25]Can any of you by worrying add a moment to your life-span? [26]If even the smallest things are beyond your control, why are you anxious about the rest? [27]Notice how the flowers grow. They do not toil or spin. But I tell you, not even Solomon in all his splendor was dressed like one of them.[v] [28]If God so clothes the grass in the field that grows today and is thrown into the oven tomorrow, will he not much more provide for you, O you of little faith? [29]As for you, do not seek what you are to eat and what you are to drink, and do not worry anymore. [30]All the nations of the world seek for these things, and your Father knows that you need them. [31]Instead, seek his kingdom, and these other things will be given you besides. [32]Do not be afraid any longer, little flock, for your Father is pleased to give you the kingdom.[w] [33]Sell your belongings and give alms. Provide money bags for yourselves that do not wear out, an inexhaustible treasure in heaven that no thief can reach nor moth destroy.[x] [34]For where your treasure is, there also will your heart be.

Vigilant and Faithful Servants.[§] [35]"Gird your loins and light your lamps [36]and be like servants who await their master's return from a wedding, ready to open immediately when he comes and knocks.[z] [37]Blessed are those servants whom the master finds vigilant on his arrival. Amen, I say to you, he will gird himself, have them recline at table, and proceed to wait on them. [38]And should he come in the second or third watch and find them prepared in this way, blessed are those servants. [39a]Be sure of this: if the master of the house had known the hour when the thief was coming, he would not have let his house be broken into. [40]You also must be prepared, for at an hour you do not expect, the Son of Man will come."

[41]Then Peter said, "Lord, is this parable meant for us or for everyone?" [42]And the Lord replied, "Who, then, is the faithful and prudent steward whom the master will put in charge of his servants to distribute [the] food allowance at the proper time? [43]Blessed is that servant whom his master on arrival finds doing so. [44]Truly, I say to you, he will put him in charge of all his property. [45]But if that servant says to himself, 'My master is delayed in coming,'[¶] and begins to beat the menservants and the maidservants, to eat and drink and get drunk, [46]then that servant's master will come on an unexpected day and at

---

[*][12:10–12] The sayings about the holy Spirit are set in the context of fearlessness in the face of persecution (Lk 12:2–9; cf. Mt 12:31–32). The holy Spirit will be presented in Luke's second volume, the Acts of the Apostles, as the power responsible for the guidance of the Christian mission and the source of courage in the face of persecution.

†[12:13–34] Luke has joined together sayings contrasting those whose focus and trust in life is on material possessions, symbolized here by the rich fool of the parable (Lk 12:16–21), with those who recognize their complete dependence on God (Lk 12:21), those whose radical detachment from material possessions symbolizes their heavenly treasure (Lk 12:33–34).

‡[12:21] **Rich in what matters to God:** literally, "rich for God."

l. [12:7] 12:24; 21:18; Acts 27:34.   m. [12:9] 9:26; Mk 8:38; 2 Tm 2:12.   n. [12:10] Mt 12:31–32; Mk 3:28–29.   o. [12:11–12] 21:12–15; Mt 10:17–20; Mk 13:11.   p. [12:14] Ex 2:14; Acts 7:27.   q. [12:15] 1 Tm 6:9–10.   r. [12:19–21] Mt 6:19–21; 1 Tm 6:17.   s. [12:19–20] Sir 11:19.   t. [12:22–32] Mt 6:25–34.

§[12:35–48] This collection of sayings relates to Luke's understanding of the end time and the return of Jesus. Luke emphasizes for his readers the importance of being faithful to the instructions of Jesus in the period before the parousia.

¶[12:45] **My master is delayed in coming:** this statement indicates that early Christian expectations for the imminent return of Jesus had undergone some modification. Luke cautions his readers against counting on such a delay and acting irresponsibly. Cf. the similar warning in Mt 24:48.

u. [12:24] 12:7.   v. [12:27] 1 Kgs 10:4–7; 2 Chr 9:3–6.   w. [12:32] 22:29; Rev 1:6.   x. [12:33] 18:22; Mt 6:20–21; Mk 10:21.   y. [12:35–46] Mt 24:45–51.   z. [12:36] Mt 25:1–13; Mk 13:35–37.   a. [12:39–40] Mt 24:43–44; 1 Thes 5:2.

an unknown hour and will punish him severely and assign him a place with the unfaithful. ⁴⁷That servant who knew his master's will but did not make preparations nor act in accord with his will shall be beaten severely;ᵇ ⁴⁸and the servant who was ignorant of his master's will but acted in a way deserving of a severe beating shall be beaten only lightly. Much will be required of the person entrusted with much, and still more will be demanded of the person entrusted with more.

Jesus: A Cause of Division.* ⁴⁹"I have come to set the earth on fire, and how I wish it were already blazing! ⁵⁰†There is a baptism with which I must be baptized, and how great is my anguish until it is accomplished!ᶜ ⁵¹Do you think that I have come to establish peace on the earth?ᵈ No, I tell you, but rather division.ᵉ ⁵²From now on a household of five will be divided, three against two and two against three; ⁵³a father will be divided against his son and a son against his father, a mother against her daughter and a daughter against her mother, a mother-in-law against her daughter-in-law and a daughter-in-law against her mother-in-law."ᶠ

Signs of the Times.ᵍ ⁵⁴He also said to the crowds, "When you see [a] cloud rising in the west you say immediately that it is going to rain—and so it does; ⁵⁵and when you notice that the wind is blowing from the south you say that it is going to be hot—and so it is. ⁵⁶You hypocrites! You know how to interpret the appearance of the earth and the sky; why do you not know how to interpret the present time?

Settlement with an Opponent.ʰ ⁵⁷"Why do you not judge for yourselves what is right? ⁵⁸If you are to go with your opponent before a magistrate, make an effort to settle the matter on the way; otherwise your opponent will turn you over to the judge, and the judge hand you over to the constable, and the constable throw you into prison. ⁵⁹I say to you, you will not be released until you have paid the last penny."‡

CHAPTER 13

A Call to Repentance.§ ¹At that time some people who were present there told him about

the Galileans whose blood Pilate⁵ had mingled with the blood of their sacrifices. ²He said to them in reply, "Do you think that because these Galileans suffered in this way they were greater sinners than all other Galileans?ⁱ ³By no means! But I tell you, if you do not repent,ʲ you will all perish as they did! ⁴Or those eighteen people who were killed when the tower at Siloam fell on them**—do you think they were more guilty than everyone else who lived in Jerusalem? ⁵By no means! But I tell you, if you do not repent, you will all perish as they did!"

The Parable of the Barren Fig Tree.†† ⁶ᵏAnd he told them this parable: "There once was a person who had a fig tree planted in his orchard, and when he came in search of fruit on it but found none, ⁷he said to the gardener, 'For three years now I have come in search of fruit on this fig tree but have found none. [So] cut it down. Why should it exhaust the soil?' ⁸He said to him in reply, 'Sir, leave it for this year also, and I shall cultivate the ground around it and fertilize it; ⁹it may bear fruit in the future. If not you can cut it down.'"

Cure of a Crippled Woman on the Sabbath.‡‡ ¹⁰He was teaching in a synagogue on the sabbath. ¹¹And a woman was there who for eighteen years had been crippled by a spirit; she was bent over, completely incapable of standing erect. ¹²When Jesus saw her, he called to her and said, "Woman, you are set free of your infirmity." ¹³He laid his hands on her, and she at once stood up straight and glorified God. ¹⁴But the leader of the synagogue, indignant that Jesus had cured on the sabbath, said to the crowd in reply, "There are six days when work should be done. Come on those days to be cured, not on the

¶[13:1] The slaughter of the Galileans by Pilate is unknown outside Luke; but from what is known about Pilate from the Jewish historian Josephus, such a slaughter would be in keeping with the character of Pilate. Josephus reports that Pilate had disrupted a religious gathering of the Samaritans on Mount Gerizim with a slaughter of the participants (*Antiquities* 18:86–87), and that on another occasion Pilate had killed many Jews who had opposed him when he appropriated money from the temple treasury to build an aqueduct in Jerusalem (*Jewish Wars* 2:175–77; *Antiquities* 18:60–62).

**[13:4] Like the incident mentioned in Lk 13:1 nothing of this accident in Jerusalem is known outside Luke and the New Testament.

††[13:6–9] Following on the call to repentance in Lk 13:1–5, the parable of the barren fig tree presents a story about the continuing patience of God with those who have not yet given evidence of their repentance (see Lk 3:8). The parable may also be alluding to the delay of the end time, when punishment will be meted out, and the importance of preparing for the end of the age because the delay will not be permanent (Lk 13:8–9).

‡‡[13:10–17] The cure of the crippled woman on the sabbath and the controversy that results furnishes a parallel to an incident that will be reported by Luke in 14:1–6, the cure of the man with dropsy on the sabbath. A characteristic of Luke's style is the juxtaposition of an incident that reveals Jesus' concern for a man with an incident that reveals his concern for a woman; cf., e.g., Lk 7:11–17 and Lk 8:49–56.

*[12:49–53] Jesus' proclamation of the kingdom is a refining and purifying fire. His message that meets with acceptance or rejection will be a source of conflict and dissension even within families.

†[12:50] **Baptism:** i.e., his death.

‡[12:59] **The last penny:** Greek, **lepton,** a very small amount. Mt 5:26 has for "the last penny" the Greek word *kodrantēs* (Latin *quadrans,* "farthing").

§[13:1–5] The death of the Galileans at the hands of Pilate (Lk 13:1) and the accidental death of those on whom the tower fell (Lk 13:4) are presented by the Lucan Jesus as timely reminders of the need for all to repent, for the victims of these tragedies should not be considered outstanding sinners who were singled out for punishment.

b. [12:47] Jas 4:17.　c. [12:50] Mk 10:38–39.　d. [12:51–53] Mt 10:34–35.　e. [12:51] 2:14.　f. [12:53] Mi 7:6.　g. [12:54–56] Mt 16:2–3.　h. [12:57–59] Mt 5:25–26.

i. [13:2] Jn 9:2.　j. [13:3–5] Jn 8:24.　k. [13:6–9] Jer 8:13; Heb 3:17; Mt 21:19; Mk 11:13.　l. [13:14] 6:7; 14:3; Ex 20:8–11; Dt 5:12–15; Mt 12:10; Mk 3:2–4; Jn 5:16; 7:23; 9:14, 16.

sabbath day." [15*]The Lord said to him in reply, "Hypocrites! Does not each one of you on the sabbath untie his ox or his ass from the manger and lead it out for watering?[m] [16†]This daughter of Abraham, whom Satan has bound for eighteen years now, ought she not to have been set free on the sabbath day from this bondage?"[n] [17]When he said this, all his adversaries were humiliated; and the whole crowd rejoiced at all the splendid deeds done by him.

The Parable of the Mustard Seed.[o] [18‡]Then he said, "What is the kingdom of God like? To what can I compare it? [19]It is like a mustard seed that a person took and planted in the garden. When it was fully grown, it became a large bush and 'the birds of the sky dwelt in its branches.'"[p]

The Parable of the Yeast.[q] [20]Again he said, "To what shall I compare the kingdom of God? [21]It is like yeast that a woman took and mixed [in] with three measures of wheat flour until the whole batch of dough was leavened."

The Narrow Door; Salvation and Rejection.[§] [22]He passed through towns and villages, teaching as he went and making his way to Jerusalem. [23]Someone asked him, "Lord, will only a few people be saved?" He answered them, [24r]"Strive to enter through the narrow door, for many, I tell you, will attempt to enter but will not be strong enough.[s] [25]After the master of the house has arisen and locked the door, then will you stand outside knocking and saying, 'Lord, open the door for us.' He will say to you in reply, 'I do not know where you are from.'[t] [26]And you will say, 'We ate and drank in your company and you taught in our streets.' [27u]Then he will say to you, 'I do not know where [you] are from. Depart from me, all you evildoers!' [28v]And there will be wailing and grinding of teeth when you see

Abraham, Isaac, and Jacob and all the prophets in the kingdom of God and you yourselves cast out. [29]And people will come from the east and the west and from the north and the south and will recline at table in the kingdom of God.[w] [30]For behold, some are last who will be first, and some are first who will be last."[x]

Herod's Desire to Kill Jesus. [31]At that time some Pharisees came to him and said, "Go away, leave this area because Herod wants to kill you." [32]He replied, "Go and tell that fox, 'Behold, I cast out demons and I perform healings today and tomorrow, and on the third day I accomplish my purpose.[¶] [33**]Yet I must continue on my way today,[y] tomorrow, and the following day, for it is impossible that a prophet should die outside of Jerusalem.'

The Lament over Jerusalem.[z] [34]"Jerusalem, Jerusalem, you who kill the prophets and stone those sent to you, how many times I yearned to gather your children together as a hen gathers her brood under her wings, but you were unwilling! [35]Behold, your house will be abandoned. [But] I tell you, you will not see me until [the time comes when] you say, 'Blessed is he who comes in the name of the Lord.'"[a]

CHAPTER 14

Healing of the Man with Dropsy on the Sabbath.[††] [1b]On a sabbath he went to dine at the home of one of the leading Pharisees, and the people there were observing him carefully.[c] [2]In front of him there was a man suffering from dropsy.[‡‡] [3]Jesus spoke to the scholars of the law and Pharisees in reply, asking, "Is it lawful to cure on the sabbath or not?"[d] [4]But they kept silent; so he took the man and, after he had healed him, dismissed him. [5]Then he said to them, "Who among you, if your son or ox[§§] falls into a cistern, would not immediately pull him out on the sabbath day?"[e] [6]But they were unable to answer his question.[f]

Conduct of Invited Guests and Hosts.[¶¶] [7g]He told a parable to those who had been invited,

---

*[13:15–16] If the law as interpreted by Jewish tradition allowed for the untying of bound animals on the sabbath, how much more should this woman who has been bound by Satan's power be freed on the sabbath from her affliction.

†[13:16] **Whom Satan has bound:** affliction and infirmity are taken as evidence of Satan's hold on humanity. The healing ministry of Jesus reveals the gradual wresting from Satan of control over humanity and the establishment of God's kingdom.

‡[13:18–21] Two parables are used to illustrate the future proportions of the kingdom of God that will result from its deceptively small beginning in the preaching and healing ministry of Jesus. They are paralleled in Mt 13:31–33 and Mk 4:30–32.

§[13:22–30] These sayings of Jesus follow in Luke upon the parables of the kingdom (Lk 13:18–21) and stress that great effort is required for entrance into the kingdom (Lk 13:24) and that there is an urgency to accept the present opportunity to enter because the narrow door will not remain open indefinitely (Lk 13:25). Lying behind the sayings is the rejection of Jesus and his message by his Jewish contemporaries (Lk 13:26) whose places at table in the kingdom will be taken by Gentiles from the four corners of the world (Lk 13:29). Those called last (the Gentiles) will precede those to whom the invitation to enter was first extended (the Jews). See also Lk 14:15–24.

¶[13:32] Nothing, not even Herod's desire to kill Jesus, stands in the way of Jesus' role in fulfilling God's will and in establishing the kingdom through his exorcisms and healings.

[13:33] **It is impossible that a prophet should die outside of Jerusalem: Jerusalem is the city of destiny and the goal of the journey of the prophet Jesus. Only when he reaches the holy city will his work be accomplished.

††[14:1–6] See note on Lk 13:10–17.

‡‡[14:2] **Dropsy:** an abnormal swelling of the body because of the retention and accumulation of fluid.

§§[14:5] **Your son or ox:** this is the reading of many of the oldest and most important New Testament manuscripts. Because of the strange collocation of **son** and **ox**, some copyists have altered it to "your ass or ox," on the model of the saying in Lk 13:15.

¶¶[14:7–14] The banquet scene found only in Luke provides the opportunity for these teachings of Jesus on humility and presents a setting to display Luke's interest in Jesus' attitude

---

m. [13:15] 14:5; Dt 22:4; Mt 12:11.   n. [13:16] 19:9.   o. [13:18–19] Mt 13:31–32; Mk 4:30–32.   p. [13:19] Ez 17:23–24; 31:6.   q. [13:20–21] Mt 13:33.   r. [13:24–30] Mt 7:13–14, 21–23.   s. [13:24] Mk 10:25.   t. [13:25] Mt 25:10–12.   u. [13:27] Ps 6:9; Mt 7:23; 25:41.   v. [13:28–29] Mt 8:11–12.

w. [13:29] Ps 107:2–3.   x. [13:30] Mt 19:20; 20:16; Mk 10:31.   y. [13:33] 2:38; Jn 6:30; 8:20.   z. [13:34–35] 19:41–44; Mt 23:37–39.   a. [13:35] 19:38; 1 Kgs 9:7–8; Ps 118:26; Jer 7:4–7, 13–15; 12:7; 22:5.   b. [14:1–6] 6:6–11; 13:10–17.   c. [14:1] 11:37.   d. [14:3] 6:9; Mk 3:4.   e. [14:5] 13:15; Dt 22:4; Mt 12:11.   f. [14:6] Mt 22:46.   g. [14:7] 11:43; Mt 23:6; Mk 12:38–39.

noticing how they were choosing the places of honor at the table. [8h]"When you are invited by someone to a wedding banquet, do not recline at table in the place of honor. A more distinguished guest than you may have been invited by him, [9]and the host who invited both of you may approach you and say, 'Give your place to this man,' and then you would proceed with embarrassment to take the lowest place. [10]Rather, when you are invited, go and take the lowest place so that when the host comes to you he may say, 'My friend, move up to a higher position.' Then you will enjoy the esteem of your companions at the table. [11]For everyone who exalts himself will be humbled, but the one who humbles himself will be exalted."[i] [12]Then he said to the host who invited him, "When you hold a lunch or a dinner, do not invite your friends or your brothers or your relatives or your wealthy neighbors, in case they may invite you back and you have repayment.[j] [13]Rather, when you hold a banquet, invite the poor, the crippled, the lame, the blind; [14]blessed indeed will you be because of their inability to repay you. For you will be repaid at the resurrection of the righteous."[k]

The Parable of the Great Feast.[*] [15]One of his fellow guests on hearing this said to him, "Blessed is the one who will dine in the kingdom of God." [16l]He replied to him, "A man gave a great dinner to which he invited many. [17]When the time for the dinner came, he dispatched his servant to say to those invited, 'Come, everything is now ready.' [18]But one by one, they all began to excuse themselves. The first said to him, 'I have purchased a field and must go to examine it; I ask you, consider me excused.' [19]And another said, 'I have purchased five yoke of oxen and am on my way to evaluate them; I ask you, consider me excused.' [20]And another said, 'I have just married a woman, and therefore I cannot come.' [21]The servant went and reported this to his master. Then the master of the house in a rage commanded his servant, 'Go out quickly into the streets and alleys of the town and bring in here the poor and the crippled, the blind and the lame.' [22]The servant reported, 'Sir, your orders have been carried out and still there is room.' [23]The master then ordered the servant, 'Go out to the highways and hedgerows and make people come in that my home may be filled. [24]For, I tell you, none of those men who were invited will taste my dinner.'"

Sayings on Discipleship.[†] [25]Great crowds were traveling with him, and he turned and addressed them, [26m]"If anyone comes to me without hating his father[‡] and mother, wife and children, brothers and sisters, and even his own life, he cannot be my disciple.[n] [27]Whoever does not carry his own cross and come after me cannot be my disciple.[o] [28]Which of you wishing to construct a tower does not first sit down and calculate the cost to see if there is enough for its completion? [29]Otherwise, after laying the foundation and finding himself unable to finish the work the onlookers should laugh at him [30]and say, 'This one began to build but did not have the resources to finish.' [31]Or what king marching into battle would not first sit down and decide whether with ten thousand troops he can successfully oppose another king advancing upon him with twenty thousand troops? [32]But if not, while he is still far away, he will send a delegation to ask for peace terms. [33]In the same way, everyone of you who does not renounce all his possessions cannot be my disciple.[p]

The Simile of Salt.[§] [34]"Salt is good, but if salt itself loses its taste, with what can its flavor be restored?[q] [35]It is fit neither for the soil nor for the manure pile; it is thrown out. Whoever has ears to hear ought to hear."[r]

CHAPTER 15

The Parable of the Lost Sheep.[s] [1]The tax collectors and sinners were all drawing near to listen to him, [2]but the Pharisees and scribes began to complain, saying, "This man welcomes sinners and eats with them."[t] [3]So to them he addressed this parable. [4u]"What man among you having a hundred sheep and losing one of them would not leave the ninety-nine in the desert and go after the lost one[v] until he finds it?[w] [5]And when

---

toward the rich and the poor (see notes on Lk 4:18; 6:20–26; 12:13–34).
*[14:15–24] The parable of the great dinner is a further illustration of the rejection by Israel, God's chosen people, of Jesus' invitation to share in the banquet in the kingdom and the extension of the invitation to other Jews whose identification as the poor, crippled, blind, and lame (Lk 14:21) classifies them among those who recognize their need for salvation, and to Gentiles (Lk 14:23). A similar parable is found in Mt 22:1–10.

h. [14:8–10]　Prv 25:6–7.　i. [14:11]　18:14.　j. [14:12]　6:32–35.
k. [14:14] Jn 5:29.　l. [14:16–24] Mt 22:2–10.

†[14:25–33] This collection of sayings, most of which are peculiar to Luke, focuses on the total dedication necessary for the disciple of Jesus. No attachment to family (Lk 14:26) or possessions (Lk 14:33) can stand in the way of the total commitment demanded of the disciple. Also, acceptance of the call to be a disciple demands readiness to accept persecution and suffering (Lk 14:27) and a realistic assessment of the hardships and costs (Lk 14:28–32).
‡[14:26] Hating his father . . . : cf. the similar saying in Mt 10:37. The disciple's family must take second place to the absolute dedication involved in following Jesus (see also Lk 9:59–62).
§[14:34–35] The simile of salt follows the sayings of Jesus that demanded of the disciple total dedication and detachment from family and possessions and illustrates the condition of one who does not display this total commitment. The halfhearted disciple is like salt that cannot serve its intended purpose. See the simile of salt in Mt 5:13 and the note there.
¶[15:1–32] To the parable of the lost sheep (Lk 15:1–7) that Luke shares with Matthew (Mt 18:12–14), Luke adds two parables (the lost coin, Lk 15:8–10; the prodigal son, Lk 15:11–32) from his own special tradition to illustrate Jesus' particular concern for the lost and God's love for the repentant sinner.

m. [14:26–27] Mt 10:37–38.　n. [14:26] 9:57–62; 18:29; Jn 12:25.
o. [14:27] 9:23; Mt 16:24; Mk 8:34.　p. [14:33] 5:11.　q. [14:34] Mt 5:13; Mk 9:50.　r. [14:35] 8:8; Mt 11:15; 13:9; Mk 4:9, 23.　s. [15:1–7] Mt 9:10–13.　t. [15:2] 5:30; 19:7.　u. [15:4–7] Mt 18:12–14.　v. [15:4–6] 19:10.　w. [15:4] Ez 34:11–12, 16.

he does find it, he sets it on his shoulders with great joy [6]and, upon his arrival home, he calls together his friends and neighbors and says to them, 'Rejoice with me because I have found my lost sheep.' [7]I tell you, in just the same way there will be more joy in heaven over one sinner who repents than over ninety-nine righteous people who have no need of repentance.[x]

The Parable of the Lost Coin. [8]"Or what woman having ten coins[*] and losing one would not light a lamp and sweep the house, searching carefully until she finds it? [9]And when she does find it, she calls together her friends and neighbors and says to them, 'Rejoice with me because I have found the coin that I lost.' [10]In just the same way, I tell you, there will be rejoicing among the angels of God over one sinner who repents."

The Parable of the Lost Son. [11]Then he said, "A man had two sons, [12]and the younger son said to his father, 'Father, give me the share of your estate that should come to me.' So the father divided the property between them. [13]After a few days, the younger son collected all his belongings and set off to a distant country where he squandered his inheritance on a life of dissipation.[y] [14]When he had freely spent everything, a severe famine struck that country, and he found himself in dire need. [15]So he hired himself out to one of the local citizens who sent him to his farm to tend the swine. [16]And he longed to eat his fill of the pods on which the swine fed, but nobody gave him any. [17]Coming to his senses he thought, 'How many of my father's hired workers have more than enough food to eat, but here am I, dying from hunger. [18]I shall get up and go to my father and I shall say to him, "Father, I have sinned against heaven and against you. [19]I no longer deserve to be called your son; treat me as you would treat one of your hired workers."' [20]So he got up and went back to his father. While he was still a long way off, his father caught sight of him, and was filled with compassion. He ran to his son, embraced him and kissed him. [21]His son said to him, 'Father, I have sinned against heaven and against you; I no longer deserve to be called your son.' [22]But his father ordered his servants, 'Quickly bring the finest robe and put it on him; put a ring on his finger and sandals on his feet. [23]Take the fattened calf and slaughter it. Then let us celebrate with a feast, [24]because this son of mine was dead, and has come to life again; he was lost, and has been found.' Then the celebration began. [25]Now the older son had been out in the field and, on his way back, as he neared the house, he heard the sound of music and dancing. [26]He called one of the servants and asked what this might mean. [27]The servant said to him, 'Your brother has returned and your father has slaughtered the fattened calf

because he has him back safe and sound.' [28]He became angry, and when he refused to enter the house, his father came out and pleaded with him. [29]He said to his father in reply, 'Look, all these years I served you and not once did I disobey your orders; yet you never gave me even a young goat to feast on with my friends. [30]But when your son returns who swallowed up your property with prostitutes, for him you slaughter the fattened calf.' [31]He said to him, 'My son, you are here with me always; everything I have is yours. [32]But now we must celebrate and rejoice, because your brother was dead and has come to life again; he was lost and has been found.'"

CHAPTER 16

The Parable of the Dishonest Steward.[†] [1]Then he also said to his disciples, "A rich man had a steward who was reported to him for squandering his property. [2]He summoned him and said, 'What is this I hear about you? Prepare a full account of your stewardship, because you can no longer be my steward.' [3]The steward said to himself, 'What shall I do, now that my master is taking the position of steward away from me? I am not strong enough to dig and I am ashamed to beg. [4]I know what I shall do so that, when I am removed from the stewardship, they may welcome me into their homes.' [5]He called in his master's debtors one by one. To the first he said, 'How much do you owe my master?' [6*]He replied, 'One hundred measures of olive oil.' He said to him, 'Here is your promissory note. Sit down and quickly write one for fifty.' [7]Then to another he said, 'And you, how much do you owe?' He replied, 'One hundred kors[§] of wheat.' He said to him, 'Here is your promissory note; write one for eighty.' [8]And the master commended that dishonest steward for acting prudently.

Application of the Parable.[¶] "For the children of this world are more prudent in dealing with their own generation than are the children of light."[z] [9]I tell you, make friends for yourselves

---

*[15:8] **Ten coins:** literally, "ten drachmas." A drachma was a Greek silver coin.

x. [15:7] Ez 18:23.   y. [15:13] Prv 29:3.

---

†[16:1–8a] The parable of the dishonest steward has to be understood in the light of the Palestinian custom of agents acting on behalf of their masters and the usurious practices common to such agents. The dishonesty of the steward consisted in the squandering of his master's property (Lk 16:1) and not in any subsequent graft. The master commends the dishonest steward who has forgone his own usurious commission on the business transaction by having the debtors write new notes that reflected only the real amount owed the master (i.e., minus the steward's profit). The dishonest steward acts in this way in order to ingratiate himself with the debtors because he knows he is being dismissed from his position (Lk 16:3). The parable, then, teaches the prudent use of one's material goods in light of an imminent crisis.

‡[16:6] **One hundred measures:** literally, "one hundred baths." A bath is a Hebrew unit of liquid measurement equivalent to eight or nine gallons.

§[16:7] **One hundred kors:** a **kor** is a Hebrew unit of dry measure for grain or wheat equivalent to ten or twelve bushels.

¶[16:8b–13] Several originally independent sayings of Jesus are gathered here by Luke to form the concluding application of the parable of the dishonest steward.

**[16:8b–9] The first conclusion recommends the prudent use of one's wealth (in the light of the coming of the end of

z. [16:8] Eph 5:8; 1 Thes 5:5.

with dishonest wealth,* so that when it fails, you will be welcomed into eternal dwellings.*[a] 10†The person who is trustworthy in very small matters is also trustworthy in great ones; and the person who is dishonest in very small matters is also dishonest in great ones.[b] 11If, therefore, you are not trustworthy with dishonest wealth, who will trust you with true wealth? 12If you are not trustworthy with what belongs to another, who will give you what is yours? 13No servant can serve two masters.‡ He will either hate one and love the other, or be devoted to one and despise the other. You cannot serve God and mammon."[c]

A Saying Against the Pharisees. 14¶The Pharisees, who loved money,¶ heard all these things and sneered at him. 15And he said to them, "You justify yourselves in the sight of others, but God knows your hearts; for what is of human esteem is an abomination in the sight of God.[d]

Sayings About the Law. 16"The law and the prophets lasted until John;** but from then on the kingdom of God is proclaimed, and everyone who enters does so with violence.[e] 17It is easier for heaven and earth to pass away than for the smallest part of a letter of the law to become invalid.[f]

Sayings About Divorce. 18"Everyone who divorces his wife and marries another commits adultery, and the one who marries a woman divorced from her husband commits adultery.[g]

The Parable of the Rich Man and Lazarus.†† 19"There was a rich man‡‡ who dressed in purple garments and fine linen and dined sumptuously each day. 20And lying at his door was a poor man named Lazarus, covered with sores,[h] 21who would gladly have eaten his fill of the scraps that fell from the rich man's table. Dogs even used to come and lick his sores. 22When the poor man died, he was carried away by angels to the bosom of Abraham. The rich man also died and was buried, 23and from the netherworld,§§ where he was in torment, he raised his eyes and saw Abraham far off and Lazarus at his side. 24And he cried out, 'Father Abraham, have pity on me. Send Lazarus to dip the tip of his finger in water and cool my tongue, for I am suffering torment in these flames.' 25Abraham replied, 'My child, remember that you received what was good during your lifetime while Lazarus likewise received what was bad; but now he is comforted here, whereas you are tormented.[i] 26Moreover, between us and you a great chasm is established to prevent anyone from crossing who might wish to go from our side to yours or from your side to ours.' 27He said, 'Then I beg you, father, send him to my father's house, 28for I have five brothers, so that he may warn them, lest they too come to this place of torment.' 29But Abraham replied, 'They have Moses and the prophets. Let them listen to them.' 30¶¶He said, 'Oh no, father Abraham, but if someone from the dead goes to them, they will repent.' 31Then Abraham said, 'If they will not listen to Moses and the prophets, neither will they be persuaded if someone should rise from the dead.'"[j]

CHAPTER 17

Temptations to Sin. 1kHe said to his disciples, "Things that cause sin will inevitably occur, but woe to the person through whom they occur. 2It would be better for him if a millstone were put around his neck and he be thrown into the sea than for him to cause one of these little ones to sin. 3Be on your guard!*** If your brother sins, rebuke him; and if he repents, forgive him.[l] 4And if he wrongs you seven times in one day and returns to you seven times saying, 'I am sorry,' you should forgive him."[m]

Saying of Faith. 5And the apostles said to the Lord, "Increase our faith." 6The Lord replied, "If you have faith the size of a mustard seed, you

---

the age) after the manner of the children of this world, represented in the parable by the dishonest steward.

* [16:9] **Dishonest wealth**: literally, "mammon of iniquity." Mammon is the Greek transliteration of a Hebrew or Aramaic word that is usually explained as meaning "that in which one trusts." The characterization of this wealth as **dishonest** expresses a tendency of wealth to lead one to dishonesty. **Eternal dwellings**: or, "eternal tents," i.e., heaven.

† [16:10–12] The second conclusion recommends constant fidelity to those in positions of responsibility.

‡ [16:13] The third conclusion is a general statement about the incompatibility of serving God and being a slave to riches. To be dependent upon wealth is opposed to the teachings of Jesus who counseled complete dependence on the Father as one of the characteristics of the Christian disciple (Lk 12:22–39). **God and mammon**: see note on Lk 16:9. Mammon is used here as if it were itself a god.

§ [16:14–18] The two parables about the use of riches in chap. 16 are separated by several isolated sayings of Jesus on the hypocrisy of the Pharisees (Lk 16:14–15), on the law (Lk 16:16–17), and on divorce (Lk 16:18).

¶ [16:14–15] The Pharisees are here presented as examples of those who are slaves to wealth (see Lk 16:13) and, consequently, they are unable to serve God.

** [16:16] John the Baptist is presented in Luke's gospel as a transitional figure between the period of Israel, the time of promise, and the period of Jesus, the time of fulfillment. With John, the fulfillment of the Old Testament promises has begun.

†† [16:19–31] The parable of the rich man and Lazarus again illustrates Luke's concern with Jesus' attitude toward the rich and the poor. The reversal of the fates of the rich man and Lazarus (Lk 16:22–23) illustrates the teachings of Jesus in Luke's "Sermon on the Plain" (Lk 6:20–21, 24–25).

‡‡ [16:19] The oldest Greek manuscript of Luke dating from ca. A.D. 175–225 records the name of the rich man as an abbreviated form of "Nineveh," but there is very little textual support in other manuscripts for this reading. "Dives" of popular tradition is the Latin Vulgate's translation for "rich man" (Lk 16:19–31).

§§ [16:23] **The netherworld**: see note on Lk 10:15.

¶¶ [16:30–31] A foreshadowing in Luke's gospel of the rejection of the call to repentance even after Jesus' resurrection.

*** [17:3] **Be on your guard**: the translation takes Lk 17:3a as the conclusion to the saying on scandal in Lk 17:1–2. It is not impossible that it should be taken as the beginning of the saying on forgiveness in Lk 17:3b–4.

---

a. [16:9] 12:33. b. [16:10] 19:17; Mt 25:20–23. c. [16:13] Mt 6:24. d. [16:15] 18:9–14. e. [16:16] Mt 11:12–13. f. [16:17] Mt 5:18. g. [16:18] Mt 5:32; 19:9; Mk 10:11–12; 1 Cor 7:10–11. h. [16:20] Mt 15:27; Mk 7:28. i. [16:25] 6:24–25. j. [16:31] Jn 5:46–47; 11:44–48. k. [17:1–2] Mt 18:6–7. l. [17:3] Mt 18:15. m. [17:4] Mt 6:14; 18:21–22, 35; Mk 11:25.

would say to [this] mulberry tree, 'Be uprooted and planted in the sea,' and it would obey you."
Attitude of a Servant.* ⁷"Who among you would say to your servant who has just come in from plowing or tending sheep in the field, 'Come here immediately and take your place at table'? ⁸Would he not rather say to him, 'Prepare something for me to eat. Put on your apron and wait on me while I eat and drink. You may eat and drink when I am finished'? ⁹Is he grateful to that servant because he did what was commanded? ¹⁰So should it be with you. When you have done all you have been commanded, say, 'We are unprofitable servants; we have done what we were obliged to do.'"
The Cleansing of Ten Lepers.† ¹¹As he continued his journey to Jerusalem,ᵒ he traveled through Samaria and Galilee.‡ ¹²As he was entering a village, ten lepers met [him]. They stood at a distance from him ¹³and raised their voice, saying, "Jesus, Master! Have pity on us!"ᵖ ¹⁴And when he saw them, he said, "Go show yourselves to the priests."§ As they were going they were cleansed.�q ¹⁵And one of them, realizing he had been healed, returned, glorifying God in a loud voice; ¹⁶and he fell at the feet of Jesus and thanked him. He was a Samaritan. ¹⁷Jesus said in reply, "Ten were cleansed, were they not? Where are the other nine? ¹⁸Has none but this foreigner returned to give thanks to God?" ¹⁹Then he said to him, "Stand up and go; your faith has saved you."ʳ
The Coming of the Kingdom of God. ²⁰¶Asked by the Pharisees when the kingdom of God would come, he said in reply, "The coming of the kingdom of God cannot be observed,ˢ ²¹**"and

no one will announce, 'Look, here it is,' or, 'There it is.'ᵗ For behold, the kingdom of God is among you."
The Day of the Son of Man. ²²Then he said to his disciples, "The days will come when you will long to see one of the days of the Son of Man, but you will not see it. ²³There will be those who will say to you, 'Look, there he is,' [or] 'Look, here he is.' Do not go off, do not run in pursuit.ᵘ ²⁴For just as lightning flashes and lights up the sky from one side to the other, so will the Son of Man be [in his day].ᵛ ²⁵But first he must suffer greatly and be rejected by this generation.ʷ ²⁶As it was in the days of Noah,ˣ so it will be in the days of the Son of Man; ²⁷they were eating and drinking, marrying and giving in marriage up to the day that Noah entered the ark, and the flood came and destroyed them all. ²⁸ʸSimilarly, as it was in the days of Lot: they were eating, drinking, buying, selling, planting, building; ²⁹on the day when Lot left Sodom, fire and brimstone rained from the sky to destroy them all. ³⁰So it will be on the day the Son of Man is revealed. ³¹‡On that day, a person who is on the housetop and whose belongings are in the house must not go down to get them, and likewise a person in the field must not return to what was left behind.ᵃ ³²Remember the wife of Lot. ³³Whoever seeks to preserve his life will lose it, but whoever loses it will save it.ᵇ ³⁴I tell you, on that night there will be two people in one bed; one will be taken, the other left. ³⁵ᶜAnd there will be two women grinding meal together; one will be taken, the other left." ³⁶†† ³⁷They said to him in reply, "Where, Lord?" He said to them, "Where the body is, there also the vultures will gather."ᵈ

CHAPTER 18

The Parable of the Persistent Widow. ¹‡‡Then he told them a parable about the necessity for them to pray always without becoming weary.ᵉ He said, ²"There was a judge in a certain town who

---

*[17:7–10] These sayings of Jesus, peculiar to Luke, which continue his response to the apostles' request to increase their faith (Lk 17:5–6), remind them that Christian disciples can make no claim on God's graciousness; in fulfilling the exacting demands of discipleship, they are only doing their duty.
†[17:11–19] This incident recounting the thankfulness of the cleansed Samaritan leper is narrated only in Luke's gospel and provides an instance of Jesus holding up a non-Jew (Lk 17:18) as an example to his Jewish contemporaries (cf. Lk 10:33 where a similar purpose is achieved in the story of the good Samaritan). Moreover, it is the faith in Jesus manifested by the foreigner that has brought him salvation (Lk 17:19; cf. the similar relationship between faith and salvation in Lk 7:50; 8:48, 50).
‡[17:11] **Through Samaria and Galilee:** or, "between Samaria and Galilee."
§[17:14] See note on Lk 5:14.
¶[17:20–37] To' the question of the Pharisees about the time of the coming of God's kingdom, Jesus replies that the kingdom is **among you** (Lk 17:20–21). The emphasis has thus been shifted from an imminent observable coming of the kingdom to something that is already present in Jesus' preaching and healing ministry. Luke has also appended further traditional sayings of Jesus about the unpredictable suddenness of the day of the Son of Man, and assures his readers that in spite of the delay of that day (Lk 12:45), it will bring judgment unexpectedly on those who do not continue to be vigilant.
[17:21] **Among you: the Greek preposition translated as **among** can also be translated as "within." In the light of other statements in Luke's gospel about the presence of the kingdom (see Lk 10:9, 11; 11:20) "among" is to be preferred.

††[17:36] The inclusion of Lk 17:36, "There will be two men in the field; one will be taken, the other left behind," in some Western manuscripts appears to be a scribal assimilation to Mt 24:40.
‡‡[18:1–14] The particularly Lucan material in the travel narrative concludes with two parables on prayer. The first (Lk 18:1–8) teaches the disciples the need of persistent prayer so that they not fall victims to apostasy (Lk 18:8). The second (Lk 18:9–14) condemns the self-righteous, critical attitude of the Pharisee and teaches that the fundamental attitude of the Christian disciple must be the recognition of sinfulness and complete dependence on God's graciousness. The second parable recalls the story of the pardoning of the sinful woman (Lk 7:36–50) where a similar contrast is presented between the critical attitude of the Pharisee Simon and the love shown by the pardoned sinner.

---

n. [17:6] Mt 17:20; 21:21; Mk 11:23. o. [17:11] 9:51–53; 13:22, 33; 18:31; 19:28; Jn 4:4. p. [17:13] 18:38; Mk 9:27; 15:22. q. [17:14] 5:14; Lv 14:2–32; Mt 8:4; Mk 1:44. r. [17:19] 7:50; 18:42. s. [17:20] Jn 3:3.

t. [17:21] 17:23; Mt 24:23; Mk 13:21. u. [17:23] 17:21; Mt 24:23, 26; Mk 13:21. v. [17:24] Mt 24:27. w. [17:25] 9:22; 18:32–33; Mt 16:21; 17:22–23; 20:18–19; Mk 8:31; 9:31; 10:33–34. x. [17:26–27] Gn 6–8; Mt 24:37–39. y. [17:28–29] Gn 18:20–21; 19:1–29. z. [17:31–32] Gn 19:17, 26. a. [17:31] Mt 24:17–18; Mk 13:15–16. b. [17:33] 9:24; Mt 10:39; 16:25; Mk 8:35; Jn 12:25. c. [17:35] Mt 24:40–41. d. [17:37] Jb 39:30; Mt 24:28. e. [18:1] Rom 12:12; Col 4:2; 1 Thes 5:17.

neither feared God nor respected any human being. [3]And a widow in that town used to come to him and say, 'Render a just decision for me against my adversary.' [4]For a long time the judge was unwilling, but eventually he thought, 'While it is true that I neither fear God nor respect any human being, [5*f]because this widow keeps bothering me I shall deliver a just decision for her lest she finally come and strike me.'" [6]The Lord said, "Pay attention to what the dishonest judge says. [7]Will not God then secure the rights of his chosen ones who call out to him day and night? Will he be slow to answer them? [8]I tell you, he will see to it that justice is done for them speedily. But when the Son of Man comes, will he find faith on earth?"

The Parable of the Pharisee and the Tax Collector. [9]He then addressed this parable to those who were convinced of their own righteousness and despised everyone else.[g] [10]"Two people went up to the temple area to pray; one was a Pharisee and the other a tax collector. [11]The Pharisee took up his position and spoke this prayer to himself, 'O God, I thank you that I am not like the rest of humanity—greedy, dishonest, adulterous—or even like this tax collector. [12]I fast twice a week, and I pay tithes on my whole income.'[h] [13]But the tax collector stood off at a distance and would not even raise his eyes to heaven but beat his breast and prayed, 'O God, be merciful to me a sinner.'[i] [14]I tell you, the latter went home justified, not the former; for everyone who exalts himself will be humbled, and the one who humbles himself will be exalted."[j]

Saying on Children and the Kingdom. [15†]People were bringing even infants to him that he might touch them,[‡] and when the disciples saw this, they rebuked them.[k] [16]Jesus, however, called the children to himself and said, "Let the children come to me and do not prevent them; for the kingdom of God belongs to such as these. [17]Amen, I say to you, whoever does not accept the kingdom of God like a child will not enter it."[l]

The Rich Official. [18m]An official asked him this question, "Good teacher, what must I do

to inherit eternal life?"[n] [19]Jesus answered him, "Why do you call me good? No one is good but God alone. [20]You know the commandments, 'You shall not commit adultery; you shall not kill; you shall not steal; you shall not bear false witness; honor your father and your mother.'"[o] [21]And he replied, "All of these I have observed from my youth." [22§p]When Jesus heard this he said to him, "There is still one thing left for you: sell all that you have and distribute it to the poor, and you will have a treasure in heaven. Then come, follow me." [23]But when he heard this he became quite sad, for he was very rich.

On Riches and Renunciation. [24]Jesus looked at him [now sad] and said, "How hard it is for those who have wealth to enter the kingdom of God! [25]For it is easier for a camel to pass through the eye of a needle than for a rich person to enter the kingdom of God." [26]Those who heard this said, "Then who can be saved?" [27]And he said, "What is impossible for human beings is possible for God."[q] [28]Then Peter said, "We have given up our possessions and followed you." [29]He said to them, "Amen, I say to you, there is no one who has given up house or wife or brothers or parents or children for the sake of the kingdom of God [30]who will not receive [back] an overabundant return in this present age and eternal life in the age to come."

The Third Prediction of the Passion.[s] [31¶]Then he took the Twelve aside and said to them, "Behold, we are going up to Jerusalem and everything written by the prophets about the Son of Man will be fulfilled." [32]He will be handed over to the Gentiles and he will be mocked and insulted and spat upon; [33]and after they have scourged him they will kill him, but on the third day he will rise." [34]But they understood nothing of this; the word remained hidden from them and they failed to comprehend what he said.[u]

The Healing of the Blind Beggar.[v] [35]Now as he approached Jericho a blind man was sitting by the roadside begging, [36]and hearing a crowd going by, he inquired what was happening.

---

*[18:5] **Strike me:** the Greek verb translated as strike means "to strike under the eye" and suggests the extreme situation to which the persistence of the widow might lead. It may, however, be used here in the much weaker sense of "to wear one out."

†[18:15–19:27] Luke here includes much of the material about the journey to Jerusalem found in his Marcan source (Lk 10:1–52) and adds to it the story of Zacchaeus (Lk 19:1–10) from his own particular tradition and the parable of the gold coins (minas) (Lk 19:11–27) from Q, the source common to Luke and Matthew.

‡[18:15–17] The sayings on children furnish a contrast to the attitude of the Pharisee in the preceding episode (Lk 18:9–14) and that of the wealthy official in the following one (Lk 18:18–23) who think that they can lay claim to God's favor by their own merit. The attitude of the disciple should be marked by the receptivity and trustful dependence characteristic of the child.

§[18:22] Detachment from material possessions results in the total dependence on God demanded of one who would inherit eternal life. **Sell all that you have:** the original saying (cf. Mk 10:21) has characteristically been made more demanding by Luke's addition of "all."

¶[18:31–33] The details included in this third announcement of Jesus' suffering and death suggest that the literary formulation of the announcement has been directed by the knowledge of the historical passion and death of Jesus.

[18:31] **Everything written by the prophets . . . will be fulfilled: this is a Lucan addition to the words of Jesus found in the Marcan source (Mk 10:32–34). Luke understands the events of Jesus' last days in Jerusalem to be the fulfillment of Old Testament prophecy, but, as is usually the case in Luke-Acts, the author does not specify which Old Testament prophets he has in mind; cf. Lk 24:25, 27, 44; Acts 3:8; 13:27; 26:22–23.

f. [18:5] 11:8.   g. [18:9] 16:5; Mt 23:25–28.   h. [18:12] Mt 23:23. i. [18:13] Ps 51:3.   j. [18:14] 14:11; Mt 23:12.   k. [18:15–17] Mt 19:13–15; Mk 10:13–16.   l. [18:17] Mt 18:3.   m. [18:18–30] Mt 19:16–30; Mk 10:17–31.

n. [18:18] 10:25.   o. [18:20] Ex 20:12–16; Dt 5:16–20.   p. [18:22] 12:33; Sir 29:11; Mt 6:20.   q. [18:27] Mk 14:36.   r. [18:29–30] 14:26.   s. [18:31–34] 24:25–27, 44; Mt 20:17–19; Mk 10:32–34; Acts 3:18.   t. [18:32–33] 9:22, 44.   u. [18:34] Mk 9:32.   v. [18:35–43] Mt 20:29–34; Mk 10:46–52.

³⁷They told him, "Jesus of Nazareth is passing by." ³⁸ʷHe shouted, "Jesus, Son of David,˙ have pity on me!" ³⁹The people walking in front rebuked him, telling him to be silent, but he kept calling out all the more, "Son of David, have pity on me!" ⁴⁰Then Jesus stopped and ordered that he be brought to him; and when he came near, Jesus asked him, ⁴¹"What do you want me to do for you?" He replied, "Lord, please let me see."ˣ ⁴²Jesus told him, "Have sight; your faith has saved you."ʸ ⁴³He immediately received his sight and followed him, giving glory to God. When they saw this, all the people gave praise to God.

CHAPTER 19

Zacchaeus the Tax Collector.† ¹He came to Jericho and intended to pass through the town. ²Now a man there named Zacchaeus, who was a chief tax collector and also a wealthy man, ³was seeking to see who Jesus was; but he could not see him because of the crowd, for he was short in stature. ⁴So he ran ahead and climbed a sycamore tree in order to see Jesus, who was about to pass that way. ⁵When he reached the place, Jesus looked up and said to him, "Zacchaeus, come down quickly, for today I must stay at your house." ⁶And he came down quickly and received him with joy. ⁷When they all saw this, they began to grumble, saying, "He has gone to stay at the house of a sinner."ᶻ ⁸But Zacchaeus stood there and said to the Lord, "Behold, half of my possessions, Lord, I shall give to the poor, and if I have extorted anything from anyone I shall repay it four times over."ᵃ ⁹‡And Jesus said to him, "Today salvationᵇ has come to this house because this man too is a descendant of Abraham. ¹⁰§ᶜFor the Son of Man has come to seek and to save what was lost."

---

*[18:38] **Son of David:** the blind beggar identifies Jesus with a title that is related to Jesus' role as Messiah (see note on Lk 2:11). Through this Son of David, salvation comes to the blind man. Note the connection between salvation and house of David mentioned earlier in Zechariah's canticle (Lk 1:69). See also note on Mt 9:27.

†[19:1–10] The story of the tax collector Zacchaeus is unique to this gospel. While a rich man (Lk 19:2), Zacchaeus provides a contrast to the rich man of Lk 18:18–23 who cannot detach himself from his material possessions to become a follower of Jesus. Zacchaeus, according to Luke, exemplifies the proper attitude toward wealth: he promises to give half of his possessions to the poor (Lk 19:8) and consequently is the recipient of salvation (Lk 19:9–10).

‡[19:9] **A descendant of Abraham:** literally, "a son of Abraham." The tax collector Zacchaeus, whose repentance is attested by his determination to amend his former ways, shows himself to be a true descendant of Abraham, the true heir to the promises of God in the Old Testament. Underlying Luke's depiction of Zacchaeus as a descendant of Abraham, the father of the Jews (Lk 1:73; 16:22–31), is his recognition of the central place occupied by Israel in the plan of salvation.

§[19:10] This verse sums up for Luke his depiction of the role of Jesus as savior in this gospel.

w. [18:38–39] 17:13; Mt 9:27; 15:22.   x. [18:41] Mk 10:36.   y. [18:42] 7:50; 17:19.   z. [19:7] 5:30; 15:2. - a. [19:8] Ex 21:37; Nm 5:6–7; 2 Sm 12:6.   b. [19:9] 13:16; Mt 21:31.   c. [19:10] 15:4–10; Ez 34:16.

The Parable of the Ten Gold Coins.¶ ¹¹ᵈWhile they were listening to him speak, he proceeded to tell a parable because he was near Jerusalem and they thought that the kingdom of God would appear there immediately. ¹²So he said, "A nobleman went off to a distant country to obtain the kingship for himself and then to return.ᵉ ¹³He called ten of his servants and gave them ten gold coins** and told them, 'Engage in trade with these until I return.' ¹⁴His fellow citizens, however, despised him and sent a delegation after him to announce, 'We do not want this man to be our king.' ¹⁵But when he returned after obtaining the kingship, he had the servants called, to whom he had given the money, to learn what they had gained by trading. ¹⁶The first came forward and said, 'Sir, your gold coin has earned ten additional ones.' ¹⁷He replied, 'Well done, good servant! You have been faithful in this very small matter; take charge of ten cities.'ᶠ ¹⁸Then the second came and reported, 'Your gold coin, sir, has earned five more.' ¹⁹And to this servant too he said, 'You, take charge of five cities.' ²⁰Then the other servant came and said, 'Sir, here is your gold coin; I kept it stored away in a handkerchief, ²¹for I was afraid of you, because you are a demanding person; you take up what you did not lay down and you harvest what you did not plant.' ²²He said to him, 'With your own words I shall condemn you, you wicked servant. You knew I was a demanding person, taking up what I did not lay down and harvesting what I did not plant; ²³why did you not put my money in a bank? Then on my return I would have collected it with interest.' ²⁴And to those standing by he said, 'Take the gold coin from him and give it to the servant who has ten.' ²⁵But they said to him, 'Sir, he has ten gold coins.' ²⁶'I tell you, to everyone who has, more will be given, but from the one who has not, even what he has will be taken away.ᵍ ²⁷Now as for those enemies of mine who did not want me as their king, bring them here and slay them before me.'"

¶[19:11–27] In this parable Luke has combined two originally distinct parables: (1) a parable about the conduct of faithful and productive servants (Lk 19:13, 15b–26) and (2) a parable about a rejected king (Lk 19:12, 14–15a, 27). The story about the conduct of servants occurs in another form in Mt 25:14–20. The story about the rejected king may have originated with a contemporary historical event. After the death of Herod the Great, his son Archelaus traveled to Rome to receive the title of king. A delegation of Jews appeared in Rome before Caesar Augustus to oppose the request of Archelaus. Although not given the title of king, Archelaus was made ruler over Judea and Samaria. As the story is used by Luke, however, it furnishes a correction to the expectation of the imminent end of the age and of the establishment of the kingdom in Jerusalem (Lk 19:11). Jesus is not on his way to Jerusalem to receive the kingly power; for that, he must go away and only after returning from the distant country (a reference to the parousia) will reward and judgment take place.

[19:13] **Ten gold coins: literally, "ten minas." A mina was a monetary unit that in ancient Greece was the equivalent of one hundred drachmas.

---

d. [19:11–27] Mt 25:14–30.   e. [19:12] Mk 13:34.   f. [19:17] 16:10.   g. [19:26] 8:18; Mt 13:12; Mk 4:25.

VI. THE TEACHING MINISTRY
IN JERUSALEM*

The Entry into Jerusalem.^h ²⁸After he had said this, he proceeded on his journey up to Jerusalem. ²⁹As he drew near to Bethphage and Bethany at the place called the Mount of Olives, he sent two of his disciples.^i ³⁰He said, "Go into the village opposite you, and as you enter it you will find a colt tethered on which no one has ever sat. Untie it and bring it here.^j ³¹And if anyone should ask you, 'Why are you untying it?' you will answer, 'The Master has need of it.'" ³²So those who had been sent went off and found everything just as he had told them.^k ³³And as they were untying the colt, its owners said to them, "Why are you untying this colt?" ³⁴They answered, "The Master has need of it." ³⁵So they brought it to Jesus, threw their cloaks over the colt, and helped Jesus to mount. ³⁶As he rode along, the people were spreading their cloaks on the road; ³⁷and now as he was approaching the slope of the Mount of Olives, the whole multitude of his disciples began to praise God aloud with joy for all the mighty deeds they had seen. ³⁸They proclaimed:

"Blessed is the king who comes
in the name of the Lord.†
Peace in heaven
and glory in the highest."^m

³⁹Some of the Pharisees in the crowd said to him, "Teacher, rebuke your disciples."‡ ⁴⁰He said in reply, "I tell you, if they keep silent, the stones will cry out!"

The Lament for Jerusalem.§ ⁴¹ⁿAs he drew near, he saw the city and wept over it,^o ⁴²saying, "If this day you only knew what makes for peace—but now it is hidden from your eyes.^p ⁴³¶For the days are coming upon you when your enemies will raise a palisade against you; they will encircle you and hem you in on all sides.^q ⁴⁴They will smash you to the ground and your children within you, and they will not leave one stone upon another within you because you did not recognize the time of your visitation."^r

The Cleansing of the Temple. ⁴⁵ˢThen Jesus entered the temple area** and proceeded to drive out those who were selling things,^t ⁴⁶saying to them, "It is written, 'My house shall be a house of prayer, but you have made it a den of thieves.'"^u ⁴⁷And every day he was teaching in the temple area.^v The chief priests, the scribes, and the leaders of the people, meanwhile, were seeking to put him to death,^w ⁴⁸but they could find no way to accomplish their purpose because all the people were hanging on his words.

CHAPTER 20††
The Authority of Jesus Questioned.^x ¹One day as he was teaching the people in the temple area and proclaiming the good news, the chief priests and scribes, together with the elders, approached him ²and said to him, "Tell us, by what authority are you doing these things? Or who is the one who gave you this authority?"^y ³He said to them in reply, "I shall ask you a question. Tell me, ⁴was John's baptism of heavenly or of human origin?"^z ⁵They discussed this among themselves, and said, "If we say, 'Of heavenly origin,' he will say, 'Why did you not believe him?'^a ⁶But if we say, 'Of human origin,' then all the people will stone us, for they are convinced that John was a prophet." ⁷So they answered that they did not know from where it came. ⁸Then Jesus said to them, "Neither shall I tell you by what authority I do these things."

The Parable of the Tenant Farmers.‡‡ ⁹ᵇThen he proceeded to tell the people this parable. "[A]

---

*[19:28–21:38] With the royal entry of Jesus into Jerusalem, a new section of Luke's gospel begins, the ministry of Jesus in Jerusalem before his death and resurrection. Luke suggests that this was a lengthy ministry in Jerusalem (Lk 19:47; 20:1; 21:37–38; 22:53) and it is characterized by Jesus' daily teaching in the temple (Lk 21:37–38). For the story of the entry of Jesus into Jerusalem, see also Mt 21:1–11; Mk 11:1–10; Jn 12:12–19 and the notes there.

†[19:38] **Blessed is the king who comes in the name of the Lord:** only in Luke is Jesus explicitly given the title **king** when he enters Jerusalem in triumph. Luke has inserted this title into the words of Ps 118:26 that heralded the arrival of the pilgrims coming to the holy city and to the temple. Jesus is thereby acclaimed as **king** (see Lk 1:32) and as the one **who comes** (see Mal 3:1; Lk 7:19). **Peace in heaven . . . :** the acclamation of the disciples of Jesus in Luke echoes the announcement of the angels at the birth of Jesus (Lk 2:14). The peace Jesus brings is associated with the salvation to be accomplished here in Jerusalem.

‡[19:39] **Rebuke your disciples:** this command, found only in Luke, was given so that the Roman authorities would not interpret the acclamation of Jesus as king as an uprising against them; cf. Lk 23:2–3.

§[19:41–44] The lament for Jerusalem is found only in Luke. By not accepting Jesus (the one who mediates peace), Jerusalem will not find peace but will become the victim of devastation.

¶[19:43–44] Luke may be describing the actual disaster that befell Jerusalem in A.D. 70 when it was destroyed by the Romans during the First Revolt.

**[19:45–46] Immediately upon entering the holy city, Jesus in a display of his authority enters the temple (see Mal 3:1–3) and lays claim to it after cleansing it that it might become a proper place for his teaching ministry in Jerusalem (Lk 19:47; 20:1; 21:37; 22:53). See Mt 21:12–17; Mk 11:15–19; Jn 2:13–17 and the notes there.

††[20:1–47] The Jerusalem religious leaders or their representatives, in an attempt to incriminate Jesus with the Romans and to discredit him with the people, pose a number of questions to him (about his authority, Lk 20:2; about payment of taxes, Lk 20:22; about the resurrection, Lk 20:28–33).

‡‡[20:9–19] This parable about an absentee landlord and a tenant farmers' revolt reflects the social and economic

---

h. [19:28–40] Mt 21:1–11; Mk 11:1–11; Jn 12:12–19.   i. [19:29] Zec 14:4.   j. [19:30] Nm 19:2; Dt 21:3; 1 Sm 6:7; Zec 9:9.   k. [19:32] 22:13.   l. [19:35–36] 2 Kgs 9:13.   m. [19:38] 2:14; Ps 118:26.   n. [19:41–44] 13:34–35.   o. [19:41] 2 Kgs 8:11–12; Jer 14:17; 15:5.

p. [19:42] 8:10; Is 6:9–10; Mt 13:14; Mk 4:12; Acts 28:26–27; Rom 11:8, 10.   q. [19:43] Is 29:3.   r. [19:44] 1:68; 21:6; Ps 137:9; Mt 24:2; Mk 13:2.   s. [19:45–46] Mt 21:12–13; Mk 11:15–17; Jn 2:13–17.   t. [19:45] 3:1 / Hos 9:15.   u. [19:46] Is 56:7; Jer 7:11.   v. [19:47–48] 20:19; 22:2; Mt 21:46; Mk 11:18; 12:12; 14:1–2; Jn 5:18; 7:30.   w. [19:47] 21:37; 22:53; Jn 18:20.   x. [20:1–8] Mt 21:23–27; Mk 11:27–33.   y. [20:2] Acts 4:7.   z. [20:4] 3:3, 16.   a. [20:5] Mt 21:32.   b. [20:9–19] Mt 21:33–46; Mk 12:1–12.

man planted a vineyard, leased it to tenant farmers, and then went on a journey for a long time.[c] [10]At harvest time he sent a servant[d] to the tenant farmers to receive some of the produce of the vineyard. But they beat the servant and sent him away empty-handed. [11]So he proceeded to send another servant, but him also they beat and insulted and sent away empty-handed. [12]Then he proceeded to send a third, but this one too they wounded and threw out. [13]The owner of the vineyard said, 'What shall I do? I shall send my beloved son; maybe they will respect him.'[e] [14]But when the tenant farmers saw him they said to one another, 'This is the heir. Let us kill him that the inheritance may become ours.' [15]So they threw him out of the vineyard and killed him.* What will the owner of the vineyard do to them? [16]He will come and put those tenant farmers to death and turn over the vineyard to others." When the people heard this, they exclaimed, "Let it not be so!" [17]But he looked at them and asked, "What then does this scripture passage mean:

'The stone which the builders rejected
has become the cornerstone'?[f]

[18]Everyone who falls on that stone will be dashed to pieces; and it will crush anyone on whom it falls." [19]The scribes and chief priests sought to lay their hands on him at that very hour, but they feared the people, for they knew that he had addressed this parable to them.[g]

Paying Taxes to the Emperor.[h] [20†]They watched him closely and sent agents pretending to be righteous who were to trap him in speech,[i] in order to hand him over to the authority and power of the governor. [21]They posed this question to him, "Teacher, we know that what you say and teach is correct, and you show no partiality, but teach the way of God in accordance with the truth.[j] [22]Is it lawful for us to pay tribute to Caesar or not?"‡ [23]Recognizing their craftiness

he said to them, [24]"Show me a denarius;[§] whose image and name does it bear?" They replied, "Caesar's." [25]So he said to them, "Then repay to Caesar what belongs to Caesar and to God what belongs to God."[k] [26]They were unable to trap him by something he might say before the people, and so amazed were they at his reply that they fell silent.

The Question About the Resurrection.[l] [27]Some Sadducees,[¶] those who deny that there is a resurrection, came forward and put this question to him,[m] [28]saying, "Teacher, Moses wrote for us, 'If someone's brother dies leaving a wife but no child, his brother must take the wife and raise up descendants for his brother.'[n] [29]Now there were seven brothers; the first married a woman but died childless. [30]Then the second [31]and the third married her, and likewise all the seven died childless. [32]Finally the woman also died. [33]Now at the resurrection whose wife will that woman be? For all seven had been married to her." [34]Jesus said to them, "The children of this age marry and are given in marriage; [35]but those who are deemed worthy to attain to the coming age and to the resurrection of the dead neither marry nor are given in marriage. [36]They can no longer die, for they are like angels; and they are the children of God because they are the ones who will rise.†† [37]That the dead will rise even Moses made known in the passage about the bush, when he called 'Lord' the God of Abraham, the God of Isaac, and the God of Jacob;[o] [38]and he is not God of the dead, but of the living, for to him all are alive."[p] [39]Some of the scribes said in reply, "Teacher, you have answered well." [40]And they no longer dared to ask him anything.[q]

The Question About David's Son.†† [41]Then he said to them, "How do they claim that the Messiah is the Son of David? [42]For David himself in the Book of Psalms says:[s]

'The Lord said to my lord,
"Sit at my right hand

<hr>

conditions of rural Palestine in the first century. The synoptic gospel writers use the parable to describe how the rejection of the landlord's son becomes the occasion for the vineyard to be taken away from those to whom it was entrusted (the religious leadership of Judaism that rejects the teaching and preaching of Jesus; Lk 20:19).

*[20:15] **They threw him out of the vineyard and killed him:** cf. Mk 12:8. Luke has altered his Marcan source and reports that the murder of the son takes place outside the vineyard to reflect the tradition of Jesus' death outside the walls of the city of Jerusalem (see Heb 13:12).

†[20:20] **The governor:** i.e., Pontius Pilate, the Roman administrator responsible for the collection of taxes and maintenance of order in Palestine.

‡[20:22] Through their question the agents of the Jerusalem religious leadership hope to force Jesus to take sides on one of the sensitive political issues of first-century Palestine. The issue of nonpayment of taxes to Rome becomes one of the focal points of the First Jewish Revolt (A.D. 66–70) that resulted in the Roman destruction of Jerusalem and the temple. See also note on Mt 22:15–22.

§[20:24] **Denarius:** a Roman silver coin (see note on Lk 7:41).
¶[20:27] **Sadducees:** see note on Mt 3:7.
**[20:28–33] The Sadducees' question, based on the law of levirate marriage recorded in Dt 25:5–10, ridicules the idea of the resurrection. Jesus rejects their naive understanding of the resurrection (Lk 20:35–36) and then argues on behalf of the resurrection of the dead on the basis of the written law (Lk 20:37–38) that the Sadducees accept. See also notes on Mt 22:23–33.

††[20:36] **Because they are the ones who will rise:** literally, "being sons of the resurrection."

‡‡[20:41–44] After successfully answering the three questions of his opponents, Jesus now asks them a question. Their inability to respond implies that they have forfeited their position and authority as the religious leaders of the people because they do not understand the scriptures. This series of controversies between the religious leadership of Jerusalem and Jesus reveals Jesus as the authoritative teacher whose words are to be listened to (see Lk 9:35). See also notes on Mt 22:41–46.

<hr>

c. [20:9] Is 5:1–7. d. [20:10–12] 2 Chr 36:15–16. e. [20:13] 3:22. f. [20:17] Ps 118:22; Is 28:16. g. [20:19] 19:47–48; 22:2; Mt 21:46; Mk 11:18; 12:12; 14:1–2; Jn 5:18; 7:30. h. [20:20–26] Mt 22:15–22; Mk 12:13–17. i. [20:20] 11:54. j. [20:21] Jn 3:2.

k. [20:25] Rom 13:6–7. l. [20:27–40] Mt 22:23–33; Mk 12:18–27. m. [20:27] Acts 23:8. n. [20:28] Gn 38:8; Dt 25:5. o. [20:37] Ex 3:2, 6, 15–16. p. [20:38] Rom 14:8–9. q. [20:40] Mt 22:46; Mk 12:34. r. [20:41–44] Mt 22:41–45; Mk 12:35–37. s. [20:42–43] Ps 110:1.

43   till I make your enemies your
                             footstool.'"

44Now if David calls him 'lord,' how can he be
his son?"
Denunciation of the Scribes.[t] 45Then, within
the hearing of all the people, he said to [his] disciples, 46"Be on guard against the scribes, who
like to go around in long robes and love greetings in marketplaces, seats of honor in synagogues, and places of honor at banquets.[u] 47They
devour the houses of widows and, as a pretext,
recite lengthy prayers. They will receive a very
severe condemnation."

CHAPTER 21
The Poor Widow's Contribution.[*] 1vWhen he
looked up he saw some wealthy people putting
their offerings into the treasury 2and he noticed
a poor widow putting in two small coins. 3He
said, "I tell you truly, this poor widow put in
more than all the rest; 4for those others have all
made offerings from their surplus wealth, but
she, from her poverty, has offered her whole
livelihood."
The Destruction of the Temple Foretold.[w]
5†While some people were speaking about how
the temple was adorned with costly stones
and votive offerings, he said, 6"All that you see
here—the days will come when there will not be
left a stone upon another stone that will not be
thrown down."[x]
The Signs of the End. 7yThen they asked him,
"Teacher, when will this happen? And what sign
will there be when all these things are about to
happen?" 8He answered, "See that you not be
deceived, for many will come in my name, saying, 'I am he,' and 'The time has come.'‡ Do not

follow them![z] 9When you hear of wars and insur-
rections, do not be terrified; for such things must
happen first, but it will not immediately be the
end." 10Then he said to them, "Nation will rise
against nation, and kingdom against kingdom.[a]
11There will be powerful earthquakes, famines,
and plagues from place to place; and awesome
sights and mighty signs will come from the sky.
The Coming Persecution. 12b"Before all this
happens,§ however, they will seize and persecute
you, they will hand you over to the synagogues
and to prisons, and they will have you led before
kings and governors because of my name.[c] 13It
will lead to your giving testimony. 14Remember,
you are not to prepare your defense beforehand,
15dfor I myself shall give you a wisdom in speak-
ing¶ that all your adversaries will be powerless to
resist or refute. 16e'You will even be handed over
by parents, brothers, relatives, and friends, and
they will put some of you to death.[f] 17You will
be hated by all because of my name, 18but not a
hair on your head will be destroyed.[g] 19By your
perseverance you will secure your lives.[h]
The Great Tribulation.[*] 20i"When you see Jerusalem surrounded by armies, know that its desolation is at hand.[j] 21Then those in Judea must
flee to the mountains. Let those within the city
escape from it, and let those in the countryside
not enter the city,[k] 22for these days are the time of
punishment when all the scriptures are fulfilled.
23Woe to pregnant women and nursing mothers
in those days, for a terrible calamity will come
upon the earth and a wrathful judgment upon
this people.[l] 24They will fall by the edge of the
sword and be taken as captives to all the Gentiles; and Jerusalem will be trampled underfoot
by the Gentiles until the times of the Gentiles††
are fulfilled.[m]
The Coming of the Son of Man.[n] 25"There will
be signs in the sun, the moon, and the stars, and
on earth nations will be in dismay, perplexed by
the roaring of the sea and the waves.[o] 26People

---

*[21:1–4] The widow is another example of the poor ones
in this gospel whose detachment from material possessions
and dependence on God leads to their blessedness (Lk 6:20).
Her simple offering provides a striking contrast to the pride
and pretentiousness of the scribes denounced in the preceding
section (Lk 20:45–47). The story is taken from Mk 12:41–44.

†[21:5–36] Jesus' eschatological discourse in Luke is
inspired by Mk 13 but Luke has made some significant
alterations to the words of Jesus found there. Luke maintains,
though in a modified form, the belief in the early expectation
of the end of the age (see Lk 21:27, 28, 31, 32, 36), but, by
focusing attention throughout the gospel on the importance
of the day-to-day following of Jesus and by reinterpreting
the meaning of some of the signs of the end from Mk 13 he
has come to terms with what seemed to the early Christian
community to be a delay of the parousia. Mark, for example,
described the desecration of the Jerusalem temple by the
Romans (Mk 13:14) as the apocalyptic symbol (see Dn 9:27;
12:11) accompanying the end of the age and the coming of
the Son of Man. Luke (Lk 21:20–24), however, removes the
apocalyptic setting and separates the historical destruction of
Jerusalem from the signs of the coming of the Son of Man by
a period that he refers to as "the times of the Gentiles" (Lk
21:24). See also notes on Mt 24:1–36 and Mk 13:1–37.

‡[21:8] **The time has come:** in Luke, the proclamation of
the imminent end of the age has itself become a false teaching.

§[21:12] **Before all this happens . . . :** to Luke and his
community, some of the signs of the end just described (Lk
21:10–11) still lie in the future. Now in dealing with the persecution of the disciples (Lk 21:12–19) and the destruction
of Jerusalem (Lk 21:20–24) Luke is pointing to eschatological
signs that have already been fulfilled.

¶[21:15] **A wisdom in speaking:** literally, "a mouth and
wisdom."

**[21:20–24] The actual destruction of Jerusalem by Rome
in A.D. 70 upon which Luke and his community look back
provides the assurance that, just as Jesus' prediction of Jerusalem's destruction was fulfilled, so too will be his announcement of their final redemption (Lk 21:27–28).

††[21:24] **The times of the Gentiles:** a period of indetermi-
nate length separating the destruction of Jerusalem from the
cosmic signs accompanying the coming of the Son of Man.

---

t. [20:45–47] 11:37–54; Mt 23:1–36; Mk 12:38–40.   u. [20:46] 14:7–
11.   v. [21:1–4] Mk 12:41–44.   w. [21:5–6] Mt 24:1–2; Mk 13:1–
2.   x. [21:6] 19:44.   y. [21:7–19] Mt 24:3–14; Mk 13:3–13.

z. [21:8] 17:23; Mk 13:5, 6, 21; 1 Jn 2:18.   a. [21:10] 2 Chr 15:6; Is
19:2.   b. [21:12–15] 12:11–12; Mt 10:17–20; Mk 13:9–11.   c. [21:12]
Jn 16:2; Acts 25:24.   d. [21:15] Acts 6:10.   e. [21:16–18] Mt 10:21–
22.   f. [21:16] 12:52–53.   g. [21:18] 12:7; 1 Sm 14:45; Mt 10:30;
Acts 27:34.   h. [21:19] 8:15.   i. [21:20–24] Mt 24:15–21; Mk 13:14–
19.   j. [21:20–22] 19:41–44.   k. [21:21] 17:31.   l. [21:23] 1 Cor
7:26.   m. [21:24] Tb 14:5; Ps 79:1; Is 63:18; Jer 21:7; Rom 11:25; Rev
11:2.   n. [21:25–28] Mt 24:29–31; Mk 13:24–27.   o. [21:25] Wis
5:22; Is 13:10; Ez 32:7; Jl 2:10; 3:3–4; 4:15; Rev 6:12–14.

will die of fright in anticipation of what is coming upon the world, for the powers of the heavens* will be shaken.*P* [27]And then they will see the Son of Man coming in a cloud with power and great glory.*q* [28]But when these signs begin to happen, stand erect and raise your heads because your redemption is at hand."*r*

The Lesson of the Fig Tree.*s* [29]He taught them a lesson. "Consider the fig tree and all the other trees. [30]When their buds burst open, you see for yourselves and know that summer is now near; [31]in the same way, when you see these things happening, know that the kingdom of God is near. [32]Amen, I say to you, this generation will not pass away until all these things have taken place.*t* [33]Heaven and earth will pass away, but my words will not pass away."*u*

Exhortation to Be Vigilant. [34]"Beware that your hearts do not become drowsy from carousing and drunkenness and the anxieties of daily life, and that day catch you by surprise*v* [35]like a trap. For that day will assault everyone who lives on the face of the earth. [36]Be vigilant at all times and pray that you have the strength to escape the tribulations that are imminent and to stand before the Son of Man."*w*

Ministry in Jerusalem. [37]During the day, Jesus was teaching in the temple area, but at night he would leave and stay at the place called the Mount of Olives.*x* [38]And all the people would get up early each morning to listen to him in the temple area.

VII. THE PASSION NARRATIVE[†]

CHAPTER 22

The Conspiracy Against Jesus. [1]*y*Now the feast of Unleavened Bread, called the Passover,[‡] was drawing near, [2]*z*and the chief priests and the scribes were seeking a way to put him to death, for they were afraid of the people. [3]*a*Then Satan entered into Judas,[§] the one surnamed Iscariot, who was counted among the Twelve,*b* [4]and he went to the chief priests and temple guards to discuss a plan for handing him over to them. [5]They were pleased and agreed to pay him money. [6]He accepted their offer and sought a favorable opportunity to hand him over to them in the absence of a crowd.

Preparations for the Passover.*c* [7]When the day of the feast of Unleavened Bread arrived, the day for sacrificing the Passover lamb,*d* [8]he sent out Peter and John, instructing them, "Go and make preparations for us to eat the Passover." [9]They asked him, "Where do you want us to make the preparations?" [10]And he answered them, "When you go into the city, a man will meet you carrying a jar of water.[¶] Follow him into the house that he enters [11]and say to the master of the house, 'The teacher says to you, "Where is the guest room where I may eat the Passover with my disciples?"' [12]He will show you a large upper room that is furnished. Make the preparations there." [13]Then they went off and found everything exactly as he had told them, and there they prepared the Passover.*e*

The Last Supper.*f* [14]When the hour came, he took his place at table with the apostles. [15]He said to them, "I have eagerly desired to eat this Passover** with you before I suffer, [16]for, I tell you, I shall not eat it [again] until there is fulfillment in the kingdom of God."*g* [17]Then he took a cup,[††] gave thanks, and said, "Take this and share it among yourselves; [18]for I tell you [that] from this time on I shall not drink of the fruit of the vine until the kingdom of God comes." [19]*‡‡h*Then he took the bread, said the blessing, broke it, and

---

*[21:26] **The powers of the heavens**: the heavenly bodies mentioned in Lk 21:25 and thought of as cosmic armies.

[†][22:1–23:56a] The passion narrative. Luke is still dependent upon Mark for the composition of the passion narrative but has incorporated much of his own special tradition into the narrative. Among the distinctive sections in Luke are: (1) the tradition of the institution of the Eucharist (Lk 22:15–20); (2) Jesus' farewell discourse (Lk 22:21–38); (3) the mistreatment and interrogation of Jesus (Lk 22:63–71); (4) Jesus before Herod and his second appearance before Pilate (Lk 23:6–16); (5) words addressed to the women followers on the way to the crucifixion (Lk 23:27–32); (6) words to the penitent thief (Lk 23:39–41); (7) the death of Jesus (Lk 23:46, 47b–49). Luke stresses the innocence of Jesus (Lk 23:4, 14–15, 22) who is the victim of the powers of evil (Lk 22:3, 31, 53) and who goes to his death in fulfillment of his Father's will (Lk 22:42, 46). Throughout the narrative Luke emphasizes the mercy, compassion, and healing power of Jesus (Lk 22:51; 23:43) who does not go to death lonely and deserted, but is accompanied by others who follow him on the way of the cross (Lk 23:26–31, 49).

[‡][22:1] **Feast of Unleavened Bread, called the Passover**: see note on Mk 14:1.

[§][22:3] **Satan entered into Judas**: see note on Lk 4:13.

[¶][22:10] **A man will meet you carrying a jar of water**: see note on Mk 14:13.

[22:15] **This Passover: Luke clearly identifies this last supper of Jesus with the apostles as a Passover meal that commemorated the deliverance of the Israelites from slavery in Egypt. Jesus reinterprets the significance of the Passover by setting it in the context of the kingdom of God (Lk 22:16). The "deliverance" associated with the Passover finds its new meaning in the blood that will be shed (Lk 22:20).

[††][22:17] Because of a textual problem in Lk 22:19–20 some commentators interpret this cup as the eucharistic cup.

[‡‡][22:19c–20] **Which will be given . . . do this in memory of me**: these words are omitted in some important Western text manuscripts and a few Syriac manuscripts. Other ancient text types, including the oldest papyrus manuscript of Luke dating from the late second or early third century, contain the longer reading presented here. The Lucan account of the words of institution of the Eucharist bears a close resemblance to the words of institution in the Pauline tradition (see 1 Cor 11:23–26). See also notes on Mt 26:26–29; 26:27–28; and Mk 14:22–24.

p. [21:26] Hg 2:6, 21.   q. [21:27] Dn 7:13–14; Mt 26:64; Rev 1:7.   r. [21:28] 2:38.   s. [21:29–33] Mt 24:32–35; Mk 13:28–31.   t. [21:32] 9:27; Mt 16:28.   u. [21:33] 16:17.   v. [21:34] 12:45–46; Mt 24:48–50; 1 Thes 5:3, 6–7.   w. [21:36] Mk 13:33.   x. [21:37] 19:47; 22:39.   y. [22:1–2] Mt 26:1–5; Mk 14:1–2; Jn 11:47–53.

z. [22:2] 19:47–48; 20:19; Mt 21:46; Mk 12:12; Jn 5:18; 7:30.   a. [22:3–6] Mt 26:14–16; Mk 14:10–11; Jn 13:2, 27.   b. [22:3] Acts 1:17.   c. [22:7–13] Mt 26:17–19; Mk 14:12–16.   d. [22:7] Ex 12:6, 14–20.   e. [22:13] 19:32.   f. [22:14–20] Mt 26:20, 26–30; Mk 14:17, 22–26; 1 Cor 11:23–25.   g. [22:16] 13:29.   h. [22:19] 24:30; Acts 27:35.

gave it to them, saying, "This is my body, which will be given for you; do this in memory of me." [20]And likewise the cup after they had eaten, saying, "This cup is the new covenant in my blood, which will be shed for you.[i]

The Betrayal Foretold.[j] [21]"And yet behold, the hand of the one who is to betray me is with me on the table; [22]for the Son of Man indeed goes as it has been determined; but woe to that man by whom he is betrayed." [23]And they began to debate among themselves who among them would do such a deed.

The Role of the Disciples. [24]Then an argument broke out among them[k] about which of them should be regarded as the greatest. [25†]He said to them, "The kings of the Gentiles lord it over them and those in authority over them are addressed as 'Benefactors'; [26]but among you it shall not be so. Rather, let the greatest among you be as the youngest, and the leader as the servant.[m] [27]For who is greater: the one seated at table or the one who serves? Is it not the one seated at table? I am among you as the one who serves. [28]It is you who have stood by me in my trials; [29]and I confer a kingdom on you, just as my Father has conferred one on me,[n] [30]that you may eat and drink at my table in my kingdom; and you will sit on thrones judging the twelve tribes of Israel.[o]

Peter's Denial Foretold.[p] [31‡]"Simon, Simon, behold Satan has demanded to sift all of you[§] like wheat,[q] [32]but I have prayed that your own faith may not fail; and once you have turned back, you must strengthen your brothers." [33]He said to him, "Lord, I am prepared to go to prison and to die with you."[r] [34]But he replied, "I tell you, Peter, before the cock crows this day, you will deny three times that you know me."[s]

Instructions for the Time of Crisis. [35†]He said to them, "When I sent you forth without a money bag or a sack or sandals, were you in need of anything?" "No, nothing," they replied. [36u]He said to them,[¶] "But now one who has a money

bag should take it, and likewise a sack, and one who does not have a sword should sell his cloak and buy one. [37]For I tell you that this scripture must be fulfilled in me, namely, 'He was counted among the wicked'; and indeed what is written about me is coming to fulfillment."[v] [38]Then they said, "Lord, look, there are two swords here." But he replied, "It is enough!"[**]

The Agony in the Garden.[w] [39]Then going out he went, as was his custom, to the Mount of Olives, and the disciples followed him. [40]When he arrived at the place he said to them, "Pray that you may not undergo the test."[x] [41]After withdrawing about a stone's throw from them and kneeling, he prayed,[y] [42]saying, "Father, if you are willing, take this cup away from me; still, not my will but yours be done."[z] [43]And to strengthen him an angel from heaven appeared to him. [44]He was in such agony and he prayed so fervently that his sweat became like drops of blood falling on the ground.] [45]When he rose from prayer and returned to his disciples, he found them sleeping from grief. [46]He said to them, "Why are you sleeping? Get up and pray that you may not undergo the test."[a]

The Betrayal and Arrest of Jesus.[b] [47]While he was still speaking, a crowd approached and in front was one of the Twelve, a man named Judas. He went up to Jesus to kiss him. [48]Jesus said to him, "Judas, are you betraying the Son of Man with a kiss?" [49]His disciples realized what was about to happen, and they asked, "Lord, shall we strike with a sword?"[c] [50]And one of them struck the high priest's servant and cut off his right ear.[d] [51‡]But Jesus said in reply, "Stop, no more of this!" Then he touched the servant's ear and healed him. [52]And Jesus said to the chief priests and temple guards and elders who had come for him, "Have you come out as against a robber, with swords and clubs?[e] [53]Day after day I was with you in the temple area, and you did not seize me; but this is your hour, the time for the power of darkness."[f]

Peter's Denial of Jesus. [54g]After arresting him they led him away and took him into the house of the high priest; Peter was following at a

---

*[22:24–38] The Gospel of Luke presents a brief farewell discourse of Jesus; compare the lengthy farewell discourses and prayer in Jn 13–17.

†[22:25] 'Benefactors': this word occurs as a title of rulers in the Hellenistic world.

‡[22:31–32] Jesus' prayer for Simon's faith and the commission to strengthen his brothers anticipates the postresurrectional prominence of Peter in the first half of Acts, where he appears as the spokesman for the Christian community and the one who begins the mission to the Gentiles (Acts 10–11).

§[22:31] All of you: literally, "you." The translation reflects the meaning of the Greek text that uses a second person plural pronoun here.

¶[22:36] In contrast to the ministry of the Twelve and of the seventy-two during the period of Jesus (Lk 9:3; 10:4), in

the future period of the church the missionaries must be prepared for the opposition they will face in a world hostile to their preaching.

**[22:38] It is enough!: the farewell discourse ends abruptly with these words of Jesus spoken to the disciples when they take literally what was intended as figurative language about being prepared to face the world's hostility.

††[22:43–44] These verses, though very ancient, were probably not part of the original text of Luke. They are absent from the oldest papyrus manuscripts of Luke and from manuscripts of wide geographical distribution.

‡‡[22:51] And healed him: only Luke recounts this healing of the injured servant.

i. [22:20] Ex 24:8; Jer 31:31; 32:40; Zec 9:11.   j. [22:21–23] Ps 41:10; Mt 26:21–25; Mk 14:18–21; Jn 13:21–30.   k. [22:24] 9:46; Mt 18:1; Mk 9:34.   l. [22:25–27] Mt 20:25–27; Mk 10:42–44; Jn 13:3–16.   m. [22:26] Mt 23:11; Mk 9:35.   n. [22:29] 12:32.   o. [22:30] Mt 19:28.   p. [22:31–34] Mt 26:33–35; Mk 14:29–31; Jn 13:37–38.   q. [22:31] Jb 1:6–12; Am 9:9.   r. [22:33] 22:54.   s. [22:34] 22:54–62.   t. [22:35] 9:3; 10:4; Mt 10:9–10; Mk 6:7–9.   u. [22:36] 22:49.

v. [22:37] Is 53:12.   w. [22:39–46] Mt 26:30, 36–46; Mk 14:26, 32–42; Jn 18:1–2.   x. [22:40] 22:46.   y. [22:41] Heb 5:7–8.   z. [22:42] Mt 6:10.   a. [22:46] 22:40.   b. [22:47–53] Mt 26:47–56; Mk 14:43–50; Jn 18:3–4.   c. [22:49] 22:36.   d. [22:50] Jn 18:26.   e. [22:52] 22:37.   f. [22:53] 19:47; 21:37; Jn 7:30; 8:20; Col 1:13.   g. [22:54–62] Mt 26:57–58, 69–75; Mk 14:53–54, 66–72; Jn 18:12–18, 25–27.

distance.[h] [55]They lit a fire in the middle of the courtyard and sat around it, and Peter sat down with them. [56]When a maid saw him seated in the light, she looked intently at him and said, "This man too was with him." [57]But he denied it saying, "Woman, I do not know him." [58]A short while later someone else saw him and said, "You too are one of them"; but Peter answered, "My friend, I am not." [59]About an hour later, still another insisted, "Assuredly, this man too was with him, for he also is a Galilean." [60]But Peter said, "My friend, I do not know what you are talking about." Just as he was saying this, the cock crowed, [61]and the Lord turned and looked at Peter;* and Peter remembered the word of the Lord, how he had said to him, "Before the cock crows today, you will deny me three times."[i] [62]He went out and began to weep bitterly. [63]The men who held Jesus in custody were ridiculing and beating him. [64]They blindfolded him and questioned him, saying, "Prophesy! Who is it that struck you?" [65]And they reviled him in saying many other things against him.

Jesus Before the Sanhedrin.[†] [66k]When day came the council of elders of the people met, both chief priests and scribes,[l] and they brought him before their Sanhedrin.[‡] [67]They said, "If you are the Messiah, tell us," but he replied to them, "If I tell you, you will not believe,[m] [68]and if I question, you will not respond. [69]But from this time on the Son of Man will be seated at the right hand of the power of God."[n] [70]They all asked, "Are you then the Son of God?" He replied to them, "You say that I am." [71]Then they said, "What further need have we for testimony? We have heard it from his own mouth."

CHAPTER 23

Jesus Before Pilate.[o] [1]Then the whole assembly of them arose and brought him before Pilate.

---

*[22:61] Only Luke recounts that **the Lord turned and looked at Peter**. This look of Jesus leads to Peter's weeping bitterly over his denial (Lk 22:62).

†[22:66–71] Luke recounts one daytime trial of Jesus (Lk 22:66–71) and hints at some type of preliminary nighttime investigation (Lk 22:54–65). Mark (and Matthew who follows Mark) has transferred incidents of this day into the nighttime interrogation with the result that there appear to be two Sanhedrin trials of Jesus in Mark (and Matthew); see note on Mk 14:53.

‡[22:66] **Sanhedrin**: the word is a Hebraized form of a Greek word meaning a "council," and refers to the elders, chief priests, and scribes who met under the high priest's leadership to decide religious and legal questions that did not pertain to Rome's interests. Jewish sources are not clear on the competence of the Sanhedrin to sentence and to execute during this period.

§[23:1–5, 13–25] Twice Jesus is brought before Pilate in Luke's account, and each time Pilate explicitly declares Jesus innocent of any wrongdoing (Lk 23:4, 14, 22). This stress on the innocence of Jesus before the Roman authorities is also characteristic of John's gospel (Jn 18:38; 19:4, 6). Luke presents the Jerusalem Jewish leaders as the ones who force the hand of the Roman authorities (Lk 23:1–2, 5, 10, 13, 18, 21, 23–25).

h. [22:54] 22:33. i. [22:61] 22:34. j. [22:63–65] Mt 26:67–68; Mk 14:65. k. [22:66–71] Mt 26:59–66; Mk 14:55–64. l. [22:66] Mt 27:1; Mk 15:1. m. [22:67] Jn 3:12; 8:45; 10:24. n. [22:69] Ps 110:1; Dn 7:13–14; Acts 7:56. o. [23:1–5] Mt 27:1–2, 11–14; Mk 15:1–5; Jn 18:28–38.

[2]They brought charges against him, saying, "We found this man misleading our people; he opposes the payment of taxes to Caesar and maintains that he is the Messiah, a king."[p] [3]Pilate asked him, "Are you the king of the Jews?" He said to him in reply, "You say so."[q] [4]Pilate then addressed the chief priests and the crowds, "I find this man not guilty." [5]But they were adamant and said, "He is inciting the people with his teaching throughout all Judea, from Galilee where he began even to here."[r]

Jesus Before Herod. [6¶]On hearing this Pilate asked if the man was a Galilean; [7]and upon learning that he was under Herod's jurisdiction, he sent him to Herod who was in Jerusalem at that time.[s] [8]Herod was very glad to see Jesus; he had been wanting to see him for a long time, for he had heard about him and had been hoping to see him perform some sign.[t] [9]He questioned him at length, but he gave him no answer.[u] [10]The chief priests and scribes, meanwhile, stood by accusing him harshly.[v] [11][Even] Herod and his soldiers treated him contemptuously and mocked him, and after clothing him in resplendent garb, he sent him back to Pilate.[w] [12]Herod and Pilate became friends that very day, even though they had been enemies formerly. [13]Pilate then summoned the chief priests, the rulers, and the people [14]and said to them, "You brought this man to me and accused him of inciting the people to revolt. I have conducted my investigation in your presence and have not found this man guilty of the charges you have brought against him,[x] [15]nor did Herod, for he sent him back to us. So no capital crime has been committed by him. [16]Therefore I shall have him flogged and then release him." [[17]]**

The Sentence of Death.[z] [18]But all together they shouted out, "Away with this man! Release Barabbas to us." [19](Now Barabbas had been imprisoned for a rebellion that had taken place in the city and for murder.) [20]Again Pilate addressed them, still wishing to release Jesus, [21]but they continued their shouting, "Crucify him! Crucify him!" [22]Pilate addressed them a third time, "What evil has this man done? I found him guilty of no

---

¶[23:6–12] The appearance of Jesus before Herod is found only in this gospel. Herod has been an important figure in Luke (Lk 9:7–9; 13:31–33) and has been presented as someone who has been curious about Jesus for a long time. His curiosity goes unrewarded. It is faith in Jesus, not curiosity, that is rewarded (Lk 7:50; 8:48, 50; 17:19).

**[23:17] This verse, "He was obliged to release one prisoner for them at the festival," is not part of the original text of Luke. It is an explanatory gloss from Mk 15:6 (also Mt 27:15) and is not found in many early and important Greek manuscripts. On its historical background, see notes on Mt 27:15–26.

p. [23:2] 20:22–25; Acts 17:7; 24:5. q. [23:3] 22:70; 1 Tm 6:13. r. [23:5] 23:14, 22, 41; Mt 27:24; Jn 19:4, 6; Acts 13:28. s. [23:7] 3:1; 9:7. t. [23:8] 9:9; Acts 4:27–28. u. [23:9] Mk 15:5. v. [23:10] Mt 27:12; Mk 15:3. w. [23:11] Mt 27:28–30; Mk 15:17–19; Jn 19:2–3. x. [23:14] 23:4, 22, 41. y. [23:16] 23:22; Jn 19:12–14. z. [23:18–25] Mt 27:20–26; Mk 15:6–7, 11–15; Jn 18:38b–40; 19:14–16; Acts 3:13–14.

capital crime. Therefore I shall have him flogged and then release him." [23]With loud shouts, however, they persisted in calling for his crucifixion, and their voices prevailed. [24]The verdict of Pilate was that their demand should be granted. [25]So he released the man who had been imprisoned for rebellion and murder, for whom they asked, and he handed Jesus over to them to deal with as they wished.

The Way of the Cross.[*] [26a]As they led him away they took hold of a certain Simon, a Cyrenian, who was coming in from the country; and after laying the cross on him, they made him carry it behind Jesus. [27]A large crowd of people followed Jesus, including many women who mourned and lamented him. [28b]Jesus turned to them and said, "Daughters of Jerusalem, do not weep for me; weep instead for yourselves and for your children, [29]for indeed, the days are coming when people will say, 'Blessed are the barren, the wombs that never bore and the breasts that never nursed.' [30]At that time people will say to the mountains, 'Fall upon us!' and to the hills, 'Cover us!'[c] [31]for if these things are done when the wood is green what will happen when it is dry?" [32]Now two others, both criminals, were led away with him to be executed.

The Crucifixion.[d] [33]When they came to the place called the Skull, they crucified him and the criminals there, one on his right, the other on his left.[e] [34][Then Jesus said, "Father, forgive them, they know not what they do."][†] They divided his garments by casting lots.[f] [35]The people stood by and watched; the rulers, meanwhile, sneered at him and said,[g] "He saved others, let him save himself if he is the chosen one, the Messiah of God."[h] [36]Even the soldiers jeered at him. As they approached to offer him wine[i] [37]they called out, "If you are King of the Jews, save yourself." [38]Above him there was an inscription that read, "This is the King of the Jews."

[39‡]Now one of the criminals hanging there reviled Jesus, saying, "Are you not the Messiah? Save yourself and us." [40]The other, however, rebuking him, said in reply, "Have you no fear

of God, for you are subject to the same condemnation? [41]And indeed, we have been condemned justly, for the sentence we received corresponds to our crimes, but this man has done nothing criminal."[j] [42]Then he said, "Jesus, remember me when you come into your kingdom."[k] [43]He replied to him, "Amen, I say to you, today you will be with me in Paradise."[l]

The Death of Jesus.[m] [44§]It was now about noon[n] and darkness came over the whole land until three in the afternoon [45]because of an eclipse of the sun. Then the veil of the temple was torn down the middle.[o] [46]Jesus cried out in a loud voice, "Father, into your hands I commend my spirit"; and when he had said this he breathed his last.[p] [47]The centurion who witnessed what had happened glorified God and said, "This man was innocent[¶] beyond doubt." [48]When all the people who had gathered for this spectacle saw what had happened, they returned home beating their breasts;[q] [49]but all his acquaintances stood at a distance, including the women who had followed him from Galilee and saw these events.[r]

The Burial of Jesus.[s] [50]Now there was a virtuous and righteous man named Joseph who, though he was a member of the council, [51]had not consented to their plan of action. He came from the Jewish town of Arimathea and was awaiting the kingdom of God.[t] [52]He went to Pilate and asked for the body of Jesus. [53]After he had taken the body down, he wrapped it in a linen cloth and laid him in a rock-hewn tomb in which no one had yet been buried.[u] [54]It was the day of preparation, and the sabbath was about to begin. [55]The women who had come from Galilee with him followed behind, and when they had seen the tomb and the way in which his body was laid in it,[v] [56]they returned and prepared spices and perfumed oils. Then they rested on the sabbath according to the commandment.[w]

VIII. THE RESURRECTION NARRATIVE[**]

CHAPTER 24

The Resurrection of Jesus. [1x]But at daybreak on the first day of the week they took the spices they

---

*[23:26–32] An important Lucan theme throughout the gospel has been the need for the Christian disciple to follow in the footsteps of Jesus. Here this theme comes to the fore with the story of Simon of Cyrene who takes up the cross and follows Jesus (see Lk 9:23; 14:27) and with the large crowd who likewise follow Jesus on the way of the cross. See also note on Mk 15:21.

†[23:34] [Then Jesus said, "Father, forgive them, they know not what they do."]: this portion of Lk 23:34 does not occur in the oldest papyrus manuscript of Luke and in other early Greek manuscripts and ancient versions of wide geographical distribution.

‡[23:39–43] This episode is recounted only in this gospel. The penitent sinner receives salvation through the crucified Jesus. Jesus' words to the penitent thief reveal Luke's understanding that the destiny of the Christian is "to be with Jesus."

a. [23:26–32] Mt 27:32, 38; Mk 15:21, 27; Jn 19:17.   b. [23:28–31] 19:41–44; 21:23–24.   c. [23:30] Hos 10:8; Rev 6:16.   d. [23:33–43] Mt 27:33–44; Mk 15:22–32; Jn 19:17–24.   e. [23:33] 22:37; Is 53:12.   f. [23:34] Nm 15:27–31; Ps 22:19; Mt 5:44; Acts 7:60.   g. [23:35–36] Ps 22:8–9.   h. [23:35] 4:23.   i. [23:36] Ps 69:22; Mt 27:48; Mk 15:36.

§[23:44] **Noon . . . three in the afternoon**: literally, the sixth and ninth hours. See note on Mk 15:25.

¶[23:47] **This man was innocent**: or, "This man was righteous."

**[24:1–53] The resurrection narrative in Luke consists of five sections: (1) the women at the empty tomb (Lk 23:56b–24:12); (2) the appearance to the two disciples on the way to Emmaus (Lk 24:13–35); (3) the appearance to the disciples in Jerusalem (Lk 24:36–43); (4) Jesus' final instructions (Lk 24:44–49); (5) the ascension (Lk 24:50–53). In Luke, all the

j. [23:41] 23:4, 14, 22.   k. [23:42] 9:27; 23:2, 3, 38.   l. [23:43] 2 Cor 12:3; Rev 2:7.   m. [23:44–49] Mt 27:45–56; Mk 15:33–41; Jn 19:25–30.   n. [23:44–45] Am 8:9.   o. [23:45] Ex 26:31–33; 36:35.   p. [23:46] Ps 31:6; Acts 7:59.   q. [23:48] 18:13; Zec 12:10.   r. [23:49] 8:1–3; 23:55–56; 24:10; Ps 38:12.   s. [23:50–56] Mt 27:57–61; Mk 15:42–47; Jn 19:38–42; Acts 13:29.   t. [23:51] 2:25, 38.   u. [23:53] 19:30; Acts 13:29.   v. [23:55] 8:2; 23:49; 24:10.   w. [23:56] Ex 12:16; 20:10; Dt 5:14.   x. [24:1–8] Mt 28:1–8; Mk 16:1–8; Jn 20:1–17.

had prepared and went to the tomb. [2]They found the stone rolled away from the tomb; [3]but when they entered, they did not find the body of the Lord Jesus. [4]While they were puzzling over this, behold, two men in dazzling garments appeared to them.[y] [5]They were terrified and bowed their faces to the ground. They said to them, "Why do you seek the living one among the dead?[z] [6]He is not here, but he has been raised.[*] Remember what he said to you while he was still in Galilee, [7]that the Son of Man must be handed over to sinners and be crucified, and rise on the third day."[a] [8]And they remembered his words.[b] [9]†Then they returned from the tomb and announced all these things to the eleven and to all the others. [10]The women were Mary Magdalene, Joanna, and Mary the mother of James; the others who accompanied them also told this to the apostles,[d] [11]but their story seemed like nonsense and they did not believe them. [12]‡eBut Peter got up and ran to the tomb, bent down, and saw the burial cloths alone; then he went home amazed at what had happened.

The Appearance on the Road to Emmaus.[§] [13]Now that very day two of them were going to a village seven miles[¶] from Jerusalem called Emmaus,[f] [14]and they were conversing about all the things that had occurred. [15]And it happened that while they were conversing and debating, Jesus himself drew near and walked with them, [16]**gbut their eyes were prevented from recognizing him.

resurrection appearances take place in and around Jerusalem; moreover, they are all recounted as having taken place on Easter Sunday. A consistent theme throughout the narrative is that the suffering, death, and resurrection of Jesus are accomplished in fulfillment of Old Testament promises and of Jewish hopes (Lk 24:19a, 21, 26–27, 44, 46). In his second volume, Acts, Luke will argue that Christianity is the fulfillment of the hopes of Pharisaic Judaism and its logical development (see Acts 24:10–21).

*[24:6] **He is not here, but he has been raised**: this part of the verse is omitted in important representatives of the Western text tradition, but its presence in other text types and the slight difference in wording from Mt 28:6 and Mk 16:6 argue for its retention.

†[24:9] The women in this gospel do not flee from the tomb and tell no one, as in Mk 16:8 but return and tell the disciples about their experience. The initial reaction to the testimony of the women is disbelief (Lk 24:11).

‡[24:12] This verse is missing from the Western textual tradition but is found in the best and oldest manuscripts of other text types.

§[24:13–35] This episode focuses on the interpretation of scripture by the risen Jesus and the recognition of him in the breaking of the bread. The references to the quotations of scripture and explanation of it (Lk 24:25–27), the kerygmatic proclamation (Lk 24:34), and the liturgical gesture (Lk 24:30) suggest that the episode is primarily catechetical and liturgical rather than apologetic.

¶[24:13] **Seven miles**: literally, "sixty stades." A stade was 607 feet. Some manuscripts read "160 stades" or more than eighteen miles. The exact location of Emmaus is disputed.

**[24:16] A consistent feature of the resurrection stories is that the risen Jesus was different and initially unrecognizable (Lk 24:37; Mk 16:12; Jn 20:14; 21:4).

[17]He asked them, "What are you discussing as you walk along?" They stopped, looking downcast. [18]One of them, named Cleopas, said to him in reply, "Are you the only visitor to Jerusalem who does not know of the things that have taken place there in these days?" [19]And he replied to them, "What sort of things?" They said to him, "The things that happened to Jesus the Nazarene, who was a prophet mighty in deed and word before God and all the people,[h] [20]how our chief priests and rulers both handed him over to a sentence of death and crucified him. [21]But we were hoping that he would be the one to redeem Israel; and besides all this, it is now the third day since this took place. [22]Some women from our group, however, have astounded us: they were at the tomb early in the morning [23]and did not find his body; they came back and reported that they had indeed seen a vision of angels who announced that he was alive. [24]kThen some of those with us went to the tomb and found things just as the women had described, but him they did not see." [25]lAnd he said to them, "Oh, how foolish you are! How slow of heart to believe all that the prophets spoke! [26]Was it not necessary that the Messiah should suffer†† these things and enter into his glory?" [27]Then beginning with Moses and all the prophets, he interpreted to them what referred to him in all the scriptures.[m] [28]As they approached the village to which they were going, he gave the impression that he was going on farther. [29]But they urged him, "Stay with us, for it is nearly evening and the day is almost over." So he went in to stay with them. [30]And it happened that, while he was with them at table, he took bread, said the blessing, broke it, and gave it to them. [31]With that their eyes were opened and they recognized him, but he vanished from their sight. [32]Then they said to each other, "Were not our hearts burning [within us] while he spoke to us on the way and opened the scriptures to us?" [33]So they set out at once and returned to Jerusalem where they found gathered together the eleven and those with them [34]who were saying, "The Lord has truly been raised and has appeared to Simon!"[n] [35]Then the two recounted what had taken place on the way and how he was made known to them in the breaking of the bread.

††[24:26] **That the Messiah should suffer . . .**: Luke is the only New Testament writer to speak explicitly of a suffering Messiah (Lk 24:26, 46; Acts 3:18; 17:3; 26:23). The idea of a suffering Messiah is not found in the Old Testament or in other Jewish literature prior to the New Testament period, although the idea is hinted at in Mk 8:31–33. See notes on Mt 26:63 and 26:67–68.

y. [24:4] 2 Mc 3:26; Acts 1:10.   z. [24:5] Acts 2:9.   a. [24:7] 9:22, 44; 17:25; 18:32–33; Mt 16:21; 17:22–23; Mk 9:31; Acts 17:3.   b. [24:8] Jn 2:22.   c. [24:9–11] Mk 16:10–11; Jn 20:18.   d. [24:10] 8:2–3; Mk 16:9.   e. [24:12] Jn 20:3–7.   f. [24:13] Mk 16:12–13.   g. [24:16] Jn 20:14; 21:4.

h. [24:19] Mt 2:23; 21:11; Acts 2:22.   i. [24:21] 1:54, 68; 2:38.   j. [24:22–23] 24:1–11; Mt 28:1–8; Mk 16:1–8.   k. [24:24] Jn 20:3–10.   l. [24:25–26] 9:22; 18:31; 24:44; Acts 3:24; 17:3.   m. [24:27] 24:44; Dt 18:15; Ps 22:1–18; Is 53; 1 Pt 1:10–11.   n. [24:34] 1 Cor 15:4–5.

The Appearance to the Disciples in Jerusalem. ³⁶*While they were still speaking about this,ᵒ he stood in their midst and said to them, "Peace be with you."ᵖ ³⁷But they were startled and terrified and thought that they were seeing a ghost.�q ³⁸Then he said to them, "Why are you troubled? And why do questions arise in your hearts? ³⁹†Look at my hands and my feet, that it is I myself. Touch me and see, because a ghost does not have flesh and bones as you can see I have." ⁴⁰ʳAnd as he said this, he showed them his hands and his feet. ⁴¹While they were still incredulous for joy and were amazed, he asked them, "Have you anything here to eat?" ⁴²They gave him a piece of baked fish;ˢ ⁴³he took it and ate it in front of them.

⁴⁴He said to them, "These are my words that I spoke to you while I was still with you, that everything written about me in the law of Moses and in the prophets and psalms must be fulfilled."ᵗ ⁴⁵Then he opened their minds to understand the scriptures.ᵘ ⁴⁶‡And he said

to them,ᵛ "Thus it is written that the Messiah would suffer and rise from the dead on the third day ⁴⁷and that repentance, for the forgiveness of sins, would be preached in his name to all the nations, beginning from Jerusalem.ʷ ⁴⁸You are witnesses of these things.ˣ ⁴⁹And [behold] I am sending the promise of my Fatherˢ upon you; but stay in the city until you are clothed with power from on high."ʸ

The Ascension.⁵ ⁵⁰ᶻThen he led them [out] as far as Bethany, raised his hands, and blessed them. ⁵¹As he blessed them he parted from them and was taken up to heaven. ⁵²They did him homage and then returned to Jerusalem with great joy,ᵃ ⁵³and they were continually in the temple praising God.**

---

§[24:49] **The promise of my Father**: i.e., the gift of the holy Spirit.

¶[24:50–53] Luke brings his story about the time of Jesus to a close with the report of the ascension. He will also begin the story of the time of the church with a recounting of the ascension. In the gospel, Luke recounts the ascension of Jesus on Easter Sunday night, thereby closely associating it with the resurrection. In Acts 1:3, 9–11; 13:31 he historicizes the ascension and the ascension. The Western text omits some phrases in Lk 24:51, 52 perhaps to avoid any chronological conflict with Acts 1 about the time of the ascension.

**[24:53] The Gospel of Luke ends as it began (Lk 1:9), in the Jerusalem temple.

---

*[24:36–43, 44–49] The Gospel of Luke, like each of the other gospels (Mt 28:16–20; Mk 16:14–15; Jn 20:19–23), focuses on an important appearance of Jesus to the Twelve in which they are commissioned for their future ministry. As in Lk 24:6, 12, so in Lk 24:36, 40 there are omissions in the Western text.

†[24:39–42] The apologetic purpose of this story is evident in the concern with the physical details and the report that Jesus ate food.

‡[24:46] See note on Lk 24:26.

---

o. [24:36–53] Mk 16:14–19; Jn 20:19–20.   p. [24:36] 1 Cor 15:5.
q. [24:37] Mt 14:26.   r. [24:40–41] Jn 21:5, 9–10, 13.   s. [24:42] Acts 10:41.   t. [24:44] 18:31; 24:27; Mt 16:21; Jn 5:39, 46.
u. [24:45] Jn 20:9.

v. [24:46] 9:22; Is 53; Hos 6:2.   w. [24:47] Mt 3:2; 28:19–20; Mk 16:15–16; Acts 10:41.   x. [24:48] Acts 1:8.   y. [24:49] Jn 14:26; Acts 1:4; 2:3–4.   z. [24:50–51] Mk 16:19; Acts 1:9–11.   a. [24:52] Acts 1:12.

THE GOSPEL ACCORDING TO
JOHN

∼ᘓᕯᘔ∼

The Gospel according to John is quite different in character from the three synoptic gospels. It is highly literary and symbolic. It does not follow the same order or reproduce the same stories as the synoptic gospels. To a much greater degree, it is the product of a developed theological reflection and grows out of a different circle and tradition. It was probably written in the 90s of the first century.

The Gospel of John begins with a magnificent prologue, which states many of the major themes and motifs of the gospel, much as an overture does for a musical work. The prologue proclaims Jesus as the preexistent and incarnate Word of God who has revealed the Father to us. The rest of the first chapter forms the introduction to the gospel proper and consists of the Baptist's testimony about Jesus (there is no baptism of Jesus in this gospel—John simply points him out as the Lamb of God), followed by stories of the call of the first disciples, in which various titles predicated of Jesus in the early church are presented.

The gospel narrative contains a series of "signs"—the gospel's word for the wondrous deeds of Jesus. The author is primarily interested in the significance of these deeds, and so interprets them for the reader by various reflections, narratives, and discourses. The first sign is the transformation of water into wine at Cana (Jn 2:1–11); this represents the replacement of the Jewish ceremonial washings and symbolizes the entire creative and transforming work of Jesus. The second sign, the cure of the royal official's son (Jn 4:46–54) simply by the word of Jesus at a distance, signifies the power of Jesus' life-giving word. The same theme is further developed by other signs, probably for a total of seven. The third sign, the cure of the paralytic at the pool with five porticoes in chap. 5, continues the theme of water offering newness of life. In the preceding chapter, to the woman at the well in Samaria Jesus had offered living water springing up to eternal life, a symbol of the revelation that Jesus brings; here Jesus' life-giving word replaces the water of the pool that failed to bring life. Jn 6 contains two signs, the multiplication of loaves and the walking on the waters of the Sea of Galilee. These signs are connected much as the manna and the crossing of the Red Sea are in the Passover narrative and symbolize a new exodus. The multiplication of the loaves is interpreted for the reader by the discourse that follows, where the bread of life is used first as a figure for the revelation of God in Jesus and then for the Eucharist. After a series of dialogues reflecting Jesus' debates with the Jewish authorities at the Feast of Tabernacles in Jn 7; 8, the sixth sign is presented in Jn 9, the sign of the young man born blind. This is a narrative illustration of the theme of conflict in the preceding two chapters; it proclaims the triumph of light over darkness, as Jesus is presented as the Light of the world. This is interpreted by a narrative of controversy between the Pharisees and the young man who had been given his sight by Jesus, ending with a discussion of spiritual blindness and spelling out the symbolic meaning of the cure. And finally, the seventh sign, the raising of Lazarus in chap. 11, is the climax of signs. Lazarus is presented as a token of the real life that Jesus, the Resurrection and the Life, who will now ironically be put to death because of his gift of life to Lazarus, will give to all who believe in him once he has been raised from the dead.

After the account of the seven signs, the "hour" of Jesus arrives, and the author passes from sign to reality, as he moves into the discourses in the upper room that interpret the meaning of the passion, death, and resurrection narratives that follow. The whole gospel of John is a progressive revelation of the glory of God's only Son, who comes to reveal the Father and then returns in glory to the Father. The author's purpose is clearly expressed in what must have been the original ending of the gospel at the end of Jn 20: "Now Jesus did many other signs in the presence of [his] disciples that are not written in this book. But these are written that you may [come to] believe that Jesus is the Messiah, the Son of God, and that through this belief you may have life in his name."

Critical analysis makes it difficult to accept the idea that the gospel as it now stands was written by one person. Jn 21 seems to have been added after the gospel was completed; it exhibits a Greek style somewhat different from that of the rest of the work. The prologue (Jn 1:1–18) apparently contains an independent hymn, subsequently adapted to serve as a preface to the gospel. Within the gospel itself there are also some inconsistencies, e.g., there are two endings of Jesus' discourse in the upper room (Jn 14:31; 18:1). To solve these problems, scholars have proposed various rearrangements that would produce a smoother order. However, most have come to the conclusion that the inconsistencies were probably produced by subsequent editing in which homogeneous materials were added to a shorter original.

Other difficulties for any theory of eyewitness authorship of the gospel in its present form are presented by its highly developed theology and by certain elements of its literary style. For instance, some of the wondrous deeds of Jesus have been worked into highly effective dramatic scenes (Jn 9); there has been a careful attempt to have these followed by discourses that explain them (Jn 5; 6); and the sayings of Jesus have been oven into long discourses of a quasi-poetic form resembling the speeches of personified Wisdom in the Old Testament.

The gospel contains many details about Jesus not found in the synoptic gospels, e.g., that Jesus engaged in a baptizing ministry (Jn 3:22) before he changed to one of preaching and signs; that Jesus' public ministry lasted for several years (see note on Jn 2:13); that he traveled to Jerusalem for various festivals and met serious opposition long before his death (Jn 2:14–25; 5; 7–8); and that he was put to death on the day before Passover (Jn 18:28). These events are not always in chronological order because of the development and editing that took place. However, the accuracy of much of the detail of the fourth gospel constitutes a strong argument that the Johannine tradition rests upon the testimony of an eyewitness. Although tradition identified this person as John, the son of Zebedee, most modern scholars find that the evidence does not support this.

The fourth gospel is not simply history; the narrative has been organized and adapted to serve the evangelist's theological purposes as well. Among them are the opposition to the synagogue of the day and to John the Baptist's followers, who tried to exalt their master at Jesus' expense, the desire to show that Jesus was the Messiah, and the desire to convince Christians that their religious belief and practice must be rooted in Jesus. Such theological purposes have impelled the evangelist to emphasize motifs that were not so clear in the synoptic account of Jesus' ministry, e.g., the explicit emphasis on his divinity.

The polemic between synagogue and church produced bitter and harsh invective, especially regarding the hostility toward Jesus of the authorities—Pharisees and Sadducees—who are combined and referred to frequently as "the Jews" (see note on Jn 1:19). These opponents are even described in Jn 8:44 as springing from their father the devil, whose conduct they imitate in opposing God by rejecting Jesus, whom God has sent. On the other hand, the author of this gospel seems to take pains to show that women are not inferior to men in the Christian community: the woman at the well in Samaria (Jn 4) is presented as a prototype of a missionary (Jn 4:4–42), and the first witness of the resurrection is a woman (Jn 20:11–18).

The final editing of the gospel and arrangement in its present form probably dates from between A.D. 90 and 100. Traditionally, Ephesus has been favored as the place of composition, though many support a location in Syria, perhaps the city of Antioch, while some have suggested other places, including Alexandria.

The principal divisions of the Gospel according to John are the following:

I. Prologue (1:1–18)
II. The Book of Signs (1:19–12:50)
III. The Book of Glory (13:1–20:31)
IV. Epilogue: The Resurrection Appearance in Galilee (21:1–25)

I. PROLOGUE*

CHAPTER 1

1 In the beginning† was the Word,
  and the Word was with God,
  and the Word was God.ᵃ
2 He was in the beginning with God.
3 ‡All things came to be through him,
  and without him nothing came to be.ᵇ
  What came to be ⁴through him was life,
  and this life was the light of the
    human race;ᶜ
5 ⁵the light shines in the darkness,ᵈ
  and the darkness has not overcome it.

⁶§A man named John was sent from God.ᵉ ⁷He came for testimony,** to testify to the light, so that all might believe through him.ᶠ ⁸He was not the light, but came to testify to the light.ᵍ ⁹The true light, which enlightens everyone, was coming into the world.ʰ

10 He was in the world,
  and the world came to be through him,
  but the world did not know him.
11 He came to what was his own,
  but his own people†† did not accept
    him.

¹²ᶦBut to those who did accept him he gave power to become children of God, to those who believe in his name, ¹³‡‡ʲwho were born not by natural generation nor by human choice nor by a man's decision but of God.

14 And the Word became flesh§§
  and made his dwelling among us,
  and we saw his glory,
  the glory as of the Father's only Son,
  full of grace and truth.ᵏ

¹⁵¶¶John testified to him and cried out, saying, "This was he of whom I said,ᶦ 'The one who is coming after me ranks ahead of me because he existed before me.'" ¹⁶From his fullness we have all received, grace in place of grace,*** ¹⁷because while the law was given through Moses, grace and truth came through Jesus Christ.ᵐ ¹⁸No one has ever seen God. The only Son, God,††† who is at the Father's side, has revealed him.ⁿ

II. THE BOOK OF SIGNS

John the Baptist's Testimony to Himself.
¹⁹‡‡‡And this is the testimony of John. When the

---

*[1:1–18] The prologue states the main themes of the gospel: life, light, truth, the world, testimony, and the preexistence of Jesus Christ, the incarnate *Logos*, who reveals God the Father. In origin, it was probably an early Christian hymn. Its closest parallel is in other christological hymns, Col 1:15–20 and Phil 2:6–11. Its core (Jn 1:1–5, 10–11, 14) is poetic in structure, with short phrases linked by "staircase parallelism," in which the last word of one phrase becomes the first word of the next. Prose inserts (at least Jn 1:6–8, 15) deal with John the Baptist.

†[1:1] **In the beginning**: also the first words of the Old Testament (Gn 1:1). **Was**: this verb is used three times with different meanings in this verse: existence, relationship, and predication. **The Word** (Greek *logos*): this term combines God's dynamic, creative word (Genesis), personified preexistent Wisdom as the instrument of God's creative activity (Proverbs), and the ultimate intelligibility of reality (Hellenistic philosophy). **With God**: the Greek preposition here connotes communication with another. **Was God**: lack of a definite article with "God" in Greek signifies predication rather than identification.

‡[1:3] **What came to be**: while the oldest manuscripts have no punctuation here, the corrector of Bodmer Papyrus P⁷⁵, some manuscripts, and the Ante-Nicene Fathers take this phrase with what follows, as staircase parallelism. Connection with Jn 1:3 reflects fourth-century anti-Arianism.

§[1:5] The ethical dualism of light and darkness is paralleled in intertestamental literature and in the Dead Sea Scrolls. **Overcome**: "comprehend" is another possible translation, but cf. Jn 12:35; Wis 7:29–30.

¶[1:6] John was **sent** just as Jesus was "sent" (Jn 4:34) in divine mission. Other references to John the Baptist in this gospel emphasize the differences between them and John's subordinate role.

[1:7] **Testimony: the testimony theme of John is introduced, which portrays Jesus as if on trial throughout his ministry. All testify to Jesus: John the Baptist, the Samaritan woman, scripture, his works, the crowds, the Father, and his disciples.

††[1:11] **What was his own . . . his own people**: first a neuter, literally, "his own property/possession" (probably = Israel), then a masculine, "his own people" (the Israelites).

‡‡[1:13] Believers in Jesus become children of God not through any of the three natural causes mentioned but through God who is the immediate cause of the new spiritual life. **Were born**: the Greek verb can mean "begotten" (by a male) or "born" (from a female or of parents). The variant "he who was begotten," asserting Jesus' virginal conception, is weakly attested in Old Latin and Syriac versions.

§§[1:14] **Flesh**: the whole person, used probably against docetic tendencies (cf. 1 Jn 4:2; 2 Jn 7). **Made his dwelling**: literally, "pitched his tent/tabernacle." Cf. the tabernacle or tent of meeting that was the place of God's presence among his people (Ex 25:8–9). The incarnate Word is the new mode of God's presence among his people. The Greek verb has the same consonants as the Aramaic word for God's presence (Shekinah). **Glory**: God's visible manifestation of majesty in power, which once filled the tabernacle (Ex 40:34) and the temple (1 Kgs 8:10–11, 27), is now centered in Jesus. **Only Son**: Greek, *monogenēs*, but see note on Jn 1:18. **Grace and truth**: these words may represent two Old Testament terms describing Yahweh in covenant relationship with Israel (cf. Ex 34:6), thus God's "love" and "fidelity." The Word shares Yahweh's covenant qualities.

¶¶[1:15] This verse, interrupting Jn 1:14, 16 seems drawn from Jn 1:30.

***[1:16] **Grace in place of grace**: replacement of the Old Covenant with the New (cf. Jn 1:17). Other possible translations are "grace upon grace" (accumulation) and "grace for grace" (correspondence).

†††[1:18] **The only Son, God**: while the vast majority of later textual witnesses have another reading, "the Son, the only one" or "the only Son," the translation above follows the best and earliest manuscripts, *monogenēs theos*, but takes the first term to mean not just "Only One" but to include a filial relationship with the Father, as at Lk 9:38 ("only child") or Heb 11:17 ("only son") and as translated at Jn 1:14. The Logos is thus "only Son" and God but not Father/God.

‡‡‡[1:19–51] The testimony of John the Baptist about the Messiah and Jesus' self-revelation to the first disciples. This section constitutes the introduction to the gospel proper and is connected with the prose inserts in the prologue. It develops the major theme of testimony in four scenes: John's negative testimony about himself; his positive testimony about Jesus;

---

a. [1:1] 10:30; Gn 1:1–5; Jb 28:12–27; Prv 8:22–25; Wis 9:1–2; 1 Jn 1:1–2; Col 1:1, 15; Rev 3:14; 19:13. b. [1:3] Ps 33:9; Wis 9:1; Sir 42:15; 1 Cor 8:6; Col 1:16; Heb 1:2; Rev 3:14. c. [1:4] 5:26; 8:12; 1 Jn 1:2. d. [1:5] 3:19; 8:12; 9:5; 12:35, 46; Wis 7:29–30; 1 Thes 5:4; 1 Jn 2:8. e. [1:6] Mt 3:1; Mk 1:4; Lk 3:2–3. f. [1:7] 1:19–34; 5:33. g. [1:8] 5:35. h. [1:9] 3:19; 8:12; 9:39; 12:46. i. [1:12] 3:11–12; 5:43–44; 12:46–50; Gal 3:26; 4:6–7; Eph 1:5; 1 Jn 3:2. j. [1:13] 3:5–6. k. [1:14] Ex 16:10; 24:17; 25:8–9; 33:22; 34:6; Sir 24:4, 8; Is 60:1; Ez 43:7; Jl 4:17; Heb 2:14; 1 Jn 1:2; 4:2; 2 Jn 7. l. [1:15] 1:30; 3:27–30. m. [1:17] 7:19; Ex 31:18; 34:28. n. [1:18] 5:37; 6:46; Ex 33:20; Jgs 13:21–22; 1 Tm 6:16; 1 Jn 4:12.

Jews* from Jerusalem sent priests and Levites [to him] to ask him, "Who are you?" [20†]he admitted and did not deny it, but admitted,[o] "I am not the Messiah." [21]So they asked him, "What are you then? Are you Elijah?"[‡] And he said, "I am not." "Are you the Prophet?" He answered, "No."[p] [22]So they said to him, "Who are you, so we can give an answer to those who sent us? What do you have to say for yourself?" [23]He said:

"I am 'the voice of one crying out in the
desert,[q]
"Make straight the way of the Lord,'"[§]

as Isaiah the prophet said." [24]Some Pharisees[¶] were also sent. [25]They asked him, "Why then do you baptize if you are not the Messiah or Elijah or the Prophet?"[r] [26]John answered them, "I baptize with water;[**] but there is one among you whom you do not recognize,[s] [27]the one who is coming after me, whose sandal strap I am not worthy to untie." [28]This happened in Bethany across the Jordan,[††] where John was baptizing. **John the Baptist's Testimony to Jesus.** [29]The next day he saw Jesus coming toward him and said, "Behold, the Lamb of God,[‡‡] who takes away the sin of the world.[t] [30§§]He is the one of whom I said,[u] 'A man is coming after me who ranks

ahead of me because he existed before me.' [31]I did not know him,[¶¶] but the reason why I came baptizing with water was that he might be made known to Israel." [32]John testified further, saying, "I saw the Spirit come down like a dove[***] from the sky and remain upon him. [33]I did not know him,[v] but the one who sent me to baptize with water told me, 'On whomever you see the Spirit come down and remain, he is the one who will baptize with the holy Spirit.'[w] [34†††]Now I have seen and testified that he is the Son of God."

The First Disciples.[y] [35]The next day John was there again with two of his disciples, [36]and as he watched Jesus walk by, he said, "Behold, the Lamb of God."[‡‡‡] [37]The two disciples[§§§] heard what he said and followed Jesus. [38]Jesus turned and saw them following him and said to them, "What are you looking for?" They said to him, "Rabbi" (which translated means Teacher), "where are you staying?" [39]He said to them, "Come, and you will see." So they went and saw where he was staying, and they stayed with him that day. It was about four in the afternoon.[¶¶¶] [40]Andrew, the brother of Simon Peter, was one of the two who heard John and followed Jesus. [41]He first found his own brother Simon and told him, "We have found the Messiah"[****] (which is translated Anointed).[z] [42]Then he brought him to Jesus. Jesus looked at him and said, "You are Simon the son of John;[††††] you will be called Cephas" (which is translated Peter).[a]

the revelation of Jesus to Andrew and Peter; the revelation of Jesus to Philip and Nathanael.

*[1:19] **The Jews:** throughout most of the gospel, the "Jews" does not refer to the Jewish people as such but to the hostile authorities, both Pharisees and Sadducees, particularly in Jerusalem, who refuse to believe in Jesus. The usage reflects the atmosphere, at the end of the first century, of polemics between church and synagogue, or possibly it refers to Jews as representative of a hostile world (Jn 1:10–11).

†[1:20] **Messiah:** the anointed agent of Yahweh, usually considered to be of Davidic descent. See further the note on Jn 1:41.

‡[1:21] **Elijah:** the Baptist did not claim to be Elijah returned to earth (cf. Mal 3:19; Mt 11:14). **The Prophet:** probably the prophet like Moses (Dt 18:15; cf. Acts 3:22).

§[1:23] This is a repunctuation and reinterpretation (as in the synoptic gospels and Septuagint) of the Hebrew text of Is 40:3 which reads, "A voice cries out: In the desert prepare the way of the LORD."

¶[1:24] **Some Pharisees:** other translations, such as "Now they had been sent from the Pharisees," misunderstand the grammatical construction. This is a different group from that in Jn 1:19; the priests and Levites would have been Sadducees, not Pharisees.

[1:26] **I baptize with water: the synoptics add "but he will baptize you with the holy Spirit" (Mk 1:8) or ". . . holy Spirit and fire" (Mt 3:11; Lk 3:16). John's emphasis is on purification and preparation for a better baptism.

††[1:28] **Bethany across the Jordan:** site unknown. Another reading is "Bethabara."

‡‡[1:29] **The Lamb of God:** the background for this title may be the victorious apocalyptic lamb who would destroy evil in the world (Rev 5–7; 17:14); the paschal lamb, whose blood saved Israel (Ex 12); and/or the suffering servant led like a lamb to the slaughter as a sin-offering (Is 53:7, 10).

§§[1:30] **He existed before me:** possibly as Elijah (to come, Jn 1:27); for the evangelist and his audience, Jesus' preexistence would be implied (see note on Jn 1:1).

¶¶[1:31] **I did not know him:** this gospel shows no knowledge of the tradition (Lk 1) about the kinship of Jesus and John the Baptist. **The reason why I came baptizing with water:** in this gospel, John's baptism is not connected with forgiveness of sins; its purpose is revelatory, that Jesus may be made known to Israel.

***[1:32] **Like a dove:** a symbol of the new creation (Gn 8:8) or the community of Israel (Hos 11:11). **Remain:** the first use of a favorite verb in John, emphasizing the permanency of the relationship between Father and Son (as here) and between the Son and the Christian. Jesus is the permanent bearer of the Spirit.

†††[1:34] **The Son of God:** this reading is supported by good Greek manuscripts, including the Chester Beatty and Bodmer Papyri and the Vatican Codex, but is suspect because it harmonizes this passage with the synoptic version: "This is my beloved Son" (Mt 3:17; Mk 1:11; Lk 3:22). The poorly attested alternate reading, "God's chosen One," is probably a reference to the Servant of Yahweh (Is 42:1).

‡‡‡[1:36] John the Baptist's testimony makes his disciples' following of Jesus plausible.

§§§[1:37] **The two disciples:** Andrew (Jn 1:40) and, traditionally, John, son of Zebedee (see note on Jn 13:23).

¶¶¶[1:39] **Four in the afternoon:** literally, the tenth hour, from sunrise, in the Roman calculation of time. Some suggest that the next day, beginning at sunset, was the sabbath; they would have stayed with Jesus to avoid travel on it.

****[1:41] **Messiah:** the Hebrew word *māšîaḥ*, "anointed one" (see note on Lk 2:11), appears in Greek as the transliterated *messias* only here and in Jn 4:25. Elsewhere the Greek translation *christos* is used.

††††[1:42] **Simon, the son of John:** in Mt 16:17, Simon is called *Bariōna*, "son of Jonah," a different tradition for the name of Simon's father. **Cephas:** in Aramaic = the Rock; cf. Mt 16:18. Neither the Greek equivalent **Petros** nor, with one

o. [1:20] 3:28; Lk 3:15; Acts 13:25.   p. [1:21] Dt 18:15, 18; 2 Kgs 2:11; Sir 48:10; Mal 3:1, 23; Mt 11:14; 17:11–13; Mk 9:13; Acts 3:22.   q. [1:23] Is 40:3; Mt 3:3; Mk 1:2; Lk 3:4.   r. [1:25] Ez 36:25; Zec 13:1; Mt 16:14.   s. [1:26] Mt 3:11; Mk 1:7–8; Lk 3:16; Acts 13:25.   t. [1:29] 1:36; Ex 12; Is 53:7; Rev 5–7; 17:14.   u. [1:30] 1:15; Mt 3:11; Mk 1:7; Lk 3:16.

v. [1:33] Sg 5:2; Is 11:2; Hos 11:11; Mt 3:16; Mk 1:10; Lk 3:21–22.   w. [1:33] Is 42:1; Mt 3:11; Mk 1:8; Lk 3:16.   x. [1:34] Is 42:1; Mt 3:17; Mk 1:11; Jn 9:35.   y. [1:35–51] Mt 4:18–22; Mk 1:16–20; Lk 5:1–11.   z. [1:41] 4:25.   a. [1:42] Mt 16:18; Mk 3:16.

⁴³The next day he˙ decided to go to Galilee, and he found Philip. And Jesus said to him, "Follow me." ⁴⁴Now Philip was from Bethsaida, the town of Andrew and Peter. ⁴⁵Philip found Nathanael and told him, "We have found the one about whom Moses wrote in the law, and also the prophets, Jesus son of Joseph, from Nazareth."ᵇ ⁴⁶But Nathanael said to him, "Can anything good come from Nazareth?" Philip said to him, "Come and see." ⁴⁷Jesus saw Nathanael coming toward him and said of him, "Here is a true Israelite.† There is no duplicity in him." ⁴⁸†ᶜNathanael said to him, "How do you know me?" Jesus answered and said to him, "Before Philip called you, I saw you under the fig tree." ⁴⁹Nathanael answered him, "Rabbi, you are the Son of God;⁵ you are the King of Israel."ᵈ ⁵⁰Jesus answered and said to him, "Do you believe because I told you that I saw you under the fig tree?⁵ You will see greater things than this." ⁵¹And he said to him, "Amen, amen,˙˙ I say to you, you will see the sky opened and the angels of God ascending and descending on the Son of Man."ᵉ

CHAPTER 2

The Wedding at Cana. ¹††On the third day there was a wedding‡‡ in Cana§§ in Galilee, and the mother of Jesus was there.ᶠ ²Jesus and his disciples were also invited to the wedding. ³When the wine ran short, the mother of Jesus said to him, "They have no wine." ⁴¶¶[And] Jesus said to her,

"Woman, how does your concern affect me? My hour has not yet come."ᵍ ⁵His mother said to the servers, "Do whatever he tells you."ʰ ⁶˙˙˙Now there were six stone water jars there for Jewish ceremonial washings,ⁱ each holding twenty to thirty gallons. ⁷Jesus told them, "Fill the jars with water." So they filled them to the brim. ⁸Then he told them, "Draw some out now and take it to the headwaiter."††† So they took it. ⁹And when the headwaiter tasted the water that had become wine, without knowing where it came from (although the servers who had drawn the water knew), the headwaiter called the bridegroom ¹⁰and said to him, "Everyone serves good wine first, and then when people have drunk freely, an inferior one; but you have kept the good wine until now." ¹¹Jesus did this as the beginning of his signs‡‡‡ in Cana in Galilee and so revealed his glory, and his disciples began to believe in him.ʲ

¹²§§§After this, he and his mother, [his] brothers, and his disciples went down to Capernaum and stayed there only a few days.¶¶¶

Cleansing of the Temple. ¹³˙˙˙˙Since the Passover†††† of the Jews was near,ᵏ Jesus went up to Jerusalem. ¹⁴‡‡‡‡He found in the temple area those who sold oxen, sheep, and doves,§§§§ as well

isolated exception, **Cephas** is attested as a personal name before Christian times.
*[1:43] **He:** grammatically, could be Peter, but logically is probably Jesus.
†[1:47] **A true Israelite. There is no duplicity in him:** Jacob was the first to bear the name "Israel" (Gn 32:29), but Jacob was a man of duplicity (Gn 27:35–36).
‡[1:48] **Under the fig tree:** a symbol of messianic peace (cf. Mi 4:4; Zec 3:10).
§[1:49] **Son of God:** this title is used in the Old Testament, among other ways, as a title of adoption for the Davidic king (2 Sm 7:14; Ps 2:7; 89:27), and thus here, with **King of Israel**, in a messianic sense. For the evangelist, **Son of God** also points to Jesus' divinity (cf. Jn 20:28).
¶[1:50] Possibly a statement: "You [singular] believe because I saw you under the fig tree."
[1:51] The double "Amen" is characteristic of John. **You is plural in Greek. The allusion is to Jacob's ladder (Gn 28:12).
††[2:1–6:71] Signs revealing Jesus as the Messiah to all Israel. "Sign" (*sēmeion*) is John's symbolic term for Jesus' wondrous deeds (see Introduction). The Old Testament background lies in the Exodus story (cf. Dt 11:3; 29:2). John is interested primarily in what the *sēmeia* signify: God's intervention in human history in a new way through Jesus.
‡‡[2:1–11] The first sign. This story of replacement of Jewish ceremonial washings (Jn 2:6) presents the initial revelation about Jesus at the outset of his ministry. He manifests his glory; the disciples believe. There is no synoptic parallel.
§§[2:1] **Cana:** unknown from the Old Testament. **The mother of Jesus:** she is never named in John.
¶¶[2:4] This verse may seek to show that Jesus did not work miracles to help his family and friends, as in the apocryphal gospels. **Woman:** a normal, polite form of address, but

unattested in reference to one's mother. Cf. also Jn 19:26. **How does your concern affect me?:** literally, "What is this to me and to you?"—a Hebrew expression of either hostility (Jgs 11:12; 2 Chr 35:21; 1 Kgs 17:18) or denial of common interest (Hos 14:9; 2 Kgs 3:13). Cf. Mk 1:24; 5:7 used by demons to Jesus. **My hour has not yet come:** the translation as a question ("Has not my hour now come?"), while preferable grammatically and supported by Greek Fathers, seems unlikely from a comparison with Jn 7:6, 30. The "hour" is that of Jesus' passion, death, resurrection, and ascension (Jn 13:1).
***[2:6] **Twenty to thirty gallons:** literally, "two or three measures"; the Attic liquid measure contained 39.39 liters. The vast quantity recalls prophecies of abundance in the last days; cf. Am 9:13–14; Hos 14:7; Jer 31:12.
†††[2:8] **Headwaiter:** used of the official who managed a banquet, but there is no evidence of such a functionary in Palestine. Perhaps here a friend of the family acted as master of ceremonies; cf. Sir 32:1.
‡‡‡[2:11] **The beginning of his signs:** the first of seven (see Introduction).
§§§[2:12–3:21] The next three episodes take place in Jerusalem. Only the first is paralleled in the synoptic gospels.
¶¶¶[2:12] This transitional verse may be a harmonization with the synoptic tradition in Lk 4:31 and Mt 4:13. There are many textual variants. John depicts no extended ministry in Capernaum as do the synoptics.
****[2:13–22] This episode indicates the post-resurrectional replacement of the temple by the person of Jesus.
††††[2:13] **Passover:** this is the first Passover mentioned in John; a second is mentioned in Jn 6:4 a third in Jn 13:1. Taken literally, they point to a ministry of at least two years.
‡‡‡‡[2:14–22] The other gospels place the cleansing of the temple in the last days of Jesus' life (Matthew, on the day Jesus entered Jerusalem; Mark, on the next day). The order of events in the gospel narratives is often determined by theological motives rather than by chronological data.
§§§§[2:14] **Oxen, sheep, and doves:** intended for sacrifice. The doves were the offerings of the poor (Lv 5:7). **Money-changers:** for a temple tax paid by every male Jew more than nineteen years of age, with a half-shekel coin (Ex 30:11–16), in Syrian currency. See note on Mt 17:24.

b. [1:45] 21:2.   c. [1:48] Mi 4:4; Zec 3:10.   d. [1:49] 12:13; Ex 4:22; Dt 14:1; 2 Sm 7:14; Jb 1:6; 2:1; 38:7; Ps 2:7; 29:1; 89:27; Wis 2:18; Sir 4:10; Dn 3:92; Hos 11:1; Mt 14:33; 16:16; Mk 13:32.   e. [1:51] Gn 28:10–17; Dn 7:13.   f. [2:1] 4:46; Jgs 14:12; Tb 11:8.

g. [2:4] 7:30; 8:20; 12:23; 13:1; Jgs 11:12; 1 Kgs 17:18; 2 Kgs 3:13; 2 Chr 35:21; Hos 14:9; Mk 1:24; 5:7; 7:30; 8:20; 12:23; 13:1.   h. [2:5] Gn 41:55.   i. [2:6] 3:25; Lv 11:33; Am 9:13–14; Mt 15:2; 23:25–26; Mk 7:2–4; Lk 11:38.   j. [2:11] 4:54.   k. [2:13–22] Mt 21:12–13; Mk 11:15–17; Lk 19:45–46.

as the money changers seated there.[l] [15]He made a whip out of cords and drove them all out of the temple area, with the sheep and oxen, and spilled the coins of the money changers and overturned their tables, [16]and to those who sold doves he said, "Take these out of here, and stop making my Father's house a marketplace."[m] [17]His disciples recalled the words of scripture,[n] "Zeal for your house will consume me." [18]At this the Jews answered and said to him, "What sign can you show us for doing this?"[o] [19]Jesus answered and said to them,[†p] "Destroy this temple and in three days I will raise it up." [20]The Jews said, "This temple has been under construction for forty-six years,[‡] and you will raise it up in three days?" [21]But he was speaking about the temple of his body. [22]Therefore, when he was raised from the dead, his disciples remembered that he had said this, and they came to believe the scripture and the word Jesus had spoken.[q]

[23]While he was in Jerusalem for the feast of Passover, many began to believe in his name when they saw the signs he was doing.[r] [24]But Jesus would not trust himself to them because he knew them all, [25]and did not need anyone to testify about human nature. He himself understood it well.[s]

CHAPTER 3

Nicodemus.[§] [1]*Now there was a Pharisee named Nicodemus, a ruler of the Jews.[t] [2]He came to Jesus at night and said to him, "Rabbi, we know that you are a teacher who has come from God, for no one can do these signs that you are doing unless God is with him."[u] [3]Jesus answered and said to him, "Amen, amen, I say to you, no one

can see the kingdom of God without being born** from above." [4]Nicodemus said to him, "How can a person once grown old be born again? Surely he cannot reenter his mother's womb and be born again, can he?"[v] [5]Jesus answered, "Amen, amen, I say to you, no one can enter the kingdom of God without being born of water and Spirit.[w] [6]What is born of flesh is flesh and what is born of spirit is spirit.[x] [7]Do not be amazed that I told you, 'You must be born from above.' [8]The wind[††] blows where it wills, and you can hear the sound it makes, but you do not know where it comes from or where it goes; so it is with everyone who is born of the Spirit."[y] [9]Nicodemus answered and said to him, "How can this happen?" [10]Jesus answered and said to him, "You are the teacher of Israel and you do not understand this? [11]Amen, amen, I say to you, we speak of what we know and we testify to what we have seen, but you people do not accept our testimony.[z] [12]If I tell you about earthly things and you do not believe, how will you believe if I tell you about heavenly things?[a] [13]No one has gone up to heaven except the one who has come down from heaven, the Son of Man.[b] [14]And just as Moses lifted up[‡‡] the serpent in the desert, so must the Son of Man be lifted up,[c] [15§§]so that everyone who believes in him may have eternal life."

[16]For God so loved the world that he gave[¶¶] his only Son, so that everyone who believes in him might not perish but might have eternal life.[d] [17]For God did not send his Son into the world to condemn*** the world, but that the world might be saved through him.[e] [18]Whoever believes in him will not be condemned, but whoever does not believe has already been condemned, because he has not believed in the name of the only Son of God.[f] [19†††]And this is the verdict,[g] that the light came into the world,

---

*[2:17] Ps 69:10, changed to future tense to apply to Jesus.

†[2:19] This saying about the destruction of the temple occurs in various forms (Mt 24:2; 27:40; Mk 13:2; 15:29; Lk 21:6; cf. Acts 6:14). Mt 26:61 has: "I *can* destroy the temple of God . . ."; see note there. In Mk 14:58, there is a metaphorical contrast with a new temple: "I will destroy this temple *made with hands* and within three days I will build another *not made with hands*." Here it is symbolic of Jesus' resurrection and the resulting community (see Jn 2:21 and Rev 21:2). In **three days**: an Old Testament expression for a short, indefinite period of time; cf. Hos 6:2.

‡[2:20] **Forty-six years**: based on references in Josephus (*Jewish Wars* 1:401; *Antiquities* 15:380), possibly the spring of A.D. 28. Cf. note on Lk 3:1.

§[3:1–21] Jesus instructs Nicodemus on the necessity of a new birth from above. This scene in Jerusalem at Passover exemplifies the faith engendered by signs (Jn 2:23). It continues the self-manifestation of Jesus in Jerusalem begun in Jn 2. This is the first of the Johannine discourses, shifting from dialogue to monologue (Jn 3:11–15) to reflection of the evangelist (Jn 3:16–21). The shift from singular through Jn 3:10 to plural in Jn 3:11 may reflect the early church's controversy with the Jews.

¶[3:1] **A ruler of the Jews**: most likely a member of the Jewish council, the Sanhedrin; see note on Mk 8:31.

[3:3] **Born: see note on Jn 1:13. **From above**: the Greek adverb *anōthen* means both "from above" and "again." Jesus means "from above" (see Jn 3:31) but Nicodemus misunderstands it as "again." This misunderstanding serves as a springboard for further instruction.

††[3:8] **Wind**: the Greek word *pneuma* (as well as the Hebrew *rûah*) means both "wind" and "spirit." In the play on the double meaning, "wind" is primary.

‡‡[3:14] **Lifted up**: in Nm 21:9, Moses simply "mounted" a serpent upon a pole. John here substitutes a verb implying glorification. Jesus, exalted to glory at his cross and resurrection, represents healing for all.

§§[3:15] **Eternal life**: used here for the first time in John, this term stresses quality of life rather than duration.

¶¶[3:16] **Gave**: as a gift in the incarnation, and also "over to death" in the crucifixion; cf. Rom 8:32.

***[3:17–19] **Condemn**: the Greek root means both judgment and condemnation. Jesus' purpose is to save, but his coming provokes judgment; some condemn themselves by turning from the light.

†††[3:19] Judgment is not only future but is partially realized here and now.

---

l. [2:14] Ex 30:11–16; Lv 5:7. m. [2:16] Zec 14:21. n. [2:17] Ps 69:9. o. [2:18] 6:30. p. [2:19] Mt 24:2; 26:61; 27:40; Mk 13:2; 14:58; 15:29; Lk 21:6; Acts 6:14. q. [2:22] 5:39; 12:16; 14:26; 20:9; Mt 12:6; Lk 24:6–8; Rev 21:22. r. [2:23] 4:45. s. [2:25] 1 Kgs 8:39; Ps 33:15; 94:11; Sir 42:18; Jer 17:10; 20:12. t. [3:1] 7:50–51; 19:39. u. [3:2] 9:4, 16, 33; 10:21; 11:10; 13:30; Mt 22:16; Mk 12:14; Lk 20:21.

v. [3:4] 1:13. w. [3:5] 1:32; 7:39; 19:30, 34–35; Is 32:15; 44:3; Ez 36:25–27; Jl 3:1–2. x. [3:6] 6:63; 1 Cor 15:44–50. y. [3:8] Eccl 11:4–5; Acts 2:2–4. z. [3:11] 3:32, 34; 8:14; Mt 11:27. a. [3:12] 6:62–65; Wis 9:16–17; 1 Cor 15:40; 2 Cor 5:1; Phil 2:10; 3:19–20. b. [3:13] 1:18; 6:62; Dn 7:13; Rom 10:6; Eph 4:9. c. [3:14] 8:28; 12:32, 34; Nm 21:4–9; Wis 16:5–7. d. [3:16] 1 Jn 4:9. e. [3:17] 5:22, 30; 8:15–18; 12:47. f. [3:18] 5:24; Mk 16:16. g. [3:19] 1:5, 9–11; 8:12; 9:5.

but people preferred darkness to light, because their works were evil. [20]For everyone who does wicked things hates the light and does not come toward the light, so that his works might not be exposed.[h] [21]But whoever lives the truth comes to the light, so that his works may be clearly seen as done in God.[i]

Final Witness of the Baptist. [22]*After this, Jesus and his disciples went into the region of Judea, where he spent some time with them baptizing.[j] [23]John was also baptizing in Aenon near Salim,[†] because there was an abundance of water there, and people came to be baptized, [24]‡[k]for John had not yet been imprisoned. [25]Now a dispute arose between the disciples of John and a Jew[§] about ceremonial washings. [26]So they came to John and said to him, "Rabbi, the one who was with you across the Jordan, to whom you testified, here he is baptizing and everyone is coming to him."[l] [27]John answered and said, "No one can receive anything except what has been given him from heaven.[m] [28]You yourselves can testify that I said [that] I am not the Messiah, but that I was sent before him.[n] [29]The one who has the bride is the bridegroom; the best man,[§] who stands and listens to him, rejoices greatly at the bridegroom's voice. So this joy of mine has been made complete.[o] [30]He must increase; I must decrease."[p]

The One from Heaven.[**] [31]The one who comes from above is above all. The one who is of the earth is earthly and speaks of earthly things. But the one who comes from heaven [is above all].[q] [32]He testifies to what he has seen and heard, but no one accepts his testimony.[r] [33]Whoever does accept his testimony certifies that God is trustworthy.[s] [34]For the one whom God sent speaks the words of God. He does not ration his gift[††] of the Spirit. [35]The Father loves the Son and

has given everything over to him.[t] [36]Whoever believes in the Son has eternal life, but whoever disobeys the Son will not see life, but the wrath of God remains upon him.[u]

CHAPTER 4

[1]‡‡Now when Jesus learned that the Pharisees had heard that Jesus was making and baptizing more disciples than John [2](although Jesus himself was not baptizing, just his disciples),[§§] [3]he left Judea and returned to Galilee.

The Samaritan Woman. [4]He had to[¶¶] pass through Samaria. [5]So he came to a town of Samaria called Sychar,[***] near the plot of land that Jacob had given to his son Joseph.[v] [6]Jacob's well was there. Jesus, tired from his journey, sat down there at the well. It was about noon.

[7]A woman of Samaria came to draw water. Jesus said to her, "Give me a drink." [8]His disciples had gone into the town to buy food. [9]†††The Samaritan woman said to him, "How can you, a Jew, ask me, a Samaritan woman, for a drink?"[w] (For Jews use nothing in common with Samaritans.) [10]‡‡‡Jesus answered and said to her,[x] "If you knew the gift of God and who is saying to you, 'Give me a drink,' you would have asked him and he would have given you living water." [11][The woman] said to him, "Sir,[§§§] you do not even have a bucket and the well is deep; where then can you get this living water? [12]Are you greater than our father Jacob, who gave us this well and drank from it himself with his children and his flocks?"[y] [13]Jesus answered and said to her, "Everyone who drinks this water will be thirsty again; [14]but whoever drinks the water I shall give will never thirst; the water I shall give will become in him a spring of water welling up to eternal life."[z] [15]The woman said to him, "Sir,

---

* [3:22–26] Jesus' ministry in Judea is only loosely connected with Jn 2:13–3:21; cf. Jn 1:19–36. Perhaps John the Baptist's further testimony was transposed here to give meaning to "water" in Jn 3:5. Jesus is depicted as baptizing (Jn 3:22); contrast Jn 4:2.

† [3:23] **Aenon near Salim**: site uncertain, either in the upper Jordan valley or in Samaria.

‡ [3:24] A remark probably intended to avoid objections based on a chronology like that of the synoptics (Mt 4:12; Mk 1:14).

§ [3:25] **A Jew**: some think Jesus is meant. Many manuscripts read "Jews."

¶ [3:29] **The best man**: literally, "the friend of the groom," the *shoshben* of Jewish tradition, who arranged the wedding. Competition between him and the groom would be unthinkable.

** [3:31–36] It is uncertain whether these are words by the Baptist, Jesus, or the evangelist. They are reflections on the two preceding scenes.

†† [3:34] **His gift**: of God or to Jesus, perhaps both. This verse echoes Jn 3:5, 8.

‡‡ [4:1–42] Jesus in Samaria. The self-revelation of Jesus continues with his second discourse, on his mission to "half-Jews." It continues the theme of replacement, here with regard to cult (Jn 4:21). Water (Jn 4:7–15) serves as a symbol (as at Cana and in the Nicodemus episode).

§§ [4:2] An editorial refinement of Jn 3:22, perhaps directed against followers of John the Baptist who claimed that Jesus imitated him.

¶¶ [4:4] **He had to**: a theological necessity; geographically, Jews often bypassed Samaria by taking a route across the Jordan.

*** [4:5] **Sychar**: Jerome identifies this with Shechem, a reading found in Syriac manuscripts.

††† [4:9] Samaritan women were regarded by Jews as ritually impure, and therefore Jews were forbidden to drink from any vessel they had handled.

‡‡‡ [4:10] **Living water**: the water of life, i.e., the revelation that Jesus brings; the woman thinks of "flowing water," so much more desirable than stagnant well water. On John's device of such misunderstanding, cf. note on Jn 3:3.

§§§ [4:11] **Sir**: the Greek *kyrios* means "master" or "lord," as a respectful mode of address for a human being or a deity; cf. Jn 4:19. It is also the word used in the Septuagint for the Hebrew *'adônai*, substituted for the tetragrammaton YHWH.

---

h. [3:20] Jb 24:13–17.   i. [3:21] Gn 47:29 LXX; Jos 2:14 LXX; 2 Sm 2:6 LXX; 15:20 LXX; Tb 4:6 LXX; 13:6; Is 26:10 LXX; Mt 5:14–16.   j. [3:22–23] 4:1–2.   k. [3:24] Mt 4:12; 14:3; Mk 1:14; 6:17; Lk 3:20.   l. [3:26] 1:26, 32–34, 36.   m. [3:27] 19:11; 1 Cor 4:7; 2 Cor 3:5; Heb 5:4.   n. [3:28] 1:20–23; Lk 3:15.   o. [3:29] 15:11; 17:13; Mt 9:15.   p. [3:30] 2 Sm 3:1.   q. [3:31] 8:23.   r. [3:32] 3:11.   s. [3:33–34] 8:26; 12:44–50; 1 Jn 5:10.

t. [3:35] 13:3; Mt 11:27; 28:18; Lk 10:22.   u. [3:36] 3:16; 1 Jn 5:13.   v. [4:5] Gn 33:18–19; 48:22; Jos 24:32.   w. [4:9] Sir 50:25–26; Mt 10:5.   x. [4:10] Sir 24:20–21; Is 55:1; Jer 2:13.   y. [4:12] 8:53; Mt 12:41.   z. [4:14] 6:35, 58; 7:37–39; Is 44:3; 49:10; Jl 4:18; Rev 7:16; 21:6.

give me this water, so that I may not be thirsty or have to keep coming here to draw water." ¹⁶Jesus said to her, "Go call your husband and come back." ¹⁷The woman answered and said to him, "I do not have a husband." Jesus answered her, "You are right in saying, 'I do not have a husband.' ¹⁸For you have had five husbands, and the one you have now is not your husband. What you have said is true."ᵃ ¹⁹The woman said to him, "Sir, I can see that you are a prophet.ᵇ ²⁰Our ancestors worshiped on this mountain;* but you people say that the place to worship is in Jerusalem."ᶜ ²¹Jesus said to her, "Believe me, woman, the hour is coming when you will worship the Father neither on this mountain nor in Jerusalem. ²²You people worship what you do not understand; we worship what we understand, because salvation is from the Jews.ᵈ ²³But the hour is coming, and is now here, when true worshipers will worship the Father in Spirit and truth;† and indeed the Father seeks such people to worship him. ²⁴God is Spirit, and those who worship him must worship in Spirit and truth."ᵉ ²⁵†The woman said to him, "I know that the Messiah is coming,ᶠ the one called the Anointed; when he comes, he will tell us everything." ²⁶Jesus said to her, "I am he,§ the one who is speaking with you."ᵍ

²⁷At that moment his disciples returned, and were amazed that he was talking with a woman,¶ but still no one said, "What are you looking for?" or "Why are you talking with her?" ²⁸The woman left her water jar and went into the town and said to the people, ²⁹"Come see a man who told me everything I have done. Could he possibly be the Messiah?" ³⁰They went out of the town and came to him. ³¹Meanwhile, the disciples urged him, "Rabbi, eat." ³²But he said to them, "I have food to eat of which you do not know." ³³So the disciples said to one another, "Could someone have brought him something to eat?" ³⁴Jesus said to them, "My food is to do the will of the one who sent me and to finish his work.ʰ ³⁵Do you not say, 'In four months"

the harvest will be here'? I tell you, look up and see the fields ripe for the harvest.ⁱ ³⁶The reaper is already†† receiving his payment and gathering crops for eternal life, so that the sower and reaper can rejoice together.ʲ ³⁷For here the saying is verified that 'One sows and another reaps.'ᵏ ³⁸I sent you to reap what you have not worked for; others have done the work, and you are sharing the fruits of their work."

³⁹Many of the Samaritans of that town began to believe in him because of the word of the woman‡‡ who testified, "He told me everything I have done." ⁴⁰When the Samaritans came to him, they invited him to stay with them; and he stayed there two days. ⁴¹Many more began to believe in him because of his word, ⁴²and they said to the woman, "We no longer believe because of your word; for we have heard for ourselves, and we know that this is truly the savior of the world."ˡ

Return to Galilee. ⁴³§§After the two days, he left there for Galilee. ⁴⁴¶¶ᵐFor Jesus himself testified that a prophet has no honor in his native place. ⁴⁵When he came into Galilee, the Galileans welcomed him, since they had seen all he had done in Jerusalem at the feast; for they themselves had gone to the feast.

Second Sign at Cana.*** ⁴⁶ⁿThen he returned to Cana in Galilee, where he had made the water wine. Now there was a royal official whose son was ill in Capernaum. ⁴⁷When he heard that Jesus had arrived in Galilee from Judea, he went to him and asked him to come down and heal his son, who was near death. ⁴⁸Jesus said to him, "Unless you people see signs and wonders, you will not believe."ᵒ ⁴⁹The royal official said to him, "Sir, come down before my child dies." ⁵⁰Jesus said to him, "You may go; your son will live." The man believed what Jesus said to him and left.ᵖ ⁵¹While he was on his way back, his slaves met him and told him that his boy would live. ⁵²He asked them when he began to recover. They told him, "The fever left him yesterday, about one in the afternoon." ⁵³The father realized that just at

---

*[4:20] **This mountain:** Gerizim, on which a temple was erected in the fourth century B.C. by Samaritans to rival Mount Zion in Jerusalem; cf. Dt 27:4 (Mount Ebal = the Jews' term for Gerizim).

†[4:23] **In Spirit and truth:** not a reference to an interior worship within one's own spirit. The Spirit is the spirit given by God that reveals truth and enables one to worship God appropriately (Jn 14:16–17). Cf. "born of water and Spirit" (Jn 3:5).

‡[4:25] The expectations of the Samaritans are expressed here in Jewish terminology. They did not expect a messianic king of the house of David but a prophet like Moses (Dt 18:15).

§[4:26] **I am he:** it could also be translated "I am," an Old Testament self-designation of Yahweh (Is 43:3, etc.); cf. Jn 6:20; 8:24, 28, 58; 13:19; 18:5–6, 8. See note on Mk 6:50.

¶[4:27] **Talking with a woman:** a religious and social restriction that Jesus is pictured treating as unimportant.

[4:35] **'In four months . . .': probably a proverb; cf. Mt 9:37–38.

a. [4:18] 2 Kgs 17:24–34.   b. [4:19] 9:17; Hos 1:3.   c. [4:20] Dt 11:29; 27:4; Jos 8:33; Ps 122:1–5.   d. [4:22] 2 Kgs 17:27; Ps 76:2–3.   e. [4:24] 2 Cor 3:17.   f. [4:25] 1:41.   g. [4:26] 9:37.   h. [4:34] 5:30; 36; 6:38; 9:4; 17:4.

††[4:36] **Already:** this word may go with the preceding verse rather than with Jn 4:36.

‡‡[4:39] The woman is presented as a missionary, described in virtually the same words as the disciples are in Jesus' prayer (Jn 17:20).

§§[4:43–54] Jesus' arrival in Cana in Galilee; the second sign. This section introduces another theme, that of the life-giving word of Jesus. It is explicitly linked to the first sign (Jn 2:11). The royal official believes (Jn 4:50). The natural life given his son is a sign of eternal life.

¶¶[4:44] Probably a reminiscence of a tradition as in Mk 6:4. Cf. Gospel of Thomas 31: "No prophet is acceptable in his village, no physician heals those who know him."

***[4:46–54] The story of the cure of the royal official's son may be a third version of the cure of the centurion's son (Mt 8:5–13) or servant (Lk 7:1–10). Cf. also Mt 15:21–28; Mk 7:24–30.

i. [4:35] Mt 9:37–38; Lk 10:2; Rev 14:15.   j. [4:36] Ps 126:5–6; Am 9:13–14.   k. [4:37] Dt 20:6; 28:30; Jb 31:8; Mi 6:15.   l. [4:42] 1 Jn 4:14.   m. [4:44] Mt 13:57; Mk 6:4; Lk 4:24.   n. [4:46–54] 2:1–11; Mt 8:5–13; 15:21–28; Mk 7:24–30; Lk 7:1–10.   o. [4:48] 2:18, 23; Wis 8:8; Mt 12:38; 1 Cor 1:22.   p. [4:50] 1 Kgs 17:23.

that time Jesus had said to him, "Your son will live," and he and his whole household came to believe. ⁵⁴[Now] this was the second sign Jesus did when he came to Galilee from Judea.�q

CHAPTER 5*

Cure on a Sabbath. ¹After this, there was a feast† of the Jews, and Jesus went up to Jerusalem.ʳ ²Now there is in Jerusalem at the Sheep [Gate]‡ a pool called in Hebrew Bethesda, with five porticoes.ˢ ³In these lay a large number of ill, blind, lame, and crippled.§ [4]§ ⁵One man was there who had been ill for thirty-eight years. ⁶When Jesus saw him lying there and knew that he had been ill for a long time, he said to him, "Do you want to be well?" ⁷The sick man answered him, "Sir, I have no one to put me into the pool when the water is stirred up; while I am on my way, someone else gets down there before me." ⁸Jesus said to him, "Rise, take up your mat, and walk."ᵗ ⁹Immediately the man became well, took up his mat, and walked.ᵘ

Now that day was a sabbath. ¹⁰So the Jews said to the man who was cured, "It is the sabbath, and it is not lawful for you to carry your mat."ᵛ ¹¹He answered them, "The man who made me well told me, 'Take up your mat and walk.'" ¹²They asked him, "Who is the man who told you, 'Take it up and walk'?" ¹³The man who was healed did not know who it was, for Jesus had slipped away, since there was a crowd there.ʷ

---

*[5:1–47] The self-revelation of Jesus continues in Jerusalem at a feast. The third sign (cf. Jn 2:11; 4:54) is performed, the cure of a paralytic by Jesus' life-giving word. The water of the pool fails to bring life; Jesus' word does.

†[5:1] The reference in Jn 5:45–46 to Moses suggests that the feast was Pentecost. The connection of that feast with the giving of the law to Moses on Sinai, attested in later Judaism, may already have been made in the first century. The feast could also be Passover (cf. Jn 6:4). John stresses that the day was a sabbath (Jn 5:9).

‡[5:2] There is no noun with **Sheep**. "Gate" is supplied on the grounds that there must have been a gate in the NE wall of the temple area where animals for sacrifice were brought in; cf. Neh 3:1, 32; 12:39. **Hebrew:** more precisely, Aramaic. **Bethesda:** preferred to variants "Be(th)zatha" and "Bethsaida"; *bêt-'eśdatayin* is given as the name of a double pool northeast of the temple area in the Qumran Copper Roll. **Five porticoes:** a pool excavated in Jerusalem actually has five porticoes.

§[5:3] The Caesarean and Western recensions, followed by the Vulgate, add "waiting for the movement of the water." Apparently an intermittent spring in the pool bubbled up occasionally (see Jn 5:7). This turbulence was believed to cure.

¶[5:4] Toward the end of the second century in the West and among the fourth-century Greek Fathers, an additional verse was known: "For [from time to time] an angel of the Lord used to come down into the pool; and the water was stirred up, so the first one to get in [after the stirring of the water] was healed of whatever disease afflicted him." The angel was a popular explanation of the turbulence and the healing powers attributed to it. This verse is missing from all early Greek manuscripts and the earliest versions, including the original Vulgate. Its vocabulary is markedly non-Johannine.

---

q. [4:54] 2:11. r. [5:1] 6:4. s. [5:2] Neh 3:1, 32; 12:39. t. [5:8] Mt 9:6; Mk 2:11; Lk 5:24; Acts 3:6. u. [5:9] Mk 2:12; Lk 5:25; 9:14. v. [5:10] Ex 20:8; Jer 17:21–27; Mk 3:2; Lk 13:10 / 14:1. w. [5:13] Mt 8:18; 13:36; Mk 4:36; 7:17.

¹⁴***After this Jesus found him in the temple area and said to him,ˣ "Look, you are well; do not sin any more, so that nothing worse may happen to you." ¹⁵The man went and told the Jews that Jesus was the one who had made him well. ¹⁶Therefore, the Jews began to persecute Jesus because he did this on a sabbath.ʸ ¹⁷††But Jesus answered them,ᶻ "My Father is at work until now, so I am at work." ¹⁸For this reason the Jews tried all the more to kill him, because he not only broke the sabbath but he also called God his own father, making himself equal to God.ᵃ

The Work of the Son. ¹⁹‡‡Jesus answered and said to them, "Amen, amen, I say to you, a son cannot do anything on his own, but only what he sees his father doing;ᵇ for what he does, his son will do also. ²⁰For the Father loves his Son and shows him everything that he himself does, and he will show him greater works than these, so that you may be amazed.ᶜ ²¹For just as the Father raises the dead and gives life,§§ so also does the Son give life to whomever he wishes.ᵈ ²²Nor does the Father judge anyone, but he has given all judgment¶¶ to his Son,ᵉ ²³so that all may honor the Son just as they honor the Father. Whoever does not honor the Son does not honor the Father who sent him. ²⁴Amen, amen, I say to you, whoever hears my word and believes in the one who sent me has eternal life and will not come to condemnation, but has passed from death to life.ᶠ ²⁵Amen, amen, I say to you, the hour is coming and is now here when the dead will hear the voice of the Son of God, and those who hear will live.ᵍ ²⁶For just as the Father has life in himself, so also he gave to his Son the possession of life in himself.ʰ ²⁷And he gave him power to exercise judgment, because he is the Son of Man.ⁱ

**[5:14] While the cure of the paralytic in Mk 2:1–12 is associated with the forgiveness of sins, Jesus never drew a one-to-one connection between sin and suffering (cf. Jn 9:3; Lk 12:1–5), as did Ez 18:20.

††[5:17] Sabbath observance (Jn 5:10) was based on God's resting on the seventh day (cf. Gn 2:2–3; Ex 20:11). Philo and some rabbis insisted that God's providence remains active on the sabbath, keeping all things in existence, giving life in birth and taking it away in death. Other rabbis taught that God rested from creating, but not from judging (= ruling, governing). Jesus here claims the same authority to work as the Father, and, in the discourse that follows, the same divine prerogatives: power over life and death (Jn 5:21, 24–26) and judgment (Jn 5:22, 27).

‡‡[5:19] This proverb or parable is taken from apprenticeship in a trade: the activity of a son is modeled on that of his father. Jesus' dependence on the Father is justification for doing what the Father does.

§§[5:21] **Gives life:** in the Old Testament, a divine prerogative (Dt 32:39; 1 Sm 2:6; 2 Kgs 5:7; Tb 13:2; Is 26:19; Dn 12:2).

¶¶[5:22] **Judgment:** another divine prerogative, often expressed as acquittal or condemnation (Dt 32:36; Ps 43:1).

---

x. [5:14] 8:11; 9:2; Ez 18:20. y. [5:16] 7:23; Mt 12:8. z. [5:17] Ex 20:11. a. [5:18] 7:1, 25; 8:37, 40; 10:33, 36; 14:28; Gn 3:5–6; Wis 2:16; Mt 26:4; 2 Thes 2:4. b. [5:19] 3:34; 8:26; 12:49; 9:4; 10:30. c. [5:20] 3:35. d. [5:21] 11:25; Dt 32:39; 1 Sm 2:6; 2 Kgs 5:7; Tb 13:2; Wis 16:13; Is 26:19; Dn 7:10, 13; 12:2; Rom 4:17; 2 Cor 1:9. e. [5:22] Acts 10:42; 17:31. f. [5:24] 3:18; 8:51; 1 Jn 3:14. g. [5:25] 5:28; 8:51; 11:25–26; Eph 2:1; 5:14; Rev 3:1. h. [5:26] 1:4; 1 Jn 5:11. i. [5:27] 5:22; Dn 7:13, 22; Mt 25:31; Lk 21:36.

28*Do not be amazed at this, because the hour is coming in which all who are in the tombs will hear his voice[j] 29and will come out, those who have done good deeds to the resurrection of life, but those who have done wicked deeds to the resurrection of condemnation.[k]

30"I cannot do anything on my own; I judge as I hear, and my judgment is just, because I do not seek my own will but the will of the one who sent me.[l]

Witnesses to Jesus. 31m"If I testify on my own behalf, my testimony cannot be verified. 32But there is another[†] who testifies on my behalf, and I know that the testimony he gives on my behalf is true. 33You sent emissaries to John, and he testified to the truth.[n] 34I do not accept testimony from a human being, but I say this so that you may be saved.[o] 35He was a burning and shining lamp,[‡] and for a while you were content to rejoice in his light.[p] 36But I have testimony greater than John's. The works that the Father gave me to accomplish, these works that I perform testify on my behalf that the Father has sent me.[q] 37Moreover, the Father who sent me has testified on my behalf. But you have never heard his voice nor seen his form,[r] 38and you do not have his word remaining in you, because you do not believe in the one whom he has sent.[s] 39You search[§] the scriptures, because you think you have eternal life through them; even they testify on my behalf.[t] 40But you do not want to come to me to have life.

Unbelief of Jesus' Hearers. 41"I do not accept human praise;[¶] 42moreover, I know that you do not have the love of God in you.[u] 43I came in the name of my Father, but you do not accept me; yet if another comes in his own name, you will accept him.[v] 44How can you believe, when you accept praise from one another and do not seek the praise that comes from the only God?[w] 45Do not think that I will accuse you before the Father: the one who will accuse you is Moses, in whom you have placed your hope.[x] 46For if you had believed Moses, you would have believed

me, because he wrote about me.[y] 47But if you do not believe his writings, how will you believe my words?"

CHAPTER 6

Multiplication of the Loaves.[**] 1zAfter this, Jesus went across the Sea of Galilee [of Tiberias].[††] 2A large crowd followed him, because they saw the signs he was performing on the sick. 3Jesus went up on the mountain, and there he sat down with his disciples. 4The Jewish feast of Passover was near.[a] 5‡‡When Jesus raised his eyes and saw that a large crowd was coming to him, he said to Philip,[b] "Where can we buy enough food for them to eat?" 6§§He said this to test him, because he himself knew what he was going to do. 7Philip answered him, "Two hundred days' wages¶¶ worth of food would not be enough for each of them to have a little [bit]."[c] 8One of his disciples, Andrew, the brother of Simon Peter, said to him, 9"There is a boy here who has five barley loaves*** and two fish; but what good are these for so many?"[d] 10Jesus said, "Have the people recline." Now there was a great deal of grass††† in that place. So the men reclined, about five thousand in number.[e] 11Then Jesus took the loaves, gave thanks, and distributed them to those who were reclining, and also as much of the fish as they wanted.[f] 12When they had had their fill, he said to his disciples, "Gather the fragments left over, so that nothing will be wasted." 13So they collected them, and filled twelve wicker baskets‡‡‡ with fragments from the five barley loaves that had been more than they could eat. 14When the people saw the sign he had done, they said, "This is truly the Prophet,§§§

---

*[5:28–29] While Jn 5:19–27 present realized eschatology, Jn 5:28–29 are future eschatology; cf. Dn 12:2.

†[5:32] **Another:** likely the Father, who in four different ways gives testimony to Jesus, as indicated in the verse groupings Jn 5:33–34, 36, 37–38, 39–40.

‡[5:35] **Lamp:** cf. Ps 132:17—"I will place a lamp for my anointed (= David)," and possibly the description of Elijah in Sir 48:1. But only **for a while,** indicating the temporary and subordinate nature of John's mission.

§[5:39] **You search:** this may be an imperative: "Search the scriptures, because you think that you have eternal life through them."

¶[5:41] **Praise:** the same Greek word means "praise" or "honor" (from others) and "glory" (from God). There is a play on this in Jn 5:44.

**[6:1–15] This story of the multiplication of the loaves is the fourth sign (cf. note on Jn 5:1–47). It is the only miracle story found in all four gospels (occurring twice in Mark and Matthew). See notes on Mt 14:13–21; 15:32–39. John differs on the roles of Philip and Andrew, the proximity of Passover (Jn 6:4), and the allusion to Elisha (see Jn 6:9). The story here symbolizes the food that is really available through Jesus. It connotes a new exodus and has eucharistic overtones.

††[6:1] **[Of Tiberias]:** the awkward apposition represents a later name of the Sea of Galilee. It was probably originally a marginal gloss.

‡‡[6:5] Jesus takes the initiative (in the synoptics, the disciples do), possibly pictured as (cf. Jn 6:14) the new Moses (cf. Nm 11:13).

§§[6:6] Probably the evangelist's comment; in this gospel Jesus is never portrayed as ignorant of anything.

¶¶[6:7] **Days' wages:** literally, "denarii"; a Roman denarius is a day's wage in Mt 20:2.

***[6:9] **Barley loaves:** the food of the poor. There seems an allusion to the story of Elisha multiplying the barley bread in 2 Kgs 4:42–44.

†††[6:10] **Grass:** implies springtime, and therefore Passover. **Five thousand:** so Mk 6:39, 44 and parallels.

‡‡‡[6:13] **Baskets:** the word describes the typically Palestinian wicker basket, as in Mk 6:43 and parallels.

§§§[6:14] **The Prophet:** probably the prophet like Moses (see note on Jn 1:21). **The one who is to come into the world:** probably Elijah; cf. Mal 3:1, 23.

---

j. [5:28] 11:43. k. [5:29] Dn 12:2; Mt 16:27; 25:46; Acts 24:15; 2 Cor 5:10. l. [5:30] 6:38. m. [5:31–32] 8:13–14, 18. n. [5:33] 1:19–27; Mt 11:10–11. o. [5:34] 1 Jn 5:9. p. [5:35] 1:8; Ps 132:17; Sir 48:1. q. [5:36] 10:25. r. [5:37] 8:18; Dt 4:12, 15; 1 Jn 5:9. s. [5:38] 1 Jn 2:14. t. [5:39] 12:16; 19:28; 20:9; Lk 24:27, 44; 1 Pt 1:10. u. [5:42] 1 Jn 2:15. v. [5:43] Mt 24:5, 24. w. [5:44] 12:43. x. [5:45] Dt 31:26.

y. [5:46] 5:39; Dt 18:15; Lk 16:31; 24:44. z. [6:1–13] Mt 14:13–21; Mk 6:32–44; Lk 9:10–17. a. [6:4] 2:13; 11:55. b. [6:5] Nm 11:13. c. [6:7] Mt 20:2. d. [6:9] 2 Kgs 4:42–44. e. [6:10] Mt 14:21; Mk 6:44. f. [6:11] 21:13.

the one who is to come into the world."[g] [15]Since Jesus knew that they were going to come and carry him off to make him king, he withdrew again to the mountain alone.[h]

Walking on the Water.[*] [16]When it was evening, his disciples went down to the sea, [17]embarked in a boat, and went across the sea to Capernaum. It had already grown dark, and Jesus had not yet come to them. [18]The sea was stirred up because a strong wind was blowing. [19]When they had rowed about three or four miles, they saw Jesus walking on the sea[†] and coming near the boat, and they began to be afraid.[j] [20]But he said to them, "It is I.[‡] Do not be afraid." [21]They wanted to take him into the boat, but the boat immediately arrived at the shore to which they were heading.

The Bread of Life Discourse. [22][§]The next day, the crowd that remained across the sea saw that there had been only one boat there, and that Jesus had not gone along with his disciples in the boat, but only his disciples had left. [23][¶]Other boats came from Tiberias near the place where they had eaten the bread when the Lord gave thanks. [24]When the crowd saw that neither Jesus nor his disciples were there, they themselves got into boats and came to Capernaum looking for Jesus. [25]And when they found him across the sea they said to him, "Rabbi, when did you get here?" [26]Jesus answered them and said, "Amen, amen, I say to you, you are looking for me not because you saw signs but because you ate the loaves and were filled. [27]Do not work for food that perishes but for the food that endures for eternal life,[**] which the Son of Man will give you. For on him the Father, God, has set his seal."[k] [28]So they said to him, "What can we do to accomplish the works of God?" [29]Jesus answered and said to them, "This is the work of God, that you believe in the one he sent." [30]So they said to him, "What sign can you do, that we may see and believe in you? What can you do?[l] [31][††]Our ancestors ate manna in the desert, as it is written:[m]

---

*[6:16–21] The fifth sign is a nature miracle, portraying Jesus sharing Yahweh's power. Cf. the parallel stories following the multiplication of the loaves in Mk 6:45–52 and Mt 14:22–33.

†[6:19] **Walking on the sea**: although the Greek (cf. Jn 6:16) could mean "on the seashore" or "by the sea" (cf. Jn 21:1), the parallels, especially Mt 14:25, make clear that Jesus walked upon the water. John may allude to Jb 9:8: God "treads upon the crests of the sea."

‡[6:20] **It is I**: literally, "I am." See also notes on Jn 4:26 and Mk 6:50.

§[6:22–71] Discourse on the bread of life; replacement of the manna. Jn 6:22–34 serve as an introduction, Jn 6:35–59 constitute the discourse proper, Jn 6:60–71 portray the reaction of the disciples and Peter's confession.

¶[6:23] Possibly a later interpolation, to explain how the crowd got to Capernaum.

[6:27] **The food that endures for eternal life: cf. Jn 4:14, on water "springing up to eternal life."

††[6:31] **Bread from heaven**: cf. Ex 16:4, 15, 32–34 and the notes there; Ps 78:24. The manna, thought to have been

g. [6:14] Dt 18:15, 18; Mal 3:1, 23; Acts 3:22.   h. [6:15] 18:36.   i. [6:16–21] Mt 14:22–27; Mk 6:45–52.   j. [6:19] Jb 9:8; Ps 29:3–4; 77:20; Is 43:16.   k. [6:27] 6:50, 51, 54, 58.   l. [6:30] Mt 16:1–4; Lk 11:29–30.   m. [6:31] Ex 16:4–5; Nm 11:7–9; Ps 78:24.

'He gave them bread from heaven to eat.'"

[32]So Jesus said to them, "Amen, amen, I say to you, it was not Moses who gave the bread from heaven; my Father gives you the true bread from heaven.[n] [33]For the bread of God is that which comes down from heaven and gives life to the world."

[34]So they said to him, "Sir, give us this bread always." [35][‡‡]Jesus said to them, "I am the bread of life; whoever comes to me will never hunger, and whoever believes in me will never thirst.[p] [36]But I told you that although you have seen [me], you do not believe.[q] [37]Everything that the Father gives me will come to me, and I will not reject anyone who comes to me, [38]because I came down from heaven not to do my own will but the will of the one who sent me.[r] [39]And this is the will of the one who sent me, that I should not lose anything of what he gave me, but that I should raise it [on] the last day.[s] [40]For this is the will of my Father, that everyone who sees the Son and believes in him may have eternal life, and I shall raise him [on] the last day."[t]

[41]The Jews murmured about him because he said, "I am the bread that came down from heaven," [42]and they said, "Is this not Jesus, the son of Joseph? Do we not know his father and mother? Then how can he say, 'I have come down from heaven'?"[u] [43]Jesus answered and said to them, "Stop murmuring[§§] among yourselves.[v] [44]No one can come to me unless the Father who sent me draw him, and I will raise him on the last day. [45]It is written in the prophets:

'They shall all be taught by God.'

Everyone who listens to my Father and learns from him comes to me.[w] [46]Not that anyone has seen the Father except the one who is from God; he has seen the Father.[x] [47]Amen, amen, I say to you, whoever believes has eternal life. [48]I am the bread of life. [49]Your ancestors ate the manna in the desert, but they died;[y] [50]this is the bread that comes down from heaven so that one may eat it and not die. [51]I am the living bread that came down from heaven; whoever eats this bread will live forever; and the bread that I will give is my flesh for the life of the world."[z]

[52]The Jews quarreled among themselves, saying, "How can this man give us [his] flesh

---

hidden by Jeremiah (2 Mc 2:5–8), was expected to reappear miraculously at Passover, in the last days.

‡‡[6:35–59] Up to Jn 6:50 "bread of life" is a figure for God's revelation in Jesus; in Jn 6:51–58, the eucharistic theme comes to the fore. There may thus be a break between Jn 6:50–51.

§§[6:43] **Murmuring**: the word may reflect the Greek of Ex 16:2, 7–8.

n. [6:32] Mt 6:11.   o. [6:34] 4:15.   p. [6:35] Is 55:1–3; Am 8:11–13.   q. [6:36] 20:29.   r. [6:38] 4:34; Mt 26:39; Heb 10:9.   s. [6:39] 10:28–29; 17:12; 18:9.   t. [6:40] 1 Jn 2:25.   u. [6:42] Mt 13:54–57; Mk 6:1–4; Lk 4:22.   v. [6:43] Ex 16:2, 7, 8; Lk 4:22.   .w. [6:45] Is 54:13; Jer 31:33–34.   x. [6:46] 1:18; 7:29; Ex 33:20.   y. [6:49] 1 Cor 10:3, 5.   z. [6:51] Mt 26:26–27; Lk 22:19.

to eat?" [53]Jesus said to them, "Amen, amen, I say to you, unless you eat the flesh of the Son of Man and drink his blood, you do not have life within you. [54]Whoever eats* my flesh and drinks my blood has eternal life, and I will raise him on the last day. [55]For my flesh is true food, and my blood is true drink. [56]Whoever eats my flesh and drinks my blood remains in me and I in him. [57]Just as the living Father sent me and I have life because of the Father, so also the one who feeds on me will have life because of me.[a] [58]This is the bread that came down from heaven. Unlike your ancestors who ate and still died, whoever eats this bread will live forever." [59]These things he said while teaching in the synagogue in Capernaum.

The Words of Eternal Life.[†] [60]Then many of his disciples who were listening said, "This saying is hard; who can accept it?" [61]Since Jesus knew that his disciples were murmuring about this, he said to them, "Does this shock you? [62]What if you were to see the Son of Man ascending to where he was before?[‡] [63]It is the spirit that gives life, while the flesh[§] is of no avail. The words I have spoken to you are spirit and life. [64]But there are some of you who do not believe." Jesus knew from the beginning the ones who would not believe and the one who would betray him.[b] [65]And he said, "For this reason I have told you that no one can come to me unless it is granted him by my Father."

[66]As a result of this, many [of] his disciples returned to their former way of life and no longer accompanied him. [67]Jesus then said to the Twelve, "Do you also want to leave?" [68]Simon Peter answered him, "Master, to whom shall we go? You have the words of eternal life. [69]We have come to believe and are convinced that you are the Holy One of God."[c] [70]Jesus answered them, "Did I not choose you twelve? Yet is not one of you a devil?" [71]He was referring to Judas, son of Simon the Iscariot; it was he who would betray him, one of the Twelve.[d]

---

*[6:54–58] **Eats**: the verb used in these verses is not the classical Greek verb used of human eating, but that of animal eating: "munch," "gnaw." This may be part of John's emphasis on the reality of the flesh and blood of Jesus (cf. Jn 6:55), but the same verb eventually became the ordinary verb in Greek meaning "eat."

†[6:60–71] These verses refer more to themes of Jn 6:35–50 than to those of Jn 6:51–58 and seem to be addressed to members of the Johannine community who found it difficult to accept the high christology reflected in the bread of life discourse.

‡[6:62] This unfinished conditional sentence is obscure. Probably there is a reference to Jn 6:49–51. Jesus claims to be **the bread that comes down from heaven** (Jn 6:50); this claim provokes incredulity (Jn 6:60); and so Jesus is pictured as asking what his disciples will say when he goes up to heaven.

§[6:63] **Spirit . . . flesh**: probably not a reference to the eucharistic body of Jesus but to the supernatural and the natural, as in Jn 3:6. **Spirit and life**: all Jesus said about the bread of life is the revelation of the Spirit.

a. [6:57] 5:26. b. [6:64] 13:11. c. [6:69] 11:27; Mt 16:16; Mk 1:24; Lk 4:34. d. [6:71] 12:4; 13:2, 27.

CHAPTER 7

The Feast of Tabernacles. [1¶]After this, Jesus moved about within Galilee; but he did not wish to travel in Judea, because the Jews were trying to kill him.[e] [2]But the Jewish feast of Tabernacles was near.[f] [3]So his brothers** said to him, "Leave here and go to Judea, so that your disciples also may see the works you are doing. [4]No one works in secret if he wants to be known publicly. If you do these things, manifest yourself to the world."[g] [5]For his brothers did not believe in him. [6††]So Jesus said to them, "My time is not yet here, but the time is always right for you. [7]The world cannot hate you, but it hates me, because I testify to it that its works are evil.[h] [8]You go up to the feast. I am not going up[‡‡] to this feast, because my time has not yet been fulfilled." [9]After he had said this, he stayed on in Galilee.

[10]But when his brothers had gone up to the feast, he himself also went up, not openly but [as it were] in secret. [11]The Jews were looking for him at the feast and saying, "Where is he?" [12]And there was considerable murmuring about him in the crowds. Some said, "He is a good man," [while] others said, "No; on the contrary, he misleads the crowd." [13]Still, no one spoke openly about him because they were afraid of the Jews.[i] **The First Dialogue.**[§§] [14]When the feast was already half over, Jesus went up into the temple area and began to teach. [15¶¶]The Jews were amazed and said, "How does he know scripture without having studied?" [16]Jesus answered them and said, "My teaching is not my own but is from

---

¶[7–8] These chapters contain events about the feast of Tabernacles (Sukkoth, Ingathering: Ex 23:16; Tents, Booths: Dt 16:13–16), with its symbols of booths (originally built to shelter harvesters), rain (water from Siloam poured on the temple altar), and lights (illumination of the four torches in the Court of the Women). They continue the theme of the replacement of feasts (Passover, Jn 2:13; 6:4; Hanukkah, Jn 10:22; Pentecost, Jn 5:1), here accomplished by Jesus as the Living Water. These chapters comprise seven miscellaneous controversies and dialogues. There is a literary inclusion with Jesus in hiding in Jn 7:4, 10; 8:59. There are frequent references to attempts on his life: Jn 7:1, 13, 19, 25, 30, 32, 44; 8:37, 40, 59.

[7:3] **Brothers: these relatives (cf. Jn 2:12 and see note on Mk 6:3) are never portrayed as disciples until after the resurrection (Acts 1:14). Mt 13:55 and Mk 6:3 give the names of four of them. Jesus has already performed works/signs in Judea; cf. Jn 2:23; 3:2; 4:45; 5:8.

††[7:6] **Time**: the Greek word means "opportune time," here a synonym for Jesus' "hour" (see note on Jn 2:4), his death and resurrection. In the wordplay, any time is suitable for Jesus' brothers, because they are not dependent on God's will.

‡‡[7:8] **I am not going up**: an early attested reading "not yet" seems a correction, since Jesus in the story does go up to the feast. "Go up," in a play on words, refers not only to going up to Jerusalem but also to exaltation at the cross, resurrection, and ascension; cf. Jn 3:14; 6:62; 20:17.

§§[7:14–31] Jesus teaches in the temple; debate with the Jews.

¶¶[7:15] **Without having studied**: literally, "How does he know letters without having learned?" Children were taught to read and write by means of the scriptures. But here more than Jesus' literacy is being discussed; the people are wondering how he can teach like a rabbi. Rabbis were trained by other rabbis and traditionally quoted their teachers.

e. [7:1] 5:18; 8:37, 40. f. [7:2] Ex 23:16; Lv 23:34; Nm 29:12; Dt 16:13–16; Zec 14:16–19. g. [7:4] 14:22. h. [7:7] 15:18. i. [7:13] 9:22; 19:38; 20:19. j. [7:15] Lk 2:47.

the one who sent me. [17]Whoever chooses to do his will[*] shall know whether my teaching is from God or whether I speak on my own.[k] [18]Whoever speaks on his own seeks his own glory, but whoever seeks the glory of the one who sent him is truthful, and there is no wrong in him. [19]Did not Moses give you the law? Yet none of you keeps the law. Why are you trying to kill me?"[l] [20]The crowd answered, "You are possessed![†] Who is trying to kill you?"[m] [21]Jesus answered and said to them, "I performed one work[‡] and all of you are amazed[n] [22]because of it. Moses gave you circumcision—not that it came from Moses but rather from the patriarchs—and you circumcise a man on the sabbath.[o] [23]If a man can receive circumcision on a sabbath so that the law of Moses may not be broken, are you angry with me because I made a whole person well on a sabbath?[p] [24]Stop judging by appearances, but judge justly."[q]

[25]So some of the inhabitants of Jerusalem said, "Is he not the one they are trying to kill? [26]And look, he is speaking openly and they say nothing to him. Could the authorities[§] have realized that he is the Messiah? [27]But we know where he is from. When the Messiah comes, no one will know where he is from."[r] [28]So Jesus cried out in the temple area as he was teaching and said, "You know me and also know where I am from. Yet I did not come on my own, but the one who sent me, whom you do not know, is true.[s] [29]I know him, because I am from him, and he sent me."[t] [30]So they tried to arrest him, but no one laid a hand upon him, because his hour had not yet come.[u] [31]But many of the crowd began to believe in him, and said, "When the Messiah comes, will he perform more signs than this man has done?"[v]

Officers Sent to Arrest Jesus.[5] [32]The Pharisees heard the crowd murmuring about him to this effect, and the chief priests and the Pharisees sent guards to arrest him. [33]So Jesus said, "I will be with you only a little while longer, and then I will go to the one who sent me.[w] [34]You will look for me but not find [me], and where I am you cannot come."[x] [35]So the Jews said to one another,

"Where is he going that we will not find him? Surely he is not going to the dispersion[**] among the Greeks to teach the Greeks, is he? [36]What is the meaning of his saying, 'You will look for me and not find [me], and where I am you cannot come'?"

Rivers of Living Water.[††] [37]On the last and greatest day of the feast, Jesus stood up and exclaimed, "Let anyone who thirsts come to me and drink.[y] [38]Whoever believes in me, as scripture says:

'Rivers of living water[‡‡] will flow from
within him.'"[z]

[39]He said this in reference to the Spirit that those who came to believe in him were to receive. There was, of course, no Spirit yet,[§§] because Jesus had not yet been glorified.[a]

Discussion About the Origins of the Messiah.[¶¶] [40]Some in the crowd who heard these words said, "This is truly the Prophet."[b] [41]Others said, "This is the Messiah." But others said, "The Messiah will not come from Galilee, will he? [42]Does not scripture say that the Messiah will be of David's family and come from Bethlehem, the village where David lived?"[c] [43]So a division occurred in the crowd because of him. [44]Some of them even wanted to arrest him, but no one laid hands on him.

[45]So the guards went to the chief priests and Pharisees, who asked them, "Why did you not bring him?" [46]The guards answered, "Never before has anyone spoken like this one." [47]So the Pharisees answered them, "Have you also been deceived? [48]Have any of the authorities or the Pharisees believed in him?[d] [49]But this crowd, which does not know the law, is accursed." [50]Nicodemus, one of their members who had come to him earlier, said to them,[e] [51]"Does our law condemn a person before it first hears him and finds out what he is doing?"[f] [52]They answered and said to him, "You are not from Galilee also, are you? Look and see that no prophet arises from Galilee."

---

* [7:17] **To do his will**: presumably a reference back to the "work" of Jn 6:29: belief in the one whom God has sent.

† [7:20] **You are possessed**: literally, "You have a demon." The insane were thought to be possessed by a demoniacal spirit.

‡ [7:21] **One work**: the cure of the paralytic (Jn 5:1–9) because of the reference to the sabbath (Jn 7:22; 5:9–10).

§ [7:26] **The authorities**: the members of the Sanhedrin (same term as Jn 3:1).

¶ [7:32–36] Jesus announces his approaching departure (cf. also Jn 8:21; 12:36; 13:33) and complete control over his destiny.

** [7:35] **Dispersion**: or "diaspora": Jews living outside Palestine. **Greeks**: probably refers to the Gentiles in the Mediterranean area; cf. Jn 12:20.

†† [7:37, 39] Promise of living water through the Spirit.

‡‡ [7:38] **Living water**: not an exact quotation from any Old Testament passage; in the gospel context the gift of the Spirit is meant; cf. Jn 3:5. **From within him**: either Jesus or the believer; if Jesus, it continues the Jesus-Moses motif (water from the rock, Ex 17:6; Nm 20:11) as well as Jesus as the new temple (cf. Ez 47:1). Grammatically, it goes better with the believer.

§§ [7:39] **No Spirit yet**: Codex Vaticanus and early Latin, Syriac, and Coptic versions add "given." In this gospel, the sending of the Spirit cannot take place until Jesus' glorification through his death, resurrection, and ascension; cf. Jn 20:22.

¶¶ [7:40–53] Discussion of the Davidic lineage of the Messiah.

---

k. [7:17] 6:29. l. [7:19] Acts 7:53. m. [7:20] 8:48–49; 10:20. n. [7:21] 5:1–9. o. [7:22] Gn 17:10; Lv 12:3. p. [7:23] 5:2–9, 16; Mt 12:11–12; Lk 14:5. q. [7:24] 8:15; Lv 19:15; Is 11:3–4. r. [7:27] Heb 7:3. s. [7:28] 8:19. t. [7:29] 6:46; 8:55. u. [7:30] 7:44; 8:20; Lk 4:29–30. v. [7:31] 2:11; 10:42; 11:45. w. [7:33] 13:33; 16:16. x. [7:34] 8:21; 12:36; 13:33, 36; 16:5; Dt 4:29; Prv 1:28; Is 55:6; Hos 5:6.

y. [7:37] Rev 21:6. z. [7:38] 4:10, 14; 19:34; Is 12:3; Ez 47:1. a. [7:39] 16:7. b. [7:40] Dt 18:15, 18. c. [7:42] 2 Sm 7:12–14; Ps 89:3–4; 132:11; Mi 5:1; Mt 2:5–6. d. [7:48] 12:42. e. [7:50] 3:1; 19:39. f. [7:51] Dt 1:16–17.

CHAPTER 8

A Woman Caught in Adultery.[*] [7:53]Then each went to his own house, [1]while Jesus went to the Mount of Olives.[†g] [2]But early in the morning he arrived again in the temple area, and all the people started coming to him, and he sat down and taught them. [3]Then the scribes and the Pharisees brought a woman who had been caught in adultery and made her stand in the middle. [4]They said to him, "Teacher, this woman was caught in the very act of committing adultery. [5]Now in the law, Moses commanded us to stone such women.[‡] So what do you say?"[h] [6]They said this to test him, so that they could have some charge to bring against him. Jesus bent down and began to write on the ground with his finger.[§] [7]But when they continued asking him, he straightened up and said to them,[i] "Let the one among you who is without sin be the first to throw a stone at her." [8]Again he bent down and wrote on the ground. [9]And in response, they went away one by one, beginning with the elders. So he was left alone with the woman before him. [10]Then Jesus straightened up and said to her, "Woman, where are they? Has no one condemned you?"[j] [11]She replied, "No one, sir." Then Jesus said, "Neither do I condemn you. Go, [and] from now on do not sin any more."][k]

The Light of the World.[**] [12]Jesus spoke to them again, saying, "I am the light of the world. Whoever follows me will not walk in darkness, but will have the light of life."[l] [13]So the Pharisees said to him, "You testify on your own behalf, so your testimony cannot be verified." [14]Jesus answered and said to them, "Even if I do testify on my own behalf, my testimony can be verified,[††] because I know where I came from and where I am going.

But you do not know where I come from or where I am going.[m] [15]You judge by appearances,[‡‡] but I do not judge anyone.[n] [16]And even if I should judge, my judgment is valid, because I am not alone, but it is I and the Father who sent me.[o] [17]Even in your law[§§] it is written that the testimony of two men can be verified.[p] [18]I testify on my behalf and so does the Father who sent me."[q] [19]So they said to him, "Where is your father?" Jesus answered, "You know neither me nor my Father. If you knew me, you would know my Father also."[r] [20]He spoke these words while teaching in the treasury in the temple area. But no one arrested him, because his hour had not yet come.[s]

Jesus, the Father's Ambassador.[¶¶] [21]He said to them again, "I am going away and you will look for me, but you will die in your sin.[***] Where I am going you cannot come."[t] [22][†††]So the Jews said, "He is not going to kill himself, is he, because he said, 'Where I am going you cannot come'?" [23]He said to them, "You belong to what is below, I belong to what is above. You belong to this world, but I do not belong to this world.[u] [24]That is why I told you that you will die in your sins. For if you do not believe that I AM,[‡‡‡] you will die in your sins."[v] [25][§§§]So they said to him, "Who are you?"[w] Jesus said to them, "What I told you from the beginning. [26]I have much to say about you in condemnation. But the one who sent me is true, and what I heard from him I tell the world."[x] [27]They did not realize that he was speaking to them of the Father. [28]So Jesus said [to them], "When you lift up the Son of Man, then you will realize that I AM, and that I do nothing on my own, but I say only what the Father taught me.[y] [29]The one who sent me is with me. He has not left me alone, because I always do what is pleasing to

---

*[7:53–8:11] The story of the woman caught in adultery is a later insertion here, missing from all early Greek manuscripts. A Western text-type insertion, attested mainly in Old Latin translations, it is found in different places in different manuscripts: here, or after Jn 7:36 or at the end of this gospel, or after Lk 21:38, or at the end of that gospel. There are many non-Johannine features in the language, and there are also many doubtful readings within the passage. The style and motifs are similar to those of Luke, and it fits better with the general situation at the end of Lk 21, but it was probably inserted here because of the allusion to Jer 17:13 (cf. note on Jn 8:6) and the statement, "I do not judge anyone," in Jn 8:15. The Catholic Church accepts this passage as canonical scripture.

†[8:1] **Mount of Olives:** not mentioned elsewhere in gospel tradition outside of passion week.

‡[8:5] Lv 20:10 and Dt 22:22 mention only death, but Dt 22:23–24 prescribes stoning for a betrothed virgin.

§[8:6] Cf. Jer 17:13 (RSV): "Those who turn away from thee shall be written in the earth, for they have forsaken the LORD, the fountain of living water"; cf. Jn 7:38.

¶[8:7] The first stones were to be thrown by the witnesses (Dt 17:7).

**[8:12–20] Jesus the light of the world. Jesus replaces the four torches of the illumination of the temple as the light of joy.

††[8:14] **My testimony can be verified:** this seems to contradict Jn 5:31, but the emphasis here is on Jesus' origin from the Father and his divine destiny. **Where I am going:** indicates Jesus' passion and glorification.

‡‡[8:15] **By appearances:** literally, "according to the flesh." **I do not judge anyone:** superficial contradiction of Jn 5:22, 27, 30; here the emphasis is that the judgment is not by material standards.

§§[8:17] **Your law:** a reflection of later controversy between church and synagogue.

¶¶[8:21–30] He whose ambassador I am is with me. Jesus' origin is from God; he can reveal God.

***[8:21] **You will die in your sin:** i.e., of disbelief; cf. Jn 8:24. **Where I am going you cannot come:** except through faith in Jesus' passion-resurrection.

†††[8:22] The Jews suspect that he is referring to his death. Johannine irony is apparent here; Jesus' death will not be self-inflicted but destined by God.

‡‡‡[8:24, 28] **I AM:** an expression that late Jewish tradition understood as Yahweh's own self-designation (Is 43:10); see note on Jn 4:26. Jesus is here placed on a par with Yahweh.

§§§[8:25] **What I told you from the beginning:** this verse seems textually corrupt, with several other possible translations: "(I am) what I say to you"; "Why do I speak to you at all?" The earliest attested reading (Bodmer Papyrus P⁶⁶) has (in a second hand), "I told you at the beginning what I also telling you (now)." The answer here (cf. Prv 8:22) seems to hinge on a misunderstanding of Jn 8:24 "that I AM" as "*what* I am."

---

g. [8:1–2] Lk 21:37–38. h. [8:5] Lv 20:10; Dt 22:22–29. i. [8:7] Dt 17:7. j. [8:10] Ez 33:11. k. [8:11] 5:14. l. [8:12] 1:4–5, 9; 12:46; Ex 13:22; Is 42:6; Zec 14:8.

m. [8:14] 5:31. n. [8:15] 12:47; 1 Sm 16:7. o. [8:16] 5:30. p. [8:17] Dt 17:6; 19:15; Nm 35:30. q. [8:18] 5:23, 37. r. [8:19] 7:28; 14:7; 15:21. s. [8:20] 7:30. t. [8:21] 7:34; 13:33. u. [8:23] 3:31; 17:14; 18:36. v. [8:24] Ex 3:14; Dt 32:39; Is 43:10. w. [8:25] 10:24. x. [8:26] 12:44–50. y. [8:28] 3:14; 12:32, 34.

him." ³⁰Because he spoke this way, many came to believe in him.

Jesus and Abraham.˙ ³¹Jesus then said to those Jews who believed in him,† "If you remain in my word, you will truly be my disciples, ³²and you will know the truth, and the truth will set you free."ᶻ ³³They answered him, "We are descendants of Abraham and have never been enslaved to anyone.‡ How can you say, 'You will become free'?"ᵃ ³⁴Jesus answered them, "Amen, amen, I say to you, everyone who commits sin is a slave of sin.ᵇ ³⁵A slave does not remain in a household forever, but a son§ always remains.ᶜ ³⁶So if a son frees you, then you will truly be free. ³⁷I know that you are descendants of Abraham. But you are trying to kill me, because my word has no room among you. ³⁸˹I tell you what I have seen in the Father's presence; then do what you have heard from the Father."

³⁹˹˹They answered and said to him, "Our father is Abraham." Jesus said to them,ᵈ "If you were Abraham's children, you would be doing the works of Abraham. ⁴⁰But now you are trying to kill me, a man who has told you the truth that I heard from God; Abraham did not do this. ⁴¹You are doing the works of your father!" [So] they said to him, "We are not illegitimate. We have one Father, God."ᵉ ⁴²Jesus said to them, "If God were your Father, you would love me, for I came from God and am here; I did not come on my own, but he sent me.ᶠ ⁴³Why do you not understand what I am saying? Because you cannot bear to hear my word. ⁴⁴You belong to your father the devil and you willingly carry out your father's desires. He was a murderer from the beginning and does not stand in truth, because there is no truth in him. When he tells a lie, he speaks in character, because he is a liar and the father of lies.ᵍ ⁴⁵But because I speak the truth, you do not believe me. ⁴⁶Can any of you charge me with sin? If I am telling the truth, why do you not believe me?ʰ ⁴⁷Whoever belongs to God

hears the words of God; for this reason you do not listen, because you do not belong to God."ⁱ

⁴⁸The Jews answered and said to him, "Are we not right in saying that you are a Samaritan†† and are possessed?" ⁴⁹Jesus answered, "I am not possessed; I honor my Father, but you dishonor me. ⁵⁰I do not seek my own glory; there is one who seeks it and he is the one who judges.ʲ ⁵¹Amen, amen, I say to you, whoever keeps my word will never see death."ᵏ ⁵²[So] the Jews said to him, "Now we are sure that you are possessed. Abraham died, as did the prophets, yet you say, 'Whoever keeps my word will never taste death.' ⁵³Are you greater than our father Abraham,‡‡ who died? Or the prophets, who died? Who do you make yourself out to be?"ˡ ⁵⁴Jesus answered, "If I glorify myself, my glory is worth nothing; but it is my Father who glorifies me, of whom you say, 'He is our God.' ⁵⁵You do not know him, but I know him. And if I should say that I do not know him, I would be like you a liar. But I do know him and I keep his word.ᵐ ⁵⁶Abraham your father rejoiced to see my day; he saw it§§ and was glad.ⁿ ⁵⁷So the Jews said to him, "You are not yet fifty years old and you have seen Abraham?"¶¶ ⁵⁸˹˹Jesus said to them,ᵒ "Amen, amen, I say to you, before Abraham came to be, I AM." ⁵⁹So they picked up stones to throw at him; but Jesus hid and went out of the temple area.ᵖ

CHAPTER 9
The Man Born Blind. ¹†††As he passed by he saw a man blind from birth.�q ²‡‡‡His disciples asked him,ʳ "Rabbi, who sinned, this man or his parents, that he was born blind?" ³Jesus answered, "Neither he nor his parents sinned; it is so that the works of God might be made visible through him.ˢ ⁴We have to do the works of the one who

---

*[8:31–59] Jesus' origin ("before Abraham") and destiny are developed; the truth will free them from sin (Jn 8:34) and death (Jn 8:51).

†[8:31] Those Jews who believed in him: a rough editorial suture, since in Jn 8:37 they are described as trying to kill Jesus.

‡[8:33] Have never been enslaved to anyone: since, historically, the Jews were enslaved almost continuously, this verse is probably Johannine irony, about slavery to sin.

§[8:35] A slave . . . a son: an allusion to Ishmael and Isaac (Gn 16; 21), or to the release of a slave after six years (Ex 21:2; Dt 15:12).

¶[8:38] The Father: i.e., God. It is also possible, however, to understand the second part of the verse as a sarcastic reference to descent of the Jews from the devil (Jn 8:44), "You do what you have heard from [your] father."

**[8:39] The works of Abraham: Abraham believed; cf. Rom 4:11–17; Jas 2:21–23.

††[8:48] Samaritan: therefore interested in magical powers; cf. Acts 7:14–24.

‡‡[8:53] Are you greater than our father Abraham?: cf. Jn 4:12.

§§[8:56] He saw it: this seems a reference to the birth of Isaac (Gn 17:7; 21:6), the beginning of the fulfillment of promises about Abraham's seed.

¶¶[8:57] The evidence of the third-century Bodmer Papyrus P⁷⁵ and the first hand of Codex Sinaiticus indicates that the text originally read: "How can Abraham have seen you?"

***[8:58] Came to be, I AM: the Greek word used for "came to be" is the one used of all creation in the prologue, while the word used for "am" is the one reserved for the Logos.

†††[9:1–10:21] Sabbath healing of the man born blind. This sixth sign is introduced to illustrate the saying, "I am the light of the world" (Jn 8:12; 9:5). The narrative of conflict about Jesus contrasts Jesus (light) with the Jews (blindness, Jn 9:39–41). The theme of water is reintroduced in the reference to the pool of Siloam. Ironically, Jesus is being judged by the Jews, yet the Jews are judged by the Light of the world; cf. Jn 3:19–21.

‡‡‡[9:2] See note on Jn 5:14, and Ex 20:5, that parents' sins were visited upon their children. Jesus denies such a cause and emphasizes the purpose: the infirmity was providential.

---

z. [8:32] Is 42:7; Gal 4:31. a. [8:33] Mt 3:9. b. [8:34] Rom 6:16–17. c. [8:35] Gn 21:10; Gal 4:30; Heb 3:5–6. d. [8:39] Gn 26:5; Rom 4:11–17; Jas 2:21–23. e. [8:41] Mal 2:10. f. [8:42] 1 Jn 5:1. g. [8:44] Gn 3:4; Wis 1:13; 2:24; Acts 13:10; 1 Jn 3:8–15. h. [8:46] Heb 4:15; 1 Pt 2:22; 1 Jn 3:5.

i. [8:47] 10:26; 1 Jn 4:6. j. [8:50] 7:18. k. [8:51] 5:24–29; 6:40, 47; 11:25–26. l. [8:53] 4:12. m. [8:55] 7:28–29. n. [8:56] Gn 17:17; Mt 13:17; Lk 17:22. o. [8:58] 1:30; 17:5. p. [8:59] 10:31, 39; 11:8; Lk 4:29–30. q. [9:1–2] Is 42:7. r. [9:2] Ex 20:5; Ez 18:20; Lk 13:2. s. [9:3] 5:14; 11:4.

sent me while it is day. Night is coming when no one can work.[t] [5]While I am in the world, I am the light of the world."[u] [6]When he had said this, he spat on the ground and made clay with the saliva, and smeared the clay on his eyes,[v] [7]and said to him, "Go wash* in the Pool of Siloam" (which means Sent). So he went and washed, and came back able to see.[w]

[8]His neighbors and those who had seen him earlier as a beggar said, "Isn't this the one who used to sit and beg?" [9]Some said, "It is," but others said, "No, he just looks like him." He said, "I am." [10]So they said to him, "[So] how were your eyes opened?" [11]He replied, "The man called Jesus made clay and anointed my eyes and told me, 'Go to Siloam and wash.' So I went there and washed and was able to see." [12]And they said to him, "Where is he?" He said, "I don't know."

[13]They brought the one who was once blind to the Pharisees. [14]Now Jesus had made clay[†] and opened his eyes on a sabbath.[x] [15]So then the Pharisees also asked him how he was able to see. He said to them, "He put clay on my eyes, and I washed, and now I can see." [16]So some of the Pharisees said, "This man is not from God, because he does not keep the sabbath." [But] others said, "How can a sinful man do such signs?" And there was a division among them.[y] [17]So they said to the blind man again, "What do you have to say about him, since he opened your eyes?" He said, "He is a prophet."[z]

[18]Now the Jews did not believe that he had been blind and gained his sight until they summoned the parents of the one who had gained his sight. [19]They asked them, "Is this your son, who you say was born blind? How does he now see?" [20]His parents answered and said, "We know that this is our son and that he was born blind. [21]We do not know how he sees now, nor do we know who opened his eyes. Ask him, he is of age; he can speak for himself." [22]‡[a]His parents said this because they were afraid of the Jews, for the Jews had already agreed that if anyone acknowledged him as the Messiah, he would be expelled from the synagogue. [23]For this reason his parents said, "He is of age; question him."[b]

[24]So a second time they called the man who had been blind and said to him, "Give God the praise![§] We know that this man is a sinner."[c] [25]He replied, "If he is a sinner, I do not know. One thing I do know is that I was blind and now I see." [26]So they said to him, "What did he do to you? How did he open your eyes?" [27]He answered them, "I told you already and you did not listen. Why do you want to hear it again? Do you want to become his disciples, too?" [28]They ridiculed him and said, "You are that man's disciple; we are disciples of Moses! [29]We know that God spoke to Moses, but we do not know where this one is from."[d] [30]The man answered and said to them, "This is what is so amazing, that you do not know where he is from, yet he opened my eyes. [31]We know that God does not listen to sinners, but if one is devout and does his will, he listens to him.[e] [32]¶It is unheard of that anyone ever opened the eyes of a person born blind. [33]If this man were not from God, he would not be able to do anything."[f] [34]They answered and said to him, "You were born totally in sin, and are you trying to teach us?" Then they threw him out.

[35]When Jesus heard that they had thrown him out, he found him and said, "Do you believe in the Son of Man?" [36]He answered and said, "Who is he, sir, that I may believe in him?" [37]Jesus said to him, "You have seen him and the one speaking with you is he."[g] [38]He said, "I do believe, Lord," and he worshiped him. [39]**Then Jesus said, "I came into this world for judgment, so that those who do not see might see, and those who do see might become blind."[h]

[40]Some of the Pharisees who were with him heard this and said to him, "Surely we are not also blind, are we?"[i] [41]Jesus said to them, "If you were blind, you would have no sin; but now you are saying, 'We see,' so your sin remains.[j]

CHAPTER 10

The Good Shepherd. [1]††"Amen, amen, I say to you,[k] whoever does not enter a sheepfold[‡‡] through the gate but climbs over elsewhere is a thief and a robber. [2]But whoever enters through the gate is the shepherd of the sheep. [3]The gatekeeper opens it for him, and the sheep hear his

§[9:24] **Give God the praise!:** an Old Testament formula of adjuration to tell the truth; cf. Jos 7:19; 1 Sm 6:5 LXX. Cf. Jn 5:41.

¶[9:32] **A person born blind:** the only Old Testament cure from blindness is found in Tobit (cf. Tb 7:7; 11:7–13; 14:1–2), but Tobit was not born blind.

**[9:39–41] These verses spell out the symbolic meaning of the cure; the Pharisees are not the innocent blind, willing to accept the testimony of others.

††[10:1–21] The good shepherd discourse continues the theme of attack on the Pharisees that ends Jn 9. The figure is allegorical: the hired hands are the Pharisees who excommunicated the cured blind man. It serves as a commentary on Jn 9. For the shepherd motif, used of Yahweh in the Old Testament, cf. Ex 34; Gn 48:15; 49:24; Mi 7:14; Ps 23:1–4; 80:1.

‡‡[10:1] **Sheepfold:** a low stone wall open to the sky.

*[9:7] **Go wash:** perhaps a test of faith; cf. 2 Kgs 5:10–14. The water tunnel Siloam (= Sent) is used as a symbol of Jesus, sent by his Father.

†[9:14] In using spittle, kneading clay, and healing, Jesus had broken the sabbath rules laid down by Jewish tradition.

‡[9:22] This comment of the evangelist (in terms used again in Jn 12:42; 16:2) envisages a situation after Jesus' ministry. Rejection/excommunication from the synagogue of Jews who confessed Jesus as Messiah seems to have begun ca. A.D. 85, when the curse against the *minîm* or heretics was introduced into the "Eighteen Benedictions."

t. [9:4] 11:9–10; 12:35–36.   u. [9:5] 8:12.   v. [9:6] 5:11; Mk 7:33; 8:23.   w. [9:7] 2 Kgs 5:10–14.   x. [9:14] 5:9.   y. [9:16] 3:2; Mt 12:10–11; Lk 13:10–11; 14:1–4.   z. [9:17] 4:19.   a. [9:22] 7:13; 12:42; 16:2; 19:38.   b. [9:23] 12:42.

c. [9:24] Jos 7:19; 1 Sm 6:5 LXX.   d. [9:29] Ex 33:11.   e. [9:31] 10:21; Ps 34:16; 66:18; Prv 15:29; Is 1:15.   f. [9:33] 3:2.   g. [9:37] 4:26; Dn 7:13.   h. [9:39] Mt 13:33–35.   i. [9:40] Mt 15:14; 23:26; Rom 2:19.   j. [9:41] 15:22.   k. [10:1–5] Gn 48:15; 49:24; Ps 23:1–4; 80:2; Jer 23:1–4; Ez 34:1–31; Mi 7:14.

voice, as he calls his own sheep by name and leads them out. [4]*When he has driven out all his own, he walks ahead of them, and the sheep follow him,[l] because they recognize his voice. [5]But they will not follow a stranger; they will run away from him, because they do not recognize the voice of strangers." [6]Although Jesus used this figure of speech,[†] they did not realize what he was trying to tell them.

[7]†So Jesus said again, "Amen, amen, I say to you, I am the gate for the sheep. [8]§All who came [before me] are thieves and robbers, but the sheep did not listen to them. [9]I am the gate. Whoever enters through me will be saved, and will come in and go out and find pasture. [10]A thief comes only to steal and slaughter and destroy; I came so that they might have life and have it more abundantly. [11]I am the good shepherd. A good shepherd lays down his life for the sheep.[m] [12]A hired man, who is not a shepherd and whose sheep are not his own, sees a wolf coming and leaves the sheep and runs away, and the wolf catches and scatters them.[n] [13]This is because he works for pay and has no concern for the sheep. [14]I am the good shepherd, and I know mine and mine know me, [15]just as the Father knows me and I know the Father; and I will lay down my life for the sheep.[o] [16]I have other sheep[s] that do not belong to this fold. These also I must lead, and they will hear my voice, and there will be one flock, one shepherd.[p] [17]This is why the Father loves me, because I lay down my life in order to take it up again.[q] [18]No one takes it from me, but I lay it down on my own. I have power to lay it down, and power to take it up again.** This command I have received from my Father."[r]

[19]Again there was a division among the Jews because of these words.[s] [20]Many of them said, "He is possessed and out of his mind; why listen to him?"[t] [21]Others said, "These are not the words of one possessed; surely a demon cannot open the eyes of the blind, can he?"[u]

Feast of the Dedication. [22]The feast of the Dedication†† was then taking place in Jerusalem. It was winter.[v] [23]‡‡And Jesus walked about in the temple area on the Portico of Solomon. [24]So the Jews gathered around him and said to him, "How long are you going to keep us in suspense?§§ If you are the Messiah, tell us plainly."[w] [25]Jesus answered them, "I told you¶¶ and you do not believe. The works I do in my Father's name testify to me.[x] [26]But you do not believe, because you are not among my sheep.[y] [27]My sheep hear my voice; I know them, and they follow me. [28]I give them eternal life, and they shall never perish. No one can take them out of my hand.[z] [29]My Father, who has given them to me, is greater than all,*** and no one can take them out of the Father's hand.[a] [30]†††The Father and I are one."[b]

[31]The Jews again picked up rocks to stone him.[c] [32]Jesus answered them, "I have shown you many good works from my Father. For which of these are you trying to stone me?" [33]The Jews answered him, "We are not stoning you for a good work but for blasphemy. You, a man, are making yourself God."[d] [34]‡‡‡Jesus answered them,[e] "Is it not written in your law, 'I said, "You are gods"'? [35]If it calls them gods to whom the word of God came, and scripture cannot be set aside, [36]can you say that the one whom the Father has consecrated§§§ and sent into the world blasphemes because I said, 'I am the Son of God'?[f] [37]If I do not perform my Father's works, do not believe me; [38]but if I perform them, even if you do not believe me, believe the works, so that you may realize [and understand] that the Father is in me and I am in the Father."[g] [39][Then] they

---

*[10:4] **Recognize his voice:** the Pharisees do not recognize Jesus, but the people of God, symbolized by the blind man, do.

†[10:6] **Figure of speech:** John uses a different word for illustrative speech than the "parable" of the synoptics, but the idea is similar.

‡[10:7–10] In Jn 10:7–8, the figure is of a gate for the shepherd to come to the sheep; in Jn 10:9–10, the figure is of a gate for the sheep to **come in and go out.**

§[10:8] **[Before me]:** these words are omitted in many good early manuscripts and versions.

¶[10:16] **Other sheep:** the Gentiles, possibly a reference to "God's dispersed children" of Jn 11:52 destined to be gathered into one, or "apostolic Christians" at odds with the community of the beloved disciple.

[10:18] **Power to take it up again: contrast the role of the Father as the efficient cause of the resurrection in Acts 2:24; 4:10; etc.; Rom 1:4; 4:24. Yet even here is added: **This command I have received from my Father.**

††[10:22] **Feast of the Dedication:** an eight-day festival of lights (Hebrew, Hanukkah) held in December, three months after the feast of Tabernacles (Jn 7:2), to celebrate the Maccabees' rededication of the altar and reconsecration of the temple in 164 B.C., after their desecration by Antiochus IV Epiphanes (Dn 8:13; 9:27; cf. 1 Mc 4:36–59; 2 Mc 1:18–2:19; 10:1–8).

‡‡[10:23] **Portico of Solomon:** on the east side of the temple area, offering protection against the cold winds from the desert.

§§[10:24] **Keep us in suspense:** literally, "How long will you take away our life?" Cf. Jn 11:48–50. **If you are the Messiah, tell us plainly:** cf. Lk 22:67. This is the climax of Jesus' encounters with the Jewish authorities. There has never yet been an open confession before them.

¶¶[10:25] **I told you:** probably at Jn 8:25 which was an evasive answer.

***[10:29] The textual evidence for the first clause is very divided; it may also be translated: "As for the Father, what he has given me is greater than all," or "My Father is greater than all, in what he has given me."

†††[10:30] This is justification for Jn 10:29; it asserts unity of power and reveals that the words and deeds of Jesus are the words and deeds of God.

‡‡‡[10:34] This is a reference to the judges of Israel who, since they exercised the divine prerogative to judge (Dt 1:17), were called "gods"; cf. Ex 21:6, besides Ps 82:6, from which the quotation comes.

§§§[10:36] **Consecrated:** this may be a reference to the rededicated altar at the Hanukkah feast; see note on Jn 10:22.

---

l. [10:4] Mi 2:12–13.   m. [10:11] Ps 23:1–4; Is 40:11; 49:9–10; Heb 13:20; Rev 7:17.   n. [10:12] Zec 11:17.   o. [10:15] 15:13; 1 Jn 3:16.   p. [10:16] 11:52; Is 56:8; Jer 23:3; Ez 34:23; 37:24; Mi 2:12.   q. [10:17] Heb 10:10.   r. [10:18] 19:11.   s. [10:19] 7:43; 9:16.   t. [10:20] 7:20; 8:48.   u. [10:21] 3:2.

v. [10:22] 1 Mc 4:54, 59.   w. [10:24] Lk 22:67.   x. [10:25] 8:25 / 5:36; 10:38.   y. [10:26] 8:45, 47.   z. [10:28] Dt 32:39.   a. [10:29] Wis 3:1; Is 43:13.   b. [10:30] 1:1; 12:45; 14:9; 17:21.   c. [10:31] 8:59.   d. [10:33] 5:18; 19:7; Lv 24:16.   e. [10:34] Ps 82:6.   f. [10:36] 5:18.   g. [10:38] 14:10–11, 20.

tried again to arrest him; but he escaped from their power.

⁴⁰He went back across the Jordan to the place where John first baptized, and there he remained.*ʰ* ⁴¹Many came to him and said, "John performed no sign,* but everything John said about this man was true." ⁴²And many there began to believe in him.*ⁱ*

CHAPTER 11
The Raising of Lazarus.† ¹Now a man was ill, Lazarus from Bethany,ʲ the village of Mary and her sister Martha. ²Mary was the one who had anointed the Lord with perfumed oil and dried his feet with her hair; it was her brother Lazarus who was ill. ³So the sisters sent word to him, saying, "Master, the one you love is ill." ⁴When Jesus heard this he said, "This illness is not to end in death,‡ but is for the glory of God, that the Son of God may be glorified through it."ᵏ ⁵Now Jesus loved Martha and her sister and Lazarus. ⁶So when he heard that he was ill, he remained for two days in the place where he was. ⁷Then after this he said to his disciples, "Let us go back to Judea." ⁸The disciples said to him, "Rabbi, the Jews were just trying to stone you, and you want to go back there?"ˡ ⁹Jesus answered, "Are there not twelve hours in a day? If one walks during the day,ᵐ he does not stumble, because he sees the light of this world."ⁿ ¹⁰But if one walks at night, he stumbles, because the light is not in him."ˢ ¹¹He said this, and then told them, "Our friend Lazarus is asleep, but I am going to awaken him." ¹²So the disciples said to him, "Master, if he is asleep, he will be saved." ¹³But Jesus was talking about his death, while they thought that he meant ordinary sleep.ᵒ ¹⁴So then Jesus said to them clearly, "Lazarus has died.

*[10:41] **Performed no sign:** this is to stress the inferior role of John the Baptist. The Transjordan topography recalls the great witness of John the Baptist to Jesus, as opposed to the hostility of the authorities in Jerusalem.

†[11:1–44] The raising of Lazarus, the longest continuous narrative in John outside of the passion account, is the climax of the signs. It leads directly to the decision of the Sanhedrin to kill Jesus. The theme of life predominates. Lazarus is a token of the real life that Jesus dead and raised will give to all who believe in him. Johannine irony is found in the fact that Jesus' gift of life leads to his own death. The story is not found in the synoptics, but cf. Mk 5:21 and parallels; Lk 7:11–17. There are also parallels between this story and Luke's parable of the rich man and poor Lazarus (Lk 16:19–31). In both a man named Lazarus dies; in Luke, there is a request that he return to convince his contemporaries of the need for faith and repentance, while in John, Lazarus does return and some believe but others do not.

‡[11:4] **Not to end in death:** this is misunderstood by the disciples as referring to physical death, but it is meant as spiritual death.

§[11:10] **The light is not in him:** the ancients apparently did not grasp clearly the entry of light *through* the eye; they seem to have thought of it as being *in* the eye; cf. Lk 11:34; Mt 6:23.

¹⁵And I am glad for you that I was not there, that you may believe. Let us go to him." ¹⁶So Thomas, called Didymus,⁵ said to his fellow disciples, "Let us also go to die with him."ᵖ

¹⁷When Jesus arrived, he found that Lazarus had already been in the tomb for four days. ¹⁸Now Bethany was near Jerusalem, only about two miles** away. ¹⁹And many of the Jews had come to Martha and Mary to comfort them about their brother.�q ²⁰When Martha heard that Jesus was coming, she went to meet him; but Mary sat at home. ²¹Martha said to Jesus, "Lord, if you had been here, my brother would not have died."ʳ ²²[But] even now I know that whatever you ask of God, God will give you." ²³Jesus said to her, "Your brother will rise." ²⁴Martha said to him, "I know he will rise, in the resurrection on the last day."ˢ ²⁵Jesus told her, "I am the resurrection and the life; whoever believes in me, even if he dies, will live,ᵗ ²⁶and everyone who lives and believes in me will never die. Do you believe this?" ²⁷††ᵘShe said to him, "Yes, Lord. I have come to believe that you are the Messiah, the Son of God, the one who is coming into the world."

²⁸When she had said this, she went and called her sister Mary secretly, saying, "The teacher is here and is asking for you." ²⁹As soon as she heard this, she rose quickly and went to him. ³⁰For Jesus had not yet come into the village, but was still where Martha had met him. ³¹So when the Jews who were with her in the house comforting her saw Mary get up quickly and go out, they followed her, presuming that she was going to the tomb to weep there. ³²When Mary came to where Jesus was and saw him, she fell at his feet and said to him, "Lord, if you had been here, my brother would not have died." ³³When Jesus saw her weeping and the Jews who had come with her weeping, he became perturbed‡‡ and deeply troubled, ³⁴and said, "Where have you laid him?" They said to him, "Sir, come and see." ³⁵And Jesus wept.ᵛ ³⁶So the Jews said, "See how he loved him." ³⁷But some of them said, "Could not the one who opened the eyes of the blind man have done something so that this man would not have died?"

³⁸So Jesus, perturbed again, came to the tomb. It was a cave, and a stone lay across it. ³⁹Jesus said, "Take away the stone." Martha, the

¶[11:16] **Called Didymus: Didymus** is the Greek word for twin. Thomas is derived from the Aramaic word for twin; in an ancient Syriac version and in the Gospel of Thomas (80:11–12) his given name, Judas, is supplied.

[11:18] **About two miles: literally, "about fifteen stades"; a stade was 607 feet.

††[11:27] The titles here are a summary of titles given to Jesus earlier in the gospel.

‡‡[11:33] **Became perturbed:** a startling phrase in Greek, literally, "He snorted in spirit," perhaps in anger at the presence of evil (death).

h. [10:40] 1:28. i. [10:42] 2:23; 7:31; 8:30. j. [11:1–2] 12:1–8; Lk 10:38–42; 16:19–31. k. [11:4] 9:3, 24. l. [11:8] 8:59; 10:31. m. [11:9–10] 12:35; 1 Jn 2:10. n. [11:9] 8:12; 9:4. o. [11:13] Mt 9:24.

p. [11:16] 14:5, 22. q. [11:19] 12:9, 17–18. r. [11:21] 11:32. s. [11:24] 5:29; 6:39–40, 44, 54; 12:48; Is 2:2; Mi 4:1; Acts 23:8; 24:15. t. [11:25] 5:24; 8:51; 14:6; Dn 12:2. u. [11:27] 1:9; 6:69. v. [11:35] Lk 19:41.

dead man's sister, said to him, "Lord, by now there will be a stench; he has been dead for four days." [40]Jesus said to her, "Did I not tell you that if you believe you will see the glory of God?" [41]So they took away the stone. And Jesus raised his eyes and said, "Father,* I thank you for hearing me. [42]I know that you always hear me; but because of the crowd here I have said this, that they may believe that you sent me."[w] [43]And when he had said this, he cried out in a loud voice,[†] "Lazarus, come out!" [44]The dead man came out, tied hand and foot with burial bands, and his face was wrapped in a cloth. So Jesus said to them, "Untie him and let him go."

Session of the Sanhedrin. [45]Now many of the Jews who had come to Mary and seen what he had done began to believe in him.[x] [46]But some of them went to the Pharisees and told them what Jesus had done. [47]So the chief priests and the Pharisees convened the Sanhedrin and said, "What are we going to do? This man is performing many signs.[y] [48]If we leave him alone, all will believe in him, and the Romans will come[‡] and take away both our land and our nation." [49=]But one of them, Caiaphas, who was high priest that year,[§] said to them, "You know nothing, [50]nor do you consider that it is better for you that one man should die instead of the people, so that the whole nation may not perish." [51]He did not say this on his own, but since he was high priest for that year, he prophesied that Jesus was going to die for the nation, [52]and not only for the nation, but also to gather into one the dispersed children of God.[§] [53]So from that day on they planned to kill him.[a]

[54]So Jesus no longer walked about in public among the Jews, but he left for the region near the desert, to a town called Ephraim,** and there he remained with his disciples.

The Last Passover. [55]Now the Passover of the Jews was near, and many went up from the country to Jerusalem before Passover to purify[††] themselves.[b] [56]They looked for Jesus and said to one another as they were in the temple area, "What do you think? That he will not come to the feast?" [57]For the chief priests and the Pharisees had given orders that if anyone knew where he was, he should inform them, so that they might arrest him.

CHAPTER 12

The Anointing at Bethany.[c] [1‡‡]Six days before Passover Jesus came to Bethany, where Lazarus was, whom Jesus had raised from the dead.[d] [2]They gave a dinner for him there, and Martha served, while Lazarus was one of those reclining at table with him.[e] [3]Mary took a liter of costly perfumed oil made from genuine aromatic nard and anointed the feet of Jesus[§§] and dried them with her hair; the house was filled with the fragrance of the oil.[f] [4]Then Judas the Iscariot, one [of] his disciples, and the one who would betray him, said, [5]"Why was this oil not sold for three hundred days' wages[¶¶] and given to the poor?" [6]He said this not because he cared about the poor but because he was a thief and held the money bag and used to steal the contributions.[g] [7]So Jesus said, "Leave her alone. Let her keep this for the day of my burial.*** [8]You always have the poor with you, but you do not always have me."[h]

[9][The] large crowd of the Jews found out that he was there and came, not only because of Jesus, but also to see Lazarus, whom he had raised from the dead.[i] [10]And the chief priests plotted to kill Lazarus too, [11]because many of the Jews were turning away and believing in Jesus because of him.[j]

The Entry into Jerusalem.[†††] [12k]On the next day, when the great crowd that had come to the feast heard that Jesus was coming to Jerusalem, [13]they took palm branches[‡‡‡] and went out to meet him, and cried out:

‡‡[12:1–8] This is probably the same scene of anointing found in Mk 14:3–9 (see note there) and Mt 26:6–13. The anointing by a penitent woman in Lk 7:36–38 is different. Details from these various episodes have become interchanged.

§§[12:3] **The feet of Jesus:** so Mk 14:3; but in Mt 26:6, Mary anoints Jesus' head as a sign of regal, messianic anointing.

¶¶[12:5] **Days' wages:** literally, "denarii." A denarius is a day's wage in Mt 20:2; see note on Jn 6:7.

***[12:7] Jesus' response reflects the rabbinical discussion of what was the greatest act of mercy, almsgiving or burying the dead. Those who favored proper burial of the dead thought it an essential condition for sharing in the resurrection.

†††[12:12–19] In John, the entry into Jerusalem follows the anointing whereas in the synoptics it precedes. In John, the crowd, not the disciples, are responsible for the triumphal procession.

‡‡‡[12:13] **Palm branches:** used to welcome great conquerors; cf. 1 Mc 13:51; 2 Mc 10:7. They may be related to the *lûlāb*, the twig bundles used at the feast of Tabernacles. **Hosanna:** see Ps 118:25–26. The Hebrew word means: "(O Lord), grant salvation." **He who comes in the name of the Lord:** referred in Ps 118:26 to a pilgrim entering the temple gates, but here a title for Jesus (see notes on Mt 11:3 and Jn 6:14; 11:27). **The king of Israel:** perhaps from Zep 3:14–15, in connection with the next quotation from Zec 9:9.

---

*[11:41] **Father:** in Aramaic, *'abbā'*. See note on Mk 14:36.

†[11:43] **Cried out in a loud voice:** a dramatization of Jn 5:28; "the hour is coming when all who are in the tombs will hear his voice."

‡[11:48] **The Romans will come:** Johannine irony; this is precisely what happened after Jesus' death.

§[11:49] **That year:** emphasizes the conjunction of the office and the year. Actually, Caiaphas was high priest A.D. 18–36. The Jews attributed a gift of prophecy, sometimes unconscious, to the high priest.

¶[11:52] **Dispersed children of God:** perhaps the "other sheep" of Jn 10:16.

**[11:54] Ephraim is usually located about twelve miles northeast of Jerusalem, where the mountains descend into the Jordan valley.

††[11:55] **Purify:** prescriptions for purity were based on Ex 19:10–11, 15; Nm 9:6–14; 2 Chr 30:1–3, 15–18.

---

w. [11:42] 12:30. x. [11:45] Lk 16:31. y. [11:47] 12:19; Mt 26:3–5; Lk 22:2; Acts 4:16. z. [11:49–50] 18:13–14. a. [11:53] 5:18; 7:1; Mt 12:14. b. [11:55] 2:13; 5:1; 6:4; 18:28; Ex 19:10–11, 15; Nm 9:6–14; 19:12; Dt 16:6; 2 Chr 30:1–3, 15–18.

c. [12:1–11] Mt 26:6–13; Mk 14:3–9. d. [12:1–2] 11:1. e. [12:2] Lk 10:38–42. f. [12:3] 11:2. g. [12:6] 13:29. h. [12:8] Dt 15:11. i. [12:9] 11:19. j. [12:11] 11:45. k. [12:12–19] Mt 21:1–16; Mk 11:1–10; Lk 19:28–40.

"Hosanna!
Blessed is he who comes in the name of
the Lord,
[even] the king of Israel."*l*

¹⁴Jesus found an ass and sat upon it, as is written:

¹⁵ "Fear no more, O daughter Zion;ˑ
see, your king comes, seated upon
an ass's colt."*m*

¹⁶His disciples did not understand this at first, but when Jesus had been glorified they remembered that these things were written about him and that they had done this† for him.*n* ¹⁷‡So the crowd that was with him when he called Lazarus from the tomb and raised him from death continued to testify. ¹⁸This was [also] why the crowd went to meet him, because they heard that he had done this sign. ¹⁹So the Pharisees said to one another, "You see that you are gaining nothing. Look, the whole world§ has gone after him."*o*
The Coming of Jesus' Hour.¶ ²⁰Now there were some Greeks** among those who had come up to worship at the feast.*p* ²¹†††They came to Philip, who was from Bethsaida in Galilee, and asked him, "Sir, we would like to see Jesus."*q* ²²Philip went and told Andrew; then Andrew and Philip went and told Jesus.*r* ²³‡‡Jesus answered them,*s* "The hour has come for the Son of Man to be glorified. ²⁴§§Amen, amen, I say to you, unless a grain of wheat falls to the ground and dies, it remains just a grain of wheat;*t* but if it dies, it produces much fruit. ²⁵Whoever loves his life¶¶ loses it, and

---

*[12:15] **Daughter Zion:** Jerusalem. **Ass's colt:** symbol of peace, as opposed to the war horse.
†[12:16] **They had done this:** the antecedent of they is ambiguous.
‡[12:17–18] There seem to be two different crowds in these verses. There are some good witnesses to the text that have another reading for Jn 12:17: "Then the crowd that was with him began to testify that he had called Lazarus out of the tomb and raised him from the dead."
§[12:19] **The whole world:** the sense is that everyone is following Jesus, but John has an ironic play on **world;** he alludes to the universality of salvation (Jn 3:17; 4:42).
¶[12:20–36] This announcement of glorification by death is an illustration of "the whole world" (Jn 12:19) going after him.
[12:20] **Greeks: not used here in a nationalistic sense. These are probably Gentile proselytes to Judaism; cf. Jn 7:35.
††[12:21–22] **Philip . . . Andrew:** the approach is made through disciples who have distinctly Greek names, suggesting that access to Jesus was mediated to the Greek world through his disciples. Philip and Andrew were from Bethsaida (Jn 1:44); Galileans were mostly bilingual. **See:** here seems to mean "have an interview with."
‡‡[12:23] Jesus' response suggests that only after the crucifixion could the gospel encompass both Jew and Gentile.
§§[12:24] This verse implies that through his death Jesus will be accessible to all. **It remains just a grain of wheat:** this saying is found in the synoptic triple and double traditions (Mk 8:35; Mt 16:25; Lk 9:24; Mt 10:39; Lk 17:33). John adds the phrases (Jn 12:25) **in this world** and **for eternal life.**
¶¶[12:25] **His life:** the Greek word *psychē* refers to a person's natural life. It does not mean "soul," for Hebrew anthropol-

---

whoever hates his life in this world will preserve it for eternal life.*u* ²⁶Whoever serves me must follow me, and where I am, there also will my servant be. The Father will honor whoever serves me.*v*
²⁷"I am troubled*** now. Yet what should I say? 'Father, save me from this hour'? But it was for this purpose that I came to this hour.*w* ²⁸Father, glorify your name." Then a voice came from heaven, "I have glorified it and will glorify it again."*x* ²⁹The crowd there heard it and said it was thunder; but others said, "An angel has spoken to him."*y* ³⁰Jesus answered and said, "This voice did not come for my sake but for yours.*z* ³¹Now is the time of judgment on this world; now the ruler of this world††† will be driven out.*a* ³²And when I am lifted up from the earth, I will draw everyone to myself."*b* ³³He said this indicating the kind of death he would die. ³⁴So the crowd answered him, "We have heard from the law that the Messiah remains forever.‡‡‡ Then how can you say that the Son of Man must be lifted up? Who is this Son of Man?"*c* ³⁵Jesus said to them, "The light will be among you only a little while. Walk while you have the light, so that darkness may not overcome you. Whoever walks in the dark does not know where he is going.*d* ³⁶While you have the light, believe in the light, so that you may become children of the light."*e*
Unbelief and Belief Among the Jews. After he had said this, Jesus left and hid from them. ³⁷§§§Although he had performed so many signs in their presence they did not believe in him, ³⁸¶¶¶in order that the word which Isaiah the prophet spoke might be fulfilled:

"Lord, who has believed our preaching,
to whom has the might of the Lord
been revealed?"*g*

³⁹For this reason they could not believe, because again Isaiah said:

---

ogy did not postulate body/soul dualism in the way that is familiar to us.
***[12:27] **I am troubled:** perhaps an allusion to the Gethsemane agony scene of the synoptics.
†††[12:31] **Ruler of this world:** Satan.
‡‡‡[12:34] There is no passage in the Old Testament that states precisely that the **Messiah remains forever.** Perhaps the closest is Ps 89:37.
§§§[12:37–50] These verses, on unbelief of the Jews, provide an epilogue to the Book of Signs.
¶¶¶[12:38–41] John gives a historical explanation of the disbelief of the Jewish people, not a psychological one. The Old Testament had to be fulfilled; the disbelief that met Isaiah's message was a foreshadowing of the disbelief that Jesus encountered. In Jn 12:42 and also in Jn 3:20 we see that there is no negation of freedom.

---

u. [12:25] Mt 10:39; 16:25; Mk 8:35; Lk 9:24; 17:33. v. [12:26] 14:3; 17:24; Mt 16:24; Mk 8:34; Lk 9:23. w. [12:27] 6:38; 18:11; Mt 26:38–39; Mk 14:34–36; Lk 22:42; Heb 5:7–8. x. [12:28] 2:11; 17:5; Dn 4:31, 34. y. [12:29] Ex 9:28; 2 Sm 22:14; Jb 37:4; Ps 29:3; Lk 22:43; Acts 23:9. z. [12:30] 11:42. a. [12:31] 16:11; Lk 10:18; Rev 12:9. b. [12:32] 3:14; 8:28; Is 52:13. c. [12:34] Ps 89:5; 110:4; Is 9:7; Dn 7:13–14; Rev 20:1–6. d. [12:35] 9:4; 11:10; Jb 5:14. e. [12:36] Eph 5:8. f. [12:37–43] Dt 29:2–4; Mk 4:11–12; Rom 9–11. g. [12:38] Is 53:1; Rom 10:16.

l. [12:13] 1:49; Lv 23:40; 1 Mc 13:51; 2 Mc 10:7; Rev 7:9. m. [12:15] Is 40:9; Zec 9:9. n. [12:16] 2:22. o. [12:19] 11:47–48. p. [12:20] Acts 10:2. q. [12:21] 1:44. r. [12:22] 1:40. s. [12:23] 2:4. t. [12:24] Is 53:10–12; 1 Cor 15:36.

[40] "He blinded their eyes
and hardened their heart,
so that they might not see with their eyes
and understand with their heart and
be converted,
and I would heal them."[h]

[41]Isaiah said this because he saw his glory* and spoke about him.[i] [42]Nevertheless, many, even among the authorities, believed in him, but because of the Pharisees they did not acknowledge it openly in order not to be expelled from the synagogue.[j] [43]For they preferred human praise to the glory of God.[k]

Recapitulation. [44]Jesus cried out and said, "Whoever believes in me believes not only in me but also in the one who sent me,[l] [45]and whoever sees me sees the one who sent me.[m] [46]I came into the world as light, so that everyone who believes in me might not remain in darkness.[n] [47]And if anyone hears my words and does not observe them, I do not condemn him, for I did not come to condemn the world but to save the world.[o] [48]Whoever rejects me and does not accept my words has something to judge him: the word that I spoke, it will condemn him on the last day,[p] [49]because I did not speak on my own, but the Father who sent me commanded me what to say and speak.[q] [50]And I know that his commandment is eternal life. So what I say, I say as the Father told me."

III. THE BOOK OF GLORY[†]

CHAPTER 13

The Washing of the Disciples' Feet.[‡] [1]Before the feast of Passover,[§] Jesus knew that his hour had come to pass from this world to the Father. He loved his own in the world and he loved them to the end.[r] [2]The devil had already induced[¶]

Judas, son of Simon the Iscariot, to hand him over. So, during supper,[s] [3]fully aware that the Father had put everything into his power and that he had come from God and was returning to God,[t] [4]he rose from supper and took off his outer garments. He took a towel and tied it around his waist. [5]**Then he poured water into a basin and began to wash the disciples' feet[u] and dry them with the towel around his waist. [6]He came to Simon Peter, who said to him, "Master, are you going to wash my feet?" [7]Jesus answered and said to him, "What I am doing, you do not understand now, but you will understand later." [8]Peter said to him, "You will never wash my feet." Jesus answered him, "Unless I wash you, you will have no inheritance with me."[v] [9]Simon Peter said to him, "Master, then not only my feet, but my hands and head as well." [10]Jesus said to him, "Whoever has bathed[††] has no need except to have his feet washed, for he is clean all over; so you are clean, but not all."[w] [11]For he knew who would betray him; for this reason, he said, "Not all of you are clean."[x]

[12]So when he had washed their feet [and] put his garments back on and reclined at table again, he said to them, "Do you realize what I have done for you? [13]You call me 'teacher' and 'master,' and rightly so, for indeed I am.[y] [14]If I, therefore, the master and teacher, have washed your feet, you ought to wash one another's feet. [15]I have given you a model to follow, so that as I have done for you, you should also do.[z] [16]Amen, amen, I say to you, no slave is greater than his master nor any messenger[‡‡] greater than the one who sent him.[a] [17]If you understand this, blessed are you if you do it. [18]I am not speaking of all of you. I know those whom I have chosen. But so that the scripture might be fulfilled, 'The one who ate my food has raised his heel against me.'[b] [19]From now on I am telling you before it happens, so that when it happens you may believe that I AM. [20]Amen, amen, I say to you, whoever receives the one I send receives me, and whoever receives me receives the one who sent me."[c]

Announcement of Judas's Betrayal.[d] [21]When he had said this, Jesus was deeply troubled and testified, "Amen, amen, I say to you, one of you will betray me." [22]The disciples looked at one

---

*[12:41] **His glory**: Isaiah saw the glory of Yahweh enthroned in the heavenly temple, but in John the antecedent of **his** is Jesus.

†[13:1–19:42] The Book of Glory. There is a major break here; the word "sign" is used again only in Jn 20:30. In this phase of Jesus' return to the Father, the discourses (Jn 13–17) precede the traditional narrative of the passion (Jn 18–20) to interpret them for the Christian reader. This is the only extended example of esoteric teaching of disciples in John.

‡[13:1–20] Washing of the disciples' feet. This episode occurs in John at the place of the narration of the institution of the Eucharist in the synoptics. It may be a dramatization of Lk 22:27—"I am your servant." It is presented as a "model" ("pattern") of the crucifixion. It symbolizes cleansing from sin by sacrificial death.

§[13:1] **Before the feast of Passover**: this would be Thursday evening, before the day of preparation; in the synoptics, the Last Supper is a Passover meal taking place, in John's chronology, on Friday evening. **To the end**: or, "completely."

¶[13:2] **Induced**: literally, "The devil put into the heart that Judas should hand him over."

**[13:5] The act of washing another's feet was one that could not be required of the lowliest Jewish slave. It is an allusion to the humiliating death of the crucifixion.

††[13:10] **Bathed**: many have suggested that this passage is a symbolic reference to baptism. The Greek root involved is used in baptismal contexts in 1 Cor 6:11; Eph 5:26; Ti 3:5; Heb 10:22.

‡‡[13:16] **Messenger**: the Greek has *apostolos*, the only occurrence of the term in John. It is not used in the technical sense here.

---

h. [12:40] Is 6:9–10; Mt 13:13–15; Mk 4:12. i. [12:41] 5:39; Is 6:1, 4. j. [12:42] 9:22. k. [12:43] 5:44. l. [12:44] 13:20; 14:1. m. [12:45] 14:7–9. n. [12:46] 1:9; 8:12. o. [12:47] 3:17. p. [12:48] Lk 10:16; Heb 4:12. q. [12:49] 14:10, 31; Dt 18:18–19. r. [13:1] 2:4; 7:30; 8:20; Mt 26:17, 45; Mk 14:12, 41; Lk 22:7.

s. [13:2] 6:71; 17:12; Mt 26:20–21; Mk 14:17–18; Lk 22:3. t. [13:3] 3:35. u. [13:5] 1 Sm 25:41. v. [13:8] 2 Sm 20:1. w. [13:10] 15:3. x. [13:11] 6:70. y. [13:13] Mt 23:8, 10. z. [13:15] Lk 22:27; 1 Pt 2:21. a. [13:16] 15:20; Mt 10:24; Lk 6:40. b. [13:18] Ps 41:10. c. [13:20] Mt 10:40; Mk 9:37; Lk 9:48. d. [13:21–30] Mt 26:21–25; Mk 14:18–21; Lk 22:21–23.

another, at a loss as to whom he meant. [23]One of his disciples, the one whom Jesus loved,* was reclining at Jesus' side.[e] [24]So Simon Peter nodded to him to find out whom he meant. [25]He leaned back against Jesus' chest and said to him, "Master, who is it?"[f] [26]Jesus answered, "It is the one to whom I hand the morsel[†] after I have dipped it." So he dipped the morsel and [took it and] handed it to Judas, son of Simon the Iscariot. [27]After he took the morsel, Satan entered him. So Jesus said to him, "What you are going to do, do quickly."[g] [28][Now] none of those reclining at table realized why he said this to him. [29]Some thought that since Judas kept the money bag, Jesus had told him, "Buy what we need for the feast," or to give something to the poor.[h] [30]So he took the morsel and left at once. And it was night.

The New Commandment. [31‡]When he had left, Jesus said,[§] "Now is the Son of Man glorified, and God is glorified in him. [32][If God is glorified in him,] God will also glorify him in himself, and he will glorify him at once.[i] [33]My children, I will be with you only a little while longer. You will look for me, and as I told the Jews, 'Where I go you cannot come,' so now I say it to you.[j] [34]I give you a new commandment:[¶] love one another. As I have loved you, so you also should love one another.[k] [35]This is how all will know that you are my disciples, if you have love for one another."

Peter's Denial Predicted. [36]Simon Peter said to him, "Master, where are you going?" Jesus answered [him], "Where I am going, you cannot follow me now, though you will follow later."[l] [37]Peter said to him, "Master, why can't I follow you now? I will lay down my life for you." [38]Jesus answered, "Will you lay down your life for me? Amen, amen, I say to you, the cock will not crow before you deny me three times."[m]

---

*[13:23] **The one whom Jesus loved**: also mentioned in Jn 19:26; 20:2; 21:7. A disciple, called "another disciple" or "the other disciple," is mentioned in Jn 18:15 and Jn 20:2; in the latter reference he is identified with the disciple whom Jesus loved. There is also an unnamed disciple in Jn 1:35–40; see note on Jn 1:37.

†[13:26] **Morsel**: probably the bitter herb dipped in salt water.

‡[13:31–17:26] Two farewell discourses and a prayer. These seem to be Johannine compositions, including sayings of Jesus at the Last Supper and on other occasions, modeled on similar farewell discourses in Greek literature and the Old Testament (of Moses, Joshua, David).

§[13:31–38] Introduction: departure and return. Terms of coming and going predominate. These verses form an introduction to the last discourse of Jesus, which extends through Jn 14–17. In it John has collected Jesus' words to his own (Jn 13:1). There are indications that several speeches have been fused together, e.g., in Jn 14:31 and Jn 17:1.

¶[13:34] **I give you a new commandment**: this puts Jesus on a par with Yahweh. The commandment itself is not new; cf. Lv 19:18 and the note there.

---

e. [13:23]19:26;20:2;21:7,20; Mt10:37.   f. [13:25]21:20.   g. [13:27] 13:2; Lk 22:3.   h. [13:29] 12:5–6.   i. [13:32] 17:1–5.   j. [13:33] 7:33; 8:21.   k. [13:34] 15:12–13, 17; Lv 19:18; 1 Thes 4:9; 1 Jn 2:7–10; 3:23; 2 Jn 5.   l. [13:36] Mk 14:27; Lk 22:23.   m. [13:38] 18:27; Mt 26:33–35; Mk 14:29–31; Lk 22:33–34.

CHAPTER 14

Last Supper Discourses. [1]""Do not let your hearts be troubled. You have faith[††] in God; have faith also in me. [2]In my Father's house there are many dwelling places. If there were not, would I have told you that I am going to prepare a place for you? [3‡‡]And if I go and prepare a place for you, I will come back again and take you to myself, so that where I am you also may be.[n] [4]Where [I] am going you know the way."[§§] [5]Thomas said to him, "Master, we do not know where you are going; how can we know the way?" [6]Jesus said to him, "I am the way and the truth[¶¶] and the life. No one comes to the Father except through me.[o] [7]If you know me, then you will also know my Father.[***] From now on you do know him and have seen him."[p] [8]Philip said to him, "Master, show us the Father,[†††] and that will be enough for us."[q] [9]Jesus said to him, "Have I been with you for so long a time and you still do not know me, Philip? Whoever has seen me has seen the Father. How can you say, 'Show us the Father'?[r] [10]Do you not believe that I am in the Father and the Father is in me? The words that I speak to you I do not speak on my own. The Father who dwells in me is doing his works.[s] [11]Believe me that I am in the Father and the Father is in me, or else, believe because of the works themselves.[t] [12]Amen, amen, I say to you, whoever believes in me will do the works that I do, and will do greater ones than these, because I am going to the Father.[u] [13]And whatever you ask in my name, I will do, so that the Father may be glorified in the Son.[v] [14]If you ask anything of me in my name, I will do it.

The Advocate. [15]"If you love me, you will keep my commandments.[w] [16]And I will ask the Father, and he will give you another Advocate[‡‡‡]

**[14:1–31] Jesus' departure and return. This section is a dialogue marked off by a literary inclusion in Jn 14:1, 27: "Do not let your hearts be troubled."

††[14:1] **You have faith**: could also be imperative: "Have faith."

‡‡[14:3] **Come back again**: a rare Johannine reference to the parousia; cf. 1 Jn 2:28.

§§[14:4] **The way**: here, of Jesus himself; also a designation of Christianity in Acts 9:2; 19:9, 23; 22:4; 24:14, 22.

¶¶[14:6] **The truth**: in John, the divinely revealed reality of the Father manifested in the person and works of Jesus. The possession of truth confers knowledge and liberation from sin (Jn 8:32).

***[14:7] An alternative reading, "If you knew me, then you would have known my Father also," would be a rebuke, as in Jn 8:19.

†††[14:8] **Show us the Father**: Philip is pictured asking for a theophany like Ex 24:9–10; 33:18.

‡‡‡[14:16] **Another Advocate**: Jesus is the first advocate (*paraclete*); see 1 Jn 2:1, where Jesus is an advocate in the sense of intercessor in heaven. The Greek term derives from legal terminology for an advocate or defense attorney, and can mean spokesman, mediator, intercessor, comforter, consoler, although no one of these terms encompasses the meaning in John. The Paraclete in John is a teacher, a witness to Jesus,

---

n. [14:3] 12:26; 17:24; 1 Jn 2:28.   o. [14:6] 8:31–47.   p. [14:7] 8:19; 12:45.   q. [14:8] Ex 24:9–10; 33:18.   r. [14:9] 1:18; 10:30; 12:45; 2 Cor 4:4; Col 1:15; Heb 1:3.   s. [14:10] 1:1; 10:37–38; 12:49.   t. [14:11] 10:38.   u. [14:12] 1:50; 5:20.   v. [14:13] 15:7, 16; 16:23–24; Mt 7:7–11.   w. [14:15] 15:10; Dt 6:4–9; Ps 119; Wis 6:18; 1 Jn 5:3; 2 Jn 6.

to be with you always,[x] [17]the Spirit of truth,[*] which the world cannot accept, because it neither sees nor knows it. But you know it, because it remains with you, and will be in you.[y] [18]I will not leave you orphans; I will come to you.[†] [19]In a little while the world will no longer see me, but you will see me, because I live and you will live.[z] [20]On that day you will realize that I am in my Father and you are in me and I in you.[a] [21]Whoever has my commandments and observes them is the one who loves me. And whoever loves me will be loved by my Father, and I will love him and reveal myself to him."[b] [22]Judas, not the Iscariot,[‡] said to him, "Master, [then] what happened that you will reveal yourself to us and not to the world?"[c] [23]Jesus answered and said to him, "Whoever loves me will keep my word, and my Father will love him, and we will come to him and make our dwelling with him.[d] [24]Whoever does not love me does not keep my words; yet the word you hear is not mine but that of the Father who sent me.

[25]"I have told you this while I am with you. [26]The Advocate, the holy Spirit that the Father will send in my name—he will teach you everything and remind you of all that [I] told you.[e] [27]Peace[§] I leave with you; my peace I give to you. Not as the world gives do I give it to you. Do not let your hearts be troubled or afraid.[f] [28]You heard me tell you, 'I am going away and I will come back to you.'[g] If you loved me, you would rejoice that I am going to the Father; for the Father is greater than I. [29]And now I have told you this before it happens, so that when it happens you may believe.[h] [30]I will no longer speak much with you, for the ruler of the world[**] is coming. He has no power over me, [31]but the world must know that I love the Father and that

I do just as the Father has commanded me. Get up, let us go.[i]

CHAPTER 15

The Vine and the Branches. [††]"I am the true vine,[‡‡] and my Father is the vine grower.[j] [2]He takes away every branch in me that does not bear fruit, and every one that does he prunes[§§] so that it bears more fruit. [3]You are already pruned because of the word that I spoke to you.[k] [4]Remain in me, as I remain in you. Just as a branch cannot bear fruit on its own unless it remains on the vine, so neither can you unless you remain in me. [5]I am the vine, you are the branches. Whoever remains in me and I in him will bear much fruit, because without me you can do nothing. [6]Anyone who does not remain in me will be thrown out like a branch and wither; people will gather them and throw them into a fire and they will be burned. [7]If you remain in me and my words remain in you, ask for whatever you want and it will be done for you.[m] [8]By this is my Father glorified, that you bear much fruit and become my disciples.[n] [9]As the Father loves me, so I also love you. Remain in my love.[o] [10]If you keep my commandments, you will remain in my love, just as I have kept my Father's commandments and remain in his love.[p]

[11]"I have told you this so that my joy may be in you and your joy may be complete.[q] [12]This is my commandment: love one another as I love you.[r] [13]"No one has greater love than this,[s] to lay down one's life for one's friends. [14]You are my friends if you do what I command you. [15]I no longer call you slaves, because a slave does not know what his master is doing. I have called you friends,[†††] because I have told you everything I have heard

---

and a prosecutor of the world, who represents the continued presence on earth of the Jesus who has returned to the Father.

[*][14:17] **The Spirit of truth:** this term is also used at Qumran, where it is a moral force put into a person by God, as opposed to the spirit of perversity. It is more personal in John; it will teach the realities of the new order (Jn 14:26), and testify to the truth (Jn 14:6). While it has been customary to use masculine personal pronouns in English for the Advocate, the Greek word for "spirit" is neuter, and the Greek text and manuscript variants fluctuate between masculine and neuter pronouns.

[†][14:18] **I will come to you:** indwelling, not parousia.

[‡][14:22] **Judas, not the Iscariot:** probably not the brother of Jesus in Mk 6:3 // Mt 13:55 or the apostle named Jude in Lk 6:16, but Thomas (see note on Jn 11:16), although other readings have "Judas the Cananean."

[§][14:27] **Peace:** the traditional Hebrew salutation šālôm; but Jesus' "Shalom" is a gift of salvation, connoting the bounty of messianic blessing.

[¶][14:28] **The Father is greater than I:** because he **sent, gave,** etc., and Jesus is "a man who has told you the truth that I heard from God" (Jn 8:40).

[**][14:30] **The ruler of the world:** Satan; cf. Jn 12:31; 16:11.

[††][15:1–16:4] Discourse on the union of Jesus with his disciples. His words become a monologue and go beyond the immediate crisis of the departure of Jesus.

[‡‡][15:1–17] Like Jn 10:1–5, this passage resembles a parable. Israel is spoken of as a vineyard at Is 5:1–7; Mt 21:33–46 and as a vine at Ps 80:9–17; Jer 2:21; Ez 15:2; 17:5–10; 19:10; Hos 10:1. The identification of the vine as the Son of Man in Ps 80:15 and Wisdom's description of herself as a vine in Sir 24:17 are further background for portrayal of Jesus by this figure. There may be secondary eucharistic symbolism here; cf. Mk 14:25, "the fruit of the vine."

[§§][15:2] **Takes away . . . prunes:** in Greek there is a play on two related verbs.

[¶¶][15:6] Branches were cut off and dried on the wall of the vineyard for later use as fuel.

[***][15:13] **For one's friends:** or: "those whom one loves." In Jn 15:9–13a, the words for love are related to the Greek agapaō. In Jn 15:13b–15, the words for love are related to the Greek phileō. For John, the two roots seem synonymous and mean "to love"; cf. also Jn 21:15–17. The word philos is used here.

[†††][15:15] **Slaves . . . friends:** in the Old Testament, Moses (Dt 34:5), Joshua (Jos 24:29), and David (Ps 89:21) were called "servants" or "slaves of Yahweh"; only Abraham (Is 41:8; 2 Chr 20:7; cf. Jas 2:23) was called a "friend of God."

---

x. [14:16] 15:26; Lk 24:49; 1 Jn 2:1.   y. [14:17] 16:13; Mt 28:20; 2 Jn 1–2.   z. [14:19] 16:16.   a. [14:20] 10:38; 17:21; Is 2:17; 4:2–3. b. [14:21] 16:27; 1 Jn 2:5; 3:24.   c. [14:22] 7:4; Acts 10:40–41. d. [14:23] Rev 3:20.   e. [14:26] 15:26; 16:7, 13–14; Ps 51:13; Is 63:10.   f. [14:27] 16:33; Eph 2:14–18.   g. [14:28] 8:40.   h. [14:29] 13:19; 16:4.

i. [14:31] 6:38.   j. [15:1] Ps 80:9–17; Is 5:1–7; Jer 2:21; Ez 15:2; 17:5–10; 19:10.   k. [15:3] 13:10.   l. [15:6] Ez 15:6–7; 19:10– 14.   m. [15:7] 14:13; Mt 7:7; Mk 11:24; 1 Jn 5:14.   n. [15:8] Mt 5:16.   o. [15:9] 17:23.   p. [15:10] 8:29; 14:15.   q. [15:11] 16:22; 17:13.   r. [15:12] 13:34.   s. [15:13] Rom 5:6–8; 1 Jn 3:16.

from my Father.^{t} ^{16}It was not you who chose me, but I who chose you and appointed you to go and bear fruit that will remain, so that whatever you ask the Father in my name he may give you.^{u} ^{17}This I command you: love one another.^{v}

The World's Hatred.* ^{18}"If the world hates you, realize that it hated me first.^{w} ^{19}If you belonged to the world, the world would love its own; but because you do not belong to the world, and I have chosen you out of the world, the world hates you.^{x} ^{20}Remember the word I spoke to you,† 'No slave is greater than his master.' If they persecuted me, they will also persecute you. If they kept my word, they will also keep yours.^{y} ^{21}And they will do all these things to you on account of my name,‡ because they do not know the one who sent me.^{z} ^{22}If I had not come and spoken§ to them, they would have no sin; but as it is they have no excuse for their sin.^{a} ^{23}Whoever hates me also hates my Father.^{b} ^{24}If I had not done works among them that no one else ever did, they would not have sin; but as it is, they have seen and hated both me and my Father.^{c} ^{25}But in order that the word written in their law¶ might be fulfilled, 'They hated me without cause.'^{d}

^{26}"When the Advocate comes whom I will send** you from the Father, the Spirit of truth that proceeds from the Father, he will testify to me.^{e} ^{27}And you also testify, because you have been with me from the beginning.^{f}

CHAPTER 16

^{1}"I have told you this so that you may not fall away. ^{2}They will expel you from the synagogues; in fact, the hour†† is coming when everyone who kills you will think he is offering worship to God.^{g} ^{3}They will do this because they have not known either the Father or me.^{h} ^{4}I have told you this so that when their hour comes you may remember that I told you.^{i}

Jesus' Departure; Coming of the Advocate.‡‡ "I did not tell you this from the beginning, because I was with you. ^{5}But now I am going to the one who sent me, and not one of you asks me,§§ 'Where are you going?'^{j} ^{6}But because I told you this, grief has filled your hearts. ^{7}But I tell you the truth, it is better for you that I go. For if I do not go, the Advocate will not come to you.^{k} But if I go, I will send him to you. ^{8}And when he comes he will convict the world in regard to sin and righteousness and condemnation: ^{9}sin, because they do not believe in me;^{l} ^{10}righteousness, because I am going to the Father and you will no longer see me; ^{11}condemnation, because the ruler of this world has been condemned.^{m}

^{12}"I have much more to tell you, but you cannot bear it now. ^{13}But when he comes, the Spirit of truth, he will guide you to all truth.^{n} He will not speak on his own, but he will speak what he hears, and will declare to you the things that are coming. ^{14}He will glorify me, because he will take from what is mine and declare it to you. ^{15}Everything that the Father has is mine; for this reason I told you that he will take from what is mine and declare it to you.

^{16}"A little while and you will no longer see me, and again a little while later and you will see me."^{o} ^{17}So some of his disciples said to one another, "What does this mean that he is saying to us, 'A little while and you will not see me, and again a little while and you will see me,' and 'Because I am going to the Father'?" ^{18}So they said, "What is this 'little while' [of which he speaks]? We do not know what he means." ^{19}Jesus knew that they wanted to ask him, so he said to them, "Are you discussing with one another what I said, 'A little while and you will not see me, and again a little while and you will see me'? ^{20}Amen, amen, I say to you, you will weep and mourn, while the world rejoices; you will grieve, but your grief will become joy.^{p}

---

*[15:18–16:4] The hostile reaction of the world. There are synoptic parallels, predicting persecution, especially at Mt 10:17–25; 24:9–10.

†[15:20] **The word I spoke to you:** a reference to Jn 13:16.

‡[15:21] **On account of my name:** the idea of persecution for Jesus' name is frequent in the New Testament (Mt 10:22; 24:9; Acts 9:14). For John, association with Jesus' name implies union with Jesus.

§[15:22, 24] Jesus' words (**spoken**) and deeds (**works**) are the great motives of credibility. **They have seen and hated:** probably means that they have seen his works and still have hated; but the Greek can be read: "have seen both me and my Father and still have hated both me and my Father." **Works . . . that no one else ever did:** so Yahweh in Dt 4:32–33.

¶[15:25] **In their law:** law is here used as a larger concept than the Pentateuch, for the reference is to Ps 35:19 or Ps 69:5. See notes on Jn 10:34; 12:34. **Their** law reflects the argument of the church with the synagogue.

[15:26] **Whom I will send: in Jn 14:16, 26, the Paraclete is to be sent by the Father, at the request of Jesus. Here the Spirit comes from both Jesus and the Father in mission; there is no reference here to the eternal procession of the Spirit.

††[16:2] **Hour:** of persecution, not Jesus' "hour" (see note on Jn 2:4).

‡‡[16:4b–33] A duplicate of Jn 14:1–31 on departure and return.

§§[16:5] **Not one of you asks me:** the difficulty of reconciling this with Simon Peter's question in Jn 13:36 and Thomas' words in Jn 14:5 strengthens the supposition that the last discourse has been made up of several collections of Johannine material.

¶¶[16:8–11] These verses illustrate the forensic character of the Paraclete's role: in the forum of the disciples' conscience he prosecutes the world. He leads believers to see (a) that the basic sin was and is refusal to believe in Jesus; (b) that, although Jesus was found guilty and apparently died in disgrace, in reality righteousness has triumphed, for Jesus has returned to his Father; (c) finally, that it is the ruler of this world, Satan, who has been condemned through Jesus' death (Jn 12:32).

***[16:13] **Declare to you the things that are coming:** not a reference to new predictions about the future, but interpretation of what has already occurred or been said.

t. [15:15] Dt 34:5; Jos 24:29; 2 Chr 20:7; Ps 89:21; Is 41:8; Rom 8:15; Gal 4:7; Jas 2:23.   u. [15:16] 14:13; Dt 7:6.   v. [15:17] 13:34; 1 Jn 3:23; 4:21.   w. [15:18] 7:7; 14:17; Mt 10:22; 24:9; Mk 13:13; Lk 6:22; 1 Jn 3:13.   x. [15:19] 17:14–16; 1 Jn 4:5.   y. [15:20] 13:16; Mt 10:24.   z. [15:21] 8:19; 16:3.   a. [15:22] 8:21, 24; 9:41.   b. [15:23] 5:23; Lk 10:16; 1 Jn 2:23.   c. [15:24] 3:2; 9:32; Dt 4:32–33.   d. [15:25] Ps 35:19; 69:4.   e. [15:26] 14:16, 26; Mt 10:19–20.   f. [15:27] Lk 1:2; Acts 1:8.

g. [16:2] 9:22; 12:42; Mt 10:17; Lk 21:12; Acts 26:11.   h. [16:3] 15:21.   i. [16:4] 13:19; 14:29.   j. [16:5] 7:33; 13:36; 14:5.   k. [16:7] 7:39; 14:16–17, 26; 15:26.   l. [16:9] 8:21–24; 15:22.   m. [16:11] 12:31.   n. [16:13] 14:17, 26; 15:26; Ps 25:5; 143:10; 1 Jn 2:27; Rev 7:17.   o. [16:16] 7:33; 14:19.   p. [16:20] Ps 126:6.

²¹When a woman is in labor, she is in anguish because her hour has arrived; but when she has given birth to a child, she no longer remembers the pain because of her joy that a child has been born into the world.�q ²²So you also are now in anguish. But I will see you again, and your hearts will rejoice, and no one will take your joy away from you.ʳ ²³On that day you will not question me about anything. Amen, amen, I say to you, whatever you ask the Father in my name he will give you.ˢ ²⁴Until now you have not asked anything in my name; ask and you will receive, so that your joy may be complete.

²⁵*"I have told you this in figures of speech. The hour is coming when I will no longer speak to you in figures but I will tell you clearly about the Father. ²⁶On that day you will ask in my name, and I do not tell you that I will ask the Father for you.ᵘ ²⁷For the Father himself loves you, because you have loved me and have come to believe that I came from God. ²⁸I came from the Father and have come into the world. Now I am leaving the world and going back to the Father."ᵛ ²⁹His disciples said, "Now you are talking plainly, and not in any figure of speech. ³⁰Now we realize that you know everything and that you do not need to have anyone question you. Because of this we believe that you came from God."† ³¹Jesus answered them, "Do you believe now? ³²Behold, the hour is coming and has arrived when each of you will be scattered‡ to his own home and you will leave me alone. But I am not alone, because the Father is with me."ʷ ³³I have told you this so that you might have peace in me. In the world you will have trouble, but take courage, I have conquered the world."ˣ

CHAPTER 17

The Prayer of Jesus.§ ¹When Jesus had said this, he raised his eyes to heavenˢ and said, "Father,

the hour has come. Give glory to your son, so that your son may glorify you,ʸ ²**just as you gave him authority over all people,ᶻ so that he may give eternal life to all you gave him. ³††Now this is eternal life,ᵃ that they should know you, the only true God, and the one whom you sent, Jesus Christ. ⁴I glorified you on earth by accomplishing the work that you gave me to do. ⁵Now glorify me, Father, with you, with the glory that I had with you before the world began.ᵇ

⁶"I revealed your name‡‡ to those whom you gave me out of the world. They belonged to you, and you gave them to me, and they have kept your word. ⁷Now they know that everything you gave me is from you, ⁸because the words you gave to me I have given to them, and they accepted them and truly understood that I came from you, and they have believed that you sent me. ⁹I pray for them. I do not pray for the world but for the ones you have given me, because they are yours,ᶜ ¹⁰and everything of mine is yours and everything of yours is mine, and I have been glorified in them.ᵈ ¹¹And now I will no longer be in the world, but they are in the world, while I am coming to you. Holy Father, keep them in your name that you have given me, so that they may be one just as we are. ¹²When I was with them I protected them in your name that you gave me, and I guarded them, and none of them was lost except the son of destruction, in order that the scripture might be fulfilled.ᵉ ¹³But now I am coming to you. I speak this in the world so that they may share my joy completely.ᶠ ¹⁴I gave them your word, and the world hated them, because they do not belong to the world any more than I belong to the world.ᵍ ¹⁵§§I do not ask that you take them out of the world ʰ but that you keep them from the evil one. ¹⁶They do not belong to the world any more than I belong to the world. ¹⁷Consecrate them in the truth. Your word is truth.ⁱ ¹⁸As you sent me into the world, so I sent them into the world.ʲ ¹⁹And I consecrate myself for them, so that they also may be consecrated in truth.

²⁰"I pray not only for them, but also for those who will believe in me through their word, ²¹so

---

*[16:25] See note on Jn 10:6. Here, possibly a reference to Jn 15:1–16 or Jn 16:21.

†[16:30] The reference is seemingly to the fact that Jesus could anticipate their question in Jn 16:19. The disciples naively think they have the full understanding that is the climax of "the hour" of Jesus' death, resurrection, and ascension (Jn 16:25), but the only part of the hour that is at hand for them is their share in the passion (Jn 16:32).

‡[16:32] **You will be scattered:** cf. Mk 14:27 and Mt 26:31, where both cite Zec 13:7 about the sheep being dispersed.

§[17:1–26] Climax of the last discourse(s). Since the sixteenth century, this chapter has been called the "high priestly prayer" of Jesus. He speaks as intercessor, with words addressed directly to the Father and not to the disciples, who supposedly only overhear. Yet the prayer is one of petition, for immediate (Jn 17:6–19) and future (Jn 17:20–21) disciples. Many phrases reminiscent of the Lord's Prayer occur. Although still in the world (Jn 17:13), Jesus looks on his earthly ministry as a thing of the past (Jn 17:4, 12). Whereas Jesus has up to this time stated that the disciples could follow him (Jn 13:33, 36), now he wishes them to be with him in union with the Father (Jn 17:12–14).

¶[17:1] The action of looking up to heaven and the address Father are typical of Jesus at prayer; cf. Jn 11:41 and Lk 11:2.

[17:2] Another possible interpretation is to treat the first line of the verse as parenthetical and the second as an appositive to the clause that ends v 1: **so that your son may glorify you (just as . . . all people), so that he may give eternal life . . . .

††[17:3] This verse was clearly added in the editing of the gospel as a reflection on the preceding verse; Jesus nowhere else refers to himself as Jesus Christ.

‡‡[17:6] **I revealed your name:** perhaps the name **I AM;** cf. Jn 8:24, 28, 58; 13:19.

§§[17:15] Note the resemblance to the petition of the Lord's Prayer, "deliver us from the evil one." Both probably refer to the devil rather than to abstract evil.

---

q. [16:21] Is 26:17–18; Jer 31:13; Mi 4:9.   r. [16:22] 14:19; 15:11; 20:20.   s. [16:23] 14:13.   t. [16:25] Mt 13:34–35.   u. [16:26] 14:13.   v. [16:28] 1:1.   w. [16:32] 8:29; Zec 13:7; Mt 26:31; Mk 14:27.   x. [16:33] 14:27.

y. [17:1] 13:31.   z. [17:2] 3:35; Mt 28:18.   a. [17:3] 1:17; Wis 14:7; 15:3; 1 Jn 5:20.   b. [17:5] 1:1, 2; 12:28; Phil 2:6, 9–11.   c. [17:9] 17:20.   d. [17:10] 16:15; 2 Thes 1:10, 12.   e. [17:12] 13:18; 18:9; Ps 41:10; Mt 26:24; Acts 1:16.   f. [17:13] 15:11.   g. [17:14] 15:19.   h. [17:15] Mt 6:13; 2 Thes 3:3; 1 Jn 5:18.   i. [17:17] 1 Pt 1:22.   j. [17:18] 20:21–22.

that they may all be one, as you, Father, are in me and I in you, that they also may be in us, that the world may believe that you sent me.ᵏ ²²And I have given them the glory you gave me, so that they may be one, as we are one, ²³I in them and you in me, that they may be brought to perfection as one, that the world may know that you sent me, and that you loved them even as you loved me. ²⁴Father, they are your gift to me. I wish that where I am* they also may be with me, that they may see my glory that you gave me, because you loved me before the foundation of the world.ˡ ²⁵Righteous Father, the world also does not know you, but I know you, and they know that you sent me.ᵐ ²⁶I made known to them your name and I will make it known,† that the love with which you loved me may be in them and I in them."

CHAPTER 18

Jesus Arrested.‡ ¹When he had said this, Jesus went out§ with his disciples across the Kidron valley to where there was a garden, into which he and his disciples entered.ⁿ ²Judas his betrayer also knew the place, because Jesus had often met there with his disciples. ³So Judas got a band of soldiers¶ and guards from the chief priests and the Pharisees and went there with lanterns, torches, and weapons.º ⁴Jesus, knowing everything that was going to happen to him, went out and said to them, "Whom are you looking for?" ⁵They answered him, "Jesus the Nazorean."** He said to them, "I AM." Judas his betrayer was also with them. ⁶When he said to them, "I AM," they turned away and fell to the ground. ⁷So he again asked them, "Whom are you looking for?" They said, "Jesus the Nazorean." ⁸Jesus answered, "I told you that I AM. So if you are looking for me, let these men go." ⁹††ᵖThis was to fulfill what he had said, "I have not lost any of those you gave me."

¹⁰Then Simon Peter, who had a sword, drew it, struck the high priest's slave, and cut off his right ear. The slave's name was Malchus.‡‡ ¹¹Jesus said to Peter, "Put your sword into its scabbard. Shall I not drink the cup§§ that the Father gave me?"�q

¹²ʳSo the band of soldiers, the tribune, and the Jewish guards seized Jesus, bound him, ¹³and brought him to Annas¶¶ first. He was the father-in-law of Caiaphas, who was high priest that year.ˢ ¹⁴It was Caiaphas who had counseled the Jews that it was better that one man should die rather than the people.ᵗ

Peter's First Denial.ᵘ ¹⁵Simon Peter and another disciple*** followed Jesus. Now the other disciple was known to the high priest, and he entered the courtyard of the high priest with Jesus. ¹⁶But Peter stood at the gate outside. So the other disciple, the acquaintance of the high priest, went out and spoke to the gatekeeper and brought Peter in. ¹⁷Then the maid who was the gatekeeper said to Peter, "You are not one of this man's disciples, are you?" He said, "I am not." ¹⁸Now the slaves and the guards were standing around a charcoal fire that they had made, because it was cold, and were warming themselves. Peter was also standing there keeping warm.

The Inquiry Before Annas.ᵛ ¹⁹The high priest questioned Jesus about his disciples and about his doctrine. ²⁰Jesus answered him, "I have spoken publicly to the world. I have always taught in a synagogue or in the temple area††† where all the Jews gather, and in secret I have said nothing.ʷ ²¹Why ask me? Ask those who heard me what I said to them. They know what I said." ²²When he had said this, one of the temple guards standing there struck Jesus and said, "Is this the way you answer the high priest?"ˣ ²³Jesus answered him, "If I have spoken wrongly, testify to the wrong; but if I have spoken rightly, why do you strike me?" ²⁴Then Annas sent him bound to Caiaphas‡‡‡ the high priest.ʸ

Peter Denies Jesus Again.ᶻ ²⁵Now Simon Peter was standing there keeping warm. And they

---

*[17:24] **Where I am:** Jesus prays for the believers ultimately to join him in heaven. Then they will not see his glory as in a mirror but clearly (2 Cor 3:18; 1 Jn 3:2).

†[17:26] **I will make it known:** through the Advocate.

‡[18:1–14] John does not mention the agony in the garden and the kiss of Judas, nor does he identify the place as Gethsemane or the Mount of Olives.

§[18:1] **Jesus went out:** see Jn 14:31, where it seems he is leaving the supper room. **Kidron valley:** literally, "the winter-flowing Kidron"; this wadi has water only during the winter rains.

¶[18:3] **Band of soldiers:** seems to refer to Roman troops, either the full cohort of 600 men (1/10 of a legion), or more likely the maniple of 200 under their tribune (Jn 18:12). In this case, John is hinting at Roman collusion in the action against Jesus before he was brought to Pilate. The lanterns and torches may be symbolic of the hour of darkness.

[18:5] **Nazorean: the form found in Mt 26:71 (see note on Mt 2:23) is here used, not Nazarene of Mark. **I AM:** or "I am he," but probably intended by the evangelist as an expression of divinity (cf. their appropriate response in Jn 18:6); see note on Jn 8:24. John sets the confusion of the arresting party against the background of Jesus' divine majesty.

††[18:9] The citation may refer to Jn 6:39; 10:28; or 17:12.

‡‡[18:10] Only John gives the names of the two antagonists; both John and Luke mention the right ear.

§§[18:11] The theme of the cup is found in the synoptic account of the agony (Mk 14:36 and parallels).

¶¶[18:13] **Annas:** only John mentions an inquiry before Annas; cf. Jn 18:16, 19–24; see note on Lk 3:2. It is unlikely that this nighttime interrogation before Annas is the same as the trial before Caiaphas placed by Matthew and Mark at night and by Luke in the morning.

***[18:15–16] **Another disciple . . . the other disciple:** see note on Jn 13:23.

†††[18:20] **I have always taught . . . in the temple area:** cf. Mk 14:49 for a similar statement.

‡‡‡[18:24] **Caiaphas:** see Mt 26:3, 57; Lk 3:2; and the notes there. John may leave room here for the trial before Caiaphas described in the synoptic gospels.

---

k. [17:21] 10:30; 14:10–11, 20. l. [17:24] 14:3; 1 Thes 4:17. m. [17:25] 1:10. n. [18:1] 2 Sm 15:23; Mt 26:30, 36; Mk 14:26, 32; Lk 22:39. o. [18:3] Mt 26:47–51; Mk 14:43–44; Lk 22:47. p. [18:9] 6:39; 10:28; 17:12.

q. [18:11] Mt 20:22; 26:39; Mk 10:38; Lk 22:42. r. [18:12–14] Mt 26:57–58; Mk 14:53–54; Lk 22:54–55. s. [18:13] Lk 3:2. t. [18:14] 11:49–50. u. [18:15–18] Mt 26:58, 69–70; Mk 14:54, 66–68; Lk 22:54–57. v. [18:19–24] Mt 26:59–66; Mk 14:55–64; Lk 22:66–71. w. [18:20] 6:59; 7:14, 26; Is 48:16; Mt 26:55; Mk 4:23; Lk 19:47; 22:53. x. [18:22] Acts 23:2. y. [18:24] Mt 26:57. z. [18:25–27] Mt 26:71–75; Mk 14:69–72; Lk 22:58–62.

said to him, "You are not one of his disciples, are you?" He denied it and said, "I am not." [26]One of the slaves of the high priest, a relative of the one whose ear Peter had cut off, said, "Didn't I see you in the garden with him?" [27]Again Peter denied it. And immediately the cock crowed.[*]

The Trial Before Pilate. [28a]Then they brought Jesus from Caiaphas to the praetorium.[†] It was morning. And they themselves did not enter the praetorium, in order not to be defiled so that they could eat the Passover. [29]So Pilate came out to them and said, "What charge do you bring [against] this man?" [30]They answered and said to him, "If he were not a criminal, we would not have handed him over to you." [31]At this, Pilate said to them, "Take him yourselves, and judge him according to your law." The Jews answered him, "We do not have the right to execute anyone,"[‡] [32§]in order that the word of Jesus might be fulfilled that he said indicating the kind of death[b] he would die. [33]So Pilate went back into the praetorium and summoned Jesus and said to him, "Are you the King of the Jews?" [34]Jesus answered, "Do you say this on your own or have others told you about me?" [35]Pilate answered, "I am not a Jew, am I? Your own nation and the chief priests handed you over to me. What have you done?"[c] [36]Jesus answered, "My kingdom does not belong to this world. If my kingdom did belong to this world, my attendants [would] be fighting to keep me from being handed over to the Jews. But as it is, my kingdom is not here."[d] [37]So Pilate said to him, "Then you are a king?" Jesus answered, "You say I am a king.[ʼ] For this I was born and for this I came into the world, to testify to the truth. Everyone who belongs to the truth listens to my voice."[ʰ] [38]Pilate said to him, "What is truth?"[f]

When he had said this, he again went out to the Jews and said to them, "I find no guilt in him. [39]But you have a custom that I release one prisoner to you at Passover.[**] Do you want me to release to you the King of the Jews?" [40]They cried out again, "Not this one but Barabbas!"[††] Now Barabbas was a revolutionary.

CHAPTER 19

[1‡‡§]Then Pilate took Jesus and had him scourged. [2]And the soldiers wove a crown out of thorns and placed it on his head, and clothed him in a purple cloak, [3]and they came to him and said, "Hail, King of the Jews!" And they struck him repeatedly. [4]Once more Pilate went out and said to them, "Look, I am bringing him out to you, so that you may know that I find no guilt in him."[ʰ] [5]So Jesus came out, wearing the crown of thorns and the purple cloak. And he said to them, "Behold, the man!"[ⁱ] [6]When the chief priests and the guards saw him they cried out, "Crucify him, crucify him!" Pilate said to them, "Take him yourselves and crucify him. I find no guilt in him."[ʲ] [7§§]The Jews answered,[k] "We have a law, and according to that law he ought to die, because he made himself the Son of God." [8]Now when Pilate heard this statement, he became even more afraid, [9]and went back into the praetorium and said to Jesus, "Where are you from?" Jesus did not answer him.[ʲ] [10]So Pilate said to him, "Do you not speak to me? Do you not know that I have power to release you and I have power to crucify you?" [11]Jesus answered [him], "You would have no power over me if it had not been given to you from above. For this reason the one who handed me over to you has the greater sin."[ᵐ] [12]Consequently, Pilate tried to release him; but the Jews cried out, "If you release him, you are not a Friend of Caesar.[¶¶] Everyone who makes himself a king opposes Caesar."[ⁿ] [13]When Pilate heard these words he brought Jesus out and seated him[***] on the judge's bench in the place called Stone Pavement, in Hebrew, Gabbatha. [14]It was preparation day for Passover, and it was about noon.[†††] And he said to the Jews,

---

[*][18:27] Cockcrow was the third Roman division of the night, lasting from midnight to 3 a.m.

[†][18:28] **Praetorium:** see note on Mt 27:27. **Morning:** literally, "the early hour," or fourth Roman division of the night, 3 to 6 a.m.. **The Passover:** the synoptic gospels give the impression that the Thursday night supper was the Passover meal (Mk 14:12); for John that meal is still to be eaten Friday night.

[‡][18:31] **We do not have the right to execute anyone:** only John gives this reason for their bringing Jesus to Pilate. Jewish sources are not clear on the competence of the Sanhedrin at this period to sentence and to execute for political crimes.

[§][18:32] The Jewish punishment for blasphemy was stoning (Lv 24:16). In coming to the Romans to ensure that Jesus would be crucified, the Jewish authorities fulfilled his prophecy that he would be exalted (Jn 3:14; 12:32–33). There is some historical evidence, however, for Jews crucifying Jews.

[¶][18:37] **You say I am a king:** see Mt 26:64 for a similar response to the high priest. It is at best a reluctant affirmative.

[**][18:39] See note on Mt 27:15.

[††][18:40] **Barabbas:** see note on Mt 27:16–17. **Revolutionary:** a guerrilla warrior fighting for nationalistic aims, though the term can also denote a robber. See note on Mt 27:38.

[‡‡][19:1] Luke places the mockery of Jesus at the midpoint in the trial when Jesus was sent to Herod. Mark and Matthew place the scourging and mockery at the end of the trial after the sentence of death. Scourging was an integral part of the crucifixion penalty.

[§§][19:7] **Made himself the Son of God:** this question was not raised in John's account of the Jewish interrogations of Jesus as it was in the synoptic account. Nevertheless, see Jn 5:18; 8:53; 10:36.

[¶¶][19:12] **Friend of Caesar:** a Roman honorific title bestowed upon high-ranking officials for merit.

[***][19:13] **Seated him:** others translate "(Pilate) sat down." In John's thought, Jesus is the real judge of the world, and John may here be portraying him seated on the judgment bench. **Stone Pavement:** in Greek *lithostrotos*; under the fortress Antonia, one of the conjectured locations of the praetorium, a massive stone pavement has been excavated. **Gabbatha** (Aramaic rather than Hebrew) probably means "ridge, elevation."

[†††][19:14] **Noon:** Mk 15:25 has Jesus crucified "at the third hour," which means either 9 a.m. or the period from 9 to 12

---

a. [18:28–38a] Mt 27:1–2, 11–25; Mk 15:1–5; Lk 23:1–5.   b. [18:32] 3:14;   8:28;   12:32–33.   c. [18:35]   1:11.   d. [18:36]   1:10; 8:23.   e. [18:37] 8:47; 1 Tm 6:13.   f. [18:38b–40] Mt 27:15–26; Mk 15:6–15; Lk 23:18–25; Acts 3:14.

g. [19:1–16] Mt 27:27–31; Mk 15:16–20; Lk 23:13–25.   h. [19:4] 18:38.   i. [19:5] Is 52:14.   j. [19:6] 18:31; 19:15.   k. [19:7] 10:33–36; Lv 24:16.   l. [19:9] 7:28.   m. [19:11] 3:27; 10:18; Rom 13:1.   n. [19:12] Acts 17:7.

"Behold, your king!" [15]They cried out, "Take him away, take him away! Crucify him!" Pilate said to them, "Shall I crucify your king?" The chief priests answered, "We have no king but Caesar." [16]Then he handed him over to them to be crucified.*

The Crucifixion of Jesus. So they took Jesus, [17o]and carrying the cross himself[†] he went out to what is called the Place of the Skull, in Hebrew, Golgotha. [18]There they crucified him, and with him two others, one on either side, with Jesus in the middle. [19‡]Pilate also had an inscription written and put on the cross. It read, "Jesus the Nazorean, the King of the Jews." [20]Now many of the Jews read this inscription, because the place where Jesus was crucified was near the city; and it was written in Hebrew, Latin, and Greek. [21]So the chief priests of the Jews said to Pilate, "Do not write 'The King of the Jews,' but that he said, 'I am the King of the Jews.'"[p] [22]Pilate answered, "What I have written, I have written."

[23§]When the soldiers had crucified Jesus,[q] they took his clothes and divided them into four shares, a share for each soldier.[r] They also took his tunic, but the tunic was seamless, woven in one piece from the top down. [24]So they said to one another, "Let's not tear it, but cast lots for it to see whose it will be," in order that the passage of scripture might be fulfilled [that says]:

"They divided my garments among them,
and for my vesture they cast lots."

This is what the soldiers did. [25§]Standing by the cross of Jesus were his mother and his mother's

sister, Mary the wife of Clopas, and Mary of Magdala. [26]When Jesus saw his mother** and the disciple there whom he loved, he said to his mother, "Woman, behold, your son."[t] [27]Then he said to the disciple, "Behold, your mother." And from that hour the disciple took her into his home.

[28u]After this, aware that everything was now finished, in order that the scripture might be fulfilled,[††] Jesus said, "I thirst."[v] [29]There was a vessel filled with common wine.[‡‡] So they put a sponge soaked in wine on a sprig of hyssop and put it up to his mouth. [30§§]When Jesus had taken the wine, he said, "It is finished."[w] And bowing his head, he handed over the spirit.

The Blood and Water. [31]Now since it was preparation day, in order that the bodies might not remain on the cross on the sabbath, for the sabbath day of that week was a solemn one, the Jews asked Pilate that their legs be broken and they be taken down.[x] [32]So the soldiers came and broke the legs of the first and then of the other one who was crucified with Jesus. [33]But when they came to Jesus and saw that he was already dead, they did not break his legs, [34¶¶]but one soldier thrust his lance into his side, and immediately blood and water flowed out. [35]An eyewitness has testified, and his testimony is true; he knows*** that he is speaking the truth, so that you

---

noon, the time when, according to John, Jesus was sentenced to death, was the hour at which the priests began to slaughter Passover lambs in the temple; see Jn 1:29.

*[19:16] **He handed him over to them to be crucified:** in context this would seem to mean "handed him over to the chief priests." Lk 23:25 has a similar ambiguity. There is a polemic tendency in the gospels to place the guilt of the crucifixion on the Jewish authorities and to exonerate the Romans from blame. But John later mentions the Roman soldiers (Jn 19:23), and it was to these soldiers that Pilate handed Jesus over.

†[19:17] **Carrying the cross himself:** a different picture from that of the synoptics, especially Lk 23:26, where Simon of Cyrene is made to carry the cross, walking behind Jesus. In John's theology, Jesus remained in complete control and master of his destiny (cf. Jn 10:18). **Place of the Skull:** the Latin word for skull is *Calvaria*; hence "Calvary." **Golgotha** is actually an Aramaic rather than a Hebrew word.

‡[19:19] The inscription differs with slightly different words in each of the four gospels. John's form is fullest and gives the equivalent of the Latin *INRI* = *Iesus Nazarenus Rex Iudaeorum.* Only John mentions its polyglot character (Jn 19:20) and Pilate's role in keeping the title unchanged (Jn 19:21–22).

§[19:23–25a] While all four gospels describe the soldiers casting lots to divide Jesus' garments (see note on Mt 27:35), only John quotes the underlying passage from Ps 22:19, and only John sees each line of the poetic parallelism literally carried out in two separate actions (Jn 19:23–24).

¶[19:25] It is not clear whether four women are meant, or three (i.e., **Mary the wife of Cl[e]opas** [cf. Lk 24:18] is in apposition with **his mother's sister**) or two (his mother

and his mother's sister, i.e., Mary of Cl[e]opas and Mary of Magdala). Only John mentions the mother of Jesus here. The synoptics have a group of women looking on from a distance at the cross (Mk 15:40).

[19:26–27] This scene has been interpreted literally, of Jesus' concern for his mother; and symbolically, e.g., in the light of the Cana story in Jn 2 (the presence of the mother of Jesus, the address **woman, and the mention of the **hour**) and of the upper room in Jn 13 (the presence of the beloved disciple; the **hour**). Now that the hour has come (Jn 19:28), Mary (a symbol of the church?) is given a role as the mother of Christians (personified by the beloved disciple); or, as a representative of those seeking salvation, she is supported by the disciple who interprets Jesus' revelation; or Jewish and Gentile Christianity (or Israel and the Christian community) are reconciled.

††[19:28] **The scripture . . . fulfilled:** either in the scene of Jn 19:25–27, or in the **I thirst** of Jn 19:28. If the latter, Ps 22:16; 69:22 deserve consideration.

‡‡[19:29] **Wine:** John does not mention the drugged wine, a narcotic that Jesus refused as the crucifixion began (Mk 15:23), but only this final gesture of kindness at the end (Mk 15:36). **Hyssop,** a small plant, is scarcely suitable for carrying a sponge (Mark mentions a reed) and may be a symbolic reference to the hyssop used to daub the blood of the paschal lamb on the doorpost of the Hebrews (Ex 12:22).

§§[19:30] **Handed over the spirit:** there is a double nuance of dying (giving up the last breath or spirit) and that of passing on the holy Spirit; see Jn 7:39, which connects the giving of the Spirit with Jesus' glorious return to the Father, and Jn 20:22, where the author portrays the conferral of the Spirit.

¶¶[19:34–35] John probably emphasizes these verses to show the reality of Jesus' death, against the docetic heretics. In the blood and water there may also be a symbolic reference to the Eucharist and baptism.

***[19:35] **He knows:** it is not certain from the Greek that this **he** is the **eyewitness** of the first part of the sentence. **May [come to] believe:** see note on Jn 20:31.

---

o. [19:17–22] Mt 27:32–37; Mk 15:21–26; Lk 23:26–35. p. [19:21] 18:33; Lk 19:14. q. [19:23–27] Mt 27:38–44; Mk 15:27–32; Lk 23:36–43. r. [19:23–24] Ps 22:19; Mt 27:35; Mk 15:24; Lk 23:34. s. [19:25] Mt 27:55; Mk 15:40–41; Lk 8:2; 23:49.

t. [19:26] 13:23. u. [19:28–30] Mt 27:45–56; Mk 15:33–41; Lk 23:44–49. v. [19:28] Ps 22:16; 69:22. w. [19:30] 4:34; 10:18; 17:4; Lk 23:46. x. [19:31] Ex 12:16; Dt 21:23. y. [19:34] Nm 20:11; 1 Jn 5:6.

also may [come to] believe.[z] [36]For this happened so that the scripture passage might be fulfilled:

"Not a bone of it will be broken."[a]

[37]And again another passage says:

"They will look upon him whom they
     have pierced."[b]

The Burial of Jesus.[*] [38c]After this, Joseph of Arimathea, secretly a disciple of Jesus for fear of the Jews, asked Pilate if he could remove the body of Jesus. And Pilate permitted it. So he came and took his body. [39]Nicodemus, the one who had first come to him at night, also came bringing a mixture of myrrh and aloes weighing about one hundred pounds.[d] [40]They took the body of Jesus and bound it with burial cloths along with the spices, according to the Jewish burial custom. [41]Now in the place where he had been crucified there was a garden, and in the garden a new tomb, in which no one had yet been buried. [42]So they laid Jesus there because of the Jewish preparation day; for the tomb was close by.

CHAPTER 20[†]
The Empty Tomb.[‡] [1]On the first day of the week,[e] Mary of Magdala came to the tomb early in the morning, while it was still dark,[§] and saw the stone removed from the tomb. [f] [2]So she ran[¶] and went to Simon Peter and to the other disciple whom Jesus loved, and told them, "They have taken the Lord from the tomb, and we don't know where they put him." [3]**So Peter and the other disciple went out and came to the tomb. [4]They both ran, but the other disciple ran faster than Peter and arrived at the tomb first; [5]he bent down and saw the burial cloths there, but did not go in. [6g]When Simon Peter arrived

after him, he went into the tomb and saw the burial cloths[††] there, [7]and the cloth that had covered his head, not with the burial cloths but rolled up in a separate place.[h] [8]Then the other disciple also went in, the one who had arrived at the tomb first, and he saw and believed. [9‡‡]For they did not yet understand the scripture that he had to rise from the dead. [10]Then the disciples returned home.

The Appearance to Mary of Magdala.[§§] [11]But Mary stayed outside the tomb weeping.[j] And as she wept, she bent over into the tomb [12]and saw two angels in white sitting there, one at the head and one at the feet where the body of Jesus had been. [13]And they said to her, "Woman, why are you weeping?" She said to them, "They have taken my Lord, and I don't know where they laid him." [14]When she had said this, she turned around and saw Jesus there, but did not know it was Jesus.[k] [15]Jesus said to her, "Woman, why are you weeping? Whom are you looking for?"[l] She thought it was the gardener and said to him, "Sir, if you carried him away, tell me where you laid him, and I will take him." [16]Jesus said to her, "Mary!" She turned and said to him in Hebrew, "Rabbouni,"[¶¶] which means Teacher. [17]Jesus said to her, "Stop holding on to me,[***] for I have not yet ascended to the Father. But go to my brothers and tell them, 'I am going to my Father and your Father, to my God and your God.'"[m] [18]Mary of Magdala went and announced to the disciples, "I have seen the Lord," and what he told her.

Appearance to the Disciples.[†††] [19]On the evening of that first day of the week,[n] when the doors

††[20:6–8] Some special feature about the state of the burial cloths caused the beloved disciple to believe. Perhaps the details emphasized that the grave had not been robbed.
‡‡[20:9] Probably a general reference to the scriptures is intended, as in Lk 24:26 and 1 Cor 15:4. Some individual Old Testament passages suggested are Ps 16:10; Hos 6:2; Jon 2:1, 2, 10.
§§[20:11–18] This appearance to Mary is found only in John, but cf. Mt 28:8–10 and Mk 16:9–11.
¶¶[20:16] **Rabbouni:** Hebrew or Aramaic for "my master."
***[20:17] **Stop holding on to me:** see Mt 28:9, where the women take hold of his feet. **I have not yet ascended:** for John and many of the New Testament writers, the ascension in the theological sense of going to the Father to be glorified took place with the resurrection as one action. This scene in John dramatizes such an understanding, for by Easter night Jesus is glorified and can give the Spirit. Therefore his ascension takes place immediately after he has talked to Mary. In such a view, the ascension after forty days described in Acts 1:1–11 would be simply a termination of earthly appearances or, perhaps better, an introduction to the conferral of the Spirit upon the early church, modeled on Elisha's being able to have a (double) share in the spirit of Elijah if he saw him being taken up (same verb as ascending) into heaven (2 Kgs 2:9–12). **To my Father and your Father, to my God and your God:** this echoes Ru 1:16: "Your people shall be my people, and your God my God." The Father of Jesus will now become the Father of the disciples because, once ascended, Jesus can give them the Spirit that comes from the Father and they can be reborn as God's children (Jn 3:5). That is why he calls them **my brothers.**
†††[20:19–29] The appearances to the disciples, without or with Thomas (cf. Jn 11:16; 14:5), have rough parallels in

*[19:38–42] In the first three gospels there is no anointing on Friday. In Matthew and Luke the women come to the tomb on Sunday morning precisely to anoint Jesus.
†[20:1–31] The risen Jesus reveals his glory and confers the Spirit. This story fulfills the basic need for testimony to the resurrection. What we have here is not a record but a series of single stories.
‡[20:1–10] The story of the empty tomb is found in both the Matthean and the Lucan traditions; John's version seems to be a fusion of the two.
§[20:1] **Still dark:** according to Mark the sun had risen, Matthew describes it as "dawning," and Luke refers to early dawn. Mary sees the stone removed, not the empty tomb.
¶[20:2] Mary runs away, not directed by an angel/young man as in the synoptic accounts. The plural "we" in the second part of her statement might reflect a tradition of more women going to the tomb.
**[20:3–10] The basic narrative is told of Peter alone in Lk 24:12, a verse missing in important manuscripts and which may be borrowed from tradition similar to John. Cf. also Lk 24:24.

z. [19:35] 7:37–39; 21:24.   a. [19:36] Ex 12:46; Nm 9:12; Ps 34:21.   b. [19:37] Nm 21:9; Zec 12:10; Rev 1:7.   c. [19:38–42] Mt 27:57–60; Mk 15:42–46; Lk 23:46–49.   d. [19:39] 3:1–2; 7:50; Ps 45:9.   e. [20:1–10] Mt 28:1–10; Mk 16:1–11; Lk 24:1–12.   f. [20:1] 19:25.   g. [20:6] Lk 24:12.

h. [20:7] 11:44; 19:40.   i. [20:9] Acts 2:26–27; 1 Cor 15:4.   j. [20:11–18] Mk 16:9–11.   k. [20:14] 21:4; Mk 16:12; Lk 24:16; 1 Cor 15:43–44.   l. [20:15–17] Mt 28:9–10.   m. [20:17] Acts 1:9.   n. [20:19–23] Mt 28:16–20; Mk 16:14–18; Lk 24:36–44.

were locked, where the disciples' were, for fear of the Jews, Jesus came and stood in their midst and said to them, "Peace be with you." [20]When he had said this, he showed them his hands and his side.[†] The disciples rejoiced when they saw the Lord.[o] [21][Jesus] said to them again,[p] "Peace be with you. As the Father has sent me, so I send you." [22]And when he had said this, he breathed on them and said to them,[q] "Receive the holy Spirit. [23]Whose sins you forgive are forgiven them, and whose sins you retain are retained."
Thomas. [24]Thomas, called Didymus, one of the Twelve, was not with them when Jesus came. [25]So the other disciples said to him, "We have seen the Lord." But he said to them, "Unless I see the mark of the nails in his hands and put my finger into the nailmarks and put my hand into his side, I will not believe."[s] [26]Now a week later his disciples were again inside and Thomas was with them. Jesus came, although the doors were locked, and stood in their midst and said, "Peace be with you."[t] [27]Then he said to Thomas, "Put your finger here and see my hands, and bring your hand and put it into my side, and do not be unbelieving, but believe." [28]*u*Thomas answered and said to him, "My Lord and my God!" [29][†][†]Jesus said to him, "Have you come to believe because you have seen me?[v] Blessed are those who have not seen and have believed."
Conclusion.[‡][‡] [30]Now Jesus did many other signs in the presence of [his] disciples that are not written in this book.[w] [31]But these are written

that you may [come to] believe that Jesus is the Messiah, the Son of God, and that through this belief you may have life in his name.[x]

IV. EPILOGUE: THE RESURRECTION APPEARANCE IN GALILEE

CHAPTER 21

The Appearance to the Seven Disciples. [1]After this, Jesus revealed himself again to his disciples at the Sea of Tiberias. He revealed himself in this way.[y] [2]Together were Simon Peter, Thomas called Didymus, Nathanael from Cana in Galilee, Zebedee's sons,[¶][¶] and two others of his disciples. [3]***Simon Peter said to them, "I am going fishing." They said to him, "We also will come with you." So they went out and got into the boat, but that night they caught nothing.[z] [4]When it was already dawn, Jesus was standing on the shore; but the disciples did not realize that it was Jesus.[a] [5]Jesus said to them, "Children, have you caught anything to eat?" They answered him, "No."[b] [6]So he said to them, "Cast the net over the right side of the boat and you will find something." So they cast it, and were not able to pull it in because of the number of fish. [7]So the disciple whom Jesus loved said to Peter, "It is the Lord." When Simon Peter heard that it was the Lord, he tucked in his garment, for he was lightly clad, and jumped into the sea. [8]The other disciples came in the boat, for they were not far from shore, only about a hundred yards, dragging the net with the fish. [9][†][†][†]*c*When they climbed out on shore, they saw a charcoal fire with fish on it and bread. [10]Jesus said to them, "Bring some of the fish you just caught." [11]So Simon Peter went over and dragged the net ashore full of one hundred fifty-three[‡][‡][‡] large fish. Even though there were so

---

the other gospels only for Jn 20:19–23; cf. Lk 24:36–39; Mk 16:14–18.

[*][20:19] **The disciples:** by implication from Jn 20:24 this means ten of the Twelve, presumably in Jerusalem. **Peace be with you:** although this could be an ordinary greeting, John intends here to echo Jn 14:27. The theme of rejoicing in Jn 20:20 echoes Jn 16:22.

[†][20:20] **Hands and . . . side:** Lk 24:39–40 mentions "hands and feet," based on Ps 22:17.

[‡][20:21] By means of this sending, the Eleven were made apostles, that is, "those sent" (cf. Jn 17:18), though John does not use the noun in reference to them (see note on Jn 13:16). A solemn mission or "sending" is also the subject of the post-resurrection appearances to the Eleven in Mt 28:19; Lk 24:47; Mk 16:15.

[§][20:22] This action recalls Gn 2:7, where God breathed on the first man and gave him life; just as Adam's life came from God, so now the disciples' new spiritual life comes from Jesus. Cf. also the revivification of the dry bones in Ez 37. This is the author's version of Pentecost. Cf. also the note on Jn 19:30.

[¶][20:23] The Council of Trent defined that this power to forgive sins is exercised in the sacrament of penance. See Mt 16:19; 18:18.

[**][20:28] **My Lord and my God:** this forms a literary inclusion with the first verse of the gospel: "and the Word was God."

[††][20:29] This verse is a beatitude on future generations; faith, not sight, matters.

[‡‡][20:30–31] These verses are clearly a conclusion to the gospel and express its purpose. While many manuscripts read **come to believe,** possibly implying a missionary purpose for John's gospel, a small number of quite early ones read "continue to believe," suggesting that the audience consists of Christians whose faith is to be deepened by the book; cf. Jn 19:35.

[§§][21:1–23] There are many non-Johannine peculiarities in this chapter, some suggesting Lucan Greek style; yet this passage is closer to John than Jn 7:53–8:11. There are many Johannine features as well. Its closest parallels are in the synoptic gospels are found in Lk 5:1–11 and Mt 14:28–31. Perhaps the tradition was ultimately derived from John but preserved by some disciple other than the writer of the rest of the gospel. The appearances narrated seem to be independent of those in Jn 20. Even if a later addition, the chapter was added before publication of the gospel, for it appears in all manuscripts.

[¶¶][21:2] **Zebedee's sons:** the only reference to James and John in this gospel (but see note on Jn 1:37). Perhaps the phrase was originally a gloss to identify, among the five, the **two others of his disciples.** The anonymity of the latter phrase is more Johannine (Jn 1:35). The total of seven may suggest the community of the disciples in its fullness.

[***][21:3–6] This may be a variant of Luke's account of the catch of fish; see note on Lk 5:1–11.

[†††][21:9, 12–13] It is strange that Jesus already has fish since none have yet been brought ashore. This meal may have had eucharistic significance for early Christians since Jn 21:13 recalls Jn 6:11 which uses the vocabulary of Jesus' action at the Last Supper; but see also note on Mt 14:19.

[‡‡‡][21:11] The exact number 153 is probably meant to have a symbolic meaning in relation to the apostles' universal

---

o. [20:20] 14:27.   p. [20:21] 17:18; Mt 28:19; Mk 16:15; Lk 24:47–48.   q. [20:22] Gn 2:7; Ez 37:9; 1 Cor 15:45.   r. [20:23] Mt 16:19; 18:18.   s. [20:25] 1 Jn 1:1.   t. [20:26] 21:14.   u. [20:28] 1:1.   v. [20:29] 4:48; Lk 1:45; 1 Pt 1:8.   w. [20:30] 21:25.

x. [20:31] 3:14, 15; 1 Jn 5:13.   y. [21:1] Mt 26:32; 28:7.   z. [21:3] Mt 4:18; Lk 5:4–10.   a. [21:4] 20:14; Mt 28:17; Lk 24:16.   b. [21:5] Lk 24:41.   c. [21:9] Lk 24:41–43.

many, the net was not torn.[d] [12]Jesus said to them, "Come, have breakfast." And none of the disciples dared to ask him,* "Who are you?" because they realized it was the Lord. [13]Jesus came over and took the bread and gave it to them, and in like manner the fish.[e] [14†]This was now the third time[f] Jesus was revealed to his disciples after being raised from the dead.

Jesus and Peter.[‡] [15]When they had finished breakfast, Jesus said to Simon Peter,[g] "Simon, son of John, do you love me more than these?"[¶] He said to him, "Yes, Lord, you know that I love you." He said to him, "Feed my lambs." [16]He then said to him a second time, "Simon, son of John, do you love me?" He said to him, "Yes, Lord, you know that I love you." He said to him, "Tend my sheep." [17]He said to him the third time, "Simon, son of John, do you love me?" Peter was distressed that he had said to him a third time, "Do you love me?" and he said to him, "Lord, you know everything; you know that I love you." [Jesus] said to him, "Feed my sheep.[g] [18**]Amen, amen, I say to you,[h] when you were younger, you used to dress yourself and go where you wanted; but when you grow old, you will stretch out your hands, and someone else will dress you and lead you where you do not want to go." [19]He said this signifying by what kind of death he would glorify God. And when he had said this, he said to him, "Follow me."[i]

The Beloved Disciple. [20]Peter turned and saw the disciple following whom Jesus loved, the one who had also reclined upon his chest during the supper and had said, "Master, who is the one who will betray you?"[j] [21]When Peter saw him, he said to Jesus, "Lord, what about him?" [22]Jesus said to him, "What if I want him to remain until I come?[††] What concern is it of yours? You follow me."[k] [23‡‡]So the word spread among the brothers that that disciple would not die. But Jesus had not told him that he would not die, just "What if I want him to remain until I come? [What concern is it of yours?]"

Conclusion. [24]It is this disciple who testifies to these things and has written them,[§§] and we know that his testimony is true.[l] [25]There are also many other things that Jesus did, but if these were to be described individually, I do not think the whole world would contain the books that would be written.[m]

---

mission; Jerome claims that Greek zoologists catalogued 153 species of fish. Or 153 is the sum of the numbers from 1 to 17. Others invoke Ez 47:10.

*[21:12] **None . . . dared to ask him**: is Jesus' appearance strange to them? Cf. Lk 24:16; Mk 16:12; Jn 20:14. The disciples do, however, recognize Jesus **before** the breaking of the bread (opposed to Lk 24:35).

†[21:14] This verse connects Jn 20 and 21; cf. Jn 20:19, 26.

‡[21:15–23] This section constitutes Peter's rehabilitation and emphasizes his role in the church.

§[21:15–17] In these three verses there is a remarkable variety of synonyms: two different Greek verbs for **love** (see note on Jn 15:13); two verbs for **feed/tend**; two nouns for **sheep**; two verbs for **know**. But apparently there is no difference of meaning. The threefold confession of Peter is meant to counteract his earlier threefold denial (Jn 18:17, 25, 27). The First Vatican Council cited these verses in defining that Jesus after his resurrection gave Peter the jurisdiction of supreme shepherd and ruler over the whole flock.

¶[21:15] **More than these**: probably "more than these disciples do" rather than "more than you love them" or "more than you love these things [fishing, etc.]."

**[21:18] Originally probably a proverb about old age, now used as a figurative reference to the crucifixion of Peter.

††[21:22] **Until I come**: a reference to the parousia.

‡‡[21:23] This whole scene takes on more significance if the disciple is already dead. The death of the apostolic generation caused problems in the church because of a belief that Jesus was to have returned first. Loss of faith sometimes resulted; cf. 2 Pt 3:4.

§§[21:24] **Who . . . has written them**: this does not necessarily mean he wrote them with his own hand. The same expression is used in Jn 19:22 of Pilate, who certainly would not have written the inscription himself. **We know**: i.e., the Christian community; cf. Jn 1:14, 16.

---

d. [21:11] 2 Chr 2:16.   e. [21:13] Lk 24:42.   f. [21:14] 20:19, 26. g. [21:17] 13:37–38; 18:15–18, 25–27; Mt 26:69–75; Mk 14:66–72; Lk 22:55–62.

h. [21:18] Acts 21:11, 14; 2 Pt 1:14.   i. [21:19] 13:36.   j. [21:20] 13:25. k. [21:22] Mt 16:28.   l. [21:24] 19:35.   m. [21:25] 20:30.

THE ACTS OF THE
APOSTLES

The Acts of the Apostles, the second volume of Luke's two-volume work, continues Luke's presentation of biblical history, describing how the salvation promised to Israel in the Old Testament and accomplished by Jesus has now under the guidance of the holy Spirit been extended to the Gentiles. This was accomplished through the divinely chosen representatives (Acts 10:41) whom Jesus prepared during his historical ministry (Acts 1:21–22) and commissioned after his resurrection as witnesses to all that he taught (Acts 1:8; 10:37–43; Lk 24:48). Luke's preoccupation with the Christian community as the Spirit-guided bearer of the word of salvation rules out of his book detailed histories of the activity of most of the preachers. Only the main lines of the roles of Peter and Paul serve Luke's interest.

Peter was the leading member of the Twelve (Acts 1:13, 15), a miracle worker like Jesus in the gospel (Acts 3:1–10; 5:1–11, 15; 9:32–35, 36–42), the object of divine care (Acts 5:17–21; 12:6–11), and the spokesman for the Christian community (Acts 2:14–36; 3:12–26; 4:8–12; 5:29–32; 10:34–43; 15:7–11), who, according to Luke, was largely responsible for the growth of the community in the early days (Acts 2:4; 4:4). Paul eventually joined the community at Antioch (Acts 11:25–26), which subsequently commissioned him and Barnabas to undertake the spread of the gospel to Asia Minor. This missionary venture generally failed to win the Jews of the diaspora to the gospel but enjoyed success among the Gentiles (Acts 13:14–14:27).

Paul's refusal to impose the Mosaic law upon his Gentile converts provoked very strong objection among the Jewish Christians of Jerusalem (Acts 15:1), but both Peter and James supported his position (Acts 15:6–21). Paul's second and third missionary journeys (Acts 16:36–21:16) resulted in the same pattern of failure among the Jews generally but of some success among the Gentiles. Paul, like Peter, is presented as a miracle worker (Acts 14:8–18; 19:12; 20:7–12; 28:7–10) and the object of divine care (Acts 16:25–31).

In Acts, Luke has provided a broad survey of the church's development from the resurrection of Jesus to Paul's first Roman imprisonment, the point at which the book ends. In telling this story, Luke describes the emergence of Christianity from its origins in Judaism to its position as a religion of worldwide status and appeal. Originally a Jewish Christian community in Jerusalem, the church was placed in circumstances impelling it to include within its membership people of other cultures: the Samaritans (Acts 8:4–25), at first an occasional Gentile (Acts 8:26–30; 10:1–48), and finally the Gentiles on principle (Acts 11:20–21). Fear on the part of the Jewish people that Christianity, particularly as preached to the Gentiles, threatened their own cultural heritage caused them to be suspicious of Paul's gospel (Acts 13:42–45; 15:1–5; 28:17–24). The inability of Christian missionaries to allay this apprehension inevitably created a situation in which the gospel was preached more and more to the Gentiles. Toward the end of Paul's career, the Christian communities, with the exception of those in Palestine itself (Acts 9:31), were mainly of Gentile membership. In tracing the emergence of Christianity from Judaism, Luke is insistent upon the prominence of Israel in the divine plan of salvation (see note on Acts 1:26; see also Acts 2:5–6; 3:13–15; 10:36; 13:16–41; 24:14–15) and that the extension of salvation to the Gentiles has been a part of the divine plan from the beginning (see Acts 15:13–18; 26:22–23).

In the development of the church from a Jewish Christian origin in Jerusalem, with its roots in Jewish religious tradition, to a series of Christian communities among the Gentiles of the Roman empire, Luke perceives the action of God in history laying open the heart of all humanity to the divine message of salvation. His approach to the history of the church is motivated by his theological interests. His history of the apostolic church is the story of a Spirit-guided community and a Spirit-guided spread of the Word of God (Acts 1:8). The travels of Peter and Paul are in reality the travels of the Word of God as it spreads from Jerusalem, the city of destiny for Jesus, to Rome, the capital of the civilized world of Luke's day. Nonetheless, the historical data he utilizes are of value for the understanding of the church's early life and development and as general background to the Pauline epistles. In the interpretation of Acts, care must be exercised to determine Luke's theological aims and interests and to evaluate his historical data without either exaggerating their literal accuracy or underestimating their factual worth.

Finally, an apologetic concern is evident throughout Acts. By stressing the continuity between Judaism and Christianity (Acts 13:16–41; 23:6–9; 24:10–21; 26:2–23), Luke argues that Christianity is deserving of the same toleration accorded Judaism by Rome. Part of Paul's defense before Roman authorities is to show that Christianity is not a disturber of the peace of the Roman Empire (Acts 24:5, 12–13; 25:7–8). Moreover, when he stands before Roman authorities, he is declared innocent of any crime against the empire (Acts 18:13–15; 23:29; 25:25–27; 26:31–32). Luke tells his story with the hope that Christianity will be treated as fairly.

Concerning the date of Acts, see the Introduction to the Gospel according to Luke.

The principal divisions of the Acts of the Apostles are the following:

I. The Preparation for the Christian Mission (1:1–2:13)
II. The Mission in Jerusalem (2:14–8:3)
III. The Mission in Judea and Samaria (8:4–9:43)
IV. The Inauguration of the Gentile Mission (10:1–15:35)
V. The Mission of Paul to the Ends of the Earth (15:36–28:31)

I. THE PREPARATION FOR THE CHRISTIAN MISSION

CHAPTER 1*

The Promise of the Spirit. ¹In the first book,ᵃ Theophilus, I dealt with all that Jesus did and taught ²until the day he was taken up, after giving instructions through the holy Spirit to the apostles whom he had chosen.ᵇ ³He presented himself alive to them by many proofs after he had suffered, appearing to them during forty days† and speaking about the kingdom of God.ᶜ

⁴While meeting with them, he enjoined them not to depart from Jerusalem, but to wait for "the promise of the Father‡ about which you have heard me speak;ᵈ ⁵for John baptized with water, but in a few days you will be baptized with the holy Spirit."ᵉ

The Ascension of Jesus. ⁶When they had gathered together they asked him, "Lord, are you at this time going§ to restore the kingdom to Israel?" ⁷*He answered them,ᶠ "It is not for you to know the times or seasons that the Father

---

*[1:1–26] This introductory material (Acts 1:1–2) connects Acts with the Gospel of Luke, shows that the apostles were instructed by the risen Jesus (Acts 1:3–5), points out that the parousia or second coming in glory of Jesus will occur as certainly as his ascension occurred (Acts 1:6–11), and lists the members of the Twelve, stressing their role as a body of divinely mandated witnesses to his life, teaching, and resurrection (Acts 1:12–26).

†[1:3] **Appearing to them during forty days:** Luke considered especially sacred the interval in which the appearances and instructions of the risen Jesus occurred and expressed it therefore in terms of the sacred number forty (cf. Dt 8:2). In his gospel, however, Luke connects the ascension of Jesus with the resurrection by describing the ascension on Easter Sunday evening (Lk 24:50–53). What should probably be understood as one event (resurrection, glorification, ascension, sending of the Spirit—the paschal mystery) has been historicized by Luke when he writes of a visible ascension of Jesus after forty

days and the descent of the Spirit at Pentecost. For Luke, the ascension marks the end of the appearances of Jesus except for the extraordinary appearance to Paul. With regard to Luke's understanding of salvation history, the ascension also marks the end of the time of Jesus (Lk 24:50–53) and signals the beginning of the time of the church.

‡[1:4] **The promise of the Father:** the holy Spirit, as is clear from the next verse. This gift of the Spirit was first promised in Jesus' final instructions to his chosen witnesses in Luke's gospel (Lk 24:49) and formed part of the continuing instructions of the risen Jesus on the kingdom of God, of which Luke speaks in Acts 1:3.

§[1:6] The question of the disciples implies that in believing Jesus to be the Christ (see note on Lk 2:11) they had expected him to be a political leader who would restore self-rule to Israel during his historical ministry. When this had not taken place, they ask if it is to take place at this time, the period of the church.

¶[1:7] This verse echoes the tradition that the precise time of the parousia is not revealed to human beings; cf. Mk 13:32; 1 Thes 5:1–3.

---

a. [1:1] Lk 1:1–4. b. [1:2] Mt 28:19–20; Lk 24:44–49; Jn 20:22; 1 Tm 3:16. c. [1:3] 10:41; 13:31.

d. [1:4] Jn 14:16, 17, 26. e. [1:5] 11:16; Mt 3:11; Mk 1:8; Lk 3:16; Jn 1:26; Eph 1:13. f. [1:7] Mt 24:36; 1 Thes 5:1–2.

has established by his own authority. [8]*But you will receive power when the holy Spirit comes upon you,[g] and you will be my witnesses in Jerusalem, throughout Judea and Samaria, and to the ends of the earth." [9]When he had said this, as they were looking on, he was lifted up, and a cloud took him from their sight.[h] [10]While they were looking intently at the sky as he was going, suddenly two men dressed in white garments stood beside them.[i] [11]They said, "Men of Galilee, why are you standing there looking at the sky? This Jesus who has been taken up from you into heaven will return in the same way as you have seen him going into heaven."[j] [12k]Then they returned to Jerusalem from the mount called Olivet, which is near Jerusalem, a sabbath day's journey away.

The First Community in Jerusalem. [13]When they entered the city they went to the upper room where they were staying, Peter and John and James and Andrew, Philip and Thomas, Bartholomew and Matthew, James son of Alphaeus, Simon the Zealot, and Judas son of James. [14]All these devoted themselves with one accord to prayer, together with some women, and Mary the mother of Jesus, and his brothers.[l]

The Choice of Judas's Successor. [15]During those days Peter stood up in the midst of the brothers (there was a group of about one hundred and twenty persons in the one place). He said, [16]"My brothers, the scripture had to be fulfilled which the holy Spirit spoke beforehand through the mouth of David, concerning Judas, who was the guide for those who arrested Jesus.[m] [17]He was numbered among us and was allotted a share in this ministry. [18n]He bought a parcel of land with the wages of his iniquity, and falling headlong, he burst open in the middle, and all his insides spilled out.† [19]This became known to everyone who lived in Jerusalem, so that the parcel of land was called in their language 'Akeldama,' that is, Field of Blood. [20]For it is written in the Book of Psalms:

'Let his encampment become desolate,
    and may no one dwell in it.'

And:

'May another take his office.'[o]

[21]Therefore, it is necessary that one of the men who accompanied us the whole time the Lord Jesus came and went among us, [22]beginning from the baptism of John until the day on which he was taken up from us, become with us a witness to his resurrection."[p] [23]So they proposed two, Joseph called Barsabbas, who was also known as Justus, and Matthias. [24]Then they prayed, "You, Lord, who know the hearts of all, show which one of these two you have chosen [25]to take the place in this apostolic ministry from which Judas turned away to go to his own place." [26‡q]Then they gave lots to them, and the lot fell upon Matthias, and he was counted with the eleven apostles.

CHAPTER 2
The Coming of the Spirit. [1§]When the time for Pentecost was fulfilled, they were all in one place together.[r] [2]And suddenly there came from the sky a noise like a strong driving wind,[¶] and it filled the entire house in which they were.[s] [3]Then there appeared to them tongues as of fire,** which parted and came to rest on each one of them.[t] [4]And they were all filled with the holy Spirit and began to speak in different tongues,†† as the Spirit enabled them to proclaim.[u]

[5]Now there were devout Jews from every nation under heaven staying in Jerusalem. [6]At this sound, they gathered in a large crowd, but they were confused because each one heard them speaking in his own language. [7]They were

---

‡[1:26] The need to replace Judas was probably dictated by the symbolism of the number twelve, recalling the twelve tribes of Israel. This symbolism also indicates that for Luke (see Lk 22:30) the Christian church is a reconstituted Israel.

§[2:1–41] Luke's pentecostal narrative consists of an introduction (Acts 2:1–13), a speech ascribed to Peter declaring the resurrection of Jesus and its messianic significance (Acts 2:14–36), and a favorable response from the audience (Acts 2:37–41). It is likely that the narrative telescopes events that took place over a period of time and on a less dramatic scale. The Twelve were not originally in a position to proclaim publicly the messianic office of Jesus without incurring immediate reprisal from those religious authorities in Jerusalem who had brought about Jesus' death precisely to stem the rising tide in his favor.

¶[2:2] **There came from the sky a noise like a strong driving wind:** wind and spirit are associated in Jn 3:8. The sound of a great rush of wind would herald a new action of God in the history of salvation.

[2:3] **Tongues as of fire: see Ex 19:18 where fire symbolizes the presence of God to initiate the covenant on Sinai. Here the holy Spirit acts upon the apostles, preparing them to proclaim the new covenant with its unique gift of the Spirit (Acts 2:38).

††[2:4] **To speak in different tongues:** ecstatic prayer in praise of God, interpreted in Acts 2:6, 11 as speaking in foreign languages, symbolizing the worldwide mission of the church.

---

*[1:8] Just as Jerusalem was the city of destiny in the Gospel of Luke (the place where salvation was accomplished), so here at the beginning of Acts, Jerusalem occupies a central position. It is the starting point for the mission of the Christian disciples to "the ends of the earth," the place where the apostles were situated and the doctrinal focal point in the early days of the community (Acts 15:2, 6). **The ends of the earth:** for Luke, this means Rome.

†[1:18] Luke records a popular tradition about the death of Judas that differs from the one in Mt 27:5, according to which Judas hanged himself. Here, although the text is not certain, Judas is depicted as purchasing a piece of property with the betrayal money and being killed on it in a fall.

---

g. [1:8] 2:1–13; 10:39; Is 43:10; Mt 28:19; Lk 24:47–48. h. [1:9] 2 Kgs 2:11; Mk 16:19; Lk 24:51. i. [1:10] Jn 20:17. j. [1:11] Lk 24:51; Eph 4:8–10; 1 Pt 3:22; Rev 1:7. k. [1:12–14] Lk 6:14–16. l. [1:14] Lk 23:49. m. [1:16] Ps 41:10; Lk 22:47. n. [1:18] Mt 27:3–10.

o. [1:20] Ps 69:26; 109:8; Jn 17:12. p. [1:22] 1:8–9; 10:39. q. [1:26] Prv 16:33. r. [2:1] Lv 23:15–21; Dt 16:9–11. s. [2:2–3] Jn 3:8. t. [2:3] Lk 3:16. u. [2:4] 1:5; 4:31; 8:15, 17; 10:44; 11:15–16; 15:8; 19:6; Ps 104:30; Jn 20:33.

astounded, and in amazement they asked, "Are not all these people who are speaking Galileans?[v] [8]Then how does each of us hear them in his own native language? [9]We are Parthians, Medes, and Elamites, inhabitants of Mesopotamia, Judea and Cappadocia, Pontus and Asia, [10]Phrygia and Pamphylia, Egypt and the districts of Libya near Cyrene, as well as travelers from Rome, [11]both Jews and converts to Judaism, Cretans and Arabs, yet we hear them speaking in our own tongues of the mighty acts of God."[w] [12]They were all astounded and bewildered, and said to one another, "What does this mean?" [13]But others said, scoffing, "They have had too much new wine."[x]

II. THE MISSION IN JERUSALEM

Peter's Speech at Pentecost. [14]*Then Peter stood up with the Eleven, raised his voice, and proclaimed to them, "You who are Jews, indeed all of you staying in Jerusalem. Let this be known to you, and listen to my words. [15]These people are not drunk, as you suppose, for it is only nine o'clock in the morning. [16]No, this is what was spoken through the prophet Joel:

[17] 'It will come to pass in the last days,' God says,
        'that I will pour out a portion of my
              spirit upon all flesh.
      Your sons and your daughters shall
              prophesy,
          your young men shall see visions,
          your old men shall dream dreams.[y]
[18] Indeed, upon my servants and my handmaids
          I will pour out a portion of my spirit
              in those days,
          and they shall prophesy.
[19] And I will work wonders in the heavens
              above
          and signs on the earth below:
              blood, fire, and a cloud of
              smoke.
[20] The sun shall be turned to darkness,
          and the moon to blood,
              before the coming of the great
              and splendid day of the Lord,
[21] and it shall be that everyone shall be
              saved who calls on the name of
              the Lord.'[z]

[22]You who are Israelites, hear these words. Jesus the Nazorean was a man commended to you by God with mighty deeds, wonders, and signs, which God worked through him in your midst, as you yourselves know.[a] [23]This man, delivered up by the set plan and foreknowledge of God, you killed, using lawless men to crucify him.[b] [24]But God raised him up, releasing him from the throes of death, because it was impossible for him to be held by it.[c] [25]For David says of him:

'I saw the Lord ever before me,[d]
        with him at my right hand I shall
              not be disturbed.
[26] Therefore my heart has been glad and my
              tongue has exulted;
          my flesh, too, will dwell in hope,
[27] because you will not abandon my soul to
              the netherworld,
          nor will you suffer your holy one to
              see corruption.[e]
[28] You have made known to me the paths of
              life;
          you will fill me with joy in your
              presence.'

[29]My brothers, one can confidently say to you about the patriarch David that he died and was buried, and his tomb is in our midst to this day. [30]But since he was a prophet and knew that God had sworn an oath to him that he would set one of his descendants upon his throne,[f] [31]he foresaw and spoke of the resurrection of the Messiah, that neither was he abandoned to the netherworld nor did his flesh see corruption.[g] [32]God raised this Jesus; of this we are all witnesses. [33]Exalted at the right hand of God,[†] he received the promise of the holy Spirit from the Father and poured it forth, as you [both] see and hear.[h] [34]For David did not go up into heaven, but he himself said:

'The Lord said to my Lord,
        "Sit at my right hand[i]
[35]   until I make your enemies your
              footstool."'

[36]Therefore let the whole house of Israel know for certain that God has made him both Lord and Messiah, this Jesus whom you crucified."[j] [37]Now when they heard this, they were cut to the heart, and they asked Peter and the other apostles, "What are we to do, my brothers?"[k] [38]Peter [said] to them, "Repent and be baptized,[‡]

[†][2:33] **At the right hand of God:** or "by the right hand of God."

[‡][2:38] **Repent and be baptized:** repentance is a positive concept, a change of mind and heart toward God reflected in the actual goodness of one's life. It is in accord with the apostolic teaching derived from Jesus (Acts 2:42) and ultimately recorded in the four gospels. Luke presents baptism in Acts as the expected response to the apostolic preaching about Jesus

a. [2:22] 10:38; Lk 24:19.   b. [2:23] 1 Thes 2:15.   c. [2:24] 13:34. d. [2:25–28] Ps 16:8–11.   e. [2:27] 13:35.   f. [2:30] 2 Sm 7:12; Ps 132:11.   g. [2:31] 13:35; Ps 16:10.   h. [2:33] 1:4–5.   i. [2:34–35] Ps 110:1.   j. [2:36] 9:22; Rom 10:9; Phil 2:11.   k. [2:37] Lk 3:10.

---

*[2:14–36] The first of six discourses in Acts (along with Acts 3:12–26; 4:8–12; 5:29–32; 10:34–43; 13:16–41) dealing with the resurrection of Jesus and its messianic import. Five of these are attributed to Peter, the final one to Paul. Modern scholars term these discourses in Acts the "kerygma," the Greek word for proclamation (cf. 1 Cor 15:11).

v. [2:7] 1:11.   w. [2:11] 10:46.   x. [2:13] 1 Cor 14:23.   y. [2:17] Is 2:2; 44:3; Jl 3:1–5.   z. [2:21] Rom 10:13.

every one of you, in the name of Jesus Christ for the forgiveness of your sins; and you will receive the gift of the holy Spirit.[l] [39]For the promise is made to you and to your children and to all those far off, whomever the Lord our God will call."[m] [40]He testified with many other arguments, and was exhorting them, "Save yourselves from this corrupt generation."[n] [41]Those who accepted his message were baptized, and about three thousand persons were added that day.[o]

Communal Life. [42p]They devoted themselves to the teaching of the apostles and to the communal life, to the breaking of the bread and to the prayers.[q] [43]Awe came upon everyone, and many wonders and signs were done through the apostles.[r] [44]All who believed were together and had all things in common;[s] [45]they would sell their property and possessions and divide them among all according to each one's need. [46]Every day they devoted themselves to meeting together in the temple area and to breaking bread in their homes. They ate their meals with exultation and sincerity of heart, [47]praising God and enjoying favor with all the people. And every day the Lord added to their number those who were being saved.

CHAPTER 3

Cure of a Crippled Beggar. [1†]Now Peter and John were going up to the temple area for the three o'clock hour of prayer.[‡] [2†]And a man crippled

---

and associates it with the conferring of the Spirit (Acts 1:5; 10:44–48; 11:16).

*[2:42–47] The first of three summary passages (along with Acts 4:32–37; 5:12–16) that outline, somewhat idyllically, the chief characteristics of the Jerusalem community: adherence to the teachings of the Twelve and the centering of its religious life in the eucharistic liturgy (Acts 2:42); a system of distribution of goods that led wealthier Christians to sell their possessions when the needs of the community's poor required it (Acts 2:44 and the note on Acts 4:32–37); and continued attendance at the temple, since in this initial stage there was little or no thought of any dividing line between Christianity and Judaism (Acts 2:46).

†[3:1–4:31] This section presents a series of related events: the dramatic cure of a lame beggar (Acts 3:1–10) produces a large audience for the kerygmatic discourse of Peter (Acts 3:11–26). The Sadducees, taking exception to the doctrine of resurrection, have Peter, John, and apparently the beggar as well, arrested (Acts 4:1–4) and brought to trial before the Sanhedrin. The issue concerns the authority by which Peter and John publicly teach religious doctrine in the temple (Acts 4:5–7). Peter replies with a brief summary of the kerygma, implying that his authority is prophetic (Acts 4:8–12). The court warns the apostles to abandon their practice of invoking prophetic authority in the name of Jesus (Acts 4:13–18). When Peter and John reply that the prophetic role cannot be abandoned to satisfy human objections, the court nevertheless releases them, afraid to do otherwise since the beggar, lame from birth and over forty years old, is a well-known figure in Jerusalem and the facts of his cure are common property (Acts 4:19–22). The narrative concludes with a prayer of the Christian community imploring divine aid against threats of persecution (Acts 4:23–31).

‡[3:1] For the three o'clock hour of prayer: literally, "at the ninth hour of prayer." With the day beginning at 6 a.m., the ninth hour would be 3 p.m.

l. [2:38] 3:19; 16:31; Lk 3:3. m. [2:39] Is 57:19; Jl 3:5; Eph 2:17.
n. [2:40] Dt 32:5; Ps 78:8; Lk 9:41; Phil 2:15. o. [2:41] 2:47; 4:4; 5:14; 6:7; 11:21, 24; 21:20. p. [2:42–47] 4:32–35. q. [2:42] 1:14; 6:4.
r. [2:43] 5:12–16. s. [2:44] 4:32, 34–35. t. [3:2–8] 14:8–10.

---

from birth was carried and placed at the gate of the temple called "the Beautiful Gate" every day to beg for alms from the people who entered the temple. [3]When he saw Peter and John about to go into the temple, he asked for alms. [4]But Peter looked intently at him, as did John, and said, "Look at us." [5]He paid attention to them, expecting to receive something from them. [6§]Peter said, "I have neither silver nor gold, but what I do have I give you: in the name of Jesus Christ the Nazorean, [rise and] walk."[u] [7]Then Peter took him by the right hand and raised him up, and immediately his feet and ankles grew strong. [8]He leaped up, stood, and walked around, and went into the temple with them, walking and jumping and praising God.[v] [9]When all the people saw him walking and praising God, [10]they recognized him as the one who used to sit begging at the Beautiful Gate of the temple, and they were filled with amazement and astonishment at what had happened to him.

Peter's Speech. [11]As he clung to Peter and John, all the people hurried in amazement toward them in the portico called "Solomon's Portico."[w] [12]When Peter saw this, he addressed the people, "You Israelites, why are you amazed at this, and why do you look so intently at us as if we had made him walk by our own power or piety?[x] [13]The God of Abraham, [the God] of Isaac, and [the God] of Jacob, the God of our ancestors, has glorified¶ his servant Jesus whom you handed over and denied in Pilate's presence, when he had decided to release him.[y] [14]You denied the Holy and Righteous One** and asked that a murderer be released to you.[z] [15††]The author of life you put to death, but God raised him from the dead; of this we are witnesses.[a] [16]And by faith in his name, this man, whom you see and know, his name has made strong, and the faith that comes through it has given him this perfect health, in the presence of all of you. [17]Now I know, brothers, that you acted

---

§[3:6–10] The miracle has a dramatic cast; it symbolizes the saving power of Christ and leads the beggar to enter the temple, where he hears Peter's proclamation of salvation through Jesus.

¶[3:13] Has glorified: through the resurrection and ascension of Jesus, God reversed the judgment against him on the occasion of his trial. Servant: the Greek word can also be rendered as "son" or even "child" here and also in Acts 3:26; 4:25 (applied to David); Acts 4:27; and Acts 4:30. Scholars are of the opinion, however, that the original concept reflected in the words identified Jesus with the suffering Servant of the Lord of Is 52:13–53:12.

**[3:14] The Holy and Righteous One: so designating Jesus emphasizes his special relationship to the Father (see Lk 1:35; 4:34) and emphasizes his sinlessness and religious dignity that are placed in sharp contrast with the guilt of those who rejected him in favor of Barabbas.

††[3:15] The author of life: other possible translations of the Greek title are "leader of life" or "pioneer of life." The title clearly points to Jesus as the source and originator of salvation.

u. [3:6] 4:10. v. [3:8] Is 35:6; Lk 7:22. w. [3:11] 5:12; Jn 10:23.
x. [3:12] 14:15. y. [3:13] Ex 3:6, 15; Is 52:13; Lk 23:14–25.
z. [3:14] Mt 27:20–21; Mk 15:11; Lk 23:18; Jn 18:40. a. [3:15] 4:10;
5:31 / 1:8; 2:32.

out of ignorance,* just as your leaders did;ᵇ ¹⁸but God has thus brought to fulfillment what he had announced beforehand through the mouth of all the prophets,† that his Messiah would suffer.ᶜ ¹⁹Repent, therefore, and be converted, that your sins may be wiped away,ᵈ ²⁰and that the Lord may grant you times of refreshment and send you the Messiah already appointed for you, Jesus,‡ ²¹whom heaven must receive until the times of universal restoration§ of which God spoke through the mouth of his holy prophets from of old. ²²For Moses said:¶

'A prophet like me will the Lord, your
    God, raise up for you
from among your own kinsmen;
to him you shall listen in all that he may
    say to you.ᵉ
²³ Everyone who does not listen to that
    prophet
will be cut off from the people.'ᶠ

²⁴Moreover, all the prophets who spoke, from Samuel and those afterwards, also announced these days. ²⁵You are the children of the prophets and of the covenant that God made with your ancestors when he said to Abraham, 'In your offspring all the families of the earth shall be blessed.'ᵍ ²⁶For you first, God raised up his servant and sent him to bless you by turning each of you from your evil ways."ʰ

---

*[3:17] **Ignorance:** a Lucan motif, explaining away the actions not only of the people but also of their leaders in crucifying Jesus. On this basis the presbyters in Acts could continue to appeal to the Jews in Jerusalem to believe in Jesus, even while affirming their involvement in his death because they were unaware of his messianic dignity. See also Acts 13:27 and Lk 23:34.

†[3:18] **Through the mouth of all the prophets:** Christian prophetic insight into the Old Testament saw the crucifixion and death of Jesus as the main import of messianic prophecy. The Jews themselves did not anticipate a suffering Messiah; they usually understood the Servant Song in Is 52:13–53:12 to signify their own suffering as a people. In his typical fashion (cf. Lk 18:31; 24:25, 27, 44), Luke does not specify the particular Old Testament prophecies that were fulfilled by Jesus. See also note on Lk 24:26.

‡[3:20] **The Lord . . . and send you the Messiah already appointed for you, Jesus:** an allusion to the parousia or second coming of Christ, judged to be imminent in the apostolic age. This reference to its nearness is the only explicit one in Acts. Some scholars believe that this verse preserves a very early christology, in which the title "Messiah" (Greek "Christ") is applied to him as of his parousia, his second coming (contrast Acts 2:36). This view of a future messiahship of Jesus is not found elsewhere in the New Testament.

§[3:21] **The times of universal restoration:** like "the times of refreshment" (Acts 3:20), an apocalyptic designation of the messianic age, fitting in with the christology of Acts 3:20 that associates the messiahship of Jesus with his future coming.

¶[3:22] A loose citation of Dt 18:15, which teaches that the Israelites are to learn the will of Yahweh from no one but their prophets. At the time of Jesus, some Jews expected a unique prophet to come in fulfillment of this text. Early Christianity applied this tradition and text to Jesus and used them especially in defense of the divergence of Christian teaching from traditional Judaism.

---

b. [3:17] 13:27; Lk 23:34; 1 Cor 2:8; 1 Tm 1:13.   c. [3:18] Lk 18:31.
d. [3:19] 2:38.   e. [3:22] 7:37; Dt 18:15, 18.   f. [3:23] Lv 23:29; Dt 18:19.   g. [3:25] Gn 12:3; 18:18; 22:18; Sir 44:19–21; Gal 3:8–9.
h. [3:26] 13:46; Rom 1:16.

CHAPTER 4

¹While they were still speaking to the people, the priests, the captain of the temple guard, and the Sadducees** confronted them, ²disturbed that they were teaching the people and proclaiming in Jesus the resurrection of the dead.ⁱ ³They laid hands on them and put them in custody until the next day, since it was already evening. ⁴But many of those who heard the word came to believe and [the] number of men grew to [about] five thousand.

Before the Sanhedrin. ⁵On the next day, their leaders, elders, and scribes were assembled in Jerusalem, ⁶with Annas the high priest, Caiaphas, John, Alexander, and all who were of the high-priestly class. ⁷They brought them into their presence and questioned them, "By what power or by what name have you done this?" ⁸Then Peter, filled with the holy Spirit, answered them, "Leaders of the people and elders:ʲ ⁹If we are being examined today about a good deed done to a cripple, namely, by what means he was saved, ¹⁰then all of you and all the people of Israel should know that it was in the name of Jesus Christ the Nazorean whom you crucified, whom God raised from the dead; in his name this man stands before you healed. ¹¹ᵏHe is 'the stone rejected by you,†† the builders, which has become the cornerstone.' ¹²‡‡There is no salvation through anyone else, nor is there any other name under heaven given to the human race by which we are to be saved."

¹³Observing the boldness of Peter and John and perceiving them to be uneducated, ordinary men, they were amazed, and they recognized them as the companions of Jesus. ¹⁴Then when they saw the man who had been cured standing there with them, they could say nothing in reply. ¹⁵So they ordered them to leave the Sanhedrin, and conferred with one another, saying, ¹⁶"What are we to do with these men? Everyone living in Jerusalem knows that a remarkable sign was done through them, and we cannot deny it. ¹⁷But so that it may not be spread any further among the people, let us give them a stern warning never again to speak to anyone in this name."ᵐ ¹⁸So they called them back and ordered them not to speak or teach at all in the name of Jesus.

[4:1] **The priests, the captain of the temple guard, and the Sadducees: the priests performed the temple liturgy; the temple guard was composed of Levites, whose captain ranked next after the high priest. The Sadducees, a party within Judaism at this time, rejected those doctrines, including bodily resurrection, which they believed alien to the ancient Mosaic religion. The Sadducees were drawn from priestly families and from the lay aristocracy.

††[4:11] Early Christianity applied this citation from Ps 118:22 to Jesus; cf. Mk 12:10; 1 Pt 2:7.

‡‡[4:12] In the Roman world of Luke's day, salvation was often attributed to the emperor who was hailed as "savior" and "god." Luke, in the words of Peter, denies that deliverance comes through anyone other than Jesus.

---

i. [4:2] 23:6–8; 24:21.   j. [4:8] Mt 10:20.   k. [4:11] Ps 118:22; Is 28:16; Mt 21:42; Mk 12:10; Lk 20:17; Rom 9:33; 1 Pt 2:7.   l. [4:12] Mt 1:21; 1 Cor 3:11.   m. [4:17] 5:28.

[19]Peter and John, however, said to them in reply, "Whether it is right in the sight of God for us to obey you rather than God, you be the judges."[n] [20]It is impossible for us not to speak about what we have seen and heard." [21]After threatening them further, they released them, finding no way to punish them, on account of the people who were all praising God for what had happened. [22]For the man on whom this sign of healing had been done was over forty years old.

Prayer of the Community. [23]After their release they went back to their own people and reported what the chief priests and elders had told them. [24]And when they heard it, they raised their voices to God with one accord and said, "Sovereign Lord, maker of heaven and earth and the sea and all that is in them, [25]you said by the holy Spirit through the mouth of our father David, your servant:

'Why did the Gentiles rage[o]
    and the peoples entertain folly?
[26]   The kings of the earth took their stand
    and the princes gathered together
        against the Lord and against his
        anointed.'

[27]Indeed they gathered in this city against your holy servant Jesus whom you anointed, Herod* and Pontius Pilate, together with the Gentiles and the peoples of Israel,[p] [28]to do what your hand and [your] will had long ago planned to take place. [29]And now, Lord, take note of their threats, and enable your servants to speak your word with all boldness, [30]as you stretch forth [your] hand to heal, and signs and wonders are done through the name of your holy servant Jesus." [31]†As they prayed, the place where they were gathered shook, and they were all filled with the holy Spirit and continued to speak the word of God with boldness.[q]

Life in the Christian Community.‡ [32]The community of believers was of one heart and mind, and no one claimed that any of his possessions was his own, but they had everything in common. [33]With great power the apostles bore witness to the resurrection of the Lord Jesus, and great favor was accorded them all. [34]There was no needy person among them, for those who owned property or houses would sell them, bring the proceeds of the sale, [35]and put them at the feet of the apostles, and they were distributed to each according to need.

[36]Thus Joseph, also named by the apostles Barnabas (which is translated "son of encouragement"), a Levite, a Cypriot by birth, [37]sold a piece of property that he owned, then brought the money and put it at the feet of the apostles.

CHAPTER 5

Ananias and Sapphira.§ [1]A man named Ananias, however, with his wife Sapphira, sold a piece of property. [2]He retained for himself, with his wife's knowledge, some of the purchase price, took the remainder, and put it at the feet of the apostles. [3]But Peter said, "Ananias, why has Satan filled your heart so that you lied to the holy Spirit and retained part of the price of the land?[r] [4]While it remained unsold, did it not remain yours? And when it was sold, was it not still under your control? Why did you contrive this deed? You have lied not to human beings, but to God." [5]When Ananias heard these words, he fell down and breathed his last, and great fear came upon all who heard of it. [6]The young men came and wrapped him up, then carried him out and buried him.

[7]After an interval of about three hours, his wife came in, unaware of what had happened. [8]Peter said to her, "Tell me, did you sell the land for this amount?" She answered, "Yes, for that amount." [9]Then Peter said to her, "Why did you agree to test the Spirit of the Lord? Listen, the footsteps of those who have buried your husband are at the door, and they will carry you out." [10]At once, she fell down at his feet and breathed her last. When the young men entered they found her dead, so they carried her out and buried her beside her husband. [11]And great fear came upon the whole church and upon all who heard of these things.[u]

Signs and Wonders of the Apostles.¶ [12]Many signs and wonders were done among the people at the hands of the apostles. They were all together in Solomon's portico.[v] [13]None of the others dared

---

*[4:27] **Herod**: Herod Antipas, ruler of Galilee and Perea from 4 B.C. to A.D. 39, who executed John the Baptist and before whom Jesus was arraigned; cf. Lk 23:6–12.

†[4:31] **The place . . . shook**: the earthquake is used as a sign of the divine presence in Ex 19:18; Is 6:4. Here the shaking of the building symbolizes God's favorable response to the prayer. Luke may have had as an additional reason for using the symbol in this sense the fact that it was familiar in the Hellenistic world. Ovid and Virgil also employ it.

‡[4:32–37] This is the second summary characterizing the Jerusalem community (see note on Acts 2:42–47). It emphasizes the system of the distribution of goods and introduces Barnabas, who appears later in Acts as the friend and companion of Paul, and who, as noted here (Acts 4:37), endeared himself to the community by a donation of money through the sale of property. This sharing of material possessions continues a practice that Luke describes during the historical ministry of Jesus (Lk 8:3) and is in accord with the sayings of Jesus in Luke's gospel (Lk 12:33; 16:9, 11, 13).

n. [4:19] 5:29–32.   o. [4:25–26] Ps 2:1–2.   p. [4:27] Lk 23:12–13.   q. [4:31] 2:4.

§[5:1–11] The sin of Ananias and Sapphira did not consist in the withholding of part of the money but in their deception of the community. Their deaths are ascribed to a lie to the holy Spirit (Acts 5:3, 9), i.e., they accepted the honor accorded them by the community for their generosity, but in reality they were not deserving of it.

¶[5:12–16] This, the third summary portraying the Jerusalem community, underscores the Twelve as its bulwark, especially because of their charismatic power to heal the sick; cf. Acts 2:42–47; 4:32–37.

r. [4:34–35] 2:44–45.   s. [4:36–37] 9:27; 11:22, 30; 12:25; 13:15; 1 Cor 9:6; Gal 2:1, 9, 13; Col 4:10.   t. [5:3] Lk 22:3; Jn 13:2.   u. [5:11] 2:43; 5:5; 19:17.   v. [5:12] 2:43; 6:8; 14:3; 15:12.

to join them, but the people esteemed them. [14]Yet more than ever, believers in the Lord, great numbers of men and women, were added to them. [15]Thus they even carried the sick out into the streets and laid them on cots and mats so that when Peter came by, at least his shadow might fall on one or another of them.[w] [16]A large number of people from the towns in the vicinity of Jerusalem also gathered, bringing the sick and those disturbed by unclean spirits, and they were all cured.

Trial Before the Sanhedrin. [17]Then the high priest rose up and all his companions, that is, the party of the Sadducees, and, filled with jealousy,[x] [18]laid hands upon the apostles and put them in the public jail. [19]But during the night, the angel of the Lord opened the doors of the prison, led them out, and said,[y] [20]"Go and take your place in the temple area, and tell the people everything about this life." [21]When they heard this, they went to the temple early in the morning and taught. When the high priest and his companions arrived, they convened the Sanhedrin, the full senate of the Israelites, and sent to the jail to have them brought in. [22]But the court officers who went did not find them in the prison, so they came back and reported, [23]"We found the jail securely locked and the guards stationed outside the doors, but when we opened them, we found no one inside." [24]When they heard this report, the captain of the temple guard and the chief priests were at a loss about them, as to what this would come to. [25]Then someone came in and reported to them, "The men whom you put in prison are in the temple area and are teaching the people." [26]Then the captain and the court officers went and brought them in, but without force, because they were afraid of being stoned by the people.[z]

[27]When they had brought them in and made them stand before the Sanhedrin, the high priest questioned them, [28]"We gave you strict orders [did we not?] to stop teaching in that name. Yet you have filled Jerusalem with your teaching and want to bring this man's blood upon us."[a] [29]But

Peter and the apostles said in reply, "We must obey God rather than men.[b] [30†]The God of our ancestors raised Jesus,[c] though you had him killed by hanging him on a tree. [31]God exalted him at his right hand[‡] as leader and savior to grant Israel repentance and forgiveness of sins.[d] [32]We are witnesses of these things, as is the holy Spirit that God has given to those who obey him."[e]

[33]When they heard this, they became infuriated and wanted to put them to death. [34]But a Pharisee in the Sanhedrin named Gamaliel, a teacher of the law, respected by all the people, stood up, ordered the men to be put outside for a short time,[f] [35]and said to them, "Fellow Israelites, be careful what you are about to do to these men. [36†]Some time ago, Theudas appeared, claiming to be someone important, and about four hundred men joined him, but he was killed, and all those who were loyal to him were disbanded and came to nothing. [37]After him came Judas the Galilean at the time of the census. He also drew people after him, but he too perished and all who were loyal to him were scattered. [38]So now I tell you, have nothing to do with these men, and let them go. For if this endeavor or this activity is of human origin, it will destroy itself. [39]But if it comes from God, you will not be able to destroy them; you may even find yourselves fighting against God." They were persuaded by him. [40]After recalling the apostles, they had them flogged, ordered them to stop speaking in the name of Jesus, and dismissed them.[g] [41]So they left the presence of the Sanhedrin, rejoicing that they had been found worthy to suffer dishonor for the sake of the name.[h] [42]And all day long, both at the temple and in their homes, they did not stop teaching and proclaiming the Messiah, Jesus.[i]

CHAPTER 6

The Need for Assistants. [1]"At that time, as the number of disciples continued to grow, the

*[5:17–42] A second action against the community is taken by the Sanhedrin in the arrest and trial of the Twelve; cf. Acts 4:1–3. The motive is the jealousy of the religious authorities over the popularity of the apostles (Acts 5:17) who are now charged with the defiance of the Sanhedrin's previous order to them to abandon their prophetic role (Acts 5:28; cf. Acts 4:18). In this crisis the apostles are favored by a miraculous release from prison (Acts 5:18–24). (For similar incidents involving Peter and Paul, see Acts 12:6–11; 16:25–29.) The real significance of such an event, however, would be manifest only to people of faith, not to unbelievers; since the Sanhedrin already judged the Twelve to be inauthentic prophets, it could disregard reports of their miracles. When the Twelve immediately resumed public teaching, the Sanhedrin determined to invoke upon them the penalty of death (Acts 5:33) prescribed in Dt 13:6–10. Gamaliel's advice against this course finally prevailed, but it did not save the Twelve from the punishment of scourging (Acts 5:40) in a last endeavor to shake their conviction of their prophetic mission.

†[5:30] **Hanging him on a tree:** that is, crucifying him (cf. also Gal 3:13).

‡[5:31] **At his right hand:** see note on Acts 2:33.

§[5:34] **Gamaliel:** in Acts 22:3, Paul identifies himself as a disciple of this Rabbi Gamaliel I who flourished in Jerusalem between A.D. 25 and 50.

¶[5:36–37] Gamaliel offers examples of unsuccessful contemporary movements to argue that if God is not the origin of this movement preached by the apostles it will perish by itself. The movement initiated by Theudas actually occurred when C. Cuspius Fadus was governor, A.D. 44–46. Luke's placing of Judas the Galilean after Theudas and at the time of the census (see note on Lk 2:1–2) is an indication of the vagueness of his knowledge of these events.

[6:1–7] The Hellenists . . . the Hebrews: the Hellenists were not necessarily Jews from the diaspora, but were more probably Palestinian Jews who spoke only Greek. The Hebrews were Palestinian Jews who spoke Hebrew or Aramaic and who may also have spoken Greek. Both groups belong to the Jerusalem Jewish Christian community. The

w. [5:15] 19:11–12; Mk 6:56.   x. [5:17] 4:1–3, 6.   y. [5:19] 12:7–10; 16:25–26.   z. [5:26] Lk 20:19.   a. [5:28] Mt 27:25.

b. [5:29]4:19.   c. [5:30]2:23–24.   d. [5:31]2:38.   e. [5:32]Lk24:48; Jn 15:26.   f. [5:34] 22:3.   g. [5:40] Mt 10:17; Acts 4:17–18.   h. [5:41] Mt 5:10–11; 1 Pt 4:13.   i. [5:42] 2:46; 5:20–21, 25; 8:35; 17:3; 18:5, 28; 19:4–5.

Hellenists complained against the Hebrews because their widows were being neglected in the daily distribution.^{j} ^{2}"So the Twelve called together the community of the disciples and said, "It is not right for us to neglect the word of God to serve at table.† ^{3}Brothers, select from among you seven reputable men, filled with the Spirit and wisdom, whom we shall appoint to this task, ^{4}whereas we shall devote ourselves to prayer and to the ministry of the word." ^{5}The proposal was acceptable to the whole community, so they chose Stephen, a man filled with faith and the holy Spirit, also Philip, Prochorus, Nicanor, Timon, Parmenas, and Nicholas of Antioch, a convert to Judaism. ^{6k}They presented these men to the apostles who prayed and laid hands on them.‡ ^{7}The word of God continued to spread, and the number of the disciples in Jerusalem increased greatly; even a large group of priests were becoming obedient to the faith.^{l}
Accusation Against Stephen. ^{8§}Now Stephen, filled with grace and power, was working great wonders and signs among the people. ^{9}Certain members of the so-called Synagogue of Freedmen, Cyrenians, and Alexandrians, and people from Cilicia and Asia, came forward and debated with Stephen, ^{10}but they could not withstand the wisdom and the spirit with which he spoke.^{m} ^{11}Then they instigated some men

to say, "We have heard him speaking blasphemous words against Moses and God."^{n} ^{12}They stirred up the people, the elders, and the scribes, accosted him, seized him, and brought him before the Sanhedrin. ^{13}They presented false witnesses¶ who testified, "This man never stops saying things against [this] holy place and the law. ^{14}For we have heard him claim that this Jesus the Nazorean will destroy this place and change the customs that Moses handed down to us."^{o} ^{15}All those who sat in the Sanhedrin looked intently at him and saw that his face was like the face of an angel.

CHAPTER 7

Stephen's Discourses. ^{1}Then the high priest asked, "Is this so?" ^{2p}And he replied," "My brothers and fathers, listen. The God of glory appeared to our father Abraham while he was in Mesopotamia,†† before he had settled in Haran, ^{3}and said to him, 'Go forth from your land and [from] your kinsfolk to the land that I will show you.'^{q} ^{4}So he went forth from the land of the Chaldeans and settled in Haran. And from there, after his father died, he made him migrate to this land where you now dwell.^{r} ^{5}Yet he gave him no inheritance in it, not even a foot's length, but he did promise to give it to him and his descendants as a possession, even though he was childless.^{s} ^{6}And God spoke thus,^{t} 'His descendants shall be aliens in a land not their own, where they shall be enslaved and oppressed for four hundred years; ^{7}but I will bring judgment on the nation they serve,' God said, 'and after that they will come out and worship me in this place.'^{u} ^{8}Then he gave him the covenant of circumcision, and so he became the father of Isaac, and circumcised him on the eighth day, as Isaac did Jacob, and Jacob the twelve patriarchs.^{v}
^{9}"And the patriarchs, jealous of Joseph, sold him into slavery in Egypt; but God was with him^w ^{10}and rescued him from all his afflictions.

conflict between them leads to a restructuring of the community that will better serve the community's needs. The real purpose of the whole episode, however, is to introduce Stephen as a prominent figure in the community whose long speech and martyrdom will be recounted in Acts 7.

* [6:2–4] The essential function of the Twelve is the "service of the word," including development of the kerygma by formulation of the teachings of Jesus.

† [6:2] **To serve at table:** some commentators think that it is not the serving of food that is described here but rather the keeping of the accounts that recorded the distribution of food to the needy members of the community. In any case, after Stephen and the others are chosen, they are never presented carrying out the task for which they were appointed (Acts 6:2–3). Rather, two of their number, Stephen and Philip, are presented as preachers of the Christian message. They, the Hellenist counterpart of the Twelve, are active in the ministry of the word.

‡ [6:6] **They . . . laid hands on them:** the customary Jewish way of designating persons for a task and invoking upon them the divine blessing and power to perform it.

§ [6:8–8:1] The summary (Acts 6:7) on the progress of the Jerusalem community, illustrated by the conversion of the priests, is followed by a lengthy narrative regarding Stephen. Stephen's defense is not a response to the charges made against him but takes the form of a discourse that reviews the fortunes of God's word to Israel and leads to a prophetic declaration: a plea for the hearing of that word as announced by Christ and now possessed by the Christian community.

The charges that Stephen depreciated the importance of the temple and the Mosaic law and elevated Jesus to a stature above Moses (Acts 6:13–14) were in fact true. Before the Sanhedrin, no defense against them was possible. With Stephen, who thus perceived the fuller implications of the teachings of Jesus, the differences between Judaism and Christianity began to appear. Luke's account of Stephen's martyrdom and its aftermath shows how the major impetus behind the Christian movement passed from Jerusalem, where the temple and law prevailed, to Antioch in Syria, where these influences were less pressing.

¶ [6:13] **False witnesses:** here, and in his account of Stephen's execution (Acts 7:54–60), Luke parallels the martyrdom of Stephen with the death of Jesus.

** [7:2–53] Stephen's speech represents Luke's description of Christianity's break from its Jewish matrix. Two motifs become prominent in the speech: (1) Israel's reaction to God's chosen leaders in the past reveals that the people have consistently rejected them; and (2) Israel has misunderstood God's choice of the Jerusalem temple as the place where he is to be worshiped.

†† [7:2] **God . . . appeared to our father Abraham . . . in Mesopotamia:** the first of a number of minor discrepancies between the data of the Old Testament and the data of Stephen's discourse. According to Gn 12:1, God first spoke to Abraham in Haran. The main discrepancies are these: in Acts 7:16 it is said that Jacob was buried in Shechem, whereas Gn 50:13 says he was buried at Hebron; in the same verse it is said that the tomb was purchased by Abraham, but in Gn 33:19 and Jos 24:32 the purchase is attributed to Jacob himself.

n. [6:11] Mt 26:59–61; Mk 14:55–58; Acts 21:21. o. [6:14] Mt 26:59–61; 27:40; Jn 2:19. p. [7:2] Gn 11:31; 12:1; Ps 29:3. q. [7:3] Gn 12:1. r. [7:4] Gn 12:5; 15:7. s. [7:5] Gn 12:7; 13:15; 15:2; 16:1; Dt 2:5. t. [7:6–7] Gn 15:13–14. u. [7:7] Ex 3:12. v. [7:8] Gn 17:10–14; 21:2–4. w. [7:9] Gn 37:11, 28; 39:2, 3, 21, 23.

j. [6:1] 2:45; 4:34–35. k. [6:6] 1:24; 13:3; 14:23. l. [6:7] 9:31; 12:24; 16:5; 19:20; 28:30–31. m. [6:10] Lk 21:15.

He granted him favor and wisdom before Pharaoh, the king of Egypt, who put him in charge of Egypt and [of] his entire household.[x] [11]Then a famine and great affliction struck all Egypt and Canaan, and our ancestors could find no food;[y] [12]but when Jacob heard that there was grain in Egypt, he sent our ancestors there a first time.[z] [13]The second time, Joseph made himself known to his brothers, and Joseph's family became known to Pharaoh.[a] [14]Then Joseph sent for his father Jacob, inviting him and his whole clan, seventy-five persons;[b] [15]and Jacob went down to Egypt. And he and our ancestors died[c] [16]and were brought back to Shechem and placed in the tomb that Abraham had purchased for a sum of money from the sons of Hamor at Shechem.[d]

[17]"When the time drew near for the fulfillment of the promise that God pledged to Abraham, the people had increased and become very numerous in Egypt,[e] [18]until another king who knew nothing of Joseph came to power [in Egypt].[f] [19]He dealt shrewdly with our people and oppressed [our] ancestors by forcing them to expose their infants, that they might not survive. [20]At this time Moses was born, and he was extremely beautiful. For three months he was nursed in his father's house;[g] [21]but when he was exposed, Pharaoh's daughter adopted him and brought him up as her own son.[h] [22]Moses was educated [in] all the wisdom of the Egyptians and was powerful in his words and deeds.

[23]"When he was forty years old, he decided to visit his kinsfolk, the Israelites. [24]When he saw one of them treated unjustly, he defended and avenged the oppressed man by striking down the Egyptian. [25]He assumed [his] kinsfolk would understand that God was offering them deliverance through him, but they did not understand. [26]The next day he appeared to them as they were fighting and tried to reconcile them peacefully, saying, 'Men, you are brothers. Why are you harming one another?' [27]Then the one who was harming his neighbor pushed him aside, saying, 'Who appointed you ruler and judge over us? [28]Are you thinking of killing me as you killed the Egyptian yesterday?' [29]Moses fled when he heard this and settled as an alien in the land of Midian, where he became the father of two sons.[k]

[30]"Forty years later, an angel appeared to him in the desert near Mount Sinai in the flame of a burning bush. [31]When Moses saw it, he was amazed at the sight, and as he drew near to look at it, the voice of the Lord came, [32]'I am the God of your fathers, the God of Abraham, of Isaac, and of Jacob.' Then Moses, trembling, did not dare to look at it. [33]But the Lord said to

him, 'Remove the sandals from your feet, for the place where you stand is holy ground. [34]I have witnessed the affliction of my people in Egypt and have heard their groaning, and I have come down to rescue them. Come now, I will send you to Egypt.' [35]This Moses, whom they had rejected with the words, 'Who appointed you ruler and judge?' God sent as [both] ruler and deliverer, through the angel who appeared to him in the bush.[m] [36]This man led them out, performing wonders and signs in the land of Egypt, at the Red Sea, and in the desert for forty years.[n] [37]It was this Moses who said to the Israelites, 'God will raise up for you, from among your own kinsfolk, a prophet like me.'[o] [38]It was he who, in the assembly in the desert, was with the angel who spoke to him on Mount Sinai and with our ancestors, and he received living utterances to hand on to us.[p]

[39]"Our ancestors were unwilling to obey him; instead, they pushed him aside and in their hearts turned back to Egypt,[q] [40]saying to Aaron, 'Make us gods who will be our leaders. As for that Moses who led us out of the land of Egypt, we do not know what has happened to him.'[r] [41]So they made a calf in those days, offered sacrifice to the idol, and reveled in the works of their hands. [42]Then God turned and handed them over to worship the host of heaven, as it is written in the book of the prophets:[s]

'Did you bring me sacrifices and offerings
　for forty years in the desert, O house
　　of Israel?[u]
[43]　No, you took up the tent of Moloch
　　and the star of [your] god Rephan,
　　　the images that you made to
　　　worship.
So I shall take you into exile beyond
　Babylon.'

[44]"Our ancestors had the tent of testimony in the desert just as the One who spoke to Moses directed him to make it according to the pattern he had seen.[v] [45]Our ancestors who inherited it brought it with Joshua when they dispossessed the nations that God drove out from before our ancestors, up to the time of David,[w] [46]who found favor in the sight of God and asked that he might find a dwelling place for the house of Jacob.[x] [47]But Solomon built a house for him.[y] [48]Yet the Most High does not dwell in houses made by human hands. As the prophet says:[z]

[49]　'The heavens are my throne,
　　the earth is my footstool.

x. [7:10] Gn 41:37–43; Ps 105:21; Wis 10:13–14.　y. [7:11] Gn 41:54–57; 42:5.　z. [7:12] Gn 42:1–2.　a. [7:13] Gn 45:3–4, 16.　b. [7:14] Gn 45:9–11, 18–19; 46:27; Ex 1:5 LXX; Dt 10:22.　c. [7:15] Gn 46:5–6; 49:33.　d. [7:16] Gn 23:3–20; 33:19; 49:29–30; 50:13; Jos 24:32.　e. [7:17] Ex 1:7.　f. [7:18] Ex 1:8.　g. [7:20] Ex 2:2; Heb 11:23.　h. [7:21] Ex 2:3–10.　i. [7:23–24] Ex 2:11–12.　j. [7:26–28] Ex 2:13–14.　k. [7:29] Ex 2:15, 21–22; 18:3–4.　l. [7:30–34] Ex 3:2–3.　m. [7:35] Ex 2:14.　n. [7:36] Ex 7:3, 10; 14:21; Nm 14:33.　o. [7:37] Dt 18:15; Acts 3:22.　p. [7:38] Ex 19:3; 20:1–17; Dt 5:4–22; 6:4–25.　q. [7:39] Nm 14:3.　r. [7:40] Ex 32:1, 23.　s. [7:41] Ex 32:4–6.　t. [7:42–43] Am 5:25–27.　u. [7:42] Jer 7:18; 8:2; 19:13.　v. [7:44] Ex 25:9, 40.　w. [7:45] Jos 3:14–17; 18:1; 2 Sm 7:5–7.　x. [7:46] 2 Sm 7:1–2; 1 Kgs 8:17; Ps 132:1–5.　y. [7:47] 1 Kgs 6:1; 1 Chr 17:12.　z. [7:48] 17:24.

What kind of house can you build for me?
says the Lord,
or what is to be my resting place?^{a}
50 Did not my hand make all these things?'

Conclusion. 51"You stiff-necked people, uncircumcised in heart and ears, you always oppose the holy Spirit; you are just like your ancestors. 52Which of the prophets did your ancestors not persecute? They put to death those who foretold the coming of the righteous one, whose betrayers and murderers you have now become.^{b} 53You received the law as transmitted by angels, but you did not observe it."^{c}
Stephen's Martyrdom. 54When they heard this, they were infuriated, and they ground their teeth at him. 55dBut he, filled with the holy Spirit, looked up intently to heaven and saw the glory of God and Jesus standing at the right hand of God,* 56and he said, "Behold, I see the heavens opened and the Son of Man standing at the right hand of God." 57But they cried out in a loud voice, covered their ears,† and rushed upon him together. 58They threw him out of the city, and began to stone him. The witnesses laid down their cloaks at the feet of a young man named Saul.^{e} 59As they were stoning Stephen,^{f} he called out, "Lord Jesus, receive my spirit."‡ 60Then he fell to his knees and cried out in a loud voice, "Lord, do not hold this sin against them"; and when he said this, he fell asleep.^{g}

CHAPTER 8

1Now Saul was consenting to his execution.^{h}
Persecution of the Church. On that day, there broke out a severe persecution§ of the church in Jerusalem, and all were scattered throughout the countryside of Judea and Samaria, except the apostles.¶ 2Devout men buried Stephen and made a loud lament over him. 3Saul, meanwhile,

was trying to destroy the church;** entering house after house and dragging out men and women, he handed them over for imprisonment.^{i}

III. THE MISSION IN JUDEA AND SAMARIA

Philip in Samaria. 4Now those who had been scattered went about preaching the word.^{j} 5Thus Philip went down to [the] city of Samaria and proclaimed the Messiah to them.^{k} 6With one accord, the crowds paid attention to what was said by Philip when they heard it and saw the signs he was doing. 7For unclean spirits, crying out in a loud voice, came out of many possessed people, and many paralyzed and crippled people were cured.^{l} 8There was great joy in that city.
Simon the Magician. 9A man named Simon used to practice magic†† in the city and astounded the people of Samaria, claiming to be someone great. 10All of them, from the least to the greatest, paid attention to him, saying, "This man is the 'Power of God' that is called 'Great.'" 11They paid attention to him because he had astounded them by his magic for a long time, 12but once they began to believe Philip as he preached the good news about the kingdom of God and the name of Jesus Christ, men and women alike were baptized.^{m} 13Even Simon himself believed and, after being baptized, became devoted to Philip; and when he saw the signs and mighty deeds that were occurring, he was astounded.
14Now when the apostles in Jerusalem heard that Samaria had accepted the word of God, they sent them Peter and John, 15who went down and prayed for them, that they might receive the holy Spirit, 16for it had not yet fallen upon any of them; they had only been baptized in the name of the Lord Jesus.‡‡ 17Then they laid hands on them and they received the holy Spirit.^{n}

---

*[7:55] He . . . saw . . . Jesus standing at the right hand of God: Stephen affirms to the Sanhedrin that the prophecy Jesus made before them has been fulfilled (Mk 14:62).

†[7:57] Covered their ears: Stephen's declaration, like that of Jesus, is a scandal to the court, which regards it as blasphemy.

‡[7:59] Compare Lk 23:34, 46.

§[8:1–40] Some idea of the severity of the persecution that now breaks out against the Jerusalem community can be gathered from Acts 22:4 and Acts 26:9–11. Luke, however, concentrates on the fortunes of the word of God among people, indicating how the dispersal of the Jewish community resulted in the conversion of the Samaritans (Acts 8:4–17, 25). His narrative is further expanded to include the account of Philip's acceptance of an Ethiopian (Acts 8:26–39).

¶[8:1] All were scattered . . . except the apostles: this observation leads some modern scholars to conclude that the persecution was limited to the Hellenist Christians and that the Hebrew Christians were not molested, perhaps because their attitude toward the law and temple was still more in line with that of their fellow Jews (see the charge leveled against the Hellenist Stephen in Acts 6:13–14). Whatever the facts, it appears that the Twelve took no public stand regarding Ste-

phen's position, choosing, instead, to await the development of events.

**[8:3] Saul . . . was trying to destroy the church: like Stephen, Saul was able to perceive that the Christian movement contained the seeds of doctrinal divergence from Judaism. A pupil of Gamaliel, according to Acts 22:3, and totally dedicated to the law as the way of salvation (Gal 1:13–14), Saul accepted the task of crushing the Christian movement, at least insofar as it detracted from the importance of the temple and the law. His vehement opposition to Christianity reveals how difficult it was for a Jew of his time to accept a messianism that differed so greatly from the general expectation.

††[8:9–13, 18–24] Sorcerers were well known in the ancient world. Probably the incident involving Simon and his altercation with Peter is introduced to show that the miraculous charisms possessed by members of the Christian community (Acts 8:6–7) were not to be confused with the magic of sorcerers.

‡‡[8:16] Here and in Acts 10:44–48 and Acts 19:1–6, Luke distinguishes between baptism in the name of the Lord Jesus and the reception of the Spirit. In each case, the Spirit is conferred through members of the Twelve (Peter and John) or their representative (Paul). This may be Luke's way of describing the role of the church in the bestowal of the Spirit. Elsewhere in Acts, baptism and the Spirit are more closely related (Acts 1:5; 11:16).

---

a. [7:49] Is 66:1–2. b. [7:52] 2 Chr 36:16; Mt 23:31, 34. c. [7:53] Gal 3:19; Heb 2:2. d. [7:55–56] Mt 26:64; Mk 14:62; Lk 22:69; Acts 2:34. e. [7:58] 22:20. f. [7:59] Ps 31:6; Lk 23:46. g. [7:60] Mt 27:46, 50; Mk 15:34; Lk 23:46. h. [8:1] 22:20.

i. [8:3] 9:1, 13; 22:4; 26:9–11; 1 Cor 5:9; Gal 1:13. j. [8:4] 11:19. k. [8:5] 6:5; 21:8–9. l. [8:7] Mk 16:17. m. [8:12] 1:3; 19:8; 28:23, 31. n. [8:17] 2:4; 4:31; 10:44–47; 15:8–9; 19:2, 6.

^{18*}When Simon saw that the Spirit was conferred by the laying on of the apostles' hands, he offered them money ¹⁹and said, "Give me this power too, so that anyone upon whom I lay my hands may receive the holy Spirit." ²⁰But Peter said to him, "May your money perish with you, because you thought that you could buy the gift of God with money. ²¹You have no share or lot in this matter, for your heart is not upright before God. ²²Repent of this wickedness of yours and pray to the Lord that, if possible, your intention may be forgiven. ²³For I see that you are filled with bitter gall and are in the bonds of iniquity." ²⁴Simon said in reply, "Pray for me to the Lord, that nothing of what you have said may come upon me." ²⁵So when they had testified and proclaimed the word of the Lord, they returned to Jerusalem and preached the good news to many Samaritan villages.

Philip and the Ethiopian.[†] ²⁶Then the angel of the Lord spoke to Philip, "Get up and head south on the road that goes down from Jerusalem to Gaza, the desert route." ²⁷So he got up and set out. Now there was an Ethiopian eunuch, a court official of the Candace,[‡] that is, the queen of the Ethiopians, in charge of her entire treasury, who had come to Jerusalem to worship,^o ²⁸and was returning home. Seated in his chariot, he was reading the prophet Isaiah. ²⁹The Spirit said to Philip, "Go and join up with that chariot." ^{30§}Philip ran up and heard him reading Isaiah the prophet and said, "Do you understand what you are reading?" ³¹He replied, "How can I, unless someone instructs me?" So he invited Philip to get in and sit with him.^p ³²This was the scripture passage he was reading:^q

"Like a sheep he was led to the slaughter,
    and as a lamb before its shearer is
        silent,
    so he opened not his mouth.
³³ In [his] humiliation justice was denied
        him.

Who will tell of his posterity?
    For his life is taken from the
        earth."

³⁴Then the eunuch said to Philip in reply, "I beg you, about whom is the prophet saying this? About himself, or about someone else?" ³⁵Then Philip opened his mouth and, beginning with this scripture passage, he proclaimed Jesus to him. ^{36r}As they traveled along the road they came to some water, and the eunuch said, "Look, there is water. What is to prevent my being baptized?" [³⁷]^s ³⁸Then he ordered the chariot to stop, and Philip and the eunuch both went down into the water, and he baptized him. ³⁹When they came out of the water, the Spirit of the Lord snatched Philip away, and the eunuch saw him no more, but continued on his way rejoicing.^s ⁴⁰Philip came to Azotus, and went about proclaiming the good news to all the towns until he reached Caesarea.^t

CHAPTER 9

Saul's Conversion. ^{1**}Now Saul, still breathing murderous threats against the disciples of the Lord,^u went to the high priest^v ²and asked him for letters to the synagogues in Damascus, that, if he should find any men or women who belonged to the Way,^{††} he might bring them back to Jerusalem in chains. ³On his journey, as he was nearing Damascus, a light from the sky suddenly flashed around him.^w ⁴He fell to the ground and heard a voice saying to him, "Saul, Saul, why are you persecuting me?"^x ⁵He said, "Who are you, sir?" The reply came, "I am Jesus, whom you are persecuting.^y ⁶Now get up and go into the city and you will be told what you must do."^z ⁷The men who were traveling with

¶[8:37] The oldest and best manuscripts of Acts omit this verse, which is a Western text reading: "And Philip said, 'If you believe with all your heart, you may.' And he said in reply, 'I believe that Jesus Christ is the Son of God.'"

**[9:1–19] This is the first of three accounts of Paul's conversion (with Acts 22:3–16 and Acts 26:2–18) with some differences of detail owing to Luke's use of different sources. Paul's experience was not visionary but was precipitated by the appearance of Jesus, as he insists in 1 Cor 15:8. The words of Jesus, "Saul, Saul, why are you persecuting me?" related by Luke with no variation in all three accounts, exerted a profound and lasting influence on the thought of Paul. Under the influence of this experience he gradually developed his understanding of justification by faith (see the letters to the Galatians and Romans) and of the identification of the Christian community with Jesus Christ (see 1 Cor 12:27). That Luke would narrate this conversion three times is testimony to the importance he attaches to it. This first account occurs when the word is first spread to the Gentiles. At this point, the conversion of the hero of the Gentile mission is recounted. The emphasis in the account is on Paul as a divinely chosen instrument (Acts 9:15).

††[9:2] The Way: a name used by the early Christian community for itself (Acts 18:26; 19:9, 23; 22:4; 24:14, 22). The Essene community at Qumran used the same designation to describe its mode of life.

---

*[8:18–20] Simon attempts to buy the gift of God (Acts 8:20) with money. Peter's cursing of Simon's attempt so to use his money expresses a typically Lucan attitude toward material wealth (cf. Lk 6:24; 12:16–21; 16:13).

†[8:26–40] In the account of the conversion of the Ethiopian eunuch, Luke adduces additional evidence to show that the spread of Christianity outside the confines of Judaism itself was in accord with the plan of God. He does not make clear whether the Ethiopian was originally a convert to Judaism or, as is more probable, a "God-fearer" (Acts 10:1), i.e., one who accepted Jewish monotheism and ethic and attended the synagogue but did not consider himself bound by other regulations such as circumcision and observance of the dietary laws. The story of his conversion to Christianity is given a strong supernatural cast by the introduction of an angel (Acts 8:26), instruction from the holy Spirit (Acts 8:29), and the strange removal of Philip from the scene (8:39).

‡[8:27] The Candace: Candace is not a proper name here but the title of a Nubian queen.

§[8:30–34] Philip is brought alongside the carriage at the very moment when the Ethiopian is pondering the meaning of Is 53:7–8, a passage that Christianity, from its earliest origins, has applied to Jesus; cf. note on Acts 3:13.

---

o. [8:27] Is 56:3–5. p. [8:31] Jn 16:13. q. [8:32–33] Is 53:7–8 LXX.

r. [8:36] 10:47. s. [8:39] 1 Kgs 18:12. t. [8:40] 21:8. u. [9:1] 8:3; 9:13; 22:4; 1 Cor 15:9; Gal 1:13–14. v. [9:1–2] 9:14; 26:10. w. [9:3] 1 Cor 9:1; 15:8; Gal 1:16. x. [9:4] 22:6; 26:14. y. [9:5] 22:8; 26:15; Mt 25:40. z. [9:6] 22:10; 26:16.

him stood speechless, for they heard the voice but could see no one.[a] [8]Saul got up from the ground, but when he opened his eyes he could see nothing;[*] so they led him by the hand and brought him to Damascus.[b] [9]For three days he was unable to see, and he neither ate nor drank. **Saul's Baptism.** [10c]There was a disciple in Damascus named Ananias, and the Lord said to him in a vision, "Ananias." He answered, "Here I am, Lord." [11]The Lord said to him, "Get up and go to the street called Straight and ask at the house of Judas for a man from Tarsus named Saul. He is there praying,[d] [12]and [in a vision] he has seen a man named Ananias come in and lay [his] hands on him, that he may regain his sight." [13]But Ananias replied, "Lord, I have heard from many sources about this man, what evil things he has done to your holy ones[†] in Jerusalem.[e] [14]And here he has authority from the chief priests to imprison all who call upon your name."[f] [15]But the Lord said to him, "Go, for this man is a chosen instrument of mine to carry my name before Gentiles, kings, and Israelites,[g] [16]and I will show him what he will have to suffer for my name." [17]So Ananias went and entered the house; laying his hands on him, he said, "Saul, my brother, the Lord has sent me, Jesus who appeared to you on the way by which you came, that you may regain your sight and be filled with the holy Spirit." [18]Immediately things like scales fell from his eyes and he regained his sight. He got up and was baptized, [19]and when he had eaten, he recovered his strength.[‡] **Saul Preaches in Damascus.** He stayed some days with the disciples in Damascus, [20]and he began at once to proclaim Jesus in the synagogues, that he is the Son of God.[§] [21]All who heard him were astounded and said, "Is not this the man who in Jerusalem ravaged those who call upon this name, and came here expressly to take them back in chains to the chief priests?" [22]But Saul grew all the stronger and confounded [the] Jews who lived in Damascus, proving that this is the Messiah. **Saul Visits Jerusalem.** [23]After a long time had passed, the Jews conspired to kill him, [24h]but their plot became known to Saul. Now they were keeping watch on the gates day and night

so as to kill him, [25]but his disciples took him one night and let him down through an opening in the wall, lowering him in a basket.
[26i]When he arrived in Jerusalem[¶] he tried to join the disciples, but they were all afraid of him, not believing that he was a disciple. [27]Then Barnabas took charge of him and brought him to the apostles, and he reported to them how on the way he had seen the Lord and that he had spoken to him, and how in Damascus he had spoken out boldly in the name of Jesus. [28]He moved about freely with them in Jerusalem, and spoke out boldly in the name of the Lord. [29]He also spoke and debated with the Hellenists,[**] but they tried to kill him. [30]And when the brothers learned of this, they took him down to Caesarea and sent him on his way to Tarsus.[j]
The Church at Peace. [31††]The church throughout all Judea, Galilee, and Samaria was at peace. It was being built up and walked in the fear of the Lord, and with the consolation of the holy Spirit it grew in numbers.
Peter Heals Aeneas at Lydda. [32]As Peter was passing through every region, he went down to the holy ones living in Lydda. [33]There he found a man named Aeneas, who had been confined to bed for eight years, for he was paralyzed. [34]Peter said to him, "Aeneas, Jesus Christ heals you. Get up and make your bed." He got up at once. [35]And all the inhabitants of Lydda and Sharon saw him, and they turned to the Lord.
Peter Restores Tabitha to Life. [36]Now in Joppa there was a disciple named Tabitha (which translated means Dorcas).[‡‡] She was completely occupied with good deeds and almsgiving. [37]Now during those days she fell sick and died, so after washing her, they laid [her] out in a room upstairs. [38]Since Lydda was near Joppa, the disciples, hearing that Peter was there, sent two men to him with the request, "Please come to us without delay." [39]So Peter got up and went with them. When he arrived, they took him to the room upstairs where all the widows came to him weeping and showing him the tunics and cloaks that Dorcas had made while she was with them. [40]Peter sent them all out and knelt down and prayed. Then he turned to her body and said, "Tabitha, rise up." She opened her eyes, saw Peter, and sat up.[k] [41]He gave her his hand and raised her up, and when he had called

---

*[9:8] **He could see nothing:** a temporary blindness (Acts 9:18) symbolizing the religious blindness of Saul as persecutor (cf. Acts 26:18).

†[9:13] **Your holy ones:** literally, "your saints."

‡[9:19–30] This is a brief resume of Paul's initial experience as an apostolic preacher. At first he found himself in the position of being regarded as an apostate by the Jews and suspect by the Christian community of Jerusalem. His acceptance by the latter was finally brought about through his friendship with Barnabas (Acts 9:27).

§[9:20] **Son of God:** the title "Son of God" occurs in Acts only here, but cf. the citation of Ps 2:7 in Paul's speech at Antioch in Pisidia (Acts 13:33).

¶[9:26] This visit of Paul to Jerusalem is mentioned by Paul in Gal 1:18.

[9:29] **Hellenists: see note on Acts 6:1–7.

††[9:31–43] In the context of the period of peace enjoyed by the community through the cessation of Paul's activities against it, Luke introduces two traditions concerning the miraculous power exercised by Peter as he was making a tour of places where the Christian message had already been preached. The towns of Lydda, Sharon, and Joppa were populated by both Jews and Gentiles and their Christian communities may well have been mixed.

‡‡[9:36] **Tabitha (Dorcas),** respectively the Aramaic and Greek words for "gazelle," exemplifies the right attitude toward material possessions expressed by Jesus in the Lucan Gospel (Lk 6:30; 11:41; 12:33; 18:22; 19:8).

---

a. [9:7] 22:9; 26:13–14. b. [9:8] 22:11. c. [9:10–19] 22:12–16. d. [9:11] 21:39. e. [9:13] 8:3; 9:1. f. [9:14] 9:1–2; 26:10; 1 Cor 1:2; 2 Tm 2:22. g. [9:15] 22:15; 26:1; 27:24. h. [9:24–25] 2 Cor 11:32–33.

i. [9:26–27] Gal 1:18. j. [9:30] 11:25. k. [9:40] Mk 5:40–41.

the holy ones and the widows, he presented her alive. [42]This became known all over Joppa, and many came to believe in the Lord. [43]*And he stayed a long time in Joppa with Simon, a tanner.

IV. THE INAUGURATION OF THE GENTILE MISSION

CHAPTER 10

The Vision of Cornelius.[m] [1]†Now in Caesarea there was a man named Cornelius, a centurion of the Cohort called the Italica,‡ [2]devout and God-fearing along with his whole household, who used to give alms generously§ to the Jewish people and pray to God constantly. [3]One afternoon about three o'clock,¶ he saw plainly in a vision an angel of God come in to him and say to him, "Cornelius." [4]He looked intently at him and, seized with fear, said, "What is it, sir?" He said to him, "Your prayers and almsgiving have ascended as a memorial offering before God. [5]Now send some men to Joppa and summon one Simon who is called Peter. [6]He is staying with another Simon, a tanner, who has a house by the sea."[n] [7]When the angel who spoke to him had left, he called two of his servants and a devout soldier** from his staff, [8]explained everything to them, and sent them to Joppa.

The Vision of Peter. [9]††The next day, while they were on their way and nearing the city, Peter went up to the roof terrace to pray at about noontime.‡‡ [10]He was hungry and wished to eat, and while they were making preparations

he fell into a trance. [11]He saw heaven opened and something resembling a large sheet coming down, lowered to the ground by its four corners. [12]In it were all the earth's four-legged animals and reptiles and the birds of the sky. [13]A voice said to him, "Get up, Peter. Slaughter and eat." [14]But Peter said, "Certainly not, sir. For never have I eaten anything profane and unclean."[p] [15]The voice spoke to him again, a second time, "What God has made clean, you are not to call profane."[q] [16]This happened three times, and then the object was taken up into the sky.

[17]§§While Peter was in doubt about the meaning of the vision he had seen, the men sent by Cornelius asked for Simon's house and arrived at the entrance. [18]They called out inquiring whether Simon, who is called Peter, was staying there. [19]As Peter was pondering the vision, the Spirit said [to him], "There are three men here looking for you.[r] [20]So get up, go downstairs, and accompany them without hesitation, because I have sent them." [21]Then Peter went down to the men and said, "I am the one you are looking for. What is the reason for your being here?" [22]They answered, "Cornelius, a centurion, an upright and God-fearing man, respected by the whole Jewish nation, was directed by a holy angel to summon you to his house and to hear what you have to say."[s] [23]So he invited them in and showed them hospitality.

The next day he got up and went with them, and some of the brothers from Joppa went with him. [24]¶¶On the following day he entered Caesarea. Cornelius was expecting them and had called together his relatives and close friends. [25]rWhen Peter entered, Cornelius met him and, falling at his feet, paid him homage. [26]Peter, however, raised him up, saying, "Get up. I myself am also a human being." [27]While he conversed with him, he went in and found many people gathered together [28]uand said to them, "You know that it is unlawful for a Jewish man to associate with, or visit, a Gentile, but God has shown me that I should not call any person profane or unclean.*** [29]And that is why I came without objection when sent for. May I ask, then, why you summoned me?"

[30]Cornelius replied, "Four days ago††† at this hour, three o'clock in the afternoon, I was at

*[9:43] The fact that Peter lodged with a tanner would have been significant to both the Gentile and Jewish Christians, for Judaism considered the tanning occupation unclean.

†[10:1–48] The narrative centers on the conversion of Cornelius, a Gentile and a "God-fearer" (see note on Acts 8:26–40). Luke considers the event of great importance, as is evident from his long treatment of it. The incident is again related in Acts 11:1–18 where Peter is forced to justify his actions before the Jerusalem community and alluded to in Acts 15:7–11 where at the Jerusalem "Council" Peter supports Paul's missionary activity among the Gentiles. The narrative divides itself into a series of distinct episodes, concluding with Peter's presentation of the Christian kerygma (Acts 10:4–43) and a pentecostal experience undergone by Cornelius' household preceding their reception of baptism (Acts 10:44–48).

‡[10:1] The Cohort called the Italica: this battalion was an auxiliary unit of archers formed originally in Italy but transferred to Syria shortly before A.D. 69.

§[10:2] Used to give alms generously: like Tabitha (Acts 9:36), Cornelius exemplifies the proper attitude toward wealth (see note on Acts 9:36).

¶[10:3] About three o'clock: literally, "about the ninth hour." See note on Acts 3:1.

**[10:7] A devout soldier: by using this adjective, Luke probably intends to classify him as a "God-fearer" (see note on Acts 8:26–40).

††[10:9–16] The vision is intended to prepare Peter to share the food of Cornelius' household without qualms of conscience (Acts 10:48). The necessity of such instructions to Peter reveals that at first not even the apostles fully grasped the implications of Jesus' teaching on the law. In Acts, the initial insight belongs to Stephen.

‡‡[10:9] At about noontime: literally, "about the sixth hour."

§§[10:17–23] The arrival of the Gentile emissaries with their account of the angelic apparition illuminates Peter's vision: he is to be prepared to admit Gentiles, who were considered unclean like the animals of his vision, into the Christian community.

¶¶[10:24–27] So impressed is Cornelius with the apparition that he invites close personal friends to join him in his meeting with Peter. But his understanding of the person he is about to meet is not devoid of superstition, suggested by his falling down before him. For a similar experience of Paul and Barnabas, see Acts 14:11–18.

***[10:28] Peter now fully understands the meaning of his vision; see note on Acts 10:17–23.

†††[10:30] Four days ago: literally, "from the fourth day up to this hour."

o. [10:11–20] 11:5–12.   p. [10:14] Lv 11:1–47; Ez 4:14.   q. [10:15] Mk 7:15–19; Gal 2:12.   r. [10:19] 13:2.   s. [10:22] Lk 7:4–5.
t. [10:25–26] 14:13–15; Rev 19:10.   u. [10:28] Gal 2:11–16.

l. [9:43] 10:6.   m. [10:1–8] 10:30–33.   n. [10:6] 9:43.

prayer in my house when suddenly a man in dazzling robes stood before me and said, ³¹"Cornelius, your prayer has been heard and your almsgiving remembered before God. ³²Send therefore to Joppa and summon Simon, who is called Peter. He is a guest in the house of Simon, a tanner, by the sea.' ³³So I sent for you immediately, and you were kind enough to come. Now therefore we are all here in the presence of God to listen to all that you have been commanded by the Lord."

Peter's Speech. ³⁴Then Peter proceeded to speak and said,† "In truth, I see that God shows no partiality.ᵛ ³⁵Rather, in every nation whoever fears him and acts uprightly is acceptable to him. ³⁶‡You know the word [that] he sent to the Israelites§ as he proclaimed peace through Jesus Christ, who is Lord of all,ʷ ³⁷what has happened all over Judea, beginning in Galilee after the baptism that John preached,ˣ ³⁸how God anointed Jesus of Nazareth¶ with the holy Spirit and power. He went about doing good and healing all those oppressed by the devil, for God was with him.ʸ ³⁹We are witnesses** of all that he did both in the country of the Jews and [in] Jerusalem. They put him to death by hanging him on a tree. ⁴⁰This man God raised [on] the third day and granted that he be visible, ⁴¹not to all the people, but to us, the witnesses chosen by God in advance, who ate and drank with him after he rose from the dead.ᶻ ⁴²He commissioned usᵃ to preach to the people and testify that he is the one appointed by God as judge of the living and

the dead.†† ⁴³To him all the prophets bear witness, that everyone who believes in him will receive forgiveness of sins through his name."

The Baptism of Cornelius. ⁴⁴ᵇWhile Peter was still speaking these things, the holy Spirit fell upon all who were listening to the word.‡‡ ⁴⁵The circumcised believers who had accompanied Peter were astounded that the gift of the holy Spirit should have been poured out on the Gentiles also, ⁴⁶for they could hear them speaking in tongues and glorifying God. Then Peter responded, ⁴⁷"Can anyone withhold the water for baptizing these people, who have received the holy Spirit even as we have?"ᶜ ⁴⁸He ordered them to be baptized in the name of Jesus Christ. ⁴⁹Then they invited him to stay for a few days.

CHAPTER 11

The Baptism of the Gentiles Explained.§§ ¹Now the apostles and the brothers who were in Judea heard that the Gentiles too had accepted the word of God. ²So when Peter went up to Jerusalem the circumcised believers confronted him, ³saying, "You entered¶¶ the house of uncircumcised people and ate with them." ⁴Peter began and explained it to them step by step, saying, ⁵ᵈ"I was at prayer in the city of Joppa when in a trance I had a vision, something resembling a large sheet coming down, lowered from the sky by its four corners, and it came to me. ⁶Looking intently into it, I observed and saw the four-legged animals of the earth, the wild beasts, the reptiles, and the birds of the sky. ⁷I also heard a voice say to me, 'Get up, Peter. Slaughter and eat.' ⁸But I said, 'Certainly not, sir, because nothing profane or unclean has ever entered my mouth.' ⁹But a second time a voice from heaven answered, 'What God has made clean, you are not to call profane.' ¹⁰This happened three times, and then everything was drawn up again into the sky. ¹¹Just then three men appeared at the house where we were, who had been sent to me from Caesarea. ¹²The Spirit told me to accompany them without discriminating. These six brothers*** also went with me, and we entered the

---

*[10:34–43] Peter's speech to the household of Cornelius typifies early Christian preaching to Gentiles.

†[10:34–35] The revelation of God's choice of Israel to be the people of God did not mean he withheld the divine favor from other people.

‡[10:36–43] These words are more directed to Luke's Christian readers than to the household of Cornelius, as indicated by the opening words, "You know." They trace the continuity between the preaching and teaching of Jesus of Nazareth and the proclamation of Jesus by the early community. The emphasis on this divinely ordained continuity (Acts 10:41) is meant to assure Luke's readers of the fidelity of Christian tradition to the words and deeds of Jesus.

§[10:36] **To the Israelites:** Luke, in the words of Peter, speaks of the prominent position occupied by Israel in the history of salvation.

¶[10:38] **Jesus of Nazareth:** God's revelation of his plan for the destiny of humanity through Israel culminated in Jesus of Nazareth. Consequently, the ministry of Jesus is an integral part of God's revelation. This viewpoint explains why the early Christian communities were interested in conserving the historical substance of the ministry of Jesus, a tradition leading to the production of the four gospels.

[10:39] **We are witnesses: the apostolic testimony was not restricted to the resurrection of Jesus but also included his historical ministry. This witness, however, was theological in character; the Twelve, divinely mandated as prophets, were empowered to interpret his sayings and deeds in the light of his redemptive death and resurrection. The meaning of these words and deeds was to be made clear to the developing Christian community as the bearer of the word of salvation (cf. Acts 1:21–26). **Hanging him on a tree:** see note on Acts 5:30.

††[10:42] **As judge of the living and the dead:** the apostolic preaching to the Jews appealed to their messianic hope, while the preaching to Gentiles stressed the coming divine judgment; cf. 1 Thes 1:10.

‡‡[10:44] Just as the Jewish Christians received the gift of the Spirit, so too do the Gentiles.

§§[11:1–18] The Jewish Christians of Jerusalem were scandalized to learn of Peter's sojourn in the house of the Gentile Cornelius. Nonetheless, they had to accept the divine directions given to both Peter and Cornelius. They concluded that the setting aside of the legal barriers between Jew and Gentile was an exceptional ordinance of God to indicate that the apostolic kerygma was also to be directed to the Gentiles. Only in Acts 15 at the "Council" in Jerusalem does the evangelization of the Gentiles become the official position of the church leadership in Jerusalem.

¶¶[11:3] **You entered . . . :** alternatively, this could be punctuated as a question.

***[11:12] **These six brothers:** companions from the Christian community of Joppa (see Acts 10:23).

---

v. [10:34] Dt 10:17; 2 Chr 19:7; Jb 34:19; Wis 6:7; Rom 2:11; Gal 2:6; Eph 6:9; 1 Pt 1:17.   w. [10:36] Is 52:7; Na 2:1.   x. [10:37] Mt 4:12; Mk 1:14; Lk 4:14.   y. [10:38] Is 61:1; Lk 4:18.   z. [10:41] Lk 24:41–43.   a. [10:42] 1:8; 3:15; 17:31; Lk 24:48; Rom 14:9; 2 Tm 4:1.

b. [10:44] 11:15; 15:8.   c. [10:47] 8:36.   d. [11:5–12] 10:11–20.

man's house. [13]He related to us how he had seen [the] angel standing in his house, saying, 'Send someone to Joppa and summon Simon, who is called Peter,[e] [14]who will speak words to you by which you and all your household will be saved.' [15]As I began to speak, the holy Spirit fell upon them as it had upon us at the beginning,[f] [16]and I remembered the word of the Lord, how he had said, 'John baptized with water but you will be baptized with the holy Spirit.'[g] [17]If then God gave them the same gift he gave to us when we came to believe in the Lord Jesus Christ, who was I to be able to hinder God?"[h] [18]When they heard this, they stopped objecting and glorified God, saying, "God has then granted life-giving repentance to the Gentiles too."

The Church at Antioch.[*] [19]Now those who had been scattered by the persecution that arose because of Stephen went as far as Phoenicia, Cyprus, and Antioch, preaching the word to no one but Jews.[i] [20]There were some Cypriots and Cyrenians among them, however, who came to Antioch and began to speak to the Greeks as well, proclaiming the Lord Jesus. [21]The hand of the Lord was with them and a great number who believed turned to the Lord. [22]The news about them reached the ears of the church in Jerusalem, and they sent Barnabas [to go] to Antioch. [23]When he arrived and saw the grace of God, he rejoiced and encouraged them all to remain faithful to the Lord in firmness of heart, [24]for he was a good man, filled with the holy Spirit and faith. And a large number of people was added to the Lord. [25]Then he went to Tarsus to look for Saul, [26]and when he had found him he brought him to Antioch. For a whole year they met with the church and taught a large number of people, and it was in Antioch that the disciples were first called Christians.[†]

The Prediction of Agabus.[‡] [27]At that time some prophets came down from Jerusalem to Antioch, [28]and one of them named Agabus stood up and

predicted by the Spirit that there would be a severe famine all over the world, and it happened under Claudius.[j] [29]So the disciples determined that, according to ability,[k] each should send relief to the brothers who lived in Judea. [30]§This they did, sending it to the presbyters in care of Barnabas and Saul.

CHAPTER 12

Herod's Persecution of the Christians.[§] [1]About that time King Herod laid hands upon some members of the church to harm them. [2]He had James, the brother of John,[**] killed by the sword, [3]††and when he saw that this was pleasing to the Jews he proceeded to arrest Peter also. (It was [the] feast of Unleavened Bread.) [4]He had him taken into custody and put in prison under the guard of four squads of four soldiers each. He intended to bring him before the people after Passover. [5]Peter thus was being kept in prison, but prayer by the church was fervently being made to God on his behalf.[l]

[6]On the very night before Herod was to bring him to trial, Peter, secured by double chains, was sleeping between two soldiers, while outside the door guards kept watch on the prison. [7]Suddenly the angel of the Lord stood by him and a light shone in the cell. He tapped Peter on the side and awakened him, saying, "Get up quickly." The chains fell from his wrists. [8]The angel said to him, "Put on your belt and your sandals." He did so. Then he said to him, "Put on your cloak and follow me." [9]So he followed him out, not realizing that what was happening through the angel was real; he thought he was seeing a vision. [10]They passed the first guard, then the second, and came to the iron gate leading out to the city, which opened for them by itself. They emerged and made their way down an alley, and suddenly the angel left him. [11]Then Peter recovered his senses and said, "Now I know for certain that [the] Lord sent his angel and rescued me from the hand of Herod and from all that the Jewish people had been expecting." [12]When he realized this, he went to the house of Mary, the mother of John who is called Mark, where there were many people gathered in prayer.[m] [13]When he knocked on the gateway door, a maid

*[11:19–26] The Jewish Christian antipathy to the mixed community was reflected by the early missionaries generally. The few among them who entertained a different view succeeded in introducing Gentiles into the community at Antioch (in Syria). When the disconcerted Jerusalem community sent Barnabas to investigate, he was so favorably impressed by what he observed that he persuaded his friend Saul to participate in the Antioch mission.

†[11:26] **Christians:** "Christians" is first applied to the members of the community at Antioch because the Gentile members of the community enable it to stand out clearly from Judaism.

‡[11:27–30] It is not clear whether the prophets from Jerusalem came to Antioch to request help in view of the coming famine or whether they received this insight during their visit there. The former supposition seems more likely. Suetonius and Tacitus speak of famines during the reign of Claudius (A.D. 41–54), while the Jewish historian Josephus mentions a famine in Judea in A.D. 46–48. Luke is interested, rather, in showing the charity of the Antiochene community toward the Jewish Christians of Jerusalem despite their differences on mixed communities.

§[11:30] **Presbyters:** this is the same Greek word that elsewhere is translated "elders," primarily in reference to the Jewish community.

§[12:1–19] Herod Agrippa ruled Judea A.D. 41–44. While Luke does not assign a motive for his execution of James and his intended execution of Peter, the broad background lies in Herod's support of Pharisaic Judaism. The Jewish Christians had lost the popularity they had had in Jerusalem (Acts 2:47), perhaps because of suspicions against them traceable to the teaching of Stephen.

[12:2] **James, the brother of John: this James, the son of Zebedee, was beheaded by Herod Agrippa ca. A.D. 44.

††[12:3–4] **Feast of Unleavened Bread . . . Passover:** see note on Lk 22:1.

e. [11:13] 10:3–5, 22, 30–32.   f. [11:15] 10:44.   g. [11:16] 1:5; 19:4; Lk 3:16.   h. [11:17] 15:8–9.   i. [11:19] 8:1–4.

j. [11:28]21:10.   k. [11:29–30]12:25.   l. [12:5]Jas 5:16.   m. [12:12] 12:25; 15:37.

named Rhoda came to answer it. ¹⁴She was so overjoyed when she recognized Peter's voice that, instead of opening the gate, she ran in and announced that·Peter was standing at the gate. ¹⁵They told her, "You are out of your mind," but she insisted that it was so. But they kept saying, "It is his angel." ¹⁶But Peter continued to knock, and when they opened it, they saw him and were astounded. ¹⁷He motioned to them with his hand to be quiet and explained [to them] how the Lord had led him out of the prison, and said, "Report this to James* and the brothers." Then he left and went to another place. ¹⁸At daybreak there was no small commotion among the soldiers over what had become of Peter." ¹⁹Herod, after instituting a search but not finding him, ordered the guards tried and executed. Then he left Judea to spend some time in Caesarea.

Herod's Death. ²⁰†He had long been very angry with the people of Tyre and Sidon, who now came to him in a body. After winning over Blastus, the king's chamberlain, they sued for peace because their country was supplied with food from the king's territory. ²¹On an appointed day, Herod, attired in royal robes, [and] seated on the rostrum, addressed them publicly. ²²The assembled crowd cried out, "This is the voice of a god, not of a man." ²³At once the angel of the Lord struck him down because he did not ascribe the honor to God, and he was eaten by worms and breathed his last. ²⁴But the word of God continued to spread and grow.º

Mission of Barnabas and Saul. ²⁵After Barnabas and Saul completed their relief mission, they returned to Jerusalem,‡ taking with them John, who is called Mark.ᵖ

CHAPTER 13

¹Now there were in the church at Antioch prophets and teachers: Barnabas, Symeon who was called Niger, Lucius of Cyrene, Manaen

who was a close friend of Herod the tetrarch, and Saul. ²While they were worshiping the Lord and fasting, the holy Spirit said, "Set apart for me Barnabas and Saul for the work to which I have called them." ³Then, completing their fasting and prayer, they laid hands on them and sent them off.

First Mission Begins in Cyprus. ⁴¶So they, sent forth by the holy Spirit, went down to Seleucia and from there sailed to Cyprus. ⁵When they arrived in Salamis, they proclaimed the word of God in the Jewish synagogues. They had John** also as their assistant. ⁶When they had traveled through the whole island as far as Paphos, they met a magician named Bar-Jesus who was a Jewish false prophet.†† ⁷He was with the proconsul Sergius Paulus, a man of intelligence, who had summoned Barnabas and Saul and wanted to hear the word of God. ⁸But Elymas the magician (for that is what his name means) opposed them in an attempt to turn the proconsul away from the faith. ⁹But Saul, also known as Paul,‡‡ filled with the holy Spirit, looked intently at him ¹⁰and said, "You son of the devil, you enemy of all that is right, full of every sort of deceit and fraud. Will you not stop twisting the straight paths of [the] Lord? ¹¹Even now the hand of the Lord is upon you. You will be blind, and unable to see the sun for a time." Immediately a dark mist fell upon him, and he went about seeking people to lead him by the hand. ¹²When the proconsul saw what had happened, he came to believe, for he was astonished by the teaching about the Lord.

Paul's Arrival at Antioch in Pisidia. ¹³From Paphos, Paul and his companions set sail and arrived at Perga in Pamphylia. But John left them and returned to Jerusalem.ᵠ ¹⁴They continued on from Perga and reached Antioch in Pisidia. On the sabbath they entered [into] the synagogue and took their seats. ¹⁵After the reading of the law and the prophets, the synagogue officials sent word to them, "My brothers, if one

---

*[12:17] **To James**: this James is not the son of Zebedee mentioned in Acts 12:2, but is James, the "brother of the Lord" (Gal 1:19), who in Acts 15; 21 is presented as leader of the Jerusalem Christian community. **He left and went to another place**: the conjecture that Peter left for Rome at this time has nothing to recommend it. His chief responsibility was still the leadership of the Jewish Christian community in Palestine (see Gal 2:7). The concept of the great missionary effort of the church was yet to come (see Acts 13:1–3).

†[12:20–23] Josephus gives a similar account of Herod's death that occurred in A.D. 44. Early Christian tradition considered the manner of it to be a divine punishment upon his evil life. See 2 Kgs 19:35 for the figure of the angel of the Lord in such a context.

‡[12:25] **They returned to Jerusalem**: many manuscripts read "from Jerusalem," since Acts 11:30 implies that Paul and Barnabas are already in Jerusalem. This present verse could refer to a return visit or subsequent relief mission.

§[13:1–3] The impulse for the first missionary effort in Asia Minor is ascribed to the prophets of the Antiochene community, under the inspiration of the holy Spirit. Just as the Jerusalem community had earlier been the center of missionary activity, so too Antioch becomes the center from which the missionaries Barnabas and Saul are sent out.

¶[13:4–14:27] The key event in Luke's account of the first missionary journey is the experience of Paul and Barnabas at Pisidian Antioch (Acts 13:14–52). The Christian kerygma proclaimed by Paul in the synagogue was favorably received. Some Jews and "God-fearers" (see note on Acts 8:26–40) became interested and invited the missionaries to speak again on the following sabbath (Acts 13:42). By that time, however, the appearance of a large number of Gentiles from the city had so disconcerted the Jews that they became hostile toward the apostles (Acts 13:44–50). This hostility of theirs appears in all three accounts of Paul's missionary journeys in Acts, the Jews of Iconium (Acts 14:1–2) and Beroea (Acts 17:11) being notable exceptions.

[13:5] **John: that is, John Mark (see Acts 12:12, 25).

††[13:6] **A magician named Bar-Jesus who was a Jewish false prophet**: that is, he posed as a prophet. Again Luke takes the opportunity to dissociate Christianity from the magical acts of the time (Acts 13:7–11); see also Acts 8:18–24.

‡‡[13:9] **Saul, also known as Paul**: there is no reason to believe that his name was changed from Saul to Paul upon his conversion. The use of a double name, one Semitic (Saul), the other Greco-Roman (Paul), is well attested (cf. Acts 1:23, Joseph Justus; Acts 12:12, 25, John Mark).

---

n. [12:18] 5:22–24.　o. [12:24] 6:7.　p. [12:25] 11:29–30.

q. [13:13] 15:38.

of you has a word of exhortation for the people, please speak."

Paul's Address in the Synagogue. [16]*So Paul got up, motioned with his hand, and said, "Fellow Israelites and you others who are God-fearing,[†] listen. [17]The God of this people Israel chose our ancestors and exalted the people during their sojourn in the land of Egypt.[r] With uplifted arm he led them out of it [18]and for about forty years he put up with[‡] them in the desert.[s] [19]When he had destroyed seven nations in the land of Canaan, he gave them their land as an inheritance[t] [20]at the end of about four hundred and fifty years.[§] After these things he provided judges up to Samuel [the] prophet.[u] [21]Then they asked for a king. God gave them Saul, son of Kish, a man from the tribe of Benjamin, for forty years.[v] [22]Then he removed him and raised up David as their king; of him he testified, 'I have found David, son of Jesse, a man after my own heart; he will carry out my every wish.'[w] [23]From this man's descendants God, according to his promise, has brought to Israel a savior, Jesus.[x] [24]John heralded his coming by proclaiming a baptism of repentance to all the people of Israel;[y] [25]and as John was completing his course, he would say, 'What do you suppose that I am? I am not he. Behold, one is coming after me; I am not worthy to unfasten the sandals of his feet.'[z]

[26]"My brothers, children of the family of Abraham, and those others among you who are God-fearing, to us this word of salvation has been sent. [27]The inhabitants of Jerusalem and their leaders failed to recognize him, and by condemning him they fulfilled the oracles of the prophets that are read sabbath after sabbath. [28]For even though they found no grounds for a death sentence, they asked Pilate to have him put to death,[a] [29]and when they had accomplished all that was written about him, they took him down from the tree and placed him in a tomb.[b] [30]But God raised him from the dead,[c] [31]and for many days he appeared to those who had come up with him from Galilee to Jerusalem.[d] These are [now] his witnesses before the people.[¶] [32]We ourselves are proclaiming this good news to you that what God promised our ancestors [33]he has brought to fulfillment for us, [their] children, by raising up Jesus, as it is written in the second psalm, 'You are my son; this day I have begotten you.'[e] [34]And that he raised him from the dead never to return to corruption he declared in this way, 'I shall give you the benefits assured to David.'[f] [35]That is why he also says in another psalm, 'You will not suffer your holy one to see corruption.'[g] [36]Now David, after he had served the will of God in his lifetime, fell asleep, was gathered to his ancestors, and did see corruption.[h] [37]But the one whom God raised up did not see corruption. [38]You must know, my brothers, that through him forgiveness of sins is being proclaimed to you, [and] in regard to everything from which you could not be justified[**] under the law of Moses, [39]in him every believer is justified.[i] [40]Be careful, then, that what was said in the prophets not come about:

[41] 'Look on, you scoffers,
          be amazed and disappear.
     For I am doing a work in your days,
          a work that you will never believe
              even if someone tells you.'"[j]

[42]As they were leaving, they invited them to speak on these subjects the following sabbath. [43]After the congregation had dispersed, many Jews and worshipers who were converts to Judaism followed Paul and Barnabas, who spoke to them and urged them to remain faithful to the grace of God.

Address to the Gentiles. [44]On the following sabbath almost the whole city gathered to hear the word of the Lord. [45]When the Jews saw the crowds, they were filled with jealousy and with violent abuse contradicted what Paul said. [46]k Both Paul and Barnabas spoke out boldly and said, "It was necessary that the word of God be spoken to you first, but since you reject it and condemn yourselves as unworthy of eternal life,

---

*[13:16–41] This is the first of several speeches of Paul to Jews proclaiming that the Christian church is the logical development of Pharisaic Judaism (see also Acts 24:10–21; 26:2–23).

†[13:16] **Who are God-fearing:** see note on Acts 8:26–40.

‡[13:18] **Put up with:** some manuscripts read "sustained."

§[13:20] **At the end of about four hundred and fifty years:** the manuscript tradition makes it uncertain whether the mention of four hundred and fifty years refers to the sojourn in Egypt before the Exodus, the wilderness period and the time of the conquest (see Ex 12:40–41), as the translation here suggests, or to the time between the conquest and the time of Samuel, the period of the judges, if the text is read, "After these things, for about four hundred and fifty years, he provided judges."

¶[13:31] The theme of the Galilean witnesses is a major one in the Gospel of Luke and in Acts and is used to signify the continuity between the teachings of Jesus and the teachings of the church and to guarantee the fidelity of the church's teachings to the words of Jesus.

[13:38–39] **Justified: the verb is the same as that used in Paul's letters to speak of the experience of justification and, as in Paul, is here connected with the term "to have faith" ("every believer"). But this seems the only passage about Paul in Acts where justification is mentioned. In Lucan fashion it is paralleled with "forgiveness of sins" (a theme at Acts 2:38; 3:19; 5:31; 10:43) based on Jesus' resurrection (Acts 13:37) rather than his cross, and is put negatively (Acts 13:38). Therefore, some would translate, "in regard to everything from which you could not be acquitted . . . every believer is acquitted."

---

r. [13:17] Ex 6:1,6; 12:51.   s. [13:18] Ex 16:1,35; Nm 14:34.   t. [13:19] Dt 7:1; Jos 14:1–2.   u. [13:20] Jgs 2:16; 1 Sm 3:20.   v. [13:21] 1 Sm 8:5, 19; 9:16; 10:1, 20–21, 24; 11:15.   w. [13:22] 1 Sm 13:14; 16:12–13; Ps 89:20–21.   x. [13:23] Is 11:1.   y. [13:24] Mt 3:1–2; Mk 1:4–5; Lk 3:2–3.   z. [13:25] Mt 3:11; Mk 1:7; Lk 3:16; Jn 1:20, 27.   a. [13:28] Mt 27:20, 22–23; Mk 15:13–14; Lk 23:4, 14–15, 21–23; Jn 19:4–6, 15.   b. [13:29] Mt 27:59–60; Mk 15:46; Lk 23:53; Jn 19:38, 41–42.   c. [13:30] 2:24, 32; 3:15; 4:10; 17:31.

d. [13:31] 1:3, 8; 10:39, 41; Mt 28:8–10, 16–20; Mk 16:9, 12–20; Lk 24:13–53; Jn 20:11–29; 21:1–23.   e. [13:33] Ps 2:7.   f. [13:34] Is 55:3.   g. [13:35] Ps 16:10.   h. [13:36] 2:29; 1 Kgs 2:10.   i. [13:39] Rom 3:20.   j. [13:41] Hab 1:5.   k. [13:46] 3:26; Rom 1:16.

we now turn to the Gentiles.' ⁴⁷For so the Lord has commanded us, 'I have made you a light to the Gentiles, that you may be an instrument of salvation to the ends of the earth.'"¹

⁴⁸The Gentiles were delighted when they heard this and glorified the word of the Lord. All who were destined for eternal life came to believe, ⁴⁹and the word of the Lord continued to spread through the whole region. ⁵⁰The Jews, however, incited the women of prominence who were worshipers and the leading men of the city, stirred up a persecution against Paul and Barnabas, and expelled them from their territory. ⁵¹ᵐSo they shook the dust from their feet in protest against them and went to Iconium.† ⁵²The disciples were filled with joy and the holy Spirit.

CHAPTER 14

Paul and Barnabas at Iconium. ¹In Iconium they entered the Jewish synagogue together and spoke in such a way that a great number of both Jews and Greeks came to believe, ²although the disbelieving Jews stirred up and poisoned the minds of the Gentiles against the brothers. ³So they stayed for a considerable period, speaking out boldly for the Lord, who confirmed the word about his grace by granting signs and wonders to occur through their hands.ⁿ ⁴The people of the city were divided: some were with the Jews; others, with the apostles. ⁵When there was an attempt by both the Gentiles and the Jews, together with their leaders, to attack and stone them,° ⁶they realized it and fled to the Lycaonian cities of Lystra and Derbe and to the surrounding countryside, ⁷where they continued to proclaim the good news.

Paul and Barnabas at Lystra. ⁸‡At Lystra there was a crippled man, lame from birth, who had never walked. ⁹He listened to Paul speaking, who looked intently at him, saw that he had the faith to be healed, ¹⁰and called out in a loud voice, "Stand up straight on your feet." He jumped up and began to walk about. ¹¹When the crowds saw what Paul had done, they cried out in Lycaonian, "The gods have come down to us in human form."ᵖ ¹²They called Barnabas "Zeus"§ and Paul "Hermes," because he was the

chief speaker. ¹³And the priest of Zeus, whose temple was at the entrance to the city, brought oxen and garlands to the gates, for he together with the people intended to offer sacrifice.

¹⁴The apostles Barnabas and Paul tore their garments¶ when they heard this and rushed out into the crowd, shouting, ¹⁵**"Men, why are you doing this? We are of the same nature as you, human beings. We proclaim to you good news that you should turn from these idols to the living God, 'who made heaven and earth and sea and all that is in them.'�q ¹⁶In past generations he allowed all Gentiles to go their own ways;ʳ ¹⁷yet, in bestowing his goodness, he did not leave himself without witness, for he gave you rains from heaven and fruitful seasons, and filled you with nourishment and gladness for your hearts."ˢ ¹⁸Even with these words, they scarcely restrained the crowds from offering sacrifice to them.

¹⁹However, some Jews from Antioch and Iconium arrived and won over the crowds. They stoned Paul and dragged him out of the city, supposing that he was dead. ²⁰But when the disciples gathered around him, he got up and entered the city. On the following day he left with Barnabas for Derbe.

End of the First Mission. ²¹After they had proclaimed the good news to that city and made a considerable number of disciples, they returned to Lystra and to Iconium and to Antioch. ²²They strengthened the spirits of the disciples and exhorted them to persevere in the faith, saying, "It is necessary for us to undergo many hardships to enter the kingdom of God."ᵘ ²³They appointed presbyters†† for them in each church and, with prayer and fasting, commended them to the Lord in whom they had put their faith. ²⁴Then they traveled through Pisidia and reached Pamphylia. ²⁵After proclaiming the word at Perga they went down to Attalia. ²⁶From there they sailed to Antioch, where they had been commended to the grace of God for the work they had now accomplished.ᵛ ²⁷And when they arrived, they called the church together and reported what God had done with them and how he had opened the door of faith to the Gentiles. ²⁸Then they spent no little time with the disciples.

---

*[13:46] The refusal to believe frustrates God's plan for his chosen people; however, no adverse judgment is made here concerning their ultimate destiny. Again, Luke, in the words of Paul, speaks of the priority of Israel in the plan for salvation (see Acts 10:36).

†[13:51] See note on Lk 9:5.

‡[14:8–18] In an effort to convince his hearers that the divine power works through his word, Paul cures the cripple. However, the pagan tradition of the occasional appearance of gods among human beings leads the people astray in interpreting the miracle. The incident reveals the cultural difficulties with which the church had to cope. Note the similarity of the miracle worked here by Paul to the one performed by Peter in Acts 3:2–10.

§[14:12] **Zeus . . . Hermes**: in Greek religion, Zeus was the chief of the Olympian gods, the "father of gods and men";

Hermes was a son of Zeus and was usually identified as the herald and messenger of the gods.

¶[14:14] **Tore their garments**: a gesture of protest.

**[14:15–17] This is the first speech of Paul to Gentiles recorded by Luke in Acts (cf. Acts 17:22–31). Rather than showing how Christianity is the logical outgrowth of Judaism, as he does in speeches before Jews, Luke says that God excuses past Gentile ignorance and then presents a natural theology arguing for the recognition of God's existence and presence through his activity in natural phenomena.

††[14:23] **They appointed presbyters**: the communities are given their own religious leaders by the traveling missionaries. The structure in these churches is patterned on the model of the Jerusalem community (Acts 11:30; 15:2, 5, 22; 21:18).

q. [14:15]3:12;10:26;Ex 20:11; Ps146:6.   r. [14:16]17:30.   s. [14:17] Wis 13:1.   t. [14:19–20]2 Cor11:25; 2Tm3:11.   u. [14:22]1Thes 3:3. v. [14:26] 13:1–3.

l. [13:47] Is 49:6.   m. [13:51] Mt 10:14; Mk 6:11; Lk 9:5; 10:11. n. [14:3] Mk 16:17–20.   o. [14:5] 2 Tm 3:11.   p. [14:11] 28:6.

CHAPTER 15

Council of Jerusalem. [1]"Some who had come down from Judea were instructing the brothers,[w] "Unless you are circumcised according to the Mosaic practice,[x] you cannot be saved."[†] [2]Because there arose no little dissension and debate by Paul and Barnabas with them, it was decided that Paul, Barnabas, and some of the others should go up to Jerusalem to the apostles and presbyters about this question. [3]They were sent on their journey by the church, and passed through Phoenicia and Samaria telling of the conversion of the Gentiles, and brought great joy to all the brothers. [4]When they arrived in Jerusalem, they were welcomed by the church, as well as by the apostles and the presbyters, and they reported what God had done with them. [5]But some from the party of the Pharisees who had become believers stood up and said, "It is necessary to circumcise them and direct them to observe the Mosaic law."

[6]‡The apostles and the presbyters met together to see about this matter. [7]§After much debate had taken place, Peter got up and said to them, "My brothers, you are well aware that from early days God made his choice among you that through my mouth the Gentiles would hear the word of the gospel and believe.[y] [8]And God, who knows the heart, bore witness by granting them the holy Spirit just as he did us.[z] [9]He made no distinction between us and them, for by faith he purified their hearts.[a] [10]Why, then, are you now putting God to the test by placing on the shoulders of the disciples a yoke that neither our ancestors nor we have been able to bear?[b] [11]On the contrary, we believe that we are saved through the grace of the Lord Jesus,[c] in the same way as they."[¶] [12]The whole assembly fell silent, and they listened while Paul and Barnabas described the signs and wonders God had worked among the Gentiles through them.

James on Dietary Law. [13]**After they had fallen silent, James responded, "My brothers, listen to me. [14]Symeon[††] has described how God first concerned himself with acquiring from among the Gentiles a people for his name. [15]The words of the prophets agree with this, as is written:

[16] 'After this I shall return[d]
      and rebuild the fallen hut of David;
   from its ruins I shall rebuild it
      and raise it up again,
[17] so that the rest of humanity may seek out
         the Lord,
      even all the Gentiles on whom my
         name is invoked.
   Thus says the Lord who accomplishes
         these things,
[18]   known from of old.'

[19]eIt is my judgment, therefore, that we ought to stop troubling the Gentiles who turn to God, [20]but tell them by letter to avoid pollution from idols, unlawful marriage, the meat of strangled animals, and blood.[f] [21]For Moses, for generations now, has had those who proclaim him in every town, as he has been read in the synagogues every sabbath."

Letter of the Apostles. [22]Then the apostles and presbyters, in agreement with the whole church, decided to choose representatives and to send them to Antioch with Paul and Barnabas. The ones chosen were Judas, who was called Barsabbas, and Silas, leaders among the brothers. [23]This is the letter delivered by them: "The apostles and the presbyters, your brothers, to the brothers in Antioch, Syria, and Cilicia of Gentile origin: greetings. [24]Since we have heard that some of our number [who went out] without

---

*[15:1–35] The Jerusalem "Council" marks the official rejection of the rigid view that Gentile converts were obliged to observe the Mosaic law completely. From here to the end of Acts, Paul and the Gentile mission become the focus of Luke's writing.

†[15:1–5] When some of the converted Pharisees of Jerusalem discover the results of the first missionary journey of Paul, they urge that the Gentiles be taught to follow the Mosaic law. Recognizing the authority of the Jerusalem church, Paul and Barnabas go there to settle the question of whether Gentiles can embrace a form of Christianity that does not include this obligation.

‡[15:6–12] The gathering is possibly the same as that recalled by Paul in Gal 2:1–10. Note that in Acts 15:2 it is only the apostles and presbyters, a small group, with whom Paul and Barnabas are to meet. Here Luke gives the meeting a public character because he wishes to emphasize its doctrinal significance (see Acts 15:22).

§[15:7–11] Paul's refusal to impose the Mosaic law on the Gentile Christians is supported by Peter on the ground that within his own experience God bestowed the holy Spirit upon Cornelius and his household without preconditions concerning the adoption of the Mosaic law (see Acts 10:44–47).

¶[15:11] In support of Paul, Peter formulates the fundamental meaning of the gospel: that all are invited to be saved through faith in the power of Christ.

**[15:13–35] Some scholars think that this apostolic decree suggested by James, the immediate leader of the Jerusalem community, derives from another historical occasion than the meeting in question. This seems to be the case if the meeting is the same as the one related in Gal 2:1–10. According to that account, nothing was imposed upon Gentile Christians in respect to Mosaic law; whereas the decree instructs Gentile Christians of mixed communities to abstain from meats sacrificed to idols and from blood-meats, and to avoid marriage within forbidden degrees of consanguinity and affinity (Lv 18), all of which practices were especially abhorrent to Jews. Luke seems to have telescoped two originally independent incidents: the first a Jerusalem "Council" that dealt with the question of circumcision, and the second a Jerusalem decree dealing mainly with Gentile observance of dietary laws (see Acts 21:25 where Paul seems to be learning of the decree for the first time).

††[15:14] **Symeon:** elsewhere in Acts he is called either Peter or Simon. The presence of the name Symeon here suggests that, in the source Luke is using for this part of the Jerusalem "Council" incident, the name may have originally referred to someone other than Peter (see Acts 13:1 where the Antiochene Symeon Niger is mentioned). As the text now stands, however, it is undoubtedly a reference to Simon Peter (Acts 15:7).

---

w. [15:1–4] Gal 2:1–9.   x. [15:1] Lv 12:3; Gal 5:2.   y. [15:7] 10:27–43.   z. [15:8] 10:44–48.   a. [15:9] 10:34–35.   b. [15:10] Mt 23:4; Gal 5:1.   c. [15:11] Gal 2:16; 3:11; Eph 2:5–8.

d. [15:16–17] Am 9:11–12.   e. [15:19–20] 15:28–29; 21:25.   f. [15:20] Gn 9:4; Lv 3:17; 17:10–14.

any mandate from us have upset you with their teachings and disturbed your peace of mind, [25]we have with one accord decided to choose representatives and to send them to you along with our beloved Barnabas and Paul, [26]who have dedicated their lives to the name of our Lord Jesus Christ. [27]So we are sending Judas and Silas who will also convey this same message by word of mouth: [28g]'It is the decision of the holy Spirit and of us not to place on you any burden beyond these necessities, [29]namely, to abstain from meat sacrificed to idols, from blood, from meats of strangled animals, and from unlawful marriage. If you keep free of these, you will be doing what is right. Farewell.'"[h]

Delegates at Antioch. [30]And so they were sent on their journey. Upon their arrival in Antioch they called the assembly together and delivered the letter. [31]When the people read it, they were delighted with the exhortation. [32]Judas and Silas, who were themselves prophets, exhorted and strengthened the brothers with many words. [33]After they had spent some time there, they were sent off with greetings of peace from the brothers to those who had commissioned them. [[34]]* [35]But Paul and Barnabas remained in Antioch, teaching and proclaiming with many others the word of the Lord.

V. THE MISSION OF PAUL TO THE ENDS OF THE EARTH

Paul and Barnabas Separate. [36†]After some time, Paul said to Barnabas, "Come, let us make a return visit to see how the brothers are getting on in all the cities where we proclaimed the word of the Lord." [37]Barnabas wanted to take with them also John, who was called Mark, [38]but Paul insisted that they should not take with them someone who had deserted them at Pamphylia and who had not continued with them in their work.[i] [39]So sharp was their disagreement that they separated. Barnabas took Mark and sailed to Cyprus. [40]But Paul chose Silas and departed after being commended by the brothers to the grace of the Lord. [41]He traveled through Syria and Cilicia bringing strength to the churches.

CHAPTER 16

Paul in Lycaonia: Timothy. [1]He reached [also] Derbe and Lystra where there was a disciple named Timothy, the son of a Jewish woman who was a believer, but his father was a Greek.[j] [2]The brothers in Lystra and Iconium spoke highly of him,[k] [3]and Paul wanted him to come along with him. On account of the Jews of that region, Paul had him circumcised,[‡] for they all knew that his father was a Greek. [4]As they traveled from city to city, they handed on to the people for observance the decisions reached by the apostles and presbyters in Jerusalem. [5]Day after day the churches grew stronger in faith and increased in number.

Through Asia Minor. [6]They traveled through the Phrygian and Galatian territory because they had been prevented by the holy Spirit from preaching the message in the province of Asia. [7]When they came to Mysia, they tried to go on into Bithynia, but the Spirit of Jesus[§] did not allow them, [8]so they crossed through Mysia and came down to Troas. [9]During [the] night Paul had a vision. A Macedonian stood before him and implored him with these words, "Come over to Macedonia and help us." [10]When he had seen the vision, we[¶] sought passage to Macedonia at once, concluding that God had called us to proclaim the good news to them.

Into Europe. [11]We set sail from Troas, making a straight run for Samothrace, and on the next day to Neapolis, [12]and from there to Philippi, a leading city in that district of Macedonia and a Roman colony. We spent some time in that city. [13]On the sabbath we went outside the city gate along the river where we thought there would be a place of prayer. We sat and spoke with the women who had gathered there. [14]One of them, a woman named Lydia, a dealer in purple cloth, from the city of Thyatira, a worshiper of

---

*[15:34] Some manuscripts add, in various wordings, "But Silas decided to remain there."

†[15:36–18:22] This continuous narrative recounts Paul's second missionary journey. On the internal evidence of the Lucan account, it lasted about three years. Paul first visited the communities he had established on his first journey (Acts 16:1–5), then pushed on into Macedonia, where he established communities at Philippi, Thessalonica, and Beroea (Acts 16:7–17:5). To escape the hostility of the Jews of Thessalonica, he left for Greece and while resident in Athens attempted, without success, to establish an effective Christian community there. From Athens he proceeded to Corinth and, after a stay of a year and a half, returned to Antioch by way of Ephesus and Jerusalem (Acts 17:16–18:22). Luke does not concern himself with the structure or statistics of the communities but aims to show the general progress of the gospel in the Gentile world as well as its continued failure to take root in the Jewish community.

g. [15:28–29] 15:19–20.   h. [15:29] Gn 9:4; Lv 3:17; 17:10–14.
i. [15:38] 13:13.

‡[16:3] **Paul had him circumcised:** he did this in order that Timothy might be able to associate with the Jews and so perform a ministry among them. Paul did not object to the Jewish Christians' adherence to the law. But he insisted that the law could not be imposed on the Gentiles. Paul himself lived in accordance with the law, or as exempt from the law, according to particular circumstances (see 1 Cor 9:19–23).

§[16:7] **The Spirit of Jesus:** this is an unusual formulation in Luke's writings. The parallelism with Acts 16:6 indicates its meaning, the holy Spirit.

¶[16:10–17] This is the first of the so-called "we-sections" in Acts, where Luke writes as one of Paul's companions. The other passages are Acts 20:5–15; 21:1–18; 27:1–28:16. Scholars debate whether Luke may not have used the first person plural simply as a literary device to lend color to the narrative. The realism of the narrative, however, lends weight to the argument that the "we" includes Luke or another companion of Paul whose data Luke used as a source.

**[16:11–40] The church at Philippi became a flourishing community to which Paul addressed one of his letters (see Introduction to the Letter to the Philippians).

j. [16:1] 1 Tm 1:2; 2 Tm 1:5.   k. [16:2] Phil 2:20.

God,* listened, and the Lord opened her heart to pay attention to what Paul was saying. ¹⁵After she and her household had been baptized, she offered us an invitation, "If you consider me a believer in the Lord, come and stay at my home," and she prevailed on us.

Imprisonment at Philippi. ¹⁶As we were going to the place of prayer, we met a slave girl with an oracular spirit,† who used to bring a large profit to her owners through her fortune-telling. ¹⁷She began to follow Paul and us, shouting, "These people are slaves of the Most High God, who proclaim to you a way of salvation." ¹⁸She did this for many days. Paul became annoyed, turned, and said to the spirit, "I command you in the name of Jesus Christ to come out of her." Then it came out at that moment.

¹⁹When her owners saw that their hope of profit was gone, they seized Paul and Silas and dragged them to the public square before the local authorities. ²⁰They brought them before the magistrates‡ and said, "These people are Jews and are disturbing our city ²¹and are advocating customs that are not lawful for us Romans to adopt or practice." ²²ˡThe crowd joined in the attack on them, and the magistrates had them stripped and ordered them to be beaten with rods. ²³After inflicting many blows on them, they threw them into prison and instructed the jailer to guard them securely. ²⁴When he received these instructions, he put them in the innermost cell and secured their feet to a stake.

Deliverance from Prison. ²⁵About midnight, while Paul and Silas were praying and singing hymns to God as the prisoners listened, ²⁶there was suddenly such a severe earthquake that the foundations of the jail shook; all the doors flew open, and the chains of all were pulled loose. ²⁷When the jailer woke up and saw the prison doors wide open, he drew [his] sword and was about to kill himself, thinking that the prisoners had escaped. ²⁸But Paul shouted out in a loud voice, "Do no harm to yourself; we are all here." ²⁹He asked for a light and rushed in and, trembling with fear, he fell down before Paul and Silas. ³⁰Then he brought them out and said, "Sirs, what must I do to be saved?" ³¹And they said, "Believe in the Lord Jesus and you and your household will be saved." ³²So they spoke the word of the Lord to him and to everyone in his house. ³³He took them in at that hour of the night and bathed their wounds; then he and all

his family were baptized at once. ³⁴He brought them up into his house and provided a meal and with his household rejoiced at having come to faith in God.

³⁵But when it was day, the magistrates sent the lictors§ with the order, "Release those men." ³⁶The jailer reported the[se] words to Paul, "The magistrates have sent orders that you be released. Now, then, come out and go in peace." ³⁷But Paul said to them, "They have beaten us publicly, even though we are Roman citizens and have not been tried, and have thrown us into prison.ᵐ And now, are they going to release us secretly? By no means. Let them come themselves and lead us out."¶ ³⁸The lictors reported these words to the magistrates, and they became alarmed when they heard that they were Roman citizens.ⁿ ³⁹So they came and placated them, and led them out and asked that they leave the city. ⁴⁰When they had come out of the prison, they went to Lydia's house where they saw and encouraged the brothers, and then they left.

CHAPTER 17

Paul in Thessalonica. ¹When they took the road through Amphipolis and Apollonia, they reached Thessalonica, where there was a synagogue of the Jews.ᵒ ²Following his usual custom, Paul joined them, and for three sabbaths he entered into discussions with them from the scriptures, ³expounding and demonstrating that the Messiah had to suffer and rise from the dead, and that "This is the Messiah, Jesus, whom I proclaim to you."ᵖ ⁴Some of them were convinced and joined Paul and Silas; so, too, a great number of Greeks who were worshipers, and not a few of the prominent women. ⁵But the Jews became jealous and recruited some worthless men loitering in the public square, formed a mob, and set the city in turmoil. They marched on the house of Jason,�q intending to bring them before the people's assembly. ⁶**When they could not find them, they dragged Jason and some of the brothers before the city magistrates, shouting, "These people who have been creating a disturbance all over the world have now come here, ⁷and Jason has welcomed them.ʳ They all act in opposition to the decrees of Caesar and claim instead that there is another king, Jesus."††

§[16:35] **The lictors:** the equivalent of police officers, among whose duties were the apprehension and punishment of criminals.

¶[16:37] Paul's Roman citizenship granted him special privileges in regard to criminal process. Roman law forbade under severe penalty the beating of Roman citizens (see also Acts 22:25).

**[17:6–7] The accusations against Paul and his companions echo the charges brought against Jesus in Lk 23:2.

††[17:7] **There is another king, Jesus:** a distortion into a political sense of the apostolic proclamation of Jesus and the kingdom of God (see Acts 8:12).

*[16:14] **A worshiper of God:** a "God-fearer." See note on Acts 8:26–40.

†[16:16] **With an oracular spirit:** literally, "with a Python spirit." The Python was the serpent or dragon that guarded the Delphic oracle. It later came to designate a "spirit that pronounced oracles" and also a ventriloquist who, it was thought, had such a spirit in the belly.

‡[16:20] **Magistrates:** in Greek, *stratēgoi*, the popular designation of the *duoviri*, the highest officials of the Roman colony of Philippi.

l. [16:22–23] 2 Cor 11:25; Phil 1:30; 1 Thes 2:2.

m. [16:37] 22:25.   n. [16:38] 22:29.   o. [17:1] 1 Thes 2:1–2.   p. [17:3] 3:18; Lk 24:25–26, 46.   q. [17:5] Rom 16:21.   r. [17:7] Lk 23:2; Jn 19:12–15.

[8]They stirred up the crowd and the city magistrates who, upon hearing these charges, [9]took a surety payment from Jason and the others before releasing them.

Paul in Beroea. [10]The brothers immediately sent Paul and Silas to Beroea during the night. Upon arrival they went to the synagogue of the Jews. [11]These Jews were more fair-minded than those in Thessalonica, for they received the word with all willingness and examined the scriptures daily to determine whether these things were so.[s] [12]Many of them became believers, as did not a few of the influential Greek women and men. [13]But when the Jews of Thessalonica learned that the word of God had now been proclaimed by Paul in Beroea also, they came there too to cause a commotion and stir up the crowds. [14]So the brothers at once sent Paul on his way to the seacoast, while Silas and Timothy remained behind.[t] [15]After Paul's escorts had taken him to Athens, they came away with instructions for Silas and Timothy to join him as soon as possible.

Paul in Athens.[*] [16]While Paul was waiting for them in Athens, he grew exasperated at the sight of the city full of idols. [17]So he debated in the synagogue with the Jews and with the worshipers, and daily in the public square with whoever happened to be there. [18]Even some of the Epicurean and Stoic philosophers[†] engaged him in discussion. Some asked, "What is this scavenger trying to say?" Others said, "He sounds like a promoter of foreign deities," because he was preaching about 'Jesus' and 'Resurrection.' [19]They took him and led him to the Areopagus[‡] and said, "May we learn what this new teaching is that you speak of?[u] [20]For you bring some strange notions to our ears; we should like to know what these things mean." [21]Now all the Athenians as well as the foreigners residing there used their time for nothing else but telling or hearing something new.

Paul's Speech at the Areopagus. [22]Then Paul stood up at the Areopagus and said:[§]

"You Athenians, I see that in every respect you are very religious. [23]For as I walked around looking carefully at your shrines, I even discovered an altar inscribed, 'To an Unknown God.'[¶] What therefore you unknowingly worship, I proclaim to you. [24]The God who made the world and all that is in it, the Lord of heaven and earth, does not dwell in sanctuaries made by human hands,[v] [25]nor is he served by human hands because he needs anything. Rather it is he who gives to everyone life and breath and everything. [26]He made from one[**] the whole human race to dwell on the entire surface of the earth, and he fixed the ordered seasons and the boundaries of their regions, [27]so that people might seek God, even perhaps grope for him and find him, though indeed he is not far from any one of us.[w] [28]For 'In him we live and move and have our being,'[††] as even some of your poets have said, 'For we too are his offspring.' [29]Since therefore we are the offspring of God, we ought not to think that the divinity is like an image fashioned from gold, silver, or stone by human art and imagination.[x] [30]God has overlooked the times of ignorance, but now he demands that all people everywhere repent [31]because he has established a day on which he will 'judge the world with justice' through a man he has appointed, and he has provided confirmation for all by raising him from the dead."[y]

[32]When they heard about resurrection of the dead, some began to scoff, but others said, "We should like to hear you on this some other time." [33]And so Paul left them. [34]But some did join him, and became believers. Among them were Dionysius, a member of the Court of the

---

*[17:16–21] Paul's presence in Athens sets the stage for the great discourse before a Gentile audience in Acts 17:22–31. Although Athens was a politically insignificant city at this period, it still lived on the glories of its past and represented the center of Greek culture. The setting describes the conflict between Christian preaching and Hellenistic philosophy.

†[17:18] **Epicurean and Stoic philosophers:** for the followers of Epicurus (342–271 B.C.), the goal of life was happiness attained through sober reasoning and the searching out of motives for all choice and avoidance. The Stoics were followers of Zeno, a younger contemporary of Alexander the Great. Zeno and his followers believed in a type of pantheism that held that the spark of divinity was present in all reality and that, in order to be free, each person must live "according to nature." **This scavenger:** literally, "seed-picker," as of a bird that picks up grain. The word is later used of scrap collectors and of people who take other people's ideas and propagate them as if they were their own. **Promoter of foreign deities:** according to Xenophon, Socrates was accused of promoting new deities. The accusation against Paul echoes the charge against Socrates. **'Jesus' and 'Resurrection':** the Athenians are presented as misunderstanding Paul from the outset; they think he is preaching about Jesus and a goddess named *Anastasis*, i.e., Resurrection.

‡[17:19] **To the Areopagus:** the "Areopagus" refers either to the Hill of Ares west of the Acropolis or to the Council of Athens, which at one time met on the hill but which at this time assembled in the Royal Colonnade (**Stoa Basileios**).

§[17:22–31] In Paul's appearance at the Areopagus he preaches his climactic speech to Gentiles in the cultural center of the ancient world. The speech is more theological than christological. Paul's discourse appeals to the Greek world's belief in divinity as responsible for the origin and existence of the universe. It contests the common belief in a multiplicity of gods supposedly exerting their powers through their images. It acknowledges that the attempt to find God is a constant human endeavor. It declares, further, that God is the judge of the human race, that the time of the judgment has been determined, and that it will be executed through a man whom God raised from the dead. The speech reflects sympathy with pagan religiosity, handles the subject of idol worship gently, and appeals for a new examination of divinity, not from the standpoint of creation but from the standpoint of judgment.

¶[17:23] **'To an Unknown God':** ancient authors such as Pausanias, Philostratus, and Tertullian speak of Athenian altars with no specific dedication as altars of "unknown gods" or "nameless altars."

[17:26] **From one: many manuscripts read "from one blood." **Fixed . . . seasons:** or "fixed limits to the epochs."

††[17:28] **'In him we live and move and have our being':** some scholars understand this saying to be based on an earlier saying of Epimenides of Knossos (6th century B.C.). **'For we too are his offspring':** here Paul is quoting Aratus of Soli, a third-century B.C. poet from Cilicia.

v. [17:24] 7:48–50; Gn 1:1; 1 Kgs 8:27; Is 42:5.   w. [17:27] Jer 23:23; Wis 13:6; Rom 1:19.   x. [17:29] 19:26; Is 40:18–20; 44:10–17; Rom 1:22–23.   y. [17:31] 10:42.

s. [17:11] Jn 5:39.   t. [17:14] 1 Thes 3:1–2.   u. [17:19] 1 Cor 1:22.

Areopagus, a woman named Damaris, and others with them.

CHAPTER 18

Paul in Corinth. ¹After this he left Athens and went to Corinth. ²There he met a Jew named Aquila,ᶻ a native of Pontus, who had recently come from Italy with his wife Priscilla* because Claudius had ordered all the Jews to leave Rome. He went to visit them ³and, because he practiced the same trade, stayed with them and worked, for they were tentmakers by trade. ⁴Every sabbath, he entered into discussions in the synagogue, attempting to convince both Jews and Greeks.

⁵When Silas and Timothy came down from Macedonia, Paul began to occupy himself totally with preaching the word, testifying to the Jews that the Messiah was Jesus. ⁶When they opposed him and reviled him, he shook out his garments† and said to them, "Your blood be on your heads! I am clear of responsibility. From now on I will go to the Gentiles."ᵃ ⁷So he left there and went to a house belonging to a man named Titus Justus, a worshiper of God;‡ his house was next to a synagogue.ᵇ ⁸Crispus,§ the synagogue official,ᶜ came to believe in the Lord along with his entire household, and many of the Corinthians who heard believed and were baptized. ⁹ᵈOne night in a vision the Lord said to Paul, "Do not be afraid. Go on speaking, and do not be silent, ¹⁰for I am with you. No one will attack and harm you, for I have many people in this city." ¹¹He settled there for a year and a half and taught the word of God among them.

Accusations Before Gallio. ¹²But when Gallio was proconsul of Achaia,⁵ the Jews rose up together against Paul and brought him to the tribunal, ¹³saying, "This man is inducing people to worship God contrary to the law."** ¹⁴When Paul was about to reply, Gallio spoke to the Jews, "If it were a matter of some crime or malicious fraud, I should with reason hear the complaint of you Jews; ¹⁵but since it is a question

of arguments over doctrine and titles and your own law, see to it yourselves. I do not wish to be a judge of such matters." ¹⁶And he drove them away from the tribunal. ¹⁷They all seized Sosthenes, the synagogue official, and beat him in full view of the tribunal. But none of this was of concern to Gallio.

Return to Syrian Antioch. ¹⁸Paul remained for quite some time, and after saying farewell to the brothers he sailed for Syria, together with Priscilla and Aquila. At Cenchreae he had his hair cutᵉ because he had taken a vow.†† ¹⁹When they reached Ephesus, he left them there, while he entered the synagogue and held discussions with the Jews. ²⁰Although they asked him to stay for a longer time, he did not consent, ²¹but as he said farewell he promised, "I shall come back to you again, God willing." Then he set sail from Ephesus. ²²Upon landing at Caesarea, he went up and greeted the church‡‡ and then went down to Antioch. ²³§§After staying there some time, he left and traveled in orderly sequence through the Galatian country and Phrygia, bringing strength to all the disciples.

Apollos. ²⁴A Jew named Apollos,ᶠ a native of Alexandria, an eloquent speaker, arrived in Ephesus. He was an authority on the scriptures.⁵⁵ ²⁵He had been instructed in the Way of the Lord and, with ardent spirit, spoke and taught accurately about Jesus, although he knew only the baptism of John. ²⁶He began to speak boldly in the synagogue; but when Priscilla and Aquila heard him, they took him aside and explained to him the Way [of God]*** more accurately. ²⁷And when he wanted to cross to Achaia, the brothers encouraged him and wrote to the disciples there to welcome him. After his arrival he gave great assistance to those who had come to believe through grace. ²⁸He vigorously refuted the Jews in public, establishing from the scriptures that the Messiah is Jesus.

CHAPTER 19

Paul in Ephesus. ¹†††While Apollos was in Corinth, Paul traveled through the interior of

---

*[18:2] **Aquila . . . Priscilla**: both may already have been Christians at the time of their arrival in Corinth (see Acts 18:26). According to 1 Cor 16:19, their home became a meeting place for Christians. **Claudius**: the Emperor Claudius expelled the Jews from Rome ca. A.D. 49. The Roman historian Suetonius gives as reason for the expulsion disturbances among the Jews "at the instigation of Chrestos," probably meaning disputes about the messiahship of Jesus.

†[18:6] **Shook out his garments**: a gesture indicating Paul's repudiation of his mission to the Jews there; cf. Acts 28:17–31.

‡[18:7] **A worshiper of God**: see note on Acts 8:26–40.

§[18:8] **Crispus**: in 1 Cor 1:14 Paul mentions that Crispus was one of the few he himself baptized at Corinth.

⁵[18:12] **When Gallio was proconsul of Achaia**: Gallio's proconsulship in Achaia is dated to A.D. 51–52 from an inscription discovered at Delphi. This has become an important date in establishing a chronology of the life and missionary work of Paul.

[18:13] **Contrary to the law: Gallio (Acts 18:15) understands this to be a problem of Jewish, not Roman, law.

††[18:18] **He had his hair cut because he had taken a vow**: a reference to a Nazirite vow (see Nm 6:1–21, especially Nm 6:18) taken by Paul (see also Acts 21:23–27).

‡‡[18:22] **He went up and greeted the church**: "going up" suggests a visit to the church in Jerusalem.

§§[18:23–21:16] Luke's account of Paul's third missionary journey devotes itself mainly to his work at Ephesus (Acts 19:1–20:1). There is a certain restiveness on Paul's part and a growing conviction that the Spirit bids him return to Jerusalem and prepare to go to Rome (Acts 19:21).

⁵⁵[18:24–25] Apollos appears as a preacher who knows the teaching of Jesus in the context of John's baptism of repentance. Aquila and Priscilla instruct him more fully. He is referred to in 1 Cor 1:12; 3:5–6, 22.

***[18:26] **The Way [of God]**: for the Way, see note on Acts 9:2. Other manuscripts here read "the way of the Lord," "the word of the Lord," or simply "the Way."

†††[19:1–6] Upon his arrival in Ephesus, Paul discovers other people at the same religious stage as Apollos, though they seem to have considered themselves followers of Christ,

---

z. [18:2]. Rom 16:3.   a. [18:6] 13:51; Mt 10:14; 27:24–25; Mk 6:11; Lk 9:5; 10:10–11.   b. [18:7] 13:46–47; 28:28.   c. [18:8] 1 Cor 1:14. d. [18:9–10] Jer 1:8.

e. [18:18] 21:24; Nm 6:18.   f. [18:24] 1 Cor 1:12.

the country and came [down] to Ephesus where he found some disciples. ²He said to them, "Did you receive the holy Spirit when you became believers?" They answered him, "We have never even heard that there is a holy Spirit." ³He said, "How were you baptized?" They replied, "With the baptism of John." ⁴Paul then said, "John baptized with a baptism of repentance, telling the people to believe in the one who was to come after him, that is, in Jesus."ᵍ ⁵When they heard this, they were baptized in the name of the Lord Jesus. ⁶And when Paul laid [his] hands on them, the holy Spirit came upon them, and they spoke in tongues and prophesied.ʰ ⁷Altogether there were about twelve men.

⁸He entered the synagogue, and for three months debated boldly with persuasive arguments about the kingdom of God. ⁹But when some in their obstinacy and disbelief disparaged the Way before the assembly, he withdrew and took his disciples with him and began to hold daily discussions in the lecture hall of Tyrannus. ¹⁰This continued for two years with the result that all the inhabitants of the province of Asia heard the word of the Lord, Jews and Greeks alike. ¹¹So extraordinary were the mighty deeds God accomplished at the hands of Paul ¹²that when face cloths or aprons that touched his skin were applied to the sick, their diseases left them and the evil spirits came out of them.ⁱ

The Jewish Exorcists. ¹³Then some itinerant Jewish exorcists tried to invoke the name of the Lord Jesus over those with evil spirits, saying, "I adjure you by the Jesus whom Paul preaches." ¹⁴When the seven sons of Sceva, a Jewish high priest, tried to do this, ¹⁵the evil spirit said to them in reply, "Jesus I recognize, Paul I know, but who are you?" ¹⁶The person with the evil spirit then sprang at them and subdued them all. He so overpowered them that they fled naked and wounded from that house. ¹⁷When this became known to all the Jews and Greeks who lived in Ephesus, fear fell upon them all, and the name of the Lord Jesus was held in great esteem. ¹⁸Many of those who had become believers came forward and openly acknowledged their former practices. ¹⁹Moreover, a large number of those who had practiced magic collected their books and burned them in public. They calculated their value and found it to be fifty thousand silver pieces. ²⁰Thus did the word of the Lord continue to spread with influence and power.

Paul's Plans. ²¹When this was concluded, Paul made up his mind to travel through Macedonia and Achaia, and then to go on to Jerusalem, saying, "After I have been there, I must visit Rome also."ʲ ²²Then he sent to Macedonia two of his assistants, Timothy and Erastus, while he himself stayed for a while in the province of Asia.

The Riot of the Silversmiths. ²³About that time a serious disturbance broke out concerning the Way. ²⁴There was a silversmith named Demetrius who made miniature silver shrines of Artemis* and provided no little work for the craftsmen. ²⁵He called a meeting of these and other workers in related crafts and said, "Men, you know well that our prosperity derives from this work. ²⁶As you can now see and hear, not only in Ephesus but throughout most of the province of Asia this Paul has persuaded and misled a great number of people by saying that gods made by hands are not gods at all.ᵏ ²⁷The danger grows, not only that our business will be discredited, but also that the temple of the great goddess Artemis will be of no account, and that she whom the whole province of Asia and all the world worship will be stripped of her magnificence."

²⁸When they heard this, they were filled with fury and began to shout, "Great is Artemis of the Ephesians!" ²⁹The city was filled with confusion, and the people rushed with one accord into the theater, seizing Gaius and Aristarchus, the Macedonians, Paul's traveling companions.ˡ ³⁰Paul wanted to go before the crowd, but the disciples would not let him, ³¹and even some of the Asiarchs† who were friends of his sent word to him advising him not to venture into the theater. ³²Meanwhile, some were shouting one thing, others something else; the assembly was in chaos, and most of the people had no idea why they had come together. ³³Some of the crowd prompted Alexander, as the Jews pushed him forward, and Alexander signaled with his hand that he wished to explain something to the gathering. ³⁴But when they recognized that he was a Jew, they all shouted in unison, for about two hours, "Great is Artemis of the Ephesians!" ³⁵Finally the town clerk restrained the crowd and said, "You Ephesians, what person is there who does not know that the city of the Ephesians is the guardian of the temple‡ of the great Artemis and of her image that fell from the sky? ³⁶Since these things are undeniable, you must

---

* [19:24] **Miniature silver shrines of Artemis**: the temple of Artemis at Ephesus was one of the seven wonders of the ancient world. Artemis, originally the Olympian virgin hunter, moon goddess, and goddess of wild nature, was worshiped at Ephesus as an Asian mother goddess and goddess of fertility. She was one of the most widely worshiped female deities in the Hellenistic world (see Acts 18:27).

† [19:31] **Asiarchs**: the precise status and role of the Asiarchs is disputed. They appear to have been people of wealth and influence who promoted the Roman imperial cult and who may also have been political representatives in a league of cities in the Roman province of Asia.

‡ [19:35] **Guardian of the temple**: this title was accorded by Rome to cities that provided a temple for the imperial cult. Inscriptional evidence indicates that Ephesus was acknowledged as the temple keeper of Artemis and of the imperial cult. **That fell from the sky**: many scholars think that this refers to a meteorite that was worshiped as an image of the goddess.

---

not of the Baptist. On the relation between baptism and the reception of the Spirit, see note on Acts 8:16.

g. [19:4] 1:5; 11:16; 13:24–25; Mt 3:11; Mk 1:8; Lk 3:16.　h. [19:6] 8:15–17; 10:44, 46.　i. [19:12] 5:15–16; Lk 8:44–47.　j. [19:21] 23:11; Rom 1:13; 15:22–32.

k. [19:26] 17:29.　l. [19:29] Col 4:10.

calm yourselves and not do anything rash. [37]The men you brought here are not temple robbers, nor have they insulted our goddess. [38]If Demetrius and his fellow craftsmen have a complaint against anyone, courts are in session, and there are proconsuls. Let them bring charges against one another. [39]If you have anything further to investigate, let the matter be settled in the lawful assembly, [40]for, as it is, we are in danger of being charged with rioting because of today's conduct. There is no cause for it. We shall [not]* be able to give a reason for this demonstration." With these words he dismissed the assembly.

CHAPTER 20
Journey to Macedonia and Greece. [1]When the disturbance was over, Paul had the disciples summoned and, after encouraging them, he bade them farewell and set out on his journey to Macedonia.*m* [2]As he traveled throughout those regions, he provided many words of encouragement for them. Then he arrived in Greece, [3]where he stayed for three months. But when a plot was made against him by the Jews as he was about to set sail for Syria, he decided to return by way of Macedonia.
Return to Troas. [4]"Sopater, the son of Pyrrhus, from Beroea, accompanied him, as did Aristarchus and Secundus from Thessalonica, Gaius from Derbe, Timothy, and Tychicus and Trophimus from Asia [5]who went on ahead and waited for us† at Troas.*o* [6]We sailed from Philippi after the feast of Unleavened Bread,‡ and rejoined them five days later in Troas, where we spent a week.
Eutychus Restored to Life. [7]On the first day of the week§ when we gathered to break bread, Paul spoke to them because he was going to leave on the next day, and he kept on speaking until midnight. [8]There were many lamps in the upstairs room where we were gathered, [9]and a young man named Eutychus who was sitting on the window sill was sinking into a deep sleep as Paul talked on and on. Once overcome by sleep, he fell down from the third story and when he was picked up, he was dead. [10p]Paul went down,¶ threw himself upon him, and said as he embraced him, "Don't be alarmed; there is

life in him." [11]Then he returned upstairs, broke the bread, and ate; after a long conversation that lasted until daybreak, he departed. [12]And they took the boy away alive and were immeasurably comforted.
Journey to Miletus. [13]We went ahead to the ship and set sail for Assos where we were to take Paul on board, as he had arranged, since he was going overland. [14]When he met us in Assos, we took him aboard and went on to Mitylene. [15]We sailed away from there on the next day and reached a point off Chios, and a day later we reached Samos, and on the following day we arrived at Miletus. [16]**Paul had decided to sail past Ephesus in order not to lose time in the province of Asia, for he was hurrying to be in Jerusalem, if at all possible, for the day of Pentecost.
Paul's Farewell Speech at Miletus. [17]From Miletus he had the presbyters of the church at Ephesus summoned. [18]When they came to him, he addressed them, "You know how I lived among you the whole time from the day I first came to the province of Asia. [19]I served the Lord with all humility and with the tears and trials that came to me because of the plots of the Jews, [20]and I did not at all shrink from telling you what was for your benefit, or from teaching you in public or in your homes. [21]I earnestly bore witness for both Jews and Greeks to repentance before God and to faith in our Lord Jesus. [22]But now, compelled by the Spirit, I am going to Jerusalem. What will happen to me there I do not know, [23]except that in one city after another the holy Spirit has been warning me that imprisonment and hardships await me.*q* [24]Yet I consider life of no importance to me, if only I may finish my course and the ministry that I received from the Lord Jesus, to bear witness to the gospel of God's grace.*r*
[25]"But now I know that none of you to whom I preached the kingdom during my travels will ever see my face again. [26]And so I solemnly declare to you this day that I am not responsible for the blood of any of you, [27]for I did not shrink from proclaiming to you the entire plan of God. [28]Keep watch over yourselves and over the whole flock of which the holy Spirit has appointed you overseers,†† in which you tend the church of God

---

*[19:40] Some manuscripts omit the negative in [not] be able, making the meaning, "There is no cause for which we shall be able to give a reason for this demonstration."
†[20:5] The second "we-section" of Acts begins here. See note on Acts 16:10–17.
‡[20:6] Feast of Unleavened Bread: see note on Lk 22:1.
§[20:7] The first day of the week: the day after the sabbath and the first day of the Jewish week, apparently chosen originally by the Jerusalem community for the celebration of the liturgy of the Eucharist in order to relate it to the resurrection of Christ.
¶[20:10] The action of Paul in throwing himself upon the dead boy recalls that of Elijah in 1 Kgs 17:21 where the son of the widow of Zarephath is revived and that of Elisha in 2 Kgs 4:34 where the Shunamite woman's son is restored to life.

**[20:16–35] Apparently aware of difficulties at Ephesus and neighboring areas, Paul calls the presbyters together at Miletus, about thirty miles from Ephesus. He reminds them of his dedication to the gospel (Acts 20:18–21), speaks of what he is about to suffer for the gospel (Acts 20:22–27), and admonishes them to guard the community against false prophets, sure to arise upon his departure (Acts 20:28–31). He concludes by citing a saying of Jesus (Acts 20:35) not recorded in the gospel tradition. Luke presents this farewell to the Ephesian presbyters as Paul's last will and testament.
††[20:28] Overseers: see note on Phil 1:1. The church of God: because the clause "that he acquired with his own blood" following "the church of God" suggests that "his own blood" refers to God's blood, some early copyists changed "the church of God" to "the church of the Lord." Some prefer the translation "acquired with the blood of his own," i.e., Christ.

---

m. [20:1] 1 Cor 16:1.   n. [20:4] Rom 16:21.   o. [20:5] 21:29; 2 Tm 4:20.
p. [20:10] 1 Kgs 17:17–24; 2 Kgs 4:30–37; Mt 9:24; Mk 5:39; Lk 8:52.   q. [20:23] 9:16.   r. [20:24] 2 Tm 4:7.   s. [20:28] Jn 21:15–17; 1 Pt 5:2.

that he acquired with his own blood. [29]I know that after my departure savage wolves will come among you, and they will not spare the flock.[t] [30]And from your own group, men will come forward perverting the truth to draw the disciples away after them.[u] [31]So be vigilant and remember that for three years, night and day, I unceasingly admonished each of you with tears.[v] [32]And now I commend you to God and to that gracious word of his that can build you up and give you the inheritance among all who are consecrated. [33]I have never wanted anyone's silver or gold or clothing. [34]You know well that these very hands have served my needs and my companions.[w] [35]In every way I have shown you that by hard work of that sort we must help the weak, and keep in mind the words of the Lord Jesus who himself said, 'It is more blessed to give than to receive.'"[x]

[36]When he had finished speaking he knelt down and prayed with them all. [37]They were all weeping loudly as they threw their arms around Paul and kissed him, [38]for they were deeply distressed that he had said that they would never see his face again. Then they escorted him to the ship.

CHAPTER 21

Arrival at Tyre. [1]*When we had taken leave of them we set sail, made a straight run for Cos, and on the next day for Rhodes, and from there to Patara. [2]Finding a ship crossing to Phoenicia, we went on board and put out to sea. [3]We caught sight of Cyprus but passed by it on our left and sailed on toward Syria and put in at Tyre where the ship was to unload cargo. [4]There we sought out the disciples and stayed for a week. They kept telling Paul through the Spirit not to embark for Jerusalem. [5]At the end of our stay we left and resumed our journey. All of them, women and children included, escorted us out of the city, and after kneeling on the beach to pray, [6]we bade farewell to one another. Then we boarded the ship, and they returned home.

Arrival at Ptolemais and Caesarea. [7]We continued the voyage and came from Tyre to Ptolemais, where we greeted the brothers and stayed a day with them. [8]On the next day we resumed the trip and came to Caesarea, where we went to the house of Philip the evangelist, who was one of the Seven,[†] and stayed with him.[y] [9]He had four virgin daughters gifted with prophecy. [10]We had been there several days when a prophet named Agabus[‡] came down from Judea. [11z]He came up to us, took Paul's belt, bound

his own feet and hands with it, and said, "Thus says the holy Spirit: This is the way the Jews will bind the owner of this belt in Jerusalem, and they will hand him over to the Gentiles."[§] [12]When we heard this, we and the local residents begged him not to go up to Jerusalem. [13]Then Paul replied, "What are you doing, weeping and breaking my heart? I am prepared not only to be bound but even to die in Jerusalem for the name of the Lord Jesus." [14a]Since he would not be dissuaded we let the matter rest, saying,[b] "The Lord's will be done."[¶]

Paul and James in Jerusalem. [15]After these days we made preparations for our journey, then went up to Jerusalem. [16]Some of the disciples from Caesarea came along to lead us to the house of Mnason, a Cypriot, a disciple of long standing, with whom we were to stay. [17]*When we reached Jerusalem the brothers welcomed us warmly. [18]The next day, Paul accompanied us on a visit to James, and all the presbyters were present. [19]He greeted them, then proceeded to tell them in detail what God had accomplished among the Gentiles through his ministry. [20]They praised God when they heard it but said to him, "Brother, you see how many thousands of believers there are from among the Jews, and they are all zealous observers of the law. [21]They have been informed that you are teaching all the Jews who live among the Gentiles to abandon Moses and that you are telling them not to circumcise their children or to observe their customary practices. [22]What is to be done? They will surely hear that you have arrived. [23††]So do what we tell you. We have four men who have taken a vow.[c] [24]Take these men and purify yourself with them, and pay their expenses[‡‡] that they may have their heads shaved. In this way everyone will know that there is nothing to the reports they have been given about you but that you yourself live in observance of the law.

§[21:11] The symbolic act of Agabus recalls those of Old Testament prophets. Compare Is 20:2; Ez 4:1; Jer 13:1.

¶[21:14] The Christian disciples' attitude reflects that of Jesus (see Lk 22:42).

**[21:17–26] The leaders of the Jewish Christians of Jerusalem inform Paul that the Jews there believe he has encouraged the Jews of the diaspora to abandon the Mosaic law. According to Acts, Paul had no objection to the retention of the law by the Jewish Christians of Jerusalem and left the Jews of the diaspora who accepted Christianity free to follow the same practice.

††[21:23–26] The leaders of the community suggest that Paul, on behalf of four members of the Jerusalem community, make the customary payment for the sacrifices offered at the termination of the Nazirite vow (see Nm 6:1–24) in order to impress favorably the Jewish Christians in Jerusalem with his high regard for the law. Since Paul himself had once made this vow (Acts 18:18), his respect for the law would be on public record.

‡‡[21:24] **Pay their expenses**: according to Nm 6:14–15 the Nazirite had to present a yearling lamb for a holocaust, a yearling ewe lamb for a sin offering, and a ram for a peace offering, along with food and drink offerings, upon completion of the period of the vow.

*[21:1–18] The third "we-section" of Acts (see note on Acts 16:10–17).

†[21:8] **One of the Seven**: see note on Acts 6:2–4.

‡[21:10] **Agabus**: mentioned in Acts 11:28 as the prophet who predicted the famine that occurred when Claudius was emperor.

t. [20:29] Jn 10:12. u. [20:30] Mt 7:15; 2 Pt 2:1–3; 1 Jn 2:18–19. v. [20:31] 1 Thes 2:11. w. [20:34] 1 Cor 4:12; 1 Thes 2:9; 2 Thes 3:8. x. [20:35] Sir 4:31. y. [21:8] 6:5; 8:5–6. z. [21:11] 11:28; 20:23.

a. [21:14] 19:15–16. b. [21:14] Mt 6:10; 26:39; Mk 14:36; Lk 22:42. c. [21:23–27] 18:18; Nm 6:1–21.

^{25d}As for the Gentiles who have come to believe, we sent them our decision that they abstain from meat sacrificed to idols, from blood, from the meat of strangled animals, and from unlawful marriage." ²⁶So Paul took the men, and on the next day after purifying himself together with them entered the temple to give notice of the day when the purification would be completed and the offering made for each of them.^e

Paul's Arrest. ²⁷When the seven days were nearly completed, the Jews from the province of Asia noticed him in the temple, stirred up the whole crowd, and laid hands on him, ^{28f}shouting, "Fellow Israelites, help us. This is the man who is teaching everyone everywhere against the people and the law and this place, and what is more, he has even brought Greeks into the temple and defiled this sacred place."[†] ²⁹For they had previously seen Trophimus the Ephesian in the city with him and supposed that Paul had brought him into the temple. ³⁰The whole city was in turmoil with people rushing together. They seized Paul and dragged him out of the temple, and immediately the gates were closed. ³¹While they were trying to kill him, a report reached the cohort commander[‡] that all Jerusalem was rioting. ³²He immediately took soldiers and centurions and charged down on them. When they saw the commander and the soldiers they stopped beating Paul. ³³The cohort commander came forward, arrested him, and ordered him to be secured with two chains; he tried to find out who he might be and what he had done. ³⁴Some in the mob shouted one thing, others something else; so, since he was unable to ascertain the truth because of the uproar, he ordered Paul to be brought into the compound. ³⁵When he reached the steps, he was carried by the soldiers because of the violence of the mob, ^{36g}for a crowd of people followed and shouted, "Away with him!"

³⁷Just as Paul was about to be taken into the compound, he said to the cohort commander, "May I say something to you?" He replied, "Do you speak Greek? ³⁸So then you are not the Egyptian[¶] who started a revolt some time ago and led the four thousand assassins into the desert?"^h ³⁹Paul answered, "I am a Jew, of Tarsus in Cilicia, a citizen of no mean city; I request you to permit me to speak to the people." ⁴⁰When he had given his permission, Paul stood on the steps and motioned with his hand to the people; and when all was quiet he addressed them in Hebrew."

CHAPTER 22

Paul's Defense Before the Jerusalem Jews.^{††} ¹"My brothers and fathers, listen to what I am about to say to you in my defense." ²When they heard him addressing them in Hebrew they became all the more quiet. And he continued, ³"I am a Jew, born in Tarsus in Cilicia, but brought up in this city. At the feet of Gamaliel I was educated strictly in our ancestral law and was zealous for God, just as all of you are today.ⁱ ⁴I persecuted this Way to death, binding both men and women and delivering them to prison.^j ⁵Even the high priest and the whole council of elders can testify on my behalf. For from them I even received letters to the brothers and set out for Damascus to bring back to Jerusalem in chains for punishment those there as well.

⁶"On that journey as I drew near to Damascus, about noon a great light from the sky suddenly shone around me.^k ⁷I fell to the ground and heard a voice saying to me, 'Saul, Saul, why are you persecuting me?'^l ⁸I replied, 'Who are you, sir?' And he said to me, 'I am Jesus the Nazorean whom you are persecuting.'^m ⁹My companions saw the light but did not hear the voice of the one who spoke to me.ⁿ ¹⁰I asked, 'What shall I do, sir?' The Lord answered me, 'Get up and go into Damascus, and there you will be told about everything appointed for you to do.'^o ¹¹Since I could see nothing because of the brightness of that light, I was led by hand by my companions and entered Damascus.^p

^{12q}"A certain Ananias, a devout observer of the law, and highly spoken of by all the Jews who

---

*[21:25] Paul is informed about the apostolic decree, seemingly for the first time (see note on Acts 15:13–35). The allusion to the decree was probably introduced here by Luke to remind his readers that the Gentile Christians themselves were asked to respect certain Jewish practices deriving from the law.

†[21:28] The charges against Paul by the diaspora Jews are identical to the charges brought against Stephen by diaspora Jews in Acts 6:13. **Brought Greeks into the temple:** non-Jews were forbidden, under penalty of death, to go beyond the Court of the Gentiles. Inscriptions in Greek and Latin on a stone balustrade marked off the prohibited area.

‡[21:31] **Cohort commander:** literally, "the leader of a thousand in a cohort." At this period the Roman cohort commander usually led six hundred soldiers, a tenth of a legion; but the number in a cohort varied.

§[21:36] **"Away with him!":** at the trial of Jesus before Pilate in Lk 23:18, the people similarly shout, "Away with this man."

d. [21:25] 15:19–20, 28–29. e. [21:26] 1 Cor 9:20. f. [21:28] Rom 15:31. g. [21:36] 22:22; Lk 23:18; Jn 19:15.

¶[21:38] **The Egyptian:** according to the Jewish historian Josephus, an Egyptian gathered a large crowd on the Mount of Olives to witness the destruction of the walls of Jerusalem that would fall at the Egyptian "prophet's" word. The commotion was put down by the Roman authorities and the Egyptian escaped, but only after thousands had been killed. **Four thousand assassins:** literally, *sicarii.* According to Josephus, these were political nationalists who removed their opponents by assassination with a short dagger, called in Latin a *sica.*

[21:40] **In Hebrew: meaning, perhaps, in Aramaic, which at this time was the Semitic tongue in common use.

††[22:1–21] Paul's first defense speech is presented to the Jerusalem crowds. Luke here presents Paul as a devout Jew (Acts 22:3) and zealous persecutor of the Christian community (Acts 22:4–5), and then recounts the conversion of Paul for the second time in Acts (see note on Acts 9:1–19).

h. [21:38] 5:36–37. i. [22:3] 5:34; 26:4–5; 2 Cor 11:22; Gal 1:13–14; Phil 3:5–6. j. [22:4] 8:3; 9:1–2; 22:19; 26:9–11; Phil 3:6. k. [22:6] 9:3; 26:13; 1 Cor 15:8. l. [22:7] 9:4; 26:14. m. [22:8] 9:5; 26:15; Mt 25:40. n. [22:9] 9:7; 26:13–14. o. [22:10] 9:6; 26:16. p. [22:11] 9:8. q. [22:12–16] 9:10–19.

lived there, [13]came to me and stood there and said, 'Saul, my brother, regain your sight.' And at that very moment I regained my sight and saw him. [14]Then he said, "The God of our ancestors designated you to know his will, to see the Righteous One, and to hear the sound of his voice; [15]for you will be his witness* before all to what you have seen and heard. [16]Now, why delay? Get up and have yourself baptized and your sins washed away, calling upon his name.'

[17]"After I had returned to Jerusalem and while I was praying in the temple, I fell into a trance [18]and saw the Lord saying to me, 'Hurry, leave Jerusalem at once, because they will not accept your testimony about me.' [19]But I replied, 'Lord, they themselves know that from synagogue to synagogue I used to imprison and beat those who believed in you.[r] [20]And when the blood of your witness Stephen was being shed, I myself stood by giving my approval and keeping guard over the cloaks of his murderers.'[s] [21]Then he said to me,[t] 'Go, I shall send you far away to the Gentiles.'"†

Paul Imprisoned. [22]"They listened to him until he said this, but then they raised their voices and shouted, "Take such a one as this away from the earth. It is not right that he should live."‡ [23]And as they were yelling and throwing off their cloaks and flinging dust into the air, [24]the cohort commander ordered him to be brought into the compound and gave instruction that he be interrogated under the lash to determine the reason why they were making such an outcry against him. [25]"But when they had stretched him out for the whips, Paul said to the centurion on duty, "Is it lawful for you to scourge a man who is a Roman citizen and has not been tried?"§ [26]When the centurion heard this, he went to the cohort commander and reported it, saying, "What are you going to do? This man is a Roman citizen." [27]Then the commander came and said to him, "Tell me, are you a Roman citizen?" "Yes," he answered. [28]The commander replied, "I acquired this citizenship for a large sum of money." Paul said, "But I was born one." [29]At once those who were going to interrogate him backed away from him, and the commander became alarmed

when he realized that he was a Roman citizen and that he had had him bound.

Paul Before the Sanhedrin. [30]The next day, wishing to determine the truth about why he was being accused by the Jews, he freed him and ordered the chief priests and the whole Sanhedrin to convene. Then he brought Paul down and made him stand before them.

CHAPTER 23

[1]Paul looked intently at the Sanhedrin and said, "My brothers, I have conducted myself with a perfectly clear conscience before God to this day."[w] [2]The high priest Ananias§ ordered his attendants to strike his mouth. [3]Then Paul said to him, "God will strike you," you whitewashed wall. Do you indeed sit in judgment upon me according to the law and yet in violation of the law order me to be struck?"[x] [4]The attendants said, "Would you revile God's high priest?" [5]Paul answered, "Brothers, I did not realize he was the high priest. For it is written,[y] 'You shall not curse a ruler of your people.'"††

[6]Paul was aware that some were Sadducees and some Pharisees, so he called out before the Sanhedrin, "My brothers, I am a Pharisee, the son of Pharisees; [I] am on trial for hope in the resurrection of the dead."[z] [7]When he said this, a dispute broke out between the Pharisees and Sadducees, and the group became divided. [8]For the Sadducees say that there is no resurrection or angels or spirits, while the Pharisees acknowledge all three.[a] [9]A great uproar occurred, and some scribes belonging to the Pharisee party stood up and sharply argued, "We find nothing wrong with this man. Suppose a spirit or an angel has spoken to him?" [10]The dispute was so serious that the commander, afraid that Paul would be torn to pieces by them, ordered his troops to go down and rescue him from their midst and take him into the compound. [11]‡‡[b]The following night the Lord stood by him and said, "Take courage. For just as you have borne witness to my cause in Jerusalem, so you must also bear witness in Rome."

Transfer to Caesarea. [12]When day came, the Jews made a plot and bound themselves by oath

---

*[22:15] **His witness:** like the Galilean followers during the historical ministry of Jesus, Paul too, through his experience of the risen Christ, is to be a witness to the resurrection (compare Acts 1:8; 10:39–41; Lk 24:48).

†[22:21] Paul endeavors to explain that his position on the law has not been identical with that of his audience because it has been his prophetic mission to preach to the Gentiles to whom the law was not addressed and who had no faith in it as a way of salvation.

‡[22:22] Paul's suggestion that his prophetic mission to the Gentiles did not involve his imposing the law on them provokes the same opposition as occurred in Pisidian Antioch (Acts 13:45).

§[22:25] **Is it lawful for you to scourge a man who is a Roman citizen and has not been tried?:** see note on Acts 16:37.

§[23:2] **The high priest Ananias:** Ananias, son of Nedebaeus, was high priest from A.D. 47 to 59.

[23:3] **God will strike you: Josephus reports that Ananias was later assassinated in A.D. 66 at the beginning of the First Revolt.

††[23:5] Luke portrays Paul as a model of one who is obedient to the Mosaic law. Paul, because of his reverence for the law (Ex 22:27), withdraws his accusation of hypocrisy, "whitewashed wall" (cf. Mt 23:27), when he is told Ananias is the high priest.

‡‡[23:11] The occurrence of the vision of Christ consoling Paul and assuring him that he will be his witness in Rome prepares the reader for the final section of Acts: the journey of Paul and the word he preaches to Rome under the protection of the Romans.

---

r. [22:19] 8:3; 9:1–2; 22:4–5; 26:9–11.   s. [22:20] 7:58; 8:1. t. [22:21] 9:15; Gal 2:7–9.   u. [22:22] 21:36; Lk 23:18; Jn 19:15. v. [22:25] 16:37.

w. [23:1] 24:16.   x. [23:3] Ez 13:10–15; Mt 23:27.   y. [23:5] Ex 22:27.   z. [23:6] 24:15, 21; 26:5; Phil 3:5.   a. [23:8] Mt 22:23; Lk 20:27.   b. [23:11] 19:21.

not to eat or drink until they had killed Paul. [13]There were more than forty who formed this conspiracy. [14]They went to the chief priests and elders and said, "We have bound ourselves by a solemn oath to taste nothing until we have killed Paul. [15]You, together with the Sanhedrin, must now make an official request to the commander to have him bring him down to you, as though you meant to investigate his case more thoroughly. We on our part are prepared to kill him before he arrives." [16]The son of Paul's sister, however, heard about the ambush; so he went and entered the compound and reported it to Paul. [17]Paul then called one of the centurions* and requested, "Take this young man to the commander; he has something to report to him." [18]So he took him and brought him to the commander and explained, "The prisoner Paul called me and asked that I bring this young man to you; he has something to say to you." [19]The commander took him by the hand, drew him aside, and asked him privately, "What is it you have to report to me?" [20]He replied, "The Jews have conspired to ask you to bring Paul down to the Sanhedrin tomorrow, as though they meant to inquire about him more thoroughly, [21]but do not believe them. More than forty of them are lying in wait for him; they have bound themselves by oath not to eat or drink until they have killed him. They are now ready and only wait for your consent." [22]As the commander dismissed the young man he directed him, "Tell no one that you gave me this information."

[23]Then he summoned two of the centurions and said, "Get two hundred soldiers ready to go to Caesarea by nine o'clock tonight,[†] along with seventy horsemen and two hundred auxiliaries. [24]Provide mounts for Paul to ride and give him safe conduct to Felix the governor." [25]Then he wrote a letter with this content: [26]‡"Claudius Lysias to his excellency the governor Felix, greetings.[§] [27]This man, seized by the Jews and about to be murdered by them, I rescued after intervening with my troops when I learned that he was a Roman citizen.[c] [28]I wanted to learn the reason for their accusations against him

so I brought him down to their Sanhedrin. [29]I discovered that he was accused in matters of controversial questions of their law and not of any charge deserving death or imprisonment.[d] [30]Since it was brought to my attention that there will be a plot against the man, I am sending him to you at once, and have also notified his accusers to state [their case] against him before you."

[31]So the soldiers, according to their orders, took Paul and escorted him by night to Antipatris. [32]The next day they returned to the compound, leaving the horsemen to complete the journey with him. [33]When they arrived in Caesarea they delivered the letter to the governor and presented Paul to him. [34]When he had read it and asked to what province he belonged, and learned that he was from Cilicia, [35]he said, "I shall hear your case when your accusers arrive." Then he ordered that he be held in custody in Herod's praetorium.

CHAPTER 24

Trial Before Felix. [1]Five days later the high priest Ananias came down with some elders and an advocate, a certain Tertullus, and they presented formal charges against Paul to the governor. [2]When he was called, Tertullus began to accuse him, saying, "Since we have attained much peace through you, and reforms have been accomplished in this nation through your provident care, [3]we acknowledge this in every way and everywhere, most excellent Felix, with all gratitude. [4]But in order not to detain you further, I ask you to give us a brief hearing with your customary graciousness. [5]We found this man to be a pest; he creates dissension among Jews all over the world and is a ringleader of the sect of the Nazoreans.[¶] [6]He even tried to desecrate our temple, but we arrested him.[f] [[7]]** [8]If you examine him you will be able to learn from him for yourself about everything of which we are accusing him." [9]The Jews also joined in the attack and asserted that these things were so.

[10]††Then the governor motioned to him to speak and Paul replied, "I know that you have been a judge over this nation for many years and so I am pleased to make my defense before you. [11]As you can verify, not more than twelve days have passed since I went up to Jerusalem to worship. [12]Neither in the temple, nor in the

---

*[23:17] **Centurions:** a centurion was a military officer in charge of one hundred soldiers.

†[23:23] **By nine o'clock tonight:** literally, "by the third hour of the night." The night hours began at 6 p.m. **Two hundred auxiliaries:** the meaning of the Greek is not certain. It seems to refer to spearmen from the local police force and not from the cohort of soldiers, which would have numbered only 500–1000 men.

‡[23:26–30] The letter emphasizes the fact that Paul is a Roman citizen and asserts the lack of evidence that he is guilty of a crime against the empire. The tone of the letter implies that the commander became initially involved in Paul's case because of his Roman citizenship, but this is not an exact description of what really happened (see Acts 21:31–33; 22:25–29).

§[23:26] M. Antonius Felix was procurator of Judea from A.D. 52 to 60. His procuratorship was marked by cruelty toward and oppression of his Jewish subjects.

c. [23:27] 21:30–34; 22:27.

¶[24:5] **Nazoreans:** that is, followers of Jesus of Nazareth.

**[24:7] The Western text has added here a verse (really Acts 24:6b–8a) that is not found in the best Greek manuscripts. It reads, "and would have judged him according to our own law, but the cohort commander Lysias came and violently took him out of our hands and ordered his accusers to come before you."

††[24:10–21] Whereas the advocate Tertullus referred to Paul's activities on his missionary journeys, the apostle narrowed the charges down to the riot connected with the incident in the temple (see Acts 21:27–30; 24:17–20). In his defense, Paul stresses the continuity between Christianity and Judaism.

d. [23:29] 18:14–15; 25:18–19.   e. [24:5] 24:14; Lk 23:2.   f. [24:6] 21:28.

synagogues, nor anywhere in the city did they find me arguing with anyone or instigating a riot among the people. [13]Nor can they prove to you the accusations they are now making against me. [14]But this I do admit to you, that according to the Way, which they call a sect, I worship the God of our ancestors and I believe everything that is in accordance with the law and written in the prophets.[g] [15]I have the same hope in God as they themselves have that there will be a resurrection of the righteous and the unrighteous.[h] [16]Because of this, I always strive to keep my conscience clear before God and man.[i] [17]After many years, I came to bring alms for my nation and offerings.[j] [18]While I was so engaged, they found me, after my purification, in the temple without a crowd or disturbance.[k] [19]But some Jews from the province of Asia, who should be here before you to make whatever accusation they might have against me— [20]or let these men themselves state what crime they discovered when I stood before the Sanhedrin, [21]unless it was my one outcry as I stood among them, that 'I am on trial before you today for the resurrection of the dead.'"[l]

[22]Then Felix, who was accurately informed about the Way, postponed the trial, saying, "When Lysias the commander comes down, I shall decide your case." [23]He gave orders to the centurion that he should be kept in custody but have some liberty, and that he should not prevent any of his friends from caring for his needs. **Captivity in Caesarea.** [24]Several days later Felix came with his wife Drusilla, who was Jewish. He had Paul summoned and listened to him speak about faith in Christ Jesus. [25]But as he spoke about righteousness and self-restraint and the coming judgment, Felix became frightened and said, "You may go for now; when I find an opportunity I shall summon you again." [26]At the same time he hoped that a bribe would be offered him by Paul, and so he sent for him very often and conversed with him.

[27]Two years passed and Felix was succeeded by Porcius Festus. Wishing to ingratiate himself with the Jews, Felix left Paul in prison.[†]

CHAPTER 25

Appeal to Caesar. [1]Three days after his arrival in the province, Festus went up from Caesarea to Jerusalem [2]where the chief priests and Jewish leaders presented him their formal charges

against Paul.[‡] They asked him [3]as a favor to have him sent to Jerusalem, for they were plotting to kill him along the way. [4]Festus replied that Paul was being held in custody in Caesarea and that he himself would be returning there shortly. [5]He said, "Let your authorities come down with me, and if this man has done something improper, let them accuse him."

[6]After spending no more than eight or ten days with them, he went down to Caesarea, and on the following day took his seat on the tribunal and ordered that Paul be brought in. [7]When he appeared, the Jews who had come down from Jerusalem surrounded him and brought many serious charges against him, which they were unable to prove. [8]In defending himself Paul said, "I have committed no crime either against the Jewish law or against the temple or against Caesar." [9]Then Festus, wishing to ingratiate himself with the Jews, said to Paul in reply, "Are you willing to go up to Jerusalem and there stand trial before me on these charges?" [10]Paul answered, "I am standing before the tribunal of Caesar; this is where I should be tried. I have committed no crime against the Jews, as you very well know. [11]If I have committed a crime or done anything deserving death, I do not seek to escape the death penalty; but if there is no substance to the charges they are bringing against me, then no one has the right to hand me over to them. I appeal to Caesar." [12]Then Festus, after conferring with his council, replied, "You have appealed to Caesar. To Caesar you will go." **Paul Before King Agrippa.** [13]When a few days had passed, King Agrippa and Bernice[¶] arrived in Caesarea on a visit to Festus. [14]Since they spent several days there, Festus referred Paul's case to the king, saying, "There is a man here left in custody by Felix.[m] [15]When I was in Jerusalem the chief priests and the elders of the Jews brought charges against him and demanded his condemnation. [16]I answered them that it was not Roman practice to hand over an accused person before he has faced his accusers and had the opportunity to defend himself against their charge. [17]So when [they] came together here, I made no delay; the next day I took my seat on the tribunal and ordered the man to be brought in. [18n]His accusers stood around him, but did

---

*[24:24–25] The way of Christian discipleship greatly disquiets Felix, who has entered into an adulterous marriage with Drusilla, daughter of Herod Agrippa I. This marriage provides the background for the topics Paul speaks about and about which Felix does not want to hear.

†[24:27] Very little is known of Porcius Festus who was a procurator of Judea from A.D. 60 to 62.

g. [24:14] 24:5. h. [24:15] Dn 12:2; Jn 5:28–29. i. [24:16] 23:1.
j. [24:17] Rom 15:25–26; Gal 2:10. k. [24:18–19] 21:26–30.
l. [24:21] 23:6; 24:15.

‡[25:2] Even after two years the animosity toward Paul in Jerusalem had not subsided (see Acts 24:27).

§[25:9–12] Paul refuses to acknowledge that the Sanhedrin in Jerusalem has any jurisdiction over him now (Acts 25:11). Paul uses his right as a Roman citizen to appeal his case to the jurisdiction of the Emperor (Nero, ca. A.D. 60) (Acts 25:12). This move broke the deadlock between Roman protective custody of Paul and the plan of his enemies to kill him (25:3).

¶[25:13] **King Agrippa and Bernice**: brother and sister, children of Herod Agrippa I whose activities against the Jerusalem community are mentioned in Acts 12:1–19. Agrippa II was a petty ruler over small areas in northern Palestine and some villages in Perea. His influence on the Jewish population of Palestine was insignificant.

m. [25:14] 24:27. n. [25:18–19] 18:14–15; 23:29.

not charge him with any of the crimes I suspected. [19]Instead they had some issues with him about their own religion and about a certain Jesus who had died but who Paul claimed was alive. [20]Since I was at a loss how to investigate this controversy, I asked if he were willing to go to Jerusalem and there stand trial on these charges. [21]And when Paul appealed that he be held in custody for the Emperor's decision, I ordered him held until I could send him to Caesar." [22]Agrippa said to Festus, "I too should like to hear this man." He replied, "Tomorrow you will hear him."

[23]The next day Agrippa and Bernice came with great ceremony and entered the audience hall in the company of cohort commanders and the prominent men of the city and, by command of Festus, Paul was brought in. [24]And Festus said, "King Agrippa and all you here present with us, look at this man about whom the whole Jewish populace petitioned me here and in Jerusalem, clamoring that he should live no longer. [25]I found, however, that he had done nothing deserving death, and so when he appealed to the Emperor, I decided to send him. [26]But I have nothing definite to write about him to our sovereign; therefore I have brought him before all of you, and particularly before you, King Agrippa, so that I may have something to write as a result of this investigation. [27]For it seems senseless to me to send up a prisoner without indicating the charges against him."

CHAPTER 26
King Agrippa Hears Paul. [1]Then Agrippa said to Paul, "You may now speak on your own behalf." So Paul stretched out his hand and began his defense. [2]*"I count myself fortunate, King Agrippa, that I am to defend myself before you today against all the charges made against me by the Jews, [3]especially since you are an expert in all the Jewish customs and controversies. And therefore I beg you to listen patiently. [4]My manner of living from my youth, a life spent from the beginning among my people[†] and in Jerusalem, all [the] Jews know. [5o]They have known about me from the start, if they are willing to testify, that I have lived my life as a Pharisee, the strictest party of our religion. [6p]But now I am standing trial because of my hope in the promise made by God to our ancestors. [7]Our twelve tribes hope to attain to that promise as they fervently worship God day and night; and

on account of this hope I am accused by Jews, O king. [8]Why is it thought unbelievable among you that God raises the dead? [9q]I myself once thought that I had to do many things against the name of Jesus the Nazorean, [10]and I did so in Jerusalem. I imprisoned many of the holy ones with the authorization I received from the chief priests, and when they were to be put to death I cast my vote against them.[r] [11]Many times, in synagogue after synagogue, I punished them in an attempt to force them to blaspheme; I was so enraged against them that I pursued them even to foreign cities.

[12]"On one such occasion I was traveling to Damascus with the authorization and commission of the chief priests. [13s]At midday, along the way, O king, I saw a light from the sky, brighter than the sun, shining around me and my traveling companions.[t] [14]We all fell to the ground and I heard a voice saying to me in Hebrew, 'Saul, Saul, why are you persecuting me?[u] It is hard for you to kick against the goad.'[‡] [15]And I said, 'Who are you, sir?' And the Lord replied, 'I am Jesus whom you are persecuting.[v] [16]Get up now, and stand on your feet.[w] I have appeared to you for this purpose, to appoint you as a servant and witness of what you have seen [of me] and what you will be shown.[§] [17]I shall deliver you from this people and from the Gentiles to whom I send you,[x] [18]to open their eyes[¶] that they may turn from darkness to light and from the power of Satan to God, so that they may obtain forgiveness of sins and an inheritance among those who have been consecrated by faith in me.'[y]

[19]"And so, King Agrippa, I was not disobedient to the heavenly vision. [20]On the contrary, first to those in Damascus and in Jerusalem and throughout the whole country of Judea, and then to the Gentiles, I preached the need to repent and turn to God, and to do works giving evidence of repentance. [21z]That is why the Jews seized me [when I was] in the temple and tried to kill me. [22a]But I have enjoyed God's help to this very day, and so I stand here testifying to small and great alike, saying nothing different

---

‡[26:14] **In Hebrew:** see note on Acts 21:40. **It is hard for you to kick against the goad:** this proverb is commonly found in Greek literature and in this context signifies the senselessness and ineffectiveness of any opposition to the divine influence in his life.

§[26:16] The words of Jesus directed to Paul here reflect the dialogues between Christ and Ananias (Acts 9:15) and between Ananias and Paul (Acts 22:14–15) in the two previous accounts of Paul's conversion.

¶[26:18] **To open their eyes:** though no mention is made of Paul's blindness in this account (cf. Acts 9:8–9, 12, 18; 22:11–13), the task he is commissioned to perform is the removal of other people's spiritual blindness.

---

*[26:2–23] Paul's final defense speech in Acts is now made before a king (see Acts 9:15). In the speech Paul presents himself as a zealous Pharisee and Christianity as the logical development of Pharisaic Judaism. The story of his conversion is recounted for the third time in Acts in this speech (see note on Acts 9:1–19).

†[26:4] **Among my people:** that is, among the Jews.

o. [26:5] Phil 3:5–6; Gal 1:13–14; 2 Cor 11:22.   p. [26:6–8] 23:6; 24:15, 21; 28:20.

q. [26:9–11] 8:3; 9:1–2; 22:19; Phil 3:6.   r. [26:10] 9:14.   s. [26:13–14] 9:7.   t. [26:13] 9:3; 22:6.   u. [26:14] 9:4; 22:7.   v. [26:15] 9:5; 22:8; Mt 25:40.   w. [26:16] 9:6; 22:10; Ez 2:1.   x. [26:17] Jer 1:7.   y. [26:18] Is 42:7, 16; 61:1 LXX; Col 1:13.   z. [26:21] 21:31.   a. [26:22–23] 3:18; Lk 24:26–27, 44–47.

from what the prophets and Moses foretold,[*] [23]that the Messiah must suffer[†] and that, as the first to rise from the dead, he would proclaim light both to our people and to the Gentiles."[b]

Reactions to Paul's Speech. [24]While Paul was so speaking in his defense, Festus said in a loud voice, "You are mad, Paul; much learning is driving you mad." [25]But Paul replied, "I am not mad, most excellent Festus; I am speaking words of truth and reason. [26]The king knows about these matters and to him I speak boldly, for I cannot believe that [any] of this has escaped his notice; this was not done in a corner.[‡] [27]King Agrippa, do you believe the prophets?[§] I know you believe." [28]Then Agrippa said to Paul, "You will soon persuade me to play the Christian." [29]Paul replied, "I would pray to God that sooner or later not only you but all who listen to me today might become as I am except for these chains."

[30]Then the king rose, and with him the governor and Bernice and the others who sat with them. [31§]And after they had withdrawn they said to one another, "This man is doing nothing [at all] that deserves death or imprisonment." [32]And Agrippa said to Festus, "This man could have been set free if he had not appealed to Caesar."[c]

CHAPTER 27

Departure for Rome. [1**]When it was decided that we should sail to Italy, they handed Paul and some other prisoners over to a centurion named Julius of the Cohort Augusta.[††] [2]We went on board a ship from Adramyttium bound for ports in the province of Asia and set sail. Aristarchus, a Macedonian from Thessalonica, was with us.[d] [3]On the following day we put in at Sidon where Julius was kind enough to allow Paul to visit his friends who took care of him. [4]From there we put out to sea and sailed around the sheltered side of Cyprus because of the headwinds, [5]and crossing the open sea off the coast of Cilicia and Pamphylia we came to Myra in Lycia.

Storm and Shipwreck. [6]There the centurion found an Alexandrian ship that was sailing to Italy and put us on board. [7]For many days we made little headway, arriving at Cnidus only with difficulty, and because the wind would not permit us to continue our course we sailed for the sheltered side of Crete off Salmone. [8]We sailed past it with difficulty and reached a place called Fair Havens, near which was the city of Lasea.

[9]Much time had now passed and sailing had become hazardous because the time of the fast[‡‡] had already gone by, so Paul warned them,[e] [10]"Men, I can see that this voyage will result in severe damage and heavy loss not only to the cargo and the ship, but also to our lives." [11]The centurion, however, paid more attention to the pilot and to the owner of the ship than to what Paul said. [12]Since the harbor was unfavorably situated for spending the winter, the majority planned to put out to sea from there in the hope of reaching Phoenix, a port in Crete facing west-northwest, there to spend the winter.

[13]A south wind blew gently, and thinking they had attained their objective, they weighed anchor and sailed along close to the coast of Crete. [14]Before long an offshore wind of hurricane force called a "Northeaster" struck. [15]Since the ship was caught up in it and could not head into the wind we gave way and let ourselves be driven. [16]We passed along the sheltered side of an island named Cauda and managed only with difficulty to get the dinghy under control. [17]They hoisted it aboard, then used cables to undergird the ship. Because of their fear that they would run aground on the shoal of Syrtis, they lowered the drift anchor and were carried along in this way. [18]We were being pounded by the storm so violently that the next day they jettisoned some cargo, [19]and on the third day with their own hands they threw even the ship's tackle overboard. [20]Neither the sun nor the stars were visible for many days, and no small storm raged. Finally, all hope of our surviving was taken away.

[21]When many would no longer eat, Paul stood among them and said, "Men, you should have taken my advice and not have set sail from Crete and you would have avoided this disastrous loss. [22]I urge you now to keep up your courage; not one of you will be lost, only the ship. [23]For last night an angel of the God to whom [I] belong and whom I serve stood by

---

*[26:22] **Saying nothing different from what the prophets and Moses foretold**: see note on Lk 18:31.

†[26:23] **That the Messiah must suffer**: see note on Lk 24:26.

‡[26:26] **Not done in a corner**: for Luke, this Greek proverb expresses his belief that he is presenting a story about Jesus and the church that is already well known. As such, the entire history of Christianity is public knowledge and incontestable. Luke presents his story in this way to provide "certainty" to his readers about the instructions they have received (Lk 1:4).

§[26:2728] If the Christian missionaries proclaim nothing different from what the Old Testament prophets had proclaimed (Acts 26:22–23), then the logical outcome for the believing Jew, according to Luke, is to become a Christian.

¶[26:31–32] In recording the episode of Paul's appearance before Agrippa, Luke wishes to show that, when Paul's case was judged impartially, no grounds for legal action against him were found (see Acts 23:29; 25:25).

**[27:1–28:16] Here Luke has written a stirring account of adventure on the high seas, incidental to his main purpose of showing how well Paul got along with his captors and how his prophetic influence saved the lives of all on board. The recital also establishes the existence of Christian communities in Puteoli and Rome. This account of the voyage and shipwreck also constitutes the final "we-section" in Acts (see note on Acts 16:10–17).

††[27:1] **Cohort Augusta**: the presence of a Cohort Augusta in Syria during the first century A.D. is attested in inscriptions. Whatever the historical background to this information given by Luke may be, the name Augusta serves to increase the prominence and prestige of the prisoner Paul whose custodians bear so important a Roman name.

b. [26:23] Is 42:6; 49:6; Lk 2:32; 1 Cor 15:20–23.   c. [26:32] 25:11–12.   d. [27:2] 19:29; 20:4.

‡‡[27:9] **The time of the fast**: the fast kept on the occasion of the Day of Atonement (Lv 16:29–31), which occurred in late September or early October.

e. [27:9] Lv 16:29–31.

me [24]and said, 'Do not be afraid, Paul. You are destined to stand before Caesar; and behold, for your sake, God has granted safety to all who are sailing with you.'[f] [25]Therefore, keep up your courage, men; I trust in God that it will turn out as I have been told. [26]We are destined to run aground on some island."

[27]On the fourteenth night, as we were still being driven about on the Adriatic Sea, toward midnight the sailors began to suspect that they were nearing land. [28]They took soundings and found twenty fathoms; a little farther on, they again took soundings and found fifteen fathoms. [29]Fearing that we would run aground on a rocky coast, they dropped four anchors from the stern and prayed for day to come. [30]The sailors then tried to abandon ship; they lowered the dinghy to the sea on the pretext of going to lay out anchors from the bow. [31]But Paul said to the centurion and the soldiers, "Unless these men stay with the ship, you cannot be saved." [32]So the soldiers cut the ropes of the dinghy and set it adrift.

[33]Until the day began to dawn, Paul kept urging all to take some food. He said, "Today is the fourteenth day that you have been waiting, going hungry and eating nothing. [34]I urge you, therefore, to take some food; it will help you survive. Not a hair of the head of anyone of you will be lost." [35]When he said this, he took bread,[*] gave thanks to God in front of them all, broke it, and began to eat.[g] [36]They were all encouraged, and took some food themselves. [37]In all, there were two hundred seventy-six of us on the ship. [38]After they had eaten enough, they lightened the ship by throwing the wheat into the sea.

[39]When day came they did not recognize the land, but made out a bay with a beach. They planned to run the ship ashore on it, if they could. [40]So they cast off the anchors and abandoned them to the sea, and at the same time they unfastened the lines of the rudders, and hoisting the foresail into the wind, they made for the beach. [41]But they struck a sandbar and ran the ship aground. The bow was wedged in and could not be moved, but the stern began to break up under the pounding [of the waves]. [42]The soldiers planned to kill the prisoners so that none might swim away and escape, [43]but the centurion wanted to save Paul and so kept them from carrying out their plan. He ordered those who could swim to jump overboard first and get to the shore, [44]and then the rest, some on planks, others on debris from the ship. In this way, all reached shore safely.

CHAPTER 28

Winter in Malta. [1]Once we had reached safety we learned that the island was called Malta. [2]The natives showed us extraordinary hospitality; they lit a fire and welcomed all of us because it had begun to rain and was cold. [3]Paul had gathered a bundle of brushwood and was putting it on the fire when a viper, escaping from the heat, fastened on his hand. [4]When the natives saw the snake hanging from his hand, they said to one another, "This man must certainly be a murderer; though he escaped the sea, Justice[†] has not let him remain alive." [5]But he shook the snake off into the fire and suffered no harm. [6]They were expecting him to swell up or suddenly to fall down dead but, after waiting a long time and seeing nothing unusual happen to him, they changed their minds and began to say that he was a god.[h] [7]In the vicinity of that place were lands belonging to a man named Publius, the chief of the island. He welcomed us and received us cordially as his guests for three days. [8]It so happened that the father of Publius was sick with a fever and dysentery. Paul visited him and, after praying, laid his hands on him and healed him. [9]After this had taken place, the rest of the sick on the island came to Paul and were cured. [10]They paid us great honor and when we eventually set sail they brought us the provisions we needed.

Arrival in Rome. [11]Three months later we set sail on a ship that had wintered at the island. It was an Alexandrian ship with the Dioscuri[‡] as its figurehead. [12]We put in at Syracuse and stayed there three days, [13]and from there we sailed round the coast and arrived at Rhegium. After a day, a south wind came up and in two days we reached Puteoli. [14]There we found some brothers and were urged to stay with them for seven days. And thus we came to Rome. [15]The brothers from there heard about us and came as far as the Forum of Appius and Three Taverns to meet us. On seeing them, Paul gave thanks to God and took courage. [16]When he entered Rome,[§] Paul was allowed to live by himself, with the soldier who was guarding him.

Testimony to Jews in Rome. [17]Three days later he called together the leaders of the Jews. When they had gathered he said to them, "My brothers, although I had done nothing against our people or our ancestral customs, I was handed over to the Romans as a prisoner from Jerusalem.[i]

---

†[28:4] **Justice:** in Greek mythology, the pursuing goddess of vengeance and justice.

‡[28:11] **Dioscuri:** that is, the Twin Brothers, Castor and Pollux, the sons of Zeus and the patrons of the sailors.

§[28:16] With Paul's arrival in Rome, the programmatic spread of the word of the Lord to "the ends of the earth" (Acts 1:8) is accomplished. In Rome, Paul is placed under house arrest, and under this mild form of custody he is allowed to proclaim the word in the capital of the civilized world of his day.

¶[28:17–22] Paul's first act in Rome is to learn from the leaders of the Jewish community whether the Jews of Jerusalem plan to pursue their case against him before the Roman jurisdiction. He is informed that no such plan is afoot, but that the Jews of Rome have heard the Christian teaching denounced. Paul's offer to explain it to them is readily accepted.

---

*[27:35] **He took bread**...: the words recall the traditional language of the celebration of the Eucharist (see Lk 22:19).

f. [27:24] 23:11.   g. [27:35] Mt 15:36; Mk 6:41; 8:6; Lk 22:19; 1 Cor 11:23–24.

h. [28:6] 14:11.   i. [28:17] 24:12–13; 25:8.

[18]After trying my case the Romans wanted to release me, because they found nothing against me deserving the death penalty.[j] [19]But when the Jews objected, I was obliged to appeal to Caesar, even though I had no accusation to make against my own nation.[k] [20]This is the reason, then, I have requested to see you and to speak with you, for it is on account of the hope of Israel* that I wear these chains." [21]They answered him, "We have received no letters from Judea about you, nor has any of the brothers arrived with a damaging report or rumor about you. [22]But we should like to hear you present your views, for we know that this sect is denounced everywhere."[m]

[23]So they arranged a day with him and came to his lodgings in great numbers. From early morning until evening, he expounded his position to them, bearing witness to the kingdom of God and trying to convince them about Jesus from the law of Moses and the prophets. [24]Some were convinced by what he had said, while others did not believe. [25†]Without reaching any agreement among themselves they began to leave; then Paul made one final statement. "Well did the holy Spirit speak to your ancestors through the prophet Isaiah, saying:

[26] 'Go to this people and say:[n]
    You shall indeed hear but not understand.
      You shall indeed look but never see.
[27] Gross is the heart of this people;
      they will not hear with their ears;
        they have closed their eyes,
    so they may not see with their eyes
      and hear with their ears
    and understand with their heart and be
      converted,
    and I heal them.'

[28o]Let it be known to you that this salvation of God has been sent to the Gentiles; they will listen."[29][‡]

[30§]He remained for two full years in his lodgings. He received all who came to him, [31]and with complete assurance and without hindrance he proclaimed the kingdom of God and taught about the Lord Jesus Christ.

---

*[28:20] **The hope of Israel**: in the words of Paul (Acts 23:6), Luke has identified this hope as hope in the resurrection of the dead.

†[28:25–28] Paul's final words in Acts reflect a major concern of Luke's writings: how the salvation promised in the Old Testament, accomplished by Jesus, and offered first to Israel (Acts 13:26), has now been offered to and accepted by the Gentiles. Quoting Is 6:9–10, Paul presents the scriptural support for his indictment of his fellow Jews who refuse to accept the message he proclaims. Their rejection leads to its proclamation among the Gentiles.

j. [28:18] 23:29; 25:25; 26:31–32.   k. [28:19] 25:11.   l. [28:20] 23:6; 24:15, 21; 26:6–8.   m. [28:22] 24:5, 14.

‡[28:29] The Western text has added here a verse that is not found in the best Greek manuscripts: "And when he had said this, the Jews left, seriously arguing among themselves."

§[28:30–31] Although the ending of Acts may seem to be abrupt, Luke has now completed his story with the establishment of Paul and the proclamation of Christianity in Rome. Paul's confident and unhindered proclamation of the gospel in Rome forms the climax to the story whose outline was provided in Acts 1:8—"You will be my witnesses in Jerusalem . . . and to the ends of the earth."

n. [28:26] Is 6:9–10; Mt 13:14–15; Mk 4:12; Lk 8:10; Jn 12:40; Rom 11:8.   o. [28:28] 13:46; 18:6; Ps 67:2; Is 40:5 LXX; Lk 3:6.

NEW TESTAMENT LETTERS

In the New Testament canon, between the Acts of the Apostles and Revelation, there are twenty-one documents that take the form of letters or epistles. Most of these are actual letters, but some are more like treatises in the guise of letters. In a few cases even some of the more obvious elements of the letter form are absent; see the Introductions to Hebrews and to 1 John.

The virtually standard form found in these documents, though with some variation, is dependent upon the conventions of letter writing common in the ancient world, but these were modified to suit the purposes of Christian writers. The New Testament letters usually begin with a greeting including an identification of the sender or senders and of the recipients. Next comes a prayer, usually in the form of a thanksgiving. The body of the letter provides an exposition of Christian teaching, usually provoked by concrete circumstances, and generally also draws conclusions regarding ethical behavior. There often follows a discussion of practical matters, such as the writer's travel plans, and the letter concludes with further advice and a formula of farewell.

Fourteen of the twenty-one letters have been traditionally attributed to Paul. One of these, the Letter to the Hebrews, does not itself claim to be the work of Paul; when it was accepted into the canon after much discussion, it was attached at the very end of the Pauline corpus. The other thirteen identify Paul as their author, but most scholars believe that some of them were actually written by his disciples; see the Introductions to Ephesians, Colossians, 2 Thessalonians, and 1 Timothy.

Four of the letters in the Pauline corpus (Ephesians, Philippians, Colossians, and Philemon) are called the "Captivity Epistles" because in each of them the author speaks of being in prison at the time of writing. Three others (1–2 Timothy and Titus) are known as the "Pastoral Epistles" because, addressed to individuals rather than communities, they give advice to disciples about caring for the flock. The letters of the Pauline corpus are arranged in roughly descending order of length from Romans to Philemon, with Hebrews added at the end.

The other seven letters of the New Testament that follow the Pauline corpus are collectively referred to as the "Catholic Epistles." This term, which means "universal," refers to the fact that most of them are directed not to a single Christian community, as are most of the Pauline letters, but to a wider audience; see the Introduction to the catholic letters. Three of them (1–2–3 John) are closely related to the fourth gospel and thus belong to the Johannine corpus. The catholic letters, like those of the Pauline corpus, are also arranged in roughly descending order of length, but the three Johannine letters are kept together and Jude is placed at the end.

The genuine letters of Paul are earlier in date than any of our written gospels. The dates of the other New Testament letters are more difficult to determine, but for the most part they belong to the second and third Christian generations rather than to the first.

THE LETTER TO THE
ROMANS

Of all the letters of Paul, that to the Christians at Rome has long held pride of place. It is the longest and most systematic unfolding of the apostle's thought, expounding the gospel of God's righteousness that saves all who believe (Rom 1:16–17); it reflects a universal outlook, with special implications for Israel's relation to the church (Rom 9–11). Yet, like all Paul's letters, Romans too arose out of a specific situation, when the apostle wrote from Greece, likely Corinth, between A.D. 56 and 58 (cf. Acts 20:2–3).

Paul at that time was about to leave for Jerusalem with a collection of funds for the impoverished Jewish Christian believers there, taken up from his predominantly Gentile congregations (Rom 15:25–27). He planned then to travel on to Rome and to enlist support there for a mission to Spain (Rom 15:24, 28). Such a journey had long been on his mind (Rom 1:9–13; 15:23). Now, with much missionary preaching successfully accomplished in the East (Rom 15:19), he sought new opportunities in the West (Rom 15:20–21), in order to complete the divine plan of evangelization in the Roman world. Yet he recognized that the visit to Jerusalem would be hazardous (Rom 15:30–32), and we know from Acts that Paul was arrested there and came to Rome only in chains, as a prisoner (Acts 21–28, especially Acts 21:30–33 and Acts 28:14, 30–31).

The existence of a Christian community in Rome antedates Paul's letter there. When it arose, likely within the sizable Jewish population at Rome, and how, we do not know. The Roman historian Suetonius mentions an edict of the Emperor Claudius about A.D. 49 ordering the expulsion of Jews from Rome in connection with a certain "Chrestus," probably involving a dispute in the Jewish community over Jesus as the Messiah ("Christus"). According to Acts 18:2, Aquila and Priscilla (or Prisca, as in Rom 16:3) were among those driven out; from them, in Corinth, Paul may have learned about conditions in the church at Rome.

Opinions vary as to whether Jewish or Gentile Christians predominated in the house churches (cf. Rom 16:5) in the capital city of the empire at the time Paul wrote. Perhaps already by then Gentile Christians were in the majority. Paul speaks in Romans of both Jews and Gentiles (Rom 3:9, 29; see note on Rom 1:14). The letter also refers to those "weak in faith" (Rom 14:1) and those "who are strong" (Rom 15:1); this terminology may reflect not so much differences between believers of Jewish and of Gentile background, respectively, as an ascetic tendency in some converts (Rom 14:2) combined with Jewish laws about clean and unclean foods (Rom 14:14, 20). The issues were similar to problems that Paul had faced in Corinth (1 Cor 8). If Rom 16 is part of the letter to Rome (see note on Rom 16:1–23), then Paul had considerable information about conditions in Rome through all these people there whom he knew, and our letter does not just reflect a generalized picture of an earlier situation in Corinth.

In any case, Paul writes to introduce himself and his message to the Christians at Rome, seeking to enlist their support for the proposed mission to Spain. He therefore employs formulations likely familiar to the Christians at Rome; see note on the confessional material at Rom 1:3–4 and compare Rom 3:25–26; 4:25. He cites the Old Testament frequently (Rom 1:17; 3:10–18; 4; 9:7, 12–13, 15, 17, 25–29, 33; 10:5–13, 15–21; 15:9–12). The gospel Paul presents is meant to be a familiar one to those in Rome, even though they heard it first from other preachers.

As the outline below shows, this gospel of Paul (see Rom 16:25) finds its center in salvation and justification through faith in Christ (Rom 1:16–17). While God's wrath is revealed against all sin and wickedness of Gentile and Jew alike (Rom 1:18–3:20), God's power to save by divine righteous or justifying action in Christ is also revealed (Rom 1:16–17; 3:21–5:21). The consequences and implications for those who believe are set forth (Rom 6:1–8:39), as are results for those in Israel (Rom 9–11) who, to Paul's great sorrow (Rom 9:1–5), disbelieve. The apostle's hope is that, just as rejection of the gospel by some in Israel has led to a ministry of salvation for non-Jews, so one day, in God's mercy, "all Israel" will be saved (Rom 11:11–15, 25–29, 30–32). The fuller ethical response of believers is also drawn out, both with reference to life in Christ's body (Rom 12) and with regard to the world (Rom 13:1–7), on the basis of the eschatological situation (Rom 13:11–14) and conditions in the community (Rom 14:1–15:13).

Others have viewed Romans more in the light of Paul's earlier, quite polemical Letter to the Galatians and so see the theme as the relationship between Judaism and Christianity, a topic judged to be much in the minds of the Roman Christians. Each of these religious faiths claimed to be the way of salvation based upon a covenant between God and a people chosen and made the beneficiary of divine gifts. But Christianity regarded itself as the prophetic development and fulfillment of the faith of the Old Testament, declaring that the preparatory Mosaic covenant must now give way to the new and more perfect covenant in Jesus Christ. Paul himself had been the implacable advocate of freedom of Gentiles from the laws of the Mosaic covenant and, especially in Galatia, had refused to allow attempts to impose them on Gentile converts to the gospel. He had witnessed the personal hostilities that developed between the adherents of the two faiths and had written his strongly worded Letter to the Galatians against those Jewish Christians who were seeking to persuade Gentile Christians to adopt the religious practices of Judaism. For him, the purity of the religious understanding of Jesus as the source of salvation would be seriously impaired if Gentile Christians were obligated to amalgamate the two religious faiths.

Still others find the theme of Israel and the church as expressed in Rom 9–11 to be the heart of Romans. Then the implication of Paul's exposition of justification by faith rather than by means of law is that the divine plan of salvation works itself out on a broad theological plane to include the whole of humanity, despite the differences in the content of the given religious system to which a human culture is heir. Romans presents a plan of salvation stretching from Adam through Abraham and Moses to Christ (Rom 4; 5) and on to the future revelation at Christ's parousia (Rom 8:18–25). Its outlook is universal.

Paul's Letter to the Romans is a powerful exposition of the doctrine of the supremacy of Christ and of faith in Christ as the source of salvation. It is an implicit plea to the Christians at Rome, and to all Christians, to hold fast to that faith. They are to resist any pressure put on them to accept a doctrine of salvation through works of the law (see note on Rom 10:4). At the same time they are not to exaggerate Christian freedom as an abdication of responsibility for others (Rom 12:1–2) or as a repudiation of God's law and will (see notes on Rom 3:9–26; 3:31; 7:7–12, 13–25).

The principal divisions of the Letter to the Romans are the following:

I. Address (1:1–15)
II. Humanity Lost Without the Gospel (1:16–3:20)
III. Justification Through Faith in Christ (3:21–5:21)
IV. Justification and the Christian Life (6:1–8:39)
V. Jews and Gentiles in God's Plan (9:1–11:36)
VI. The Duties of Christians (12:1–15:13)
VII. Conclusion (15:14–16:27)

I. ADDRESS

CHAPTER 1

Greeting.[*] [1]Paul, a slave of Christ Jesus,[†] called to be an apostle and set apart for the gospel of God,[a] [2]which he promised previously through his prophets in the holy scriptures,[b] [3+]the gospel about his Son, descended from David according to the flesh,[c] [4]but established as Son of God in power according to the spirit of holiness through resurrection from the dead, Jesus Christ our Lord.[d] [5+]Through him we have received the grace of apostleship, to bring about the obedience of faith, for the sake of his name, among all the Gentiles,[e] [6]among whom are you also, who are called to belong to Jesus Christ;[f] [7]to all the beloved of God in Rome, called to be holy.[‡] Grace to you and peace from God our Father and the Lord Jesus Christ.[g]

---

*[1:1-7] In Paul's letters the greeting or *praescriptio* follows a standard form, though with variations. It is based upon the common Greco-Roman epistolary practice, but with the addition of Semitic and specifically Christian elements. The three basic components are: name of sender; name of addressee; greeting. In identifying himself, Paul often adds phrases to describe his apostolic mission; this element is more developed in Romans than in any other letter. Elsewhere he associates co-workers with himself in the greeting: Sosthenes (1 Corinthians), Timothy (2 Corinthians; Philippians; Philemon) Silvanus (1 Thessalonians–2 Thessalonians). The standard secular greeting was the infinitive *chairein*, "greetings." Paul uses instead the similar-sounding *charis*, "grace," together with the Semitic greeting *šālôm* (Greek *eirēnē*), "peace." These gifts, foreshadowed in God's dealings with Israel (see Nm 6:24–26), have been poured out abundantly in Christ, and Paul wishes them to his readers. In Romans the Pauline *praescriptio* is expanded and expressed in a formal tone; it emphasizes Paul's office as apostle to the Gentiles. Rom 1:3–4 stress the gospel or *kerygma*, Rom 1:2 the fulfillment of God's promise, and Rom 1:1, 5 Paul's office. On his call, see Gal 1:15–16; 1 Cor 9:1; 15:8–10; Acts 9:1–22; 22:3–16; 26:4–18.

†[1:1] **Slave of Christ Jesus**: Paul applies the term slave to himself in order to express his undivided allegiance to the Lord of the church, the Master of all, including slaves and masters. "No one can serve (i.e., be a slave to) two masters," said Jesus (Mt 6:24). It is this aspect of the slave-master relationship rather than its degrading implications that Paul emphasizes when he discusses Christian commitment.

‡[1:3–4] Paul here cites an early confession that proclaims Jesus' sonship as messianic descendant of David (cf. Mt 22:42; 2 Tm 2:8; Rev 22:16) and as Son of God by the resurrection. As "life-giving spirit" (1 Cor 15:45), Jesus Christ is able to communicate the Spirit to those who believe in him.

§[1:5] Paul recalls his apostolic office, implying that the Romans know something of his history. **The obedience of faith**: as Paul will show at length in chaps. 6–8 and 12–15, faith in God's justifying action in Jesus Christ relates one to God's gift of the new life that is made possible through the death and resurrection of Jesus Christ and the activity of the holy Spirit (see especially Rom 8:1–11).

¶[1:7] **Called to be holy**: Paul often refers to Christians as "the holy ones" or "the saints." The Israelite community was called a "holy assembly" because they had been separated for the worship and service of the Lord (see Lv 11:44; 23:1–44). The Christian community regarded its members as sanctified by baptism (Rom 6:22; 15:16; 1 Cor 6:11; Eph 5:26–27). Christians are called to holiness (1 Cor 1:2; 1 Thes 4:7), that

Thanksgiving. [8]First, I give thanks[**] to my God through Jesus Christ for all of you, because your faith is heralded throughout the world.[h] [9]God is my witness, whom I serve with my spirit in proclaiming the gospel of his Son, that I remember you constantly,[i] [10††]always asking in my prayers that somehow by God's will I may at last find my way clear to come to you.[j] [11]For I long to see you, that I may share with you some spiritual gift so that you may be strengthened,[k] [12]that is, that you and I may be mutually encouraged by one another's faith, yours and mine. [13]I do not want you to be unaware, brothers,[‡‡] that I often planned to come to you, though I was prevented until now, that I might harvest some fruit among you, too, as among the rest of the Gentiles.[l] [14]To Greeks[§§] and non-Greeks alike, to the wise and the ignorant, I am under obligation, [15]that is why I am eager to preach the gospel also to you in Rome.[m]

II. HUMANITY LOST WITHOUT THE GOSPEL

God's Power for Salvation.[¶¶] [16]For I am not ashamed of the gospel. It is the power of God for the salvation of everyone who believes: for Jew first, and then Greek.[n] [17]For in it is revealed

---

is, they are called to make their lives conform to the gift they have already received.

**[1:8] In Greco-Roman letters, the greeting was customarily followed by a prayer. The Pauline letters usually include this element (except Gal 1 and 2 Timothy) expressed in Christian thanksgiving formulas and usually stating the principal theme of the letter. In 2 Corinthians the thanksgiving becomes a blessing, and in Ephesians it is preceded by a lengthy blessing. Sometimes the thanksgiving is blended into the body of the letter, especially in 1 Thessalonians. In Romans it is stated briefly.

††[1:10–12] Paul lays the groundwork for his more detailed statement in Rom 15:22–24 about his projected visit to Rome.

‡‡[1:13] **Brothers** is idiomatic for all Paul's "kin in Christ," all those who believe in the gospel; it includes women as well as men (cf. Rom 4:3).

§§[1:14] **Greeks and non-Greeks**: literally, "Greeks and barbarians." As a result of Alexander's conquests, Greek became the standard international language of the Mediterranean world. **Greeks** in Paul's statement therefore means people who know Greek or who have been influenced by Greek culture. **Non-Greeks** were people whose cultures remained substantially unaffected by Greek influences. Greeks called such people "barbarians" (cf. Acts 28:2), meaning people whose speech was foreign. Roman citizens would scarcely classify themselves as such, and Nero, who was reigning when Paul wrote this letter, prided himself on his admiration for Greek culture. **Under obligation**: Paul will expand on the theme of obligation in Rom 13:8; 15:1, 27.

¶¶[1:16–17] The principal theme of the letter is salvation through faith. **I am not ashamed of the gospel**: Paul is not ashamed to proclaim the gospel, despite the criticism that Jews and Gentiles leveled against the proclamation of the crucified savior; cf. 1 Cor 1:23–24. Paul affirms, however, that it is precisely through the crucifixion and resurrection of Jesus that God's saving will and power become manifest. **Jew first** (cf. Rom 2:9–10) means that Jews especially, in view of the example of Abraham (Rom 4), ought to be the leaders in the response of faith.

---

a. [1:1] Gal 1:10; Phil 1:1; Jas 1:1 / Acts 9:15; 13:2; 1 Cor 1:1; Gal 1:15; Ti 1:1.   b. [1:2] 16:25–26; Ti 1:2.   c. [1:3] 9:5; 2 Sm 7:12; Mt 1:1; Mk 12:35; Jn 7:42; Acts 13:22–23; 2 Tm 2:8; Rev 22:16.   d. [1:4] 10:9; Acts 13:33; Phil 3:10.   e. [1:5] 15:15; Gal 2:7, 9 / 15:18; Acts 9:15; 26:16–18; Gal 1:16; 2:7, 9.   f. [1:6] 1 Cor 1:9.   g. [1:7] Nm 6:25–26; 1 Cor 1:2–3; 2 Cor 1:1–2.

h. [1:8] 16:19; 1 Thes 1:8.   i. [1:9] 2 Cor 1:23; Eph 1:16; Phil 1:8; 1 Thes 1:2; 2:5, 10; 2 Tm 1:3.   j. [1:10] 15:23, 32; Acts 18:21; 1 Cor 4:19; 1 Thes 2:17.   k. [1:11] 1 Thes 2:17; 3:10.   l. [1:13] 15:22; Jn 15:16; Acts 19:21.   m. [1:15] Acts 28:30–31.   n. [1:16] Ps 119:46; 1 Cor 1:18, 24 / Rom 2:9; Acts 3:26; 13:46.

the righteousness of God from faith to faith;* as it is written, "The one who is righteous by faith will live."*ᵒ

Punishment of Idolaters. [18†]The wrath‡ of God§ is indeed being revealed from heaven against every impiety and wickednessᵖ of those who suppress the truth by their wickedness. [19]For what can be known about God is evident to them, because God made it evident to them.�q [20]Ever since the creation of.the world, his invisible attributes of eternal power and divinity have been able to be understood and perceived in what he has made.ʳ As a result, they have no excuse; [21]for although they knew God they did not accord him glory as God or give him thanks. Instead, they became vain in their reasoning, and their senseless minds were darkened.ˢ [22]While claiming to be wise,ᵗ they became fools [23]and exchanged the glory of the immortal God for the likeness of an image of mortal man or of birds or of four-legged animals or of snakes.ᵘ

[24]Therefore, God handed them over to impurity through the lusts of their hearts¶ for

the mutual degradation of their bodies.ᵛ [25]They exchanged the truth of God for a lie and revered and worshiped the creature rather than the creator, who is blessed forever. Amen.ʷ [26]Therefore, God handed them over to degrading passions. Their females exchanged natural relations for unnatural, [27]and the males likewise gave up natural relations with females and burned with lust for one another. Males did shameful things with males and thus received in their own persons the due penalty for their perversity.ˣ [28]And since they did not see fit to acknowledge God, God handed them over to their undiscerning mind to do what is improper. [29]They are filled with every form of wickedness, evil, greed, and malice; full of envy, murder, rivalry, treachery, and spite. They are gossips [30]and scandalmongers and they hate God. They are insolent, haughty, boastful, ingenious in their wickedness, and rebellious toward their parents. [31]They are senseless, faithless, heartless, ruthless. [32]Although they know the just decree of God that all who practice such things deserve death, they not only do them but give approval to those who practice them.ᶻ

CHAPTER 2

God's Just Judgment. [1]**Therefore, you are without excuse,ᵃ every one of you who passes judgment.†† For by the standard by which you judge another you condemn yourself, since you, the judge, do the very same things. [2]We know that the judgment of God on those who do such things is true. [3]Do you suppose, then, you who judge those who engage in such things and yet do them yourself, that you will escape the judgment of God?ᵇ [4]Or do you hold his priceless kindness, forbearance, and patience in low esteem, unaware that the kindness of God would lead you to repentance?ᶜ [5]By your stubbornness and impenitent heart,ᵈ you are storing up wrath for yourself for the day of wrath and revelation of the just judgment of God, [6]who will repay

---

*[1:17] **In it is revealed the righteousness of God from faith to faith**: the gospel centers in Jesus Christ, in whom God's saving presence and righteousness in history have been made known. Faith is affirmation of the basic purpose and meaning of the Old Testament as proclamation of divine promise (Rom 1:2; 4:13) and exposure of the inability of humanity to effect its salvation even through covenant law. Faith is the gift of the holy Spirit and denotes acceptance of salvation as God's righteousness, that is, God's gift of a renewed relationship in forgiveness and power for a new life. Faith is response to God's total claim on people and their destiny. **The one who is righteous by faith will live**: see note on Heb 2:4.

†[1:18–3:20] Paul aims to show that all humanity is in a desperate plight and requires God's special intervention if it is to be saved.

‡[1:18–32] In this passage Paul uses themes and rhetoric common in Jewish-Hellenistic mission proclamation (cf. Wis 13:1–14:31) to indict especially the non-Jewish world. The close association of idolatry and immorality is basic, but the generalization needs in all fairness to be balanced against the fact that non-Jewish Christian society on many levels displayed moral attitudes and performance whose quality would challenge much of contemporary Christian culture. Romans themselves expressed abhorrence over devotion accorded to animals in Egypt. Paul's main point is that the wrath of God does not await the end of the world but goes into action at each present moment in humanity's history when misdirected piety serves as a facade for self-interest.

§[1:18] **The wrath of God**: God's reaction to human sinfulness, an Old Testament phrase that expresses the irreconcilable opposition between God and evil (see Is 9:11, 16, 18, 20; 10:4; 30:27). It is not contrary to God's universal love for his creatures, but condemns Israel's turning aside from the covenant obligations. Hosea depicts Yahweh as suffering intensely at the thought of having to punish Israel (Hos 11:8–9). God's wrath was to be poured forth especially on the "Day of Yahweh" and thus took on an eschatological connotation (see Zep 1:15).

¶[1:24] In order to expose the depth of humanity's rebellion against the Creator, **God handed them over to impurity through the lusts of their hearts**. Instead of curbing people's evil interests, God abandoned them to self-indulgence, thereby removing the facade of apparent conformity to the

divine will. Subsequently Paul will show that the Mosaic law produces the same effect; cf. Rom 5:20; 7:13–24. The divine judgment expressed here is related to the theme of hardness of heart described in Rom 9:17–18.

**[2:1–3:20] After his general indictment of the Gentile, Paul shows that in spite of special revelation Jews enjoy no advantage in moral status before God (Rom 3:1–8). With the entire human race now declared guilty before God (Rom 3:9–20), Paul will then be able to display the solution for the total problem: salvation through God's redemptive work that is revealed in Christ Jesus for all who believe (Rom 3:21–31).

††[2:1–11] As a first step in his demonstration that Jews enjoy no real moral supremacy over Gentiles, Paul explains that the final judgment will be a review of performance, not of privilege. From this perspective Gentiles stand on an equal footing with Jews, and Jews cannot condemn the sins of Gentiles without condemning themselves.

---

o. [1:17] 3:21–22; Heb 2:4; Gal 3:11; Heb 10:38.   p. [1:18] 2:5, 8–9; Is 66:15; Eph 5:6; Col 3:6.   q. [1:19–32] Wis 13–19; Acts 14:15–17; 17:23–29.   r. [1:20] Jb 12:7–9; Ps 8:4; 19:2; Sir 17:7–9; Is 40:26; Acts 14:17; 17:25–28.   s. [1:21] Eph 4:17–18.   t. [1:22] Wis 13:1–9; Is 5:21; Jer 10:14; Acts 17:29–30; 1 Cor 1:19–21.   u. [1:23] Dt 4:15–19; Ps 106:20; Wis 11:15; 12:24; 13:10–19; Jer 2:11.

v. [1:24] Wis 12:25; 14:22–31; Acts 7:41–42; Eph 4:19.   w. [1:25] 9:5; Jer 13:25–27.   x. [1:27] Lv 18:22; 20:13; Wis 14:26; 1 Cor 6:9; 1 Tm 1:10.   y. [1:29–31] 13:13; Mt 15:19; Mk 7:21–22; Gal 5:19–21; 2 Tm 3:2–4.   z. [1:32] Acts 8:1; 2 Thes 2:12.   a. [2:1] Mt 7:1–2.   b. [2:3] Wis 16:15–16.   c. [2:4] 3:25–26; 9:22; Wis 11:23; 15:1; 2 Pt 3:9, 15.   d. [2:5] Ex 33:3; Acts 7:51; Rev 6:17; 11:18.   e. [2:6] Ps 62:12; Prv 24:12; Sir 16:14; Mt 16:27; Jn 5:29; 2 Cor 5:10.

everyone according to his works:* [7]eternal life to those who seek glory, honor, and immortality through perseverance in good works, [8]but wrath and fury to those who selfishly disobey the truth and obey wickedness.[f] [9]Yes, affliction and distress will come upon every human being who does evil, Jew first and then Greek. [10g]But there will be glory, honor, and peace for everyone who does good, Jew first and then Greek. [11th]There is no partiality with God.

Judgment by the Interior Law.[‡] [12]All who sin outside the law will also perish without reference to it, and all who sin under the law will be judged in accordance with it.[i] [13]For it is not those who hear the law who are just in the sight of God; rather, those who observe the law will be justified.[j] [14]For when the Gentiles who do not have the law by nature observe the prescriptions of the law, they are a law for themselves even though they do not have the law.[k] [15]They show that the demands of the law are written in their hearts,[§] while their conscience also bears witness and their conflicting thoughts accuse or even defend them [16]on the day when, according to my gospel, God will judge people's hidden works through Christ Jesus.[l]

Judgment by the Mosaic Law.[¶] [17]Now if you call yourself a Jew and rely on the law and boast of God[m] [18]and know his will and are able to discern what is important since you are instructed from the law,[n] [19]and if you are confident that you are a guide for the blind and a light for those in darkness,[o] [20]that you are a trainer of the foolish and teacher of the simple,[p] because in the law you have the formulation of knowledge and truth— [21]then you who teach another, are you failing to teach yourself? You who preach against stealing, do you steal?[q] [22]You who forbid adultery, do you commit adultery? You who detest idols, do you rob temples? [23]You who boast of the law, do you dishonor God by breaking the law? [24r]For, as it is written, "Because of you the name of God is reviled among the Gentiles."** [25s]Circumcision, to be sure, has value if you observe the law; but if you break the law, your circumcision has become uncircumcision.[t] [26]Again, if an uncircumcised man keeps the precepts of the law, will he not be considered circumcised?[u] [27]Indeed, those who are physically uncircumcised but carry out the law will pass judgment on you, with your written law and circumcision, who break the law. [28]One is not a Jew outwardly. True circumcision is not outward, in the flesh.[v] [29]Rather, one is a Jew inwardly, and circumcision is of the heart, in the spirit, not the letter; his praise is not from human beings but from God.[w]

CHAPTER 3

Answers to Objections. [1††]What advantage is there then in being a Jew? Or what is the value of circumcision? [2]Much, in every respect. [For] in the first place, they were entrusted with the utterances of God.[x] [3]What if some were unfaithful? Will their infidelity nullify the fidelity of God?[y] [4]Of course not! God must be true, though every human being is a liar,[‡‡] as it is written:

> "That you may be justified in your words,
>   and conquer when you are judged."[z]

[5]But if our wickedness provides proof of God's righteousness, what can we say? Is God unjust, humanly speaking, to inflict his wrath?[a] [6]Of course not! For how else is God to judge the world? [7]But if God's truth redounds to his glory through my falsehood, why am I still being condemned as a sinner? [8]And why not say—as we are accused and as some claim we say—that we should do evil that good may come of it? Their penalty is what they deserve.[b]

Universal Bondage to Sin.[§§] [9]Well, then, are we better off? Not entirely, for we have already

---

*[2:6] **Will repay everyone according to his works:** Paul reproduces the Septuagint text of Ps 62:12 and Prv 24:12.

†[2:11] **No partiality with God:** this sentence is not at variance with the statements in Rom 2:9–10. Since Jews are the first to go under indictment, it is only fair that they be given first consideration in the distribution of blessings. Basic, of course, is the understanding that God accepts no bribes (Dt 10:17).

‡[2:12–16] Jews cannot reasonably demand from Gentiles the standard of conduct inculcated in the Old Testament since God did not address its revelation to them. Rather, God made it possible for Gentiles to know instinctively the difference between right and wrong. But, as Paul explained in Rom 1:18–32, humanity misread the evidence of God's existence, power, and divinity, and "while claiming to be wise, they became fools" (Rom 1:22).

§[2:15] Paul expands on the thought of Jer 31:33; Wis 17:11.

¶[2:17–29] Mere possession of laws is no evidence of virtue. By eliminating circumcision as an elitist moral sign, Paul clears away the last obstacle to his presentation of justification through faith without claims based on the receipt of circumcision and its attendant legal obligations.

**[2:24] According to Is 52:5 the suffering of Israel prompts her enemies to revile God. Paul uses the passage in support of his point that the present immorality of Israelites is the cause of such defamation.

††[3:1–4] In keeping with the popular style of diatribe, Paul responds to the objection that his teaching on the sinfulness of all humanity detracts from the religious prerogatives of Israel. He stresses that Jews have remained the vehicle of God's revelation despite their sins, though this depends on the fidelity of God.

‡‡[3:4] **Though every human being is a liar:** these words reproduce the Greek text of Ps 116:11. The rest of the verse is from Ps 51:6.

§§[3:9–20] **Well, then, are we better off?:** this phrase can also be translated "Are we at a disadvantage?" but the latter

---

f. [2:8] 2 Thes 1:8.   g. [2:10] 1:16; 3:9.   h. [2:11] Dt 10:17; 2 Chr 19:7; Sir 35:12–13; Acts 10:34; Gal 2:6; Eph 6:9; Col 3:25; 1 Pt 1:17. i. [2:12] 3:19.   j. [2:13] Mt 7:21; Lk 6:46–49; 8:21; Jas 1:22–25; 1 Jn 3:7.   k. [2:14] Acts 10:35.   l. [2:16] Acts 10:42; 17:31.   m. [2:17] Is 48:1–2; Mi 3:11; Phil 3:4–6.   n. [2:18] Phil 1:10.   o. [2:19] Mt 15:14; Lk 6:39.   p. [2:20] 2 Tm 3:15.   q. [2:21] Ps 50:16–21; Mt 23:3–4.

r. [2:24] Is 52:5; Ez 36:20; 2 Pt 2:2.   s. [2:25–29] Jer 4:4; 9:24–25.   t. [2:25] 1 Cor 7:19; Gal 5:3.   u. [2:26] Gal 5:6.   v. [2:28] Jn 7:24; 8:15, 39.   w. [2:29] Dt 30:6; Jer 4:4; 9:25; Col 2:11 / 1 Cor 4:5; 2 Cor 10:18.   x. [3:2] 9:4; Dt 4:7–8; Ps 103:7; 147:19–20.   y. [3:3] Rom 9:6; 11:1, 29; Ps 89:30–37; 2 Tm 2:13.   z. [3:4] Ps 116:11 / Ps 51:6. a. [3:5] 9:14; Jb 34:12–17.   b. [3:8] 6:1.

brought the charge against Jews and Greeks alike that they are all under the domination of sin,*c* *10*as it is written:*d*

"There is no one just, not one,
11   there is no one who understands,
        there is no one who seeks God.
12 All have gone astray; all alike are worthless;
        there is not one who does good,
        [there is not] even one.
13 Their throats are open graves;
        they deceive with their tongues;
        the venom of asps is on their lips;*e*
14   their mouths are full of bitter
    ,   cursing.*f*
15 Their feet are quick to shed blood;*g*
16   ruin and misery are in their ways,
17 and the way of peace they know not.
18   There is no fear of God before their
        eyes."*h*

*19*Now we know that what the law* says is addressed to those under the law, so that every mouth may be silenced and the whole world stand accountable to God,*i* *20*since no human being will be justified in his sight† by observing the law; for through the law comes consciousness of sin.*j*

III. JUSTIFICATION THROUGH FAITH IN CHRIST

Justification Apart from the Law.‡ *21*But now§ the righteousness of God has been manifested apart from the law, though testified to by the law

and the prophets,*k* *22*the righteousness of God through faith in Jesus Christ for all who believe. For there is no distinction;*l* *23*all have sinned and are deprived of the glory of God.*m* *24*They are justified freely by his grace through the redemption in Christ Jesus,*n* *25*whom God set forth as an expiation,¶ through faith, by his blood, to prove his righteousness because of the forgiveness of sins previously committed,*o* *26*through the forbearance of God—to prove his righteousness in the present time, that he might be righteous and justify the one who has faith in Jesus.

*27p*What occasion is there then for boasting?** It is ruled out. On what principle, that of works? No, rather on the principle of faith.†† *28*For we consider that a person is justified by faith apart from works of the law.*q* *29*Does God belong to Jews alone? Does he not belong to Gentiles, too? Yes, also to Gentiles,*r* *30*for God is one and will justify the circumcised on the basis of faith and the uncircumcised through faith.*s* *31*Are we then annulling the law by this faith? Of course not!*t* On the contrary, we are supporting the law.‡‡

CHAPTER 4§§
Abraham Justified by Faith. *1*What then can we say that Abraham found, our ancestor according to the flesh?*u* *2*¶¶Indeed, if Abraham was justified

---

expressions indicate that Rom 3:21–26 are the consolatory answer to Rom 3:9–20.

¶[3:25] **Expiation**: this rendering is preferable to "propitiation," which suggests hostility on the part of God toward sinners. As Paul will be at pains to point out (Rom 5:8–10), it is humanity that is hostile to God.

**[3:27–31] People cannot boast of their own holiness, since it is God's free gift (Rom 3:27), both to the Jew who practices circumcision out of faith and to the Gentile who accepts faith without the Old Testament religious culture symbolized by circumcision (Rom 3:29–30).

††[3:27] **Principle of faith**: literally, "law of faith." Paul is fond of wordplay involving the term "law"; cf. Rom 7:21, 23; 8:2. Since "law" in Greek may also connote "custom" or "principle," his readers and hearers would have sensed no contradiction in the use of the term after the negative statement concerning law in Rom 3:20.

‡‡[3:31] **We are supporting the law**: giving priority to God's intentions. God is the ultimate source of law, and the essence of law is fairness. On the basis of the Mosaic covenant, God's justice is in question if those who sinned against the law are permitted to go free (see Rom 3:23–26). In order to rescue all humanity rather than condemn it, God thinks of an alternative: the law or "principle" of faith (Rom 3:27). What can be more fair than to admit everyone into the divine presence on the basis of forgiveness grasped by faith? Indeed, this principle of faith antedates the Mosaic law, as Paul will demonstrate in Rom 4, and does not therefore mark a change in divine policy.

§§[4:1–25] This is an expanded treatment of the significance of Abraham's faith, which Paul discusses in Gal 3:6–18; see notes there.

¶¶[4:2–5] Rom 4:2 corresponds to Rom 4:4, and Rom 4:3–5. The Greek term here rendered **credited** means "made an entry." The context determines whether it is credit or debit. Rom 4:8 speaks of "recording sin" as a debit. Paul's repeated use of accountants' terminology in this and other passages can

---

version does not substantially change the overall meaning of the passage. Having explained that Israel's privileged status is guaranteed by God's fidelity, Paul now demonstrates the infidelity of the Jews by a catena of citations from scripture, possibly derived from an existing collection of *testimonia*. These texts show that all human beings share the common burden of sin. They are linked together by mention of organs of the body: throat, tongue, lips, mouth, feet, eyes.

*[3:19] **The law**: Paul here uses the term in its broadest sense to mean all of the scriptures; none of the preceding texts is from the Torah or Pentateuch.

†[3:20] **No human being will be justified in his sight**: these words are freely cited from Ps 143:2. In place of the psalmist's "no living person," Paul substitutes "no human being" (literally "no flesh," a Hebraism), and he adds "by observing the law."

‡[3:21–31] These verses provide a clear statement of Paul's "gospel," i.e., the principle of justification by faith in Christ. God has found a means of rescuing humanity from its desperate plight: Paul's general term for this divine initiative is the righteousness of God (Rom 3:21). Divine mercy declares the guilty innocent and makes them so. God does this not as a result of the law but apart from it (Rom 3:21), and not because of any merit in human beings but through forgiveness of their sins (Rom 3:24), in virtue of the redemption wrought in Christ Jesus for all who believe (Rom 3:22, 24–25). God has manifested his righteousness in the coming of Jesus Christ, whose saving activity inaugurates a new era in human history.

§[3:21] **But now**: Paul adopts a common phrase used by Greek authors to describe movement from disaster to prosperity. The

---

c. [3:9] 1:18–2:25; 3:23; Sir 8:5.   d. [3:10–11] Ps 14:1–3; 53:2–4; Eccl 7:20.   e. [3:13] Ps 5:10; 140:4.   f. [3:14] Ps 10:7.   g. [3:15–17] Prv 1:16; Is 59:7–8.   h. [3:18] Ps 36:2.   i. [3:19] 7:7.   j. [3:20] Ps 143:2; Gal 2:16 / 7:7.

k. [3:21] Is 51:6–8; Acts 10:43.   l. [3:22] 1:17; Gal 2:16; Phil 3:9.   m. [3:23] 3:9; 5:12.   n. [3:24] Eph 2:8; Ti 3:7 / Rom 5:1–2; Eph 1:7.   o. [3:25] Lv 16:12–15; Acts 17:31; 1 Jn 4:10.   p. [3:27] 8:2; 1 Cor 1:29–31.   q. [3:28] 5:1; Gal 2:16.   r. [3:29] 10:12.   s. [3:30] Dt 6:4; Gal 3:20; Jas 2:19 / Rom 4:11–12.   t. [3:31] 8:4; Mt 5:17.   u. [4:1] Gal 3:6–9.

on the basis of his works, he has reason to boast; but this was not so in the sight of God. [3v]For what does the scripture say? "Abraham believed God, and it was credited to him as righteousness." [4]A worker's wage is credited not as a gift, but as something due.[w] [5]But when one does not work, yet believes in the one who justifies the ungodly, his faith is credited as righteousness. [6]So also David declares the blessedness of the person to whom God credits righteousness apart from works:

[7] "Blessed are they whose iniquities are
    forgiven[x]
  and whose sins are covered.
[8] Blessed is the man whose sin the Lord
  does not record."

[9]Does this blessedness[†] apply only to the circumcised, or to the uncircumcised as well? Now we assert that "faith was credited to Abraham as righteousness."[y] [10]Under what circumstances was it credited? Was he circumcised or not? He was not circumcised, but uncircumcised. [11]And he received the sign of circumcision as a seal on the righteousness received through faith while he was uncircumcised. Thus he was to be the father of all the uncircumcised who believe, so that to them [also] righteousness might be credited,[z] [12]as well as the father of the circumcised who not only are circumcised but also follow the path of faith that our father Abraham walked while still uncircumcised.
Inheritance Through Faith. [13]It was not through the law that the promise was made to Abraham and his descendants that he would inherit the world, but through the righteousness that comes from faith.[a] [14]For if those who adhere to the law are the heirs, faith is null and the promise is void.[b] [15]For the law produces wrath;[c] but where there is no law, neither is there violation.[‡] [16]For this reason, it depends on faith, so that it may be a gift, and the promise may be guaranteed to all his descendants, not to those who only adhere to

the law but to those who follow the faith of Abraham, who is the father of all of us,[d] [17]as it is written, "I have made you father of many nations." He is our father in the sight of God, in whom he believed, who gives life to the dead and calls into being what does not exist.[e] [18]He believed, hoping against hope,[f] that he would become "the father of many nations," according to what was said, "Thus shall your descendants be." [19g]He did not weaken in faith when he considered his own body as [already] dead (for he was almost a hundred years old) and the dead womb of Sarah. [20]He did not doubt God's promise in unbelief;[§] rather, he was empowered by faith and gave glory to God [21]and was fully convinced that what he had promised he was also able to do.[h] [22]That is why "it was credited to him as righteousness."[i] [23]But it was not for him alone that it was written that "it was credited to him"; [24]it was also for us, to whom it will be credited, who believe in the one who raised Jesus our Lord from the dead,[j] [25]who was handed over for our transgressions and was raised for our justification.[k]

CHAPTER 5
Faith, Hope, and Love.[¶] [1]Therefore, since we have been justified by faith, we have peace** with God through our Lord Jesus Christ,[l] [2]through whom we have gained access [by faith] to this grace in which we stand, and we boast in hope of the glory of God.[m] [3]Not only that, but we even boast of our afflictions, knowing that affliction produces endurance, [4]and endurance, proven character, and proven character, hope,[n] [5]and hope

§[4:20] **He did not doubt God's promise in unbelief:** any doubts Abraham might have had were resolved in commitment to God's promise. Heb 11:8–12 emphasizes the faith of Abraham and Sarah.

¶[5:1–11] Popular piety frequently construed reverses and troubles as punishment for sin; cf. Jn 9:2. Paul therefore assures believers that God's justifying action in Jesus Christ is a declaration of peace. The crucifixion of Jesus Christ displays God's initiative in certifying humanity for unimpeded access into the divine presence. Reconciliation is God's gift of pardon to the entire human race. Through faith one benefits personally from this pardon or, in Paul's term, is justified. The ultimate aim of God is to liberate believers from the pre-Christian self as described in Rom 1–3. Since this liberation will first find completion in the believer's resurrection, salvation is described as future in Rom 5:10. Because this fullness of salvation belongs to the future it is called the Christian hope. Paul's Greek term for hope does not, however, suggest a note of uncertainty, to the effect: "I wonder whether God really means it." Rather, God's promise in the gospel fills believers with expectation and anticipation for the climactic gift of unalloyed commitment in the holy Spirit to the performance of the will of God. The persecutions that attend Christian commitment are to teach believers patience and to strengthen this hope, which will not disappoint them because the holy Spirit dwells in their hearts and imbues them with God's love (Rom 5:5).

[5:1] **We have peace: a number of manuscripts, versions, and church Fathers read "Let us have peace"; cf. Rom 14:19.

---

be traced both to the Old Testament texts he quotes and to his business activity as a tentmaker. The commercial term in Gn 15:6, "attributed it to him," reminds Paul in Rom 4:7–8 of Ps 32:2, in which the same term is used and applied to forgiveness of sins. Thus Paul is able to argue that Abraham's faith involved receipt of forgiveness of sins and that all believers benefit as he did through faith.

*[4:3] Jas 2:24 appears to conflict with Paul's statement. However, James combats the error of extremists who used the doctrine of justification through faith as a screen for moral self-determination. Paul discusses the subject of holiness in greater detail than does James and beginning with Rom 6 shows how justification through faith introduces one to the gift of a new life in Christ through the power of the holy Spirit.

†[4:9] **Blessedness:** evidence of divine favor.

‡[4:15] Law has the negative function of bringing the deep-seated rebellion against God to the surface in specific sins; see note on Rom 1:18–32.

---

v. [4:3] Gn 15:6; Gal 3:6; Jas 2:14, 20–24. w. [4:4] 11:6. x. [4:7–8] Ps 32:1–2. y. [4:9] 4:3. z. [4:11] Gn 17:10–11; Gal 3:6–8. a. [4:13] Gn 12:7; 18:18; 22:17–18; Sir 44:21; Gal 3:16–18, 29. b. [4:14] Gal 3:18. c. [4:15] 3:20; 5:13; 7:8; Gal 3:19.

d. [4:16] Sir 44:19; Gal 3:7–9. e. [4:17] Gn 17:5; Heb 11:19 / Is 48:13. f. [4:18] Gn 15:5. g. [4:19–20] Gn 17:17; Heb 11:11. h. [4:21] Gn 18:14; Lk 1:37. i. [4:22] Gn 15:6. j. [4:24] 10:9; 1 Pt 1:21. k. [4:25] Is 53:4–5, 12; 1 Cor 15:17; 1 Pt 1:3 / 8:11. l. [5:1] 3:24–28; Gal 2:16. m. [5:2] Eph 2:18; 3:12. n. [5:4] 2 Cor 12:9–10; Jas 1:2–4; 1 Pt 1:5–7; 4:12–14.

does not disappoint, because the love of God has been poured out into our hearts through the holy Spirit that has been given to us.° 6For Christ, while we were still helpless, yet died at the appointed time for the ungodly. 7Indeed, only with difficulty does one die for a just person, though perhaps for a good person one might even find courage to die.* 8But God proves his love for us in that while we were still sinners Christ died for us.ᵖ 9How much more then, since we are now justified by his blood, will we be saved through him from the wrath.�q 10Indeed, if, while we were enemies, we were reconciled to God through the death of his Son, how much more, once reconciled, will we be saved by his life.ʳ 11Not only that, but we also boast of God through our Lord Jesus Christ, through whom we have now received reconciliation.

Humanity's Sin Through Adam. 12†Therefore, just as through one person sin entered the world,ˢ and through sin, death, and thus death came to all, inasmuch as all sinned‡— 13for up to the time of the law, sin was in the world, though sin is not accounted when there is no law.ᵗ 14But death reigned from Adam to Moses, even over those who did not sin after the pattern of the trespass of Adam, who is the type of the one who was to come.ᵘ

Grace and Life Through Christ. 15But the gift is not like the transgression. For if by that one person's transgression the many died, how much more did the grace of God and the gracious gift of the one person Jesus Christ overflow for the many. 16And the gift is not like the result of the one person's sinning. For after one sin there was the judgment that brought condemnation; but the gift, after many transgressions, brought acquittal. 17For if, by the transgression of one person, death came to reign through that one, how much more will those who receive the abundance of grace and of the gift of justification come to reign in life through the one

person Jesus Christ. 18In conclusion, just as through one transgression condemnation came upon all, so through one righteous act acquittal and life came to all.ᵛ 19For just as through the disobedience of one person the many were made sinners, so through the obedience of one the many will be made righteous.ʷ 20The law entered inˢ so that transgression might increase but, where sin increased, grace overflowed all the more,ˣ 21so that, as sin reigned in death, grace also might reign through justification for eternal life through Jesus Christ our Lord.ʸ

IV. JUSTIFICATION AND THE CHRISTIAN LIFE

CHAPTER 6

Freedom from Sin; Life in God. 1¶What then shall we say? Shall we persist in sin that grace may abound? Of course not!ᶻ 2How can we who died to sin yet live in it?ᵃ 3Or are you unaware that we who were baptized into Christ Jesus were baptized into his death?ᵇ 4We were indeed buried with him through baptism into death, so that, just as Christ was raised from the dead by the glory of the Father, we too might live in newness of life.ᶜ

5For if we have grown into union with him through a death like his, we shall also be united with him in the resurrection.ᵈ 6We know that our old self was crucified with him, so that our sinful body might be done away with, that we might no longer be in slavery to sin.ᵉ 7For a dead person has been absolved from sin. 8If, then, we have died with Christ, we believe that we shall also live with him.ᶠ 9We know that Christ, raised from the dead, dies no more; death no longer has power over him.ᵍ 10As to his death, he died to sin once and for all; as to his life, he lives for God.ʰ 11Consequently, you too must think of

---

*[5:7] In the world of Paul's time the **good person** is especially one who is magnanimous to others.

†[5:12–21] Paul reflects on the sin of Adam (Gn 3:1–13) in the light of the redemptive mystery of Christ. Sin, as used in the singular by Paul, refers to the dreadful power that has gripped humanity, which is now in revolt against the Creator and engaged in the exaltation of its own desires and interests. But no one has a right to say, "Adam made me do it," for all are culpable (Rom 5:12): Gentiles under the demands of the law written in their hearts (Rom 2:14–15), and Jews under the Mosaic covenant. Through the Old Testament law, the sinfulness of humanity that was operative from the beginning (Rom 5:13) found further stimulation, with the result that sins were generated in even greater abundance. According to Rom 5:15–21, God's act in Christ is in total contrast to the disastrous effects of the virus of sin that invaded humanity through Adam's crime.

‡[5:12] **Inasmuch as all sinned:** others translate "because all sinned," and understand Rom 5:13 as a parenthetical remark. Unlike Wis 2:24, Paul does not ascribe the entry of death to the devil.

o. [5:5] 8:14–16; Ps 22:5–6; 25:20. p. [5:8] Jn 3:16; 1 Jn 4:10, 19. q. [5:9] 1:18; 1 Thes 1:10. r. [5:10] 8:7–8; 2 Cor 5:18; Col 1:21–22. s. [5:12] Gn 2:17; 3:1–19; Wis 2:24 / Rom 3:19, 23. t. [5:13] 4:15. u. [5:14] 1 Cor 15:21.

§[5:20] **The law entered in:** sin had made its entrance (Rom 5:12); now the law comes in alongside sin. See notes on Rom 1:18–32; 5:12–21. **Where sin increased, grace overflowed all the more:** Paul declares that grace outmatches the productivity of sin.

¶[6:1–11] To defend the gospel against the charge that it promotes moral laxity (cf. Rom 3:5–8), Paul expresses himself in the typical style of spirited diatribe. God's display of generosity or grace is not evoked by sin but, as stated in Rom 5:8 is the expression of God's love, and this love pledges eternal life to all believers (Rom 5:21). Paul views the present conduct of the believers from the perspective of God's completed salvation when the body is resurrected and directed totally by the holy Spirit. Through baptism believers share the death of Christ and thereby escape from the grip of sin. Through the resurrection of Christ the power to live anew becomes reality for them, but the fullness of participation in Christ's resurrection still lies in the future. But life that is lived in dedication to God now is part and parcel of that future. Hence anyone who sincerely claims to be interested in that future will scarcely be able to say, "Let us sin so that grace may prosper" (cf. Rom 6:1).

v. [5:18] 1 Cor 15:21–22. w. [5:19] Is 53:11; Phil 2:8–9. x. [5:20] 4:15;7:7–8;Gal3:19. y. [5:21]6:23. z. [6:1]3:5–8. a. [6:2]1Pt4:1. b. [6:3] Gal 3:27. c. [6:4] Col 2:12; 1 Pt 3:21–22. d. [6:5] Phil 3:10–11; 2 Tm 2:11. e. [6:6] Gal 5:24; 6:14; Eph 4:22–23. f. [6:8] 1 Thes 4:17. g. [6:9] Acts 13:34; 1 Cor 15:26; 2 Tm 1:10; Rev 1:18. h. [6:10] Heb 9:26–28; 1 Pt 3:18.

yourselves as [being] dead to sin and living for God in Christ Jesus.[i]

[12]"Therefore, sin must not reign over your mortal bodies so that you obey their desires.[j] [13]And do not present the parts of your bodies to sin as weapons for wickedness, but present yourselves to God as raised from the dead to life and the parts of your bodies to God as weapons for righteousness.[k] [14]For sin is not to have any power over you, since you are not under the law but under grace.[l]

[15]What then? Shall we sin because we are not under the law but under grace? Of course not![m] [16]Do you not know that if you present yourselves to someone as obedient slaves,[n] you are slaves of the one you obey, either of sin, which leads to death, or of obedience, which leads to righteousness?[o] [17]But thanks be to God that, although you were once slaves of sin, you have become obedient from the heart to the pattern of teaching to which you were entrusted.[†] [18]Freed from sin, you have become slaves of righteousness. [19]I am speaking in human terms because of the weakness of your nature. For just as you presented the parts of your bodies as slaves to impurity and to lawlessness for lawlessness, so now present them as slaves to righteousness for sanctification. [20p]For when you were slaves of sin, you were free from righteousness.[‡] [21]But what profit did you get then from the things of which you are now ashamed? For the end of those things is death.[q] [22]But now that you have been freed from sin and have become slaves of God, the benefit that you have leads to sanctification,[§] and its end is eternal life.[r] [23]For the wages of sin is death, but the gift of God is eternal life in Christ Jesus our Lord.[s]

CHAPTER 7
Freedom from the Law.[¶] [1]Are you unaware, brothers (for I am speaking to people who know

the law), that the law has jurisdiction over one as long as one lives? [2]Thus a married woman is bound by law to her living husband; but if her husband dies, she is released from the law in respect to her husband.[t] [3]Consequently, while her husband is alive she will be called an adulteress if she consorts with another man. But if her husband dies she is free from that law, and she is not an adulteress if she consorts with another man.

[4]In the same way, my brothers, you also were put to death to the law through the body of Christ, so that you might belong to another, to the one who was raised from the dead in order that we might bear fruit for God. [5]For when we were in the flesh, our sinful passions, awakened by the law, worked in our members to bear fruit for death.[u] [6]But now we are released from the law, dead to what held us captive, so that we may serve in the newness of the spirit and not under the obsolete letter.[v]

Acquaintance with Sin Through the Law. [7]"What then can we say? That the law is sin? Of course not![††] Yet I did not know sin except through the law, and I did not know what it is to covet except that the law said, "You shall not covet."[w] [8]But sin, finding an opportunity in the commandment, produced in me every kind of covetousness. Apart from the law sin is dead.[x] [9]I once lived outside the law, but when the commandment came, sin became alive; [10]then I died, and the commandment that was for life turned out to be death for me.[y] [11]For sin, seizing an opportunity in the commandment, deceived me and through it put me to death.[z] [12]So then the law is holy, and the commandment is holy and righteous and good.[a]

Sin and Death. [‡‡] [13]Did the good, then, become death for me? Of course not! Sin, in order that

---

*[6:12–19] Christians have been released from the grip of sin, but sin endeavors to reclaim its victims. The antidote is constant remembrance that divine grace has claimed them and identifies them as people who are alive only for God's interests.

†[6:17] In contrast to humanity, which was handed over to self-indulgence (Rom 1:24–32), believers are **entrusted** ("handed over") to God's **pattern of teaching**, that is, the new life God aims to develop in Christians through the productivity of the holy Spirit. Throughout this passage Paul uses the slave-master model in order to emphasize the fact that one cannot give allegiance to both God and sin.

‡[6:20] **You were free from righteousness:** expressed ironically, for such freedom is really tyranny. The commercial metaphors in Rom 6:21–23 add up only one way: sin is a bad bargain.

§[6:22] **Sanctification:** or holiness.

¶[7:1–6] Paul reflects on the fact that Christians have a different understanding of the law because of their faith in Christ. Law binds the living, not the dead, as exemplified in

marriage, which binds in life but is dissolved through death. Similarly, Christians who through baptism have died with Christ to sin (cf. Rom 6:2–4) are freed from the law that occasioned transgressions, which in turn were productive of death. Now that Christians are joined to Christ, the power of Christ's resurrection makes it possible for them to bear the fruit of newness of life for God.

**[7:7–25] In this passage Paul uses the first person singular in the style of diatribe for the sake of argument. He aims to depict the disastrous consequences when a Christian reintroduces the law as a means to attain the objective of holiness pronounced in Rom 6:22.

††[7:7–12] The apostle defends himself against the charge of identifying the law with sin. Sin does not exist in law but in human beings, whose sinful inclinations are not overcome by the proclamation of law.

‡‡[7:13–25] Far from improving the sinner, law encourages sin to expose itself in transgressions or violations of specific commandments (see Rom 1:24; 5:20). Thus persons who do not experience the justifying grace of God, and Christians who revert to dependence on law as the criterion for their relationship with God, will recognize a rift between their reasoned desire for the goodness of the law and their actual performance that is contrary to the law. Unable to free themselves from the slavery of sin and the power of death, they can only be rescued from defeat in the conflict by the power of God's grace working through Jesus Christ.

---

i. [6:11] 2 Cor 5:15; 1 Pt 2:24. j. [6:12] Gn 4:7. k. [6:13] 12:1; Eph 2:5; 5:14/Col 3:5. l. [6:14] Gal 5:18; 1 Jn 3:6. m. [6:15] 5:17, 21. n. [6:16–18] Jn 8:32–36. o. [6:16] Jn 8:31–34; 2 Pt 2:19. p. [6:20] Jn 8:34. q. [6:21] 8:6, 13; Prv 12:28; Ez 16:61, 63. r. [6:22] 1 Pt 1:9. s. [6:23] Gn 2:17; Gal 6:7–9; Jas 1:15.

t. [7:2] 1 Cor 7:39. u. [7:5] 6:21; 8:6, 13. v. [7:6] 8:2; 2 Cor 3:6. w. [7:7] 3:20; Ex 20:17; Dt 5:21. x. [7:8] 5:13,20; 1 Cor 15:56 / Rom 4:15. y. [7:10] Lv 18:5. z. [7:11] Gn 3:13; Heb 3:13. a. [7:12] 1 Tm 1:8.

it might be shown to be sin, worked death in me through the good, so that sin might become sinful beyond measure through the commandment.[b] [14]We know that the law is spiritual; but I am carnal, sold into slavery to sin.[c] [15]What I do, I do not understand. For I do not do what I want, but I do what I hate. [16]Now if I do what I do not want, I concur that the law is good. [17]So now it is no longer I who do it, but sin that dwells in me. [18]For I know that good does not dwell in me, that is, in my flesh. The willing is ready at hand, but doing the good is not.[d] [19]For I do not do the good I want, but I do the evil I do not want. [20]Now if [I] do what I do not want, it is no longer I who do it, but sin that dwells in me. [21]So, then, I discover the principle that when I want to do right, evil is at hand. [22]For I take delight in the law of God, in my inner self, [23e]but I see in my members another principle at war with the law of my mind, taking me captive to the law of sin that dwells in my members.* [24]Miserable one that I am! Who will deliver me from this mortal body? [25]Thanks be to God through Jesus Christ our Lord. Therefore, I myself, with my mind, serve the law of God but, with my flesh, the law of sin.[f]

CHAPTER 8
The Flesh and the Spirit.[†] [1]Hence, now there is no condemnation for those who are in Christ Jesus. [2]For the law of the spirit of life in Christ Jesus has freed you from the law of sin and death.[g] [3]For what the law, weakened by the flesh, was powerless to do, this God has done: by sending his own Son in the likeness of sinful flesh and for the sake of sin, he condemned sin in the flesh,[h] [4]so that the righteous decree of the law might be fulfilled in us, who live not according to the flesh but according to the spirit.[i] [5]For those who live according to the flesh are

concerned with the things of the flesh, but those who live according to the spirit with the things of the spirit. [6]The concern of the flesh is death, but the concern of the spirit is life and peace.[j] [7]For the concern of the flesh is hostility toward God; it does not submit to the law of God, nor can it;[k] [8]and those who are in the flesh cannot please God.[l] [9]But you are not in the flesh; on the contrary, you are in the spirit, if only the Spirit of God dwells in you. Whoever does not have the Spirit of Christ does not belong to him.[m] [10]But if Christ is in you, although the body is dead because of sin, the spirit is alive because of righteousness.[n] [11]If the Spirit of the one who raised Jesus from the dead dwells in you, the one who raised Christ from the dead will give life to your mortal bodies also, through his Spirit that dwells in you. [12]Consequently, brothers, we are not debtors to the flesh, to live according to the flesh. [13]For if you live according to the flesh, you will die, but if by the spirit you put to death the deeds of the body, you will live.[o]

Children of God Through Adoption.[‡] [14]For those who are led by the Spirit of God are children of God.[p] [15]For you did not receive a spirit of slavery to fall back into fear, but you received a spirit of adoption, through which we cry, "Abba,[§] Father!"[q] [16]The Spirit itself bears witness with our spirit that we are children of God,[r] [17]and if children, then heirs, heirs of God and joint heirs with Christ, if only we suffer with him so that we may also be glorified with him.[s]

Destiny of Glory.[¶] [18]I consider that the sufferings of this present time as nothing compared with the glory to be revealed for us.[t] [19]For creation awaits with eager expectation the revelation of the children of God; [20]for creation was made subject to futility, not of its own accord but because of the one who subjected it,[u] in hope [21]that creation itself would be set free from slavery to corruption and share in the glorious freedom of the children of God.[v] [22]We know that all creation is groaning in labor pains even until

---

*[7:23] As in Rom 3:27, Paul plays on the term **law**, which in Greek can connote custom, system, or **principle**.

†[8:1–13] After his warning in Rom 7 against the wrong route to fulfillment of the objective of holiness expressed in Rom 6:22, Paul points his addressees to the correct way. Through the redemptive work of Christ, Christians have been liberated from the terrible forces of sin and death. Holiness was impossible so long as the **flesh** (or our "old self"), that is, self-interested hostility toward God (Rom 8:7), frustrated the divine objectives expressed in the law. What is worse, sin used the law to break forth into all manner of lawlessness (Rom 8:8). All this is now changed. At the cross God broke the power of sin and pronounced sentence on it (Rom 8:3). Christians still retain the flesh, but it is alien to their new being, which is life in the spirit, namely the new self, governed by the holy Spirit. Under the direction of the holy Spirit Christians are able to fulfill the divine will that formerly found expression in the law (Rom 8:4). The same Spirit who enlivens Christians for holiness will also resurrect their bodies at the last day (Rom 8:11). Christian life is therefore the experience of a constant challenge to put to death the evil deeds of the body through life of the spirit (Rom 8:13).

b. [7:13] 4:15; 5:20.   c. [7:14] 8:7–8; Ps 51:7.   d. [7:18] Gn 6:5; 8:21; Phil 2:13.   e. [7:23] Gal 5:17; 1 Pt 2:11.   f. [7:25] 1 Cor 15:57.   g. [8:2] 7:23–24; 2 Cor 3:17.   h. [8:3] Acts 13:38; 15:10 / Jn 3:16–17; 2 Cor 5:21; Gal 3:13; 4:4; Phil 2:7; Col 1:22; Heb 2:17; 4:15; 1 Jn 4:9.   i. [8:4] Gal 5:16–25.

‡[8:14–17] Christians, by reason of the Spirit's presence within them, enjoy not only new life but also a new relationship to God, that of adopted children and heirs through Christ, whose sufferings and glory they share.

§[8:15] **Abba:** see note on Mk 14:36.

¶[8:18–27] The glory that believers are destined to share with Christ far exceeds the sufferings of the present life. Paul considers the destiny of the created world to be linked with the future that belongs to the believers. As it shares in the penalty of corruption brought about by sin, so also will it share in the benefits of redemption and future glory that comprise the ultimate liberation of God's people (Rom 8:19–22). After patient endurance in steadfast expectation, the full harvest of the Spirit's presence will be realized. On earth believers enjoy the firstfruits, i.e., the Spirit, as a guarantee of the total liberation of their bodies from the influence of the rebellious old self (Rom 8:23).

j. [8:6] 6:21; 7:5; 8:13; Gal 6:8.   k. [8:7] 5:10; Jas 4:4.   l. [8:8] 1 Jn 2:16.   m. [8:9] 1 Cor 3:16.   n. [8:10] Gal 2:20; 1 Pt 4:6.   o. [8:13] Gal 5:24; 6:8; Eph 4:22–24.   p. [8:14] Gal 5:18.   q. [8:15] Mk 14:36; Gal 4:5–6; 2 Tm 1:7.   r. [8:16] Jn 1:12; Gal 3:26–29.   s. [8:17] Gal 4:7; 1 Pt 4:13; 5:1.   t. [8:18] 2 Cor 4:17.   u. [8:20] Gn 3:17–19.   v. [8:21] 2 Pt 3:12–13; Rev 21:1.

now;[w] [23]and not only that, but we ourselves, who have the firstfruits of the Spirit, we also groan within ourselves as we wait for adoption, the redemption of our bodies.[x] [24]For in hope we were saved. Now hope that sees for itself is not hope. For who hopes for what one sees?[y] [25]But if we hope for what we do not see, we wait with endurance.

[26]In the same way, the Spirit too comes to the aid of our weakness; for we do not know how to pray as we ought, but the Spirit itself intercedes with inexpressible groanings. [27]And the one who searches hearts knows what is the intention of the Spirit, because it intercedes for the holy ones according to God's will.[z]

God's Indomitable Love in Christ. [28*]We know that all things work for good for those who love God,[†] who are called according to his purpose.[a] [29*]For those he foreknew he also predestined to be conformed to the image of his Son, so that he might be the firstborn among many brothers.[b] [30]And those he predestined he also called; and those he called he also justified; and those he justified he also glorified.[c]

[31§]What then shall we say to this? If God is for us, who can be against us?[d] [32]He who did not spare his own Son but handed him over for us all, how will he not also give us everything along with him?[e] [33]Who will bring a charge against God's chosen ones? It is God who acquits us.[f] [34]Who will condemn? It is Christ [Jesus] who died, rather, was raised, who also is at the right hand of God, who indeed intercedes for us.[g] [35]What will separate us from the love of Christ? Will anguish, or distress, or persecution, or famine, or nakedness, or peril, or the sword? [36]As it is written:[h]

"For your sake we are being slain all the day;
    we are looked upon as sheep to be slaughtered."

[37]No, in all these things we conquer overwhelmingly through him who loved us.[i] [38]For I am convinced that neither death, nor life, nor angels, nor principalities, nor present things,[¶] nor future things, nor powers,[j] [39]nor height, nor depth,[**] nor any other creature will be able to separate us from the love of God in Christ Jesus our Lord.

V. JEWS AND GENTILES IN GOD'S PLAN[††]

CHAPTER 9

Paul's Love for Israel.[‡‡] [1]I speak the truth in Christ, I do not lie; my conscience joins with the holy Spirit in bearing me witness[k] [2]that I have great sorrow and constant anguish in my heart. [3]For I could wish that I myself were accursed and separated from Christ for the sake of my brothers, my kin according to the flesh.[l] [4]They are Israelites; theirs the adoption, the glory, the covenants, the giving of the law, the worship, and the promises;[m] [5]theirs the patriarchs, and from them, according to the flesh, is the Messiah. God who is over all[§§] be blessed forever. Amen.[n]

God's Free Choice. [6]But it is not that the word of God has failed. For not all who are of Israel

---

*[8:28–30] These verses outline the Christian vocation as it was designed by God: **to be conformed to the image of his Son**, who is to **be the firstborn among many brothers** (Rom 8:29). God's redemptive action on behalf of the believers has been in process before the beginning of the world. Those whom God chooses are **those he foreknew** (Rom 8:29) or elected. Those who are **called** (Rom 8:30) are **predestined** or predetermined. These expressions do not mean that God is arbitrary. Rather, Paul uses them to emphasize the thought and care that God has taken for the Christian's salvation.

†[8:28] **We know that all things work for good for those who love God:** a few ancient authorities have God as the subject of the verb, and some translators render: "We know that God makes everything work for good for those who love God . . . ."

‡[8:29] **Image:** while man and woman were originally created in God's image (Gn 1:26–27), it is through baptism into Christ, the image of God (2 Cor 4:4; Col 1:15), that we are renewed according to the image of the Creator (Col 3:10).

§[8:31–39] The all-conquering power of God's love has overcome every obstacle to Christians' salvation and every threat to separate them from God. That power manifested itself fully when God's own Son was delivered up to death for their salvation. Through him Christians can overcome all their afflictions and trials.

¶[8:38] **Present things** and **future things** may refer to astrological data. Paul appears to be saying that the gospel liberates believers from dependence on astrologers.

[8:39] **Height, depth may refer to positions in the zodiac, positions of heavenly bodies relative to the horizon. In astrological documents the term for "height" means "exaltation" or the position of greatest influence exerted by a planet. Since hostile spirits were associated with the planets and stars, Paul includes **powers** (Rom 8:38) in his list of malevolent forces.

††[9:1–11:36] Israel's unbelief and its rejection of Jesus as savior astonished and puzzled Christians. It constituted a serious problem for them in view of God's specific preparation of Israel for the advent of the Messiah. Paul addresses himself here to the essential question of how the divine plan could be frustrated by Israel's unbelief. At the same time, he discourages both complacency and anxiety on the part of Gentiles. To those who might boast of their superior advantage over Jews, he warns that their enjoyment of the blessings assigned to Israel can be terminated. To those who might anxiously ask, "How can we be sure that Israel's fate will not be ours?" he replies that only unbelief can deprive one of salvation.

‡‡[9:1–5] The apostle speaks in strong terms of the depth of his grief over the unbelief of his own people. He would willingly undergo a curse himself for the sake of their coming to the knowledge of Christ (Rom 9:3; cf. Lv 27:28–29). His love for them derives from God's continuing choice of them and from the spiritual benefits that God bestows on them and through them on all of humanity (Rom 9:4–5).

§§[9:5] Some editors punctuate this verse differently and prefer the translation, "Of whom is Christ according to the flesh, who is God over all." However, Paul's point is that God **who is over all** aimed to use Israel, which had been entrusted with every privilege, in outreach to the entire world through the Messiah.

---

w. [8:22] 2 Cor 5:2–5.   x. [8:23] 2 Cor 1:22; Gal 5:5.   y. [8:24] 2 Cor 5:7; Heb 11:1.   z. [8:27] Ps 139:1; 1 Cor 4:5.   a. [8:28–29] Eph 1:4–14; 3:11.   b. [8:29] Eph 1:5; 1 Pt 1:2.   c. [8:30] Is 45:25; 2 Thes 2:13–14.   d. [8:31] Ps 118:6; Heb 13:6.   e. [8:32] Jn 3:16.   f. [8:33–34] Is 50:8.   g. [8:34] Ps 110:1; Heb 7:25; 1 Jn 2:1.   h. [8:36] Ps 44:23; 1 Cor 4:9; 15:30; 2 Cor 4:11; 2 Tm 3:12.

i. [8:37] 1 Jn 5:4.   j. [8:38–39] 1 Cor 3:22; Eph 1:21; 1 Pt 3:22.   k. [9:1] 2 Cor 11:31; 1 Tm 2:7.   l. [9:3] Ex 32:32.   m. [9:4–5] 3:2; Ex 4:22; Dt 7:6; 14:1–2.   n. [9:5] Mt 1:1–16; Lk 3:23–38 / Rom 1:25; Ps 41:14.

are Israel,[o] [7]nor are they all children of Abraham because they are his descendants; but "It is through Isaac that descendants shall bear your name."[p] [8]This means that it is not the children of the flesh who are the children of God, but the children of the promise are counted as descendants.[q] [9]For this is the wording of the promise, "About this time I shall return and Sarah will have a son."[r] [10]And not only that,[s] but also when Rebecca had conceived children by one husband, our father Isaac*—[11]before they had yet been born or had done anything, good or bad, in order that God's elective plan might continue, [12]not by works but by his call—she was told, "The older shall serve the younger."[t] [13]As it is written:[u]

"I loved Jacob
    but hated Esau."[†]

[14‡]What then are we to say? Is there injustice on the part of God? Of course not![v] [15]For he says to Moses:

"I will show mercy to whom I will,
    I will take pity on whom I will."[w]

[16]So it depends not upon a person's will or exertion, but upon God, who shows mercy.[x] [17]For the scripture says to Pharaoh, "This is why I have raised you up, to show my power through you that my name may be proclaimed throughout the earth."[y] [18]Consequently, he has mercy upon whom he wills,[z] and he hardens whom he wills.[§]

*[9:10] **Children by one husband, our father Isaac:** Abraham had two children, Ishmael and Isaac, by two wives, Hagar and Sarah, respectively. In that instance Isaac, although born later than Ishmael, became the bearer of the messianic promise. In the case of twins born to Rebecca, God's elective procedure is seen even more dramatically, and again the younger, contrary to Semitic custom, is given the preference.

†[9:13] The literal rendering, **"Jacob I loved, but Esau I hated,"** suggests an attitude of divine hostility that is not implied in Paul's statement. In Semitic usage "hate" means to love less; cf. Lk 14:26 with Mt 10:37. Israel's unbelief reflects the mystery of the divine election that is always operative within it. Mere natural descent from Abraham does not ensure the full possession of the divine gifts; it is God's sovereign prerogative to bestow this fullness upon, or to withhold it from, whomsoever he wishes; cf. Mt 3:9; Jn 8:39. The choice of Jacob over Esau is a case in point.

‡[9:14–18] The principle of divine election does not invite Christians to theoretical inquiry concerning the nonelected, nor does this principle mean that God is unfair in his dealings with humanity. The instruction concerning divine election is a part of the gospel and reveals that the gift of faith is the enactment of God's mercy (Rom 9:16). God raised up Moses to display that mercy, and Pharaoh to display divine severity in punishing those who obstinately oppose their Creator.

§[9:18] The basic biblical principle is: those who will not see or hear *shall* not see or hear. On the other hand, the same God who thus makes stubborn or hardens the heart can reconstruct it through the work of the holy Spirit.

[19]You will say to me then, "Why [then] does he still find fault? For who can oppose his will?"[a] [20]But who indeed are you, a human being, to talk back to God?[b] Will what is made say to its maker, "Why have you created me so?" [21]Or does not the potter have a right over the clay, to make out of the same lump one vessel for a noble purpose and another for an ignoble one? [22]What if God, wishing to show his wrath and make known his power, has endured with much patience the vessels of wrath made for destruction?[c] [23]This was to make known the riches of his glory to the vessels of mercy, which he has prepared previously for glory, [24]namely, us whom he has called, not only from the Jews but also from the Gentiles. **Witness of the Prophets.** [25]As indeed he says in Hosea:

"Those who were not my people I will call
    'my people,'
    and her who was not beloved" I will
        call 'beloved.'[d]
[26] And in the very place where it was said to
        them, 'You are not my people,'
    there they shall be called children of
        the living God."[e]

[27f]And Isaiah cries out concerning Israel, "Though the number of the Israelites were like the sand of the sea, only a remnant will be saved; [28]for decisively and quickly will the Lord execute sentence upon the earth." [29]And as Isaiah predicted:

"Unless the Lord of hosts had left us
        descendants,
    we would have become like Sodom
    and have been made like
        Gomorrah."[g]

Righteousness Based on Faith.[††] [30]What then shall we say? That Gentiles, who did not pursue

¶[9:19–29] The apostle responds to the objection that if God rules over faith through the principle of divine election, God cannot then accuse unbelievers of sin (Rom 9:19). For Paul, this objection is in the last analysis a manifestation of human insolence, and his "answer" is less an explanation of God's ways than the rejection of an argument that places humanity on a level with God. At the same time, Paul shows that God is far less arbitrary than appearances suggest, for God endures **with much patience** (Rom 9:22) a person like the Pharaoh of the Exodus.

[9:25] Beloved: in Semitic discourse means "preferred" or "favorite" (cf. Rom 9:13). See Hos 2:1.

††[9:30–33] In the conversion of the Gentiles and, by contrast, of relatively few Jews, the Old Testament prophecies are seen to be fulfilled; cf. Rom 9:25–29. Israel feared that the doctrine of justification through faith would jeopardize the validity of the Mosaic law, and so they never reached their goal of righteousness that they had sought to attain through meticulous observance of the law (Rom 9:31). Since Gentiles, including especially Greeks and Romans, had a great regard

o. [9:6] Nm 23:19 / Mt 3:9.   p. [9:7] Gn 21:12; Gal 3:29.   q. [9:8] Gal 4:23,28.   r. [9:9] Gn 18:10,14.   s. [9:10] Gn 25:21.   t. [9:12] 11:5–6 / Gn 25:23–24.   u. [9:13] Mal 1:3.   v. [9:14] Dt 32:4.   w. [9:15] Ex 33:19.   x. [9:16] Eph 2:8; Ti 3:5.   y. [9:17] Ex 9:16.   z. [9:18] 11:30–32; Ex 4:21; 7:3.

a. [9:19] 3:7; Wis 12:12.   b. [9:20–21] Wis 15:7; Is 29:16; 45:9; Jer 18:6.   c. [9:22] 2:4; Wis 12:20–21; Jer 50:25.   d. [9:25] Hos 2:25.   e. [9:26] Hos 2:1.   f. [9:27–28] Is 10:22–23; Hos 2:1 / Rom 11:5 / Is 28:22.   g. [9:29] Is 1:9; Mt 10:15.

righteousness, have achieved it, that is, righteousness that comes from faith;[h] [31]but that Israel, who pursued the law of righteousness, did not attain to that law?[i] [32]Why not? Because they did it not by faith, but as if it could be done by works.[j] They stumbled over the stone that causes stumbling,* [33]as it is written:

"Behold, I am laying a stone in Zion
that will make people stumble
and a rock that will make them fall,
and whoever believes in him shall not be
put to shame."[k]

CHAPTER 10

[1†]Brothers, my heart's desire and prayer to God on their behalf is for salvation.[l] [2]I testify with regard to them that they have zeal for God, but it is not discerning.[m] [3]For, in their unawareness of the righteousness that comes from God and their attempt to establish their own [righteousness], they did not submit to the righteousness of God.[n] [4]For Christ is the end[‡] of the law for the justification of everyone who has faith.[o]

[5§]Moses writes about the righteousness that comes from [the] law, "The one who does these things will live by them."[p] [6]But the righteousness that comes from faith says,[q] "Do not say in your heart, 'Who will go up into heaven?' (that is, to bring Christ down) [7¶]or 'Who will go down into the abyss?' (that is, to bring Christ up from the dead)."[r] [8]But what does it say?

"The word is near you,
in your mouth and in your heart"[s]

(that is, the word of faith that we preach), [9]for, if you confess** with your mouth that Jesus is Lord and believe in your heart that God raised him from the dead, you will be saved.[t] [10]For one believes with the heart and so is justified, and one confesses with the mouth and so is saved. [11]For the scripture says, "No one who believes in him will be put to shame."[u] [12]For there is no distinction between Jew and Greek; the same Lord is Lord of all, enriching all who call upon him.[v] [13]For "everyone who calls on the name of the Lord will be saved."[w]

[14††]But how can they call on him in whom they have not believed? And how can they believe in him of whom they have not heard? And how can they hear without someone to preach?[x] [15]And how can people preach unless they are sent? As it is written,[y] "How beautiful are the feet of those who bring [the] good news!"[‡‡] [16]But not everyone has heeded the good news; for Isaiah says, "Lord, who has believed what was heard from us?"[z] [17]Thus faith comes from what is heard, and what is heard comes through the word of Christ.[a] [18]But I ask, did they not hear? Certainly they did; for

"Their voice has gone forth to all the earth,
and their words to the ends of the
world."[b]

[19]But I ask, did not Israel understand?[c] First Moses says:

"I will make you jealous of those who are
not a nation;
with a senseless nation I will make
you angry."

[20d]Then Isaiah speaks boldly and says:

"I was found [by] those who were not
seeking me;
I revealed myself to those who were
not asking for me."

for righteousness, Paul's statement concerning Gentiles in Rom 9:30 is to be understood from a Jewish perspective: quite evidently they had not been interested in "God's" righteousness, for it had not been revealed to them; but now in response to the proclamation of the gospel they respond in faith.

*[9:32] Paul discusses Israel as a whole from the perspective of contemporary Jewish rejection of Jesus as Messiah. The Old Testament and much of Jewish noncanonical literature in fact reflect a fervent faith in divine mercy.

†[10:1–13] Despite Israel's lack of faith in God's act in Christ, Paul does not abandon hope for her salvation (Rom 10:1). However, Israel must recognize that the Messiah's arrival in the person of Jesus Christ means the termination of the Mosaic law as the criterion for understanding oneself in a valid relationship to God. Faith in God's saving action in Jesus Christ takes precedence over any such legal claim (Rom 10:6).

‡[10:4] The Mosaic legislation has been superseded by God's action in Jesus Christ. Others understand end here in the sense that Christ is the goal of the law, i.e., the true meaning of the Mosaic law, which cannot be correctly understood apart from him. Still others believe that both meanings are intended.

§[10:5–6] The subject of the verb says (Rom 10:6) is righteousness personified. Both of the statements in Rom 10:5–6 derive from Moses, but Paul wishes to contrast the language of law and the language of faith.

¶[10:7] Here Paul blends Dt 30:13 and Ps 107:26.

[10:9–11] To confess Jesus as Lord was frequently quite hazardous in the first century (cf. Mt 10:18; 1 Thes 2:2; 1 Pt 2:18–21; 3:14). For a Jew it could mean disruption of normal familial and other social relationships, including great economic sacrifice. In the face of penalties imposed by the secular world, Christians are assured that **no one who believes in Jesus will be put to shame (Rom 10:11).

††[10:14–21] The gospel has been sufficiently proclaimed to Israel, and Israel has adequately understood God's plan for the messianic age, which would see the gospel brought to the uttermost parts of the earth. As often in the past, Israel has not accepted the prophetic message; cf. Acts 7:51–53.

‡‡[10:15] **How beautiful are the feet of those who bring [the] good news**: in Semitic fashion, the parts of the body that bring the messenger with welcome news are praised; cf. Lk 11:27.

h. [9:30] 10:4, 20. i. [9:31] 10:3. j. [9:32] Is 8:14. k. [9:33] Is 28:16; 1 Pt 2:6–8. l. [10:1] 9:1, 3. m. [10:2] Acts 22:3. n. [10:3] 9:31–32; Phil 3:9. o. [10:4] Acts 13:38–39; 2 Cor 3:14; Heb 8:13. p. [10:5] Lv 18:5; Gal 3:12. q. [10:6] Dt 9:4; 30:12. r. [10:7] Dt 30:13; 1 Pt 3:19. s. [10:8] Dt 30:14.

t. [10:9] 1 Cor 12:3. u. [10:11] 9:33; Is 28:16. v. [10:12] 1:16; 3:22, 29; Acts 10:34; 15:9, 11; Gal 3:28; Eph 2:14. w. [10:13] Jl 3:5; Acts 2:21. x. [10:14] Acts 8:31. y. [10:15] Is 52:7; Na 2:1; Eph 6:15. z. [10:16] Is 53:1; Jn 12:38. a. [10:17] Jn 17:20. b. [10:18] Ps 19:5; Mt 24:14. c. [10:19] 11:11, 14; Dt 32:21. d. [10:20–21] 9:30; Is 65:1–2.

²¹But regarding Israel he says, "All day long I stretched out my hands to a disobedient and contentious people."

CHAPTER 11

The Remnant of Israel. * ¹I ask, then, has God rejected his people? Of course not!ᵉ For I too am an Israelite, a descendant of Abraham, of the tribe of Benjamin.ᶠ ²God has not rejected his people whom he foreknew. Do you not know what the scripture says about Elijah, how he pleads with God against Israel? ³"Lord, they have killed your prophets, they have torn down your altars, and I alone am left, and they are seeking my life."ᵍ ⁴But what is God's response to him? "I have left for myself seven thousand men who have not knelt to Baal."ʰ ⁵So also at the present time there is a remnant, chosen by grace.ⁱ ⁶But if by grace, it is no longer because of works; otherwise grace would no longer be grace.ʲ ⁷What then? What Israel was seeking it did not attain, but the elect attained it; the rest were hardened,ᵏ ⁸as it is written:

"God gave them a spirit of deep sleep,
    eyes that should not see
    and ears that should not hear,
down to this very day."ˡ

⁹And David says:ᵐ

"Let their table become a snare and a trap,
    a stumbling block and a retribution
        for them;
¹⁰ let their eyes grow dim so that they may
        not see,
    and keep their backs bent forever."

The Gentiles' Salvation. ¹¹†Hence I ask, did they stumble so as to fall? Of course not! But through their transgression salvation has come to the Gentiles, so as to make them jealous.ⁿ ¹²Now if their transgression is enrichment for the world, and if their diminished number is enrichment for the Gentiles, how much more their full number.

¹³Now I am speaking to you Gentiles. Inasmuch then as I am the apostle to the Gentiles, I glory in my ministryᵒ ¹⁴in order to make my race jealous and thus save some of them. ¹⁵For if their rejection is the reconciliation of the world, what will their acceptance be but life from the dead? ¹⁶‡If the firstfruits are holy, so is the whole batch of dough; and if the root is holy, so are the branches.ᵖ

¹⁷But if some of the branches were broken off, and you, a wild olive shoot, were grafted in their place and have come to share in the rich root of the olive tree,�q ¹⁸do not boast against the branches. If you do boast, consider that you do not support the root; the root supports you.ʳ ¹⁹Indeed you will say, "Branches were broken off so that I might be grafted in." ²⁰That is so. They were broken off because of unbelief, but you are there because of faith. So do not become haughty, but stand in awe.ˢ ²¹For if God did not spare the natural branches, [perhaps] he will not spare you either.ᵗ ²²See, then, the kindness and severity of God: severity toward those who fell, but God's kindness to you, provided you remain in his kindness; otherwise you too will be cut off.ᵘ ²³And they also, if they do not remain in unbelief, will be grafted in, for God is able to graft them in again.ᵛ ²⁴For if you were cut from what is by nature a wild olive tree, and grafted, contrary to nature, into a cultivated one, how much more will they who belong to it by nature be grafted back into their own olive tree. **God's Irrevocable Call.** § ²⁵I do not want you to be unaware of this mystery, brothers, so that you will not become wise [in] your own estimation: a hardening has come upon Israel in part, until the full number of the Gentiles comes in,ʷ ²⁶and thus all Israel will be saved,ˣ as it is written:ʸ

"The deliverer will come out of Zion,
    he will turn away godlessness from
        Jacob;
²⁷ and this is my covenant with them
    when I take away their sins."ᶻ

---

*[11:1–10] Although Israel has been unfaithful to the prophetic message of the gospel (Rom 10:14–21), God remains faithful to Israel. Proof of the divine fidelity lies in the existence of Jewish Christians like Paul himself. The unbelieving Jews, says Paul, have been blinded by the Christian teaching concerning the Messiah.

†[11:11–15] The unbelief of the Jews has paved the way for the preaching of the gospel to the Gentiles and for their easier acceptance of it outside the context of Jewish culture. Through his mission to the Gentiles Paul also hopes to fill his fellow Jews with jealousy. Hence he hastens to fill the entire Mediterranean world with the gospel. Once all the Gentile nations have heard the gospel, Israel as a whole is expected to embrace it. This will be tantamount to resurrection of the dead, that is, the reappearance of Jesus Christ with all the believers at the end of time.

‡[11:16–24] Israel remains holy in the eyes of God and stands as a witness to the faith described in the Old Testament because of **the firstfruits** (or the first piece baked) (Rom 11:16), that is, the converted remnant, and **the root** that is holy, that is, the patriarchs (Rom 11:16). The Jews' failure to believe in Christ is a warning to Gentile Christians to be on guard against any semblance of anti-Jewish arrogance, that is, failure to recognize their total dependence on divine grace.

§[11:25–29] In God's design, Israel's unbelief is being used to grant the light of faith to the Gentiles. Meanwhile, Israel remains dear to God (cf. Rom 9:13), still the object of special providence, the mystery of which will one day be revealed.

e. [11:1–2] 1 Sm 12:22; Ps 94:14.   f. [11:1] 2 Cor 11:22; Phil 3:5.
g. [11:3] 1 Kgs 19:10, 14.   h. [11:4] 1 Kgs 19:18.   i. [11:5] 9:27.
j. [11:6] 4:4; Gal 3:18.   k. [11:7] 9:31.   l. [11:8] Dt 29:3; Is 29:10;
Mt 13:13–15; Acts 28:26–27.   m. [11:9–10] Ps 69:23–24; 35:8.
n. [11:11] Acts 13:46; 18:6; 28:28 / Rom 10:19; Dt 32:21.

o. [11:13] 1:5.   p. [11:16] Nm 15:17–21; Ez 44:30; Neh 10:36–38.
q. [11:17] Eph 2:11–19.   r. [11:18] 1 Cor 1:31.   s. [11:20] 12:16.
t. [11:21] 1 Cor 10:12.   u. [11:22] Jn 15:2, 4; Heb 3:14.   v. [11:23]
2 Cor 3:16.   w. [11:25] Prv 3:7 / Rom 12:16; Mk 13:10; Lk 21:24;
Jn 10:16.   x. [11:26–27] Ps 14:7; Is 59:20–21.   y. [11:26] Mt
23:39.   z. [11:27] Is 27:9; Jer 31:33–34.

²⁸In respect to the gospel, they are enemies on your account; but in respect to election, they are beloved because of the patriarchs.ᵃ ²⁹For the gifts and the call of God are irrevocable.ᵇ

Triumph of God's Mercy. ³⁰Just as you once disobeyed God but have now received mercy because of their disobedience, ³¹so they have now disobeyed in order that, by virtue of the mercy shown to you, they too may [now] receive mercy. ³²For God delivered all to disobedience, that he might have mercy upon all.ᶜ

³³Oh, the depth of the riches and wisdom and knowledge of God! How inscrutable are his judgments and how unsearchable his ways!ᵈ

³⁴ "For who has known the mind of the
        Lord‡
   or who has been his counselor?"ᵉ
³⁵ §"Or who has given him anythingᶠ
   that he may be repaid?"

³⁶For from him and through him and for him are all things. To him be glory forever. Amen.ᵍ

VI. THE DUTIES OF CHRISTIANS¹

CHAPTER 12
Sacrifice of Body and Mind. ¹*"I urge you therefore, brothers, by the mercies of God,

to offer your bodies as a living sacrifice, holy and pleasing to God, your spiritual worship.ʰ ²Do not conform yourselves to this age but be transformed by the renewal of your mind, that you may discern what is the will of God, what is good and pleasing and perfect.ⁱ

Many Parts in One Body. ³For by the grace given to me I tell everyone among you not to think of himself more highly than one ought to think, but to think soberly, each according to the measure of faith that God has apportioned. ⁴ᵏFor as in one body we have many parts, and all the parts do not have the same function, ⁵so we, though many, are one body in Christ†† and individually parts of one another. ⁶ˡSince we have gifts that differ according to the grace given to us, let us exercise them:‡‡ if prophecy, in proportion to the faith; ⁷if ministry, in ministering; if one is a teacher, in teaching; ⁸if one exhorts, in exhortation; if one contributes, in generosity; if one is over others,§§ with diligence; if one does acts of mercy, with cheerfulness.

Mutual Love. ⁹Let love be sincere; hate what is evil, hold on to what is good;ᵐ ¹⁰love one another with mutual affection; anticipate one another in showing honor.ⁿ ¹¹Do not grow slack in zeal, be fervent in spirit, serve the Lord.ᵒ ¹²Rejoice in hope, endure in affliction, persevere in prayer.ᵖ ¹³Contribute to the needs of the holy ones,ᑫ exercise hospitality. ¹⁴§Bless those who persecute [you],ʳ bless and do not curse them.ˢ ¹⁵Rejoice with those who rejoice, weep with those who weep.ᵗ ¹⁶Have the same regard for one another; do not be haughty but associate with the lowly;

---

*[11:30–32] Israel, together with the Gentiles who have been handed over to all manner of vices (Rom 1), **has been delivered . . . to disobedience.** The conclusion of Rom 11:32 repeats the thought of Rom 5:20, "Where sin increased, grace overflowed all the more."

†[11:33–36] This final reflection celebrates the wisdom of God's plan of salvation. As Paul has indicated throughout these chapters, both Jew and Gentile, despite the religious recalcitrance of each, have received the gift of faith. The methods used by God in making this outreach to the world stagger human comprehension but are at the same time a dazzling invitation to abiding faith.

‡[11:34] The citation is from the Greek text of Is 40:13. Paul does not explicitly mention Isaiah in this verse, nor Job in Rom 11:35.

§[11:35] Paul quotes from an old Greek version of Jb 41:3a, which differs from the Hebrew text (Jb 41:11a).

¶[12:1–13:14] Since Christ marks the termination of the Mosaic law as the primary source of guidance for God's people (Rom 10:4), the apostle explains how Christians can function, in the light of the gift of justification through faith, in their relation to one another and the state.

[12:1–8] The Mosaic code included elaborate directions on sacrifices and other cultic observances. The gospel, however, invites believers to present their **bodies as a living sacrifice (Rom 12:1). Instead of being limited by specific legal maxims, Christians are liberated for the exercise of good judgment as they are confronted with the many and varied decisions required in the course of daily life. To assist them, God distributes a variety of gifts to the fellowship of believers, including those of prophecy, teaching, and exhortation (Rom 12:6–8). Prophets assist the community to understand the will of God as it applies to the present situation (Rom 12:6). Teachers help people to understand themselves and their responsibilities in relation to others (Rom 12:7). One who **exhorts**

offers encouragement to the community to exercise their faith in the performance of all that is pleasing to God (Rom 12:8). Indeed, this very section, beginning with Rom 12:1, is a specimen of Paul's own style of exhortation.

††[12:5] **One body in Christ:** on the church as the body of Christ, see 1 Cor 12:12–27.

‡‡[12:6] Everyone has some gift that can be used for the benefit of the community. When the instruction on justification through faith is correctly grasped, the possessor of a gift will understand that it is not an instrument of self-aggrandizement. Possession of a gift is not an index to quality of faith. Rather, the gift is a challenge to faithful use.

§§[12:8] **Over others:** usually taken to mean "rule over" but possibly "serve as a patron." Wealthier members in Greco-Roman communities were frequently asked to assist in public service projects. In view of the references to contributing **in generosity** and to **acts of mercy,** Paul may have in mind people like Phoebe (Rom 16:1–2), who is called a **benefactor** (or "patron") because of the services she rendered to many Christians, including Paul.

¶¶[12:14–21] Since God has justified the believers, it is not necessary for them to take justice into their own hands by taking vengeance. God will ultimately deal justly with all, including those who inflict injury on the believers. This question of personal rights as a matter of justice prepares the way for more detailed consideration of the state as adjudicator.

---

h. [12:1] 2 Cor 1:3 / Rom 6:13; 1 Pt 2:5.   i. [12:2] Eph 4:17, 22–23; 1 Pt 1:14 / Eph 5:10, 17; Phil 1:10.   j. [12:3] 15:15 / Phil 2:3 / 1 Cor 12:11; Eph 4:7.   k. [12:4–5] 1 Cor 12:12, 27; Eph 4:25.   l. [12:6–8] 1 Cor 12:4–11, 28–31; Eph 4:7–12; 1 Pt 4:10–11 / 2 Cor 9:7.   m. [12:9] 2 Cor 6:6; 1 Tm 1:5; 1 Pt 1:22 / Am 5:15.   n. [12:10] Jn 13:34; 1 Thes 4:9; 1 Pt 2:17; 2 Pt 1:7 / Phil 2:3.   o. [12:11] Acts 18:25.   p. [12:12] 5:2–3; Col 4:2; 1 Thes 5:17.   q. [12:13] Heb 13:2; 1 Pt 4:9.   r. [12:14–21] Mt 5:38–48; 1 Cor 4:12; 1 Pt 3:9.   s. [12:14] Lk 6:27–28.   t. [12:15] Ps 35:13; Sir 7:34; 1 Cor 12:26.

a. [11:28] 15:8; 1 Thes 2:15–16.   b. [11:29] 9:6; Nm 23:19; Is 54:10.   c. [11:32] Gal 3:22; 1 Tm 2:4.   d. [11:33] Jb 11:7–8; Ps 139:6, 17–18; Wis 17:1; Is 55:8–9.   e. [11:34] Jb 15:8; Wis 9:13; Is 40:13; Jer 23:18; 1 Cor 2:11–16.   f. [11:35] Jb 41:3; Is 40:14.   g. [11:36] 1 Cor 8:6; Col 1:16–17.

do not be wise in your own estimation.[u] [17]Do not repay anyone evil for evil; be concerned for what is noble in the sight of all.[v] [18]If possible, on your part, live at peace with all.[w] [19]Beloved, do not look for revenge but leave room for the wrath; for it is written, "Vengeance is mine, I will repay, says the Lord."[x] [20]Rather, "if your enemy is hungry, feed him; if he is thirsty, give him something to drink; for by so doing you will heap burning coals upon his head."[y] [21]Do not be conquered by evil but conquer evil with good.

CHAPTER 13

Obedience to Authority.[*] [1]Let every person be subordinate to the higher authorities, for there is no authority except from God, and those that exist have been established by God.[z] [2]Therefore, whoever resists authority opposes what God has appointed, and those who oppose it will bring judgment upon themselves. [3]For rulers are not a cause of fear to good conduct, but to evil.[a] Do you wish to have no fear of authority? Then do what is good and you will receive approval from it, [4]for it is a servant of God for your good. But if you do evil, be afraid, for it does not bear the sword without purpose; it is the servant of God to inflict wrath on the evildoer.[b] [5]Therefore, it is necessary to be subject not only because of the wrath but also because of conscience.[c] [6]This is why you also pay taxes, for the authorities are ministers of God, devoting themselves to this very thing. [7]Pay to all their dues, taxes to whom taxes are due, toll to whom toll is due, respect to whom respect is due, honor to whom honor is due.[d]

Love Fulfills the Law.[†] [8]Owe nothing to anyone, except to love one another; for the one who loves another has fulfilled the law.[e] [9]The

commandments, "You shall not commit adultery; you shall not kill; you shall not steal; you shall not covet," and whatever other commandment there may be, are summed up in this saying, [namely] "You shall love your neighbor as yourself."[f] [10]Love does no evil to the neighbor; hence, love is the fulfillment of the law.[g]

Awareness of the End of Time.[‡] [11]And do this because you know the time; it is the hour now for you to awake from sleep. For our salvation is nearer now than when we first believed;[h] [12]the night is advanced, the day is at hand. Let us then throw off the works of darkness [and] put on the armor of light;[i] [13]let us conduct ourselves properly as in the day,[§] not in orgies and drunkenness, not in promiscuity and licentiousness, not in rivalry and jealousy.[j] [14]But put on the Lord Jesus Christ, and make no provision for the desires of the flesh.[k]

CHAPTER 14

To Live and Die for Christ.[¶] [1]Welcome anyone who is weak in faith,[l] but not for disputes over opinions.[m] [2]One person believes that one may eat anything, while the weak person eats only vegetables.[n] [3]The one who eats must not despise the one who abstains, and the one who abstains must not pass judgment on the one who eats; for God has welcomed him.[o] [4]Who are you to pass judgment on someone else's servant? Before his own master he stands or falls. And he will be upheld, for the Lord is able to make him stand.[p] [5][For] one person considers one day more important than another, while another person considers all days alike.[q] Let everyone be fully persuaded in his own mind." [6]Whoever observes the day, observes it for the Lord. Also

---

*[13:1–7] Paul must come to grips with the problem raised by a message that declares people free from the law. How are they to relate to Roman authority? The problem was exacerbated by the fact that imperial protocol was interwoven with devotion to various deities. Paul builds on the traditional instruction exhibited in Wis 6:1–3, according to which kings and magistrates rule by consent of God. From this perspective, then, believers who render obedience to the governing authorities are obeying the one who is highest in command. At the same time, it is recognized that Caesar has the responsibility to make just ordinances and to commend uprightness; cf. Wis 6:4–21. That Caesar is not entitled to obedience when such obedience would nullify God's prior claim to the believers' moral decision becomes clear in the light of the following verses.

†[13:8–10] When love directs the Christian's moral decisions, the interest of law in basic concerns, such as familial relationships, sanctity of life, and security of property, is safeguarded (Rom 13:9). Indeed, says Paul, the same applies to any **other commandment** (Rom 13:9), whether one in the Mosaic code or one drawn up by local magistrates under imperial authority. Love anticipates the purpose of public legislation, namely, to secure the best interests of the citizenry. Since Caesar's obligation is to punish the wrongdoer (Rom 13:4), the Christian who acts in love is free from all legitimate indictment.

‡[13:11–14] These verses provide the motivation for the love that is encouraged in Rom 13:8–10.

§[13:13] **Let us conduct ourselves properly as in the day**: the behavior described in Rom 1:29–30 is now to be reversed. Secular moralists were fond of making references to people who could not wait for nightfall to do their carousing. Paul says that Christians claim to be people of the new day that will dawn with the return of Christ. Instead of planning for nighttime behavior they should be concentrating on conduct that is consonant with avowed interest in the Lord's return.

¶[14:1–15:6] Since Christ spells termination of the law, which included observance of specific days and festivals as well as dietary instruction, the jettisoning of long-practiced customs was traumatic for many Christians brought up under the Mosaic code. Although Paul acknowledges that in principle no food is a source of moral contamination (Rom 14:14), he recommends that the consciences of Christians who are scrupulous in this regard be respected by other Christians (Rom 14:21). On the other hand, those who have scruples are not to sit in judgment on those who know that the gospel has liberated them from such ordinances (Rom 14:10). See 1 Cor 8; 10.

**[14:5] Since the problem to be overcome was humanity's perverted mind or judgment (Rom 1:28), Paul indicates

u. [12:16] 15:5; Phil 2:2–3 / Rom 11:20; Prv 3:7; Is 5:21.   v. [12:17] Prv 3:4; 1 Thes 5:15; 1 Pt 3:9.   w. [12:18] Heb 12:14.   x. [12:19] Lv 19:18; Dt 32:35, 41; Mt 5:39; 1 Cor 6:6–7; Heb 10:30.   y. [12:20] Prv 25:21–22; Mt 5:44.   z. [13:1] Prv 8:15–16; Wis 6:3; Jn 19:11; 1 Pt 2:13–17; Ti 3:1.   a. [13:3] 1 Pt 2:13–14; 3:13.   b. [13:4] 12:19.   c. [13:5] 1 Pt 2:19.   d. [13:7] Mt 22:21; Mk 12:17; Lk 20:25.   e. [13:8] Jn 13:34; Gal 5:14.

f. [13:9] Ex 20:13–17 / Lv 19:18; Dt 5:17–21; Mt 5:43–44; 19:18–19; 22:39; Mk 12:31; Lk 10:27; Gal 5:14; Jas 2:8.   g. [13:10] Mt 22:40; 1 Cor 13:4–7.   h. [13:11] Eph 5:8–16; 1 Thes 5:5–7.   i. [13:12] Jn 8:12; 1 Thes 5:4–8; 1 Jn 2:8 / 2 Cor 6:7; 10:4; Eph 5:11; 6:13–17.   j. [13:13] Lk 21:34; Eph 5:18.   k. [13:14] Gal 3:27; 5:16; Eph 4:24; 6:11.   l. [14:1–23] 1 Cor 8:1–13.   m. [14:1] 15:1, 7; 1 Cor 9:22.   n. [14:2] Gn 1:29; 9:3; 1 Cor 8:1–13; 10:14–33.   o. [14:3] Col 2:16.   p. [14:4] 2:1; Mt 7:11; Jas 4:11–12.   q. [14:5] Gal 4:10.

whoever eats, eats for the Lord, since he gives thanks to God; while whoever abstains, abstains for the Lord and gives thanks to God. [7]None of us lives for oneself, and no one dies for oneself. [8]For if we live, we live for the Lord,* and if we die, we die for the Lord; so then, whether we live or die, we are the Lord's.[r] [9]For this is why Christ died and came to life, that he might be Lord of both the dead and the living.[s] [10]Why then do you judge your brother? Or you, why do you look down on your brother? For we shall all stand before the judgment seat of God;[t] [11]for it is written:

"As I live, says the Lord, every knee shall
      bend before me,
   and every tongue shall give praise
      to God."[u]

[12]So [then] each of us shall give an account of himself [to God].[v]
Consideration for the Weak Conscience. [13]Then let us no longer judge one another, but rather resolve never to put a stumbling block or hindrance in the way of a brother.[w] [14]I know and am convinced in the Lord Jesus that nothing is unclean in itself; still, it is unclean for someone who thinks it unclean.[x] [15]If your brother is being hurt by what you eat, your conduct is no longer in accord with love. Do not because of your food destroy him for whom Christ died.[y] [16]So do not let your good be reviled.[z] [17]For the kingdom of God is not a matter of food and drink, but of righteousness, peace, and joy in the holy Spirit;[a] [18]whoever serves Christ in this way is pleasing to God and approved by others. [19]Let us[†] then pursue what leads to peace and to building up one another.[b] [20]For the sake of food, do not destroy the work of God.[c] Everything is indeed clean, but it is wrong for anyone to become a stumbling block by eating; [21]it is good not to eat meat or drink wine or do anything that causes your brother to stumble. [22]Keep the faith [that] you have to yourself in the presence of God; blessed is the one who does not condemn himself for what he approves. [23][d]But whoever has doubts is condemned if he eats, because this is not from faith; for whatever is not from faith is sin.[‡]

CHAPTER 15

Patience and Self-Denial. [1]We who are strong ought to put up with the failings of the weak and not to please ourselves;[e] [2]let each of us please our neighbor for the good, for building up.[f] [3]For Christ did not please himself; but, as it is written,[g] "The insults of those who insult you fall upon me."[§] [4]For whatever was written previously was written for our instruction, that by endurance and by the encouragement of the scriptures we might have hope.[h] [5]May the God of endurance and encouragement grant you to think in harmony[¶] with one another, in keeping with Christ Jesus,[i] [6]that with one accord you may with one voice glorify the God and Father of our Lord Jesus Christ.
God's Fidelity and Mercy.[**] [7]Welcome one another, then, as Christ welcomed you, for the glory of God.[j] [8]For I say that Christ became a minister of the circumcised to show God's truthfulness, to confirm the promises to the patriarchs,[k] [9]but so that the Gentiles might glorify God for his mercy. As it is written:

"Therefore, I will praise you among the
      Gentiles
   and sing praises to your name."[l]

[10]And again it says:[m]

"Rejoice, O Gentiles, with his people."[††]

[11]And again:

"Praise the Lord, all you Gentiles,
   and let all the peoples praise him."[n]

[12]And again Isaiah says:

"The root of Jesse shall come,
      raised up to rule the Gentiles;
   in him shall the Gentiles hope."[o]

---

that the **mind** of the Christian is now able to function with appropriate discrimination (cf. Rom 12:2).
* [14:8] **The Lord:** Jesus, our Master. The same Greek word, *kyrios*, was applied to both rulers and holders of slaves. Throughout the Letter to the Romans Paul emphasizes God's total claim on the believer; see note on Rom 1:1.
† [14:19] Some manuscripts, versions, and church Fathers read, "We then pursue . . ."; cf. Rom 5:1.
‡ [14:23] **Whatever is not from faith is sin:** Paul does not mean that all the actions of unbelievers are sinful. He addresses

himself to the question of intracommunity living. **Sin** in the singular is the dreadful power described in Rom 5:12–14.
§ [15:3] Liberation from the law of Moses does not make the scriptures of the old covenant irrelevant. Much consolation and motivation for Christian living can be derived from the Old Testament, as in the citation from Ps 69:10. Because this psalm is quoted several times in the New Testament, it has been called indirectly messianic.
¶ [15:5] **Think in harmony:** a Greco-Roman ideal. Not rigid uniformity of thought and expression but thoughtful consideration of other people's views finds expression here.
** [15:7–13] True oneness of mind is found in pondering the ultimate mission of the church: to bring it about that God's name be glorified throughout the world and that Jesus Christ be universally recognized as God's gift to all humanity. Paul here prepares his addressees for the climactic appeal he is about to make.
†† [15:10] Paul's citation of Dt 32:43 follows the Greek version.

---

r. [14:8] Lk 20:38; 2 Cor 5:15; Gal 2:20; 1 Thes 5:10.   s. [14:9] Acts 10:42.   t. [14:10] Acts 17:31; 2 Cor 5:10.   u. [14:11] Is 49:18 / Is 45:23; Phil 2:10–11.   v. [14:12] Gal 6:5.   w. [14:13] 1 Cor 8:9, 13.   x. [14:14] Mk 7:5, 20; Acts 10:15; 1 Cor 10:25–27; 1 Tm 4:4.   y. [14:15] 1 Cor 8:11–13.   z. [14:16] 2:24; Ti 2:5.   a. [14:17] 1 Cor 8:8.   b. [14:19] 12:18 / 15:2.   c. [14:20–21] 1 Cor 8:11–13; 10:28–29; Ti 1:15.   d. [14:23] Ti 1:15; Jas 4:17.

e. [15:1] 14:1–2.   f. [15:2] 14:1, 19; 1 Cor 9:19; 10:24, 33.   g. [15:3] Ps 69:10.   h. [15:4] 4:23–24; 1 Mc 12:9; 1 Cor 10:11; 2 Tm 3:16.   i. [15:5] 12:16; Phil 2:2; 4:2.   j. [15:7] 14:1.   k. [15:8] Mt 15:24 / Mi 7:20; Acts 3:25.   l. [15:9] 11:30 / 2 Sm 22:50; Ps 18:50.   m. [15:10] Dt 32:43.   n. [15:11] Ps 117:1.   o. [15:12] Is 11:10; Rev 5:5; 22:16.

¹³May the God of hope fill you with all joy and peace in believing, so that you may abound in hope by the power of the holy Spirit.^p

VII. CONCLUSION

Apostle to the Gentiles. ^{14*}I myself am convinced about you, my brothers, that you yourselves are full of goodness,[†] filled with all knowledge, and able to admonish one another. ¹⁵But I have written to you rather boldly in some respects to remind you, because of the grace given me by God^q ¹⁶to be a minister of Christ Jesus to the Gentiles in performing the priestly service of the gospel of God, so that the offering up of the Gentiles may be acceptable, sanctified by the holy Spirit.^r ¹⁷In Christ Jesus, then, I have reason to boast in what pertains to God. ¹⁸For I will not dare to speak of anything except what Christ has accomplished through me to lead the Gentiles to obedience by word and deed,^s ¹⁹by the power of signs and wonders, by the power of the Spirit [of God], so that from Jerusalem all the way around to Illyricum[‡] I have finished preaching the gospel of Christ. ²⁰Thus I aspire[§] to proclaim the gospel not where Christ has already been named, so that I do not build on another's foundation,^t ²¹but as it is written:^u

"Those who have never been told of him
shall see,
and those who have never heard of
him shall understand."[¶]

Paul's Plans; Need for Prayers. ²²That is why I have so often been prevented from coming to you. ²³But now, since I no longer have any opportunity in these regions and since I have desired to come to you for many years,^v

²⁴I hope to see you in passing as I go to Spain and to be sent on my way there by you, after I have enjoyed being with you for a time.^w ^{25**}Now, however, I am going to Jerusalem to minister to the holy ones.^x ²⁶For Macedonia and Achaia^{††} have decided to make some contribution for the poor among the holy ones in Jerusalem;^y ²⁷they decided to do it, and in fact they are indebted to them, for if the Gentiles have come to share in their spiritual blessings, they ought also to serve them in material blessings.^z ²⁸So when I have completed this and safely handed over this contribution to them, I shall set out by way of you to Spain; ²⁹and I know that in coming to you I shall come in the fullness of Christ's blessing.

³⁰I urge you, [brothers,] by our Lord Jesus Christ and by the love of the Spirit, to join me in the struggle by your prayers to God on my behalf,^a ³¹that I may be delivered from the disobedient in Judea, and that my ministry for Jerusalem may be acceptable to the holy ones, ³²so that I may come to you with joy by the will of God and be refreshed together with you. ³³The God of peace be with all of you. Amen.^b

CHAPTER 16

Phoebe Commended. ^{1‡‡}I commend to you Phoebe our sister, who is [also] a minister^{§§} of the church at Cenchreae,^c ²that you may receive her in the Lord in a manner worthy of the holy ones, and help her in whatever she may need from you, for she has been a benefactor to many and to me as well.

Paul's Greetings. ³Greet Prisca and Aquila,^{¶¶} my co-workers in Christ Jesus,^d ⁴who risked their necks for my life, to whom not only I am grateful but also all the churches of the Gentiles; ⁵greet also the church at their house.*** Greet my beloved Epaenetus, who was the firstfruits in

---

*[15:14–33] Paul sees himself as apostle and benefactor in the priestly service of the gospel and so sketches plans for a mission in Spain, supported by those in Rome.

†[15:14] **Full of goodness:** the opposite of what humanity was filled with according to Rom 1:29–30.

‡[15:19] **Illyricum:** Roman province northwest of Greece on the eastern shore of the Adriatic.

§[15:20] **I aspire:** Paul uses terminology customarily applied to philanthropists. Unlike some philanthropists of his time, Paul does not engage in cheap competition for public acclaim. This explanation of his missionary policy is to assure the Christians in Rome that he is also not planning to remain in that city and build on other people's foundations (cf. 2 Cor 10:12–18). However, he does solicit their help in sending him on his way to Spain, which was considered the limit of the western world. Thus Paul's addressees realize that evangelization may be understood in the broader sense of mission or, as in Rom 1:15, of instruction within the Christian community that derives from the gospel.

¶[15:21] The citation from Is 52:15 concerns the Servant of the Lord. According to Isaiah, the Servant is first of all Israel, which was to bring the knowledge of Yahweh to the nations. In Rom 9–11 Paul showed how Israel failed in this mission. Therefore, he himself undertakes almost singlehandedly Israel's responsibility as the Servant and moves as quickly as possible with the gospel through the Roman empire.

**[15:25–27] Paul may have viewed the contribution he was gathering from Gentile Christians for the poor in Jerusalem (cf. 2 Cor 8–9) as a fulfillment of the vision of Is 60:5–6. In confidence that the messianic fulfillment was taking place, Paul stresses in Rom 14–16 the importance of harmonious relationships between Jews and Gentiles.

††[15:26] **Achaia:** the Roman province of southern Greece.

‡‡[16:1–23] Some authorities regard these verses as a later addition to the letter, but in general the evidence favors the view that they were included in the original. Paul endeavors through the long list of greetings (Rom 16:3–16, 21–23) to establish strong personal contact with congregations that he has not personally encountered before. The combination of Jewish and Gentile names dramatically attests the unity in the gospel that transcends previous barriers of nationality, religious ceremony, or racial status.

§§[16:1] **Minister:** in Greek, *diakonos*; see note on Phil 1:1.

¶¶[16:3] **Prisca and Aquila:** presumably the couple mentioned at Acts 18:2; 1 Cor 16:19; 2 Tm 4:19.

***[16:5] **The church at their house:** i.e., that meets there. Such local assemblies (cf. 1 Cor 16:19; Col 4:15; Phlm 2) might consist of only one or two dozen Christians each. It is understandable, therefore, that such smaller groups might

w. [15:24] 1 Cor 16:6.   x. [15:25] Acts 19:21; 20:22.   y. [15:26] 1 Cor 16:1; 2 Cor 8:1–4; 9:2, 12.   z. [15:27] 9:4 / 1 Cor 9:11.   a. [15:30] 2 Cor 1:11; Phil 1:27; Col 4:3; 2 Thes 3:1.   b. [15:33] 16:20; 2 Cor 13:11; Phil 4:9; 1 Thes 5:23; 2 Thes 3:16; Heb 13:20.   c. [16:1] Acts 18:18.   d. [16:3] Acts 18:2, 18–26; 1 Cor 16:19; 2 Tm 4:19.

---

p. [15:13] 5:1–2.   q. [15:15] 1:5; 12:3.   r. [15:16] 11:13; Phil 2:17.   s. [15:18] Acts 15:12; 2 Cor 12:12.   t. [15:20] 2 Cor 10:13–18.   u. [15:21] Is 52:15.   v. [15:23] 1:10–13; Acts 19:21–22.

Asia for Christ.[e] [6]Greet Mary, who has worked hard for you. [7]Greet Andronicus and Junia,[*] my relatives and my fellow prisoners; they are prominent among the apostles and they were in Christ before me. [8]Greet Ampliatus, my beloved in the Lord. [9]Greet Urbanus, our co-worker in Christ, and my beloved Stachys. [10]Greet Apelles, who is approved in Christ. Greet those who belong to the family of Aristobulus. [11]Greet my relative Herodion. Greet those in the Lord who belong to the family of Narcissus. [12]Greet those workers in the Lord, Tryphaena and Tryphosa. Greet the beloved Persis, who has worked hard in the Lord. [13]Greet Rufus,[†] chosen in the Lord, and his mother and mine.[f] [14]Greet Asyncritus, Phlegon, Hermes, Patrobas, Hermas, and the brothers who are with them. [15]Greet Philologus, Julia, Nereus and his sister, and Olympas, and all the holy ones who are with them. [16]Greet one another with a holy kiss. All the churches of Christ greet you.[g]

Against Factions. [17‡]I urge you, brothers, to watch out for those who create dissensions and obstacles, in opposition to the teaching that you learned; avoid them.[h] [18]For such people do not serve our Lord Christ but their own appetites, and by fair and flattering speech they deceive the hearts of the innocent.[i] [19]For while your obedience is known to all, so that I rejoice over you, I want you to be wise as to what is good, and simple as to what is evil;[j] [20]then the God of peace will quickly crush Satan[§] under your feet. The grace of our Lord Jesus be with you.[k]

Greetings from Corinth. [21]Timothy, my co-worker, greets you; so do Lucius and Jason and Sosipater, my relatives.[l] [22]I, Tertius, the writer of this letter, greet you in the Lord. [23m]Gaius, who is host to me and to the whole church, greets you. Erastus,[¶] the city treasurer, and our brother Quartus greet you. [[24]][**]

Doxology.[††] [[25]Now to him who can strengthen you, according to my gospel and the proclamation of Jesus Christ,[n] according to the revelation of the mystery kept secret for long ages[‡‡] [26]but now manifested through the prophetic writings and, according to the command of the eternal God, made known to all nations to bring about the obedience of faith,[o] [27]to the only wise God, through Jesus Christ be glory forever and ever. Amen.][p]

§[16:20] This verse contains the only mention of Satan in Romans.

¶[16:23] This Erastus is not necessarily to be identified with the Erastus of Acts 19:22 or of 2 Tm 4:20.

**[16:24] Some manuscripts add, similarly to Rom 16:20, "The grace of our Lord Jesus Christ be with you all. Amen."

††[16:25–27] This doxology is assigned variously to the end of Rom 14; 15; 16 in the manuscript tradition. Some manuscripts omit it entirely. Whether written by Paul or not, it forms an admirable conclusion to the letter at this point.

‡‡[16:25] Paul's gospel reveals **the mystery kept secret for long ages**: justification and salvation through faith, with all the implications for Jews and Gentiles that Paul has developed in the letter.

experience difficulty in relating to one another on certain issues. **Firstfruits**: cf. Rom 8:23; 11:16; 1 Cor 16:15.

*[16:7] The name Junia is a woman's name. One ancient Greek manuscript and a number of ancient versions read the name "Julia." Most editors have interpreted it as a man's name, Junias.

†[16:13] This Rufus cannot be identified to any degree of certainty with the Rufus of Mk 15:21.

‡[16:17–18] Paul displays genuine concern for the congregations in Rome by warning them against self-seeking teachers. It would be a great loss, he intimates, if their obedience, which is known to all (cf. Rom 1:8), would be diluted.

e. [16:5] 1 Cor 16:19; Col 4:15; Phlm 2 / 1 Cor 16:15. f. [16:13] Mk 15:21. g. [16:16] 1 Cor 16:20; 2 Cor 13:12; 1 Thes 5:26; 1 Pt 5:14. h. [16:17] Mt 7:15; Ti 3:10.

i. [16:18] Phil 3:18–19; Col 2:4; 2 Pt 2:3. j. [16:19] 1:8; Mt 10:16; 1 Cor 14:20. k. [16:20] 15:33; Gn 3:15; Lk 10:19 / 1 Cor 16:23; 1 Thes 5:28; 2 Thes 3:18. l. [16:21] Acts 16:1–2; 19:22; 20:4; 1 Cor 4:17; 16:10; Phil 2:19–22; Heb 13:23. m. [16:23] Acts 19:29; 1 Cor 1:14 / 2 Tm 4:20. n. [16:25] 1 Cor 2:7; Eph 1:9; 3:3–9; Col 1:26. o. [16:26] 2 Tm 1:10 / Rom 1:5; Eph 3:4–5, 9; 1 Pt 1:20. p. [16:27] 11:36; Gal 1:5; Eph 3:20–21; Phil 4:20; 1 Tm 1:17; 2 Tm 4:18; Heb 13:21; 1 Pt 4:11; 2 Pt 3:18; Jude 25; Rev 1:6.

THE FIRST LETTER TO THE
CORINTHIANS

〜❧〜

Paul's first letter to the church of Corinth provides us with a fuller insight into the life of an early Christian community of the first generation than any other book of the New Testament. Through it we can glimpse both the strengths and the weaknesses of this small group in a great city of the ancient world, men and women who had accepted the good news of Christ and were now trying to realize in their lives the implications of their baptism. Paul, who had founded the community and continued to look after it as a father, responds both to questions addressed to him and to situations of which he had been informed. In doing so, he reveals much about himself, his teaching, and the way in which he conducted his work of apostleship. Some things are puzzling because we have the correspondence only in one direction. For the person studying this letter, it seems to raise as many questions as it answers, but without it our knowledge of church life in the middle of the first century would be much poorer.

Paul established a Christian community in Corinth about the year 51, on his second missionary journey. The city, a commercial crossroads, was a melting pot full of devotees of various pagan cults and marked by a measure of moral depravity not unusual in a great seaport. The Acts of the Apostles suggests that moderate success attended Paul's efforts among the Jews in Corinth at first, but that they soon turned against him (Acts 18:1–8). More fruitful was his year and a half spent among the Gentiles (Acts 18:11), which won to the faith many of the city's poor and underprivileged (1 Cor 1:26). After his departure the eloquent Apollos, an Alexandrian Jewish Christian, rendered great service to the community, expounding "from the scriptures that the Messiah is Jesus" (Acts 18:24–28).

While Paul was in Ephesus on his third journey (1 Cor 16:8; Acts 19:1–20), he received disquieting news about Corinth. The community there was displaying open factionalism, as certain members were identifying themselves exclusively with individual Christian leaders and interpreting Christian teaching as a superior wisdom for the initiated few (1 Cor 1:10–4:21). The community lacked the decisiveness to take appropriate action against one of its members who was living publicly in an incestuous union (1 Cor 5:1–13). Other members engaged in legal conflicts in pagan courts of law (1 Cor 6:1–11); still others may have participated in religious prostitution (1 Cor 6:12–20) or temple sacrifices (1 Cor 10:14–22).

The community's ills were reflected in its liturgy. In the celebration of the Eucharist certain members discriminated against others, drank too freely at the agape, or fellowship meal, and denied Christian social courtesies to the poor among the membership (1 Cor 11:17–22). Charisms such as ecstatic prayer, attributed freely to the impulse of the holy Spirit, were more highly prized than works of charity (1 Cor 13:1–2, 8), and were used at times in a disorderly way (1 Cor 14:1–40). Women appeared at the assembly without the customary head-covering (1 Cor 11:3–16), and perhaps were quarreling over their right to address the assembly (1 Cor 14:34–35).

Still other problems with which Paul had to deal concerned matters of conscience discussed among the faithful members of the community: the eating of meat that had been sacrificed to idols (1 Cor 8:1–13), the use of sex in marriage (1 Cor 7:1–7), and the attitude to be taken by the unmarried toward marriage in view of the possible proximity of Christ's second coming (1 Cor 7:25–40). There was also a doctrinal matter that called for Paul's attention, for some members of the community, despite their belief in the resurrection of Christ, were denying the possibility of general bodily resurrection.

To treat this wide spectrum of questions, Paul wrote this letter from Ephesus about the year A.D. 56. The majority of the Corinthian Christians may well have been quite faithful. Paul writes on their behalf to guard against the threats posed to the community by the views and conduct of various minorities. He writes with confidence in the authority of his apostolic mission, and he presumes that the Corinthians, despite their deficiencies, will recognize and accept it. On the other hand, he does not hesitate to exercise his authority as his judgment dictates in each situation, even going so far as to promise a direct confrontation with recalcitrants, should the abuses he scores remain uncorrected (1 Cor 4:18–21).

The letter illustrates well the mind and character of Paul. Although he is impelled to insist on his office as founder of the community, he recognizes that he is only one servant of God among many and generously acknowledges the labors of Apollos (1 Cor 3:5–8). He provides us in this letter with many valuable examples of his method of theological reflection and exposition. He always treats the questions at issue on the level of the purity of Christian teaching and conduct. Certain passages of the letter are of the greatest importance for the understanding of early Christian teaching on the Eucharist (1 Cor 10:14–22; 11:17–34) and on the resurrection of the body (1 Cor 15:1–58).

Paul's authorship of 1 Corinthians, apart from a few verses that some regard as later interpolations, has never been seriously questioned. Some scholars have proposed, however, that the letter as we have it contains portions of more than one original Pauline letter. We know that Paul wrote at least two other letters to Corinth (see 1 Cor 5:9; 2 Cor 2:3–4) in addition to the two that we now have; this theory holds that the additional letters are actually contained within the two canonical ones. Most commentators, however, find 1 Corinthians quite understandable as a single coherent work.

The principal divisions of the First Letter to the Corinthians are the following:

I. Address (1:1–9)
II. Disorders in the Corinthian Community (1:10–6:20)
    A. Divisions in the Church (1:10–4:21)
    B. Moral Disorders (5:1–6:20)
III. Answers to the Corinthians' Questions (7:1–11:1)
    A. Marriage and Virginity (7:1–40)
    B. Offerings to Idols (8:1–11:1)
IV. Problems in Liturgical Assemblies (11:2–14:40)
    A. Women's Headdresses (11:3–16)
    B. The Lord's Supper (11:17–34)
    C. Spiritual Gifts (12:1–14:40)
V. The Resurrection (15:1–58)
    A. The Resurrection of Christ (15:1–11)
    B. The Resurrection of the Dead (15:12–34)
    C. The Manner of the Resurrection (15:35–58)
VI. Conclusion (16:1–24)

I. ADDRESS*

CHAPTER 1

Greeting. ¹Paul, called to be an apostle of Christ Jesus by the will of God,† and Sosthenes our brother,ᵃ ²to the church of God that is in Corinth, to you who have been sanctified in Christ Jesus, called to be holy, with all those everywhere who call upon the name of our Lord Jesus Christ, their Lord and ours.ᵇ ³Grace to you and peace from God our Father and the Lord Jesus Christ.

Thanksgiving. ⁴I give thanks to my God always on your account for the grace of God bestowed on you in Christ Jesus, ⁵that in him you were enriched in every way, with all discourse and all knowledge, ⁶as the testimony‡ to Christ was confirmed among you, ⁷so that you are not lacking in any spiritual gift as you wait for the revelation of our Lord Jesus Christ.ᶜ ⁸He will keep you firm

---

*[1:1–9] Paul follows the conventional form for the opening of a Hellenistic letter (cf. Rom 1:1–7), but expands the opening with details carefully chosen to remind the readers of their situation and to suggest some of the issues the letter will discuss.

†[1:1] **Called . . . by the will of God:** Paul's mission and the church's existence are grounded in God's initiative. God's call, grace, and fidelity are central ideas in this introduction, emphasized by repetition and wordplays in the Greek.

a. [1:1] Rom 1:1.

‡[1:6] **The testimony:** this defines the purpose of Paul's mission (see also 1 Cor 15:15 and the note on 1 Cor 2:1). The forms of his testimony include oral preaching and instruction, his letters, and the life he leads as an apostle.

b. [1:2] Acts 18:1–11.   c. [1:7] Ti 2:13.

to the end, irreproachable on the day of our Lord Jesus [Christ].[d] [9]God is faithful, and by him you were called to fellowship with his Son, Jesus Christ our Lord.[e]

II. DISORDERS IN THE CORINTHIAN COMMUNITY

A. Divisions in the Church[*]

Groups and Slogans. [10]I urge you, brothers, in the name of our Lord Jesus Christ, that all of you agree in what you say, and that there be no divisions among you, but that you be united in the same mind and in the same purpose.[f] [11]For it has been reported to me about you, my brothers, by Chloe's people, that there are rivalries among you. [12]I mean that each of you is saying, "I belong to[†] Paul," or "I belong to Apollos," or "I belong to Cephas," or "I belong to Christ."[g] [13*]Is Christ divided? Was Paul crucified for you? Or were you baptized in the name of Paul? [14]I give thanks [to God] that I baptized none of you except Crispus and Gaius,[h] [15]so that no one can say you were baptized in my name. [16](I baptized the household of Stephanas also; beyond that I do not know whether I baptized anyone else.)[i] [17§]For Christ did not send me to baptize but to preach the gospel, and not with the wisdom of human eloquence,[¶] so that the cross of Christ might not be emptied of its meaning.[j]

─────────

*[1:10–4:21] The first problem Paul addresses is that of divisions within the community. Although we are unable to reconstruct the situation in Corinth completely, Paul clearly traces the divisions back to a false self-image on the part of the Corinthians, coupled with a false understanding of the apostles who preached to them (cf. 1 Cor 4:6, 9; 9:1–5) and of the Christian message itself. In these chapters he attempts to deal with those underlying factors and to bring the Corinthians back to a more correct perspective.

†[1:12] **I belong to**: the activities of Paul and Apollos in Corinth are described in Acts 18. **Cephas** (i.e., "the Rock," a name by which Paul designates Peter also in 1 Cor 3:22; 9:5; 15:5 and in Gal 1:18; 2:9, 11, 14) may well have passed through Corinth; he could have baptized some members of the community either there or elsewhere. The reference to **Christ** may be intended ironically here.

‡[1:13–17] The reference to baptism and the contrast with preaching the gospel in v 17a suggest that some Corinthians were paying special allegiance to the individuals who initiated them into the community.

§[1:17b–18] The basic theme of 1 Cor 1–4 is announced. Adherence to individual leaders has something to do with differences in rhetorical ability and also with certain presuppositions regarding wisdom, eloquence, and effectiveness (power), which Paul judges to be in conflict with the gospel and the cross.

¶[1:17b] **Not with the wisdom of human eloquence**: both of the nouns employed here involve several levels of meaning, on which Paul deliberately plays as his thought unfolds. **Wisdom** (*sophia*) may be philosophical and speculative, but in biblical usage the term primarily denotes practical knowledge such as is demonstrated in the choice and effective application of means to achieve an end. The same term can designate the arts of building (cf. 1 Cor 3:10) or of persuasive speaking (cf. 1 Cor 2:4) or effectiveness in achieving salvation. **Eloquence** (*logos*): this translation emphasizes one possible meaning of the term *logos* (cf. the references to rhetorical style and persuasiveness in 1 Cor 2:1, 4). But the term itself may denote an internal reasoning process,

─────────

Paradox of the Cross. [18]The message of the cross is foolishness to those who are perishing, but to us who are being saved it is the power of God.[k] [19]For it is written:

"I will destroy the wisdom of the wise,
   and the learning of the learned I will set aside."[l]

[20]Where is the wise one? Where is the scribe? Where is the debater of this age? Has not God made the wisdom of the world foolish?[m] [21**]For since in the wisdom of God the world did not come to know God through wisdom, it was the will of God through the foolishness of the proclamation to save those who have faith. [22]For Jews demand signs and Greeks look for wisdom,[n] [23]but we proclaim Christ crucified, a stumbling block to Jews and foolishness to Gentiles,[o] [24]but to those who are called, Jews and Greeks alike, Christ the power of God and the wisdom of God. [25]For the foolishness of God is wiser than human wisdom, and the weakness of God is stronger than human strength.

The Corinthians and Paul.[††] [26]Consider your own calling, brothers. Not many of you were wise by human standards, not many were powerful, not many were of noble birth. [27]Rather, God chose the foolish of the world to shame the wise, and God chose the weak of the world to shame the strong,[p] [28]and God chose the lowly and despised of the world, those who count for nothing, to reduce to nothing those who are something, [29]so that no human being might boast[‡‡] before God.[q] [30]It is due to him that you are in Christ Jesus, who became for us wisdom from God, as well as righteousness, sanctification, and redemption,[r] [31]so that, as it is written, "Whoever boasts, should boast in the Lord."[s]

─────────

plan, or intention, as well as an external word, speech, or message. So by his expression *ouk en sophia logou* in the context of gospel preaching, Paul may intend to exclude both human ways of reasoning or thinking about things and human rhetorical technique. **Human**: this adjective does not stand in the Greek text but is supplied from the context. Paul will begin immediately to distinguish between *sophia* and *logos* from their divine counterparts and play them off against each other.

**[1:21–25] True wisdom and power are to be found paradoxically where one would least expect them, in the place of their apparent negation. To human eyes the crucified Christ symbolizes impotence and absurdity.

††[1:26–2:5] The pattern of God's wisdom and power is exemplified in their own experience, if they interpret it rightly (1 Cor 1:26–31), and can also be read in their experience of Paul as he first appeared among them preaching the gospel (1 Cor 2:1–5).

‡‡[1:29–31] "Boasting (about oneself)" is a Pauline expression for the radical sin, the claim to autonomy on the part of a creature, the illusion that we live and are saved by our own resources. "Boasting in the Lord" (1 Cor 1:31), on the other hand, is the acknowledgment that we live only from God and for God.

─────────

k. [1:18] 2:14 / Rom 1:16. l. [1:19] Is 29:14. m. [1:20] Is 19:12. n. [1:22] Mt 12:38; 16:1 / Acts 17:18–21. o. [1:23] 2:2; Gal 3:1 / Gal 5:11. p. [1:27] Jas 2:5. q. [1:29] Eph 2:9. r. [1:30] Rom 4:17 / 6:11; Rom 3:24–26; 2 Cor 5:21 / Eph 1:7; Col 1:14; 1 Thes 5:23. s. [1:31] Jer 9:23; 2 Cor 10:17.

d. [1:8] Phil 1:6. e. [1:9] 1 Jn 1:3. f. [1:10] Phil 2:2. g. [1:12] 3:4, 22; 16:12; Acts 18:24–28. h. [1:14] Acts 18:8 / Rom 16:23. i. [1:16] 16:15–17. j. [1:17] 2:1, 4.

CHAPTER 2

¹When I came to you, brothers, proclaiming the mystery of God,* I did not come with sublimity of words or of wisdom.ᵗ ²For I resolved to know nothing while I was with you except Jesus Christ, and him crucified.ᵘ ³I came to you in weakness† and fear and much trembling, ⁴and my message and my proclamation were not with persuasive [words of] wisdom,‡ but with a demonstration of spirit and power,ᵛ ⁵so that your faith might rest not on human wisdom but on the power of God.ʷ

The True Wisdom.§ ⁶Yet we do speak a wisdom to those who are mature, but not a wisdom of this age, nor of the rulers of this age who are passing away. ⁷Rather, we speak God's wisdom,⁵ mysterious, hidden, which God predetermined before the ages for our glory, ⁸and which none of the rulers of this age** knew; for if they had known it, they would not have crucified the Lord of glory. ⁹But as it is written:

"What eye has not seen, and ear has not
　　heard,
and what has not entered the human
　　heart,
what God has prepared for those
　　who love him,"ˣ

¹⁰ʸthis God has revealed to us through the Spirit. For the Spirit scrutinizes everything, even the depths of God. ¹¹Among human beings, who knows what pertains to a person except the spirit of the person that is within? Similarly, no one knows what pertains to God except the Spirit of God. ¹²We have not received the spirit of the world but the Spirit that is from God, so that we may understand the things freely given us by God. ¹³And we speak about them not with words taught by human wisdom, but with words taught by the Spirit, describing spiritual realities in spiritual terms.††

¹⁴Now the natural person‡‡ does not accept what pertains to the Spirit of God, for to him it is foolishness, and he cannot understand it, because it is judged spiritually. ¹⁵The spiritual person, however, can judge everything but is not subject to judgment§§ by anyone.

¹⁶For "who has known the mind of the Lord, so as to counsel him?" But we have the mind of Christ.ᶻ

CHAPTER 3

¹⁵⁵Brothers, I could not talk to you as spiritual people, but as fleshly people,*** as infants in Christ. ²I fed you milk, not solid food, because you were unable to take it. Indeed, you are still not able, even now,ᵃ ³for you are still of the flesh. While there is jealousy and rivalry among you,†††

---

*[2:1] **The mystery of God:** God's secret, known only to himself, is his plan for the salvation of his people; it is clear from 1 Cor 1:18–25; 2:2, 8–10 that this secret involves Jesus and the cross. In place of **mystery**, other good manuscripts read "testimony" (cf. 1 Cor 1:6).

†[2:3] The **weakness** of the crucified Jesus is reflected in Paul's own bearing (cf. 2 Cor 10–13). **Fear and much trembling:** reverential fear based on a sense of God's transcendence permeates Paul's existence and preaching. Compare his advice to the Philippians to work out their salvation with "fear and trembling" (Phil 2:12), because God is at work in them just as his exalting power was paradoxically at work in the emptying, humiliation, and obedience of Jesus to death on the cross (Phil 2:6–11).

‡[2:4] Among many manuscript readings here the best is either "not with the persuasion of wisdom" or "not with persuasive words of wisdom," which differ only by a nuance. Whichever reading is accepted, the inefficacy of human wisdom for salvation is contrasted with the power of the cross.

§[2:6–3:4] Paul now asserts paradoxically what he has previously been denying. To the Greeks who "are looking for wisdom" (1 Cor 1:22), he does indeed bring a wisdom, but of a higher order and an entirely different quality, the only wisdom really worthy of the name. The Corinthians would be able to grasp Paul's preaching as wisdom and enter into a wisdom-conversation with him if they were more open to the Spirit and receptive to the new insight and language that the Spirit teaches.

⁵[2:7–10a] **God's wisdom:** his plan for our salvation. This was his own eternal secret that no one else could fathom, but in this new age of salvation he has graciously revealed it to us. For the pattern of God's secret, hidden to others and now revealed to the Church, cf. also Rom 11:25–36; 16:25–27; Eph 1:3–10; 3:3–11; Col 1:25–28.

[2:8] **The rulers of this age: this suggests not only the political leaders of the Jews and Romans under whom Jesus was crucified (cf. Acts 4:25–28) but also the cosmic powers behind them (cf. Eph 1:20–23; 3:10). **They would not have crucified the Lord of glory:** they became the unwitting executors of God's plan, which will paradoxically bring about their own conquest and submission (1 Cor 15:24–28).

††[2:13] **In spiritual terms:** the Spirit teaches spiritual people a new mode of perception (1 Cor 2:12) and an appropriate language by which they can share their self-understanding, their knowledge about what God has done in them. The final phrase in 1 Cor 2:13 can also be translated "describing spiritual realities to spiritual people," in which case it prepares for 1 Cor 2:14–16.

‡‡[2:14] **The natural person:** see note on 1 Cor 3:1.

§§[2:15] **The spiritual person . . . is not subject to judgment:** since spiritual persons have been given knowledge of what pertains to God (1 Cor 2:11–12), they share in God's own capacity to judge. One to whom the mind of the Lord (and of Christ) is revealed (1 Cor 2:16) can be said to share in some sense in God's exemption from counseling and criticism.

⁵⁵[3:1–4] The Corinthians desire a sort of wisdom dialogue or colloquy with Paul; they are looking for solid, adult food, and he appears to disappoint their expectations. Paul counters: if such a dialogue has not yet taken place, the reason is that they are still at an immature stage of development (cf. 1 Cor 2:6).

***[3:1] **Spiritual people . . . fleshly people:** Paul employs two clusters of concepts and terms to distinguish what later theology will call the "natural" and the "supernatural." (1) The natural person (1 Cor 2:14) is one whose existence, perceptions, and behavior are determined by purely natural principles, the *psychē* (1 Cor 2:14) and the *sarx* (flesh, a biblical term that connotes creatureliness, 1 Cor 3:1, 3). Such persons are only infants (1 Cor 3:1); they remain on a purely human level (*anthrōpoi*, 1 Cor 3:4). (2) On the other hand, they are called to be animated by a higher principle, the *pneuma*, God's spirit. They are to become spiritual (*pneumatikoi*, 1 Cor 3:1) and mature (1 Cor 2:6) in their perceptions and behavior (cf. Gal 5:16–26). The culmination of existence in the Spirit is described in 1 Cor 15:44–49.

†††[3:3–4] Jealousy, rivalry, and divisions in the community are symptoms of their arrested development; they reveal the immaturity both of their self-understanding (1 Cor 3:4) and of the judgments about their apostles (1 Cor 3:21).

---

t. [2:1] 1:17.　u. [2:2] 1:23; Gal 6:14.　v. [2:4] 4:20; Rom 15:19; 1 Thes 1:5.　w. [2:5] 2 Cor 4:7.　x. [2:9] Is 64:3.

y. [2:10] Mt 11:25; 13:11; 16:17.　z. [2:16] Wis 9:13; Is 40:13; Rom 11:34.　a. [3:2] Heb 5:12–14.

are you not of the flesh and behaving in an ordinary human way?[b] [4]Whenever someone says, "I belong to Paul," and another, "I belong to Apollos," are you not merely human?[c]
The Role of God's Ministers.[*] [5]What is Apollos, after all, and what is Paul? Ministers[†] through whom you became believers, just as the Lord assigned each one. [6]I planted, Apollos watered, but God caused the growth.[d] [7]Therefore, neither the one who plants nor the one who waters is anything, but only God, who causes the growth. [8]The one who plants and the one who waters are equal, and each will receive wages in proportion to his labor. [9]For we are God's co-workers; you are God's field, God's building.[e]
[10‡]According to the grace of God given to me, like a wise master builder I laid a foundation, and another is building upon it. But each one must be careful how he builds upon it, [11]for no one can lay a foundation other than the one that is there, namely, Jesus Christ. [12]If anyone builds on this foundation with gold, silver, precious stones, wood, hay, or straw, [13]the work of each will come to light, for the Day[§] will disclose it. It will be revealed with fire, and the fire [itself] will test the quality of each one's work.[f] [14]If the work stands that someone built upon the foundation, that person will receive a wage. [15]But if someone's work is burned up, that one will suffer loss; the person will be saved,[¶] but only as through fire. [16]Do you not know that you are the temple of God, and that the Spirit of God dwells in you?[g] [17]If anyone destroys God's temple, God will destroy that person; for the temple of God, which you are, is holy.[**]

[18]Let no one deceive himself. If anyone among you considers himself wise in this age, let him become a fool so as to become wise.[h] [19]For the wisdom of this world is foolishness in the eyes of God, for it is written:[i] ·

"He catches the wise in their own ruses,"

[20]and again:

"The Lord knows the thoughts of the wise,
      that they are vain."[j]

[21††]So let no one boast about human beings, for everything belongs to you,[k] [22]Paul or Apollos or Cephas, or the world or life or death, or the present or the future: all belong to you, [23]and you to Christ, and Christ to God.

CHAPTER 4 ·
[1]Thus should one regard us: as servants of Christ and stewards of the mysteries of God.[l] [2]Now it is of course required of stewards that they be found trustworthy. [3]It does not concern me in the least that I be judged by you or any human tribunal; I do not even pass judgment on myself; [4]I am not conscious of anything against me, but I do not thereby stand acquitted; the one who judges me is the Lord.[m] [5]Therefore, do not make any judgment before the appointed time, until the Lord comes, for he will bring to light what is hidden in darkness and will manifest the motives of our hearts, and then everyone will receive praise from God.
Paul's Life as Pattern.[‡‡] [6]I have applied these things to myself and Apollos for your benefit, brothers, so that you may learn from us not to go beyond what is written,[§§] so that none of you

---

*[3:5–4:5] The Corinthians tend to evaluate their leaders by the criteria of human wisdom and to exaggerate their importance. Paul views the role of the apostles in the light of his theology of spiritual gifts (cf. 1 Cor 12–14, where the charism of the apostle heads the lists). The essential aspects of all spiritual gifts (1 Cor 12:4–6 presents them as gifts of grace, as services, and as modes of activity) are exemplified by the apostolate, which is a gift of grace (1 Cor 3:10) through which God works (1 Cor 3:9) and a form of service (1 Cor 3:5) for the common good (elsewhere expressed by the verb "build up," suggested here by the image of the building, 1 Cor 3:9). The apostles serve the church, but their accountability is to God and to Christ (1 Cor 4:1–5).
†[3:5] **Ministers**: for other expressions of Paul's understanding of himself as minister or steward to the church, cf. 1 Cor 4:1; 9:17, 19–27; 2 Cor 3:6–9; 4:1; 5:18; 6:3–4; and 2 Cor 11:23 (the climax of Paul's defense).
‡[3:10–11] There are diverse functions in the service of the community, but each individual's task is serious, and each will stand accountable for the quality of his contribution.
§[3:13] **The Day**: the great day of Yahweh, the day of judgment, which can be a time of either gloom or joy. **Fire** both destroys and purifies.
¶[3:15] **Will be saved**: although Paul can envision very harsh divine punishment (cf. 1 Cor 3:17), he appears optimistic about the success of divine corrective means both here and elsewhere (cf. 1 Cor 5:5; 11:32 [discipline]). The text of 1 Cor 3:15 has sometimes been used to support the notion of purgatory, though it does not envisage this.
[3:17] **Holy: i.e., "belonging to God." The cultic sanctity of the community is a fundamental theological reality to which Paul frequently alludes (cf. 1 Cor 1:2, 30; 6:11; 7:14).

††[3:21–23] These verses pick up the line of thought of 1 Cor 1:10–13. If the Corinthians were genuinely wise (1 Cor 3:18–20), their perceptions would be reversed, and they would see everything in the world and all those with whom they exist in the church in their true relations with one another. Paul assigns all the persons involved in the theological universe a position on a scale: God, Christ, church members, church leaders. Read from top to bottom, the scale expresses ownership; read from bottom to top, the obligation to serve. This picture should be complemented by similar statements such as those in 1 Cor 8:6 and 1 Cor 15:20–28.
‡‡[4:6–21] This is an emotionally charged peroration to the discussion about divisions. It contains several exhortations and statements of Paul's purpose in writing (cf. 1 Cor 4:6, 14–17, 21) that counterbalance the initial exhortation at 1 Cor 1:10.
§§[4:6] **That you may learn from us not to go beyond what is written**: the words "to go" are not in the Greek, but have here been added as the minimum necessary to elicit sense from this difficult passage. It probably means that the Corinthians should avoid the false wisdom of vain speculation, contenting themselves with Paul's proclamation of the cross, which is the fulfillment of God's promises in the Old Testament (what is written). **Inflated with pride**: literally, "puffed up," i.e., arrogant, filled with a sense of self-importance. The term is particularly Pauline, found in the New

---

b. [3:3] Jas 3:13–16.   c. [3:4] 1:12.   d. [3:6] Acts 18:1–11, 24–28.
e. [3:9] Eph 2:20–22; 1 Pt 2:5.   f. [3:13] Mt 3:11–12; 2 Thes 1:7–10.
g. [3:16] 6:19; 2 Cor 6:16; Eph 2:20–22.
h. [3:18] 8:2; Is 5:21; Gal 6:3.   i. [3:19] 1:20 / Jb 5:13.   j. [3:20] Ps 94:11.   k. [3:21] 4:6 / Rom 8:32.   l. [4:1] Ti 1:7; 1 Pt 4:10.   m. [4:4] 2 Cor 1:12 / Rom 2:16; 2 Cor 5:10.

will be inflated with pride in favor of one person over against another. [7]Who confers distinction upon you? What do you possess that you have not received? But if you have received it, why are you boasting as if you did not receive it? [8]You are already satisfied; you have already grown rich; you have become kings* without us! Indeed, I wish that you had become kings, so that we also might become kings with you.

[9†]For as I see it, God has exhibited us apostles as the last of all, like people sentenced to death, since we have become a spectacle to the world, to angels and human beings alike.[n] [10]We are fools on Christ's account, but you are wise in Christ; we are weak, but you are strong; you are held in honor, but we in disrepute.[o] [11]To this very hour we go hungry and thirsty, we are poorly clad and roughly treated, we wander about homeless[p] [12]and we toil, working with our own hands. When ridiculed, we bless; when persecuted, we endure;[q] [13]when slandered, we respond gently. We have become like the world's rubbish, the scum of all, to this very moment.

[14]I am writing you this not to shame you, but to admonish you as my beloved children.[‡] [15]Even if you should have countless guides to Christ, yet you do not have many fathers, for I became your father in Christ Jesus through the gospel.[r] [16]Therefore, I urge you, be imitators of me.[s] [17]For this reason I am sending you Timothy,

who is my beloved and faithful son in the Lord; he will remind you of my ways in Christ [Jesus], just as I teach them everywhere in every church.[t]

[18§]Some have become inflated with pride, as if I were not coming to you. [19]But I will come to you soon, if the Lord is willing, and I shall ascertain not the talk of these inflated people but their power. [20]For the kingdom of God is not a matter of talk but of power.[u] [21]Which do you prefer? Shall I come to you with a rod, or with love and a gentle spirit?[v]

B. Moral Disorders[¶]

CHAPTER 5

A Case of Incest.[**] [1]It is widely reported that there is immorality among you, and immorality of a kind not found even among pagans— a man living with his father's wife.[w] [2]And you are inflated with pride.[††] Should you not rather have been sorrowful? The one who did this deed should be expelled from your midst. [3]I, for my part, although absent in body but present in spirit, have already, as if present, pronounced judgment on the one who has committed this deed,[x] [4]in the name of [our] Lord Jesus: when you have gathered together and I am with you in spirit with the power of the Lord Jesus, [5]you are to deliver this man to Satan[‡‡] for the destruction of his flesh, so that his spirit may be saved on the day of the Lord.[y]

[6z]Your boasting is not appropriate. Do you not know that a little yeast[§§] leavens all the

---

Testament only in 1 Cor 4:6, 18–19; 5:2; 8:1; 13:4; Col 2:18 (cf. the related noun at 2 Cor 12:20). It sometimes occurs in conjunction with the theme of "boasting," as in 1 Cor 4:6–7 here.

*[4:8] **Satisfied . . . rich . . . kings**: these three statements could also be punctuated as questions continuing the series begun in v 7. In any case these expressions reflect a tendency at Corinth toward an overrealized eschatology, a form of self-deception that draws Paul's irony. The underlying attitude has implications for the Corinthians' thinking about other issues, notably morality and the resurrection, that Paul will address later in the letter.

†[4:9–13] A rhetorically effective catalogue of the circumstances of apostolic existence, in the course of which Paul ironically contrasts his own sufferings with the Corinthians' illusion that they have passed beyond the folly of the passion and have already reached the condition of glory. His language echoes that of the beatitudes and woes, which assert a future reversal of present conditions. Their present sufferings ("to this very hour," 11) place the apostles in the class of those to whom the beatitudes promise future relief (Mt 5:3–11; Lk 6:20–23); whereas the Corinthians' image of themselves as "already" filled, rich, ruling (1 Cor 4:8), as wise, strong, and honored (1 Cor 4:10) places them paradoxically in the position of those whom the woes threaten with future undoing (Lk 6:24–26). They have lost sight of the fact that the reversal is predicted for the future.

‡[4:14–17] **My beloved children**: the close of the argument is dominated by the tender metaphor of the father who not only gives his children life but also educates them. Once he has begotten them through his preaching, Paul continues to present the gospel to them existentially, by his life as well as by his word, and they are to learn, as children do, by imitating their parents (1 Cor 4:16). The reference to the **rod** in 1 Cor 4:21 belongs to the same image-complex. So does the image of the **ways** in 1 Cor 4:17: the ways that Paul teaches everywhere, "his ways in Christ Jesus," mean a behavior pattern quite different from the human ways along which the Corinthians are walking (1 Cor 3:3).

§[4:18–21] 1 Cor 4:20 picks up the contrast between a certain kind of talk (*logos*) and true power (*dynamis*) from 1 Cor 1:17–18 and 1 Cor 2:4–5. The kingdom, which many of them imagine to be fully present in their lives (1 Cor 4:8), will be rather unexpectedly disclosed in the strength of Paul's encounter with them, if they make a powerful intervention on his part necessary. Compare the similar ending to an argument in 2 Cor 13:1–4, 10.

¶[5:1–6:20] Paul now takes up a number of other matters that require regulation. These have come to his attention by hearsay (1 Cor 5:1), probably in reports brought by "Chloe's people" (1 Cor 1:11).

**[5:1–13] Paul first deals with the incestuous union of a man with his stepmother (1 Cor 5:1–8) and then attempts to clarify general admonitions he has given about associating with fellow Christians guilty of immorality (1 Cor 5:9–13). Each of these three brief paragraphs expresses the same idea: the need of separation between the holy and the unholy.

††[5:2] **Inflated with pride**: this remark and the reference to **boasting** in 1 Cor 5:6 suggest that they are proud of themselves despite the infection in their midst, tolerating and possibly even approving the situation. The attitude expressed in 1 Cor 6:2, 13 may be influencing their thinking in this case.

‡‡[5:5] **Deliver this man to Satan**: once the sinner is expelled from the church, the sphere of Jesus' lordship and victory over sin, he will be in the region outside over which Satan is still master. **For the destruction of his flesh**: the purpose of the penalty is medicinal: through affliction, sin's grip over him may be destroyed and the path to repentance and reunion laid open. With Paul's instructions for an excommunication ceremony here, contrast his recommendations for the reconciliation of a sinner in 2 Cor 2:5–11.

§§[5:6] **A little yeast**: yeast, which induces fermentation, is a natural symbol for a source of corruption that becomes all-pervasive. The expression is proverbial.

---

n. [4:9] 15:31; Rom 8:36; 2 Cor 4:8–12; 11:23 / Heb 10:33.   o. [4:10] 1:18; 3:18; 2 Cor 11:19 / 1 Cor 2:3; 2 Cor 13:9.   p. [4:11] Rom 8:35; 2 Cor 11:23–27.   q. [4:12] Acts 9:6–14; 18:3; 20:34; 1 Thes 2:9 / 1 Pt 3:9.   r. [4:15] Gal 4:19; Phlm 10.   s. [4:16] 11:1; Phil 3:17; 4:9; 1 Thes 1:6; 2 Thes 3:7, 9.

t. [4:17] 16:10; Acts 19:22.   u. [4:20] 2:4; 1 Thes 1:5.   v. [4:21] 2 Cor 1:23; 10:2.   w. [5:1] Lv 18:7–8; 20:11; Dt 27:20.   x. [5:3] Col 2:5.   y. [5:5] 1 Tm 1:20.   z. [5:6] Gal 5:9.

dough? [7c]Clear out the old yeast, so that you may become a fresh batch of dough, inasmuch as you are unleavened. For our paschal lamb, Christ, has been sacrificed.[a] [8]Therefore, let us celebrate the feast, not with the old yeast, the yeast of malice and wickedness, but with the unleavened bread of sincerity and truth.[b]

[9†]I wrote you in my letter not to associate with immoral people, [10]not at all referring to the immoral of this world or the greedy and robbers or idolaters; for you would then have to leave the world.[c] [11]But I now write to you not to associate with anyone named a brother, if he is immoral, greedy, an idolater, a slanderer, a drunkard, or a robber, not even to eat with such a person.[d] [12]For why should I be judging outsiders? Is it not your business to judge those within? [13]God will judge those outside. "Purge the evil person from your midst."[e]

CHAPTER 6

Lawsuits Before Unbelievers.[‡] [1]How can any one of you with a case against another dare to bring it to the unjust for judgment instead of to the holy ones? [2§§]Do you not know that the holy ones will judge the world? If the world is to be judged by you, are you unqualified for the lowest law courts?[f] [3]Do you not know that we will judge angels? Then why not everyday matters? [4]If, therefore, you have courts for everyday matters, do you seat as judges people of no standing in the church? [5]I say this to shame you. Can it be that there is not one among you wise enough to be able to settle a case between brothers? [6]But rather brother goes to court against brother, and that before unbelievers?

[7]Now indeed [then] it is, in any case, a failure on your part that you have lawsuits against one another. Why not rather put up with injustice? Why not rather let yourselves be cheated?[g] [8]Instead, you inflict injustice and cheat, and this to brothers. [9§]Do you not know that the unjust will not inherit the kingdom of God? Do not be deceived; neither fornicators nor idolaters nor adulterers nor boy prostitutes[¶] nor sodomites[h] [10]nor thieves nor the greedy nor drunkards nor slanderers nor robbers will inherit the kingdom of God. [11]That is what some of you used to be; but now you have had yourselves washed, you were sanctified, you were justified in the name of the Lord Jesus Christ and in the Spirit of our God.[i]

Sexual Immorality.[*] [12]"Everything is lawful for me,"[††] but not everything is beneficial. "Everything is lawful for me," but I will not let myself be dominated by anything.[j] [13]"Food for the stomach and the stomach for food," but God will do away with both the one and the other. The body, however, is not for immorality, but for the Lord, and the Lord is for the body; [14]God raised the Lord and will also raise us by his power.[k]

[15]Do you not know that your bodies are members of Christ? Shall I then take Christ's members and make them the members of a prostitute?[‡‡] Of course not![l] [16][Or] do you not

§[6:9–10] A catalogue of typical vices that exclude from the kingdom of God and that should be excluded from God's church. Such lists (cf. 1 Cor 5:10) reflect the common moral sensibility of the New Testament period.

¶[6:9] The Greek word translated as **boy prostitutes** may refer to catamites, i.e., boys or young men who were kept for purposes of prostitution, a practice not uncommon in the Greco-Roman world. In Greek mythology this was the function of Ganymede, the "cupbearer of the gods," whose Latin name was Catamitus. The term translated **sodomites** refers to adult males who indulged in homosexual practices with such boys. See similar condemnations of such practices in Rom 1:26–27; 1 Tm 1:10.

**[6:12–20] Paul now turns to the opinion of some Corinthians that sexuality is a morally indifferent area (1 Cor 6:12–13). This leads him to explain the mutual relation between the Lord Jesus and our bodies (1 Cor 6:13b) in a densely packed paragraph that contains elements of a profound theology of sexuality (1 Cor 6:15–20).

††[6:12–13] **Everything is lawful for me**: the Corinthians may have derived this slogan from Paul's preaching about Christian freedom, but they mean something different by it: they consider sexual satisfaction a matter as indifferent as food, and they attribute no lasting significance to bodily functions (1 Cor 6:13a). Paul begins to deal with the slogan by two qualifications, which suggest principles for judging sexual activity. **Not everything is beneficial**: cf. 1 Cor 10:23, and the whole argument of 1 Cor 8–10 on the finality of freedom and moral activity. **Not let myself be dominated**: certain apparently free actions may involve in fact a secret servitude in conflict with the lordship of Jesus.

‡‡[6:15b–16] **A prostitute**: the reference may be specifically to religious prostitution, an accepted part of pagan culture at Corinth and elsewhere; but the prostitute also serves as a symbol for any sexual relationship that conflicts with Christ's claim over us individually. **The two . . . will become one flesh**: the text of Gn 2:24 is applied positively to human marriage in Matthew and Mark, and in Eph 5:29–32: love of husband and wife reflect the love of Christ for his church. The application of the text to union with a prostitute is jarring, for such a union is a parody, an antitype of marriage, which does conflict with Christ's claim over us. This explains the horror expressed in 1 Cor 6:15b.

---

*[5:7–8] In the Jewish calendar, Passover was followed immediately by the festival of Unleavened Bread. In preparation for this feast all traces of old bread were removed from the house, and during the feast only unleavened bread was eaten. The sequence of these two feasts provides Paul with an image of Christian existence: Christ's death (the true Passover celebration) is followed by the life of the Christian community, marked by newness, purity, and integrity (a perpetual feast of unleavened bread). Paul may have been writing around Passover time (cf. 1 Cor 16:5); this is a little Easter homily, the earliest in Christian literature.

†[5:9–13] Paul here corrects a misunderstanding of his earlier directives against associating with immoral fellow Christians. He concedes the impossibility of avoiding contact with sinners in society at large but urges the Corinthians to maintain the inner purity of their own community.

‡[6:1–11] Christians at Corinth are suing one another before pagan judges in Roman courts. A barrage of rhetorical questions (1 Cor 6:1–9) betrays Paul's indignation over this practice, which he sees as an infringement upon the holiness of the Christian community.

§§[6:2–3] The principle to which Paul appeals is an eschatological prerogative promised to Christians: they are to share with Christ the judgment of the world (cf. Dn 7:22, 27). Hence they ought to be able to settle minor disputes within the community.

---

a. [5:7] Ex 12:1–13; Dt 1:6–2; 1 Pt 1:19. b. [5:8] Ex 12:15–20; 13:7; Dt 16:3. c. [5:10] 10:27; Jn 17:15. d. [5:11] Mt 18:17; 2 Thes 3:6, 14; 2 Jn 10. e. [5:13] Dt 13:6; 17:7; 22:24. f. [6:2] Wis 3:8; Mt 19:28; Rev 20:4.

g. [6:7] Mt 5:38–42; Rom 12:17–21; 1 Thes 5:15. h. [6:9] 15:50; Gal 5:19–21; Eph 5:5. i. [6:11] Ti 3:3–7. j. [6:12] 10:23. k. [6:14] Rom 8:11; 2 Cor 4:14. l. [6:15] 12:27; Rom 6:12–13; 12:5; Eph 5:30.

know that anyone who joins himself to a prostitute becomes one body with her? For "the two," it says, "will become one flesh."^m ^17But whoever is joined to the Lord becomes one spirit with him.^n ^18Avoid immorality. Every other sin a person commits is outside the body, but the immoral person sins against his own body.* ^19Do you not know that your body is a temple† of the holy Spirit within you, whom you have from God, and that you are not your own?* ^20For you have been purchased at a price. Therefore glorify God in your body.^p

III. ANSWERS TO THE CORINTHIANS' QUESTIONS

A. Marriage and Virginity‡

CHAPTER 7

Advice to the Married.^§ ^1Now in regard to the matters about which you wrote: "It is a good thing for a man not to touch a woman,"^¶ ^2but because of cases of immorality every man should have his own wife, and every woman her own husband. ^3The husband should fulfill his duty toward his wife, and likewise the wife toward her husband. ^4A wife does not have authority over her own body, but rather her husband, and

similarly a husband does not have authority over his own body, but rather his wife. ^5Do not deprive each other, except perhaps by mutual consent for a time, to be free for prayer, but then return to one another, so that Satan may not tempt you through your lack of self-control. ^6This I say by way of concession,** however, not as a command. ^7Indeed, I wish everyone to be as I am, but each has a particular gift from God,†† one of one kind and one of another.^q

^8‡‡Now to the unmarried and to widows I say: it is a good thing for them to remain as they are, as I do, ^9but if they cannot exercise self-control they should marry, for it is better to marry than to be on fire. ^10§§To the married, however, I give this instruction (not I, but the Lord):§§ A wife should not separate from her husband ^11— and if she does separate she must either remain single or become reconciled to her husband— and a husband should not divorce his wife.

^12To the rest¶¶ I say (not the Lord): if any brother has a wife who is an unbeliever, and she is willing to go on living with him, he should not divorce her; ^13and if any woman has a husband who is an unbeliever, and he is willing to go on living with her, she should not divorce her husband. ^14For the unbelieving husband is made holy through his wife, and the unbelieving wife is made holy through the brother. Otherwise your children would be unclean, whereas in fact they are holy.^t

^15If the unbeliever separates,*** however, let him separate. The brother or sister is not bound in such cases; God has called you to peace. ^16For how do you know, wife, whether you will save your husband; or how do you know, husband, whether you will save your wife?

The Life That the Lord Has Assigned.††† ^17Only, everyone should live as the Lord has assigned,

---

*[6:18] **Against his own body**: expresses the intimacy and depth of sexual disorder, which violates the very orientation of our bodies.

†[6:19–20] Paul's vision becomes trinitarian. **A temple**: sacred by reason of God's gift, his indwelling Spirit. **Not your own**: but "for the Lord," who acquires ownership by the act of redemption. **Glorify God in your body**: the argument concludes with a positive imperative to supplement the negative "avoid immorality" of 1 Cor 6:18. Far from being a terrain that is morally indifferent, the area of sexuality is one in which our relationship with God (and his Christ and his Spirit) is very intimately expressed: he is either highly glorified or deeply offended.

‡[7:1–40] Paul now begins to answer questions addressed to him by the Corinthians (1 Cor 7:1–11:1). The first of these concerns marriage. This chapter contains advice both to the married (1–16) and to the unmarried (1 Cor 7:25–38) or widowed (1 Cor 7:39–40); these two parts are separated by 1 Cor 7:17–24, which enunciate a principle applicable to both.

§[7:1–16] It seems that some Christians in Corinth were advocating asceticism in sexual matters. The pattern **it is a good thing . . . , but** occurs twice (1 Cor 7:1–2, 8–9; cf. 1 Cor 7:26), suggesting that in this matter as in others the Corinthians have seized upon a genuine value but are exaggerating or distorting it in some way. Once again Paul calls them to a more correct perspective and a better sense of their own limitations. The phrase it is a **good thing** (1 Cor 7:1) may have been the slogan of the ascetic party at Corinth.

¶[7:1–7] References to Paul's own behavior (1 Cor 7:7–8) suggest that his celibate way of life and his preaching to the unmarried (cf. 1 Cor 7:25–35) have given the impression that asceticism within marriage, i.e., suspension of normal sexual relations, would be a laudable ideal. Paul points to their experience of widespread immorality to caution them against overestimating their own strength (1 Cor 7:2); as individuals they may not have the particular gift that makes such asceticism feasible (1 Cor 7:7) and hence are to abide by the principle to be explained in 1 Cor 7:17–24.

[7:6] **By way of concession: this refers most likely to the concession mentioned in 1 Cor 7:5a: temporary interruption of relations for a legitimate purpose.

††[7:7] **A particular gift from God**: use of the term *charisma* suggests that marriage and celibacy may be viewed in the light of Paul's theology of spiritual gifts (1 Cor 7:12–14).

‡‡[7:8] Paul was obviously unmarried when he wrote this verse. Some interpreters believe that he had previously been married and widowed; there is no clear evidence either for or against this view, which was expressed already at the end of the second century by Clement of Alexandria.

§§[7:10–11] (**Not I, but the Lord**): Paul reminds the married of Jesus' principle of nonseparation (Mk 10:9). This is one of his rare specific references to the teaching of Jesus.

¶¶[7:12–14] **To the rest**: marriages in which only one partner is a baptized Christian. Jesus' prohibition against divorce is not addressed to them, but Paul extends the principle of nonseparation to such unions, provided they are marked by peacefulness and shared sanctification.

***[7:15–16] **If the unbeliever separates**: the basis of the "Pauline privilege" in Catholic marriage legislation.

†††[7:17–24] On the ground that distinct human conditions are less significant than the whole new existence opened up by God's call, Paul urges them to be less concerned with changing their states of life than with answering God's call where it finds them. The principle applies both to the married state (1 Cor 7:1–16) and to the unmarried (1 Cor 7:25–38).

---

m. [6:16] Gn 2:24; Mt 19:5; Mk 10:8; Eph 5:31.   n. [6:17] Rom 8:9–10; 2 Cor 3:17.   o. [6:19] 3:16–17; Rom 5:5.   p. [6:20] 3:23; 7:23; Acts 20:28 / Rom 12:1; Phil 1:20.

q. [7:7] Mt 19:11–12.   r. [7:8] 1 Tm 5:11–16 / 9:5.   s. [7:10–11] Mt 5:32; 19:9.   t. [7:14] Rom 11:16.

just as God called each one. I give this order in all the churches. ¹⁸Was someone called after he had been circumcised? He should not try to undo his circumcision. Was an uncircumcised person called? He should not be circumcised.ᵘ ¹⁹Circumcision means nothing, and uncircumcision means nothing; what matters is keeping God's commandments.ᵛ ²⁰Everyone should remain in the state in which he was called.

²¹Were you a slave when you were called? Do not be concerned but, even if you can gain your freedom, make the most of it. ²²For the slave called in the Lord is a freed person in the Lord, just as the free person who has been called is a slave of Christ.ʷ ²³You have been purchased at a price. Do not become slaves to human beings.ˣ ²⁴Brothers, everyone should continue before God in the state in which he was called.

Advice to Virgins and Widows. ²⁵Now in regard to virgins I have no commandment from the Lord, but I give my opinion as one who by the Lord's mercy is trustworthy. ²⁶So this is what I think best because of the present distress: that it is a good thing for a person to remain as he is.ʸ ²⁷Are you bound to a wife? Do not seek a separation. Are you free of a wife? Then do not look for a wife. ²⁸If you marry, however, you do not sin, nor does an unmarried woman sin if she marries; but such people will experience affliction in their earthly life, and I would like to spare you that.

²⁹†I tell you, brothers, the time is running out. From now on, let those having wives act as not having them,ᶻ ³⁰those weeping as not weeping, those rejoicing as not rejoicing, those buying as not owning, ³¹those using the world as not using it fully. For the world in its present form is passing away.

³²I should like you to be free of anxieties. An unmarried man is anxious about the things of the Lord, how he may please the Lord. ³³But a married man is anxious about the things of the world, how he may please his wife,ᵃ ³⁴and he is divided. An unmarried woman or a virgin is anxious about the things of the Lord, so that she may be holy in both body and spirit. A married woman, on the other hand, is anxious about the things of the world, how she may please her husband.ᵇ ³⁵I am telling you this for your own benefit, not to impose a restraint upon you, but for the sake of propriety and adherence to the Lord without distraction.ᶜ

³⁶‡If anyone thinks he is behaving improperly toward his virgin, and if a critical moment has come§ and so it has to be, let him do as he wishes. He is committing no sin; let them get married. ³⁷The one who stands firm in his resolve, however, who is not under compulsion but has power over his own will, and has made up his mind to keep his virgin, will be doing well. ³⁸So then, the one who marries his virgin does well; the one who does not marry her will do better.

³⁹¶A wife is bound to her husband as long as he lives. But if her husband dies, she is free to be married to whomever she wishes, provided that it be in the Lord.ᵈ ⁴⁰She is more blessed, though, in my opinion, if she remains as she is, and I think that I too have the Spirit of God.ᵉ

*B. Offerings to Idols***

CHAPTER 8
Knowledge Insufficient. ¹Now in regard to meat sacrificed to idols:†† we realize that "all of us have knowledge"; knowledge inflates with pride, but love builds up.ᶠ ²If anyone supposes he knows something, he does not yet know as he ought to know. ³But if one loves God, one is known by him.ᵍ

‡[7:36–38] The passage is difficult to interpret, because it is unclear whether Paul is thinking of a father and his unmarried daughter (or slave), or of a couple engaged in a betrothal or spiritual marriage. The general principles already enunciated apply: there is no question of sin, even if they should marry, but staying as they are is "better" (for the reasons mentioned in 1 Cor 7:28–35). Once again the *charisma* of 1 Cor 7:7 which applies also to the unmarried (1 Cor 7:8–9), is to be presupposed.

§[7:36] **A critical moment has come:** either because the woman will soon be beyond marriageable age, or because their passions are becoming uncontrollable (cf. 1 Cor 7:9).

¶[7:39–40] Application of the principles to the case of widows. If they do choose to remarry, they ought to prefer Christian husbands.

**[8:1–11:1] The Corinthians' second question concerns meat that has been sacrificed to idols; in this area they were exhibiting a disordered sense of liberation that Paul here tries to rectify. These chapters contain a sustained and unified argument that illustrates Paul's method of theological reflection on a moral dilemma. Although the problem with which he is dealing is dated, the guidelines for moral decisions that he offers are of lasting validity. Essentially Paul urges them to take a communitarian rather than an individualistic view of their Christian freedom. Many decisions that they consider pertinent only to their private relationship with God have, in fact, social consequences. Nor can moral decisions be determined by merely theoretical considerations; they must be based on concrete circumstances, specifically on the value and needs of other individuals and on mutual responsibility within the community. Paul here introduces the theme of "building up" (*oikodomē*), i.e., of contributing by individual action to the welfare and growth of the community. This theme will be further developed in 1 Cor 14; see note on 1 Cor 14:3b–5. Several years later Paul would again deal with the problem of meat sacrificed to idols in Rom 14:1–15:6.

††[8:1a] **Meat sacrificed to idols:** much of the food consumed in the city could have passed through pagan religious ceremonies before finding its way into markets and homes. **"All of us have knowledge":** a slogan, similar to 1 Cor 6:12, which reveals the self-image of the Corinthians. 1 Cor 8:4 will specify the content of this knowledge.

*[7:25–28] Paul is careful to explain that the principle of 1 Cor 7:17 does not bind under sin but that present earthly conditions make it advantageous for the unmarried to remain as they are (1 Cor 7:28). These remarks must be complemented by the statement about "particular gifts" from 1 Cor 7:7.

†[7:29–31] **The world . . . is passing away:** Paul advises Christians to go about the ordinary activities of life in a manner different from those who are totally immersed in them and unaware of their transitoriness.

u. [7:18] 1 Mc 1:15 / Acts 15:1–2.   v. [7:19] Rom 2:25, 29; Gal 5:6; 6:15.   w. [7:22] Eph 6:5–9; Col 3:11; Phlm 16.   x. [7:23] 6:20.   y. [7:26] 7:8.   z. [7:29] Rom 13:11.   a. [7:33] Lk 14:20.   b. [7:34] 1 Tm 5:5.   c. [7:35] Lk 10:39–42.

d. [7:39] Rom 7:2.   e. [7:40] 7:25.   f. [8:1] Rom 15:14 / 1 Cor 13:1–13; Rom 14:15, 19.   g. [8:3] Rom 8:29; Gal 4:9.

⁴So about the eating of meat sacrificed to idols: we know that "there is no idol in the world," and that "there is no God but one."ʰ ⁵Indeed, even though there are so-called gods in heaven and on earth (there are, to be sure, many "gods" and many "lords"), ⁶*yet for us there is

> one God, the Father,
> from whom all things are and for
>   whom we exist,
> and one Lord, Jesus Christ,
> through whom all things are and
>   through whom we exist.ⁱ

Practical Rules. ⁷But not all have this knowledge. There are some who have been so used to idolatry up until now that, when they eat meat sacrificed to idols, their conscience, which is weak, is defiled.ʲ ⁸†Now food will not bring us closer to God. We are no worse off if we do not eat, nor are we better off if we do.ᵏ ⁹But make sure that this liberty of yours in no way becomes a stumbling block to the weak.ˡ ¹⁰If someone sees you, with your knowledge, reclining at table in the temple of an idol, may not his conscience too, weak as it is, be "built up" to eat the meat sacrificed to idols? ¹¹Thus through your knowledge, the weak person is brought to destruction, the brother for whom Christ died.ᵐ ¹²When you sin in this way against your brothers and wound their consciences, weak as they are, you are sinning against Christ. ¹³†*Therefore, if food causes my brother to sin, I will never eat meat again, so that I may not cause my brother to sin.

CHAPTER 9§

Paul's Rights as an Apostle. ¹Am I not free? Am I not an apostle? Have I not seen Jesus our Lord?

Are you not my work in the Lord?ᵒ ²Although I may not be an apostle for others, certainly I am for you, for you are the seal of my apostleship in the Lord. ³My defense against those who would pass judgment on me¶ is this. ⁴"Do we not have the right to eat and drink? ⁵Do we not have the right to take along a Christian wife, as do the rest of the apostles, and the brothers of the Lord, and Cephas? ⁶Or is it only myself and Barnabas who do not have the right not to work?ᵖ ⁷Who ever serves as a soldier at his own expense? Who plants a vineyard without eating its produce? Or who shepherds a flock without using some of the milk from the flock?�q ⁸Am I saying this on human authority, or does not the law also speak of these things? ⁹It is written in the law of Moses, "You shall not muzzle an ox while it is treading out the grain."ʳ Is God concerned about oxen, ¹⁰or is he not really speaking for our sake? It was written for our sake, because the plowman should plow in hope, and the thresher in hope of receiving a share.ˢ ¹¹If we have sown spiritual seed for you, is it a great thing that we reap a material harvest from you?ᵗ ¹²If others share this rightful claim on you, do not we still more?ᵘ **Reason for Not Using His Rights.** Yet we have not used this right.†† On the contrary, we endure everything so as not to place an obstacle to the gospel of Christ. ¹³‡‡Do you not know that those

---

and his apostleship (1 Cor 9:1), themes that the chapter will develop in reverse order, 1 Cor 9:1–18 treating the question of his apostleship and the rights that flow from it, and 1 Cor 9:19–27 exploring dialectically the nature of Paul's freedom. The language is highly rhetorical, abounding in questions, wordplays, paradoxes, images, and appeals to authority and experience. The argument is unified by repetitions; its articulations are highlighted by inclusions and transitional verses.

¶[9:3] **My defense against those who would pass judgment on me:** the reference to a defense (*apologia*) is surprising, and suggests that Paul is incorporating some material here that he has previously used in another context. The defense will touch on two points: the fact of Paul's rights as an apostle (1 Cor 9:4–12a and 1 Cor 9:13–14) and his nonuse of those rights (1 Cor 9:12b and 1 Cor 9:15–18).

**[9:4–12a] Apparently some believe that Paul is not equal to the other apostles and therefore does not enjoy equal privileges. His defense on this point (here and in 1 Cor 9:13–14) reinforces the assertion of his apostolic character in 1 Cor 9:2. It consists of a series of analogies from natural equity (1 Cor 9:7) and religious custom (1 Cor 9:13) designed to establish his equal right to support from the churches (1 Cor 9:4–6, 11–12a); these analogies are confirmed by the authority of the law (1 Cor 9:8–10) and of Jesus himself (1 Cor 9:14).

††[9:12b] It appears, too, that suspicion or misunderstanding has been created by Paul's practice of not living from his preaching. The first reason he asserts in defense of this practice is an entirely apostolic one; it anticipates the developments to follow in 1 Cor 9:19–22. He will give a second reason in 1 Cor 9:15–18.

‡‡[9:13–14] The position of these verses produces an interlocking of the two points of Paul's defense. These arguments by analogy (1 Cor 9:13) and from authority (1 Cor 9:14) belong with those of 1 Cor 9:7–10 and ground the first point. But Paul defers them until he has had a chance to mention "the gospel of Christ" (1 Cor 9:12b), after which it is more appropriate to mention Jesus' injunction to his preachers and to argue by

---

*[8:6] This verse rephrases the monotheistic confession of 1 Cor 8:4 in such a way as to contrast it with polytheism (1 Cor 8:5) and to express our relationship with the one God in concrete, i.e., in personal and Christian terms. **And for whom we exist:** since the Greek contains no verb here and the action intended must be inferred from the preposition *eis*, another translation is equally possible: "toward whom we return." **Through whom all things:** the earliest reference in the New Testament to Jesus' role in creation.

†[8:8–9] Although the food in itself is morally neutral, extrinsic circumstances may make the eating of it harmful. **A stumbling block:** the image is that of tripping or causing someone to fall (cf. 1 Cor 8:13; 9:12; 10:12, 32; 2 Cor 6:3; Rom 14:13, 20–1). This is a basic moral imperative for Paul, a counterpart to the positive imperative to "build one another up"; compare the expression "giving offense" as opposed to "pleasing" in 1 Cor 10:32–33.

‡[8:13] His own course is clear: he will avoid any action that might harm another Christian. This statement prepares for the paradigmatic development in 1 Cor 9.

§[9:1–27] This chapter is an emotionally charged expansion of Paul's appeal to his own example in 1 Cor 8:13; its purpose is to reinforce the exhortation of 1 Cor 8:9. The two opening questions introduce the themes of Paul's freedom

---

h. [8:4] 10:19; Dt 6:4.   i. [8:6] Mal 2:10 / Rom 11:36; Eph 4:5–6 / 1 Cor 1:2–3 / Jn 1:3; Col 1:16.   j. [8:7] 10:28; Rom 14:23 / Rom 14:1; 15:1.   k. [8:8] Rom 14:17.   l. [8:9] Rom 14:13, 20–21.   m. [8:11] Rom 14:15, 20.   n. [8:13] Mt 18:6; Rom 14:20–21.

o. [9:1] 1 Cor 9:19 / 2 Cor 12:12 / 1 Cor 15:8–9 / Acts 9:17; 26:16.   p. [9:6] Acts 4:36–37; 13:1–2; Gal 2:1, 9, 13; Col 4:10.   q. [9:7] 2 Tm 2:3–4.   r. [9:9] Dt 25:4; 1 Tm 5:18.   s. [9:10] 2 Tm 2:6.   t. [9:11] Rom 15:27.   u. [9:12] 2 Cor 11:7–12; 12:13–18; 2 Thes 3:6–12.

who perform the temple services eat [what] belongs to the temple, and those who minister at the altar share in the sacrificial offerings?[v] [14]In the same way, the Lord ordered that those who preach the gospel should live by the gospel.[w]

[15]"I have not used any of these rights, however, nor do I write this that it be done so in my case. I would rather die. Certainly no one is going to nullify my boast.[x] [16]If I preach the gospel, this is no reason for me to boast, for an obligation has been imposed on me, and woe to me if I do not preach it![y] [17]If I do so willingly, I have a recompense, but if unwillingly, then I have been entrusted with a stewardship.[z] [18]What then is my recompense? That, when I preach, I offer the gospel free of charge so as not to make full use of my right in the gospel.[a]

All Things to All. [19†]Although I am free in regard to all, I have made myself a slave to all so as to win over as many as possible.[b] [20]To the Jews I became like a Jew to win over Jews; to those under the law I became like one under the law—though I myself am not under the law—to win over those under the law. [21]To those outside the law I became like one outside the law—though I am not outside God's law but within the law of Christ—to win over those outside the law. [22]To the weak I became weak, to win over the weak. I have become all things to all, to save at least some.[c] [23]All this I do for the sake of the gospel, so that I too may have a share in it.

[24†]Do you not know that the runners in the stadium all run in the race, but only one wins the prize? Run so as to win.[d] [25]Every athlete exercises discipline in every way. They do it to win a perishable crown, but we an imperishable one.[e] [26]Thus I do not run aimlessly; I do not fight as if I were shadowboxing. [27]No, I drive my body and train it, for fear that, after having preached to others, I myself should be disqualified.[s]

CHAPTER 10

Warning Against Overconfidence. [1]I do not want you to be unaware, brothers, that our ancestors were all under the cloud and all passed through the sea,[f] [2]and all of them were baptized into Moses in the cloud and in the sea.[g] [3]All ate the same spiritual food, [4]and all drank the same spiritual drink, for they drank from a spiritual rock that followed them,[**] and the rock was the Christ.[h] [5]Yet God was not pleased with most of them, for they were struck down in the desert.[i]

[6††]These things happened as examples for us, so that we might not desire evil things, as they did.[j] [7]And do not become idolaters, as some of them did, as it is written, "The people sat down to eat and drink, and rose up to revel."[k] [8]Let us not indulge in immorality as some of them did; and twenty-three thousand fell within a single day.[l] [9]Let us not test Christ[‡‡] as some of them did, and suffered death by serpents.[m] [10]Do not grumble as some of them did, and suffered death by the destroyer.[n] [11]These things happened to them as an example, and they have been written down as a warning to us, upon whom the end of the ages has come.[§§] [12]Therefore, whoever thinks he is standing secure should take care not to fall.[¶¶] [13]No trial has come to you but what is human. God is faithful and will not let you be tried beyond your strength; but with the trial he will also provide a way out, so that you may be able to bear it.[o]

---

analogy from the sacred temple service to his own liturgical service, the preaching of the gospel (cf. Rom 1:9; 15:16).

*[9:15–18] Paul now assigns a more personal motive to his renounce of his right to support. His preaching is not a service spontaneously undertaken on his part but a stewardship imposed by a sort of divine compulsion. Yet to merit any reward he must bring some spontaneous quality to his service, and this he does by freely renouncing his right to support. The material here is quite similar to that contained in Paul's "defense" at 2 Cor 11:5–12; 12:11–18.

†[9:19–23] In a rhetorically balanced series of statements Paul expands and generalizes the picture of his behavior and explores the paradox of apostolic freedom. It is not essentially freedom from restraint but freedom for service—a possibility of constructive activity.

‡[9:24–27] A series of miniparables from sports, appealing to readers familiar with Greek gymnasia and the nearby Isthmian games.

§[9:27] **For fear that . . . I myself should be disqualified:** a final paradoxical turn to the argument: what appears at first a free, spontaneous renunciation of rights (1 Cor 9:12–18) seems subsequently to be required for fulfillment of Paul's stewardship (to preach effectively he must reach his hearers wherever

they are, 1 Cor 9:19–22), and finally is seen to be necessary for his own salvation (1 Cor 9:23–27). Mention of the possibility of disqualification provides a transition to 1 Cor 10.

¶[10:1–5] Paul embarks unexpectedly upon a panoramic survey of the events of the Exodus period. The privileges of Israel in the wilderness are described in terms that apply strictly only to the realities of the new covenant ("baptism," "spiritual food and drink"); interpreted in this way they point forward to the Christian experience (1 Cor 10:1–4). But those privileges did not guarantee God's permanent pleasure (1 Cor 10:5).

[10:4] **A spiritual rock that followed them: the Torah speaks only about a rock from which water issued, but rabbinic legend amplified this into a spring that followed the Israelites throughout their migration. Paul uses this legend as a literary type: he makes the rock itself accompany the Israelites, and he gives it a spiritual sense. **The rock was the Christ:** in the Old Testament, Yahweh is the Rock of his people (cf. Dt 32, Moses' song to Yahweh the Rock). Paul now applies this image to the Christ, the source of the living water, the true Rock that accompanied Israel, guiding their experiences in the desert.

††[10:6–13] This section explicitates the typological value of these Old Testament events: the desert experiences of the Israelites are examples, meant as warnings, to deter us from similar sins (idolatry, immorality, etc.) and from a similar fate.

‡‡[10:9] **Christ:** to avoid Paul's concept of Christ present in the wilderness events, some manuscripts read "the Lord."

§§[10:11] **Upon whom the end of the ages has come:** it is our period in time toward which past ages have been moving and in which they arrive at their goal.

¶¶[10:12–13] **Take care not to fall:** the point of the whole comparison with Israel is to caution against overconfidence, a sense of complete security (1 Cor 10:12). This warning is immediately balanced by a reassurance, based, however, on God (1 Cor 10:13).

---

v. [9:13] Nm 18:8, 31; Dt 18:1–5. w. [9:14] Mt 10:10; Lk 10:7–8. x. [9:15] 2 Cor 11:9–10. y. [9:16] Acts 26:14–18. z. [9:17] 4:1; Gal 2:7. a. [9:18] 2 Cor 11:7–12. b. [9:19] Mt 20:26–27. c. [9:22] 10:33; Rom 15:1; 2 Cor 11:29. d. [9:24] Heb 12:1. e. [9:25] 2 Tm 2:5 / 2 Tm 4:7–8; Jas 1:12; 1 Pt 5:4.

f. [10:1] Ex 13:21–22; 14:19–20 / Ex 14:21–22, 26–30. g. [10:2] Rom 6:3; Gal 3:27 / Ex 16:4–35. h. [10:4] Ex 17:1–7; Nm 20:7–11; Dt 8:15. i. [10:5] Nm 14:28–38; Jude 5. j. [10:6] Nm 11:4, 34. k. [10:7] Ex 32:6. l. [10:8] Nm 25:1–9. m. [10:9] Nm 21:5–9. n. [10:10] Nm 14:2–37; 16:1–35. o. [10:13] Mt 6:13; Jas 1:13–14 / 1 Cor 1:9.

Warning Against Idolatry. ⸰ ¹⁴Therefore, my beloved, avoid idolatry.ᵖ ¹⁵I am speaking as to sensible people; judge for yourselves what I am saying. ¹⁶The cup of blessing that we bless, is it not a participation in the blood of Christ? The bread that we break, is it not a participation in the body of Christ?�q ,¹⁷Because the loaf of bread is one, we, though many, are one body, for we all partake of the one loaf.ʳ

¹⁸Look at Israel according to the flesh; are not those who eat the sacrifices participants in the altar?ˢ ¹⁹So what am I saying? That meat sacrificed to idols is anything? Or that an idol is anything? ²⁰No, I mean that what they sacrifice, [they sacrifice] to demons,† not to God, and I do not want you to become participants with demons.ᵗ ²¹You cannot drink the cup of the Lord and also the cup of demons. You cannot partake of the table of the Lord and of the table of demons.ᵘ ²²Or are we provoking the Lord to jealous anger? Are we stronger than he?ᵛ

Seek the Good of Others. ‡ ²³"Everything is lawful," but not everything is beneficial.§ "Everything is lawful," but not everything builds up.ʷ ²⁴No one should seek his own advantage, but that of his neighbor.ˣ ²⁵¶Eat anything sold in the market, without raising questions on grounds of

conscience, ²⁶for "the earth and its fullness are the Lord's."ʸ ²⁷If an unbeliever invites you and you want to go, eat whatever is placed before you, without raising questions on grounds of conscience. ²⁸But if someone says to you, "This was offered in sacrifice," do not eat it on account of the one who called attention to it and on account of conscience; ²⁹I mean not your own conscience, but the other's. For why should my freedom be determined by someone else's conscience? ³⁰If I partake thankfully, why am I reviled for that over which I give thanks?ᶻ

³¹So whether you eat or drink, or whatever you do, do everything for the glory of God. ³²**Avoid giving offense, whether to Jews or Greeks or the church of God, ³³just as I try to please everyone in every way, not seeking my own benefit but that of the many, that they may be saved.ᵃ

CHAPTER 11
¹Be imitators of me, as I am of Christ.ᵇ

IV. PROBLEMS IN LITURGICAL ASSEMBLIES††

²I praise you because you remember me in everything and hold fast to the traditions, just as I handed them on to you.ᶜ

A. Women's Headdresses‡‡

Man and Woman. ³But I want you to know that Christ is the head of every man, and a husband the head of his wife,§§ and God the head

---

*[10:14–22] The warning against idolatry from 1 Cor 10:7 is now repeated (1 Cor 10:14) and explained in terms of the effect of sacrifices: all sacrifices, Christian (1 Cor 10:16–17), Jewish (1 Cor 10:18), or pagan (1 Cor 10:20), establish communion. But communion with Christ is exclusive, incompatible with any other such communion (1 Cor 10:21). Compare the line of reasoning at 1 Cor 6:15.

†[10:20] **To demons**: although Jews denied divinity to pagan gods, they often believed that there was some nondivine reality behind the idols, such as the dead, or angels, or demons. The explanation Paul offers in 1 Cor 10:20 is drawn from Dt 32:17: the power behind the idols, with which the pagans commune, consists of demonic powers hostile to God.

‡[10:23–11:1] By way of peroration Paul returns to the opening situation (1 Cor 8) and draws conclusions based on the intervening considerations (1 Cor 9–10).

§[10:23–24] He repeats in the context of this new problem the slogans of liberty from 1 Cor 6:12, with similar qualifications. Liberty is not merely an individual perfection, nor an end in itself, but is to be used for the common good. The language of 1 Cor 10:24 recalls the descriptions of Jesus' self-emptying in Phil 2.

¶[10:25–30] A summary of specific situations in which the eating of meat sacrificed to idols could present problems of conscience. Three cases are considered. In the first (the marketplace, 1 Cor 10:25–26) and the second (at table, 1 Cor 10:27), there is no need to be concerned with whether food has passed through a pagan sacrifice or not, for the principle of 1 Cor 8:4–6 still stands, and the whole creation belongs to the one God. But in the third case (1 Cor 10:28), the situation changes if someone present explicitly raises the question of the sacrificial origin of the food; eating in such circumstances may be subject to various interpretations, some of which could be harmful to individuals. Paul is at pains to insist that the enlightened Christian conscience need not change its judgment about the neutrality, even the goodness, of the food in itself (1 Cor 10:29–30); yet the total situation is altered to the extent that others are potentially endangered, and this calls for a different response, for the sake of others.

**[10:32–11:1] In summary, the general rule of mutually responsible use of their Christian freedom is enjoined first negatively (1 Cor 10:32), then positively, as exemplified in Paul (1 Cor 10:33), and finally grounded in Christ, the pattern for Paul's behavior and theirs (1 Cor 11:1; cf. Rom 15:1–3).

††[11:2–14:40] This section of the letter is devoted to regulation of conduct at the liturgy. The problems Paul handles have to do with the dress of women in the assembly (1 Cor 11:3–16), improprieties in the celebration of community meals (1 Cor 11:17–34), and the use of charisms or spiritual gifts (1 Cor 12:1–14:40). The statement in 1 Cor 11:2 introduces all of these discussions, but applies more appropriately to the second (cf. the mention of praise in 1 Cor 11:17 and of tradition in 1 Cor 11:23).

‡‡[11:3–16] Women have been participating in worship at Corinth without the head-covering normal in Greek society of the period. Paul's stated goal is to bring them back into conformity with contemporary practice and propriety. In his desire to convince, he reaches for arguments from a variety of sources, though he has space to develop them only sketchily and is perhaps aware that they differ greatly in persuasiveness.

§§[11:3] **A husband the head of his wife**: the specific problem suggests to Paul the model of the head as a device for clarifying relations within a hierarchical structure. The model is similar to that developed later in greater detail and nuance in Eph 5:21–33. It is a hybrid model, for it grafts onto a strictly theological scale of existence (cf. 1 Cor 3:21–23) the hierarchy of sociosexual relations prevalent in the ancient world: men, dominant, reflect the active function of Christ in relation to his church; women, submissive, reflect the passive role of the church with respect to its savior. This gives us the functional scale: God, Christ, man, woman.

---

p. [10:14] 1 Jn 5:21.   q. [10:16] Mt 26:26–29; Acts 2:42.   r. [10:17] Rom 12:5; Eph 4:4.   s. [10:18] Lv 7:6.   t. [10:20] Dt 32:17.   u. [10:21] 2 Cor 6:14–18.   v. [10:22] Dt 32:21 / Eccl 6:10.   w. [10:23] 6:12.   x. [10:24] Rom 15:2; Phil 2:4, 21.

y. [10:26] Ps 24:1; 50:12. z. [10:30] Rom 14:6; 1 Tm 4:3–4. a. [10:33] 9:22; Rom 15:2.   b. [11:1] 4:16; Phil 3:17.   c. [11:2] 15:3; 2 Thes 2:15.

of Christ.*d* ⁴"Any man who prays or prophesies with his head covered brings shame upon his head. ⁵But any woman who prays or prophesies with her head unveiled brings shame upon her head, for it is one and the same thing as if she had had her head shaved. ⁶For if a woman does not have her head veiled, she may as well have her hair cut off. But if it is shameful for a woman to have her hair cut off or her head shaved, then she should wear a veil.

⁷†A man, on the other hand, should not cover his head, because he is the image and glory of God, but woman is the glory of man.*e* ⁸For man did not come from woman, but woman from man;*f* ⁹nor was man created for woman, but woman for man;*g* ¹⁰for this reason a woman should have a sign of authority‡ on her head, because of the angels. ¹¹§Woman is not independent of man or man of woman in the Lord.*h* ¹²For just as woman came from man, so man is born of woman; but all things are from God.*i*

¹³¶Judge for yourselves: is it proper for a woman to pray to God with her head unveiled? ¹⁴Does not nature itself teach you that if a man wears his hair long it is a disgrace to him, ¹⁵whereas if a woman has long hair it is her glory, because long hair has been given [her]

---

*[11:4–6] From man's direct relation to Christ, Paul infers that his head should not be covered. But woman, related not directly to Christ on the scale but to her husband, requires a covering as a sign of that relationship. **Shameful . . . to have her hair cut off:** certain less honored classes in society, such as lesbians and prostitutes, are thought to have worn their hair close-cropped.

†[11:7–9] The hierarchy of v 3 is now expressed in other metaphors: the image (*eikōn*) and the reflected glory (*doxa*). Paul is alluding basically to the text of Gn 1:27, in which mankind as a whole, the male female couple, is created in God's image and given the command to multiply and together dominate the lower creation. But Gn 1:24 is interpreted here in the light of the second creation narrative in Gn 2, in which each of the sexes is created separately (first the man and then the woman from man and for him, to be his helpmate, Gn 2:20–23), and under the influence of the story of the fall, as a result of which the husband rules over the woman (Gn 3:16). This interpretation splits the single image of God into two, at different degrees of closeness.

‡[11:10] **A sign of authority:** "authority" (*exousia*) may possibly be due to mistranslation of an Aramaic word for "veil"; in any case, the connection with 1 Cor 11:9 indicates that the covering is a sign of woman's subordination. **Because of the angels:** a surprising additional reason, which the context does not clarify. Presumably the reference is to cosmic powers who might inflict harm on women or whose function is to watch over women or the cult.

§[11:11–12] These parenthetical remarks relativize the argument from Gn 2–3. **In the Lord:** in the Christian economy the relation between the sexes is characterized by a mutual dependence, which is not further specified. And even in the natural order conditions have changed: the mode of origin described in Gn 2 has been reversed (1 Cor 11:12a). But the ultimately significant fact is the origin that all things have in common (1 Cor 11:12b).

¶[11:13–16] The argument for conformity to common church practice is summed up and pressed home. 1 Cor 11:14–15 contain a final appeal to the sense of propriety that contemporary Greek society would consider "natural" (cf. 1 Cor 11:5–6).

d. [11:3] Eph 5:23.   e. [11:7] Gn 1:26–27;5:1.   f. [11:8] Gn 2:21–23.
g. [11:9] Gn 2:18.   h. [11:11] Gal 3:27–28.   i. [11:12] 8:6; Rom 11:36.

---

for a covering? ¹⁶But if anyone is inclined to be argumentative, we do not have such a custom, nor do the churches of God.

B. The Lord's Supper**

An Abuse at Corinth. ¹⁷In giving this instruction, I do not praise the fact that your meetings are doing more harm than good. ¹⁸First of all, I hear that when you meet as a church there are divisions among you, and to a degree I believe it;*j* ¹⁹there have to be factions among you in order that [also] those who are approved among you may become known.†† ²⁰When you meet in one place, then, it is not to eat the Lord's supper, ²¹for in eating, each one goes ahead with his own supper, and one goes hungry while another gets drunk. ²²Do you not have houses in which you can eat and drink? Or do you show contempt for the church of God and make those who have nothing feel ashamed? What can I say to you? Shall I praise you? In this matter I do not praise you.*k*

Tradition of the Institution. ²³‡‡For I received from the Lord what I also handed on to you,*l* that the Lord Jesus, on the night he was handed over, took bread, ²⁴and, after he had given thanks, broke it and said, "This is my body that is for you. Do this in remembrance of me." ²⁵In the same way also the cup, after supper, saying, "This cup is the new covenant in my blood. Do this, as often as you drink it, in remembrance of me."*m* ²⁶For as often as you eat this bread and drink the cup, you proclaim the death of the Lord until he comes.

²⁷Therefore whoever eats the bread or drinks the cup of the Lord unworthily will have to answer for the body and blood of the Lord.§§ ²⁸A person should examine himself,¶¶ and so eat the

---

**[11:17–34] Paul turns to another abuse connected with the liturgy, and a more serious one, for it involves neglect of basic Christian tradition concerning the meaning of the Lord's Supper. Paul recalls that tradition for them and reminds them of its implications.

††[11:19] **That . . . those who are approved among you may become known:** Paul situates their divisions within the context of the eschatological separation of the authentic from the inauthentic and the final revelation of the difference. The notion of authenticity-testing recurs in the injunction to self-examination in view of present and future judgment (1 Cor 11:28–32).

‡‡[11:23–25] This is the earliest written account of the institution of the Lord's Supper in the New Testament. The narrative emphasizes Jesus' action of self-giving (expressed in the words over the bread and the cup) and his double command to repeat his own action.

§§[11:27] It follows that the only proper way to celebrate the Eucharist is one that corresponds to Jesus' intention, which fits with the meaning of his command to reproduce his action in the proper spirit. If the Corinthians eat and drink unworthily, i.e., without having grasped and internalized the meaning of his death for them, **they will have to answer for the body and blood,** i.e., will be guilty of a sin against the Lord himself (cf. 1 Cor 8:12).

¶¶[11:28] **Examine himself:** the Greek word is similar to that for "approved" in 1 Cor 11:19, which means "having been

j. [11:18] 1:10–12; Gal 5:20.   k. [11:22] Jas 2:1–7.   l. [11:23] 11:2; 15:3 / 10:16–17; Mt 26:26–29; Mk 14:22–25; Lk 22:14–20.   m. [11:25] Ex 24:8; 2 Cor 3:6; Heb 8:6–13.

bread and drink the cup. [29]For anyone who eats and drinks without discerning the body, eats and drinks judgment* on himself. [30]That is why many among you are ill and infirm, and a considerable number are dying. [31]If we discerned ourselves, we would not be under judgment; [32]but since we are judged by [the] Lord, we are being disciplined so that we may not be condemned along with the world.*

[33]Therefore, my brothers, when you come together to eat, wait for one another. [34]If anyone is hungry, he should eat at home, so that your meetings may not result in judgment. The other matters I shall set in order when I come.

C. Spiritual Gifts†

CHAPTER 12

Unity and Variety. [1]Now in regard to spiritual gifts, brothers, I do not want you to be unaware. [2‡]You know how, when you were pagans, you were constantly attracted and led away to mute idols.° [3]Therefore, I tell you that nobody speaking by the spirit of God says, "Jesus be accursed." And no one can say, "Jesus is Lord," except by the holy Spirit.ᵖ

[4§]There are different kinds of spiritual gifts but the same Spirit;�q [5]there are different forms of service but the same Lord; [6]there are different workings but the same God who produces all of them in everyone. [7]To each individual the manifestation of the Spirit is given for some benefit. [8]To one is given through the Spirit the expression of wisdom; to another the expression of knowledge according to the same Spirit;ʳ [9]to another faith by the same Spirit; to another gifts of healing by the one Spirit; [10]to another mighty deeds; to another prophecy; to another discernment of spirits; to another varieties of tongues; to another interpretation of tongues.ˢ [11]But one and the same Spirit produces all of these, distributing them individually to each person as he wishes.ᵗ

One Body, Many Parts.¶ [12]As a body is one though it has many parts, and all the parts of the body, though many, are one body, so also Christ.ᵘ [13]For in one Spirit we were all baptized into one body, whether Jews or Greeks, slaves or free persons, and we were all given to drink of one Spirit.ᵛ

[14]Now the body is not a single part, but many. [15]If a foot should say, "Because I am not a hand I do not belong to the body," it does not for this reason belong any less to the body. [16]Or if an ear should say, "Because I am not an eye I do not belong to the body," it does not for this reason belong any less to the body. [17]If the whole body were an eye, where would the hearing be? If the whole body were hearing, where would the sense of smell be? [18]But as it is, God placed the parts, each one of them, in the body as he intended. [19]If they were all one part, where would the body be? [20]But as it is, there are many parts, yet one body. [21]The eye cannot say to the hand, "I do not need you," nor again the head to the feet, "I do not need you." [22]Indeed, the parts of the body that seem to be weaker are all the more necessary, [23]and those parts of the body that we consider less honorable we surround with greater honor, and our less presentable parts are treated with greater propriety, [24]whereas our more presentable parts do not need this. But God has so constructed the body as to give greater honor to a part that is without it, [25]so that there may be no division in the body, but that the parts may have the same concern for one another. [26]If [one] part suffers, all the parts suffer with it; if one part is honored, all the parts share its joy.

Application to Christ.** [27]Now you are Christ's body, and individually parts of it.ʷ [28]Some

tested and found true." The self-testing required for proper eating involves **discerning the body** (1 Cor 11:29), which, from the context, must mean understanding the sense of Jesus' death (1 Cor 11:26), perceiving the imperative to unity that follows from the fact that Jesus gives himself to all and requires us to repeat his sacrifice in the same spirit (1 Cor 11:18–25).

*[11:29–32] **Judgment:** there is a series of wordplays in these verses that would be awkward to translate literally into English; it includes all the references to judgment (*krima*, 1 Cor 11:29, 34; *krinō*, 1 Cor 11:31, 32) discernment (*diakrinō*, 1 Cor 11:29, 31), and condemnation (*katakrinō*, 1 Cor 11:32). The judgment is concretely described as the illness, infirmity, and death that have visited the community. These are signs that the power of Jesus' death is not yet completely recognized and experienced. Yet even the judgment incurred is an expression of God's concern; it is a medicinal measure meant to rescue us from condemnation with God's enemies.

†[12:1–14:40] Ecstatic and charismatic activity were common in early Christian experience, as they were in other ancient religions. But the Corinthians seem to have developed a disproportionate esteem for certain phenomena, especially tongues, to the detriment of order in the liturgy. Paul's response to this development provides us with the fullest exposition we have of his theology of the charisms.

‡[12:2–3] There is an experience of the Spirit and an understanding of ecstatic phenomena that are specifically Christian and that differ, despite apparent similarities, from those of the pagans. It is necessary to discern which spirit is leading one; ecstatic phenomena must be judged by their effect (1 Cor 12:2). 1 Cor 12:3 illustrates this by an example: power to confess Jesus as Lord can come only from the Spirit, and it is inconceivable that the Spirit would move anyone to curse the Lord.

§[12:4–6] There are some features common to all charisms, despite their diversity: all are **gifts** (*charismata*), grace from outside ourselves; all are **forms of service** (*diakoniai*), an expression of their purpose and effect; and all are workings (*energēmata*), in which God is at work. Paul associates each

of these aspects with what later theology will call one of the persons of the Trinity, an early example of "appropriation."

¶[12:12–26] The image of **a body** is introduced to explain Christ's relationship with believers (1 Cor 12:12). 1 Cor 12:13 applies this model to the church: by baptism all, despite diversity of ethnic or social origins, are integrated into one organism. 1 Cor 12:14–26 then develop the need for diversity of function among the parts of a body without threat to its unity.

**[12:27–30] Paul now applies the image again to the church as a whole and its members (1 Cor 12:27). The lists

n. [11:32] Dt 8:5; Heb 12:5–11. o. [12:2] Eph 2:11–18. p. [12:3] Rom 10:9; 1 Jn 4:2–3. q. [12:4] Rom 12:6; Eph 4:7, 11.

r. [12:8] 2:6–13. s. [12:10] 14:5, 26, 39; Acts 2:4. t. [12:11] 7:7; Eph 4:7. u. [12:12] 10:17; Rom 12:4–5; Eph 2:16; Col 3:15. v. [12:13] Gal 3:28; Eph 2:13–18; Col 3:11 / Jn 7:37–39. w. [12:27] Rom 12:5–8; Eph 1:23; 4:12; 5:30; Col 1:18, 24.

people God has designated in the church to be, first, apostles;* second, prophets; third, teachers; then, mighty deeds; then gifts of healing, assistance, administration, and varieties of tongues.*
²⁹Are all apostles? Are all prophets? Are all teachers? Do all work mighty deeds? ³⁰Do all have gifts of healing? Do all speak in tongues? Do all interpret? ³¹Strive eagerly for the greatest spiritual gifts.
The Way of Love. But I shall show you a still more excellent way.

CHAPTER 13†

¹If I speak in human and angelic tongues‡ but do not have love, I am a resounding gong or a clashing cymbal.ʸ ²And if I have the gift of prophecy and comprehend all mysteries and all knowledge; if I have all faith so as to move mountains but do not have love, I am nothing.ᶻ ³If I give away everything I own, and if I hand my body over so that I may boast but do not have love, I gain nothing.ᵃ

⁴§Love is patient, love is kind. It is not jealous, [love] is not pompous, it is not inflated,ᵇ ⁵it is not rude, it does not seek its own interests, it is not quick-tempered, it does not brood over injury,ᶜ ⁶it does not rejoice over wrongdoing but rejoices with the truth. ⁷It bears all things, believes all things, hopes all things, endures all things.ᵈ

⁸¶Love never fails. If there are prophecies, they will be brought to nothing; if tongues, they will cease; if knowledge, it will be brought to nothing. ⁹For we know partially and we prophesy partially, ¹⁰but when the perfect comes, the partial will pass away. ¹¹When I was a child, I used to talk as a child, think as a child, reason as a child; when I became a man, I put aside childish things. ¹²At present we see indistinctly, as in a mirror, but then face to face. At present I know partially; then I shall know fully, as I am fully known.ᵉ ¹³**So faith, hope, love remain, these three;ᶠ but the greatest of these is love.

CHAPTER 14

Prophecy Greater than Tongues. ¹††Pursue love, but strive eagerly for the spiritual gifts, above all that you may prophesy.ᵍ ²‡‡For one who speaks in a tongue does not speak to human beings but to God, for no one listens; he utters mysteries in spirit. ³On the other hand, one who prophesies does speak to human beings, for their building up,§§ encouragement, and solace.ʰ ⁴Whoever speaks in a tongue builds himself up, but whoever prophesies builds up the church. ⁵Now I should like all of you to speak in tongues, but even more to prophesy. One who prophesies is greater than one who speaks in tongues, unless he interprets, so that the church may be built up.

⁶¶¶Now, brothers, if I should come to you speaking in tongues, what good will I do you if I do not speak to you by way of revelation, or

---

in 1 Cor 12:28–30 spell out the parallelism by specifying the diversity of functions found in the church (cf. Rom 12:6–8; Eph 4:11).
*[12:28] **First, apostles:** apostleship was not mentioned in 1 Cor 12:8–10, nor is it at issue in these chapters, but Paul gives it pride of place in his listing. It is not just one gift among others but a prior and fuller gift that includes the others. They are all demonstrated in Paul's apostolate, but he may have developed his theology of charisms by reflecting first of all on his own grace of apostleship (cf. 1 Cor 3:5–4:14; 9:1–27; 2 Cor 2:14–6:13; 10:1–13:30, esp. 1 Cor 11:23 and 12:12).
†[13:1–13] This chapter involves a shift of perspective and a new point. All or part of the material may once have been an independent piece in the style of Hellenistic eulogies of virtues, but it is now integrated, by editing, into the context of 1 Cor 12–14 (cf. the reference to tongues and prophecy) and into the letter as a whole (cf. the references to knowledge and to behavior). The function of 1 Cor 13 within the discussion of spiritual gifts is to relativize all the charisms by contrasting them with the more basic, pervasive, and enduring value that gives them their purpose and their effectiveness. The rhetoric of this chapter is striking.
‡[13:1–3] An inventory of gifts, arranged in careful gradation: neither tongues (on the lowest rung), nor prophecy, knowledge, or faith, nor even self-sacrifice has value unless informed by love.
§[13:4–7] This paragraph is developed by personification and enumeration, defining love by what it does or does not do. The Greek contains fifteen verbs; it is natural to translate many of them by adjectives in English.
¶[13:8–13] The final paragraph announces its topic, **Love never fails** (1 Cor 13:8), then develops the permanence of love in contrast to the charisms (1 Cor 13:9–12), and finally asserts

love's superiority even over the other "theological virtues" (1 Cor 13:13).
[13:13] In speaking of love, Paul is led by spontaneous association to mention faith and hope as well. They are already a well-known triad (cf. 1 Thes 1:3), three interrelated (cf. 1 Cor 13:7) features of Christian life, more fundamental than any particular charism. **The greatest . . . is love: love is operative even within the other members of the triad (1 Cor 13:7), so that it has a certain primacy among them. Or, if the perspective is temporal, love will remain (cf. "never fails," 1 Cor 13:8) even when faith has yielded to sight and hope to possession.
††[14:1–5] 1 Cor 14:1b returns to the thought of 1 Cor 12:31a and reveals Paul's primary concern. The series of contrasts in 1 Cor 14:2–5 discloses the problem at Corinth: a disproportionate interest in tongues, with a corresponding failure to appreciate the worth of prophecy. Paul attempts to clarify the relative values of those gifts by indicating the kind of communication achieved in each and the kind of effect each produces.
‡‡[14:2–3a] They involve two kinds of communication: tongues, private speech toward God in inarticulate terms that need interpretation to be intelligible to others (see 1 Cor 14:27–28); prophecy, communication with others in the community.
§§[14:3b–5] They produce two kinds of effect. One who speaks in tongues **builds himself up;** it is a matter of individual experience and personal perfection, which inevitably recalls Paul's previous remarks about being inflated, seeking one's own good, pleasing oneself. But a prophet **builds up the church:** the theme of "building up" or "edifying" others, the main theme of the letter, comes to clearest expression in this chapter (1 Cor 14:3, 4, 5, 12, 17). It has been anticipated at 1 Cor 8:1 and 1 Cor 10:23, and by the related concept of "the beneficial" in 1 Cor 6:12; 10:23; 12:7; etc.
¶¶[14:6–12] Sound, in order to be useful, must be intelligible. This principle is illustrated by a series of analogies from music (1 Cor 14:7–8) and from ordinary human speech (1 Cor 14:10–11); it is applied to the case at hand in 1 Cor 14:9, 12.

---

x. [12:28] Eph 2:20; 3:5; 4:11. y. [13:1] 8:1; 16:14; Rom 12:9–10; 13:8–10. z. [13:2] 4:1; 14:2 / 1:5; 8:1–3; 12:8 / Mt 17:20; 21:21; Col 2:3. a. [13:3] Mt 6:2. b. [13:4] Eph 4:2 / 1 Cor 4:6, 18; 5:2; 8:1. c. [13:5] 10:24, 33; Phil 2:4, 21; 1 Thes 5:15. d. [13:7] Prv 10:12; 1 Pt 4:8.

e. [13:12] 2 Cor 5:7; Heb 11:1 / 2 Tm 2:19; 1 Jn 3:2. f. [13:13] Col 1:4; 1 Thes 1:3; 5:8. g. [14:1] 14:5, 12, 39. h. [14:3] 14:4–5, 12, 17, 26; 3:9; 8:1, 10; 10:23.

knowledge, or prophecy, or instruction? [7]Likewise, if inanimate things that produce sound, such as flute or harp, do not give out the tones distinctly, how will what is being played on flute or harp be recognized? [8]And if the bugle gives an indistinct sound, who will get ready for battle? [9]Similarly, if you, because of speaking in tongues, do not utter intelligible speech, how will anyone know what is being said? For you will be talking to the air. [10]It happens that there are many different languages in the world, and none is meaningless; [11]but if I do not know the meaning of a language, I shall be a foreigner to one who speaks it, and one who speaks it a foreigner to me. [12]So with yourselves: since you strive eagerly for spirits, seek to have an abundance of them for building up the church.
Need for Interpretation.[*] [13]Therefore, one who speaks in a tongue should pray to be able to interpret. [14][For] if I pray in a tongue, my spirit[†] is at prayer but my mind is unproductive. [15]So what is to be done? I will pray with the spirit, but I will also pray with the mind. I will sing praise with the spirit, but I will also sing praise with the mind.[i] [16]Otherwise, if you pronounce a blessing [with] the spirit, how shall one who holds the place of the uninstructed say the "Amen" to your thanksgiving, since he does not know what you are saying? [17]For you may be giving thanks very well, but the other is not built up. [18]I give thanks to God that I speak in tongues more than any of you, [19]but in the church I would rather speak five words with my mind, so as to instruct others also, than ten thousand words in a tongue.
Functions of These Gifts. [20‡]Brothers, stop being childish in your thinking. In respect to evil be like infants, but in your thinking be mature.[j] [21]It is written in the law:

"By people speaking strange tongues
　　and by the lips of foreigners
I will speak to this people,
　　and even so they will not listen to me,[k]

says the Lord." [22]Thus, tongues are a sign not for those who believe but for unbelievers, whereas prophecy is not for unbelievers but for those who believe.
[23§]So if the whole church meets in one place and everyone speaks in tongues, and then uninstructed people or unbelievers should come in, will they not say that you are out of your minds?[l] [24]But if everyone is prophesying, and an unbeliever or uninstructed person should come in, he will be convinced by everyone and judged by everyone, [25]and the secrets of his heart will be disclosed, and so he will fall down and worship God, declaring, "God is really in your midst."[m]
Rules of Order. [26¶]So what is to be done, brothers? When you assemble, one has a psalm, another an instruction, a revelation, a tongue, or an interpretation. Everything should be done for building up.[n] [27]If anyone speaks in a tongue, let it be two or at most three, and each in turn, and one should interpret. [28]But if there is no interpreter, the person should keep silent in the church and speak to himself and to God.
[29]Two or three prophets should speak, and the others discern. [30]But if a revelation is given to another person sitting there, the first one should be silent. [31]For you can all prophesy one by one, so that all may learn and all be encouraged. [32]Indeed, the spirits of prophets are under the prophets' control, [33]since he is not the God of disorder but of peace.
As in all the churches of the holy ones,[**] [34]women should keep silent in the churches, for they are not allowed to speak, but should be

---

*[14:13–19] The charism of interpretation lifts tongues to the level of intelligibility, enabling them to produce the same effect as prophecy (cf. 1 Cor 14:5, 26–28).
†[14:14–15] **My spirit:** Paul emphasizes the exclusively ecstatic, nonrational quality of tongues. The tongues at Pentecost are also described as an ecstatic experience (Acts 2:4, 12–13), though Luke superimposes further interpretations of his own. **My mind:** the ecstatic element, dominant in earliest Old Testament prophecy as depicted in 1 Sm 10:5–13; 19:20–24, seems entirely absent from Paul's notion of prophecy and completely relegated to tongues. He emphasizes the role of reason when he specifies instruction as a function of prophecy (1 Cor 14:6, 19, 31). But he does not exclude intuition and emotion; cf. references to encouragement and consolation (1 Cor 14:3, 31) and the scene describing the ideal exercise of prophecy (1 Cor 14:24–25).
‡[14:20–22] The Corinthians pride themselves on tongues as a sign of God's favor, a means of direct communication with him (2:28). To challenge them to a more mature appraisal, Paul draws from scripture a less flattering explanation of what speaking in tongues may signify. Isaiah threatened the people that if they failed to listen to their prophets, the Lord would speak to them (in punishment) through the lips of Assyrian conquerors (Is 28:11–12). Paul compresses Isaiah's text and makes God address his people directly. Equating tongues with foreign languages (cf. 1 Cor 14:10–11), Paul concludes from Isaiah that **tongues are a sign not for those who believe,** i.e., not a mark of God's pleasure for those who listen to him but a mark of his displeasure with those in the community who are faithless, who have not heeded the message that he has sent through the prophets.

§[14:23–25] Paul projects the possible missionary effect of two hypothetical liturgical experiences, one consisting wholly of tongues, the other entirely of prophecy. **Uninstructed** (*idiōtai*): the term may simply mean people who do not speak or understand tongues, as in 1 Cor 14:16, where it seems to designate Christians. But coupled with the term "unbelievers" it may be another way of designating those who have not been initiated into the community of faith; some believe it denotes a special class of non-Christians who are close to the community, such as catechumens. **Unbelievers** (*apistoi*): he has shifted from the inner-community perspective of 1 Cor 14:22; the term here designates non-Christians (cf. 1 Cor 6:6; 7:15; 10:27).
¶[14:26–33a] Paul concludes with specific directives regarding exercise of the gifts in their assemblies. Verse 26 enunciates the basic criterion in the use of any gift: it must contribute to "building up."
**[14:33b–36] Verse 33b may belong with what precedes, so that the new paragraph would begin only with 1 Cor 14:34. 1 Cor 14:34–35 change the subject. These two verses have the theme of submission in common with 1 Cor 14:11 despite differences in vocabulary, and a concern with what is or is not becoming; but it is difficult to harmonize the injunction to silence here with 1 Cor 11 which appears to take it for granted that women do pray and prophesy aloud in the assembly (cf. 1 Cor 11:5, 13). Hence the verses are often considered an interpolation, reflecting the discipline of later churches; such an interpolation would have to have antedated our manuscripts,

---

i. [14:15] Eph 5:19; Col 3:16. 　j. [14:20] Mt 10:16; Rom 16:19; Eph 4:14.

k. [14:21] Is 28:11–12; Dt 28:49. 　l. [14:23] Acts 2:6, 13. 　m. [14:25] 4:5 / Is 45:14; Zec 8:23. 　n. [14:26] Eph 4:12.

subordinate, as even the law says.° ³⁵But if they want to learn anything, they should ask their husbands at home. For it is improper for a woman to speak in the church. ³⁶Did the word of God go forth from you? Or has it come to you alone?

³⁷If anyone thinks that he is a prophet or a spiritual person, he should recognize that what I am writing to you is a commandment of the Lord. ³⁸If anyone does not acknowledge this, he is not acknowledged. ³⁹So, [my] brothers, strive eagerly to prophesy, and do not forbid speaking in tongues, ⁴⁰but everything must be done properly and in order.

V. THE RESURRECTION

A. The Resurrection of Christ

CHAPTER 15*
The Gospel Teaching.† ¹Now I am reminding you, brothers, of the gospel I preached to you, which you indeed received and in which you also stand. ²Through it you are also being saved, if you hold fast to the word I preached to you, unless you believed in vain. ³‡For I handed on to you as of first importance what I also received: that Christ died for our sins in accordance with the scriptures;ᵖ ⁴that he was buried; that he was raised on the third day in accordance with the scriptures;�q ⁵that he appeared to Cephas, then to the Twelve.ʳ ⁶After that, he appeared to more than five hundred brothers at once, most of whom are still living, though some have fallen asleep. ⁷After that he appeared to James, then to all the apostles. ⁸Last of all, as to one born abnormally, he appeared to me.ˢ ⁹For I am the least§ of the apostles, not fit to be called an apostle, because I persecuted the church of God.ᵗ ¹⁰But by the grace of God I am what I am, and his grace to me has not been ineffective. Indeed, I have toiled harder than all of them; not I, however, but the grace of God [that is] with me. ¹¹Therefore, whether it be I or they, so we preach and so you believed.

B. The Resurrection of the Dead

Results of Denial.§ ¹²But if Christ is preached as raised from the dead, how can some among you say there is no resurrection of the dead? ¹³If there is no resurrection of the dead, then neither has Christ been raised.ᵘ ¹⁴And if Christ has not been raised, then empty [too] is our preaching; empty, too, your faith. ¹⁵Then we are also false witnesses to God, because we testified against God that he raised Christ, whom he did not raise if in fact the dead are not raised.ᵛ ¹⁶For if the dead are not raised, neither has Christ been raised, ¹⁷and if Christ has not been raised," your faith is vain; you are still in your sins. ¹⁸Then those who have fallen asleep in Christ have perished. ¹⁹If for this life only we have hoped in Christ, we are the most pitiable people of all. **Christ the Firstfruits.**†† ²⁰ʷBut now Christ has been raised from the dead, the firstfruits‡‡ of those who have fallen asleep. ²¹§§For since death

---

all of which contain them, though some transpose them to the very end of the chapter.

*[15:1–58] Some consider this chapter an earlier Pauline composition inserted into the present letter. The problem that Paul treats is clear to a degree: some of the Corinthians are denying the resurrection of the dead (1 Cor 15:12), apparently because of their inability to imagine how any kind of bodily existence could be possible after death (1 Cor 15:35). It is plausibly supposed that their attitude stems from Greek anthropology, which looks with contempt upon matter and would be content with the survival of the soul, and perhaps also from an overrealized eschatology of gnostic coloration, such as that reflected in 2 Tm 2:18, which considers the resurrection a purely spiritual experience already achieved in baptism and in the forgiveness of sins. Paul, on the other hand, will affirm both the essential corporeity of the resurrection and its futurity. His response moves through three steps: a recall of the basic kerygma about Jesus' resurrection (1 Cor 15:1–11), an assertion of the logical inconsistencies involved in denial of the resurrection (1 Cor 15:12–34), and an attempt to perceive theologically what the properties of the resurrected body must be (1 Cor 15:35–58).

†[15:1–11] Paul recalls the tradition (1 Cor 15:3–7), which he can presuppose as common ground and which provides a starting point for his argument. This is the fundamental content of all Christian preaching and belief (1 Cor 15:1–2, 11).

‡[15:3–7] The language by which Paul expresses the essence of the "gospel" (1 Cor 15:1) is not his own but is drawn from older credal formulas. This credo highlights Jesus' death for our sins (confirmed by his burial) and Jesus' resurrection (confirmed by his appearances) and presents both of them as fulfillment of prophecy. **In accordance with the scriptures:** conformity of Jesus' passion with the scriptures is asserted in Mt 16:1; Lk 24:25–27, 32, 44–46. Application of some Old Testament texts (Ps 2:7; 16:8–11) to his resurrection is illustrated by Acts 2:27–31; 13:29–39; and Is 52:13–53:12 and Hos 6:2 may also have been envisaged.

§[15:9–11] A persecutor may have appeared disqualified (ouk . . . hikanos) from apostleship, but in fact God's grace has qualified him. Cf. the remarks in 2 Corinthians about his qualifications (2 Cor 2:16; 3:5) and his greater labors (2 Cor 11:23). These verses are parenthetical, but a nerve has been touched (the references to his abnormal birth and his activity as a persecutor may echo taunts from Paul's opponents), and he is instinctively moved to self-defense.

¶[15:12–19] Denial of the resurrection (1 Cor 15:12) involves logical inconsistencies. The basic one, stated twice (1 Cor 15:13, 16), is that if there is no such thing as (bodily) resurrection, then it has not taken place even in Christ's case.

**[15:17–18] The consequences for the Corinthians are grave: both forgiveness of sins and salvation are an illusion, despite their strong convictions about both. Unless Christ is risen, their faith does not save.

††[15:20–28] After a triumphant assertion of the reality of Christ's resurrection (1 Cor 15:20a), Paul explains its positive implications and consequences. As a soteriological event of both human (1 Cor 15:20–23) and cosmic (1 Cor 15:24–28) dimensions, Jesus' resurrection logically and necessarily involves ours as well.

‡‡[15:20] **The firstfruits:** the portion of the harvest offered in thanksgiving to God implies the consecration of the entire harvest to come. Christ's resurrection is not an end in itself; its finality lies in the whole harvest, ourselves.

§§[15:21–22] Our human existence, both natural and supernatural, is corporate, involves solidarity. **In Adam . . . in Christ:** the Hebrew word *ādām* in Genesis is both a common noun for mankind and a proper noun for the first man. Paul here presents Adam as at least a literary type of Christ; the

---

o. [14:34] 1 Tm 2:11–15; 1 Pt 3:1.   p. [15:3] 11:23 / 1 Pt 2:24; 3:18 / Is 53:4–12.   q. [15:4] Acts 2:23–24 / Ps 16:8–11; Hos 6:1–2; Jon 2:1. r. [15:5] Mk 16:14; Mt 28:16–17; Lk 24:36; Jn 20:19.

s. [15:8] 9:1; Acts 9:3–6; Gal 1:16.   t. [15:9] Acts 8:3; 9:1–2; Gal 1:23; Eph 3:8; 1 Tm 1:15.   u. [15:13] 1 Thes 4:14.   v. [15:15] Acts 5:32.   w. [15:20] Rom 8:11; Col 1:18; 1 Thes 4:14.

came through a human being, the resurrection of the dead came also through a human being. ²²For just as in Adam all die, so too in Christ shall all be brought to life,^x ²³but each one in proper order: Christ the firstfruits; then, at his coming, those who belong to Christ;^y ²⁴then comes the end,* when he hands over the kingdom to his God and Father, when he has destroyed every sovereignty and every authority and power.^z ²⁵For he must reign until he has put all his enemies under his feet.^a ^{26†}The last enemy^b to be destroyed is death, ^{27‡}for "he subjected everything under his feet."^c But when it says that everything has been subjected, it is clear that it excludes the one who subjected everything to him. ²⁸When everything is subjected to him, then the Son himself will [also] be subjected to the one who subjected everything to him, so that God may be all in all.^d

Practical Arguments.[§] ²⁹Otherwise, what will people accomplish by having themselves baptized for the dead?[¶] If the dead are not raised at all, then why are they having themselves baptized for them?

^{30**}Moreover, why are we endangering ourselves all the time?^e ³¹Every day I face death; I swear it by the pride in you [brothers] that I have in Christ Jesus our Lord.^f ³²If at Ephesus I fought with beasts, so to speak, what benefit was it to me? If the dead are not raised:

"Let us eat and drink,
    for tomorrow we die."^g

³³Do not be led astray:

"Bad company corrupts good morals."

³⁴Become sober as you ought and stop sinning. For some have no knowledge of God; I say this to your shame.^h

C. The Manner of the Resurrection^{††}

^{35‡‡}But someone may say, "How are the dead raised? With what kind of body will they come back?"

The Resurrection Body. ^{36§§}You fool! What you sow is not brought to life unless it dies.ⁱ ³⁷And what you sow is not the body that is to be but a bare kernel of wheat, perhaps, or of some other kind; ^{38¶}but God gives it a body as he chooses, and to each of the seeds its own body. ^{39¶¶}Not all flesh is the same, but there is one kind for human beings, another kind of flesh for animals, another kind of flesh for birds, and another for fish. ⁴⁰There are both heavenly bodies and earthly bodies, but the brightness of the heavenly is one kind and that of the earthly another. ⁴¹The brightness of the sun is one kind, the brightness of the moon another, and the brightness of the stars another. For star differs from star in brightness.

^{42***}So also is the resurrection of the dead. It is sown corruptible; it is raised incorruptible. ⁴³It

---

parallelism and contrast between them will be developed further in 1 Cor 15:45–49 and in Rom 5:12–21.

*[15:24–28] Paul's perspective expands to cosmic dimensions, as he describes the climax of history, **the end.** His viewpoint is still christological, as in 1 Cor 15:20–23. 1 Cor 15:24, 28 describe Christ's final relations to his enemies and his Father in language that is both royal and military; 1 Cor 15:25–28 insert a proof from scripture (Ps 110:1; 8:6) into this description. But the viewpoint is also theological, for God is the ultimate agent and end, and likewise soteriological, for we are the beneficiaries of all the action.

†[15:26] **The last enemy . . . is death:** a parenthesis that specifies the final fulfillment of the two Old Testament texts just referred to, Ps 110:1 and Ps 8:7. Death is not just one cosmic power among many, but the ultimate effect of sin in the universe (cf. 1 Cor 15:56; Rom 5:12). Christ defeats death where it prevails, in our bodies. The destruction of the last enemy is concretely the "coming to life" (1 Cor 15:22) of "those who belong to Christ" (1 Cor 15:23).

‡[15:27b–28] **The one who subjected everything to him:** the Father is the ultimate agent in the drama, and the final end of the process, to whom the Son and everything else is ordered (1 Cor 15:24, 28). **That God may be all in all:** his reign is a dynamic exercise of creative power, an outpouring of life and energy through the universe, with no further resistance. This is the supremely positive meaning of "subjection": that God may fully be God.

§[15:29–34] Paul concludes his treatment of logical inconsistencies with a listing of miscellaneous Christian practices that would be meaningless if the resurrection were not a fact.

¶[15:29] **Baptized for the dead:** this practice is not further explained here, nor is it necessarily mentioned with approval, but Paul cites it as something in their experience that attests in one more way to belief in the resurrection.

[15:30–34] A life of sacrifice, such as Paul describes in 1 Cor 4:9–13 and 2 Corinthians, would be pointless without the prospect of resurrection; a life of pleasure, such as that expressed in the Epicurean slogan of 1 Cor 15:32, would be far more consistent. **I fought with beasts: since Paul does not elsewhere mention a combat with beasts at Ephesus, he may be speaking figuratively about struggles with adversaries.

††[15:35–58] Paul imagines two objections that the Corinthians could raise: one concerning the manner of the resurrection (**how?**), the other pertaining to the qualities of the risen body (**what kind?**). These questions probably lie behind their denial of the resurrection (1 Cor 15:12), and seem to reflect the presumption that no kind of body other than the one we now possess would be possible. Paul deals with these objections in inverse order, in 1 Cor 15:36–49 and 1 Cor 15:50–58. His argument is fundamentally theological and its appeal is to the understanding.

‡‡[15:35–49] Paul approaches the question of the nature of the risen body (**what kind of body?**) by means of two analogies: the seed (1 Cor 15:36–44) and the first man, Adam (1 Cor 15:45–49).

§§[15:36–38] The analogy of the seed: there is a change of attributes from seed to plant; the old life-form must be lost for the new to emerge. By speaking about the seed as a **body** that dies and comes to life, Paul keeps the point of the analogy before the reader's mind.

¶¶[15:39–41] The expression "its own body" (1 Cor 15:38) leads to a development on the marvelous diversity evident in bodily life.

***[15:42–44] The principles of qualitative difference before and after death (1 Cor 15:36–38) and of diversity on different levels of creation (1 Cor 15:39–41) are now applied to the human body. Before: a body animated by a lower, natural life-principle (*psychē*) and endowed with the properties of natural

---

x. [15:22] Gn 3:17–19; Rom 5:12–19.   y. [15:23] 1 Thes 4:15–17.
z. [15:24] Eph 1:22.   a. [15:25] Ps 110:1.   b. [15:26] Rom 6:9;
2 Tm 1:10; Rev 20:14; 21:4.   c. [15:27] Ps 8:7; Eph 1:22; Phil 3:21.
d. [15:28] Eph 4:6; Col 3:11.   e. [15:30] 2 Cor 4:8–12; 11:23–27.

f. [15:31] Ps 44:23; Rom 8:36.   g. [15:32] 4:9; 2 Cor 4:10–11 / Wis
2:5–7; Is 22:13.   h. [15:34] Mt 22:29; Mk 12:24.   i. [15:36] Jn
12:24.   j. [15:38] Gn 1:11.

is sown dishonorable; it is raised glorious. It is sown weak; it is raised powerful.[k] [44]It is sown a natural body; it is raised a spiritual body. If there is a natural body, there is also a spiritual one. [45]So, too, it is written, "The first man, Adam,* became a living being," the last Adam a life-giving spirit.[l] [46]But the spiritual was not first; rather the natural and then the spiritual. [47]The first man was from the earth, earthly; the second man, from heaven. [48]As was the earthly one, so also are the earthly, and as is the heavenly one, so also are the heavenly. [49]Just as we have borne the image[†] of the earthly one, we shall also bear the image[†] of the heavenly one.[m]

The Resurrection Event. [50‡]This I declare, brothers: flesh and blood cannot inherit the kingdom of God, nor does corruption[§] inherit incorruption.[n] [51§]Behold, I tell you a mystery. We shall not all fall asleep, but we will all be changed,[o] [52]in an instant, in the blink of an eye, at the last trumpet. For the trumpet will sound, the dead will be raised incorruptible, and we shall be changed.[p] [53]For that which is corruptible must clothe itself with incorruptibility, and that which is mortal must clothe itself with immortality.[q] [54**]And when this which

is corruptible clothes itself with incorruptibility and this which is mortal clothes itself with immortality, then the word that is written shall come about:[r]

"Death is swallowed up in victory.
[55] Where, O death, is your victory?
Where, O death, is your sting?"[s]

[56]The sting of death is sin,[††] and the power of sin is the law.[t] [57]But thanks be to God who gives us the victory through our Lord Jesus Christ.[u]

[58]Therefore, my beloved brothers, be firm, steadfast, always fully devoted to the work of the Lord, knowing that in the Lord your labor is not in vain.

VI. CONCLUSION

CHAPTER 16

The Collection.[‡‡] [1]Now in regard to the collection[§§] for the holy ones, you also should do as I ordered the churches of Galatia.[v] [2]On the first day of the week each of you should set aside and save whatever he can afford, so that collections will not be going on when I come. [3]And when I arrive, I shall send those whom you have approved with letters of recommendation to take your gracious gift to Jerusalem. [4]If it seems fitting that I should go also,[¶¶] they will go with me. **Paul's Travel Plans.***** [5]I shall come to you after I pass through Macedonia (for I am going to pass through Macedonia),[w] [6]and perhaps I shall stay or even spend the winter with you, so that you may send me on my way wherever I may go. [7]For I do not wish to see you now just in passing, but I hope to spend some time with you, if the Lord permits.[x] [8†††]I shall stay in Ephesus[y]

---

existence (corruptibility, lack of glory, weakness). After: a body animated by a higher life-principle (*pneuma*; cf. 1 Cor 15:45) and endowed with other qualities (incorruptibility, glory, power, spirituality), which are properties of God himself.

*[15:45] The analogy of **the first man, Adam**, is introduced by a citation from Gn 2:7. Paul alters the text slightly, adding the adjective **first**, and translating the Hebrew *ādām* twice, so as to give it its value both as a common noun (**man**) and as a proper name (**Adam**). 1 Cor 15:45b then specifies similarities and differences between the two Adams. The last **Adam**, Christ (cf. 1 Cor 15:21–22) has become a . . . **spirit** (*pneuma*), a life-principle transcendent with respect to the natural soul (*psychē*) of the first Adam (on the terminology here, cf. note on 1 Cor 3:1). Further, he is not just alive, but life-giving, a source of life for others.

†[15:49] **We shall also bear the image**: although it has less manuscript support, this reading better fits the context's emphasis on futurity and the transforming action of God; on future transformation as conformity to the image of the Son, cf. Rom 8:29; Phil 3:21. The majority reading, "let us bear the image," suggests that the image of the heavenly man is already present and exhorts us to conform to it.

‡[15:50–57] These verses, an answer to the first question of 1 Cor 15:35, explain theologically how the change of properties from one image to another will take place: God has the power to transform, and he will exercise it.

§[15:50–53] **Flesh and blood . . . corruption**: living persons and the corpses of the dead, respectively. In both cases, the gulf between creatures and God is too wide to be bridged unless God himself transforms us.

¶[15:51–52] **A mystery**: the last moment in God's plan is disclosed; cf. notes on 1 Cor 2:1, 7–10a. The final trumpet and the awakening of the dead are stock details of the apocalyptic scenario. **We shall not all fall asleep**: Paul expected that some of his contemporaries might still be alive at Christ's return; after the death of Paul and his whole generation, copyists altered this statement in various ways. **We will all be changed**: the statement extends to all Christians, for Paul is not directly speaking about anyone else. Whether they have died before the end or happen still to be alive, all must be transformed.

[15:54–55] **Death is swallowed up in victory: scripture itself predicts death's overthrow. **O death**: in his prophetic

vision Paul may be making Hosea's words his own, or imagining this cry of triumph on the lips of the risen church.

††[15:56] **The sting of death is sin**: an explanation of Hosea's metaphor. Death, scorpion-like, is equipped with a sting, sin, by which it injects its poison. Christ defeats sin, the cause of death (Gn 3:19; Rom 5:12).

‡‡[16:1–4] This paragraph contains our earliest evidence for a project that became a major undertaking of Paul's ministry. The collection for the church at Jerusalem was a symbol in his mind for the unity of Jewish and Gentile Christianity. Cf. Gal 2:10; Rom 15:25–29; 2 Cor 8–9 and the notes to this last passage.

§§[16:1] **In regard to the collection**: it has already begun in Galatia and Macedonia (cf. 2 Cor 8), and presumably he has already instructed the Corinthians about its purpose.

¶¶[16:4] **That I should go also**: presumably Paul delivered the collection on his final visit to Jerusalem; cf. Rom 15:25–32; Acts 24:14.

***[16:5–12] The travel plans outlined here may not have materialized precisely as Paul intended; cf. 2 Cor 1:8–2:13; 7:4–16.

†††[16:8] **In Ephesus until Pentecost**: this tells us the place from which he wrote the letter and suggests he may have composed it about Easter time (cf. 1 Cor 5:7–8).

---

r. [15:54] Is 25:8; 2 Cor 5:4; 2 Tm 1:10; Heb 2:14–15.   s. [15:55] Hos 13:14.   t. [15:56] Rom 4:15; 7:7, 13.   u. [15:57] Jn 16:33; 1 Jn 5:4.   v. [16:1] Acts 24:17; Rom 15:25–32; 2 Cor 8–9; Gal 2:10.   w. [16:5] Acts 19:21; Rom 15:26; 2 Cor 1:15–16.   x. [16:7] Acts 18:21.   y. [16:8] 15:32; Acts 18:19; 19:1–10.

k. [15:43] Phil 3:20–21; Col 3:4.   l, [15:45] Gn 2:7 / Jn 5:21–29; 2 Cor 3:6, 17.   m. [15:49] Gn 5:3 / Rom 8:29; Phil 3:21.   n. [15:50] Jn 3:3–6.   o. [15:51] 1 Thes 4:14–17.   p. [15:52] Jl 2:1; Zec 9:14; Mt 24:31; Rev 11:15–18.   q. [15:53] 2 Cor 5:2–4.

until Pentecost, ⁹because a door has opened for me wide and productive for work, but there are many opponents.ᶻ

¹⁰If Timothy comes, see that he is without fear in your company, for he is doing the work of the Lord just as I am.ᵃ ¹¹Therefore, no one should disdain him. Rather, send him on his way in peace that he may come to me, for I am expecting him with the brothers. ¹²Now in regard to our brother Apollos, I urged him strongly to go to you with the brothers, but it was not at all his will that he go now. He will go when he has an opportunity.ᵇ

Exhortation and Greetings. ¹³Be on your guard, stand firm in the faith, be courageous, be strong. ¹⁴Your every act should be done with love.

¹⁵I urge you, brothers—you know that the household of Stephanasᶜ is the firstfruits of Achaia and that they have devoted themselves to the service of the holy ones— ¹⁶be subordinate to such people and to everyone who works and toils with them. ¹⁷I rejoice in the arrival of Stephanas, Fortunatus, and Achaicus, because they made up for your absence, ¹⁸for they refreshed my spirit as well as yours. So give recognition to such people.ᵈ

¹⁹*The churches of Asia send you greetings. Aquila and Prisca together with the church at their house send you many greetings in the Lord.ᵉ ²⁰All the brothers greet you. Greet one another with a holy kiss.ᶠ

²¹I, Paul, write you this greeting in my own hand.ᵍ ²²If anyone does not love the Lord, let him be accursed.† *Marana tha.*ʰ ²³The grace of the Lord Jesus be with you.ⁱ ²⁴My love to all of you in Christ Jesus.

---

*[16:19–24] These paragraphs conform to the normal epistolary conclusion, but their language is overlaid with liturgical coloration as well. The **greetings** of the Asian churches are probably to be read, along with the letter, in the liturgy at Corinth, and the union of the church is to be expressed by a holy kiss (1 Cor 16:19–20). Paul adds to this his own greeting (1 Cor 16:21) and blessings (1 Cor 16:23–24).

†[16:22] **Accursed:** literally, "anathema." This expression (cf. 1 Cor 12:3) is a formula for exclusion from the community; it may imply here a call to self-examination before celebration of the Eucharist, in preparation for the Lord's coming and judgment (cf. 1 Cor 11:17–34). *Marana tha:* an Aramaic expression, probably used in the early Christian liturgy. As understood here ("O Lord, come!"), it is a prayer for the early return of Christ. If the Aramaic words are divided differently (*Maran atha,* "Our Lord has come"), it becomes a credal declaration. The former interpretation is supported by what appears to be a Greek equivalent of this acclamation in Rev 22:20 "Amen. Come, Lord Jesus!"

---

z. [16:9] Acts 14:27; 2 Cor 2:12.   a. [16:10] 4:17; Acts 16:1; 19:22; Phil 2:19–23.   b. [16:12] 1:12; 3:4–6, 22; Acts 18:24–28.   c. [16:15] 1:16.   d. [16:18] 1 Thes 5:12–13.

e. [16:19] Acts 18:2, 18, 26; Rom 16:3–5.   f. [16:20] Rom 16:16; 2 Cor 13:12; 1 Thes 5:26; 1 Pt 5:14.   g. [16:21] Gal 6:11; Col 4:18; 2 Thes 3:17.   h. [16:22] 12:3; Rom 9:3; Gal 1:8–9; Rev 22:20.   i. [16:23] Rom 16:20.

THE SECOND LETTER TO THE
CORINTHIANS

～∾⁊～

The Second Letter to the Corinthians is the most personal of all of Paul's extant writings, and it reveals much about his character. In it he deals with one or more crises that have arisen in the Corinthian church. The confrontation with these problems caused him to reflect deeply on his relationship with the community and to speak about it frankly. One moment he is venting his feelings of frustration and uncertainty, the next he is pouring out his relief and affection. The importance of the issues at stake between them calls forth from him an enormous effort of personal persuasion, as well as doctrinal considerations that are of great value for us. Paul's ability to produce profound theological foundations for what may at first sight appear to be rather commonplace circumstances is perhaps nowhere better exemplified than in Second Corinthians. The emotional tone of the letter, its lack of order, and our ignorance of some of its background do not make it easy to follow, but it amply repays the effort required of the reader.

Second Corinthians is rich and varied in content. The interpretation of Exodus in chapter 3, for instance, offers a striking example of early apologetic use of the Old Testament. Paul's discussion of the collection in chaps. 8–9 contains a theology of sharing of possessions, of community of goods among Christian churches, which is both balanced and sensitive. Furthermore, the closing chapters provide an illustration of early Christian invective and polemic, because the conflict with intruders forces Paul to assert his authority. But in those same chapters Paul articulates the vision and sense of values that animate his own apostolate, revealing his faith that Jesus' passion and resurrection are the pattern for all Christian life and expressing a spirituality of ministry unsurpassed in the New Testament.

The letter is remarkable for its rhetoric. Paul falls naturally into the style and argumentation of contemporary philosophic preachers, employing with ease the stock devices of the "diatribe." By a barrage of questions, by challenges both serious and ironic, by paradox heaped upon paradox, even by insults hurled at his opponents, he strives to awaken in his hearers a true sense of values and an appropriate response. All his argument centers on the destiny of Jesus, in which a paradoxical reversal of values is revealed. But Paul appeals to his own personal experience as well. In passages of great rhetorical power (2 Cor 4:7–15; 6:3–10; 11:21–29; 12:5–10; 13:3–4) he enumerates the circumstances of his ministry and the tribulations he has had to endure for Jesus and the gospel, in the hope of illustrating the pattern of Jesus' existence in his own and of drawing the Corinthians into a reappraisal of the values they cherish. Similar passages in the same style in his other letters (cf. especially Rom 8:31–39; 1 Cor 1:26–31; 4:6–21; 9:1–27; 13:1–13; Phil 4:10–19) confirm Paul's familiarity with contemporary rhetoric and demonstrate how effectively it served to express his vision of Christian life and ministry.

Second Corinthians was occasioned by events and problems that developed after Paul's first letter reached Corinth. We have no information about these circumstances except what is contained in the letter itself, which of course supposes that they are known to the readers. Consequently the reconstruction of the letter's background is an uncertain enterprise about which there is not complete agreement.

The letter deals principally with these three topics: (1) a crisis between Paul and the Corinthians, occasioned at least partially by changes in his travel plans (2 Cor 1:12–2:13), and the successful resolution of that crisis (2 Cor 7:5–16); (2) further directives and encouragement in regard to the collection for the church in Jerusalem (2 Cor 8:1–9:15); (3) the definition and defense of Paul's ministry as an apostle. Paul's reflections on this matter are occasioned by visitors from other churches who passed through Corinth, missionaries who differed from Paul in a variety of ways, both in theory and in practice. Those differences led to comparisons. Either the visitors themselves or some of the local church members appear to have sown confusion among the Corinthians with regard to Paul's authority or his style, or both. Paul deals at length with aspects of this situation in 2 Cor 2:14–7:4 and again in 2 Cor 10:1–13:10, though the manner of treatment and the thrust of the argument differ in each of these sections.

Scholars have noticed a lack of continuity in this document. For example, the long section of 2 Cor 2:14–7:4 seems abruptly spliced into the narrative of a crisis and its resolution. Identical or similar topics, moreover, seem to be treated several times during the letter (compare 2 Cor 2:14–7:4 with 2 Cor 10:1–13:10, and 2 Cor 8:1–24 with 2 Cor 9:1–15). Many judge, therefore, that this letter as it stands incorporates several briefer letters sent to Corinth over a certain span of time. If this is so, then Paul himself or, more likely, some other editor clearly took care to gather those letters together and impose some literary unity upon the collection, thus producing the document that has come down to us as the Second Letter to the Corinthians. Others continue to regard it as a single letter, attributing its inconsistencies to changes of perspective in Paul that may have been occasioned by the arrival of fresh news from Corinth during its composition. The letter, or at least some sections of it, appears to have been composed in Macedonia (2 Cor 2:12–13; 7:5–6; 8:1–4; 9:2–4). It is generally dated about the autumn of A.D. 57; if it is a compilation, of course, the various parts may have been separated by intervals of at least some months.

The principal divisions of the Second Letter to the Corinthians are the following:

I. Address (1:1–11)
II. The Crisis Between Paul and the Corinthians (1:12–7:16)
    A. Past Relationships (1:12–2:13)
    B. Paul's Ministry (2:14–7:4)
    C. Resolution of the Crisis (7:5–16)
III. The Collection for Jerusalem (8:1–9:15)
IV. Paul's Defense of His Ministry (10:1–13:10)
V. Conclusion (13:11–13)

I. ADDRESS

CHAPTER 1

Greeting. [1]Paul, an apostle of Christ Jesus by the will of God, and Timothy our brother, to the church of God that is in Corinth, with all the holy ones throughout Achaia:[a] [2]grace to you and peace from God our Father and the Lord Jesus Christ.

Thanksgiving. [3b]Blessed be the God and Father of our Lord Jesus Christ, the Father of compassion and God of all encouragement,[†] [4]who encourages us in our every affliction, so that we may be able to encourage those who are in any affliction with the encouragement with which we ourselves are encouraged by God.[c] [5]For as Christ's sufferings overflow to us, so through Christ[‡] does our encouragement also overflow. [6]If we are afflicted, it is for your encouragement and salvation; if we are encouraged, it is for your encouragement, which enables you to endure the same sufferings that we suffer. [7]Our hope for you is firm, for we know that as you share in the sufferings, you also share in the encouragement.[§]

[8]We do not want you to be unaware, brothers, of the affliction that came to us in the province of Asia;[¶] we were utterly weighed down beyond our strength, so that we despaired even of life.[d] [9]Indeed, we had accepted within ourselves the

*[1:1–11] The opening follows the usual Pauline form, except that the thanksgiving takes the form of a doxology or glorification of God (2 Cor 1:3). This introduces a meditation on the experience of suffering and encouragement shared by Paul and the Corinthians (2 Cor 1:4–7), drawn, at least in part, from Paul's reflections on a recent affliction (2 Cor 1:8–10). The section ends with a modified and delayed allusion to thanksgiving (2 Cor 1:11).

†[1:3] **God of all encouragement:** Paul expands a standard Jewish blessing so as to state the theme of the paragraph. The theme of "encouragement" or "consolation" (*paraklēsis*) occurs ten times in this opening, against a background formed by multiple references to "affliction" and "suffering."

‡[1:5] **Through Christ:** the Father of compassion is the Father of our Lord Jesus (2 Cor 1:3); Paul's sufferings and encouragement (or "consolation") are experienced in union with Christ. Cf. Lk 2:25: the "consolation of Israel" is Jesus himself.

§[1:7] **You also share in the encouragement:** the eschatological reversal of affliction and encouragement that Christians expect (cf. Mt 5:4; Lk 6:24) permits some present experience of reversal in the Corinthians' case, as in Paul's.

¶[1:8] **Asia:** a Roman province in western Asia Minor, the capital of which was Ephesus.

a. [1:1] Eph 1:1; Col 1:1 / 2 Cor 1:19; Acts 16 / Rom 1:7; 1 Cor 1:2.   b. [1:3] 1 Cor 15:24; Eph 1:3; 1 Pt 1:3 / Rom 15:5.   c. [1:4] 7:6–7, 13; 1 Thes 3:6–8; 2 Thes 2:16.   d. [1:8] Acts 20:18–19; 1 Cor 15:32.

sentence of death,* that we might trust not in ourselves but in God who raises the dead.*e 10He rescued us from such great danger of death, and he will continue to rescue us; in him we have put our hope [that] he will also rescue us again,f 11as you help us with prayer, so that thanks may be given by many on our behalf for the gift granted us through the prayers of many.g

II. THE CRISIS BETWEEN PAUL AND THE CORINTHIANS

A. Past Relationships†

Paul's Sincerity and Constancy. 12‡For our boast is this, the testimony of our conscience that we have conducted ourselves in the world, and especially toward you, with the simplicity and sincerity of God, [and] not by human wisdom but by the grace of God. 13For we write you nothing but what you can read and understand, and I hope that you will understand completely, 14as you have come to understand us partially, that we are your boast as you also are ours, on the day of [our] Lord Jesus.h

15With this confidence I formerly intended to come§ to you so that you might receive a double favor, 16namely, to go by way of you to Macedonia, and then to come to you again on my return from Macedonia, and have you send me on my way to Judea.i 17So when I intended this, did I act lightly?¶ Or do I make my plans according to human considerations, so that

with me it is "yes, yes" and "no, no"?j 18As God is faithful,** our word to you is not "yes" and "no." 19For the Son of God, Jesus Christ, who was proclaimed to you by us, Silvanus and Timothy and me, was not "yes" and "no," but "yes" has been in him.k 20For however many are the promises of God, their Yes is in him; therefore, the Amen from us also goes through him to God for glory.l 21††But the one who gives us security with you in Christ and who anointed us is God;m 22he has also put his seal upon us and given the Spirit in our hearts as a first installment.n

Paul's Change of Plan. 23oBut I call upon God as witness, on my life, that it is to spare you that I have not yet gone to Corinth.‡‡ 24Not that we lord it over your faith; rather, we work together for your joy, for you stand firm in the faith.

CHAPTER 2
1For I decided not to come to you again in painful circumstances. 2For if I inflict pain upon you, then who is there to cheer me except the one pained by me? 3And I wrote as I did§§ so that when I came I might not be pained by those in whom I should have rejoiced, confident about all of you that my joy is that of all of you. 4For

---

*[1:9–10] **The sentence of death:** it is unclear whether Paul is alluding to a physical illness or to an external threat to life. The result of the situation was to produce an attitude of faith in God alone. **God who raises the dead:** rescue is the constant pattern of God's activity; his final act of encouragement is the resurrection.

†[1:12–2:13] The autobiographical remarks about the crisis in Asia Minor lead into consideration of a crisis that has arisen between Paul and the Corinthians. Paul will return to this question, after a long digression, in 2 Cor 7:5–16. Both of these sections deal with travel plans Paul had made, changes in the plans, alternative measures adopted, a breach that opened between him and the community, and finally a reconciliation between them.

‡[1:12–14] Since Paul's own conduct will be under discussion here, he prefaces the section with a statement about his habitual behavior and attitude toward the community. He protests his openness, single-mindedness, and conformity to God's grace; he hopes that his relationship with them will be marked by mutual understanding and pride, which will constantly increase until it reaches its climax at the judgment. Two references to boasting frame this paragraph (2 Cor 1:12, 14), the first appearances of a theme that will be important in the letter, especially in 2 Cor 10–13; the term is used in a positive sense here (cf. note on 1 Cor 1:29–31).

§[1:15] **I formerly intended to come:** this plan reads like a revision of the one mentioned in 1 Cor 16:5. Not until 2 Cor 1:23–2:1 will Paul tell us something his original readers already knew, that he has canceled one or the other of these projected visits.

¶[1:17] **Did I act lightly?:** the subsequent change of plans casts suspicion on the original intention, creating the impression that Paul is vacillating and inconsistent or that **human considerations** keep dictating shifts in his goals and projects (cf. the counterclaim of 2 Cor 1:12). **"Yes, yes" and "no, no":** stating something and denying it in the same or the next breath; being of two minds at once, or from one moment to the next.

[1:18–22] **As God is faithful: unable to deny the change in plans, Paul nonetheless asserts the firmness of the original plan and claims a profound constancy in his life and work. He grounds his defense in God himself, who is firm and reliable; this quality can also be predicated in various ways of those who are associated with him. Christ, Paul, and the Corinthians all participate in analogous ways in the constancy of God. A number of the terms here, which appear related only conceptually in Greek or English, would be variations of the same root, *'mn*, in a Semitic language, and thus naturally associated in a Semitic mind, such as Paul's. These include the words **yes** (2 Cor 1:17–20), **faithful** (2 Cor 1:18), **Amen** (2 Cor 1:20), **gives us security** (2 Cor 1:21), **faith, stand firm** (2 Cor 1:24).

††[1:21–22] The commercial terms **gives us security, seal, first installment** are here used analogously to refer to the process of initiation into the Christian life, perhaps specifically to baptism. The passage is clearly trinitarian. The Spirit is the **first installment** or "down payment" of the full messianic benefits that God guarantees to Christians. Cf. Eph 1:13–14.

‡‡[1:23–24] **I have not yet gone to Corinth:** some suppose that Paul received word of some affair in Corinth, which he decided to regulate by letter even before the first of his projected visits (cf. 2 Cor 1:16). Others conjecture that he did pay the first visit, was offended there (cf. 2 Cor 2:5), returned to Ephesus, and sent a letter (2 Cor 2:3–9) in place of the second visit. The expressions **to spare you** (2 Cor 1:23) and **work together for your joy** (2 Cor 1:24) introduce the major themes of the next two paragraphs, which are remarkable for insistent repetition of key words and ideas. These form two clusters of terms in the English translation: (1) cheer, rejoice, encourage, joy; (2) pain, affliction, anguish. These clusters reappear when Paul resumes treatment of this subject in 2 Cor 7:5–16.

§§[2:3–4] **I wrote as I did:** we learn for the first time about the sending of a letter in place of the proposed visit. Paul mentions the letter in passing, but emphasizes his motivation in sending it: to avoid being saddened by them (cf. 1 Cor 2:1), and to help them realize the depth of his love. Another motive will be added in 2 Cor 7:12: to bring to light their own concern for him. **With many tears:** it has been suggested that we may have all or part of this "tearful letter" somewhere in the Corinthian correspondence, either in 1 Cor 5 (the case of the incestuous man), or in 1 Corinthians as a whole, or in 2 Cor 2:10–13. None of these hypotheses is entirely convincing. See note on 2 Cor 13:1.

---

e. [1:9] 4:7–11; Rom 4:17.   f. [1:10] 2 Tm 4:18.   g. [1:11] 4:15; 9:12.   h. [1:14] Phil 2:16; 1 Thes 2:19–20.   i. [1:16] 1 Cor 16:5–9; Acts 19:21.

j. [1:17] Mt 5:37; Jas 5:12.   k. [1:19] Acts 16:1–3; 1 Thes 1:1; 2 Thes 1:1.   l. [1:20] 1 Cor 14:16; Rev 3:14.   m. [1:21] 1 Jn 2:20, 27.   n. [1:22] Eph 1:13–14; 4:30 / 2 Cor 5:5; Rom 5:5; 8:16, 23.   o. [1:23] 13:2.

out of much affliction and anguish of heart I wrote to you with many tears, not that you might be pained but that you might know the abundant love I have for you.
The Offender.* ⁵If anyone has caused pain, he has caused it not to me, but in some measure (not to exaggerate) to all of you. ⁶This punishment by the majority is enough for such a person, ⁷so that on the contrary you should forgive and encourage him instead, or else the person may be overwhelmed by excessive pain.ᵖ ⁸Therefore, I urge you to reaffirm your love for him. ⁹For this is why I wrote, to know your proven character, whether you were obedient in everything.�q ¹⁰Whomever you forgive anything, so do I. For indeed what I have forgiven, if I have forgiven anything, has been for you in the presence of Christ, ¹¹so that we might not be taken advantage of by Satan, for we are not unaware of his purposes.ʳ
Paul's Anxiety.† ¹²When I went to Troas for the gospel of Christ, although a door was opened for me in the Lord,ˢ ¹³*I had no relief in my spirit because I did not find my brother Titus.ᵗ So I took leave of them and went on to Macedonia.

B. Paul's Ministry§

Ministers of a New Covenant. ¹⁴*But thanks be to God,** who always leads us in triumph in

---

*[2:5–11] The nature of the **pain** (2 Cor 2:5) is unclear, though some believe an individual at Corinth rejected Paul's authority, thereby scandalizing many in the community. In any case, action has been taken, and Paul judges the measures adequate to right the situation (2 Cor 2:6). The follow-up directives he now gives are entirely positive: forgive, encourage, love. **Overwhelmed** (2 Cor 2:7): a vivid metaphor (literally "swallowed") that Paul employs positively at 2 Cor 5:4 and in 1 Cor 15:54 (2 Cor 2:7). It is often used to describe satanic activity (cf. 1 Pt 5:8); note the reference to Satan here in 2 Cor 2:11.

†[2:12–13] **I had no relief:** Paul does not explain the reason for his anxiety until he resumes the thread of his narrative at 2 Cor 7:5: he was waiting to hear how the Corinthians would respond to his letter. Since 2 Cor 7:5–16 describes their response in entirely positive terms, we never learn in detail why he found it necessary to defend and justify his change of plans, as in 2 Cor 1:15–24. Was this portion of the letter written before the arrival of Titus with his good news (2 Cor 7:6–7)?

‡[2:13] **Macedonia:** a Roman province in northern Greece.

§[2:14–7:4] This section constitutes a digression within the narrative of the crisis and its resolution (2 Cor 1:12–2:13 and 2 Cor 7:5–16). The main component (2 Cor 2:14–6:10) treats the nature of Paul's ministry and his qualifications for it; this material bears some similarity to the defense of his ministry in chaps. 10–13, but it may well come from a period close to the crisis. This is followed by a supplementary block of material quite different in character and tone (2 Cor 6:14–7:1). These materials may have been brought together into their present position during final editing of the letter; appeals to the Corinthians link them to one another (2 Cor 6:11–13) and lead back to the interrupted narrative (2 Cor 7:2–4).

¶[2:14–6:10] The question of Paul's adequacy (2 Cor 2:16; cf. 2 Cor 3:5) and his credentials (2 Cor 3:1–2) has been raised. Paul responds by an extended treatment of the nature of his ministry. It is a ministry of glory (2 Cor 3:7–4:6), of life (2 Cor 4:7–5:10), of reconciliation (2 Cor 5:11–6:10).

**[2:14–16a] The initial statement plunges us abruptly into another train of thought. Paul describes his personal existence and his function as a preacher in two powerful images (2 Cor 2:14) that constitute a prelude to the development to follow.

p. [2:7] Col 3:13.   q. [2:9] 7:15.   r. [2:11] Eph 4:27.   s. [2:12] Acts 16:8.   t. [2:13] 7:6; 1 Tm 1:3.

Christ†† and manifests through us the odor of the knowledge of him‡‡ in every place. ¹⁵For we are the aroma of Christ for God among those who are being saved and among those who are perishing,ᵘ ¹⁶to the latter an odor of death that leads to death, to the former an odor of life that leads to life. Who is qualified§§ for this? ¹⁷For we are not like the many who trade on the word of God; but as out of sincerity, indeed as from God and in the presence of God, we speak in Christ.ᵛ

CHAPTER 3

¹¶¶*Are we beginning to commend ourselves again? Or do we need, as some do, letters of recommendation to you or from you? ²You are our letter,*** written on our hearts, known and read by all, ³†††ˣshown to be a letter of Christ administered

---

††[2:14a] **Leads us in triumph in Christ:** this metaphor of a festive parade in honor of a conquering military hero can suggest either a positive sharing in Christ's triumph or an experience of defeat, being led in captivity and submission (cf. 2 Cor 4:8–11; 1 Cor 4:9). Paul is probably aware of the ambiguity, as he is in the case of the next metaphor.

‡‡[2:14b–16a] **The odor of the knowledge of him:** incense was commonly used in triumphal processions. The metaphor suggests the gradual diffusion of the knowledge of God through the apostolic preaching. **The aroma of Christ:** the image shifts from the fragrance Paul diffuses to the aroma that he is. Paul is probably thinking of the "sweet odor" of the sacrifices in the Old Testament (e.g., Gn 8:21; Ex 29:18) and perhaps of the metaphor of wisdom as a sweet odor (Sir 24:15). **Death . . . life:** the aroma of Christ that comes to them through Paul is perceived differently by various classes of people. To some his preaching and his life (cf. 1 Cor 1:17–2:6) are perceived as death, and the effect is death for them; others perceive him, despite appearances, as **life,** and the effect is life for them. This fragrance thus produces a separation and a judgment (cf. the function of the "light" in John's gospel).

§§[2:16b–17] **Qualified:** Paul may be echoing either the self-satisfied claims of other preachers or their charges about Paul's deficiencies. No one is really qualified, but the apostle contrasts himself with those who dilute or falsify the preaching for personal advantage and insists on his totally good conscience: his ministry is from God, and he has exercised it with fidelity and integrity (cf. 2 Cor 3:5–6).

¶¶[3:1] Paul seems to allude to certain preachers who pride themselves on their written credentials. Presumably they reproach him for not possessing similar credentials and compel him to spell out his own qualifications (2 Cor 4:2; 5:12; 6:4). The Corinthians themselves should have performed this function for Paul (2 Cor 5:12; cf. 2 Cor 12:11). Since he is forced to find something that can recommend him, he points to them: their very existence constitutes his **letter** of recommendation (2 Cor 3:1–2). Others who engage in self-commendation will also be mentioned in 2 Cor 10:12–18.

***[3:2–3] Mention of "letters of recommendation" generates a series of metaphors in which Paul plays on the word "letter": (1) the community is Paul's letter of recommendation (2 Cor 3:2a); (2) they are a letter engraved on his affections for all to see and read (2 Cor 3:2b); (3) they are a letter from Christ that Paul merely delivers (2 Cor 3:3a); (4) they are a letter written by the Spirit on the tablets of human hearts (2 Cor 3:3b). One image dissolves into another.

†††[3:3b] This verse contrasts Paul's letter with those **written . . . in ink** (like the credentials of other preachers) and those **written . . . on tablets of stone** (like the law of Moses). These contrasts suggest that the other preachers may have claimed special relationship with Moses. If they were Judaizers zealous for the Mosaic law, that would explain the detailed contrast between the old and the new covenants (2 Cor 3:6; 4:7–6:10). If they were charismatics who claimed Moses as

u. [2:15] 4:3; 1 Cor 1:18.   v. [2:17] 4:2; 1 Cor 5:8.   w. [3:1] Acts 18:27; Rom 16:1; 1 Cor 16:3.   x. [3:3] Ex 24:12; 31:18; 32:15–19 / Jer 31:33; Ez 11:19; 36:26–27.

by us, written not in ink but by the Spirit of the living God, not on tablets of stone but on tablets that are hearts of flesh.

⁴*Such confidence we have through Christ toward God. ⁵Not that of ourselves we are qualified to take credit for anything as coming from us; rather, our qualification comes from God,ʸ ⁶who has indeed qualified us as ministers of a new covenant, not of letter but of spirit;ᶻ for the letter brings death, but the Spirit gives life.†

Contrast with the Old Covenant. ⁷‡Now if the ministry of death,§ carved in letters on stone, was so glorious that the Israelites could not look intently at the face of Moses because of its glory that was going to fade,ᵃ ⁸how much moreˢ will the ministry of the Spirit be glorious? ⁹For if the ministry of condemnation was glorious, the ministry of righteousness will abound much more in glory. ¹⁰Indeed, what was endowed with glory has come to have no glory in this respect because of the glory that surpasses it. ¹¹For if what was going to fade was glorious, how much more will what endures be glorious.

¹²Therefore, since we have such hope,** we act very boldly ¹³and not like Moses,†† who put a veil over his face so that the Israelites could not look intently at the cessation of what was fading. ¹⁴Rather, their thoughts were rendered dull, for to this present day‡‡ the same veil remains unlifted when they read the old covenant, because through Christ it is taken away. ¹⁵To this day, in fact, whenever Moses is read, a veil lies over their hearts,ᵇ ¹⁶but whenever a person turns to the Lord the veil is removed.ᶜ ¹⁷Now the Lord is the Spirit,§§ and where the Spirit of the Lord is, there is freedom. ¹⁸¶¶All of us, gazing with unveiled face on the glory of the Lord, are being transformed into the same image from glory to glory, as from the Lord who is the Spirit.ᵈ

CHAPTER 4

Integrity in the Ministry. ¹***Therefore, since we have this ministry through the mercy shown us, we are not discouraged. ²Rather, we have renounced shameful, hidden things; not acting deceitfully or falsifying the word of God, but by

Without impugning Moses' sincerity, Paul attributes another effect to the veil. Since it lies between God's glory and the Israelites, it explains how they could fail to notice the glory disappearing. **Their thoughts were rendered dull:** the problem lay with their understanding. This will be expressed in 2 Cor 3:14b–16 by a shift in the place of the veil: it is no longer over Moses' face but over their perception.

‡‡[3:14b–16] The parallelism in these verses makes it necessary to interpret corresponding parts in relation to one another. **To this present day:** this signals the shift of Paul's attention to his contemporaries; his argument is typological, as in 1 Cor 10. The Israelites of Moses' time typify the Jews of Paul's time, and perhaps also Christians of Jewish origin or mentality who may not recognize the temporary character of Moses' glory. **When they read the old covenant:** the lasting dullness prevents proper appraisal of Moses' person and covenant. When his writings are read in the synagogue, a veil still impedes their understanding. **Through Christ:** i.e., in the new covenant. **Whenever a person turns to the Lord:** Moses in Exodus appeared before God without the veil and gazed on his face unprotected. Paul applies that passage to converts to Christianity: when they turn to the Lord fully and authentically, the impediment to their understanding is removed.

§§[3:17] **The Lord is the Spirit:** the "Lord" to whom the Christian turns (2 Cor 3:16) is the Spirit of whom Paul has been speaking, the life-giving Spirit of the living God (2 Cor 3:6, 8), the inaugurator of the new covenant and ministry, who is also the Spirit of Christ. **The Spirit of the Lord:** the Lord here is the living God (2 Cor 3:3), but there may also be an allusion to Christ as Lord (2 Cor 3:14, 16). **Freedom:** i.e., from the ministry of death (2 Cor 3:7) and the covenant that condemned (2 Cor 3:9).

¶¶[3:18] Another application of the veil image. **All of us . . . with unveiled face:** Christians (Israelites from whom the veil has been removed) are like Moses, standing in God's presence, beholding and reflecting his glory. **Gazing:** the verb may also be translated "contemplating as in a mirror"; 2 Cor 4:6 would suggest that the mirror is Christ himself. **Are being transformed:** elsewhere Paul speaks of transformation, conformity to Jesus, God's image, as a reality of the end time, and even 2 Cor 3:12 speaks of the glory as an object of hope. But the life-giving Spirit, the distinctive gift of the new covenant, is already present in the community (cf. 2 Cor 1:22, the "first installment"), and the process of transformation has already begun. **Into the same image:** into the image of God, which is Christ (2 Cor 4:4).

***[4:1–2] A ministry of this sort generates confidence and forthrightness; cf. 2 Cor 1:12–14; 2:17.

their model, that would explain the extended treatment of Moses himself and his glory (2 Cor 3:7–4:6). **Hearts of flesh:** cf. Ezekiel's contrast between the heart of flesh that the Spirit gives and the heart of stone that it replaces (Ez 36:26); the context is covenant renewal and purification that makes observance of the law possible.

*[3:4–6] These verses resume 2 Cor 2:1–3:3. Paul's confidence (2 Cor 3:4) is grounded in his sense of God-given mission (2 Cor 2:17), the specifics of which are described in 2 Cor 3:1–3. 2 Cor 3:5–6 return to the question of his qualifications (2 Cor 2:16), attributing them entirely to God. 2 Cor 3:6 further spells out the situation described in 2 Cor 3:3b and "names" it: Paul is living within a **new covenant**, characterized by the Spirit, which **gives life.** The usage of a **new covenant** is derived from Jer 31:31–33 a passage that also speaks of writing on the heart; cf. 2 Cor 3:2.

†[3:6b] This verse serves as a topic sentence for 2 Cor 3:7–6:10. For the contrast between **letter** and **spirit,** cf. Rom 2:29; 7:5–6.

‡[3:7–4:6] Paul now develops the contrast enunciated in 2 Cor 3:6b in terms of the relative glory of the two covenants, insisting on the greater glory of the new. His polemic seems directed against individuals who appeal to the glorious Moses and fail to perceive any comparable glory either in Paul's life as an apostle or in the gospel he preaches. He asserts in response that Christians have a glory of their own that far surpasses that of Moses.

§[3:7] **The ministry of death:** from his very first words, Paul describes the Mosaic covenant and ministry from the viewpoint of their limitations. They lead to **death** rather than life (2 Cor 3:6–7; cf. 2 Cor 4:7–5:10), to **condemnation** rather than reconciliation (2 Cor 3:9; cf. 2 Cor 5:11–6:10). **Was so glorious:** the basic text to which Paul alludes is Ex 34:29–35 to which his opponents have undoubtedly laid claim. **Going to fade:** Paul concedes the glory of Moses' covenant and ministry, but grants them only temporary significance.

¶[3:8–11] **How much more:** the argument "from the less to the greater" is repeated three times (2 Cor 3:8, 9, 11). 2 Cor 3:10 expresses another point of view: the difference in glory is so great that only the new covenant and ministry can properly be called "glorious" at all.

[3:12] **Such hope: the glory is not yet an object of experience, but that does not lessen Paul's confidence. **Boldly:** the term *parrēsia* expresses outspoken declaration of Christian conviction (cf. 2 Cor 4:1–2). Paul has nothing to hide and no reason for timidity.

††[3:13–14a] **Not like Moses:** in Exodus Moses veiled his face to protect the Israelites from God's reflected glory.

y. [3:5] Jn 3:27.   z. [3:6] Eph 3:7 / Jer 31:31–34.   a. [3:7] Ex 34:29–35.

b. [3:15] Rom 11:7–10.   c. [3:16] Ex 34:34.   d. [3:18] Rom 8:29–30; 12:2; Gal 4:19; Phil 3:10, 20–21 / 2 Cor 4:4–6; 1 Cor 15:49; Col 1:15; 3:9–11; 1 Jn 3:2.

the open declaration of the truth we commend ourselves to everyone's conscience in the sight of God.ᵉ ³And even though our gospel is veiled,⁎ it is veiled for those who are perishing,ᶠ ⁴in whose case the god of this age has blinded the minds of the unbelievers, so that they may not see the light of the gospel of the glory of Christ, who is the image of God.ᵍ ⁵For we do not preach ourselves† but Jesus Christ as Lord, and ourselves as your slaves for the sake of Jesus. ⁶†For God who said, "Let light shine out of darkness," has shone in our hearts to bring to light the knowledge of the glory of God on the face of [Jesus] Christ.ʰ

The Paradox of the Ministry. ⁷§But we hold this treasure⁵ in earthen vessels, that the surpassing power may be of God and not from us. ⁸⁎⁎We are afflicted in every way, but not constrained; perplexed, but not driven to despair;ⁱ ⁹persecuted, but not abandoned; struck down, but not destroyed; ¹⁰††always carrying about in the body the dying of Jesus, so that the life of Jesus may also be manifested in our body. ¹¹For we who live are constantly being given up to death for the sake of Jesus, so that the life of Jesus may be manifested in our mortal flesh.ᵏ

¹²‡‡So death is at work in us, but life in you. ¹³§§Since, then, we have the same spirit of faith, according to what is written, "I believed, therefore I spoke," we too believe and therefore speak,ˡ ¹⁴knowing that the one who raised the Lord Jesus will raise us also with Jesus and place us with you in his presence.ᵐ ¹⁵Everything indeed is for you, so that the grace bestowed in abundance on more and more people may cause the thanksgiving to overflow for the glory of God.ⁿ

¹⁶¶¶Therefore, we are not discouraged;⁎⁎⁎ rather, although our outer self is wasting away, our inner self is being renewed day by day.ᵒ ¹⁷For this momentary light affliction is producing for us an eternal weight of glory beyond all comparison,ᵖ ¹⁸as we look not to what is seen but to what is unseen; for what is seen is transitory, but what is unseen is eternal.�q

CHAPTER 5

Our Future Destiny. ¹ʳFor we know that if our earthly dwelling,††† a tent, should be destroyed, we have a building from God, a dwelling not made with hands, eternal in heaven. ²‡‡‡For in

---

⁎[4:3–4] **Though our gospel is veiled**: the final application of the image. Paul has been reproached either for obscurity in his preaching or for his manner of presenting the gospel. But he confidently asserts that there is no veil over his gospel. If some fail to perceive its light, that is because of unbelief. The veil lies over their eyes (2 Cor 3:14), a blindness induced by Satan, and a sign that they are headed for destruction (cf. 2 Cor 2:15).

†[4:5] **We do not preach ourselves**: the light seen in his gospel is the glory of Christ (2 Cor 4:4). Far from preaching himself, the preacher should be a transparent medium through whom Jesus is perceived (cf. 2 Cor 4:10–11). **Your slaves**: Paul draws attention away from individuals as such and toward their role in relation to God, Christ, and the community; cf. 1 Cor 3:5; 2 Cor 4:1.

‡[4:6] Autobiographical allusion to the episode at Damascus clarifies the origin and nature of Paul's service; cf. Acts 9:1–19; 22:3–16; 26:2–18. **"Let light shine out of darkness"**: Paul seems to be thinking of Gn 1:3 and presenting his apostolic ministry as a new creation. There may also be an allusion to Is 9:1 suggesting his prophetic calling as servant of the Lord and light to the nations; cf. Is 42:6, 16; 49:6; 60:1–2, and the use of light imagery in Acts 26:13–23. **To bring to light the knowledge**: Paul's role in the process of revelation, expressed at the beginning under the image of the odor and aroma (2 Cor 2:14–15), is restated now, at the end of this first moment of the development, in the imagery of light and glory (2 Cor 4:3–6).

§[4:7–5:10] Paul now confronts the difficulty that his present existence does not appear glorious at all; it is marked instead by suffering and death. He deals with this by developing the topic already announced in 2 Cor 3:3, 6, asserting his faith in the presence and ultimate triumph of life, in his own and every Christian existence, despite the experience of death.

¶[4:7] **This treasure**: the glory that he preaches and into which they are being transformed. **In earthen vessels**: the instruments God uses are human and fragile; some imagine small terracotta lamps in which light is carried.

⁎⁎[4:8–9] A catalogue of his apostolic trials and afflictions. Yet in these the negative never completely prevails; there is always some experience of rescue, of salvation.

††[4:10–11] Both the negative and the positive sides of the experience are grounded christologically. The logic is similar to that of 2 Cor 1:3–11. His sufferings are connected with Christ's, and his deliverance is a sign that he is to share in Jesus' resurrection.

‡‡[4:12–15] His experience does not terminate in himself, but in others (2 Cor 4:12, 15; cf. 2 Cor 1:4–5). Ultimately, everything is ordered even beyond the community, toward God (2 Cor 4:15; cf. 2 Cor 1:11).

§§[4:13–14] Like the psalmist, Paul clearly proclaims his faith, affirming life within himself despite death (2 Cor 4:10–11) and the life-giving effect of his experience upon the church (2 Cor 4:12, 14–15). **And place us with you in his presence**: Paul imagines God presenting him and them to Jesus at the parousia and the judgment; cf. 2 Cor 11:2; Rom 14:10.

¶¶[4:16–18] In a series of contrasts Paul explains the extent of his faith in life. Life is not only already present and revealing itself (2 Cor 4:8–11, 16) but will outlast his experience of affliction and dying: it is eternal (2 Cor 4:17–18).

⁎⁎⁎[4:16] **Not discouraged**: i.e., despite the experience of death. Paul is still speaking of himself personally, but he assumes his faith and attitude will be shared by all Christians. **Our outer self**: the individual subject of ordinary perception and observation, in contrast to the interior and hidden self, which undergoes renewal. **Is being renewed day by day**: this suggests a process that has already begun; cf. 2 Cor 3:18. The renewal already taking place even in Paul's dying is a share in the life of Jesus, but this is recognized only by faith (2 Cor 4:13, 18; 2 Cor 5:7).

†††[5:1] **Our earthly dwelling**: the same contrast is restated in the imagery of a dwelling. The language recalls Jesus' saying about the destruction of the temple and the construction of another building **not made with hands** (Mk 14:58), a prediction later applied to Jesus' own body (Jn 2:20).

‡‡‡[5:2–5] 2 Cor 5:2–3 and 4 are largely parallel in structure. **We groan, longing**: see note on 2 Cor 5:5. **Clothed with our heavenly habitation**: Paul mixes his metaphors, adding the image of the garment to that of the building. **Further clothed**: the verb means strictly "to put one garment on over another." Paul may desire to put the resurrection body on over his mortal body, without dying; 2 Cor 5:2, 4 permit this meaning but do not impose it. Or perhaps he imagines the resurrection body as a garment put on over the Christ-garment first received in baptism (Gal 3:27) and preserved by moral behavior (Rom 13:12–14; Col 3:12; cf. Mt 22:11–13). Some support for this interpretation may be found in the context; cf. the

---

e. [4:2] 2:17; 1 Thes 2:4–7. f. [4:3] 2:15–16; 2 Thes 2:10. g. [4:4] Jn 12:31–36 / 1 Tm 1:11. h. [4:6] Gn 1:3; Is 9:1; Acts 26:13–23; Gal 1:15–16 / Jn 8:12; Heb 1:3. i. [4:8] 6:4–10; 1 Cor 4:9–13. j. [4:10] Col 1:24.

k. [4:11] Rom 8:36; 1 Cor 15:31. l. [4:13] Ps 116:10. m. [4:14] Rom 4:24–25; 8:11; 1 Cor 6:14; 1 Thes 4:14. n. [4:15] 1:11. o. [4:16] 4:1. p. [4:17] Mt 5:11–12; Rom 8:18. q. [4:18] Rom 8:24–25; Heb 11:1. r. [5:1] Is 38:12 / Col 3:1–4 / Mk 14:58; Col 2:11; Heb 9:11, 24.

this tent we groan, longing to be further clothed with our heavenly habitation[s] [3]if indeed, when we have taken it off,[*] we shall not be found naked. [4]For while we are in this tent we groan and are weighed down, because we do not wish to be unclothed[†] but to be further clothed, so that what is mortal may be swallowed up by life.[t] [5]Now the one who has prepared us for this very thing is God,[u] who has given us the Spirit as a first installment.[‡]

[6]So we are always courageous, although we know that while we are at home in the body we are away from the Lord, [7]for we walk by faith, not by sight. [8]Yet we are courageous, and we would rather leave the body and go home to the Lord.[v] [9]Therefore, we aspire to please him, whether we are at home or away. [10]For we must all appear[§] before the judgment seat of Christ, so that each one may receive recompense, according to what he did in the body, whether good or evil.[w]

The Ministry of Reconciliation. [11**]Therefore, since we know the fear of the Lord, we try to persuade others; but we are clearly apparent to God, and I hope we are also apparent to your consciousness.[x] [12]We are not commending ourselves to you again but giving you an opportunity to boast of us, so that you may have something to say to those who boast of external appearance rather than of the heart.[y] [13]For if we are out of our minds,[††] it is for God; if we are rational, it is for you. [14‡‡]For the love of Christ impels us, once we have come to the conviction that one died for all; therefore, all have died.[z] [15]He indeed died for all, so that those who live might no longer live for themselves but for him who for their sake died and was raised.[a]

[16]Consequently,[§§] from now on we regard no one according to the flesh; even if we once knew Christ according to the flesh, yet now we know him so no longer. [17b]So whoever is in Christ is a new creation: the old things have passed away; behold, new things have come. [18¶¶]And all this is from God, who has reconciled us to himself through Christ and given us the ministry of reconciliation, [19]namely, God was reconciling the world to himself in Christ, not counting their trespasses against them and entrusting to us the message of reconciliation.[c] [20]So we are ambassadors for Christ, as if God were appealing through us. We implore you on behalf of Christ, be reconciled to God.[d] [21***]For our sake he made

---

references to baptism (2 Cor 5:5), to judgment according to works (2 Cor 5:10), and to present renewal (2 Cor 4:16), an idea elsewhere combined with the image of "putting on" a new nature (Eph 4:22–24; Col 3:1–5, 9–10).

*[5:3] **When we have taken it off**: the majority of witnesses read "when we have put it on," i.e., when we have been clothed (in the resurrection body), then we shall not be without a body (naked). This seems mere tautology, though some understand it to mean: whether we are "found" (by God at the judgment) clothed or naked depends upon whether we have preserved or lost our original investiture in Christ (cf. the previous note). In this case "put it on" does not refer to the resurrection body, but to keeping intact the Christ-garment of baptism. The translation follows the western reading (Codex Bezae, Tertullian), the sense of which is clear: to "take it off" is to shed our mortal body in death, after which we shall be clothed in the resurrection body and hence not "naked" (cf. 1 Cor 15:51–53).

†[5:4] **We do not wish to be unclothed**: a clear allusion to physical death (2 Cor 4:16; 5:1). Unlike the Greeks, who found dissolution of the body desirable (cf. Socrates), Paul has a Jewish horror of it. He seems to be thinking of the "intermediate period," an interval between death and resurrection. **Swallowed up by life**: cf. 1 Cor 15:54.

‡[5:5] God has created us for resurrected bodily life and already prepares us for it by the gift of the Spirit in baptism. **The Spirit as a first installment**: the striking parallel to 2 Cor 5:1–5 in Rom 8:17–30 describes Christians who have received the "firstfruits" (cf. "first installment" here) of the Spirit as "groaning" (cf. 2 Cor 5:2, 4 here) for the resurrection, the complete redemption of their bodies. In place of clothing and building, Rom 8 uses other images for the resurrection: adoption and conformity to the image of the Son.

§[5:6–9] Tension between present and future is expressed by another spatial image, the metaphor of the country and its citizens. At present we are like citizens in exile or far away from home. The Lord is the distant homeland, believed in but unseen (2 Cor 5:7).

¶[5:10] **We must all appear**: the verb is ambiguous: we are scheduled to "appear" for judgment, at which we will be "revealed" as we are (cf. 2 Cor 11; 2:14; 4:10–11).

**[5:11–15] This paragraph is transitional. Paul sums up much that has gone before. Still playing on the term "appearance," he reasserts his transparency before God and the Corinthians, in contrast to the self-commendation, boasting, and preoccupation with externals that characterize some others (cf. 2 Cor 1:12–14; 2:14; 3:1; 3:7–4:6). 2 Cor 5:14 recalls 2 Cor 3:7–4:6, and sums up 2 Cor 4:7–5:10.

††[5:13] **Out of our minds**: this verse confirms that a concern for ecstasy and charismatic experience may lie behind the discussion about "glory" in 2 Cor 3:7–4:6. Paul also enjoys such experiences but, unlike others, does not make a public display of them or consider them ends in themselves. **Rational**: the Greek virtue *sōphrosynē*, to which Paul alludes, implies reasonableness, moderation, good judgment, self-control.

‡‡[5:14–15] These verses echo 2 Cor 4:14 and resume the treatment of "life despite death" from 2 Cor 4:7–5:10.

§§[5:16–17] **Consequently**: the death of Christ described in 2 Cor 5:14–15 produces a whole new order (2 Cor 5:17) and a new mode of perception (2 Cor 5:16). **According to the flesh**: the natural mode of perception, characterized as "fleshly," is replaced by a mode of perception proper to the Spirit. Elsewhere Paul contrasts what Christ looks like according to the old criteria (weakness, powerlessness, folly, death) and according to the new (wisdom, power, life); cf. 2 Cor 5:15, 21; 1 Cor 1:17–3:3. Similarly, he describes the paradoxical nature of Christian existence, e.g., in 2 Cor 4:10–11, 14. **A new creation**: rabbis used this expression to describe the effect of the entrance of a proselyte or convert into Judaism or of the remission of sins on the Day of Atonement. The new order created **in Christ** is the new covenant (2 Cor 3:6).

¶¶[5:18–21] Paul attempts to explain the meaning of God's action by a variety of different categories; his attention keeps moving rapidly back and forth from God's act to his own ministry as well. **Who has reconciled us to himself**: i.e., he has brought all into oneness. **Not counting their trespasses**: the reconciliation is described as an act of justification (cf. "righteousness," 2 Cor 5:21); this contrasts with the covenant that condemned (2 Cor 3:8). **The ministry of reconciliation**: Paul's role in the wider picture is described: entrusted with the message of reconciliation (2 Cor 5:19), he is Christ's ambassador, through whom God appeals (2 Cor 5:20a). In v 20b Paul acts in the capacity just described.

***[5:21] This is a statement of God's purpose, expressed paradoxically in terms of sharing and exchange of attributes.

s. [5:2] Rom 8:23 / 1 Cor 15:51–54. t. [5:4] Is 25:8; 1 Cor 15:54. u. [5:5] 1:22. v. [5:8] Phil 1:21–23. w. [5:10] Mt 16:27; 25:31–46; Rom 2:16; 14:10–11.

x. [5:11] 1:12–14. y. [5:12] 3:1 / 2 Cor 1:14; Phil 1:26. z. [5:14] Rom 6:1–6. a. [5:15] Rom 4:25; 6:4–11; 14:9; Col 3:3–4. b. [5:17] Gal 6:15; Eph 2:15 / Is 43:18–21; Rev 21:5. c. [5:19] Rom 5:10–11; Col 1:20. d. [5:20] Eph 6:20; Phlm 9.

him to be sin who did not know sin,[e] so that we might become the righteousness of God in him.

CHAPTER 6

The Experience of the Ministry. [1*]Working together,[f] then, we appeal to you not to receive the grace of God in vain.[†] [2]For he says:

"In an acceptable time[‡] I heard you,
    and on the day of salvation I helped you."[g]

Behold, now is a very acceptable time; behold, now is the day of salvation. [3h]We cause no one to stumble[§] in anything, in order that no fault may be found with our ministry; [4§§]on the contrary, in everything we commend ourselves as ministers of God, through much endurance,[**] in afflictions, hardships, constraints,[i] [5]beatings, imprisonments, riots, labors, vigils, fasts;[j] [6††]by purity, knowledge, patience, kindness, in a holy spirit, in unfeigned love,[k] [7]in truthful speech, in the power of God; with weapons of righteousness at the right and at the left;[l] [8]through glory and dishonor, insult and praise. We are treated as deceivers and yet are truthful;[‡‡] [9]as unrec-

ognized and yet acknowledged; as dying and behold we live; as chastised and yet not put to death;[m] [10]as sorrowful yet always rejoicing; as poor yet enriching many; as having nothing and yet possessing all things.[n]

[11§§]We have spoken frankly to you, Corinthians; our heart is open wide. [12]You are not constrained by us; you are constrained by your own affections.[o] [13]As recompense in kind (I speak as to my children), be open yourselves.[p]

Call to Holiness. [14***]Do not be yoked with those who are different, with unbelievers.*** For what partnership do righteousness and lawlessness have? Or what fellowship does light have with darkness? [15]What accord has Christ with Beliar? Or what has a believer in common with an unbeliever? [16q]What agreement has the temple of God with idols? For we are the temple of the living God; as God said:

"I will live with them and move among them,[†††]
    and I will be their God
    and they shall be my people.
[17] Therefore, come forth from them
    and be separate," says the Lord,
    "and touch nothing unclean;
    then I will receive you[r]
[18] and I will be a father to you,

As Christ became our righteousness (1 Cor 1:30), we become God's righteousness (cf. 2 Cor 5:14–15).

*[6:1–10] This paragraph is a single sentence in the Greek, interrupted by the parentheses of 2 Cor 5:2. The one main verb is "we appeal." In this paragraph Paul both exercises his ministry of reconciliation (cf. 2 Cor 5:20) and describes how his ministry is exercised: the "message of reconciliation" (2 Cor 5:19) is lived existentially in his apostolic experience.

†[6:1] **Not to receive . . . in vain:** i.e., conform to the gift of justification and new creation. The context indicates how this can be done concretely: become God's righteousness (2 Cor 5:21), not live for oneself (2 Cor 5:15) be reconciled with Paul (2 Cor 6:11–13; 7:2–3).

‡[6:2] **In an acceptable time:** Paul cites the Septuagint text of Is 49:8; the Hebrew reads "in a time of favor"; it is parallel to "on the day of salvation." **Now:** God is bestowing favor and salvation at this very moment, as Paul is addressing his letter to them.

§[6:3] **Cause no one to stumble:** the language echoes that of 1 Cor 8–10 as does the expression "no longer live for themselves" in 2 Cor 5:15. **That no fault may be found:** i.e., at the eschatological judgment (cf. 1 Cor 4:2–5).

¶[6:4a] This is the central assertion, the topic statement for the catalogue that follows. **We commend ourselves:** Paul's self-commendation is ironical (with an eye on the charges mentioned in 2 Cor 3:1–3) and paradoxical (pointing mostly to experiences that would not normally be considered points of pride but are perceived as such by faith). Cf. also the self-commendation in 2 Cor 11:23–29. **As ministers of God:** the same Greek word, *diakonos*, means "minister" and "servant"; cf. 2 Cor 11:23, the central assertion in a similar context, and 1 Cor 3:5.

[6:4b–5] Through much endurance: this phrase functions as a subtitle; it is followed by an enumeration of nine specific types of trials endured.

††[6:6–7a] A list of virtuous qualities in two groups of four, the second fuller than the first.

‡‡[6:8b–10] A series of seven rhetorically effective antitheses, contrasting negative external impressions with positive inner reality. Paul perceives his existence as a reflection of

Jesus' own and affirms an inner reversal that escapes outward observation. The final two members illustrate two distinct kinds of paradox or apparent contradiction that are characteristic of apostolic experience.

§§[6:11–13] Paul's tone becomes quieter, but his appeal for acceptance and affection is emotionally charged. References to the heart and their mutual relations bring the development begun in 2 Cor 2:14–3:3 to an effective conclusion.

¶¶[6:14–7:1] Language and thought shift noticeably here. Suddenly we are in a different atmosphere, dealing with a quite different problem. Both the vocabulary and the thought, with their contrast between good and evil, are more characteristic of Qumran documents or the Book of Revelation than they are of Paul. Hence, critics suspect that this section was inserted by another hand.

***[6:14–16a] The opening injunction to separate from unbelievers is reinforced by five rhetorical questions to make the point that Christianity is not compatible with paganism. Their opposition is emphasized also by the accumulation of five distinct designations for each group. These verses are a powerful statement of God's holiness and the exclusiveness of his claims.

†††[6:16c–18] This is a chain of scriptural citations carefully woven together. God's covenant relation to his people and his presence among them (2 Cor 6:16) is seen as conditioned on cultic separation from the profane and cultically impure (2 Cor 6:17); that relation is translated into the personal language of the parent-child relationship, an extension to the community of the language of 2 Sm 7:14 (2 Cor 6:18). Some remarkable parallels to this chain are found in the final chapters of Revelation. God's presence among his people (Rev 21:22) is expressed there, too, by applying 2 Sm 7:14 to the community (Rev 21:7). There is a call to separation (Rev 18:4) and exclusion of the unclean from the community and its liturgy (Rev 21:27). The title "Lord Almighty" (*Pantokratōr*) occurs in the New Testament only here in 2 Cor 6:18 and nine times in Revelation.

---

e. [5:21] Is 53:6–9; Gal 3:13 / Rom 3:24–26; 1 Cor 1:30; 1 Pt 2:24; 1 Jn 3:5–8. f. [6:1] 1 Cor 3:9; 1 Thes 3:2. g. [6:2] Is 49:8. h. [6:3] 1 Cor 9:12; 10:32 / 2 Cor 8:20–21. i. [6:4] 4:8–11; 11:23–27; 1 Cor 4:9–13. j. [6:5] Acts 16:23. k. [6:6] Gal 5:22–23. l. [6:7] 10:4; Rom 13:12; Eph 6:11–17.

m. [6:9] 4:10–11; Rom 8:36. n. [6:10] Rom 8:32; 1 Cor 3:21. o. [6:12] 7:3. p. [6:13] Gal 4:19. q. [6:16] 1 Cor 10:20–21 / 1 Cor 3:16–17; 6:19 / Ex 25:8; 29:45; Lv 26:12; Jer 31:1; 32:38; Ez 37:27. r. [6:17] Is 52:11; Ez 20:34, 41; Rev 18:4; 21:27.

and you shall be sons and daughters
to me,
says the Lord Almighty."*

CHAPTER 7

[1]Since we have these promises, beloved, let us cleanse ourselves from every defilement of flesh and spirit, making holiness perfect in the fear of God.

[2]*Make room for us; we have not wronged anyone, or ruined anyone, or taken advantage of anyone. [3]I do not say this in condemnation, for I have already said that you are in our hearts, that we may die together and live together.[t] [4]I have great confidence in you, I have great pride in you; I am filled with encouragement, I am overflowing with joy all the more because of all our affliction.

C. Resolution of the Crisis[t]

Paul's Joy in Macedonia. [5]*For even when we came into Macedonia,[§] our flesh had no rest, but we were afflicted in every way—external conflicts, internal fears.[u] [6]But God, who encourages the downcast, encouraged us by the arrival of Titus,[v] [7]and not only by his arrival but also by the encouragement with which he was encouraged in regard to you, as he told us of your yearning, your lament, your zeal for me, so that I rejoiced even more. [8]*For even if I saddened you by my letter, I do not regret it; and if I did regret it ([for] I see that that letter saddened you, if only for a while),[w] [9]I rejoice now, not because you were saddened, but because you were saddened into repentance; for you were saddened

in a godly way, so that you did not suffer loss in anything because of us. [10]For godly sorrow produces a salutary repentance without regret, but worldly sorrow produces death. [11]For behold what earnestness this godly sorrow has produced for you, as well as readiness for a defense, and indignation, and fear, and yearning, and zeal, and punishment. In every way you have shown yourselves to be innocent in the matter. [12]So then even though I wrote to you, it was not on account of the one who did the wrong, or on account of the one who suffered the wrong, but in order that your concern for us might be made plain to you in the sight of God.[x] [13]For this reason we are encouraged.

And besides our encouragement,** we rejoice even more because of the joy of Titus, since his spirit has been refreshed by all of you. [14]For if I have boasted to him about you, I was not put to shame. No, just as everything we said to you was true, so our boasting before Titus proved to be the truth. [15]And his heart goes out to you all the more, as he remembers the obedience of all of you, when you received him with fear and trembling.[y] [16]I rejoice, because I have confidence in you in every respect.

III. THE COLLECTION FOR JERUSALEM[tt]

CHAPTER 8

Generosity in Giving. [1]‡‡We want you to know, brothers,[§§] of the grace of God** that has been

---

* [7:2–4] These verses continue the thought of 2 Cor 6:11–13, before the interruption of 2 Cor 6:14–7:1. 2 Cor 7:4 serves as a transition to the next section: the four themes it introduces (confidence; pride or "boasting"; encouragement; joy in affliction) are developed in 2 Cor 7:5–16. All have appeared previously in the letter.

† [7:5–16] This section functions as a peroration or formal summing up of the whole first part of the letter, 2 Cor 1–7. It deals with the restoration of right relations between Paul and the Corinthians, and it is marked by fullness and intensity of emotion.

‡ [7:5–7] Paul picks up the thread of the narrative interrupted at 2 Cor 2:13 (2 Cor 7:5) and describes the resolution of the tense situation there depicted (2 Cor 7:6–7). Finally Titus arrives and his coming puts an end to Paul's restlessness (2 Cor 2:13; 2 Cor 7:5), casts out his fears, and reverses his mood. The theme of encouragement and affliction is reintroduced (cf. 2 Cor 1:3–11); here, too, encouragement is traced back to God and is described as contagious (2 Cor 7:6). The language of joy and sorrow also reappears in 2 Cor 7:7 (cf. 2 Cor 1:23–2:1 and the note on 2 Cor 1:23–24).

§ [7:5] **Macedonia:** see note on 2 Cor 2:13.

¶ [7:8–12] Paul looks back on the episode from the viewpoint of its ending. The goal of their common activity, promotion of their joy (2 Cor 1:24), has been achieved, despite and because of the sorrow they felt. That sorrow was God-given. Its salutary effects are enumerated fully and impressively in 2 Cor 7:10–11; not the least important of these is that it has revealed to them the attachment they have to Paul.

** [7:13–16] Paul summarizes the effect of the experience on Titus: encouragement, joy, love, relief. Finally, he describes its effects on himself: encouragement, joy, confidence, pride or "boasting" (i.e., the satisfaction resulting from a boast that proves well-founded; cf. 2 Cor 7:4; 1:12, 14).

†† [8:1–9:15] Paul turns to a new topic, the collection for the church in Jerusalem. There is an early precedent for this project in the agreement mentioned in Gal 2:6–10. According to Acts, the church at Antioch had sent Saul and Barnabas to Jerusalem with relief (Acts 11:27–30). Subsequently Paul organized a project of relief for Jerusalem among his own churches. Our earliest evidence for it comes in 1 Cor 16:1–4—after it had already begun (see notes there); by the time Paul wrote Rom 15:25–28 the collection was completed and ready for delivery. 2 Cor 8–9 contain what appear to be two letters on the subject. In them Paul gives us his fullest exposition of the meaning he sees in the enterprise, presenting it as an act of Christian charity and as an expression of the unity of the church, both present and eschatological. These chapters are especially rich in the recurrence of key words, on which Paul plays; it is usually impossible to do justice to these wordplays in the translation.

‡‡ [8:1–24] This is a letter of recommendation for Titus and two unnamed companions, written from Macedonia probably at least a year later than 1 Cor 16. The recommendation proper is prefaced by remarks about the ideals of sharing and equality within the Christian community (2 Cor 8:1–15). Phil 4:10–20 shows that Paul has reflected on his personal experience of need and relief in his relations with the community at Philippi; he now develops his reflections on the larger scale of relations between his Gentile churches and the mother church in Jerusalem.

§§ [8:1–5] The example of the Macedonians, a model of what ought to be happening at Corinth, provides Paul with the occasion for expounding his theology of "giving."

¶¶ [8:1] **The grace of God:** the fundamental theme is expressed by the Greek noun *charis*, which will be variously

s. [6:18] 2 Sm 7:14; Ps 2:7; Is 43:6; Jer 31:9; Rev 21:7 / Rev 4:8; 11:17; 15:3;21:22.   t. [7:3] 6:11–13.   u. [7:5] 2:13.   v. [7:6] 7:13–14;1 Thes 3:6–8.   w. [7:8] 2:2–4; Heb 12:11.

x. [7:12] 2:3, 9; 7:8.   y. [7:15] 2:9.

given to the churches of Macedonia,^{z} ^{2}for in a severe test of affliction, the abundance of their joy and their profound poverty overflowed in a wealth of generosity on their part. ^{3}†For according to their means, I can testify, and beyond their means, spontaneously, ^{4}they begged us insistently for the favor of taking part in the service to the holy ones,^{a} ^{5}and this, not as we expected, but they gave themselves first to the Lord and to us‡ through the will of God, ^{6}so that we urged Titus§ that, as he had already begun, he should also complete for you this gracious act also.^{b} ^{7¶}Now as you excel in every respect, in faith, discourse, knowledge, all earnestness, and in the love we have for you,^{c} may you excel in this gracious act also.

^{8}I say this not by way of command, but to test the genuineness of your love by your concern for others. ^{9**d}For you know the gracious act of our Lord Jesus Christ, that for your sake he became poor although he was rich, so that by his poverty you might become rich. ^{10}And I am giving counsel in this matter, for it is appropriate for you who began not only to act but to act willingly last year:^{e} ^{11}complete it now, so that your eager†† willingness may be matched by your completion of it out of what you have. ^{12‡‡}For if the eagerness is there, it is acceptable according to what one has, not according to what one does not have; ^{13}not that others should have relief while you are burdened, but that as a matter of equality ^{14}your surplus at the present time should supply their needs, so that their surplus may also supply your needs, that there may be equality. ^{15}As it is written:

"Whoever had much did not have more,
    and whoever had little did not have
    less."^{f}

Titus and His Collaborators.§§ ^{16}But thanks be to God who put the same concern for you into the heart of Titus, ^{17}for he not only welcomed our appeal but, since he is very concerned, he has gone to you of his own accord. ^{18}With him we have sent the brother¶¶ who is praised in all the churches for his preaching of the gospel.^{g} ^{19}And not only that, but he has also been appointed our traveling companion by the churches in this gracious work administered by us for the glory of the Lord [himself] and for the expression of our eagerness.^{h} ^{20}This we desire to avoid, that anyone blame us*** about this lavish gift administered by us, ^{21}for we are concerned for what is honorable not only in the sight of the Lord but also in the sight of others.^{i} ^{22}And with them we have sent our brother whom we often tested in many ways and found earnest, but who is now much more earnest because of his great confidence in you. ^{23}As for Titus, he is my partner and co-worker for you; as for our brothers, they are apostles of the churches, the glory of Christ.

---

translated throughout these chapters as "grace" (2 Cor 8:1; 9:8, 14), "favor" (2 Cor 8:4), "gracious act" (2 Cor 8:6, 7, 9) or "gracious work" (2 Cor 8:19), to be compared to "gracious gift" (1 Cor 16:3). The related term, *eucharistia*, "thanksgiving," also occurs at 2 Cor 9:11, 12. The wordplay is not superficial; various mutations of the same root signal inner connection between aspects of a single reality, and Paul consciously exploits the similarities in vocabulary to highlight that connection.

*[8:2] Three more terms are now introduced. **Test** (*dokimē*): the same root is translated as "to test" (2 Cor 8:8) and "evidence" (2 Cor 9:13); it means to be tried and found genuine. **Abundance**: variations on the same root lie behind "overflow" (2 Cor 8:2; 9:12), "excel" (2 Cor 8:7), "surplus" (2 Cor 8:14), "superfluous" (2 Cor 9:1) "make abundant" and "have an abundance" (2 Cor 9:8). These expressions of fullness contrast with references to need (2 Cor 8:14; 9:12). **Generosity**: the word *haplotēs* has nuances of both simplicity and sincerity; here and in 2 Cor 9:11, 13 it designates the singleness of purpose that manifests itself in generous giving.

†[8:3–4] Paul emphasizes the spontaneity of the Macedonians and the nature of their action. **They begged us insistently**: the same root is translated as "urge," "appeal," "encourage" (2 Cor 8:6, 17; 9:5). **Taking part**: the same word is translated "contribution" in 2 Cor 9:13 and a related term as "partner" in 2 Cor 8:23. **Service** (*diakonia*): this word occurs also in 2 Cor 9:1, 13 as "service"; in 2 Cor 9:12 it is translated "administration," and in 2 Cor 8:19, 20 the corresponding verb is rendered "administer."

‡[8:5] **They gave themselves . . . to the Lord and to us**: on its deepest level their attitude is one of self-giving.

§[8:6] **Titus**: 1 Cor 16 seemed to leave the organization up to the Corinthians, but apparently Paul has sent Titus to initiate the collection as well; 2 Cor 8:16–17 will describe Titus' attitude as one of shared concern and cooperation.

¶[8:7] The charitable service Paul is promoting is seen briefly and in passing within the perspective of Paul's theology of the charisms. **Earnestness** (*spoudē*): this or related terms occur also in 2 Cor 8:22 ("earnest") and 2 Cor 8:8, 16, 17 ("concern").

**[8:9] The dialectic of Jesus' experience, expressed earlier in terms of life and death (2 Cor 5:15), sin and righteousness (2 Cor 5:21), is now rephrased in terms of poverty and wealth. Many scholars think this is a reference to Jesus' preexistence with God (his "wealth") and to his incarnation and death (his "poverty"), and they point to the similarity between this verse and Phil 2:6–8. Others interpret the wealth and poverty as succeeding phases of Jesus' earthly existence, e.g., his sense of intimacy with God and then the desolation and the feeling of abandonment by God in his death (cf. Mk 15:34).

††[8:11] **Eager**: the word *prothymia* also occurs in 2 Cor 8:12, 19; 9:2.

‡‡[8:12–15] Paul introduces the principle of **equality** into the discussion. The goal is not impoverishment but sharing of resources; balance is achieved at least over the course of time. In 2 Cor 8:15 Paul grounds his argument unexpectedly in the experience of Israel gathering manna in the desert: equality was achieved, independently of personal exertion, by God, who gave with an even hand according to need. Paul touches briefly here on the theme of "living from God."

§§[8:16–24] In recommending Titus and his companions, Paul stresses their personal and apostolic qualities, their good dispositions toward the Corinthians, and their authority as messengers of the churches and representatives of Christ.

¶¶[8:18] **The brother**: we do not know the identity of this co-worker of Paul, nor of the third companion mentioned below in 2 Cor 8:22.

***[8:20–22] **That anyone blame us**: 2 Cor 12:16–18 suggests that misunderstandings may indeed have arisen concerning Paul's management of the collection through the messengers mentioned here, but those same verses seem to imply that the Corinthians by and large would recognize the honesty of Paul's conduct in this area as in others (cf. 2 Cor 6:3).

---

z. [8:1] 11:9; Rom 15:26.   a. [8:4] Acts 24:17; Rom 15:31.   b. [8:6] 2:13; 7:6–7, 13–14; 8:16, 23; 12:18.   c. [8:7] 1 Cor 1:5.   d. [8:9] 6:10; Phil 2:6–8.

e. [8:10] 9:2; 1 Cor 16:1–4.   f. [8:15] Ex 16:18.   g. [8:18] 12:18.   h. [8:19] 1 Cor 16:3–4.   i. [8:21] Rom 12:17.

²⁴So give proof before the churches of your love and of our boasting about you to them.*

CHAPTER 9

God's Indescribable Gift.† ¹Now about the service to the holy ones, it is superfluous for me to write to you, ²for I know your eagerness, about which I boast of you to the Macedonians, that Achaia‡ has been ready since last year; and your zeal has stirred up most of them.ʲ ³Nonetheless, I sent the brothers§ so that our boast about you might not prove empty in this case, so that you might be ready, as I said, ⁴for fear that if any Macedonians come with me and find you not ready we might be put to shame (to say nothing of you) in this conviction. ⁵So I thought it necessary to encourage the brothers to go on ahead to you and arrange in advance for your promised gift, so that in this way it might be ready as a bountiful gift and not as an exaction.

⁶Consider this: whoever sows sparingly will also reap sparingly, and whoever sows bountifully will also reap bountifully.ᵏ ⁷Each must do as already determined, without sadness or compulsion, for God loves a cheerful giver.ˡ ⁸Moreover, God is able to make every grace abundant for you, so that in all things, always having all you need, you may have an abundance for every good work. ⁹As it is written:

"He scatters abroad, he gives to the poor;
    his righteousness endures forever."ᵐ

¹⁰The one who supplies seed to the sower and bread for food will supply and multiply your seed and increase the harvest of your righteousness.ⁿ ¹¹**You are being enriched in every way for all generosity, which through us produces

thanksgiving to God, ¹²for the administration of this public service is not only supplying the needs of the holy ones but is also overflowing in many acts of thanksgiving to God. ¹³Through the evidence of this service, you are glorifying God for your obedient confession of the gospel of Christ and the generosity of your contribution to them and to all others,ᵒ ¹⁴while in prayer on your behalf they long for you, because of the surpassing grace of God upon you. ¹⁵Thanks be to God for his indescribable gift!ᵖ

IV. PAUL'S DEFENSE OF HIS MINISTRY††

CHAPTER 10

Accusation of Weakness.‡‡ ¹Now I myself, Paul, urge you through the gentleness and clemency of Christ,§§ I who am humble when face to face with you, but brave toward you when absent, ²¶¶ᑫI

---

*[8:24] As Paul began by holding up the Macedonians as examples to be imitated, he closes by exhorting the Corinthians to show their love (by accepting the envoys and by cooperating as the Macedonians do), thus justifying the pride Paul demonstrates because of them before other churches.

†[9:1–15] Quite possibly this was originally an independent letter, though it deals with the same subject and continues many of the same themes. In that case, it may have been written a few weeks later than 2 Cor 8, while the delegation there mentioned was still on its way.

‡[9:2] **Achaia**: see note on Rom 15:26.

§[9:3] **I sent the brothers**: the Greek aorist tense here could be epistolary, referring to the present; in that case Paul would be sending them now, and 2 Cor 9 would merely conclude the letter of recommendation begun in 2 Cor 8. But the aorist may also refer to a sending that is past as Paul writes; then 2 Cor 9, with its apparently fresh beginning, is a follow-up message entrusted to another carrier.

¶[9:8–10] The behavior to which he exhorts them is grounded in God's own pattern of behavior. God is capable of overwhelming generosity, as scripture itself attests (2 Cor 9:9), so that they need not fear being short. He will provide in abundance, both supplying their natural needs and increasing their righteousness. Paul challenges them to godlike generosity and reminds them of the fundamental motive for encouragement: God himself cannot be outdone.

**[9:11–15] Paul's vision broadens to take in all the interested parties in one dynamic picture. His language becomes

liturgically colored and conveys a sense of fullness. With a final play on the words *charis* and *eucharistia* (see note on 2 Cor 8:1), he describes a circle that closes on itself: the movement of grace overflowing from God to them and handed on from them through Paul to others is completed by the prayer of praise and thanksgiving raised on their behalf to God.

††[10:1–13:10] These final chapters have their own unity of structure and theme and could well have formed the body of a separate letter. They constitute an *apologia* on Paul's part, i.e., a legal defense of his behavior and his ministry; the writing is emotionally charged and highly rhetorical. In the central section (2 Cor 11:16–12:10), the *apologia* takes the form of a boast. This section is prepared for by a prologue (2 Cor 11:1–15) and followed by an epilogue (2 Cor 12:11–18), which are similar in content and structure. These sections, in turn, are framed by an introduction (2 Cor 10:1–18) and a conclusion (2 Cor 12:19–13:10), both of which assert Paul's apostolic authority and confidence and define the purpose of the letter. The structure that results from this disposition of the material is chiastic, i.e., the first element corresponds to the last, the second to the second last, etc., following the pattern a b c b¹, a¹.

‡‡[10:1–18] Paul asserts his apostolic authority and expresses the confidence this generates in him. He writes in response to certain opinions that have arisen in the community and certain charges raised against him and in preparation for a forthcoming visit in which he intends to set things in order. This section gives us an initial glimpse of the situation in Corinth that Paul must address; much of its thematic material will be taken up again in the finale (2 Cor 12:19–13:10).

§§[10:1–2] A strong opening plunges us straight into the conflict. Contrasts dominate here: presence versus absence, gentleness-clemency-humility versus boldness-confidence-bravery. **Through the gentleness and clemency of Christ**: the figure of the gentle Christ, presented in a significant position before any specifics of the situation are suggested, forms a striking contrast to the picture of the bold and militant Paul (2 Cor 10:2–6); this tension is finally resolved in 2 Cor 13:3–4. **Absent . . . present**: this same contrast, with a restatement of the purpose of the letter, recurs in 2 Cor 13:10, which forms an inclusion with 2 Cor 10:1–2.

¶¶[10:2b–4a] **Flesh**: the Greek word *sarx* can express both the physical life of the body without any pejorative overtones (as in "we are in the flesh," 3) and our natural life insofar as it is marked by limitation and weakness (as in the other expressions) in contrast to the higher life and power conferred by the Spirit; cf. note on 1 Cor 3:1. The wordplay is intended to express the paradoxical situation of a life already taken over by the Spirit but not yet seen as such except by faith. Lack of empirical evidence of the Spirit permits misunderstanding and misjudgment, but Paul resolutely denies that his behavior and effectiveness are as limited as some suppose.

---

j. [9:2] 8:10; Rom 15:26. k. [9:6] Prv 11:24–25. l. [9:7] Prv 22:8 LXX. m. [9:9] Ps 112:9. n. [9:10] Is 55:10.

o. [9:13] 8:4; Rom 15:31. p. [9:15] Rom 5:15–16. q. [10:2] 13:2, 10; 1 Cor 4:21.

beg you that, when present, I may not have to be brave with that confidence with which I intend to act boldly against some who consider us as acting according to the flesh. ³For, although we are in the flesh, we do not battle according to the flesh,* ⁴for the weapons of our battle are not of flesh but are enormously powerful, capable of destroying fortresses. We destroy arguments ʳ ⁵and every pretension raising itself against the knowledge of God, and take every thought captive in obedience to Christ, ⁶and we are ready to punish every disobedience, once your obedience is complete.ˢ

⁷ᵗLook at what confronts you. Whoever is confident of belonging to Christ should consider that as he belongs to Christ, so do we.† ⁸ᵘAnd even if I should boast a little too much of our authority, which the Lord gave for building you up and not for tearing you down, I shall not be put to shame. ⁹ᵗMay I not seem as one frightening you through letters. ¹⁰For someone will say, "His letters are severe and forceful, but his bodily presence is weak, and his speech contemptible." ᵛ ¹¹Such a person must understand that what we are in word through letters when absent, that we also are in action when present.ʷ

¹²§Not that we dare to class or compare ourselves with some of those who recommend themselves. But when they measure themselves by one another and compare themselves with one another, they are without understanding.ˣ ¹³But we will not boast beyond measure but will keep to the limits⁵ God has apportioned us, namely, to reach even to you. ¹⁴For we are not overreaching ourselves, as though we did not reach you; we indeed first came to you with the gospel of Christ. ¹⁵We are not boasting beyond measure, in other people's labors; yet our hope is that, as your faith increases, our influence among you may be greatly enlarged, within our proper limits, ¹⁶so that we may preach the gospel even beyond you, not boasting of work already done in another's sphere.ʸ ¹⁷ᶻ**Whoever boasts, should boast in the Lord.'"* ¹⁸For it is not the one who recommends himself who is approved,†† but the one whom the Lord recommends.ᵃ

CHAPTER 11

Preaching Without Charge.‡‡ ¹If only you would put up with a little foolishness from me!§§ Please put up with me.ᵇ ²¶¶For I am jealous of you with the jealousy of God, since I betrothed you to one husband to present you as a chaste virgin to Christ.ᶜ ³But I am afraid that, as the serpent deceived Eve*** by his cunning, your thoughts may be corrupted from a sincere [and pure] commitment to Christ.ᵈ ⁴For if someone comes and preaches another Jesus††† than the one we preached,ᵉ or if you receive a different spirit

---

*[10:3b–6] Paul is involved in combat. The strong military language and imagery are both an assertion of his confidence in the divine power at his disposal and a declaration of war against those who underestimate his resources. The threat is echoed in 2 Cor 13:2–3.

†[10:7–8] Belonging to Christ . . . so do we: these phrases already announce the pattern of Paul's boast in 2 Cor 11:21b–29, especially 2 Cor 11:22–23. **For building you up and not for tearing you down:** Paul draws on the language by which Jeremiah described the purpose of the prophetic power the Lord gave to him (Jer 1:9–10; 12:16–17; 24:6). Though Paul's power may have destructive effects on others (2 Cor 10:2–6), its intended effect on the community is entirely constructive (cf. 2 Cor 13:10). **I shall not be put to shame:** his assertions will not be refuted; they will be revealed as true at the judgment.

‡[10:9–10] Paul cites the complaints of some who find him lacking in personal forcefulness and holds out the threat of a personal *parousia* (both "return" and "presence") that will be forceful, indeed will be a demonstration of Christ's own power (cf. 2 Cor 13:2–4).

§[10:12–18] Paul now qualifies his claim to boldness, indicating its limits. He distinguishes his own behavior from that of others, revealing those "others" as they appear to him: as self-recommending, immoderately boastful, encroaching on territory not assigned to them, and claiming credit not due to them.

⁵[10:13] Will keep to the limits: the notion of proper limits is expressed here by two terms with overlapping meanings, *metron* and *kanōn*, which are played off against several expressions denoting overreaching or expansion beyond a legitimate sphere.

**[10:17] Boast in the Lord: there is a legitimate boasting, in contrast to the immoderate boasting to which 2 Cor 10:13, 15 allude. God's work through Paul in the community is the object of his boast (2 Cor 10:13–16; 2 Cor 1:12–14) and constitutes his recommendation (2 Cor 3:1–3). Cf. notes on 2 Cor 1:12–14 and 1 Cor 1:29–31.

††[10:18] Approved: to be approved is to come successfully through the process of testing for authenticity (cf. 2 Cor 13:3–7 and the note on 2 Cor 8:2). **Whom the Lord recommends:** self-commendation is a premature and unwarranted anticipation of the final judgment, which the Lord alone will pass (cf. 1 Cor 4:3–5). Paul alludes to this judgment throughout 2 Cor 10–13, frequently in final or transitional positions; cf. 2 Cor 11:15; 12:19a; 13:3–7.

‡‡[11:1–15] Although these verses continue to reveal information about Paul's opponents and the differences he perceives between them and himself, 2 Cor 11:1 signals a turn in Paul's thought. This section constitutes a prologue to the boasting that he will undertake in 2 Cor 11:16–12:10, and it bears remarkable similarities to the section that follows the central boast, 2 Cor 12:11–18.

§§[11:1] Put up with a little foolishness from me: this verse indicates more clearly than the general statement of intent in 2 Cor 10:13 the nature of the project Paul is about to undertake. He alludes ironically to the Corinthians' toleration for others. **Foolishness:** Paul qualifies his project as folly from beginning to end; see note on 2 Cor 11:16–12:10.

¶¶[11:2] Paul gives us a sudden glimpse of the theological values that are at stake. **The jealousy of God:** the perspective is that of the covenant, described in imagery of love and marriage, as in the prophets; cf. 1 Cor 10:22. **I betrothed you:** Paul, like a father (cf. 2 Cor 12:14), betroths the community to Christ as his bride (cf. Eph 5:21–33) and will present her to him at his second coming. Cf. Mt 25:1–13 and the nuptial imagery in Rev 21.

***[11:3] As the serpent deceived Eve: before Christ can return for the community Paul fears a repetition of the primal drama of seduction. Corruption of minds is satanic activity (see 2 Cor 2:11; 4:4). Satanic imagery recurs in 2 Cor 11:13–15, 20; 12:7b, 16–17; see notes on these passages.

†††[11:4] Preaches another Jesus: the danger is specified, and Paul's opponents are identified with the cunning serpent. The battle for minds has to do with the understanding of Jesus, the Spirit, the gospel; the Corinthians have flirted with another understanding than the one that Paul handed on to them as traditional and normative.

---

r. [10:4] 6:7; 13:2–3; 1 Cor 1:25; Eph 6:10–14. s. [10:6] 2:9. t. [10:7] 1 Cor 1:12. u. [10:8] 13:10. v. [10:10] 1 Cor 2:3. w. [10:11] 13:1–2. x. [10:12] 3:1–2; 4:2; 5:12; 6:4; 10:18; 12:11.

y. [10:16] Rom 15:20–21. z. [10:17] Jer 9:22–23; 1 Cor 1:31. a. [10:18] 13:3–9. b. [11:1] 11:21; 12:11. c. [11:2] Hos 2:21–22; Eph 5:26–27. d. [11:3] Gn 3:1–6. e. [11:4] Gal 1:6–9.

from the one you received or a different gospel from the one you accepted, you put up with it well enough. [5]*For I think that I am not in any way inferior to these "superapostles." [6]Even if I am untrained in speaking, I am not so in knowledge;[g] in every way we have made this plain to you in all things.[†]

[7‡]Did I make a mistake when I humbled myself so that you might be exalted, because I preached the gospel of God to you without charge?[h] [8]I plundered other churches by accepting from them in order to minister to you. [9]And when I was with you and in need, I did not burden anyone, for the brothers who came from Macedonia supplied my needs. So I refrained and will refrain from burdening you in any way.[i] [10]By the truth of Christ in me, this boast of mine shall not be silenced in the regions of Achaia.[j] [11§]And why? Because I do not love you? God knows I do![k]

[12]And what I do I will continue to do, in order to end this pretext of those who seek a pretext for being regarded as we are in the mission of which they boast. [13¶]For such people are false apostles, deceitful workers, who masquerade as apostles of Christ. [14]And no wonder, for even Satan masquerades as an angel of light. [15]So it is not strange that his ministers also masquerade as ministers of righteousness. Their end will correspond to their deeds.

Paul's Boast: His Labors. [16**]"I repeat, no one should consider me foolish;[††] but if you do, accept me as a fool, so that I too may boast a little.[‡‡] [17]What I am saying I am not saying according to the Lord but as in foolishness, in this boastful state. [18]Since many boast according to the flesh, I too will boast. [19]For you gladly put up with fools, since you are wise yourselves. [20§§]For you put up with it if someone enslaves you, or devours you, or gets the better of you, or puts on airs, or slaps you in the face. [21]To my shame I say that we were too weak!¶¶

But what anyone dares to boast of (I am speaking in foolishness) I also dare. [22***]Are they Hebrews? So am I. Are they Israelites? So am I. Are they descendants of Abraham? So am I.[l] [23†††]Are they ministers of Christ? (I am talking like an insane person.)[m] I am still more,[‡‡‡] with

---

*[11:5] These "superapostles": this term, employed again in 2 Cor 12:11b, designates the opponents of whom Paul has spoken in 2 Cor 10 and again in 2 Cor 11:4. They appear to be intruders at Corinth. Their preaching is marked at least by a different emphasis and style, and they do not hesitate to accept support from the community. Perhaps these itinerants appeal to the authority of church leaders in Jerusalem and even carry letters of recommendation from them. But it is not those distant leaders whom Paul is attacking here. The intruders are "superapostles" not in the sense of the "pillars" at Jerusalem (Gal 2), but in their own estimation. They consider themselves superior to Paul as apostles and ministers of Christ, and they are obviously enjoying some success among the Corinthians. Paul rejects their claim to be apostles in any superlative sense (hyperlian), judging them bluntly as "false apostles," ministers of Satan masquerading as apostles of Christ (2 Cor 11:13–15). On the contrary, he himself will claim to be a superminister of Christ (hyper egō, 2 Cor 11:23).

†[11:6] Apparently found deficient in both rhetorical ability (cf. 2 Cor 10:10) and knowledge (cf. 2 Cor 10:5), Paul concedes the former charge but not the latter. In every way: in all their contacts with him revelation has been taking place. Paul, through whom God reveals the knowledge of himself (2 Cor 2:14), and in whom the death and life of Jesus are revealed (2 Cor 4:10–11; cf. 2 Cor 6:4), also demonstrates his own role as the bearer of true knowledge. Cf. 1 Cor 1:18–2:16.

‡[11:7–10] Abruptly Paul passes to another reason for complaints: his practice of preaching without remuneration (cf. 1 Cor 9:3–18). He deftly defends his practice by situating it from the start within the pattern of Christ's own self-humiliation (cf. 2 Cor 10:1) and reduces objections to absurdity by rhetorical questions (cf. 2 Cor 12:13).

§[11:11–12] Paul rejects lack of affection as his motive (possibly imputed to him by his opponents) and states his real motive, a desire to emphasize the disparity between himself and the others (cf. 2 Cor 11:19–21). The topic of his gratuitous service will be taken up once more in 2 Cor 12:13–18. 1 Cor 9:15–18 gives a different but complementary explanation of his motivation.

¶[11:13–15] Paul picks up again the imagery of 2 Cor 11:3 and applies it to the opponents: they are false apostles of Christ, really serving another master. Deceitful . . . masquerade: deception and simulation, like cunning (2 Cor 11:3), are marks of the satanic. Angel of light: recalls the contrast between light and darkness, Christ and Beliar at 2 Cor 6:14–15. Ministers of righteousness: recalls the earlier contrast between the

ministry of condemnation and that of righteousness (2 Cor 3:9). Their end: the section closes with another allusion to the judgment, when all participants in the final conflict will be revealed or unmasked and dealt with as they deserve.

**[11:16–12:10] Paul now accepts the challenge of his opponents and indulges in boasting similar to theirs, but with differences that he has already signaled in 2 Cor 10:12–18 and that become clearer as he proceeds. He defines the nature of his project and unmistakably labels it as folly at the beginning and the end (2 Cor 11:16–23; 12:11). Yet his boast does not spring from ignorance (2 Cor 11:21; 12:6) nor is it concerned merely with human distinctions (2 Cor 11:18). Paul boasts "in moderation" (2 Cor 10:13, 15) and "in the Lord" (2 Cor 10:17).

††[11:16–29] The first part of Paul's boast focuses on labors and afflictions, in which authentic service of Christ consists.

‡‡[11:16–21] These verses recapitulate remarks already made about the foolishness of boasting and the excessive toleration of the Corinthians. They form a prelude to the boast proper.

§§[11:20] Paul describes the activities of the "others" in terms that fill out the picture drawn in vv 3–4, 13–15. Much of the vocabulary suggests fleshly or even satanic activity. Enslaves: cf. Gal 2:4. Devours: cf. 1 Pt 5:8. Gets the better: the verb lambanō means "to take," but is used in a variety of senses; here it may imply financial advantage, as in the English colloquialism "to take someone." It is similarly used at 2 Cor 12:16 and is there connected with cunning and deceit. Puts on airs: the same verb is rendered "raise oneself" (2 Cor 10:5) and "be too elated" (2 Cor 12:7).

¶¶[11:21] Paul ironically concedes the charge of personal weakness from 2 Cor 10:1–18 but will refute the other charge there mentioned, that of lack of boldness, accepting the challenge to demonstrate it by his boast.

***[11:22] The opponents apparently pride themselves on their "Jewishness." Paul, too, can claim to be a Jew by race, religion, and promise. Descendants of Abraham: elsewhere Paul distinguishes authentic from inauthentic heirs of Abraham and the promise (Rom 4:13–18; 9:7–13; 11:1; Gal 3:9, 27–29; cf. Jn 8:33–47). Here he grants his opponents this title in order to concentrate on the principal claim that follows.

†††[11:23a] Ministers of Christ . . . I am still more: the central point of the boast (cf. note on 2 Cor 11:5). Like an insane person: the climax of his folly.

‡‡‡[11:23b–29] Service of the humiliated and crucified Christ is demonstrated by trials endured for him. This rhetorically impressive catalogue enumerates many of the labors and perils Paul encountered on his missionary journeys.

---

f. [11:5] 12:11..   g. [11:6] 1 Cor 1:5, 17; 2:1–5.   h. [11:7] 12:13–18; Acts 18:3; 1 Cor 9:6–18.   i. [11:9] Phil 4:15, 18.   j. [11:10] 1 Cor 9:15.   k. [11:11] 12:15.

l. [11:22] Acts 22:3 / Rom 11:1; Phil 3:5–6.   m. [11:23] 6:5; Acts 16:22–24; 1 Cor 15:31–32.

far greater labors, far more imprisonments, far worse beatings, and numerous brushes with death. ²⁴Five times at the hands of the Jews I received forty lashes minus one.ⁿ ²⁵Three times I was beaten with rods, once I was stoned, three times I was shipwrecked, I passed a night and a day on the deep;ᵒ ²⁶on frequent journeys, in dangers from rivers, dangers from robbers, dangers from my own race, dangers from Gentiles, dangers in the city, dangers in the wilderness, dangers at sea, dangers among false brothers; ²⁷in toil and hardship, through many sleepless nights, through hunger and thirst, through frequent fastings, through cold and exposure.ᵖ ²⁸And apart from these things, there is the daily pressure upon me of my anxiety for all the churches. ²⁹Who is weak, and I am not weak? Who is led to sin, and I am not indignant?�q

Paul's Boast: His Weakness. * ³⁰If I must boast, I will boast of the things that show my weakness. ³¹⁺The God and Father of the Lord Jesus knows, he who is blessed forever, that I do not lie. ³²At Damascus, the governor under King Aretas guarded the city of Damascus, in order to seize me, ³³but I was lowered in a basket through a window in the wall and escaped his hands.ʳ

CHAPTER 12

¹I⁺ must boast; not that it is profitable, but I will go on to visions and revelations of the Lord. ²I know someone in Christ who, fourteen years ago (whether in the body or out of the body I do not know, God knows), was caught up to the third heaven. ³And I know that this person (whether in the body or out of the body I do not know, God knows) ⁴was caught up into Paradise and heard ineffable things, which no one may utter.ˢ ⁵About this personˢ I will boast,

but about myself I will not boast, except about my weaknesses. ⁶Although if I should wish to boast, I would not be foolish, for I would be telling the truth. But I refrain, so that no one may think more of me than what he sees in me or hears from me ⁷because of the abundance of the revelations. Therefore, that I might not become too elated,⁵ a thorn in the flesh was given to me, an angel of Satan, to beat me, to keep me from being too elated.ᵗ ⁸Three times⁎⁎ I begged the Lord about this, that it might leave me,ᵘ ⁹⁺⁺but he said to me, "My grace is sufficient for you, for power is made perfect in weakness." I will rather boast most gladly of my weaknesses,⁺⁺ in order that the power of Christ may dwell with me.ᵛ ¹⁰Therefore, I am content with weaknesses, insults, hardships, persecutions, and constraints, for the sake of Christ;ʷ for when I am weak, then I am strong.§§

Selfless Concern for the Church. ¶⁶ ¹¹I have been foolish. You compelled me, for I ought to have

revelations were not a personal achievement, nor were they meant to draw attention to any quality of his own.

¶[12:7] **That I might not become too elated:** God assures that there is a negative component to his experience, so that he cannot lose proper perspective; cf. 2 Cor 1:9; 4:7–11. **A thorn in the flesh:** variously interpreted as a sickness or physical disability, a temptation, or a handicap connected with his apostolic activity. But since Hebrew "thorn in the flesh," like English "thorn in my side," refers to persons (cf. Nm 33:55; Ez 28:24), Paul may be referring to some especially persistent and obnoxious opponent. The language of 2 Cor 12:7–8 permits this interpretation. If this is correct, the frequent appearance of singular pronouns in depicting the opposition may not be merely a stylistic variation; the singular may be provoked and accompanied by the image of one individual in whom criticism of Paul's preaching, way of life, and apostolic consciousness is concentrated, and who embodies all the qualities Paul attributes to the group. **An angel of Satan:** a personal messenger from Satan; cf. the satanic language already applied to the opponents in 2 Cor 11:3, 13–15, 20.

⁎⁎[12:8] **Three times:** his prayer was insistent, like that of Jesus in Gethsemane, a sign of how intolerable he felt the thorn to be.

⁺⁺[12:9] **But he said to me:** Paul's petition is denied; release and healing are withheld for a higher purpose. The Greek perfect tense indicates that Jesus' earlier response still holds at the time of writing. **My grace is sufficient for you:** this is not a statement about the sufficiency of grace in general. Jesus speaks directly to Paul's situation. **Is made perfect:** i.e., is given most fully and manifests itself fully.

⁺⁺[12:9b–10a] Paul draws the conclusion from the autobiographical anecdote and integrates it into the subject of this part of the boast. **Weaknesses:** the apostolic hardships he must endure, including active personal hostility, as specified in a final catalogue (2 Cor 12:10a). **That the power of Christ may dwell with me:** Paul pinpoints the ground for the paradoxical strategy he has adopted in his self-defense.

§§[12:10] **When I am weak, then I am strong:** Paul recognizes a twofold pattern in the resolution of the weakness-power (and death-life) dialectic, each of which looks to Jesus as the model and is experienced in him. The first is personal, involving a reversal in himself (Jesus, 2 Cor 13:4a; Paul, 2 Cor 1:9–10; 4:10–11; 6:9). The second is apostolic, involving an effect on others (Jesus, 2 Cor 5:14–15; Paul, 2 Cor 1:6; 4:12; 13:9). The specific kind of "effectiveness in ministry" that Paul promises to demonstrate on his arrival (2 Cor 13:4b; cf. 2 Cor 10:1–11) involves elements of both; this, too, will be modeled on Jesus' experience and a participation in that experience (2 Cor 9; 13:3b).

¶¶[12:11–18] This brief section forms an epilogue or concluding observation to Paul's boast, corresponding to the prologue in 2 Cor 11:1–15. A four-step sequence of ideas is

*[11:30–12:10] The second part of Paul's boast, marked by a change of style and a shift in focus. After recalling the project in which he is engaged, he states a new topic: his weaknesses as matter for boasting. Everything in this section, even the discussion of privileges and distinctions, will be integrated into this perspective.

†[11:31–32] The episode at Damascus is symbolic. It aptly illustrates Paul's weakness but ends in deliverance (cf. 2 Cor 4:7–11).

‡[12:1–4] **In the body or out of the body:** he seemed no longer confined to bodily conditions, but he does not claim to understand the mechanics of the experience. **Caught up:** i.e., in ecstasy. **The third heaven . . . Paradise:** ancient cosmologies depicted a multitiered universe. Jewish intertestamental literature contains much speculation about the number of heavens. Seven is the number usually mentioned, but the Testament of Levi (2:7–10; 3:1–4) speaks of three; God himself dwelt in the third of these. Without giving us any clear picture of the cosmos, Paul indicates a mental journey to a nonearthly space, set apart by God, in which secrets were revealed to him. **Ineffable things:** i.e., privileged knowledge, which it was not possible or permitted to divulge.

§[12:5–7] **This person:** the indirect way of referring to himself has the effect of emphasizing the distance between that experience and his everyday life, just as the indirect **someone in Christ** (2 Cor 12:2) and all the passive verbs emphasize his passivity and receptivity in the experience. The

n. [11:24] Dt 25:2–3.   o. [11:25] Acts 14:19; 27:43–44.   p. [11:27] 1 Cor 4:11.   q. [11:29] 1 Cor 9:22.   r. [11:33] Acts 9:23–25. s. [12:4] Lk 23:43; Rev 2:7.

t. [12:7] Nm 33:55; Jos 23:13; Ez 28:24.   u. [12:8] Mt 26:39–44. v. [12:9] 4:7.   w. [12:10] 6:4–5; Rom 5:3 / Phil 4:13.

been commended by you. For I am in no way inferior to these "superapostles,"ˣ even though I am nothing. ¹²˙The signs of an apostle were performed among you with all endurance, signs and wonders, and mighty deeds.ʸ ¹³†In what way were you less privileged than the rest of the churches, except that on my part I did not burden you? Forgive me this wrong!ᶻ

¹⁴Now I am ready to come to you this third time. And I will not be a burden, for I want not what is yours, but you. Children ought not to save for their parents, but parents for their children. ¹⁵I will most gladly spend and be utterly spent for your sakes. If I love you more, am I to be loved less? ¹⁶But granted that I myself did not burden you, yet I was crafty and got the better of you by deceit.ᵃ ¹⁷Did I take advantage of you through any of those I sent to you? ¹⁸I urged Titus to go and sent the brother with him. Did Titus take advantage of you? Did we not walk in the same spirit? And in the same steps?ᵇ

Final Warnings and Appeals.‡ ¹⁹Have you been thinking all along that we are defending§ ourselves before you? In the sight of God we are speaking in Christ, and all for building you up, beloved. ²⁰For I fear that⁵ when I come I may find you not such as I wish, and that you may find me not as you wish; that there may be rivalry, jealousy, fury, selfishness, slander, gossip, conceit, and disorder.ᶜ ²¹I fear that when I

come again‧‧ my God may humiliate me before you, and I may have to mourn over many of those who sinned earlier and have not repented of the impurity, immorality, and licentiousness they practiced.

CHAPTER 13

¹This third time I am coming†† to you. "On the testimony of two or three witnesses a fact shall be established."ᵈ ²I warned those who sinned earlier‡‡ and all the others, and I warn them now while absent, as I did when present on my second visit, that if I come again I will not be lenient, ³§§since you are looking for proof of Christ speaking in me. He is not weak toward you but powerful in you. ⁴For indeed he was crucified out of weakness, but he lives by the power of God. So also we are weak in him, but toward you we shall live with him by the power of God.

⁵¶¶Examine yourselves to see whether you are living in faith. Test yourselves. Do you not

---

‧‧[12:21] **Again**: one can also translate, "I fear that when I come my God may again humiliate me." Paul's allusion to the humiliation and mourning that may await him recall the mood he described in 2 Cor 2:1–4, but there is no reference here to any individual such as there is in 2 Cor 2:5–11. The crisis of 2 Cor 2 has happily been resolved by integration of the offender and repentance (2 Cor 7:4–16), whereas 2 Cor 12:21 is preoccupied with still unrepentant sinners. The sexual sins recall 1 Cor 5–7.

††[13:1] **This third time I am coming**: designation of the forthcoming visit as the "third" (cf. 2 Cor 12:14) may indicate that, in addition to his founding sojourn in Corinth, Paul had already made the first of two visits mentioned as planned in 2 Cor 1:15, and the next visit will be the long-postponed second of these. If so, the materials in 2 Cor 1:12–2:13 plus 2 Cor 7:4–16 and 2 Cor 10–13 may date from the same period of time, presumably of some duration, between Paul's second and third visit, though it is not clear that they are addressing the same crisis. The chronology is too unsure and the relations between sections of 2 Corinthians too unclear to yield any certainty. The hypothesis that 2 Cor 10–13 are themselves the "tearful letter" mentioned at 2 Cor 2:3–4 creates more problems than it solves.

‡‡[13:2] **I warned those who sinned earlier**: mention of unrepentant sinners (2 Cor 12:21 and here) and of an oral admonition given them on an earlier visit complicates the picture at the very end of Paul's development. It provides, in fact, a second explanation for the show of power that has been threatened from the beginning (2 Cor 10:1–6), but a different reason for it, quite unsuspected until now. It is not clear whether Paul is merely alluding to a dimension of the situation that he has not previously had occasion to mention, or whether some other community crisis, not directly connected with that behind 2 Cor 10–13, has influenced the final editing. **I will not be lenient**: contrast Paul's hesitation and reluctance to inflict pain in 2 Cor 1:23 and 2 Cor 2:1–4. The next visit will bring the showdown.

§§[13:3–4] Paul now gives another motive for severity when he comes, the charge of weakness leveled against him as an apostle. The motive echoes more closely the opening section (2 Cor 10:1–18) and the intervening development (especially 2 Cor 11:30–12:10). **Proof of Christ speaking in me**: the threat of 2 Cor 10:1–2 is reworded to recall Paul's conformity with the pattern of Christ, his insertion into the interplay of death and life, weakness and power (cf. note on 2 Cor 12:10b).

¶¶[13:5–9] Paul turns the challenge mentioned in 2 Cor 13:3 on them: they are to put themselves to the test to demonstrate whether Christ is in them. These verses involve a complicated series of plays on the theme of *dokimē* (testing, proof,

---

common to these two sections: Paul qualifies his boast as folly (2 Cor 11:1; 12:11a), asserts his noninferiority to the "superapostles" (2 Cor 11:5; 12:11b), exemplifies this by allusion to charismatic endowments (2 Cor 11:6; 12:12), and finally denies that he has been a financial burden to the community (2 Cor 11:7–12; 12:13–18).

*[12:12] Despite weakness and affliction (suggested by the mention of **endurance**), his ministry has been accompanied by demonstrations of power (cf. 1 Cor 2:3–4). **Signs of an apostle**: visible proof of belonging to Christ and of mediating Christ's power, which the opponents require as touchstones of apostleship (2 Cor 12:11; cf. 2 Cor 13:3).

†[12:13–18] Paul insists on his intention to continue refusing support from the community (cf. 2 Cor 11:8–12). In defending his practice and his motivation, he once more protests his love (cf. 2 Cor 11:11) and rejects the suggestion of secret self-enrichment. He has recourse here again to language applied to his opponents earlier: "cunning" (2 Cor 11:3), "deceit" (2 Cor 11:13), "got the better of you" (see note on 2 Cor 11:20), "take advantage" (2 Cor 2:11).

‡[12:19–13:10] This concludes the development begun in 2 Cor 10. In the chiastic arrangement of the material (see note on 2 Cor 10:1–13:10), this final part corresponds to the opening; there are important similarities of content between the two sections as well.

§[12:19] This verse looks back at the previous chapters and calls them by their proper name, a defense, an *apologia* (cf. 1 Cor 9:3). Yet Paul insists on an important distinction: he has indeed been speaking for their benefit, but the ultimate judgment to which he submits is God's (cf. 1 Cor 4:3–5). This verse also leads into the final section, announcing two of its themes: judgment and building up.

¶[12:20] **I fear that . . .** : earlier Paul expressed fear that the Corinthians were being victimized, exploited, seduced from right thinking by his opponents (2 Cor 11:3–4, 19–21). Here he alludes unexpectedly to moral disorders among the Corinthians themselves. The catalogue suggests the effects of factions that have grown up around rival apostles.

---

x. [12:11] 11:5. y. [12:12] Rom 15:19; 1 Thes 1:5. z. [12:13] 11:9–12. a. [12:16] 11:3, 13. b. [12:18] 2:13; 8:16, 23. c. [12:20] 1 Cor 1:11; 3:3.

d. [13:1] Dt 19:15; Mt 18:16; Jn 8:17; Heb 10:28.

realize that Jesus Christ is in you?—unless, of course, you fail the test. ⁶I hope you will discover that we have not failed. ⁷But we pray to God that you may not do evil, not that we may appear to have passed the test but that you may do what is right, even though we may seem to have failed. ⁸For we cannot do anything against the truth, but only for the truth. ⁹For we rejoice when we are weak but you are strong. What we pray for is your improvement.

¹⁰*ᵉI am writing this while I am away, so that when I come I may not have to be severe in virtue of the authority that the Lord has given me to build up and not to tear down.

V. CONCLUSION†

¹¹Finally, brothers, rejoice. Mend your ways, encourage one another, agree with one another, live in peace, and the God of love and peace will be with you. ¹²Greet one another with a holy kiss. All the holy ones greet you.ᶠ

¹³The grace of the Lord Jesus Christ and the love of God and the fellowship of the holy Spirit be with all of you.ᵍ

---

passing and failing a test). Behind this stands the familiar distinction between present human judgment and final divine judgment. This is the final appearance of the theme (cf. 2 Cor 10:18; 11:15; 12:19).

*[13:10] **Authority . . . to build up and not to tear down:** Paul restates the purpose of his letter in language that echoes 2 Cor 10:2, 8, emphasizing the positive purpose of his authority in their regard. This verse forms an inclusion with the topic sentence of the section (2 Cor 12:19), as well as with the opening of this entire portion of the letter (2 Cor 10:1–2).

e. [13:10] 10:8.

---

†[13:11–13] These verses may have originally concluded 2 Cor 10–13, but they have nothing specifically to do with the material of that section. It is also possible to consider them a conclusion to the whole of 2 Corinthians in its present edited form. The exhortations are general, including a final appeal for peace in the community. The letter ends calmly, after its many storms, with the prospect of ecclesial unity and divine blessing. The final verse is one of the clearest trinitarian passages in the New Testament.

f. [13:12] Rom 16:16; 1 Cor 16:20 / Phil 4:22; 1 Thes 5:26; 1 Pt 5:14.   g. [13:13] Rom 16:20; 1 Cor 16:23.

THE LETTER TO THE
GALATIANS

⟿

The Galatians to whom the letter is addressed were Paul's converts, most likely among the descendants of Celts who had invaded western and central Asia Minor in the third century B.C. and had settled in the territory around Ancyra (modern Ankara, Turkey). Paul had passed through this area on his second missionary journey (Acts 16:6) and again on his third (Acts 18:23). It is less likely that the recipients of this letter were Paul's churches in the southern regions of Pisidia, Lycaonia, and Pamphylia where he had preached earlier in the Hellenized cities of Perge, Iconium, Pisidian Antioch, Lystra, and Derbe (Acts 13:13–14:27); this area was part of the Roman province of Galatia, and some scholars think that South Galatia was the destination of this letter.

If it is addressed to the Galatians in the north, the letter was probably written around A.D. 54 or 55, most likely from Ephesus after Paul's arrival there for a stay of several years on his third missionary journey (Acts 19; 20:31). On the South Galatian theory, the date would be earlier, perhaps A.D. 48–50. Involved is the question of how one relates the events of Gal 2:1–10 to the "Council of Jerusalem" described in Acts 15 (see notes on each passage).

In any case, the new Christians whom Paul is addressing were converts from paganism (Gal 4:8–9) who were now being enticed by other missionaries to add the observances of the Jewish law, including the rite of circumcision, to the cross of Christ as a means of salvation. For, since Paul's visit, some other interpretation of Christianity had been brought to these neophytes, probably by converts from Judaism (the name "Judaizers" is sometimes applied to them); it has specifically been suggested that they were Jewish Christians who had come from the austere Essene sect.

These interlopers insisted on the necessity of following certain precepts of the Mosaic law along with faith in Christ. They were undermining Paul's authority also, asserting that he had not been trained by Jesus himself, that his gospel did not agree with that of the original and true apostles in Jerusalem, that he had kept from his converts in Galatia the necessity of accepting circumcision and other key obligations of the Jewish law, in order more easily to win them to Christ, and that his gospel was thus not the full and authentic one held by "those of repute" in Jerusalem (Gal 2:2). Some scholars also see in Galatians 5; 6 another set of opponents against whom Paul writes, people who in their emphasis on the Spirit set aside all norms for conduct and became libertines in practice.

When Paul learned of the situation, he wrote this defense of his apostolic authority and of the correct understanding of the faith. He set forth the unique importance of Christ and his redemptive sacrifice on the cross, the freedom that Christians enjoy from the old burdens of the law, the total sufficiency of Christ and of faith in Christ as the way to God and to eternal life, and the beauty of the new life of the Spirit. Galatians is thus a summary of basic Pauline theology. Its themes were more fully and less polemically developed in the Letter to the Romans.

Autobiographically, the letter gives us Paul's own accounts of how he came to faith (Gal 1:15–24), the agreement in "the truth of the gospel" (Gal 2:5, 14) that he shared with the Jewish Christian leaders in Jerusalem, James, Cephas, and John (Gal 2:1–10), and the rebuke he had to deliver to Cephas in Antioch for inconsistency, contrary to the gospel, on the issue of table fellowship in the racially mixed church of Jewish and Gentile Christians in Antioch (Gal 2:11–14; cf. Gal 2:15–21). At the conclusion of the letter (Gal 6:11–18), Paul wrote in his own hand (cf. 2 Thes 3:17–18) a vivid summary of the message to the Galatians.

In his vigorous emphasis on the absolute preeminence of Christ and his cross as God's way to salvation and holiness, Paul stresses Christian freedom and the ineffectiveness of the Mosaic law for gaining divine favor and blessings (Gal 3:19–29). The pious Jew saw in the law a way established by God to win divine approval by a life of meticulous observance of ritual, social, and moral regulations. But Paul's profound insight into the higher designs of God in Christ led him to understand and welcome the priority of promise and faith (shown in the experience of Abraham, Gal 3:6–18) and the supernatural gifts of the Spirit (Gal 3:2–5; 5:16–6:10). His enthusiasm for this new vision of the life of grace in Christ and of the uniquely salvific role of Christ's redemptive death on the cross shines through this whole letter.

The principal divisions of the Letter to the Galatians are the following:

I. Address (1:1–5)
II. Loyalty to the Gospel (1:6–10)
III. Paul's Defense of His Gospel and His Authority (1:11–2:21)
IV. Faith and Liberty (3:1–4:31)
V. Exhortation to Christian Living (5:1–6:10)
VI. Conclusion (6:11–18)

I. ADDRESS

CHAPTER 1

Greeting.[*] [1a]Paul, an apostle[†] not from human beings nor through a human being but through Jesus Christ and God the Father who raised him from the dead,[b] [2‡]and all the brothers who are with me, to the churches of Galatia: [3]grace to you and peace from God our Father and the Lord Jesus Christ, [4§]who gave himself for our sins that he might rescue us from the present evil age in accord with the will of our God and Father,[c] [5]to whom be glory forever and ever. Amen.[d]

II. LOYALTY TO THE GOSPEL[¶]

[6e]I am amazed that you are so quickly forsaking the one who called you[**] by [the] grace [of Christ] for a different gospel [7](not that there is another). But there are some who are disturbing you and wish to pervert the gospel of Christ.

[8f]But even if we or an angel from heaven should preach [to you] a gospel other than the one that we preached to you, let that one be accursed![††] [9]As we have said before, and now I say again, if anyone preaches to you a gospel other than the one that you received, let that one be accursed! [10g]Am I now currying favor with human beings or God? Or am I seeking to please people? If I were still trying to please people, I would not be a slave of Christ.[‡‡]

III. PAUL'S DEFENSE OF HIS GOSPEL AND HIS AUTHORITY[§§]

His Call by Christ. [11h]Now I want you to know, brothers, that the gospel preached by me is not of human origin. [12]For I did not receive it from a human being, nor was I taught it, but it came through a revelation of Jesus Christ.[¶¶]

---

*[1:1–5] See note on Rom 1:1–7, concerning the greeting.

†[1:1] **Apostle**: because of attacks on his authority in Galatia, Paul defends his apostleship. He is not an apostle commissioned by a congregation (Phil 2:25; 2 Cor 8:23) or even by prophets (1 Tm 1:18; 4:14) but **through Jesus Christ and God the Father**.

‡[1:2] **All the brothers**: fellow believers in Christ, male and female; cf. Gal 3:27–28. Paul usually mentions the cosender(s) at the start of a letter, but the use of **all** is unique, adding weight to the letter. **Galatia**: central Turkey more likely than the Roman province of Galatia; see Introduction.

§[1:4] The greeting in Gal 1:3 is expanded by a christological formula that stresses deliverance through the Lord Jesus from a world dominated by Satan; cf. 2 Cor 4:4; Eph 2:2; 6:12.

¶[1:6–10] In place of the usual thanksgiving (see note on Rom 1:8), Paul, with little to be thankful for in the Galatian situation, expresses amazement at the way his converts are deserting the gospel of Christ for a perverted message. He reasserts the one gospel he has preached (Gal 1:7–9) and begins to defend himself (Gal 1:10).

[1:6] **The one who called you: God or Christ, though in actuality Paul was the divine instrument to call the Galatians.

††[1:8] **Accursed**: in Greek, *anathema*; cf. Rom 9:3; 1 Cor 12:3; 16:22.

‡‡[1:10] This charge by Paul's opponents, that he sought to conciliate people with flattery and to curry favor with God, might refer to his mission practices (cf. 1 Cor 9:19–23) but the word **still** suggests it refers to his pre-Christian days (cf. Gal 1:14; Phil 3:6). The self-description **slave of Christ** is one Paul often uses in a greeting (Rom 1:1).

§§[1:11–2:21] Paul's presentation on behalf of his message and of his apostleship reflects rhetorical forms of his day: he first narrates the facts about certain past events (Gal 1:12–2:14) and then states his contention regarding justification by faith as the gospel message (Gal 2:15–21). Further arguments follow from both experience and scripture in Galatians 3; 4, before he draws out the ethical consequences (Gal 5:1–6:10). The specific facts that he takes up here to show that his gospel is not a human invention (Gal 1:11) but **came through a revelation of Jesus Christ** (Gal 1:12) deal with his own calling as a Christian missionary (Gal 1:13–17), his initial relations with the apostles in Jerusalem (Gal 1:18–24), a later journey to Jerusalem (Gal 2:1–10), and an incident in Antioch involving Cephas and persons from James (Gal 2:11–14). The content of Paul's revealed gospel is then set forth in the heart of the letter (Gal 2:15–21).

¶¶[1:12] Although Paul received his gospel **through a revelation** from Christ, this did not exclude his use of early Christian confessional formulations. See note on Gal 1:4.

---

a. [1:1–3] Rom 1:1–7; 1 Cor 1:1–3. b. [1:1] 1:11–12. c. [1:4] 2:20; Eph 5:2; 1 Tm 2:6 / 1 Jn 5:19 / Rom 12:2; Eph 5:16; Heb 10:10. d. [1:5] Rom 16:27; 2 Tm 4:18. e. [1:6–7] 5:8, 10; Acts 15:1, 24; 2 Cor 11:4.

f. [1:8–9] 1 Cor 16:22 / Gal 5:3, 21; 2 Cor 13:2. g. [1:10] 2 Cor 5:11 / 1 Thes 2:4. h. [1:11–12] 1 Cor 15:1 / Gal 1:1; Eph 3:3.

[13]"For you heard of my former way of life in Judaism, how I persecuted the church of God beyond measure and tried to destroy it,[i] [14]and progressed in Judaism beyond many of my contemporaries among my race, since I was even more a zealot for my ancestral traditions.[j] [15]But when [God], who from my mother's womb had set me apart and called me through his grace, was pleased[k] [16]to reveal his Son to me,[l] so that I might proclaim him to the Gentiles, I did not immediately consult flesh and blood,[†] [17]nor did I go up to Jerusalem to those who were apostles before me; rather, I went into Arabia[‡] and then returned to Damascus.

[18§]Then after three years[l] I went up to Jerusalem to confer with Cephas and remained with him for fifteen days.[m] [19]But I did not see any other of the apostles,[n] only James the brother of the Lord.[**] [20](As to what I am writing to you, behold, before God, I am not lying.)[o] [21]Then I went into the regions of Syria and Cilicia.[p] [22]And I was unknown personally to the churches of Judea that are in Christ; [23]they only kept hearing that "the one who once was persecuting us is now preaching the faith he once tried to destroy."[q] [24]So they glorified God because of me.

CHAPTER 2
The Council of Jerusalem.[††] [1]Then after fourteen years I again went up to Jerusalem with

Barnabas,[‡‡] taking Titus along also.[r] [2]I went up in accord with a revelation,[§§] and I presented to them the gospel that I preach to the Gentiles—but privately to those of repute—so that I might not be running, or have run, in vain.[s] [3]Moreover, not even[¶¶] Titus, who was with me, although he was a Greek, was compelled to be circumcised,[t] [4]but because of the false brothers[***] secretly brought in, who slipped in to spy on our freedom that we have in Christ Jesus,[u] that they might enslave us— [5]to them we did not submit even for a moment, so that the truth of the gospel[†††] might remain intact for you.[v] [6]But from those who were reputed to be important (what they once were makes no difference to me; God shows no partiality)—those of repute made me add nothing.[w] [7‡‡‡]On the contrary, when they saw that I had been entrusted with the gospel to the uncircumcised, just as Peter to the circumcised,[x] [8]for the one who worked in Peter for an apostolate to the circumcised worked also in me for the Gentiles, [9]and when they recognized the grace bestowed upon me, James and Cephas and

---

*[1:13–17] Along with Phil 3:4–11, which also moves from autobiography to its climax in a discussion on justification by faith (cf. Gal 2:15–21), this passage is Paul's chief account of the change from his **former way of life** (Gal 1:13) to service as a Christian missionary (Gal 1:16); cf. Acts 9:1–22; 22:4–16; 26:9–18. Paul himself does not use the term "conversion" but stresses revelation (Gal 1:12, 16). In Gal 1:15 his language echoes the Old Testament prophetic call of Jeremiah. Unlike the account in Acts (cf. Acts 22:4–16), the calling of Paul here includes the mission to proclaim Christ **to the Gentiles** (Gal 1:16).

†[1:16] **Flesh and blood:** human authorities (cf. Mt 16:17; 1 Cor 15:50). Paul's apostleship comes from God (Gal 1:1).

‡[1:17] **Arabia:** probably the region of the Nabataean Arabs, east and south of Damascus.

§[1:18–24] Paul's first journey to Jerusalem as a Christian, according to Galatians (cf. Acts 9:23–31 and the note on Acts 22:5). He is quite explicit about contacts there, testifying under oath (Gal 1:20). On returning to **Syria** (perhaps specifically Damascus, cf. Gal 1:17) **and Cilicia** (including his home town Tarsus, cf. Acts 9:30; 22:3), Paul most likely engaged in missionary work. He underscores the fact that Christians in Judea knew of him only by reputation.

¶[1:18] **After three years:** two years and more, since Paul's call. To **confer with** Cephas may mean simply "pay a visit" or more specifically "get information from" him about Jesus, over a two-week period. **Cephas:** Aramaic name of Simon (Peter); cf. Mt 16:16–18 and the notes there.

[1:19] **James the brother of the Lord: not one of the Twelve, but a brother of Jesus (see note on Mk 6:3). He played an important role in the Jerusalem church (see note on Gal 2:9), the leadership of which he took over from Peter (Acts 12:17). Paul may have regarded James as an apostle.

††[2:1–10] Paul's second journey to Jerusalem, according to Galatians, involved a private meeting with **those of repute** (Gal 2:2). At issue was a Gentile, Titus, and the question

of circumcision, which **false brothers** (Gal 2:4) evidently demanded for him. Paul insists that the gospel he preaches (Gal 2:2; cf. Gal 1:9, 11) remained intact with no addition by those of repute (Gal 2:6); that **Titus** was not **compelled** to accept circumcision (Gal 2:3); and that he and the reputed **pillars** in Jerusalem agreed on how each would advance the missionary task (Gal 1:7–10). Usually, Gal 1:1–10 is equated with the "Council of Jerusalem," as it is called, described in Acts 15. See notes on Acts 15:6–12, 13–35, the latter concerning the "decree" that Paul does not mention.

‡‡[2:1] **After fourteen years:** thirteen or more years, probably reckoned from the return to Syria and Cilicia (Gal 1:21), though possibly from Paul's calling as a Christian (Gal 1:15). **Barnabas:** cf. Gal 2:9, 13; 1 Cor 9:6. A Jewish Christian missionary, with whom Paul worked (Acts 4:36–37; 11:22, 25, 30; 12:25; 13:1–3; 15:2). **Titus:** a missionary companion of Paul (2 Cor 2:13; 7:6, 13–15; 8:6, 16, 23; 12:18), non-Jewish (Gal 2:3), never mentioned in Acts.

§§[2:2] **A revelation:** cf. Gal 1:1, 12. Paul emphasizes it was God's will, not Jerusalem authority, that led to the journey. Acts 15:2 states that the church in Antioch appointed Paul and Barnabas for the task. **Those of repute:** leaders of the Jerusalem church; the term, while positive, may be slightly ironic (cf. Gal 1:6, 9). **Run, in vain:** while Paul presents a positive picture in what follows, his missionary work in Galatia would have been to no purpose if his opponents were correct that circumcision is needed for complete faith in Christ.

¶¶[2:3] **Not even** a Gentile Christian like Titus was compelled to receive the rite of circumcision. The Greek text could be interpreted that he voluntarily accepted circumcision, but this is unlikely in the overall argument.

***[2:4] **False brothers:** Jewish Christians who took the position that Gentile Christians must first become Jews through circumcision and observance of the Mosaic law in order to become Christians; cf. Acts 15:1.

†††[2:5] **The truth of the gospel:** the true gospel, in contrast to the false one of the opponents (Gal 1:6–9); the gospel of grace, used as a norm (Gal 2:14).

‡‡‡[2:7–9] Some think that actual "minutes" of the meeting are here quoted. Paul's apostleship to the Gentiles (Gal 1:16) is recognized alongside that of Peter to the Jews. Moreover, the right to proclaim the gospel without requiring circumcision and the Jewish law is sealed by a handshake. That Paul and colleagues **should go to the Gentiles** did not exclude his preaching to the Jews as well (Rom 1:13–16) or Cephas to Gentile areas.

---

i. [1:13] Acts 8:1–3; 9:1–2; 1 Cor 15:9.   j. [1:14] Acts 26:4–5.   k. [1:15] Is 49:1; Jer 1:4.   l. [1:16] 1:11–12; Rom 1:5; 1 Cor 15:10; Acts 9:3–9 / Gal 2:2, 7 / Mt 16:17.   m. [1:18] Acts 9:26–30 / Jn 1:42.   n. [1:19] 2:9; Mt 13:55; Acts 12:17.   o. [1:20] Rom 9:1; 2 Cor 11:31.   p. [1:21] Acts 9:30.   q. [1:23] 1:13.

r. [2:1] Acts 15:2.   s. [2:2] 1:11–12, 16 / 1:16 / Phil 2:16.   t. [2:3] 2 Cor 2:13; 7:6–7; 8:16–17; 12:18; Ti 1:4 / Gal 2:14; 6:12.   u. [2:4] 5:1; Acts 15:1, 24.   v. [2:5] 2:14; 4:16.   w. [2:6] Dt 10:17; Rom 2:11.   x. [2:7] 1:15–16; Acts 9:15; 15:12; 22:21; Rom 1:5.

John,* who were reputed to be pillars, gave me and Barnabas their right hands in partnership, that we should go to the Gentiles and they to the circumcised.ʸ ¹⁰Only, we were to be mindful of the poor,† which is the very thing I was eager to do.ᶻ

Peter's Inconsistency at Antioch.‡ ¹¹ᵃAnd when Cephas came to Antioch, I opposed him to his face because he clearly was wrong.§ ¹²For, until some people came from James,⁵ he used to eat with the Gentiles; but when they came, he began to draw back and separated himself, because he was afraid of the circumcised.ᵇ ¹³And the rest of the Jews** [also] acted hypocritically along with him, with the result that even Barnabas was carried away by their hypocrisy.ᶜ ¹⁴But when I saw that they were not on the right road in line with the truth of the gospel, I said to Cephas in front of all,ᵈ "If you, though a Jew, are living like a Gentile and not like a Jew, how can you compel the Gentiles to live like Jews?"††

Faith and Works.‡‡ ¹⁵We, who are Jews by nature and not sinners from among the Gentiles, ¹⁶ᵉ[yet]

---

*[2:9] **James and Cephas and John:** see notes on Gal 1:18, 19; on Peter and John as leaders in the Jerusalem church, cf. Acts 3:1 and 8:14. The order here, with James first, may reflect his prominence·in Jerusalem after Peter (Cephas) departed (Acts 12:17).

†[2:10] **The poor:** Jerusalem Christians or a group within the church there (cf. Rom 15:26). The collection for them was extremely important in Paul's thought and labor (cf. Rom 15:25–28; 1 Cor 16:1–4; 2 Cor 8–9).

‡[2:11–14] The decision reached in Jerusalem (Gal 2:3–7) recognized the freedom of Gentile Christians from the Jewish law. But the problem of table fellowship between Jewish Christians, who possibly still kept kosher food regulations, and Gentile believers was not yet settled. When Cephas first came to the racially mixed community of Jewish and Gentile Christians in Antioch (Gal 2:12), he ate with non-Jews. Pressure from persons arriving later from Jerusalem caused him and Barnabas to draw back. Paul therefore publicly rebuked Peter's inconsistency toward the gospel (Gal 2:14). Some think that what Paul said on that occasion extends through Gal 2:16 or 2:21.

§[2:11] **Clearly was wrong:** literally, "stood condemned," by himself and also by Paul. His action in breaking table fellowship was especially grievous if the eating involved the meal at the Lord's supper (cf. 1 Cor 11:17–25).

¶[2:12] **Some people came from James:** strict Jewish Christians (cf. Acts 15:1, 5; 21:20–21), either sent by James (Gal 1:19; 2:9) or claiming to be from the leader of the Jerusalem church. The **circumcised:** presumably Jewish Christians, not Jews.

[2:13] The Jews: Jewish Christians, like Barnabas. **Hypocrisy:** literally, "pretense," "play-acting"; moral insincerity.

††[2:14] **Compel the Gentiles to live like Jews:** that is, conform to Jewish practices, such as circumcision (Gal 2:3–5) or regulations about food (Gal 2:12).

‡‡[2:15–21] Following on the series of incidents cited above, Paul's argument, whether spoken to Cephas at Antioch or only now articulated, is pertinent to the Galatian situation, where believers were having themselves circumcised (Gal 6:12–13) and obeying other aspects of Jewish law (Gal 4:9–10; 5:1–4). He insists that salvation is by faith in Christ, not by works of the law. His teaching on the gospel concerns justification by faith (Gal 2:16) in relation to sin (Gal 2:17), law (Gal 2:19), life in Christ (Gal 2:19–20), and grace (Gal 2:21).

y. [2:9] Rom 15:15 / Gal 1:18–19; Jn 1:42; Acts 12:17 / Gal 2:1.
z. [2:10] Acts 11:29–30; Rom 15:25–28; 1 Cor 16:1–4; 2 Cor 8:9. a. [2:11] 1:18 / Acts 11:19–30; 15:1–2. b. [2:12] Acts 10:15, 28; 11:3. c. [2:13] 2:1, 9. d. [2:14] 2:5 / 1:18; 2:9 / 2:3. e. [2:16] 3:2, 11; Ps 143:1–2; Rom 3:20, 28; 4:5; 11:6; Eph 2:8–9; Phil 3:9.

---

who know that a person is not justified by works of the law but through faith in Jesus Christ, even we have believed in Christ Jesus that we may be justified by faith in Christ and not by works of the law, because by works of the law no one will be justified.§§ ¹⁷But if, in seeking to be justified in Christ, we ourselves are found to be sinners, is Christ then a minister of sin?¶¶ Of course not! ¹⁸But if I am building up again those things that I tore down, then I show myself to be a transgressor.*** ¹⁹For through the law I died to the law,††† that I might live for God. I have been crucified with Christ;ᶠ ²⁰yet I live, no longer I, but Christ lives in me; insofar as I now live in the flesh, I live by faith in the Son of God who has loved me and given himself up for me.ᵍ ²¹I do not nullify the grace of God; for if justification comes through the law, then Christ died for nothing.ʰ

IV. FAITH AND LIBERTY

CHAPTER 3

Justification by Faith.‡‡‡ ¹O stupid§§§ Galatians! Who has bewitched you, before whose eyes Jesus Christ was publicly portrayed as crucified?ⁱ ²I want to learn only this from you:ʲ did you receive the Spirit from works of the law, or from faith in what you heard?¶¶¶ ³Are you so stupid?ᵏ After beginning with the Spirit, are you now ending with the flesh?**** ⁴Did you experience so

---

§§[2:16] **No one will be justified:** Ps 143:2 is reflected.

¶¶[2:17] **A minister of sin:** literally, "a servant of sin" (cf. Rom 15:8), an agent of sin, one who promotes it. This is possibly a claim by opponents that justification on the basis of faith in Christ makes Christ an abettor of sin when Christians **are found to be sinners.** Paul denies the conclusion (cf. Rom 6:1–4).

***[2:18] To return to observance of the law as the means to salvation would entangle one not only in inevitable transgressions of it but also in the admission that it was wrong to have abandoned the law in the first place.

†††[2:19] **Through the law I died to the law:** this is variously explained: the law revealed sin (Rom 7:7–9) and led to death and then to belief in Christ; or, the law itself brought the insight that law cannot justify (Gal 2:16; Ps 143:2); or, the "law of Christ" (Gal 6:2) led to abandoning the Mosaic law; or, the law put Christ to death (cf. Gal 3:13) and so provided a way to our salvation, through baptism into Christ, through which we die (**crucified with Christ;** see Rom 6:6). Cf. also Gal 3:19–25 on the role of the law in reference to salvation.

‡‡‡[3:1–14] Paul's contention that justification comes not through the law or the works of the law but by faith in Christ and in his death (Gal 2:16, 21) is supported by appeals to Christian experience (Gal 3:1–5) and to scripture (Gal 3:6–14). The gift of God's Spirit to the Galatians came from the gospel received in faith, not from doing what the law enjoins. The story of Abraham shows that faith in God brings **righteousness** (Gal 3:6; Gn 15:6). The promise to Abraham (Gal 3:8; Gn 12:3) extends to the Gentiles (Gal 3:14)

§§§[3:1] **Stupid:** not just senseless, for they were in danger of deserting their salvation.

¶¶¶[3:2] **Faith in what you heard:** Paul's message received with faith. The Greek can also mean "the proclamation of the faith" or "a hearing that comes from faith."

****[3:3] On the contrast of **Spirit and flesh,** cf. Rom 8:1–11. Having received the Spirit, they need not be circumcised now.

f. [2:19] 6:14; Rom 6:6, 8, 10; 7:6. g. [2:20] 1:4; Rom 8:10–11; Col 3:3–4. h. [2:21] 5:2. i. [3:1] 5:7; 1 Cor 1:23. j. [3:2] 2:16 / 3:14; Rom 10:17. k. [3:3] 5:16–18.

many things* in vain?—if indeed it was in vain.
[5]Does, then, the one who supplies the Spirit to
you and works mighty deeds among you do so
from works of the law or from faith in what you
heard?[l] [6]Thus Abraham "believed God,"[m] and it
was credited to him as righteousness."[†]

[7†]Realize then that it is those who have
faith who are children of Abraham.[n] [8]Scripture,
which saw in advance that God would justify
the Gentiles by faith, foretold the good news
to Abraham, saying, "Through you shall all the
nations be blessed."[o] [9]Consequently, those who
have faith are blessed along with Abraham who
had faith.[p] [10§]For all who depend on works of the
law are under a curse; for it is written, "Cursed
be everyone who does not persevere in doing all
the things written in the book of the law."[q] [11]And
that no one is justified before God by the law is
clear, for "the one who is righteous by faith will
live."[r] [12]But the law does not depend on faith;
rather, "the one who does these things will live
by them."[s] [13]Christ ransomed us from the curse
of the law by becoming a curse for us, for it is
written, "Cursed be everyone who hangs on a
tree,"[t] [14]that the blessing of Abraham might be
extended to the Gentiles through Christ Jesus,
so that we might receive the promise of the
Spirit through faith.[u]

The Law Did Not Nullify the Promise. [15¶]Broth-
ers, in human terms I say that no one can annul
or amend even a human will once ratified.[v]
[16]Now the promises were made to Abraham
and to his descendant.** It does not say, "And to
descendants," as referring to many, but as referring to one, "And to your descendant," who is
Christ.[w] [17]This is what I mean: the law, which
came four hundred and thirty years afterward,[††]
does not annul a covenant previously ratified by
God, so as to cancel the promise.[x] [18]For if the
inheritance comes from the law,[y] it is no longer
from a promise; but God bestowed it on Abraham through a promise.[‡‡]

[19§§]Why, then, the law? It was added for transgressions, until the descendant¶¶ came to whom
the promise had been made; it was promulgated
by angels at the hand of a mediator.[z] [20]Now there
is no mediator when only one party is involved,
and God is one.[a] [21]Is the law then opposed to the
promises [of God]? Of course not! For if a law
had been given that could bring life, then righteousness would in reality come from the law.[b]
[22]But scripture confined all things under the
power of sin, that through faith in Jesus Christ
the promise might be given to those who believe.[c]
What Faith Has Brought Us.[***] [23]Before faith
came, we were held in custody under law,
confined for the faith that was to be revealed.[d]

---

*[3:4] **Experience so many things**: probably the **mighty deeds** of Gal 1:5 but possibly the experience of sufferings.

†[3:6] **Abraham . . . righteousness**: see Gn 15:6; Rom 4:3. The Galatians like Abraham heard with faith and experienced justification. This first argument forms the basis for the further scriptural evidence that follows.

‡[3:7–9] **Faith** is what matters, for **Abraham** and the **children of Abraham**, in contrast to the claims of the oppo- nents that circumcision and observance of the law are needed to bring the promised blessing of Gn 12:3; cf. Gn 18:18; Sir 44:21; Acts 3:25.

§[3:10–14] Those **who depend** not on promise and faith but **on works of the law are under a curse** because they do **not persevere in doing all the things written in the book of the law** (Gal 3:10; Dt 27:26) in order to gain life (Gal 3:12; Lv 18:5; cf. Rom 10:5). But scripture teaches that **no one is justified before God by the law** (Gal 3:11; Heb 2:4, adapted from the Greek version of Habakkuk; cf. Rom 1:17; Heb 10:38). Salvation, then, depends on faith in Christ who died on the cross (Gal 3:13), taking upon himself a curse found in Dt 21:23 (about executed criminals hanged in public view), to free us from **the curse of the law** (Gal 3:13). That the Gentile Galatians have received the promised Spirit (Gal 3:14) by faith and in no other way returns the argument to the experience cited in Gal 3:1–5.

¶[3:15–18] A third argument to support Paul's position that salvation is not through the law but by promise (Gal 3:1–14) comes from legal practice and scriptural history. A legal agreement or **human will**, duly ratified, is unalterable (Gal 3:15). God's **covenant** with **Abraham** and its repeated promises (Gn 12:2–3, 7; 13:15; 17:7–8; 22:16–18; 24:7) is not superseded by **the law**, which came much later, in the time of Moses. **The inheritance** (of the Spirit and the blessings) is by promise, not by law (Gal 3:18). Paul's argument hinges on

the fact that the same Greek word, *diathēkē*, can be rendered as **will** or testament (Gal 3:15) and as **covenant** (Gal 3:17).

[3:16] **Descendant: literally, "and to his seed." The Hebrew, as in Gn 12:7; 15:18; 22:17–18, is a collective singular, traditionally rendered as a plural, **descendants**, but taken by Paul in its literal number to refer to **Christ** as descendant of Abraham.

††[3:17] **Four hundred and thirty years afterward**: fol- lows Ex 12:40 in the Greek (Septuagint) version, in contrast to Gn 15:13 and Acts 7:6, for chronology.

‡‡[3:18] This refutes the opponents' contention that the promises of God are fulfilled only as a reward for human observance of the law.

§§[3:19–22] A digression: if the Mosaic law, then, does not save or **bring life**, why was it given? Elsewhere, Paul says the law served to show what sin is (Rom 3:20; 7:7–8). Here the further implication is that the law in effect served to produce transgressions. Moreover, it was received at second hand **by angels**, through a **mediator**, not directly from God (Gal 3:19). The law does not, however, oppose God's purposes, for it car- ries out its function (Gal 3:22), so that **righteousness** comes by **faith** and **promise**, not by human works of the law.

¶¶[3:19] **The descendant**: Christ (Gal 3:16). **By angels**: Dt 33:2–4 stressed their presence as enhancing the importance of the law; Paul uses their role to diminish its significance (cf. Acts 7:38, 53). **A mediator**: Moses. But in a covenant of promise, where all depends on the one God, no mediator is needed (Gal 3:20).

***[3:23–29] Paul adds a further argument in support of righteousness or justification by faith and through God's promise rather than by works of the law (Gal 2:16; 3:22): as **children of God, baptized into Christ**, the Galatians are all **Abraham's descendant** and **heirs of the promise** to Abra- ham (Gal 3:8, 14, 16–18, 29). The teaching in Gal 3:23–25, that since **faith** (Christianity) **has come, we are no longer under** the law, could be taken with the previous paragraph on the role of the Mosaic law, but it also fits here as a contrast between the situation **before faith** (Gal 3:23) and the results after faith has come (Gal 3:25–29).

---

l. [3:5] 2:16.   m. [3:6] Gn 15:6; Rom 4:3; Jas 2:23.   n. [3:7] 3:29; Rom 4:11–12 / Sir 44:19–21.   o. [3:8] Gn 12:3; 18:17–19; Acts 3:25.   p. [3:9] Rom 4:16.   q. [3:10] Dt 27:26; Jas 2:10.   r. [3:11] 2:16; Heb 2:4; Rom 1:17.   s. [3:12] Lv 18:5; Rom 10:5.   t. [3:13] Dt 21:23; Rom 8:3; 2 Cor 5:21.   u. [3:14] 3:2–3, 5; Is 44:3; Jl 3:1–2; Acts 2:33.

v. [3:15] Rom 3:5 / Heb 9:16–17.   w. [3:16] Gn 12:7; 13:15; 17:8; 22:17; 24:7; Mt 1:1.   x. [3:17] Ex 12:40.   y. [3:18] Rom 4:16; 11:6.   z. [3:19] Rom 4:15; 5:20; 7:7, 13 / Acts 7:38, 53.   a. [3:20] Dt 6:4.   b. [3:21] Rom 7:7, 10; 8:2–4.   c. [3:22] Rom 3:9–20, 23; 11:32.   d. [3:23] 4:3–5; 5:18.

²⁴Consequently, the law was our disciplinarian* for Christ, that we might be justified by faith.ᵉ ²⁵But now that faith has come, we are no longer under a disciplinarian.ᶠ ²⁶For through faith you are all children of God† in Christ Jesus.ᵍ ²⁷‡For all of you who were baptized into Christʰ have clothed yourselves with Christ.§ ²⁸There is neither Jew nor Greek, there is neither slave nor free person, there is not male and female; for you are all one in Christ Jesus.ⁱ ²⁹And if you belong to Christ, then you are Abraham's descendant, heirs according to the promise.ʲ

CHAPTER 4
God's Free Children in Christ.¶ ¹I mean that as long as the heir is not of age,** he is no different from a slave, although he is the owner of everything, ²but he is under the supervision of guardians and administrators until the date set by his father. ³‡In the same way we also, when we were not of age, were enslaved to the elemental powers of the world.†† ⁴But when the fullness of time had come, God sent his Son, born of a woman, born under the law,ⁱ ⁵to ransom those under the law, so that we might receive adoption.ᵐ ⁶As proof that you are children,‡‡ God sent the spirit of his Son into our hearts, crying out, "Abba, Father!"ⁿ ⁷So you are no longer a slave but a child, and if a child then also an heir, through God.ᵒ
Do Not Throw This Freedom Away.§§ ⁸ᵖAt a time when you did not know God, you became slaves

to things that by nature are not gods;¶¶ ⁹but now that you have come to know God, or rather to be known by God, how can you turn back again to the weak and destitute elemental powers? Do you want to be slaves to them all over again?�q ¹⁰You are observing days,ʳ months, seasons, and years.*** ¹¹I am afraid on your account that perhaps I have labored for you in vain.†††
Appeal to Former Loyalty.‡‡‡ ¹²I implore you, brothers, be as I am, because I have also become as you are.§§§ You did me no wrong;ˢ ¹³you know that it was because of a physical illness¶¶¶ that I originally preached the gospel to you, ¹⁴and you did not show disdain or contempt because of the trial caused you by my physical condition, but rather you received me as an angel of God, as Christ Jesus. ¹⁵Where now is that blessedness of yours?**** Indeed, I can testify to you that, if it had been possible, you would have torn out your eyes and given them to me. ¹⁶So now have I become your enemy by telling you the truth? ¹⁷They show interest in you, but not in a good way; they want to isolate you,†††† so that you may show interest in them.ᵗ ¹⁸Now it is good to be shown interest for good reason at all times, and not only when I am with you. ¹⁹My children, for whom I am again in labor until Christ be formed in you!ᵘ ²⁰I would like to be with you now and to change my tone, for I am perplexed because of you.

---

*[3:24–25] **Disciplinarian**: the Greek *paidagōgos* referred to a slave who escorted a child to school but did not teach or tutor; hence, a guardian or monitor. Applying this to the law fits the role of the law described in Gal 3:19–25.

†[3:26] **Children of God**: literally "sons," in contrast to the young child under the disciplinarian in Gal 3:24–25. The term includes males and females (Gal 3:28).

‡[3:27–28] Likely a formula used at baptism that expresses racial, social-economic, and sexual equality in Christ (cf. Col 3:11).

§[3:27] **Clothed yourselves with Christ**: literally, "have put on Christ"; cf. Rom 13:14; Eph 4:24; Col 3:10. Baptismal imagery, traceable to the Old Testament (Jb 29:14; Is 59:17) but also found in pagan mystery cults.

¶[4:1–7] What Paul has argued in Gal 3:26–29 is now elaborated in terms of the Christian as **the heir** (Gal 4:1, 7; cf. Gal 3:18, 29) freed from control by others. Again, as in Gal 3:2–5, the proof that Christians are children of God is the gift of the Spirit of Christ relating them intimately to God.

[4:1, 3] **Not of age: an infant or minor.

††[4:3] **The elemental powers of the world**: while the term can refer to the "elements" like earth, air, fire, and water or to elementary forms of religion, the sense here is more likely that of celestial beings that were thought in pagan circles to control the world; cf. Gal 4:8; Col 2:8, 20.

‡‡[4:6] **Children**: see note on Gal 3:26; here in contrast to the infant or young person **not of age** (Gal 3:1, 3). **Abba**: cf. Mk 14:36 and the note; Rom 8:15.

§§[4:8–11] On the basis of the arguments advanced from Gal 3:1 through Gal 4:7, Paul now launches his appeal to the Galatians with the question, **how can you turn back** to the slavery of the law (Gal 4:9)? The question is posed with

reference to bondage to the **elemental powers** (see note on Gal 4:3) because the Galatians had originally been converted to Christianity from paganism, not Judaism (Gal 4:8). The use of the direct question is like Gal 3:3–5.

¶¶[4:8] **Things that by nature are not gods**: or "gods that by nature do not exist."

***[4:10] This is likely a reference to ritual observances from the Old Testament, promoted by opponents: sabbaths or Yom Kippur, new moon, Passover or Pentecost, sabbatical years.

†††[4:11] Cf. Gal 2:2. If the Galatians become **slaves . . . all over again** to the law (Gal 4:9), Paul will have worked in vain among them.

‡‡‡[4:12–20] A strongly personal section. Paul appeals to past ties between the Galatians and himself. He speaks sharply of the opponents (Gal 4:17–18) and pastorally to the Galatians (Gal 4:19–20).

§§§[4:12] **Because I have also become as you are**: a terse phrase in Greek, meaning "Be as I, Paul, am," i.e., living by faith, independent of the law, for, in spite of my background in Judaism (Gal 1:13), I have become as you Galatians are now, a brother in Christ.

¶¶¶[4:13] **Physical illness**: because its nature is not described, some assume an eye disease (Gal 4:15); others, epilepsy; some relate it to 2 Cor 12:7–9. **Originally**: this may also be translated "formerly" or "on the first (of two) visit(s)"; cf. Acts 16:6; 18:23.

****[4:15] **That blessedness of yours**: possibly a reference to the Galatians' initial happy reception of Paul (Gal 4:14) and of his gospel (Gal 1:6; 3:1–4) and their felicitation at such blessedness, but the phrase could also refer ironically to earlier praise by Paul of the Galatians, no longer possible when they turn from the gospel to the claims of the opponents (Gal 4:17–18; 1:7). If the word is a more literal reference to a beatitude, Gal 3:26–28 may be in view.

††††[4:17] **Isolate you**: that is, from the blessings of the gospel and/or from Paul.

---

e. [3:24] 2:16. f. [3:25] Rom 10:4. g. [3:26] 4:5–7; Jn 1:12; Rom 8:14–17. h. [3:27] Rom 6:3; 13:14; Eph 4:24. i. [3:28] Rom 10:12; 1 Cor 12:13; Col 3:11. j. [3:29] 3:7, 14, 16, 18; Rom 4:16–17; 9:7 / Gal 4:1, 7; Rom 4:13–14; 8:17; Heb 6:12; Jas 2:5. k. [4:3] 3:23 / 4:9; Col 2:20. l. [4:4] Mk 1:15. m. [4:5] 3:13, 26. n. [4:6] 3:26; Rom 8:15. o. [4:7] 3:29; Rom 8:16–17. p. [4:8] 1 Cor 12:2.

q. [4:9] 4:3; Col 2:20. r. [4:10] Col 2:16–20. s. [4:12] 1 Cor 11:1. t. [4:17] 1:7; 6:12; Acts 20:30. u. [4:19] 1 Cor 4:14–15; 2 Cor 6:13; 1 Thes 2:7–8.

An Allegory on Christian Freedom. [*] ²¹Tell me, you who want to be under the law, do you not listen to the law? ²²For it is written that Abraham had two sons, one by the slave woman and the other by the freeborn woman.[v] ²³The son of the slave woman was born naturally, the son of the freeborn through a promise.[w] ²⁴Now this is an allegory. These women represent two covenants. One was from Mount Sinai, bearing children for slavery; this is Hagar.[x] ²⁵Hagar represents Sinai,[†] a mountain in Arabia; it corresponds to the present Jerusalem, for she is in slavery along with her children. ²⁶But the Jerusalem above is freeborn, and she is our mother.[y] ²⁷For it is written:

"Rejoice, you barren one who bore no
        children;[z]
    break forth and shout, you who were
        not in labor;
for more numerous are the children of the
        deserted one
    than of her who has a husband."[‡]

²⁸Now you, brothers, like Isaac, are children of the promise.[a] ²⁹But just as then the child of the flesh persecuted the child of the spirit, it is the same now. ³⁰But what does the scripture say?

"Drive out the slave woman and her son!
    For the son of the slave woman shall
        not share the inheritance with
        the son"[b]

of the freeborn. ³¹Therefore, brothers, we are children not of the slave woman but of the freeborn woman.[c]

V. EXHORTATION
TO CHRISTIAN LIVING

CHAPTER 5
The Importance of Faith.[§] ¹For freedom[*] Christ set us free; so stand firm and do not submit again to the yoke of slavery.[d] ²It is I, Paul, who am telling you that if you have yourselves circumcised, Christ will be of no benefit to you.[e] ³Once again I declare to every man who has himself circumcised[f] that he is bound to observe the entire law.[**] ⁴You are separated from Christ, you who are trying to be justified by law; you have fallen from grace. ⁵For through the Spirit, by faith, we await the hope of righteousness. ⁶For in Christ Jesus, neither circumcision nor uncircumcision counts for anything, but only faith working through love.[††]
Be Not Misled.[‡‡] ⁷You were running well;[§§] who hindered you from following [the] truth? ⁸That enticement does not come from the one who called you.[¶¶] ⁹A little yeast leavens the whole batch of dough.[j] ¹⁰I am confident of you in the Lord that you will not take a different view, and that the one who is troubling you will bear the condemnation, whoever he may be.[k] ¹¹As for me, brothers, if I am still preaching circumcision,[***] why am I still being persecuted? In that case, the stumbling block of the cross has been abolished.[l] ¹²Would that those who are upsetting you might also castrate themselves![†††]
Freedom for Service.[‡‡‡] ¹³For you were called for freedom, brothers.[m] But do not use this freedom

---

a [4:21–31] Paul supports his appeal for the gospel (Gal 4:9; 1:6–9; 2:16; 3:2) by a further argument from scripture (cf. Gal 3:6–18). It involves the relationship of **Abraham** (Gal 3:6–16) to his wife, Sarah, the **freeborn woman**, and to Hagar, **the slave woman**, and the contrast between the sons born to each, **Isaac**, child of promise, and Ishmael, son of Hagar (Gn 16; 21). Only through Isaac is the promise of God preserved. This **allegory** (Gal 4:24), with its equation of the Sinai covenant and Mosaic law with slavery and of the promise of God with freedom, Paul uses only in light of previous arguments. His quotation of Gn 21:10 at Gal 4:30 suggests on a scriptural basis that the Galatians should expel those who are troubling them (Gal 1:7).
†[4:25] **Hagar represents Sinai . . . :** some manuscripts have what seems a geographical note, "For Sinai is a mountain in Arabia."
‡[4:27] Is 54:1 in the Septuagint translation is applied to Sarah as the **barren one** (in Gn 15) who ultimately becomes the mother not only of Isaac but now of numerous children, i.e., of all those who believe, the **children of the promise** (Gal 4:28).

§[5:1–6] Paul begins the exhortations, continuing through Gal 6:10, with an appeal to the Galatians to side with freedom instead of slavery (Gal 5:1). He reiterates his message of justification or righteousness by faith instead of law and circumcision (Gal 5:2–5); cf. Gal 2:16; 3:3. Faith, not circumcision, is what counts (Gal 5:6).
¶[5:1] **Freedom:** Paul stresses as the conclusion from the allegory in Gal 4:21–31 this result of Christ's work for us. It is a principle previously mentioned (Gal 2:4), the responsible use of which Gal 5:13 will emphasize.
**[5:3] Cf. Gal 3:10–12. Just as those who seek to live by the law must carry out all its contents, so those who have faith and live by promise must stand firm in their freedom (Gal 5:1, 13).
††[5:6] Cf. Rom 2:25–26; 1 Cor 7:19; Gal 6:15. The Greek for **faith working through love** or "faith expressing itself through love" can also be rendered as "faith energized by (God's) love."
‡‡[5:7–12] Paul addresses the Galatians directly: with questions (Gal 5:7, 11), a proverb (Gal 5:9), a statement (Gal 5:8), and biting sarcasm (Gal 5:12), seeking to persuade the Galatians to break with those trying to add law and circumcision to Christ as a basis for salvation.
§§[5:7] **Running well:** as in an athletic contest; cf. Gal 2:2; 1 Cor 9:24–26; Phil 2:16; 3:14.
¶¶[5:8] **The one who called you:** see note on Gal 1:6.
***[5:11] **Preaching circumcision:** this could refer to Paul's pre-Christian period (possibly as a missionary for Judaism); more probably it arose as a charge from opponents, based perhaps on the story in Acts 16:1–3 that Paul had circumcised Timothy "on account of the Jews." Unlike the Gentile Titus in Gal 2:3, Timothy was the son of a Jewish mother. The **stumbling block of the cross:** cf. 1 Cor 1:23.
†††[5:12] A sarcastic half-wish that their knife would go beyond mere circumcision; cf. Phil 3:2 and the note there.
‡‡‡[5:13–26] In light of another reminder of the freedom of the gospel (Gal 5:13; cf. Gal 5:1), Paul elaborates on what

d. [5:1] 2:4; 4:5, 9; Jn 8:32, 36.   e. [5:2] 2:21; Acts 15:1–29.   f. [5:3] 3:10; Rom 2:25; Jas 2:10.   g. [5:5] Rom 8:23, 25.   h. [5:6] 3:28; 6:15; 1 Cor 7:19.   i. [5:8] 1:6.   j. [5:9] 1 Cor 5:6.   k. [5:10] 1:7.   l. [5:11] 6:12, 14; 1 Cor 1:23.   m. [5:13] 5:1 / Rom 6:18; 1 Cor 8:9; 1 Pt 2:16.

v. [4:22] Gn 16:15; 21:2–3.   w. [4:23] Gn 17:16; Rom 4:19–20; 9:7–9.   x. [4:24] 3:17 / Ex 19:20 / Gn 16:1.   y. [4:26] Heb 12:22; Rev 21:2.   z. [4:27] Is 54:1.   a. [4:28] Rom 9:8.   b. [4:30] Gn 21:10.   c. [4:31] 3:29; Jn 8:35.

as an opportunity for the flesh; rather, serve* one another through love. [14]For the whole law" is fulfilled in one statement, namely, "You shall love your neighbor as yourself."[†] [15]But if you go on biting and devouring one another, beware that you are not consumed by one another.

[16o]I say, then: live by the Spirit and you will certainly not gratify the desire of the flesh.[‡] [17]For the flesh has desires against the Spirit, and the Spirit against the flesh; these are opposed to each other, so that you may not do what you want.[p] [18]But if you are guided by the Spirit, you are not under the law.[q] [19§]Now the works of the flesh are obvious: immorality, impurity, licentiousness,[r] [20]idolatry, sorcery, hatreds, rivalry, jealousy, outbursts of fury, acts of selfishness, dissensions, factions,[s] [21]occasions of envy,[¶] drinking bouts, orgies, and the like. I warn you, as I warned you before, that those who do such things will not inherit the kingdom of God. [22]In contrast, the fruit of the Spirit is love, joy, peace, patience, kindness, generosity, faithfulness,[t] [23]gentleness, self-control. Against such there is no law.[u] [24]Now those who belong to Christ [Jesus] have crucified their flesh with its passions and desires.[v] [25]If we live in the Spirit, let us also follow the Spirit.[w] [26]Let us not be conceited, provoking one another, envious of one another.[x]

CHAPTER 6
Life in the Community of Christ.[**] [1]Brothers, even if a person is caught in some transgression, you who are spiritual should correct that one in a gentle spirit, looking to yourself, so that you also may not be tempted.[y] [2]Bear one another's burdens,[z] and so you will fulfill the law of

Christ.[††] [3a]For if anyone thinks he is something when he is nothing, he is deluding himself. [4‡‡]Each one must examine his own work, and then he will have reason to boast with regard to himself alone, and not with regard to someone else; [5]for each will bear his own load.[b]

[6]One who is being instructed in the word should share all good things with his instructor.[§§] [7]Make no mistake: God is not mocked, for a person will reap only what he sows, [8]because the one who sows for his flesh will reap corruption from the flesh, but the one who sows for the spirit will reap eternal life from the spirit.[d] [9]Let us not grow tired of doing good, for in due time we shall reap our harvest, if we do not give up.[e] [10]So then, while we have the opportunity, let us do good to all,[f] but especially to those who belong to the family of the faith.[¶¶]

VI. CONCLUSION

Final Appeal.[***] [11]See with what large letters[†††] I am writing to you in my own hand![g] [12‡‡‡]It is those who want to make a good appearance in the flesh who are trying to compel you to have yourselves circumcised, only that they may not be persecuted for the cross of Christ.[h] [13]Not even those having themselves circumcised[§§§] observe the law themselves; they only want you to be circumcised so that they may boast of your flesh.

---

believers are called to do and be: they fulfill the law by love of neighbor (Gal 5:14–15), walking in the Spirit (Gal 5:16–26), as is illustrated by concrete **fruit of the Spirit** in their lives.

*[5:13] **Serve . . . through love**: cf. Gal 5:6.

†[5:14] Lv 19:18, emphasized by Jesus (Mt 22:39; Lk 10:27); cf. Rom 13:8–10.

‡[5:16–25] **Spirit . . . flesh**: cf. Gal 3:3 and the note on Rom 8:1–13.

§[5:19–23] Such lists of vices and virtues (cf. Rom 1:29–31; 1 Cor 6:9–10) were common in the ancient world. Paul contrasts **works of the flesh** (Gal 5:19) with **fruit** (not "works") **of the Spirit** (Gal 5:22). Not law, but the Spirit, leads to such traits.

¶[5:21] **Occasions of envy**: after the Greek word *phthonoi*, "envies," some manuscripts add a similar sounding one, *phonoi*, "murders."

[6:1–10] The ethical exhortations begun at Gal 5:1 continue with a variety of admonitions to the community (brothers**: see note on Gal 1:2). Nearly every sentence contains a separate item of practical advice; the faith and freedom of the gospel underlie each maxim. Tensions and temptation within communal life have previously been addressed in Gal 5:15, 26, and Gal 6:1 continues with a case in which a **person is caught in some transgression** such as those in Gal 5:19–21; cf. Gal 2:17.

n. [5:14] Lv 19:18; Mt 22:39; Rom 13:8–10. o. [5:16] 5:24–25; Rom 8:5. p. [5:17] Rom 7:15, 23; 8:6. q. [5:18] Rom 6:14; 8:14. r. [5:19–21] Rom 1:29–31; 1 Cor 6:9–10; Col 3:5–6, 8. s. [5:20] Rev 22:15. t. [5:22] Eph 5:9 / 1 Cor 13:4–7; 2 Cor 6:6; 1 Tm 4:12; 2 Pt 1:6. u. [5:23] 1 Tm 1:9. v. [5:24] 2:19; Rom 6:6; 8:13. w. [5:25] 5:16. x. [5:26] Phil 2:3. y. [6:1] Mt 18:15; Jas 5:19 / 1 Cor 10:12–13. z. [6:2] Col 3:13 / 1 Cor 9:21.

---

††[6:2] **The law of Christ**: cf. Rom 8:2; 1 Cor 9:21; Gal 5:14. The principle of love for others is meant. To **bear one another's burdens** is to "serve one another through love" (Gal 5:13).

‡‡[6:4–5] Self-examination is the cure for self-deception. Compare what you are with what you were before, and give the glory to God; cf. Rom 6:19–22. **Load**: used elsewhere of a soldier's pack. Correcting one's own conduct avoids burdening others with it.

§§[6:6] Implies oral instruction in the faith by catechists; these are to be remunerated for their service; cf. Rom 15:27.

¶¶[6:10] **The family of the faith**: the Christian household or church. Doing good has a universal object (**to all**), but the local community makes specific the reality of those to be served.

***[6:11–18] A postscript in Paul's own hand, as was his practice (see 1 Cor 16:21; 2 Thes 3:17). Paul summarizes his appeal against his opponents (Gal 6:12–13), then returns to his message of glorying in the cross, not in circumcision, as the means of salvation (Gal 6:14–15; cf. Gal 5:11). A benediction follows at Gal 6:16. In the polemical spirit that the attack on his apostleship called forth (Gal 1:11–2:21), Paul reasserts his missionary credentials (Gal 6:17) before giving a final benediction (Gal 6:18).

†††[6:11] **Large letters**: in contrast to the finer hand of the scribe who wrote the letter up to this point. The larger Greek letters make Paul's message even more emphatic. Some find a hint of poor eyesight on Paul's part. See note on Gal 4:13.

‡‡‡[6:12–15] The Jewish Christian opponents wished **not** to **be persecuted**, possibly by Jews. But since Judaism seems to have had a privileged status as a religion in the Roman empire, circumcised Christians might, if taken as Jews, thereby avoid persecution from the Romans. In any case, Paul instead stresses conformity with **the cross of our Lord Jesus Christ**; cf. Gal 2:19–21; 5:11.

§§§[6:13] **Those having themselves circumcised**: other manuscripts read, "those who have had themselves circumcised."

---

a. [6:3–4] 1 Cor 3:18; 8:2; 2 Cor 12:11. b. [6:5] Rom 14:12. c. [6:6] 1 Cor 9:14. d. [6:8] Prv 11:18; Rom 8:6, 13. e. [6:9] 2 Thes 3:13; Heb 12:1–3. f. [6:10] 1 Thes 5:15. g. [6:11] 1 Cor 16:21. h. [6:12] 5:2, 11.

[14] But may I never boast except in the cross of our Lord Jesus Christ, through which* the world has been crucified to me, and I to the world.[i] [15] For neither does circumcision mean anything, nor does uncircumcision,[j] but only a new creation.[†] [16] Peace and mercy be to all who follow this rule‡ and to the Israel of God.[k]

---

*[6:14] **Through which**: or "through whom."
†[6:15] **New creation**: or "new creature"; cf. 2 Cor 5:17.
‡[6:16] **This rule**: the principle in Gal 6:14–15. **The Israel of God**: while the church may be meant (the phrase can be translated "to all who follow this rule, even the Israel of God";

i. [6:14] 2:20; 1 Cor 2:2.   j. [6:15] 5:6; 1 Cor 7:19 / 2 Cor 5:17.   k. [6:16] Ps 125:5; 128:6.

[17] From now on, let no one make troubles for me; for I bear the marks of Jesus§ on my body.[l] [18] The grace of our Lord Jesus Christ be with your spirit, brothers. Amen.[m]

---

cf. Gal 6:10; 1 Cor 10:18), the reference may also be to God's ancient people, Israel; cf. Ps 125:5; 128:6.
§[6:17] **The marks of Jesus**: slaves were often branded by marks (stigmata) burned into their flesh to show to whom they belonged; so also were devotees of pagan gods. Paul implies that instead of outdated circumcision, his body bears the scars of his apostolic labors (2 Cor 11:22–31), such as floggings (Acts 16:22; 2 Cor 11:25) and stonings (Acts 14:19), that mark him as belonging to the Christ who suffered (cf. Rom 6:3; 2 Cor 4:10; Col 1:24) and will protect his own.

l. [6:17] 2 Cor 4:10.   m. [6:18] Phil 4:23; 2 Tm 4:22; Phlm 25.

THE LETTER TO THE
EPHESIANS

❧

Ephesians is the great Pauline letter about the church. It deals, however, not so much with a congregation in the city of Ephesus in Asia Minor as with the worldwide church, the head of which is Christ (Eph 4:15), the purpose of which is to be the instrument for making God's plan of salvation known throughout the universe (Eph 3:9–10). Yet this ecclesiology is anchored in God's saving love, shown in Jesus Christ (Eph 2:4–10), and the whole of redemption is rooted in the plan and accomplishment of the triune God (Eph 1:3–14). The language is often that of doxology (Eph 1:3–14) and prayer (cf. Eph 1:15–23; 3:14–19), indeed of liturgy and hymns (Eph 3:20–21; 5:14).

The majestic chapters of Ephesians emphasize the unity in the church of Christ that has come about for both Jews and Gentiles within God's household (Eph 1:15–2:22, especially Eph 2:11–22) and indeed the "seven unities" of church, Spirit, hope; one Lord, faith, and baptism; and the one God (Eph 4:4–6). Yet the concern is not with the church for its own sake but rather as the means for mission in the world (Eph 3:1–4:24). The gifts Christ gives its members are to lead to growth and renewal (Eph 4:7–24). Ethical admonition is not lacking either; all aspects of human life and relationships are illumined by the light of Christ (Eph 4:25–6:20).

The letter is seemingly addressed by Paul to Christians in Ephesus (Eph 1:1), a place where the apostle labored for well over two years (Acts 19:10). Yet there is a curiously impersonal tone to the writing for a community with which Paul was so intimately acquainted (cf. Eph 3:2 and Eph 4:21). There are no personal greetings (cf. Eph 6:23). More significantly, important early manuscripts omit the words "in Ephesus" (see note on Eph 1:1). Many therefore regard the letter as an encyclical or "circular letter" sent to a number of churches in Asia Minor, the addressees to be designated in each place by its bearer, Tychicus (Eph 6:21–22). Others think that Ephesians is the letter referred to in Col 4:16 as "to the Laodiceans."

Paul, who is designated as the sole author at Eph 1:1, is described in almost unparalleled terms with regard to the significant role he has in God's plan for bringing the Gentiles to faith in Christ (Eph 3:1–12). Yet at the time of writing he is clearly in prison (Eph 3:1; 4:1; 6:20), suffering afflictions (Eph 3:13). Traditionally this "Captivity Epistle" has, along with Colossians, Philippians, and Philemon, been dated to an imprisonment in Rome, likely in A.D. 61–63. Others appeal to an earlier imprisonment, perhaps in Caesarea (Acts 23:27–27:2). Since the early nineteenth century, however, much of critical scholarship has considered the letter's style and use of words (especially when compared with Colossians), its concept of the church, and other points of doctrine put forward by the writer as grounds for serious doubt about authorship by Paul. The letter may then be the work of a secretary writing at the apostle's direction or of a later disciple who sought to develop Paul's ideas for a new situation around A.D. 80–100.

The principal divisions of the Letter to the Ephesians are the following:

I. Address (1:1–14)
II. Unity of the Church in Christ (1:15–2:22)
III. World Mission of the Church (3:1–4:24)
IV. Daily Conduct, an Expression of Unity (4:25–6:20)
V. Conclusion (6:21–24).

I. ADDRESS

CHAPTER 1

Greeting.' [1]Paul, an apostle of Christ Jesus by the will of God, to the holy ones who are [in Ephesus][†] faithful in Christ Jesus:[a] [2]grace to you and peace from God our Father and the Lord Jesus Christ.[b]

The Father's Plan of Salvation. [3‡]Blessed be the God and Father of our Lord Jesus Christ,[c] who has blessed us in Christ with every spiritual blessing in the heavens,[§] [4]as he chose us in him, before the foundation of the world, to be holy and without blemish before him.[d] In love [5]he destined us for adoption to himself through Jesus Christ, in accord with the favor of his will,[e] [6]for the praise of the glory of his grace that he granted us in the beloved.[f]

Fulfillment Through Christ. [7]In him we have redemption by his blood, the forgiveness of transgressions, in accord with the riches of his grace[g] [8]that he lavished upon us. In all wisdom and insight,[h] [9]he has made known to us the mystery[§] of his will in accord with his favor that he

set forth in him[i] [10]as a plan for the fullness of times, to sum up all things in Christ, in heaven and on earth.[j]

Inheritance Through the Spirit. [11]In him we were also chosen, destined in accord with the purpose of the One who accomplishes all things according to the intention of his will,[k] [12]so that we might exist for the praise of his glory, we who first hoped[**] in Christ. [13]In him you also, who have heard the word of truth, the gospel of your salvation, and have believed in him, were sealed[††] with the promised holy Spirit,[l] [14]which is the first installment[‡‡] of our inheritance toward redemption as God's possession, to the praise of his glory.[m]

II. UNITY OF THE CHURCH IN CHRIST

The Church as Christ's Body.[§§] [15]Therefore, I, too, hearing of your faith in the Lord Jesus and of your love[¶¶] for all the holy ones,[n] [16]do not cease giving thanks for you, remembering you in my prayers,[o] [17]that the God of our Lord Jesus Christ, the Father of glory, may give you a spirit of wisdom and revelation resulting in knowledge of him.[p] [18]May the eyes of [your] hearts be enlightened, that you may know what is the hope that belongs to his call, what are the riches of glory in his inheritance among the holy ones,[q] [19]and what is the surpassing greatness of his power for us who believe, in accord with the exercise of his great might,[r] [20]which he worked in Christ, raising him from the dead and seating him at his right hand in the heavens,[s] [21]far above every principality, authority, power, and dominion, and every name that is named not only in this age but also in the one to come.[t] [22]And he put all things beneath his feet and gave him as head

---

*[1:1–2] For the epistolary form used at the beginning of letters, see note on Rom 1:1–7. Twenty-two of the thirty Greek words in Eph 1:1–2 also occur in Col 1:1–2.

†[1:1] **[In Ephesus]**: the phrase is lacking in important early witnesses such as P⁴⁶ (3rd cent.), and Sinaiticus and Vaticanus (4th cent.), appearing in the latter two as a fifth-century addition. Basil and Origen mention its absence from manuscripts. See Introduction. Without the phrase, the Greek can be rendered, as in Col 1:2, "to the holy ones and faithful brothers in Christ."

‡[1:3–14] While a Pauline letter usually continues after the greeting with a prayer of thanksgiving, as in Eph 1:15–23 below, Ephesians first inserts a blessing of God for the blessings Christians have experienced, as in 2 Cor 1:3–4 and 1 Pt 1:3–12. The blessing here, akin to a Jewish *berakah*, is rich in images almost certainly drawn from hymns and liturgy. Many ideas here are also found in Col 1:3–23. Certain phrases are frequently repeated, such as **in Christ** (Eph 1:3, 10, 12) or **in him** (Eph 1:4, 7, 9, 11, 13) or **in the beloved** (Eph 1:6) and **(for) the praise of (his) glory** (Eph 1:6, 12, 14). Some terms like **chose** (Eph 1:4) and **destined** (Eph 1:5) reflect Old Testament theology (Dt 7:7; 9:4–6; 23:5) or Pauline themes (**redemption**, Eph 1:7, 14; **grace**, Eph 1:6, 7) or specific emphases in Colossians (**forgiveness**, Col 1:14). A triadic structure is discernible in Eph 1:3–14: God the **Father** (Eph 1:3–6, 8, 11), **Christ** (Eph 1:3, 5, 7–10, 12), and the **Spirit** (Eph 1:13–14). The spiritual blessings Christians have received through Christ (Eph 1:3) are gratefully enumerated: the call to holiness (Eph 1:4; cf. Col 1:22); the gift of divine **adoption** establishing a unique spiritual relationship with God the Father through Christ (Eph 1:5; cf. Gal 4:5); liberation from sin through Christ's sacrificial death (Eph 1:7); revelation of God's plan of salvation in Christ (Eph 1:9; cf. Eph 3:3–4; Rom 16:25); the gift of election and faith in Christ bestowed upon Jewish Christians (see note on Eph 1:12, **we who first hoped in Christ**); and finally, the same gift granted to Gentiles (Eph 1:13, **you also**). In the Christ-centered faith and existence of the Christian communities the apostle sees the predetermined **plan** of God to bring all creation under the final rule of Christ (Eph 1:4–5, 9–10) being **made known** (Eph 1:9) and carried through, to God's **glory** (Eph 1:6, 12, 14).

§[1:3] **In the heavens**: literally, "in the heavenlies" or "in the heavenly places," a term in Ephesians for the divine realm.

¶[1:9] **Mystery**: as in Rom 16:25; Col 1:26–27 and elsewhere, a secret of God now revealed in the **plan** to save and **sum up all things in Christ** (Eph 1:10); cf. Eph 3:3–6.

[1:12] **We who first hoped: probably Jewish Christians (contrast Eph 1:13, **you**, the Gentiles); possibly the people of Israel, "we who already enjoyed the hope of Christ," or perhaps present hope in contrast to future redemption (cf. Eph 1:14).

††[1:13] **Sealed**: by God, in baptism; cf. Eph 4:30; 2 Cor 1:22.

‡‡[1:14] **First installment**: down payment by God on full salvation, as at 2 Cor 1:22.

§§[1:15–23] See note on Rom 1:8 for the thanksgiving form in a letter. Much of the content parallels thoughts in Col 1:3–20. The prayer moves from God and Christ (Eph 1:17, 20–21) to the Ephesians (Eph 1:17–19) and the church (Eph 1:22–23). Paul asks that the blessing imparted by God the Father (Eph 1:3) to the Ephesians will be strengthened in them through the message of the gospel (Eph 1:13, 17–19), Those blessings are seen in the context of God's **might** in establishing the sovereignty of Christ over all other creatures (Eph 1:19–21) and in appointing him **head** of the church (Eph 1:22–23). For the allusion to angelic spirits in Eph 1:21, see Rom 8:38 and Col 1:16. Here, as in 1 Cor 15:24–25 and Col 2:15, every such **principality** and **power** is made subject to Christ.

¶¶[1:15] **Your faith . . . your love**: some manuscripts omit the latter phrase, but cf. Col 1:4.

---

i. [1:9] 3:3, 9; Rom 16:25.   j. [1:10] Gal 4:4; Col 1:16, 20.   k. [1:11] Is 46:10; Rom 8:28; Col 1:12; Rev 4:11.   l. [1:13] 4:30; Acts 2:33; Col 1:5–6.   m. [1:14] 2 Cor 1:22; 5:5.   n. [1:15] Col 1:3–4; Phlm 4–5.   o. [1:16] Col 1:3, 9.   p. [1:17] 3:14, 16; Col 1:9–10; 1 Jn 5:20.   q. [1:18] 4:4; Col 1:12, 27.   r. [1:19] 2 Cor 13:4; Col 1:11; 2:12.   s. [1:20] Ps 110:1; Heb 1:3.   t. [1:21] Phil 2:9; Col 1:16; 1 Pt 3:22.

a. [1:1] Rom 1:7; 1 Cor 1:1–2; Col 1:1.   b. [1:2] Col 1:2.   c. [1:3] 2:6; 2 Cor 1:3.   d. [1:4] 5:27; Jn 15:16; 17:24; Rom 8:29; 2 Thes 2:13.   e. [1:5] Jn 1:12; 1 Jn 3:1.   f. [1:6] Mt 3:17; Col 1:13.   g. [1:7] 2:7–13; Rom 3:24; Col 1:14, 20.   h. [1:8] Col 1:9.

over all things to the church,ᵘ ²³which is his body,* the fullness of the one who fills all things in every way.ᵛ

CHAPTER 2†
Generosity of God's Plan.‡ ¹ᵂYou were dead in your transgressions and sins§ ²in which you once lived following the age of this world,¶ following the ruler of the power of the air, the spirit that is now at work in the disobedient.ˣ ³All of us once lived among them in the desires of our flesh, following the wishes of the flesh and the impulses, and we were by nature children of wrath, like the rest.ʸ ⁴But God, who is rich in mercy, because of the great love he had for us, ⁵ᵉeven when we were dead in our transgressions, brought us to life with Christ** (by grace you have been saved),

⁶raised us up with him, and seated us with him in the heavens in Christ Jesus,ᵃ ⁷that in the ages to come he might show the immeasurable riches of his grace in his kindness to us in Christ Jesus.ᵇ ⁸For by grace you have been saved through faith, and this is not from you; it is the gift of God;ᶜ ⁹it is not from works, so no one may boast.ᵈ ¹⁰For we are his handiwork, created in Christ Jesus for the good works that God has prepared in advance, that we should live in them.ᵉ

One in Christ.†† ¹¹Therefore, remember that at one time you, Gentiles in the flesh, called the uncircumcision by those called the circumcision, which is done in the flesh by human hands, ¹²were at that time without Christ, alienated from the community of Israel‡‡ and strangers to the covenants of promise, without hope and without God in the world.ᶠ ¹³But now in Christ Jesus you who once were far off have become near by the blood of Christ.ᵍ

¹⁴§§For he is our peace, he who made both one and broke down the dividing wall of enmity, through his flesh,ʰ ¹⁵abolishing the law with its commandments and legal claims, that he might create in himself one new person¶¶ in place of the two, thus establishing peace,ⁱ ¹⁶and might reconcile both with God, in one body, through the cross, putting that enmity to death by it.ʲ ¹⁷He came and preached peace to you who were far off and peace to those who were near,ᵏ ¹⁸for through him we both have access in one Spirit to the Father.ˡ

¹⁹So then you are no longer strangers and sojourners, but you are fellow citizens with the holy ones and members of the household of God,ᵐ ²⁰built upon the foundation of the

---

*[1:23] **His body**: the church (Eph 1:22); cf. note on Col 1:18. Only in Ephesians and Colossians is Christ the **head** of the **body**, in contrast to the view in 1 Cor 12 and Rom 12:4–8 where Christ is equated with the entire body or community. **Fullness**: see note on Col 1:19. Some take **the one who fills** as God, others as Christ (cf. Eph 4:10). If in Christ "dwells the fullness of the deity bodily" (Col 2:9), then, as God "fills" Christ, Christ in turn fills the church and the believer (Eph 3:19; 5:18). But the difficult phrases here may also allow the church to be viewed as the "complement" of Christ who is "being filled" as God's plan for the universe is carried out through the church (cf. Eph 3:9–10).

†[2:1–22] The gospel of **salvation** (Eph 1:13) that God **worked in Christ** (Eph 1:20) is reiterated in terms of what God's **great love** (Eph 2:4), expressed in Christ, means for us. The passage sometimes addresses **you**, Gentiles (Eph 2:1–2, 8, 11–13, 19, 22), but other times speaks of **all of us** who believe (Eph 2:3–7, 10, 14, 18). In urging people to **remember** their grim past when they were **dead** in sins (Eph 2:1–3, 11–12) and what they are **now in Christ** (Eph 2:4–10, 13), the author sees both Jew and Gentile reconciled with God, now **one new person**, a new humanity, **one body, the household of God, a temple** and **dwelling place** of God's Spirit (Eph 2:15–16, 19–22). The presentation falls into two parts, the second stressing more the meaning for the church.

‡[2:1–10] The recipients of Paul's letter have experienced, in their redemption from **transgressions and sins**, the effect of Christ's supremacy over the power of the devil (Eph 2:1–2; cf. Eph 6:11–12), who rules not from the netherworld but from the **air** between God in heaven and human beings on earth. Both Jew and Gentile have experienced, through Christ, God's free gift of salvation that already marks them for a future heavenly destiny (Eph 2:3–7). The language **dead, raised us up**, and **seated us . . . in the heavens** closely parallels Jesus' own passion and Easter experience. The terms in Eph 2:8–9 describe salvation in the way Paul elsewhere speaks of justification: **by grace, through faith, the gift of God, not from works**; cf. Gal 2:16–21; Rom 3:24–28. Christians are a newly created people in Christ, fashioned by God for a life of goodness (Eph 2:10).

§[2:1–7] These verses comprise one long sentence in Greek, the main verb coming in Eph 2:5, God **brought us to life**, the object you/us dead in a . . . **transgressions** being repeated in Eph 2:1, 5; cf. Col 2:13.

¶[2:2] **Age of this world**: or "aeon," a term found in gnostic thought, possibly synonymous with the **rulers of this world**, but also reflecting the Jewish idea of "two ages," this present evil age and "the age to come"; cf. 1 Cor 3:19; 5:10; 7:31; Gal 1:4; Ti 2:12. **The disobedient**: literally, "the sons of disobedience," a Semitism as at Is 30:9.

[2:5] Our relation through baptism **with Christ, the risen Lord, is depicted in terms of realized eschatology, as already exaltation, though Eph 2:7 brings in the future aspect too.

††[2:11–22] The Gentiles lacked Israel's messianic expectation, lacked the various **covenants** God made with **Israel**, lacked **hope** of salvation and knowledge of the true **God** (Eph 2:11–12); but through Christ all these religious barriers between Jew and Gentile have been transcended (Eph 2:13–14) by the abolition of the Mosaic covenant-law (Eph 2:15) for the sake of uniting Jew and Gentile into a single religious community (Eph 2:15–16), imbued with the same holy **Spirit** and worshiping the same **Father** (Eph 2:18). The Gentiles are now included in God's **household** (Eph 2:19) as it arises upon the **foundation** of **apostles** assisted by those endowed with the prophetic gift (Eph 3:5), the preachers of Christ (Eph 2:20; cf. 1 Cor 12:28). With Christ as the **capstone** (Eph 2:20; cf. Is 28:16; Mt 21:42), they are being built into the holy **temple** of God's people where the divine presence dwells (Eph 2:21–22).

‡‡[2:12] **The community of Israel**: or "commonwealth"; cf. Eph 4:18. **The covenants**: cf. Rom 9:4: with Abraham, with Moses, with David.

§§[2:14–16] The elaborate imagery here combines pictures of Christ as **our peace** (Is 9:5), his crucifixion, the ending of the Mosaic law (cf. Col 2:14), reconciliation (2 Cor 5:18–21), and the destruction of **the dividing wall** such as kept people from God in the temple or a barrier in the heavens.

¶¶[2:15] **One new person**: a corporate body, the Christian community, made up of Jews and Gentiles, replacing ancient divisions; cf. Rom 1:16.

---

u. [1:22] 4:15; Ps 8:7; Mt 28:18; Col 1:18.   v. [1:23] 4:10, 12; Rom 12:5; 1 Cor 12:27; Col 1:19.   w. [2:1] Col 1:21; 2:13.   x. [2:2] 6:12; Jn 12:31; Col 1:13.   y. [2:3] Col 3:6–7.   z. [2:5] Rom 5:8; 6:13; Col 2:13.

a. [2:6] Rom 8:10–11; Phil 3:20; Col 2:12.   b. [2:7] 1:7.   c. [2:8] Rom 3:24; Gal 2:16.   d. [2:9] 1 Cor 1:29.   e. [2:10] 4:24; Ti 2:14. f. [2:12] Rom 9:4; Col 1:21, 27.   g. [2:13] 2:17; Is 57:19; Col 1:20.   h. [2:14] Gal 3:28.   i. [2:15] 2 Cor 5:17; Col 2:14. j. [2:16] Col 1:20, 22.   k. [2:17] Is 57:19; Zec 9:10.   l. [2:18] 3:12. m. [2:19] Heb 12:22–23.

apostles and prophets,[n] with Christ Jesus himself as the capstone.[*] [21]Through him the whole structure is held together and grows into a temple sacred in the Lord;[o] [22]in him you also are being built together into a dwelling place of God in the Spirit.[p]

III. WORLD MISSION OF THE CHURCH

CHAPTER 3

Commission to Preach God's Plan.[†] [1]Because of this,[q] I, Paul, a prisoner of Christ[‡] [Jesus] for you Gentiles— [2]if, as I suppose, you have heard of the stewardship[§] of God's grace that was given to me for your benefit,[r] [3][namely, that] the mystery[¶] was made known to me by revelation, as I have written briefly earlier.[s] [4]When you read this you can understand my insight into the mystery of Christ, [5]which was not made known to human beings in other generations as it has now been revealed to his holy apostles and prophets by the Spirit,[t] [6]that the Gentiles are coheirs, members of the same body, and copartners in the promise in Christ Jesus through the gospel.[u] [7]Of this I became a minister by the gift of God's grace that was granted me in accord with the exercise of his power.[v] [8]To me, the very least of all the holy ones, this grace was given, to preach to the Gentiles the inscrutable riches of Christ,[w] [9]and to bring to light [for all][**] what is the plan of the mystery hidden from ages past in God who

created all things,[x] [10]so that the manifold wisdom of God might now be made known through the church to the principalities and authorities[††] in the heavens.[y] [11]This was according to the eternal purpose that he accomplished in Christ Jesus our Lord, [12]in whom we have boldness of speech and confidence of access through faith in him.[z] [13]So I ask you not to lose heart over my afflictions for you; this is your glory.[a]

Prayer for the Readers.[‡‡] [14]For this reason I kneel before the Father, [15]from whom every family[§§] in heaven and on earth is named, [16]that he may grant you in accord with the riches of his glory to be strengthened with power through his Spirit in the inner self,[b] [17]and that Christ may dwell in your hearts through faith; that you, rooted and grounded in love,[c] [18]may have strength to comprehend with all the holy ones what is the breadth and length and height and depth,[d] [19]and to know the love of Christ that surpasses knowledge, so that you may be filled with all the fullness of God.[e]

[20]Now to him who is able to accomplish far more than all we ask or imagine, by the power at work within us,[f] [21]to him be glory in the church and in Christ Jesus to all generations, forever and ever. Amen.

CHAPTER 4

Unity in the Body. [1][¶¶]I, then, a prisoner for the Lord, urge you to live in a manner worthy of

---

*[2:20] **Capstone**: the Greek can also mean cornerstone or keystone.

†[3:1–13] Paul reflects on his mission to the Gentiles. He alludes to his call and appointment to the apostolic office (Eph 3:2–3) and how his **insight** through revelation, as well as that of the other apostles and charismatic prophets in the church (Eph 3:4–5), has deepened understanding of God's plan of salvation in Christ. Paul is the special herald (Eph 3:7) of a new **promise** to the **Gentiles** (Eph 3:6): that the divine plan includes them in the spiritual benefits promised to Israel. Not only is this unique apostolic role his; Paul also has been given the task of explaining to all the divine **plan** of salvation (Eph 3:8–9), once **hidden**. Through **the church**, God's plan to save through Christ is becoming manifest to angelic beings (Eph 3:10; cf. Eph 1:21), in accord with God's **purpose** (Eph 3:11). The fulfillment of the plan in Christ gives the whole church more **confidence** through **faith** in God (Eph 3:12). The readers of this letter are also thereby encouraged to greater confidence despite Paul's imprisonment (Eph 3:13).

‡[3:1] **A prisoner of Christ**: see Introduction. Paul abruptly departs from his train of thought at the end of Eph 3:1, leaving an incomplete sentence.

§[3:2] **Stewardship**: the Greek is the same term employed at Eph 1:10 for the **plan** that God administers (Col 1:25) and in which Paul plays a key role.

¶[3:3–4] **The mystery**: God's resolve to deliver Gentiles along with Israel through Christ; cf. notes on Eph 1:10; 3:9.

[3:9] [For all]: while some think this phrase was added so as to yield the sense "to enlighten all about the plan . . . ," it is more likely that some manuscripts and Fathers omitted it accidentally or to avoid the idea that **all** conflicted with Paul's assignment to preach to **the Gentiles** (Eph 3:8) specifically.

††[3:10] **Principalities and authorities**: see note on Eph 1:15–23 regarding Eph 3:21.

‡‡[3:14–21] The apostle prays that those he is addressing may, like the rest of the church, deepen their understanding of God's plan of salvation in Christ. It is a plan that affects the whole universe (Eph 3:15) with **the breadth and length and height and depth** of God's love in Christ (Eph 3:18) or possibly the universe in all its dimensions. The apostle prays that they may perceive the redemptive love of Christ for them and be completely immersed in the fullness of God (Eph 3:19). The prayer concludes with a doxology to God (Eph 3:20–21).

§§[3:14–15] **Every family**: in the Greek there is wordplay on the word for the **Father** (*patria, patēr*). The phrase could also mean "God's whole family" (cf. Eph 2:21).

¶¶[4:1–16] A general plea for unity in the church. Christians have been fashioned through the **Spirit** into a single harmonious religious community (**one body**, Eph 4:4, 12; cf. Eph 4:16), belonging to a single **Lord** (in contrast to the many gods of the pagan world), and by one way of salvation through **faith**, brought out especially by the significance of **baptism** (Eph 4:1–6; cf. Rom 6:1–11). But Christian unity is more than adherence to a common belief. It is manifested in the exalted Christ's gifts to individuals to serve so as to make the community more Christlike (Eph 4:11–16). This teaching on Christ as the source of the gifts is introduced in Eph 4:8 by a citation of Ps 68:18, which depicts Yahweh triumphantly leading Israel to salvation in Jerusalem. It is here understood of Christ, ascending **above all the heavens**, the **head** of the church; through his redemptive death, resurrection, and ascension he has become the source of the church's spiritual gifts. The "descent" of Christ (Eph 4:9–10) refers more probably to the incarnation (cf. Phil 2:6–8) than to Christ's presence after his death in the world of the dead (cf. 1 Pt 3:19).

---

n. [2:20] Is 28:16; Rev 21:14.   o. [2:21] 1 Cor 3:16; Col 2:19. p. [2:22] 1 Pt 2:5.   q. [3:1] Phil 1:7, 13; Col 1:24–29; 4:18; Phlm 9; 2 Tm 2:9.   r. [3:2] Col 1:25.   s. [3:3] 1:9–10; Col 1:26.   t. [3:5] Col 1:26.   u. [3:6] 2:13, 18–19.   v. [3:7] Rom 15:15; Col 1:25, 29. w. [3:8] 1 Cor 15:8–10; Gal 1:16; 2:7–9.

x. [3:9] Rom 16:25; Col 1:26–27.   y. [3:10] 1 Pt 1:12.   z. [3:12] Rom 5:1–2; Heb 4:16.   a. [3:13] Col 1:22, 24; 2 Tm 2:10.   b. [3:16] 6:10; Rom 7:22; 2 Cor 4:16; Col 1:11.   c. [3:17] Jn 14:23; Col 1:23; 2:7.   d. [3:18] Col 2:2.   e. [3:19] Col 2:3, 9.   f. [3:20] Rom 16:25–27; Col 1:29.

the call you have received,[g] [2]with all humility and gentleness, with patience, bearing with one another through love,[h] [3]striving to preserve the unity of the spirit through the bond of peace:[i] [4]one body and one Spirit, as you were also called to the one hope of your call;[j] [5]one Lord, one faith, one baptism;[k] [6]one God and Father of all, who is over all and through all and in all.[l] **Diversity of Gifts.** [7]But grace was given to each of us according to the measure of Christ's gift.[m] [8]Therefore, it says:

"He ascended[†] on high and took prisoners captive;
he gave gifts to men."[n]

[9]What does "he ascended" mean except that he also descended into the lower [regions] of the earth? [10]The one who descended is also the one who ascended far above all the heavens, that he might fill all things.

[11‡]And he gave some as apostles, others as prophets, others as evangelists, others as pastors and teachers,[o] [12]to equip the holy ones for the work of ministry,[§] for building up the body of Christ, [13]until we all attain to the unity of faith and knowledge of the Son of God, to mature manhood,[¶] to the extent of the full stature of Christ,[p] [14]so that we may no longer be infants, tossed by waves and swept along by every wind of teaching arising from human trickery, from their cunning in the interests of deceitful scheming.[q] [15]Rather, living the truth in love, we should grow in every way into him who is the head,[r] Christ,** [16]from whom the whole body, joined and held together by every supporting ligament, with the proper functioning of each part, brings about the body's growth and builds itself up in love.[s]

Renewal in Christ.[††] [17]So I declare and testify in the Lord that you must no longer live as the Gentiles do, in the futility of their minds;[t] [18]darkened in understanding, alienated from the life of God because of their ignorance, because of their hardness of heart,[u] [19]they have become callous and have handed themselves over to licentiousness for the practice of every kind of impurity to excess.[v] [20]That is not how you learned Christ, [21]assuming that you have heard of him and were taught in him, as truth is in Jesus, [22]that you should put away the old self of your former way of life, corrupted through deceitful desires,[w] [23]and be renewed in the spirit of your minds,[x] [24]and put on[‡‡] the new self, created in God's way in righteousness and holiness of truth.[y]

IV. DAILY CONDUCT,
AN EXPRESSION OF UNITY[§§]

Rules for the New Life. [25]Therefore, putting away falsehood, speak the truth, each one to his neighbor, for we are members one of another.[z] [26]Be angry but do not sin;[a] do not let the sun set on your anger,[¶¶] [27]and do not leave room for the devil.[b] [28]The thief must no longer steal, but rather labor, doing honest work*** with his [own] hands, so that he may have something to share with one in need.[c] [29]No foul language should come out of your mouths, but only such as is good for needed edification, that it may impart grace to those who hear.[d] [30]And do not grieve the holy Spirit of God, with which you were sealed for the day of redemption.[†††] [31]All bitterness, fury, anger, shouting, and reviling must be removed from you, along with all malice.[e] [32][And] be kind to one another, compassionate, forgiving one another as God has forgiven you in Christ.[f]

CHAPTER 5
[1]So be imitators of God,[‡‡‡] as beloved children,[g] [2]and live in love, as Christ loved us and handed

---

*[4:4–6] The "seven unities" (church, **Spirit, hope; Lord, faith** in Christ [Eph 1:13], **baptism; one God**) reflect the triune structure of later creeds in reverse.

†[4:8–10] While the emphasis is on an ascension and gift-giving by Christ, there is also a reference in taking **prisoners captive** to the aeons and powers mentioned at Eph 1:21; 2:2; 3:10; 6:12.

‡[4:11] Concerning this list of ministers, cf. 1 Cor 12:28 and Rom 12:6–8. **Evangelists:** missionary preachers (cf. Acts 21:8; 2 Tm 4:5), not those who wrote gospels. **Pastors and teachers:** a single group in the Greek, shepherding congregations.

§[4:12] The ministerial leaders in Eph 4:11 are to equip the whole people of God for their **work of ministry.**

¶[4:13] **Mature manhood:** literally, "a perfect man" (cf. Col 1:28), possibly the "one new person" of Eph 2:15, though there *anthrōpos* suggests humanity, while here *anēr* is the term for male. This personage becomes visible in the church's growing to its fullness in the unity of those who believe in Christ.

[4:15–16] **The head, Christ: cf. Col 1:18 and contrast 1 Cor 12:12–27 and Rom 12:4–5 where Christ is identified with the whole body, including the head. The imagery may derive from ancient views in medicine, the **head** coordinating and caring for the body, each **ligament** (perhaps the ministers of Eph 4:11) supporting the whole. But as at Eph 2:19–22, where the temple is depicted as a growing organism, there may also be the idea here of growth toward the capstone, Christ.

††[4:17–24] Paul begins to indicate how the new life in Christ contrasts with the Gentiles' old way of existence. Literally, **the old self** (Eph 4:22) and **the new self** (Eph 4:24) are "the old man" and "the new man" (*anthrōpos*, person), as at Eph 2:15; cf. note on Eph 4:13.

‡‡[4:24] **Put on:** in baptism. See note on Gal 3:27.

§§[4:25–6:20] For similar exhortations to a morally good life in response to God's gift of faith, see notes on Rom 12:1–13:14 and Gal 5:13–26.

¶¶[4:26] If angry, seek reconciliation that day, not giving the devil (Eph 6:11) opportunity to lead into sin.

***[4:28] **Honest work:** literally, "the good." **His [own] hands:** some manuscripts have the full phrase as in 1 Cor 4:12.

†††[4:30] See note on Eph 1:13.

‡‡‡[5:1] **Imitators of God:** in forgiving (Eph 4:32) and in loving (as exhibited in how **Christ loved us**).

---

g. [4:1] 3:1; Col 1:10. h. [4:2] Col 3:12–13. i. [4:3] Col 3:14–15. j. [4:4] Rom 12:5; 1 Cor 10:17; 12:12–13. k. [4:5] 1 Cor 8:6. l. [4:6] 1 Cor 12:6. m. [4:7] Rom 12:3, 6; 1 Cor 12:28. n. [4:8] Ps 68:19; Col 2:15. o. [4:11] 1 Cor 12:28. p. [4:13] Col 1:28. q. [4:14] 1 Cor 14:20; Col 2:4, 8; Heb 13:9; Jas 1:6. r. [4:15] 1 Cor 11:3; Col 1:18; 2:19.
s. [4:16] Col 2:19. t. [4:17] Rom 1:21. u. [4:18] Col 1:21; 1 Pt 1:14. v. [4:19] Col 3:5. w. [4:22] Rom 8:13; Gal 6:8; Col 3:9. x. [4:23] Rom 12:2. y. [4:24] Gn 1:26–27; Col 3:10. z. [4:25] Zec 8:16. a. [4:26] Ps 4:5 LXX; Mt 5:22. b. [4:27] 2 Cor 2:11. c. [4:28] 1 Thes 4:11. d. [4:29] 5:4; Col 3:16; 4:6. e. [4:31] Col 3:8. f. [4:32] Mt 6:14; Col 3:12–13. g. [5:1] Mt 5:45, 48.

himself over for us as a sacrificial offering to God for a fragrant aroma.[h] [3]Immorality or any impurity or greed must not even be mentioned among you, as is fitting among holy ones,[i] [4]no obscenity or silly or suggestive talk, which is out of place, but instead, thanksgiving.[j] [5]Be sure of this, that no immoral or impure or greedy person, that is, an idolater, has any inheritance in the kingdom of Christ and of God.[k]

Duty to Live in the Light. [6]Let no one deceive you with empty arguments, for because of these things the wrath of God is coming upon the disobedient.[*] [7]So do not be associated with them. [8]For you were once darkness, but now you are light in the Lord. Live as children of light,[m] [9]for light produces every kind of goodness and righteousness and truth.[n] [10]Try to learn what is pleasing to the Lord.[o] [11]Take no part in the fruitless works of darkness; rather expose them,[p] [12]for it is shameful even to mention the things done by them in secret; [13]but everything exposed by the light becomes visible,[q] [14]for everything that becomes visible is light. Therefore, it says:[r]

"Awake, O sleeper,
        and arise from the dead,
and Christ will give you light."[†]

[15‡]Watch carefully then how you live, not as foolish persons but as wise,[s] [16]making the most of the opportunity, because the days are evil. [17]Therefore, do not continue in ignorance, but try to understand what is the will of the Lord. [18]And do not get drunk on wine, in which lies debauchery, but be filled with the Spirit,[t] [19]addressing one another [in] psalms and hymns and spiritual songs, singing and playing to the Lord in your hearts,[u] [20]giving thanks always and for everything in the name of our Lord Jesus Christ to God the Father.[v]

Wives and Husbands. [21§]Be subordinate to one

another[w] out of reverence for Christ.[¶] [22]Wives should be subordinate to their husbands as to the Lord.[x] [23]For the husband is head of his wife just as Christ is head of the church, he himself the savior of the body.[y] [24]As the church is subordinate to Christ, so wives should be subordinate to their husbands in everything. [25]Husbands, love your wives, even as Christ loved the church and handed himself over for her[z] [26]to sanctify her, cleansing her by the bath of water with the word,[a] [27]that he might present to himself the church in splendor, without spot or wrinkle or any such thing, that she might be holy and without blemish.[b] [28]So [also] husbands should love their wives as their own bodies. He who loves his wife loves himself. [29]For no one hates his own flesh but rather nourishes and cherishes it, even as Christ does the church, [30]because we are members of his body.[c]

[31] "For this reason a man shall leave [his]
            father and [his] mother
      and be joined to his wife,
   and the two shall become one flesh."[d]

[32]This is a great mystery, but I speak in reference to Christ and the church.[e] [33]In any case, each one of you should love his wife as himself, and the wife should respect her husband.

CHAPTER 6

Children and Parents. [1]Children, obey your parents [in the Lord], for this is right.[f] [2]"Honor your father and mother."[g] This is the first commandment with a promise, [3]"that it may go well with you and that you may have a long life on earth." [4]Fathers, do not provoke your children to anger, but bring them up with the training and instruction of the Lord.[h]

Slaves and Masters. [5]Slaves, be obedient to your human masters with fear and trembling, in sincerity of heart, as to Christ,[i] [6]not only when being watched, as currying favor, but as slaves of Christ, doing the will of God from the heart,[j] [7]willingly serving the Lord and not human beings, [8]knowing that each will be requited from

---

*[5:6] See note on Eph 2:2.

†[5:14] An early Christian hymn, possibly from a baptismal liturgy. For the content compare Eph 2:5–6; 3:9 and Is 60:1.

‡[5:15–16, 19–20] The wording is similar to Col 4:5 and Eph 3:16–17.

§[5:21–6:9] Cf. notes on Col 3:18–4:1 and 1 Pt 2:18–3:7 for a similar listing of household duties where the inferior is admonished first (**wives**, Eph 5:22; **children**, Eph 6:1; **slaves**, Eph 6:5), then the superior (**husbands**, Eph 5:25; **fathers**, Eph 6:4; **masters**, Eph 6:9). Paul varies this pattern by an emphasis on mutuality (see Eph 5:20); use of Old Testament material about **father and mother** in Eph 6:2; the judgment to come for slave-owners (**you have a Master in heaven**, Eph 6:9); and above all the initial principle of subordination **to one another** under **Christ**, thus effectively undermining exclusive claims to domination by one party. Into the section on **wives and husbands** an elaborate teaching on **Christ** and **the church** has been woven (Eph 5:22–33).

¶[5:21–33] The apostle exhorts married Christians to a strong mutual love. Holding with Gn 2:24 that marriage is a divine institution (Eph 5:31), Paul sees Christian marriage as taking on a new meaning symbolic of the intimate relationship of love between Christ and the church. The wife should serve her husband in the same spirit as that of the church's service to Christ (Eph 5:22, 24), and the husband should care for his wife with the devotion of Christ to the church (Eph 5:25–30). Paul gives to the Genesis passage its highest meaning in the light of the union of Christ and the church, of which Christlike loyalty and devotion in Christian marriage are a clear reflection (Eph 5:31–33).

---

h. [5:2] Ex 29:18; Ps 40:7; Gal 2:20; 1 Jn 3:16.   i. [5:3] Gal 5:19; Col 3:5.
j. [5:4] 4:29; Col 3:8.   k. [5:5] 1 Cor 6:9–10; Gal 5:21; Col 3:5.
l. [5:6] Rom 1:18; Col 2:4, 8.   m. [5:8] 2:11–13; Jn 12:36; Col 1:12–13.
n. [5:9] Gal 5:22.   o. [5:10] Rom 12:2.   p. [5:11] Rom 13:12.
q. [5:13] Jn 3:20–21.   r. [5:14] Is 26:19; 60:1.   s. [5:15–16] Col 4:5.
t. [5:18] Prv 23:31 LXX; Lk 21:34.   u. [5:19] Ps 33:2–3; Col 3:16.
v. [5:20] Col 3:17.

w. [5:21] 1 Pt 5:5.   x. [5:22] Col 3:18–4:1; 1 Pt 3:1–7.   y. [5:23] 1 Cor 11:3; Col 1:18.   z. [5:25] Col 3:19; 1 Tm 2:6.   a. [5:26] Rom 6:4; Ti 3:5–7.   b. [5:27] 2 Cor 11:2; Col 1:22.   c. [5:30] Rom 12:5; 1 Cor 6:15.   d. [5:31] Gn 2:24; Mt 19:5; Mk 10:7–8.   e. [5:32] Rev 19:7.   f. [6:1] Prv 6:20; Sir 3:1–6; Col 3:20.   g. [6:2–3] Ex 20:12; Dt 5:16.   h. [6:4] Col 3:21–22.   i. [6:5] Col 3:22–25; 1 Tm 6:1–2; Ti 2:9–10.   j. [6:6] 1 Pt 2:18.

the Lord for whatever good he does, whether he is slave or free. [9]Masters, act in the same way toward them, and stop bullying, knowing that both they and you have a Master in heaven and that with him there is no partiality.[k]

Battle Against Evil. [10*]Finally, draw your strength from the Lord and from his mighty power. [11]Put on the armor of God so that you may be able to stand firm against the tactics of the devil.[l] [12]For our struggle is not with flesh and blood but with the principalities, with the powers, with the world rulers of this present darkness, with the evil spirits in the heavens.[m] [13]Therefore, put on the armor of God, that you may be able to resist on the evil day and, having done everything, to hold your ground.[n] [14]So stand fast with your loins girded in truth, clothed with righteousness as a breastplate,[o] [15]and your feet shod in readiness for the gospel of peace.[p] [16]In all circumstances, hold faith as a shield, to quench all [the] flaming arrows of the evil one.[q] [17]And take the helmet of salvation and the sword of the Spirit, which is the word of God.[r]

Constant Prayer. [18]With all prayer and supplication, pray at every opportunity in the Spirit. To that end, be watchful with all perseverance and supplication for all the holy ones[s] [19]and also for me, that speech may be given me to open my mouth, to make known with boldness the mystery of the gospel[t] [20]for which I am an ambassador in chains, so that I may have the courage to speak as I must.[u]

V. CONCLUSION

A Final Message.[†] [21]So that you also may have news of me and of what I am doing, Tychicus, my beloved brother and trustworthy minister in the Lord, will tell you everything.[v] [22]I am sending him to you for this very purpose, so that you may know about us and that he may encourage your hearts.[w]

[23]Peace be to the brothers, and love with faith, from God the Father and the Lord Jesus Christ. [24]Grace be with all who love our Lord Jesus Christ in immortality.[x]

---

*[6:10–20] A general exhortation to courage and prayer. Drawing upon the imagery and ideas of Is 11:5; 59:16–17; and Wis 5:17–23, Paul describes the Christian in terms of the dress and equipment of Roman soldiers. He observes, however, that the Christian's readiness for combat is not directed against human beings but against the spiritual powers of evil (Eph 6:10–17; cf. Eph 1:21; 2:2; 3:10). Unique importance is placed upon prayer (Eph 6:18–20).

†[6:21–24] **Tychicus:** the bearer of the letter; see note on Col 4:7. Eph 6:21–22 parallel Col 4:7–8, often word for word. If Ephesians is addressed to several Christian communities (see Introduction), it is understandable that no greetings to individual members of these communities should have been included in it.

k. [6:9] Col 4:1. l. [6:11] Rom 13:12; 2 Cor 6:7; 10:4; Jas 4:7. m. [6:12] 1:21; 2:2; Col 1:13. n. [6:13] Rom 13:12. o. [6:14] Wis 5:17–20; Is 11:5; Lk 12:35; 1 Thes 5:8. p. [6:15] Is 52:7. q. [6:16] 1 Pt 5:9.

r. [6:17] Is 59:17; 1 Thes 5:8. s. [6:18] Mt 26:41; Col 4:2–3. t. [6:19] Acts 4:29; Col 4:3; 2 Thes 3:1. u. [6:20] 2 Cor 5:20; Col 4:4. v. [6:21] Acts 20:4; Col 4:7; 2 Tm 4:12. w. [6:22] Col 4:8. x. [6:24] 1 Pt 1:8.

PHILIPPIANS

～❧～

Philippi, in northeastern Greece, was a city of some importance in the Roman province of Macedonia. Lying on the great road from the Adriatic coast to Byzantium, the Via Egnatia, and in the midst of rich agricultural plains near the gold deposits of Mt. Pangaeus, it was in Paul's day a Roman town (Acts 16:21), with a Greek-Macedonian population and a small group of Jews (see Acts 16:13). Originally founded in the sixth century B.C. as Krenides by the Thracians, the town was taken over after 360 B.C. by Philip II of Macedon, the father of Alexander the Great, and was renamed for himself, "Philip's City." The area became Roman in the second century B.C. On the plains near Philippi in October 42 B.C., Antony and Octavian decisively defeated the forces of Brutus and Cassius, the slayers of Julius Caesar. Octavian (Augustus) later made Philippi a Roman colony and settled many veterans of the Roman armies there.

Paul, according to Acts (Acts 16:9–40), established at Philippi the first Christian community in Europe. He came to Philippi, via its harbor town of Neapolis (modern Kavalla), on his second missionary journey, probably in A.D. 49 or 50, accompanied by Silas and Timothy (Acts 15:40; 16:3; cf. Phil 1:1) and Luke, if he is to be included in the "we" references of Acts 16:10–17. The Acts account tells of the conversion of a business woman, Lydia; the exorcism of a slave girl; and, after an earthquake, while Paul and Silas were imprisoned in Philippi, the faith and baptism of a jailer and his family. None of these persons, however, is directly mentioned in Philippians (cf. the notes on Phil 4:2 and Phil 4:3). Acts 16 concludes its account by describing how Paul (and Silas), asked by the magistrates to leave Philippi, went on to Thessalonica (Acts 17:1–10), where several times his loyal Philippians continued to support him with financial aid (Phil 4:16). Later, Paul may have passed through Philippi on his way from Ephesus to Greece (Acts 20:1–2), and he definitely stopped there on his fateful trip to Jerusalem (Acts 20:6).

Paul's letter to the Christians at Philippi was written while he was in a prison somewhere (Phil 1:7, 13, 14, 17), indeed in danger of death (Phil 1:20–23). Although under guard for preaching Christ, Paul rejoices at the continuing progress of the gospel (Phil 1:12–26) and expresses gratitude for the Philippians' renewed concern and help in an expression of thanks most clearly found at Phil 4:10–20. Much of the letter is devoted to instruction about unity and humility within the Christian community at Philippi (Phil 1:27–2:18) and exhortations to growth, joy, and peace in their life together (Phil 4:1–9). The letter seems to be drawing to a close at the end of what we number as Phil 2, as Paul reports the plans of his helper Timothy and of Epaphroditus (whom the Philippians had sent to aid Paul) to come to Philippi (Phil 2:19–3:1), and even Paul's own expectation that he will go free and come to Philippi (Phil 1:25–26; 2:24). Yet quite abruptly at Phil 3:2, Paul erupts into warnings against false teachers who threaten to impose on the Philippians the burdens of the Mosaic law, including circumcision. The section that follows, Phil 3:2–21, is a vigorous attack on these Judaizers (cf. Gal 2:11–3:29) or Jewish Christian teachers (cf. 2 Cor 11:12–23), giving us insights into Paul's own life story (Phil 3:4–6) and into the doctrine of justification, the Christian life, and ultimate hope (Phil 3:7–21).

The location of Paul's imprisonment when he wrote to the Philippians, and thus the date of the letter, are uncertain. The traditional view has been that it stems from Paul's confinement in Rome, between A.D. 59 and 63 (cf. Acts 28:14–31). One modern view suggests the period when he was imprisoned at Caesarea, on the coast of Palestine, A.D. 57 or 58 (Acts 23:23–26:32); another suggests Corinth (cf. 2 Cor 11:9). Much recent scholarship favors Ephesus, around A.D. 55, a situation referred to in 2 Cor 1:8 concerning "the affliction that came to us" in Asia Minor (cf. also 1 Cor 15:32). The reference at Phil 1:13 to the "praetorium" (cf. also Phil 4:22) can be understood to mean the imperial guard or government house at Ephesus (or Caesarea), or the praetorian camp in Rome. Involved in a decision are the several journeys back and forth between Philippi and wherever Paul is imprisoned, mentioned in the letter (Phil 2:25–28; 4:14); this factor causes many to prefer Ephesus because of its proximity to Philippi. The Ephesian hypothesis dates the composition of Philippians to the mid-50s when most of Paul's major letters were written.

There is also a likelihood, according to some scholars, that the letter as we have it is a composite from parts of three letters by Paul to the Philippians. Seemingly Phil 4:10–20 is a brief note of appreciation for help sent through Epaphroditus. The long section from Phil 1:3 to Phil 3:1 is then another letter, with news of Paul's imprisonment and reports on Timothy and Epaphroditus (who has fallen ill while with Paul), along with exhortations to the Philippians about Christian conduct; and Phil 3:2–21 a third communication warning about threats to Philippian Christianity. The other verses in Phil 4 and Phil 1:1–2, are variously assigned by critics to these three underlying letters, which an editor presumably put together to produce a picture of Paul writing earnestly from prison (Phil 1–2), facing opponents of the faith (Phil 3), and with serene joy advising and thanking his Philippians (Phil 4). If all four chapters were originally a unity, then one must assume that a break occurred between the writing of Phil 3:1 and Phil 3:2, possibly involving the receipt of bad news from Philippi, and that Paul had some reasons for delaying his words of thanks for the aid brought by Epaphroditus till the end of his letter.

This beautiful letter is rich in insights into Paul's theology and his apostolic love and concern for the gospel and his converts. In Philippians, Paul reveals his human sensitivity and tenderness, his enthusiasm for Christ as the key to life and death (Phil 1:21), and his deep feeling for those in Christ who dwell in Philippi. With them he shares his hopes and convictions, his anxieties and fears, revealing the total confidence in Christ that constitutes faith (Phil 3:8–10). The letter incorporates a hymn about the salvation that God has brought about through Christ (Phil 2:6–11), applied by Paul to the relations of Christians with one another (Phil 2:1–5). Philippians has been termed "the letter of joy" (Phil 4:4, 10). It is the rejoicing of faith, based on true understanding of Christ's unique role in the salvation of all who profess his lordship (Phil 2:11; 3:8–12, 14, 20–21).

The principal divisions of the Letter to the Philippians are the following:

I.   Address (1:1–11)
II. Progress of the Gospel (1:12–26)
III. Instructions for the Community (1:27–2:18)
IV. Travel Plans of Paul and His Assistants (2:19–3:1)
V.   Polemic: Righteousness and the Goal in Christ (3:2–21)
VI. Instructions for the Community (4:1–9)
VII. Gratitude for the Philippians' Generosity (4:10–20)
VIII. Farewell (4:21–23)

I. ADDRESS

CHAPTER 1

Greeting.* ¹Paul and Timothy, slaves† of Christ Jesus, to all the holy ones in Christ Jesus who are in Philippi, with the overseers and ministers:ᵃ ²ᵇgrace to you and peace from God our Father and the Lord Jesus Christ.‡

Thanksgiving.§ ³I give thanks to my God at every remembrance of you,ᶜ ⁴praying always with joy in my every prayer for all of you, ⁵because of your partnership for the gospel from the first day until now. ⁶ᵈI am confident of this, that the one who began a good work in you will continue to complete it until the day of Christ Jesus.⁵ ⁷It is right that I should think this way about all of you, because I hold you in my heart, you who are all partners with me in grace, both in my imprisonment and in the defense and confirmation of the gospel. ⁸For God is my witness, how I long for all of you with the affection of Christ Jesus.ᵉ ⁹And this is my prayer: that your love may increase ever more and more in knowledge and every kind of perception,ᶠ ¹⁰to discern what is of value, so that you may be pure and blameless for the day of Christ,ᵍ ¹¹filled with the fruit of righteousness that comes through Jesus Christ for the glory and praise of God.ʰ

II. PROGRESS OF THE GOSPEL**

¹²ⁱI want you to know, brothers, that my situation has turned out rather to advance the gospel, ¹³so that my imprisonment has become well known in Christ throughout the whole praetorium†† and to all the rest,ʲ ¹⁴‡‡and so that the majority of the brothers, having taken encouragement in the Lord from my imprisonment, dare more than ever to proclaim the word fearlessly.

¹⁵Of course, some preach Christ from envy and rivalry, others from good will. ¹⁶The latter act out of love, aware that I am here for the defense of the gospel; ¹⁷the former proclaim Christ out of selfish ambition, not from pure motives, thinking that they will cause me trouble in my imprisonment. ¹⁸What difference does it make, as long as in every way, whether in pretense or in truth, Christ is being proclaimed?ᵏ And in that I rejoice.§§

Indeed I shall continue to rejoice, ¹⁹¶¶for I know that this will result in deliverance for me*** through your prayers and support from the Spirit of Jesus Christ.ˡ ²⁰My eager expectation and hope is that I shall not be put to shame in any way, but that with all boldness, now as always, Christ will be magnified in my body, whether by life or by death.ᵐ ²¹For to me life is

---

*[1:1–2] See note on Rom 1:1–7, concerning the greeting.

†[1:1] **Slaves:** Paul usually refers to himself at the start of a letter as an apostle. Here he substitutes a term suggesting the unconditional obligation of himself and Timothy to the service of Christ, probably because, in view of the good relationship with the Philippians, he wishes to stress his status as a co-servant rather than emphasize his apostolic authority. Reference to Timothy is a courtesy: Paul alone writes the letter, as the singular verb throughout shows (Phil 1:3–26), and the reference (Phil 2:19–24) to Timothy in the third person. **Overseers:** the Greek term *episkopos* literally means "one who oversees" or "one who supervises," but since the second century it has come to designate the "bishop," the official who heads a local church. In New Testament times this office had not yet developed into the form that it later assumed, though it seems to be well on the way to such development in the Pastorals; see 1 Tm 3:2 and Ti 1:7, where it is translated bishop. At Philippi, however (and at Ephesus, according to Acts 20:28), there was more than one *episkopos*, and the precise function of these officials is uncertain. In order to distinguish this office from the later stages into which it developed, the term is here translated as **overseers.** **Ministers:** the Greek term *diakonoi* is used frequently in the New Testament to designate "servants," "attendants," or "ministers." Paul refers to himself and to other apostles as "ministers of God" (2 Cor 6:4) or "ministers of Christ" (2 Cor 11:23). In the Pastorals (1 Tm 3:8, 12) the *diakonos* has become an established official in the local church; hence the term is there translated as **deacon.** The *diakonoi* at Philippi seem to represent an earlier stage of development of the office; we are uncertain about their precise functions. Hence the term is here translated as **ministers.** See Rom 16:1, where Phoebe is described as a *diakonos* (minister) of the church of Cenchreae.

‡[1:2] The gifts come **from** Christ the Lord, not simply through him from the Father; compare the christology in Phil 2:6–11.

§[1:3–11] As in Rom 1:8–15 and all the Pauline letters except Galatians, a thanksgiving follows, including a direct prayer for the Philippians (Phil 1:9–11); see note on Rom 1:8. On their **partnership for the gospel** (Phil 1:5), cf. Phil 1:29–30; 4:10–20. Their devotion to the faith and to Paul made them his pride and joy (Phil 4:1). The characteristics thus manifested are evidence of the community's continuing preparation for the Lord's parousia (Phil 1:6, 10). Paul's especially warm relationship with the Philippians is suggested here (Phil 1:7–8) as elsewhere in the letter. The eschatology serves to underscore a concern for ethical growth (Eph 1:9–11), which appears throughout the letter.

¶[1:6] **The day of Christ Jesus:** the parousia or triumphant return of Christ, when those loyal to him will be with him and share in his eternal glory; cf. Phil 1:10; 2:16; 3:20–21; 1 Thes 4:17; 5:10; 2 Thes 1:10; 1 Cor 1:8.

[1:12–26] The body of the letter begins with an account of Paul's present **situation, i.e., his **imprisonment** (Phil 1:12–13; see Introduction), and then goes on with advice for the Philippians (Phil 1:27–2:18). The **advance** of the gospel (Phil 1:12) and the **progress** of the Philippians **in the faith** (Phil 1:25) frame what is said.

††[1:13] **Praetorium:** either the praetorian guard in the city where Paul was imprisoned or the governor's official residence in a Roman province (cf. Mk 15:16; Acts 23:35). See Introduction on possible sites.

‡‡[1:14–18] Although Paul is imprisoned, Christians there nonetheless go on preaching Christ. But they do so with varied motives, **some** with personal hostility toward Paul, others out of personal ambition.

§§[1:18] **Rejoice:** a major theme in the letter; see Introduction.

¶¶[1:19–25] Paul earnestly debates his prospects of martyrdom or continued missionary labor. While he may **long to depart this life** and thus **be with Christ** (Phil 1:23), his overall and final expectation is that he will be delivered from this imprisonment and **continue in the service** of the Philippians and of others (Phil 1:19, 25; Phil 2:24). In either case, Christ is central (Phil 1:20–21); if to live means Christ for Paul, death means to be united with Christ in a deeper sense.

***[1:19] **Result in deliverance for me:** an echo of Jb 13:16, hoping that God will turn suffering to ultimate good and deliverance from evil.

e. [1:8] Rom 1:9; 2 Cor 1:23; 1 Thes 2:5. f. [1:9] Eph 3:14–19; Col 1:9–10; Phlm 6. g. [1:10] Rom 2:18; 12:2 / 1:6. h. [1:11] Jn 15:8.
i. [1:12–13] Eph 3:1; 6:20; 2 Tm 2:9; Phlm 9. j. [1:13] 4:22. k. [1:18] 4:10. l. [1:19] Jb 13:16 / 2 Cor 1:11. m. [1:20] 1 Cor 6:20; 1 Pt 4:16.

a. [1:1] Rom 1:1; 2 Cor 1:1; 1 Thes 1:1; Phlm 1 / 1 Tm 3:1–13.
b. [1:2] Rom 1:7; Gal 1:3; Phlm 3.   c. [1:3] Rom 1:8; 1 Cor 1:4; 1 Thes 1:2.   d. [1:6] 2:13 / 1:10; 2:16; 1 Cor 1:8.

Christ, and death is gain.[n] [22]If I go on living in the flesh, that means fruitful labor for me. And I do not know which I shall choose.[o] [23]I am caught between the two. I long to depart this life and be with Christ, [for] that is far better.[p] [24]Yet that I remain [in] the flesh is more necessary for your benefit. [25]And this I know with confidence, that I shall remain and continue in the service of all of you for your progress and joy in the faith, [26]so that your boasting in Christ Jesus may abound on account of me when I come to you again.

III. INSTRUCTIONS FOR THE COMMUNITY

Steadfastness in Faith.[*] [27]Only, conduct yourselves in a way worthy of the gospel of Christ, so that, whether I come and see you or am absent, I may hear news of you, that you are standing firm in one spirit, with one mind struggling together for the faith of the gospel,[q] [28]not intimidated in any way by your opponents. This is proof to them of destruction, but of your salvation. And this is God's doing. [29]For to you has been granted, for the sake of Christ, not only to believe in him but also to suffer for him.[r] [30]Yours is the same struggle[s] as you saw in me and now hear about me.[t]

CHAPTER 2

Plea for Unity and Humility.[‡] [1]If there is any encouragement in Christ, any solace in love, any participation in the Spirit, any compassion and mercy, [2]complete my joy by being of the same mind, with the same love, united in heart, thinking one thing.[t] [3]Do nothing out of selfishness or out of vainglory; rather, humbly regard others as more important than yourselves,[u] [4]each looking out not for his own interests, but [also] everyone for those of others.[v]

[5]Have among yourselves the same attitude that is also yours in Christ Jesus,[§]

[6]   Who,¶ though he was in the form of God,[w]
        did not regard equality with God
            something to be grasped.**
[7]   Rather, he emptied himself,
        taking the form of a slave,
        coming in human likeness;††
        and found human in appearance,[x]
[8]   he humbled himself,[y]
            becoming obedient to death,
            even death on a cross.‡‡
[9]   Because of this, God greatly exalted him
        and bestowed on him the name§§
        that is above every name;[z]
[10]   that at the name of Jesus
        every knee should bend,¶¶
        of those in heaven and on earth and
            under the earth,[a]
[11]   and every tongue confess that
        Jesus Christ is Lord,***
        to the glory of God the Father.[b]

Obedience and Service in the World.††† [12c]So then, my beloved, obedient as you have always

---

held that Christ here functions as a model for moral imitation, it is not the historical Jesus but the entire Christ event that Phil 2:6–11 depict. Therefore, the appeal is to have in relations among yourselves that same relationship you have in Jesus Christ, i.e., serving one another as you serve Christ (Phil 2:4).

¶[2:6–11] Perhaps an early Christian hymn quoted here by Paul. The short rhythmic lines fall into two parts, Phil 2:6–8 where the subject of every verb is Christ, and Phil 2:9–11 where the subject is God. The general pattern is thus of Christ's humiliation and then exaltation. More precise analyses propose a division into six three-line stanzas (Phil 2:6; 7abc, 7d–8, 9, 10, 11) or into three stanzas (Phil 2:6–7ab, 7cd–8, 9–11). Phrases such as **even death on a cross** (Phil 2:8c) are considered by some to be additions (by Paul) to the hymn, as are Phil 2:10c, 11c.

[2:6] Either a reference to Christ's preexistence and those aspects of divinity that he was willing to give up in order to serve in human form, or to what the man Jesus refused to grasp at to attain divinity. Many see an allusion to the Genesis story: unlike Adam, Jesus, **though . . . in the form of God (Gn 1:26–27), did not reach out for **equality with God**, in contrast with the first Adam in Gn 3:5–6.

††[2:7] **Taking the form of a slave, coming in human likeness:** or ". . . taking the form of a slave. // Coming in human likeness, and found human in appearance." While it is common to take Phil 2:6–7 as dealing with Christ's preexistence and Phil 2:8 with his incarnate life, so that lines Phil 2:7b–7c are parallel, it is also possible to interpret so as to exclude any reference to preexistence (see note on Phil 2:6) and to take Phil 2:6–8 as presenting two parallel stanzas about Jesus' human state (Phil 2:6–7b; 7cd–8); in the latter alternative, **coming in human likeness** begins the second stanza and parallels Phil 2:6a to some extent.

‡‡[2:8] There may be reflected here language about the servant of the Lord, Is 52:13–53:12 especially Is 53:12.

§§[2:9] **The name:** "Lord" (Phil 2:11), revealing the true nature of the one who is named.

¶¶[2:10–11] **Every knee should bend . . . every tongue confess:** into this language of Is 45:23 there has been inserted a reference to the three levels in the universe, according to ancient thought, **heaven, earth, under the earth**.

***[2:11] **Jesus Christ is Lord:** a common early Christian acclamation; cf. 1 Cor 12:3; Rom 10:9. But doxology to God the Father is not overlooked here (Phil 2:11c) in the final version of the hymn.

†††[2:12–18] Paul goes on to draw out further ethical implications for daily life (Phil 2:14–18) from the salvation God works in Christ.

---

*[1:27–30] Ethical admonition begins at this early point in the letter, emphasizing steadfastness and congregational unity in the face of possible suffering. The **opponents** (Phil 1:28) are those in Philippi, probably pagans, who oppose the gospel cause. **This is proof . . .** (Phil 1:28) may refer to the whole outlook and conduct of the Philippians, turning out for their salvation but to the judgment of the opponents (cf. 2 Cor 2:15–16), or possibly the sentence refers to the opinion of the opponents, who hold that the obstinacy of the Christians points to the destruction of such people as defy Roman authority (though in reality, Paul holds, such faithfulness leads to salvation).

†[1:30] A reference to Paul's earlier imprisonment in Philippi (Acts 16:19–24; 1 Thes 2:2) and to his present confinement.

‡[2:1–11] The admonition to likemindedness and unity (Phil 2:2–5) is based on the believers' threefold experience with Christ, God's love, and the Spirit. The appeal to humility (Phil 2:3) and to obedience (Phil 2:12) is rooted in christology, specifically in a statement about Christ Jesus (Phil 2:6–11) and his humbling of self and obedience to the point of death (Phil 2:8).

§[2:5] **Have . . . the same attitude that is also yours in Christ Jesus:** or, "that also Christ Jesus had." While it is often

n. [1:21] Gal 2:20.   o. [1:22] Rom 1:13.   p. [1:23] 2 Cor 5:8. q. [1:27] Eph 4:1; Col 1:10; 1 Thes 2:12 / 4:3.   r. [1:29] Mt 5:10; 10:38; Mk 8:34; Acts 5:41.   s. [1:30] 1:13; Acts 16:22–24.   t. [2:2] Rom 15:5; 1 Cor 1:10.   u. [2:3] Rom 12:3, 10; Gal 5:26.   v. [2:4] 1 Cor 10:24, 33; 13:5.

w. [2:6] Jn 1:1–2; 17:5; Col 2:9; Heb 1:3.   x. [2:7] Is 53:3, 11; Jn 1:14; Rom 8:3; 2 Cor 8:9; Gal 4:4; Heb 2:14, 17.   y. [2:8] Mt 26:39; Jn 10:17; Heb 5:8; 12:2.   z. [2:9] Acts 2:33; Mt 23:12; Eph 1:20–21; Heb 1:3–4. a. [2:10] Is 45:23; Jn 5:23; Rom 14:11; Rev 5:13.   b. [2:11] Acts 2:36; Rom 10:9; 1 Cor 12:3.   c. [2:12] Ps 2:11; 1 Cor 2:3; 2 Cor 7:15.

been, not only when I am present but all the more now when I am absent, work out your salvation with fear and trembling.* ¹³For God is the one who, for his good purpose, works in you both to desire and to work.ᵈ ¹⁴Do everything without grumbling or questioning,ᵉ ¹⁵that you may be blameless and innocent, children of God without blemish in the midst of a crooked and perverse generation,† among whom you shine like lights in the world,ᶠ ¹⁶as you hold on to the word of life, so that my boast for the day of Christ may be that I did not run in vain or labor in vain.ᵍ ¹⁷But, even if I am poured out as a libation‡ upon the sacrificial service of your faith, I rejoice and share my joy with all of you.ʰ ¹⁸In the same way you also should rejoice and share your joy with me.ⁱ

IV. TRAVEL PLANS OF PAUL AND HIS ASSISTANTS§

Timothy and Paul. ¹⁹I hope, in the Lord Jesus, to send Timothy¶ to you soon, so that I too may be heartened by hearing news of you.ʲ ²⁰For I have no one comparable to him for genuine interest in whatever concerns you. ²¹For they all seek their own interests, not those of Jesus Christ.ᵏ ²²But you know his worth, how as a child with a father he served along with me in the cause of the gospel. ²³He it is, then, whom I hope to send as soon as I see how things go with me, ²⁴but I am confident in the Lord that I myself will also come soon.**

Epaphroditus. ²⁵With regard to Epaphroditus,†† my brother and co-worker and fellow soldier, your messenger and minister in my need, I consider it necessary to send him to you.ˡ ²⁶For he has been longing for all of you and was distressed because you heard that he was ill. ²⁷He was indeed ill, close to death; but God had mercy on him, not just on him but also on me, so that I might not have sorrow upon sorrow. ²⁸I

send him therefore with the greater eagerness, so that, on seeing him, you may rejoice again, and I may have less anxiety. ²⁹Welcome him then in the Lord with all joy and hold such people in esteem,ᵐ ³⁰because for the sake of the work of Christ he came close to death, risking his life to make up for those services to me that you could not perform.

CHAPTER 3

Concluding Admonitions. ¹Finally, my brothers, rejoice‡‡ in the Lord. Writing the same things to you is no burden for me but is a safeguard for you.ⁿ

V. POLEMIC: RIGHTEOUSNESS AND THE GOAL IN CHRIST§§

Against Legalistic Teachers. ²¶Beware of the dogs! Beware of the evil-workers!º Beware of the mutilation!*** ³For we are the circumcision,††† we who worship through the Spirit of God, who boast in Christ Jesus and do not put our confidence in flesh,ᵖ ⁴although I myself have grounds for confidence even in the flesh.�q
Paul's Autobiography. If anyone else thinks he can be confident in flesh, all the more can I.

---

*[2:12] **Fear and trembling**: a common Old Testament expression indicating awe and seriousness in the service of God (cf. Ex 15:16; Jdt 2:28; Ps 2:11; Is 19:16).

†[2:15–16] **Generation . . . as you hold on to . . . :** or ". . . generation. Among them shine like lights in the world because you hold the word of life. . . ."

‡[2:17] **Libation**: in ancient religious ritual, the pouring out on the ground of a liquid offering as a sacrifice. Paul means that he may be facing death.

§[2:19–3:1] The plans of Paul and his assistants for future travel are regularly a part of a Pauline letter near its conclusion; cf. Rom 15:22–29; 1 Cor 16:5–12.

¶[2:19] **Timothy**: already known to the Philippians (Acts 16:1–15; cf. 1 Cor 4:17; 16:10).

[2:24] **I myself will also come soon: cf. Phil 1:19–25 for the significance of this statement.

††[2:25] **Epaphroditus**: sent by the Philippians as their **messenger** (literally, "apostle") to aid Paul in his imprisonment, he had fallen seriously ill; Paul commends him as he sends him back to Philippi.

‡‡[3:1] **Finally . . . rejoice:** the adverb often signals the close of a letter; cf. Phil 4:8; 2 Cor 13:11. While the verb could also be translated "good-bye" or "farewell," although it is never so used in Greek epistolography, the theme of joy has been frequent in the letter (Phil 1:18; 2:2, 18); note also Phil 4:4 and the addition of "always" there as evidence for the meaning "rejoice." To write **the same things** may refer to what Paul has previously taught in Philippi or to what he has just written or to what follows.

§§[3:2–21] An abrupt change in content and tone, either because Paul at this point responds to disturbing news he has just heard about a threat to the faith of the Philippians in the form of false teachers, or because part of another Pauline letter was inserted here; see Introduction. The chapter describes these teachers in strong terms as **dogs**. The persons meant are evidently different from the rival preachers of Phil 1:14–18 and the opponents of Phil 1:28. Since Phil 3:2–4 emphasize Jewish terms like **circumcision** (Phil 3:2–3, 5), some relate them to the "Judaizers" of the Letter to the Galatians. Other phrases make them appear more like the false teachers of 2 Cor 11:12–15, the **evil-workers**. The latter part of the chapter depicts the **many** who are **enemies** of Christ's cross in terms that may sound even more Gentile or even "gnostic" than Jewish (Phil 3:18–19). Accordingly, some see two groups of false teachers in Phil 3, others one group characterized by a claim of having attained "perfect maturity" (Phil 3:12–15).

¶¶[3:2–11] Paul sets forth the Christian claim, especially using personal, autobiographical terms that are appropriate to the situation. He presents his own experience in coming to know Christ Jesus in terms of **righteousness** or justification (cf. Rom 1:16–17; 3:21–5:11; Gal 2:5–11), contrasting the **righteousness from God** through faith and that of one's own **based on the law** as two exclusive ways of pleasing God.

***[3:2] **Beware of the mutilation**: literally, "incision," an ironic wordplay on "circumcision"; cf. Gal 5:12. There may be an association with the self-inflicted mutilations of the prophets of Baal (1 Kgs 18:28) and of devotees of Cybele who slashed themselves in religious frenzy.

†††[3:3] **We are the circumcision**: the true people of God, seed and offspring of Abraham (Gal 3:7, 29; 6:15). **Spirit of God**: some manuscripts read "worship God by the Spirit."

---

d. [2:13] 1:6; 1 Cor 12:6; 15:10; 2 Cor 3:5.　e. [2:14] 1 Cor 10:10; 1 Pt 4:9.　f. [2:15] 1 Thes 3:13 / Dt 32:5; Mt 10:16; Acts 2:40 / Dn 12:3; Mt 5:14, 16; Eph 5:8.　g. [2:16] 1 Thes 2:19 / Is 49:4; 65:23; Gal 2:2.　h. [2:17] Rom 15:16; 2 Tm 4:6.　i. [2:18] 3:1; 4:4.　j. [2:19] Acts 16:1–3; 17:14–15; 1 Cor 4:17; 16:10.　k. [2:21] 1 Cor 13:5; 2 Tm 4:10.　l. [2:25] 4:10–11, 15–16, 18.

m. [2:29] 1 Cor 16:18.　n. [3:1] 2:18; 4:4.　o. [3:2] Ps 22:17, 21; Rev 22:15 / 2 Cor 11:13 / Gal 5:6, 12.　p. [3:3] Rom 2:28–29; Col 2:11.　q. [3:4] 2 Cor 11:18, 21–23.

[5]Circumcised on the eighth day,* of the race of Israel, of the tribe of Benjamin, a Hebrew of Hebrew parentage, in observance of the law a Pharisee,[r] [6]in zeal I persecuted the church, in righteousness based on the law I was blameless.[s] **Righteousness from God.** [7][But] whatever gains I had, these I have come to consider a loss[t] because of Christ.[t] [8]More than that, I even consider everything as a loss because of the supreme good of knowing Christ Jesus my Lord. For his sake I have accepted the loss of all things and I consider them so much rubbish, that I may gain Christ [9]and be found in him, not having any righteousness of my own based on the law but that which comes through faith in Christ,[u] the righteousness from God, depending on faith [10]to know him and the power of his resurrection and [the] sharing of his sufferings by being conformed to his death,[v] [11]if somehow I may attain the resurrection from the dead.[w] **Forward in Christ.**[‡] [12x]It is not that I have already taken hold of it or have already attained perfect maturity,[§] but I continue my pursuit in hope that I may possess it, since I have indeed been taken possession of by Christ [Jesus]. [13]Brothers, I for my part do not consider myself to have taken possession. Just one thing: forgetting what lies behind but straining forward to what lies ahead, [14]I continue my pursuit toward the goal, the prize of God's upward calling, in Christ Jesus.[y] [15]Let us, then, who are "perfectly mature" adopt this attitude. And if you have a different attitude, this too God will reveal to you. [16]Only, with regard to what we have attained, continue on the same course.[§] **Wrong Conduct and Our Goal.**[**] [17]Join with others in being imitators of me,[††] brothers, and observe those who thus conduct themselves according to the model you have in us.[z] [18]For

many, as I have often told you and now tell you even in tears, conduct themselves as enemies of the cross of Christ.[a] [19]Their end is destruction. Their God is their stomach; their glory is in their "shame." Their minds are occupied with earthly things.[b] [20]But our citizenship[‡‡] is in heaven, and from it we also await a savior, the Lord Jesus Christ.[c] [21]He will change our lowly body to conform with his glorified body by the power that enables him also to bring all things into subjection to himself.[d]

VI. INSTRUCTIONS FOR THE COMMUNITY[§§]

CHAPTER 4

Live in Concord. [1]Therefore, my brothers, whom I love and long for, my joy and crown, in this way stand firm in the Lord, beloved.[e]

[2]I urge Euodia and I urge Syntyche[¶¶] to come to a mutual understanding in the Lord. [3]Yes, and I ask you also, my true yokemate,[***] to help them, for they have struggled at my side in promoting the gospel, along with Clement and my other co-workers, whose names are in the book of life.[f] **Joy and Peace.** [4]Rejoice[†††] in the Lord always. I shall say it again: rejoice![g] [5]Your kindness[‡‡‡] should be known to all. The Lord is near.[h] [6]Have no anxiety at all, but in everything, by prayer and petition, with thanksgiving, make your requests known to God.[i] [7]Then the peace of God that surpasses all understanding will guard your hearts and minds in Christ Jesus.[j]

[8k]Finally, brothers, whatever is true, whatever is honorable, whatever is just, whatever is pure, whatever is lovely, whatever is gracious, if there is any excellence and if there is anything worthy of praise, think about these things.[§§§]

---

*[3:5] **Circumcised on the eighth day**: as the law required (Gn 17:12; Lv 12:3).

†[3:7] **Loss**: his knowledge of Christ led Paul to reassess the ways of truly pleasing and serving God. His reevaluation indicates the profound and lasting effect of his experience of the meaning of Christ on the way to Damascus some twenty years before (Gal 1:15–16; Acts 9:1–22).

‡[3:12–16] To be **taken possession of by Christ** does not mean that one has already arrived at perfect spiritual maturity. Paul and the Philippians instead press on, trusting in God.

§[3:12] **Attained perfect maturity**: possibly an echo of the concept in the mystery religions of being an initiate, admitted to divine secrets.

¶[3:16] Some manuscripts add, probably to explain Paul's cryptic phrase, "thinking alike."

**[3:17–21] Paul and those who live a life centered in Christ, envisaging both his suffering and resurrection, provide a model that is the opposite of opponents who reject Christ's cross (cf. 1 Cor 1:23).

††[3:17] **Being imitators of me**: not arrogance, but humble simplicity, since all his converts know that Paul is wholly dedicated to imitating Christ (1 Cor 11:1; cf. also Phil 4:9; 1 Thes 1:6; 2 Thes 3:7, 9; 1 Cor 4:6).

‡‡[3:20] **Citizenship**: Christians constitute a colony of heaven, as Philippi was a *colonia* of Rome (Acts 16:12). The hope Paul expresses involves the final coming of Christ, not a status already attained, such as the opponents claim.

§§[4:1–9] This series of ethical admonitions rests especially on the view of Christ and his coming (cf. Phil 4:5) in Phil 3:20–21. Paul's instructions touch on unity within the congregation, joy, prayer, and the Christian outlook on life.

¶¶[4:2] **Euodia . . . Syntyche**: two otherwise unknown women in the Philippian congregation; on the advice to them, cf. Phil 2:2–4.

***[4:3] **Yokemate**: or "comrade," although the Greek *syzygos* could also be a proper name. **Clement**: otherwise unknown, although later writers sought to identify him with Clement, bishop of Rome (Eusebius, *Ecclesiastical History* 3.15.1).

†††[4:4] **Rejoice**: see note on Phil 3:1.

‡‡‡[4:5] **Kindness**: considerateness, forbearance, fairness. **The Lord is near**: most likely a reference to Christ's parousia (Phil 1:6, 10; 3:20–21; 1 Cor 16:22), although some sense an echo of Ps 119:151 and the perpetual presence of the Lord.

§§§[4:8] The language employs terms from Roman Stoic thought.

a. [3:18] 1 Cor 1:17, 23; Gal 6:12.   b. [3:19] Rom 8:5–6; 16:18.
c. [3:20] Eph 2:6, 19; Col 3:1–3; Heb 12:22.   d. [3:21] Rom 8:23, 29;
1 Cor 15:42–57; 2 Cor 3:18; 5:1–5 / 1 Cor 15:27–28.   e. [4:1] 1 Thes
2:19–20.   f. [4:3] Ex 32:32–33; Ps 69:29; Dn 12:1; Lk 10:20; Rev 3:5;
13:8; 17:8; 20:12, 15; 21:27.   g. [4:4] 2:18; 3:1.   h. [4:5] Ti 3:2 / Ps
145:18; Heb 10:37; Jas 5:8–9.   i. [4:6] Mt 6:25–34; 1 Pt 5:7 / Col
4:2.   j. [4:7] Jn 14:27; Col 3:15.   k. [4:8] Rom 12:17.

r. [3:5] Lk 1:59; 2:21 / Acts 22:3; 23:6; 26:5.   s. [3:6] Acts 8:3; 22:4;
26:9–11.   t. [3:7] Mt 13:44, 46; Lk 14:33.   u. [3:9] Rom 3:21–
22.   v. [3:10] Rom 6:3–5; 8:17; Gal 6:17.   w. [3:11] Jn 11:23–26;
Acts 4:2; Rev 20:5–6.   x. [3:12] 1 Tm 6:12, 19.   y. [3:14] 1 Cor
9:24–25; 2 Tm 4:7.   z. [3:17] 1 Cor 4:16; 11:1; 1 Thes 1:7; 1 Pt 5:3.

⁹Keep on doing what you have learned and received and heard and seen in me.ˡ Then the God of peace will be with you.ˑ

VII. GRATITUDE FOR THE PHILIPPIANS' GENEROSITY†

¹⁰I rejoice greatly in the Lord that now at last you revived your concern for me. You were, of course, concerned about me but lacked an opportunity.ᵐ ¹¹Not that I say this because of need, for I have learned, in whatever situation I find myself, to be self-sufficient.ⁿ ¹²I know indeed how to live in humble circumstances; I know also how to live with abundance. In every circumstance and in all things I have learned the secret of being well fed and of going hungry, of living in abundance and of being in need. ¹³I have the strength for everything through him who empowers me.º ¹⁴Still, it was kind of you to share in my distress.

---

*[4:9] Cf. note on Phil 3:17.

†[4:10–20] Paul, more directly than anywhere else in the letter (cf. Phil 1:3–5), here thanks the Philippians for their gift of money sent through Epaphroditus (Phil 2:25). Paul's own policy was to be self-sufficient as a missionary, supporting himself by his own labor (1 Thes 2:5–9; 1 Cor 9:15–18; cf. Acts 18:2–3). In spite of this reliance on self and on God to provide (Phil 4:11–13) Paul accepted gifts from the Philippians not only once but more than once (Phil 4:16) when he was in Thessalonica (Acts 17:1–9), as he does now, in prison (my distress, Phil 4:14). While commercial terms appear in the passage, like an account of giving and receiving (Phil 4:15) and received full payment (Phil 4:18), Paul is most concerned about the spiritual growth of the Philippians (Phil 4:10, 17, 19); he emphasizes that God will care for their needs, through Christ.

l. [4:9] 1 Thes 4:1 / Rom 15:33; 16:20; 1 Cor 14:33; 1 Thes 5:23. m. [4:10] 1:18; 2:25; 1 Cor 9:11; 2 Cor 11:9. n. [4:11–12] 1 Cor 4:11; 2 Cor 6:10; 11:27 / 2 Cor 12:9–10. o. [4:13] Col 1:29; 2 Tm 4:17.

---

¹⁵You Philippians indeed know that at the beginning of the gospel,‡ when I left Macedonia, not a single church shared with me in an account of giving and receiving, except you alone. ¹⁶For even when I was at Thessalonica you sent me something for my needs, not only once but more than once. ¹⁷It is not that I am eager for the gift; rather, I am eager for the profit that accrues to your account. ¹⁸I have received full payment and I abound. I am very well supplied because of what I received from you through Epaphroditus, "a fragrant aroma," an acceptable sacrifice,§ pleasing to God.ᵖ ¹⁹My God will fully supply whatever you need, in accord with his glorious riches in Christ Jesus.�q ²⁰To our God and Father, glory forever and ever. Amen.ʳ

VIII. FAREWELL⁵

²¹Give my greetings to every holy one in Christ Jesus. The brothers who are with me send you their greetings; ²²all the holy ones send you their greetings, especially those of Caesar's household.** ²³The grace of the Lord Jesus Christ be with your spirit.

---

‡[4:15] The beginning of the gospel: it was at Philippi that Paul first preached Christ in Europe, going on from there to Thessalonica and Beroea (Acts 16:9–17:14).

§[4:18] Aroma . . . sacrifice: Old Testament cultic language (cf. Gn 8:21; Ex 29:18, 25, 41; Lv 1:9, 13; Ez 20:41) applied to the Philippians' gift; cf. Eph 5:2; 2 Cor 2:14–16.

⁵[4:21–23] On the usual greetings at the conclusion of a letter, see note on 1 Cor 16:19–24. Inclusion of greetings from all the holy ones in the place from which Paul writes would involve even the Christians of Phil 1:14–18 who had their differences with Paul.

**[4:22] Those of Caesar's household: minor officials or even slaves and freedmen, found in Ephesus or Rome, among other places.

p. [4:18] Gn 8:21; Ex 29:18; Eph 5:2; Heb 13:16.   q. [4:19] 1 Thes 3:11, 13.   r. [4:20] Rom 16:27; Eph 5:20.   s. [4:22] 1:13.

THE LETTER TO THE
COLOSSIANS

This letter is addressed to a congregation at Colossae in the Lycus Valley in Asia Minor, east of Ephesus. At the time of writing, Paul had not visited there, the letter says (Col 1:4; 2:1). The community had apparently been established by Epaphras of Colossae (Col 1:7; 4:12; Phlm 23). Problems, however, had arisen, brought on by teachers who emphasized Christ's relation to the universe (cosmos). Their teachings stressed angels (Col 2:18; "principalities and powers," Col 2:15), which were connected with astral powers and cultic practices (see note on Col 2:16) and rules about food and drink and ascetical disciplines (Col 2:16, 18). These teachings, Paul insists, detract from the person and work of Christ for salvation as set forth magnificently in a hymnic passage at Col 1:15–20 and reiterated throughout the letter. Such teachings are but "shadows"; Christ is "reality" (Col 2:17).

For help in dealing with these problems that the new teachers posed at Colossae, Epaphras sought out Paul, who was then imprisoned (Col 4:10, 18) at a place that the letter does not mention. Paul, without entering into debate over the existence of angelic spirits or their function, simply affirms that Christ possesses the sum total of redemptive power (Col 1:19) and that the spiritual renewal of the human person occurs through contact in baptism with the person of Christ, who died and rose again (Col 2:9–14). It is unnecessary for the Christian to be concerned about placating spirits (Col 2:15) or avoiding imagined defilement through ascetical practices in regard to food and drink (Col 2:20–23). True Christian asceticism consists in the conquering of personal sins (Col 3:5–10) and the practice of love of neighbor in accordance with the standard set by Christ (Col 3:12–16).

Paul commends the community as a whole (Col 1:3–8); this seems to indicate that, though the Colossians have been under pressure to adopt the false doctrines, they have not yet succumbed. The apostle expresses his prayerful concern for them (Col 1:9–14). His preaching has cost him persecution, suffering, and imprisonment, but he regards these as reflective of the sufferings of Christ, a required discipline for the sake of the gospel (see note on 1:24; cf. 1:29; 2:1). His instructions to the Christian family and to slaves and masters require a new spirit of reflection and action. Love, obedience, and service are to be rendered "in the Lord" (Col 3:18–4:1).

Colossians follows the outline of a typical Pauline letter. It is distinguished by the poetic lines in Col 1:15–20 concerning who Christ is and what Christ means in creation and redemption. This hymn may be compared with similar passages in Phil 2:6–11; 1 Tm 3:16; and Jn 1:1–18. It was apparently familiar liturgical material to the author, the audience, and the false teachers. In Col 1:21–2:7, however, Paul interprets the relation between the body of Christ, which he insists is the church (Col 1:18), and the world or cosmos to be one not simply of Christ's preexistence and rule but one of missionary advance into the world by the spreading of the word (Col 1:25, 28). In this labor of the missionary body of Christ, Paul as a minister plays a prime part in bringing Christ and the gospel as hope to the Gentiles (Col 1:23, 25, 27). To "every creature under heaven" the word is to be proclaimed, so that everyone receives Christ, is established in faith, and walks in Christ (Col 1:28; 2:6, 7).

Paul wrote the Letter to the Colossians while in prison, but his several imprisonments leave the specific place and date of composition uncertain. On this point the same problem exists as with Ephesians and Philippians (see the Introductions to these letters). Traditionally the house arrest at Rome, in which Paul enjoyed a certain restricted freedom in preaching (see Acts 28:16–28), or a second Roman imprisonment has been claimed as the setting. Others suggest a still earlier imprisonment at Caesarea (see Acts 23:12–27:1) or in Ephesus (see Acts 19). Still others regard the letter as the work of some pupil or follower of Paul, writing in his name. In any case, the contents are often closely paralleled by thoughts in Ephesians.

The principal divisions of the Letter to the Colossians are the following:

I. Address (1:1–14)
II. The Preeminence of Christ (1:15–2:3)
III. Warnings Against False Teachers (2:4–23)
IV. The Ideal Christian Life in the World (3:1–4:6)
V. Conclusion (4:7–18)

I. ADDRESS

CHAPTER 1

Greeting.* ¹Paul, an apostle of Christ Jesus by the will of God, and Timothy our brother,ᵃ ²to the holy ones and faithful brothers in Christ in Colossae: grace to you and peace from God our Father.
Thanksgiving.† ³We always give thanks to God, the Father of our Lord Jesus Christ, when we pray for you,ᵇ ⁴for we have heard of your faith in Christ Jesus and the love that you have for all the holy ones ⁵because of the hope reserved for you in heaven. Of this you have already heard through the word of truth, the gospel,ᶜ ⁶that has come to you. Just as in the whole world it is bearing fruit and growing, so also among you, from the day you heard it and came to know the grace of God in truth, ⁷ᵈas you learned it from Epaphras‡ our beloved fellow slave, who is a trustworthy minister of Christ on your behalf ⁸and who also told us of your love in the Spirit.
Prayer for Continued Progress.§ ⁹Therefore, from the day we heard this, we do not cease praying for you and asking that you may be filled with the knowledge of his will through all spiritual wisdom and understandingᵉ ¹⁰to live in a manner worthy of the Lord, so as to be fully pleasing, in every good work bearing fruit and growing in the knowledge of God, ¹¹strengthened with every power, in accord with his glorious might, for all endurance and patience, with joy ¹²⁵giving thanks to the Father, who has made you fit to share in the inheritance of the holy ones in light.ᶠ ¹³He delivered us from the power of darkness and transferred us to the kingdom of his beloved Son, ¹⁴in whom we have redemption, the forgiveness of sins.ᵍ

II. THE PREEMINENCE OF CHRIST

His Person and Work

15 "He is the image†† of the invisible God,
    the firstborn of all creation.ʰ
16 For in him‡‡ were created all things
    heaven and on earth,
    the visible and the invisible,
    whether thrones or dominions or
    principalities or powers;

---

*[1:1–2] For the epistolary form used by Paul at the beginning of his letters, see note on Rom 1:1–7. On **holy ones** or "God's people," see note on Rom 1:7. Awareness of their calling helps this group to be **faithful brothers** and sisters in Christ, i.e., dedicated to the tasks implied in their calling.

†[1:3–8] On thanksgiving at the start of a letter, see note on Rom 1:8. The apostle, recalling his own prayers for them and the good report about them he has received (Col 1:3–4), congratulates the Colossians upon their acceptance of Christ and their faithful efforts to live the gospel (Col 3:6–8). To encourage them he mentions the success of the gospel elsewhere (Col 1:6) and assures them that his knowledge of their community is accurate, since he has been in personal contact with Epaphras (Col 1:7–8), who likely had evangelized Colossae and other cities in the Lycus Valley of Asia Minor (cf. Col 4:12, 13; Phlm 23). On **faith, love,** and **hope** (Col 1:4, 5, 8), see note on 1 Cor 13:13; cf. 1 Thes 1:3; 5:8.

‡[1:7] **Epaphras:** now with Paul but a Colossian, founder of the church there.

§[1:9–14] Moved by Epaphras' account, the apostle has prayed and continues to pray fervently for the Colossians that, in their response to the gospel, they **may be filled with the knowledge of** God's **will** (Col 1:9; cf. Col 3:10). Paul expects a mutual interaction between their life according to the gospel and this knowledge (Col 1:10), yielding results (**fruit,** Col 1:10; cf. Col 1:6) **in every good work:** growth, strength, **endurance, patience, with joy** (Col 1:11), and the further giving of thanks (Col 1:12).

¶[1:12–14] A summary about **redemption** by **the Father** precedes the statement in Col 1:15–20 about the **beloved Son** who is God's love in person (Col 1:13). Christians share **the inheritance . . . in light** with **the holy ones,** here probably the angels (Col 1:12). The imagery reflects the Exodus (**delivered . . . transferred**) and Jesus' theme of the **kingdom.** Redemption is explained as **forgiveness of sins** (cf. Acts 2:38; Rom 3:24–25; Eph 1:7).

[1:15–20] As the poetic arrangement indicates, these lines are probably an early Christian hymn, known to the Colossians and taken up into the letter from liturgical use (cf. Phil 2:6–11; 1 Tm 3:16). They present Christ as the mediator of creation (Col 1:15–18a) and of redemption (Col 1:18b–20). There is a parallelism between **firstborn of all creation (Col 1:15) and **firstborn from the dead** (Col 1:18). While many of the phrases were at home in Greek philosophical use and even in gnosticism, the basic ideas also reflect Old Testament themes about Wisdom found in Prv 8:22–31; Wis 7:22–8:1; and Sir 1:4. See also notes on what is possibly a hymn in Jn 1:1–18.

††[1:15] **Image:** cf. Gn 1:27. Whereas the man and the woman were originally created in the image and likeness of God (see also Gn 1:26), Christ as image (2 Cor 4:4) of **the invisible God** (Jn 1:18) now shares this new nature in baptism with those redeemed (cf. Col 3:10–11).

‡‡[1:16–17] Christ (though not mentioned by name) is preeminent and supreme as God's agent in the creation of **all things** (cf. Jn 1:3), as prior to **all things** (Col 1:17; cf. Heb 1:3).

---

a. [1:1] Eph 1:1. b. [1:3] Eph 1:15–16; Phlm 4–5. c. [1:5] Eph 1:13, 18; 1 Pt 1:4. d. [1:7] Phlm 23.

e. [1:9] Eph 1:15–17; 5:17; Phil 1:9. f. [1:12] 3:17; Jn 8:12; Acts 26:18; 1 Tm 6:16; 1 Pt 2:9. g. [1:14] Eph 1:7. h. [1:15] Ps 89:28; Jn 1:3, 18; 2 Cor 4:4.

all things were created through him
and for him.[i]

[17] He is before all things,
and in him all things hold together.

[18] He is the head of the body, the church.[*]
He is the beginning, the firstborn from
the dead,
that in all things he himself might be
preeminent.[j]

[19] For in him all the fullness[†] was pleased to
dwell,

[20]   and through him to reconcile all
things for him,
making peace by the blood of his
cross[‡]
[through him], whether those on
earth or those in heaven.[k]

[21§]And you who once were alienated and hostile in mind because of evil deeds[l] [22]he has now reconciled in his fleshly body through his death, to present you holy, without blemish, and irreproachable before him, [23]provided that you persevere in the faith, firmly grounded, stable, and not shifting from the hope of the gospel that you heard, which has been preached to every creature under heaven, of which I, Paul, am a minister. **Christ in Us.[¶]** [24]Now I rejoice in my sufferings for your sake, and in my flesh I am filling

up what is lacking[**] in the afflictions of Christ on behalf of his body, which is the church, [25]of which I am a minister in accordance with God's stewardship given to me to bring to completion for you the word of God, [26]the mystery hidden from ages and from generations past. But now it has been manifested to his holy ones,[m] [27]to whom God chose to make known the riches of the glory of this mystery among the Gentiles; it is Christ in you, the hope for glory.[n] [28]It is he whom we proclaim, admonishing everyone and teaching everyone with all wisdom, that we may present everyone perfect in Christ.[o] [29]For this I labor and struggle, in accord with the exercise of his power working within me.[p]

CHAPTER 2

[1]For I want you to know how great a struggle I am having for you and for those in Laodicea[††] and all who have not seen me face to face, [2]that their hearts may be encouraged as they are brought together in love, to have all the richness of fully assured understanding, for the knowledge of the mystery of God, Christ,[q] [3]in whom are hidden all the treasures of wisdom and knowledge.[r]

III. WARNINGS AGAINST FALSE TEACHERS[‡‡]

*[1:18] **Church**: such a reference seemingly belongs under "redemption" in the following lines, not under the "creation" section of the hymn. Stoic thought sometimes referred to the world as "the body of Zeus." Pauline usage is to speak of the church as the body of Christ (1 Cor 12:12–27; Rom 12:4–5). Some think that the author of Colossians has inserted the reference to the church here so as to define "head of the body" in Paul's customary way. See Col 1:24. **Preeminent**: when Christ was raised by God as **firstborn from the dead** (cf. Acts 26:23; Rev 1:5), he was placed over the community, the church, that he had brought into being, but he is also indicated as crown of the whole new creation, over **all things**. His further role is to **reconcile all things** (Col 1:20) for God or possibly "to himself."

†[1:19] **Fullness**: in gnostic usage this term referred to a spiritual world of beings above, between God and the world; many later interpreters take it to refer to **the fullness of the deity** (Col 2:9); the reference could also be to the fullness of grace (cf. Jn 1:16).

‡[1:20] **The blood of his cross**: the most specific reference in the hymn to redemption through Christ's death, a central theme in Paul; cf. Col 2:14–15; 1 Cor 1:17, 18, 23. [**Through him**]: the phrase, lacking in some manuscripts, seems superfluous but parallels the reference to reconciliation through Christ earlier in the verse.

§[1:21–23] Paul, in applying this hymn to the Colossians, reminds them that they have experienced the reconciling effect of Christ's death. He sees the effects of the cross in the redemption of human beings, not of cosmic powers such as those referred to in Col 1:16, 20 (**all things**). Paul also urges adherence to Christ in faith and begins to point to his own role as minister (Col 1:23), sufferer (Col 1:24), and proclaimer (Col 1:27–28) of this gospel.

¶[1:24–2:3] As the community at Colossae was not personally known to Paul (see Introduction), he here invests his teaching with greater authority by presenting a brief sketch of his apostolic ministry and sufferings as they reflect those of Christ on behalf of the church (Col 1:24). The preaching of God's word (Col 1:25) carries out the divine plan (**the mystery**, Col 1:26) to make Christ known to the Gentiles (Col

1:27). It teaches the God-given wisdom about Christ (Col 1:28), whose power works mightily in the apostle (Col 1:29). Even in those communities that do not know him personally (Col 2:1), he can increase the perception of God in Christ, unite the faithful more firmly in love, and so bring encouragement to them (Col 2:2). He hopes that his apostolic authority will make the Colossians perceive more readily the defects in the teaching of others who have sought to delude them, the next concern in the letter.

[1:24] **What is lacking: although variously interpreted, this phrase does not imply that Christ's atoning death on the cross was defective. It may refer to the apocalyptic concept of a quota of "messianic woes" to be endured before the end comes; cf. Mk 13:8, 19–20, 24 and the note on Mt 23:29–32. Others suggest that Paul's mystical unity with Christ allowed him to call his own **sufferings the afflictions of Christ**.

††[2:1] **Laodicea**: chief city in Phrygia, northwest of Colossae; cf. Col 4:13, 16; Rev 3:14–22.

‡‡[2:4–23] In face of the threat posed by false teachers (Col 2:4), the Colossians are admonished to adhere to the gospel as it was first preached to them (Col 2:6), steeping themselves in it with grateful hearts (Col 2:7). They must reject religious teachings originating in any source except the gospel (Col 2:8) because in Christ alone will they have access to God, **the deity** (Col 2:9). So fully has Christ enlightened them that they need no other source of religious knowledge or virtue (Col 2:10). They do not require **circumcision** (Col 2:11), for **in baptism** their whole being has been affected by Christ (Col 2:12) through forgiveness of sin and resurrection to a new life (Col 2:13; cf. Col 3:1 and Rom 6:1–11).

On the cross Christ canceled the record of the debt that stood against us with all its claims (Col 2:14), i.e., he eliminated the law (cf. Eph 2:15) that human beings could not observe—and that could not save them. He forgave sins against the law (Col 2:14) and exposed as false and misleading (Col 2:15) all other powers (cf. Col 1:16) that purport to offer salvation. Therefore, the Colossians are not to accept judgments from such teachers on **food and drink** or to keep certain religious festivals or engage in certain cultic practices (Col 2:16), for the Colossians would thereby risk severing themselves from

i. [1:16] 1 Cor 8:6; Eph 1:10, 21.   j. [1:18] 1 Cor 11:3; 12:12, 27; 15:20; Eph 1:22–23; Rev 1:5.   k. [1:20] 2 Cor 5:18–19; Eph 1:10.   l. [1:21] Eph 2:14–16.

m. [1:26] Rom 16:25–26; 1 Cor 2:7; Eph 3:3,9.   n. [1:27] 3:4; Rom 8:10.   o. [1:28] Eph 4:13.   p. [1:29] 2:1; 4:12; Phil 4:13.   q. [2:2] 1:26–27; Eph 3:18–19.   r. [2:3] Prv 2:4–5; Is 45:3; Rom 11:33; 1 Cor 1:30.

A General Admonition. [4]I say this so that no one may deceive you by specious arguments.[s] [5]For even if I am absent in the flesh, yet I am with you in spirit, rejoicing as I observe your good order and the firmness of your faith in Christ.[t] [6]So, as you received Christ Jesus the Lord, walk in him, [7]rooted in him and built upon him and established in the faith as you were taught, abounding in thanksgiving.[u] [8]See to it that no one captivate you with an empty, seductive philosophy according to human tradition, according to the elemental powers of the world[*] and not according to Christ.[v]

Sovereign Role of Christ. [9*]For in him dwells the whole fullness of the deity[†] bodily, [10]and you share in this fullness in him, who is the head of every principality and power. [11x]In him[‡] you were also circumcised with a circumcision not administered by hand, by stripping off the carnal body, with the circumcision of Christ. [12]You were buried with him in baptism, in which you were also raised with him through faith in the power of God, who raised him from the dead.[y] [13z]And even when you were dead [in] transgressions and the uncircumcision of your flesh, he brought you to life along with him, having forgiven us all our transgressions; [14§]obliterating the bond against us, with its legal claims, which was opposed to us, he also removed it from our midst, nailing it to the cross;[a] [15]despoiling the principalities and the powers, he made a public spectacle of them,[b] leading them away in triumph by it.[¶]

Practices Contrary to Faith. [16c]Let no one, then, pass judgment on you in matters of food and drink or with regard to a festival or new moon or sabbath.[**] [17]These are shadows of things to come; the reality belongs to Christ.[d] [18]Let no one disqualify you, delighting in self-abasement

and worship of angels, taking his stand on visions,[††] inflated without reason by his fleshly mind,[e] [19]and not holding closely to the head, from whom the whole body, supported and held together by its ligaments and bonds, achieves the growth that comes from God.[f]

[20]If you died with Christ to the elemental powers of the world, why do you submit to regulations as if you were still living in the world? [21]"Do not handle! Do not taste! Do not touch!" [22]These are all things destined to perish with use; they accord with human precepts and teachings.[g] [23]While they have a semblance of wisdom in rigor of devotion and self-abasement [and] severity to the body, they are of no value against gratification of the flesh.

IV. THE IDEAL CHRISTIAN LIFE IN THE WORLD

CHAPTER 3

Mystical Death and Resurrection.[‡‡] [1]If then you were raised with Christ, seek what is above, where Christ is seated at the right hand of God.[h] [2]Think of what is above, not of what is on earth. [3]For you have died, and your life is hidden with Christ in God.[i] [4]When Christ your life appears, then you too will appear with him in glory.

Renunciation of Vice.[§§] [5]Put to death, then, the parts of you that are earthly:[j] immorality, impurity, passion, evil desire, and the greed that is idolatry.[¶¶] [6]Because of these the wrath of God[***] is coming [upon the disobedient].[k] [7]By these you too once conducted yourselves, when you lived in that way. [8]But now you must put them all away:[†††] anger, fury, malice, slander, and obscene language out of your mouths.[l] [9]Stop lying to one another, since you have taken off the old self with its practices[m] [10‡‡‡]and have put on the new

---

Christ (Col 2:19). If, when they accepted the gospel, they believed in Christ as their savior, they must be convinced that their salvation cannot be achieved by appeasing ruling spirits through dietary practices or through a wisdom gained simply by means of harsh asceticism (Col 2:20–23).

*[2:8] **Elemental powers of the world**: see note on Gal 4:3.

†[2:9] **Fullness of the deity**: the divine nature, not just attributes; see note on Col 1:19.

‡[2:11] A description of baptism (Col 2:12) in symbolic terms of the Old Testament rite for entry into the community. The false teachers may have demanded physical circumcision of the Colossians.

§[2:14] The elaborate metaphor here about how God canceled the legal claims against us through Christ's cross depicts not Christ being nailed to the cross by men but the **bond . . . with its legal claims** being nailed to the cross by God.

¶[2:15] The picture derives from the **public spectacle** and **triumph** of a Roman emperor's victory parade, where captives marched in subjection. The **principalities and the powers** are here conquered, not reconciled (cf. Col 1:16, 20). An alternate rendering for **by it** (the cross) is "by him" (Christ).

[2:16] **Festival or new moon or sabbath: yearly, monthly, and weekly observances determined by religious powers associated with a calendar set by the heavenly bodies, sun, moon, and stars (cf. Col 2:8).

††[2:18] Ascetic practices encouraged by the false teachers included subjection of self humbly to their rules, worship of angels, and cultivation of visions, though exact details are unclear.

‡‡[3:1–4] By retaining the message of the gospel that the risen, living Christ is the source of their salvation, the Colossians will be free from false religious evaluations of the things of the world (Col 3:1–2). They have died to these; but one day when Christ . . . appears, they will live with Christ in the presence of God (Col 3:3–4).

§§[3:5–17] In lieu of false asceticism and superstitious festivals, the apostle reminds the Colossians of the moral life that is to characterize their response to God through Christ. He urges their participation in the liturgical hymns and prayers that center upon God's plan of salvation in Christ (Col 3:16).

¶¶[3:5, 8] The two lists of five vices each are similar to enumerations at Rom 1:29–31 and Gal 5:19–21.

***[3:6] **The wrath of God**: see note on Rom 1:18. Many manuscripts add, as at Eph 5:6, "upon the disobedient."

†††[3:8–10] Put . . . away; have taken off; have put on: the terms may reflect baptismal practice, taking off garments and putting on new ones after being united with Christ, here translated into ethical terms.

‡‡‡[3:10] **Image**: see note on Col 1:15.

---

s. [2:4] Eph 4:14.   t. [2:5] 1 Cor 5:3; Phil 1:27.   u. [2:7] Eph 2:20–22; 3:17.   v. [2:8] Gal 4:3; Eph 5:6.   w. [2:9] 1:19; Eph 3:19.   x. [2:11] 1:22; Jer 4:4; Rom 2:25–29; Phil 3:3.   y. [2:12] Rom 6:3–4.   z. [2:13] Eph 2:1, 5.   a. [2:14] Eph 2:14–15.   b. [2:15] 1:16, 20; 2 Cor 2:14; Eph 1:21.   c. [2:16] Rom 14:3–4; 1 Tm 4:3.   d. [2:17] Heb 8:5; 10:1.

e. [2:18] 2:23; Mt 24:4.   f. [2:19] Eph 2:21–22; 4:16.   g. [2:22] Is 29:13.   h. [3:1] 2:12; Ps 110:1; Phil 3:20; Eph 2:6.   i. [3:3] Rom 6:2–5.   j. [3:5] Mt 15:19; Rom 1:29–30; Gal 5:19–21; Eph 5:3, 5.   k. [3:6] Rom 1:18.   l. [3:8] Eph 4:22, 25, 31.   m. [3:9] Rom 6:4, 6; Eph 4:22–25; Heb 12:1; 1 Pt 2:1; 4:2.

self, which is being renewed, for knowledge, in the image of its creator." [11]Here there is not Greek and Jew, circumcision and uncircumcision, barbarian, Scythian,* slave, free; but Christ is all and in all.[o]

[12]Put on then, as God's chosen ones, holy and beloved, heartfelt compassion, kindness, humility, gentleness, and patience,[p] [13]bearing with one another and forgiving one another, if one has a grievance against another; as the Lord has forgiven you, so must you also do.[q] [14]And over all these put on love, that is, the bond of perfection.[r] [15]And let the peace of Christ control your hearts, the peace into which you were also called in one body. And be thankful.[s] [16]Let the word of Christ dwell in you richly, as in all wisdom you teach and admonish one another, singing psalms, hymns, and spiritual songs with gratitude in your hearts to God.[t] [17]And whatever you do, in word or in deed, do everything in the name of the Lord Jesus, giving thanks to God the Father through him.[u]

The Christian Family. [18†]Wives, be subordinate to your husbands, as is proper in the Lord.[v] [19]Husbands, love your wives, and avoid any bitterness toward them. [20]Children, obey your parents in everything, for this is pleasing to the Lord.[w] [21]Fathers, do not provoke your children, so they may not become discouraged.[x]

Slaves and Masters. [22]Slaves,‡ obey your human masters in everything, not only when being watched, as currying favor, but in simplicity of heart, fearing the Lord.[y] [23]Whatever you do, do from the heart, as for the Lord and not for others, [24]knowing that you will receive from the Lord the due payment of the inheritance; be slaves of the Lord Christ. [25]For the wrongdoer will receive recompense for the wrong he committed, and there is no partiality.[z]

CHAPTER 4

[1]Masters, treat your slaves justly and fairly, realizing that you too have a Master in heaven.

Prayer and Apostolic Spirit. [2]Persevere in prayer, being watchful in it with thanksgiving;[a] [3]at the same time, pray for us, too, that God may open a door to us for the word, to speak of the mystery of Christ, for which I am in prison,[b] [4]that I may make it clear, as I must speak. [5]Conduct yourselves wisely toward outsiders, making the most of the opportunity.[c] [6]Let your speech always be gracious, seasoned with salt, so that you know how you should respond to each one.

V. CONCLUSION[§]

Tychicus and Onesimus. [7]Tychicus,¶ my beloved brother, trustworthy minister, and fellow slave in the Lord, will tell you all the news of me.[d] [8]I am sending him to you for this very purpose, so that you may know about us and that he may encourage your hearts, [9]together with Onesimus, a trustworthy and beloved brother, who is one of you. They will tell you about everything here.[e]

From Paul's Co-Workers. [10]Aristarchus,** my fellow prisoner, sends you greetings, as does Mark the cousin of Barnabas (concerning whom you have received instructions; if he comes to you, receive him),[f] [11]and Jesus,†† who is called Justus, who are of the circumcision; these alone are my co-workers for the kingdom of God, and they have been a comfort to me. [12]Epaphras‡‡ sends you greetings; he is one of you, a slave of Christ [Jesus], always striving for you in his prayers so that you may be perfect and fully assured in all the will of God.[g] [13]For I can testify that he works very hard for you and for those in Laodicea[§§] and those in Hierapolis. [14]Luke¶¶ the beloved physician sends greetings, as does Demas.[h]

A Message for the Laodiceans. [15]Give greetings to the brothers in Laodicea and to Nympha and to the church in her house.*** [16]And when this

---

§[4:7–18] Paul concludes with greetings and information concerning various Christians known to the Colossians.

¶[4:7] **Tychicus:** Acts 20:4 mentions his role in the collection for Jerusalem; Eph 6:21 repeats what is said here; see also 2 Tm 4:12; Ti 3:12.

[4:10] **Aristarchus: a Thessalonian who was with Paul at Ephesus and Caesarea and on the voyage to Rome (Acts 19:29; 20:4; 27:2). **Mark:** also referred to at Phlm 24 and 2 Tm 4:11 and, as "John Mark," in Acts (Acts 12:12, 25; 13:13; 15:37–40). See also 1 Pt 5:13 and the note there. Traditionally the author of the second gospel.

††[4:11] **Jesus:** a then common Jewish name, the Greek form of Joshua.

‡‡[4:12] **Epaphras:** see notes on Col 1:3–8 and Col 1:7.

§§[4:13] **Laodicea:** see note on Col 2:1. **Hierapolis:** a city northeast of Laodicea and northwest of Colossae.

¶¶[4:14] **Luke:** only here described as a medical doctor; cf. Phlm 24 and 2 Tm 4:11. Traditionally the author of the third gospel. **Demas:** cf. Phlm 24; he later deserted Paul (2 Tm 4:10).

***[4:15] **Nympha and . . . her house:** some manuscripts read a masculine for the house-church leader, "Nymphas and . . . his house."

---

*[3:11] **Scythian:** a barbarous people from north of the Black Sea.

†[3:18–4:6] After general recommendations that connect family life and the social condition of slavery with the service of Christ (Col 3:18–4:1), Paul requests prayers for himself, especially in view of his imprisonment (Col 3:2–3), and recommends friendly relations and meaningful discussions of Christian teaching with **outsiders**, i.e., non-Christians (Col 3:5–6). See note on Eph 5:21–6:9.

‡[3:22–25] **Slaves:** within this table of duties in family and societal relations, involving wives and husbands, children and parents (Col 3:18–21), such as also appears in Eph 5:22–6:9, slaves here receive special attention because of the case of Onesimus the slave returning to his master (Col 4:9; Phlm 10–12).

---

n. [3:10] Gn 1:26–27.   o. [3:11] 1 Cor 12:13; Gal 3:27–28.   p. [3:12] Eph 4:1–2, 32; 1 Thes 5:15.   q. [3:13] Mt 6:14; 18:21–35; Eph 4:32.   r. [3:14] Rom 13:8–10.   s. [3:15] Rom 12:5; 1 Cor 12:12; Eph 2:16; 4:3–4; Phil 4:7.   t. [3:16] Eph 5:19–20.   u. [3:17] 1 Cor 10:31.   v. [3:18] Eph 5:22; Ti 2:5; 1 Pt 3:1.   w. [3:20] Eph 6:1.   x. [3:21] Eph 6:4.   y. [3:22] Eph 6:5; 1 Tm 6:1; Ti 2:9–10; 1 Pt 2:18.   z. [3:25] Rom 2:11.

a. [4:2] Lk 18:1; Rom 12:12; Eph 6:18–20; 1 Thes 5:17.   b. [4:3] Rom 15:30; 1 Cor 16:9; Eph 6:19; 2 Thes 3:1.   c. [4:5] Eph 5:15–16.   d. [4:7] Acts 20:4; Eph 6:21–22; Phil 1:12.   e. [4:9] Phlm 10–11.   f. [4:10] Acts 19:29; 20:4; 27:2 / Acts 12:12, 25; 13:13; 15:37, 40; 2 Tm 4:11; Phlm 24; 1 Pt 5:13.   g. [4:12] 1:7; Rom 15:30.   h. [4:14] Phlm 24; 2 Tm 4:10–11.

letter is read before you, have it read also in the church of the Laodiceans, and you yourselves read the one from Laodicea.* 17And tell Archippus, "See that you fulfill the ministry† that you received in the Lord."i

18The greeting is in my own hand,‡ Paul's. Remember my chains. Grace be with you.j

---

*[4:16] The one from Laodicea: either a letter by Paul that has been lost or the Letter to the Ephesians (cf. note on Eph 1:1 in Ephesus).

†[4:17] Fulfill the ministry: usually taken to mean that Archippus, the son of Philemon and Apphia (Phlm 1–2),

is "pastor" at Colossae. An alternate interpretation is that Archippus, not Philemon, is the owner of the slave Onesimus and that Paul is asking Archippus to complete the service he has received in the Lord by sending Onesimus back to minister to Paul in his captivity (cf. Phlm 20).

‡[4:18] My own hand: a postscript in Paul's own hand was his custom; cf. Gal 6:11–18 and 2 Thes 3:17–18.

i. [4:17] Phlm 2.

j. [4:18] 1 Cor 16:21; Gal 6:11; Eph 3:1; 2 Thes 3:17.

THE FIRST LETTER TO THE
THESSALONIANS

࿇

When Paul parted from Barnabas (Acts 15:36–41) at the beginning of what is called his second missionary journey, he chose Silvanus (Silas) as his traveling companion. Soon afterwards he took Timothy along with him (Acts 16:1–3). Paul was now clearly at the head of his own missionary band. About A.D. 50, he arrived in Greece for the first time. In making converts in Philippi and, soon afterwards, in Thessalonica, he was beset by persecution from Jews and Gentiles alike. Moving on to Beroea, he was again harassed by enemies from Thessalonica and hurriedly left for Athens (Acts 16:11–17:15). Silvanus and Timothy remained behind for a while. Paul soon sent Timothy back to Thessalonica to strengthen that community in its trials (1 Thes 3:1–5). Timothy and Silvanus finally returned to Paul when he reached Corinth (Acts 18:1–18), probably in the early summer of A.D. 51. Timothy's return with a report on conditions at Thessalonica served as the occasion for Paul's first letter (1 Thes 3:6–8).

The letter begins with a brief address (1 Thes 1:1) and concludes with a greeting (1 Thes 5:26–28). The body of the letter consists of two major parts. The first (1 Thes 1:2–3:13) is a set of three sections of thanksgiving connected by two *apologiae* (defenses) dealing, respectively, with the missionaries' previous conduct and their current concerns. Paul's thankful optimism regarding the Thessalonians' spiritual welfare is tempered by his insistence on their recognition of the selfless love shown by the missionaries. In an age of itinerant peddlers of new religions, Paul found it necessary to emphasize not only the content of his gospel but also his manner of presenting it, for both attested to God's grace as freely bestowed and powerfully effected.

The second part of the letter (1 Thes 4:1–5:25) is specifically hortatory or parenetic. The superabundant love for which Paul has just prayed (1 Thes 3:12–13) is to be shown practically by living out the norms of conduct that he has communicated to them. Specific "imperatives" of Christian life, principles for acting morally, stem from the "indicative" of one's relationship to God through Christ by the sending of the holy Spirit. Thus, moral conduct is the practical, personal expression of one's Christian faith, love, and hope.

The principal divisions of the First Letter to the Thessalonians are the following:

I. Address (1:1–10)
II. Previous Relations with the Thessalonians (2:1–3:13)
III. Specific Exhortations (4:1–5:25)
IV. Final Greeting (5:26–28)

I. ADDRESS

CHAPTER 1

Greeting. [1] *[a]*Paul, Silvanus, and Timothy to the church of the Thessalonians in God the Father and the Lord Jesus Christ: grace to you and peace.
Thanksgiving for Their Faith. [2]We give thanks to God always for all of you, remembering you in our prayers, unceasingly*[b]* [3]calling to mind

your work of faith and labor of love and endurance in hope[†] of our Lord Jesus Christ, before our God and Father, [4]knowing, brothers loved by God, how you were chosen.*[c]* [5]For our gospel did not come to you in word alone, but also in power and in the holy Spirit and [with] much conviction. You know what sort of people we were [among] you for your sake.*[d]* [6]And you

---

*[1:1] On the address, see note on Rom 1:1–7.

a. [1:1] Acts 15:40; 16:1–3, 19; 17:14–15; 2 Thes 1:1–2.   b. [1:2] 2 Thes 1:3.

[†][1:3] **Faith . . . love . . . hope:** this, along with 1 Thes 5:8, is the earliest mention in Christian literature of the three "theological virtues" (see 1 Cor 13:13). The order here stresses eschatological hope, in line with the letter's emphasis on the Lord's second, triumphal coming, or parousia (1 Thes 1:10; 2:12, 19; 3:13; 4:13–5:11; 5:23).

c. [1:4] 2 Thes 2:13.   d. [1:5] Acts 13:52; 17:1–9.

became imitators* of us and of the Lord, receiving the word in great affliction, with joy from the holy Spirit, [7]so that you became a model for all the believers in Macedonia and in Achaia.[e] [8]For from you the word of the Lord has sounded forth not only in Macedonia and [in] Achaia, but in every place your faith in God has gone forth, so that we have no need to say anything.[f] [9]For they themselves openly declare about us what sort of reception we had among you, and how you turned to God from idols to serve the living and true God[g] [10]and to await his Son from heaven, whom he raised from [the] dead, Jesus, who delivers us from the coming wrath.[h]

II. PREVIOUS RELATIONS WITH THE THESSALONIANS

CHAPTER 2

Paul's Ministry Among Them. [1]For you yourselves know, brothers, that our reception among you was not without effect. [2]Rather, after we had suffered and been insolently treated, as you know, in Philippi, we drew courage through our God to speak to you the gospel of God with much struggle.[i] [3]Our exhortation was not from delusion or impure motives, nor did it work through deception. [4]But as we were judged worthy[†] by God to be entrusted with the gospel, that is how we speak, not as trying to please human beings, but rather God, who judges our hearts.[j] [5]Nor, indeed, did we ever appear with flattering speech, as you know, or with a pretext for greed—God is witness— [6]nor did we seek praise from human beings, either from you or from others,[k] [7]although we were able to impose our weight as apostles of Christ. Rather, we were gentle[‡] among you, as a nursing mother cares for her children. [8]With such affection for you, we were determined to share with you not only the gospel of God, but our very selves as well, so dearly beloved had you become to us. [9]You recall, brothers, our toil and drudgery. Working night and day in order not to burden any of you, we proclaimed to you the gospel of God.[l] [10]You are witnesses, and so is God, how devoutly and justly and blamelessly we behaved toward you believers. [11]As you know, we treated each one of you as a father treats his children,[m] [12]exhorting and encouraging you and insisting that you conduct yourselves as worthy of the God who calls you into his kingdom and glory.[n]

Further Thanksgiving. [13]And for this reason we too give thanks to God unceasingly, that, in receiving the word of God from hearing us, you received not a human word but, as it truly is, the word of God, which[‡] is now at work in you who believe. [14]§For you, brothers, have become imitators of the churches of God that are in Judea in Christ Jesus. For you suffer the same things from your compatriots as they did from the Jews, [15]¶who killed both the Lord Jesus and the prophets and persecuted us; they do not please God, and are opposed to everyone,[o] [16]trying to prevent us from speaking to the Gentiles that they may be saved, thus constantly filling up the measure of their sins. But the wrath of God has finally begun to come upon them.[p]

Paul's Recent Travel Plans. [17]Brothers, when we were bereft of you for a short time, in person, not in heart, we were all the more eager in our great desire to see you in person.[q] [18]We decided to go to you—I, Paul, not only once but more than once—yet Satan thwarted us.[r] [19]For what is our hope or joy or crown to boast of in the presence of our Lord Jesus at his coming if not you yourselves?[s] [20]For you are our glory and joy.

CHAPTER 3

[1]That is why, when we could bear it no longer, we decided to remain alone in Athens[t] [2]and sent Timothy, our brother and co-worker for God in the gospel of Christ, to strengthen and encourage you in your faith,[u] [3]so that no one be disturbed in these afflictions. For you yourselves know that we are destined** for this. [4]For even when we were among you, we used to warn you in advance that we would undergo affliction,

§[2:14] Luke's picture of the persecutions at Philippi (by Gentiles) and in Thessalonica and Beroea (by Jews) seems to be considerably schematized (Acts 16:11–40; 17:1–15). Paul pictures the Thessalonian community as composed of converts from paganism (1 Thes 1:9) and speaks here of persecution by their (pagan) compatriots rather than by Jews.

¶[2:15–16] Paul is speaking of historical opposition on the part of Palestinian Jews in particular and does so only some twenty years after Jesus' crucifixion. Even so, he quickly proceeds to depict the persecutors typologically, in apocalyptic terms. His remarks give no grounds for anti-Semitism to those willing to understand him, especially in view of Paul's pride in his own ethnic and religious background (Rom 9:1–5; 10:1; 11:1–3; Phil 3:4–6). Sinful conduct (1 Thes 2:16) is itself an anticipation of the ultimate wrath or judgment of God (Rom 1:18–2:5), whether or not it is perceived as such.

[3:3] We are destined: the Greek phraseology and the context suggest Paul's concern to alert his readers to difficulties he knew they would necessarily face and to enable them to see their present experience in the light of what he warned them would happen in the future. This line of thought is followed in 2 Thes 2:1–15.

*[1:6] **Imitators:** the Pauline theme of "imitation" (see 1 Thes 2:14; 1 Cor 4:16; 11:1; 2 Thes 3:9) is rooted in Paul's view of solidarity in Christ through sharing in Jesus' cross and in the Spirit of the risen Lord.

†[2:4] **Judged worthy:** Paul regards "worthiness" not as grounded in one's own talent or moral self-righteousness but in God's discernment of genuinely selfless attitudes and actions (see 2 Cor 10:17–18).

‡[2:7] **Gentle:** many excellent manuscripts read "infants" (*nēpioi*), but "gentle" (*ēpioi*) better suits the context here.

e. [1:7] 2 Thes 1:4; 1 Cor 4:16; 11:1 / 2:14; Phil 3:17.   f. [1:8] Rom 1:8.   g. [1:9] Acts 14:15; Gal 4:8 / 4:5.   h. [1:10] Rom 2:1–16; 5:9; 13:4 / 5:9.   i. [2:2] Acts 16:19–17:10.   j. [2:4] Gal 1:10.   k. [2:6] Jn 5:41, 44; 1 Cor 10:31; 2 Cor 4:17.   l. [2:9] Acts 20:34; 1 Cor 4:12; 9:3–18; 2 Thes 3:7–9.

m. [2:11] Acts 20:31.   n. [2:12] 1 Pt 5:10 / 4:7; 2 Thes 2:14.   o. [2:15] Acts 2:23; 7:52.   p. [2:16] Gn 15:16; 2 Mc 6:14 / Rom 1:18; 2:5–6.   q. [2:17] 3:10; Rom 1:10–11.   r. [2:18] Rom 15:22.   s. [2:19] 2 Cor 1:14; Phil 2:16; 4:1.   t. [3:1] Acts 17:14.   u. [3:2] Acts 16:1–2; 1 Cor 3:5–9.

just as has happened, as you know.*v* *5*For this reason, when I too could bear it no longer, I sent to learn about your faith, for fear that somehow the tempter had put you to the test and our toil might come to nothing.

*6*But just now Timothy has returned to us from you, bringing us the good news of your faith and love, and that you always think kindly of us and long to see us as' we long to see you. *7*Because of this, we have been reassured about you, brothers, in our every distress and affliction, through your faith. *8*For we now live, if you stand firm in the Lord.

Concluding Thanksgiving and Prayer. *9*What thanksgiving, then, can we render to God for you, for all the joy we feel on your account before our God? *10*Night and day we pray beyond measure to see you in person and to remedy the deficiencies of your faith. *11*Now may God himself, our Father, and our Lord Jesus direct our way to you, *12*and may the Lord make you increase and abound in love for one another and for all, just as we have for you,*w* *13*so as to strengthen your hearts, to be blameless in holiness before our God and Father at the coming of our Lord Jesus with all his holy ones. [Amen.]*x* •

III. SPECIFIC EXHORTATIONS

CHAPTER 4

General Exhortations. *1*Finally, brothers, we earnestly ask and exhort you in the Lord Jesus that, as you received from us how you should conduct yourselves to please God—and as you are conducting yourselves—you do so even more. *2*For you know what instructions† we gave you through the Lord Jesus.

Holiness in Sexual Conduct.‡ *3*This is the will of God, your holiness: that you refrain from immorality, *4*that each of you know how to acquire a wife for himself in holiness and honor, *5*not in lustful passion as do the Gentiles who do not know God;*y* *6*not to take advantage of or exploit a brother in this matter, for the Lord is an avenger in all these things, as we told you before and solemnly affirmed. *7*For God did not call us to impurity but to holiness. *8*Therefore, whoever disregards this, disregards not a human being but God, who [also] gives his holy Spirit to you.*z*

Mutual Charity. *9*On the subject of mutual charity you have no need for anyone to write you, for you yourselves have been taught by God to love one another.*a* *10*Indeed, you do this for all the brothers throughout Macedonia. Nevertheless we urge you, brothers, to progress even more,*b* *11*and to aspire to live a tranquil life, to mind your own affairs, and to work with your [own] hands, as we instructed you, *12*that you may conduct yourselves properly toward outsiders and not depend on anyone.

Hope for the Christian Dead. *13*We do not want you to be unaware, brothers, about those who have fallen asleep, so that you may not grieve like the rest, who have no hope. *14*For if we believe that Jesus died and rose, so too will God, through Jesus, bring with him those who have fallen asleep.*c* *15*Indeed, we tell you this, on the word of the Lord, that we who are alive, who are left until the coming of the Lord,§ will surely not precede those who have fallen asleep.*d* *16*For the Lord himself, with a word of command, with the voice of an archangel and with the trumpet of God, will come down from heaven, and the dead in Christ will rise first.*e* *17*Then we who are alive, who are left, will be caught up together§ with them in the clouds to meet the Lord in the air. Thus we shall always be with the Lord. *18*Therefore, console one another with these words.

CHAPTER 5

Vigilance. *1*Concerning times and seasons, brothers, you have no need for anything to be written to you.*f* *2*For you yourselves know very well that the day of the Lord will come like a thief at night.*g* *3*When people are saying, "Peace

---

*[3:9–10] The tension between Paul's optimism concerning the Thessalonians' faith and his worries about their perseverance remains unresolved. Perhaps this is accounted for not only by the continuing harassment but also by the shortness of his own stay in Thessalonica (even if that were over twice as long as the conventional three weeks that Luke assigns to it, Acts 17:2).

†[4:2] **Instructions**: these include specific guidelines on the basis of the Lord's authority, not necessarily sayings Jesus actually uttered. More profoundly, as 1 Thes 4:8 implies, the instructions are practical principles that Paul worked out in accordance with his understanding of the role of the Spirit.

‡[4:3–8] Many think that this passage deals with a variety of moral regulations (fornication, adultery, sharp business practices). It can be more specifically interpreted as bringing general norms to bear on a specific problem, namely, marriage within degrees of consanguinity (as between uncle and niece) forbidden in Jewish law but allowed according to a Greek heiress law, which would insure retention of an inheritance within the family and would perhaps thereby occasion divorce. In that case, "immorality" (1 Thes 4:3) should be rendered as "unlawful marriage" and "this matter" (1 Thes 4:6) as "a lawsuit." The phrase in 1 Thes 4:4, "acquire a wife for himself," has often been interpreted to mean "control one's body."

§[4:15] **Coming of the Lord**: Paul here assumes that the second coming, or parousia, will occur within his own lifetime but insists that the time or season is unknown (1 Thes 5:1–2). Nevertheless, the most important aspect of the parousia for him was the fulfillment of union with Christ. His pastoral exhortation focuses first on hope for the departed faithful, then (1 Thes 5:1–3) on the need of preparedness for those who have to achieve their goal.

§[4:17] **Will be caught up together**: literally, snatched up, carried off; cf. 2 Cor 12:2; Rev 12:5. From the Latin verb here used, *rapiemur*, has come the idea of "the rapture," when believers will be transported away from the woes of the world; this construction combines this verse with Mt 24:40–41 (see note there) // Lk 17:34–35 and passages from Revelation in a scheme of millennial dispensationalism.

v. [3:4] Acts 14:22; 2 Thes 2:5–7; 2 Tm 3:12.   w. [3:12] 4:9–10; 2 Thes 1:3.   x. [3:13] 5:23; 1 Cor 1:8.

y. [4:5] Ps 79:6; Jer 10:25; 2 Thes 1:8; 1 Pt 3:7.   z. [4:8] Lk 10:16.   a. [4:9] Jn 6:45; 13:34; 1 Jn 2:20–21, 27; 4:7.   b. [4:10] 2 Thes 3:6–12.   c. [4:14] 1 Cor 15:3–4, 12, 20.   d. [4:15] 1 Cor 15:51; Rev 14:13; 20:4–6.   e. [4:16] Mt 24:31; 1 Cor 15:23, 52.   f. [5:1] Mt 24:36–45.   g. [5:2] 2 Pt 3:10.

and security," then sudden disaster comes upon them, like labor pains upon a pregnant woman, and they will not escape. ⁴But you, brothers, are not in darkness, for that day to overtake you like a thief.ʰ ⁵For all of you are children of the light* and children of the day. We are not of the night or of darkness. ⁶Therefore, let us not sleep as the rest do, but let us stay alert and sober.ⁱ ⁷Those who sleep go to sleep at night, and those who are drunk get drunk at night. ⁸But since we are of the day, let us be sober, putting on the breastplate of faith and love and the helmet that is hope for salvation.ʲ ⁹For God did not destine us for wrath, but to gain salvation through our Lord Jesus Christ, ¹⁰who died for us, so that whether we are awake or asleep we may live together with him.† ¹¹Therefore, encourage one another and build one another up, as indeed you do.ᵏ

Church Order. ¹²We ask you, brothers, to respect those who are laboring among you and who are over you in the Lord and who admonish you, ¹³and to show esteem for them with special love on account of their work. Be at peace among yourselves.

¹⁴We urge you, brothers, admonish the idle, cheer the fainthearted, support the weak, be patient with all. ¹⁵See that no one returns evil for evil; rather, always seek what is good [both] for each other and for all.ˡ ¹⁶Rejoice always. ¹⁷Pray without ceasing. ¹⁸In all circumstances give thanks, for this is the will of God for you in Christ Jesus.ᵐ ¹⁹‡Do not quench the Spirit. ²⁰Do not despise prophetic utterances. ²¹Test everything; retain what is good. ²²Refrain from every kind of evil.

Concluding Prayer. ²³§May the God of peace himself make you perfectly holy and may you entirely, spirit, soul, and body, be preserved blameless for the coming of our Lord Jesus Christ.ⁿ ²⁴The one who calls you is faithful, and he will also accomplish it. ²⁵Brothers, pray for us [too].

IV. FINAL GREETING

²⁶Greet all the brothers with a holy kiss.¶ ²⁷I adjure you by the Lord that this letter be read to all the brothers. ²⁸The grace of our Lord Jesus Christ be with you.

---

*[5:5] **Children of the light**: that is, belonging to the daylight of God's personal revelation and expected to achieve it (an analogous development of imagery that appears in Jn 12:36).

†[5:10] Characteristically, Paul plays on words suggesting ultimate and anticipated death and life. Union with the crucified and risen Lord at his parousia is anticipated in some measure in contrasted states of our temporal life. The essential element he urges is our indestructible personal union in Christ's own life (see Rom 5:1 10).

‡[5:19–21] Paul's buoyant encouragement of charismatic freedom sometimes occasioned excesses that he or others had to remedy (see 1 Cor 14; 2 Thes 2:1–15; 2 Pt 3:1–16).

§[5:23] Another possible translation is, "May the God of peace himself make you perfectly holy and sanctify your spirit fully, and may both soul and body be preserved blameless for the coming of our Lord Jesus Christ." In either case, Paul is not offering an anthropological or philosophical analysis of human nature. Rather, he looks to the wholeness of what may be called the supernatural and natural aspects of a person's service of God.

¶[5:26] **Kiss**: the holy embrace (see Rom 16:16; 1 Cor 16:20; 2 Cor 13:12; 1 Pt 5:14) was a greeting of respect and affection, perhaps given during a liturgy at which Paul's letter would have been read.

---

h. [5:4] Eph 5:8–9.   i. [5:6] Mt 24:42; Rom 13:12–13; 1 Pt 5:8.   j. [5:8] Is 59:17; Rom 13:11–14; Eph 6:11, 14–17.   k. [5:11] Rom 15:2; 1 Cor 8:1; 14:12, 26; Eph 4:29.

l. [5:15] Prv 20:22; Mt 5:38–42; Rom 12:17.   m. [5:18] Eph 5:20.   n. [5:23] 2 Thes 3:16.

THESSALONIANS

‿␣‿

This letter is addressed to the same church as the letter that precedes it in the canon and contains many expressions parallel to those in the First Letter to the Thessalonians, indeed verbatim with them. Yet other aspects of the contents of the Second Letter to the Thessalonians suggest a more impersonal tone and changed circumstances in the situation at Thessalonica.

The letter begins with an address (2 Thes 1:1–2) that expands only slightly on that of 1 Thes 1:1. It ends with a greeting insisting on its Pauline authority in the face of false claims made in Paul's name (see note on 2 Thes 2:2). The body of the letter falls into three short parts, of which the second is notoriously difficult (2 Thes 2).

The opening thanksgiving and prayer (2 Thes 1:3–12) speak of the Thessalonians' increasing faith and love in the face of outside persecution. God's eventual judgment against persecutors and his salvation for the faithful are already evidenced by the very fact of persecution. The second part (2 Thes 2:1–17), the heart of the letter, deals with a problem threatening the faith of the community. A message involving a prophetic oracle and apparently a forged letter, possibly presented at a liturgical gathering (cf. 2 Thes 2:2 and 1 Cor 14:26–33), to the effect that the day of the Lord and all that it means have already come, has upset the life of the Thessalonian church.

The writer counters their preoccupation with the date of the parousia (or coming again of the Lord Jesus from heaven, 2 Thes 2:1) by recalling Paul's teaching concerning what must happen first and by going on to describe what will happen at the Lord's coming (2 Thes 2:8); he indicates the twofold process by which the "activity of Satan" and God's actions (2 Thes 2:9–11) are working out, namely, a growing division between believers and those who succumb to false prophecy and "the lie." He concludes by insisting on Pauline traditions and by praying for divine strength (2 Thes 2:13–17). The closing part of the letter (2 Thes 3:1–16) deals in particular with the apostle's directives and model style of life and with correction of disorderly elements within the community.

Traditional opinion holds that this letter was written shortly after 1 Thessalonians. Occasionally it has been argued that 2 Thessalonians was written first or that the two letters are addressed to different segments within the church at Thessalonica (2 Thessalonians being directed to the Jewish Christians there) or even that 2 Thessalonians was originally written to some other nearby place where Paul carried out mission work, such as Philippi or Beroea. Increasingly in recent times, however, the opinion has been advanced that 2 Thessalonians is a pseudepigraph, that is, a letter written authoritatively in Paul's name, to maintain apostolic traditions in a later period, perhaps during the last two decades of the first century.

In any case, the presumed audience of Second Thessalonians and certain features of its style and content require that it be read and studied in a Pauline context, particularly that provided by 1 Thessalonians. At the same time, and especially if the letter is regarded as not by Paul himself, its apocalyptic presentation of preconditions for the parousia (2 Thes 2:1–12) may profit from and require recourse to a wider biblical basis for interpretation, namely Old Testament books such as Daniel and Isaiah and especially, in the New Testament, the synoptic apocalyptic discourse (Mk 13; Mt 24–25; Lk 21:5–36) and the Book of Revelation.

The principal divisions of the Second Letter to the Thessalonians are the following:

I. Address (1:1–12)
II. Warning Against Deception Concerning the Parousia (2:1–17)
III. Concluding Exhortations (3:1–16)
IV. Final Greetings (3:17–18)

I. ADDRESS

CHAPTER 1

Greeting.[*] [1]Paul, Silvanus, and Timothy to the church of the Thessalonians in God our Father and the Lord Jesus Christ:[a] [2]grace to you and peace from God [our] Father and the Lord Jesus Christ.

Thanksgiving. [3†]We ought to thank God always for you, brothers, as is fitting, because your faith flourishes ever more, and the love of every one of you for one another grows ever greater.[b] [4]Accordingly, we ourselves boast of you in the churches of God regarding your endurance and faith in all your persecutions and the afflictions you endure. [5]This is evidence of the just judgment of God, so that you may be considered worthy of the kingdom of God for which you are suffering.[c] [6]For it is surely just on God's part to repay with afflictions those who are afflicting you, [7]and to grant rest along with us to you who are undergoing afflictions, at the revelation of the Lord Jesus from heaven with his mighty angels, [8]in blazing fire, inflicting punishment on those who do not acknowledge God and on those who do not obey the gospel of our Lord Jesus.[d] [9]These will pay the penalty of eternal ruin, separated from the presence of the Lord and from the glory of his power,[e] [10]when he comes to be glorified among his holy ones[‡] and to be marveled at on that day among all who have believed, for our testimony to you was believed.[f]

Prayer. [11]To this end, we always pray for you, that our God may make you worthy of his calling and powerfully bring to fulfillment every good purpose and every effort of faith,[g] [12§]that the name of our Lord Jesus may be glorified in you, and you in him,[h] in accord with the grace of our God and Lord Jesus Christ.

II. WARNING AGAINST DECEPTION CONCERNING THE PAROUSIA

CHAPTER 2

Christ and the Lawless One.[¶] [1]We ask you, brothers, with regard to the coming of our Lord Jesus Christ and our assembling with him,[i] [2]not to be shaken out of your minds suddenly, or to be alarmed either by a "spirit,"[**] or by an oral statement, or by a letter allegedly from us to the effect that the day of the Lord is at hand.[j] [3]Let no one deceive you in any way. For unless the apostasy comes first and the lawless one is revealed,[††] the one doomed to perdition, [4k]who opposes and exalts himself above every so-called god and object of worship, so as to seat himself in the temple of God,[‡‡] claiming that he

---

[¶][2:1–17] The Thessalonians have been **shaken** by a message purporting to come from Paul himself that **the day of the Lord** is already present. He warns against this deception in eschatology by citing a scenario of events that must first occur (2 Thes 2:3–12) before the end will come. The overall point Paul makes is the need to reject such lies as Satan sends; he also reaffirms the Thessalonians in their calling (2 Thes 2:13–14). They are to uphold what Paul himself has taught (2 Thes 2:15). There is a concluding prayer for their strengthening (2 Thes 2:16–17). As in 2 Thes 1:8–10, the Old Testament provides a good deal of coloring; cf. especially Is 14:13–14; 66:15, 18–21; Ez 28:2–9; Dn 11:36–37. The contents of 2 Thes 2:3b–8 may come from a previously existing apocalypse. The details have been variously interpreted.

An alternative to the possibilities noted below understands that an oracular utterance, supposedly coming from a prophetic spirit (2 Thes 2:2–3a), has so disrupted the community's thinking that its effects may be compared to those of the mania connected with the worship of the Greek god Dionysus. On this view, the writer seems to allude in 2 Thes 2:6–8 to Dionysiac "seizure," although, of course, ironically, somewhat as Paul alludes to witchcraft ("an evil eye") in Gal 3:1 in speaking of the threat to faith posed by those disturbing the Galatians (Gal 1:6–7; 5:10b). On this view of 2 Thes 2, the Greek participles *katechon* (rendered above as **what is restraining**) and *katechōn* (**the one who restrains**) are to be translated "the seizing power" in 2 Thes 2:6 and "the seizer" in 2 Thes 2:7. They then allude to a pseudocharismatic force or spirit of Dionysiac character that has suddenly taken hold of the Thessalonian community (see 2 Thes 2:2). The addressees **know** (2 Thes 2:6) this force or spirit because of the problem it is causing. This pseudocharismatic force or spirit is a kind of anticipation and advance proof of the ultimate, climactic figure (**the lawless one** or the rebel, 2 Thes 2:3), of which the community has been warned (see note on 1 Thes 3:3). It is, however, only the beginning of the end that the latter's manifestation entails; the end is not yet. For in the course of the **mystery of lawlessness** (2 Thes 2:7), false prophetism, after it ceases in the Thessalonian community, will be manifested in the world at large (2 Thes 2:8–12), where it will also be eliminated in turn by the Lord Jesus.

[**][2:2] "**Spirit**": a Spirit-inspired utterance or ecstatic revelation. **An oral statement**: literally, a "word" or pronouncement, not necessarily of ecstatic origin. **A letter allegedly sent by us**: possibly a forged letter, so that Paul calls attention in 2 Thes 3:17 to his practice of concluding a genuine letter with a summary note or greeting in his own hand, as at Gal 6:11–18 and elsewhere.

[††][2:3b–5] This incomplete sentence (anacoluthon, 2 Thes 2:4) recalls what the Thessalonians had already been taught, an apocalyptic scenario depicting, in terms borrowed especially from Dn 11:36–37 and related verses, human self-assertiveness against God in the **temple of God** itself. **The lawless one** represents the climax of such activity in this account.

[‡‡][2:4] **Seat himself in the temple of God**: a reflection of the language in Dn 7:23–25; 8:9–12; 9:27; 11:36–37; 12:11 about the attempt of Antiochus IV Epiphanes to set up a statue of Zeus in the Jerusalem temple and possibly of the Roman emperor Caligula to do a similar thing (Mk 13:14). Here the imagery suggests an attempt to install someone in the place of

---

[*][1:1–2] On the address, see note on Rom 1:1–7 and cf. 1 Thes 1:1.

[†][1:3–12] On the thanksgiving, see note on Rom 1:8 and cf. 1 Thes 1:2–10. Paul's gratitude to God for the faith and love of the Thessalonians (2 Thes 1:3) and his Christian pride in their faithful endurance (2 Thes 1:4–5) contrast with the condemnation announced for those who afflict them, a judgment to be carried out at the parousia (2 Thes 1:6–10), which is described in vivid language drawn from Old Testament apocalyptic. A prayer for the fulfillment of God's purpose in the Thessalonians (2 Thes 1:11–12) completes the section, as is customary in a Pauline letter (cf. 1 Thes 1:2–3).

[‡][1:10] **Among his holy ones**: in the Old Testament, this term can refer to an angelic throng (cf. also Jude 14), but here, in parallel with **among all who have believed**, it can refer to the triumphant people of God.

[§][1:12] **The grace of our God and Lord Jesus Christ**: the Greek can also be translated, "the grace of our God and of the Lord Jesus Christ."

---

a. [1:1] 1 Thes 1:1.   b. [1:3] 1 Cor 1:4; 1 Thes 1:2; 3:12.   c. [1:5] Phil 1:28; 1 Thes 2:12.   d. [1:8] Ps 79:5–6; Is 66:15; Jer 10:25.   e. [1:9] Is 2:10, 19, 21.   f. [1:10] Ps 89:8; Dn 7:18–22, 27; 1 Thes 3:13.   g. [1:11] 1 Thes 1:2–3.   h. [1:12] Is 66:5.

i. [2:1] 1 Thes 4:13–17.   j. [2:2] Mt 24:6; 1 Cor 14:26, 32–33; 1 Thes 5:1–2.   k. [2:4] Dn 11:36–37; Ez 28:2.

is a god— [5]do you not recall that while I was still with you I told you these things? [6]And now you know what is restraining,* that he may be revealed in his time. [7†]For the mystery of lawlessness is already at work. But the one who restrains is to do so only for the present, until he is removed from the scene.[1] [8]And then the lawless one will be revealed, whom the Lord [Jesus] will kill with the breath of his mouth and render powerless by the manifestation of his coming,[m] [9]the one whose coming springs from the power of Satan in every mighty deed and in signs and wonders that lie,[n] [10]and in every wicked deceit for those who are perishing because they have not accepted the love of truth so that they may be saved. [11]Therefore, God is sending them a deceiving power so that they may believe the lie, [12]that all who have not believed the truth but have approved wrongdoing may be condemned.

[13]But we ought to give thanks to God for you always, brothers loved by the Lord, because God chose you as the firstfruits[‡] for salvation through sanctification by the Spirit and belief in truth.[o] [14]To this end he has [also] called you through our gospel to possess the glory of our Lord Jesus Christ.[p] [15]Therefore, brothers, stand firm and hold fast to the traditions that you were taught, either by an oral statement or by a letter of ours.[§]

[16]May our Lord Jesus Christ himself and God our Father, who has loved us and given us everlasting encouragement and good hope through his grace, [17]encourage your hearts and strengthen them in every good deed and word.

III. CONCLUDING EXHORTATIONS

CHAPTER 3[¶]

Request for Prayers. [1]Finally, brothers, pray for us, so that the word of the Lord may speed forward and be glorified, as it did among you,[q] [2]and that we may be delivered from perverse and wicked people, for not all have faith. [3]But the Lord is faithful; he will strengthen you and guard you from the evil one.[r] [4]We are confident of you in the Lord that what we instruct you, you [both] are doing and will continue to do.[s] [5]May the Lord direct your hearts to the love of God and to the endurance of Christ.

Neglect of Work. [6]We instruct you, brothers, in the name of [our] Lord Jesus Christ, to shun any brother who conducts himself in a disorderly way and not according to the tradition they received from us.** [7]For you know how one must imitate us. For we did not act in a disorderly way among you, [8]nor did we eat food received free from anyone. On the contrary, in toil and drudgery, night and day we worked, so as not to burden any of you.[t] [9]Not that we do not have the right. Rather, we wanted to present ourselves as a model for you, so that you might imitate us.[u] [10]In fact, when we were with you, we instructed you that if anyone was unwilling to work, neither should that one eat.[v] [11]We hear that some are conducting themselves among you in a disorderly way, by not keeping busy but minding the business of others.[w] [12]Such people we instruct and urge in the Lord Jesus Christ to work quietly and to eat their own food. [13]But

---

God, **claiming that he is a god** (cf. Ez 28:2). Usually, it is the Jerusalem temple that is assumed to be meant; on the alternative view sketched above (see note on 2 Thes 2:1–17), **the temple** refers to the Christian community.

*[2:6–7] **What is restraining . . . the one who restrains**: neuter and masculine, respectively, of a force and person holding back the lawless one. The Thessalonians know what is meant (2 Thes 2:6), but the terms, seemingly found only in this passage and in writings dependent on it, have been variously interpreted. Traditionally, 2 Thes 2:6 has been applied to the Roman empire and 2 Thes 2:7 to the Roman emperor (in Paul's day, Nero) as bulwarks holding back chaos (cf. Rom 13:1–7). A second interpretation suggests that cosmic or angelic powers are binding Satan (2 Thes 2:9) and so restraining him; some relate this to an anti-Christ figure (1 Jn 2:18) or to Michael the archangel (Rev 12:7–9; 20:1–3). A more recent view suggests that it is the preaching of the Christian gospel that restrains the end, for in God's plan the end cannot come until the gospel is preached to all nations (Mk 13:10); in that case, Paul as missionary preacher par excellence is "the one who restrains," whose removal (death) will bring the end (2 Thes 2:7). On the alternative view (see note on 2 Thes 2:1–17), the phrases should be referred to that which and to him who seizes (a prophet) in ecstasy so as to have him speak pseudo-oracles.

†[2:7–12] **The lawless one** and **the one who restrains** are involved in an activity or process, **the mystery of lawlessness**, behind which **Satan** stands (2 Thes 2:9). The action of the **Lord [Jesus]** in overcoming the lawless one is described in Old Testament language (**with the breath of his mouth**; cf. Is 11:4; Jb 4:9; Rev 19:15). His **coming** is literally the Lord's "parousia." The biblical concept of the "holy war," eschatologically conceived, may underlie the imagery.

‡[2:13] **As the firstfruits**: there is also strong manuscript evidence for the reading, "God chose you from the beginning," thus providing a focus on God's activity from beginning to end; **firstfruits** is a Pauline term, however; cf. Rom 8:23; 11:16; 16:5 among other references.

§[2:15] Reference to **an oral statement** and a **letter** (2 Thes 2:2) and the content here, including a formula of conclusion

(cf. 1 Cor 16:13; Gal 5:1), suggest that 2 Thes 2:1–15 or even 2 Thes 2:1–17 are to be taken as a literary unit, notwithstanding the incidental thanksgiving formula in 2 Thes 2:13.

¶[3:1–18] The final chapter urges the Thessalonians to pray for Paul and his colleagues (2 Thes 3:1–2) and reiterates confidence in the Thessalonians (2 Thes 3:3–5), while admonishing them about a specific problem in their community that has grown out of the intense eschatological speculation, namely, not to work but to become instead disorderly busybodies (2 Thes 3:6–15). A benediction (2 Thes 3:16) and postscript in Paul's own hand round out the letter. On 2 Thes 3:17–18, cf. note on 2 Thes 2:2.

**[3:6] Some members of the community, probably because they regarded the parousia as imminent or the new age of the Lord to be already here (2 Thes 2:2), had apparently ceased to work for a living. The disciplinary problem they posed could be rooted in distorted thinking about Paul's own teaching (cf. 1 Thes 2:16; 3:3–4; 5:4–5) or, more likely, in a forged letter (2 Thes 2:2) and the type of teaching dealt with in 2 Thes 2:1–15. The apostle's own moral teaching, reflected in his selfless labors for others, was rooted in a deep doctrinal concern for the gospel message (cf. 1 Thes 2:3–10).

---

l. [2:7] Mt 13:36–43; Acts 20:29; Gal 5:10; 2 Pt 2:1; Rev 22:11.
m. [2:8] Is 11:4; Rev 19:15.   n. [2:9] Mt 24:24; Rev 13:13.   o. [2:13] 1 Thes 2:13; 5:9.   p. [2:14] Rom 5:1–10; 8:29–30; 1 Thes 4:7; 5:9.

q. [3:1] Eph 6:19; Col 4:3.   r. [3:3] 1 Thes 5:24 / 1 Cor 16:13 / Mt 6:13.
s. [3:4] 2 Cor 7:16; 1 Thes 4:1–2.   t. [3:8] 1 Thes 2:9.   u. [3:9] Mt 10:10; Phil 3:17.   v. [3:10] 1 Thes 4:11.   w. [3:11] 1 Thes 5:14.

you, brothers, do not be remiss in doing good. [14]If anyone does not obey our word as expressed in this letter, take note of this person not to associate with him, that he may be put to shame. [15]Do not regard him as an enemy but admonish him as a brother.[x] [16]May the Lord of peace himself give you peace at all times and in every way. The Lord be with all of you.[y]

IV. FINAL GREETINGS

[17]This greeting is in my own hand, Paul's. This is the sign in every letter; this is how I write.[z] [18]The grace of our Lord Jesus Christ be with all of you.

---

x. [3:15] 2 Cor 2:7; Gal 6:1.   y. [3:16] Jn 14:27; Rom 15:33.

z. [3:17] 1 Cor 16:21; Gal 6:11.

THE FIRST LETTER TO
TIMOTHY

~~∾⌣∾~~

The three letters, First and Second Timothy and Titus, form a distinct group within the Pauline corpus. In the collection of letters by the Apostle to the Gentiles, they differ from the others in form and contents. All three suggest they were written late in Paul's career. The opponents are not "Judaizers" as in Galatians but false teachers stressing "knowledge" (*gnōsis*; see note on 1 Tm 6:20–21). Attention is given especially to correct doctrine and church organization. Jesus' second coming recedes into the background compared to references in Paul's earlier letters (though not Colossians and Ephesians). The three letters are addressed not to congregations but to those who shepherd congregations (Latin, *pastores*). These letters were first named "Pastoral Epistles" in the eighteenth century because they all are concerned with the work of a pastor in caring for the community or communities under his charge.

The first of the Pastorals, 1 Timothy, is presented as having been written from Macedonia. Timothy, whom Paul converted, was of mixed Jewish and Gentile parentage (Acts 16:1–3). He was the apostle's companion on both the second and the third missionary journeys (Acts 16:3; 19:22) and was often sent by him on special missions (Acts 19:22; 1 Cor 4:17; 1 Thes 3:2). In 1 Timothy (1 Tm 1:3), he is described as the administrator of the entire Ephesian community.

The letter instructs Timothy on his duty to restrain false and useless teaching (1 Tm 1:3–11; 4:1–5; 6:3–16) and proposes principles pertaining to his relationship with the older members of the community (1 Tm 5:1–2) and with the presbyters (1 Tm 5:17–22). It gives rules for aid to widows (1 Tm 5:3–8) and their selection for charitable ministrations (1 Tm 5:9–16) and also deals with liturgical celebrations (1 Tm 2:1–15), selections for the offices of bishop and deacon (1 Tm 3:1–13), relation of slaves with their masters (1 Tm 6:1–2), and obligations of the wealthier members of the community (1 Tm 6:17–19). This letter also reminds Timothy of the prophetic character of his office (1 Tm 1:12–20) and encourages him in his exercise of it (1 Tm 4:6–16). The central passage of the letter (1 Tm 3:14–16) expresses the principal motive that should guide the conduct of Timothy— preservation of the purity of the church's doctrine against false teaching. On this same note the letter concludes (1 Tm 6:20–21).

From the late second century to the nineteenth, Pauline authorship of the three Pastoral Epistles went unchallenged. Since then, the attribution of these letters to Paul has been questioned. Most scholars are convinced that Paul could not have been responsible for the vocabulary and style, the concept of church organization, or the theological expressions found in these letters. A second group believes, on the basis of statistical evidence, that the vocabulary and style are Pauline, even if at first sight the contrary seems to be the case. They state that the concept of church organization in the letters is not as advanced as the questioners of Pauline authorship hold since the notion of hierarchical order in a religious community existed in Israel before the time of Christ, as evidenced in the Dead Sea Scrolls. Finally, this group sees affinities between the theological thought of the Pastorals and that of the unquestionably genuine letters of Paul. Other scholars, while conceding a degree of validity to the positions mentioned above, suggest that the apostle made use of a secretary who was responsible for the composition of the letters. A fourth group of scholars believes that these letters are the work of a compiler, that they are based on traditions about Paul in his later years, and that they include, in varying amounts, actual fragments of genuine Pauline correspondence.

If Paul is considered the more immediate author, the Pastorals are to be dated between the end of his first Roman imprisonment (Acts 28:16) and his execution under Nero (A.D. 63–67); if they are regarded as only more remotely Pauline, their date may be as late as the early second century. In spite of these problems of authorship and dating, the Pastorals are illustrative of early Christian life and remain an important element of canonical scripture.

The principal divisions of the First Letter to Timothy are the following:

I. Address (1:1–2)
II. Sound Teaching (1:3–20)
III. Problems of Discipline (2:1–4:16)
IV. Duties Toward Others (5:1–6:2a)
V. False Teaching and True Wealth (6:2b–19)
VI. Final Recommendation and Warning (6:20–21)

I. ADDRESS

CHAPTER 1

Greeting.[*] [1]Paul, an apostle of Christ Jesus by command of God our savior and of Christ Jesus our hope,[a] [2]to Timothy, my true child in faith: grace, mercy, and peace from God the Father and Christ Jesus our Lord.[b]

II. SOUND TEACHING

Warning Against False Doctrine. [3†]I repeat the request I made of you when I was on my way to Macedonia,[c] that you stay in Ephesus to instruct certain people not to teach false doctrines [4†]or to concern themselves with myths and endless genealogies, which promote speculations rather than the plan of God that is to be received by faith.[d] [5]The aim of this instruction is love from a pure heart, a good conscience, and a sincere faith.[e] [6]Some people have deviated from these and turned to meaningless talk,[f] [7]wanting to be teachers of the law, but without understanding either what they are saying or what they assert with such assurance.

[8§]We know that the law is good, provided that one uses it as law,[g] [9]with the understanding that law is meant not for a righteous person but for the lawless and unruly, the godless and sinful, the unholy and profane, those who kill their fathers or mothers, murderers, [10]the unchaste,

sodomites,[¶] kidnappers, liars, perjurers, and whatever else is opposed to sound teaching,[h] [11]according to the glorious gospel of the blessed God, with which I have been entrusted.[i]

Gratitude for God's Mercy.[**] [12]I am grateful to him who has strengthened me, Christ Jesus our Lord, because he considered me trustworthy in appointing me to the ministry.[j] [13]I was once a blasphemer and a persecutor and an arrogant man, but I have been mercifully treated because I acted out of ignorance in my unbelief.[k] [14]Indeed, the grace of our Lord has been abundant, along with the faith and love that are in Christ Jesus.[l] [15]This saying is trustworthy[††] and deserves full acceptance: Christ Jesus came into the world to save sinners. Of these I am the foremost.[m] [16]But for that reason I was mercifully treated, so that in me, as the foremost, Christ Jesus might display all his patience as an example for those who would come to believe in him for everlasting life. [17]To the king of ages,[‡‡] incorruptible, invisible, the only God, honor and glory forever and ever. Amen.[n]

Responsibility of Timothy.[§§] [18]I entrust this charge to you, Timothy, my child, in accordance

¶[1:10] **Sodomites:** see 1 Cor 6:9 and the note there.
**[1:12–17] Present gratitude for the Christian apostleship leads Paul to recall an earlier time when he had been a fierce persecutor of the Christian communities (cf. Acts 26:9–11) until his conversion by intervention of divine mercy through the appearance of Jesus. This and his subsequent apostolic experience testify to the saving purpose of Jesus' incarnation. The fact of his former ignorance of the truth has not kept the apostle from regarding himself as having been the worst of sinners (1 Tm 1:15). Yet he was chosen to be an apostle, that God might manifest his firm will to save sinful humanity through Jesus Christ (1 Tm 1:16). The recounting of so great a mystery leads to a spontaneous outpouring of adoration (1 Tm 1:17).
††[1:15] **This saying is trustworthy:** this phrase regularly introduces in the Pastorals a basic truth of early Christian faith; cf. 1 Tm 3:1; 4:9; 2 Tm 2:11; Ti 3:8.
‡‡[1:17] **King of ages:** through Semitic influence, the Greek expression could mean "everlasting king"; it could also mean "king of the universe."
§§[1:18–20] Timothy is to be mindful of his calling, which is here compared to the way Barnabas and Saul were designated by Christ as prophets for missionary service; cf. Acts 13:1–3. Such is probably the sense of the allusion to the prophetic words (1 Tm 1:18). His task is not to yield, whether in doctrine or in conduct, to erroneous opinions, taking warning

*[1:1–2] For the Pauline use of the conventional epistolary form, see note on Rom 1:1–7.
†[1:3–7] Here Timothy's initial task in Ephesus (cf. Acts 20:17–35) is outlined: to suppress the idle religious speculations, probably about Old Testament figures (1 Tm 1:3–4, but see note on 1 Tm 6:20–21), which do not contribute to the development of love within the community (1 Tm 1:5) but rather encourage similar useless conjectures (1 Tm 1:6–7).
‡[1:4] The **plan of God that is to be received by faith:** the Greek may also possibly mean "God's trustworthy plan" or "the training in faith that God requires."
§[1:8–11] Those responsible for the speculations that are to be suppressed by Timothy do not present the Old Testament from the Christian viewpoint. The Christian values the Old Testament not as a system of law but as the first stage in God's revelation of his saving plan, which is brought to fulfillment in the good news of salvation through faith in Jesus Christ.

a. [1:1] 2:3; Lk 1:47; Ti 1:3; 2:10 / Col 1:27.　b. [1:2] 2 Tm 1:2; Ti 1:4.　c. [1:3] Acts 20:1.　d. [1:4] 4:7; Ti 1:14; 3:9; 2 Pt 1:16.　e. [1:5] Rom 13:10.　f. [1:6] 6:4, 20; Ti 1:10.　g. [1:8] Rom 7:12, 16.

h. [1:10] 4:6; 6:3; 2 Tm 4:3; Ti 1:9; 2:1.　i. [1:11] Ti 1:3.　j. [1:12] Phil 4:13 / Acts 9:15; Gal 1:15–16.　k. [1:13] Acts 8:3; 9:1–2; 1 Cor 15:9; Gal 1:13.　l. [1:14] Rom 5:20; 2 Tm 1:13.　m. [1:15] Lk 15:2; 19:10.　n. [1:17] Rom 16:27.

with the prophetic words once spoken about you. Through them may you fight a good fight[o] [19]by having faith and a good conscience. Some, by rejecting conscience, have made a shipwreck of their faith,[p] [20]among them Hymenaeus[†] and Alexander, whom I have handed over to Satan to be taught not to blaspheme.[q]

III. PROBLEMS OF DISCIPLINE

CHAPTER 2
Prayer and Conduct. [1‡]First of all, then, I ask that supplications, prayers, petitions, and thanksgivings be offered for everyone,[r] [2]for kings and for all in authority, that we may lead a quiet and tranquil life in all devotion and dignity. [3]This is good and pleasing to God our savior,[s] [4]who wills everyone to be saved and to come to knowledge of the truth.[t]

[5]　For there is one God.
　There is also one mediator between God
　　　and the human race,
　Christ Jesus, himself human,[u]
[6]　who gave himself as ransom for all.

This was the testimony[§] at the proper time.[v] [7]For this I was appointed preacher and apostle (I am speaking the truth, I am not lying), teacher of the Gentiles in faith and truth.[w]

----

from what has already happened at Ephesus in the case of Hymenaeus and Alexander (1 Tm 1:19–20).

*[1:18] **The prophetic words once spoken about you:** the Greek may also be translated, "the prophecies that led (me) to you." It probably refers to testimonies given by charismatic figures in the Christian communities. **Fight a good fight:** this translation preserves the play on words in Greek. The Greek terms imply a lengthy engagement in battle and might well be translated "wage a good campaign."

†[1:20] **Hymenaeus:** mentioned in 2 Tm 2:17 as saying that the resurrection has already taken place (in baptism). **Alexander:** probably the Alexander mentioned in 2 Tm 4:14 as the coppersmith who "did me a great deal of harm." **Whom I have handed over to Satan:** the same terms are used in the condemnation of the incestuous man in 1 Cor 5:5.

‡[2:1–7] This marked insistence that the liturgical prayer of the community concern itself with the needs of all, whether Christian or not, and especially of those in authority, may imply that a disposition existed at Ephesus to refuse prayer for pagans. In actuality, such prayer aids the community to achieve peaceful relationships with non-Christians (1 Tm 2:2) and contributes to salvation, since it derives its value from the presence within the community of Christ, who is the one and only savior of all (1 Tm 2:3–6). The vital apostolic mission to the Gentiles (1 Tm 2:7) reflects Christ's purpose of universal salvation. 1 Tm 2:5 contains what may well have been a very primitive creed. Some interpreters have called it a Christian version of the Jewish *shema*: "Hear, O Israel! The LORD is our God, the LORD alone . . ." (Dt 6:4–5). The assertion in 1 Tm 2:7, "I am speaking the truth, I am not lying," reminds one of similar affirmations in Rom 9:1; 2 Cor 11:31; and Gal 1:20.

§[2:6] **The testimony:** to make sense of this overly concise phrase, many manuscripts supply "to which" (or "to whom"); two others add "was given." The translation has supplied "this was."

o. [1:18] 4:14 / 6:12; 2 Tm 4:7; Jude 3.　p. [1:19] 3:9.　q. [1:20] 2 Tm 2:17; 4:14 / 1 Cor 5:5.　r. [2:1] Eph 6:18; Phil 4:6.　s. [2:3] 1:1; 4:10.　t. [2:4] 2 Tm 3:7; 2 Pt 3:9.　u. [2:5] 1 Cor 8:6; Heb 8:6; 9:15; 12:24 / Rom 5:15.　v. [2:6] Mk 10:45; Gal 1:4; 2:20; Eph 5:25; Ti 2:14.　w. [2:7] Acts 9:15; 1 Cor 9:1; Gal 2:7–8.

[8¶]It is my wish, then, that in every place the men should pray, lifting up holy hands, without anger or argument. [9]Similarly, [too,] women should adorn themselves with proper conduct, with modesty and self-control, not with braided hairstyles and gold ornaments, or pearls, or expensive clothes,[x] [10]but rather, as befits women who profess reverence for God, with good deeds.[y] [11]A woman must receive instruction silently and under complete control.[z] [12]I do not permit a woman to teach or to have authority over a man.** She must be quiet. [13]For Adam was formed first, then Eve.[a] [14]Further, Adam was not deceived, but the woman was deceived and transgressed.[b] [15]But she will be saved through motherhood, provided women persevere in faith and love and holiness, with self-control.[c]

CHAPTER 3
Qualifications of Various Ministers. [1††]This saying is trustworthy:[‡‡] whoever aspires to the office of bishop desires a noble task.[d] [2]Therefore, a bishop must be irreproachable, married only once, temperate, self-controlled, decent, hospitable, able to teach, [3]not a drunkard, not aggressive, but gentle, not contentious, not a lover of money.[e] [4]He must manage his own household well, keeping his children under control with perfect dignity; [5]for if a man does not know how to manage his own household, how can he take care of the church of God? [6]He should not be a recent convert, so that he may not become

----

¶[2:8–15] The prayer of the community should be unmarred by internal dissension (1 Tm 2:8); cf. Mt 5:21–26; 6:14; Mk 11:25. At the liturgical assembly the dress of women should be appropriate to the occasion (1 Tm 2:9); their chief adornment is to be reputation for good works (1 Tm 2:10). Women are not to take part in the charismatic activity of the assembly (1 Tm 2:11–12; cf. 1 Cor 14:34) or exercise authority; their conduct there should reflect the role of man's helpmate (1 Tm 2:13; cf. Gn 2:18) and not the later relationship of Eve to Adam (1 Tm 2:14; cf. Gn 3:6–7). As long as women perform their role as wives and mothers in faith and love, their salvation is assured (1 Tm 2:15).

[2:12] **A man: this could also mean "her husband."

††[3:1–7] The passage begins by commending those who aspire to the office of bishop (*episkopos*; see note on Phil 1:1) within the community, but this first sentence (1 Tm 3:1) may also imply a warning about the great responsibilities involved. The writer proceeds to list the qualifications required: personal stability and graciousness; talent for teaching (1 Tm 3:2); moderation in habits and temperament (1 Tm 3:3); managerial ability (1 Tm 3:4); and experience in Christian living (1 Tm 3:5–6). Moreover, the candidate's previous life should provide no grounds for the charge that he did not previously practice what he now preaches. No list of qualifications for presbyters appears in 1 Timothy. The presbyter-bishops here and in Titus (see note on Ti 1:5–9) lack certain functions reserved here for Paul and Timothy.

‡‡[3:1] **This saying is trustworthy:** the saying introduced is so unlike others after this phrase that some later Western manuscripts read, "This saying is popular." It is understood by some interpreters as concluding the preceding section (1 Tm 2:8–15). **Bishop:** literally, "overseer"; see note on Phil 1:1.

----

x. [2:9] 1 Pt 3:3–5.　y. [2:10] 5:10; 1 Pt 3:1.　z. [2:11–12] 1 Cor 14:34–35.　a. [2:13] Gn 1:27; 2:7, 22; 1 Cor 11:8–9.　b. [2:14] Gn 3:6, 13; 2 Cor 11:3.　c. [2:15] 5:14.　d. [3:1–7] Ti 1:6–9.　e. [3:3] Heb 13:5.

conceited and thus incur the devil's punishment.* [7]He must also have a good reputation among outsiders, so that he may not fall into disgrace, the devil's trap.[f]

[8†]Similarly, deacons must be dignified, not deceitful, not addicted to drink, not greedy for sordid gain, [9]holding fast to the mystery of the faith with a clear conscience. [10]Moreover, they should be tested first; then, if there is nothing against them, let them serve as deacons. [11]Women,[‡] similarly, should be dignified, not slanderers, but temperate and faithful in everything.[g] [12]Deacons may be married only once and must manage their children and their households well. [13]Thus those who serve well as deacons gain good standing and much confidence in their faith in Christ Jesus.

The Mystery of Our Religion.[§] [14]I am writing you about these matters, although I hope to visit you soon. [15]But if I should be delayed, you should know how to behave in the household of God, which is the church of the living God, the pillar and foundation of truth.[h] [16]Undeniably great is the mystery of devotion,

Who[¶] was manifested in the flesh,
vindicated in the spirit,

seen by angels,
proclaimed to the Gentiles,
believed in throughout the world,
taken up in glory.[i]

CHAPTER 4

False Asceticism.[**] [1]Now the Spirit explicitly says that in the last times some will turn away from the faith by paying attention to deceitful spirits and demonic instructions[j] [2]through the hypocrisy of liars with branded consciences. [3]They forbid marriage and require abstinence from foods that God created to be received with thanksgiving by those who believe and know the truth.[k] [4]For everything created by God is good, and nothing is to be rejected when received with thanksgiving,[l] [5]for it is made holy by the invocation of God in prayer.[††]

Counsel to Timothy. [6‡‡]If you will give these instructions to the brothers, you will be a good minister of Christ Jesus, nourished on the words of the faith and of the sound teaching you have followed. [7]Avoid profane and silly myths. Train yourself for devotion,[m] [8]for, while physical training is of limited value, devotion is valuable in every respect, since it holds a promise of life both for the present and for the future.[n] [9]This saying is trustworthy and deserves full acceptance.[o] [10]For this we toil and struggle,[§§] because we have set our hope on the living God, who is the savior of all, especially of those who believe.[p]

[11¶¶]Command and teach these things. [12]Let no one have contempt for your youth,[***] but set an example for those who believe, in speech, conduct, love, faith, and purity.[q] [13]Until I arrive, attend to the reading,[†††] exhortation, and teaching. [14]Do not neglect the gift you have, which

---

*[3:6] **The devil's punishment**: this phrase could mean the punishment once incurred by the devil (objective genitive) or a punishment brought about by the devil (subjective genitive).

†[3:8–13] Deacons, besides possessing the virtue of moderation (1 Tm 3:8), are to be outstanding for their faith (1 Tm 3:9) and well respected within the community (1 Tm 3:10). Women in the same role, although some interpreters take them to mean wives of deacons, must be dignified, temperate, dedicated, and not given to malicious talebearing (1 Tm 3:11). Deacons must have shown stability in marriage and have a good record with their families (1 Tm 3:12), for such experience prepares them well for the exercise of their ministry on behalf of the community (1 Tm 3:13). See further the note on Phil 1:1.

‡[3:11] **Women**: this seems to refer to women deacons but may possibly mean wives of deacons. The former is preferred because the word is used absolutely; if deacons' wives were meant, a possessive "their" would be expected. Moreover, they are also introduced by the word "similarly," as in 1 Tm 3:8; this parallel suggests that they too exercised ecclesiastical functions.

§[3:14–16] In case there is some delay in the visit to Timothy at Ephesus planned for the near future, the present letter is being sent on ahead to arm and enlighten him in his task of preserving sound Christian conduct in the Ephesian church. The care he must exercise over this community is required by the profound nature of Christianity. It centers in Christ, appearing in human flesh, vindicated by the holy Spirit; the mystery of his person was revealed to the angels, announced to the Gentiles, and accepted by them in faith. He himself was taken up (through his resurrection and ascension) to the divine glory (1 Tm 3:16). This passage apparently includes part of a liturgical hymn used among the Christian communities in and around Ephesus. It consists of three couplets in typical Hebrew balance: flesh-spirit (contrast), seen-proclaimed (complementary), world-glory (contrast).

¶[3:16] **Who**: the reference is to Christ, who is himself "the mystery of our devotion." Some predominantly Western manuscripts read "which," harmonizing the gender of the pronoun with that of the Greek word for mystery; many later (eighth/ninth century on), predominantly Byzantine manuscripts read "God," possibly for theological reasons.

f. [3:7] 2 Cor 8:21; 2 Tm 2:26. g. [3:11] Ti 2:3. h. [3:15] Eph 2:19–22.

**[4:1–5] Doctrinal deviations from the true Christian message within the church have been prophesied, though the origin of the prophecy is not specified (1 Tm 4:1–2); cf. Acts 20:29–30. The letter warns against a false asceticism that prohibits marriage and regards certain foods as forbidden, though they are part of God's good creation (1 Tm 4:3).

††[4:5] **The invocation of God in prayer**: literally, "the word of God and petition." The use of "word of God" without an article in Greek suggests that it refers to the name of God being invoked in blessing rather than to the "word of God" proclaimed to the community.

‡‡[4:6–10] Timothy is urged to be faithful, both in his teaching and in his own life, as he looks only to God for salvation.

§§[4:10] **Struggle**: other manuscripts and patristic witnesses read "suffer reproach."

¶¶[4:11–16] Timothy is urged to preach and teach with confidence, relying on the gifts and the mission that God has bestowed on him.

***[4:12] **Youth**: some commentators find this reference a sign of pseudepigraphy. Timothy had joined Paul as a missionary already in A.D. 49, some fifteen years before the earliest supposed date of composition.

†††[4:13] **Reading**: the Greek word refers to private or public reading. Here, it probably designates the public reading of scripture in the Christian assembly.

i. [3:16] Jn 1:14; Rom 1:3–4. j. [4:1] 2 Tm 3:1; 4:3; 2 Pt 3:3; Jude 18. k. [4:3] Gn 9:3; Rom 14:6; 1 Cor 10:30–31. l. [4:4] Gn 1:31; Acts 10:15. m. [4:7] 1:4; 2 Tm 2:16; Ti 1:14. n. [4:8] 6:6. o. [4:9] 1:15; 2 Tm 2:11; Ti 3:8. p. [4:10] 2:4; Ti 2:11. q. [4:12] 1 Cor 16:11; Ti 2:15 / Phil 3:17.

was conferred on you through the prophetic word* with the imposition of hands of the presbyterate.^r [15]Be diligent in these matters, be absorbed in them, so that your progress may be evident to everyone. [16]Attend to yourself and to your teaching; persevere in both tasks, for by doing so you will save both yourself and those who listen to you.

IV. DUTIES TOWARD OTHERS

CHAPTER 5

[1†]Do not rebuke an older man, but appeal to him as a father. Treat younger men as brothers,[s] [2]older women as mothers, and younger women as sisters with complete purity.

Rules for Widows. [3]Honor widows who are truly widows. [4]But if a widow has children or grandchildren, let these first learn to perform their religious duty to their own family and to make recompense to their parents, for this is pleasing to God. [5]The real widow, who is all alone, has set her hope on God and continues in supplications and prayers night and day.[t] [6]But the one who is self-indulgent is dead while she lives. [7]Command this, so that they may be irreproachable. [8]And whoever does not provide for relatives and especially family members has denied the faith and is worse than an unbeliever.

[9]Let a widow be enrolled if she is not less than sixty years old, married only once, [10]with a reputation for good works, namely, that she has raised children, practiced hospitality, washed the feet of the holy ones, helped those in distress, involved herself in every good work.[u] [11]But exclude younger widows, for when their sensuality estranges them from Christ, they want to marry [12]and will incur condemnation for

breaking their first pledge. [13]And furthermore, they learn to be idlers, going about from house to house, and not only idlers but gossips and busybodies as well, talking about things that ought not to be mentioned.[v] [14]So I would like younger widows to marry, have children, and manage a home, so as to give the adversary no pretext for maligning us.[w] [15]For some have already turned away to follow Satan. [16]If any woman believer[‡] has widowed relatives, she must assist them; the church is not to be burdened, so that it will be able to help those who are truly widows.

Rules for Presbyters.[§] [17]Presbyters who preside well deserve double honor, especially those who toil in preaching and teaching.[x] [18]For the scripture says, "You shall not muzzle an ox when it is threshing," and, "A worker deserves his pay."[y] [19]Do not accept an accusation against a presbyter unless it is supported by two or three witnesses.[z] [20]Reprimand publicly those who do sin, so that the rest also will be afraid.[a] [21]I charge you before God and Christ Jesus and the elect angels to keep these rules without prejudice, doing nothing out of favoritism. [22]Do not lay hands too readily on anyone, and do not share in another's sins. Keep yourself pure.[b] [23]Stop drinking only water, but have a little wine for the sake of your stomach and your frequent illnesses.

[24]Some people's sins are public, preceding them to judgment; but other people are followed by their sins. [25]Similarly, good works are also public; and even those that are not cannot remain hidden.

CHAPTER 6

Rules for Slaves. [1†]Those who are under the yoke of slavery must regard their masters as worthy

---

*[4:14] **Prophetic word**: this may mean the utterance of a Christian prophet designating the candidate or a prayer of blessing accompanying the rite. **Imposition of hands**: this gesture was used in the Old Testament to signify the transmission of authority from Moses to Joshua (Nm 27:18–23; Dt 34:9). The early Christian community used it as a symbol of installation into an office: the Seven (Acts 6:6) and Paul and Barnabas (Acts 13:3). **Of the presbyterate**: this would mean that each member of the college of presbyters imposed hands and appears to contradict 2 Tm 1:6, in which Paul says that he imposed hands on Timothy. This latter text, however, does not exclude participation by others in the rite. Some prefer to translate "for the presbyterate," and thus understand it to designate the office into which Timothy was installed rather than the agents who installed him.

†[5:1–16] After a few words of general advice based on common sense (1 Tm 5:1–2), the letter takes up, in its several aspects, the subject of widows. The first responsibility for their care belongs to the family circle, not to the Christian community as such (1 Tm 5:3–4, 16). The widow left without the aid of relatives may benefit the community by her prayer, and the community should consider her material sustenance its responsibility (1 Tm 5:5–8). Widows who wish to work directly for the Christian community should not be accepted unless they are well beyond the probability of marriage, i.e., sixty years of age, married only once, and with a reputation for good works (1 Tm 5:9–10). Younger widows are apt to be troublesome and should be encouraged to remarry (1 Tm 5:11–15).

‡[5:16] **Woman believer**: some early Latin manuscripts and Fathers have a masculine here, while most later manuscripts and patristic quotations conflate the two readings, perhaps to avoid unfair restriction to women.

§[5:17–25] The function of presbyters is not exactly the same as that of the *episkopos*, "bishop" (1 Tm 3:1); in fact, the relation of the two at the time of this letter is obscure (but cf. note on Ti 1:5–9). The Pastorals seem to reflect a transitional stage that developed in many regions of the church into the monarchical episcopate of the second and third centuries. The presbyters possess the responsibility of preaching and teaching, for which functions they are supported by the community (1 Tm 5:17–18). The realization that their position subjects them to adverse criticism is implied in the direction to Timothy (1 Tm 5:19–20) to make sure of the truth of any accusation against them before public reproof is given. He must be as objective as possible in weighing charges against presbyters (1 Tm 5:21), learning from his experience to take care in selecting them (1 Tm 5:22). Some scholars take 1 Tm 5:22 as a reference not to ordination of presbyters but to reconciliation of public sinners. The letter now sounds an informal note of personal concern in its advice to Timothy not to be so ascetic that he even avoids wine (1 Tm 5:23). Judgment concerning the fitness of candidates to serve as presbyters is easy with persons of open conduct, more difficult and prolonged with those of greater reserve (1 Tm 5:24–25).

¶[6:1–2] Compare the tables for household duties, such as that of Col 3:18–4:1. Domestic relationships derive new meaning from the Christian faith.

---

r. [4:14] 5:22; Acts 6:6; 8:17; 2 Tm 1:6.   s. [5:1] Lv 19:32; Ti 2:2.   t. [5:5] Jer 49:11; Lk 2:37; 18:7.   u. [5:10] Jn 13:14; Heb 13:2.

v. [5:13] 2 Thes 3:11.   w. [5:14] 1 Cor 7:9.   x. [5:17] 1 Cor 16:18; Phil 2:29.   y. [5:18] Dt 25:4; 1 Cor 9:8 / Mt 10:10; Lk 10:7.   z. [5:19] Dt 17:6; 19:15; Mt 18:16; 2 Cor 13:1.   a. [5:20] Gal 2:14; Eph 5:11; 2 Tm 4:2; Ti 1:9, 13.   b. [5:22] 4:14; 2 Tm 1:6.

of full respect, so that the name of God and our teaching* may not suffer abuse.[c] [21†]Those whose masters are believers must not take advantage of them because they are brothers but must give better service because those who will profit from their work are believers and are beloved.[d]

V. FALSE TEACHING AND TRUE WEALTH

Teach and urge these things. [3]Whoever teaches something different and does not agree with the sound words of our Lord Jesus Christ and the religious teaching[e] [4]is conceited, understanding nothing, and has a morbid disposition for arguments and verbal disputes. From these come envy, rivalry, insults, evil suspicions, [5]and mutual friction among people with corrupted minds, who are deprived of the truth, supposing religion to be a means of gain.[f] [6‡]Indeed, religion with contentment is a great gain.[g] [7]For we brought nothing into the world, just as we shall not be able to take anything out of it.[h] [8]If we have food and clothing, we shall be content with that.[i] [9]Those who want to be rich are falling into temptation and into a trap and into many foolish and harmful desires, which plunge them into ruin and destruction.[j] [10]For the love of money is the root of all evils, and some people in their desire for it have strayed from the faith and have pierced themselves with many pains.

Exhortations to Timothy.[§] [11]But you, man of God,[t] avoid all this. Instead, pursue righteousness, devotion, faith, love, patience, and gentleness.[k] [12]Compete well for the faith. Lay hold of eternal life, to which you were called when you made the noble confession in the presence of many witnesses.[l] [13]I charge [you] before God, who gives life to all things, and before Christ Jesus, who gave testimony under Pontius Pilate for the noble confession,[m] [14]to keep the commandment without stain or reproach until the appearance of our Lord Jesus Christ [15]that the blessed and only ruler will make manifest at the proper time, the King of kings and Lord of lords,[n] [16]who alone has immortality, who dwells in unapproachable light, and whom no human being has seen or can see. To him be honor and eternal power. Amen.[o]

Right Use of Wealth.[**] [17]Tell the rich in the present age not to be proud and not to rely on so uncertain a thing as wealth but rather on God, who richly provides us with all things for our enjoyment.[p] [18]Tell them to do good, to be rich in good works, to be generous, ready to share, [19]thus accumulating as treasure a good foundation for the future, so as to win the life that is true life.[q]

VI. FINAL RECOMMENDATION AND WARNING[††]

[20]O Timothy, guard what has been entrusted to you. Avoid profane babbling and the absurdities of so-called knowledge.[r] [21]By professing it, some people have deviated from the faith.

Grace be with all of you.[s]

---

*[6:1] **Our teaching**: this refers to the teaching of the Christian community.

†[6:2b–10] Timothy is exhorted to maintain steadfastly the position outlined in this letter, not allowing himself to be pressured into any other course. He must realize that false teachers can be discerned by their pride, envy, quarrelsomeness, and greed for material gain. 1 Tm 6:6 is rather obscure and is interpreted, and therefore translated, variously. The suggestion seems to be that the important gain that religion brings is spiritual, but that there is material gain, too, up to the point of what is needed for physical sustenance (cf. 1 Tm 6:17–19).

‡[6:6] **Contentment**: the word *autarkeia* is a technical Greek philosophical term for the virtue of independence from material goods (Aristotle, Cynics, Stoics).

§[6:11–16] Timothy's position demands total dedication to God and faultless witness to Christ (1 Tm 6:11–14) operating from an awareness, through faith, of the coming revelation in Jesus of the invisible God (1 Tm 6:15–16).

¶[6:11] **Man of God**: a title applied to Moses and the prophets (Dt 33:1; 1 Sm 2:27; 1 Kgs 12:22; 13:1; etc.).

**[6:17–19] Timothy is directed to instruct the rich, advising them to make good use of their wealth by aiding the poor.

††[6:20–21] A final solemn warning against the heretical teachers, with what seems to be a specific reference to gnosticism, the great rival and enemy of the church for two centuries and more (the Greek word for "knowledge" is *gnōsis*). If gnosticism is being referred to here, it is probable that the warnings against "speculations" and "myths and genealogies" (cf. especially 1 Tm 1:4; Ti 3:9) involve allusions to that same kind of heresy. Characteristic of the various gnostic systems of speculation was an elaborate mythology of innumerable superhuman intermediaries, on a descending scale ("genealogies"), between God and the world. Thus would be explained the emphasis upon Christ's being the one mediator (as in 1 Tm 2:5). Although fully developed gnosticism belonged to the second and later centuries, there are signs that incipient forms of it belonged to Paul's own period.

---

c. [6:1] Eph 6:5; Ti 2:9–10. d. [6:2] Phlm 16. e. [6:3] Gal 1:6–9; 2 Tm 1:13; Ti 1:1. f. [6:5] 2 Tm 3:8; 4:4; Ti 1:14. g. [6:6] 4:8; Phil 4:11–12; Heb 13:5. h. [6:7] Jb 1:21; Eccl 5:14. i. [6:8] Prv 30:8. j. [6:9] Prv 23:4; 28:22.

k. [6:11] 2 Tm 2:22. l. [6:12] 1 Cor 9:26; 2 Tm 4:7. m. [6:13] Jn 18:36–37; 19:11. n. [6:15] 2 Mc 13:4; Rev 17:14. o. [6:16] Ex 33:20; Ps 104:2. p. [6:17] Ps 62:11; Lk 12:20. q. [6:19] Mt 6:20. r. [6:20] 2 Tm 1:14 / 1 Tm 4:7. s. [6:21] 1:6; 2 Tm 2:18.

THE SECOND LETTER TO
TIMOTHY

The authorship and date of this letter, as one of the Pastoral Epistles, are discussed in the Introduction to the First Letter to Timothy.

The tone here is more personal than in First Timothy, for this letter addresses Timothy in vivid terms (2 Tm 1:6–14; 2:1–13) and depicts Paul's courage and hope in the face of discouragements late in the course of his apostolic ministry (2 Tm 1:15–18; 3:10–17; 4:9–18). Indeed, the letter takes on the character of a final exhortation and testament from Paul to the younger Timothy (2 Tm 4:1–8). Paul is portrayed as a prisoner (2 Tm 1:8, 16; 2:9) in Rome (2 Tm 1:17), and there is a hint that Timothy may be in Ephesus (2 Tm 2:17). The letter reveals that, with rare exceptions, Christians have not rallied to Paul's support (2 Tm 1:15–18) and takes a pessimistic view of the outcome of his case (2 Tm 4:6). It describes Paul as fully aware of what impends, looking to God, not to human beings, for his deliverance (2 Tm 4:3–8, 18). It recalls his mission days with Timothy (2 Tm 1:3–5; cf. Acts 16:1–4). It points to his preaching of the gospel as the reason for his imprisonment and offers Timothy, as a motive for steadfastness, his own example of firmness in faith despite adverse circumstances (2 Tm 1:6–14). The letter suggests that Timothy should prepare others to replace himself as Paul has prepared Timothy to replace him (2 Tm 2:1–2). Paul urges him not to desist out of fear from preserving and spreading the Christian message (2 Tm 2:3–7). It presents the resurrection of Jesus and his messianic role as the heart of the gospel for which Paul has been ready to lay down his life (2 Tm 2:8–9) and thus not only to express his own conviction fully but to support the conviction of others (2 Tm 2:10–13).

This letter, like the preceding one, urges Timothy to protect the community from the inevitable impact of false teaching (2 Tm 2:14–3:9), without fear of the personal attacks that may result (2 Tm 3:10–13). It recommends that he rely on the power of the scriptures, on proclamation of the word, and on sound doctrine (2 Tm 3:14–4:2), without being troubled by those who do not accept him (2 Tm 4:3–5). The letter poignantly observes in passing that Paul has need of his reading materials and his cloak (2 Tm 4:13) and, what will be best of all, a visit from Timothy.

On the theory of authorship by Paul himself, Second Timothy appears to be the last of the three Pastoral Epistles. The many scholars who argue that the Pastorals are products of the Pauline school often incline toward Second Timothy as the earliest of the three and the one most likely to have actual fragments of material from Paul himself.

The principal divisions of the Second Letter to Timothy are the following:

I. Address (1:1–5)
II. Exhortations to Timothy (1:6–2:13)
III. Instructions Concerning False Teaching (2:14–4:8)
IV. Personal Requests and Final Greetings (4:9–22)

I. ADDRESS

CHAPTER 1

Greeting. [1] Paul, an apostle of Christ Jesus by the will of God[a] for the promise of life in Christ Jesus,[†] [2] to Timothy, my dear child: grace, mercy, and peace from God the Father and Christ Jesus our Lord.

Thanksgiving. [3b] I am grateful to God, whom I worship with a clear conscience as my ancestors

---

*[1:1–2] For the formula of address and greeting, see note on Rom 1:1–7.

†[1:1] **The promise of life in Christ Jesus:** that God grants through union with Christ in faith and love; cf. Col 3:4; 1 Tm 4:8.

a. [1:1] 1 Tm 4:8.

b. [1:3] 1 Tm 3:9 / Phil 3:5.

did,ᵃ as I remember you constantly in my prayers, night and day. ⁴ᵗI yearn to see you again, recalling your tears, so that I may be filled with joy, ⁵as I recall your sincere faith that first lived in your grandmother Lois and in your mother Eunice and that I am confident lives also in you.ᶜ

II. EXHORTATIONS TO TIMOTHY

The Gifts Timothy Has Received. ⁶For this reason, I remind you to stir into flame the gift of God‡ that you have through the imposition of my hands.ᵈ ⁷For God did not give us a spirit of cowardice but rather of power and love and self-control.ᵉ ⁸So do not be ashamed of your testimony to our Lord,§ nor of me, a prisoner for his sake; but bear your share of hardship for the gospel with the strength that comes from God.ᶠ

⁹¶He saved us and called us to a holy life, not according to our works but according to his own design and the grace bestowed on us in Christ Jesus before time began,ᵍ ¹⁰but now made manifest through the appearance of our savior Christ Jesus, who destroyed death and brought life and immortality to light through the gospel,ʰ ¹¹**for which I was appointed preacher and apostle and teacher. ¹²ᵗᵗOn this account I am suffering these things; but I am not ashamed,ʲ for I know him in whom I have believed and am confident that he is able to guard what has been entrusted to me until that day. ¹³Take as your norm the sound words that you heard from me, in the faith and love that are in Christ Jesus.ᵏ ¹⁴Guard this rich trust with the help of the holy Spirit that dwells within us.ˡ

Paul's Suffering. ¹⁵‡‡ᵐYou know that everyone in Asia deserted me, including Phygelus and

Hermogenes. ¹⁶§§May the Lord grant mercy to the family of Onesiphorusⁿ because he oftenⁿ gave me new heart and was not ashamed of my chains. ¹⁷But when he came to Rome, he promptly searched for me and found me. ¹⁸May the Lord grant him to find mercy from the Lord¶¶ on that day. And you know very well the services he rendered in Ephesus.ᵒ

CHAPTER 2

Timothy's Conduct. ¹***So you, my child, be strong in the grace that is in Christ Jesus. ²And what you heard from me through many witnesses entrust to faithful people who will have the ability to teach others as well. ³Bear your share of hardship along with me like a good soldier of Christ Jesus.ᵖ ⁴To satisfy the one who recruited him, a soldier does not become entangled in the business affairs of life.�q ⁵Similarly, an athlete cannot receive the winner's crown except by competing according to the rules.ʳ ⁶The hardworking farmer ought to have the first share of the crop.ˢ ⁷Reflect on what I am saying, for the Lord will give you understanding in everything.ᵗ

⁸ᵗᵗᵗRemember Jesus Christ, raised from the dead, a descendant of David: such is my gospel,ᵘ ⁹for which I am suffering, even to the point of chains, like a criminal. But the word of God is not chained.ᵛ ¹⁰Therefore, I bear with everything for the sake of those who are chosen, so

---

*[1:3] **As my ancestors did:** this emphasizes the continuity of Judaism and Christianity; for a similar view, see Rom 9:3–5; Phil 3:4–6.

†[1:4–5] Purportedly written from prison in Rome (2 Tm 1:8, 17; 4:6–8) shortly before the writer's death, the letter recalls the earlier sorrowful parting from Timothy, commending him for his faith and expressing the longing to see him again.

‡[1:6] **The gift of God:** the grace resulting from the conferral of an ecclesiastical office. **The imposition of my hands:** see note on 1 Tm 4:14.

§[1:8] **Do not be ashamed of your testimony to our Lord:** i.e., of preaching and suffering for the sake of the gospel.

¶[1:9–10] Redemption from sin and the call to holiness of life are not won by personal deeds but are freely and graciously bestowed according to God's eternal plan; cf. Eph 1:4.

[1:11] **Teacher: the overwhelming majority of manuscripts and Fathers read "teacher of the nations," undoubtedly a harmonization with 1 Tm 2:7.

††[1:12] **He is able to guard . . . until that day:** the intervening words can also be translated "what I have entrusted to him" (i.e., the fruit of his ministry) as well as "what has been entrusted to me" (i.e., the faith). The same difficult term occurs in 2 Tm 1:14, where it is modified by the adjective "rich" and used without a possessive.

‡‡[1:15] Keen disappointment is expressed, here and later (2 Tm 4:16), that the Christians of the province of Asia,

especially Phygelus and Hermogenes, should have abandoned the writer and done nothing to defend his case in court.

§§[1:16–18] **The family of Onesiphorus because he . . . of my chains:** Onesiphorus seems to have died before this letter was written. His family is mentioned twice (here and in 2 Tm 4:19), though it was Onesiphorus himself who was helpful to Paul in prison and rendered much service to the community of Ephesus. Because the apostle complains of abandonment by all in Asia during his second imprisonment and trial, the assistance of Onesiphorus seems to have been given to Paul during his first Roman imprisonment (A.D. 61–63).

¶¶[1:18] **Lord . . . Lord:** the first "Lord" here seems to refer to Christ, the second "Lord" to the Father.

***[2:1–7] This passage manifests a characteristic deep concern for safeguarding the faith and faithfully transmitting it through trustworthy people (2 Tm 2:1–2; cf. 2 Tm 1:14; 1 Tm 6:20; Ti 1:9). Comparisons to the soldier's detachment, the athlete's sportsmanship, and the farmer's arduous work as the price of recompense (2 Tm 2:4–6) emphasize the need of singleness of purpose in preaching the word, even at the cost of hardship, for the sake of Christ (2 Tm 2:3).

†††[2:8–13] The section begins with a sloganlike summary of Paul's gospel about Christ (2 Tm 2:8) and concludes with what may be part of an early Christian hymn (2 Tm 2:11b–12a; most exegetes include the rest of 2 Tm 2:12 and all of 2 Tm 2:13 as part of the quotation). The poetic lines suggest that through baptism Christians die spiritually with Christ and hope to live with him and reign with him forever, but the Christian life includes endurance, witness, and even suffering, as the final judgment will show and as Paul's own case makes clear; while he is imprisoned for preaching the gospel (2 Tm 2:9), his sufferings are helpful to the elect for obtaining the salvation and glory available in Christ (2 Tm 2:10), who will be true to those who are faithful and will disown those who deny him (2 Tm 2:12–13).

---

c. [1:5] 1 Tm 1:5 / Acts 16:1.   d. [1:6] 1 Tm 4:14; 5:22 / Acts 6:6; 8:17.   e. [1:7] Rom 5:5; 8:15; 1 Cor 2:4.   f. [1:8] 2:3, 15; Rom 1:16.   g. [1:9] Eph 2:8–9; Ti 3:5 / Eph 1:4; Ti 1:2.   h. [1:10] Rom 16:26; 1 Pt 1:20 / 1 Tm 6:14 / Phil 3:20; Ti 1:4; 2:13; 2 Pt 1:11 / 1 Cor 15:54–55; Heb2:14/1Cor15:53–54.   i. [1:11]1Tm2:7.   j. [1:12]1Pt4:16/1Tm 1:10–11.   k. [1:13] 1 Tm 1:14.   l. [1:14] 1 Tm 6:20 / Rom 8:11.

m. [1:15] 4:16.   n. [1:16] 4:19.   o. [1:18] Jude 21.   p. [2:3] 1:8; 4:5; Phlm 2.   q. [2:4] 1 Cor 9:25.   r. [2:5] 1 Cor 9:25.   s. [2:6] 1 Cor 9:7–10.   t. [2:7] Prv 2:6.   u. [2:8] Rom 1:3; 1 Cor 15:4, 20 / Rom 2:16; Gal 1:11; 2:2.   v. [2:9] Phil 1:12–14.

that they too may obtain the salvation that is in Christ Jesus, together with eternal glory.ʷ ¹¹This saying is trustworthy:

If we have died with him
    we shall also live with him;ˣ
¹² if we persevere
    we shall also reign with him.
But if we deny him
    he will deny us.ʸ
¹³ If we are unfaithful
    he remains faithful,
    for he cannot deny himself.ᶻ

III. INSTRUCTIONS CONCERNING FALSE TEACHING

Warning Against Useless Disputes. ¹⁴*Remind people of these things and charge them before God† to stop disputing about words. This serves no useful purpose since it harms those who listen.ᵃ ¹⁵Be eager to present yourself as acceptable to God, a workman who causes no disgrace, imparting the word of truth without deviation.ᵇ ¹⁶Avoid profane, idle talk, for such people will become more and more godless,ᶜ ¹⁷and their teaching will spread like gangrene. Among them are Hymenaeus and Philetus,ᵈ ¹⁸who have deviated from the truth by saying that [the] resurrection has already taken place and are upsetting the faith of some.ᵉ ¹⁹Nevertheless, God's solid foundation stands, bearing this inscription, "The Lord knows those who are his"; and, "Let everyone who calls upon the name of the Lord avoid evil."ᶠ
    ²⁰In a large household there are vessels not only of gold and silver but also of wood and clay, some for lofty and others for humble use. ²¹If anyone cleanses himself of these things, he will be a vessel for lofty use, dedicated, beneficial to the master of the house, ready for every good work.ᵍ ²²So turn from youthful desires and pursue righteousness, faith, love, and peace, along with those who call on the Lord‡ with purity of heart.ʰ ²³Avoid foolish and ignorant debates, for

you know that they breed quarrels.ⁱ ²⁴A slave of the Lord should not quarrel, but should be gentle with everyone, able to teach, tolerant,ʲ ²⁵correcting opponents with kindness. It may be that God will grant them repentance that leads to knowledge of the truth,ᵏ ²⁶§and that they may return to their senses out of the devil's snare,ˡ where they are entrapped by him, for his will.

CHAPTER 3

The Dangers of the Last Days.§ ¹But understand this: there will be terrifying times in the last days.ᵐ ²People will be self-centered and lovers of money, proud, haughty, abusive, disobedient to their parents, ungrateful, irreligious,ⁿ ³callous, implacable, slanderous, licentious, brutal, hating what is good, ⁴traitors, reckless, conceited, lovers of pleasure rather than lovers of God, ⁵as they make a pretense of religion but deny its power. Reject them.ᵒ ⁶For some of these slip into homes and make captives of women weighed down by sins, led by various desires,ᵖ ⁷always trying to learn but never able to reach a knowledge of the truth.�q ⁸Just as Jannes and Jambres opposed Moses, so they also oppose the truth—people of depraved mind, unqualified in the faith.ʳ ⁹But they will not make further progress, for their foolishness will be plain to all, as it was with those two.
Paul's Example and Teaching.** ¹⁰You have followed my teaching, way of life, purpose, faith, patience, love, endurance, ¹¹persecutions, and sufferings, such as happened to me in Antioch, Iconium, and Lystra, persecutions that I endured. Yet from all these things the Lord delivered me.ˢ ¹²In fact, all who want to live religiously in Christ Jesus will be persecuted.ᵗ ¹³But wicked people and charlatans will go from bad to worse, deceivers and deceived. ¹⁴But you, remain faithful to what you have learned and believed,

20–21; Rom 10:12–13; cf. 2 Tm 2:19, literally, "Everyone who names the name of the Lord").
    §[2:26] Some interpreters would render this passage, "Thus they may come to their senses and, forced to do his (i.e., God's) will, may escape the devil's trap." This interpretation of the Greek is possible, but the one accepted in the text seems more likely.
    §[3:1–9] The moral depravity and false teaching that will be rampant in the last days are already at work (2 Tm 3:1–5). The frivolous and superficial, too, devoid of the true spirit of religion, will be easy victims of those who pervert them by falsifying the truth (2 Tm 3:6–8), just as Jannes and Jambres, Pharaoh's magicians of Egypt (Ex 7:11–12, 22), discredited the truth in Moses' time. Exodus does not name the magicians, but the two names are widely found in much later Jewish, Christian, and even pagan writings. Their origins are legendary.
    **[3:10–17] Paul's example for Timothy includes persecution, a frequent emphasis in the Pastorals. Timothy is to be steadfast to what he has been taught and to scripture. The scriptures are the source of wisdom, i.e., of belief in and loving fulfillment of God's word revealed in Christ, through whom salvation is given.

---

*[2:14–19] For those who dispute about mere words (cf. 2 Tm 2:23–24) and indulge in irreligious talk to the detriment of their listeners (2 Tm 2:16–19), see notes on 1 Tm 1:3–7; 6:20–21. Hymenaeus and Philetus (2 Tm 2:17), while accepting the Christian's mystical death and resurrection in Christ through baptism, claimed that baptized Christians are already risen with Christ in this life and thus that there is no future bodily resurrection or eternal glory to come. The first quotation in 2 Tm 2:19 is from Nm 16:5; the other quotation is from some unidentified Jewish or Christian writing.
    †[2:14] **Before God:** many ancient manuscripts read "before the Lord."
    ‡[2:22] **Those who call on the Lord:** those who believe in Christ and worship him as Lord, i.e., Christians (Acts 9:14–16,

---

w. [2:10] Col 1:24; 1 Tm 1:15.   x. [2:11] Rom 6:8.   y. [2:12] Mt 10:22, 33; Lk 12:9.   z. [2:13] Nm 23:19; Rom 3:3–4; 1 Cor 10:13; Ti 1:2.   a. [2:14] 1 Tm 6:4.   b. [2:15] 1:8; 2 Cor 6:7; Eph 1:13; Col 1:5.   c. [2:16] 1 Tm 4:7.   d. [2:17] 1 Tm 1:20.   e. [2:18] 2 Thes 2:2.   f. [2:19] Is 28:16; 1 Cor 3:10–15 / Nm 16:5; Jn 10:14.   g. [2:21] 3:17.   h. [2:22] Gal 5:22; 1 Tm 6:11 / Rom 10:13; 1 Cor 1:2.

i. [2:23] 1 Tm 1:4; 4:7; 6:4; Ti 3:9.   j. [2:24] 1 Tm 3:2–3.   k. [2:25] 3:7; 1 Tm 2:4.   l. [2:26] 1 Tm 3:7.   m. [3:1] 1 Tm 4:1; 2 Pt 3:3; Jude 18.   n. [3:2–4] Rom 1:29–31.   o. [3:5] Rom 2:20–22; Ti 1:16.   p. [3:6] Ti 1:11.   q. [3:7] 2:25.   r. [3:8] Ex 7:11, 22; 1 Tm 6:5.   s. [3:11] Acts 13:50; 14:5, 19 / Ps 34:20.   t. [3:12] Jn 15:20; Acts 14:22.

because you know from whom you learned it,[u] [15]and that from infancy you have known [the] sacred scriptures, which are capable of giving you wisdom for salvation through faith in Christ Jesus.[v] [16*]All scripture[w] is inspired by God and is useful for teaching, for refutation, for correction, and for training in righteousness,[†] [17]so that one who belongs to God may be competent, equipped for every good work.[x]

CHAPTER 4

Solemn Charge.[‡] [1]I charge you in the presence of God and of Christ Jesus, who will judge the living and the dead, and by his appearing and his kingly power:[y] [2]proclaim the word; be persistent whether it is convenient or inconvenient; convince, reprimand, encourage through all patience and teaching.[z] [3]For the time will come when people will not tolerate sound doctrine but, following their own desires and insatiable curiosity,[§] will accumulate teachers[a] [4]and will stop listening to the truth and will be diverted to myths.[b] [5]But you, be self-possessed in all circumstances; put up with hardship; perform the work of an evangelist; fulfill your ministry.

Reward for Fidelity. [6‡]For I am already being poured out like a libation, and the time of my departure is at hand. [7**]I have competed well; I have finished the race;[d] I have kept the faith. [8††]From now on the crown of righteousness awaits me, which the Lord, the just judge, will award to me on that day,[e] and not only to me, but to all who have longed for his appearance.

---

*[3:16–17] **Useful for teaching . . . every good work**: because as God's word the scriptures share his divine authority. It is exercised through those who are ministers of the word.

†[3:16] **All scripture is inspired by God**: this could possibly also be translated, "All scripture inspired by God is useful for . . . ." In this classic reference to inspiration, God is its principal author, with the writer as the human collaborator. Thus the scriptures are the word of God in human language. See also 2 Pt 1:20–21.

‡[4:1–5] The gravity of the obligation incumbent on Timothy to preach the word can be gauged from the solemn adjuration: in the presence of God, and of Christ coming as universal judge, and by his appearance and **his kingly power** (2 Tm 4:1). Patience, courage, constancy, and endurance are required despite the opposition, hostility, indifference, and defection of many to whom the truth has been preached (2 Tm 4:2–5).

§[4:3] **Insatiable curiosity**: literally, "with itching ears."

¶[4:6] The apostle recognizes his death through martyrdom to be imminent. He regards it as an act of worship in which his blood will be poured out in sacrifice; cf. Ex 29:38–40; Phil 2:17.

**[4:7] At the close of his life Paul could testify to the accomplishment of what Christ himself foretold concerning him at the time of his conversion, "I will show him what he will have to suffer for my name" (Acts 9:16).

††[4:8] When the world is judged at the parousia, all who have eagerly looked for the Lord's appearing and have sought to live according to his teachings will be rewarded. The crown is a reference to the laurel wreath placed on the heads of victorious athletes and conquerors in war; cf. 2 Tm 2:5; 1 Cor 9:25.

---

u. [3:14] 2:2.   v. [3:15] Jn 5:39.   w. [3:16] Rom 15:4; 2 Pt 1:19–21.
x. [3:17] 2:21.   y. [4:1] 1 Tm 5:21; 6:14 / Acts 10:42; Rom 14:9–10;
1 Pt 4:5.   z. [4:2] Acts 20:20, 31; 1 Tm 5:20.   a. [4:3] 1 Tm 4:1.
b. [4:4] 1 Tm 1:4; 4:7; Ti 1:14.   c. [4:6] Phil 2:17.   d. [4:7] 1 Tm
1:18; 6:12; Jude 3 / Acts 20:24; 1 Cor 9:24; Heb 12:1.   e. [4:8] 2:5;
Wis 5:16; 1 Cor 9:25; Phil 3:14; Jas 1:12; 1 Pt 5:4; Rev 2:10.

IV. PERSONAL REQUESTS AND FINAL GREETINGS

Paul's Loneliness. [9‡‡]Try to join me soon, [10]for Demas, enamored of the present world, deserted me and went to Thessalonica, Crescens to Galatia,[§§] and Titus to Dalmatia.[f] [11]Luke is the only one with me. Get Mark and bring him with you, for he is helpful to me in the ministry.[g] [12]I have sent Tychicus to Ephesus.[h] [13]When you come, bring the cloak I left with Carpus in Troas, the papyrus rolls, and especially the parchments.[i]

[14]Alexander[¶¶] the coppersmith did me a great deal of harm; the Lord will repay him according to his deeds.[j] [15]You too be on guard against him, for he has strongly resisted our preaching.

[16]At my first defense no one appeared on my behalf, but everyone deserted me. May it not be held against them![k] [17]But the Lord stood by me and gave me strength, so that through me the proclamation might be completed and all the Gentiles might hear it. And I was rescued from the lion's mouth.[l] [18]The Lord will rescue me from every evil threat and will bring me safe to his heavenly kingdom. To him be glory forever and ever. Amen.[m]

Final Greeting. [19]Greet Prisca and Aquila[***] and the family of Onesiphorus.[n] [20]Erastus[†††] remained in Corinth, while I left Trophimus sick at Miletus.[o] [21]Try to get here before winter. Eubulus, Pudens, Linus,[‡‡‡] Claudia, and all the brothers send greetings.

[22]The Lord be with your spirit. Grace be with all of you.[p]

---

‡‡[4:9–13] Demas either abandoned the work of the ministry for worldly affairs or, perhaps, gave up the faith itself (2 Tm 4:10). Luke (2 Tm 4:11) may have accompanied Paul on parts of his second and third missionary journeys (Acts 16:10–12; 20:5–7). Notice the presence of the first personal pronoun "we" in these Acts passages, suggesting to some that Luke (or at least some traveling companion of Paul's) was the author of Acts. Mark, once rejected by Paul (Acts 13:13; 15:39), is now to render him a great service (2 Tm 4:11); cf. Col 4:10; Phlm 24. For Tychicus, see Eph 6:21; cf. also Acts 20:4; Col 4:7.

§§[4:10] **Galatia**: some manuscripts read "Gaul" or "Gallia."

¶¶[4:14–18] **Alexander**: an opponent of Paul's preaching (2 Tm 4:14–15), perhaps the one who is mentioned in 1 Tm 1:20. Despite Paul's abandonment by his friends in the province of Asia (cf. 2 Tm 1:15–16), the divine assistance brought this first trial to a successful issue, even to the point of making the gospel message known to those who participated in or witnessed the trial (2 Tm 4:16–17).

***[4:19] **Prisca and Aquila**: they assisted Paul in his ministry in Corinth (Acts 18:2–3) and Ephesus (Acts 18:19, 26; 1 Cor 16:19). They risked death to save his life, and all the Gentile communities are indebted to them (Rom 16:3–5).

†††[4:20] **Erastus**: he was the treasurer of the city of Corinth (Rom 16:24); cf. also Acts 19:22. **Trophimus**: from the province of Asia, he accompanied Paul from Greece to Troas (Acts 20:4–5).

‡‡‡[4:21] **Linus**: Western tradition sometimes identified this Linus with the supposed successor of Peter as bishop of Rome, and Claudia as the mother of Linus (*Apostolic Constitutions*, fourth century).

---

f. [4:10] Col 4:14; Phlm 24 / 2 Cor 2:13; 7:6–7; 8:23; Gal 2:3; Ti
1:4.   g. [4:11] Col 4:14; Phlm 24 / Col 4:10; Phlm 24.   h. [4:12]
Acts 20:4; Eph 6:21; Col 4:7.   i. [4:13] Acts 16:8; 20:6.   j. [4:14]
1 Tm 1:20 / 2 Sm 3:39; Ps 28:4; 62:12; Prv 24:12; Rom 2:6.   k. [4:16]
1:15.   l. [4:17] Acts 23:11; 27:23; Phil 4:13 / 1 Mc 2:60; Ps 22:22; Dn
6:23.   m. [4:18] 2 Cor 1:10 / Rom 16:27.   n. [4:19] Acts 18:2; Rom
16:3; 1 Cor 16:19 / 2 Tm 1:16.   o. [4:20] Acts 19:22; Rom 16:24 / Acts
20:4; 21:29.   p. [4:22] Gal 6:18; Phil 4:23; Col 4:18; 1 Tm 6:21; Ti 3:15.

THE LETTER TO
TITUS

ᘒᓭᕲ

The third of the Pastoral Epistles in the New Testament is addressed to a different co-worker of Paul than are First and Second Timothy. The situation is different, too, for Titus is addressed as the person in charge of developing the church on the large Mediterranean island of Crete (Ti 1:5), a place Paul had never, according to the New Testament, visited. The tone is closer to that of First Timothy as three topics of church life and structure are discussed: presbyter-bishops (see note on Ti 1:5–9), groups with which one must work in the church (Ti 2:1–10), and admonitions for conduct based on the grace and love of God that appeared in Jesus Christ (Ti 2:11–3:10). The warmer personal tone of Second Timothy is replaced by emphasis on church office and on living in the society of the day, in which deceivers and heretics abound (Ti 1:10–16; 3:9–10).

The Pauline assistant who is addressed, Titus, was a Gentile Christian, but we are nowhere informed of his place of birth or residence. He went from Antioch with Paul and Barnabas to Jerusalem (Gal 2:1; cf. Acts 15:2). According to 2 Corinthians (2 Cor 2:13; 7:6, 13–14), he was with Paul on his third missionary journey; his name, however, does not appear in Acts. Besides being the bearer of Paul's severe letter to the Corinthians (2 Cor 7:6–8), he had the responsibility of taking up the collection in Corinth for the Christian community of Jerusalem (2 Cor 8:6, 16–19, 23). In the present letter (Ti 1:5), he is mentioned as the administrator of the Christian community in Crete, charged with the task of organizing it through the appointment of presbyters and bishops (Ti 1:5–9; here the two terms refer to the same personages).

The letter instructs Titus about the character of the assistants he is to choose in view of the pastoral difficulties peculiar to Crete (Ti 1:5–16). It suggests the special individual and social virtues that the various age groups and classes in the Christian community should be encouraged to acquire (Ti 2:1–10). The motivation for transformation of their lives comes from christology, especially the redemptive sacrifice of Christ and his future coming, as applied through baptism and justification (Ti 2:11–14; 3:4–8). The community is to serve as a leaven for Christianizing the social world about it (Ti 3:1–3). Good works are to be the evidence of their faith in God (Ti 3:8); those who engage in religious controversy are, after suitable warning, to be ignored (Ti 3:9–11).

The authorship and date of the Letter to Titus are discussed in the Introduction to 1 Timothy. Those who assume authorship by Paul himself usually place Titus after 1 Timothy and before 2 Timothy. Others see it as closely related to 1 Timothy, in a growing emphasis on church structure and opposition to heresy, later than the letters of Paul himself and 2 Timothy. It has also been suggested that, if the three Pastorals once circulated as a literary unit, Titus was meant to be read ahead of 1 and 2 Timothy.

The principal divisions of the Letter to Titus are the following:

I. Address (1:1–4)
II. Pastoral Charge (1:5–16)
III. Teaching the Christian Life (2:1–3:15)

I. ADDRESS

CHAPTER 1

Greeting.[*] [1]Paul, a slave of God and apostle of Jesus Christ for the sake of the faith of God's chosen ones and the recognition of religious truth,[a] [2]in the hope of eternal life that God, who does not lie, promised before time began,[b] [3]who indeed at the proper time revealed his word in the proclamation with which I was entrusted by the command of God our savior,[c] [4]to Titus, my true child in our common faith: grace and peace from God the Father and Christ Jesus our savior.[d]

II. PASTORAL CHARGE

Titus in Crete. [5†]For this reason I left you in Crete so that you might set right what remains to be done and appoint presbyters in every town, as I directed you, [6]on condition that a man be blameless, married only once, with believing children who are not accused of licentiousness or rebellious. [7]For a bishop as God's steward must be blameless, not arrogant, not irritable, not a drunkard, not aggressive, not greedy for sordid gain, [8]but hospitable, a lover of goodness, temperate, just, holy, and self-controlled, [9]holding fast to the true message as taught so that he will be able both to exhort with sound doctrine and to refute opponents.[f] [10‡]For there are also many rebels, idle talkers and deceivers, especially the Jewish Christians.[§] [11]It is imperative to silence them, as they are upsetting whole families by teaching for sordid gain what they should not. [12]One of them, a prophet of their own, once said, "Cretans have always been liars, vicious beasts, and lazy gluttons."[¶] [13]That testimony is true. Therefore, admonish them sharply, so that they may be sound in the faith,[g] [14]instead of paying attention to Jewish myths and regulations of people who have repudiated

the truth.[h] [15]To the clean all things are clean, but to those who are defiled and unbelieving nothing is clean; in fact, both their minds and their consciences are tainted.[i] [16]They claim to know God, but by their deeds they deny him. They are vile and disobedient and unqualified for any good deed.

III. TEACHING THE CHRISTIAN LIFE

CHAPTER 2

Christian Behavior.[**] [1]As for yourself, you must say what is consistent with sound doctrine, namely,[j] [2]that older men should be temperate, dignified, self-controlled, sound in faith, love, and endurance. [3]Similarly, older women should be reverent in their behavior, not slanderers, not addicted to drink, teaching what is good, [4]so that they may train younger women to love their husbands and children, [5]to be self-controlled, chaste, good homemakers, under the control of their husbands, so that the word of God may not be discredited.[k] [6]Urge the younger men, similarly, to control themselves, [7]showing yourself as a model of good deeds in every respect, with integrity in your teaching, dignity, [8]and sound speech that cannot be criticized, so that the opponent will be put to shame without anything bad to say about us. [9]Slaves are to be under the control of their masters in all respects, giving them satisfaction, not talking back to them[l] [10]or stealing from them, but exhibiting complete good faith, so as to adorn the doctrine of God our savior in every way.[m] **Transformation of Life.** [11††]For the grace of God has appeared, saving all[n] [12]and training us to reject godless ways and worldly desires and to live temperately, justly, and devoutly in this age, [13]as we await the blessed hope, the appearance[‡‡] of the glory of the great God and of our savior Jesus Christ,[o] [14]who gave himself for us to

---

*[1:1–4] On the epistolary form, see note on Rom 1:1–7. The apostolate is the divinely appointed mission to lead others to the true faith and through it to eternal salvation (Ti 1:1–3).

†[1:5–9] This instruction on the selection and appointment of presbyters, substantially identical with that in 1 Tm 3:1–7 on a bishop (see note there), was aimed at strengthening the authority of Titus by apostolic mandate; cf. Ti 2:15. In Ti 1:5, 7 and Acts 20:17, 28, the terms *episkopos* and *presbyteros* ("bishop" and "presbyter") refer to the same persons. Deacons are not mentioned in Titus. See also note on Phil 1:1.

‡[1:10–16] This adverse criticism of the defects within the community is directed especially against certain Jewish Christians, who busy themselves with useless speculations over persons mentioned in the Old Testament, insist on the observance of Jewish ritual purity regulations, and thus upset whole families by teaching things they have no right to teach; cf. Ti 3:9; 1 Tm 1:3–10.

§[1:10] Jewish Christians: literally, "those of the circumcision."

¶[1:12] Cretans . . . gluttons: quoted from Epimenides, a Cretan poet of the sixth century B.C.

**[2:1–10] One of Titus' main tasks in Crete is to become acquainted with the character of the Cretans and thereby learn to cope with its deficiencies (see Ti 1.12). The counsel is not only for Titus himself but for various classes of people with whom he must deal: older men and women (Ti 2:2–4), younger women and men (Ti 2:4–7), and slaves (Ti 2:9–10); cf. Eph 6:1–9; Col 3:18–4:1.

††[2:11–15] Underlying the admonitions for moral improvement in Ti 2:1–10 as the moving force is the constant appeal to God's revelation of salvation in Christ, with its demand for transformation of life.

‡‡[2:13] The blessed hope, the appearance: literally, "the blessed hope and appearance," but the use of a single article in Greek strongly suggests an epexegetical, i.e., explanatory sense. Of the great God and of our savior Jesus Christ: another possible translation is "of our great God and savior Jesus Christ."

---

a. [1:1] 1 Tm 2:4; 4:3; 2 Tm 2:25; 3:7; Heb 10:26.   b. [1:2] 3:7; 2 Tm 1:1; 1 Jn 2:25.   c. [1:3] 2:10; 3:4; Ps 24:5; 1 Tm 1:1; 2:3; 4:10; Jude 25.   d. [1:4] 2:13; 3:6; Phil 3:20; 2 Tm 1:10; 2 Pt 1:1, 11; 2:20; 3:2, 18.   e. [1:6–7] 1 Tm 3:2–7; 2 Tm 2:24–26.   f. [1:9] 1:13; 2:1–2, 8; 1 Tm 1:10; 6:3; 2 Tm 1:13; 4:3.   g. [1:13] 1:9.

h. [1:14] 3:9; 1 Tm 1:4; 4:7; 2 Tm 4:4; 2 Pt 1:16.   i. [1:15] Mk 7:18–23; Acts 10:15; Rom 14:14–23.   j. [2:1] 1:9, 13; 2:8; 1 Tm 1:10; 6:3; 2 Tm 1:13; 4:3.   k. [2:5] 1 Cor 11:3; 14:34; Eph 5:22–24; Col 3:18; 1 Tm 2:11–15; 1 Pt 3:1–6.   l. [2:9] 1 Cor 7:21–22; Eph 6:5–8; Col 3:22–25; 1 Tm 6:1–2; 1 Pt 2:18.   m. [2:10] 1:3; 3:4; Ps 24:5; 1 Tm 1:1; 2:3; 4:10; Jude 25.   n. [2:11] 1 Tm 2:4; 4:10.   o. [2:13] 1 Cor 1:7; Phil 3:20; 1 Thes 1:10 / 2 Tm 1:10 / Ti 1:4; 3:6; 2 Pt 1:11; 2:20; 3:2, 18.

deliver us from all lawlessness and to cleanse for himself a people as his own, eager to do what is good.[p]

[15]Say these things. Exhort and correct with all authority. Let no one look down on you.[q]

CHAPTER 3

[1]*Remind them to be under the control of magistrates and authorities,[t] to be obedient, to be open to every good enterprise.[r] [2]They are to slander no one, to be peaceable, considerate, exercising all graciousness toward everyone. [3]For we ourselves were once foolish, disobedient, deluded, slaves to various desires and pleasures, living in malice and envy, hateful ourselves and hating one another.[s]

[4] But when the kindness and generous love
    of God our savior appeared,[t]
[5] not because of any righteous deeds we
        had done
    but because of his mercy,
    he saved us through the bath of rebirth
        and renewal by the holy Spirit,[u]
[6] whom he richly poured out on us

---

*[3:1–8] The list of Christian duties continues from Ti 2:9–10, undergirded again as in Ti 2:11–13 by appeal to what God in Christ has done (Ti 2:4–7; cf. Ti 2:11–14). The spiritual renewal of the Cretans, signified in God's merciful gift of baptism (Ti 3:4–7), should be reflected in their improved attitude toward civil authority and in their Christian relationship with all (Ti 3:1–3).

†[3:1] **Magistrates and authorities:** some interpreters understand these terms as referring to the principalities and powers of the heavenly hierarchy. **To be open to every good enterprise:** this implies being good citizens. It could also be translated "ready to do every sort of good work" (as Christians); cf. Ti 3:14.

p. [2:14] Gal 1:4; 2:20; Eph 5:2, 25; 1 Tm 2:6; 1 Pt 1:18–19 / Ps 130:8.   q. [2:15] 1 Tm 4:12.   r. [3:1] Rom 13:1–7; 1 Tm 2:1–2; 1 Pt 2:13–14.   s. [3:3] 1 Cor 6:9–11; Eph 2:1–3; 5:8; Col 3:5–7; 1 Pt 4:3.   t. [3:4] 1:3; 2:10; Ps 24:5; 1 Tm 1:1; 2:3; 4:10; Jude 25.   u. [3:5] Dt 9:5; Eph 2:4–5, 8–9; 2 Tm 1:9.

---

    through Jesus Christ our savior,[v]
[7] so that we might be justified by his grace
    and become heirs in hope of eternal
        life.[w]

[8]This saying is trustworthy.

Advice to Titus.[‡] I want you to insist on these points, that those who have believed in God be careful to devote themselves to good works; these are excellent and beneficial to others.[x] [9§]Avoid foolish arguments, genealogies, rivalries, and quarrels about the law,[y] for they are useless and futile. [10]After a first and second warning, break off contact with a heretic,[z] [11]realizing that such a person is perverted and sinful and stands self-condemned.

Directives, Greetings, and Blessing.[¶] [12]When I send Artemas to you, or Tychicus, try to join me at Nicopolis, where I have decided to spend the winter.[a] [13]Send Zenas the lawyer and Apollos on their journey soon, and see to it that they have everything they need.[b] [14]But let our people, too, learn to devote themselves to good works to supply urgent needs, so that they may not be unproductive.[c]

[15]All who are with me send you greetings. Greet those who love us in the faith.
    Grace be with all of you.[d]

---

‡[3:8–11] In matters of good conduct and religious doctrine, Titus is to stand firm.

§[3:9] See note on 1 Tm 6:20–21.

¶[3:12–15] **Artemas** or **Tychicus** (2 Tm 4:12) is to replace Titus, who will join Paul in his winter sojourn at Nicopolis in Epirus, on the western coast of Greece.

v. [3:6] 1:4; 2:13; Phil 3:20; 2 Tm 1:10; 2 Pt 1:1, 11; 2:20; 3:2, 18.   w. [3:7] 1:2; 2 Tm 1:1; 1 Jn 2:25.   x. [3:8] 1 Tm 1:15; 3:1; 4:9; 2 Tm 2:11.   y. [3:9] 1 Tm 1:4; 4:7; 2 Tm 2:23.   z. [3:10] Mt 18:15–18; Rom 16:17; 1 Cor 5:11; 2 Thes 3:6, 14–15.   a. [3:12] Acts 20:4; Eph 6:21; Col 4:7; 2 Tm 4:12.   b. [3:13] Acts 18:24–26; 1 Cor 1:12; 3:4–6, 22; 4:6; 16:12.   c. [3:14] 2:14; 3:8; Heb 10:24; 1 Pt 3:13.   d. [3:15] Heb 13:25.

THE LETTER TO
PHILEMON

This short letter addressed to three specific individuals was written by Paul during an imprisonment, perhaps in Rome between A.D. 61 and 63 (see the Introduction to Colossians for other possible sites). It concerns Onesimus, a slave from Colossae (Col 4:9), who had run away from his master, perhaps guilty of theft in the process (Phlm 18). Onesimus was converted to Christ by Paul (Phlm 10). Paul sends him back to his master (Phlm 12) with this letter asking that he be welcomed willingly by his old master (Phlm 8–10, 14, 17) not just as a slave but as a brother in Christ (Phlm 16). Paul uses very strong arguments (especially Phlm 19) in his touching appeal on behalf of Onesimus. It is unlikely that Paul is subtly hinting that he would like to retain Onesimus as his own slave, lent to Paul by his master. Rather, he suggests he would like to have Onesimus work with him for the gospel (Phlm 13, 20–21). There is, however, little evidence connecting this Onesimus with a bishop of Ephesus of the same name mentioned by Ignatius of Antioch (ca. A.D. 110).

Paul's letter deals with an accepted institution of antiquity, human slavery. But Paul breathes into this letter the spirit of Christ and of equality within the Christian community. He does not attack slavery directly, for this is something the Christian communities of the first century were in no position to do, and the expectation that Christ would soon come again militated against social reforms. Yet Paul, by presenting Onesimus as "brother, beloved . . . to me, but even more so to you" (Phlm 16), voiced an idea revolutionary in that day and destined to break down worldly barriers of division "in the Lord."

Address and Greeting. [1]"Paul, a prisoner for Christ Jesus, and Timothy our brother, to Philemon, our beloved and our co-worker,[a] [2]to Apphia our sister,[†] to Archippus our fellow soldier, and to the church at your house.[b] [3]Grace to you and peace[‡] from God our Father and the Lord Jesus Christ.[c]

Thanksgiving. [4s–d]I give thanks to my God always, remembering you in my prayers, [5]as I hear of the love and the faith you have in the Lord Jesus and for all the holy ones,[¶] [6]so that your partnership in the faith may become effective in recognizing every good there is in us" that leads to Christ.[e]

Plea for Onesimus. [7]For I have experienced much joy and encouragement[††] from your love, because the hearts of the holy ones have been refreshed by you, brother.[f] [8]Therefore, although I have the full right[‡‡] in Christ to order you to do what is proper, [9]I rather urge you out of love, being as I am, Paul, an old man,[§§] and now also a prisoner for Christ Jesus.[g] [10]I urge you on behalf of my child Onesimus, whose father I have become in my imprisonment,[h] [11]who was once

---

*[1] **Prisoner**: as often elsewhere (cf. Romans, 1 Corinthians, Galatians especially), the second word in Greek enunciates the theme and sets the tone of the letter. Here it is the prisoner appealing rather than the apostle commanding.

†[2] **Apphia our sister**: sister is here used (like brother) to indicate a fellow Christian. **The church at your house**: your here is singular. It more likely refers to Philemon than to the last one named, Archippus; Philemon is then the owner of the slave Onesimus (Phlm 10). An alternate view is that the actual master of the slave is Archippus and that the one to whom the letter is addressed, Philemon, is the most prominent Christian there; see note on Col 4:17.

‡[3] **Grace . . . and peace**: for this greeting, which may be a combination of Greek and Aramaic epistolary formulae, see note on Rom 1:1–7.

§[4] **In my prayers**: literally, "at the time of my prayers."

¶[5] **Holy ones**: a common term for members of the Christian community (so also Phlm 7).

[6] **In us: some good ancient manuscripts have *in you* (plural). **That leads to Christ**: leads to translates the Greek preposition *eis*, indicating direction or purpose.

††[7] **Encouragement**: the Greek word *paraklēsis* is cognate with the verb translated "urge" in Phlm 9–10, and serves as an introduction to Paul's plea. **Hearts**: literally, "bowels," expressing in Semitic fashion the seat of the emotions, one's "inmost self." The same Greek word is used in Phlm 12 and again in Phlm 20, where it forms a literary inclusion marking off the body of the letter.

‡‡[8] **Full right**: often translated "boldness," the Greek word *parrēsia* connotes the full franchise of speech, as the right of a citizen to speak before the body politic, claimed by the Athenians as their privilege (Euripides).

§§[9] **Old man**: some editors conjecture that Paul here used a similar Greek word meaning "ambassador" (cf. Eph 6:20). This conjecture heightens the contrast with "prisoner" but is totally without manuscript support.

---

a. [1] 9; Eph 3:1; 4:1; Phil 1:7, 13.   b. [2] Col 4:17.   c. [3] Rom 1:7; Gal 1:3; Phil 1:2.   d. [4–5] Rom 1:8–9; Eph 1:15–16.   e. [6] Phil 1:9; Col 1:9.   f. [7] 2 Cor 7:4.   g. [9] 1; Eph 3:1; 4:1; Phil 1:7, 13.   h. [10] 1 Cor 4:14–15; Gal 4:19; Col 4:9.

useless to you but is now useful* to [both] you and me. [12]I am sending him, that is, my own heart, back to you. [13]I should have liked to retain him for myself, so that he might serve† me on your behalf in my imprisonment for the gospel,[i] [14]but I did not want to do anything without your consent, so that the good you do might not be ‘forced but voluntary.[j] [15]Perhaps this is why he was away from‡ you for a while, that you might have him back forever, [16]no longer as a slave but more than a slave, a brother, beloved especially to me, but even more so to you, as a man§ and in the Lord.[k] [17]So if you regard me as a partner, welcome him as you would me. [18]And if he has done you any injustice or owes you anything, charge it to me. [19]I, Paul, write this in my own hand: I will pay. May I not tell you that you owe me your very self.[l] [20]Yes, brother, may I profit from you in the Lord. Refresh my heart in Christ.

[21]With trust in your compliance I write to you, knowing that you will do even more than I say. [22]At the same time prepare a guest room for me, for I hope to be granted to you through your prayers.[m]

Final Greetings. [23]Epaphras,** my fellow prisoner in Christ Jesus, greets you,[n] [24]as well as Mark, Aristarchus, Demas, and Luke, my coworkers. [25]The grace of the Lord Jesus Christ be with your spirit.[o]

---

*[11] **Useless . . . useful**: here Paul plays on the name Onesimus, which means "useful" or "beneficial." The verb translated "profit" in Phlm 20 is cognate.

†[13] **Serve**: the Greek *diakoneō* could connote a ministry.

‡[15] **Was away from**: literally, "was separated from," but the same verb means simply "left" in Acts 18:1. It is a euphemism for his running away.

§[16] **As a man**: literally, "in the flesh." With this and the following phrase, Paul describes the natural and spiritual orders.

¶[18–19] **Charge it to me . . . I will pay**: technical legal and commercial terms in account keeping and acknowledgment of indebtedness.

i. [13] Phil 2:30.   j. [14] 2 Cor 9:7; 1 Pt 5:2.   k. [16] 1 Tm 6:2.

[23–24] **Epaphras: a Colossian who founded the church there (Col 1:7) and perhaps also in Laodicea and Hierapolis (Col 2:1; 4:12–13). **Aristarchus**: a native of Thessalonica and fellow worker of Paul (Acts 19:29; 20:4; 27:2). For Mark, Demas, and Luke, see 2 Tm 4:9–13 and the note there.

l. [19] Gal 6:11; 2 Thes 3:17.   m. [22] Heb 13:19.   n. [23] Col 1:7; 4:12–13.   o. [25] Acts 12:12, 15; 13:13; 15:37–39; 19:29; 20:4; 27:2; Col 4:10, 14; 2 Tm 4:10–13.

THE LETTER TO THE
HEBREWS

As early as the second century, this treatise, which is of great rhetorical power and force in its admonition to faithful pilgrimage under Christ's leadership, bore the title "To the Hebrews." It was assumed to be directed to Jewish Christians. Usually Hebrews was attached in Greek manuscripts to the collection of letters by Paul. Although no author is mentioned (for there is no address), a reference to Timothy (Heb 13:23) suggested connections to the circle of Paul and his assistants. Yet the exact audience, the author, and even whether Hebrews is a letter have long been disputed.

The author saw the addressees in danger of apostasy from their Christian faith. This danger was due not to any persecution from outsiders but to a weariness with the demands of Christian life and a growing indifference to their calling (Heb 2:1; 4:14; 6:1-12; 10:23-32). The author's main theme, the priesthood and sacrifice of Jesus (Heb 3-10), is not developed for its own sake but as a means of restoring their lost fervor and strengthening them in their faith. Another important theme of the letter is that of the pilgrimage of the people of God to the heavenly Jerusalem (Heb 11:10; 12:1-3, 18-29; 13:14). This theme is intimately connected with that of Jesus' ministry in the heavenly sanctuary (Heb 9:11-10:22).

The author calls this work a "message of encouragement" (Heb 13:22), a designation that is given to a synagogue sermon in Acts 13:15. Hebrews is probably therefore a written homily, to which the author gave an epistolary ending (Heb 13:22-25).

The author begins with a reminder of the preexistence, incarnation, and exaltation of Jesus (Heb 1:3) that proclaimed him the climax of God's word to humanity (Heb 1:1-3). He dwells upon the dignity of the person of Christ, superior to the angels (Heb 1:4-2:2). Christ is God's final word of salvation communicated (in association with accredited witnesses to his teaching: cf. Heb 2:3-4) not merely by word but through his suffering in the humanity common to him and to all others (Heb 2:5-16). This enactment of salvation went beyond the pattern known to Moses, faithful prophet of God's word though he was, for Jesus as high priest expiated sin and was faithful to God with the faithfulness of God's own Son (Heb 2:17-3:6).

Just as the infidelity of the people thwarted Moses' efforts to save them, so the infidelity of any Christian may thwart God's plan in Christ (Heb 3:6-4:13). Christians are to reflect that it is their humanity that Jesus took upon himself, with all its defects save sinfulness, and that he bore the burden of it until death out of obedience to God. God declared this work of his Son to be the cause of salvation for all (Heb 4:14-5:10). Although Christians recognize this fundamental teaching, they may grow weary of it and of its implications, and therefore require other reflections to stimulate their faith (Heb 5:11-6:20).

Therefore, the author presents to the readers for their reflection the everlasting priesthood of Christ (Heb 7:1-28), a priesthood that fulfills the promise of the Old Testament (Heb 8:1-13). It also provides the meaning God ultimately intended in the sacrifices of the Old Testament (Heb 9:1-28): these pointed to the unique sacrifice of Christ, which alone obtains forgiveness of sins (Heb 10:1-18). The trial of faith experienced by the readers should resolve itself through their consideration of Christ's ministry in the heavenly sanctuary and his perpetual intercession there on their behalf (Heb 7:25; 8:1-13). They should also be strengthened by the assurance of his foreordained parousia, and by the fruits of faith that they have already enjoyed (Heb 10:19-39).

It is in the nature of faith to recognize the reality of what is not yet seen and is the object of hope, and the saints of the Old Testament give striking example of that faith (Heb 11:1-40). The perseverance to which the author exhorts the readers is shown forth in the early life of Jesus. Despite the afflictions of his ministry and the supreme trial of his suffering and death, he remained confident of the triumph that God would bring him (Heb 12:1-3). The difficulties of human life have meaning when they are accepted as God's discipline (Heb 12:4-13), and if Christians persevere in fidelity to the word in which they have believed, they are assured of possessing forever the unshakable kingdom of God (Heb 12:14-29).

The letter concludes with specific moral commandments (Heb 13:1-17), in the course of which the author recalls again his central theme of the sacrifice of Jesus and the courage needed to associate oneself with it in faith (Heb 13:9-16).

As early as the end of the second century, the church of Alexandria in Egypt accepted Hebrews as a letter of Paul, and that became the view commonly held in the East. Pauline authorship was contested in the West into the fourth century, but then accepted. In the sixteenth century, doubts about that position were again raised, and the modern consensus is that the letter was not written by Paul. There is, however, no widespread agreement on any of the other suggested authors, e.g., Barnabas, Apollos, or Prisc(ill)a and Aquila. The document itself has no statement about its author.

Among the reasons why Pauline authorship has been abandoned are the great difference of vocabulary and style between Hebrews and Paul's letters, the alternation of doctrinal teaching with moral exhortation, the different manner of citing the Old Testament, and the resemblance between the thought of Hebrews and that of Alexandrian Judaism. The Greek of the letter is in many ways the best in the New Testament.

Since the letter of Clement of Rome to the Corinthians, written about A.D. 96, most probably cites Hebrews, the upper limit for the date of composition is reasonably certain. While the letter's references in the present tense to the Old Testament sacrificial worship do not necessarily show that temple worship was still going on, many older commentators and a growing number of recent ones favor the view that it was and that the author wrote before the destruction of the temple of Jerusalem in A.D. 70. In that case, the argument of the letter is more easily explained as directed toward Jewish Christians rather than those of Gentile origin, and the persecutions they have suffered in the past (cf. Heb 10:32-34) may have been connected with the disturbances that preceded the expulsion of the Jews from Rome in A.D. 49 under the emperor Claudius. These were probably caused by disputes between Jews who accepted Jesus as the Messiah and those who did not.

The principal divisions of the Letter to the Hebrews are the following:

I. Introduction (1:1-4)
II. The Son Higher Than the Angels (1:5-2:18)
III. Jesus, Faithful and Compassionate High Priest (3:1-5:10)
IV. Jesus' Eternal Priesthood and Eternal Sacrifice (5:11-10:39)
V. Examples, Discipline, Disobedience (11:1-12:29)
VI. Final Exhortation, Blessing, Greetings (13:1-25)

I. INTRODUCTION*

CHAPTER 1

[1]In times past, God spoke in partial and various ways to our ancestors through the prophets; [2]in these last days, he spoke to us through a son, whom he made heir of all things and through whom he created the universe,[a]

[3] who is the refulgence of his glory,
     the very imprint of his being,
* and who sustains all things by his mighty
     word.
     When he had accomplished purification
          from sins,
     he took his seat at the right hand of the
          Majesty on high,[b]
[4]   as far superior to the angels
     as the name he has inherited is more
          excellent than theirs.[c]

II. THE SON HIGHER THAN THE ANGELS

Messianic Enthronement.[†] [5]For to which of the angels did God ever say:

"You are my son; this day I have begotten you"?[d]

Or again:

"I will be a father to him, and he shall be a son to me"?

[6]And again, when he leads[‡] the first-born into the world, he says:

"Let all the angels of God worship him."[e]

[7]Of the angels he says:

"He makes his angels winds
     and his ministers a fiery flame";[f]

[8]but of the Son:

"Your throne, O God,[§] stands forever and
     ever;
     and a righteous scepter is the scepter
          of your kingdom.[g]
[9] You loved justice and hated wickedness;
     therefore God, your God, anointed
          you
     with the oil of gladness above your
          companions";

[10]and:

"At the beginning, O Lord, you
          established the earth,[h]
     and the heavens are the works of
          your hands.
[11] They will perish, but you remain;
     and they will all grow old like a
          garment.
[12] You will roll them up like a cloak,
     and like a garment they will be
          changed.
     But you are the same, and your years will
          have no end."

[13]But to which of the angels has he ever said:

"Sit at my right hand
     until I make your enemies your
          footstool"?[i]

---

*[1:1–4] The letter opens with an introduction consisting of a reflection on the climax of God's revelation to the human race in his Son. The divine communication was initiated and maintained during Old Testament times in fragmentary and varied ways through **the prophets** (Heb 1:1), including Abraham, Moses, and all through whom God spoke. But now **in these last days** (Heb 1:2) the final age, God's revelation of his saving purpose is achieved **through a son**, i.e., one who is Son, whose role is redeemer and mediator of creation. He was made **heir of all things** through his death and exaltation to glory, yet he existed before he appeared as man; through him God **created the universe**. Heb 1:3–4, which may be based upon a liturgical hymn, assimilate the Son to the personified Wisdom of the Old Testament as **refulgence of** God's **glory** and **imprint of his being** (Heb 1:3; cf. Wis 7:26). These same terms are used of the Logos in Philo. The author now turns from the cosmological role of the preexistent Son to the redemptive work of Jesus: he brought about purification from sins and has been exalted to the right hand of God (see Ps 110:1). The once-humiliated and crucified Jesus has been declared God's Son, and this name shows his superiority to the angels. The reason for the author's insistence on that superiority is, among other things, that in some Jewish traditions angels were mediators of the old covenant (see Acts 7:53; Gal 3:19). Finally, Jesus' superiority to the angels emphasizes the superiority of the new covenant to the old because of the heavenly priesthood of Jesus.

†[1:5–14] Jesus' superiority to the angels is now demonstrated by a series of seven Old Testament texts. Some scholars see in the stages of Jesus' exaltation an order corresponding to that of enthronement ceremonies in the ancient Near East, especially in Egypt, namely, elevation to divine status (Heb 1:5–6); presentation to the angels and proclamation of everlasting lordship (Heb 1:7–12); enthronement and conferral of royal power (Heb 1:13). The citations from the Psalms in Heb 1:5, 13 were traditionally used of Jesus' messianic sonship (cf. Acts 13:33) through his resurrection and exaltation (cf. Acts 2:33–35); those in Heb 1:8, 10–12 are concerned with his divine kingship and his creative function. The central quotation in Heb 1:7 serves to contrast the angels with the Son. The author quotes it according to the Septuagint translation, which is quite different in meaning from that of the Hebrew

("You make the winds your messengers, and flaming fire your ministers"). The angels are only **sent to serve . . . those who are to inherit salvation** (Heb 1:14).

‡[1:6] **And again, when he leads**: the Greek could also be translated "And when he again leads" in reference to the parousia.

§[1:8–12] **O God**: the application of the name "God" to the Son derives from the preexistence mentioned in Heb 1:2–3; the psalmist had already used it of the Hebrew king in the court style of the original. See note on Ps 45:7. It is also important for the author's christology that in Heb 1:10–12 an Old Testament passage addressed to God is redirected to Jesus.

---

a. [1:2] Is 2:2; Jer 23:20; Ez 38:16; Dn 10:14 / Jn 3:17; Rom 8:3; Gal 4:4 / Prv 8:30; Wis 7:22; Jn 1:3; 1 Cor 8:6; Col 1:16. b. [1:3] Wis 7:26; 2 Cor 4:4; Col 1:15 / Heb 8:1; 10:12; 12:2; Mk 16:19; Acts 2:33; 7:55–56; Rom 8:34; Eph 1:20; Col 3:1; 1 Pt 3:22. c. [1:4] Eph 1:21; Phil 2:9–11.

d. [1:5] Ps 2:7 / 2 Sm 7:14. e. [1:6] Dt 32:43 LXX; Ps 97:7. f. [1:7] Ps 104:4 LXX. g. [1:8] Ps 45:7–8. h. [1:10–12] Ps 102:26–28. i. [1:13] Ps 110:1.

¹⁴Are they not all ministering spirits sent to serve, for the sake of those who are to inherit salvation?ʲ

CHAPTER 2

Exhortation to Faithfulness.* ¹Therefore, we must attend all the more to what we have heard, so that we may not be carried away. ²For if the word announced through angels proved firm, and every transgression and disobedience received its just recompense,ᵏ ³how shall we escape if we ignore so great a salvation? Announced originally through the Lord, it was confirmed for us by those who had heard.ˡ ⁴God added his testimony by signs, wonders, various acts of power, and distribution of the gifts of the holy Spirit according to his will.ᵐ

Exaltation Through Abasement.† ⁵For it was not to angels that he subjected the world to come, of

which we are speaking. ⁶Instead, someone has testified somewhere:

> "What is man that you are mindful of
>   him,
>   or the son of man that you care for
>   him?"ⁿ

⁷ You made him for a little while lower than
>   the angels;
>   you crowned him with glory and
>   honor,

⁸   subjecting all things under his feet."

In "subjecting" all things [to him], he left nothing not "subject to him." Yet at present we do not see "all things subject to him,"ᵒ ⁹but we do see Jesus "crowned with glory and honor" because he suffered death, he who "for a little while" was made "lower than the angels," that by the grace of God he might taste death for everyone.ᵖ

¹⁰For it was fitting that he, for whom and through whom all things exist, in bringing many children to glory, should make the leader to their salvation perfect through suffering.�q ¹¹He who consecrates and those who are being consecrated all have one origin. Therefore, he is not ashamed to call them "brothers," ¹²saying:

> "I will proclaim your name to my
>   brothers,
>   in the midst of the assembly I will
>   praise you";ʳ

¹³and again:

> "I will put my trust in him";

and again:

> "Behold, I and the children God has given
>   me."ˢ

¹⁴Now since the children share in blood and flesh, he likewise shared in them, that through death he might destroy the one who has the power of death, that is, the devil,ᵗ ¹⁵and free those who through fear of death had been subject to slavery all their life. ¹⁶Surely he did not help angels but rather the descendants of Abraham; ¹⁷therefore, he had to become like his brothers in every way, that he might be a merciful and faithful high priest before God to expiate the sins of the people.ᵘ ¹⁸Because he himself was tested through what he suffered, he is able to help those who are being tested.

---

*[2:1–4] The author now makes a transition into exhortation, using an a fortiori argument (as at Heb 7:21–22; 9:13–14; 10:28–29; 12:25). The **word announced through angels** (Heb 2:2), the Mosaic law, is contrasted with the more powerful word that Christians have received (Heb 2:3–4). Christ's supremacy strengthens Christians against being **carried away** from their faith.

†[2:5–18] The humanity and the suffering of Jesus do not constitute a valid reason for relinquishing the Christian faith. Ps 8:6–7 is also applied to Jesus in 1 Cor 15:27; Eph 1:22; and probably 1 Pt 3:22. This christological interpretation, therefore, probably reflects a common early Christian tradition, which may have originated in the expression **the son of man** (Heb 2:6). The psalm contrasts God's greatness with man's relative insignificance but also stresses the superiority of man to the rest of creation, of which he is lord. Hebrews applies this christologically: Jesus lived a truly human existence, **lower than the angels**, in the days of his earthly life, particularly in his suffering and death; now, **crowned with glory and honor**, he is raised above all creation. The author considers all things as already **subject to him** because of his exaltation (Heb 2:8–9), though **we do not see** this yet. The reference to Jesus as **leader** (Heb 2:10) sounds the first note of an important leitmotif in Hebrews: the journey of the people of God to the sabbath rest (Heb 4:9), the heavenly sanctuary, following Jesus, their "forerunner" (Heb 6:20). It was fitting that God should make him **perfect through suffering**, consecrated by obedient suffering. Because he is perfected as high priest, Jesus is then able to consecrate his people (Heb 2:11); access to God is made possible by each of these two consecrations. If Jesus is able to help human beings, it is because he has become one of us; we are his "brothers." The author then cites three Old Testament texts as proofs of this unity between ourselves and the Son. Ps 22:23 is interpreted so as to make Jesus the singer of this lament, which ends with joyful praise of the Lord in the assembly of "brothers." The other two texts are from Is 8:17–18. The first of these seems intended to display in Jesus an example of the trust in God that his followers should emulate. The second curiously calls these followers "children"; probably this is to be understood to mean children of Adam, but the point is our solidarity with Jesus. By sharing human nature, including the ban on death, Jesus broke the power of the devil over death (Heb 2:14); the author shares the view of Hellenistic Judaism that death was not intended by God and that it had been introduced into the world by the devil. The **fear of death** (Heb 2:15) is a religious fear based on the false conception that death marks the end of a person's relations with God (cf. Ps 115:17–18; Is 38:18). Jesus deliberately allied himself with the **descendants of Abraham** (Heb 2:16) in order to be a **merciful and faithful high priest**. This is the first appearance of the central theme of Hebrews, Jesus the

great high priest expiating the **sins of the people** (Heb 2:17), as one who experienced the same tests as they (Heb 2:18).

n. [2:6] Ps 8:5–7.   o. [2:8] Mt 28:18; 1 Cor 15:25–28; Eph 1:20–23; Phil 3:21; 1 Pt 3:22.   p. [2:9] Phil 2:6–11.   q. [2:10] 12:2; Is 53:4 / Rom 11:36; 1 Cor 8:6.   r. [2:12] Ps 22:23.   s. [2:13] Is 8:17, 18.   t. [2:14] Is 25:8; Hos 13:14; Jn 12:31; Rom 6:9; 1 Cor 15:54–55; 2 Tm 1:10; Rev 12:10.   u. [2:17] 4:15; 5:1–3.

j. [1:14] Ps 91:11; Dn 7:10.   k. [2:2] Acts 7:38, 53; Gal 3:19.   l. [2:3] 10:29; 12:25.   m. [2:4] Mk 16:20; Acts 14:3; 19:11.

III. JESUS, FAITHFUL AND COMPASSIONATE HIGH PRIEST

CHAPTER 3

Jesus, Superior to Moses.[*] [1]Therefore, holy "brothers," sharing in a heavenly calling, reflect on Jesus, the apostle and high priest of our confession, [2]who was faithful to the one who appointed him, just as Moses was "faithful in [all] his house."[y] [3]But he is worthy of more "glory" than Moses, as the founder of a house has more "honor" than the house itself.[w] [4]Every house is founded by someone, but the founder of all is God. [5]Moses was "faithful in all his house" as a "servant" to testify to what would be spoken, [6†x]but Christ was faithful as a son placed over his house. We are his house, if [only] we hold fast to our confidence and pride in our hope.

Israel's Infidelity a Warning. [7‡]Therefore, as the holy Spirit says:

"Oh, that today you would hear his voice,[y]
[8]   'Harden not your hearts as at the rebellion
        in the day of testing in the desert,
[9]   where your ancestors tested and tried me
        and saw my works[z] [10]for forty years.
    Because of this I was provoked with that generation
        and I said, "They have always been of erring heart,
        and they do not know my ways."
[11]   As I swore in my wrath,
        "They shall not enter into my rest."'"

[12]Take care, brothers, that none of you may have an evil and unfaithful heart, so as to forsake the living God. [13]Encourage yourselves daily while it is still "today," so that none of you may grow hardened by the deceit of sin. [14]We have become partners of Christ if only we hold the beginning of the reality firm until the end,[a] [15]for it is said:

"Oh, that today you would hear his voice:
'Harden not your hearts as at the rebellion.'"[b]

[16]Who were those who rebelled when they heard? Was it not all those who came out of Egypt under Moses? [17]With whom was he "provoked for forty years"? Was it not those who had sinned, whose corpses fell in the desert?[d] [18]And to whom did he "swear that they should not enter into his rest," if not to those who were disobedient?[e] [19]And we see that they could not enter for lack of faith.

CHAPTER 4

The Sabbath Rest. [1]Therefore, let us be on our guard while the promise of entering into his rest remains, that none of you seem to have failed. [2]For in fact we have received the good news just as they did. But the word that they heard did not profit them, for they were not united in faith with those who listened. [3]For we who believed enter into [that] rest, just as he has said:[f]

"As I swore in my wrath,
'They shall not enter into my rest,'"

and yet his works were accomplished at the foundation of the world. [4]For he has spoken somewhere about the seventh day in this manner,

---

*[3:1–6] The author now takes up the two qualities of Jesus mentioned in Heb 2:17, but in inverse order: faithfulness (Heb 3:1–4:13) and mercy (Heb 4:14–5:10). Christians are called **holy "brothers"** because of their common relation to him (Heb 2:11), **the apostle,** a designation for Jesus used only here in the New Testament (cf. Jn 13:16; 17:3), meaning one sent as God's final word to us (Heb 1:2). He is compared with Moses probably because he is seen as mediator of the new covenant (Heb 9:15) just as Moses was of the old (Heb 9:19–22, including his sacrifice). But when the author of Hebrews speaks of Jesus' sacrifice, he does not consider Moses as the Old Testament antitype, but rather the high priest on the Day of Atonement (Heb 9:6–15). Moses' faithfulness **"in [all] his house"** refers back to Nm 12:7, on which this section is a midrashic commentary. In Heb 3:3–6, the author does not indicate that he thinks of either Moses or Christ as the founder of the household. **His house** (Heb 3:2, 5, 6) means God's house, not that of Moses or Christ; in the case of Christ, compare Heb 3:6 with Heb 10:21. The **house** of Heb 3:6 is the Christian community; the author suggests its continuity with Israel by speaking not of two houses but of only one. Heb 3:6 brings out the reason why Jesus is superior to Moses: the latter was the faithful **servant** laboring in the house founded by God, but Jesus is God's **son,** placed **over** the house.

†[3:6] The majority of manuscripts add "firm to the end," but these words are not found in the three earliest and best witnesses and are probably an interpolation derived from Heb 3:14.

‡[3:7–4:13] The author appeals for steadfastness of faith in Jesus, basing his warning on the experience of Israel during the Exodus. In the Old Testament the Exodus had been invoked as a symbol of the return of Israel from the Babylonian exile (Is 42:9; 43:16–21; 51:9–11). In the New Testament the redemption was similarly understood as a new exodus, both in the experience of Jesus himself (Lk 9:31) and in that of his followers (1 Cor 10:1–4). The author cites Ps 95:7–11, a salutary example of hardness of heart, as a warning against the danger of growing weary and giving up the journey. To call God **living** (Heb 3:12) means that he reveals himself in his works (cf. Jos 3:10; Jer 10:11). The **rest** (Heb 3:11) into which Israel was to enter was only a foreshadowing of that rest to which Christians are called. They are to remember the example of Israel's revolt in the desert that cost a whole generation the loss of the promised land (Heb 3:15–19; cf. Nm 14:20–29). In Heb 4:1–11, the symbol of **rest** is seen in deeper dimension: because the promise to the ancient Hebrews foreshadowed that given to Christians, it is **good news;** and because the promised land was the place of rest that God provided for his people, it was a share in his own rest, which he enjoyed after he had finished his creative work (Heb 3:3–4; cf. Gn 2:2). The author attempts to read this meaning of God's rest into Ps 95:7–11 (Heb 3:6–9). The Greek form of the name of Joshua, who led Israel into the promised land, is Jesus (Heb 3:8). The author plays upon the name but stresses the superiority of

---

Jesus, who leads his followers into heavenly rest. Heb 3:12–13 are meant as a continuation of the warning, for the word of God brings judgment as well as salvation. Some would capitalize **the word of God** and see it as a personal title of Jesus, comparable to that of Jn 1:1–18.

y. [3:2] Nm 12:7.   w. [3:3] 2 Cor 3:7–8.   x. [3:6] 10:21; Eph 2:19; 1 Tm 3:15; 1 Pt 4:17.

y. [3:7–11] Ps 95:7–11.   z. [3:9] Ex 17:7; Nm 20:2–5.   a. [3:14] Rom 8:17.   b. [3:15] Ps 95:7–8.   c. [3:16–19] Nm 14:1–38; Dt 1:19–40.   d. [3:17] Nm 14:29.   e. [3:18] Nm 14:22–23; Dt 1:35.   f. [4:3] 3:11; Ps 95:11.

"And God rested on the seventh day from all his works";[g] [5]and again, in the previously mentioned place, "They shall not enter into my rest."[h] [6]Therefore, since it remains that some will enter into it, and those who formerly received the good news did not enter because of disobedience, [7]he once more set a day, "today," when long afterwards he spoke through David, as already quoted:[i]

"Oh, that today you would hear his voice:
'Harden not your hearts.'"

[8]Now if Joshua had given them rest, he would not have spoken afterwards of another day.[j] [9]Therefore, a sabbath rest still remains for the people of God. [10]And whoever enters into God's rest, rests from his own works as God did from his. [11]Therefore, let us strive to enter into that rest, so that no one may fall after the same example of disobedience.

[12]Indeed, the word of God is living and effective, sharper than any two-edged sword, penetrating even between soul and spirit, joints and marrow, and able to discern reflections and thoughts of the heart.[k] [13]No creature is concealed from him, but everything is naked and exposed to the eyes of him to whom we must render an account.[l]

Jesus, Compassionate High Priest. [14]*Therefore, since we have a great high priest who has passed through the heavens, Jesus, the Son of God, let us hold fast to our confession.[m] [15]For we do not have a high priest who is unable to sympathize with our weaknesses, but one who has similarly been tested in every way, yet without sin.[n] [16]So let us confidently approach the throne of grace to receive mercy and to find grace for timely help.[o]

CHAPTER 5

[1†]Every high priest is taken from among men and made their representative before God, to offer gifts and sacrifices for sins.[‡] [2]He is able to deal patiently[§] with the ignorant and erring, for he himself is beset by weakness [3]and so, for this reason, must make sin offerings for himself as well as for the people.[p] [4]No one takes this honor upon himself but only when called by God, just as Aaron was.[q] [5]In the same way, it was not Christ who glorified himself in becoming high priest, but rather the one who said to him:

"You are my son;
    this day I have begotten you";[r]

[6]just as he says in another place:[s]

"You are a priest forever
    according to the order of
    Melchizedek."[s]

[7]In the days when he was in the flesh, he offered prayers and supplications with loud cries and tears to the one who was able to save him from death," and he was heard because of his reverence.[t] [8]Son though he was,[††] he learned obedience from what he suffered;[u] [9]and when he was made perfect, he became the source of eternal salvation for all who obey him,[v] [10]declared by God high priest according to the order of Melchizedek.[w]

IV. JESUS' ETERNAL PRIESTHOOD AND ETERNAL SACRIFICE

Exhortation to Spiritual Renewal. [11‡‡]About this we have much to say, and it is difficult

---

*[4:14–16] These verses, which return to the theme first sounded in Heb 2:16–3:1, serve as an introduction to the section that follows. The author here alone calls Jesus **a great high priest** (Heb 4:14), a designation used by Philo for the Logos; perhaps he does so in order to emphasize Jesus' superiority over the Jewish high priest. He has **been tested in every way, yet without sin** (Heb 4:15); this indicates an acquaintance with the tradition of Jesus' temptations, not only at the beginning (as in Mk 1:13) but throughout his public life (cf. Lk 22:28). Although the reign of the exalted Jesus is a theme that occurs elsewhere in Hebrews, and Jesus' throne is mentioned in Heb 1:8, **the throne of grace** (Heb 4:16) refers to the throne of God. The similarity of Heb 4:16 to Heb 10:19–22 indicates that the author is thinking of our confident access to God, made possible by the priestly work of Jesus.

†[5:1–10] The true humanity of Jesus (see note on Heb 2:5–18) makes him a more rather than a less effective high priest to the Christian community. In Old Testament tradition, the high priest was identified with the people, guilty of personal sin just as they were (Heb 5:1–3). Even so, the office

was of divine appointment (Heb 5:4), as was also the case with the sinless Christ (Heb 5:5). For Heb 5:6, see note on Ps 110:4. Although Jesus was Son of God, he was destined as a human being to learn obedience by accepting the suffering he had to endure (Heb 5:8). Because of his perfection through this experience of human suffering, he is the cause of salvation for all (Heb 5:9), a **high priest according to the order of Melchizedek** (Heb 5:10; cf. Heb 5:6 and Heb 7:3).

‡[5:1] **To offer gifts and sacrifices for sins:** the author is thinking principally of the Day of Atonement rite, as is clear from Heb 9:7. This ritual was celebrated to atone for "all the sins of the Israelites" (Lv 16:34).

§[5:2] **Deal patiently:** the Greek word *metriopathein* occurs only here in the Bible; this term was used by the Stoics to designate the golden mean between excess and defect of passion. Here it means rather the ability to sympathize.

¶[5:6–8] The author of Hebrews is the only New Testament writer to cite Ps 110:4, here and in Heb 7:17, 21, to show that Jesus has been called by God to his role as priest. Heb 5:7–8 deal with his ability to sympathize with sinners, because of his own experience of the trials and weakness of human nature, especially fear of death. In his present exalted state, weakness is foreign to him, but he understands what we suffer because of his previous earthly experience.

[5:7] He offered prayers . . . to the one who was able to save him from death: at Gethsemane (cf. Mk 14:35), though some see a broader reference (see note on Jn 12:27).

††[5:8] **Son though he was:** two different though not incompatible views of Jesus' sonship coexist in Hebrews, one associating it with his exaltation, the other with his preexistence. The former view is the older one (cf. Rom 1:4).

‡‡[5:11–6:20] The central section of Hebrews (Heb 5:11–10:39) opens with a reprimand and an appeal. Those to whom the author directs his teaching about Jesus' priesthood, which is

---

g. [4:4] Gn 2:2.   h. [4:5] Ps 95:11.   i. [4:7] 3:7–8, 15; Ps 95:7–8.
j. [4:8] Dt 31:7; Jos 22:4.   k. [4:12] Wis 18:15–16; Is 49:2; Eph 6:17; Rev 1:16; 2:12.   l. [4:13] Jb 34:21–22; Ps 90:8; 139:2–4.   m. [4:14] 9:11, 24.   n. [4:15] 2:17–18; 5:2.   o. [4:16] 8:1; 10:19, 22, 35; 12:2; Eph 3:12.

p. [5:3] Lv 9:7; 16:15–17, 30, 34.   q. [5:4] Ex 28:1.   r. [5:5] Ps 2:7.
s. [5:6] Ps 110:4.   t. [5:7] Mt 26:38–44; Mk 14:34–40; Lk 22:41–46; Jn 12:27.   u. [5:8] Rom 5:19; Phil 2:8.   v. [5:9] 7:24–25, 28.   w. [5:10] 6:20; Ps 110:4.

to explain, for you have become sluggish in hearing. [12]Although you should be teachers by this time, you need to have someone teach you again the basic elements of the utterances of God. You need milk, [and] not solid food.[x] [13]Everyone who lives on milk lacks experience of the word of righteousness, for he is a child. [14]But solid food is for the mature, for those whose faculties are trained by practice to discern good and evil.

CHAPTER 6

[1]Therefore, let us leave behind the basic teaching about Christ and advance to maturity, without laying the foundation all over again: repentance from dead works and faith in God,[y] [2]instruction about baptisms[*] and laying on of hands, resurrection of the dead and eternal judgment.[z] [3]And we shall do this, if only God permits. [4]For it is impossible in the case of those who have once been enlightened and tasted the heavenly gift[†] and shared in the holy Spirit[a] [5]and tasted the good word of God and the powers of the age to come,[‡] [6]and then have fallen away, to bring them to repentance again, since they are recrucifying the Son of God for themselves[§] and holding him up to contempt.[b] [7]Ground that has absorbed the rain falling upon it repeatedly and brings forth crops useful to those for whom it is cultivated receives a blessing from God.[c] [8]But if it produces

thorns and thistles, it is rejected; it will soon be cursed and finally burned.[d]

[9]But we are sure in your regard, beloved, of better things related to salvation, even though we speak in this way. [10]For God is not unjust as to overlook your work and the love you have demonstrated for his name by having served and continuing to serve the holy ones. [11]We earnestly desire each of you to demonstrate the same eagerness for the fulfillment of hope until the end,[e] [12]so that you may not become sluggish, but imitators of those who, through faith and patience,[f] are inheriting the promises.[¶]

God's Promise Immutable. [13][*][g]When God made the promise to Abraham, since he had no one greater by whom to swear, "he swore by himself," [14]and said, "I will indeed bless you and multiply" you.[h] [15]And so, after patient waiting,[i] he obtained the promise.[††] [16]Human beings swear by someone greater than themselves; for them an oath serves as a guarantee and puts an end to all argument. [17]So when God wanted to give the heirs of his promise an even clearer demonstration of the immutability of his purpose, he intervened with an oath,[j] [18]so that by two immutable things,[‡‡] in which it was impossible for God to lie, we who have taken refuge might be strongly encouraged to hold fast to the hope that lies before us.[k] [19]This we have as an anchor of the soul,[l] sure and firm, which reaches into the interior behind the veil,[§§] [20]where Jesus has entered on our behalf as forerunner, becoming high priest forever according to the order of Melchizedek.[m]

CHAPTER 7

Melchizedek, a Type of Christ. [1][*]This "Melchizedek, king of Salem and priest of God Most

---

difficult to explain, have become **sluggish in hearing** and forgetful of even **the basic elements** (Heb 5:12). But rather than treating of basic teachings, the author apparently believes that the challenge of more advanced ones may shake them out of their inertia (**therefore,** Heb 6:1). The six examples of **basic teaching** in Heb 6:1–3 are probably derived from a traditional catechetical list. No effort is made to address apostates, for their very hostility to the Christian message cuts them off completely from Christ (Heb 6:4–8). This harsh statement seems to rule out repentance after apostasy, but perhaps the author deliberately uses hyperbole in order to stress the seriousness of abandoning Christ. With Heb 6:9 a milder tone is introduced, and the criticism of the community (Heb 6:1–3, 9) is now balanced by an expression of confidence that its members are living truly Christian lives, and that God will justly reward their efforts (Heb 6:10). The author is concerned especially about their persevering (Heb 6:11–12), citing in this regard the achievement of Abraham, who relied on God's promise and on God's oath (Heb 6:13–18; cf. Gn 22:16), and proposes to them as a firm anchor of Christian hope the high priesthood of Christ, who is now living with God (Heb 6:19–20).

*[6:2] **Instruction about baptisms:** not simply about Christian baptism but about the difference between it and similar Jewish rites, such as proselyte baptism, John's baptism, and the washings of the Qumran sectaries. **Laying on of hands:** in Acts 8:17; 19:6 this rite effects the infusion of the holy Spirit; in Acts 6:6; 13:3; 1 Tm 4:14; 5:22; 2 Tm 1:6 it is a means of conferring some ministry or mission in the early Christian community.

†[6:4] **Enlightened and tasted the heavenly gift:** this may refer to baptism and the Eucharist, respectively, but more probably means the neophytes' enlightenment by faith and their experience of salvation.

‡[6:5] **Tasted the good word of God and the powers of the age to come:** the proclamation of the **word of God** was accompanied by signs of the Spirit's power (1 Thes 1:5; 1 Cor 2:4).

§[6:6] **They are recrucifying the Son of God for themselves:** a colorful description of the malice of apostasy, which is portrayed as again crucifying and deriding the Son of God.

¶[6:12] **Imitators of those . . . inheriting the promises:** the author urges the addressees to imitate the faith of the holy people of the Old Testament, who now possess the promised goods of which they lived in hope. This theme will be treated fully in Heb 6:11.

[6:13] **He swore by himself: God's promise to Abraham, which he confirmed by an oath ("I swear by myself," Gn 22:16) was the basis for the hope of all Abraham's descendants.

††[6:15] **He obtained the promise:** this probably refers not to Abraham's temporary possession of the land but to the eschatological blessings that Abraham and the other patriarchs have now come to possess.

‡‡[6:18] **Two immutable things:** the promise and the oath, both made by God.

§§[6:19] **Anchor . . . into the interior behind the veil:** a mixed metaphor. The Holy of Holies, beyond the veil that separates it from the Holy Place (Ex 26:31–33), is seen as the earthly counterpart of the heavenly abode of God. This theme will be developed in Heb 9.

¶¶[7:1–3] Recalling the meeting between Melchizedek and Abraham described in Gn 14:17–20, the author enhances the significance of this priest by providing the popular etymological meaning of his name and that of the city over which he ruled (Heb 7:2). Since Genesis gives no information on the parentage or the death of Melchizedek, he is seen here as a

---

d. [6:8] Gn 3:17–18; Mt 7:16; 13:7; Mk 4:7; Lk 8:7.   e. [6:11] 3:14. f. [6:12] 5:11; Gal 3:14; Eph 1:13–14.   g. [6:13] Gn 22:16. h. [6:14] Gn 22:17.   i. [6:15] 6:12; Rom 4:20.   j. [6:17] 6:12.   k. [6:18] Nm 23:19; 1 Sm 15:29; Jn 8:17; 2 Tm 2:13.   l. [6:19] 10:20; Ex 26:31–33; Lv 16:2.   m. [6:20] 5:10; Ps 110:4.

x. [5:12] 1 Cor 3:1–3.   y. [6:1] 9:14.   z. [6:2] 9:10; Mk 7:4 / Acts 6:6; 8:17; 13:3; 19:6; 1 Tm 4:14; 5:22; 2 Tm 1:6.   a. [6:4] 10:26, 32; Ps 34:6; 2 Cor 4:6.   b. [6:6] 2 Pt 2:21.   c. [6:7] Gn 1:11–12; Dt 11:11.

High,"* "met Abraham as he returned from his defeat of the kings" and "blessed him."*ⁿ 2†And Abraham apportioned to him "a tenth of every-thing." His name first means righteous king, and he was also "king of Salem," that is, king of peace. ³Without father, mother, or ancestry, without beginning of days or end of life,‡ thus made to resemble the Son of God, he remains a priest forever.°

⁴ˢSee how great he is to whom the patriarch "Abraham [indeed] gave a tenth" of his spoils.ᵖ ⁵The descendants of Levi who receive the office of priesthood have a commandment according to the law to exact tithes from the people, that is, from their brothers, although they also have come from the loins of Abraham.�q ⁶But he who was not of their ancestry received tithes from Abraham and blessed him who had received the promises. ⁷Unquestionably, a lesser person is blessed by a greater.ˢ ⁸In the one case, mortal men receive tithes; in the other, a man of whom it is testified that he lives on. ⁹One might even say that Levi** himself, who receives tithes, was tithed through Abraham, ¹⁰for he was still in his father's loins when Melchizedek met him.

¹¹††If, then, perfection came through the levit-ical priesthood, on the basis of which the people received the law, what need would there still have been for another priest to arise according to the order of Melchizedek, and not reckoned according to the order of Aaron?ʳ ¹²When there is a change of priesthood, there is necessarily a change of law as well. ¹³Now he of whom these things are said‡‡ belonged to a different tribe, of which no member ever officiated at the altar. ¹⁴It is clear that our Lord arose from Judah,§§ and in regard to that tribe Moses said noth-ing about priests.ˢ ¹⁵¶¶It is even more obvious if another priest is raised up after the likeness of Melchizedek, ¹⁶who has become so, not by a law expressed in a commandment concerning physical descent but by the power of a life that cannot be destroyed."** ¹⁷For it is testified:

"You are a priest forever
    according to the order of
        Melchizedek."ᵗ

¹⁸On the one hand, a former command-ment is annulled because of its weakness and uselessness,ᵘ ¹⁹for the law brought nothing to perfection; on the other hand, a better hope†††
is introduced, through which we draw near to God. ²⁰‡‡‡And to the degree that this happened

---

type of Christ, representing a priesthood that is unique and eternal (Heb 7:3).

*[7:1] The author here assumes that Melchizedek was a priest of the God of Israel (cf. Gn 14:22 and the note there).

†[7:2] In Gn 14, the Hebrew text does not state explicitly who gave tithes to whom. The author of Hebrews supplies Abraham as the subject, according to a contemporary inter-pretation of the passage. This supports the argument of the midrash and makes it possible to see in Melchizedek a type of Jesus. The messianic blessings of righteousness and peace are foreshadowed in the names "Melchizedek" and "Salem."

‡[7:3] Without father, mother, or ancestry, without beginning of days or end of life: this is perhaps a quota-tion from a hymn about Melchizedek. The rabbis maintained that anything not mentioned in the Torah does not exist. Consequently, since the Old Testament nowhere mentions Melchizedek's ancestry, birth, or death, the conclusion can be drawn that he remains . . . forever.

§[7:4–10] The tithe that Abraham gave to Melchizedek (Heb 7:4), a practice later followed by the levitical priest-hood (Heb 7:5), was a gift (Heb 7:6) acknowledging a certain superiority in Melchizedek, the foreign priest (Heb 7:7). This is further indicated by the fact that the institution of the leviti-cal priesthood was sustained by hereditary succession in the tribe of Levi, whereas the absence of any mention of Melchize-dek's death in Genesis implies that his personal priesthood is permanent (Heb 7:8). The levitical priesthood itself, through Abraham, its ancestor, paid tithes to Melchizedek, thus acknowledging the superiority of his priesthood over its own (Heb 7:9–10).

¶[7:7] A lesser person is blessed by a greater: though this sounds like a principle, there are some examples in the Old Testament that do not support it (cf. 2 Sm 14:22; Jb 31:20). The author may intend it as a statement of a liturgical rule.

**[7:9] Levi: for the author this name designates not only the son of Jacob mentioned in Genesis but the priestly tribe that was thought to be descended from him.

††[7:11–14] The levitical priesthood was not typified by the priesthood of Melchizedek, for Ps 110:4 speaks of a priest-hood of a new order, the order of Melchizedek, to arise in messianic times (Heb 7:11). Since the levitical priesthood served the Mosaic law, a new priesthood (Heb 7:12) would

not come into being without a change in the law itself. Thus Jesus was not associated with the Old Testament priesthood, for he was a descendant of the tribe of Judah, which had never exercised the priesthood (Heb 7:13–14).

‡‡[7:13] He of whom these things are said: Jesus, the priest "according to the order of Melchizedek." According to the author's interpretation, Ps 110 spoke prophetically of Jesus.

§§[7:14] Judah: the author accepts the early Christian tradi-tion that Jesus was descended from the family of David (cf. Mt 1:1–2, 16, 20; Lk 1:27; 2:4; Rom 1:3). The Qumran community expected two Messiahs, one descended from Aaron and one from David; Hebrews shows no awareness of this view or at least does not accept it. Our author's view is not attested in contemporaneous Judaism.

¶¶[7:15–19] Jesus does not exercise a priesthood through family lineage but through his immortal existence (Heb 7:15–16), fulfilling Ps 110:4 (Heb 7:17; cf. Heb 7:3). Thus he abolishes forever both the levitical priesthood and the law it serves, because neither could effectively sanctify people (Heb 7:18) by leading them into direct communication with God (Heb 7:19).

***[7:16] A life that cannot be destroyed: the life to which Jesus has attained by virtue of his resurrection; it is his exalta-tion rather than his divine nature that makes him priest. The Old Testament speaks of the Aaronic priesthood as eternal (see Ex 40:15); our author does not explicitly consider this possible objection to his argument but implicitly refutes it in Heb 7:23–24.

†††[7:19] A better hope: this hope depends upon the sacri-fice of the Son of God; through it we "approach the throne of grace" (Heb 4:16); cf. Heb 6:19, 20.

‡‡‡[7:20–25] As was the case with the promise to Abraham (Heb 6:13), though not with the levitical priesthood, the eter-nal priesthood of the order of Melchizedek was confirmed by God's oath (Heb 7:20–21); cf. Ps 110:4. Thus Jesus becomes the guarantee of a permanent covenant (Heb 7:22) that does not require a succession of priests as did the levitical priest-hood (Heb 7:23) because his high priesthood is eternal and unchangeable (Heb 7:24). Consequently, Jesus is able to save all who draw near to God through him since he is their ever-living intercessor (Heb 7:25).

---

n. [7:1] Gn 14:17–20.   o. [7:3] 4:14; 6:6; 10:29.   p. [7:4] Gn 14:20.
q. [7:5] Nm 18:21 / Gn 35:11.

r. [7:11] 5:6; Ps 110:4.   s. [7:14] Gn 49:10; Is 11:1; Mt 1:1–2, 16, 20; 2:6; Lk 1:27; 2:4; Rom 1:3; Rev 5:5.   t. [7:17] 5:6; Ps 110:4. u. [7:18] 10:1.

not without the taking of an oath*—for others became priests without an oath, [21]but he with an oath, through the one who said to him:

"The Lord has sworn, and he will not repent:[v]
'You are a priest forever'"—

[22w]to that same degree has Jesus [also] become the guarantee of an [even] better covenant.[†] [23]Those priests were many because they were prevented by death from remaining in office, [24]but he, because he remains forever, has a priesthood that does not pass away.[x] [25‡]Therefore, he is always able to save those who approach God through him, since he lives forever to make intercession for them.[y]

[26z]It was fitting that we should have such a high priest:[§] holy, innocent, undefiled, separated from sinners, higher than the heavens.[¶] [27]He has no need, as did the high priests, to offer sacrifice day after day,**[a] first for his own sins and then for those of the people; he did that once for all when he offered himself. [28]For the law appoints men subject to weakness to be high priests, but the word of the oath, which was taken after the law, appoints a son, who has been made perfect forever.[b]

CHAPTER 8
Heavenly Priesthood of Jesus.[††] [1]The main point of what has been said is this: we have such a

high priest, who has taken his seat at the right hand of the throne of the Majesty in heaven,[c] [2]a minister of the sanctuary[‡‡] and of the true tabernacle that the Lord, not man, set up.[d] [3]Now every high priest is appointed to offer gifts and sacrifices; thus the necessity for this one also to have something to offer.[e] [4]If then he were on earth, he would not be a priest, since there are those who offer gifts according to the law.[f] [5]They worship in a copy and shadow of the heavenly sanctuary, as Moses was warned when he was about to erect the tabernacle. For he says, "See that you make everything according to the pattern shown you on the mountain."[g] [6]Now he has obtained so much more excellent a ministry as he is mediator of a better covenant, enacted on better promises.[h] **Old and New Covenants.**[§§] [7]For if that first covenant had been faultless, no place would have been sought for a second one. [8]But he finds fault with them and says:[¶¶]

"Behold, the days are coming, says the Lord,[i]
　　when I will conclude a new covenant
　　　with the house of Israel and
　　　the house of Judah.
[9]　It will not be like the covenant I made
　　　with their fathers
　　the day I took them by the hand to
　　　lead them forth from the land
　　　of Egypt;
　　for they did not stand by my covenant
　　　and I ignored them, says the Lord.
[10]　But this is the covenant I will establish
　　　with the house of Israel
　　after those days, says the Lord:

---

*[7:20] **An oath:** God's oath in Ps 110:4.

†[7:22] **An [even] better covenant:** better than the Mosaic covenant because it will be eternal, like the priesthood of Jesus upon which it is based. Heb 7:12 argued that a change of priesthood involves a change of law; since "law" and "covenant" are used correlatively, a new covenant is likewise instituted.

‡[7:25] **To make intercession:** the intercession of the exalted Jesus, not the sequel to his completed sacrifice but its eternal presence in heaven; cf. Rom 8:34.

§[7:26] This verse with its list of attributes is reminiscent of Heb 7:3 and is perhaps a hymnic counterpart to it, contrasting the exalted Jesus with Melchizedek.

¶[7:26–28] Jesus is precisely the high priest whom the human race requires, holy and sinless, installed far above humanity (Heb 7:26); one having no need to offer sacrifice daily for sins but making a single offering of himself (Heb 7:27) once for all. The law could only appoint high priests with human limitations, but the fulfillment of God's oath regarding the priesthood of Melchizedek (Ps 110:4) makes the Son of God the perfect priest forever (Heb 7:28).

[7:27] Such daily sacrifice is nowhere mentioned in the Mosaic law; only on the Day of Atonement is it prescribed that the high priest must **offer sacrifice . . . for his own sins and then for those of the people (Lv 16:11–19). **Once for all:** this translates the Greek words *ephapax/hapax* that occur eleven times in Hebrews.

††[8:1–6] The Christian community has in Jesus the kind of high priest described in Heb 7:26–28. In virtue of his ascension Jesus has taken his place at God's right hand in accordance with Ps 110:1 (Heb 8:1), where he presides over the heavenly sanctuary established by God himself (Heb 8:2). Like every high priest, he has his offering to make (Heb 8:3; cf. Heb 9:12, 14), but it differs from that of the levitical

priesthood in which he had no share (Heb 8:4) and which was in any case but a shadowy reflection of the true offering in the heavenly sanctuary (Heb 8:5). But Jesus' ministry in the heavenly sanctuary is that of mediator of a superior covenant that accomplishes what it signifies (Heb 8:6).

‡‡[8:2] **The sanctuary:** the Greek term could also mean "holy things" but bears the meaning "sanctuary" elsewhere in Hebrews (Heb 9:8, 12, 24, 25; 10:19; 13:11). **The true tabernacle:** the heavenly tabernacle **that the Lord . . . set up** is contrasted with the earthly tabernacle that Moses set up in the desert. **True** means "real" in contradistinction to a mere "copy and shadow" (Heb 8:5); compare the Johannine usage (e.g., Jn 1:9; 6:32; 15:1). The idea that the earthly sanctuary is a reflection of a heavenly model may be based upon Ex 25:9, but probably also derives from the Platonic concept of a real world of which our observable world is merely a shadow.

§§[8:7–13] Since the first covenant was deficient in accomplishing what it signified, it had to be replaced (Heb 8:7), as Jeremiah (Jer 31:31–34) had prophesied (Heb 8:8–12). Even in the time of Jeremiah, the first covenant was antiquated (Heb 8:13). In Heb 7:22–24, the superiority of the new covenant was seen in the permanence of its priesthood; here the superiority is based on better promises, made explicit in the citation of Jer 31:31–34 (LXX: 38), namely, in the immediacy of the people's knowledge of God (Heb 8:11) and in the forgiveness of sin (Heb 8:12).

¶¶[8:8–12] In citing Jeremiah the author follows the Septuagint; some apparent departures from it may be the result of a different Septuagintal text rather than changes deliberately introduced.

---

v. [7:21] Ps 110:4.　w. [7:22] 8:6–10; 9:15–20; 10:29; 12:24; 13:20.　x. [7:24] 5:6; 13:8.　y. [7:25] Rom 8:34; 1 Jn 2:1; Rev 1:18.　z. [7:26] 4:14, 15.　a. [7:27] 5:3; 9:12, 25–28; 10:11–14; Ex 29:38–39; Lv 16:6, 11, 15–17; Nm 28:3–4; Is 53:10; Rom 6:10.　b. [7:28] 5:1–2, 9.

c. [8:1] 1:3; 4:14; 7:26–28.　d. [8:2] 9:11; Ex 33:7; Nm 24:6 LXX.　e. [8:3] 5:1.　f. [8:4] 7:13.　g. [8:5] 9:23; Ex 25:40; Acts 7:44; Col 2:17.　h. [8:6] 7:22; 9:15.　j. [8:8] Jer 31:31–34.

I will put my laws in their minds
　　and I will write them upon their
　　hearts.
I will be their God,
　　and they shall be my people.[j]
11 And they shall not teach, each one his
　　　fellow citizen
　　and kinsman, saying, 'Know the Lord,'
　　for all shall know me,
　　　from least to greatest.
12 For I will forgive their evildoing
　　and remember their sins no more."

13*[k]When he speaks of a "new" covenant, he declares the first one obsolete. And what has become obsolete and has grown old is close to disappearing.

CHAPTER 9

The Worship of the First Covenant.[†]
1Now [even] the first covenant had regulations for worship and an earthly sanctuary. 2For a tabernacle was constructed, the outer one,[‡] in which were the lampstand, the table, and the bread of offering; this is called the Holy Place.[l] 3*Behind the second veil was the tabernacle called the Holy of Holies,[m] 4in which were the gold altar of incense[§] and the ark of the covenant entirely covered with gold. In it were the gold jar containing the manna, the staff of Aaron that had sprouted, and the tablets of the covenant.[n] 5**Above it were the cherubim of glory overshadowing the place of expiation. Now is not the time to speak of these in detail.[o]

*[8:13] Close to disappearing: from the prophet's perspective, not that of the author of Hebrews.

†[9:1–10] The regulations for worship under the old covenant permitted all the priests to enter the Holy Place (Heb 2:6), but only the high priest to enter the Holy of Holies and then only once a year (Heb 9:3–5, 7). The description of the sanctuary and its furnishings is taken essentially from Ex 25–26. This exclusion of the people from the Holy of Holies signified that they were not allowed to stand in God's presence (Heb 9:8) because their offerings and sacrifices, which were merely symbols of their need of spiritual renewal (Heb 9:10), could not obtain forgiveness of sins (Heb 9:9).

‡[9:2] The outer one: the author speaks of the outer tabernacle (Heb 9:6) and the inner one (Heb 9:7) rather than of one Mosaic tabernacle divided into two parts or sections.

§[9:3] The second veil: what is meant is the veil that divided the Holy Place from the Holy of Holies. It is here called the second, because there was another veil at the entrance to the Holy Place, or "outer tabernacle" (Ex 26:36).

¶[9:4] The gold altar of incense: Ex 30:6 locates this altar in the Holy Place, i.e., the first tabernacle, rather than in the Holy of Holies. Neither is there any Old Testament support for the assertion that the jar of manna and the staff of Aaron were in the ark of the covenant. For the tablets of the covenant, see Ex 25:16.

**[9:5] The place of expiation: the gold "mercy seat" (Greek hilastērion, as in Rom 3:25), where the blood of the sacrificial animals was sprinkled on the Day of Atonement (Lv 16:14–15). This rite achieved "expiation" or atonement for the sins of the preceding year.

6With these arrangements for worship, the priests, in performing their service,[††] go into the outer tabernacle repeatedly,[p].7but the high priest alone goes into the inner one once a year, not without blood[‡‡] that he offers for himself and for the sins of the people.[q] 8In this way the holy Spirit shows that the way into the sanctuary had not yet been revealed while the outer tabernacle still had its place. 9This is a symbol of the present time,[§§] in which gifts and sacrifices are offered that cannot perfect the worshiper in conscience 10but only in matters of food and drink and various ritual washings: regulations concerning the flesh, imposed until the time of the new order.[r]

Sacrifice of Jesus. 11¶¶But when Christ came as high priest of the good things that have come to be,[***] passing through the greater and more perfect tabernacle not made by hands, that is, not belonging to this creation,[s] 12he entered once for all into the sanctuary, not with the blood of goats and calves but with his own blood, thus obtaining eternal redemption.[t] 13For if the blood of goats and bulls and the sprinkling of a heifer's ashes[†††] can sanctify those who are defiled so that their flesh is cleansed,[u] 14how much more will the blood of Christ, who through the eternal spirit[‡‡‡] offered himself unblemished to God, cleanse our consciences from dead works to worship the living God.[v]

††[9:6] In performing their service: the priestly services that had to be performed regularly in the Holy Place or outer tabernacle included burning incense on the incense altar twice each day (Ex 30:7), replacing the loaves on the table of the bread of offering once each week (Lv 24:8), and constantly caring for the lamps on the lampstand (Ex 27:21).

‡‡[9:7] Not without blood: blood was essential to Old Testament sacrifice because it was believed that life was located in the blood. Hence blood was especially sacred, and its outpouring functioned as a meaningful symbol of cleansing from sin and reconciliation with God. Unlike Hebrews, the Old Testament never says that the blood is "offered." The author is perhaps retrojecting into his description of Mosaic ritual a concept that belongs to the New Testament antitype, as Paul does when he speaks of the Israelites' passage through the sea as a "baptism" (1 Cor 10:2).

§§[9:9] The present time: this expression is equivalent to the "present age," used in contradistinction to the "age to come."

¶¶[9:11–14] Christ, the high priest of the spiritual blessings foreshadowed in the Old Testament sanctuary, has actually entered the true sanctuary of heaven that is not of human making (Heb 9:11). His place there is permanent, and his offering is his own blood that won eternal redemption (Heb 9:12). If the sacrifice of animals could bestow legal purification (Heb 9:13), how much more effective is the blood of the sinless, divine Christ who spontaneously offered himself to purge the human race of sin and render it fit for the service of God (Heb 9:14).

***[9:11] The good things that have come to be: the majority of later manuscripts here read "the good things to come"; cf. Heb 10:1.

†††[9:13] A heifer's ashes: ashes from a red heifer that had been burned were mixed with water and used for the cleansing of those who had become ritually defiled by touching a corpse; see Nm 19:9, 14–21.

‡‡‡[9:14] Through the eternal spirit: this expression does not refer either to the holy Spirit or to the divine nature of Jesus but to the life of the risen Christ, "a life that cannot be destroyed" (Heb 7:16).

j. [8:10]　10:16–17.　k. [8:13]　Rom 10:4.　l. [9:2]　Ex 25:23–30.　m. [9:3] Ex 26:31–34.　n. [9:4] Ex 16:32–34; 25:10, 16, 21; 30:1–10; Lv 16:12–13; Nm 17:2–7, 16–26.　o. [9:5] Ex 25:16–22; 26:34; Lv 16:14–15.

p. [9:6]　Ex 27:21; 30:7; Lv 24:8.　q. [9:7]　Ex 30:10; Lv 16:1–14.　r. [9:10] 13:9; Lv 11; 14:8; Nm 19:11–21; Col 2:16.　s. [9:11] 4:14; 10:1, 20.　t. [9:12] 7:27; Mt 26:28.　u. [9:13] 10:4; Lv 16:6–16; Nm 19:9, 14–21.　v. [9:14] 10:10; Rom 5:9; 1 Tm 3:9; Ti 2:14; 1 Pt 1:18–19; 1 Jn 1:7; Rev 1:5.

¹⁵*For this reason he is mediator of a new covenant: since a death has taken place for deliverance from transgressions under the first covenant, those who are called may receive the promised eternal inheritance.ʷ ¹⁶†Now where there is a will, the death of the testator must be established. ¹⁷For a will takes effect only at death; it has no force while the testator is alive. ¹⁸Thus not even the first covenant was inaugurated without blood. ¹⁹‡When every commandment had been proclaimed by Moses to all the people according to the law, he took the blood of calves [and goats], together with water and crimson wool and hyssop, and sprinkled both the book itself and all the people,ˣ ²⁰saying, "This is 'the blood of the covenant which God has enjoined upon you.'"ʸ ²¹In the same way, he sprinkled also the tabernacle§ and all the vessels of worship with blood.ᶻ ²²§According to the law almost everything is purified by blood,ᵃ and without the shedding of blood there is no forgiveness.

²³**Therefore, it was necessary for the copies of the heavenly things to be purified by these rites, but the heavenly things themselves by better sacrifices than these.ᵇ ²⁴For Christ did not enter into a sanctuary made by hands, a copy of the true one, but heaven itself, that he might now appear before God on our behalf.ᶜ ²⁵Not that he might offer himself repeatedly, as the high priest enters each year into the sanctuary with blood that is not his own; ²⁶if that were so, he would have had to suffer repeatedly from the foundation of the world. But now once for all he has appeared at the end of the ages†† to take away sin by his sacrifice.ᵈ ²⁷Just as it is appointed that human beings die once, and after this the judgment,ᵉ ²⁸so also Christ, offered once to take away the sins of many,‡‡ will appear a second time, not to take away sin but to bring salvation to those who eagerly await him.ᶠ

CHAPTER 10

One Sacrifice Instead of Many. ¹§§Since the law has only a shadow of the good things to come,¶¶ and not the very image of them, it can never make perfect those who come to worship by the same sacrifices that they offer continually each year.ᵍ ²Otherwise, would not the sacrifices have

*[9:15–22] Jesus' role as **mediator of the new covenant** is based upon his sacrificial **death** (cf. Heb 8:6). His death has effected **deliverance from transgressions**, i.e., deliverance from sins committed under the old covenant, which the Mosaic sacrifices were incapable of effacing. Until this happened, the **eternal inheritance** promised by God could not be obtained (Heb 9:15). This effect of his work follows the human pattern by which a last will and testament becomes effective only with the death of the testator (Heb 9:16–17). The Mosaic covenant was also associated with death, for Moses made use of blood to seal the pact between God and the people (Heb 9:18–21). In Old Testament tradition, guilt could normally not be remitted without the use of blood (Heb 9:22; cf. Lv 17:11).

†[9:16–17] **A will . . . death of the testator:** the same Greek word *diathēkē*, meaning "covenant" in Heb 9:15, 18, is used here with the meaning **will**. The new covenant, unlike the old, is at the same time a will that requires the **death of the testator**. Jesus as eternal Son is the one who established the new covenant together with his Father, author of both covenants; at the same time he is the testator whose death puts his **will** into effect.

‡[9:19–20] A number of details here are different from the description of this covenant rite in Ex 24:5–8. Exodus mentions only calves ("young bulls," NAB), not goats (but this addition in Hebrews is of doubtful authenticity), says nothing of the use of **water and crimson wool and hyssop** (these features probably came from a different rite; cf. Lv 14:3–7; Nm 19:6–18), and describes Moses as splashing blood on the altar, whereas Hebrews says he sprinkled it on the book (but both book and altar are meant to symbolize the agreement of God). The words of Moses are also slightly different from those in Exodus and are closer to the words of Jesus at the Last Supper in Mk 14:24 // Mt 26:28.

§[9:21] According to Exodus, the tabernacle did not yet exist at the time of the covenant rite. Moreover, nothing is said of sprinkling it with blood at its subsequent dedication (Ex 40:9–11).

¶[9:22] **Without the shedding of blood there is no forgiveness:** in fact, ancient Israel did envisage other means of obtaining forgiveness; the Old Testament mentions contrition of heart (Ps 51:17), fasting (Jl 2:12), and almsgiving (Sir 3:29). The author is limiting his horizon to the sacrificial cult, which did always involve the shedding of blood for its expiatory and unitive value.

**[9:23–28] Since the blood of animals became a cleansing symbol among Old Testament prefigurements, it was necessary that the realities foreshadowed be brought into being by a

shedding of blood that was infinitely more effective by reason of its worth (Heb 9:23). Christ did not simply prefigure the heavenly realities (Heb 9:24) by performing an annual sacrifice with a blood not his own (Heb 9:25); he offered the single sacrifice of himself as the final annulment of sin (Heb 9:26). Just as death is the unrepeatable act that ends a person's life, so Christ's offering of himself for all is the unrepeatable sacrifice that has once for all achieved redemption (Heb 9:27–28).

††[9:26] **At the end of the ages:** the use of expressions such as this shows that the author of Hebrews, despite his interest in the Platonic concept of an eternal world above superior to temporal reality here below, nevertheless still clings to the Jewish Christian eschatology with its sequence of "the present age" and "the age to come."

‡‡[9:28] **To take away the sins of many:** the reference is to Is 53:12. Since the Greek verb *anapherō* can mean both "to take away" and "to bear," the author no doubt intended to play upon both senses: Jesus took away sin by bearing it himself. See the similar wordplay in Jn 1:29. **Many** is used in the Semitic meaning of "all" in the inclusive sense, as in Mk 14:24. **To those who eagerly await him:** Jesus will appear **a second time** at the parousia, as the high priest reappeared on the Day of Atonement, emerging from the Holy of Holies, which he had entered to **take away sin.** This dramatic scene is described in Sir 50:5–11.

§§[10:1–10] Christian faith now realizes that the Old Testament sacrifices did not effect the spiritual benefits to come but only prefigured them (Heb 10:1). For if the sacrifices had actually effected the forgiveness of sin, there would have been no reason for their constant repetition (Heb 10:2). They were rather a continual reminder of the people's sins (Heb 10:3). It is not reasonable to suppose that human sins could be removed by the blood of animal sacrifices (Heb 10:4). Christ, therefore, is here shown to understand his mission in terms of Ps 40:6–8, cited according to the Septuagint (Heb 10:5–7). Jesus acknowledged that the Old Testament sacrifices did not remit the sins of the people and so, perceiving the will of God, offered his own body for this purpose (Heb 10:8–10).

¶¶[10:1] **A shadow of the good things to come:** the term **shadow** was used in Heb 8:5 to signify the earthly counterpart of the Platonic heavenly reality. But here it means a prefiguration of what is to come in Christ, as it is used in the Pauline literature; cf. Col 2:17.

w. [9:15] 1 Tm 2:5.   x. [9:19] 9:12–13.   y. [9:20] Ex 24:3–8; Mt 26:28; Mk 14:24.   z. [9:21] Ex 40:9; Lv 8:15, 19.   a. [9:22] Lv 17:11.   b. [9:23] Jb 15:15.   c. [9:24] 7:25; Rom 8:34; 1 Jn 2:1–2.   d. [9:26] 7:27; Jn 1:29; Gal 4:4.   e. [9:27] Gn 3:19.   f. [9:28] 10:10; Is 53:12.   g. [10:1] 8:5; Col 2:17.

ceased to be offered, since the worshipers, once cleansed, would no longer have had any consciousness of sins? [3]But in those sacrifices there is only a yearly remembrance of sins,[h] [4]for it is impossible that the blood of bulls and goats take away sins.[i] [5]For this reason, when he came into the world, he said:*

"Sacrifice and offering you did not desire,[j]
     but a body you prepared for me;
[6] holocausts and sin offerings you took no
     delight in.
[7] Then I said, 'As is written of me in the
     scroll,
     Behold, I come to do your will,
     O God.'"

[8]First he says, "Sacrifices and offerings, holocausts and sin offerings,[†] you neither desired nor delighted in." These are offered according to the law.[k] [9]Then he says, "Behold, I come to do your will." He takes away the first to establish the second.[l] [10]By this "will," we have been consecrated through the offering of the body of Jesus Christ once for all.[m]

[11‡]Every priest stands daily at his ministry, offering frequently those same sacrifices that can never take away sins."[12]But this one offered one sacrifice for sins, and took his seat forever at the right hand of God;[o] [13§]now he waits until his enemies are made his footstool. [14]For by one offering he has made perfect forever those who are being consecrated.[p] [15¶]The holy Spirit also testifies to us, for after saying:

[16] "This is the covenant I will establish with
          them after those days, says the
          Lord:
     'I will put my laws in their hearts,
     and I will write them upon their
          minds,'"[q]

[17]he also says:*

     "Their sins and their evildoing
     I will remember no more."[r]

[18]Where there is forgiveness of these, there is no longer offering for sin.

Recalling the Past.[††] [19]Therefore, brothers, since through the blood of Jesus we have confidence of entrance into the sanctuary[s] [20‡‡]by the new and living way he opened for us through the veil,[t] that is, his flesh, [21§§]"and since we have "a great priest over the house of God," [22]let us approach with a sincere heart and in absolute trust, with our hearts sprinkled clean from an evil conscience[¶¶] and our bodies washed in pure water.[v]

---

*[10:5–7] A passage from Ps 40:7–9 is placed in the mouth of the Son at his incarnation. As usual, the author follows the Septuagint text. There is a notable difference in Heb 10:5 (Ps 40:7b), where the Masoretic text reads "ears you have dug for me" ("ears open to obedience you gave me," NAB), but most Septuagint manuscripts have "a body you prepared for me," a reading obviously more suited to the interpretation of Hebrews.

†[10:8] **Sacrifices and offerings, holocausts and sin offerings:** these four terms taken from the preceding passage of Ps 40 (with the first two changed to plural forms) are probably intended as equivalents to the four principal types of Old Testament sacrifices: peace offerings (Lv 3, here called **sacrifices**); cereal offerings (Lv 2, here called **offerings**); holocausts (Lv 1); and **sin offerings** (Lv 4–5). This last category includes the guilt offerings of Lv 5:14–19.

‡[10:11–18] Whereas the levitical priesthood offered daily sacrifices that were ineffectual in remitting sin (Heb 10:11), Jesus offered a single sacrifice that won him a permanent place at God's right hand. There he has only to await the final outcome of his work (Heb 10:12–13; cf. Ps 110:1). Thus he has brought into being in his own person the new covenant prophesied by Jeremiah (Jer 31:33–34) that has rendered meaningless all other offerings for sin (Heb 10:14–18).

§[10:13] **Until his enemies are made his footstool:** Ps 110:1 is again used; the reference here is to the period of time between the enthronement of Jesus and his second coming. The identity of the **enemies** is not specified; cf. 1 Cor 15:25–27.

¶[10:15–17] The testimony of the scriptures is now invoked to support what has just preceded. The passage cited

is a portion of the new covenant prophecy of Jer 31:31–34, which the author previously used in Heb 8:8–12.

[10:17] **He also says: these words are not in the Greek text, which has only *kai,* "also," but the expression **"after saying"** in Heb 10:15 seems to require such a phrase to divide the Jeremiah text into two sayings. Others understand "the Lord says" of Heb 10:16 (here rendered **says the Lord**) as outside the quotation and consider Heb 10:16b as part of the second saying. Two ancient versions and a number of minuscules introduce the words "then he said" or a similar expression at the beginning of Heb 10:17.

††[10:19–39] Practical consequences from these reflections on the priesthood and the sacrifice of Christ should make it clear that Christians may now have direct and confident access to God through the person of Jesus (Heb 10:19–20), who rules God's house as high priest (Heb 10:21). They should approach God with sincerity and faith, in the knowledge that through baptism their sins have been remitted (Heb 10:22), reminding themselves of the hope they expressed in Christ at that event (Heb 10:23). They are to encourage one another to Christian love and activity (Heb 10:24), not refusing, no matter what the reason, to participate in the community's assembly, especially in view of the parousia (Heb 10:25; cf. 1 Thes 4:13–18). If refusal to participate in the assembly indicates rejection of Christ, no sacrifice exists to obtain forgiveness for so great a sin (Heb 10:26); only the dreadful judgment of God remains (Heb 10:27). For if violation of the Mosaic law could be punished by death, how much worse will be the punishment of those who have turned their backs on Christ by despising his sacrifice and disregarding the gifts of the holy Spirit (Heb 10:28–29). Judgment belongs to the Lord, and he enacts it by his living presence (Heb 10:30–31). There was a time when the spirit of their community caused them to welcome and share their sufferings (Heb 10:32–34). To revitalize that spirit is to share in the courage of the Old Testament prophets (cf. Is 26:20; Heb 2:3–4), the kind of courage that must distinguish the faith of the Christian (Heb 10:35–39).

‡‡[10:20] **Through the veil, that is, his flesh:** the term **flesh** is used pejoratively. As the temple veil kept people from entering the Holy of Holies (it was rent at Christ's death, Mk 15:38), so the flesh of Jesus constituted an obstacle to approaching God.

§§[10:21] **The house of God:** this refers back to Heb 3:6, "we are his house."

¶¶[10:22] **With our hearts sprinkled clean from an evil conscience:** as in Heb 9:13 (see note there), the sprinkling

---

h. [10:3] Lv 16:21; Nm 5:15 LXX.   i. [10:4] Is 1:11; Mi 6:6–8. j. [10:5–7] Ps 40:7–9.   k. [10:8] 10:5–6; Ps 40:7.   l. [10:9] 7; Ps 40:8; Mt 26:39; Mk 14:36; Lk 22:42; Jn 6:38.   m. [10:10] 9:12, 14.   n. [10:11] 7:27; Dt 10:8;18:7.   o. [10:12–13] Ps 110:1.   p. [10:14] 9:28.

q. [10:16] 8:10; Jer 31:33.   r. [10:17] 8:12; Jer 31:34.   s. [10:19] 3:6; 4:16; 6:19–20; Eph 1:7; 3:12.   t. [10:20] Jn 14:6 / Heb 6:19–20; 9:8, 11–12; Mt 27:51; Mk 15:38; Lk 23:45.   u. [10:21] 3:6.   v. [10:22] 9:13–14; Ez 36:25; 1 Cor 6:11; Ti 3:5; 1 Pt 3:21.

²³Let us hold unwaveringly to our confession that gives us hope, for he who made the promise is trustworthy.ʷ ²⁴We must consider how to rouse one another to love and good works. ²⁵We should not stay away from our assembly,⋆ as is the custom of some, but encourage one another, and this all the more as you see the day drawing near.ˣ

²⁶†If we sin deliberately after receiving knowledge of the truth, there no longer remains sacrifice for sins ²⁷but a fearful prospect of judgment and a flaming fire that is going to consume the adversaries.ᶻ ²⁸Anyone who rejects the law of Moses‡ is put to death without pity on the testimony of two or three witnesses.ᵃ ²⁹Do you not think that a much worse punishment is due the one who has contempt for the Son of God, considers unclean the covenant-blood by which he was consecrated, and insults the spirit of grace?ᵇ ³⁰We know the one who said:

"Vengeance is mine; I will repay,"

and again:

"The Lord will judge his people."ᶜ

³¹It is a fearful thing to fall into the hands of the living God.ᵈ
³²Remember the days past when, after you had been enlightened,§ you endured a great contest of suffering.ᵉ ³³At times you were publicly exposed to abuse and affliction; at other times you associated yourselves with those so treated.ᶠ ³⁴You even joined in the sufferings of those in prison and joyfully accepted the confiscation of your property, knowing that you had a better and lasting possession.ᵍ ³⁵Therefore, do not throw away your confidence; it will have great recompense.ʰ ³⁶You need endurance to do the will of God and receive what he has promised.ⁱ

³⁷ "For, after just a brief moment,⁵
he who is to come shall come;
he shall not delay.ʲ
³⁸ But my just one shall live by faith,
and if he draws back I take no
pleasure in him."ᵏ

³⁹We are not among those who draw back and perish, but among those who have faith and will possess life.

V. EXAMPLES, DISCIPLINE, DISOBEDIENCE

CHAPTER 11⋆⋆

Faith of the Ancients. ¹Faith is the realization of what is hoped for and evidence†† of things not seen.ˡ ²Because of it the ancients were well attested. ³ᵐBy faith we understand that the universe was ordered by the word of God,‡‡ so that what is visible came into being through the invisible. ⁴§§By faith Abel offered to God a

---

¶[10:37–38] In support of his argument, the author uses Hb 2:3–4 in a wording almost identical with the text of the Codex Alexandrinus of the Septuagint but with the first and second lines of Heb 10:4 inverted. He introduces it with a few words from Is 26:20: **after just a brief moment.** Note the Pauline usage of Hb 2:4 in Rom 1:17; Gal 3:11.

⋆⋆[11:1–40] This chapter draws upon the people and events of the Old Testament to paint an inspiring portrait of religious faith, firm and unyielding in the face of any obstacles that confront it. These pages rank among the most eloquent and lofty to be found in the Bible. They expand the theme announced in Heb 6:12, to which the author now returns (Heb 10:39). The material of this chapter is developed chronologically. Heb 11:3–7 draw upon the first nine chapters of Genesis (Gn 1–9); Heb 11:8–22, upon the period of the patriarchs; Heb 11:23–31, upon the time of Moses; Heb 11:32–38, upon the history of the judges, the prophets, and the Maccabean martyrs. The author gives the most extensive description of faith provided in the New Testament, though his interest does not lie in a technical, theological definition. In view of the needs of his audience he describes what authentic faith does, not what it is in itself. Through faith God guarantees the blessings to be hoped for from him, providing evidence in the gift of faith that what he promises will eventually come to pass (Heb 11:1). Because they accepted in faith God's guarantee of the future, the biblical personages discussed in Heb 11:3–38 were themselves commended by God (Heb 11:2). Christians have even greater reason to remain firm in faith since they, unlike the Old Testament men and women of faith, have perceived the beginning of God's fulfillment of his messianic promises (Heb 11:39–40).

††[11:1] **Faith is the realization . . . evidence:** the author is not attempting a precise definition. There is dispute about the meaning of the Greek words *hypostasis* and *elenchos,* here translated **realization** and **evidence,** respectively. *Hypostasis* usually means "substance," "being" (as translated in Heb 1:3), or "reality" (as translated in Heb 3:14); here it connotes something more subjective, and so **realization** has been chosen rather than "assurance" (RSV). *Elenchos,* usually "proof," is used here in an objective sense and so translated **evidence** rather than the transferred sense of "(inner) conviction" (RSV).

‡‡[11:3] **By faith . . . God:** this verse does not speak of the faith of the Old Testament men and women but is in the first person plural. Hence it seems out of place in the sequence of thought.

§§[11:4] The "Praise of the Ancestors" in Sir 44:1–50:21 gives a similar list of heroes. The Cain and Abel narrative in Gn 4:1–16 does not mention Abel's faith. It says, however, that

---

motif refers to the Mosaic rite of cleansing from ritual impurity. This could produce only an external purification, whereas sprinkling with the blood of Christ (Heb 9:14) cleanses the conscience. **Washed in pure water:** baptism is elsewhere referred to as a washing; cf. 1 Cor 6:11; Eph 5:26.

⋆[10:25] **Our assembly:** the liturgical **assembly** of the Christian community, probably for the celebration of the Eucharist. **The day:** this designation for the parousia also occurs in the Pauline letters, e.g., Rom 2:16; 1 Cor 3:13; 1 Thes 5:2.

†[10:26] **If we sin deliberately:** verse 29 indicates that the author is here thinking of apostasy; cf. Heb 3:12; 6:4–8.

‡[10:28] **Rejects the law of Moses:** evidently not any sin against the law, but idolatry. Dt 17:2–7 prescribed capital punishment for idolaters who were convicted on the testimony of two or three witnesses.

§[10:32] **After you had been enlightened:** "enlightenment" is an ancient metaphor for baptism (cf. Eph 5:14; Jn 9:11), but see Heb 6:4 and the note there.

---

w. [10:23] 3:1, 6; 4:14; 1 Cor 10:13.   x. [10:25] Rom 13:12; 1 Cor 3:13.   y. [10:26] 3:12; 6:4–8.   z. [10:27] 10:31; 9:27; Is 26:11 LXX; Zep 1:18.   a. [10:28] Dt 17:6.   b. [10:29] 6:6.   c. [10:30] Dt 32:35, 36; Rom 12:19.   d. [10:31] 10:27; Mt 10:28; Lk 12:4–5.   e. [10:32] 6:4.   f. [10:33] 1 Cor 4:9.   g. [10:34] 13:3; Mt 6:19–20; Lk 12:33–34.   h. [10:35] 4:16.   i. [10:36] Lk 21:19.

j. [10:37] Is 26:20; Heb 2:3.   k. [10:38] Heb 2:4; Rom 1:17; Gal 3:11.   l. [11:1] 1:3; 3:14; Rom 8:24; 2 Cor 4:18.   m. [11:3] Gn 1:3; Ps 33:6; Wis 9:1; Jn 1:3.

sacrifice greater than Cain's. Through this he was attested to be righteous, God bearing witness to his gifts, and through this, though dead, he still speaks.*n* *5*By faith Enoch was taken up so that he should not see death, and "he was found no more because God had taken him." Before he was taken up, he was attested to have pleased God.*o* *6*But without faith it is impossible to please him,*p* for anyone who approaches God must believe that he exists and that he rewards those who seek him. *7*By faith Noah, warned about what was not yet seen, with reverence built an ark for the salvation of his household. Through this he condemned the world and inherited the righteousness that comes through faith.*q*

*8*By faith Abraham obeyed when he was called to go out to a place that he was to receive as an inheritance; he went out, not knowing where he was to go.*r* *9*By faith he sojourned in the promised land as in a foreign country, dwelling in tents with Isaac and Jacob, heirs of the same promise;*s* *10*for he was looking forward to the city with foundations, whose architect and maker is God.*t* *11*By faith he received power to generate, even though he was past the normal age—and Sarah herself was sterile—for he thought that the one who had made the promise was trustworthy.*u* *12*So it was that there came forth from one man, himself as good as dead, descendants as numerous as the stars in the sky and as countless as the sands on the seashore.*v*

*13*All these died in faith. They did not receive what had been promised but saw it and greeted it from afar and acknowledged themselves to be strangers and aliens on earth,*w* *14*for those who speak thus show that they are seeking a homeland. *15*If they had been thinking of the land from which they had come, they would have had opportunity to return. *16*But now they desire a better homeland, a heavenly one. Therefore, God is not ashamed to be called their God, for he has prepared a city for them.*x*

*17*By faith Abraham, when put to the test, offered up Isaac, and he who had received the promises was ready to offer his only son,*y* *18*of whom it was said, "Through Isaac descendants

shall bear your name."*z* *19†*He reasoned that God was able to raise even from the dead,*a* and he received Isaac back as a symbol. *20*By faith regarding things still to come Isaac‡ blessed Jacob and Esau.*b* *21*By faith Jacob, when dying, blessed each of the sons of Joseph and "bowed in worship, leaning on the top of his staff."*c* *22*By faith Joseph, near the end of his life, spoke of the Exodus of the Israelites and gave instructions about his bones.*d*

*23§*By faith Moses was hidden by his parents for three months after his birth, because they saw that he was a beautiful child, and they were not afraid of the king's edict. *24§*By faith Moses, when he had grown up, refused to be known as the son of Pharaoh's daughter;*f* *25*he chose to be ill-treated along with the people of God rather than enjoy the fleeting pleasure of sin. *26*He considered the reproach of the Anointed greater wealth than the treasures of Egypt, for he was looking to the recompense. *27*By faith he left Egypt, not fearing the king's fury, for he persevered as if seeing the one who is invisible.*g* *28*By faith he kept the Passover and sprinkled the blood, that the Destroyer of the firstborn might not touch them.*h* *29*By faith they crossed the Red Sea as if it were dry land, but when the Egyptians attempted it they were drowned.*i* *30*By faith the walls of Jericho fell after being encircled for seven days.*j* *31*By faith Rahab the harlot did not perish with the disobedient, for she had received the spies in peace.*k*

*32*What more shall I say? I have not time to tell of Gideon, Barak, Samson, Jephthah, of David and Samuel and the prophets,*l* *33*who by faith conquered kingdoms, did what was righteous, obtained the promises; they closed the mouths of lions,*m* *34*put out raging fires, escaped the devouring sword; out of weakness they were made powerful, became strong in battle, and turned back foreign invaders.*n* *35*Women received back their dead through resurrection. Some were tortured and would not accept deliverance, in order to obtain a better resurrection.*o*

---

†[11:19] **As a symbol:** Isaac's "return from death" is seen as a **symbol** of Christ's resurrection. Others understand the words *en parabolē* to mean "in figure," i.e., the word **dead** is used figuratively of Isaac, since he did not really die. But in the one other place that *parabolē* occurs in Hebrews, it means symbol (Heb 9:9).

‡[11:20–22] Each of these three patriarchs, Isaac, Jacob, and Joseph, had faith in the future fulfillment of God's promise and renewed this faith when near death.

§[11:24–27] The reason given for Moses' departure from Egypt differs from the account in Ex 2:11–15. The author also gives a christological interpretation of his decision to share the trials of his people.

God "looked with favor on Abel and his offering" (Gn 4:4); in view of Heb 11:6 the author probably understood God's favor to have been activated by Abel's faith. **Though dead, he still speaks:** possibly because his blood "cries out to me from the soil" (Gn 4:10), but more probably a way of saying that the repeated story of Abel provides ongoing witness to faith.

*[11:6] One must believe not only that God *exists* but that he is concerned about human conduct; the Old Testament defines folly as the denial of this truth; cf. Ps 52:2.

n. [11:4] 12:24; Gn 4:4, 10. o. [11:5] Sir 5:24; Sir 44:16. p. [11:6] Wis 4:10. q. [11:7] Gn 6:8–22; Sir 44:17–18; Mt 24:37–39; Lk 17:26–27; 1 Pt 3:20; 2 Pt 2:5. r. [11:8] Gn 12:1–4; 15:7–21; Sir 44:19–22; Acts 7:2–8; Rom 4:16–22. s. [11:9] Gn 12:8; 13:12; 23:4; 26:3; 35:27. t. [11:10] 12:22; 13:14; Rev 21:10–22. u. [11:11] Gn 17:19; 21:2; Rom 4:19–21 / 1 Cor 10:13. v. [11:12] Gn 15:5; 22:17; 32:13; Ex 32:13; Dt 10:22; Dn 3:36 LXX. w. [11:13] Gn 23:4; Ps 39:13. x. [11:16] 13:14; Ex 3:6. y. [11:17] Gn 22:1–10; Sir 44:20; 1 Mc 2:52; Jas 2:21.

z. [11:18] Gn 21:12 LXX; Rom 9:7. a. [11:19] Rom 4:16–22. b. [11:20] Gn 27:27–40. c. [11:21] Gn 27:38–40; 47:31 LXX; 48:15–16. d. [11:22] Gn 50:24–25. e. [11:23] Ex 2:2; Acts 7:20. f. [11:24–25] Ex 2:10–15; Acts 7:23–29. g. [11:27] Ex 2:15; Acts 7:29. h. [11:28] Ex 12:21–23; Wis 18:25; 1 Cor 10:10. i. [11:29] Ex 14:22–28. j. [11:30] Jos 6:12–21. k. [11:31] Jos 2:1–21; 6:22–25; Jas 2:25. l. [11:32] Jgs 4:6–22; 6:11–8:32; 11:1–12:7. m. [11:33] Dn 6:23. n. [11:34] Dn 3:22–25, 49–50. o. [11:35] 1 Kgs 17:17–24; 2 Kgs 4:18–37; 2 Mc 6:18–7:42.

³⁶Others endured mockery, scourging, even chains and imprisonment.ᵖ ³⁷They were stoned, sawed in two, put to death at sword's point; they went about in skins of sheep or goats, needy, afflicted, tormented.�q ³⁸The world was not worthy of them. They wandered about in deserts and on mountains, in caves and in crevices in the earth.ʳ

³⁹Yet all these, though approved because of their faith, did not receive what had been promised. ⁴⁰God had foreseen something better for us, so that without us they should not be made perfect.˙

CHAPTER 12
God Our Father.† ¹Therefore, since we are surrounded by so great a cloud of witnesses, let us rid ourselves of every burden and sin that clings to us‡ and persevere in running the race that lies before us ²while keeping our eyes fixed on Jesus, the leader and perfecter of faith. For the sake of the joy that lay before him he endured the cross, despising its shame, and has taken his seat at the right of the throne of God.ˢ ³Consider how he endured such opposition from sinners, in order that you may not grow weary and lose heart. ⁴In your struggle against sin you have not yet resisted to the point of shedding blood. ⁵You have also forgotten the exhortation addressed to you as sons:

"My son, do not disdain the discipline of
    the Lordᵗ
or lose heart when reproved by him;
⁶   for whom the Lord loves, he disciplines;
    he scourges every son he
        acknowledges."

⁷Endure your trials as "discipline"; God treats you as sons. For what "son" is there whom his father does not discipline?ᵘ ⁸If you are without discipline, in which all have shared, you are not sons but bastards. ⁹Besides this, we have had our

earthly fathers to discipline us, and we respected them. Should we not [then] submit all the more to the Father of spirits and live?ᵛ ¹⁰They disciplined us for a short time as seemed right to them, but he does so for our benefit, in order that we may share his holiness. ¹¹At the time, all discipline seems a cause not for joy but for pain, yet later it brings the peaceful fruit of righteousness to those who are trained by it.ʷ ¹²So strengthen your drooping hands and your weak knees.ˣ ¹³Make straight paths for your feet, that what is lame may not be dislocated but healed.ʸ

Penalties of Disobedience. ¹⁴ᶻStrive for peace with everyone, and for that holiness without which no one will see the Lord. ¹⁵ᵃSee to it that no one be deprived of the grace of God, that no bitter root spring up and cause trouble, through which many may become defiled,ᵃ ¹⁶that no one be an immoral or profane person like Esau, who sold his birthright for a single meal.ᵇ ¹⁷For you know that later, when he wanted to inherit his father's blessing, he was rejected because he found no opportunity to change his mind, even though he sought the blessing with tears.ᶜ

¹⁸*You have not approached that which could be touched˙ᵈ and a blazing fire and gloomy darkness and storm ¹⁹and a trumpet blast and a voice speaking words such that those who heard begged that no message be further addressed to them,ᵉ ²⁰for they could not bear to hear the command: "If even an animal touches the mountain, it shall be stoned."ᶠ ²¹Indeed, so fearful was the spectacle that Moses said, "I am terrified and trembling."ᵍ ²²No, you have approached Mount Zion and the city of the living God, the

§[12:15–17] Esau serves as an example in two ways: his **profane** attitude illustrates the danger of apostasy, and his inability to secure a blessing afterward illustrates the impossibility of repenting after falling away (see Heb 6:4–6).
¶[12:18–29] As a final appeal for adherence to Christian teaching, the two covenants, of Moses and of Christ, are compared. The Mosaic covenant, the author argues, is shown to have originated in fear of God and threats of divine punishment (Heb 12:18–21). The covenant in Christ gives us direct access to God (Heb 12:22), makes us members of the Christian community, God's children, a sanctified people (Heb 12:23), who have Jesus as mediator to speak for us (Heb 12:24). Not to heed the voice of the risen Christ is a graver sin than the rejection of the word of Moses (Heb 12:25–26). Though Christians fall away, God's kingdom in Christ will remain and his justice will punish those guilty of deserting it (Heb 12:28–29).
[12:18] This remarkably beautiful passage contrasts two great assemblies of people: that of the Israelites gathered at Mount Sinai for the sealing of the old covenant and the promulgation of the Mosaic law, and that of the followers of Jesus gathered at **Mount Zion, the heavenly Jerusalem, the assembly of the **new covenant**. This latter scene, marked by the presence of **countless angels** and of **Jesus** with his redeeming **blood**, is reminiscent of the celestial liturgies of the Book of Revelation.

*[11:40] **So that without us they should not be made perfect:** the heroes of the Old Testament obtained their recompense only after the saving work of Christ had been accomplished. Thus they already enjoy what Christians who are still struggling do not yet possess in its fullness.
†[12:1–13] Christian life is to be inspired not only by the Old Testament men and women of faith (Heb 12:1) but above all by Jesus. As the architect of Christian faith, he had himself to endure the cross before receiving the glory of his triumph (Heb 12:2). Reflection on his sufferings should give his followers courage to continue the struggle, if necessary even to the shedding of blood (Heb 12:3–4). Christians should regard their own sufferings as the affectionate correction of the Lord, who loves them as a father loves his children.
‡[12:1] **That clings to us:** the meaning is uncertain, since the Greek word *euperistatos*, translated **cling**, occurs only here. The papyrus P⁴⁶ and one minuscule read *euperispastos*, "easily distracting," which also makes good sense.

p. [11:36] 2 Chr 36:16; Jer 20:2; 37:15. q. [11:37] 2 Chr 24:21.
r. [11:38] 1 Mc 2:28–30. s. [12:2] 2:10; Ps 110:1; Phil 2:6–8. t.
[12:5–6] Prv 3:11–12 / Dt 8:5; 1 Cor 11:32. u. [12:7] Prv 13:24;
Sir 30:1.

v. [12:9] Nm 16:22; 27:16 LXX. w. [12:11] 2 Cor 4:17; Phil 1:11;
Jas 3:18. x. [12:12] Is 35:3; Sir 25:23; Jb 4:3–4. y. [12:13] Prv
4:26 LXX. z. [12:14] Rom 12:18; 14:19. a. [12:15] Dt 29:18 (17
LXX). b. [12:16] Gn 25:33. c. [12:17] Gn 27:34–38. d. [12:18]
Ex 19:12–14; Dt 4:11; 5:22–23. e. [12:19] Ex 19:16, 19; 20:18–
19. f. [12:20] Ex 19:12–13. g. [12:21] Dt 9:19.

heavenly Jerusalem, and countless angels in festal gathering,[h] [23]and the assembly of the first-born enrolled in heaven,* and God the judge of all, and the spirits of the just made perfect,[i] [24]and Jesus, the mediator of a new covenant, and the sprinkled blood that speaks more eloquently[†] than that of Abel.[j]

[25]See that you do not reject the one who speaks. For if they did not escape when they refused the one who warned them on earth, how much more in our case if we turn away from the one who warns from heaven.[k] [26]His voice shook the earth at that time, but now he has promised, "I will once more shake not only earth but heaven."[l] [27]That phrase, "once more," points to [the] removal of shaken, created things, so that what is unshaken may remain.[m] [28]Therefore, we who are receiving the unshakable kingdom should have gratitude, with which we should offer worship pleasing to God in reverence and awe.[n] [29]For our God is a consuming fire.[o]

VI. FINAL EXHORTATION, BLESSING, GREETINGS

CHAPTER 13

[1‡]Let mutual love continue. [2]Do not neglect hospitality, for through it some have unknowingly entertained angels.[p] [3]Be mindful of prisoners as if sharing their imprisonment, and of the ill-treated as of yourselves, for you also are in the body.[q] [4]Let marriage be honored among all and the marriage bed be kept undefiled, for God will judge the immoral and adulterers.[r] [5]Let your life be free from love of money but be content with what you have, for he has said, "I will never forsake you or abandon you."[s] [6]Thus we may say with confidence:

"The Lord is my helper,
[and] I will not be afraid.
What can anyone do to me?"[t]

[7]Remember your leaders who spoke the word of God to you. Consider the outcome of their way of life and imitate their faith. [8]Jesus Christ is the same yesterday, today, and forever.[u]

[9]Do not be carried away by all kinds of strange teaching.[§] It is good to have our hearts strengthened by grace and not by foods, which do not benefit those who live by them.[v] [10]We have an altar[¶] from which those who serve the tabernacle have no right to eat. [11]The bodies of the animals whose blood the high priest brings into the sanctuary as a sin offering are burned outside the camp.[w] [12]Therefore, Jesus also suffered outside the gate, to consecrate the people by his own blood.[x] [13]Let us then go to him outside the camp, bearing the reproach that he bore. [14]For here we have no lasting city, but we seek the one that is to come.[y] [15]Through him [then] let us continually offer God a sacrifice of praise, that is, the fruit of lips that confess his name.[z] [16]Do not neglect to do good and to share what you have; God is pleased by sacrifices of that kind.[a]

[17**]Obey your leaders and defer to them, for they keep watch over you and will have to give an account, that they may fulfill their task with joy and not with sorrow, for that would be of no advantage to you.

[18]Pray for us, for we are confident that we have a clear conscience, wishing to act rightly in every respect. [19]I especially ask for your prayers that I may be restored to you very soon.

[20††]May the God of peace, who brought up from the dead the great shepherd of the sheep by the blood of the eternal covenant, Jesus our Lord,[b] [21]furnish you with all that is good, that you may do his will. May he carry out in you what is pleasing to him through Jesus Christ, to whom be glory forever [and ever]. Amen.

---

*[12:23] **The assembly of the firstborn enrolled in heaven:** this expression may refer to the angels of Heb 12:22, or to the heroes of the Old Testament (see Heb 11), or to the entire assembly of the new covenant.

†[12:24] **Speaks more eloquently:** the blood of Abel, the first human blood to be shed, is contrasted with that of Jesus. Abel's blood cried out from the earth for vengeance, but the blood of Jesus has opened the way for everyone, providing cleansing and access to God (Heb 10:19).

‡[13:1–16] After recommendations on social and moral matters (Heb 13:1–6), the letter turns to doctrinal issues. The fact that the original leaders are dead should not cause the recipients of this letter to lose their faith (Heb 13:7), for Christ still lives and he remains always the same (Heb 13:8). They must not rely for their personal sanctification on regulations concerning foods (Heb 13:9), nor should they entertain the notion that Judaism and Christianity can be intermingled (Heb 13:10; cf. notes on Gal 2:11–14; 2:15–21). As Jesus died separated from his own people, so must the Christian community remain apart from the religious doctrines of Judaism (Heb 13:11–14). Christ must be the heart and center of the community (Heb 13:15–16).

§[13:9] **Strange teaching:** this doctrine about **foods** probably refers to the Jewish food laws; in view of Heb 13:10, however, the author may be thinking of the Mosaic sacrificial banquets.

¶[13:10] **We have an altar:** this does not refer to the Eucharist, which is never clearly mentioned in Hebrews, but to the sacrifice of Christ.

**[13:17–25] Recommending obedience to the leaders of the community, the author asks for prayers (Heb 13:17–19). The letter concludes with a blessing (Heb 13:20–21), a final request for the acceptance of its message (Heb 13:22), information regarding Timothy (Heb 13:23), and general greetings (Heb 13:24–25).

††[13:20–21] These verses constitute one of the most beautiful blessings in the New Testament. The resurrection of Jesus is presupposed throughout Hebrews, since it is included in the author's frequently expressed idea of his exaltation, but this is the only place where it is explicitly mentioned.

---

h. [12:22] Gal 4:26; Rev 21:2. i. [12:23] Lk 10:20; Rev 5:11. j. [12:24] 7:22; 8:6; 9:15 / 11:4; Gn 4:10. k. [12:25] Ex 20:19. l. [12:26] Ex 19:18; Jgs 5:4–5; Ps 68:9; Hg 2:6. m. [12:27] Is 66:22; Mt 24:35; Mk 13:31; Lk 21:33. n. [12:28] Dn 7:14, 18 / Rom 1:9. o. [12:29] Dt 4:24; Is 33:14. p. [13:2] Gn 18:3; 19:2–3; Jgs 6:11–22; Tb 5:4. q. [13:3] Mt 25:36. r. [13:4] 1 Cor 5:13; Eph 5:5. s. [13:5] Dt 31:6, 8; Jos 1:5.

t. [13:6] Ps 27:1–3; 118:6. u. [13:8] 1:12; 7:24; Rev 1:17. v. [13:9] Rom 14:17; 1 Cor 8:8; Eph 4:14; Col 2:16. w. [13:11] Ex 29:14; Lv 16:27. x. [13:12] Mt 21:39; Mk 12:8; Lk 20:15; Jn 19:17. y. [13:14] 11:10, 14. z. [13:15] Hos 14:3. a. [13:16] Phil 4:18. b. [13:20] Is 63:11; Zec 9:11; Jn 10:11; Acts 2:24; Rom 15:33.

²²Brothers, I ask you to bear with this message of encouragement, for I have written to you rather briefly. ²³I must let you know that our brother Timothy has been set free. If he comes soon, I shall see you together with him.ᶜ

²⁴Greetings to all your leaders and to all the holy ones. Those from Italy send you greetings. ²⁵Grace be with all of you.ᵈ

c. [13:23] Acts 16:1.

d. [13:25] Ti 3:15.

THE
CATHOLIC LETTERS

In addition to the thirteen letters attributed to Paul and the Letter to the Hebrews, the New Testament contains seven other letters. Three of these are attributed to John, two to Peter, and one each to James and Jude, all personages of the apostolic age. The term "catholic letter" first appears, with reference only to 1 John, in the writings of Apollonius of Ephesus, a second-century apologist, known only from a citation in Eusebius's *Ecclesiastical History*. Eusebius himself (A.D. 260–340) used the term to refer to all seven letters.

The reason for the term "catholic," which means "universal," was the perception that these letters, unlike those of Paul, which were directed to a particular local church, were apparently addressed more generally to the universal church. This designation is not entirely accurate, however. On the one hand, Hebrews has no specifically identified addressees, and originally this was probably true of Ephesians as well. On the other hand, 3 John is addressed to a named individual, 2 John to a specific, though unnamed, community, and 1 Peter to a number of churches that are specified as being located in Asia Minor.

While all seven of these writings begin with an epistolary formula, several of them do not appear to be real letters in the modern sense of the term. In the ancient world it was not unusual to cast an exhortation in the form of a letter for literary effect, a phenomenon comparable to the "open letter" that is sometimes used today.

With the exception of 1 Peter and 1 John, the ancient church showed reluctance to include the catholic letters in the New Testament canon. The reason for this was widespread doubt whether they had actually been written by the apostolic figures to whom they are attributed. The early Christians saw the New Testament as the depository of apostolic faith; therefore, they wished to include only the testimony of apostles. Today we distinguish more clearly between the authorship of a work and its canonicity: even though written by other, later witnesses than those whose names they bear, these writings nevertheless testify to the apostolic faith and constitute canonical scripture. By the late fourth or early fifth centuries, most objections had been overcome in both the Greek and Latin churches (though not in the Syriac), and all seven of the catholic letters have since been acknowledged as canonical.

THE LETTER OF
JAMES

The person to whom this letter is ascribed can scarcely be one of the two members of the Twelve who bore the name James (see Mt 10:2–3; Mk 3:17–18; Lk 6:14–15), for he is not identified as an apostle but only as "slave of God and of the Lord Jesus Christ" (Jas 1:1). This designation most probably refers to the third New Testament personage named James, a relative of Jesus who is usually called "brother of the Lord" (see Mt 13:55; Mk 6:3). He was the leader of the Jewish Christian community in Jerusalem whom Paul acknowledged as one of the "pillars" (Gal 2:9). In Acts he appears as the authorized spokesman for the Jewish Christian position in the early Church (Acts 12:17; 15:13–21). According to the Jewish historian Josephus (*Antiquities* 20:201–203), he was stoned to death by the Jews under the high priest Ananus II in A.D. 62.

The letter is addressed to "the twelve tribes in the dispersion." In Old Testament terminology the term "twelve tribes" designates the people of Israel; the "dispersion" or "diaspora" refers to the non-Palestinian Jews who had settled throughout the Greco-Roman world (see Jn 7:35). Since in Christian thought the church is the new Israel, the address probably designates the Jewish Christian churches located in Palestine, Syria, and elsewhere. Or perhaps the letter is meant more generally for all Christian communities, and the "dispersion" has the symbolic meaning of exile from our true home, as it has in the address of 1 Peter (1 Pt 1:1). The letter is so markedly Jewish in character that some scholars have regarded it as a Jewish document subsequently "baptized" by a few Christian insertions, but such an origin is scarcely tenable in view of the numerous contacts discernible between the Letter of James and other New Testament literature.

From the viewpoint of its literary form, James is a letter only in the most conventional sense; it has none of the characteristic features of a real letter except the address. It belongs rather to the genre of parenesis or exhortation and is concerned almost exclusively with ethical conduct. It therefore falls within the tradition of Jewish wisdom literature, such as can be found in the Old Testament (Proverbs, Sirach) and in the extracanonical Jewish literature (Testaments of the Twelve Patriarchs, the Books of Enoch, the Manual of Discipline found at Qumran). More specifically, it consists of sequences of didactic proverbs, comparable to Tb 4:5–19, to many passages in Sirach, and to sequences of sayings in the synoptic gospels. Numerous passages in James treat of subjects that also appear in the synoptic sayings of Jesus, especially in Matthew's Sermon on the Mount, but the correspondences are too general to establish any literary dependence. James represents a type of early Christianity that emphasized sound teaching and responsible moral behavior. Ethical norms are derived not primarily from christology, as in Paul, but from a concept of salvation that involves conversion, baptism, forgiveness of sin, and expectation of judgment (Jas 1:17; 4:12).

Paradoxically, this very Jewish work is written in an excellent Greek style, which ranks among the best in the New Testament and appears to be the work of a trained Hellenistic writer. Those who continue to regard James of Jerusalem as its author are therefore obliged to suppose that a secretary must have put the letter into its present literary form. This assumption is not implausible in the light of ancient practice. Some regard the letter as one of the earliest writings in the New Testament and feel that its content accurately reflects what we would expect of the leader of Jewish Christianity. Moreover, they argue that the type of Jewish Christianity reflected in the letter cannot be situated historically after the fall of Jerusalem in A.D. 70.

Others, however, believe it more likely that James is a pseudonymous work of a later period. In addition to its Greek style, they observe further that (a) the prestige that the writer is assumed to enjoy points to the later legendary reputation of James; (b) the discussion of the importance of good works seems to presuppose a debate subsequent to that in Paul's own day; (c) the author does not rely upon prescriptions of the Mosaic law, as we would expect from the historical James; (d) the letter contains no allusions to James's own history and to his relationship with Jesus or to the early Christian community of Jerusalem. For these reasons, many recent interpreters assign James to the period A.D. 90–100.

The principal divisions of the Letter of James are the following:

I. Address (1:1)
II. The Value of Trials and Temptation (1:2–18)
III. Exhortations and Warnings (1:19–5:12)
IV. The Power of Prayer (5:13–20)

I. ADDRESS

CHAPTER 1

¹*James, a slave of God and of the Lord Jesus Christ, to the twelve tribes in the dispersion, greetings.ᵃ

II. THE VALUE OF TRIALS AND TEMPTATION

Perseverance in Trial. ²ᵇConsider it all joy, my brothers, when you encounter various trials,† ³for you know that the testing‡ of your faith produces perseverance. ⁴And let perseverance be perfect, so that you may be perfect and complete, lacking in nothing. ⁵But if any of you lacks wisdom,§ he should ask God who gives to all generously and ungrudgingly, and he will be given it.ᶜ ⁶But he should ask in faith, not doubting, for the one who doubts is like a wave of the sea that is driven and tossed about by the wind.ᵈ ⁷For that person must not suppose that he will receive anything from the Lord, ⁸since he is a man of two minds, unstable in all his ways.

⁹The brother in lowly circumstances¶ should take pride in his high standing,ᵉ ¹⁰and the rich one in his lowliness, for he will pass away "like the flower of the field."ᶠ ¹¹For the sun comes up with its scorching heat and dries up the grass, its flower droops, and the beauty of its appearance vanishes. So will the rich person fade away in the midst of his pursuits.

Temptation. ¹²ᵍBlessed is the man who perseveres in temptation,** for when he has been proved he will receive the crown of life that he promised to those who love him. ¹³††No one experiencing temptation should say, "I am being tempted by God"; for God is not subject to temptation to evil, and he himself tempts no one.ʰ ¹⁴Rather, each person is tempted when he is lured and enticed by his own desire. ¹⁵Then desire conceives and brings forth sin, and when sin reaches maturity it gives birth to death.

¹⁶‡‡Do not be deceived, my beloved brothers: ¹⁷all good giving and every perfect gift§§ is from above, coming down from the Father of lights, with whom there is no alteration or shadow caused by change. ¹⁸ⁱHe willed to give us birth by the word of truth that we may be a kind of firstfruits of his creatures.¶¶

*[1:1] **James, a slave of God and of the Lord Jesus Christ**: a declaration of the writer's authority for instructing the Christian communities; cf. Rom 1:1. Regarding the identity of the author, see Introduction. **Dispersion**: see Introduction.

†[1:2] **Consider it all joy . . . various trials**: a frequent teaching of the New Testament derived from the words and sufferings of Jesus (Mt 5:10–12; Jn 10:11; Acts 5:41).

‡[1:3–8] The sequence of testing, perseverance, and being perfect and complete indicates the manner of attaining spiritual maturity and full preparedness for the coming of Christ (Jas 5:7–12; cf. 1 Pt 1:6–7; Rom 5:3–5). These steps require wisdom (Jas 1:5).

§[1:5] **Wisdom**: a gift that God readily grants to all who ask in faith and that sustains the Christian in times of trial. It is a kind of knowledge or understanding not accessible to the unbeliever or those who doubt, which gives the recipient an understanding of the real importance of events. In this way a Christian can deal with adversity with great calm and hope (cf. 1 Cor 2:6–12).

¶[1:9–11] Throughout his letter (see Jas 2:5; 4:10, 13–16; 5:1–6), the author reaffirms the teaching of Jesus that worldly prosperity is not necessarily a sign of God's favor but can even be a hindrance to proper humility before God (cf. Lk 6:20–25; 12:16–21; 16:19–31).

[1:12] **Temptation: the Greek word used here is the same one used for "trials" in Jas 1:2. **The crown of life**: in ancient Palestine, crowns or wreaths of flowers were worn at festive occasions as signs of joy and honor. In the Hellenistic world, wreaths were given as a reward to great statesmen, soldiers, athletes. **Life**: here means eternal life. **He promised**: some manuscripts read "God" or "the Lord," while the best witnesses do not specify the subject of "promised."

††[1:13–15] It is contrary to what we know of God for God to be the author of human temptation (Jas 1:13). In the commission of a sinful act, one is first beguiled by passion (Jas 1:14), then consent is given, which in turn causes the sinful act. When sin permeates the entire person, it incurs the ultimate penalty of death (Jas 1:15).

‡‡[1:16–18] The author here stresses that God is the source of all good and of good alone, and the evil of temptation does not come from him.

§§[1:17] **All good giving and every perfect gift** may be a proverb written in hexameter. **Father of lights**: God is here called the Father of the heavenly luminaries, i.e., the stars, sun, and moon that he created (Gn 1:14–18). Unlike orbs moving from nadir to zenith, he never changes or diminishes in brightness.

¶¶[1:18] Acceptance of the gospel message, **the word of truth**, constitutes new birth (Jn 3:5–6) and makes the recipient the firstfruits (i.e., the cultic offering of the earliest grains, symbolizing the beginning of an abundant harvest) of a new creation; cf. 1 Cor 15:20; Rom 8:23.

a. [1:1] Jn 7:35; 1 Pt 1:1. b. [1:2] Rom 5:3–5; 1 Pt 1:6; 4:13–16. c. [1:5] Prv 2:2–6; Wis 9:4, 9–12. d. [1:6] Mt 7:7; Mk 11:24. e. [1:9] 2:5.

f. [1:10] Is 40:6–7. g. [1:12] 1 Cor 9:25; 2 Tm 4:8; 1 Pt 5:4; Rev 2:10. h. [1:13] Sir 15:11–20; 1 Cor 10:13. i. [1:18] Jn 1:12–13; 1 Pt 1:23.

III. EXHORTATIONS AND WARNINGS

Doers of the Word. [19]Know this, my dear brothers: everyone should be quick to hear,* slow to speak, slow to wrath,[j] [20]for the wrath of a man does not accomplish the righteousness of God.[k] [21]Therefore, put away all filth and evil excess and humbly welcome the word that has been planted in you and is able to save your souls.[l]

[22]Be doers of the word and not hearers only, deluding yourselves.[m] [23]For if anyone is a hearer of the word and not a doer, he is like a man who looks at his own face in a mirror. [24]He sees himself, then goes off and promptly forgets what he looked like. [25]But the one who peers into the perfect law[†] of freedom and perseveres, and is not a hearer who forgets but a doer who acts, such a one shall be blessed in what he does.[n]

[26‡]If anyone thinks he is religious and does not bridle his tongue[§] but deceives his heart, his religion is vain.[o] [27]Religion that is pure and undefiled before God and the Father is this: to care for orphans and widows[¶] in their affliction and to keep oneself unstained by the world.[p]

CHAPTER 2

Sin of Partiality.[**] [1]My brothers, show no partiality as you adhere to the faith in our glorious Lord Jesus Christ. [2]For if a man with gold rings on his fingers and in fine clothes comes into your assembly, and a poor person in shabby clothes also comes in, [3]and you pay attention to the one wearing the fine clothes and say, "Sit here, please," while you say to the poor one, "Stand there," or "Sit at my feet," [4]have you not made distinctions among yourselves and become judges with evil designs?[††]

[5]Listen, my beloved brothers. Did not God choose those who are poor[‡‡] in the world to be rich in faith and heirs of the kingdom that he promised to those who love him?[q] [6]But you dishonored the poor person. Are not the rich oppressing you? And do they themselves not haul you off to court? [7]Is it not they who blaspheme the noble name that was invoked over you?[r] [8]However, if you fulfill the royal[§§] law according to the scripture, "You shall love your neighbor as yourself," you are doing well.[s] [9]But if you show partiality, you commit sin, and are convicted by the law as transgressors.[t] [10]For whoever keeps the whole law, but falls short in one particular, has become guilty in respect to all of it.[u] [11]For he who said, "You shall not commit adultery," also said, "You shall not kill."[v] Even if you do not commit adultery but kill, you have become a transgressor of the law. [12w]So speak and so act as people who will be judged by the law of freedom.[¶¶] [13]For the judgment is merciless to one who has not shown mercy; mercy triumphs over judgment.[x]

Faith and Works.[***] [14]What good is it, my brothers, if someone says he has faith but does not have works? Can that faith save him?[y] [15]If a brother or sister has nothing to wear and has no food for the day, [16]and one of you says to them, "Go in peace, keep warm, and eat well," but you do not give them the necessities of the body, what good is it?[z] [17]So also faith of itself, if it does not have works, is dead.

[18]Indeed someone may say, "You have faith and I have works." Demonstrate your faith to me without works, and I will demonstrate my faith to you from my works. [19]You believe that God is

---

*[1:19–25] To be quick to hear the gospel is to accept it readily and to act in conformity with it, removing from one's soul whatever is opposed to it, so that it may take root and effect salvation (Jas 1:19–21). To listen to the gospel message but not practice it is failure to improve oneself (Jas 1:22–24). Only conformity of life to the perfect law of true freedom brings happiness (Jas 1:25).

†[1:25] Peers into the perfect law: the image of a person doing this is paralleled to that of hearing God's word. The perfect law applies the Old Testament description of the Mosaic law to the gospel of Jesus Christ that brings freedom.

‡[1:26–27] A practical application of Jas 1:22 is now made.

§[1:26] For control of the tongue, see note on Jas 3:1–12.

¶[1:27] In the Old Testament, orphans and widows are classical examples of the defenseless and oppressed.

**[2:1–13] In the Christian community there must be no discrimination or favoritism based on status or wealth (Jas 2:2–4; cf. Mt 5:3; 11:5; 23:6; 1 Cor 1:27–29). Divine favor rather consists in God's election and promises (Jas 2:5). The rich who oppress the poor blaspheme the name of Christ (Jas 2:6–7). By violating one law of love of neighbor, they offend against the whole law (Jas 2:8–11). On the other hand, conscious awareness of the final judgment helps the faithful to fulfill the whole law (Jas 2:12).

††[2:4] When Christians show favoritism to the rich they are guilty of the worst kind of prejudice and discrimination. The author says that such Christians set themselves

up as judges who judge not by divine law but by the basest, self-serving motives.

‡‡[2:5] The poor, "God's poor" of the Old Testament, were seen by Jesus as particularly open to God for belief in and reliance on him alone (Lk 6:20). God's law cannot tolerate their oppression in any way (Jas 2:9).

§§[2:8] Royal: literally, "kingly"; because the Mosaic law came from God, the universal king. There may be an allusion to Jesus' uses of this commandment in his preaching of the kingdom of God (Mt 22:39; Mk 12:31; Lk 10:27).

¶¶[2:12–13] The law upon which the last judgment will be based is the law of freedom. As Jesus taught, mercy (which participates in God's own loving mercy) includes forgiveness of those who wrong us (see Mt 6:12, 14–15).

***[2:14–26] The theme of these verses is the relationship of faith and works (deeds). It has been argued that the teaching here contradicts that of Paul (see especially Rom 4:5–6). The problem can only be understood if the different viewpoints of the two authors are seen. Paul argues against those who claim to participate in God's salvation because of their good deeds as well as because they have committed themselves to trust in God through Jesus Christ (Paul's concept of faith). Paul certainly understands, however, the implications of true faith for a life of love and generosity (see Gal 5:6, 13–15). The author of James is well aware that proper conduct can only come about with an authentic commitment to God in faith (Jas 2:18, 26). Many think he was seeking to correct a misunderstanding of Paul's view.

---

j. [1:19] Prv 14:17; Sir 5:11. k. [1:20] Eph 4:26. l. [1:21] Col 3:8. m. [1:22] Mt 7:26; Rom 2:13. n. [1:25] 2:12; Ps 19:8; Rom 8:2. o. [1:26] 3:2; Ps 34:14. p. [1:27] Ex 22:21.

q. [2:5] 1 Cor 1:26–28; Rev 2:9. r. [2:7] 1 Pt 4:4. s. [2:8] Lv 19:18; Mt 22:39; Rom 13:9. t. [2:9] Dt 1:17. u. [2:10] Gal 3:10. v. [2:11] Ex 20:13–14; Dt 5:17–18. w. [2:12] 1:25; Rom 8:2. x. [2:13] Mt 5:7; 6:14–15; 18:32–33. y. [2:14] Mt 25:31–46; Gal 5:6. z. [2:16] 1 Jn 3:17.

one. You do well. Even the demons believe that and tremble. [20]Do you want proof, you ignoramus, that faith without works is useless? [21]Was not Abraham our father justified by works when he offered his son Isaac upon the altar?[a] [22]You see that faith was active along with his works, and faith was completed by the works. [23]Thus the scripture was fulfilled that says, "Abraham believed God, and it was credited to him as righteousness," and he was called "the friend of God."[b] [24]See how a person is justified by works and not by faith alone. [25]And in the same way, was not Rahab the harlot also justified by works when she welcomed the messengers and sent them out by a different route?[c] [26]For just as a body without a spirit is dead, so also faith without works is dead.

CHAPTER 3

Power of the Tongue.[*] [1]Not many of you should become teachers, my brothers, for you realize that we will be judged more strictly, [2]for we all fall short in many respects. If anyone does not fall short in speech, he is a perfect man, able to bridle his whole body also.[d] [3]If we put bits into the mouths of horses to make them obey us, we also guide their whole bodies. [4]It is the same with ships: even though they are so large and driven by fierce winds, they are steered by a very small rudder wherever the pilot's inclination wishes. [5]In the same way the tongue is a small member and yet has great pretensions.

Consider how small a fire can set a huge forest ablaze. [6]The tongue is also a fire. It exists among our members as a world of malice, defiling the whole body and setting the entire course of our lives on fire, itself set on fire by Gehenna. [7]For every kind of beast and bird, of reptile and sea creature, can be tamed and has been tamed by the human species, [8]but no human being can tame the tongue. It is a restless evil, full of deadly poison.[e] [9]With it we bless the Lord and Father, and with it we curse human beings who are made in the likeness of God. [10]From the same mouth come blessing and cursing. This need not be so, my brothers. [11]Does a spring gush forth from the same opening both pure and brackish water? [12]Can a fig tree, my brothers, produce olives, or a grapevine figs? Neither can salt water yield fresh.[f] **True Wisdom.**[†] [13]Who among you is wise and understanding? Let him show his works by a good life in the humility that comes from wisdom.[g] [14]But if you have bitter jealousy and selfish ambition in your hearts, do not boast and be false to the truth. [15]Wisdom of this kind does not come down from above but is earthly, unspiritual, demonic. [16]For where jealousy and selfish ambition exist, there is disorder and every foul practice. [17]But the wisdom from above is first of all pure, then peaceable, gentle, compliant, full of mercy and good fruits, without inconstancy or insincerity.[h] [18]And the fruit of righteousness is sown in peace for those who cultivate peace.[i]

CHAPTER 4

Causes of Division.[‡] [1]Where do the wars and where do the conflicts among you come from? Is it not from your passions[§] that make war within your members?[j] [2]You covet but do not possess. You kill and envy but you cannot obtain; you fight and wage war. You do not possess because you do not ask. [3]You ask but do not receive, because you ask wrongly, to spend it on your passions. [4]Adulterers![¶] Do you not know that to be a lover of the world means enmity with God? Therefore, whoever wants to be a lover of the world makes himself an enemy of God.[k] [5]Or do you suppose that the scripture speaks without meaning when it says, "The spirit that he has made to dwell in us tends toward jealousy"?[**] [6]But he bestows a greater grace; therefore, it says:[l]

"God resists the proud,
   but gives grace to the humble."[††]

‡[4:1–12] The concern here is with the origin of conflicts in the Christian community. These are occasioned by love **of the world**, which **means enmity with God** (Jas 4:4). Further, the conflicts are bound up with failure to pray properly (cf. Mt 7:7–11; Jn 14:13; 15:7; 16:23), that is, not asking God at all or using God's kindness only for one's pleasure (Jas 4:2–3). In contrast, the proper dispositions are submission to God, repentance, humility, and resistance to evil (Jas 4:7–10).

§[4:1–3] **Passions:** the Greek word here (literally, "pleasures") does not indicate that pleasure is evil. Rather, as the text points out (Jas 4:2–3), it is the manner in which one deals with needs and desires that determines good or bad. The motivation for any action can be wrong, especially if one does not pray properly but seeks only selfish enjoyment (Jas 4:3).

¶[4:4] **Adulterers:** a common biblical image for the covenant between God and his people is the marriage bond. In this image, breaking the covenant with God is likened to the unfaithfulness of adultery.

**[4:5] The meaning of this saying is difficult because the author of James cites, probably from memory, a passage that is not in any extant manuscript of the Bible. Other translations of the text with a completely different meaning are possible: "The Spirit that he (God) made to dwell in us yearns (for us) jealously," or, "He (God) yearns jealously for the spirit that he has made to dwell in us." If this last translation is correct, the author perhaps had in mind an apocryphal religious text that echoes the idea that God is zealous for his creatures; cf. Ex 20:5; Dt 4:24; Zec 8:2.

††[4:6] The point of this whole argument is that God wants the happiness of all, but that selfishness and pride can make that impossible. We must work with him in humility (Jas 4:10).

*[3:1–12] The use and abuse of the important role of teaching in the church (Jas 3:1) are here related to the good and bad use of the tongue (Jas 3:9–12), the instrument through which teaching was chiefly conveyed (see Sir 5:11–6:1; 28:12–26).

†[3:13–18] This discussion of true wisdom is related to the previous reflection on the role of the teacher as one who is in control of his speech. The qualities of the wise man endowed from above are detailed (Jas 3:17–18; cf. Gal 5:22–23), in contrast to the qualities of earthbound wisdom (Jas 3:14–16; cf. 2 Cor 12:20).

a. [2:21] Gn 22:9–12; Heb 11:17.   b. [2:23] Gn 15:6; Rom 4:3; Gal 3:6 / 2 Chr 20:7; Is 41:8.   c. [2:25] Jos 2:1–21.   d. [3:2] 1:26; Prv 13:3; Sir 28:12–26.   e. [3:8] Ps 140:4.   f. [3:12] Mt 7:16–17.

g. [3:13] Eph 4:1–2.   h. [3:17] 1:17; Wis 7:22–23.   i. [3:18] Mt 5:9.   j. [4:1] Rom 7:23; 1 Pt 2:11.   k. [4:4] Mt 6:24; Lk 16:13; Rom 8:7; 1 Jn 2:15–16.   l. [4:6] Jb 22:29; Prv 3:34; Mt 23:12; 1 Pt 5:5.

[7] So submit yourselves to God. Resist the devil, and he will flee from you.[m] [8] Draw near to God, and he will draw near to you. Cleanse your hands, you sinners, and purify your hearts, you of two minds.[n] [9] Begin to lament, to mourn, to weep. Let your laughter be turned into mourning and your joy into dejection. [10] Humble yourselves before the Lord and he will exalt you.[o] [11] Do not speak evil of one another, brothers. Whoever speaks evil of a brother or judges his brother speaks evil of the law and judges the law.* If you judge the law, you are not a doer of the law but a judge. [12] There is one lawgiver and judge who is able to save or to destroy. Who then are you to judge your neighbor?[p]

Warning Against Presumption.[†] [13] Come now, you who say, "Today or tomorrow we shall go into such and such a town, spend a year there doing business, and make a profit"— [14] you have no idea what your life will be like tomorrow.[‡] You are a puff of smoke that appears briefly and then disappears.[q] [15] Instead you should say, "If the Lord wills it,[§] we shall live to do this or that." [16] But now you are boasting in your arrogance. All such boasting is evil. [17] So for one who knows the right thing to do and does not do it, it is a sin.[¶]

CHAPTER 5

Warning to the Rich.[**] [1] Come now, you rich, weep and wail over your impending miseries.[s] [2] Your wealth has rotted away, your clothes have become moth-eaten,[t] [3] your gold and silver have corroded, and that corrosion will be a testimony against you; it will devour your flesh like a fire. You have stored up treasure for the last days.[u] [4] Behold, the wages you withheld from the workers who harvested your fields are crying aloud, and the cries of the harvesters have reached the ears of the Lord of hosts.[v] [5] You have lived on earth in luxury and pleasure; you have fattened your hearts for the day of slaughter.[w] [6] You have condemned; you have murdered the righteous one;[x] he offers you no resistance.[††]

Patience and Oaths. [7][‡‡] Be patient, therefore, brothers, until the coming of the Lord. See how the farmer waits for the precious fruit of the earth, being patient with it until it receives the early and the late rains.[§§] [8] You too must be patient. Make your hearts firm, because the coming of the Lord is at hand.[y] [9] Do not complain, brothers, about one another, that you may not be judged. Behold, the Judge is standing before the gates. [10] Take as an example of hardship and patience, brothers, the prophets who spoke in the name of the Lord. [11] Indeed we call blessed those who have persevered. You have heard of the perseverance of Job, and you have seen the purpose of the Lord, because "the Lord is compassionate and merciful."[z]

[12a] But above all, my brothers, do not swear, either by heaven or by earth or with any other oath, but let your "Yes" mean "Yes" and your "No" mean "No," that you may not incur condemnation.[¶¶]

IV. THE POWER OF PRAYER

Anointing of the Sick. [13] Is anyone among you suffering? He should pray. Is anyone in good spirits? He should sing praise. [14] Is anyone among you sick?[***] He should summon the presbyters of the church, and they should pray over him and anoint [him] with oil in the name of the Lord,[b] [15] and the prayer of faith will save the sick person, and the Lord will raise him up. If he has committed any sins, he will be forgiven.[†††]

---

*[4:11] Slander of a fellow Christian does not break just one commandment but makes mockery of the authority of law in general and therefore of God.

†[4:13–17] The uncertainty of life (Jas 4:14), its complete dependence on God, and the necessity of submitting to God's will (Jas 4:15) all help one know and do what is right (Jas 4:17). To disregard this is to live in pride and arrogance (Jas 4:16); failure to do what is right is a sin (Jas 4:17).

‡[4:14] Some important Greek manuscripts here have, "You who have no idea what tomorrow will bring. Why, what is your life?"

§[4:15] **If the Lord wills it:** often in piety referred to as the "*conditio Jacobaea*," the condition James says we should employ to qualify all our plans.

¶[4:17] **It is a sin:** those who live arrogantly, forgetting the contingency of life and our dependence on God (Jas 4:13–16), are guilty of sin.

**[5:1–6] Continuing with the theme of the transitory character of life on earth, the author points out the impending ruin of the godless. He denounces the unjust rich, whose victims cry to heaven for judgment on their exploiters (Jas 5:4–6). The decay and corrosion of the costly garments and metals, which symbolize wealth, prove them worthless and portend the destruction of their possessors (Jas 5:2–3).

††[5:6] The author does not have in mind any specific crime in his readers' communities but rather echoes the Old Testament theme of the harsh oppression of the righteous poor (see Prv 1:11; Wis 2:10, 12, 20).

‡‡[5:7–11] Those oppressed by the unjust rich are reminded of the need for patience, both in bearing the sufferings of human life (Jas 5:9) and in their expectation of the coming of the Lord. It is then that they will receive their reward (Jas 5:7–8, 10–11; cf. Heb 10:25; 1 Jn 2:18).

§§[5:7] **The early and the late rains:** an expression related to the agricultural season in ancient Palestine (see Dt 11:14; Jer 5:24; Jl 2:23).

¶¶[5:12] This is the threat of condemnation for the abuse of swearing oaths (cf. Mt 5:33–37). **By heaven or by earth:** these words were substitutes for the original form of an oath, to circumvent its binding force and to avoid pronouncing the holy name of God (see Ex 22:10).

***[5:14] In case of sickness a Christian should ask for the presbyters of the church, i.e., those who have authority in the church (cf. Acts 15:2, 22–23; 1 Tm 5:17; Ti 1:5). They are to pray over the person and anoint with oil; oil was used for medicinal purposes in the ancient world (see Is 1:6; Lk 10:34). In Mk 6:13, the Twelve anoint the sick with oil on their missionary journey. **In the name of the Lord:** by the power of Jesus Christ.

†††[5:15] The results of the prayer and anointing are physical health and forgiveness of sins. The Roman Catholic

---

m. [4:7] 1 Pt 5:8–9.   n. [4:8] Zec 1:3; Mal 3:7.   o. [4:10] Jb 5:11; Mt 23:12; Lk 14:11; 18:14; 1 Pt 5:6.   p. [4:12] Mt 7:1; Rom 2:1; 14:4.   q. [4:14] Prv 27:1 / Ps 39:6–7.   r. [4:17] Lk 12:47.   s. [5:1] Lk 6:24.   t. [5:2] Mt 6:19.   u. [5:3] Ps 21:10; Prv 11:4; Jdt 16:17.   v. [5:4] Lv 19:13; Dt 24:14–15; Mal 3:5.   w. [5:5] Jer 12:3; Lk 16:19–25.   x. [5:6] Wis 2:10–20.   y. [5:8] Lk 21:19; Heb 10:36 / Heb 10:25; 1 Pt 4:7.   z. [5:11] Ex 34:6; Ps 103:8.   a. [5:12] Mt 5:34–37.   b. [5:14] Mk 6:13.

Confession and Intercession. [16]Therefore, confess your sins to one another and pray for one another, that you may be healed. The fervent prayer of a righteous person is very powerful. [17]Elijah was a human being like us; yet he prayed earnestly that it might not rain, and for three years and six months it did not rain upon the land.[c] [18]Then he prayed again, and the sky gave rain and the earth produced its fruit.[d]

Conversion of Sinners. [19e]My brothers, if anyone among you should stray from the truth and someone bring him back, [20]he should know that whoever brings back a sinner from the error of his way will save his soul from death and will cover a multitude of sins.[*]

Church (Council of Trent, Session 14) declared that this anointing of the sick is a sacrament "instituted by Christ and promulgated by blessed James the apostle."

---

*[5:20] When a Christian is instrumental in the conversion of a sinner, the result is forgiveness of sins and a reinstatement of the sinner to the life of grace.

---

c. [5:17] 1 Kgs 17:1; Lk 4:25.   d. [5:18] 1 Kgs 18:45.

e. [5:19] Mt 18:15; Gal 6:1.   f. [5:20] Prv 10:12; 1 Pt 4:8.

THE FIRST LETTER OF
PETER

ᢇᢗᢦᢂ

This letter begins with an address by Peter to Christian communities located in five provinces of Asia Minor (1 Pt 1:1), including areas evangelized by Paul (Acts 16:6–7; 18:23). Christians there are encouraged to remain faithful to their standards of belief and conduct in spite of threats of persecution. Numerous allusions in the letter suggest that the churches addressed were largely of Gentile composition (1 Pt 1:14, 18; 2:9–10; 4:3–4), though considerable use is made of the Old Testament (1 Pt 1:24; 2:6–7, 9–10, 22; 3:10–12).

The contents following the address both inspire and admonish these "chosen sojourners" (1 Pt 1:1) who, in seeking to live as God's people, feel an alienation from their previous religious roots and the society around them. Appeal is made to Christ's resurrection and the future hope it provides (1 Pt 1:3–5) and to the experience of baptism as new birth (1 Pt 1:3, 23–25; 3:21). The suffering and death of Christ serve as both source of salvation and example (1 Pt 1:19; 2:21–25; 3:18). What Christians are in Christ, as a people who have received mercy and are to proclaim and live according to God's call (1 Pt 2:9–10), is repeatedly spelled out for all sorts of situations in society (1 Pt 2:11–17), work (even as slaves, 1 Pt 2:18–20), the home (1 Pt 3:1–7), and general conduct (1 Pt 3:8–12; 4:1–11). But over all hangs the possibility of suffering as a Christian (1 Pt 3:13–17). In 1 Pt 4:12–19 persecution is described as already occurring, so that some have supposed the letter was addressed both to places where such a "trial by fire" was already present and to places where it might break out.

The letter constantly mingles moral exhortation (*paraklēsis*) with its catechetical summaries of mercies in Christ. Encouragement to fidelity in spite of suffering is based upon a vision of the meaning of Christian existence. The emphasis on baptism and allusions to various features of the baptismal liturgy suggest that the author has incorporated into his exposition numerous homiletic, credal, hymnic, and sacramental elements of the baptismal rite that had become traditional at an early date.

From Irenaeus in the late second century until modern times, Christian tradition regarded Peter the apostle as author of this document. Since he was martyred at Rome during the persecution of Nero between A.D. 64 and 67, it was supposed that the letter was written from Rome shortly before his death. This is supported by its reference to "Babylon" (1 Pt 5:13), a code name for Rome in the early church.

Some modern scholars, however, on the basis of a number of features that they consider incompatible with Petrine authenticity, regard the letter as the work of a later Christian writer. Such features include the cultivated Greek in which it is written, difficult to attribute to a Galilean fisherman, together with its use of the Greek Septuagint translation when citing the Old Testament; the similarity in both thought and expression to the Pauline literature; and the allusions to widespread persecution of Christians, which did not occur until at least the reign of Domitian (A.D. 81–96). In this view the letter would date from the end of the first century or even the beginning of the second, when there is evidence for persecution of Christians in Asia Minor (the letter of Pliny the Younger to Trajan, A.D. 111–12).

Other scholars believe, however, that these objections can be met by appeal to use of a secretary, Silvanus, mentioned in 1 Pt 5:12. Such secretaries often gave literary expression to the author's thoughts in their own style and language. The persecutions may refer to local harassment rather than to systematic repression by the state. Hence there is nothing in the document incompatible with Petrine authorship in the 60s.

Still other scholars take a middle position. The many literary contacts with the Pauline literature, James, and 1 John suggest a common fund of traditional formulations rather than direct dependence upon Paul. Such liturgical and catechetical traditions must have been very ancient and in some cases of Palestinian origin.

Yet it is unlikely that Peter addressed a letter to the Gentile churches of Asia Minor while Paul was still alive. This suggests a period after the death of the two apostles, perhaps A.D. 70–90. The author would be a disciple of Peter in Rome, representing a Petrine group that served as a bridge between the Palestinian origins of Christianity and its flowering in the Gentile world. The problem addressed would not be official persecution but the difficulty of living the Christian life in a hostile, secular environment that espoused different values and subjected the Christian minority to ridicule and oppression.

The principal divisions of the First Letter of Peter are the following:

    I. Address (1:1–2)
    II. The Gift and Call of God in Baptism (1:3–2:10)
    III. The Christian in a Hostile World (2:11–4:11)
    IV. Advice to the Persecuted (4:12–5:11)
    V. Conclusion (5:12–14)

I. ADDRESS

CHAPTER 1

Greeting. [*] ¹Peter, an apostle of Jesus Christ, to the chosen sojourners of the dispersion[†] in Pontus, Galatia, Cappadocia, Asia, and Bithynia,[a] ²in the foreknowledge of God the Father, through sanctification by the Spirit, for obedience and sprinkling with the blood of Jesus Christ: may grace and peace be yours in abundance.[b]

II. THE GIFT AND CALL OF GOD IN BAPTISM

Blessing. ³[‡]Blessed be the God and Father of our Lord Jesus Christ, who in his great mercy gave us a new birth to a living hope through the resurrection of Jesus Christ from the dead,[c] ⁴to an inheritance that is imperishable, undefiled, and unfading, kept in heaven for you[d] ⁵who by the power of God are safeguarded through faith, to a salvation that is ready to be revealed in the final time. ⁶[§]In this you rejoice, although now

for a little while you may have to suffer through various trials,[e] ⁷so that the genuineness of your faith, more precious than gold that is perishable even though tested by fire, may prove to be for praise, glory, and honor at the revelation of Jesus Christ.[f] ⁸Although you have not seen him you love him; even though you do not see him now yet believe in him, you rejoice with an indescribable and glorious joy,[g] ⁹as you attain the goal of [your] faith, the salvation of your souls.

¹⁰[¶]Concerning this salvation, prophets who prophesied about the grace that was to be yours searched and investigated it, ¹¹investigating the time and circumstances that the Spirit of Christ within them indicated when it testified in advance to the sufferings destined for Christ and the glories to follow them.[h] ¹²It was revealed to them that they were serving not themselves but you with regard to the things that have now been announced to you by those who preached the good news to you [through] the holy Spirit sent from heaven, things into which angels longed to look.

Obedience. ¹³[**]Therefore, gird up the loins of your mind,[††] live soberly, and set your hopes

---

*[1:1–2] The introductory formula names **Peter** as the writer (but see Introduction). In his comments to the presbyters (1 Pt 5:1), the author calls himself a "fellow presbyter." He addresses himself to the Gentile converts of Asia Minor. Their privileged status as a **chosen** and sanctified people makes them worthy of God's **grace** and **peace**. In contrast is their actual existence as aliens and **sojourners**, scattered among pagans, far from their true country.

†[1:1] **Dispersion**: literally, diaspora; see Jas 1:1 and Introduction to that letter. **Pontus . . . Bithynia**: five provinces in Asia Minor, listed in clockwise order from the north, perhaps in the sequence in which a messenger might deliver the letter.

‡[1:3–5] A prayer of praise and thanksgiving to God who bestows the gift of new life and hope in baptism (**new birth**, 1 Pt 1:3) **through the resurrection of Jesus Christ from the dead**. The new birth is a sign of an **imperishable inheritance** (1 Pt 1:4), of **salvation** that is still in the future (**to be revealed in the final time**, 1 Pt 1:5).

§[1:6–9] As the glory of Christ's resurrection was preceded by his sufferings and death, the new life of faith that it bestows

is to be subjected to many **trials** (1 Pt 1:6) while achieving its goal: the glory of the fullness of **salvation** (1 Pt 1:9) at the coming of Christ (1 Pt 1:7).

¶[1:10–12] The **Spirit of Christ** (1 Pt 1:11) is here shown to have been present in the prophets, moving them to search, investigate, and prophesy about the **grace** of **salvation** that was to come (1 Pt 1:10), and in the apostles impelling them to preach the fulfillment of salvation in the message of Christ's sufferings and glory (1 Pt 1:12).

**[1:13–25] These verses are concerned with the call of God's people to holiness and to mutual love by reason of their redemption through the blood of Christ (1 Pt 1:18–21).

††[1:13] **Gird up the loins of your mind**: a figure reminiscent of the rite of Passover when the Israelites were in flight from their oppressors (Ex 12:11), and also suggesting the vigilance of the Christian people in expectation of the parousia of Christ (Lk 12:35).

---

a. [1:1] Jas 1:1.   b. [1:2] Rom 8:29.   c. [1:3] Ti 3:5.   d. [1:4] Mt 6:19–20.

e. [1:6] Jas 1:2–3.   f. [1:7] 1 Cor 3:13.   g. [1:8] 2 Cor 5:6–7.   h. [1:11] Is 52:13–53:12; Dn 9:24.

completely on the grace to be brought to you at the revelation of Jesus Christ. ¹⁴Like obedient children, do not act in compliance with the desires of your former ignorance* ¹⁵but, as he who called you is holy, be holy yourselves in every aspect of your conduct,ⁱ ¹⁶for it is written, "Be holy because I [am] holy."ʲ

Reverence. ¹⁷Now if you invoke as Father him who judges impartially according to each one's works, conduct yourselves with reverence during the time of your sojourning,ᵏ ¹⁸realizing that you were ransomed from your futile conduct, handed on by your ancestors, not with perishable things like silver or goldˡ ¹⁹but with the precious blood of Christᵐ as of a spotless unblemished lamb.† ²⁰He was known before the foundation of the world but revealed in the final time for you, ²¹who through him believe in God who raised him from the dead and gave him glory, so that your faith and hope are in God.

Mutual Love.‡ ²²Since you have purified yourselves by obedience to the truth for sincere mutual love, love one another intensely from a [pure] heart.ⁿ ²³You have been born anew,ᵒ not from perishable but from imperishable seed, through the living and abiding word of God,§ ²⁴for:

"All flesh is like grass,
    and all its glory like the flower of
        the field;
the grass withers,
    and the flower wilts;ᵖ
²⁵ but the word of the Lord remains forever."

This is the word that has been proclaimed to you.

CHAPTER 2

God's House and People. ¶¹Rid yourselves of all malice and all deceit, insincerity, envy, and all slander;�q ²like newborn infants, long for pure spiritual milk so that through it you may grow into salvation, ³for you have tasted that the Lord

is good.** ⁴Come to him, a living stone,†† rejected by human beings but chosen and precious in the sight of God,ˢ ⁵and, like living stones, let yourselves be built‡‡ into a spiritual house to be a holy priesthood to offer spiritual sacrifices acceptable to God through Jesus Christ.ᵗ ⁶For it says in scripture:

"Behold, I am laying a stone in Zion,
    a cornerstone, chosen and precious,
and whoever believes in it shall not be put
        to shame."ᵘ

⁷Therefore, its value is for you who have faith, but for those without faith:

"The stone which the builders rejected
    has become the cornerstone,"ᵛ

⁸and

"A stone that will make people stumble,
    and a rock that will make them fall."

They stumble by disobeying the word, as is their destiny.ʷ
⁹§§But you are "a chosen race, a royal priesthood, a holy nation, a people of his own, so that you may announce the praises" of him who called you out of darkness into his wonderful light.ˣ

¹⁰ Once you were "no people"
    but now you are God's people;
you "had not received mercy"
    but now you have received mercy.ʸ

III. THE CHRISTIAN IN
A HOSTILE WORLD

Christian Examples. ¹¹¶¶Beloved, I urge you as

---

*[1:14–16] The **ignorance** here referred to (1 Pt 1:14) was their former lack of knowledge of God, leading inevitably to godless conduct. Holiness (1 Pt 1:15–16), on the contrary, is the result of their call to the knowledge and love of God.

†[1:19] Christians have received the redemption prophesied by Isaiah (Is 52:3), through the blood (Jewish symbol of life) of the spotless lamb (Is 53:7, 10; Jn 1:29; Rom 3:24–25; cf. 1 Cor 6:20).

‡[1:22–25] The new birth of Christians (1 Pt 1:23) derives from Christ, the **imperishable seed** or sowing that produces a new and lasting existence in those who accept the gospel (1 Pt 1:24–25), with the consequent duty of loving **one another** (1 Pt 1:22).

§[1:23] **The living and abiding word of God**: or, "the word of the living and abiding God."

¶[2:1–3] Growth toward salvation is seen here as two steps: first, stripping away all that is contrary to the new life in Christ; second, the nourishment (**pure spiritual milk**) that the newly baptized have received.

[2:3] **Tasted that the Lord is good: cf. Ps 34:9.

††[2:4–8] Christ is the cornerstone (cf. Is 28:16) that is the foundation of the spiritual edifice of the Christian community (1 Pt 2:5). To unbelievers, Christ is an obstacle and a stumbling block on which they are destined to fall (1 Pt 2:8); cf. Rom 11:11.

‡‡[2:5] **Let yourselves be built**: the form of the Greek word could also be indicative passive, "you are being built" (cf. 1 Pt 2:9).

§§[2:9–10] The prerogatives of ancient Israel mentioned here are now more fully and fittingly applied to the Christian people: "a chosen race" (cf. Is 43:20–21) indicates their divine election (Eph 1:4–6); "a royal priesthood" (cf. Ex 19:6) to serve and worship God in Christ, thus continuing the priestly functions of his life, passion, and resurrection; "a holy nation" (Ex 19:6) reserved for God, a people he claims for his own (cf. Mal 3:17) in virtue of their baptism into his death and resurrection. This transcends all natural and national divisions and unites the people into one community to glorify the one who led them from the darkness of paganism to the light of faith in Christ. From being "no people" deprived of all mercy, they have become the very people of God, the chosen recipients of his mercy (cf. Hos 1:9; 2:25).

¶¶[2:11–3:12] After explaining the doctrinal basis for the Christian community, the author makes practical applications in terms of the virtues that should prevail in all the social relationships of the members of the community: good example to Gentile neighbors (1 Pt 2:11–12); respect for human authority (1 Pt 2:13–17); obedience, patience, and endurance of hardship in domestic relations (1 Pt 2:18–25); Christian

---

i. [1:15] Mt 5:48; 1 Jn 3:3.   j. [1:16] Lv 11:44; 19:2.   k. [1:17] 2:11.
l. [1:18] Is 52:3; 1 Cor 6:20.   m. [1:19] Ex 12:5; Jn 1:29; Heb 9:14.
n. [1:22] Rom 12:10.   o. [1:23] 1 Jn 3:9.   p. [1:24] Is 40:6–8.   q. [2:1–2] Jas 1:21.   r. [2:3] Ps 34:9.

s. [2:4] Ps 118:22; Mt 21:42; Acts 4:11.   t. [2:5] Eph 2:21-22.
u. [2:6] Is 28:16.   v. [2:7] Ps 118:22; Mt 21:42; Lk 20:17; Acts 4:11.
w. [2:8] Is 8:14; Rom 9:33.   x. [2:9] Ex 19:6; Is 61:6; Rev 1:6; 20:6.
y. [2:10] Hos 1:9; 2:25 / Hos 1:6.

aliens and sojourners* to keep away from worldly desires that wage war against the soul.z [12]Maintain good conduct among the Gentiles, so that if they speak of you as evildoers, they may observe your good works and glorify God on the day of visitation.

Christian Citizens.† [13]Be subject to every human institution for the Lord's sake, whether it be to the king as supreme[a] [14]or to governors as sent by him for the punishment of evildoers and the approval of those who do good. [15]For it is the will of God that by doing good you may silence the ignorance of foolish people. [16]Be free, yet without using freedom as a pretext for evil, but as slaves of God.b [17]Give honor to all, love the community, fear God, honor the king.c

Christian Slaves. [18]‡Slaves, be subject to your masters with all reverence, not only to those who are good and equitable but also to those who are perverse.d [19]For whenever anyone bears the pain of unjust suffering because of consciousness of God, that is a grace. [20]But what credit is there if you are patient when beaten for doing wrong? But if you are patient when you suffer for doing what is good, this is a grace before God. [21]For to this you have been called, because Christ also suffered§ for you, leaving you an example that you should follow in his footsteps.e

[22] "He committed no sin,f
　　and no deceit was found in his
　　　　mouth."§

[23]When he was insulted, he returned no insult; when he suffered, he did not threaten; instead,

he handed himself over to the one who judges justly.g [24]He himself bore our sins in his body upon the cross, so that, free from sin, we might live for righteousness. By his wounds you have been healed.h [25]For you had gone astray like sheep,i but you have now returned to the shepherd and guardian of your souls.**

CHAPTER 3

Christian Spouses. [1]††Likewise, you wives should be subordinate to your husbands so that, even if some disobey the word, they may be won over without a word by their wives' conduct [2]when they observe your reverent and chaste behavior.j [3]Your adornment should not be an external one: braiding the hair, wearing gold jewelry, or dressing in fine clothes,k [4]but rather the hidden character of the heart, expressed in the imperishable beauty of a gentle and calm disposition, which is precious in the sight of God. [5]For this is also how the holy women who hoped in God once used to adorn themselves and were subordinate to their husbands; [6]thus Sarah obeyed Abraham, calling him "lord." You are her children when you do what is good and fear no intimidation.

[7]Likewise, you husbands should live with your wives in understanding, showing honor to the weaker female sex, since we are joint heirs of the gift of life, so that your prayers may not be hindered.‡‡

Christian Conduct.§§ [8]Finally, all of you, be of one mind, sympathetic, loving toward one another, compassionate, humble. [9]Do not return evil for evil, or insult for insult; but, on the contrary, a blessing, because to this you were called, that you might inherit a blessing.m [10]For:

---

behavior of husbands and wives (1 Pt 3:1–7); mutual charity (1 Pt 3:8–12).

*[2:11] **Aliens and sojourners:** no longer signifying absence from one's native land (Gn 23:4), this image denotes rather their estrangement from the world during their earthly pilgrimage (see also 1 Pt 1:1, 17).

†[2:13–17] True Christian freedom is the result of being servants of God (1 Pt 2:16; see note on 1 Pt 2:18–23). It includes reverence for God, esteem for every individual, and committed love for fellow Christians (1 Pt 2:17). Although persecution may threaten, subjection to human government is urged (1 Pt 2:13, 17) and concern for the impact of Christians' conduct on those who are not Christians (1 Pt 2:12, 15).

‡[2:18–21] Most of the labor in the commercial cities of first-century Asia Minor was performed by a working class of slaves. The sense of freedom contained in the gospel undoubtedly caused great tension among Christian slaves: witness the special advice given concerning them here and in 1 Cor 7:21–24; Eph 6:5–8; Col 3:22–25; Phlm. The point made here does not have so much to do with the institution of slavery, which the author does not challenge, but with the nonviolent reaction (1 Pt 2:20) of slaves to unjust treatment. Their patient suffering is compared to that of Jesus (1 Pt 2:21), which won righteousness for all humanity.

§[2:21] **Suffered:** some ancient manuscripts and versions read "died" (cf. 1 Pt 3:18).

¶[2:22–25] After the quotation of Is 53:9b, the passage describes Jesus' passion with phrases concerning the Suffering Servant from Is 53:4–12, perhaps as employed in an early Christian confession of faith; cf. 1 Pt 1:18–21 and 1 Pt 3:18–22.

[2:25] **The shepherd and guardian of your souls: the familiar shepherd and flock figures express the care, vigilance, and love of God for his people in the Old Testament (Ps 23; Is 40:11; Jer 23:4–5; Ez 34:11–16) and of Jesus for all humanity in the New Testament (Mt 18:10–14; Lk 15:4–7; Jn 10:1–16; Heb 13:20).

††[3:1–6] The typical marital virtues of women of the ancient world, obedience, reverence, and chastity (1 Pt 3:1–2), are outlined here by the author, who gives them an entirely new motivation: Christian wives are to be virtuous so that they may be instrumental in the conversion of their husbands. In imitation of **holy women** in the past (1 Pt 3:5) they are to cultivate the interior life (1 Pt 3:4) instead of excessive concern with their appearance (1 Pt 3:3).

‡‡[3:7] Husbands who do not respect their wives will have as little success in prayer as those who, according to Paul, have no love: their prayers will be "a resounding gong or a clashing cymbal" (1 Cor 13:1). Consideration for others is shown as a prerequisite for effective prayer also in Mt 5:23–24; 1 Cor 11:20–22; Jas 4:3. After all, whatever the social position of women in the world and in the family, they are equal recipients of the gift of God's salvation. Paul is very clear on this point, too (see 1 Cor 11:11–12; Gal 3:28).

§§[3:8–12] For the proper ordering of Christian life in its various aspects as described in 1 Pt 2:11–3:9, there is promised the blessing expressed in Ps 34:13–17. In the Old Testament this refers to longevity and prosperity; here, it also refers to eternal life.

---

z. [2:11] Gal 5:24.　a. [2:13] Rom 13:1–7.　b. [2:16] Gal 5:13.　c. [2:17] Prv 24:21; Mt 22:21.　d. [2:18] Eph 6:5.　e. [2:21] Mt 16:24.　f. [2:22] Is 53:9.

g. [2:23] Mt 5:39.　h. [2:24] Is 53:4, 12 / Is 53:5.　i. [2:25] Is 53:6.　j. [3:2] 1 Cor 7:12–16; Eph 5:22–24; Col 3:18; 1 Tm 2:9–15.　k. [3:3] 1 Tm 2:9–10.　l. [3:7] Eph 5:25–33; Col 3:19.　m. [3:9] Mt 5:44; Lk 6:28; Rom 12:14.

"Whoever would love life"
and see good days
must keep the tongue from evil
and the lips from speaking deceit,
[11] must turn from evil and do good,
seek peace and follow after it.
[12] For the eyes of the Lord are on the righteous
and his ears turned to their prayer,
but the face of the Lord is against evildoers."

Christian Suffering. [13]Now who is going to harm you if you are enthusiastic for what is good? [14]But even if you should suffer because of righteousness, blessed are you. Do not be afraid or terrified with fear of them, [15]but sanctify Christ as Lord in your hearts. Always be ready to give an explanation to anyone who asks you for a reason for your hope,[o] [16]but do it with gentleness and reverence, keeping your conscience clear, so that, when you are maligned, those who defame your good conduct in Christ may themselves be put to shame. [17]For it is better to suffer for doing good, if that be the will of God, than for doing evil.

[18]For Christ also suffered[†] for sins once, the righteous for the sake of the unrighteous, that he might lead you to God. Put to death in the flesh, he was brought to life in the spirit.[p] [19]In it he also went to preach to the spirits in prison,[‡] [20]who had once been disobedient while God patiently waited in the days of Noah during the building of the ark, in which a few persons, eight in all, were saved through water.[q] [21]This prefigured baptism, which saves you now. It is not a removal of dirt from the body but an appeal to God[§] for a clear conscience, through the resurrection of Jesus Christ,[r] [22]who has gone into heaven and is at the right hand of God, with angels, authorities, and powers subject to him.[s]

CHAPTER 4

Christian Restraint.[⁵] [1]Therefore, since Christ suffered in the flesh, arm yourselves also with the same attitude (for whoever suffers in the flesh has broken with sin), [2]so as not to spend what remains of one's life in the flesh on human desires, but on the will of God. [3]For the time that has passed is sufficient for doing what the Gentiles like to do: living in debauchery, evil desires, drunkenness, orgies, carousing, and wanton idolatry.[t] [4]They are surprised that you do not plunge into the same swamp of profligacy, and they vilify you; [5]but they will give an account to him who stands ready to judge the living and the dead.[u] [6]For this is why the gospel was preached even to the dead** that, though condemned in the flesh in human estimation, they might live in the spirit in the estimation of God.

Christian Charity.[††] [7]The end of all things is at hand. Therefore, be serious and sober for prayers. [8]Above all, let your love for one another be intense, because love covers a multitude of sins.[‡‡] [9]Be hospitable to one another without complaining.[w] [10]As each one has received a gift, use it to serve one another as good stewards of God's varied grace.[x] [11]Whoever preaches, let it be with the words of God; whoever serves, let it be with the strength that God supplies, so that in all things God may be glorified through Jesus Christ,[y] to whom belong glory and dominion forever and ever. Amen.[§§]

IV. ADVICE TO THE PERSECUTED

Trial of Persecution.[¶¶] [12]Beloved, do not be surprised that a trial by fire is occurring among you, as if something strange were happening to

*[3:13–22] This exposition, centering on 1 Pt 3:17, runs as follows: by his suffering and death Christ the righteous one saved the unrighteous (1 Pt 3:18); by his resurrection he received new life in the spirit, which he communicates to believers through the baptismal bath that cleanses their consciences from sin. As Noah's family was saved **through water**, so Christians are saved through the waters of baptism (1 Pt 3:19–22). Hence they need not share the fear of sinners; they should rather rejoice in suffering because of their hope in Christ. Thus their innocence disappoints their accusers (1 Pt 3:13–16; cf. Mt 10:28; Rom 8:35–39).

†[3:18] **Suffered**: very many ancient manuscripts and versions read "died." **Put to death in the flesh**: affirms that Jesus truly died as a human being. **Brought to life in the spirit**: that is, in the new and transformed existence freed from the limitations and weaknesses of natural human life (cf. 1 Cor 15:45).

‡[3:19] **The spirits in prison**: it is not clear just who these spirits are. They may be the spirits of the sinners who died in the flood, or angelic powers, hostile to God, who have been overcome by Christ (cf. 1 Pt 3:22; Gn 6:4; Enoch 6–36, especially 21:6; 2 Enoch 7:1–5).

§[3:21] **Appeal to God**: this could also be translated "pledge," that is, a promise on the part of Christians to live with a good conscience before God, or a pledge from God of forgiveness and therefore a good conscience for us.

¶[4:1–6] Willingness to suffer with Christ equips the Christian with the power to conquer sin (1 Pt 4:1). Christ is here portrayed as the judge to whom those guilty of pagan vices must render an account (1 Pt 4:5; cf. Jn 5:22–27; Acts 10:42; 2 Tm 4:1).

[4:6] **The dead: these may be the sinners of the flood generation who are possibly referred to in 1 Pt 3:19. But many scholars think that there is no connection between these two verses, and that **the dead** here are Christians who have died since hearing the preaching of the gospel.

††[4:7–11] The inner life of the eschatological community is outlined as **the end** (the parousia of Christ) and the judgment draws near in terms of seriousness, sobriety, prayer, and love expressed through hospitality and the use of one's gifts for the glory of God and of Christ.

‡‡[4:8] **Love covers a multitude of sins**: a maxim based on Prv 10:12; see also Ps 32:1; Jas 5:20.

§§[4:11] Some scholars feel that this doxology concludes the part of the homily addressed specifically to the newly baptized, begun in 1 Pt 1:3; others that it concludes a baptismal liturgy. Such doxologies do occur within a New Testament letter, e.g., Rom 9:5. Some propose that 1 Pt 4:11 was an alternate ending, with 1 Pt 4:12–5:14 being read in places where persecution was more pressing. But such doxologies usually do not occur at the end of letters (the only examples are 2 Pt 3:18, Jude 25, and Rom 16:27, the last probably a liturgical insertion).

¶¶[4:12–19] The suffering to which the author has already frequently referred is presented in more severe terms. This has led some scholars to see these verses as referring to an actual persecution. Others see the heightening of the language

n. [3:10–12] Ps 34:13–17.   o. [3:15] Is 8:12.   p. [3:18] 1 Cor 15:45.
q. [3:20] Gn 7:7, 17; 2 Pt 2:5.   r. [3:21] Eph 5:26; Heb 10:22.
s. [3:22] Eph 1:20–21.

t. [4:3] Eph 2:2–3; 4:17–19; Col 3:7; Ti 3:3.   u. [4:5] Acts 10:42; 2 Tm 4:1.   v. [4:8] Prv 10:12; Jas 5:20.   w. [4:9] Heb 13:2.   x. [4:10] Rom 12:6–8; 1 Cor 12:4–11.   y. [4:11] 1 Cor 10:31.

you.[z] [13]But rejoice to the extent that you share in the sufferings of Christ, so that when his glory is revealed you may also rejoice exultantly.[a] [14]If you are insulted for the name of Christ, blessed are you, for the Spirit of glory and of God rests upon you.[b] [15]But let no one among you be made to suffer as a murderer, a thief, an evildoer, or as an intriguer. [16]But whoever is made to suffer as a Christian should not be ashamed but glorify God because of the name. [17]For it is time for the judgment to begin with the household of God; if it begins with us, how will it end for those who fail to obey the gospel of God?[c]

[18] "And if the righteous one is barely saved,
            where will the godless and the
                   sinner appear?"[d]

[19]As a result, those who suffer in accord with God's will hand their souls over to a faithful creator as they do good.

CHAPTER 5
Advice to Presbyters.[*] [1]So I exhort the presbyters[†] among you, as a fellow presbyter and witness to the sufferings of Christ and one who has a share in the glory to be revealed. [2]Tend the flock of God in your midst, [overseeing] not by constraint but willingly, as God would have it, not for shameful profit but eagerly.[e] [3]Do not lord it over those assigned to you, but be examples to the flock. [4]And when the chief Shepherd is revealed, you will receive the unfading crown of glory.[‡]
Advice to the Community.[§] [5]Likewise, you younger members,[¶] be subject to the presbyters.

And all of you, clothe yourselves with humility in your dealings with one another, for:

"God opposes the proud
    but bestows favor on the humble."[g]

[6]So humble yourselves under the mighty hand of God, that he may exalt you in due time.[h] [7]Cast all your worries upon him because he cares for you.[i] [8]Be sober and vigilant. Your opponent the devil is prowling around like a roaring lion looking for [someone] to devour.[j] [9]Resist him, steadfast in faith, knowing that your fellow believers throughout the world undergo the same sufferings. [10]The God of all grace who called you to his eternal glory through Christ [Jesus] will himself restore, confirm, strengthen, and establish you after you have suffered a little.[k] [11]To him be dominion forever. Amen.

V. CONCLUSION
[12]I write you this briefly through Silvanus,[**] whom I consider a faithful brother, exhorting you and testifying that this is the true grace of God. Remain firm in it. [13]The chosen one[††] at Babylon sends you greeting, as does Mark, my son. [14]Greet one another with a loving kiss. Peace to all of you who are in Christ.[l]

---

as only a rhetorical device used at the end of the letter to emphasize the suffering motif.
*[5:1–4] In imitation of Christ, the chief shepherd, those entrusted with a pastoral office are to tend the flock by their care and example.
†[5:1] **Presbyters:** the officially appointed leaders and teachers of the Christian community (cf. 1 Tm 5:17–18; Ti 1:5–8; Jas 5:14).
‡[5:4] See note on 1 Pt 2:25.
§[5:5–11] The community is to be subject to the presbyters and to show humility toward one another and trust in God's love and care (1 Pt 5:5–7). With sobriety, alertness, and steadfast faith they must resist the evil one; their sufferings are shared with Christians everywhere (1 Pt 5:8–9). They will be strengthened and called to eternal glory (1 Pt 5:10–11).
¶[5:5] **Younger members:** this may be a designation for office-holders of lesser rank.

z. [4:12] 1:6–7; 3:14, 17.   a. [4:13] Rom 5:3–5; 8:17; 2 Tm 2:12.
b. [4:14] Acts 5:41 / Is 11:2.   c. [4:17] Lk 23:31; 2 Thes 1:8.
d. [4:18] Prv 11:31 LXX.   e. [5:2] Acts 20:28; Ti 1:7.   f. [5:4] Wis 5:15–16; 1 Cor 9:25; 2 Tm 4:8; Jas 1:12.

[5:12] **Silvanus: the companion of Paul (see 2 Cor 1:19; 1 Thes 1:1; 2 Thes 1;1). Jews and Jewish Christians, like Paul, often had a Hebrew name (Saoul, Silas) and a Greek or Latin name (Paul, Silvanus). On Silvanus's possible role as amanuensis, see Introduction.
††[5:13] **The chosen one:** feminine, referring to the Christian community (*ekklēsia*) at **Babylon,** the code name for Rome in Rev 14:8; 17:5; 18:2. **Mark, my son:** traditionally a prominent disciple of Peter and co-worker at the church in Rome, perhaps the John Mark referred to in Acts 12:12, 25; 13:5, 13; and in Acts 15:37–39, a companion of Barnabas. Perhaps this is the same Mark mentioned as Barnabas's cousin in Col 4:10, a co-worker with Paul in Phlm 24 (see also 2 Tm 4:11).

g. [5:5] Prv 3:34.   h. [5:6] Jb 22:29; Jas 4:10.   i. [5:7] Ps 55:23; Mt 6:25–33; Lk 12:22–31; Phil 4:6.   j. [5:8] 1 Thes 5:6.   k. [5:10] Rom 8:18; 2 Cor 4:17.   l. [5:14] Rom 16:16; 1 Cor 16:20; 2 Cor 13:12.

THE SECOND LETTER OF
PETER

_{◦───◦───◦}

This letter can be appreciated both for its positive teachings and for its earnest warnings. It seeks to strengthen readers in faith (2 Pt 1:1), hope for the future (2 Pt 3:1-10), knowledge (2 Pt 1:2, 6, 8), love (2 Pt 1:7), and other virtues (2 Pt 1:5-6). This aim is carried out especially by warning against false teachers, the condemnation of whom occupies the long central section of the letter (2 Pt 2:1-22). A particular crisis is the claim by "scoffers" that there will be no second coming of Jesus, a doctrine that the author vigorously affirms (2 Pt 3:1-10). The concept of God's "promises" is particularly precious in the theology of 2 Peter (2 Pt 1:4; 3:4, 9, 13). Closing comments at 2 Pt 3:17-18 well sum up the twin concerns: that you not "be led into" error and "fall" but instead "grow in grace" and "knowledge" of Jesus Christ.

Second Peter is clearly structured in its presentation of these points. It reminds its readers of the divine authenticity of Christ's teaching (2 Pt 1:3-4), continues with reflections on Christian conduct (2 Pt 1:5-15), then returns to the exalted dignity of Jesus by incorporating into the text the apostolic witness to his transfiguration (2 Pt 1:16-18). It takes up the question of the interpretation of scripture by pointing out that it is possible to misunderstand the sacred writings (2 Pt 1:19-21) and that divine punishment will overtake false teachers (2 Pt 2:1-22). It proclaims that the parousia is the teaching of the Lord and of the apostles and is therefore an eventual certainty (2 Pt 3:1-13). At the same time, it warns that the meaning of Paul's writings on this question should not be distorted (2 Pt 3:14-18).

In both content and style this letter is very different from 1 Peter, which immediately precedes it in the canon. The opening verse attributes it to "Symeon Peter, a slave and apostle of Jesus Christ." Moreover, the author in 2 Pt 3:1 calls his work a "second letter," referring probably to 1 Peter as his first, and in 2 Pt 1:18 counts himself among those present at the transfiguration of Jesus.

Nevertheless, acceptance of 2 Peter into the New Testament canon met with great resistance in the early church. The oldest certain reference to it comes from Origen in the early third century. While he himself accepted both Petrine letters as canonical, he testifies that others rejected 2 Peter. As late as the fifth century some local churches still excluded it from the canon, but eventually it was universally adopted. The principal reason for the long delay was the persistent doubt that the letter stemmed from the apostle Peter.

Among modern scholars there is wide agreement that 2 Peter is a pseudonymous work, i.e., one written by a later author who attributed it to Peter according to a literary convention popular at the time. It gives the impression of being more remote in time from the apostolic period than 1 Peter; indeed, many think it is the latest work in the New Testament and assign it to the first or even the second quarter of the second century.

The principal reasons for this view are the following. The author refers to the apostles and "our ancestors" as belonging to a previous generation, now dead (2 Pt 3:2-4). A collection of Paul's letters exists and appears to be well known, but disputes have arisen about the interpretation of them (2 Pt 3:14-16). The passage about false teachers (2 Pt 2:1-18) contains a number of literary contacts with Jude 4-16, and it is generally agreed that 2 Peter depends upon Jude, not vice versa. Finally, the principal problem exercising the author is the false teaching of "scoffers" who have concluded from the delay of the parousia that the Lord is not going to return. This could scarcely have been an issue during the lifetime of Simon Peter.

The Christians to whom the letter is addressed are not identified, though it may be the intent of 2 Pt 3:1 to identify them with the churches of Asia Minor to which 1 Peter was sent. Except for the epistolary greeting in 2 Pt 1:1-2, 2 Peter does not have the features of a genuine letter at all, but is rather a general exhortation cast in the form of a letter. The author must have been a Jewish Christian of the dispersion for, while his Jewish heritage is evident in various features of his thought and style, he writes in the rather stilted literary Greek of the Hellenistic period. He appeals to tradition against the twin threat of doctrinal error and moral laxity, which appear to reflect an early stage of what later developed into full-blown gnosticism. Thus he forms a link between the apostolic period and the church of subsequent ages.

The principal divisions of the Second Letter of Peter are the following:

I. Address (1:1–2)
II. Exhortation to Christian Virtue (1:3–21)
III. Condemnation of the False Teachers (2:1–22)
IV. The Delay of the Second Coming (3:1–16)
V. Final Exhortation and Doxology (3:17–18)

I. ADDRESS

CHAPTER 1

Greeting. [1]'Symeon Peter, a slave and apostle of Jesus Christ, to those who have received a faith of equal value to ours through the righteousness of our God and savior Jesus Christ: [2]may grace and peace be yours in abundance through knowledge† of God and of Jesus our Lord.

II. EXHORTATION TO CHRISTIAN VIRTUE

The Power of God's Promise.‡ [3]His divine power has bestowed on us everything that makes for life and devotion, through the knowledge of him[a] who called us by his own glory and power.§ [4]Through these, he has bestowed on us the precious and very great promises, so that through them you may come to share in the divine nature, after escaping from the corruption that is in the world because of evil desire.[b] [5]For this very reason, make every effort to supplement your faith with virtue, virtue with knowledge,[c] [6]knowledge with self-control, self-control with endurance, endurance with devotion, [7]devotion with mutual affection, mutual affection with love. [8]If these are yours and increase in abundance, they will keep you from being idle or unfruitful in the knowledge of our Lord Jesus Christ. [9]Anyone who lacks them is blind and shortsighted, forgetful of the cleansing of his past sins. [10]*Therefore, brothers, be all the more eager to make your call and election firm, for, in doing so, you will never stumble. [11]For, in this way, entry into the eternal kingdom of our Lord and savior Jesus Christ will be richly provided for you.

Apostolic Witness. [12]††Therefore, I will always remind you of these things, even though you already know them and are established in the truth you have. [13]I think it right, as long as I am in this "tent,"‡‡ to stir you up by a reminder, [14]since I know that I will soon have to put it aside, as indeed our Lord Jesus Christ has shown me.[e] [15]I shall also make every effort to enable you always to remember these things after my departure.

[16]We did not follow cleverly devised myths when we made known to you the power and coming§§ of our Lord Jesus Christ, but we had

---

*[1:1] **Symeon Peter**: on the authorship of 2 Peter, see Introduction; on the spelling here of the Hebrew name Šim'ôn, cf. Acts 15:14. The greeting is especially similar to those in 1 Peter and Jude. The words translated **our God and savior Jesus Christ** could also be rendered "our God and the savior Jesus Christ"; cf. 2 Pt 1:11; 2:20; 3:2, 18.

†[1:2] **Knowledge**: a key term in the letter (2 Pt 1:3, 8; 2:20; 3:18), perhaps used as a Christian emphasis against gnostic claims.

‡[1:3–4] Christian life in its fullness is a gift of divine power effecting a knowledge of Christ and the bestowal of divine promises (2 Pt 3:4, 9). **To share in the divine nature**, escaping from a corrupt world, is a thought found elsewhere in the Bible but expressed only here in such Hellenistic terms, since it is said to be accomplished through knowledge (2 Pt 1:3); cf. 2 Pt 1:2; 2:20; but see also Jn 15:4; 17:22–23; Rom 8:14–17; Heb 3:14; 1 Jn 1:3; 3:2.

§[1:3] **By his own glory and power**: the most ancient papyrus and the best codex read "through glory and power."

¶[1:5–9] Note the climactic gradation of qualities (2 Pt 1:5–7), beginning with faith and leading to the fullness of Christian life, which is love; cf. Rom 5:3–4; Gal 5:6, 22 for a similar series of "virtues," though the program and sense here are different than in Paul. The fruit of these is knowledge of Christ (2 Pt 1:8) referred to in 2 Pt 1:3; their absence is spiritual blindness (2 Pt 1:9).

[1:10–11] Perseverance in the Christian vocation is the best preventative against losing it and the safest provision for attaining its goal, the kingdom. **Kingdom of . . . Christ, instead of "God," is unusual; cf. Col 1:13 and Mt 13:41, as well as the **righteousness of . . . Christ** (2 Pt 1:1).

††[1:12–19] The purpose in writing is to call to mind the apostle's witness to the truth, even as he faces the end of his life (2 Pt 1:12–15), his eyewitness testimony to Christ (1 Pt 1:16–18), and the true prophetic message (2 Pt 1:19) through the Spirit in scripture (2 Pt 1:20–21), in contrast to what false teachers are setting forth (2 Pt 2).

‡‡[1:13] **Tent**: a biblical image for transitory human life (Is 38:12), here combined with a verb that suggests not folding or packing up a tent but its being discarded in death (cf. 2 Cor 5:1–4).

§§[1:16] **Coming**: in Greek parousia, used at 2 Pt 3:4, 12 of the second coming of Christ. The word was used in the

---

a. [1:3] 2 Cor 4:6; 1 Pt 2:9.   b. [1:4] 2 Cor 7:1; 1 Jn 2:15.

c. [1:5–7] Gal 5:22–23.   d. [1:9] 1 Jn 2:9, 11.   e. [1:14] Is 38:12; Jn 21:18–19.

been eyewitnesses of his majesty.[f] [17]For he received honor and glory from God the Father* when that unique declaration came to him from the majestic glory, "This is my Son, my beloved, with whom I am well pleased."[g] [18]We[†] ourselves heard this voice come from heaven while we were with him on the holy mountain. [19h]Moreover, we possess the prophetic message that is altogether reliable. You will do well to be attentive to it, as to a lamp shining in a dark place, until day dawns and the morning star rises in your hearts. [20‡]Know this first of all, that there is no prophecy of scripture that is a matter of personal interpretation, [21]for no prophecy ever came through human will; but rather human beings moved by the holy Spirit spoke under the influence of God.

III. CONDEMNATION OF THE FALSE TEACHERS

CHAPTER 2

False Teachers.[§] [1]There were also false prophets among the people, just as there will be false teachers among you, who will introduce destructive heresies and even deny the Master who ransomed them, bringing swift destruction on themselves.[i] [2]Many will follow their licentious ways, and because of them the way of truth will be reviled.[j] [3]In their greed they will exploit you with fabrications, but from of old their condemnation has not been idle and their destruction does not sleep.[k]

Lessons from the Past. [4]For if God did not spare the angels when they sinned, but condemned them to the chains of Tartarus** and handed them over to be kept for judgment;[l] [5†]and if he did not spare the ancient world, even though he preserved Noah, a herald of righteousness, together with seven others, when he brought a flood upon the godless world;[m] [6]and if he condemned the cities of Sodom and Gomorrah [to destruction], reducing them to ashes, making them an example for the godless [people] of what is coming;[n] [7]and if he rescued Lot, a righteous man oppressed by the licentious conduct of unprincipled people [8](for day after day that righteous man living among them was tormented in his righteous soul at the lawless deeds that he saw and heard), [9]then the Lord knows how to rescue the devout from trial and to keep the unrighteous under punishment for the day of judgment,[o] [10]and especially those who follow the flesh with its depraved desire and show contempt for lordship.[p]

False Teachers Denounced.‡‡ Bold and arrogant, they are not afraid to revile glorious beings,§§ [11¶¶]whereas angels,[q] despite their superior strength and power, do not bring a reviling judgment against them from the Lord. [12]But these people, like irrational animals born by nature for capture and destruction, revile things that they do not understand, and in their destruction they will also be destroyed,[r] [13]suffering wrong*** as payment

¶[2:4–6] The false teachers will be punished just as surely and as severely as were the fallen **angels** (2 Pt 2:4; cf. Jude 6; Gn 6:1–4), the sinners of Noah's day (2 Pt 2:5; Gn 7:21–23), and the inhabitants of the cities of the Plain (2 Pt 2:6; Jude 7; Gn 19:25). Whereas there are three examples in Jude 5–7 (Exodus and wilderness; rebellious angels; Sodom and Gomorrah), 2 Peter omitted the first of these, has inserted a new illustration about Noah (2 Pt 2:5) between Jude's second and third examples, and listed the resulting three examples in their Old Testament order (Gn 6; 7; 19).

[2:4] Chains of Tartarus: cf. Jude 6; other manuscripts in 2 Peter read "pits of Tartarus." **Tartarus:** a term borrowed from Greek mythology to indicate the infernal regions.

††[2:5–10a] Although God did not spare the sinful, he kept and saved the righteous, such as **Noah** (2 Pt 2:5) and **Lot** (2 Pt 2:7), and **he knows how to rescue the devout** (2 Pt 2:9), who are contrasted with the false teachers of the author's day. On Noah, cf. Gn 5:32–9:29, especially 7:1. On Lot, cf. Gn 13 and 19.

‡‡[2:10b–22] Some take 2 Pt 2:10b, 11 with the preceding paragraph. Others begin the new paragraph with 2 Pt 2:10a, supplying from 2 Pt 2:9 **The Lord knows how . . . to keep . . . under punishment,** with reference to God and probably specifically Christ (2 Pt 2:1). The conduct of the false teachers is described and condemned in language similar to that of Jude 8–16. This arrogance knows no bounds; animallike, they are due to be caught and destroyed. They seduce even those who have knowledge of Christ (2 Pt 2:20).

§§[2:10b] **Glorious beings:** literally, "glories"; cf. Jude 8. While some think that illustrious personages are meant or even political officials behind whom (fallen) angels stand, it is more likely that the reference is to glorious angelic beings (cf. Jude 9).

¶¶[2:11] **From the Lord:** some manuscripts read "before the Lord"; cf. Jude 9.

***[2:13] **Suffering wrong:** some manuscripts read "receiving a reward." **In their deceits:** some manuscripts read "in their love feasts" (Jude 12).

---

extrabiblical writings for the visitation of someone in authority; in Greek cult and Hellenistic Judaism it was used for the manifestation of the divine presence. That the apostles **made known** has been interpreted to refer to Jesus' transfiguration (2 Pt 1:17) or to his entire first coming or to his future coming in power (2 Pt 3).

*[1:17] The author assures the readers of the reliability of the apostolic message (including Jesus' power, glory, and coming; cf. note on 2 Pt 1:16) by appeal to the transfiguration of Jesus in glory (cf. Mt 17:1–8 and parallels) and by appeal to the prophetic message (2 Pt 1:19; perhaps Nm 24:17). Here, as elsewhere, the New Testament insists on continued reminders as necessary to preserve the historical facts about Jesus and the truths of the faith; cf. 2 Pt 3:1–2; 1 Cor 11:2; 15:1–3. **My Son, my beloved:** or, "my beloved Son."

†[1:18] **We:** at Jesus' transfiguration, referring to Peter, James, and John (Mt 17:1).

‡[1:20–21] Often cited, along with 2 Tm 3:16, on the "inspiration" of scripture or against private interpretation, these verses in context are directed against the false teachers of 2 Pt 2 and clever tales (2 Pt 1:16). The prophetic word in scripture comes admittedly through **human beings** (2 Pt 1:21), but **moved by the holy Spirit,** not from their own interpretation, and is a matter of what the author and Spirit intended, not the **personal interpretation** of false teachers. Instead of **under the influence of God,** some manuscripts read "holy ones of God."

§[2:1–3] The pattern of **false prophets** among the Old Testament people of God will recur through **false teachers** in the church. Such destructive opinions of heretical sects bring loss of faith in Christ, contempt for the way of salvation (cf. 2 Pt 2:21), and immorality.

f. [1:16] Lk 9:28–36; Jn 1:14. g. [1:17] Ps 2:7; Mt 17:4–6. h. [1:19] Lk 1:78–79; Rev 2:28. i. [2:1] Mt 24:11, 24; 1 Tm 4:1; Jude 4. j. [2:2] Is 52:5. k. [2:3] Rom 16:18.

l. [2:4] Jude 6. m. [2:5] Gn 8:15–19; Heb 11:7. n. [2:6] Gn 19:24–25; Jude 7. o. [2:9] 1 Cor 10:13; Rev 3:10. p. [2:10] Jude 8. q. [2:11] Jude 9. r. [2:12] Ps 49:13–15; Jude 10.

for wrongdoing. Thinking daytime revelry a delight, they are stains and defilements as they revel in their deceits while carousing with you.[s] [14]Their eyes are full of adultery and insatiable for sin. They seduce unstable people, and their hearts are trained in greed. Accursed children! [15]Abandoning the straight road, they have gone astray, following the road of Balaam, the son of Bosor,[*] who loved payment for wrongdoing,[t] [16]but he received a rebuke for his own crime: a mute beast spoke with a human voice and restrained the prophet's madness.[u]

[17]These people are waterless springs and mists driven by a gale; for them the gloom of darkness has been reserved.[v] [18]For, talking empty bombast, they seduce with licentious desires of the flesh those who have barely escaped[t] from people who live in error.[w] [19]They promise them freedom, though they themselves are slaves of corruption, for a person is a slave of whatever overcomes him.[x] [20]For if they, having escaped the defilements of the world through the knowledge of [our] Lord and savior Jesus Christ, again become entangled and overcome by them, their last condition is worse than their first.[y] [21]For it would have been better for them not to have known the way of righteousness than after knowing it to turn back from the holy commandment handed down[‡] to them.[z] [22]What is expressed in the true proverb has happened to them,[a] "The dog returns to its own vomit," and "A bathed sow returns to wallowing in the mire."

IV. THE DELAY OF THE SECOND COMING

CHAPTER 3

Denial of the Parousia. [1]This is now, beloved, the second letter I am writing to you; through them by way of reminder I am trying to stir up your sincere disposition, [2]to recall the words previously spoken by the holy prophets and the commandment of the Lord and savior through your apostles.[b] [3]Know this first of all, that in the last days scoffers[**] will come [to] scoff, living according to their own desires[c] [4]and saying, "Where is the promise of his coming?[††] From the time when our ancestors fell asleep, everything has remained as it was from the beginning of creation."[d] [5]They deliberately ignore the fact that the heavens existed of old and earth was formed out of water and through water[‡‡] by the word of God;[e] [6]through these the world that then existed was destroyed,[f] deluged with water.[§§] [7]The present heavens and earth have been reserved by the same word for fire, kept for the day of judgment and of destruction of the godless.[g]

[8]But do not ignore this one fact, beloved, that with the Lord one day is like a thousand years[***] and a thousand years like one day.[h] [9]The Lord does not delay his promise, as some regard "delay," but he is patient with you, not wishing that any should perish but that all should come to repentance.[i] [10]But the day of the Lord will come like a thief,[†††] and then the heavens will pass away with a mighty roar and the elements will be dissolved by fire, and the earth and everything done on it will be found out.[j]

Exhortation to Preparedness.[‡‡‡] [11]Since everything is to be dissolved in this way, what sort

---

the **apostles** (2 Pt 3:1–2; cf. Jude 17); cf. 1 Pt 1:10–12, 16–21, especially 16–21; Eph 2:20.

** [3:3] **Scoffers:** cf. Jude 18, where, however, only the passions of the scoffers are mentioned, not a denial on their part of Jesus' parousia.

†† [3:4–7] The false teachers tried to justify their immorality by pointing out that the promised **coming** (*parousia*) of the Lord has not yet occurred, even though early Christians expected it in their day. They thus insinuate that God is not guiding the world's history anymore, since nothing has changed and the first generation of Christians, **our ancestors** (2 Pt 3:4), has all died by this time. The author replies that, just as God destroyed the earth by water in the flood (2 Pt 3:5–6, cf. 2 Pt 2:5), so he will destroy it along with the false teachers on judgment day (2 Pt 3:7). **The word of God**, which called the world into being (Gn 1; Ps 33:6) and **destroyed** it by the waters of a flood, will destroy it again by fire on **the day of judgment** (2 Pt 3:5–7).

‡‡ [3:5] **Formed out of water and through water:** Gn 1:2, 6–8 is reflected as well as Greek views that water was the basic element from which all is derived.

§§ [3:6] **Destroyed, deluged with water:** cf. 2 Pt 2:5; Gn 7:11–8:2.

§§ [3:8–10] The scoffers' objection (2 Pt 3:4) is refuted also by showing that **delay** of the Lord's second coming is not a failure to fulfill his word but rather a sign of his patience: God is giving time for repentance before the final judgment (cf. Wis 11:23–26; Ez 18:23; 33:11).

*** [3:8] Cf. Ps 90:4.

††† [3:10] **Like a thief:** Mt 24:43; 1 Thes 5:2; Rev 3:3. **Will be found out:** cf. 1 Cor 3:13–15. Some few versions read, as the sense may demand, "will not be found out"; many manuscripts read "will be burned up"; there are further variants in other manuscripts, versions, and Fathers. Total destruction is assumed (2 Pt 3:11).

‡‡‡ [3:11–16] The second coming of Christ and the judgment of the world are the doctrinal bases for the moral

---

* [2:15] **Balaam, the son of Bosor:** in Nm 22:5, Balaam is said to be the son of Beor, and it is this name that turns up in a few ancient Greek manuscripts by way of "correction" of the text. Balaam is not portrayed in such a bad light in Nm 22. His evil reputation and his **madness** (2 Pt 2:16), and possibly his surname Bosor, may have come from a Jewish tradition about him in the first/second century, of which we no longer have any knowledge.

† [2:18] **Barely escaped:** some manuscripts read "really escaped."

‡ [2:21] **Commandment handed down:** cf. 2 Pt 3:2 and Jude 3.

§ [2:22] The second proverb is of unknown origin, while the first appears in Prv 26:11.

¶ [3:1–4] The false teachers not only flout Christian morality (cf. Jude 8–19); they also deny the second coming of Christ and the judgment (2 Pt 3:4; cf. 2 Pt 3:7). They seek to justify their licentiousness by arguing that the promised return of Christ has not been realized and the world is the same, no better than it was before (2 Pt 3:3–4). The author wishes to strengthen the faithful against such errors by reminding them in this **second letter** of the instruction in 1 Peter and of the teaching of the **prophets** and of Christ, conveyed through

---

s. [2:13] Jude 12. t. [2:15] Nm 31:16; Jude 11. u. [2:16] Nm 22:28–33. v. [2:17] Jude 12–13. w. [2:18] Jude 16. x. [2:19] Jn 8:34; Rom 6:16–17. y. [2:20] Mt 12:45. z. [2:21] Ez 3:20. a. [2:22] Prv 26:11.

b. [3:2] Jude 17. c. [3:3] 1 Tm 4:1; 2 Tm 3:1; Jude 18. d. [3:4] Is 5:19. e. [3:5] Gn 1:2, 6, 8; Ps 24:2. f. [3:6] Gn 7:21. g. [3:7] Is 51:6; Mt 3:12. h. [3:8] Ps 90:4. i. [3:9] Ez 18:23; 1 Tm 2:4. j. [3:10] Is 66:15–16; Mt 24:29.

of persons ought [you] to be, conducting yourselves in holiness and devotion,*k* 12*waiting for and hastening the coming of the day of God,*l* because of which the heavens will be dissolved in flames and the elements melted by fire. 13But according to his promise we await new heavens and a new earth† in which righteousness dwells.*m*

14Therefore, beloved, since you await these things, be eager to be found without spot or blemish before him, at peace. 15And consider the patience of our Lord as salvation, as our beloved brother Paul, according to the wisdom

given to him, also wrote to you,*n* 16speaking of these things‡ as he does in all his letters. In them there are some things hard to understand that the ignorant and unstable distort to their own destruction, just as they do the other scriptures.

V. FINAL EXHORTATION AND DOXOLOGY§

17Therefore, beloved, since you are forewarned, be on your guard not to be led into the error of the unprincipled and to fall from your own stability.*o* 18But grow in grace and in the knowledge of our Lord and savior Jesus Christ. To him be glory now and to the day of eternity. [Amen.]*p*

exhortation to readiness through vigilance and a virtuous life; cf. Mt 24:42, 50–51; Lk 12:40; 1 Thes 5:1–11; Jude 20–21.

*[3:12] **Flames . . . fire**: although this is the only New Testament passage about a final conflagration, the idea was common in apocalyptic and Greco-Roman thought. **Hastening**: eschatology is here used to motivate ethics (2 Pt 3:11), as elsewhere in the New Testament. Jewish sources and Acts 3:19–20 assume that proper ethical conduct can help bring the promised day of the Lord; cf. 2 Pt 3:9. Some render the phrase, however, "desiring it earnestly."

†[3:13] **New heavens and a new earth**: cf. Is 65:17; 66:22. The divine promises will be fulfilled after the day of judgment will have passed. The universe will be transformed by the reign of God's **righteousness** or justice; cf. Is 65:17–18; Acts 3:21; Rom 8:18–25; Rev 21:1.

‡[3:16] **These things**: the teachings of this letter find parallels in Paul, e.g., God's will to save (Rom 2:4; 9:22–23; 1 Cor 1:7–8), the coming of Christ (1 Thes 4:16–17; 1 Cor 15:23–52), and preparedness for the judgment (Col 1:22–23; Eph 1:4–14; 4:30; 5:5–14). **Other scriptures**: used to guide the faith and life of the Christian community. The letters of Paul are thus here placed on the same level as books of the Old Testament. Possibly other New Testament writings could also be included.

§[3:17–18] To avoid the dangers **of error** and loss of **stability**, Christians are **forewarned** to be **on guard** and to **grow in grace and knowledge** (2 Pt 1:2) of Christ. The doxology (2 Pt 3:18) recalls 1 Pt 4:11. Some manuscripts add **Amen**.

k. [3:11] Acts 3:19–21. l. [3:12] Is 34:4; Heb 10:27. m. [3:13] Is 65:17; 66:22; Rom 8:21; Rev 21:1, 27.

n. [3:15] Rom 8:19; Jude 24. o. [3:17] Mk 13:5; Heb 2:1. p. [3:18] Rom 16:27.

THE FIRST LETTER OF
JOHN

Early Christian tradition identified this work as a letter of John the apostle. Because of its resemblance to the fourth gospel in style, vocabulary, and ideas, it is generally agreed that both works are the product of the same school of Johannine Christianity. The terminology and the presence or absence of certain theological ideas in 1 John suggest that it was written after the gospel; it may have been composed as a short treatise on ideas that were developed more fully in the fourth gospel. To others, the evidence suggests that 1 John was written after the fourth gospel as part of a debate on the proper interpretation of that gospel. Whatever its relation to the gospel, 1 John may be dated toward the end of the first century. Unlike 2 and 3 John, it lacks in form the salutation and epistolary conclusion of a letter. These features, its prologue, and its emphasis on doctrinal teaching make it more akin to a theological treatise than to most other New Testament letters.

The purpose of the letter is to combat certain false ideas, especially about Jesus, and to deepen the spiritual and social awareness of the Christian community (1 Jn 3:17). Some former members (1 Jn 2:19) of the community refused to acknowledge Jesus as the Christ (1 Jn 2:22) and denied that he was a true man (1 Jn 4:2). The specific heresy described in this letter cannot be identified exactly, but it is a form of docetism or gnosticism; the former doctrine denied the humanity of Christ to insure that his divinity was untainted, and the latter viewed the appearance of Christ as a mere stepping-stone to higher knowledge of God. These theological errors are rejected by an appeal to the reality and continuity of the apostolic witness to Jesus. The author affirms that authentic Christian love, ethics, and faith take place only within the historical revelation and sacrifice of Jesus Christ. The fullness of Christian life as fellowship with the Father must be based on true belief and result in charitable living; knowledge of God and love for one another are inseparable, and error in one area inevitably affects the other. Although the author recognizes that Christian doctrine presents intangible mysteries of faith about Christ, he insists that the concrete Christian life brings to light the deeper realities of the gospel.

The structure and language of the letter are straightforward yet repetitious. The author sets forth the striking contrasts between light and darkness, Christians and the world, and truth and error to illustrate the threats and responsibilities of Christian life. The result is not one of theological argument but one of intense religious conviction expressed in simple truths. The letter is of particular value for its declaration of the humanity and divinity of Christ as an apostolic teaching and for its development of the intrinsic connection between Christian moral conduct and Christian doctrine.

The principal divisions of the First Letter of John are the following:

I. Prologue (1:1–4)
II. God as Light (1:5–3:10)
III. Love for One Another (3:11–5:12)
IV. Epilogue (5:13–21)

I. PROLOGUE

CHAPTER 1
The Word of Life*

1 What was from the beginning,
   what we have heard,
   what we have seen with our eyes,
   what we looked upon
   and touched with our hands
   concerns the Word of life—*a*
2 for the life was made visible;
   we have seen it and testify to it
   and proclaim to you the eternal life
   that was with the Father and was
   made visible to us—*b*
3 what we have seen and heard
   we proclaim now to you,
   so that you too may have fellowship
   with us;
   for our fellowship is with the Father
   and with his Son, Jesus Christ.*c*
4 We are writing this so that our joy may be
   complete.*d*

II. GOD AS LIGHT

God Is Light. 5Now this is the message that we have heard from him and proclaim to you: God is light,† and in him there is no darkness at all. 6If we say, "We have fellowship with him," while we continue to walk in darkness, we lie and do not act in truth.*e* 7But if we walk in the light as he is in the light, then we have fellowship with one another, and the blood of his Son Jesus cleanses us from all sin.*f* 8If we say, "We are without sin," we deceive ourselves,* and the truth is not in us.*g* 9If we acknowledge our sins, he is faithful and just and will forgive our sins and cleanse us from every wrongdoing.*h* 10If we say, "We have

not sinned," we make him a liar, and his word is not in us.*i*

CHAPTER 2

Christ and His Commandments. 1My children,§ I am writing this to you so that you may not commit sin. But if anyone does sin, we have an Advocate with the Father, Jesus Christ the righteous one.*j* 2He is expiation for our sins, and not for our sins only but for those of the whole world.*k* 3The way we may be sure¶ that we know him is to keep his commandments.*l* 4Whoever says, "I know him," but does not keep his commandments is a liar, and the truth is not in him.*m* 5But whoever keeps his word, the love of God is truly perfected in him. This is the way we may know that we are in union with him:*n* 6whoever claims to abide in him ought to live [just] as he lived.

The New Commandment.** 7Beloved, I am writing no new commandment to you but an old commandment that you had from the beginning. The old commandment is the word that you have heard.*o* 8And yet I do write a new commandment to you, which holds true in him and among you,†† for the darkness is passing away, and the true light is already shining.*p* 9Whoever says he is in the light, yet hates his brother, is still in the darkness.*q* 10Whoever loves his brother remains in the light, and there is nothing in him to cause a fall.*r* 11Whoever hates his brother is in darkness; he walks in darkness and does not know where he is going because the darkness has blinded his eyes.

Members of the Community.‡‡ 12I am writing to you, children, because your sins have been forgiven* for his name's sake.§§

---

§[2:1] **Children**: like the term "beloved," this is an expression of pastoral love (cf. Jn 13:33; 21:5; 1 Cor 4:14). **Advocate**: for the use of the term, see Jn 14:16. Forgiveness of sin is assured through Christ's intercession and expiation or "offering"; the death of Christ effected the removal of sin.
¶[2:3–6] **The way we may be sure**: to those who claim, "I have known Christ and therefore I know him," our author insists on not mere intellectual knowledge but obedience to God's commandments in a life conformed to the example of Christ; this confirms our knowledge of him and is **the love of God . . . perfected**. Disparity between moral life and the commandments proves improper belief.
[2:7–11] The author expresses the continuity and freshness of mutual charity in Christian experience. Through Christ the commandment of love has become the **light defeating the **darkness** of evil in a new age. All hatred as darkness is incompatible with the light and Christian life. Note also the characteristic Johannine polemic in which a positive assertion is emphasized by the negative statement of its opposite.
††[2:8] **Which holds true in him and among you**: literally, "a thing that holds true in him and in you."
‡‡[2:12–17] The Christian community that has experienced the grace of God through forgiveness of sin and knowledge of Christ is armed against the evil one.
§§[2:12] **For his name's sake**: because of Christ our sins are forgiven.

---

*[1:1–4] There is a striking parallel to the prologue of the gospel of John (Jn 1:1–18), but the emphasis here is not on the preexistent Word but rather on the apostles' witness to the incarnation of life by their experience of the historical Jesus. He is **the Word of life** (1 Jn 1:1; cf. Jn 1:4), **the eternal life that was with the Father and was made visible** (1 Jn 1:2; cf. Jn 1:14), and was **heard, seen, looked upon**, and **touched** by the apostles. The purpose of their teaching is to share that life, called **fellowship . . . with the Father and with his Son, Jesus Christ**, with those who receive their witness (1 Jn 1:3; Jn 1:14, 16).
†[1:5–7] **Light** is to be understood here as truth and goodness; **darkness** here is error and depravity (cf. Jn 3:19–21; 17:17; Eph 5:8). To **walk** in light or darkness is to live according to truth or error, not merely intellectual but moral as well. Fellowship with God and with one another consists in a life according to the truth as found in God and in Christ.
‡[1:8–10] Denial of the condition of sin is self-deception and even contradictory of divine revelation; there is also the continual possibility of sin's recurrence. Forgiveness and deliverance from sin through Christ are assured through acknowledgment of them and repentance.

a. [1:1] 2:13; Jn 1:1, 14; 20:20, 25, 27.   b. [1:2] Jn 15:27; 17:5.   c. [1:3] Jn 17:21; Acts 4:20.   d. [1:4] Jn 15:11; 2 Jn 12.   e. [1:6] Jn 12:35.   f. [1:7] Mt 26:28; Rom 3:24–25; Heb 9:14; 1 Pt 1:19; Rev 1:5.   g. [1:8] 2 Chr 6:36; Prv 20:9.   h. [1:9] Prv 28:13; Jas 5:16.   i. [1:10] 5:10.   j. [2:1] Jn 14:16; Heb 7:25.   k. [2:2] 4:10.   l. [2:3] Jn 14:15; 15:10.   m. [2:4] 4:20.   n. [2:5] Jn 14:23.   o. [2:7] 3:11; Dt 6:5; Mt 22:37–40.   p. [2:8] Jn 13:34 / Jn 1:5; Rom 13:12.   q. [2:9] Jn 8:12.   r. [2:10] Eccl 2:14; Jn 11:10.   s. [2:12] 1 Cor 6:11.

¹³I am writing to you, fathers, because you know him who is from the beginning.

I am writing to you, young men, because you have conquered the evil one.ᵗ ¹⁴I write to you, children, because you know the Father.

I write to you, fathers, because you know him who is from the beginning.

I write to you, young men, because you are strong and the word of God remains in you, and you have conquered the evil one.

¹⁵Do not love the world or the things of the world.⁎ If anyone loves the world, the love of the Father is not in him.ᵘ ¹⁶For all that is in the world, sensual lust,† enticement for the eyes, and a pretentious life, is not from the Father but is from the world. ¹⁷Yet the world and its enticement are passing away. But whoever does the will of God remains forever.ᵛ

Antichrists. ¹⁸Children, it is the last hour;‡ and just as you heard that the antichrist was coming, so now many antichrists have appeared. Thus we know this is the last hour.ʷ ¹⁹They went out from us, but they were not really of our number;§ if they had been, they would have remained with us. Their desertion shows that none of them was of our number. ²⁰But you have the anointing that comes from the holy one,¶ and you all have knowledge.ˣ ²¹I write to you not because you do not know the truth but because you do, and because every lie is alien to the truth.ʸ ²²⁎⁎Who is the liar? Whoever denies that Jesus is the Christ. Whoever denies the Father and the Son, this is the antichrist.ᶻ ²³No one who denies the Son has the Father, but whoever confesses the Son has the Father as well.ᵃ

Life from God's Anointing. ²⁴ᵇLet what you heard from the beginning remain in you. If what you heard from the beginning remains in you, then you will remain in the Son and in the Father.†† ²⁵And this is the promise that he made us: eternal life.ᶜ ²⁶I write you these things about those who would deceive you. ²⁷As for you, the anointing that you received from him remains in you, so that you do not need anyone to teach you. But his anointing teaches you about everything and is true and not false; just as it taught you, remain in him.

Children of God. ²⁸‡‡And now, children, remain in him, so that when he appears we may have confidence and not be put to shame by him at his coming. ²⁹If you consider that he is righteous, you also know that everyone who acts in righteousness is begotten by him.

CHAPTER 3

¹§§See what love the Father has bestowed on us that we may be called the children of God. Yet so we are. The reason the world does not know us is that it did not know him.ᵈ ²Beloved, we are God's children now; what we shall be has not yet been revealed. We do know that when it is revealed¶¶ we shall be like him, for we shall see him as he is.ᵉ ³Everyone who has this hope based on him makes himself pure, as he is pure.ᶠ

Avoiding Sin. ⁴Everyone who commits sin commits lawlessness, for sin is lawlessness.⁎⁎⁎ ⁵You know that he was revealed to take away sins, and in him there is no sin.ᵍ ⁶No one who remains in him sins; no one who sins has seen him or known him. ⁷Children, let no one deceive you. The person who acts in righteousness is righteous, just as he is righteous. ⁸Whoever sins belongs to the devil, because the devil has sinned from the beginning. Indeed, the Son of God was revealed to destroy the works of the devil.ʰ ⁹No one who is begotten by God commits sin, because God's seed remains in him; he cannot

---

⁎[2:15] **The world**: all that is hostile toward God and alienated from him. Love of the **world** and love of God are thus mutually exclusive; cf. Jas 4:4.

†[2:16] **Sensual lust**: literally, "the lust of the flesh," inordinate desire for physical gratification. **Enticement for the eyes**: literally, "the lust of the eyes," avarice or covetousness; the eyes are regarded as the windows of the soul. **Pretentious life**: literally, "pride of life," arrogance or ostentation in one's earthly style of life that reflects a willful independence from God and others.

‡[2:18] **It is the last hour**: literally, "a last hour," the period between the death and resurrection of Christ and his second coming. **The antichrist**: opponent or adversary of Christ; the term appears only in 1 John–2 John, but "pseudochrists" (translated "false messiahs") in Mt 24:24 and Mk 13:22, and Paul's "lawless one" in 2 Thes 2:3, are similar figures. **Many antichrists**: Matthew, Mark, and Revelation seem to indicate a collectivity of persons, here related to the false teachers.

§[2:19] **Not really of our number**: the apostate teachers only proved their lack of faith by leaving the community.

¶[2:20] **The anointing that comes from the holy one**: this anointing is in the Old Testament sense of receiving the Spirit of God. The **holy one** probably refers to Christ. True knowledge is the gift of the Spirit (cf. Is 11:2), and the function of the Spirit is to lead Christians to the truth (Jn 14:17, 26; 16:13).

⁎⁎[2:22–23] Certain gnostics denied that the earthly Jesus was the Christ; to deny knowledge of the Son is to deny the Father, since only through the Son has God been fully revealed (Jn 1:18; 14:8–9).

††[2:24] Continuity with the apostolic witness as proclaimed in the prologue is the safeguard of right belief.

‡‡[2:28–29] Our confidence at his judgment is based on the daily assurance of salvation. Our actions reflect our true relation to him.

§§[3:1–3] The greatest sign of God's love is the gift of his Son (Jn 3:16) that has made Christians true children of God. This relationship is a present reality and also part of the life to come; true knowledge of God will ultimately be gained, and Christians prepare themselves now by virtuous lives in imitation of the Son.

¶¶[3:2] **When it is revealed**: or "when he is revealed" (the subject of the verb could be Christ).

⁎⁎⁎[3:4] **Lawlessness**: a reference to the activity of the antichrist, since it is expressed as hostility toward God and a rejection of Christ. The author goes on to contrast the states of sin and righteousness. Christians do not escape sin but realize that when they sin they cease to have fellowship with God. Virtue and sin distinguish the children of God from the children of the devil.

---

t. [2:13] 1:1; Jn 1:1.   u. [2:15] Rom 8:7–8; Jas 4:4; 2 Pt 1:4.   v. [2:17] Is 40:8; Mt 7:21; 1 Cor 7:31; 1 Pt 4:2.   w. [2:18] 1 Tm 4:1.   x. [2:20] Jn 14:26.   y. [2:21] 3:19; 2 Pt 1:12.   z. [2:22] 2 Thes 2:4.   a. [2:23] Jn 14:7–9.

b. [2:24] Jn 14:23.   c. [2:25] Jn 5:24; 10:28; 17:2.   d. [3:1] Jn 1:12; Eph 1:5 / Jn 15:21; 17:25.   e. [3:2] Phil 3:21.   f. [3:3] 2:6.   g. [3:5] Is 53:9; Jn 1:29; 8:46; 1 Pt 2:22.   h. [3:8] Jn 8:44; 12:31–32.

sin because he is begotten by God.* [10]In this way, the children of God and the children of the devil are made plain; no one who fails to act in righteousness belongs to God, nor anyone who does not love his brother.

III. LOVE FOR ONE ANOTHER

[11†]For this is the message you have heard from the beginning: we should love one another,[i] [12]unlike Cain who belonged to the evil one and slaughtered his brother. Why did he slaughter him? Because his own works were evil, and those of his brother righteous.[j] [13]Do not be amazed, [then,] brothers, if the world hates you.[k] [14]We know that we have passed from death to life because we love our brothers. Whoever does not love remains in death.[l] [15]Everyone who hates his brother is a murderer, and you know that no murderer has eternal life remaining in him.[m] [16]The way we came to know love was that he laid down his life for us; so we ought to lay down our lives for our brothers.[n] [17]If someone who has worldly means sees a brother in need and refuses him compassion, how can the love of God remain in him?[o] [18]Children, let us love not in word or speech but in deed and truth.[p]

Confidence Before God.[‡] [19][Now] this is how we shall know that we[§] belong to the truth and reassure our hearts before him [20]in whatever our hearts condemn, for God is greater than our hearts and knows everything. [21]Beloved, if [our] hearts do not condemn us, we have confidence in God [22]and receive from him whatever we ask, because we keep his commandments and do what pleases him.[q] [23]And his commandment is this: we should believe in the name of his Son, Jesus Christ, and love one another just as he commanded us.[r] [24]Those who keep his commandments remain in him, and he in them, and the way we know that he remains in us is from the Spirit that he gave us.[s]

CHAPTER 4

Testing the Spirits.[¶] [1]Beloved, do not trust every spirit but test the spirits to see whether they belong to God, because many false prophets have gone out into the world.[t] [2]This is how you can know the Spirit of God: every spirit that acknowledges Jesus Christ come in the flesh belongs to God,[u] [3]and every spirit that does not acknowledge Jesus** does not belong to God. This is the spirit of the antichrist that, as you heard, is to come, but in fact is already in the world.[v] [4]You belong to God, children, and you have conquered them, for the one who is in you is greater than the one who is in the world. [5]They belong to the world; accordingly, their teaching belongs to the world, and the world listens to them.[w] [6]We belong to God, and anyone who knows God listens to us, while anyone who does not belong to God refuses to hear us. This is how we know the spirit of truth and the spirit of deceit.[x]

God's Love and Christian Life.[7††]Beloved, let us love one another, because love is of God; everyone who loves is begotten by God and knows God. [8]Whoever is without love does not know God, for God is love. [9]In this way the love of God was revealed to us: God sent his only Son into the world so that we might have life through him.[y] [10]In this is love: not that we have loved God, but that he loved us and sent his Son as expiation for our sins.[z] [11]Beloved, if God so loved us, we also must love one another. [12]No one has ever seen God. Yet, if we love one another, God remains in us, and his love is brought to perfection in us.[a]

[13‡‡]This is how we know that we remain in him and he in us, that he has given us of his Spirit. [14]Moreover, we have seen and testify that the Father sent his Son as savior of the world.

¶[4:1–6] Deception is possible in spiritual phenomena and may be tested by its relation to Christian doctrine (cf. 1 Cor 12:3): those who fail to acknowledge Jesus Christ in the flesh are false prophets and belong to the antichrist. Even though these false prophets are well received in the world, the Christian who belongs to God has a greater power in the truth.

[4:3] **Does not acknowledge Jesus: some ancient manuscripts add "Christ" and/or "to have come in the flesh" (cf. 1 Jn 4:2), and others read "every spirit that annuls (or severs) Jesus."

††[4:7–12] Love as we share in it testifies to the nature of God and to his presence in our lives. One who loves shows that one is a child of God and knows God, for God's very being is love; one without love is without God. The revelation of the nature of God's love is found in the free gift of his Son to us, so that we may share life with God and be delivered from our sins. The love we have for one another must be of the same sort: authentic, merciful; this unique Christian love is our proof that we know God and can "see" the invisible God.

‡‡[4:13–21] The testimony of the Spirit and that of faith join the testimony of love to confirm our knowledge of God. Our love is grounded in the confession of Jesus as the Son of God and the example of God's love for us. Christian life is founded on the knowledge of God as love and on his continuing presence that relieves us from fear of judgment (1 Jn 4:16–18). What Christ is gives us confidence, even as we live and love in this world. Yet Christian love is not abstract but lived in the concrete manner of love for one another.

---

*[3:9] A habitual sinner is a child of the devil, while a child of God, who by definition is in fellowship with God, cannot sin. **Seed**: Christ or the Spirit who shares the nature of God with the Christian.

†[3:11–18] Love, even to the point of self-sacrifice, is the point of the commandment. The story of Cain and Abel (1 Jn 3:12–15; Gn 4:1–16) presents the rivalry of two brothers, in a contrast of evil and righteousness, where envy led to murder. For Christians, proof of deliverance is love toward others, after the example of Christ. This includes concrete acts of charity, out of our material abundance.

‡[3:19–24] Living a life of faith in Jesus and of Christian love assures us of abiding in God no matter what our feelings may at times tell us. Our obedience gives us confidence in prayer and trust in God's judgment. This obedience includes our belief in Christ and love for one another.

§[3:19b–20] This difficult passage may also be translated "we shall be at peace before him in whatever our hearts condemn, for . . ." or "and before God we shall convince our hearts, if our hearts condemn us, that God is greater than our hearts."

i. [3:11] 2:7; Jn 13:34; 15:12, 17. j. [3:12] Gn 4:8; Jude 11. k. [3:13] Mt 24:9; Jn 15:18; 17:14. l. [3:14] Lv 19:17; Jn 5:24. m. [3:15] Jn 8:44. n. [3:16] Mt 20:28; Jn 10:11; 15:13. o. [3:17] Dt 15:7, 11; Jas 2:15–16. p. [3:18] Jas 1:22. q. [3:22] 5:15; Mt 7:7–11; 21:22; Jn 14:13–14. r. [3:23] Jn 13:34; 15:17. s. [3:24] 4:13; Jn 14:21–23.

t. [4:1] 2:18; Mt 24:24. u. [4:2] 1 Cor 12:3; 1 Thes 5:21. v. [4:3] 3:22. w. [4:5] Jn 15:19. x. [4:6] Jn 8:47; 10:16. y. [4:9] Jn 3:16. z. [4:10] Rom 5:8. a. [4:12] Jn 1:18; 1 Tm 6:16.

¹⁵Whoever acknowledges that Jesus is the Son of God, God remains in him and he in God. ¹⁶We have come to know and to believe in the love God has for us.

God is love, and whoever remains in love remains in God and God in him. ¹⁷In this is love brought to perfection among us, that we have confidence on the day of judgment because as he is, so are we in this world.ᵇ ¹⁸There is no fear in love, but perfect love drives out fear because fear has to do with punishment, and so one who fears is not yet perfect in love. ¹⁹We love because he first loved us. ²⁰If anyone says, "I love God," but hates his brother, he is a liar; for whoever does not love a brother whom he has seen cannot love God* whom he has not seen.ᶜ ²¹This is the commandment we have from him: whoever loves God must also love his brother.ᵈ

CHAPTER 5

Faith Is Victory over the World. ¹†Everyone who believes that Jesus is the Christ is begotten by God, and everyone who loves the father loves [also] the one begotten by him.ᵉ ²In this way we know that we love the children of God when we love God and obey his commandments. ³For the love of God is this, that we keep his commandments. And his commandments are not burdensome,ᶠ ⁴for whoever is begotten by God conquers the world. And the victory that conquers the world is our faith.ᵍ ⁵Who [indeed] is the victor over the world but the one who believes that Jesus is the Son of God?ʰ

⁶This is the one who came through water and blood,‡ Jesus Christ, not by water alone, but by water and blood. The Spirit is the one that testifies, and the Spirit is truth.ⁱ ⁷So there are three that testify, ⁸the Spirit, the water, and the blood, and the three are of one accord.ʲ ⁹If we accept human testimony, the testimony of God is surely greater. Now the testimony of God is this, that he has testified on behalf of his Son.ᵏ ¹⁰Whoever believes in the Son of God has this testimony within himself. Whoever does not believe God has made him a liar by not believing the testimony God has given about his Son.ˡ ¹¹And this is the testimony: God gave us eternal life, and this life is in his Son.ᵐ ¹²Whoever possesses the Son has life; whoever does not possess the Son of God does not have life.

IV. EPILOGUE§

Prayer for Sinners. ¹³I write these things to you so that you may know that you have eternal life, you who believe in the name of the Son of God.ⁿ ¹⁴And we have this confidence in him, that if we ask anything according to his will, he hears us.ᵒ ¹⁵And if we know that he hears us in regard to whatever we ask, we know that what we have asked him for is ours. ¹⁶If anyone sees his brother sinning, if the sin is not deadly, he should pray to God and he will give him life. This is only for those whose sin is not deadly. There is such a thing as deadly sin, about which I do not say that you should pray.ᵖ ¹⁷All wrongdoing is sin, but there is sin that is not deadly.

¹⁸We know that no one begotten by God sins; but the one begotten by God he protects, and the evil one cannot touch him. ¹⁹We know that we belong to God, and the whole world is under the power of the evil one. ²⁰We also know that the Son of God has come and has given us discernment to know the one who is true. And we are in the one who is true, in his Son Jesus Christ. He is the true God and eternal life.�q ²¹Children, be on your guard against idols.

---

*[4:20] **Cannot love God**: some ancient manuscripts read "how can he love . . . ?"

†[5:1–5] Children of God are identified not only by their love for others (1 Jn 4:7–9) and for God (1 Jn 5:1–2) but by their belief in the divine sonship of Jesus Christ. Faith, the acceptance of Jesus in his true character and the obedience in love to God's commands (1 Jn 5:3), is the source of the Christian's power in the world and conquers the world of evil (1 Jn 5:4–5), even as Christ overcame the world (Jn 16:33).

‡[5:6–12] **Water and blood** (1 Jn 5:6) refers to Christ's baptism (Mt 3:16–17) and to the shedding of his blood on the cross (Jn 19:34). **The Spirit** was present at the baptism (Mt 3:16; Mk 1:10; Lk 3:22; Jn 1:32, 34). **The testimony** to Christ as the Son of God is confirmed by divine witness (1 Jn 5:7–9), greater by far than the two legally required human witnesses (Dt 17:6). To deny this is to deny God's truth; cf. Jn 8:17–18. The gist of the divine witness or **testimony** is that **eternal life** (1 Jn 5:11–12) is given in Christ and nowhere else. To **possess the Son** is not acceptance of a doctrine but of a person who lives now and provides life.

§[5:13–21] As children of God we have confidence in prayer because of our intimate relationship with him (1 Jn 5:14–15). In love, we pray (1 Jn 5:16–17) for those who are in **sin**, but not in **deadly sin** (literally, "sin unto death"), probably referring to apostasy or activities brought on under the antichrist; cf. Mk 3:29; Heb 6:4–6; 10:26–31. Even in the latter case, however, prayer, while not enjoined, is not forbidden. The letter concludes with a summary of the themes of the letter (1 Jn 5:18–20). There is a sharp antithesis between the children of God and those belonging to the world and to the evil one. The Son reveals the God of truth; Christians dwell in the true God, in his Son, and have eternal life. The final verse (1 Jn 5:21) voices a perennial warning about **idols**, any type of rival to God.

b. [4:17] 2:28.   c. [4:20] 2:4.   d. [4:21] Jn 13:34; 14:15, 21; 15:17.   e. [5:1] Jn 8:42; 1 Pt 1:23.   f. [5:3] Jn 14:15.   g. [5:4] Jn 16:33.   h. [5:5] 1 Cor 15:57.   i. [5:6] Jn 15:26; 19:34.

j. [5:8] Jn 5:32, 36; 15:26.   k. [5:9] Jn 5:32, 37.   l. [5:10] Jn 3:33.   m. [5:11] 1:2; Jn 1:4; 5:21, 26; 17:3.   n. [5:13] Jn 1:12; 20:31.   o. [5:14] 3:21–22; Mt 7:7; Jn 14:13–14.   p. [5:16] Mt 12:31.   q. [5:20] Jer 24:7; Jn 17:3; Eph 1:17.

THE SECOND LETTER OF
JOHN

〜❧〜

Written in response to similar problems, the Second and Third Letters of John are of the same length, perhaps determined by the practical consideration of the writing space on one piece of papyrus. In each letter the writer calls himself "the Presbyter," and their common authorship is further evidenced by internal similarities in style and wording, especially in the introductions and conclusions. The literary considerations that link 2 John and 3 John also link them with the First Letter and the Gospel of John. The concern with "truth," christology, mutual love, the new commandment, antichrist, and the integrity of witness to the earthly Jesus mark these works as products of the Johannine school. The identity of the Presbyter is problematic. The use of the title implies more than age, and refers to his position of leadership in the early church. The absence of a proper name indicates that he was well known and acknowledged in authority by the communities to which he writes. Although traditionally attributed to John the apostle, these letters were probably written by a disciple or scribe of an apostle. The traditional place and date of composition, Ephesus at the end of the first century, are plausible for both letters.

The Second Letter is addressed to "the chosen Lady" and "to her children." This literary image of a particular Christian community reflects the specific destination and purpose of the letter. Unlike 1 John, this brief letter is not a theological treatise but a reply to problems within the church. The Johannine themes of love and truth are used to support practical advice on Christian living. The Presbyter encourages community members to show their Christianity by adhering to the great commandment of mutual love and to the historical truth about Jesus. The false teaching present among them is a spiritualizing christology that may tempt some members to discount teachings about the incarnation and death of Jesus the Christ; cf. 1 Jn 4:2. For their protection the Presbyter forbids hospitality toward unknown or "progressive" Christians to prevent their infiltration of the community. The Second Letter preserves the Johannine concerns of doctrinal purity and active love in the form of pastoral advice to a threatened community.

---

1 [a]The Presbyter to the chosen Lady and to her children whom I love in truth—and not only I but also all who know the truth— 2because of the truth that dwells in us and will be with us forever. 3Grace, mercy, and peace[†] will be with us from God the Father and from Jesus Christ the Father's Son in truth and love.

4I rejoiced greatly to find some of your children[‡] walking in the truth just as we were commanded by the Father.[b] 5But now, Lady, I ask you, not as though I were writing a new commandment but the one we have had from the beginning: let us love one another.[c] 6For this is love, that we walk according to his commandments;[§] this is the commandment, as you heard from the beginning, in which you should walk.[d]

7[e]Many deceivers have gone out into the world, those who do not acknowledge Jesus

---

*[1] **The chosen Lady**: literally, "elected"; this could also be translated "Kyria (a woman's name) chosen (by God)" or "the lady Electa" or "Electa Kyria." The adjective "chosen" is applied to all Christians at the beginning of other New Testament letters (1 Pt 1:1; Ti 1:1). The description is of a specific community with "children" who are its members. **The truth**: the affirmation of Jesus in the flesh and in contrast to false teaching (2 Jn 7).

†[3] **Grace, mercy, and peace**: like 1 Timothy; 2 Timothy this letter adds **mercy** to the terms used frequently in a salutation to describe Christian blessing; it appears only here in the Johannine writings. The author also puts the blessing in relation to **truth** and **love**, the watchwords of the Johannine teaching. **The Father's Son**: the title that affirms the close relationship of Christ to God; similar variations of this title occur elsewhere (Jn 1:14; 3:35), but the precise wording is not found elsewhere in the New Testament.

‡[4] **Some of your children**: this refers to those whom the Presbyter has recently encountered, but it may also indicate the presence of false doctrine in the community: the Presbyter encourages those who have remained faithful. **Walking in the truth**: an expression used in the Johannine writings to describe a way of living in which the Christian faith is visibly expressed; cf. 1 Jn 1:6–7; 2:6, 11; 3 Jn 3.

§[6] **His commandments**: cf. 1 Jn 3:23; 2:7–8; 4:21; obedience to the commandment of faith and love includes all others.

a. [1] Jn 8:32; 3 Jn 1.
b. [4] 3 Jn 3.   c. [5] Jn 13:34; 15:12; 1 Jn 4:7.   d. [6] Jn 13:34; 14:15; 1 Jn 5:3.   e. [7] 1 Jn 2:22; 4:2.

Christ as coming in the flesh; such is the deceitful one and the antichrist.* [8]Look to yourselves that you† do not lose what we worked for but may receive a full recompense. [9f]Anyone who is so "progressive"‡ as not to remain in the teaching of the Christ does not have God; whoever remains in the teaching has the Father and the Son. [10§]If anyone comes to you and does not bring this doctrine, do not receive him in your house or even greet him;g [11]for whoever greets him shares in his evil works.

[12¶]Although I have much to write to you, I do not intend to use paper and ink. Instead, I hope to visit you and to speak face to face so that our joy may be complete.h [13]The children of your chosen sister** send you greetings.

---

*[7] **The antichrist**: see 1 Jn 2:18–19, 22; 4:3.

†[8] **You** (plural): it is not certain whether this means the Christians addressed or includes the Presbyter, since some of the ancient Greek manuscripts and Greek Fathers have "we."

‡[9] **Anyone who is so "progressive"**: literally, "Anyone who goes ahead." Some gnostic groups held the doctrine of the Christ come in the flesh to be a first step in belief, which the more advanced and spiritual believer surpassed and abandoned in his knowledge of the spiritual Christ. The author affirms that fellowship with God may be gained only by holding to the complete doctrine of Jesus Christ (1 Jn 2:22–23; 4:2; 5:5–6).

§[10–11] At this time false teachers were considered so dangerous and divisive as to be shunned completely. From this description they seem to be wandering preachers. We see here a natural suspicion of early Christians concerning such itinerants and can envisage the problems faced by missionaries such as those mentioned in 3 Jn 10.

¶[12] **Our joy**: a number of other Greek manuscripts read "your joy."

[13] **Chosen sister: the community of which the Presbyter is now a part greets you (singular), the community of the Lady addressed.

---

f. [9] Jn 8:31; 1 Jn 2:23; 4:15.

g. [10] Rom 16:17; 2 Thes 3:6.   h. [12] Jn 15:11; 1 Jn 1:4; 3 Jn 13.

THE THIRD LETTER OF

JOHN

〜✲〜

The Third Letter of John preserves a brief glimpse into the problems of missionary activity and local autonomy in the early church. In contrast to the other two letters of John, this work was addressed to a specific individual, Gaius. This letter is less theological in content and purpose. The author's goal was to secure hospitality and material support for his missionaries, and the Presbyter is writing to another member of the church who has welcomed missionaries in the past. The Presbyter commends Gaius for his hospitality and encourages his future help. He indicates he may come to challenge the policy of Diotrephes that is based on evil gossip.

The problems of the Presbyter in this short letter provide us with valuable evidence of the flexible and personal nature of authority in the early church. The Presbyter writes to Gaius, whom perhaps he had converted or instructed, on the basis of their personal links. The brothers have also confirmed him as a loyal Christian in action and belief. Gaius accepted the missionaries from the Presbyter and presumably will accept Demetrius on the Presbyter's recommendation. In contrast, Diotrephes refuses to receive either letters or friends of the Presbyter. Although he is portrayed as ambitious and hostile, he perhaps exemplifies the cautious and sectarian nature of early Christianity; for its own protection the local community mistrusted missionaries as false teachers. Most interestingly, Diotrephes seems comfortable in ignoring the requests of the Presbyter. The Presbyter seems to acknowledge that only a personal confrontation with Diotrephes will remedy the situation (3 Jn 10). The division, however, may also rest on doctrinal disagreement in which Gaius and the other "friends" accept the teaching of the Presbyter, and Diotrephes does not; the missionaries are not received for suspicion of theological error. Diotrephes has thus been viewed by some as an overly ambitious local upstart trying to thwart the advance of orthodox Christianity, by others as an orthodox church official suspicious of the teachings of the Presbyter and those in the Johannine school who think as he does, or by still others as a local leader anxious to keep the debates in the Johannine community out of his own congregation.

This brief letter and the situation that it mirrors show us how little we know about some details of early development in the church: schools of opinion existed around which questions of faith and life were discussed; and personal ties as well as doctrine and authority played a role in what happened amid divisions and unity.

---

¹*The Presbyter to the beloved Gaius whom I love in truth.ᵃ

²Beloved, I hope you are prospering in every respect and are in good health, just as your soul is prospering. ³I rejoiced greatly when some of the brothers† came and testified to how truly you walk in the truth.ᵇ ⁴Nothing gives me greater joy than to hear that my children are walking in the truth.ᶜ

⁵Beloved, you are faithful in all you do‡ for the brothers, especially for strangers;ᵈ ⁶they have testified to your love before the church.ᵉ Please help them in a way worthy of God to continue their journey.§ ⁷For they have set out for the sake of the Name¶ and are accepting nothing from

*[1] **Beloved Gaius**: a frequent form of address for fellow Christians in New Testament epistolary literature.

†[3] **The brothers**: in this letter, the term may refer to Christians who have been missionaries and received hospitality from Gaius (3 Jn 5–6). **Walk in the truth**: the common Johannine term to describe Christian living; this description presents Gaius as following the teachings of the Presbyter in contrast to Diotrephes.

‡[5] **You are faithful in all you do**: Gaius's aid to the missionaries is a manifestation of his true Christian faith.

§[6] **Help them . . . to continue their journey**: the Presbyter asks Gaius not only to continue to welcome the missionaries to his community but also to equip them for further travels.

¶[7] **The Name**: of Jesus Christ (cf. Acts 5:41; 1 Jn 2:12; 3:23; 5:13). **Accepting nothing**: not expecting support from the pagans to whom they preach the gospel, so that they will not be considered as beggars; they required support from

---

a. [1] 2 Jn 1.   b. [3] 5; Gal 6:10; 2 Jn 4.   c. [4] 1 Thes 2:11–12; 1 Tm 1:2; 2 Tm 1:2; 1 Jn 2:1; 2 Jn 4.

d. [5] Rom 12:13; Gal 6:10; Heb 13:2.   e. [6] Acts 15:3; Col 1:10; 1 Thes 2:12.

the pagans. [8]Therefore, we ought to support such persons, so that we may be co-workers in the truth.
[9]I wrote to the church, but Diotrephes, who loves to dominate,* does not acknowledge us. [10]Therefore, if I come,[†] I will draw attention to what he is doing, spreading evil nonsense about us. And not content with that, he will not receive the brothers, hindering those who wish to do so and expelling them from the church.
[11]Beloved, do not imitate evil[‡] but imitate good. Whoever does what is good is of God;

whoever does what is evil has never seen God.[f] [12]Demetrius[§] receives a good report from all, even from the truth itself. We give our testimonial as well, and you know our testimony is true.[g]
[13]I have much to write to you, but I do not wish to write with pen and ink.[h] [14]Instead, I hope to see you soon, when we can talk face to face. [15]Peace be with you. The friends greet you; greet the friends[¶] there each by name.[i]

---

other Christians; cf. Paul's complaints to the Corinthians (1 Cor 9:3–12).

*[9] **Who loves to dominate**: the Presbyter does not deny Diotrephes' place as leader but indicates that his ambition may have caused him to disregard his letter and his influence.

†[10] **If I come**: the Presbyter may visit the community to challenge the actions of Diotrephes toward himself and the missionaries. **Will not receive the brothers**: Diotrephes may have been critical of the teachings of the Presbyter and sought to maintain doctrinal purity; cf. 1 Jn 2:19 and 2 Jn 10–11.

‡[11] **Do not imitate evil**: Gaius should not be influenced by the behavior of Diotrephes.

§[12] **Demetrius**: because of the fear of false teachers, Demetrius, perhaps the bearer of the letter, is provided with a recommendation from the Presbyter; cf. 2 Cor 3:1; Rom 16:1. **Even from the truth itself**: this refers probably to the manner of Demetrius's life that testifies to his true belief; cf. Gaius above (3 Jn 3).

¶[15] **Friends**: although a Johannine term for Christians (Jn 15:15), the word here may refer to those in the community loyal to the Presbyter and to Gaius.

---

f. [11] 1 Jn 2:29; 3:6, 10.   g. [12] Jn 19:35; 21:24; 1 Tm 3:7.   h. [13] 2 Jn 12.   i. [15] Jn 20:19, 21, 26; Eph 6:23; 1 Pt 5:14.

THE LETTER OF
JUDE

꧁꧂

This letter is by its address attributed to "Jude, a slave of Jesus Christ and brother of James" (Jude 1). Since he is not identified as an apostle, this designation can hardly be meant to refer to the Jude or Judas who is listed as one of the Twelve (Lk 6:16; Acts 1:13; cf. Jn 14:22). The person intended is almost certainly the other Jude, named in the gospels among the relatives of Jesus (Mt 13:55; Mk 6:3), and the James who is listed there as his brother is the one to whom the Letter of James is attributed (see the Introduction to James). Nothing else is known of this Jude, and the apparent need to identify him by reference to his better-known brother indicates that he was a rather obscure personage in the early church.

The letter is addressed in the most general terms to "those who are called, beloved in God the Father and kept safe for Jesus Christ" (Jude 1), hence apparently to all Christians. But since its purpose is to warn the addressees against false teachers, the author must have had in mind one or more specific Christian communities located in the unidentified region where the errors in question constituted a danger. While the letter contains some Semitic features, there is nothing to identify the addressees specifically as Jewish Christians; indeed, the errors envisaged seem to reflect an early form of gnosticism, opposed to law, that points rather to the cultural context of the Gentile world. Like James and 2 Peter, the Letter of Jude manifests none of the typical features of the letter form, except the address.

There is so much similarity between Jude and 2 Peter, especially Jude 4–16 and 2 Pt 2:1–18, that there must be a literary relationship between them. Since there is no evidence for the view that both authors borrowed from the same source, it is usually supposed that one of them borrowed from the other. Most scholars believe that Jude is the earlier of the two, principally because he quotes two apocryphal Jewish works, the Assumption of Moses (Jude 9) and the Book of Enoch (Jude 14–15) as part of his structured argument, whereas 2 Peter omits both references. Since there was controversy in the early church about the propriety of citing noncanonical literature that included legendary material, it is more probable that a later writer would omit such references than that he would add them.

Many interpreters today consider Jude a pseudonymous work dating from the end of the first century or even later. In support of this view they adduce the following arguments: (a) the apostles are referred to as belonging to an age that has receded into the past (Jude 17–18); (b) faith is understood as a body of doctrine handed down by a process of tradition (Jude 3); (c) the author's competent Greek style shows that he must have had a Hellenistic cultural formation; (d) the gnostic character of the errors envisaged fits better into the early second century than into a period several decades earlier. While impressive, these arguments are not entirely compelling and do not completely rule out the possibility of composition around the year A.D. 80, when the historical Jude may still have been alive.

This little letter is an urgent note by an author who intended to write more fully about salvation to an unknown group of readers, but who was forced by dangers from false teachers worming their way into the community (Jude 3–4) to dash off a warning against them (Jude 5–16) and to deliver some pressing Christian admonitions (Jude 17–23). The letter is justly famous for its majestic closing doxology (Jude 24–25).

Address and Greeting. [1]*Jude, a slave of Jesus Christ and brother of James, to those who are called, beloved in God the Father and kept safe for Jesus Christ:[a] [2]may mercy, peace, and love be yours in abundance.[b]

Occasion for Writing. [3]Beloved, although I was making every effort to write to you about our common salvation,[†] I now feel a need to write to encourage you to contend for the faith that was once for all handed down to the holy ones.[c] [4]For there have been some intruders, who long ago were designated for this condemnation, godless persons, who pervert the grace of our God into licentiousness and who deny our only Master and Lord, Jesus Christ.[d]

The False Teachers. [5]*I wish to remind you, although you know all things, that [the] Lord who once saved a people from the land of Egypt later destroyed those who did not believe.[‡] [6]*The angels too, who did not keep to their own domain but deserted their proper dwelling, he has kept in eternal chains, in gloom, for the judgment of the great day.[§] [7]Likewise, Sodom, Gomorrah, and the surrounding towns, which, in the same manner as they, indulged in sexual promiscuity and practiced unnatural vice,[¶] serve as an example by undergoing a punishment of eternal fire.[g]

[8]Similarly, these dreamers** nevertheless also defile the flesh, scorn lordship, and revile glorious beings. [9]Yet the archangel Michael, when he argued with the devil in a dispute over the body of Moses, did not venture to pronounce a reviling judgment[††] upon him but said, "May the Lord rebuke you!"[h] [10]But these people revile what they do not understand and are destroyed by what they know by nature like irrational animals.[i] [11]Woe to them![j] They followed the way of Cain, abandoned themselves to Balaam's error for the sake of gain, and perished in the rebellion of Korah.[‡‡] [12]These are blemishes on your love feasts,[§§] as they carouse fearlessly and look after themselves. They are waterless clouds blown about by winds, fruitless trees in late autumn, twice dead and uprooted.[k] [13]They are like wild waves of the sea, foaming up their shameless deeds, wandering stars for whom the gloom of darkness has been reserved forever.

[14]¶¶Enoch, of the seventh generation from Adam, prophesied also about them when he said,[l] "Behold, the Lord has come with his countless holy ones [15]to execute judgment on all and to convict everyone for all the godless deeds that they committed and for all the harsh words godless sinners have uttered against him." [16]These people are complainers, disgruntled ones who live by their desires; their mouths utter bombast as they fawn over people to gain advantage.[m]

Exhortations. [17]But you, beloved, remember the words spoken beforehand by the apostles of our Lord Jesus Christ,[n] [18]for they told you,[o] "In [the] last time there will be scoffers who will live according to their own godless desires."*** [19]These are the ones who cause divisions; they live on the natural plane, devoid of the Spirit.[p] [20]But you, beloved, build yourselves up in your most holy faith; pray in the holy Spirit.[q] [21]Keep

---

*[1] **Jude . . . brother of James**: for the identity of the author of this letter, see Introduction. **To those who are called**: the vocation to the Christian faith is God's free gift to those whom he loves and whom he safely protects in Christ until the Lord's second coming.

†[3–4] **Our common salvation**: the teachings of the Christian faith derived from the apostolic preaching and to be kept by the Christian community.

‡[5] For this first example of divine punishment on those who had been saved but did not then keep faith, see Nm 14:28–29 and the note there. Some manuscripts have the word "once" (*hapax* as at Jude 3) after "you know"; some commentators have suggested that it means "knowing one thing" or "you know all things once for all." Instead of "[the] Lord" manuscripts vary, having "Jesus," "God," or no subject stated.

§[6] This second example draws on Gn 6:1–4 as elaborated in the apocryphal Book of Enoch (cf. Jude 14): heavenly beings came to earth and had sexual intercourse with women. God punished them by casting them out of heaven into darkness and bondage.

¶[7] **Practiced unnatural vice**: literally, "went after alien flesh." This example derives from Gn 19:1–25, especially 4–11, when the townsmen of Sodom violated both hospitality and morality by demanding that Lot's two visitors (really messengers of Yahweh) be handed over to them so that they could abuse them sexually. **Unnatural vice**: this refers to the desire for intimacies by human beings with angels (the reverse of the example in Jude 6). Sodom (whence "sodomy") and Gomorrah became proverbial as object lessons for God's punishment on sin (Is 1:9; Jer 50:40; Am 4:11; Mt 10:15; 2 Pt 2:6).

[8] **Dreamers: the writer returns to the false teachers of Jude 4, applying charges from the three examples in Jude 5, 6, 7. This may apply to claims they make for revelations they have received by night (to the author, hallucinations). **Defile the flesh**: this may mean bodily pollutions from the erotic dreams of sexual license (Jude 7). **Lordship . . . glorious beings**: these may reflect the Lord (Jude 5; Jesus, Jude 4)

whom they spurn and the angels (Jude 6; cf. note on 2 Pt 2:10, here, as there, literally, "glories").

††[9] **The archangel Michael . . . judgment**: a reference to an incident in the apocryphal Assumption of Moses. Dt 34:6 had said of Moses, literally in Greek, "they buried him" or "he (God?) buried him" (taken to mean "he was buried"). The later account tells how Michael, who was sent to bury him, was challenged by the devil's interest in the body. Our author draws out the point that if an archangel refrained from reviling even the devil, how wrong it is for mere human beings to revile glorious beings (angels).

‡‡[11] **Cain . . . Balaam . . . Korah**: examples of rebellious men and of the punishment their conduct incurred; cf. Gn 4:8–16; Nm 16:1–35; 31:16. See note on 2 Pt 2:15.

§§[12] **Blemishes on your love feasts**: or "hidden rocks" or "submerged reefs" (cf. Jude 13). The opponents engaged in scandalous conduct in connection with community gatherings called **love feasts** (agape meals), which were associated with eucharistic celebrations at certain stages of early Christian practice; cf. 1 Cor 11:18–34 and the note on 2 Pt 2:13.

¶¶[14–15] Cited from the apocryphal Book of Enoch 1:9.

***[18] This is the substance of much early Christian preaching rather than a direct quotation of any of the various New Testament passages on this theme (see Mk 13:22; Acts 20:30; 1 Tm 4:1–3; 2 Pt 3:3).

---

h. [9] Dn 10:21; 12:1. i. [10] 2 Pt 2:12. j. [11] Gn 4:8–16; 1 Jn 3:12 / Nm 31:15–16; 2 Pt 2:15; Rev 2:14 / Nm 16:19–35. k. [12] 2 Pt 2:13, 17. l. [14–15] Mt 16:27; Heb 12:22–23. m. [16] 18; 1 Cor 10:10; 2 Pt 2:10, 18. n. [17] Heb 2:3; 2 Pt 3:2. o. [18] 1 Tm 4:1; 2 Tm 3:1–5; 2 Pt 3:3. p. [19] 1 Cor 2:14; Jas 3:15. q. [20] 2; Eph 6:18; Col 2:7.

---

a. [1] Mt 13:55; Mk 6:3; Acts 12:17; Rom 1:7. b. [2] Gal 6:16; 1 Tm 1:2; 2 Pt 1:2. c. [3] 17, 20; 1 Tm 6:12. d. [4] Gal 2:4; 2 Tm 3:6; 2 Pt 2:1. e. [5] Nm 14:35; 1 Cor 10:5; Heb 3:16, 17. f. [6] 2 Pt 2:4, 9. g. [7] Dt 29:22–24; Mt 25:41; 2 Thes 1:8–9; 2 Pt 2:6; 3:7.

yourselves in the love of God and wait for the mercy of our Lord Jesus Christ that leads to eternal life.[r] [22]On those who waver, have mercy;* [23]save others by snatching them out of the fire; on others have mercy with fear,[†] abhorring even the outer garment stained by the flesh.

Doxology.[‡] [24]To the one who is able to keep you from stumbling and to present you unblemished and exultant, in the presence of his glory,[s] [25]to the only God, our savior, through Jesus Christ our Lord be glory, majesty, power, and authority from ages past, now, and for ages to come. Amen.[t]

---

*[22] **Have mercy:** some manuscripts read "convince," "confute," or "reprove." Others have "even though you waver" or "doubt" instead of **who waver.**

†[23] **With fear:** some manuscripts connect the phrase "with fear" with the imperative "save" or with the participle "snatching." Other manuscripts omit the phrase "on others have mercy," so that only two groups are envisioned. Rescue of those led astray and caution in the endeavor are both enjoined. **Outer garment stained by the flesh:** the imagery may come from Zec 3:3–5, just as that of **snatching . . . out of the fire** comes from Zec 3:2; the very garments of the godless are to be abhorred because of their contagion.

‡[24–25] With this liturgical statement about the power of God to keep the faithful from stumbling, and praise to him through Jesus Christ, the letter reaches its conclusion by returning to the themes with which it began (Jude 1–2).

---

r. [21] Ti 2:13.

s. [24] 2 Cor 4:14; 1 Pt 4:13.   t. [25] Rom 11:36; 1 Tm 1:17.

THE BOOK OF
REVELATION

The Apocalypse, or Revelation to John, the last book of the Bible, is one of the most difficult to understand because it abounds in unfamiliar and extravagant symbolism, which at best appears unusual to the modern reader. Symbolic language, however, is one of the chief characteristics of apocalyptic literature, of which this book is an outstanding example. Such literature enjoyed wide popularity in both Jewish and Christian circles from ca. 200 B.C. to A.D. 200.

This book contains an account of visions in symbolic and allegorical language borrowed extensively from the Old Testament, especially Ezekiel, Zechariah, and Daniel. Whether or not these visions were real experiences of the author or simply literary conventions employed by him is an open question.

This much, however, is certain: symbolic descriptions are not to be taken as literal descriptions, nor is the symbolism meant to be pictured realistically. One would find it difficult and repulsive to visualize a lamb with seven horns and seven eyes; yet Jesus Christ is described in precisely such words (Rev 5:6). The author used these images to suggest Christ's universal (seven) power (horns) and knowledge (eyes). A significant feature of apocalyptic writing is the use of symbolic colors, metals, garments (Rev 1:13–16; 3:18; 4:4; 6:1–8; 17:4; 19:8), and numbers (*four* signifies the world, *six* imperfection, *seven* totality or perfection, *twelve* Israel's tribes or the apostles, *one thousand* immensity). Finally the vindictive language in the book (Rev 6:9–10; 18:1–19:4) is also to be understood symbolically and not literally. The cries for vengeance on the lips of Christian martyrs that sound so harsh are in fact literary devices the author employed to evoke in the reader and hearer a feeling of horror for apostasy and rebellion that will be severely punished by God.

The lurid descriptions of the punishment of Jezebel (Rev 2:22) and of the destruction of the great harlot, Babylon (Rev 16:9–19:2), are likewise literary devices. The metaphor of Babylon as harlot would be wrongly construed if interpreted literally. On the other hand, the stylized figure of the woman clothed with the sun (Rev 12:1–6), depicting the New Israel, may seem to be a negative stereotype. It is necessary to look beyond the literal meaning to see that these images mean to convey a sense of God's wrath at sin in the former case and trust in God's providential care over the church in the latter.

The Book of Revelation cannot be adequately understood except against the historical background that occasioned its writing. Like Daniel and other apocalypses, it was composed as resistance literature to meet a crisis. The book itself suggests that the crisis was ruthless persecution of the early church by the Roman authorities; the harlot Babylon symbolizes pagan Rome, the city on seven hills (Rev 17:9). The book is, then, an exhortation and admonition to Christians of the first century to stand firm in the faith and to avoid compromise with paganism, despite the threat of adversity and martyrdom; they are to await patiently the fulfillment of God's mighty promises. The triumph of God in the world of men and women remains a mystery, to be accepted in faith and longed for in hope. It is a triumph that unfolded in the history of Jesus of Nazareth and continues to unfold in the history of the individual Christian who follows the way of the cross, even, if necessary, to a martyr's death.

Though the perspective is eschatological—ultimate salvation and victory are said to take place at the end of the present age when Christ will come in glory at the parousia—the book presents the decisive struggle of Christ and his followers against Satan and his cohorts as already over. Christ's overwhelming defeat of the kingdom of Satan ushered in the everlasting reign of God (Rev 11:15; 12:10). Even the forces of evil unwittingly carry out the divine plan (Rev 17:17), for God is the sovereign Lord of history.

The Book of Revelation had its origin in a time of crisis, but it remains valid and meaningful for Christians of all time. In the face of apparently insuperable evil, either from within or from without, all Christians are called to trust in Jesus' promise, "Behold, I am with you always, until the end of the age" (Mt 28:20). Those who remain steadfast in their faith and confidence in the risen Lord need have no fear. Suffering, persecution, even death by martyrdom, though remaining impenetrable mysteries of evil, do not comprise an absurd dead end. No matter what adversity or sacrifice Christians may endure, they will in the end triumph over Satan and his forces because of their fidelity to Christ the victor. This is the enduring message of the book; it is a message of hope and consolation and challenge for all who dare to believe.

The author of the book calls himself John (Rev 1:1, 4, 9; 22:8), who because of his Christian faith has been exiled to the rocky island of Patmos, a Roman penal colony. Although he never claims to be John the apostle, whose name is attached to the fourth gospel, he was so identified by several of the early church Fathers, including Justin, Irenaeus, Clement of Alexandria, Tertullian, Cyprian, and Hippolytus. This identification, however, was denied by other Fathers, including Denis of Alexandria, Eusebius of Caesarea, Cyril of Jerusalem, Gregory Nazianzen, and John Chrysostom. Indeed, vocabulary, grammar, and style make it doubtful that the book could have been put into its present form by the same person(s) responsible for the fourth gospel. Nevertheless, there are definite linguistic and theological affinities between the two books. The tone of the letters to the seven churches (Rev 1:4–3:22) is indicative of the great authority the author enjoyed over the Christian communities in Asia. It is possible, therefore, that he was a disciple of John the apostle, who is traditionally associated with that part of the world. The date of the book in its present form is probably near the end of the reign of Domitian (A.D. 81–96), a fierce persecutor of the Christians.

The principal divisions of the Book of Revelation are the following:

I. Prologue (1:1–3)
II. Letters to the Churches of Asia (1:4–3:22)
III. God and the Lamb in Heaven (4:1–5:14)
IV. The Seven Seals, Trumpets, and Plagues, with Interludes (6:1–16:21)
V. The Punishment of Babylon and the Destruction of Pagan Nations (17:1–20:15)
VI. The New Creation (21:1–22:5)
VII. Epilogue (22:6–21)

I. PROLOGUE*

CHAPTER 1

[1]The revelation of Jesus Christ, which God gave to him, to show his servants what must happen soon. He made it known by sending his angel to his servant John,[a] [2]who gives witness to the word of God and to the testimony of Jesus Christ by reporting what he saw. [3]Blessed is the one[†] who reads aloud and blessed are those who listen to this prophetic message and heed what is written in it, for the appointed time is near.[b]

---

*[1:1–3] This prologue describes the source, contents, and audience of the book and forms an inclusion with the epilogue (Rev 22:6–21), with its similar themes and expressions.

†[1:3] Blessed is the one: this is the first of seven beatitudes in this book; the others are in Rev 14:13; 16:15; 19:9; 20:6; 22:7, 14. This prophetic message: literally, "the words of the prophecy"; so Rev 22:7, 10, 18, 19 by inclusion. The appointed time: when Jesus will return in glory; cf. Rev 1:7; 3:11; 22:7, 10, 12, 20.

a. [1:1] 22:6–8, 20; Dn 2:28 / Rev 19:10. b. [1:3] 22:7 / Lk 11:28.

II. LETTERS TO THE CHURCHES OF ASIA

Greeting.[‡] [4]John, to the seven churches in Asia:[§] grace to you and peace from him who is and who was and who is to come, and from the seven spirits before his throne,[c] [5]and from Jesus Christ, the faithful witness, the firstborn of the dead and ruler of the kings of the earth. To him who loves us and has freed us[¶] from our sins by

---

‡[1:4–8] Although Revelation begins and ends (Rev 22:21) with Christian epistolary formulae, there is nothing between Rev 4; 22 resembling a letter. The author here employs the standard word order for greetings in Greek letter writing: "N. to N., greetings . . ."; see note on Rom 1:1.

§[1:4] Seven churches in Asia: Asia refers to the Roman province of that name in western Asia Minor (modern Turkey); these representative churches are mentioned by name in Rev 1:11, and each is the recipient of a message (Rev 2:1–3:22). Seven is the biblical number suggesting fullness and completeness; thus the seer is writing for the whole church.

¶[1:5] Freed us: the majority of Greek manuscripts and several early versions read "washed us"; but "freed us" is supported by the best manuscripts and fits well with Old Testament imagery, e.g., Is 40:2.

c. [1:4] 8; 4:8; 11:17; 16:5; Ex 3:14.

his blood,[d] [6]who has made us into a kingdom, priests for his God and Father, to him be glory and power forever [and ever]. Amen.[e]

[7] Behold, he is coming amid the clouds,
   and every eye will see him,
   even those who pierced him.
All the peoples of the earth will lament
   him.
   Yes. Amen.[f]

[8]"I am the Alpha and the Omega,"* says the Lord God, "the one who is and who was and who is to come, the almighty."[g]
The First Vision.[†] [9]I, John, your brother, who share with you the distress, the kingdom, and the endurance we have in Jesus, found myself on the island called Patmos[‡] because I proclaimed God's word and gave testimony to Jesus. [10]I was caught up in spirit on the Lord's day[§] and heard behind me a voice as loud as a trumpet, [11]which said, "Write on a scroll[¶] what you see and send it to the seven churches: to Ephesus, Smyrna, Pergamum, Thyatira, Sardis, Philadelphia, and Laodicea." [12]"Then I turned to see whose voice it was that spoke to me, and when I turned, I saw seven gold lampstands [13]and in the midst of the lampstands one like a son of man,[††] wearing an ankle-length robe, with a gold sash around his chest.[h] [14]The hair of his head was as white as white wool or as snow,[‡‡] and his eyes were like a fiery flame. [15]His feet were like polished brass refined in a furnace,[§§] and his voice was like

the sound of rushing water. [16]In his right hand he held seven stars.[¶¶] A sharp, two-edged sword came out of his mouth, and his face shone like the sun at its brightest.[i]
   [17]When I caught sight of him, I fell down at his feet as though dead.*** He touched me with his right hand and said, "Do not be afraid. I am the first and the last,[j] [18]the one who lives. Once I was dead, but now I am alive forever and ever. I hold the keys to death and the netherworld.[†††] [19]Write down, therefore, what you have seen, and what is happening, and what will happen afterwards.[‡‡‡] [20]This is the secret meaning[§§§] of the seven stars you saw in my right hand, and of the seven gold lampstands: the seven stars are the angels of the seven churches, and the seven lampstands are the seven churches.

CHAPTER 2

To Ephesus. [¶¶¶]"To the angel of the church**** in Ephesus,[††††] write this:
   "'The one who holds the seven stars in his right hand and walks in the midst of the seven gold lampstands says this: [2]"I know your works,

---

"refined" is unconnected grammatically with any other word in the sentence. **His voice . . . water:** Christ speaks with divine authority; cf. Ez 1:24.
   ¶¶[1:16] **Seven stars:** in the pagan world, Mithras and the Caesars were represented with seven stars in their right hand, symbolizing their universal dominion. **A sharp two-edged sword:** this refers to the word of God (cf. Eph 6:17; Heb 4:12) that will destroy unrepentant sinners; cf. Rev 2:16; 19:15; Wis 18:15; Is 11:4; 49:2. **His face . . . brightest:** this symbolizes the divine majesty of Christ; cf. Rev 10:1; 21:23; Jgs 5:31; Is 60:19; Mt 17:2.
   ***[1:17] It was an Old Testament belief that for sinful human beings to see God was to die; cf. Ex 19:21; 33:20; Jgs 6:22–23; Is 6:5.
   †††[1:18] **Netherworld:** Greek Hades, Hebrew Sheol, the abode of the dead; cf. Rev 20:13–14; Nm 16:33.
   ‡‡‡[1:19] **What you have seen, and what is happening, and what will happen afterwards:** the three parts of the Book of Revelation, the vision (Rev 1:10–20), the situation in the seven churches (Rev 2–3), and the events of Rev 6–22.
   §§§[1:20] **Secret meaning:** literally, "mystery." **Angels:** these are the presiding spirits of the seven churches. Angels were thought to be in charge of the physical world (cf. Rev 7:1; 14:18; 16:5) and of nations (Dn 10:13; 12:1), communities (the seven churches), and individuals (Mt 18:10; Acts 12:15). Some have seen in the "angel" of each of the seven churches its pastor or a personification of the spirit of the congregation.
   ¶¶¶[2:1–3:22] Each of the seven letters follows the same pattern: address; description of the exalted Christ; blame and/or praise for the church addressed; threat and/or admonition; final exhortation and promise to all Christians.
   ****[2:1–7] The letter to Ephesus praises the members of the church there for their works and virtues, including discerning false teachers (Rev 2:2–3), but admonishes them to repent and return to their former devotion (Rev 2:4–5). It concludes with a reference to the Nicolaitans (see note on Rev 2:6) and a promise that the victor will have access to eternal life (Rev 2:7).
   ††††[2:1] **Ephesus:** this great ancient city had a population of ca. 250,000; it was the capital of the Roman province of Asia and the commercial, cultural, and religious center of Asia. The other six churches were located in the same province, situated roughly in a circle; they were selected for geographical reasons rather than for the size of their Christian communities. **Walks in the midst of the seven gold lampstands:** this signifies that Christ is always present in the church; see note on Rev 1:4.

---

   *[1:8] **The Alpha and the Omega:** the first and last letters of the Greek alphabet. In Rev 22:13 the same words occur together with the expressions "the First and the Last, the Beginning and the End"; cf. Rev 1:17; 2:8; 21:6; Is 41:4; 44:6.
   †[1:9–20] In this first vision, the seer is commanded to write what he sees to the seven churches (Rev 1:9–11). He sees Christ in glory, whom he depicts in stock apocalyptic imagery (Rev 1:12–16), and hears him describe himself in terms meant to encourage Christians by emphasizing his victory over death (Rev 1:17–20).
   ‡[1:9] **Island called Patmos:** one of the Sporades islands in the Aegean Sea, some fifty miles south of Ephesus, used by the Romans as a penal colony. **Because I proclaimed God's word:** literally, "on account of God's word."
   §[1:10] **The Lord's day:** Sunday. **As loud as a trumpet:** the imagery is derived from the theophany at Sinai (Ex 19:16, 19; cf. Heb 12:19 and the trumpet in other eschatological settings in Is 27:13; Jl 2:1; Mt 24:31; 1 Cor 15:52; 1 Thes 4:16).
   ¶[1:11] **Scroll:** a papyrus roll.
   **[1:12–16] A symbolic description of Christ in glory. The metaphorical language is not to be understood literally; cf. Introduction.
   ††[1:13] **Son of man:** see note on Mk 8:31. **Ankle-length robe:** Christ is priest; cf. Ex 28:4; 29:5; Wis 18:24; Zec 3:4. **Gold sash:** Christ is king; cf. Ex 28:4; 1 Mc 10:89; 11:58; Dn 10:5.
   ‡‡[1:14] **Hair . . . as white as white wool or as snow:** Christ is eternal, clothed with the dignity that belonged to the "Ancient of Days"; cf. Rev 1:18; Dn 7:9. **His eyes were like a fiery flame:** Christ is portrayed as all-knowing; cf. Rev 2:23; Ps 7:10; Jer 17:10; and similar expressions in Rev 2:18; 19:12; cf. Dn 10:6.
   §§[1:15] **His feet . . . furnace:** Christ is depicted as unchangeable; cf. Ez 1:27; Dn 10:6. The Greek word translated

---

d. [1:5] 3:14; 1 Cor 15:20; Col 1:18 / Heb 9:14; 1 Pt 1:19; 1 Jn 1:7. e. [1:6] Ex 19:6; 1 Pt 2:9. f. [1:7] Dn 7:13 / Zec 12:10; Mt 24:30; Jn 19:37. g. [1:8] 17; 21:6; 22:13; Is 41:4; 44:6; 48:12. h. [1:13] Dn 7:13; 10:5.

i. [1:16] Heb 4:12. j. [1:17] Dn 8:18 / Rev 1:8.

your labor, and your endurance, and that you cannot tolerate the wicked; you have tested those who call themselves apostles but are not, and discovered that they are impostors.* ³Moreover, you have endurance and have suffered for my name, and you have not grown weary. ⁴Yet I hold this against you: you have lost the love you had at first. ⁵Realize how far you have fallen. Repent, and do the works you did at first. Otherwise, I will come to you and remove your lampstand from its place, unless you repent. ⁶But you have this in your favor: you hate the works of the Nicolaitans,† which I also hate.

⁷""Whoever has ears ought to hear what the Spirit says to the churches. To the victor‡ I will give the right to eat from the tree of life that is in the garden of God.""ᵏ

To Smyrna.§ ⁸"To the angel of the church in Smyrna,⁵ write this:

"The first and the last, who once died but came to life, says this: ⁹"I know your tribulation and poverty, but you are rich." I know the slander of those who claim to be Jews and are not, but rather are members of the assembly of Satan.ʲ ¹⁰Do not be afraid of anything that you are going to suffer. Indeed, the devil will throw some of you into prison, that you may be tested, and you will face an ordeal for ten days. Remain faithful until death, and I will give you the crown of life.

¹¹""Whoever has ears ought to hear what the Spirit says to the churches.ᵐ The victor shall not be harmed by the second death.""††

---

*[2:2] **Who call themselves . . . impostors:** this refers to unauthorized and perverse missionaries; cf. Acts 20:29–30.

†[2:6] **Nicolaitans:** these are perhaps the impostors of Rev 2:2; see note on Rev 2:14–15. There is little evidence for connecting this group with Nicolaus, the proselyte from Antioch, mentioned in Acts 6:5.

‡[2:7] **Victor:** referring to any Christian individual who holds fast to the faith and does God's will in the face of persecution. **The tree of life that is in the garden of God:** this is a reference to the tree in the primeval paradise (Gn 2:9); cf. Rev 22:2, 14, 19. The decree excluding humanity from the tree of life has been revoked by Christ.

§[2:8–11] The letter to Smyrna encourages the Christians in this important commercial center by telling them that although they are impoverished, they are nevertheless rich, and calls those Jews who are slandering them members of the assembly of Satan (Rev 2:9). There is no admonition; rather, the Christians are told that they will suffer much, even death, but the time of tribulation will be short compared to their eternal reward (Rev 2:10), and they will thus escape final damnation (Rev 2:11).

§[2:8] **Smyrna:** modern Izmir, ca. thirty miles north of Ephesus, and the chief city of Lydia, with a temple to the goddess Roma. It was renowned for its loyalty to Rome, and it also had a large Jewish community very hostile toward Christians.

**[2:9–10] The church in Smyrna was materially poor but spiritually rich. Accusations made by Jewish brethren there occasioned the persecution of Christians; cf. Acts 14:2, 19; 17:5, 13.

††[2:11] **The second death:** this refers to the eternal death, when sinners will receive their final punishment; cf. Rev 20:6, 14–15; 21:8.

---

k. [2:7] 11, 17, 29; 3:6, 13, 22; 13:9; Mt 11:15.   l. [2:9] Jas 2:5.   m. [2:11] 20:6, 14; 21:8.

To Pergamum.‡‡ ¹²"To the angel of the church in Pergamum,§§ write this:

"The one with the sharp two-edged sword says this: ¹³"I know that you live where Satan's throne⁵⁵ is, and yet you hold fast to my name and have not denied your faith in me, not even in the days of Antipas, my faithful witness, who was martyred among you, where Satan lives. ¹⁴"Yet I have a few things against you. You have some people there who hold to the teaching of Balaam, who instructed Balak to put a stumbling block before the Israelites: to eat food sacrificed to idols and to play the harlot.ⁿ ¹⁵Likewise, you also have some people who hold to the teaching of [the] Nicolaitans. ¹⁶Therefore, repent. Otherwise, I will come to you quickly and wage war against them with the sword of my mouth.

¹⁷""Whoever has ears ought to hear what the Spirit says to the churches. To the victor I shall give some of the hidden manna;††† I shall also give a white amulet upon which is inscribed a new name, which no one knows except the one who receives it.""ᵒ

To Thyatira.‡‡‡ ¹⁸"To the angel of the church in Thyatira,§§§ write this:

"The Son of God, whose eyes are like a fiery flame and whose feet are like polished brass,

---

‡‡[2:12–17] The letter to Pergamum praises the members of the church for persevering in their faith in Christ even in the midst of a pagan setting and in face of persecution and martyrdom (Rev 2:13). But it admonishes them about members who advocate an unprincipled morality (Rev 2:14; cf. 2 Pt 2:15; Jude 11) and others who follow the teaching of the Nicolaitans (Rev 2:15; see note there). It urges them to repent (Rev 2:16) and promises them the hidden manna and Christ's amulet (Rev 2:17).

§§[2:12] **Pergamum:** modern Bergama, ca. forty-five miles northeast of Smyrna, a center for various kinds of pagan worship. It also had an outstanding library (the word *parchment* is derived from its name).

§§[2:13] **Satan's throne:** the reference is to emperor worship and other pagan practices that flourished in Pergamum, perhaps specifically to the white marble altar erected and dedicated to Zeus by Eumenes II (197–160 B.C.).

***[2:14–15] Like Balaam, the biblical prototype of the religious compromiser (cf. Nm 25:1–3; 31:16; 2 Pt 2:15; Jude 11), the Nicolaitans in Pergamum and Ephesus (Rev 2:6) accommodated their Christian faith to paganism. They abused the principle of liberty enunciated by Paul (1 Cor 9:19–23).

†††[2:17] **The hidden manna:** this is the food of life; cf. Ps 78:24–25. **White amulet:** literally, "white stone," on which was written a magical name, whose power could be tapped by one who knew the secret name. It is used here as a symbol of victory and joy; cf. Rev 3:4–5. **New name:** this is a reference to the Christian's rebirth in Christ; cf. Rev 3:12; 19:12; Is 62:2; 65:15.

‡‡‡[2:18–29] The letter to Thyatira praises the progress in virtue of this small Christian community (Rev 2:19) but admonishes them for tolerating a false prophet who leads them astray (Rev 2:20). Her fate is sealed, but there is hope of repentance for her followers (Rev 2:21–22). Otherwise, they too shall die (Rev 2:23). They are warned against Satanic power or knowledge (Rev 2:24–25). Those who remain faithful will share in the messianic reign, having authority over nations (Rev 2:26–27), and will in fact possess Christ himself (Rev 2:8).

§§§[2:18] **Thyatira:** modern Akhisar, ca. forty miles southeast of Pergamum, a frontier town famous for its workers' guilds (cf. Acts 16:14), membership in which may have involved festal meals in pagan temples.

---

n. [2:14] Nm 22–24; 25:1–3; 31:16; 2 Pt 2:15; Jude 11.   o. [2:17] Is 62:2; 65:15.

says this: [19]"I know your works, your love, faith, service, and endurance, and that your last works are greater than the first. [20]Yet I hold this against you, that you tolerate the woman Jezebel, who calls herself a prophetess, who teaches and misleads my servants to play the harlot and to eat food sacrificed to idols.[*] [21]I have given her time to repent, but she refuses to repent of her harlotry. [22]So I will cast her on a sickbed and plunge those who commit adultery with her into intense suffering unless they repent of her works. [23]I will also put her children[†] to death. Thus shall all the churches come to know that I am the searcher of hearts and minds and that I will give each of you what your works deserve.[p] [24]But I say to the rest of you in Thyatira, who do not uphold this teaching and know nothing of the so-called deep secrets of Satan:[‡] on you I will place no further burden, [25]except that you must hold fast to what you have until I come.

[26] """To the victor,[§] who keeps to my ways[¶]
      until the end,
   I will give authority over the
      nations.[q]
[27] He will rule them with an iron rod.
   Like clay vessels will they be
      smashed,

[28]just as I received authority from my Father. And to him I will give the morning star. [29]"Whoever has ears ought to hear what the Spirit says to the churches.""

CHAPTER 3
To Sardis.[**] [1]"To the angel of the church in Sardis,[††] write this:
"'The one who has the seven spirits of God and the seven stars says this: "I know your works, that you have the reputation of being alive, but you are dead. [2]Be watchful and strengthen what

is left, which is going to die, for I have not found your works complete in the sight of my God. [3]Remember then how you accepted and heard; keep it, and repent. If you are not watchful, I will come like a thief, and you will never know at what hour I will come upon you.[r] [4]However, you have a few people in Sardis who have not soiled their garments; they will walk with me dressed in white, because they are worthy.[s]
[5]"'"The victor will thus be dressed in white,[‡‡] and I will never erase his name from the book of life but will acknowledge his name in the presence of my Father and of his angels.[t]
[6]"'"Whoever has ears ought to hear what the Spirit says to the churches.""
To Philadelphia.[§§] [7]"To the angel of the church in Philadelphia,[¶¶] write this:

   "'The holy one, the true,
      who holds the key of David,
      who opens and no one shall close,
      who closes and no one shall open,[u]

says this:
[8]"'"I know your works (behold, I have left an open door[***] before you, which no one can close). You have limited strength, and yet you have kept my word and have not denied my name. [9]Behold, I will make those of the assembly of Satan who claim to be Jews and are not, but are lying, behold I will make them come and fall prostrate at your feet, and they will realize that I love you.[v] [10]Because you have kept my message of endurance,[†††] I will keep you safe in the time of trial that is going to come to the whole world to test the inhabitants of the earth. [11]I am coming

---

[*][2:20] The scheming and treacherous Jezebel of old (cf. 1 Kgs 19:1–2; 21:1–14; 2 Kgs 9:22, 30–34) introduced pagan customs into the religion of Israel; this new Jezebel was doing the same to Christianity.

[†][2:23] **Children:** spiritual descendants.

[‡][2:24] **The so-called deep secrets of Satan:** literally, "the deep things of Satan," a scathing reference to the perverse teaching of the Nicolaitans (Rev 2:15).

[§][2:26–28] The Christian who perseveres in faith will share in Christ's messianic authority (cf. Ps 2:8–9) and resurrection victory over death, symbolized by the morning star; cf. Rev 22:16.

[¶][2:26] **Who keeps to my ways:** literally, "who keeps my works."

[**] The letter to Sardis does not praise the community but admonishes its members to watchfulness, mutual support, and repentance (Rev 3:2–3). The few who have remained pure and faithful will share Christ's victory and will be inscribed in the book of life (Rev 3:4–5).

[††][3:1] **Sardis:** this city, located ca. thirty miles southeast of Thyatira, was once the capital of Lydia, known for its wealth at the time of Croesus (6th century B.C.). Its citadel, reputed to be unassailable, was captured by surprise, first by Cyrus and later by Antiochus. The church is therefore warned to be on guard.

[‡‡][3:5] **In white:** white is a sign of victory and joy as well as resurrection; see note on Rev 2:17. **The book of life:** the roll in which the names of the redeemed are kept; cf. Rev 13:8; 17:8; 20:12, 15; 21:27; Phil 4:3; Dn 12:1. They will be acknowledged by Christ in heaven; cf. Mt 10:32.

[§§][3:7–13] The letter to Philadelphia praises the Christians there for remaining faithful even with their limited strength (Rev 3:8). Members of the assembly of Satan are again singled out (Rev 3:9; see Rev 2:9). There is no admonition; rather, the letter promises that they will be kept safe at the great trial (Rev 3:10–11) and that the victors will become pillars of the heavenly temple, upon which three names will be inscribed: God, Jerusalem, and Christ (Rev 3:12).

[¶¶][3:7] **Philadelphia:** modern Alasehir, ca. thirty miles southeast of Sardis, founded by Attalus II Philadelphus of Pergamum to be an "open door" (Rev 3:8) for Greek culture; it was destroyed by an earthquake in A.D. 17. Rebuilt by money from the Emperor Tiberius, the city was renamed Neo-Caesarea; this may explain the allusions to "name" in Rev 3:12. **Key of David:** to the heavenly city of David (cf. Is 22:22), "the new Jerusalem" (Rev 3:12), over which Christ has supreme authority.

[***][3:8] **An open door:** opportunities for sharing and proclaiming the faith; cf. Acts 14:27; 1 Cor 16:9; 2 Cor 2:12.

[†††][3:10] **My message of endurance:** this does not refer to a saying of Jesus about patience but to the example of Christ's patient endurance. **The inhabitants of the earth:** literally, "those who live on the earth." This expression, which also occurs in Rev 6:10; 8:13; 11:10; 13:8, 12, 14; 17:2, 8, always refers to the pagan world.

---

r. [3:3] Mt 24:42–44; Mk 13:33; 1 Thes 5:2; 2 Pt 3:10.   s. [3:4] 7:13–14.   t. [3:5] Ps 69:29; Dn 12:1 / Mt 10:32.   u. [3:7] Is 22:22; Mt 16:19.   v. [3:9] 2:9 / Is 45:14; 60:14.

---

p. [2:23] 1 Sm 16:7; Jer 11:20; 17:10.   q. [2:26] 12:5; Ps 2:8–9.

quickly. Hold fast to what you have, so that no one may take your crown."

¹²"'The victor I will make into a pillar* in the temple of my God, and he will never leave it again. On him I will inscribe the name of my God and the name of the city of my God, the new Jerusalem, which comes down out of heaven from my God, as well as my new name.ˣ ¹³"'Whoever has ears ought to hear what the Spirit says to the churches.'"

To Laodicea.† ¹⁴"To the angel of the church in Laodicea,‡ write this:

"'The Amen, the faithful and true witness, the source of God's creation, says this:ʸ ¹⁵"'I know your works; I know that you are neither cold nor hot.§ I wish you were either cold or hot. ¹⁶§So, because you are lukewarm, neither hot nor cold, I will spit you out of my mouth. ¹⁷**ᶻFor you say, 'I am rich and affluent and have no need of anything,' and yet do not realize that you are wretched, pitiable, poor, blind, and naked. ¹⁸I advise you to buy from me gold refined by fire†† so that you may be rich, and white garments to put on so that your shameful nakedness may not be exposed, and buy ointment to smear on your eyes so that you may see. ¹⁹Those whom I love, I reprove and chastise. Be earnest, therefore, and repent.ᵃ

²⁰"'Behold, I stand at the door and knock. If anyone hears my voice and opens the door, [then] I will enter his house and dine with him,

---

*[3:12] **Pillar**: this may be an allusion to the rebuilding of the city; see note on v 7. **New Jerusalem**: it is described in Rev 21:10–22:5.

†[3:14–22] The letter to Laodicea reprimands the community for being lukewarm (Rev 3:15–16), but no particular faults are singled out. Their material prosperity is contrasted with their spiritual poverty, the violet tunics that were the source of their wealth with the white robe of baptism, and their famous eye ointment with true spiritual perception (Rev 3:17–18). But Christ's chastisement is inspired by love and a desire to be allowed to share the messianic banquet with his followers in the heavenly kingdom (Rev 3:9–21).

‡[3:14] **Laodicea**: ca. forty miles southeast of Philadelphia and ca. eighty miles east of Ephesus, a wealthy industrial and commercial center, with a renowned medical school. It exported fine woolen garments and was famous for its eye salves. It was so wealthy that it was proudly rebuilt without outside aid after the devastating earthquake of A.D. 60/61. **The Amen**: this is a divine title (cf. Hebrew text of Is 65:16) applied to Christ; cf. 2 Cor 1:20. **Source of God's creation**: literally, "the beginning of God's creation," a concept found also in Jn 1:3; Col 1:16–17; Heb 1:2; cf. Prv 8:22–31; Wis 9:1–2.

§[3:15–16] Halfhearted commitment to the faith is nauseating to Christ; cf. Rom 12:11.

¶[3:16] **Spit**: literally, "vomit." The image is that of a beverage that should be either hot or cold. Perhaps there is an allusion to the hot springs of Hierapolis across the Lycus river from Laodicea, which would have been lukewarm by the time they reached Laodicea.

**[3:17] Economic prosperity occasioned spiritual bankruptcy.

††[3:18] **Gold . . . fire**: God's grace. **White garments**: symbol of an upright life; the city was noted for its violet/purple cloth. **Ointment . . . eyes**: to remove spiritual blindness; one of the city's exports was eye ointment (see note on Rev 3:14).

w. [3:11] 2:25; 22:7, 20.　x. [3:12] 21:2–3; Ez 48:35 / Rev 19:13. y. [3:14] 1:5.　z. [3:17] Prv 13:7; Lk 12:21.　a. [3:19] Prv 3:11–12; 1 Cor 11:32; Heb 12:5–11.

---

and he with me.‡‡ ²¹I will give the victor the right to sit with me on my throne, as I myself first won the victory and sit with my Father on his throne.ᵇ

²²"'Whoever has ears ought to hear what the Spirit says to the churches.'"'"

III. GOD AND THE LAMB IN HEAVEN

CHAPTER 4

Vision of Heavenly Worship.§§ ¹After this I had a vision of an open door¶¶ to heaven, and I heard the trumpetlike voice that had spoken to me before, saying, "Come up here and I will show you what must happen afterwards." ²***At once I was caught up in spirit.ᶜ A throne was there in heaven, and on the throne sat ³one whose appearance sparkled like jasper and carnelian. Around the throne was a halo as brilliant as an emerald. ⁴Surrounding the throne I saw twenty-four other thrones on which twenty-four elders††† sat, dressed in white garments and with gold crowns on their heads.ᵈ ⁵From the throne came flashes of lightning, rumblings, and peals of thunder.‡‡‡ Seven flaming torches burned in front of the throne, which are the seven spirits of God. ⁶In front of the throne was something that resembled a sea of glass like crystal.§§§

In the center and around the throne, there were four living creatures covered with eyes in front and in back. ⁷The first creature resembled a lion, the second was like a calf, the third had a face like that of a human being, and the fourth looked like an eagle¶¶¶ in flight. ⁸The four living

---

‡‡[3:20] Christ invites all to the messianic banquet in heaven; cf. Is 25:6; Lk 14:15; 22:30.

§§[4:1–11] The seer now describes a vision of the heavenly court in worship of God enthroned. He reverently avoids naming or describing God but pictures twenty-four elders in priestly and regal attire (Rev 4:4) and God's throne and its surroundings made of precious gems and other symbols that traditionally express the majesty of God (Rev 4:5–6). Universal creation is represented by the four living creatures (Rev 4:6–7). Along with the twenty-four elders, they praise God unceasingly in humble adoration (Rev 4:8–11).

¶¶[4:1] The ancients viewed heaven as a solid vault, entered by way of actual doors.

***[4:2–8] Much of the imagery here is taken from Ez 1; 10.

†††[4:4] **Twenty-four elders**: these represent the twelve tribes of Israel and the twelve apostles; cf. Rev 21:12–14.

‡‡‡[4:5] **Flashes of lightning, rumblings, and peals of thunder**: as in other descriptions of God's appearance or activity; cf. Rev 8:5; 11:19; 16:18; Ex 19:16; Ez 1:4, 13. **The seven spirits of God**: the seven "angels of the presence" as in Rev 8:2 and Tb 12:15.

§§§[4:6] **A sea of glass like crystal**: an image adapted from Ez 1:22–26. **Four living creatures**: these are symbols taken from Ez 1:5–21; they are identified as cherubim in Ez 10:20. **Covered with eyes**: these suggest God's knowledge and concern.

¶¶¶[4:7] **Lion . . . calf . . . human being . . . eagle**: these symbolize, respectively, what is noblest, strongest, wisest, and swiftest in creation. **Calf**: traditionally translated "ox," the Greek word refers to a heifer or young bull. Since the second century, these four creatures have been used as symbols of the evangelists Mark, Luke, Matthew, and John, respectively.

b. [3:21] Lk 22:28–30; Mt 19:28.　c. [4:2–3] Is 6:1 / Ez 1:26–28. d. [4:4] Is 24:23.　e. [4:6] Ex 24:10.

creatures, each of them with six wings,* were covered with eyes inside and out. Day and night they do not stop exclaiming:

> "Holy, holy, holy is the Lord God
>   almighty,
>   who was, and who is, and who is to
>   come."f

9Whenever the living creatures give glory and honor and thanks to the one who sits on the throne, who lives forever and ever, 10the twenty-four elders fall down before the one who sits on the throne and worship him, who lives forever and ever. They throw down their crowns before the throne, exclaiming:

11 "Worthy are you, Lord our God,
>   to receive glory and honor and
>   power,
>   for you created all things;
>   because of your will they came to be
>   and were created."g

CHAPTER 5

The Scroll and the Lamb.† 1I saw a scroll‡ in the right hand of the one who sat on the throne. It had writing on both sides and was sealed with seven seals.h 2Then I saw a mighty angel who proclaimed in a loud voice, "Who is worthy to open the scroll and break its seals?" 3But no one in heaven or on earth or under the earth was able to open the scroll or to examine it. 4I shed many tears because no one was found worthy to open the scroll or to examine it. 5One of the elders said to me, "Do not weep. The lion of the tribe of Judah, the root of David,§ has triumphed, enabling him to open the scroll with its seven seals."i

6Then I saw standing in the midst of the throne and the four living creatures and the

elders a Lamb⁵ that seemed to have been slain. He had seven horns and seven eyes; these are the [seven] spirits of God sent out into the whole world.j 7He came and received the scroll from the right hand of the one who sat on the throne. 8When he took it, the four living creatures and the twenty-four elders fell down before the Lamb. Each of the elders held a harp and gold bowls filled with incense, which are the prayers of the holy ones. 9They sang a new hymn:

> "Worthy are you to receive the scroll
>   and to break open its seals,
>   for you were slain and with your
>   blood you purchased for God
>   those from every tribe and tongue,
>   people and nation.
> 10 You made them a kingdom and priests for
>   our God,
>   and they will reign on earth."k

11I looked again and heard the voices of many angels who surrounded the throne and the living creatures and the elders. They were countless** in number,l 12and they cried out in a loud voice:

> "Worthy is the Lamb that was slain
>   to receive power and riches, wisdom
>   and strength,
>   honor and glory and blessing."

13Then I heard every creature in heaven and on earth and under the earth and in the sea, everything in the universe, cry out:

> "To the one who sits on the throne and to
>   the Lamb
>   be blessing and honor, glory and
>   might,
>   forever and ever."

14The four living creatures answered, "Amen," and the elders fell down and worshiped.

IV. THE SEVEN SEALS, TRUMPETS, AND PLAGUES, WITH INTERLUDES††

---

*[4:8] **Six wings:** like the seraphim of Is 6:2.

†[5:1–14] The seer now describes a papyrus roll in God's right hand (Rev 5:1) with seven seals indicating the importance of the message. A mighty angel asks who is worthy to open the scroll, i.e., who can accomplish God's salvific plan (Rev 5:2). There is despair at first when no one in creation can do it (Rev 5:3–4). But the seer is comforted by an elder who tells him that Christ, called the lion of the tribe of Judah, has won the right to open it (Rev 5:5). Christ then appears as a Lamb, coming to receive the scroll from God (Rev 5:6–7), for which he is acclaimed as at a coronation (Rev 5:8–10). This is followed by a doxology of the angels (Rev 5:11–12) and then finally by the heavenly church united with all of creation (Rev 5:13–14).

‡[5:1] **A scroll:** a papyrus roll possibly containing a list of afflictions for sinners (cf. Ez 2:9–10) or God's plan for the world. **Sealed with seven seals:** it is totally hidden from all but God. Only the Lamb (Rev 5:7–9) has the right to carry out the divine plan.

§[5:5] **The lion of the tribe of Judah, the root of David:** these are the messianic titles applied to Christ to symbolize his victory; cf. Rev 22:16; Gn 49:9; Is 11:1, 10; Mt 1:1.

f. [4:8] Is 6:2–3 / Rev 1:4, 8; 11:17; 16:5.   g. [4:11] Rom 4:17; 16:27.
h. [5:1] Is 29:11.   i. [5:5] Is 11:1, 10; Rom 15:12.

¶[5:6] Christ is the Paschal Lamb without blemish, whose blood saved the new Israel from sin and death; cf. Ex 12; Is 53:7; Jn 1:29, 36; Acts 8:32; 1 Pt 1:18–19. This is the main title for Christ in Revelation, used twenty-eight times. **Seven horns and seven eyes:** Christ has the fullness (see note on Rev 1:4) of power (horns) and knowledge (eyes); cf. Zec 4:7. **[Seven] spirits:** as in Rev 1:4; 3:1; 4:5.

[5:11] **Countless: literally, "100,000,000 plus 1,000,000," used by the author to express infinity.

††[6:1–16:21] A series of seven disasters now begins as each seal is broken (Rev 6:1–8:1), followed by a similar series as seven trumpets sound (Rev 8:2–11:19) and as seven angels pour bowls on the earth causing plagues (Rev 15:1–16:21). These gloomy sequences are interrupted by longer or shorter

j. [5:6] Jn 1:29.   k. [5:10] 1:6; Ex 19:6; Is 61:6.   l. [5:11] Dn 7:10; Jude 14–15.

CHAPTER 6*

The First Six Seals. [1*]Then I watched while the Lamb broke open the first of the seven seals, and I heard one of the four living creatures cry out in a voice like thunder, "Come forward." [2]I looked, and there was a white horse, and its rider had a bow.[‡] He was given a crown, and he rode forth victorious to further his victories.[m]

[3]When he broke open the second seal, I heard the second living creature cry out, "Come forward." [4*n]Another horse came out, a red one. Its rider was given power to take peace away from the earth, so that people would slaughter one another. And he was given a huge sword.

[5]When he broke open the third seal, I heard the third living creature cry out, "Come forward." I looked, and there was a black horse,[§] and its rider held a scale in his hand. [6]I heard what seemed to be a voice in the midst of the four living creatures. It said, "A ration of wheat costs a day's pay,** and three rations of barley cost a day's pay. But do not damage the olive oil or the wine."[o]

[7]When he broke open the fourth seal, I heard the voice of the fourth living creature cry out, "Come forward." [8]I looked, and there was a pale green[††] horse. Its rider was named Death, and Hades accompanied him. They were given authority over a quarter of the earth, to kill with sword, famine, and plague, and by means of the beasts of the earth.[p]

[9]When he broke open the fifth seal, I saw underneath the altar[‡‡] the souls of those who had been slaughtered because of the witness they bore to the word of God. [10]They cried out in a loud voice, "How long will it be, holy and true master,[§§] before you sit in judgment and avenge our blood on the inhabitants of the earth?" [11]Each of them was given a white robe, and they were told to be patient a little while longer until the number was filled of their fellow servants and brothers who were going to be killed as they had been.

[12¶]Then I watched while he broke open the sixth seal, and there was a great earthquake; the sun turned as black as dark sackcloth*** and the whole moon became like blood.[q] [13]The stars in the sky fell to the earth like unripe figs[†††] shaken loose from the tree in a strong wind. [14]Then the sky was divided[‡‡‡] like a torn scroll curling up, and every mountain and island was moved from its place.[r] [15]The kings of the earth, the nobles,[§§§] the military officers, the rich, the powerful, and every slave and free person hid themselves in caves and among mountain crags. [16]They cried out to the mountains and the rocks, "Fall on us and hide us from the face of the one who sits on the throne and from the wrath of the Lamb,[s] [17]because the great day of their[¶¶¶] wrath has come and who can withstand it?"

CHAPTER 7****

The 144,000 Sealed. [1]After this I saw four angels

---

scenes suggesting the triumph of God and his witnesses (e.g., Rev 7; 10; 11; 12; 13; 14).

*[6:1–17] This chapter provides a symbolic description of the contents of the sealed scroll. The breaking of the first four seals reveals four riders. The first rider (of a white horse) is a conquering power (Rev 6:1–2), the second (red horse) a symbol of bloody war (Rev 6:3–4), the third (black horse) a symbol of famine (Rev 6:5–6), the fourth (pale green horse) a symbol of Death himself, accompanied by Hades (the netherworld) as his page (Rev 6:7–8). Rev 6:8b summarizes the role of all four riders. The breaking of the fifth seal reveals Christian martyrs in an attitude of sacrifice as blood poured out at the foot of an altar begging God for vindication, which will come only when their quota is filled; but they are given a white robe symbolic of victory (Rev 6:9–11). The breaking of the sixth seal reveals typical apocalyptic signs in the sky and the sheer terror of all people at the imminent divine judgment (Rev 6:12–17).

†[6:1–8] The imagery is adapted from Zec 1:8–10; 6:1–8.

‡[6:2] **White horse . . . bow:** this may perhaps allude specifically to the Parthians on the eastern border of the Roman empire. Expert in the use of the bow, they constantly harassed the Romans and won a major victory in A.D. 62; see note on Rev 9:13–21. But the Old Testament imagery typifies the history of oppression of God's people at all times.

§[6:4] **Huge sword:** this is a symbol of war and violence; cf. Ez 21:14–17.

§[6:5] **Black horse:** this is a symbol of famine, the usual accompaniment of war in antiquity; cf. Lv 26:26; Ez 4:12–13. The **scale** is a symbol of shortage of food with a corresponding rise in price.

[6:6] **A day's pay: literally, "a denarius," a Roman silver coin that constitutes a day's wage in Mt 20:2. Because of the famine, food was rationed and sold at an exorbitant price. A liter of flour was considered a day's ration in the Greek historians Herodotus and Diogenes Laertius. **Barley:** food of the poor (Jn 6:9, 13; cf. 2 Kgs 7:1, 16, 18); it was also used to feed animals; cf. 1 Kgs 5:8. **Do not damage:** the olive and the vine are to be used more sparingly in time of famine.

††[6:8] **Pale green:** symbol of death and decay; cf. Ez 14:21.

‡‡[6:9] **The altar:** this altar corresponds to the altar of holocausts in the temple in Jerusalem; see also Rev 11:1. **Because of the witness . . . word of God:** literally, "because of the word of God and the witness they had borne."

§§[6:10] **Holy and true master:** Old Testament usage as well as the context indicates that this is addressed to God rather than to Christ.

¶¶[6:12–14] Symbolic rather than literal description of the cosmic upheavals attending the day of the Lord when the martyrs' prayer for vindication (Rev 6:10) would be answered; cf. Am 8:8–9; Is 34:4; 50:3; Jl 2:10; 3:3–4; Mt 24:4–36; Mk 13:5–37; Lk 21:8–36.

***[6:12] **Dark sackcloth:** for mourning, sackcloth was made from the skin of a black goat.

†††[6:13] **Unripe figs:** literally, "summer (or winter) fruit."

‡‡‡[6:14] **Was divided:** literally, "was split," like a broken papyrus roll torn in two, each half then curling up to form a roll on either side.

§§§[6:15] **Nobles:** literally, "courtiers," "grandees." **Military officers:** literally, "commanders of 1,000 men," used in Josephus and other Greek authors as the equivalent of the Roman *tribunus militum.* The listing of various ranks of society represents the universality of terror at the impending doom.

¶¶¶[6:17] **Their:** this reading is attested in the best manuscripts, but the vast majority read "his" in reference to the wrath of the Lamb in the preceding verse.

****[7:1–17] An interlude of two visions precedes the breaking of the seventh seal, just as two more will separate the sixth and seventh trumpets (Rev 10). In the first vision (Rev 7:1–8), the elect receive the seal of the living God as protection against the coming cataclysm; cf. Rev 14:1; Ez 9:4–6; 2 Cor 1:22; Eph 1:13; 4:30. The second vision (Rev 7:9–17) portrays the faithful Christians before God's throne to encourage those on earth to persevere to the end, even to death.

---

m. [6:2] Zec 1:8–10; 6:1–3.   n. [6:4] Ez 21:14–16.   o. [6:6] Lv 26:26; Ez 4:16–17.

p. [6:8] Ez 14:21.   q. [6:12] Jl 3:4; Mt 24:29.   r. [6:14] Is 34:4 / Rev 16:20.   s. [6:16] Is 2:19; Hos 10:8; Lk 23:30.

standing at the four corners of the earth,* holding back the four winds of the earth so that no wind could blow on land or sea or against any tree.[t] [2]Then I saw another angel come up from the East,[†] holding the seal of the living God. He cried out in a loud voice to the four angels who were given power to damage the land and the sea, [3]"Do not damage the land or the sea or the trees until we put the seal on the foreheads of the servants of our God."[u] [4]I heard the number of those who had been marked with the seal, one hundred and forty-four thousand marked[‡] from every tribe of the Israelites:[v] [5]twelve thousand were marked from the tribe of Judah,[§] twelve thousand from the tribe of Reuben, twelve thousand from the tribe of Gad, [6]twelve thousand from the tribe of Asher, twelve thousand from the tribe of Naphtali, twelve thousand from the tribe of Manasseh, [7]twelve thousand from the tribe of Simeon, twelve thousand from the tribe of Levi, twelve thousand from the tribe of Issachar, [8]twelve thousand from the tribe of Zebulun, twelve thousand from the tribe of Joseph, and twelve thousand were marked from the tribe of Benjamin.

Triumph of the Elect. [9]After this I had a vision of a great multitude, which no one could count, from every nation, race, people, and tongue. They stood before the throne and before the Lamb, wearing white robes and holding palm branches[ſ] in their hands. [10]They cried out in a loud voice:

"Salvation comes from** our God, who is
seated on the throne,
and from the Lamb."

[11]All the angels stood around the throne and around the elders and the four living creatures. They prostrated themselves before the throne, worshiped God, [12]and exclaimed:

"Amen. Blessing and glory, wisdom and
thanksgiving,
honor, power, and might

be to our God forever and ever.
Amen."

[13]Then one of the elders spoke up and said to me, "Who are these wearing white robes, and where did they come from?" [14]I said to him, "My lord, you are the one who knows." He said to me, "These are the ones who have survived the time of great distress;[††] they have washed their robes and made them white in the blood of the Lamb.[w]

[15] "For this reason they stand before God's
throne
and worship him day and night in
his temple.
The one who sits on the throne will
shelter them.
[16] They will not hunger or thirst anymore,
nor will the sun or any heat strike
them.[x]
[17] For the Lamb who is in the center of the
throne will shepherd them
and lead them to springs of life-
giving water,[‡‡]
and God will wipe away every tear
from their eyes."[y]

CHAPTER 8[§§]
The Seven Trumpets. [1]When he broke open the seventh seal, there was silence in heaven[ſſ] for about half an hour.[z] [2]And I saw that the seven angels who stood before God were given seven trumpets.[a]
The Gold Censer. [3]Another angel came and stood at the altar,*** holding a gold censer. He was given a great quantity of incense to offer, along with the prayers of all the holy ones, on the gold altar that was before the throne.[b] [4]The smoke of the incense along with the prayers of the holy ones went up before God from the hand of the angel. [5]Then the angel took the censer, filled it with burning coals from the altar, and

---

*[7:1] **The four corners of the earth**: the earth is seen as a table or rectangular surface.
†[7:2] **East**: literally, "rising of the sun." The east was considered the source of light and the place of paradise (Gn 2:8). **Seal**: whatever was marked by the impression of one's signet ring belonged to that person and was under his protection.
‡[7:4–9] **One hundred and forty-four thousand**: the square of twelve (the number of Israel's tribes) multiplied by a thousand, symbolic of the new Israel (cf. Rev 14:1–5; Gal 6:16; Jas 1:1) that embraces people **from every nation, race, people, and tongue** (Rev 7:9).
§[7:5–8] Judah is placed first because of Christ; cf. "the Lion of the tribe of Judah" (Rev 5:5). Dan is omitted because of a later tradition that the antichrist would arise from it.
ſ[7:9] **White robes . . . palm branches**: symbols of joy and victory; see note on Rev 3:5.
[7:10] **Salvation comes from: literally, "(let) salvation (be ascribed) to." A similar hymn of praise is found at the fall of the dragon (Rev 12:10) and of Babylon (Rev 19:1).

††[7:14] **Time of great distress**: fierce persecution by the Romans; cf. Introduction.
‡‡[7:17] **Life-giving water**: literally, "the water of life," God's grace, which flows from Christ; cf. Rev 21:6; 22:1, 17; Jn 4:10, 14.
§§[8:1–13] The breaking of the seventh seal produces at first silence and then seven symbolic disasters, each announced by a trumpet blast, of which the first four form a unit as did the first four seals. A minor liturgy (Rev 8:3–5) is enclosed by a vision of seven angels (Rev 8:2, 6). Then follow the first four trumpet blasts, each heralding catastrophes modeled on the plagues of Egypt affecting the traditional prophetic third (cf. Ez 5:12) of the earth, sea, fresh water, and stars (Rev 8:7–12). Finally, there is a vision of an eagle warning of the last three trumpet blasts (Rev 8:13).
ſſ[8:1] **Silence in heaven**: as in Zep 1:7, a prelude to the eschatological woes that are to follow; cf. Introduction.
***[8:3] **Altar**: there seems to be only one altar in the heavenly temple, corresponding to the altar of holocausts in Rev 6:9, and here to the altar of incense in Jerusalem; cf. also Rev 9:13; 11:1; 14:18; 16:7.

---

t. [7:1] Jer 49:36; Zec 6:5. u. [7:3] Ex 12:7–14; Ez 9:4; 2 Cor 1:22; Eph 1:13; 4:30. v. [7:4] 14:1.

w. [7:14] Mt 24:21. x. [7:16] Is 49:10. y. [7:17] 21:4; Is 25:8. z. [8:1] Heb 2:20; Zep 1:7; Zec 2:17. a. [8:2] 4:5; Tb 12:15. b. [8:3] Ps 141:2; Tb 12:12.

hurled it down to the earth. There were peals of thunder, rumblings, flashes of lightning, and an earthquake.*

The First Four Trumpets. ⁶The seven angels who were holding the seven trumpets prepared to blow them.*

⁷When the first one blew his trumpet, there came hail and fire mixed with blood, which was hurled down to the earth. A third of the land was burned up, along with a third of the trees and all green grass.*

⁸†When the second angel blew his trumpet, something like a large burning mountain was hurled into the sea. A third of the sea turned to blood,* ⁹a third of the creatures living in the sea‡ died, and a third of the ships were wrecked.

¹⁰When the third angel blew his trumpet, a large star burning like a torch fell from the sky. It fell on a third of the rivers and on the springs of water.* ¹¹The star was called "Wormwood,"§ and a third of all the water turned to wormwood. Many people died from this water, because it was made bitter.*

¹²When the fourth angel blew his trumpet, a third of the sun, a third of the moon, and a third of the stars were struck, so that a third of them became dark. The day lost its light for a third of the time, as did the night.*

¹³Then I looked again and heard an eagle flying high overhead cry out in a loud voice, "Woe! Woe! Woe§ to the inhabitants of the earth from the rest of the trumpet blasts that the three angels are about to blow!"

CHAPTER 9
The Fifth Trumpet.** ¹Then the fifth angel blew his trumpet, and I saw a star†† that had fallen from the sky to the earth. It was given the key

for the passage to the abyss. ²It opened the passage to the abyss,* and smoke came up out of the passage like smoke from a huge furnace. The sun and the air were darkened by the smoke from the passage.* ³Locusts came out of the smoke onto the land, and they were given the same power as scorpions‡‡ of the earth.* ⁴They were told not to harm the grass of the earth or any plant or any tree, but only those people who did not have the seal of God on their foreheads. ⁵They were not allowed to kill them but only to torment them for five months;§§ the torment they inflicted was like that of a scorpion when it stings a person. ⁶During that time these people will seek death but will not find it, and they will long to die but death will escape them.*

⁷§§The appearance of the locusts was like that of horses ready for battle. On their heads they wore what looked like crowns of gold; their faces were like human faces,* ⁸and they had hair like women's hair. Their teeth were like lions' teeth,* ⁹and they had chests like iron breastplates. The sound of their wings was like the sound of many horse-drawn chariots racing into battle. ¹⁰They had tails like scorpions, with stingers; with their tails they had power to harm people for five months. ¹¹They had as their king the angel of the abyss, whose name in Hebrew is Abaddon*** and in Greek Apollyon.

¹²The first woe has passed, but there are two more to come.

The Sixth Trumpet.††† ¹³Then the sixth angel blew his trumpet, and I heard a voice coming from the [four]‡‡‡ horns of the gold altar before God,* ¹⁴telling the sixth angel who held the trumpet, "Release the four angels§§§ who are bound at the banks of the great river Euphrates." ¹⁵So the four angels were released, who were prepared for this hour, day, month, and year to kill a third of the human race. ¹⁶The number of cavalry troops was two hundred million; I heard their number. ¹⁷Now in my vision this is how I saw the horses and their riders. They wore red,

---

*[8:7] This woe resembles the seventh plague of Egypt (Ex 9:23–24); cf. Jl 3:3.

†[8:8–11] The background of these two woes is the first plague of Egypt (Ex 7:20–21).

‡[8:9] **Creatures living in the sea**: literally, "creatures in the sea that had souls."

§[8:11] **Wormwood**: an extremely bitter and malignant plant symbolizing the punishment God inflicts on the ungodly; cf. Jer 9:12–14; 23:15.

¶[8:13] **Woe! Woe! Woe**: each of the three woes pronounced by the angel represents a separate disaster; cf. Rev 9:12; 11:14. The final woe, released by the seventh trumpet blast, includes the plagues of Rev 16.

**[9:1–12] The fifth trumpet heralds a woe containing elements from the eighth and ninth plagues of Egypt (Ex 10:12–15, 21–23) but specifically reminiscent of the invasion of locusts in Jl 1:4–2:10.

††[9:1] **A star**: late Judaism represented fallen powers as stars (Is 14:12–15; Lk 10:18; Jude 13), but a comparison with Rev 1:20 and Rev 20:1 suggests that here it means an angel. **The passage to the abyss**: referring to Sheol, the netherworld, where Satan and the fallen angels are kept for a thousand years, to be cast afterwards into the pool of fire; cf. Rev 20:7–10. The abyss was conceived of as a vast subterranean cavern full of fire. Its only link with the earth was a kind of passage or mine shaft, which was kept locked.

c. [8:5] Ez 10:2; Ps 11:6 / Rev 4:5; 11:19; 16:18.   d. [8:6] 16:1–21.
e. [8:8] Ex 7:20.   f. [8:10] Is 14:12.   g. [8:11] Jer 9:14.   h. [8:12] Ex 10:21–23.

---

††[9:3] **Scorpions**: their poisonous sting was proverbial; Ez 2:6; Lk 11:12.

§§[9:5] **For five months**: more or less corresponding to the life-span of locusts.

¶¶[9:7–10] Eight characteristics are listed to show the eschatological and diabolical nature of these locusts.

***[9:11] **Abaddon**: Hebrew (more precisely, Aramaic) for destruction or ruin. **Apollyon**: Greek for the "Destroyer."

†††[9:13–21] The sixth trumpet heralds a woe representing another diabolical attack symbolized by an invasion by the Parthians living east of the Euphrates; see note on Rev 6:2. At the appointed time (Rev 9:15), the frightful horses act as God's agents of judgment. The imaginative details are not to be taken literally; see Introduction and the note on Rev 6:12–14.

‡‡‡[9:13] **[Four]**: many Greek manuscripts and versions omit the word. The horns were situated at the four corners of the altar (Ex 27:2; 30:2–3); see note on Rev 8:3.

§§§[9:14–15] **The four angels**: they are symbolic of the destructive activity that will be extended throughout the universe.

i. [9:2] 20:1.   j. [9:2] Gn 19:28.   k. [9:3] Ex 10:12–15; Wis 16:9.
l. [9:6] Jb 3:21.   m. [9:7] Jl 2:4.   n. [9:8] Jl 1:6.   o. [9:13] Ex 30:1–3.

blue, and yellow breastplates,* and the horses' heads were like heads of lions, and out of their mouths came fire, smoke, and sulfur.* [18]By these three plagues of fire, smoke, and sulfur that came out of their mouths a third of the human race was killed. [19]For the power of the horses is in their mouths and in their tails; for their tails are like snakes, with heads that inflict harm.

[20]The rest of the human race, who were not killed by these plagues, did not repent of the works of their hands,† to give up the worship of demons and idols made from gold, silver, bronze, stone, and wood, which cannot see or hear or walk.* [21]Nor did they repent of their murders, their magic potions, their unchastity, or their robberies.

CHAPTER 10

The Angel with the Small Scroll. [1‡]Then I saw another mighty angel come down from heaven wrapped in a cloud, with a halo around his head; his face was like the sun and his feet were like pillars of fire. [2]In his hand he held a small scroll that had been opened. He placed his right foot on the sea and his left foot on the land,§ [3]and then he cried out in a loud voice as a lion roars. When he cried out, the seven thunders¶ raised their voices, too.* [4]When the seven thunders had spoken, I was about to write it down; but I heard a voice from heaven say, "Seal up what the seven thunders have spoken, but do not write it down." [5]Then the angel I saw standing on the sea and on the land raised his right hand to heaven [6]and swore by the one who lives forever and ever, who created heaven and earth and sea** and all that is in them, "There shall be no more delay.* [7]At the time when you hear the seventh angel blow his trumpet, the mysterious plan of God††

shall be fulfilled, as he promised to his servants the prophets."*

[8]Then the voice that I had heard from heaven spoke to me again and said, "Go, take the scroll that lies open in the hand of the angel who is standing on the sea and on the land." [9]So I went up to the angel and told him to give me the small scroll. He said to me, "Take and swallow it. It will turn your stomach sour, but in your mouth it will taste as sweet‡‡ as honey." [10]I took the small scroll from the angel's hand and swallowed it. In my mouth it was like sweet honey, but when I had eaten it, my stomach turned sour." [11]Then someone said to me, "You must prophesy again about many peoples, nations, tongues, and kings."§§

CHAPTER 11

The Two Witnesses. [1¶¶]Then I was given a measuring rod like a staff and I was told, "Come and measure the temple of God and the altar, and count those who are worshiping in it. [2]But exclude the outer court*** of the temple; do not measure it, for it has been handed over to the Gentiles, who will trample the holy city for forty-two months. [3]I will commission my two witnesses††† to prophesy for those twelve hundred and sixty days, wearing sackcloth." [4]These are the two olive trees and the two lampstands‡‡‡ that stand before the Lord of the earth. [5§§§]If anyone wants to harm them, fire comes out of their mouths and devours their enemies. In this way, anyone wanting to harm them is sure to be slain. [6]They have the power to close up the sky so that no rain can fall during the time of

---

‡‡[10:9–10] The small scroll was sweet because it predicted the final victory of God's people; it was sour because it also announced their sufferings. Cf. Ez 3:1–3.

§§[10:11] This further prophecy is contained in chaps. 12–22.

¶¶[11:1] The temple and altar symbolize the new Israel; see note on Rev 7:4–9. The worshipers represent Christians. The measuring of the temple (cf. Ez 40:3–42:20; 47:1–12; Zec 2:5–6) suggests that God will preserve the faithful remnant (cf. Is 4:2–3) who remain true to Christ (Rev 14:1–5).

***[11:2] The outer court: the Court of the Gentiles. Trample . . . forty-two months: the duration of the vicious persecution of the Jews by Antiochus IV Epiphanes (Dn 7:25; 12:7); this persecution of three and a half years (half of seven, counted as 1260 days in Rev 11:3; 12:6) became the prototype of periods of trial for God's people; cf. Lk 4:25; Jas 5:17. The reference here is to the persecution by the Romans; cf. Introduction.

†††[11:3] The two witnesses, wearing sackcloth symbolizing lamentation and repentance, cannot readily be identified. Do they represent Moses and Elijah, or the Law and the Prophets, or Peter and Paul? Most probably they refer to the universal church, especially the Christian martyrs, fulfilling the office of witness (two because of Dt 19:15; cf. Mk 6:7; Jn 8:17).

‡‡‡[11:4] The two olive trees and the two lampstands: the martyrs who stand in the presence of the Lord; the imagery is taken from Zec 4:8–14, where the olive trees refer to Zerubbabel and Joshua.

§§§[11:5–6] These details are derived from stories of Moses, who turned **water into blood** (Ex 7:17–20), and of Elijah, who called down fire from heaven (1 Kgs 18:36–40; 2 Kgs 1:10) and closed up the sky for three years (1 Kgs 17:1; cf. 18:1).

---

*[9:17] **Blue**: literally, "hyacinth-colored." **Yellow**: literally, "sulfurous."

†[9:20] **The works of their hands**: i.e., the gods their hands had made.

‡[10:1–11:14] An interlude in two scenes (Rev 10:1–11 and Rev 11:1–14) precedes the sounding of the seventh trumpet; cf. Rev 7:1–17. The first vision describes an angel astride sea and land like a colossus, with a small scroll open, the contents of which indicate that the end is imminent (Rev 10). The second vision is of the measuring of the temple and of two witnesses, whose martyrdom means that the kingdom of God is about to be inaugurated.

§[10:2] **He placed . . . on the land**: this symbolizes the universality of the angel's message, as does the figure of the small scroll open to be read.

¶[10:3] **The seven thunders**: God's voice announcing judgment and doom; cf. Ps 29:3–9, where thunder, as the voice of Yahweh, is praised seven times.

[10:6] **Heaven and earth and sea: the three parts of the universe. **No more delay**: cf. Dn 12:7; Heb 2:3.

††[10:7] **The mysterious plan of God**: literally, "the mystery of God," the end of the present age when the forces of evil will be put down (Rev 17:1–19:4, 11–21; 20:7–10; cf. 2 Thes 2:6–12; Rom 16:25–26), and the establishment of the reign of God when all creation will be made new (Rev 21:1–22:5).

---

p. [9:17] Jb 41:10–13.   q. [9:20] Ps 135:15–17; Is 17:8; Dn 5:4.
r. [10:3] Ps 29:3–9; Jer 25:30; Am 3:8.   s. [10:6] Dt 32:40; Dn 12:7 / Ez 12:28.

t. [10:7] Am 3:7.   u. [10:10] Ez 3:1–3.   v. [11:1] Ez 40:3–5 / Zec 2:5–9.   w. [11:4] Zec 4:3, 14.

their prophesying. They also have power to turn water into blood and to afflict the earth with any plague as often as they wish.[x] [7]When they have finished their testimony, the beast that comes up from the abyss[*] will wage war against them and conquer them and kill them.[y] [8]Their corpses will lie in the main street of the great city,[†] which has the symbolic names "Sodom" and "Egypt," where indeed their Lord was crucified. [9†]Those from every people, tribe, tongue, and nation will gaze on their corpses for three and a half days, and they will not allow their corpses to be buried. [10]The inhabitants of the earth will gloat over them and be glad and exchange gifts because these two prophets tormented the inhabitants of the earth. [11]But after the three and a half days, a breath of life from God entered them. When they stood on their feet, great fear fell on those who saw them.[z] [12]Then they heard a loud voice from heaven say to them, "Come up here." So they went up to heaven in a cloud as their enemies looked on.[a] [13]At that moment there was a great earthquake, and a tenth of the city fell in ruins. Seven thousand people[§] were killed during the earthquake; the rest were terrified and gave glory to the God of heaven.

[14]The second woe has passed, but the third is coming soon.

The Seventh Trumpet.[¶] [15]Then the seventh angel blew his trumpet. There were loud voices in heaven, saying, "The kingdom of the world now belongs to our Lord and to his Anointed, and he will reign forever and ever." [16]The twenty-four elders who sat on their thrones before God prostrated themselves and worshiped God [17]and said:

"We give thanks to you, Lord God
    almighty,
who are and who were.
For you have assumed your great power
    and have established your reign.

[18] The nations raged,
    but your wrath has come,
    and the time for the dead to be
        judged,
and to recompense your servants, the
        prophets,
    and the holy ones and those who
        fear your name,
    the small and the great alike,
    and to destroy those who destroy the
        earth."[b]

[19]Then God's temple in heaven was opened, and the ark of his covenant could be seen in the temple. There were flashes of lightning, rumblings, and peals of thunder, an earthquake, and a violent hailstorm.

CHAPTER 12

The Woman and the Dragon. [1**]A great sign appeared in the sky, a woman[††] clothed with the sun, with the moon under her feet, and on her head a crown of twelve stars.[c] [2]She was with child and wailed aloud in pain as she labored to give birth.[‡‡] [3]Then another sign appeared in the sky; it was a huge red dragon,[§§] with seven heads and ten horns, and on its heads were seven diadems.[d] [4]Its tail swept away a third of the stars in the sky and hurled them down to earth. Then the dragon stood before the woman about to give birth, to devour her child when she gave birth.[e] [5]She gave birth to a son, a male child,

---

*[11:7] **The beast . . . from the abyss**: the Roman emperor Nero, who symbolizes the forces of evil, or the antichrist (Rev 13:1, 8; 17:8); cf. Dn 7:2–8, 11–12, 19–22 and Introduction.

†[11:8] **The great city**: this expression is used constantly in Revelation for Babylon, i.e., Rome; cf. Rev 14:8; 16:19; 17:18; 18:2, 10, 21. **"Sodom" and "Egypt"**: symbols of immorality (cf. Is 1:10) and oppression of God's people (cf. Ex 1:11–14). **Where indeed their Lord was crucified**: not the geographical but the symbolic Jerusalem that rejects God and his witnesses, i.e., Rome, called Babylon in Rev 16–18; see note on Rev 17:9 and Introduction.

‡[11:9–12] Over the martyrdom (Rev 11:7) of the two witnesses, now called prophets, the ungodly rejoice **for three and a half days**, a symbolic period of time; see note on Rev 11:2. Afterwards they go in triumph to heaven, as did Elijah (2 Kgs 2:11).

§[11:13] **Seven thousand people**: a symbolic sum to represent all social classes (seven) and large numbers (thousands); cf. Introduction.

¶[11:15–19] The seventh trumpet proclaims the coming of God's reign after the victory over diabolical powers; see note on Rev 10:7.

**[12:1–14:20] This central section of Revelation portrays the power of evil, represented by a dragon, in opposition to God and his people. First, the dragon pursues the woman about to give birth, but her son is saved and "caught up to God and his throne" (Rev 12:5). Then Michael and his angels cast the dragon and his angels out of heaven (Rev 12:7–9). After this, the dragon tries to attack the boy indirectly by attacking members of his church (Rev 12:13–17). A beast, symbolizing the Roman empire, then becomes the dragon's agent, mortally wounded but restored to life and worshiped by all the world (Rev 13:1–10). A second beast arises from the land, symbolizing the antichrist, which leads people astray by its prodigies to idolize the first beast (Rev 13:11–18). This is followed by a vision of the Lamb and his faithful ones, and the proclamation of imminent judgment upon the world in terms of the wine of God's wrath (Rev 14:1–20).

††[12:1–6] The woman adorned with the sun, the moon, and the stars (images taken from Gn 37:9–10) symbolizes God's people in the Old and the New Testament. The Israel of old gave birth to the Messiah (Rev 12:5) and then became the new Israel, the church, which suffers persecution by the dragon (Rev 12:6, 13–17); cf. Is 50:1; 66:7; Jer 50:12. This corresponds to a widespread myth throughout the ancient world that a goddess pregnant with a savior was pursued by a horrible monster; by miraculous intervention, she bore a son who then killed the monster.

‡‡[12:2] Because of Eve's sin, the woman gives birth in distress and pain (Gn 3:16; cf. Is 66:7–14).

§§[12:3] **Huge red dragon**: the Devil or Satan (cf. Rev 12:9; 20:2), symbol of the forces of evil, a mythical monster known also as Leviathan (Ps 74:13–14) or Rahab (Jb 26:12–13; Ps 89:11). **Seven diadems**: these are symbolic of the fullness of the dragon's sovereignty over the kingdoms of this world; cf. Christ with many diadems (Rev 19:12).

---

x. [11:6] Ex 7:17.   y. [11:7] Dn 7:21.   z. [11:11] Ez 37:5, 10.
a. [11:12] 2 Kgs 2:11.

b. [11:18] Ps 2:1, 5 / Am 3:7.   c. [12:1] Gn 37:9.   d. [12:3] Dn 7:7.
e. [12:4] Dn 8:10.

destined to rule all the nations with an iron rod.* Her child was caught up to God and his throne.[j] [6]The woman herself fled into the desert where she had a place prepared by God, that there she might be taken care of for twelve hundred and sixty days.[†]

[7‡]Then war broke out in heaven; Michael[§] and his angels battled against the dragon. The dragon and its angels fought back, [8]but they did not prevail and there was no longer any place for them in heaven. [9]The huge dragon, the ancient serpent,[¶] who is called the Devil and Satan, who deceived the whole world, was thrown down to earth, and its angels were thrown down with it.[g]

[10]Then I heard a loud voice in heaven say:

"Now have salvation and power come,
    and the kingdom of our God
    and the authority of his Anointed.
For the accuser** of our brothers is cast
        out,
    who accuses them before our God
        day and night.
[11] They conquered him by the blood of the
        Lamb
    and by the word of their testimony;
    love for life did not deter them from
        death.
[12] Therefore, rejoice, you heavens,
    and you who dwell in them.
But woe to you, earth and sea,
    for the Devil has come down to you
        in great fury,
    for he knows he has but a short
        time."

[13]When the dragon saw that it had been thrown down to the earth, it pursued the woman who had given birth to the male child.[h] [14]But the woman was given the two wings of the great eagle,[††] so that she could fly to her place in the desert, where, far from the serpent, she was taken care of for a year, two years, and a half-year.[i] [15]The serpent,[‡‡] however, spewed a torrent of water out of his mouth after the woman to sweep her away with the current. [16]But the earth helped the woman and opened its mouth and swallowed the flood that the dragon spewed out of its mouth. [17]Then the dragon became angry with the woman and went off to wage war against the rest of her offspring, those who keep God's commandments and bear witness to Jesus.[§§] [18]It took its position[¶¶] on the sand of the sea.[j]

CHAPTER 13

The First Beast.*** [1]Then I saw a beast come out of the sea with ten horns and seven heads; on its horns were ten diadems, and on its heads blasphemous name[s].[k] [2]The beast I saw was like a leopard, but it had feet like a bear's, and its mouth was like the mouth of a lion.[†††][l] To it the dragon gave its own power and throne, along with great authority. [3]I saw that one of its heads seemed to have been mortally wounded, but this mortal wound was healed.[‡‡‡] Fascinated, the whole world followed after the beast. [4]They worshiped the dragon because it gave its authority to the beast; they also worshiped the beast[§§§] and said, "Who can compare with the beast or who can fight against it?"

[5¶¶¶]The beast was given a mouth uttering proud boasts and blasphemies,[m] and it was given authority to act for forty-two months.***** [6]It opened its mouth to utter blasphemies against God, blaspheming his name and his dwelling and those who dwell in heaven. [7]It was also allowed to wage war against the holy ones and conquer them, and it was granted authority over every tribe, people, tongue, and nation.[n] [8]All

‡‡[12:15] The serpent is depicted as the sea monster; cf. Rev 13:1; Is 27:1; Ez 32:2; Ps 74:13–14.

§§[12:17] Although the church is protected by God's special providence (Rev 12:16), the individual Christian is to expect persecution and suffering.

¶¶[12:18] **It took its position**: many later manuscripts and versions read "I took my position," thus connecting the sentence to the following paragraph.

***[13:1–10] This wild beast, combining features of the four beasts in Dn 7:2–28, symbolizes the Roman empire; the seven heads represent the emperors; see notes on Rev 17:10 and Rev 17:12–14. The blasphemous names are the divine titles assumed by the emperors.

†††[13:2] Satan (Rev 12:9), the prince of this world (Jn 12:31), commissioned the beast to persecute the church (Rev 13:5–7).

‡‡‡[13:3] This may be a reference to the popular legend that Nero would come back to life and rule again after his death (which occurred in A.D. 68 from a self-inflicted stab wound in the throat); cf. Rev 13:14; Rev 17:8. Domitian (A.D. 81–96) embodied all the cruelty and impiety of Nero. Cf. Introduction.

§§§[13:4] **Worshiped the beast**: allusion to emperor worship, which Domitian insisted upon and ruthlessly enforced. **Who can compare with the beast**: perhaps a deliberate parody of the name Michael; see note on Rev 12:7.

¶¶¶[13:5–6] Domitian, like Antiochus IV Epiphanes (Dn 7:8, 11, 25), demanded that he be called by divine titles such as "our lord and god" and "Jupiter." See note on Rev 11:2.

****[13:5] **Forty-two months**: this is the same duration as the profanation of the holy city (Rev 11:2), the prophetic mission of the two witnesses (Rev 11:3), and the retreat of the woman into the desert (Rev 12:6, 14).

*[12:5] **Rule . . . iron rod**: fulfilled in Rev 19:15; cf. Ps 2:9. **Was caught up to God**: reference to Christ's ascension.

†[12:6] God protects the persecuted church in the desert, the traditional Old Testament place of refuge for the afflicted, according to the typology of the Exodus; see note on Rev 11:2.

‡[12:7–12] Michael, mentioned only here in Revelation, wins a victory over the dragon. A hymn of praise follows.

§[12:7] **Michael**: the archangel, guardian and champion of Israel; cf. Dn 10:13, 21; 12:1; Jude 9. In Hebrew, the name Michael means "Who can compare with God?"; cf. Rev 13:4.

¶[12:9] **The ancient serpent**: who seduced Eve (Gn 3:1–6), mother of the human race; cf. Rev 20:2; Eph 6:11–12. **Was thrown down**: allusion to the expulsion of Satan from heaven; cf. Lk 10:18.

[12:10] **The accuser: the meaning of the Hebrew word "Satan," found in Rev 12:9; Jb 1–2; Zec 3:1; 1 Chr 21:1; he continues to accuse Christ's disciples.

††[12:14] **Great eagle**: symbol of the power and swiftness of divine help; cf. Ex 19:4; Dt 32:11; Is 40:31.

f. [12:5] Is 66:7 / Ps 2:9. g. [12:9] Gn 3:1–4; Lk 10:18. h. [12:13] Gn 3:15. i. [12:14] Ex 19:4; Dn 7:25; 12:7.

j. [12:18] Gn 3:15. k. [13:1] 2 Thes 2:3–12. l. [13:2] Dn 7:3–6. m. [13:5] Dn 7:8, 11, 25; 8:14; 9:27; 11:36; 12:7. n. [13:7] Dn 7:21.

the inhabitants of the earth will worship it, all whose names were not written from the foundation of the world in the book of life, which belongs to the Lamb who was slain.°

9 Whoever has ears ought to hear these words.ᵖ
10 Anyone destined for captivity goes into captivity.
Anyone destined to be slain by the sword shall be slain by the sword.�q

Such is the faithful endurance of the holy ones. **The Second Beast.*** ¹¹Then I saw another beast come up out of the earth; it had two horns like a lamb's but spoke like a dragon. ¹²It wielded all the authority of the first beast in its sight and made the earth and its inhabitants worship the first beast, whose mortal wound had been healed. ¹³It performed great signs, even making fire come down from heaven to earth in the sight of everyone.ʳ ¹⁴It deceived the inhabitants of the earth with the signs it was allowed to perform in the sight of the first beast, telling them to make an image for the beast who had been wounded by the sword and revived. ¹⁵It was then permitted to breathe life into the beast's image, so that the beast's image could speak and [could] have anyone who did not worship it put to death.ˢ ¹⁶It forced all the people, small and great, rich and poor, free and slave, to be given a stamped image on their right hands or their foreheads,ᵗ ¹⁷so that no one could buy or sell except one who had the stamped image of the beast's name or the number that stood for its name.
¹⁸†ᵘWisdom is needed here; one who understands can calculate the number of the beast, for it is a number that stands for a person. His number is six hundred and sixty-six.

CHAPTER 14
The Lamb's Companions.‡ ¹Then I looked and there was the Lamb standing on Mount Zion,§

and with him a hundred and forty-four thousand who had his name and his Father's name written on their foreheads.ᵛ ²I heard a sound from heaven like the sound of rushing water or a loud peal of thunder. The sound I heard was like that of harpists playing their harps. ³They were singing [what seemed to be] a new hymn before the throne, before the four living creatures and the elders. No one could learn this hymn except the hundred and forty-four thousand who had been ransomed from the earth.ʷ ⁴These are they who were not defiled with women; they are virginsˢ and these are the ones who follow the Lamb wherever he goes. They have been ransomed as the firstfruits of the human race for God and the Lamb.ˣ ⁵On their lips no deceit** has been found; they are unblemished.ʸ
The Three Angels.†† ⁶Then I saw another angel flying high overhead, with everlasting good news‡‡ to announce to those who dwell on earth, to every nation, tribe, tongue, and people. ⁷He said in a loud voice, "Fear God and give him glory, for his time has come to sit in judgment. Worship him who made heaven and earth and sea and springs of water."ᶻ
⁸A second angel followed, saying:

"Fallen, fallen is Babylon the great,ᵃ
    that made all the nations drink
    the wine of her licentious passion."§§

⁹A third angel followed them and said in a loud voice, "Anyone who worships the beast or its image, or accepts its mark on forehead or hand, ¹⁰will also drink the wine of God's fury,¶¶ poured

---

*[13:11–18] The second beast is described in terms of the false prophets (cf. Rev 16:13; 19:20; 20:10) who accompany the false messiahs (the first beast); cf. Mt 24:24; Mk 13:22; 2 Thes 2:9; cf. also Dt 13:2–4. Christians had either to worship the emperor and his image or to suffer martyrdom.

†[13:18] Each of the letters of the alphabet in Hebrew as well as in Greek has a numerical value. Many possible combinations of letters will add up to 666, and many candidates have been nominated for this infamous number. The most likely is the emperor Caesar Nero (see note on Rev 13:3), the Greek form of whose name in Hebrew letters gives the required sum. (The Latin form of this name equals 616, which is the reading of a few manuscripts.) Nero personifies the emperors who viciously persecuted the church. It has also been observed that "6" represents imperfection, falling short of the perfect number "7," and is represented here in a triple or superlative form.

‡[14:1–5] Now follows a tender and consoling vision of the Lamb and his companions.

§[14:1] **Mount Zion**: in Jerusalem, the traditional place where the true remnant, the Israel of faith, is to be gathered in the messianic reign; cf. 2 Kgs 19:30–31; Jl 3:5; Ob 17; Mi

4:6–8; Zep 3:12–20. **A hundred and forty-four thousand**: see note on Rev 7:4–9. **His Father's name . . . foreheads**: in contrast to the pagans who were marked with the name or number of the beast (Rev 13:16–17).

¶[14:4] **Virgins**: metaphorically, because they never indulged in any idolatrous practices, which are considered in the Old Testament to be adultery and fornication (Rev 2:14–15, 20–22; 17:1–6; cf. Ez 16:1–58; 23:1–49). The parallel passages (Rev 7:3; 22:4) indicate that the 144,000 whose foreheads are sealed represent all Christian people.

[14:5] **No deceit: because they did not deny Christ or do homage to the beast. Lying is characteristic of the opponents of Christ (Jn 8:44), but the Suffering Servant spoke no falsehood (Is 53:9; 1 Pt 2:22). **Unblemished**: a cultic term taken from the vocabulary of sacrificial ritual.

††[14:6–13] Three angels proclaim imminent judgment on the pagan world, calling all peoples to worship God the creator. Babylon (Rome) will fall, and its supporters will be tormented forever.

‡‡[14:6] **Everlasting good news**: that God's eternal reign is about to begin; see note on Rev 10:7.

§§[14:8] This verse anticipates the lengthy dirge over Babylon (Rome) in Rev 18:1–19:4. The oracle of Is 21:9 to Babylon is applied here.

¶¶[14:10–11] **The wine of God's fury**: image taken from Is 51:17; Jer 25:15–16; 49:12; 51:7; Ez 23:31–34. Eternal punishment in the fiery pool of burning sulfur (or "fire and brimstone"; cf. Gn 19:24) is also reserved for the Devil, the beast, and the false prophet (Rev 19:20; 20:10; 21:8).

---

o. [13:8] 3:5; 17:8; 20:12.   p. [13:9] Mt 13:9.   q. [13:10] Jer 15:2.
r. [13:13] Dt 13:2–4; Mt 24:24; 2 Thes 2:9–10.   s. [13:15] Dn 3:5–7,
15.   t. [13:16] 14:9; 16:2; 19:20; 20:4.   u. [13:18] 17:9.

v. [14:1] Jl 3:5; Ob 17; Acts 2:21.   w. [14:3] Ps 33:3; 96:1; 98:1; Is
42:10.   x. [14:4] Jer 2:2; Jas 1:18.   y. [14:5] Zep 3:13.   z. [14:7]
2:10; Mt 10:28.   a. [14:8] 18:2–3; Is 21:9; Jer 51:8 / Is 51:17; Jer
25:15–17.

full strength into the cup of his wrath, and will be tormented in burning sulfur before the holy angels and before the Lamb. ¹¹The smoke of the fire that torments them will rise forever and ever, and there will be no relief day or night for those who worship the beast or its image or accept the mark of its name."ᵇ ¹²Here is what sustains the holy ones who keep God's commandmentsᶜ and their faith in Jesus.*

¹³ᵈI heard a voice from heaven say, "Write this: Blessed are the dead who die in the Lord from now on." "Yes," said the Spirit, "let them find rest from their labors, for their works accompany them."†

The Harvest of the Earth.‡ ¹⁴Then I looked and there was a white cloud, and sitting on the cloud one who looked like a son of man, with a gold crown on his head and a sharp sickle in his hand.ᵉ ¹⁵Another angel came out of the temple, crying out in a loud voice to the one sitting on the cloud, "Use your sickle and reap the harvest, for the time to reap has come, because the earth's harvest is fully ripe."ᶠ ¹⁶So the one who was sitting on the cloud swung his sickle over the earth, and the earth was harvested.

¹⁷Then another angel came out of the temple in heaven who also had a sharp sickle. ¹⁸Then another angel [came] from the altar,§ [who] was in charge of the fire, and cried out in a loud voice to the one who had the sharp sickle, "Use your sharp sickle and cut the clusters from the earth's vines, for its grapes are ripe." ¹⁹So the angel swung his sickle over the earth and cut the earth's vintage. He threw it into the great wine press of God's fury.ᵍ ²⁰The wine press was trodden outside the city and blood poured out of the wine press to the height of a horse's bridle for two hundred miles.¶

CHAPTER 15

The Seven Last Plagues. ¹***Then I saw in heaven another sign,†† great and awe-inspiring: seven

angels with the seven last plagues, for through them God's fury is accomplished.

²Then I saw something like a sea of glass mingled with fire.‡‡ On the sea of glass were standing those who had won the victory over the beast and its image and the number that signified its name. They were holding God's harps,ʰ ³and they sang the song of Moses,§§ the servant of God, and the song of the Lamb:

"Great and wonderful are your works,
        Lord God almighty.
Just and true are your ways,
        O king of the nations.ⁱ
⁴ Who will not fear you, Lord,
        or glorify your name?
For you alone are holy.
        All the nations will come
        and worship before you,
        for your righteous acts have been
        revealed."ʲ

⁵¶¶After this I had another vision. The temple that is the heavenly tent of testimony*** opened, ⁶and the seven angels with the seven plagues came out of the temple. They were dressed in clean white linen, with a gold sash around their chests.ᵏ ⁷One of the four living creatures gave the seven angels seven gold bowls filled with the fury of God, who lives forever and ever. ⁸Then the temple became so filled with the smoke from God's glory and might that no one could enter it until the seven plagues of the seven angels had been accomplished.ˡ

CHAPTER 16

The Seven Bowls.††† ¹I heard a loud voice speaking from the temple to the seven angels, "Go and pour out the seven bowls of God's fury upon the earth."

²The first angel went and poured out his bowl on the earth. Festering and ugly sores broke out on those who had the mark of the beast or worshiped its image.‡‡‡

---

*[14:12] In addition to **faith in Jesus**, the seer insists upon the necessity and value of works, as in Rev 2:23; 20:12–13; 22:12; cf. Mt 16:27; Rom 2:6.

†[14:13] See note on Rev 1:3. According to Jewish thought, people's actions followed them as witnesses before the court of God.

‡[14:14–20] The reaping of the harvest symbolizes the gathering of the elect in the final judgment, while the reaping and treading of the grapes symbolizes the doom of the ungodly (cf. Jl 4:12–13; Is 63:1–6) that will come in Rev 19:11–21.

§[14:18] **Altar:** there was only one altar in the heavenly temple; see notes above on Rev 6:9; 8:3; 11:1.

¶[14:20] **Two hundred miles:** literally sixteen hundred stades. The *stadion,* a Greek unit of measurement, was about 607 feet in length, approximately the length of a furlong.

**[15:1–16:21] The seven bowls, the third and last group of seven after the seven seals and the seven trumpets, foreshadow the final cataclysm. Again, the series is introduced by a heavenly prelude, in which the victors over the beast sing the canticle of Moses (Rev 15:2–4).

††[15:1–4] A vision of the victorious martyrs precedes the vision of woe in Rev 15:5–16:21; cf. Rev 7:9–12.

‡‡[15:2] **Mingled with fire:** fire symbolizes the sanctity involved in facing God, reflected in the trials that have prepared the victorious Christians or in God's wrath.

§§[15:3] **The song of Moses:** the song that Moses and the Israelites sang after their escape from the oppression of Egypt (Ex 15:1–18). The martyrs have escaped from the oppression of the Devil. **Nations:** many other Greek manuscripts and versions read "ages."

¶¶[15:5–8] Seven angels receive the bowls of God's wrath.

***[15:5] **Tent of testimony:** the name of the meeting tent in the Greek text of Ex 40. Cf. 2 Mc 2:4–7.

†††[16:1–21] These seven bowls, like the seven seals (Rev 6:1–17; 8:1) and the seven trumpets (Rev 8:2–9:21; 11:15–19), bring on a succession of disasters modeled in part on the plagues of Egypt (Ex 7–12). See note on Rev 6:12–14.

‡‡‡[16:2] Like the sixth Egyptian plague (Ex 9:8–11).

---

b. [14:11] 19:3.   c. [14:12] 12:17.   d. [14:13] Mt 11:28–29; 2 Thes 1:7; Heb 4:10.   e. [14:14] 1:7; Dn 7:13.   f. [14:15] Jl 4:13; Mt 13:36–43.   g. [14:19] 19:15; Is 63:1–6.

h. [15:2] 7:9, 14; 13:15–18.   i. [15:3] Ps 92:6; 98:1 / Dt 32:4; Ps 145:17.   j. [15:4] Ps 86:9–10; Jer 10:7.   k. [15:6] 19:8.   l. [15:8] 1 Kgs 8:10; Is 6:4.

³*The second angel poured out his bowl on the sea. The sea turned to blood like that from a corpse; every creature living in the sea died. ⁴The third angel poured out his bowl on the rivers and springs of water. These also turned to blood.ᵐ ⁵Then I heard the angel in charge of the waters say:

"You are just, O Holy One,
 who are and who were,
 in passing this sentence."ⁿ
⁶ For they have shed the blood of the holy
   ones and the prophets,
 and you [have] given them blood
   to drink;
 it is what they deserve."ᵒ

⁷Then I heard the altar cry out,

"Yes, Lord God almighty,
 your judgments are true and just."ᵖ

⁸The fourth angel poured out his bowl on the sun. It was given the power to burn people with fire. ⁹People were burned by the scorching heat and blasphemed the name of God who had power over these plagues, but they did not repent or give him glory.�q

¹⁰*The fifth angel poured out his bowl on the throne of the beast.† Its kingdom was plunged into darkness, and people bit their tongues in pain ¹¹and blasphemed the God of heaven because of their pains and sores. But they did not repent of their works.ˢ

¹²The sixth angel emptied his bowl on the great river Euphrates. Its water was dried up to prepare the way for the kings of the East.‡ ¹³I saw three unclean spirits like frogs§ come from the mouth of the dragon, from the mouth of the beast, and from the mouth of the false prophet.ᵗ ¹⁴These were demonic spirits who performed signs. They went out to the kings of the whole world to assemble them for the battle on the great day of God the almighty.ᵘ ¹⁵("Behold, I am coming like a thief."⁵ Blessed is the one who watches and keeps his clothes ready, so that he may not go naked and people see him exposed.)ᵛ ¹⁶They then

assembled the kings in the place that is named ·Armageddon** in Hebrew.
¹⁷The seventh angel poured out his bowl into the air. A loud voice came out of the temple from the throne, saying, "It is done."ʷ ¹⁸Then there were lightning flashes, rumblings, and peals of thunder, and a great earthquake. It was such a violent earthquake that there has never been one like it since the human race began on earth.ˣ ¹⁹The great city†† was split into three parts, and the gentile cities fell. But God remembered great Babylon, giving it the cup filled with the wine of his fury and wrath. ²⁰‡‡Every island fled, and mountains disappeared. ²¹Large hailstones like huge weights came down from the sky on people, and they blasphemed God for the plague of hail because this plague was so severe.ʸ

V. THE PUNISHMENT OF BABYLON AND THE DESTRUCTION OF PAGAN NATIONS

CHAPTER 17

Babylon the Great. ¹§§Then one of the seven angels who were holding the seven bowls came and said to me, "Come here. I will show you the judgment on the great harlot⁵⁵ who lives near the many waters.ᶻ ²***The kings of the earth have had intercourse with her,ᵃ and the inhabitants of the earth became drunk on the wine of her harlotry." ³Then he carried me away in spirit to a deserted place where I saw a woman seated on a scarlet beast††† that was covered with blasphemous names, with seven heads and ten horns.ᵇ ⁴The woman was wearing purple and scarlet and adorned with gold, precious stones, and pearls.ᶜ She held in her hand a gold cup that was filled with the abominable and sordid deeds of her harlotry. ⁵On her forehead was written a name, which is a mystery, "Babylon the great, the mother of harlots and of the abominations

---

*[16:3–4] Like the first Egyptian plague (Ex 7:20–21). The same woe followed the blowing of the second trumpet (Rev 8:8–9).

†[16:10] **The throne of the beast:** symbol of the forces of evil. **Darkness:** like the ninth Egyptian plague (Ex 10:21–23); cf. Rev 9:2.

‡[16:12] **The kings of the East:** Parthians; see notes on Rev 6:2 and Rev 17:12–13. **East:** literally, "rising of the sun," as in Rev 7:2.

§[16:13] **Frogs:** possibly an allusion to the second Egyptian plague (Ex 7:26–8:11). **The false prophet:** identified with the two-horned second beast (Rev 13:11–18 and the note there).

¶[16:15] **Like a thief:** as in Rev 3:3 (cf. Mt 24:42–44; 1 Thes 5:2). **Blessed:** see note on Rev 1:3.

[16:16] **Armageddon: in Hebrew, this means "Mountain of·Megiddo." Since Megiddo was the scene of many decisive battles in antiquity (Jgs 5:19–20; 2 Kgs 9:27; 2 Chr 35:20–24), the town became the symbol of the final disastrous rout of the forces of evil.

††[16:19] **The great city:** Rome and the empire.

‡‡[16:20–21] See note on Rev 6:12–14. **Hailstones:** as in the seventh Egyptian plague (Ex 9:23–24); cf. Rev 8:7. **Like huge weights:** literally, "weighing a talent," about one hundred pounds.

§§[17:1–19:10] The punishment of Babylon is now described as a past event and, metaphorically, under the image of the great harlot who leads people astray into idolatry.

⁵⁵[17:1–6] Babylon, the symbolic name (Rev 17:5) of Rome, is graphically described as "the great harlot."

***[17:2] **Intercourse ... harlotry:** see note on Rev 14:4. The pagan kings subject to Rome adopted the cult of the emperor.

†††[17:3] **Scarlet beast:** see note on Rev 13:1–10. **Blasphemous names:** divine titles assumed by the Roman emperors; see note on Rev 13:5–6.

---

m. [16:4] Ex 7:14–24. n. [16:5] 1:4. o. [16:6] Ez 35:6; Mt 23:34–35. p. [16:7] Dn 3:27; Tb 3:2. q. [16:9] Am 4:6. r. [16:10] Ex 10:21–23. s. [16:11] Ex 9:8–11 / Jer 5:3. t. [16:13] Ex 8:2–3. u. [16:14] 1 Cor 1:8. v. [16:15] Mt 24:42–44 / 3:17.

w. [16:17] Is 66:6. x. [16:18] Mk 13:19. y. [16:21] Ex 9:22–26. z. [17:1] Jer50:38; 51:13. a. [17:2] Jer51:7. b. [17:3] 13:1. c. [17:4] 18:16.

of the earth." ⁶*I saw that the woman was drunk on the blood of the holy ones and on the blood of the witnesses to Jesus.

Meaning of the Beast and Harlot.† When I saw her I was greatly amazed. ⁷The angel said to me, "Why are you amazed? I will explain to you the mystery of the woman and of the beast that carries her, the beast with the seven heads and the ten horns. ⁸‡ᵈThe beast that you saw existed once but now exists no longer. It will come up from the abyss and is headed for destruction. The inhabitants of the earth whose names have not been written in the book of life from the foundation of the world shall be amazed when they see the beast, because it existed once but exists no longer, and yet it will come again. ⁹Here is a clue§ for one who has wisdom. The seven heads represent seven hills upon which the woman sits. They also represent seven kings:ᵉ ¹⁰five have already fallen, one still lives, and the last has not yet come,⁵ and when he comes he must remain only a short while. ¹¹The beast** that existed once but exists no longer is an eighth king, but really belongs to the seven and is headed for destruction. ¹²The ten horns that you saw represent ten kings who have not yet been crowned;†† they will receive royal authority along with the beast for one hour.ᶠ ¹³They are of one mind and will give their power and authority to the beast. ¹⁴They will fight with the Lamb, but the Lamb will conquer them, for he is Lord of lords and king of kings, and those with him are called, chosen, and faithful."ᵍ

¹⁵Then he said to me, "The waters that you saw where the harlot lives represent large numbers of peoples, nations, and tongues. ¹⁶The ten horns‡‡ that you saw and the beast will hate the harlot; they will leave her desolate and naked; they will eat her flesh and consume her with fire.ʰ ¹⁷For God has put it into their minds to carry out his purpose and to make them come to an agreement to give their kingdom to the beast until the words of God are accomplished. ¹⁸The

woman whom you saw represents the great city that has sovereignty over the kings of the earth."

CHAPTER 18

The Fall of Babylon.§§ ¹After this I saw another angel coming down from heaven, having great authority, and the earth became illumined by his splendor.ⁱ ²⁵⁵He cried out in a mighty voice:

"Fallen, fallen is Babylon the great.ʲ
    She has become a haunt for demons.
She is a cage for every unclean spirit,
    a cage for every unclean bird,
    [a cage for every unclean] and
        disgusting [beast].
3 For all the nations have drunk***
        the wine of her licentious passion.
    The kings of the earth had intercourse
        with her,
    and the merchants of the earth
        grew rich from her drive for
        luxury."ᵏ

⁴Then I heard another voice from heaven say:

"Depart from her,††† my people,
    so as not to take part in her sins
    and receive a share in her plagues,ˡ
5 for her sins are piled up to the sky,
    and God remembers her crimes.ᵐ
6 Pay her back as she has paid others.
    Pay her back double for her deeds.
    Into her cup pour double what she
        poured.ⁿ
7 To the measure of her boasting and
        wantonness
    repay her in torment and grief;
for she said to herself,
    'I sit enthroned as queen;
    I am no widow,
    and I will never know grief.'ᵒ
8 Therefore, her plagues will come in one
        day,
    pestilence, grief, and famine;
    she will be consumed by fire.

---

*[17:6] Reference to the great wealth and idolatrous cults of Rome.

†[17:6b–18] An interpretation of the vision is here given.

‡[17:8] Allusion to the belief that the dead Nero would return to power (Rev 17:11); see note on Rev 13:3.

§[17:9] **Here is a clue**: literally, "Here a mind that has wisdom." **Seven hills**: of Rome.

⁵[17:10] There is little agreement as to the identity of the Roman emperors alluded to here. The number seven (Rev 17:9) suggests that all the emperors are meant; see note on Rev 1:4.

[17:11] **The beast: Nero; see note on Rev 17:8.

††[17:12–13] **Ten kings who have not yet been crowned**: perhaps Parthian satraps who are to accompany the revived Nero (the beast) in his march on Rome to regain power; see note on Rev 13:3. In Rev 19:11–21, the Lamb and his companions will conquer them.

‡‡[17:16–18] **The ten horns**: the ten pagan kings (Rev 17:12) who unwittingly fulfill God's will against harlot Rome, the great city; cf. Ez 16:37.

§§[18:1–19:4] A stirring dirge over the fall of Babylon-Rome. The perspective is prophetic, as if the fall of Rome had already taken place. The imagery here, as elsewhere in this book, is not to be taken literally. The vindictiveness of some of the language, borrowed from the scathing Old Testament prophecies against Babylon, Tyre, and Nineveh (Is 23; 24; 27; Jer 50–51; Ez 26–27), is meant to portray symbolically the inexorable demands of God's holiness and justice; cf. Introduction. The section concludes with a joyous canticle on the future glory of heaven.

⁵⁵[18:2] Many Greek manuscripts and versions omit **a cage for every unclean . . . beast**.

***[18:3–24] Rome is condemned for her immorality, symbol of idolatry (see note on Rev 14:4), and for persecuting the church; cf. Rev 19:2.

†††[18:4] **Depart from her**: not evacuation of the city but separation from sinners, as always in apocalyptic literature.

---

d. [17:8] 13:3–4 / 3:5; 13:8; 20:12.   e. [17:9] 13:18.   f. [17:12] Dn 7:24.   g. [17:14] 19:11–21; 2 Mc 13:4; 1 Tm 6:15 / Rom 1:6; 1 Pt 2:9; Jude 1.   h. [17:16] Ez 16:37–41; 23:25–29.

i. [18:1] Ez 43:2.   j. [18:2] 14:8; Is 21:9; Jer 50:2–3; 51:8.   k. [18:3] 17:2; Jer 51:7.   l. [18:4] Is 48:20; Jer 50:8.   m. [18:5] Jer 51:9.   n. [18:6] Jer 50:15 / Jer 16:18.   o. [18:7] Is 47:8–9.

For mighty is the Lord God who judges
her."

[9]The kings of the earth who had intercourse
with her in their wantonness will weep and
mourn over her when they see the smoke of her
pyre. [10]They will keep their distance for fear of
the torment inflicted on her, and they will say:

"Alas, alas, great city,
Babylon, mighty city.
In one hour your judgment has come."

[11]The merchants of the earth will weep and
mourn for her, because there will be no more
markets* for their cargo: [12]their cargo of gold,
silver, precious stones, and pearls; fine linen,
purple silk, and scarlet cloth; fragrant wood of
every kind, all articles of ivory and all articles
of the most expensive wood, bronze, iron, and
marble; [13]cinnamon, spice,† incense, myrrh,
and frankincense; wine, olive oil, fine flour, and
wheat; cattle and sheep, horses and chariots, and
slaves, that is, human beings.

[14] "The fruit you craved
has left you.
All your luxury and splendor are gone,
never again will one find them."[p]

[15]The merchants who deal in these goods, who
grew rich from her, will keep their distance for
fear of the torment inflicted on her. Weeping
and mourning, [16]they cry out:

"Alas, alas, great city,
wearing fine linen, purple and scarlet,
adorned [in] gold, precious stones,
and pearls.[q]
[17] In one hour this great wealth has been
ruined."

Every captain of a ship, every traveler at sea, sailors, and seafaring merchants stood at a distance
[18]and cried out when they saw the smoke of her
pyre, "What city could compare with the great
city?" [19]They threw dust on their heads and
cried out, weeping and mourning:

"Alas, alas, great city,
in which all who had ships at sea
grew rich from her wealth.
In one hour she has been ruined."
[20] Rejoice over her, heaven,
you holy ones, apostles, and
prophets.

For God has judged your case against her."[s]

[21]A mighty angel picked up a stone like a huge
millstone and threw it into the sea and said:

"With such force will Babylon the great
city be thrown down,
and will never be found again.[t]
[22] No melodies of harpists and musicians,
flutists and trumpeters,
will ever be heard in you again.
No craftsmen in any trade
will ever be found in you again.
No sound of the millstone
will ever be heard in you again.[u]
[23] No light from a lamp
will ever be seen in you again.
No voices of bride and groom
will ever be heard in you again.
Because your merchants were the great
ones of the world,
all nations were led astray by your
magic potion.[v]
[24] In her was found the blood of prophets
and holy ones
and all who have been slain on the
earth."[w]

CHAPTER 19

[1]After this I heard what sounded like the loud
voice of a great multitude in heaven, saying:

"Alleluia!‡
Salvation, glory, and might belong to our
God,
[2]   for true and just are his judgments.
He has condemned the great harlot
who corrupted the earth with her
harlotry.
He has avenged on her the blood of his
servants."[x]

[3]They said a second time:

"Alleluia! Smoke will rise from her forever
and ever."[y]

[4]The twenty-four elders and the four living creatures fell down and worshiped God who sat on
the throne, saying, "Amen. Alleluia."
The Victory Song.§ [5]A voice coming from the
throne said:

---

‡[19:1, 3, 4, 6] **Alleluia:** found only here in the New Testament, this frequent exclamation of praise in the Hebrew
psalms was important in Jewish liturgy.

§[19:5–10] A victory song follows, sung by the entire
church, celebrating the marriage of the Lamb, the union of
the Messiah with the community of the elect.

*[18:11] Ironically, the merchants weep not so much for
Babylon-Rome, but for their lost markets; cf. Ez 27:36.

†[18:13] **Spice:** an unidentified spice plant called in Greek
amōmon.

p. [18:14] Hos 10:5 / Am 6:7.   q. [18:16] 17:4.   r. [18:19] Ez 27:27–32.

s. [18:20] 19:1–2; Dt 32:43.   t. [18:21] Jer 51:63–64; Ez 26:21.
u. [18:22] Is 24:8; Ez 26:13.   v. [18:23] Jer 7:34; 16:9; 25:10.
w. [18:24] 16:6.   x. [19:2] Dn 3:27 / Jer 51:48–49.   y. [19:3] 14:11;
Is 34:10.

"Praise our God, all you his servants,
[and] you who revere him, small
and great."ᶻ

⁶Then I heard something like the sound of a great multitude or the sound of rushing water or mighty peals of thunder, as they said:

"Alleluia!
The Lord has established his reign,
[our] God, the almighty.
⁷ Let us rejoice and be glad
and give him glory.
For the wedding day of the Lamb* has
come,
his bride has made herself ready.ᵃ
⁸ She was allowed to wear
a bright, clean linen garment."ᵇ

(The linen represents the righteous deeds of the holy ones.)†
⁹Then the angel said to me, "Write this: Blessed‡ are those who have been called to the wedding feast of the Lamb." And he said to me, "These words are true; they come from God."ᶜ ¹⁰I fell at his feet to worship him. But he said to me, "Don't! I am a fellow servant of yours and of your brothers who bear witness to Jesus. Worship God.ᵈ Witness to Jesus is the spirit of prophecy."§
The King of Kings. ¹¹¶Then I saw the heavens opened, and there was a white horse; its rider was [called] "Faithful and True." He judges and wages war in righteousness.ᵉ ¹²His eyes were [like] a fiery flame, and on his head were many diadems. He had a name** inscribed that no one knows except himself.ᶠ ¹³He wore a cloak that had been dipped in†† blood, and his name was called the Word of God.ᵍ ¹⁴The armies of heaven followed him, mounted on white horses and wearing clean white linen.ʰ ¹⁵Out of his mouth

came a sharp sword to strike the nations. He will rule them with an iron rod, and he himself will tread out in the wine press‡‡ the wine of the fury and wrath of God the almighty.ⁱ ¹⁶He has a name written on his cloak and on his thigh, "King of kings and Lord of lords."ʲ
¹⁷§§Then I saw an angel standing on the sun. He cried out [in] a loud voice to all the birds flying high overhead, "Come here. Gather for God's great feast, ¹⁸to eat the flesh of kings, the flesh of military officers, and the flesh of warriors, the flesh of horses and of their riders, and the flesh of all, free and slave, small and great."ᵏ ¹⁹Then I saw the beast and the kings of the earth and their armies gathered to fight against the one riding the horse and against his army. ²⁰The beast was caught and with it the false prophet¶¶ who had performed in its sight the signs by which he led astray those who had accepted the mark of the beast and those who had worshiped its image. The two were thrown alive into the fiery pool burning with sulfur.ˡ ²¹The rest were killed by the sword that came out of the mouth of the one riding the horse, and all the birds gorged themselves on their flesh.

CHAPTER 20

The Thousand-year Reign. ¹***Then I saw an angel come down from heaven, holding in his hand the key to the abyss††† and a heavy chain.ᵐ ²He seized the dragon, the ancient serpent, which is the Devil or Satan,‡‡‡ and tied it up for a thousand yearsⁿ ³and threw it into the abyss, which he locked over it and sealed, so that it could no longer lead the nations astray until the thousand years are completed. After this, it is to be released for a short time.
⁴Then I saw thrones; those who sat on them were entrusted with judgment. I also saw the souls of those who had been beheaded for their witness to Jesus and for the word of God, and who had not worshiped the beast or its image

---

*[19:7] **The wedding day of the Lamb**: symbol of God's reign about to begin (Rev 21:1–22:5); see note on Rev 10:7. **His bride**: the church; cf. 2 Cor 11:2; Eph 5:22–27. Marriage is one of the biblical metaphors used to describe the covenant relationship between God and his people; cf. Hos 2:16–22; Is 54:5–6; 62:5; Ez 16:6–14. Hence, idolatry and apostasy are viewed as adultery and harlotry (Hos 2:4–15; Ez 16:15–63); see note on Rev 14:4.
†[19:8] See note on Rev 14:12.
‡[19:9] **Blessed**: see note on Rev 1:3.
§[19:10] **The spirit of prophecy**: as the prophets were inspired to proclaim God's word, so the Christian is called to give witness to the Word of God (Rev 19:13) made flesh; cf. Rev 1:2; 6:9; 12:17.
¶[19:11–16] Symbolic description of the exalted Christ (cf. Rev 1:13–16) who together with the armies of heaven overcomes the beast and its followers; cf. Rev 17:14.
[19:12] **A name: in Semitic thought, the name conveyed the reality of the person; cf. Mt 11:27; Lk 10:22.
††[19:13] **Had been dipped in**: other Greek manuscripts and versions read "had been sprinkled with"; cf. Rev 19:15. **The Word of God**: Christ is the revelation of the Father; cf. Jn 1:1, 14; 1 Jn 2:14.

‡‡[19:15] The treading of the wine press is a prophetic symbol used to describe the destruction of God's enemies; cf. Is 63:1–6; Jl 4:13.
§§[19:17–21] The certainty of Christ's victory is proclaimed by an angel, followed by a reference to the mustering of enemy forces and a fearsome description of their annihilation. The gruesome imagery is borrowed from Ez 39:4, 17–20.
¶¶[19:20] **Beast . . . false prophet**: see notes on Rev 13. **The fiery pool . . . sulfur**: symbol of God's punishment (Rev 14:10; 20:10, 14–15), different from the abyss; see note on Rev 9:1.
***[20:1–6] Like the other numerical values in this book, the thousand years are not to be taken literally; they symbolize the long period of time between the chaining up of Satan (a symbol for Christ's resurrection-victory over death and the forces of evil) and the end of the world. During this time God's people share in the glorious reign of God that is present to them by virtue of their baptismal victory over death and sin; cf. Rom 6:1–8; Jn 5:24–25; 16:33; 1 Jn 3:14; Eph 2:1.
†††[20:1] **Abyss**: see note on Rev 9:1.
‡‡‡[20:2] **Dragon . . . serpent . . . Satan**: see notes on Rev 12:3, 9, 10, 15.

---

z. [19:5] 11:18; Ps 115:13.   a. [19:7] Mt 22:9; Eph 5:27.   b. [19:8] 15:6; Is 61:10; Mt 22:11–12.   c. [19:9] Mt 8:11; Lk 14:15.   d. [19:10] 22:8–9.   e. [19:11] Is 11:4.   f. [19:12] 1:14–16; 2:18 / Lk 10:22.   g. [19:13] Is 63:1 / Jn 1:1.   h. [19:14] 15:6; 19:8.

i. [19:15] 14:20; Is 63:3.   j. [19:16] 17:14; 2 Mc 13:4.   k. [19:18] Ez 39:17–20.   l. [19:20] 14:10.   m. [20:1] 9:1.   n. [20:2] Gn 3:1.

nor had accepted its mark* on their foreheads or hands. They came to life and they reigned with Christ for a thousand years.⁰ ⁵The rest of the dead did not come to life until the thousand years were over. This is the first resurrection. ⁶Blessed† and holy is the one who shares in the first resurrection. The second death has no power over these; they will be priests of God and of Christ, and they will reign with him for [the] thousand years.

⁷‡When the thousand years are completed, Satan will be released from his prison. ⁸He will go out to deceive the nations at the four corners of the earth, Gog and Magog,§ to gather them for battle; their number is like the sand of the sea.ᵖ ⁹They invaded the breadth of the earth⁵ and surrounded the camp of the holy ones and the beloved city. But fire came down from heaven and consumed them.�q ¹⁰The Devil who had led them astray was thrown into the pool of fire and sulfur, where the beast and the false prophet were. There they will be tormented day and night forever and ever.

The Large White Throne.** ¹¹Next I saw a large white throne and the one who was sitting on it. The earth and the sky fled from his presence and there was no place for them.ʳ ¹²I saw the dead, the great and the lowly, standing before the throne, and scrolls were opened. Then another scroll was opened, the book of life.†† The dead were judged according to their deeds, by what was written in the scrolls.ˢ ¹³The sea gave up its dead; then Death and Hades‡‡ gave up their dead. All the dead were judged according to their deeds. ¹⁴Then Death and Hades were thrown into the pool of fire. (This pool of fire is the second death.§§) ¹⁵Anyone whose name was not found written in the book of life was thrown into the pool of fire.

VI. THE NEW CREATION¶¶

CHAPTER 21

The New Heaven and the New Earth. ¹ᵃThen I saw a new heaven and a new earth. The former

heaven and the former earth had passed away, and the sea was no more.*** ²I also saw the holy city, a new Jerusalem,††† coming down out of heaven from God, prepared as a bride adorned for her husband.ᵛ ³I heard a loud voice from the throne saying, "Behold, God's dwelling is with the human race.ʷ He will dwell with them and they will be his people‡‡‡ and God himself will always be with them [as their God].§§§ ⁴He will wipe every tear from their eyes, and there shall be no more death or mourning, wailing or pain, [for] the old order has passed away."ˣ

⁵The one who sat on the throne¶¶¶ said, "Behold, I make all things new." Then he said, "Write these words down, for they are trustworthy and true."ʸ ⁶He said to me, "They are accomplished.**** I [am] the Alpha and the Omega, the beginning and the end. To the thirsty I will give a gift from the spring of life-giving water.ᶻ ⁷The victor†††† will inherit these gifts, and I shall be his God, and he will be my son.ᵃ ⁸But as for cowards,‡‡‡‡ the unfaithful, the depraved, murderers, the unchaste, sorcerers, idol-worshipers, and deceivers of every sort, their lot is in the burning pool of fire and sulfur, which is the second death."ᵇ

The New Jerusalem.§§§§ ⁹One of the seven angels who held the seven bowls filled with the seven last plagues came and said to me, "Come here. I will show you the bride, the wife of the Lamb."¶¶¶¶ ¹⁰He took me in spirit to a great, high mountain and showed me the holy city Jerusalem coming down out of heaven from God.ᶜ ¹¹It gleamed with the splendor of God. Its radiance was like that of a precious stone, like jasper, clear as crystal.ᵈ ¹²It had a massive, high wall, with twelve gates where twelve angels were stationed and on which names were inscribed, [the names] of the twelve tribes of the Israelites. ¹³There were

---

ª [20:4] **Beast . . . mark:** see Rev 13 and its notes.

† [20:6] **Blessed:** see note on Rev 1:3. **Second death:** see note on Rev 2:11. **Priests:** as in Rev 1:6; 5:10; cf. 1 Pt 2:9.

‡ [20:7–10] A description of the symbolic battle to take place when Satan is released at the end of time, when the thousand years are over; see note on Rev 20:1–6.

§ [20:8] **Gog and Magog:** symbols of all pagan nations; the names are taken from Ez 38:1–39:20.

¶ [20:9] **The breadth of the earth:** Palestine. **The beloved city:** Jerusalem; see note on Rev 14:1.

** [20:11–15] A description of the final judgment. After the intermediate reign of Christ, all the dead are raised and judged, thus inaugurating the new age.

†† [20:12] **The book of life:** see note on Rev 3:5. **Judged . . . scrolls:** see note on Rev 14:12.

‡‡ [20:13] **Hades:** the netherworld; see note on Rev 1:18.

§§ [20:14] **Second death:** see note on Rev 2:11.

¶¶ [21:1–22:5] A description of God's eternal kingdom in heaven under the symbols of a new heaven and a new earth; cf. Is 65:17–25; 66:22; Mt 19:28.

*** [21:1] **Sea . . . no more:** because as home of the dragon it was doomed to disappear; cf. Jb 7:12.

††† [21:2] **New Jerusalem . . . bride:** symbol of the church (Gal 4:26); see note on Rev 19:7.

‡‡‡ [21:3–4] Language taken from Ez 37:27; Is 25:8; 35:10; cf. Rev 7:17.

§§§ [21:3] **People:** other ancient manuscripts read a plural, "peoples."

¶¶¶ [21:5] **The one . . . on the throne:** God himself; cf. Rev 4:1–11.

**** [21:6] **They are accomplished:** God's reign has already begun; see note on Rev 20:1–6. **Alpha . . . Omega:** see note on Rev 1:8. **Life-giving water:** see note on Rev 7:17.

†††† [21:7] **The victor:** over the forces of evil; see the conclusions of the seven letters (Rev 2:7, 11, 17, 26; 3:5, 12, 21). **He will be my son:** the victorious Christian enjoys divine affiliation by adoption (Gal 4:4–7; Rom 8:14–17); see note on Rev 2:26–28.

‡‡‡‡ [21:8] **Cowards:** their conviction is so weak that they deny Christ in time of trial and become traitors. **Second death:** see note on Rev 2:11.

§§§§ [21:9–22:5] Symbolic descriptions of the new Jerusalem, the church. Most of the images are borrowed from Ez 40–48.

¶¶¶¶ [21:9] **The bride, the wife of the Lamb:** the church (Rev 21:2), the new Jerusalem (Rev 21:10); cf. 2 Cor 11:2.

---

o. [20:4] Mt 19:28.　p. [20:8] Ez 38:2, 9, 16.　q. [20:9] Ez 38:22. r. [20:11] 2 Pt 3:7, 10, 12.　s. [20:12] Rom 2:6.　t. [20:14] 1 Cor 15:26, 54–55.　u. [21:1] Is 65:17; 66:22; Rom 8:19–23; 2 Pt 3:13.

v. [21:2] 19:7–9.　w. [21:3] Ez 37:27.　x. [21:4] 7:17; Is 25:8; 35:10. y. [21:5] Is 43:19; 2 Cor 5:17.　z. [21:6] 22:17; Ps 36:8–9; Is 55:1. a. [21:7] 2 Sm 7:14.　b. [21:8] 22:15; Rom 1:29–32.　c. [21:10] Ez 40:2.　d. [21:11] Heb 11:10.

three gates facing east, three north, three south, and three west.*[e] [14]The wall of the city had twelve courses of stones as its foundation, on which were inscribed the twelve names of the twelve apostles* of the Lamb.[f]

[15†]The one who spoke to me held a gold measuring rod to measure the city, its gates, and its wall. [16]The city was square, its length the same as [also] its width. He measured the city with the rod and found it fifteen hundred miles‡ in length and width and height. [17]He also measured its wall: one hundred and forty-four cubits§ according to the standard unit of measurement the angel used. [18¶]The wall was constructed of jasper, while the city was pure gold, clear as glass. [19]The foundations of the city wall were decorated with every precious stone; the first course of stones was jasper, the second sapphire, the third chalcedony, the fourth emerald,[g] [20]the fifth sardonyx, the sixth carnelian, the seventh chrysolite, the eighth beryl, the ninth topaz, the tenth chrysoprase, the eleventh hyacinth, and the twelfth amethyst. [21]The twelve gates were twelve pearls, each of the gates made from a single pearl; and the street of the city was of pure gold, transparent as glass.

[22**h]I saw no temple in the city, for its temple is the Lord God almighty and the Lamb. [23††]The city had no need of sun or moon to shine on it,[i] for the glory of God gave it light, and its lamp was the Lamb. [24]The nations will walk by its light,‡‡ and to it the kings of the earth will bring their treasure.[j] [25]During the day its gates will never be shut, and there will be no night there. [26]The treasure and wealth of the nations will be brought there, [27]but nothing unclean will enter it, nor any[one] who does abominable things or tells lies. Only those will enter whose names are written in the Lamb's book of life.[k]

---

*[21:14] **Courses of stones . . . apostles**: literally, "twelve foundations"; cf. Eph 2:19–20.

†[21:15–17] The city is shaped like a gigantic cube, a symbol of perfection (cf. 1 Kgs 6:19–20). The measurements of the city and its wall are multiples of the symbolic number twelve; see note on Rev 7:4–9.

‡[21:16] **Fifteen hundred miles**: literally, twelve thousand stades, about 12,000 furlongs (see note on Rev 14:20); the number is symbolic: twelve (the apostles as leaders of the new Israel) multiplied by 1,000 (the immensity of Christians); cf. Introduction. **In length and width and height**: literally, "its length and width and height are the same."

§[21:17] **One hundred and forty-four cubits**: the cubit was about eighteen inches in length. **Standard unit of measurement the angel used**: literally, "by a human measure, i.e., an angel's."

¶[21:18–21] The gold and precious gems symbolize the beauty and excellence of the church; cf. Ex 28:15–21; Tb 13:16–17; Is 54:11–12.

**[21:22] Christ is present throughout the church; hence, no temple is needed as an earthly dwelling for God; cf. Mt 18:20; 28:20; Jn 4:21.

††[21:23] **Lamp . . . Lamb**: cf. Jn 8:12.

‡‡[21:24–27] All men and women of good will are welcome in the church; cf. Is 60:1, 3, 5, 11. **The . . . book of life**: see note on Rev 3:5.

e. [21:13] Ez 48:31–35. f. [21:14] Eph 2:20. g. [21:19] Is 54:11–12. h. [21:22] Jn 2:19–20. i. [21:23] Is 60:1–2, 19–20. j. [21:24] Is 60:11. k. [21:27] Is 35:8; 52:1; Zec 13:2 / Rev 3:5; 20:12.

CHAPTER 22

[1]Then the angel showed me the river of life-giving water,§§ sparkling like crystal, flowing from the throne of God and of the Lamb[l] [2]down the middle of its street. On either side of the river grew the tree of life¶¶ that produces fruit twelve times a year, once each month; the leaves of the trees serve as medicine for the nations. [3]Nothing accursed will be found there anymore. The throne of God and of the Lamb will be in it, and his servants will worship him. [4]They will look upon his face,*** and his name will be on their foreheads. [5]Night will be no more, nor will they need light from lamp or sun, for the Lord God shall give them light, and they shall reign forever and ever.[m]

VII. EPILOGUE†††

[6]And he said to me, "These words are trustworthy and true, and the Lord, the God of prophetic spirits, sent his angel to show his servants what must happen soon."[n] [7‡‡‡]"Behold, I am coming soon."§§§ Blessed is the one who keeps the prophetic message of this book.[o]

[8]It is I, John, who heard and saw these things, and when I heard and saw them I fell down to worship at the feet of the angel who showed them to me. [9]But he said to me, "Don't! I am a fellow servant of yours and of your brothers the prophets and of those who keep the message of this book. Worship God."[p]

[10]Then he said to me, "Do not seal up the prophetic words of this book, for the appointed time¶¶¶ is near. [11]Let the wicked still act wickedly, and the filthy still be filthy. The righteous must still do right, and the holy still be holy."

[12]"Behold, I am coming soon. I bring with me the recompense I will give to each according to his deeds.[q] [13]I am the Alpha and the Omega,[r] the first and the last, the beginning and the end."****

[14]Blessed are they who wash their robes so as to have the right to the tree of life and enter the city†††† through its gates.[s] [15]Outside are the dogs, the sorcerers, the unchaste, the murderers, the

---

§§[22:1, 17] **Life-giving water**: see note on Rev 7:17.

¶¶[22:2] **The tree of life**: cf. Rev 22:14; see note on Rev 2:7. **Fruit . . . medicine**: cf. Ez 47:12.

***[22:4] **Look upon his face**: cf. Mt 5:8; 1 Cor 13:12; 1 Jn 3:2.

†††[22:6–21] The book ends with an epilogue consisting of a series of warnings and exhortations and forming an inclusion with the prologue by resuming its themes and expressions; see note on Rev 1:1–3.

‡‡‡[22:7, 12, 20] **I am coming soon**: Christ is the speaker; see note on Rev 1:3.

§§§[22:7, 14] **Blessed**: see note on Rev 1:3.

¶¶¶[22:10] **The appointed time**: see note on Rev 1:3.

****[22:13] Christ applies to himself words used by God in Rev 1:8.

††††[22:14] **The city**: heavenly Jerusalem; see note on Rev 2:2.

l. [22:1] Ez 47:1–12. m. [22:5] Is 60:20. n. [22:6] 1:1. o. [22:7] 12, 20 / 1:3. p. [22:9] 19:10. q. [22:12] 7, 20 / Ps 62:12; 2 Tm 4:14. r. [22:13] 1:8; 21:6; Is 41:4; 44:6. s. [22:14] 7:14–15; 22:2.

idol-worshipers, and all who love and practice deceit.^{t}

^{16}"I, Jesus, sent my angel to give you this testimony for the churches. I am the root and offspring of David,* the bright morning star."^{u}

^{17}The Spirit and the bride† say, "Come." Let the hearer say, "Come." Let the one who thirsts come forward, and the one who wants it receive the gift of life-giving water.^{v}

^{18}I warn everyone who hears the prophetic words in this book: if anyone adds to them, God will add to him the plagues described in this book, ^{19}and if anyone takes away from the words in this prophetic book, God will take away his share in the tree of life and in the holy city described in this book.^{w}

^{20‡x}The one who gives this testimony says, "Yes, I am coming soon." Amen! Come, Lord Jesus!

^{21}The grace of the Lord Jesus be with all.

---

*[22:16] **The root . . . of David**: see note on Rev 5:5. **Morning star**: see note on Rev 2:26–28.

†[22:17] **Bride**: the church; see note on Rev 21:2.

t. [22:15] 21:8; Rom 1:29–32. u. [22:16] 1:1, 11–12; 22:6 / 2:28. v. [22:17] 21:6; Is 55:1.

‡[22:20] **Come, Lord Jesus**: a liturgical refrain, similar to the Aramaic expression *Marana tha*—"Our Lord, come!"—in 1 Cor 16:22; cf. note there. It was a prayer for the coming of Christ in glory at the parousia; see note on Rev 1:3.

w. [22:19] Dt 4:2. x. [22:20] 7, 12 / Acts 3:20–21; 1 Cor 15:23; 16:22.

THE BOOK OF
PSALMS

THE BOOK OF
PSALMS

~~~

The Hebrew Psalter numbers 150 songs. The corresponding number in the Septuagint differs because of a different division of certain Psalms. Hence the numbering in the Greek Psalter (which was followed by the Latin Vulgate) is usually one digit behind the Hebrew. In the New American Bible the numbering of the verses follows the Hebrew numbering; many of the traditional English translations are often a verse number behind the Hebrew because they do not count the superscriptions as a verse.

The superscriptions derive from pre-Christian Jewish tradition, and they contain technical terms, many of them apparently liturgical, which are no longer known to us. Seventy-three Psalms are attributed to David, but there is no sure way of dating any Psalm. Some are preexilic (before 587), and others are postexilic (after 539), but not as late as the Maccabean period (ca. 165). The Psalms are the product of many individual collections (e.g., Songs of Ascents, Ps 120–134), which were eventually combined into the present work in which one can detect five "books," because of the doxologies which occur at 41:14; 72:18–19; 89:53; 106:48.

Two important features of the Psalms deserve special notice. First, the majority were composed originally precisely for liturgical worship. This is shown by the frequent indication of liturgical leaders interacting with the community (e.g., Ps 118:1–4). Secondly, they follow certain distinct patterns or literary forms. Thus, the hymn is a song of praise, in which a community is urged joyfully to sing out the praise of God. Various reasons are given for this praise (often introduced by "for" or "because"): the divine work of creation and sustenance (Ps 135:1–12; 136). Some of the hymns have received a more specific classification, based on content. The "Songs of Zion" are so called because they exalt Zion, the city in which God dwells among the people (Ps 47; 96–99). Characteristic of the songs of praise is the joyful summons to get involved in the activity; Ps 104 is an exception to this, although it remains universal in its thrust.

Another type of Psalm is similar to the hymn: the thanksgiving Psalm. This too is a song of praise acknowledging the Lord as the rescuer of the psalmist from a desperate situation. Very often the psalmist will give a flashback, recounting the past distress, and the plea that was uttered (Ps 30; 116). The setting for such prayers seems to have been the offering of a *todah* (a "praise" sacrifice) with friends in the Temple.

There are more Psalms of lament than of any other type. They may be individual (e.g., Ps 3–7; 22) or communal (e.g., Ps 44). Although they usually begin with a cry for help, they develop in various ways. The description of the distress is couched in the broad imagery typical of the Bible (one is in Sheol, the Pit, or is afflicted by enemies or wild beasts, etc.)—in such a way that one cannot pinpoint the exact nature of the psalmist's plight. However, Ps 51 (cf. also Ps 130) seems to refer clearly to deliverance from sin. Several laments end on a note of certainty that the Lord has heard the prayer (cf. Ps 7, but contrast Ps 88), and the Psalter has been characterized as a movement from lament to praise. If this is somewhat of an exaggeration, it serves at least to emphasize the frequent expressions of trust which characterize the lament. In some cases it would seem as if the theme of trust has been lifted out to form a literary type all its own; cf. Ps 23, 62, 91. Among the communal laments can be counted Ps 74 and 79. They complain to the Lord about some national disaster, and try to motivate God to intervene in favor of the suffering people.

Other Psalms are clearly classified on account of content, and they may be in themselves laments or Psalms of thanksgiving. Among the "royal" Psalms that deal directly with the currently reigning king, are Ps 20, 21, and 72. Many of the royal Psalms were given a messianic interpretation by Christians. In Jewish tradition they were preserved, even after kingship had disappeared, because they were read in the light of the Davidic covenant reported in 2 Sm 7. Certain Psalms are called wisdom Psalms because they seem to betray the influence of the concerns of the ages (cf. Ps 37; 49), but there is no general agreement as to the number of these prayers. Somewhat related to the wisdom Psalms are the "torah" Psalms, in which the torah (instruction or law) of the Lord is glorified (Ps 1; 19:8–14; 119). Ps 78, 105, 106 can be considered as "historical" Psalms. Although the majority of the Psalms have a liturgical setting, there are certain prayers that may be termed "liturgies," so clearly does their structure reflect a liturgical incident (e.g., Ps 15; 24).

It is obvious that not all of the Psalms can be pigeon-holed into neat classifications, but even a brief sketch of these types help us to catch the structure and spirit of the Psalms we read. It has been rightly said that the Psalms are "a school of prayer." They not only provide us with models to follow, but inspire us to voice our own deepest feelings and aspirations.

First Book—Psalms 1–41

PSALM 1*
True Happiness in God's Law

I

1 Blessed is the man who does not walk
  in the counsel of the wicked,
Nor stand in the way† of sinners,
  nor sit in company with scoffers.ᵃ
2 Rather, the law of the LORD‡ is his joy;
  and on his law he meditates day and
  night.ᵇ
3 He is like a treeᶜ
  planted near streams of water,
  that yields its fruit in season;
Its leaves never wither;
  whatever he does prospers.

II

4 But not so are the wicked,§ not so!
  They are like chaff driven by the
  wind.ᵈ
5 Therefore the wicked will not arise at the
  judgment,
  nor will sinners in the assembly of
  the just.
6 Because the LORD knows the way of the
  just,ᵉ
  but the way of the wicked leads to
  ruin.

PSALM 2¶
A Psalm for a Royal Coronation

1 Why do the nations protest
  and the peoples conspire in vain?ᶠ
2 Kings on earth rise up
  and princes plot together
  against the LORD and against his
  anointed one:**ᵍ
3 "Let us break their shackles
  and cast off their chains from us!"ʰ
4 The one enthroned in heaven laughs;
  the Lord derides them,ⁱ
5 Then he speaks to them in his anger,
  in his wrath he terrifies them:
6 "I myself have installed my king
  on Zion, my holy mountain."
7 I will proclaim the decree of the LORD,
  he said to me, "You are my son;
  today I have begotten you.ʲ
8 Ask it of me,
  and I will give you the nations as
  your inheritance,
  and, as your possession, the ends of
  the earth.
9 With an iron rod you will shepherd them,
  like a potter's vessel you will shatter
  them."ᵏ
10 And now, kings, give heed;
  take warning, judges on earth.
11 Serve the LORD with fear;
  exult with trembling,
Accept correction
  lest he become angry and you perish

---

*[Psalm 1] A preface to the whole Book of Psalms, contrasting with striking similes the destiny of the good and the wicked. The Psalm views life as activity, as choosing either the good or the bad. Each "way" brings its inevitable consequences. The wise through their good actions will experience rootedness and life, and the wicked, rootlessness and death.

†[1:1] The way: a common biblical term for manner of living or moral conduct (Ps 32:8; 101:2, 6; Prv 2:20; 1 Kgs 8:36).

‡[1:2] The law of the LORD: either the Torah, the first five books of the Bible, or, more probably, divine teaching or instruction.

§[1:4] The wicked: those who by their actions distance themselves from God's life-giving presence.

¶[Psalm 2] A royal Psalm. To rebellious kings (Ps 2:1–3) God responds vigorously (Ps 2:4–6). A speaker proclaims the divine decree (in the legal adoption language of the day), making the Israelite king the earthly representative of God (Ps 2:7–9) and warning kings to obey (Ps 2:10–11). The Psalm has a messianic meaning for the Church; the New Testament understands it of Christ (Acts 4:25–27; 13:33; Heb 1:5).

**[2:2] Anointed: in Hebrew mashiah, "anointed"; in Greek christos, whence English Messiah and Christ. In Israel kings (Jgs 9:8; 1 Sm 9:16; 16:12–13) and high priests (Lv 8:12; Nm 3:3) received the power of their office through anointing.

---

a. [1:1] Ps 26:4–5; 40:5.   b. [1:2] Jos 1:8; Ps 119; Sir 9:1.   c. [1:3] Ps 52:10; 92:13–15; Jer 17:8.   d. [1:4] Ps 35:5; 83:14–16; Jb 21:18.   e. [1:6] Ps 37:18.

f. [2:1] Rev 11:18.   g. [2:2] Ps 83:6.   h. [2:3] Ps 149:8.   i. [2:4] Ps 37:13; 59:9; Wis 4:18.   j. [2:7] Ps 89:27; 110:2–3; Is 49:1.   k. [2:9] Rev 2:27; 12:5; 19:15.

along the way
when his anger suddenly blazes up.[l]
Blessed are all who take refuge in him!

PSALM 3*
Threatened but Trusting

[1]A psalm of David, when he fled from his son
Absalom.[†m]

I

[2] How many are my foes, LORD!
How many rise against me!
[3] [‡]How many say of me,
"There is no salvation for him in
God."[n]

Selah

[4] But you, LORD, are a shield around me;
my glory, you keep my head high.[o]

II

[5] With my own voice I will call out to the
LORD,
and he will answer me from his holy
mountain.

Selah

[6] I lie down and I fall asleep,
[and] I will wake up, for the LORD
sustains me.[p]
[7] I do not fear, then, thousands of people
arrayed against me on every side.

III

[8] Arise, LORD! Save me, my God!
For you strike the cheekbone of all
my foes;
you break the teeth of the wicked.[q]
[9] Salvation is from the LORD!
May your blessing be upon your
people![r]

Selah

PSALM 4[§]
Trust in God

[1]For the leader;[¶] with stringed instruments. A
psalm of David.

I

[2] Answer me when I call, my saving God.
When troubles hem me in, set me free;
take pity on me, hear my prayer.[s]

II

[3] How long, O people, will you be hard of
heart?
Why do you love what is worthless,
chase after lies?[**t]

Selah

[4] Know that the LORD works wonders for
his faithful one;
the LORD hears when I call out to him.
[5] Tremble[††] and sin no more;
weep bitterly[††] within your hearts,
wail upon your beds,[u]
[6] Offer fitting sacrifices
and trust in the LORD.[v]

III

[7] Many say, "May we see better times!
LORD, show us the light of your face!"[w]

Selah

[8] But you have given my heart more joy
than they have when grain and wine
abound.
[9] [x‡‡]In peace I will lie down and fall asleep,
for you alone, LORD, make me secure.

PSALM 5[§§]
Prayer for Divine Help

[1]For the leader; with wind instruments. A psalm
of David.

I

[2] Give ear to my words, O LORD;
understand my sighing.[y]
[3] Attend to the sound of my cry, ·
my king and my God!
For to you I will pray, LORD;
[4] in the morning you will hear my voice;
in the morning I will plead before
you and wait.[z]

---

*[Psalm 3] An individual lament complaining of enemies
who deny that God will come to the rescue (Ps 3:2–3). Despite
such taunts the psalmist hopes for God's protection even in
sleep (Ps 3:4–7). The Psalm prays for an end to the enemies'
power to speak maliciously (Ps 3:8) and closes peacefully with
an expression of trust (Ps 3:9).
†[3:1] The superscription, added later, relates the Psalm to
an incident in the life of David.
‡[3:3, 3:5, 3:9] Selah: the term is generally considered a
direction to the cantor or musicians but its exact meaning is
not known. It occurs 71 times in 39 Psalms.
§[Psalm 4] An individual lament emphasizing trust in
God. The petition is based upon the psalmist's vivid experience of God as savior (Ps 4:2). That experience of God is the
basis for the warning to the wicked: revere God who inter-
venes on the side of the faithful (Ps 4:3–6). The faithful psalmist exemplifies the blessings given to the just (Ps 4:7–8).
¶[4:1] For the leader: many Psalm headings contain
this rubric. Its exact meaning is unknown but may signify

that such Psalms once stood together in a collection of "the
choirmaster," cf. 1 Chr 15:21.
**[4:3] Love what is worthless . . . lies: these expressions
probably refer to false gods worshiped by those the psalmist
is addressing.
††[4:5] Tremble: be moved deeply with fear for failing to
worship the true God. The Greek translation understood the
emotion to be anger, and it is so cited in Eph 4:26. Weep bitterly . . . wail: weeping within one's heart and wailing upon one's
bed denote sincere repentance because these actions are not
done in public or with the community but in the privacy of one's
heart and one's home. The same idiom is found in Hos 7:14.
‡‡[4:9] In peace I will . . . fall asleep: the last verse repeats
two themes in the Psalm. One is the security of one who
trusts in the true God; the other is the interior peace of those
who sincerely repent ("on [their] beds"), whose sleep is not
disturbed by a guilty conscience.
§§[Psalm 5] A lament contrasting the security of the house of
God (Ps 5:8–9, 12–13) with the danger of the company of evildoers (Ps 5:5–7, 10–11). The psalmist therefore prays that God will
hear (Ps 5:2–4) and grant the protection and joy of the Temple.

---

l. [2:11] Ps 34:9; 146:5; Prv 16:20.   m. [3:1] 2 Sm 15:13ff.   n. [3:3]
Ps 71:11.   o. [3:4] Ps 7:11; 18:3; 62:7–8; Dt 33:29; Is 60:19.   p. [3:6]
Ps 4:9; Prv 3:24.   q. [3:8] Ps 58:7.   r. [3:9] Ps 28:9; Jon 2:10.

s. [4:2] Ps 118:5.   t. [4:3] Ps 62:4.   u. [4:5] Eph 4:26.   v. [4:6] Ps
51:19.   w. [4:7] Ps 31:17; 44:4; 67:1; 80:4; Jb 13:24; Nm 6:25; Dn
9:17.   x. [4:9] Ps 3:6.   y. [5:2] Ps 86:6; 130:1–2.   z. [5:4] Wis 16:28.

II

5 You are not a god who delights in evil;
  no wicked person finds refuge with
   you;
6   the arrogant cannot stand before
   your eyes.
 You hate all who do evil;
7   you destroy those who speak falsely.*
 A bloody and fraudulent man
  the LORD abhors.

III

8 But I, through the abundance of your mercy,*
  will enter into your house.
 I will bow down toward your holy
   sanctuary
  out of fear of you.*b*
9 LORD, guide me in your justice because of
  my foes;
  make straight your way before me.*c*

IV

10 For there is no sincerity in their mouth;
  their heart is corrupt.
 Their throat† is an open grave;*d*
  on their tongue are subtle lies.
11 Declare them guilty, God;
  make them fall by their own devices.*e*
 Drive them out for their many sins;
  for they have rebelled against you.

V

12 Then all who trust in you will be glad
  and forever shout for joy.*f*
 You will protect them and those will
   rejoice in you
  who love your name.
13 For you, LORD, bless the just one;
  you surround him with favor like a
   shield.

PSALM 6‡
Prayer in Distress

1For the leader; with stringed instruments,
"upon the eighth."§

---

*[5:8] **Mercy**: used to translate the Hebrew word, *hesed*. This term speaks to a relationship between persons. It is manifested in concrete actions to persons with some need or desire. The one who offers *hesed* has the ability to respond to that need of the other person. Other possible ways to translate *hesed* include "steadfast love" and "loving kindness."

†[5:10] **Their throat**: their speech brings harm to their hearers (cf. Jer 5:16). The verse mentions four parts of the body, each a source of evil to the innocent.

‡[Psalm 6] The first of the seven Penitential Psalms (Ps 6, 32, 38, 51, 102, 130, 143), a designation dating from the seventh century A.D. for Psalms suitable to express repentance. The psalmist does not, as in many laments, claim to be innocent but appeals to God's mercy (Ps 6:5). Sin here, as often in the Bible, is both the sinful act and its injurious conseqfences; here it is physical sickness (Ps 6:3–4, 7–8) and the attacks of enemies (Ps 6:8, 9, 11). The psalmist prays that the effects of personal and social sin be taken away.

§[6:1] **Upon the eighth**: apparently a musical notation, now lost.

a. [5:7] Ps 101:7; Wis 14:9; Heb 1:13. b. [5:8] Ps 138:2; Jon 2:5.
c. [5:9] Ps 23:3; Prv 4:11; Is 26:7. d. [5:10] Rom 3:13. e. [5:11] Ps 141:10. f. [5:12] Ps 64:11.

A psalm of David.

I

2 Do not reprove me in your anger, LORD,
  nor punish me in your wrath.*g*
3 Have pity on me, LORD, for I am weak;
  heal me, LORD, for my bones are
   shuddering.*h*
4 My soul too is shuddering greatly—
  and you, LORD, how long . . . ?§*i*
5 Turn back, LORD, rescue my soul;
  save me because of your mercy.
6 For in death there is no remembrance of
   you.
  Who praises you in Sheol?**j*

II

7 I am wearied with sighing;
  all night long I drench my bed with
   tears;
  I soak my couch with weeping.
8 My eyes are dimmed with sorrow,
  worn out because of all my foes.*k*

III

9 Away from me, all who do evil!*l*
  The LORD has heard the sound of
   my weeping.
10 The LORD has heard my plea;
  the LORD will receive my prayer.
11 My foes will all be disgraced and will
   shudder greatly;
  they will turn back in sudden
   disgrace.*m*

PSALM 7††
God the Vindicator

1A plaintive song of David, which he sang to the LORD concerning Cush, the Benjaminite.

I

2 LORD my God, in you I trusted;
  save me; rescue me from all who
   pursue me,*n*
3 Lest someone maul me like a lion,
  tear my soul apart with no one to
   deliver.

---

§[6:4] **How long?**: elliptical for "How long will it be before you answer my prayer?" cf. Ps 13:2–3.

**[6:6] A motive for God to preserve the psalmist from death: in the shadowy world of the dead no one offers you praise. Sheol is the biblical term for the underworld where the insubstantial souls of dead human beings dwelt. It was similar to the Hades of Greek and Latin literature. In the second century B.C., biblical books begin to speak positively of life with God after death (Dn 12:1–3; Wis 3).

††[Psalm 7] An individual lament. The psalmist flees to God's presence in the sanctuary for justice and protection (Ps 7:2–3) and takes an oath that only the innocent can swear (Ps 7:4–6). The innocent psalmist can thus hope for the just God's protection (Ps 7:7–14) and be confident that the actions of the wicked will come back upon their own heads (Ps 7:15–17). The justice of God leads the psalmist to praise (Ps 7:18).

g. [6:2] Ps 38:2. h. [6:3] Jer 17:14–15. i. [6:4] Ps 13:2–3; 74:10; 89:47. j. [6:6] Ps 30:10; 88:11; 115:17; Is 38:18. k. [6:8] Ps 31:10; 38:11; 40:13. l. [6:9] Ps 119:115; Mt 7:23; Lk 13:27. m. [6:11] Ps 35:4, 26; 40:15; 71:13. n. [7:2] Ps 6:5; 22:21.

II

4 LORD my God, if I have done this,*
  if there is guilt on my hands,
5 If I have maltreated someone treating me
    equitably—
  or even despoiled my oppressor
    without cause—
6 Then let my enemy pursue and overtake
    my soul,
  trample my life to the ground,
  and lay my honor in the dust.[o]

  Selah

III

7 Rise up, LORD, in your anger;
  be aroused against the outrages of
    my oppressors.[p]
  Stir up the justice, my God, you have
    commanded.
8 Have the assembly of the peoples gather
    about you;
  and return on high above them,
9   the LORD will pass judgment on the
    peoples.
  Judge me, LORD, according to my
    righteousness,
  and my integrity.
10 Let the malice of the wicked end.
  Uphold the just one,
  O just God,[q]
  who tries hearts and minds.

IV

11 God is a shield above me
  saving the upright of heart.[r]
12 God is a just judge, powerful and patient,†
  not exercising anger every day.
13 If one does not repent,
  God sharpens his sword,
  strings and readies the bow,[s]
14 Prepares his deadly shafts,
  makes arrows blazing thunderbolts.[t]

V

15 Consider how one conceives iniquity;
  is pregnant with mischief,
  and gives birth to deception.[u]
16 He digs a hole and bores it deep,
  but he falls into the pit he has made.[v]
17 His malice turns back upon his head;
  his violence falls on his own skull.

VI

18 I will thank the LORD in accordance with
    his justice;
  I will sing the name of the LORD
    Most High.[w]

---

*[7:4] **Have done this**: in the accusation the enemies have made against the psalmist.

†[7:12] **Powerful and patient**: the inclusion of these words is drawn from the Septuagint tradition concerning this verse.

o. [7:6] Ps 143:3.   p. [7:7] Ps 9:4; 19:20.   q. [7:10] Ps 17:3; 26:2; 35:24; 43:1; 139:23; Jer 17:10; 20:12.   r. [7:11] Ps 3:4.   s. [7:13] Ps 11:2.   t. [7:14] Is 50:11.   u. [7:15] Jb 15:35; Is 59:4.   v. [7:16] Ps 9:16; 35:8; 57:7; Prv 26:27; Eccl 10:8; Sir 27:26.   w. [7:18] Ps 18:50; 30:5; 135:3; 146:2.

PSALM 8‡
Divine Majesty and Human Dignity

1 For the leader; "upon the *gittith*."§ A psalm of David.

2 O LORD, our Lord,
  how awesome is your name through
    all the earth!
  I will sing of your majesty above the heavens
3   with the mouths of babes[x] and
    infants.¶
  You have established a bulwark¶ against
    your foes,
  to silence enemy and avenger.¶

4 When I see your heavens, the work of
    your fingers,
  the moon and stars that you set in
    place—
5 **What is man that you are mindful of him,[y]
  and a son of man that you care for
    him?[z]
6 Yet you have made him little less than a
    god,††
  crowned him with glory and honor.
7 You have given him rule over the works of
    your hands,[a]
  put all things at his feet:
8 All sheep and oxen,
  even the beasts of the field,
9 The birds of the air, the fish of the sea,
  and whatever swims the paths of
    the seas.

10 O LORD, our Lord,
  how awesome is your name through
    all the earth!

---

‡[Psalm 8] While marvelling at the limitless grandeur of God (Ps 8:2–3), the psalmist is struck first by the smallness of human beings in creation (Ps 8:4–5), and then by the royal dignity and power that God has graciously bestowed upon them (Ps 8:6–9).

§[8:1] **Upon the gittith**: probably the title of the melody to which the Psalm was to be sung or a musical instrument.

¶[8:3] **With the mouths of babes and infants**: the psalmist realizes that his attempts to praise such an awesome God are hopelessly inadequate and amount to little more than the sounds made by infants. **Established a bulwark**: an allusion to lost myth telling how God built a fortress for himself in the heavens in primordial times in his battle with the powers of chaos. This "bulwark" is the firmament. **Enemy and avenger**: probably cosmic enemies. The primeval powers of watery chaos are often personified in poetic texts (Ps 74:13–14; 89:11; Jb 9:13; 26:12–13; Is 51:9).

[8:5] **Man . . . a son of man: the emphasis is on the fragility and mortality of human beings to whom God has given great dignity.

††[8:6] **Little less than a god**: Hebrew *'elohim*, the ordinary word for "God" or "the gods" or members of the heavenly court. The Greek version translated *'elohim* by "angel, messenger"; several ancient and modern versions so translate. The meaning seems to be that God created human beings almost at the level of the beings in the heavenly world. Heb 2:9, translating "for a little while," finds the eminent fulfillment of this verse in Jesus Christ, who was humbled before being glorified, cf. also 1 Cor 15:27 where St. Paul applies to Christ the closing words of Ps 8:7.

x. [8:3] Mt 21:16; Wis 10:21.   y. [8:5] Ps 144:3; Jb 7:17.   z. [8:5] Heb 2:6ff.   a. [8:7ff] Gn 1:26, 28; Wis 9:2; 1 Cor 15:27.

PSALM 9*
Thanksgiving for Victory
and Prayer for Justice

[1]For the leader; according to *Muth Labben*.[†] A psalm of David.

I

[2] I will praise you, LORD, with all my heart;
  I will declare all your wondrous
    deeds.
[3] I will delight and rejoice in you;
  I will sing hymns to your name,
    Most High.
[4] When my enemies turn back,
  they stumble and perish before you.

II

[5] For you upheld my right and my cause,
  seated on your throne, judging
    justly.
[6] You rebuked the nations, you destroyed
    the wicked;
  their name you blotted out for all
    time.[b]
[7] The enemies have been ruined forever;
  you destroyed their cities;
  their memory has perished.

III

[8] The LORD rules forever,
  has set up his throne for judgment.
[9] It is he who judges the world with
    justice,[c]
  who judges the peoples with
    fairness.
[10] The LORD is a stronghold for the
    oppressed,
  a stronghold in times of trouble.[d]
[11] Those who know your name trust in you;
  you never forsake those who seek
    you, LORD.

IV

[12] Sing hymns to the LORD enthroned on
    Zion;
  proclaim his deeds among the
    nations!
[13] For the avenger of bloodshed remembers,
  does not forget the cry of the
    afflicted.[e]

V

[14] Be gracious to me, LORD;
  see how my foes afflict me!

You alone can raise me from the
    gates of death.[f]
[15] Then I will declare all your praises,
  sing joyously of your salvation
  in the gates of daughter Zion.[‡]

VI

[16] The nations fall into the pit they dig;
  in the snare they hide, their own
    foot is caught.
[17] [§]The LORD is revealed in making
    judgments:
  by the deeds they do the wicked are
    trapped.[g]

Higgaion. Selah[§]

VII

[18] To Sheol the wicked will depart,
  all the nations that forget God.
[19] For the needy will never be forgotten,
  nor will the hope of the afflicted ever
    fade.[h]
[20] Arise, LORD, let no mortal prevail;
  let the nations be judged in your
    presence.
[21] Strike them with terror, LORD;
  show the nations they are only
    human.

Selah

PSALM 10

I

[1] Why, LORD, do you stand afar
  and pay no heed in times of trouble?
[2] Arrogant scoundrels pursue the poor;
  they trap them by their cunning
    schemes.[i]

II

[3] The wicked even boast of their greed;
  these robbers curse and scorn the
    LORD.[j]
[4] In their insolence the wicked boast:
  "God does not care; there is no God."[k]
[5]   Yet their affairs always succeed;
  they ignore your judgment on high;
  they sneer at all who oppose them.
[6] They say in their hearts, "We will never
    fall;
  never will we see misfortune."
[7] Their mouths are full of oaths, violence,
    and lies;
  discord and evil are under their
    tongues.[l]

---

*[Psalms 9–10] Ps 9 and Ps 10 in the Hebrew text have been transmitted as separate poems but they actually form a single acrostic poem and are so transmitted in the Greek and Latin tradition. Each verse of the two Psalms begins with a successive letter of the Hebrew alphabet (though several letters have no corresponding stanza). The Psalm states loosely connected themes: the rescue of the helpless poor from their enemies, God's worldwide judgment and rule over the nations, the psalmist's own concern for rescue (Ps 9:14–15).

†[9:1] **Muth Labben**: probably the melodic accompaniment of the Psalm, now lost.

‡[9:15] **Daughter Zion**: an ancient Near Eastern city could sometimes be personified as a woman or a queen, the spouse of the god of the city.

§[9:17] **The LORD is revealed in making judgments**: God has so made the universe that the wicked are punished by the very actions they perform. **Selah**: see note on Ps 3:3.

---

b. [9:6] Jb 18:17.   c. [9:9] Ps 96:10; 98:9.   d. [9:10] Ps 37:39; Is 25:4.
e. [9:13] Jb 16:18.

f. [9:14] Wis 16:13.   g. [9:17] Ps 35:8; Sir 27:26.   h. [9:19] Prv 23:18.   i. [10:2] Is 32:7.   j. [10:3] Ps 36:2.   k. [10:4] Ps 14:1; Jb 22:13; Is 29:15; Jer 5:12; Zep 1:12.   l. [10:7] Is 32:7; Rom 3:14.

8 They wait in ambush near towns;
    their eyes watch for the helpless
      to murder the innocent in secret.^m
9 They lurk in ambush like lions in a
    thicket,
    hide there to trap the poor,
    snare them and close the net.ⁿ
10 The helpless are crushed, laid low;
    they fall into the power of the
      wicked,
11 Who say in their hearts, "God has
    forgotten,
    shows no concern, never bothers to
      look."^o

III

12 Rise up, LORD! God, lift up your hand!
    Do not forget the poor!
13 Why should the wicked scorn God,
    say in their hearts, "God does not
      care"?
14 But you do see;
    you take note of misery and sorrow;^p
    you take the matter in hand.
    To you the helpless can entrust their
      cause;
    you are the defender of orphans.^q
15 Break the arm of the wicked and
    depraved;
    make them account for their crimes;
    let none of them survive.

IV

16 The LORD is king forever;^r
    the nations have vanished from his
      land.
17 You listen, LORD, to the needs of the poor;
    you strengthen their heart and
      incline your ear.
18 You win justice for the orphaned and
    oppressed;^s
    no one on earth will cause terror
      again.

PSALM 11[*]
Confidence in the Presence of God

1 For the leader. Of David.

I

In the LORD I take refuge;
    how can you say to me,
    "Flee like a bird to the mountains!^t
2 See how the wicked string their bows,
    fit their arrows to the string
    to shoot from the shadows at the
      upright of heart.^u

3 †If foundations are destroyed,
    what can the just one do?"

II

4 The LORD is in his holy temple;
    the LORD's throne is in heaven.^v
    God's eyes keep careful watch;
    they test the children of Adam.
5 The LORD tests the righteous and the
    wicked,
    hates those who love violence,
6 And rains upon the wicked
    fiery coals and brimstone,
    a scorching wind their allotted cup.^{‡w}
7 The LORD is just and loves just deeds;
    the upright will see his face.

PSALM 12[§]
Prayer Against Evil Tongues

1 For the leader; "upon the eighth." A psalm of David.

I

2 Help, LORD, for no one loyal remains;
    the faithful have vanished from the
      children of men.^x
3 They tell lies to one another,
    speak with deceiving lips and a
      double heart.^y

II

4 May the LORD cut off all deceiving lips,
    and every boastful tongue,
5 Those who say, "By our tongues we
    prevail;
    when our lips speak, who can lord it
      over us?"^z

III

6 "Because they rob the weak, and the
    needy groan,
    I will now arise," says the LORD;
    "I will grant safety to whoever longs
      for it."^a

IV

7 The promises of the LORD are sure,
    silver refined in a crucible,[¶]
    silver purified seven times.^b

---

†[11:3] **Foundations:** usually understood of public order, cf. Ps 82:5.

‡[11:6] **Their allotted cup:** the cup that God gives people to drink is a common figure for their destiny, cf. Ps 16:5; 75:9; Mt 20:22; 26:39; Rev 14:10.

§[Psalm 12] A lament. The psalmist, thrown into a world where lying and violent people persecute the just (Ps 12:2–3), prays that the wicked be punished (Ps 12:4–5). The prayer is not simply for vengeance but arises from a desire to see God's justice appear on earth. Ps 12:6 preserves the word of assurance spoken by the priest to the lamenter; it is not usually transmitted in such Psalms. In Ps 12:7–8 the psalmist affirms the intention to live by the word of assurance.

¶[12:7] **A crucible:** lit., "in a crucible in the ground." The crucible was placed in the ground for support.

---

*[Psalm 11] A song of trust. Though friends counsel flight to the mountain country (a traditional hideout) to escape trouble (Ps 11:1–3), the innocent psalmist reaffirms confidence in God, who protects those who seek asylum in the Temple (Ps 11:4–7).

m. [10:8] Ps 11:2; Jb 24:14. n. [10:9] Ps 17:12; Prv 1:11; Jer 5:26. o. [10:11] Ps 44:25; 64:6; 73:11; 94:7; Ez 9:9. p. [10:14] Ps 31:8; 56:9; 2 Kgs 20:5; Is 25:8; Rev 7:17. q. [10:14] Ex 22:21–22. r. [10:16] Ps 145:13; Jer 10:10. s. [10:18] Dt 10:18. t. [11:1] Ps 55:7; 91:4. u. [11:2] Ps 7:13; 37:14; 57:5; 64:4.

v. [11:4] Ps 14:2; 102:20; Hab 2:20; Dt 26:15; Is 66:1; Mt 5:34. w. [11:6] Ps 120:4; 140:11; Prv 16:27; Ez 38:22; Rev 8:5; 20:10. x. [12:2] Ps 14:3; 116:11; Is 59:15; Mi 7:2. y. [12:3] Ps 28:3; 55:22; Is 59:3–4; Jer 9:7. z. [12:5] Sir 5:3. a. [12:6] Is 33:10. b. [12:7] Ps 18:31; 19:8; Prv 30:5.

8 You, O LORD, protect us always;
   preserve us from this generation.
9 On every side the wicked roam;
   the shameless are extolled by the
      children of men.

PSALM 13*
Prayer for Help

1 For the leader. A psalm of David.
   I
2 How long, LORD? Will you utterly forget
      me?
   How long will you hide your face
      from me?*c*
3 How long must I carry sorrow in my soul,
      grief in my heart day after day?
   How long will my enemy triumph
      over me?
   II
4 Look upon me, answer me, LORD, my
      God!
   Give light to my eyes lest I sleep in
      death,
5 Lest my enemy say, "I have prevailed,"
      lest my foes rejoice at my downfall.*d*
   III
6 But I trust in your mercy.
   Grant my heart joy in your
      salvation,
   I will sing to the LORD,
      for he has dealt bountifully with
         me!*e*

PSALM 14†
A Lament over Widespread Corruption

1 For the leader. Of David.
   I
   The fool says in his heart,
      "There is no God."
   Their deeds are loathsome and corrupt;
      not one does what is good.*f*
2 The LORD looks down from heaven
      upon the children of men,*g*
   To see if even one is wise,
      if even one seeks God.*h*
3 All have gone astray;
      all alike are perverse.
   Not one does what is good,
      not even one.*i*

   II
4 Will these evildoers never learn?
   They devour my people as they
      devour bread;*j*
   they do not call upon the LORD.*k*
5 They have good reason, then, to fear;
   God is with the company of the
      just.
6 They would crush the hopes of the poor,
   but the poor have the LORD as their
      refuge.
   III
7 *l*Oh, that from Zion might come
      the salvation of Israel!
   Jacob would rejoice, and Israel be glad
      when the LORD restores his people!‡

PSALM 15§
The Righteous Israelite

1 *m*A psalm of David.
   I
   LORD, who may abide in your tent?¶
   Who may dwell on your holy
      mountain?¶
   II
2 Whoever walks without blame,*n*
      doing what is right,
      speaking truth from the heart;
3 Who does not slander with his tongue,
      does no harm to a friend,
      never defames a neighbor;
4 Who disdains the wicked,
      but honors those who fear the LORD;
   Who keeps an oath despite the cost,
5   lends no money at interest,**
      accepts no bribe against the
         innocent.*o*
   III
   Whoever acts like this
      shall never be shaken.

*[Psalm 13] A typical lament, in which the psalmist feels forgotten by God (Ps 13:2–3)—note the force of the repetition of "How long." The references to enemies may suggest some have wished evil on the psalmist. The heartfelt prayer (Ps 13:4–5) passes on a statement of trust (Ps 13:6a), intended to reinforce the prayer, and a vow to thank God when deliverance has come (Ps 13:6b).

†[Psalm 14] The lament (duplicated in Ps 53) depicts the world as consisting of two types of people: "the fool" (equals

the wicked, Ps 14:1–3) and "the company of the just" (Ps 14:4–6; also called "my people," and "the poor"). The wicked persecute the just, but the Psalm expresses the hope that God will punish the wicked and reward the good.

‡[14:7] Jacob . . . Israel . . . his people: the righteous poor are identified with God's people.

§[Psalm 15] The Psalm records a liturgical scrutiny at the entrance to the Temple court (cf. Ps 24:3–6; Is 33:14b–16). The Israelite wishing to be admitted had to ask the Temple official what conduct was appropriate to God's precincts. Note the emphasis on virtues relating to one's neighbor.

¶[15:1] Your tent: the Temple could be referred to as "tent" (Ps 61:5; Is 33:20), a reference to the tent of the wilderness period and the tent of David (2 Sm 6:17; 7:2), predecessors of the Temple. Holy mountain: a venerable designation of the divine abode (Ps 2:6; 3:5; 43:3; 48:2, etc.).

**[15:5] Lends no money at interest: lending money in the Old Testament was often seen as assistance to the poor in their distress, not as an investment; making money off the poor by charging interest was thus forbidden (Ex 22:24; Lv 25:36–37; Dt 23:20).

c. [13:2] Ps 6:4; 44:25; 77:8; 79:5; 89:47; 94:3; Lam 5:20.
d. [13:5] Ps 38:17.   e. [13:6] Ps 116:7.   f. [14:1] Ps 10:4; 36:2; Is 32:6; Jer 5:12.   g. [14:2–3] Rom 3:11–12.   h. [14:2] Ps 11:4; 102:20.
i. [14:3] Ps 12:1.

j. [14:4] Ps 27:2; Is 9:11.   k. [14:4] Ps 79:6.   l. [14:7] Ps 85:2.
m. [15:1] Is 56:7.   n. [15:2] Ps 119:1.   o. [15:5] Ex 22:24; 23:8.

PSALM 16*
God the Supreme Good

¹ᵖA *miktam*† of David.

I

Keep me safe, O God;
    in you I take refuge.
² I say to the LORD,
    you are my Lord,
    you are my only good.
³ As for the holy ones who are in the land,
    they are noble,
    in whom is all my delight.
⁴ ‡They multiply their sorrows
    who court other gods.
Blood libations to them I will not pour
    out,
    nor will I take their names upon
    my lips.
⁵ LORD, my allotted portion and my cup,
    you have made my destiny secure.�q
⁶ §Pleasant places were measured out for
    me;
    fair to me indeed is my
    inheritance.

II

⁷ I bless the LORD who counsels me;
    even at night my heart exhorts me.
⁸ I keep the LORD always before me;
    with him at my right hand, I shall
    never be shaken.ʳ
⁹ Therefore my heart is glad, my soul
    rejoices;
    my body also dwells secure,
¹⁰ For you will not abandon my soul to
    Sheol,
    nor let your devout one see the pit.¶ˢ
¹¹ You will show me the path to life,
    abounding joy in your presence,
    the delights at your right hand
    forever.

PSALM 17**
Prayer for Rescue from Persecutors

¹A prayer of David.

I

Hear, LORD, my plea for justice;
    pay heed to my cry;
Listen to my prayer
    from lips without guile.
² From you let my vindication come;
    your eyes see what is right.
³ You have tested my heart,
    searched it in the night.ᵗ
You have tried me by fire,
    but find no malice in me.
My mouth has not transgressed
⁴   as others often do.
As your lips have instructed me,
    I have kept from the way of the
    lawless.
⁵ My steps have kept to your paths;
    my feet have not faltered.ᵘ

II

⁶ I call upon you; answer me, O God.
    Turn your ear to me; hear my
    speech.
⁷ Show your wonderful mercy,
    you who deliver with your right
    arm
    those who seek refuge from their
    foes.
⁸ ††Keep me as the apple of your eye;
    hide me in the shadow of your wings
⁹   from the wicked who despoil me.ᵛ

III

My ravenous enemies press upon me;ʷ
¹⁰   ‡‡they close their hearts,
    they fill their mouths with proud
    roaring.
¹¹ Their steps even now encircle me;
    they watch closely, keeping low to
    the ground,
¹² Like lions eager for prey,
    like a young lion lurking in
    ambush.
¹³ Rise, O LORD, confront and cast them
    down;
    rescue my soul from the wicked.
¹⁴ Slay them with your sword;
    with your hand, LORD, slay them;

---

*[Psalm 16] In the first section, the psalmist rejects the futile worship of false gods (Ps 16:2–5), preferring Israel's God (Ps 16:1), the giver of the land (Ps 16:6). The second section reflects on the wise and life-giving presence of God (Ps 16:7–11).

†[16:1] **Miktam**: a term occurring six times in Psalm superscriptions, always with "David." Its meaning is unknown.

‡[16:4] **Take their names**: to use the gods' names in oaths and hence to affirm them as one's own gods.

§[16:6] **Pleasant places were measured out for me**: the psalmist is pleased with the plot of land measured out to the family, which was to be passed on to succeeding generations ("my inheritance").

¶[16:10] **Nor let your devout one see the pit**: Hebrew *shahath* means here the pit, a synonym for Sheol, the underworld. The Greek translation derives the word here and elsewhere from the verb *shahath*, "to be corrupt." On the basis of the Greek, Acts 2:25–32; 13:35–37 apply the verse to Christ's resurrection, "Nor will you suffer your holy one to see corruption."

p. [16:1] Ps 25:20.   q. [16:5] Ps 23:5; 73:26; Nm 18:20; Lam 3:24.
r. [16:8] Ps 73:23; 121:5, 8–12; Acts 2:25–28.   s. [16:10] Ps 28:1; 30:4; 49:16; 86:13; Jon 2:7; Acts 13:35.

**[Psalm 17] A lament of an individual unjustly attacked. Confident of being found innocent, the psalmist cries out for God's just judgment (Ps 17:1–5) and requests divine help against enemies (Ps 17:6–9a). Those ravenous lions (Ps 17:9b–12) should be punished (Ps 17:13–14). The Psalm ends with a serene statement of praise (Ps 17:15). The Hebrew text of Ps 17:3–4, 14 is uncertain.

††[17:8] **Apple of your eye . . . shadow of your wings**: images of God's special care, cf. Dt 32:10; Prv 7:2; Is 49:2.

‡‡[17:10–12, 14] An extended metaphor: the enemies are lions.

t. [17:3] Ps 26:2; 139:23.   u. [17:5] Ps 18:36; Jb 23:11–12.   v. [17:9–12] Ps 10:9; 22:14, 22; 35:17; 58:7; Jb 4:10–11.   w. [17:9] Ps 36:8; 57:2; 61:5; 63:8; 91:4; Dt 32:10; Ru 2:12; Zec 2:12; Mt 23:37.

snatch them from the world in their
 prime.
Their bellies are being filled with your
 friends;
 their children are satisfied too,
 for they share what is left with their
 young.
15 I am just—let me see your face;
 when I awake, let me be filled with
 your presence.ˣ

PSALM 18*
A King's Thanksgiving for Victory

¹For the leader. Of David, the servant of the
LORD, who sang to the LORD the words of this
song after the LORD had rescued him from the
clutches of all his enemies and from the hand of
Saul. ²He said:ʸ

I

 I love you, LORD, my strength,
3 LORD, my rock, my fortress, my
   deliverer,
 My God, my rock of refuge,
  my shield, my saving horn,† my
   stronghold!ᶻ
4 Praised be the LORD, I exclaim!
  I have been delivered from my
   enemies.

II

5 The cords of death encompassed me;
  the torrents of destruction terrified
   me.
6 The cords‡ of Sheol encircled me;
  the snares of death lay in wait for me.ᵃ
7 In my distress I called out: LORD!
  I cried out to my God.ᵇ
 From his temple he heard my voice;
  my cry to him reached his ears.
8 §The earth rocked and shook;
  the foundations of the mountains
   trembled;

they shook as his wrath flared up.ᶜ
9 Smoke rose from his nostrils,
  a devouring fire from his mouth;
  it kindled coals into flame.
10 He parted the heavens and came down,
  a dark cloud under his feet.ᵈ
11 Mounted on a cherubᶴ he flew,
  borne along on the wings of the
   wind.
12 He made darkness his cloak around him;
  his canopy, water-darkened
   stormclouds.
13 From the gleam before him, his clouds
   passed,
  hail and coals of fire.ᵉ
14 The LORD thundered from heaven;
  the Most High made his voice
   resound.ᶠ
15 He let fly his arrows** and scattered them;
  shot his lightning bolts and
   dispersed them.ᵍ
16 Then the bed of the sea appeared;
  the world's foundations lay bare,ʰ
 At your rebuke, O LORD,
  at the storming breath of your
   nostrils.
17 He reached down from on high and
   seized me;
  drew me out of the deep waters.ⁱ
18 He rescued me from my mighty enemy,
  from foes too powerful for me.
19 They attacked me on my day of distress,
  but the LORD was my support.
20 He set me free in the open;
  he rescued me because he loves me.

III

21 The LORD acknowledged my
   righteousness,
  rewarded my clean hands.ʲ
22 For I kept the ways of the LORD;
  I was not disloyal to my God.
23 For his laws were all before me,
  his decrees I did not cast aside.
24 I was honest toward him;
  I was on guard against sin.
25 So the LORD rewarded my righteousness,
  the cleanness of my hands in his
   sight.
26 Toward the faithful you are faithful;
  to the honest man you are honest;ᵏ
27 Toward the pure, you are pure;
  but to the perverse you are devious.

---

*[Psalm 18] A royal thanksgiving for a military victory,
duplicated in 2 Sm 22. Thanksgiving Psalms are in essence
reports of divine rescue. The Psalm has two parallel reports of
rescue, the first told from a heavenly perspective (Ps 18:5–20),
and the second from an earthly perspective (Ps 18:36–46).
The first report adapts old mythic language of a cosmic battle
between sea and rainstorm in order to depict God's rescue of
the Israelite king from his enemies. Each report has a short
hymnic introduction (Ps 18:2–4, 32–36) and conclusion (Ps
18:21–31, 47–50).

†[18:3] **My saving horn**: my strong savior. The horn
referred to is the weapon of a bull and the symbol of fertility,
cf. 1 Sm 2:10; Ps 132:17; Lk 1:69.

‡[18:6] **Cords**: hunting imagery, the cords of a snare.

§[18:8–16] God appears in the storm, which in Palestine
comes from the west. The introduction to the theophany (Ps
18:8–9) is probably a description of a violent, hot, and dry
east-wind storm. In the fall transition period from the rainless summer to the rainy winter such storms regularly precede
the rains, cf. Ex 14:21–22.

¶[18:11] **Cherub**: a winged creature, derived from myth,
in the service of the deity (Gn 3:24; Ex 25:18–20; 37:6–9).
Cherubim were the throne bearers of the deity (Ps 80:2; 99:1;
1 Kgs 6:23–28; 8:6–8).

[18:15] **Arrows: lightning.

---

c. [18:8] Ps 97:3–4; 99:1; Jgs 5:4–5; Is 64:1; Heb 3:9–11. d. [18:10]
Ps 104:3; 144:5; Is 63:19. e. [18:13] Ex 13:21; 19:16. f. [18:14]
Ps 29; 77:19; Ex 19:19; Jb 37:3–4. g. [18:15] Ps 144:6; Wis
5:21. h. [18:16] Ps 77:17; Zec 9:14. i. [18:17] Ps 144:7. j. [18:21]
Ps 26; 1 Sm 26:23. k. [18:26] Ps 125:4.

---

x. [17:15] Ps 4:7; 31:17; 67:2; 80:4; Nm 6:25; Dn 9:17. y. [18:2–
51] 2 Sm 22:2–51. z. [18:3] Ps 3:4; 31:3–4; 42:10; Gn 49:24; Dt
32:4. a. [18:6] Ps 88:8; 93:3–4; 116:3–4. b. [18:7] Jon 2:3.

²⁸ For humble people you save;
    haughty eyes you bring low.ⁱ
²⁹ For you, LORD, give light to my lamp;
    my God brightens my
      darkness.ᵐ
³⁰ With you I can rush an armed band,
    with my God to help I can leap a
      wall.
³¹ God's way is unerring;
    the LORD's promise is refined;
    he is a shield for all who take refuge
      in him.ⁿ

IV

³² Truly, who is God except the LORD?
    Who but our God is the rock?ᵒ
³³ This God who girded me with might,
    kept my way unerring,
³⁴ Who made my feet like a deer's,
    and set me on the heights,ᵖ
³⁵ Who trained my hands for war,
    my arms to string a bow of
      bronze.*�q

V

³⁶ You have given me your saving shield;
    your right hand has upheld me;
    your favor made me great.
³⁷ You made room for my steps beneath
      me;
    my ankles never twisted.ʳ
³⁸ I pursued my enemies and overtook
      them;
    I did not turn back till I destroyed
      them.
³⁹ I decimated them; they could not rise;
    they fell at my feet.
⁴⁰ You girded me with valor for war,
    subjugated my opponents beneath
      me.
⁴¹ You made my foes expose their necks to
      me;
    those who hated me I silenced.
⁴² They cried for help, but no one saved
      them;
    cried to the LORD but received no
      answer.
⁴³ I ground them to dust before the wind;
    I left them like mud in the streets.
⁴⁴ You rescued me from the strife of
      peoples;
    you made me head over nations.
    A people I had not known served me;
⁴⁵   as soon as they heard of me they
      obeyed.
    Foreigners submitted before me;
⁴⁶   foreigners cringed;

they came cowering from their
      dungeons.ˢ

VI

⁴⁷ The LORD lives! Blessed be my rock!ᵗ
    Exalted be God, my savior!
⁴⁸ O God who granted me vengeance,
    made peoples subject to me,ᵘ
⁴⁹   and saved me from my enemies,
    Truly you have elevated me above my
      opponents,
    from a man of lawlessness you have
      rescued me.
⁵⁰ Thus I will praise you, LORD, among the
      nations;
    I will sing praises to your name.ᵛ
⁵¹ You have given great victories to your
      king,
    and shown mercy to his anointed,
    to David and his posterity forever.ʷ

PSALM 19†
God's Glory in the Heavens and in the Law

¹For the leader. A psalm of David.

I

² The heavens declare the glory of God;
    the firmament proclaims the works
      of his hands.ˣ
³ Day unto day pours forth speech;
    night unto night whispers
      knowledge.
⁴ ‡There is no speech, no words;
    their voice is not heard;
⁵ A report goes forth through all the earth,
    their messages, to the ends of the
      world.
    He has pitched in them a tent for the
      sun;§
⁶   it comes forth like a bridegroom
      from his canopy,
    and like a hero joyfully runs its
      course.
⁷ From one end of the heavens it comes
      forth;
    its course runs through to the
      other;
    nothing escapes its heat.

---

†[Psalm 19] The heavenly elements of the world, now beautifully arranged, bespeak the power and wisdom of their creator (Ps 19:2–7). The creator's wisdom is available to human beings in the law (Ps 19:8–11), toward which the psalmist prays to be open (Ps 19:12–14). The themes of light and speech unify the poem.

‡[19:4] No speech, no words: the regular functioning of the heavens and the alternation of day and night inform human beings without words of the creator's power and wisdom.

§[19:5] The sun: in other religious literature the sun is a judge and lawgiver since it sees all in its daily course; Ps 19:5b–7 form a transition to the law in Ps 19:8–11. The six synonyms for God's revelation (Ps 19:8–11) are applied to the sun in comparable literature.

*[18:35] Bow of bronze: hyperbole for a bow difficult to bend and therefore capable of propelling an arrow with great force.

l. [18:28] Jb 22:29; Prv 3:34. m. [18:29] Ps 27:1; 36:10; 43:3; 119:105; Jb 29:3; Mi 7:8. n. [18:31] Ps 12:6; 77:13; Prv 30:5. o. [18:32] Is 44:8; 45:21. p. [18:34] Heb 3:19. q. [18:35] Ps 144:1. r. [18:37] Ps 17:5.

s. [18:46] Mi 7:17. t. [18:47] Ps 144:1. u. [18:48] Ps 144:2. v. [18:50] Ps 7:18; 30:5; 57:9; 135:3; 146:2; Rom 15:9. w. [18:51] Ps 89:28–37; 144:10; 1 Sm 2:10. x. [19:2] Ps 8:1; 50:6; 97:6.

II

8 The law of the LORD is perfect,
   refreshing the soul.
The decree of the LORD is trustworthy,
   giving wisdom to the simple.^y
9 The precepts of the LORD are right,
   rejoicing the heart.
The command of the LORD is clear,
   enlightening the eye.
10 The fear of the LORD is pure,
   enduring forever.
The statutes of the LORD are true,
   all of them just;
11 More desirable than gold,
   than a hoard of purest gold,
Sweeter also than honey
   or drippings from the comb.^z
12 By them your servant is warned;*
   obeying them brings much reward.

III

13 Who can detect trespasses?
   Cleanse me from my inadvertent sins.
14 Also from arrogant ones restrain your
      servant;
   let them never control me.
Then shall I be blameless,
   innocent of grave sin.
15 Let the words of my mouth be acceptable,
   the thoughts of my heart before you,
LORD, my rock and my redeemer.

PSALM 20[†]
Prayer for the King in Time of War

1 For the leader. A psalm of David.

I

2 The LORD answer you in time of distress;
   the name of the God of Jacob defend
      you!
3 May he send you help from the sanctuary,
   from Zion be your support.^a
4 May he remember[‡] your every offering,
   graciously accept your burnt offering,
                                    Selah
5 Grant what is in your heart,
   fulfill your every plan.
6 May we shout for joy at your victory,[§]
   raise the banners in the name of our
      God.
The LORD grant your every petition!

II

7 Now I know the LORD gives victory
   to his anointed.^b
He will answer him from the holy heavens
   with a strong arm that brings victory.
8 Some rely on chariots, others on horses,
   but we on the name of the LORD our
      God.^c
9 They collapse and fall,
   but we stand strong and firm.^d
10 LORD, grant victory to the king;
   answer when we call upon you.

PSALM 21[¶]
Thanksgiving and Assurances for the King

1 For the leader. A psalm of David.

I

2 LORD, the king finds joy in your power;^e
   in your victory how greatly he
      rejoices!
3 You have granted him his heart's desire;
   you did not refuse the request of
      his lips.
                                    Selah
4 For you welcomed him with goodly
      blessings;
   you placed on his head a crown of
      pure gold.
5 He asked life of you;
   you gave it to him,
   length of days forever.^f
6 Great is his glory in your victory;
   majesty and splendor you confer
      upon him.
7 You make him the pattern of blessings
      forever,
   you gladden him with the joy of
      your face.
8 For the king trusts in the LORD,
   stands firm through the mercy of
      the Most High.

II

9 Your hand will find all your enemies;
   your right hand will find your foes!
10 At the time of your coming
   you will make them a fiery furnace.
Then the LORD in his anger will consume
      them,
   devour them with fire.
11 Even their descendants you will wipe out
      from the earth,
   their offspring from the human race.

---

*[19:12] **Warned**: the Hebrew verb means both to shine
and to warn, cf. Dn 12:3.

†[Psalm 20] The people pray for the king before battle. The
people ask for divine help (Ps 20:2–6) and express confidence
that such help will be given (Ps 20:7–10). A solemn assurance
of divine help may well have been given between the two sections in the liturgy, something like the promises of Ps 12:6;
21:9–13. The final verse (Ps 20:10) echoes the opening verse.

‡[20:4] **Remember**: God's remembering implies readiness
to act, cf. Gn 8:1; Ex 2:24.

§[20:6] **Victory**: the Hebrew root is often translated "salvation," "to save," but in military contexts it can have the specific
meaning of "victory."

y. [19:8] Ps 12:7; 119.   z. [19:11] Sir 24:19.   a. [20:3] Ps 128:5; 134:3.

¶[Psalm 21] The first part of this royal Psalm is a thanksgiving (Ps 21:2–8), and the second is a promise that the king will
triumph over his enemies (Ps 21:9–13). The king's confident
prayer (Ps 21:3–5) and trust in God (Ps 21:8) enable him to
receive the divine gifts of vitality, peace, and military success.
Ps 21:14 reprises Ps 21:2. When kings ceased in Israel after the
sixth century B.C., the Psalm was sung of a future Davidic king.

b. [20:7] Ps 18:51; 144:10; 1 Sm 2:10.   c. [20:8] Ps 147:10–11; 2 Chr
14:10; Prv 21:31; 1 Sm 17:45; Is 31:1; 36:9.   d. [20:9] Is 40:30.
e. [21:2] Ps 63:12.   f. [21:5] 1 Kgs 3:14.

¹² Though they intend evil against you,
    devising plots, they will not succeed,
¹³ For you will put them to flight;
    you will aim at their faces with your
        bow.

III

¹⁴ Arise, LORD, in your power!^{g}
    We will sing and chant the praise of
        your might.

PSALM 22*
The Prayer of an Innocent Person

¹For the leader; according to "The deer of the
dawn."† A psalm of David.

I

² My God, my God, why have you
    abandoned me?
  Why so far from my call for help,
    from my cries of anguish?^{h}
³ My God, I call by day, but you do not
    answer;
  by night, but I have no relief.^{i}
⁴ Yet you are enthroned as the Holy One;
    you are the glory of Israel.^{j}
⁵ In you our fathers trusted;
    they trusted and you rescued them.
⁶ To you they cried out and they escaped;
    in you they trusted and were not
        disappointed.^{k}
⁷ ‡But I am a worm, not a man,
    scorned by men, despised by the
        people.^{l}
⁸ All who see me mock me;
    they curl their lips and jeer;
    they shake their heads at me:^{m}
⁹ "He relied on the LORD—let him deliver
        him;
    if he loves him, let him rescue him."^{n}
¹⁰ For you drew me forth from the womb,
    made me safe at my mother's
        breasts.
¹¹ Upon you I was thrust from the womb;
    since my mother bore me you are
        my God.^{o}

¹² Do not stay far from me,
    for trouble is near,
    and there is no one to help.^{p}

II

¹³ Many bulls§ surround me;
    fierce bulls of Bashan§ encircle
        me.
¹⁴ They open their mouths against me,
    lions that rend and roar.^{q}
¹⁵ Like water my life drains away;
    all my bones are disjointed.
  My heart has become like wax,
    it melts away within me.
¹⁶ As dry as a potsherd is my throat;
    my tongue cleaves to my palate;
    you lay me in the dust of death.¶
¹⁷ Dogs surround me;
    a pack of evildoers closes in on me.
  They have pierced my hands and my feet
¹⁸ I can count all my bones.^{r}
  They stare at me and gloat;
¹⁹   they divide my garments among
        them;
    for my clothing they cast lots.^{s}
²⁰ But you, LORD, do not stay far off;
    my strength, come quickly to help
        me.
²¹ Deliver my soul from the sword,
    my life from the grip of the dog.
²² Save me from the lion's mouth,
    my poor life from the horns of wild
        bulls.^{t}

III

²³ Then I will proclaim your name to my
        brethren;
    in the assembly I will praise you:**^{u}
²⁴ "You who fear the LORD, give praise!
    All descendants of Jacob, give
        honor;
    show reverence, all descendants of
        Israel!
²⁵ For he has not spurned or disdained
    the misery of this poor wretch,
  Did not turn away†† from me,
    but heard me when I cried out.

---

*[Psalm 22] A lament unusual in structure and in inten-
sity of feeling. The psalmist's present distress is contrasted
with God's past mercy in Ps 22:2–12. In Ps 22:13–22 enemies
surround the psalmist. The last third is an invitation to praise
God (Ps 22:23–27), becoming a universal chorus of praise (Ps
22:28–31). The Psalm is important in the New Testament. Its
opening words occur on the lips of the crucified Jesus (Mk
15:34; Mt 27:46), and several other verses are quoted, or at
least alluded to, in the accounts of Jesus' passion (Mt 27:35,
43; Jn 19:24).
†[22:1] The deer of the dawn: apparently the title of the
melody.
‡[22:7] I am a worm, not a man: the psalmist's sense of
isolation and dehumanization, an important motif of Ps 22, is
vividly portrayed here.

§[22:13–14] Bulls: the enemies of the psalmist are also
portrayed in less-than-human form, as wild animals (cf. Ps
22:17, 21–22). Bashan: a grazing land northeast of the Sea of
Galilee, famed for its cattle, cf. Dt 32:14; Ez 39:18; Am 4:1.
¶[22:16] The dust of death: the netherworld, the domain
of the dead.
**[22:23] In the assembly I will praise you: the person who
offered a thanksgiving sacrifice in the Temple recounted to
the other worshipers the favor received from God and invited
them to share in the sacrificial banquet. The final section (Ps
22:24–32) may be a summary or a citation of the psalmist's
poem of praise.
††[22:25] Turn away: lit., "hides his face from me," an
important metaphor for God withdrawing from someone,
e.g., Mi 3:4; Is 8:17; Ps 27:9; 69:18; 88:15.

---

g. [21:14] Nm 10:35. h. [22:2] Is 49:14; 54:7; Mt 27:46; Mk
15:34. i. [22:3] Sir 2:10. j. [22:4] Is 6:3. k. [22:6] Ps 25:3;
Is 49:23; Dn 3:40. l. [22:7] Is 53:3. m. [22:8] Ps 109:25; Mt
27:39; Mk 15:29; Lk 23:35. n. [22:9] Ps 71:11; Wis 2:18–20; Mt
27:43. o. [22:11] Ps 71:6; Is 44:2; 46:3.

p. [22:12] Ps 35:22; 38:22; 71:12. q. [22:14] Ps 17:12; Jb 4:10;
1 Pt 5:8. r. [22:18] Ps 109:24. s. [22:19] Mt 27:35; Mk 15:24; Lk
23:34; Jn 19:24. t. [22:22] Ps 7:2–3; 17:12; 35:17; 57:5; 58:7; 2 Tm
4:17. u. [22:23] Ps 26:12; 35:18; 40:10; 109:30; 149:1; 2 Sm 22:50;
Heb 2:12.

²⁶ I will offer praise in the great assembly;
   my vows I will fulfill before those
      who fear him.
²⁷ The poor* will eat their fill;
   those who seek the LORD will offer
      praise.
   May your hearts enjoy life forever!"ᵛ
                IV
²⁸ All the ends of the earth
   will remember and turn to the
      LORD;
   All the families of nations
   will bow low before him.ʷ
²⁹ For kingship belongs to the LORD,
   the ruler over the nations.ˣ
³⁰ †All who sleep in the earth
   will bow low before God;
   All who have gone down into the dust
   will kneel in homage.
³¹ And I will live for the LORD;
   my descendants will serve you.
³² The generation to come will be told of the
      Lord,
   that they may proclaim to a people
      yet unborn
   the deliverance you have brought.ʸ

PSALM 23‡
The Lord, Shepherd and Host

¹A psalm of David.
                I
The LORD is my shepherd;§
   there is nothing I lack.ᶻ
² In green pastures he makes me lie down;
   to still waters he leads me;
³   ᵃhe restores my soul.
   He guides me along right paths¶
   for the sake of his name.
⁴ Even though I walk through the valley of
      the shadow of death,ᵇ
   I will fear no evil, for you are with
      me;

---

*[22:27] **The poor**: originally the poor, who were dependent on God; the term ('anawim) came to include the religious sense of "humble, pious, devout."

†[22:30] Hebrew unclear. The translation assumes that all on earth (Ps 22:27–28) and under the earth (Ps 22:29) will worship God.

‡[Psalm 23] God's loving care for the psalmist is portrayed under the figures of a shepherd for the flock (Ps 23:1–4) and a host's generosity toward a guest (Ps 23:5–6). The imagery of both sections is drawn from traditions of the exodus (Is 40:11; 49:10; Jer 31:10).

§[23:1] **My shepherd**: God as good shepherd is common in both the Old Testament and the New Testament (Ez 34:11–16; Jn 10:11–18).

¶[23:3] **Right paths**: connotes "right way" and "way of righteousness."

---

v. [22:27] Ps 23:5; 69:33. w. [22:28] Ps 86:9; Tb 13:11; Is 45:22; 52:10; Zec 14:16. x. [22:29] Ps 103:19; Ob 21; Zec 14:9. y. [22:32] Ps 48:14–15; 71:18; 78:6; 102:19; Is 53:10. z. [23:1] Ps 80:2; 95:7; 100:3; Dt 2:7. a. [23:3] Prv 4:11. b. [23:4] Jb 10:21–22; Is 50:10.

---

your rod and your staff comfort me.
                II
⁵ "You set a table before me
   in front of my enemies;"
   You anoint my head with oil;"ᶜ
   my cup overflows.ᵈ
⁶ Indeed, goodness and mercy†† will pursue
      me
   all the days of my life;
   I will dwell in the house of the LORDᵉ
   for endless days.

PSALM 24‡‡
The Glory of God in Procession to Zion

¹A psalm of David.
                I
The earth is the LORD's and all it holds,ᶠ
   the world and those who dwell in
      it.
² For he founded it on the seas,
   established it over the rivers.ᵍ
                II
³ Who may go up the mountain of the
      LORD?ʰ
   Who can stand in his holy place?
⁴ §§"The clean of hand and pure of heart,
   who has not given his soul to useless
      things,
   what is vain.
⁵ He will receive blessings from the LORD,
   and justice from his saving God.
⁶ Such is the generation that seeks him,
   that seeks the face of the God of
      Jacob."
                                    Selah
                III
⁷ Lift up your heads, O gates;¶¶

[23:5] **You set a table before me: this expression occurs in an exodus context in Ps 78:19. **In front of my enemies**: my enemies see that I am God's friend and guest. **Oil**: a perfumed ointment made from olive oil, used especially at banquets (Ps 104:15; Mt 26:7; Lk 7:37, 46; Jn 12:2).

††[23:6] **Goodness and mercy**: the blessings of God's covenant with Israel.

‡‡[Psalm 24] The Psalm apparently accompanied a ceremony of the entry of God (invisibly enthroned upon the ark), followed by the people, into the Temple. The Temple commemorated the creation of the world (Ps 24:1–2). The people had to affirm their fidelity before being admitted into the sanctuary (Ps 24:3–6; cf. Ps 15). A choir identifies the approaching God and invites the very Temple gates to bow down in obeisance (Ps 24:7–10).

§§[24:4–5] Lit., "the one whose hands are clean." The singular is used for the entire class of worshipers.

¶¶[24:7, 9] **Lift up your heads, O gates . . . you ancient portals**: the literal meaning would involve disassembly of the gates, since the portcullis (a gate that moves up and down) was unknown in the ancient world. Extra-biblical parallels might also suggest a full personification of the circle of gate towers: they are like a council of elders, bowed down and anxious, awaiting the return of the army and the great warrior gone to battle.

---

c. [23:5] Ps 92:11. d. [23:5] Ps 16:5. e. [23:6] Ps 27:4. f. [24:1] Ps 50:12; 89:12; Dt 10:14; 1 Cor 10:26. g. [24:2] Ps 136:6; Is 42:5. h. [24:3] Ps 15:1.

be lifted, you ancient portals,
that the king of glory may enter.[i]
8 Who is this king of glory?
The LORD, strong and mighty,
the LORD, mighty in war.
9 Lift up your heads, O gates;
rise up, you ancient portals,
that the king of glory may enter.
10 Who is this king of glory?
The LORD of hosts, he is the king of
glory.

Selah

PSALM 25*
Confident Prayer for
Forgiveness and Guidance

1Of David.

I

To you, O LORD, I lift up my soul,
2 jmy God, in you I trust;
do not let me be disgraced;[k]
do not let my enemies gloat over
me.
3 No one is disgraced who waits for you,[l]
but only those who are treacherous
without cause.
4 Make known to me your ways, LORD;
teach me your paths.[m]
5 Guide me by your fidelity and teach me,
for you are God my savior,
for you I wait all the day long.
6 Remember your compassion and your
mercy, O LORD,
for they are ages old.[n]
7 Remember no more the sins of my
youth;[o]
remember me according to your
mercy,
because of your goodness, LORD.

II

8 Good and upright is the LORD,
therefore he shows sinners the way,
9 He guides the humble in righteousness,
and teaches the humble his way.
10 All the paths of the LORD are mercy and
truth
toward those who honor his
covenant and decrees.
11 For the sake of your name, LORD,
pardon my guilt, though it is great.
12 Who is the one who fears the LORD?
God shows him the way he should
choose.[p]

13 He will abide in prosperity,
and his descendants will inherit the
land.[q]
14 The counsel of the LORD belongs to those
who fear him;
and his covenant instructs them.
15 My eyes are ever upon the LORD,
who frees my feet from the snare.[r]

III

16 Look upon me, have pity on me,
for I am alone and afflicted.[s]
17 Relieve the troubles of my heart;
bring me out of my distress.
18 Look upon my affliction and suffering;
take away all my sins.
19 See how many are my enemies,
see how fiercely they hate me.
20 Preserve my soul and rescue me;
do not let me be disgraced, for in
you I seek refuge.
21 Let integrity and uprightness preserve
me;
I wait for you, O LORD.
22 †Redeem Israel, O God,
from all its distress!

PSALM 26‡
Prayer of Innocence

1Of David.

I

Judge me, LORD!
For I have walked in my integrity.[t]
In the LORD I trust;
I do not falter.
2 Examine me, Lord, and test me;
search my heart and mind.[u]
3 Your mercy is before my eyes;
I walk guided by your faithfulness.[v]

II

4 I do not sit with worthless men,
nor with hypocrites do I mingle.
5 I hate an evil assembly;
with the wicked I do not sit.
6 I will wash my hands§ in innocence[w]
so that I may process around your
altar, Lord,

---

†[25:22] A final verse beginning with the Hebrew letter
pe is added to the normal 22-letter alphabet. Thus the letters
aleph, lamed, and *pe* open the first, middle (Ps 25:11), and last
lines of the Psalm. Together, they spell *aleph,* the first letter of
the alphabet, from a Hebrew root that means "to learn."

‡[Psalm 26] Like a priest washing before approaching
the altar (Ex 30:17–21), the psalmist seeks God's protection
upon entering the Temple. Ps 26:1–3, matched by Ps 26:11–12,
remind God of past integrity while asking for purification; Ps
26:4–5, matched by Ps 26:9–10, pray for inclusion among the
just; Ps 26:6–8, the center of the poem, express the joy in God
at the heart of all ritual.

§[26:6] **I will wash my hands:** the washing of hands was
a liturgical act (Ex 30:19, 21; 40:31–32), symbolic of inner as
well as outer cleanness, cf. Is 1:16.

---

i. [24:7] Ps 118:19–20. j. [25:2] Ps 86:4; 143:8. k. [25:2] Ps 71:1.
l. [25:3] Ps 22:6; Is 49:23; Dn 3:40. m. [25:4] Ps 27:11; 86:11;
119:12, 35; 143:8, 10. n. [25:6] Sir 51:8. o. [25:7] Jb 13:26; Is
64:8. p. [25:12] Prv 19:23.

q. [25:13] Ps 37:9, 29. r. [25:15] Ps 123:1, 2; 141:8. s. [25:16] Ps
86:16; 119:132. t. [26:1] Ps 7:9. u. [26:2] Ps 17:3; 139:23. v. [26:3]
Ps 86:11. w. [26:6] Ps 73:13.

7 To hear the sound of thanksgiving,
  and recount all your wondrous
  deeds.
8 Lord, I love the refuge of your house,
  the site of the dwelling-place of your
  glory.ˣ

III

9 Do not take me away with sinners,
  nor my life with the men of blood,ʸ
10 In whose hands there is a plot,
  their right hands full of bribery.
11 But I walk in my integrity;ᶻ
  redeem me, be gracious to me!ᵃ
12 My foot stands on level ground;*
  in assemblies I will bless the Lord.ᵇ

PSALM 27†
Trust in God

¹ᶜOf David.

A

I

The Lord is my light and my salvation;
  whom should I fear?
The Lord is my life's refuge;
  of whom should I be afraid?
2 When evildoers come at me
  to devour my flesh,‡ᵈ
These my enemies and foes
  themselves stumble and fall.
3 Though an army encamp against me,
  my heart does not fear;
Though war be waged against me,
  even then do I trust.

II

4 One thing I ask of the Lord;
  this I seek:
To dwell in the Lord's house
  all the days of my life,
To gaze on the Lord's beauty,
  to visit his temple.ᵉ
5 For God will hide me in his shelter
  in time of trouble,ᶠ
He will conceal me in the cover of his
  tent;
  and set me high upon a rock.

6 Even now my head is held high
  above my enemies on every side!
I will offer in his tent
  sacrifices with shouts of joy;
I will sing and chant praise to the
  Lord.

B

I

7 Hear my voice, Lord, when I call;
  have mercy on me and answer me.
8 "Come," says my heart, "seek his face";§
  your face, Lord, do I seek!ᵍ
9 Do not hide your face from me;
  do not repel your servant in anger.
You are my salvation; do not cast me off;
  do not forsake me, God my savior!
10 Even if my father and mother forsake me,
  the Lord will take me in.ʰ

II

11 Lord, show me your way;
  lead me on a level path
  because of my enemies.ⁱ
12 Do not abandon me to the desire of my
  foes;
  malicious and lying witnesses have
  risen against me.
13 I believe I shall see the Lord's goodness
  in the land of the living.¶ʲ
14 Wait for the Lord, take courage;
  be stouthearted, wait for the Lord!

PSALM 28**
Petition and Thanksgiving

¹Of David.

I

To you, Lord, I call;
  my Rock, do not be deaf to me,ᵏ
Do not be silent toward me,
  so that I join those who go down to
  the pit.ˡ
2 Hear the sound of my pleading when I cry
  to you for help
when I lift up my hands toward your
  holy place.††ᵐ
3 Do not drag me off with the wicked,
  with those who do wrong,ⁿ
Who speak peace to their neighbors

---

*[26:12] **On level ground**: in safety, where there is no danger of tripping and falling. **In assemblies**: at the Temple. Having walked around the altar, the symbol of God's presence, the psalmist blesses God.

†[Psalm 27] Tradition has handed down the two sections of the Psalm (Ps 27:1–6; 7–14) as one Psalm, though each part could be understood as complete in itself. Asserting boundless hope that God will bring rescue (Ps 27:1–3), the psalmist longs for the presence of God in the Temple, protection from all enemies (Ps 27:4–6). In part B there is a clear shift in tone (Ps 27:7–12); the climax of the poem comes with "I believe" (Ps 27:13), echoing "I trust" (Ps 27:3).

‡[27:2] **To devour my flesh**: the psalmist's enemies are rapacious beasts (Ps 7:3; 17:12; 22:14, 17).

§[27:8] **Seek his face**: to commune with God in the Temple. The idiom is derived from the practice of journeying to sacred places, cf. Hos 5:15; 2 Sm 21:1; Ps 24:6.

¶[27:13] **In the land of the living**: or "in the land of life," an epithet of the Jerusalem Temple (Ps 52:7; 116:9; Is 38:11), where the faithful had access to the life-giving presence of God.

**[Psalm 28] A lament asking that the psalmist, who has taken refuge in the Temple (Ps 28:2), not be punished with the wicked, who are headed inevitably toward destruction (Ps 28:1, 3–5). The statement of praise is exceptionally lengthy and vigorous (Ps 28:6–7). The Psalm ends with a prayer (Ps 28:8–9).

††[28:2] **Your holy place**: the innermost part of the Temple, the holy of holies, containing the ark, cf. 1 Kgs 6:16, 19–23; 8:6–8.

---

x. [26:12] Ps 29:9; 63:3; Ex 24:16; 25:8.   y. [26:9] Ps 28:3.   z. [26:11] Ps 101:6.   a. [26:11] Ps 25:16.   b. [26:12] Ps 22:23; 35:18; 149:1.   c. [27:1] Ps 18:29; 36:10; 43:3; Is 10:17; Mi 7:8.   d. [27:2] Ps 14:4.   e. [27:4] Ps 23:6; 61:5.   f. [27:5] Ps 31:21.

g. [27:8] Ps 24:6; Hos 5:15.   h. [27:10] Is 49:15.   i. [27:11] Ps 25:4; 86:11.   j. [27:13] Ps 116:9; Is 38:11.   k. [28:1] Ps 18:2.   l. [28:1] Ps 30:4; 88:5; 143:7; Prv 1:12.   m. [28:2] Ps 134:2.   n. [28:3] Ps 26:9.

though evil is in their hearts.[o]
4 Repay them for their deeds,
  for the evil that they do.
For the work of their hands repay them;
  give them what they deserve.[p]
5 Because they do not understand the
    LORD's works,
  the work of his hands,[q]
He will tear them down,
  never to rebuild them.

II

6 ˚Blessed be the LORD,
  who has heard the sound of my
    pleading.
7 The LORD is my strength and my shield,
  in whom my heart trusts.
I am helped, so my heart rejoices;
  with my song I praise him.

III

8 †LORD, you are a strength for your people,
  the saving refuge of your anointed.
9 Save your people, bless your inheritance;
  pasture and carry them forever!

PSALM 29[‡]
The Lord of Majesty Acclaimed
as King of the World

[1]A psalm of David.

I

Give to the LORD, you sons of God,[s]
  give to the LORD glory and might;
2 Give to the LORD the glory due his name.
  Bow down before the LORD's holy
    splendor![r]

II

3 The voice of the LORD[s] is over the waters;
  the God of glory thunders,
  the LORD, over the mighty waters.
4 The voice of the LORD is power;
  the voice of the LORD is splendor.[s]
5 The voice of the LORD cracks the cedars;

the LORD splinters the cedars of
  Lebanon,
6 Makes Lebanon leap like a calf,
  and Sirion** like a young bull.
7 The voice of the LORD strikes with fiery
    flame;
8 the voice of the LORD shakes the
    desert;
  the LORD shakes the desert of
    Kadesh.
9 ††The voice of the LORD makes the deer
    dance
  and strips the forests bare.
  All in his Temple say, "Glory!"

III

10 The LORD sits enthroned above the
     flood![‡‡t]
   The LORD reigns as king forever!
11 May the LORD give might to his people;[§§]
   may the LORD bless his people with
     peace![u]

PSALM 30[§§]
Thanksgiving for Deliverance

[1]A psalm. A song for the dedication of the Temple.*** Of David.

I

2 I praise you, LORD, for you raised me up
  and did not let my enemies rejoice
    over me.
3 O LORD, my God,
  I cried out to you for help and you
    healed††† me.
4 LORD, you brought my soul up from
    Sheol;
  you let me live, from going down to
    the pit.[‡‡‡v]

II

5 Sing praise to the LORD, you faithful;
  give thanks to his holy memory.
6 For his anger lasts but a moment;
  his favor a lifetime.

---

*[28.6] The psalmist shifts to fervent thanksgiving, prob-
ably responding to a priestly or prophetic oracle in Ps 28.5cd
(not usually transmitted) assuring the worshiper that the
prayer has been heard.

†[28:8] **Your people . . . your anointed:** salvation is more
than individual, affecting all the people and their God-given
leader.

‡[Psalm 29] The hymn invites the members of the heavenly court to acknowledge God's supremacy by ascribing
glory and might to God alone (Ps 29:1–2a, 9b). Divine glory
and might are dramatically visible in the storm (Ps 29:3–9a).
The storm apparently comes from the Mediterranean onto the
coast of Syria-Palestine and then moves inland. In Ps 29:10
the divine beings acclaim God's eternal kingship. The Psalm
concludes with a prayer that God will impart the power just
displayed to the Israelite king and through the king to Israel.

§[29:1] **Sons of God:** members of the heavenly court who
served Israel's God in a variety of capacities.

¶[29:3] **The voice of the LORD:** the sevenfold repetition of
the phrase imitates the sound of crashing thunder and may
allude to God's primordial slaying of Leviathan, the seven-
headed sea monster of Canaanite mythology.

[29:6] **Sirion: the Phoenician name for Mount Hermon,
cf. Dt 3:9.

††[29:9b–10] Having witnessed God's supreme power (Ps
29:3–9a), the gods acknowledge the glory that befits the king
of the divine and human world.

‡‡[29:10] **The flood:** God defeated the primordial waters
and made them part of the universe, cf. Ps 89:10–13; 93:3–4.

§§[29:11] **His people:** God's people, Israel.

¶¶[Psalm 30] An individual thanksgiving in four parts:
praise and thanks for deliverance and restoration (Ps 30:2–4);
an invitation to others to join in (Ps 30:5–6); a flashback to the
time before deliverance (Ps 30:7–11); a return to praise and
thanks (Ps 30:12). Two sets of images recur: 1) going down,
death, silence; 2) coming up, life, praising. God has delivered
the psalmist from one state to the other.

***[30:1] **For the dedication of the Temple:** a later adapta-
tion of the Psalm to celebrate the purification of the Temple in
164 B.C. during the Maccabean Revolt.

†††[30:3] **Healed:** for God as healer, see also Ps 103:3;
107:20; Hos 6:1; 7:1; 11:3; 14:5.

‡‡‡[30:4] **Sheol . . . pit:** the shadowy underworld residence
of the spirits of the dead, here a metaphor for near-death.

---

o. [28:3] Ps 12:2; 55:22; 62:5; Prv 26:24–28.   p. [28:4] 2 Sm
3:39.   q. [28:5] Is 5:12.   r. [29:2] Ps 68:35; 96:7–9.   s. [29:4] Ps
46:7; 77:18–19; Jb 37:4; Is 30:30.

t. [29:10] Bar 3:3.   u. [29:11] Ps 68:36.   v. [30:4] Ps 28:1; Jon 2:7.

At dusk weeping comes for the night;
    but at dawn there is rejoicing.

III

7 Complacent,* I once said,
    "I shall never be shaken."

8 LORD, you showed me favor,
    established for me mountains of
      virtue.
But when you hid your face
    I was struck with terror.[w]

9 To you, LORD, I cried out;
    with the Lord I pleaded for mercy:

10 †"What gain is there from my lifeblood,
    from my going down to the grave?
Does dust give you thanks
    or declare your faithfulness?

11 Hear, O LORD, have mercy on me;
    LORD, be my helper."

IV

12 You changed my mourning into dancing;
    you took off my sackcloth
    and clothed me with gladness.[x]

13 So that my glory may praise you
    and not be silent.
O LORD, my God,
    forever will I give you thanks.

PSALM 31‡
Prayer in Distress and
Thanksgiving for Escape

1 For the leader. A psalm of David.

I

2 In you, LORD, I take refuge;[y]
    let me never be put to shame.
In your righteousness deliver me;

3   incline your ear to me;
    make haste to rescue me!
Be my rock of refuge,
    a stronghold to save me.

4 For you are my rock and my fortress;[z]
    for your name's sake lead me and
      guide me.

5 Free me from the net they have set for me,
    for you are my refuge.

6 §Into your hands I commend my spirit;[a]

---

*[30:7] **Complacent**: untroubled existence is often seen as a source of temptation to forget God, cf. Dt 8:10–18; Hos 13:6; Prv 30:9.

†[30:10] In the stillness of Sheol no one gives you praise; let me live and be among your worshipers, cf. Ps 6:6; 88:11–13; 115:17; Is 38:18.

‡[Psalm 31] A lament (Ps 31:2–19) with a strong emphasis on trust (Ps 31:4, 6, 15–16), ending with an anticipatory thanksgiving (Ps 31:20–24). As is usual in laments, the affliction is couched in general terms. The psalmist feels overwhelmed by evil people but trusts in the "God of truth" (Ps 31:6).

§[31:6] **Into your hands I commend my spirit**: in Lk 23:46 Jesus breathes his last with this Psalm verse. Stephen in Acts 7:59 alludes to these words as he is attacked by enemies. The verse is used as an antiphon in the Divine Office at Compline, the last prayer of the day.

w. [30:8] Ps 104:29.   x. [30:12] Is 61:3; Jer 31:13.   y. [31:2–4] Ps 71:1–3.   z. [31:4] Ps 18:2.   a. [31:6] Lk 23:46; Acts 7:59.

    you will redeem me, LORD, God of
      truth.

7 You hate those who serve worthless idols,
    but I trust in the LORD.

8 I will rejoice and be glad in your mercy,
    once you have seen my misery,
    [and] gotten to know the distress of
      my soul.[b]

9 You will not abandon me into enemy
      hands,
    but will set my feet in a free and
      open space.

II

10 Be gracious to me, LORD, for I am in
      distress;
affliction is wearing down my eyes,
    my throat and my insides.

11 My life is worn out by sorrow,
    and my years by sighing.
My strength fails in my affliction;
    my bones are wearing down.[c]

12 To all my foes I am a thing of scorn,
    and especially to my neighbors
    a horror to my friends.
When they see me in public,
    they quickly shy away.[d]

13 I am forgotten, out of mind like the dead;
    I am like a worn-out tool.¶

14 I hear the whispers of the crowd;
    terrors are all around me.**
They conspire together against me;
    they plot to take my life.

15 But I trust in you, LORD;
    I say, "You are my God."[e]

16 My destiny is in your hands;
    rescue me from my enemies,
    from the hands of my pursuers.

17 Let your face shine on your servant;[f]
    save me in your mercy.

18 Do not let me be put to shame,
    for I have called to you, LORD.
Put the wicked to shame;
    reduce them to silence in Sheol.

19 Strike dumb their lying lips,
    which speak arrogantly against the
      righteous
    in contempt and scorn.[g]

III

20 How great is your goodness, Lord,
    stored up for those who fear you.
You display it for those who trust you,
    in the sight of the children of Adam.

21 You hide them in the shelter of your
      presence,
    safe from scheming enemies.

¶[31:13] **Like a worn-out tool**: a common comparison for something ruined and useless, cf. Is 30:14; Jer 19:11; 22:28.

[31:14] **Terrors are all around me: a cry used in inescapable danger, cf. Jer 6:25; 20:10; 46:5; 49:29.

b. [31:8] Ps 10:14.   c. [31:11] Ps 32:3; 38:10–11.   d. [31:12] Jb 19:13–19.   e. [31:15] Ps 140:7; Is 25:1.   f. [31:17] Ps 67:1; Nm 6:24.   g. [31:19] Ps 12:4.

You conceal them in your tent,
   away from the strife of tongues.[h]
22 Blessed be the LORD,
   marvelously he showed to me
   his mercy in a fortified city.
23 Though I had said in my alarm,
   "I am cut off from your eyes."[i]
   Yet you heard my voice, my cry for mercy,
   when I pleaded with you for help.
24 Love the LORD, all you who are faithful to
   him.
   The LORD protects the loyal,
   but repays the arrogant in full.
25 Be strong and take heart,
   all who hope in the LORD.

PSALM 32*
Remission of Sin

[1j]Of David. A *maskil.*

I
Blessed is the one whose fault is removed,
   whose sin is forgiven.
2 Blessed is the man to whom the LORD
   imputes no guilt,
   in whose spirit is no deceit.

II
3 Because I kept silent,[†] my bones wasted
   away;
   I groaned all day long.[k]
4 For day and night your hand was heavy
   upon me;
   my strength withered as in dry
   summer heat.
                              Selah
5 Then I declared my sin to you;
   my guilt I did not hide.[l]
   I said, "I confess my transgression to the
   LORD,"
   and you took away the guilt of my sin.
                              Selah
6 Therefore every loyal person should pray
   to you
   in time of distress.
   Though flood waters[‡] threaten,
   they will never reach him.[m]
7 You are my shelter; you guard me from
   distress;

with joyful shouts of deliverance you
   surround me.
                              Selah

III
8 I will instruct you and show you the way
   you should walk,
   give you counsel with my eye upon
   you.
9 Do not be like a horse or mule, without
   understanding;
   with bit and bridle their temper is
   curbed,
   else they will not come to you.

IV
10 Many are the sorrows of the wicked one,
   but mercy surrounds the one who
   trusts in the LORD.
11 Be glad in the LORD and rejoice, you
   righteous;
   exult, all you upright of heart.[n]

PSALM 33§
Praise of God's Power and Providence

I
1 Rejoice, you righteous, in the LORD;
   praise from the upright is fitting.[o]
2 Give thanks to the LORD on the harp;
   on the ten-stringed lyre offer praise.[p]
3 Sing to him a new song;
   skillfully play with joyful chant.
4 For the LORD's word is upright;
   all his works are trustworthy.
5 He loves justice and right.
   The earth is full of the mercy of the
   LORD.[q]

II
6 By the LORD's word the heavens were
   made;
   by the breath of his mouth all their
   host.[¶r]
7 **He gathered the waters of the sea as a
   mound;
   he sets the deep into storage vaults.[s]

III
8 Let all the earth fear the LORD;
   let all who dwell in the world show
   him reverence.

---

*[Psalm 32] An individual thanksgiving and the second of the seven Penitential Psalms (cf. Ps 6). The opening declaration—the forgiven are blessed (Ps 32:1–2)—arises from the psalmist's own experience. At one time the psalmist was stubborn and closed, a victim of sin's power (Ps 32:3–4), and then became open to the forgiving God (Ps 32:5–7). Sin here, as often in the Bible, is not only the personal act of rebellion against God but also the consequences of that act—frustration and waning of vitality. Having been rescued, the psalmist can teach others the joys of justice and the folly of sin (Ps 32:8–11).
†[32:3] **I kept silent:** did not confess the sin before God.
‡[32:6] **Flood waters:** the untamed waters surrounding the earth, a metaphor for danger.

§[Psalm 33] A hymn in which the just are invited (Ps 33:1–3) to praise God, who by a mere word (Ps 33:4–5) created the three-tiered universe of the heavens, the cosmic waters, and the earth (Ps 33:6–9). Human words, in contrast, effect nothing (Ps 33:10–11). The greatness of human beings consists in God's choosing them as a special people and their faithful response (Ps 33:12–22).
¶[33:6] **All their host:** the stars of the sky are commonly viewed as a vast army, e.g., Neh 9:6; Is 40:26; 45:12; Jer 33:22.
[33:7] **The waters . . . as a mound: ancients sometimes attributed the power keeping the seas from overwhelming land to a primordial victory of the storm-god over personified Sea.

---

h. [31:21] Ps 27:5.   i. [31:23] Jon 2:5.   j. [32:1] Is 1:18; Ps 65:3; Rom 4:7–8.   k. [32:3] Ps 31:11.   l. [32:5] Ps 38:19; 51:5.   m. [32:6] Ps 18:5.

n. [32:11] Ps 33:1.   o. [33:1] Ps 32:11; 147:1.   p. [33:2] Ps 92:4; 144:9.   q. [33:5] Ps 119:64.   r. [33:6] Gn 2:1.   s. [33:7] Ps 78:13; Gn 1:9–10; Ex 15:8; Jos 3:16.

⁹ For he spoke, and it came to be,
     commanded, and it stood in place.ᵗ
¹⁰ The LORD foils the plan of nations,
     frustrates the designs of peoples.
¹¹ But the plan of the LORD stands forever,
     the designs of his heart through all
     generations.ᵘ
¹² Blessed is the nation whose God is the
     LORD,
     the people chosen as his
     inheritance.ᵛ

IV

¹³ From heaven the LORD looks down
     and observes the children of Adam,ʷ
¹⁴ From his dwelling place he surveys
     all who dwell on earth.
¹⁵ The One who fashioned together their
     hearts
     is the One who knows all their
     works.

V

¹⁶ A king is not saved by a great army,
     nor a warrior delivered by great
     strength.
¹⁷ Useless is the horse for safety;
     despite its great strength, it cannot
     be saved.
¹⁸ Behold, the eye of the LORD is upon those
     who fear him,
     upon those who count on his mercy,
¹⁹ To deliver their soul from death,
     and to keep them alive through
     famine.

VI

²⁰ Our soul waits for the LORD,
     he is our help and shield.ˣ
²¹ For in him our hearts rejoice;
     in his holy name we trust.
²² May your mercy, LORD, be upon us;
     as we put our hope in you.

PSALM 34*
Thanksgiving to God Who Delivers the Just

¹Of David, when he feigned madness before
Abimelech,† who drove him out and he went
away.

I

² I will bless the LORD at all times;
     his praise shall be always in my
     mouth.ʸ

---

*[Psalm 34] A thanksgiving in acrostic form, each line
beginning with a successive letter of the Hebrew alphabet. In
this Psalm one letter is missing and two are in reverse order.
The psalmist, fresh from the experience of being rescued (Ps
34:5, 7), can teach the "poor," those who are defenseless, to
trust in God alone (Ps 34:4, 12). God will make them powerful
(Ps 34:5–11) and give them protection (Ps 34:12–22).

†[34:1] **Abimelech**: a scribal error for Achish. In 1 Sm 21:13–
16, David feigned madness before Achish, not Abimelech.

---

³ My soul will glory in the LORD;
     let the poor hear and be glad.
⁴ Magnify the LORD with me;
     and let us exalt his name together.

II

⁵ I sought the LORD, and he answered me,
     delivered me from all my fears.
⁶ Look to him and be radiant,
     and your faces may not blush for
     shame.
⁷ This poor one cried out and the LORD
     heard,
     and from all his distress he saved him.
⁸ The angel of the LORD encamps
     around those who fear him, and he
     saves them.ᶻ
⁹ ˙ Taste and see that the LORD is good;
     blessed is the stalwart one who takes
     refuge in him.ᵃ
¹⁰ Fear the LORD, you his holy ones;
     nothing is lacking to those who fear
     him.ᵇ
¹¹ The rich grow poor and go hungry,
     but those who seek the LORD lack
     no good thing.

III

¹² Come, children,‡ listen to me;ᶜ
     I will teach you fear of the LORD.
¹³ Who is the man who delights in life,ᵈ
     who loves to see the good days?
¹⁴ Keep your tongue from evil,
     your lips from speaking lies.
¹⁵ Turn from evil and do good;ᵉ
     seek peace and pursue it.
¹⁶ The eyes of the LORD are directed toward
     the righteousᶠ
     and his ears toward their cry.
¹⁷ The LORD's face is against evildoers
     to wipe out their memory from the
     earth.
¹⁸ The righteous cry out, the LORD hears
     and he rescues them from all their
     afflictions.
¹⁹ The LORD is close to the brokenhearted,
     saves those whose spirit is crushed.
²⁰ Many are the troubles of the righteous,
     but the LORD delivers him from
     them all.
²¹ He watches over all his bones;
     not one of them shall be broken.ᵍ
²² Evil will slay the wicked;
     those who hate the righteous are
     condemned.
²³ The LORD is the redeemer of the souls of
     his servants;
     and none are condemned who take
     refuge in him.

---

‡[34:12] **Children**: the customary term for students in
wisdom literature.

---

t. [33:9] Ps 148:5; Gn 1:3f; Jdt 16:14.   u. [33:11] Prv 19:21; Is
40:8.   v. [33:12] Ps 144:15; Ex 19:6; Dt 7:6.   w. [33:13] Jb 34:21;
Sir 15:19; Jer 16:17; 32:19.   x. [33:20] Ps 115:9.   y. [34:2] Ps 145:2.

z. [34:8]Ex14:19.   a. [34:9]Ps2:12.   b. [34:10]Prv3:7.   c. [34:12]
Prv 1:8; 4:1.   d. [34:13–17] 1 Pt 3:10–12.   e. [34:15] Ps 37:27.
f. [34:16] Ps 33:18.   g. [34:21] Jn 19:36.

PSALM 35*
Prayer for Help Against Unjust Enemies

¹Of David.

I

†Oppose, O Lord, those who oppose me;
  war upon those who make war upon
    me.
2 Take up the shield and buckler;
  rise up in my defense.
3 Brandish lance and battle-ax
  against my pursuers.
Say to my soul,
  "I am your salvation."
4 Let those who seek my life
  be put to shame and disgrace.
Let those who plot evil against me[h]
  be turned back and confounded.
5 Make them like chaff before the wind,[i]
  with the angel of the Lord driving
    them on.
6 Make their way slippery and dark,
  with the angel of the Lord pursuing
    them.

II

7 Without cause they set their snare for me;
  without cause they dug a pit for me.
8 Let ruin overtake them unawares;
  let the snare they have set catch them;
  let them fall into the pit they have
    dug.[j]
9 Then I will rejoice in the Lord,
  exult in God's salvation.
10 My very bones shall say,
  "O Lord, who is like you,[k]
Who rescue the afflicted from the powerful,
  the afflicted and needy from the
    despoiler?"

III

11 Malicious witnesses rise up,
  accuse me of things I do not know.
12 They repay me evil for good;
  my soul is desolate.[l]
13 ‡Yet I, when they were ill, put on
    sackcloth,
  afflicted myself with fasting,
  sobbed my prayers upon my bosom.

14 I went about in grief as for my brother,
  bent in mourning as for my mother.
15 Yet when I stumbled they gathered with
    glee,
  gathered against me and I did not
    know it.
They slandered me without ceasing;
16   without respect they mocked me,
  gnashed their teeth against me.

IV

17 O Lord, how long will you look on?
  Restore my soul from their
    destruction,
  my very life from lions![m]
18 Then I will thank you in the great
    assembly;
  I will praise you before the mighty
    throng.[n]
19 Do not let lying foes rejoice over me,
  my undeserved enemies wink
    knowingly.[o]
20 They speak no words of peace,
  but against the quiet in the land
  they fashion deceitful speech.[p]
21 They open wide their mouths against me.
  They say, "Aha! Good!
  Our eyes have seen it!"[q]
22 You see this, Lord; do not be silent;[r]
  Lord, do not withdraw from me.
23 Awake, be vigilant in my defense,
  in my cause, my God and my Lord.
24 Defend me because you are just, Lord;
  my God, do not let them rejoice
    over me.
25 Do not let them say in their hearts,
  "Aha! Our soul!"[s]
Do not let them say,
  "We have devoured that one!"
26 Put to shame and confound
  all who relish my misfortune.
Clothe with shame and disgrace
  those who lord it over me.
27 But let those who favor my just cause
  shout for joy and be glad.
May they ever say, "Exalted be the Lord
  who delights in the peace of his loyal
    servant."
28 Then my tongue shall recount your justice,
  declare your praise, all the day long.[s]

PSALM 36¶
Human Wickedness and Divine Providence

¹For the leader. Of David, the servant of the
Lord.

---

*[Psalm 35] A lament of a person betrayed by friends. The psalmist prays that the evildoers be publicly exposed as unjust (Ps 35:1–8), and gives thanks in anticipation of vindication (Ps 35:9–10). Old friends are the enemies (Ps 35:11–16). May their punishment come quickly (Ps 35:17–21)! The last part (Ps 35:22–26) echoes the opening in praying for the destruction of the psalmist's persecutors. The Psalm may appear vindictive, but one must keep in mind that the psalmist is praying for public redress now of a public injustice. There is at this time no belief in an afterlife in which justice will be redressed.

†[35:1–6] The mixture of judicial, martial, and hunting images shows that the language is figurative. The actual injustice is false accusation of serious crimes (Ps 35:11, 15, 20–21). The psalmist seeks lost honor through a trial before God.

‡[35:13, 15–17] The Hebrew is obscure.

§[35:25] **Aha! Our soul!**: an ancient idiomatic expression meaning that we have attained what we wanted.

¶[Psalm 36] A Psalm with elements of wisdom (Ps 36:2–5), the hymn (Ps 36:6–10), and the lament (Ps 36:11–13). The

h. [35:4] Ps 40:15; 71:13.   i. [35:5] Ps 1:4; 83:14; Jb 21:18.   j. [35:8] Ps 7:16; 9:16; 57:7; Prv 26:27; Eccl 10:8; Sir 27:26.   k. [35:10] Ps 86:8; 89:7, 9; Ex 15:11.   l. [35:12] Ps 27:12; 38:20–21; 109:5; Jer 18:20.

m. [35:17] Ps 17:12; 22:22; 58:7.   n. [35:18] Ps 22:23; 26:12; 35:18; 40:10; 149:1.   o. [35:19] Ps 38:17.   p. [35:20] Ps 120:6–7.   q. [35:21] Ps 40:16; Lam 2:16.   r. [35:22] Ps 22:12; 38:21; 109:1.   s. [35:28] Ps 71:15–16.

I

2 Sin directs the heart of the wicked man;
  his eyes are closed to the fear of
   God.ᵗ
3 For he lives with the delusion:
  his guilt will not be known and
   hated.*
4 Empty and false are the words of his
   mouth;
  he has ceased to be wise and do
   good.
5 On his bed he hatches plots;
  he sets out on a wicked way;
  he does not reject evil.ᵘ

II

6 †Lord, your mercy reaches to heaven;
  your fidelity, to the clouds.ᵛ
7 Your justice is like the highest mountains;
  your judgments, like the mighty
   deep;
  human being and beast you sustain,
   Lord.
8 How precious is your mercy, O God!
  The children of Adam take refuge in
   the shadow of your wings.‡ʷ
9 They feast on the rich food of your house;
  from your delightful streamˣ you
   give them drink.
10 For with you is the fountain of life,ʸ
  and in your light we see light.ᶻ
11 Show mercy on those who know you,
  your just defense to the upright of
   heart.
12 Do not let the foot of the proud overtake
   me,
  nor the hand of the wicked disturb
   me.
13 There make the evildoers fall;
  thrust them down, unable to rise.

PSALM 37§
The Fate of Sinners and
the Reward of the Just

1 Of David.

ALEPH

Do not be provoked by evildoers;
  do not envy those who do wrong.ᵃ
2 Like grass they wither quickly;
  like green plants they wilt away.ᵇ

BETH

3 Trust in the Lord and do good
  that you may dwell in the landᵗ and
   live secure.ᶜ
4 Find your delight in the Lord
  who will give you your heart's
   desire.ᵈ

GIMEL

5 Commit your way to the Lord;
  trust in him and he will actᵉ
6 And make your righteousness shine like
   the dawn,
  your justice like noonday.ᶠ

DALETH

7 Be still before the Lord;
  wait for him.
Do not be provoked by the prosperous,
  nor by malicious schemers.

HE

8 Refrain from anger; abandon wrath;
  do not be provoked; it brings only
   harm.
9 Those who do evil will be cut off,
  but those who wait for the Lord will
   inherit the earth.ᵍ

WAW

10 Wait a little, and the wicked will be no
   more;
  look for them and they will not be
   there.
11 But the poor will inherit the earth,ʰ
  will delight in great prosperity.

ZAYIN

12 The wicked plot against the righteous
  and gnash their teeth at them;
13 But my Lord laughs at them,ⁱ
  because he sees that their day is
   coming.

HETH

14 The wicked unsheath their swords;
  they string their bows
To fell the poor and oppressed,

rule of sin over the wicked (Ps 36:2–5) is contrasted with the rule of divine love and mercy over God's friends (Ps 36:6–10). The Psalm ends with a prayer that God's guidance never cease (Ps 36:11–12).

 *[36:3] **Hated:** punished by God.
 †[36:6–7] God actively controls the entire world.
 ‡[36:8] **The shadow of your wings:** metaphor for divine protection. It probably refers to the winged cherubim in the holy of holies in the Temple, cf. 1 Kgs 6:23–28, 32; 2 Chr 3:10–13; Ez 1:4–9.
 §[Psalm 37] The Psalm responds to the problem of evil, which the Old Testament often expresses as a question: why do the wicked prosper and the good suffer? The Psalm answers that the situation is only temporary. God will reverse things, rewarding the good and punishing the wicked here

on earth. The perspective is concrete and earthbound: people's very actions place them among the ranks of the good or wicked. Each group or "way" has its own inherent dynamism—eventual frustration for the wicked, eventual reward for the just. The Psalm is an acrostic, i.e., each section begins with a successive letter of the Hebrew alphabet. Each section has its own imagery and logic.
 ¶[37:3] **The land:** the promised land, Israel, which became for later interpreters a type or figure of heaven, cf. Heb 11:9–10, 13–16. The New Testament Beatitudes (Mt 5:3–12; Lk 6:20–26) have been influenced by the Psalm, especially their total reversal of the present and their interpretation of the happy future as possession of the land.

t. [36:2] Rom 3:18. u. [36:5] Mi 2:1. v. [36:6] Ps 57:11; 71:19.
w. [36:8] Ps 17:8. x. [36:9] Gn 2:8, 10. y. [36:10] Is 55:1; Jn 4:14.
z. [36:10] Ps 80:4, 8, 20.

a. [37:1] Prv 3:31; 23:17; 24:1, 19. b. [37:2] Ps 90:5–6; 102:12; 103:15–16; Jb 14:2; Is 40:7. c. [37:3] Ps 128:2. d. [37:4] Prv 10:24. e. [37:5] Ps 55:23; Prv 3:5; 16:3. f. [37:6] Wis 5:6; Is 58:10. g. [37:9] Ps 25:13; Prv 2:21; Is 57:13. h. [37:11] Mt 5:4. i. [37:13] Ps 2:4; 59:9; Wis 4:18.

to slaughter those whose way is
upright.[j]
15 Their swords will pierce their own hearts;
their bows will be broken.

TETH

16 Better the meagerness of the righteous one
than the plenty of the wicked.[k]
17 The arms of the wicked will be broken,
while the LORD will sustain the
righteous.

YODH

18 The LORD knows the days of the
blameless;
their heritage lasts forever.
19 They will not be ashamed when times are
bad;
in days of famine they will be
satisfied.

KAPH

20 The wicked perish,
enemies of the LORD;
They shall be consumed like fattened
lambs;
like smoke they disappear.[l]

LAMEDH

21 The wicked one borrows but does not
repay;
the righteous one is generous and
gives.
22 For those blessed by the Lord will inherit
the earth,
but those accursed will be cut off.

MEM

23 The valiant one whose steps are guided by
the LORD,
who will delight in his way,[m]
24 May stumble, but he will never fall,
for the LORD holds his hand.

NUN

25 Neither in my youth, nor now in old age
have I seen the righteous one
abandoned[n]
or his offspring begging for bread.
26 All day long he is gracious and lends,
and his offspring become a blessing.

SAMEKH

27 Turn from evil and do good,
that you may be settled forever.[o]
28 For the LORD loves justice
and does not abandon the faithful.

AYIN

When the unjust are destroyed,
and the offspring of the wicked cut off,
29 The righteous will inherit the earth
and dwell in it forever.[p]

PE

30 The mouth of the righteous utters
wisdom;[q]
his tongue speaks what is right.

31 God's teaching is in his heart;[r]
his steps do not falter.

SADHE

32 The wicked spies on the righteous
and seeks to kill him.
33 But the LORD does not abandon him in
his power,
nor let him be condemned when
tried.

QOPH

34 Wait eagerly for the LORD,
and keep his way;[s]
He will raise you up to inherit the earth;
you will see when the wicked are
cut off.

RESH

35 I have seen a ruthless scoundrel,
spreading out like a green cedar.[t]
36 When I passed by again, he was gone;
though I searched, he could not be
found.

SHIN

37 Observe the person of integrity and mark
the upright;
Because there is a future for a man
of peace.[u]
38 Sinners will be destroyed together;
the future of the wicked will be cut
off.

TAW

39 The salvation of the righteous is from the
LORD,
their refuge in a time of distress.[v]
40 The LORD helps and rescues them,
rescues and saves them from the
wicked,
because they take refuge in him.

PSALM 38*
Prayer of an Afflicted Sinner

1 A psalm of David. For remembrance.

I

2 LORD, do not punish me in your anger;
in your wrath do not chastise me![w]
3 Your arrows have sunk deep in me;[x]
your hand has come down upon me.
4 There is no wholesomeness in my flesh
because of your anger;
there is no health in my bones
because of my sin.[y]
5 My iniquities overwhelm me,
a burden too heavy for me.[z]

---

*[Psalm 38] In this lament, one of the Penitential Psalms
(cf. Ps 6), the psalmist acknowledges the sin that has brought
physical and mental sickness and social ostracism. There is
no one to turn to for help; only God can undo the past and
restore the psalmist.

---

j. [37:14] Ps 11:2; 57:5; 64:4.   k. [37:16] Prv 15:16; 16:8.   l. [37:20]
Wis 5:14.   m. [37:23] Prv 20:24.   n. [37:25] Jb 4:7; Sir 2:10.
o. [37:27] Ps 34:14–15; Am 5:14.   p. [37:29] Ps 25:13; Prv 2:21; Is
57:13.   q. [37:30] Prv 10:31.

r. [37:31] Ps 40:9; Dt 6:6; Is 51:7; Jer 31:33.   s. [37:34] Ps 31:24.
t. [37:35] Ps 92:8–9; Is 2:13; Ez 31:10–11.   u. [37:37] Prv 23:18;
24:14.   v. [37:39] Ps 9:10; Is 25:4.   w. [38:2] Ps 6:2.   x. [38:3] Jb 6:4;
Lam 3:12; Ps 31:11; 64:7.   y. [38:4] Is 1:5–6.   z. [38:5] Ps 40:13;
Ezr 9:6.

II

6 Foul and festering are my sores
   because of my folly.
7 I am stooped and deeply bowed;[a]
   every day I go about mourning.
8 My loins burn with fever;
   there is no wholesomeness in my
   flesh.
9 I am numb and utterly crushed;
   I wail with anguish of heart.[b]
10 My Lord, my deepest yearning is before
   you;
   my groaning is not hidden from you.
11 My heart shudders, my strength forsakes
   me;
   the very light of my eyes has failed.[c]
12 Friends and companions shun my disease;
   my neighbors stand far off.
13 Those who seek my life lay snares for me;
   they seek my misfortune, they speak
   of ruin;
   they plot treachery every day.

III

14 But I am like the deaf, hearing nothing,
   like the mute, I do not open my
   mouth,
15 I am even like someone who does not
   hear,
   who has no answer ready.
16 LORD, it is for you that I wait;
   O Lord, my God, you respond.[d]
17 For I have said that they would gloat over
   me,
   exult over me if I stumble.

IV

18 I am very near to falling;
   my wounds are with me always.
19 I acknowledge my guilt
   and grieve over my sin.[e]
20 My enemies live and grow strong,
   those who hate me grow numerous
   fraudulently,
21 Repaying me evil for good,
   accusing me for pursuing good.[f]
22 Do not forsake me, O LORD;
   my God, be not far from me![g]
23 Come quickly to help me,[h]
   my Lord and my salvation!

PSALM 39*
The Vanity of Life

¹For the leader, for Jeduthun.[i] A psalm of David.

*[Psalm 39] The lament of a mortally ill person who at
first had resolved to remain silently submissive (Ps 39:2–4).
But the grief was too much and now the psalmist laments the
brevity and vanity of life (Ps 39:5–7), yet remaining hope-
ful (Ps 39:8–10). The psalmist continues to express both
acceptance of the illness and hope for healing in Ps 39:11–13.

a. [38:7] Ps 35:14.   b. [38:9] Ps 102:4–6.   c. [38:11] Ps 6:8; 31:10.
d. [38:16] Ps 13:4.   e. [38:19] Ps 32:5; 51:5.   f. [38:21] Ps 109:5.
g. [38:22] Ps 22:2, 12, 20; 35:22.   h. [38:23] Ps 40:14.   i. [39:1]
1 Chr 16:41; Ps 62:1; 77:1.

I

2 I said, "I will watch my ways,
   lest I sin with my tongue;
   I will keep a muzzle on my mouth."
3 Mute and silent before the wicked,
   I refrain from good things.
   But my sorrow increases;
4   my heart smolders within me.[j]
   In my sighing a fire blazes up,
   and I break into speech:

II

5 LORD, let me know my end, the number
   of my days,
   that I may learn how frail I am.
6 To be sure, you establish the expanse of
   my days;
   indeed, my life is as nothing before
   you.
   Every man is but a breath.[k]
                                          Selah

III

7 Man goes about as a mere phantom;
   they hurry about, although in vain;
   he heaps up stores without knowing
   for whom.
8 And now, LORD, for what do I wait?
   You are my only hope.
9 From all my sins deliver me;
   let me not be the taunt of fools.

10 I am silent and do not open my mouth
   because you are the one who did this.
11 Take your plague away from me;
   I am ravaged by the touch of your
   hand.
12 You chastise man with rebukes for sin;
   like a moth you consume his
   treasures.
   Every man is but a breath.
                                          Selah
13 Listen to my prayer, LORD, hear my cry;
   do not be deaf to my weeping!
   For I am with you like a foreigner,
   a refugee, like my ancestors.[l]
14 Turn your gaze from me, that I may smile
   before I depart to be no more.

PSALM 40†
Gratitude and Prayer for Help

¹For the leader. A psalm of David.

†[Psalm 40] A thanksgiving (Ps 40:2–13) has been combined with a lament (Ps 40:14–17) that appears also in Ps 70.
The psalmist describes the rescue in spatial terms—being
raised up from the swampy underworld to firm earth where
one can praise God (Ps 40:2–4). All who trust God will experience like protection (Ps 40:5–6)! The Psalm stipulates the precise mode of thanksgiving: not animal sacrifice but open and
enthusiastic proclamation of the salvation just experienced
(Ps 40:7–11). A prayer for protection concludes (Ps 40:12–17).

j. [39:4] Jer 20:9.   k. [39:6] Ps 62:10; 90:9–10; 144:4; Jb 7:6, 16; 14:1,
5; Eccl 6:12; Wis 2:5.   l. [39:13] Ps 119:19; Gn 23:4; Heb 11:13; 1 Pt
2:11.

A

2 Surely, I wait for the LORD;
       who bends down to me and hears
          my cry,[m]
3 Draws me up from the pit of destruction,
       out of the muddy clay,[n]
   Sets my feet upon rock,
       steadies my steps,
4 And puts a new song* in my mouth,[o]
       a hymn to our God.
   Many shall look on in fear
       and they shall trust in the LORD.
5 Blessed the man who sets
       his security in the LORD,
   who turns not to the arrogant
       or to those who stray after falsehood.[p]
6 You, yes you, O LORD, my God,
       have done many wondrous deeds!
   And in your plans for us
       there is none to equal you.[q]
   Should I wish to declare or tell them,
       too many are they to recount.[r]
7 †Sacrifice and offering you do not want;[s]
       you opened my ears.
   Holocaust and sin-offering you do not
          request;
8   so I said, "See; I come
   with an inscribed scroll written
          upon me.
9 I delight to do your will, my God;
       your law is in my inner being!"[t]
10 When I sing of your righteousness
       in a great assembly,
    See, I do not restrain my lips;
       as you, LORD, know.[u]
11 I do not conceal your righteousness
       within my heart;
    I speak of your loyalty and your salvation.
    I do not hide your mercy or
          faithfulness from a great
          assembly.
12 LORD, may you not withhold
       your compassion from me;
    May your mercy and your faithfulness
       continually protect me.[v]

B

13 But evils surround me
       until they cannot be counted.
    My sins overtake me,
       so that I can no longer see.
    They are more numerous than the hairs of
       my head;

    my courage fails me.[w]
14 LORD, graciously rescue me![x]
       Come quickly to help me, LORD!
15 May those who seek to destroy my life
       be shamed and confounded.
    Turn back in disgrace
       those who desire my ruin.[y]
16 Let those who say to me "Aha!"[z]
       Be made desolate on account of
          their shame.
17 While those who seek you
       rejoice and be glad in you.
    May those who long for your salvation
       always say, "The LORD is great."[a]
18 Though I am afflicted and poor,
       my Lord keeps me in mind.
    You are my help and deliverer;
       my God, do not delay!

PSALM 41‡
Thanksgiving After Sickness

1 For the leader. A psalm of David.

I

2 Blessed the one concerned for the poor;[§]
       on a day of misfortune, the LORD
          delivers him.[b]
3 The LORD keeps and preserves him,
       makes him blessed in the land,
       and does not betray him to his
          enemies.
4 The LORD sustains him on his sickbed,
       you turn down his bedding
          whenever he is ill.¶

II

5 Even I have said, "LORD, take note of me;
       heal me, although I have sinned
          against you.
6 My enemies say bad things against me:
       'When will he die and his name be
          forgotten?'
7 When someone comes to visit me, he
          speaks without sincerity.
    His heart stores up malice;
       when he leaves, he gossips.[c]
8 All those who hate me whisper together
          against me;
       they imagine the worst about me:

---

‡[Psalm 41] A thanksgiving for rescue from illness (Ps 41:4, 5, 9). Many people, even friends, have interpreted the illness as a divine punishment for sin and have ostracized the psalmist (Ps 41:5–11). The healing shows the return of God's favor and rebukes the psalmist's detractors (Ps 41:12–13).

§[41:2] Blessed the one concerned for the poor: cf. Ps 32:1–2; 34:9; 40:5; 65:5. The psalmist's statement about God's love of the poor is based on the experience of being rescued (Ps 41:1–3).

¶[41:4] You turn down his bedding whenever he is ill: the Hebrew is obscure. It suggests ongoing attentive care of the one who is sick.

---

*[40:4] A new song: a song in response to the new action of God (cf. Ps 33:3; 96:1; 144:9; 149:1; Is 42:10). Giving thanks is not purely a human response but is itself a divine gift.

†[40:7–9] Obedience is better than sacrifice (cf. 1 Sm 15:22; Is 1:10–20; Hos 6:6; Am 5:22–25; Mi 6:6–8; Acts 7:42–43 [quoting Am 5:25–26]). Heb 10:5–9 quotes the somewhat different Greek version and interprets it as Christ's self-oblation.

m. [40:2] Lam 3:25.   n. [40:3] Ps 28:1; 30:4; 69:3, 15–16; 88:5; Prv 1:12; Jon 2:7.   o. [40:4] Ps 33:3.   p. [40:5] Ps 1:1; Prv 16:20; Jer 17:7.   q. [40:6] Ps 35:10.   r. [40:6] Ps 71:15; 139:17–18.   s. [40:7–9] Heb 10:5–7; Ps 51:18–19; Am 5:22; Hos 6:6; Is 1:11–15.   t. [40:9] Ps 37:31.   u. [40:10] Ps 22:23; 26:12; 35:18; 149:1.   v. [40:12] Ps 89:34.

w. [40:13] Ps 38:5, 11; Ezr 9:6.   x. [40:14–18] Ps 70:2–6; 71:12.   y. [40:15] Ps 35:4, 26.   z. [40:16] Ps 35:21, 25.   a. [40:17] Ps 35:27.   b. [41:2] Tb 4:7–11.   c. [41:7] Ps 31:12; 38:12–13; 88:8; Jb 19:13–19; Jer 20:10.

9 'He has had ruin poured over him;
 that one lying down will never rise
 again.'
10 'Even my trusted friend,
 who ate my bread,
 has raised his heel against me.*d*

III

11 "But you, LORD, take note of me to raise
 me up
 that I may repay them."†

12 By this I will know you are pleased with
 me,
 that my enemy no longer shouts in
 triumph over me.
13 In my integrity may you support me
 and let me stand in your presence
 forever.
14 ‡Blessed be the LORD, the God of Israel,
 from all eternity and forever.
 Amen. Amen.*e*

Second Book—Psalms 42–72

PSALM 42§
Longing for God's Presence in the Temple

1For the leader. A *maskil* of the Korahites.¶

I

2 As the deer longs for streams of water,*f*
 so my soul longs for you, O God.
3 My soul thirsts for God, the living God.
 When can I enter and see the face
 of God?"*g*
4 My tears have been my bread day and
 night,*h*
 as they ask me every day, "Where is
 your God?"*i*
5 Those times I recall
 as I pour out my soul,*j*

---

*[41:10] Even my trusted friend . . . has raised his heel against me: Jn 13:18 cites this verse to characterize Judas as a false friend. Raised his heel against me: an interpretation of the unclear Hebrew, "made great the heel against me."
†[41:11] That I may repay them: the healing itself is an act of judgment through which God decides for the psalmist and against the false friends. The prayer is not necessarily for strength to punish enemies.
‡[41:14] The doxology, not part of the Psalm, marks the end of the first of the five books of the Psalter, cf. Ps 72:18–20; 89:53; 106:48.
§[Psalms 42–43] Ps 42–43 form a single lament of three sections, each section ending in an identical refrain (Ps 42:6, 12; 43:5). The psalmist is far from Jerusalem, and longs for the divine presence that Israel experienced in the Temple liturgy. Despite sadness, the psalmist hopes once again to join the worshiping crowds.
¶[42:1] The Korahites: a major guild of Temple singers (2 Chr 20:19) whose name appears in the superscriptions of Ps 42; 44–49; 84–85; 87–88.
**[42:3] See the face of God: "face" designates a personal presence (Gn 33:10; Ex 10:28–29; 2 Sm 17:11). The expressions "see God/God's face" occur elsewhere (Ps 11:7; 17:15; cf. Ex 24:10; 33:7–11; Jb 33:26) for the presence of God in the Temple.

---

d. [41:10] Ps 55:14–15; Jn 13:18.   e. [41:14] Neh 9:5.   f. [42:2–3] Ps 63:2; 84:3; 143:6; Is 26:9.   g. [42:3] Ps 27:4.   h. [42:4] Ps 80:6; 102:10.   i. [42:4] Ps 79:10; Jl 2:17.   j. [42:5] Lam 3:20.

When I would cross over to the shrine of
 the Mighty One,††
 to the house of God,
 Amid loud cries of thanksgiving,
 with the multitude keeping festival.*k*
6 Why are you downcast, my soul;
 why do you groan within me?
 Wait for God, for I shall again praise him,
 my savior and my God.

II

7 My soul is downcast within me;
 therefore I remember you
 From the land of the Jordan‡‡ and
 Hermon,
 from Mount Mizar,*l*
8 §§Deep calls to deep
 in the roar of your torrents,
 and all your waves and breakers
 sweep over me.*m*
9 By day may the LORD send his mercy,
 and by night may his righteousness
 be with me!
 I will pray¶¶ to the God of my life,
10 I will say to God, my rock:
 "Why do you forget me?*n*
 Why must I go about mourning
 with the enemy oppressing me?"
11 It shatters my bones, when my adversaries
 reproach me,
 when they say to me every day:
 "Where is your God?"
12 Why are you downcast, my soul,
 why do you groan within me?
 Wait for God, for I shall again praise him,
 my savior and my God.

PSALM 43

1 Grant me justice, O God;
 defend me from a faithless people;
 from the deceitful and unjust rescue
 me.*o*
2 You, O God, are my strength.
 Why then do you spurn me?
 Why must I go about mourning,
 with the enemy oppressing me?
3 *p*Send your light and your fidelity,***
 that they may be my guide;*q*

---

††[42:5] The shrine of the Mighty One: this reading follows the tradition of the Septuagint and the Vulgate.
‡‡[42:7] From the land of the Jordan: the sources of the Jordan are in the foothills of Mount Hermon in present-day southern Lebanon. Mount Mizar is presumed to be a mountain in the same range.
§§[42:8] Deep calls to deep: to the psalmist, the waters arising in the north are overwhelming and far from God's presence, like the waters of chaos (Ps 18:5; 69:2–3, 15; Jon 2:3–6).
¶¶[42:9–10] I will pray . . . I will say: in the midst of his depression the psalmist turns to prayer. Despite his situation he trusts the Lord to deliver him from his sorrow so that he may enter the Temple precincts and praise him once again (Ps 43:3–4, 5b).
***[43:3] Your light and your fidelity: a pair of divine attributes personified as guides for the pilgrimage. As in Ps 42:9

---

k. [42:5] Ps 122:5.   l. [42:7] Ps 43:3.   m. [42:8] Ps 18:5; 32:6; 69:2; 88:8; Jon 2:4.   n. [42:10] Ps 18:2; 31:3–4.   o. [43:1] Ps 119:154.   p. [43:3] Ps 18:29; 27:1; 36:10; Mi 7:8.   q. [43:3] Ps 122:1.

Let them bring me to your holy
mountain,
to the place of your dwelling,
4 That I may come to the altar of God,
to God, my joy, my delight.
Then I will praise you with the harp,
O God, my God.
5 Why are you downcast, my soul?
Why do you groan within me?
Wait for God, for I shall again praise him,
my savior and my God.

PSALM 44*
God's Past Favor and Israel's Present Need

1 For the leader. A *maskil* of the Korahites.

I

2 O God, we have heard with our own ears;
our ancestors have told us[r]
The deeds you did in their days,
with your own hand in days of old:
3 You rooted out nations to plant them,[s]
crushed peoples and expelled them.
4 Not with their own swords did they
conquer the land,[t]
nor did their own arms bring victory;
It was your right hand, your own arm,
the light of your face for you favored
them.[u]
5 You are my king and my God,[v]
who bestows victories on Jacob.
6 Through you we batter our foes;
through your name we trample our
adversaries.
7 Not in my bow do I trust,
nor does my sword bring me victory.
8 You have brought us victory over our
enemies,
shamed those who hate us.
9 In God we have boasted all the day long;
your name we will praise forever.
Selah

II

10 [w]But now you have rejected and disgraced
us;
you do not march out with our
armies.[x]
11 You make us retreat[†] before the foe;

those who hate us plunder us at
will.[y]
12 You hand us over like sheep to be
slaughtered,
scatter us among the nations.[z]
13 You sell your people for nothing;
you make no profit from their sale.[a]
14 You make us the reproach of our
neighbors,[b]
the mockery and scorn of those
around us.
15 You make us a byword among the nations;
the peoples shake their heads at us.
16 All day long my disgrace is before me;
shame has covered my face
17 At the sound of those who taunt and
revile,
at the sight of the enemy and
avenger.

III

18 All this has come upon us,
though we have not forgotten you,
nor been disloyal to your covenant.
19 ‡Our hearts have not turned back,
nor have our steps strayed from
your path.
20 Yet you have left us crushed,
desolate in a place of jackals;§c
you have covered us with a shadow
of death.
21 If we had forgotten the name of our God,
stretched out our hands to another
god,
22 Would not God have discovered this,
God who knows the secrets of the
heart?
23 For you we are slain all the day long,
considered only as sheep to be
slaughtered.[d]

IV

24 Awake! Why do you sleep, O Lord?
Rise up! Do not reject us forever![e]
25 Why do you hide your face,[f]
why forget our pain and misery?
26 For our soul has been humiliated in the
dust;[g]
our belly is pressed to the earth.
27 Rise up, help us!
Redeem us in your mercy.

---

the psalmist prays that these divine attributes lead him back
to Jerusalem and ultimately to God's presence in the Temple.

*[Psalm 44] In this lament the community reminds God
of past favors which it has always acknowledged (Ps 44:2–9).
But now God has abandoned Israel to defeat and humiliation
(Ps 44:10–17), though the people are not conscious of any sin
against the covenant (Ps 44:18–23). They struggle with being
God's special people amid divine silence; yet they continue to
pray (Ps 44:24–26).

†[44:11] **You make us retreat**: the corollary of Ps 44:3.
Defeat, like victory, is God's doing; neither Israel nor its enemies can claim credit (Ps 44:23).

---

‡[44:19] **Our hearts have not turned back**: Israel's defeat
was not caused by its lack of fidelity.

§[44:20] **A place of jackals**: following Israel's defeat and
exile (Ps 44:11–12), the land lies desolate, inhabited only by
jackals, cf. Is 13:22; Jer 9:10; 10:22. Others take *tannim* as "sea
monster" (cf. Ez 29:3; 32:2) and render: "you crushed us as
you did the sea monster."

---

r. [44:2] Ps 78:3.   s. [44:3] Ps 78:55; 80:9f.   t. [44:4] Dt 8:17f;
Jos 24:12.   u. [44:4] Ps 4:7; 31:17; 67:2; 80:4; Nm 6:25; Dn
9:17.   v. [44:5] Ps 145:1.   w. [44:10–27] Ps 89:39–52.   x. [44:10]
Ps 60:12.

y. [44:11] Lv 26:17; Dt 28:25.   z. [44:12] Lv 26:33; Dt 28:64.
a. [44:13] Dt 32:30; Is 52:3.   b. [44:14–17] Ps 79:4; 80:7; 123:3–4;
Jb 12:4; Dn 9:16.   c. [44:20] Jer 9:10.   d. [44:23] Rom 8:36.
e. [44:24] Ps 10:1; 74:1; 77:8; 79:5; 83:2.   f. [44:25] Ps 10:11; 89:47;
Jb 13:24.   g. [44:26] Ps 119:25.

PSALM 45*
Song for a Royal Wedding

¹For the leader; according to "Lilies." A *maskil* of the Korahites. A love song.

I

² My heart is stirred by a noble theme,
    as I sing my ode to the king.
    My tongue is the pen of a nimble
        scribe.

II

³ You are the most handsome of men;
    fair speech has graced your lips,
    for God has blessed you forever.ʰ
⁴ Gird your sword upon your hip, mighty
        warrior!
    In splendor and majesty ride on
        triumphant!ⁱ
⁵ In the cause of truth, meekness, and
        justice
    may your right hand show your
        wondrous deeds.
⁶ Your arrows are sharp;
    peoples will cower at your feet;
    the king's enemies will lose heart.
⁷ Your throne, O God,† stands forever;ʲ
    your royal scepter is a scepter for
        justice.
⁸ You love justice and hate wrongdoing;
    therefore God, your God, has
        anointed you
    with the oil of gladness above your
        fellow kings.
⁹ With myrrh, aloes, and cassia
    your robes are fragrant.
    From ivory-paneled palaces‡
    stringed instruments bring you joy.
¹⁰ Daughters of kings are your lovely wives;
    a princess arrayed in Ophir's gold§
    comes to stand at your right hand.

III

¹¹ Listen, my daughter, and understand;
    pay me careful heed.
    Forget your people and your father's house,¶

¹² that the king might desire your
        beauty.
    He is your lord;
¹³ ᵏhonor him, daughter of Tyre.
    Then the richest of the people
    will seek your favor with gifts.
¹⁴ All glorious is the king's daughter as she
        enters,ˡ
    her raiment threaded with gold;
¹⁵ In embroidered apparel she is led to the
        king.
    The maids of her train are presented
        to the king.
¹⁶ They are led in with glad and joyous
        acclaim;
    they enter the palace of the king.

IV

¹⁷ The throne of your fathers your sons will
        have;
    you shall make them princes
        through all the land.ᵐ
¹⁸ I will make your name renowned through
        all generations;
    thus nations shall praise you
        forever.ⁿ

PSALM 46**
God, the Protector of Zion

¹For the leader. A song of the Korahites. According to *alamoth*.††

I

² God is our refuge and our strength,
    an ever-present help in distress.ᵒ
³ ‡‡Thus we do not fear, though earth be
        shaken
    and mountains quake to the depths
        of the sea,
⁴ Though its waters rage and foam
    and mountains totter at its surging.ᵖ
                                        Selah

II

⁵ §§Streams of the river gladden the city of
        God,
    the holy dwelling of the Most High.�q
⁶ God is in its midst; it shall not be shaken;
    God will help it at break of day.ʳ

---

*[Psalm 45] A song for the Davidic king's marriage to a foreign princess from Tyre in Phoenicia. The court poet sings (Ps 45:2, 18) of God's choice of the king (Ps 45:3, 8), of his role in establishing divine rule (Ps 45:4–8), and of his splendor as he waits for his bride (Ps 45:9–10). The woman is to forget her own house when she becomes wife to the king (Ps 45:11–13). Her majestic beauty today is a sign of the future prosperity of the royal house (Ps 45:14–17). The Psalm was retained in the collection when there was no reigning king, and came to be applied to the king who was to come, the messiah.

†[45:7] **O God**: the king, in courtly language, is called "god," i.e., more than human, representing God to the people. Heb 1:8–9 applies Ps 45:7–8 to Christ.

‡[45:9] **Ivory-paneled palaces**: lit., "palaces of ivory." Ivory paneling and furniture decoration have been found in Samaria and other ancient Near Eastern cities, cf. Am 3:15.

§[45:10] **Ophir's gold**: uncertain location, possibly a region on the coast of southern Arabia or eastern Africa, famous for its gold, cf. 1 Kgs 9:28; 10:11; Jb 22:24.

¶[45:11] **Forget your people and your father's house**: the bride should no longer consider herself a daughter of her father's house, but the wife of the king—the queen.

h. [45:3] Sg 5:10–16. i. [45:4] Ps 21:5. j. [45:7–8] Heb 1:8–9.

**[Psalm 46] A song of confidence in God's protection of Zion with close parallels to Ps 48. The dominant note in Ps 46 is sounded by the refrain, The Lord of hosts is with us (Ps 46:8, 12). The first strophe (Ps 46:2–4) sings of the security of God's presence even in utter chaos; the second (Ps 46:5–8), of divine protection of the city from its enemies; the third (Ps 46:9–11), of God's imposition of imperial peace.

††[46:1] **Alamoth**: the melody of the Psalm, now lost.

‡‡[46:3–4] Figurative ancient Near Eastern language to describe social and political upheavals.

§§[46:5] Jerusalem is not situated on a river. This description derives from mythological descriptions of the divine abode and symbolizes the divine presence as the source of all life (cf. Is 33:21; Ez 47:1–12; Jl 4:18; Zec 14:8; Rev 22:1–2).

k. [45:13] Ps 72:10–11; Is 60:5f. l. [45:14–16] Ez 16:10–13.
m. [45:17] Gn 17:6. n. [45:18] Is 60:15. o. [46:2] Ps 48:4; Is 33:2. p. [46:4] Ps 93:3–4; Jb 9:5–6; Is 24:18–20; 54:10. q. [46:5] Ps 48:2–3; 76:3. r. [46:6] Is 7:14.

7 Though nations rage and kingdoms totter,
   he utters his voice and the earth melts.[s]
8 The LORD of hosts is with us;
   our stronghold is the God of Jacob.
                                          Selah

III

9 Come and see the works of the LORD,
   who has done fearsome deeds on
   earth;[t]
10 Who stops wars to the ends of the earth,
   breaks the bow, splinters the spear,
   and burns the shields with fire;[u]
11 v"Be still and know that I am God!
   I am exalted among the nations,
   exalted on the earth."
12 The LORD of hosts is with us;
   our stronghold is the God of Jacob.
                                          Selah

PSALM 47[†]
The Ruler of All the Nations

1 For the leader. A psalm of the Korahites.

I

2 All you peoples, clap your hands;
   shout to God with joyful cries.[w]
3 For the LORD, the Most High, is to be
   feared,
   the great king over all the earth,[x]
4 Who made people subject to us,
   nations under our feet,[y]
5 ‡Who chose our heritage for us,
   the glory of Jacob, whom he loves.[z]
                                          Selah

II

6 §God has gone up with a shout;
   the LORD, amid trumpet blasts.[u]
7 Sing praise to God, sing praise;
   sing praise to our king, sing praise.

III

8 For God is king over all the earth;[b]
   sing hymns of praise.
9 God rules over the nations;
   God sits upon his holy throne.
10 The princes of the peoples assemble
   with the people of the God of
   Abraham.
   For the shields of the earth belong to God,
   highly exalted.[c]

---

*[46:8] The first line of the refrain is similar in structure and meaning to Isaiah's name for the royal child, Emmanuel, With us is God (Is 7:14; 8:8, 10).

†[Psalm 47] A hymn calling on the nations to acknowledge the universal rule of Israel's God (Ps 47:2–5) who is enthroned as king over Israel and the nations (Ps 47:6–9).

‡[47:5] Our heritage . . . the glory: the land of Israel (cf. Is 58:14), which God has given Israel in an act of sovereignty.

§[47:6] God has gone up: Christian liturgical tradition has applied the verse to the Ascension of Christ.

---

s. [46:7] Ps 2:1–5; 48:5–8; 76:7–9; Is 17:12–14.   t. [46:9] Ps 48:9–10.
u. [46:10] Ps 76:4.   v. [46:11] Ps 48:11.   w. [47:2] Ps 89:16; Zep
3:14.   x. [47:3] Ps 95:3; Ex 15:18; Is 24:23; 52:7.   y. [47:4] Ps 2:8.
z. [47:5] Is 58:14.   a. [47:6] Ps 24:8, 10; 68:18–19; 98:6.   b. [47:8–9]
Ps 72:11; 93:1; 96:10; 97:1; 99:1; Jer 10:7.   c. [47:10] Ps 89:19; Ex 3:6;
Is 2:2–4.

PSALM 48[¶]
The Splendor of the Invincible City

1 A psalm of the Korahites.[**] A song.

I

2 Great is the LORD and highly praised
   in the city of our God:[d]
   His holy mountain,
3   fairest of heights,
   the joy of all the earth,[e]
   Mount Zion, the heights of Zaphon,[††f]
   the city of the great king.

II

4 God is in its citadel,
   renowned as a stronghold.
5 See! The kings assembled,
   together they advanced.
6 ‡‡When they looked they were astounded;
   terrified, they were put to flight![g]
7 Trembling seized them there,
   anguish, like a woman's labor,[h]
8 As when the east wind wrecks
   the ships of Tarshish![§§]

III

9 §§What we had heard we have now seen
   in the city of the LORD of hosts,
   In the city of our God,
   which God establishes forever.
                                          Selah

10 We ponder, O God, your mercy
   within your temple
11 Like your name, O God,
   so is your praise to the ends of the
   earth.[i]
   Your right hand is fully victorious.
12   Mount Zion is glad!
   The daughters of Judah rejoice
   because of your judgments![j]

¶[Psalm 48] A Zion hymn, praising the holy city as the invincible dwelling place of God. Unconquerable, it is an apt symbol of God who has defeated all enemies. After seven epithets describing the city (Ps 48:2–3), the Psalm describes the victory by the Divine Warrior over hostile kings (Ps 48:4–8). The second half proclaims the dominion of the God of Zion over all the earth (Ps 48:9–12) and invites pilgrims to announce that God is eternally invincible like Zion itself (Ps 48:13–14).

**[48:1] Korahites: see note on Ps 42:1.

††[48:3] The heights of Zaphon: the mountain abode of the Canaanite storm-god Baal in comparable texts. To speak of Zion as if it were Zaphon was to claim for Israel's God what Canaanites claimed for Baal. Though topographically speaking Zion is only a hill, viewed religiously it towers over other mountains as the home of the supreme God (cf. Ps 68:16–17).

‡‡[48:6] When they looked: the kings are stunned by the sight of Zion, touched by divine splendor. The language is that of holy war, in which the enemy panics and flees at the sight of divine glory.

§§[48:8] The ships of Tarshish: large ships, named after the distant land or port of Tarshish, probably ancient Tartessus in southern Spain, although other identifications have been proposed, cf. Is 2:16; 60:9; Jon 1:3.

§§[48:9] What we had heard we have now seen: the glorious things that new pilgrims had heard about the holy city—its beauty and awesomeness—they now see with their own eyes. The seeing here contrasts with the seeing of the hostile kings in Ps 48:6.

---

d. [48:2] Ps 96:4; 145:3.   e. [48:3] Ps 50:2; Lam 2:15.   f. [48:3] Is
14:13.   g. [48:6] Jgs 5:19.   h. [48:7] Ex 15:14; Jer 4:31.   i. [48:11]
Mal 1:11.   j. [48:12] Ps 97:8.

IV
13 Go about Zion, walk all around it,
    note the number of its towers.
14 Consider the ramparts, examine its
      citadels,
    that you may tell future generations:*k*
15 That this is God,
    our God for ever and ever.*
    He will lead us until death.

PSALM 49†
Confidence in God Rather than in Riches

1 For the leader. A psalm of the Korahites.‡
2 Hear this, all you peoples!
    Give ear, all who inhabit the world,
3 You of lowly birth or high estate,
    rich and poor together.
4 My mouth shall speak words of wisdom,
    my heart shall offer insights.*l*
5 I will turn my ear to a riddle,§
    expound my question on a lyre.
        I
6 Why should I fear in evil days,
    with the iniquity of my assailants
      surrounding me,
7 Of those who trust in their wealth
    and boast of their abundant riches?*m*
8 'No man can ransom even a brother,
    or pay to God his own ransom.*n*
9 The redemption of his soul is costly;
    and he will pass away forever.
10 Will he live on forever, then,
    and never see the Pit of Corruption?
11 Indeed, he will see that the wise die,
    and the fool will perish together
      with the senseless,*o*
    and they leave their wealth to
      others.*p*
12 Their tombs are their homes forever,
    their dwellings through all
      generations,

"They named countries after
    themselves"
13 —but man does not abide in
      splendor.
    He is like the beasts—they perish.*q*
        II
14 This is the way of those who trust in
    themselves,
    and the end of those who take
      pleasure in their own mouth.
                              Selah
15 Like a herd of sheep they will be put into
      Sheol,
    and Death will shepherd them.
    Straight to the grave they descend,
      where their form will waste away,
      Sheol will be their palace.
16 But God will redeem my life,
    will take me** from the hand of
      Sheol.*r*
                              Selah
17 Do not fear when a man becomes rich,
    when the wealth of his house grows
      great.
18 At his death he will not take along
      anything,
    his glory will not go down after
      him.*s*
19 During his life his soul uttered blessings;
    "They will praise you, for you do
      well for yourself."
20 But he will join the company of his
      fathers,
    never again to see the light.*t*
21 In his prime, man does not understand.
    He is like the beasts—they perish.

PSALM 50††
The Acceptable Sacrifice

1 A psalm of Asaph.
        I
The God of gods, the LORD,
    has spoken and summoned the
      earth
    from the rising of the sun to its
      setting.*u*
2 From Zion, the perfection of beauty,
    God shines forth.*v*

---

*[48:15] **Our God for ever and ever**: Israel's God is like Zion in being eternal and invincible. The holy city is therefore a kind of "sacrament" of God.

†[Psalm 49] The Psalm affirms confidence in God (cf. Ps 23; 27:1–6; 62) in the face of the apparent good fortune of the unjust rich, cf. Ps 37; 73. Reliance on wealth is misplaced (Ps 49:8–10) for it is of no avail in the face of death (Ps 49:18–20). After inviting all to listen to this axiom of faith (Ps 49:2–5), the psalmist depicts the self-delusion of the ungodly (Ps 49:6–13), whose destiny is to die like ignorant beasts (Ps 49:13, 18; cf. Prv 7:21–23). Their wealth should occasion no alarm, for they will come to nought, whereas God will save the just (Ps 49:14–20).

‡[49:1] **Korahites**: see note on Ps 42:1.

§[49:5] **Riddle**: the psalmist's personal solution to the perennial biblical problem of the prosperity of the wicked. **Question**: parallel in meaning to problem; in wisdom literature it means the mysterious way of how the world works.

¶[49:8] **No man can ransom even a brother**: an axiom. For the practice of redemption, cf. Jb 6:21–23. A play on the first Hebrew word of Ps 49:8, 16 relates the two verses.

[49:16] **Will take me: the same Hebrew verb is used of God "taking up" a favored servant: Enoch in Gn 5:24; Elijah in 2 Kgs 2:11–12; the righteous person in Ps 73:24. The verse apparently states the hope that God will rescue the faithful psalmist in the same manner.

††[Psalm 50] A covenant lawsuit stating that the sacrifice God really wants is the sacrifice of praise accompanied by genuine obedience (cf. Mi 6:1–8). It begins with a theophany and the summoning of the court (Ps 50:1–6). Then in direct address God explains what is required of the faithful (Ps 50:7–15), rebukes the hypocritical worshiper (Ps 50:16–21), and concludes with a threat and a promise (Ps 50:22–23; cf. Is 1:19–20).

---

k. [48:14] Ps 22:31–32; 71:18. l. [49:4] Ps 78:2; Mt 13:35.
m. [49:7] Jb 31:24. n. [49:8] Prv 10:15; 11:4; Ez 7:19; Mt 16:26.
o. [49:11] Eccl 2:16. p. [49:11] Ps 39:7; Sir 11:18–19.

q. [49:13] Eccl 3:18–21. r. [49:16] Ps 16:10; 86:13; 103:4; 116:8. s. [49:18] Sir 11:18–19; Eccl 5:15; 1 Tm 6:7. t. [49:20] Jb 10:21–22. u. [50:1] Dt 10:17; Jos 22:22. v. [50:2] Ps 48:2.

³ Our God comes and will not be silent!
    Devouring fire precedes him,
    it rages strongly around him.ʷ
⁴ He calls to the heavens above
    and to the earth to judge his people:
⁵ "Gather my loyal ones to me,
    those who made a covenant with me
        by sacrifice."
⁶ The heavens proclaim his righteousness,
    for God himself is the judge.ˣ

                                              Selah

                    II
⁷ "Listen, my people, I will speak;
    Israel, I will testify against you;
    God, your God, am I.
⁸ Not for your sacrifices do I rebuke you,
    your burnt offerings are always
        before me.
⁹ I will not take a bullock from your house,
    or he-goats from your folds.ʸ
¹⁰ For every animal of the forest is mine,
    beasts by the thousands on my
        mountains.
¹¹ I know every bird in the heights;
    whatever moves in the wild is mine.
¹² Were I hungry, I would not tell you,
    for mine is the world and all that
        fills it.ᶻ
¹³ Do I eat the flesh of bulls
    or drink the blood of he-goats?
¹⁴ Offer praise as your sacrifice to God;ᵃ
    fulfill your vows to the Most High.
¹⁵ Then call on me on the day of distress;ᵇ
    I will rescue you, and you shall
        honor me."

                    III
¹⁶ But to the wicked God says:
    "Why do you recite my
        commandments
    and profess my covenant with your
        mouth?
¹⁷ You hate discipline;
    you cast my words behind you!
¹⁸ If you see a thief, you run with him;
    with adulterers you throw in your
        lot.
¹⁹ You give your mouth free rein for evil;
    you yoke your tongue to deceit.
²⁰ You sit and speak against your brother,
    slandering your mother's son.
²¹ When you do these things should I be
        silent?
    Do you think that I am like you?
    I accuse you, I lay out the matter
        before your eyes.

                    IV
²² "Now understand this, you who forget
        God,
    lest I start ripping apart and there be
        no rescuer.

²³ Those who offer praise as a sacrifice
        honor me;
    I will let him whose way is steadfast
    look upon the salvation of God."ᶜ

                PSALM 51*
        The Miserere: Prayer of Repentance

¹For the leader. A psalm of David, ²when Nathan
the prophet came to him after he had gone in to
Bathsheba.ᵈ

                    I
³ Have mercy on me, God, in accord with
        your merciful love;
    in your abundant compassion blot
        out my transgressions.
⁴ Thoroughly wash away my guilt;
    and from my sin cleanse me.
⁵ For I know my transgressions;
    my sin is always before me.ᵉ
⁶ Against you, you alone have I sinned;
    I have done what is evil in your eyes
    So that you are just in your word,
    and without reproach in your
        judgment.ᶠ
⁷ Behold, I was born in guilt,
    in sin my mother conceived me.†ᵍ
⁸ Behold, you desire true sincerity;
    and secretly you teach me wisdom.
⁹ Cleanse me with hyssop,‡ that I may be
        pure;
    wash me, and I will be whiter than
        snow.ʰ
¹⁰ You will let me hear gladness and joy;
    the bones you have crushed will
        rejoice.

---

*[Psalm 51] A lament, the most famous of the seven Peni-
tential Psalms, prays for the removal of the personal and social
disorders that sin has brought. The poem has two parts of
approximately equal length: Ps 51:3–10 and Ps 51:11–19, and
a conclusion in Ps 51:20–21. The two parts interlock by repetition of "blot out" in the first verse of each section (Ps 51:3, 11),
of "wash (away)" just after the first verse of each section (Ps
51:4) and just before the last verse (Ps 51:9) of the first section,
and of "heart," "God," and "spirit" in Ps 51:12, 19. The first part
(Ps 51:3–10) asks deliverance from sin, not just a past act but its
emotional, physical, and social consequences. The second part
(Ps 51:11–19) seeks something more profound than wiping
the slate clean: nearness to God, living by the spirit of God (Ps
51:12–13), like the relation between God and people described
in Jer 31:33–34. Nearness to God brings joy and the authority
to teach sinners (Ps 51:15–16). Such proclamation is better than
offering sacrifice (Ps 51:17–19). The last two verses express the
hope that God's good will toward those who are cleansed and
contrite will prompt him to look favorably on the acts of worship offered in the Jerusalem Temple (Ps 51:19 [20–21]).
    †[51:7] **In sin my mother conceived me:** lit., "In iniquity
was I conceived," an instance of hyperbole: at no time was the
psalmist ever without sin, cf. Ps 88:15, "I am mortally afflicted
since youth," i.e., I have always been afflicted. The verse does
not imply that the sexual act of conception is sinful.
    ‡[51:9] **Hyssop:** a small bush whose many woody twigs
make a natural sprinkler. It was prescribed in the Mosaic law
as an instrument for sprinkling sacrificial blood or lustral
water for cleansing, cf. Ex 12:22; Lv 14:4; Nm 19:18.

---

w. [50:3] Ps 97:3; Dn 7:10.   x. [50:6] Ps 19:2; 97:6.   y. [50:9] Ps
69:32; Am 5:21–22.   z. [50:12] Ps 24:1; 89:12; Dt 10:14; 1 Cor
10:26.   a. [50:14] Heb 13:15.   b. [50:15] Ps 77:3.

c. [50:23] Ps 91:16.   d. [51:2] 2 Sm 12.   e. [51:5] Ps 32:5; 38:19; Is
59:12.   f. [51:6] Rom 3:4.   g. [51:7] Jb 14:4.   h. [51:9] Jb 9:30; Is
1:18; Ez 36:25.

II
11 Turn away your face from my sins;
    blot out all my iniquities.
12 A clean heart create for me, God;
    renew within me a steadfast spirit.[i]
13 Do not drive me from before your face,
    nor take from me your holy spirit.[j]
14 Restore to me the gladness of your
    salvation;
    uphold me with a willing spirit.
15 I will teach the wicked your ways,
    that sinners may return to you.
16 Rescue me from violent bloodshed, God,
    my saving God,
    and my tongue will sing joyfully of
    your justice.[k]
17 Lord, you will open my lips;
    and my mouth will proclaim your
    praise.
18 For you do not desire sacrifice* or I would
    give it;
    a burnt offering you would not accept.[l]
19 My sacrifice, O God, is a contrite spirit;
    a contrite, humbled heart, O God,
    you will not scorn.
III
20 †Treat Zion kindly according to your good
    will;
    build up the walls of Jerusalem.[m]
21 Then you will desire the sacrifices of the
    just,
    burnt offering and whole offerings;
    then they will offer up young bulls
    on your altar.

PSALM 52‡
The Deceitful Tongue

1For the leader. A *maskil* of David, 2when Doeg
the Edomite entered and reported to Saul, saying to him: "David has entered the house of
Ahimelech."[n]

I
3 Why do you glory in what is evil, you who
    are mighty by the mercy of
    God?
    All day long
4 you are thinking up intrigues;

your tongue is like a sharpened
    razor,
    you worker of deceit.[o]
5 You love evil more than good,
    lying rather than saying what is
    right.[p]
                                    Selah
6 You love all the words that create
    confusion,
    you deceitful tongue.[q]
II
7 God too will strike you down forever,
    he will lay hold of you and pluck you
    from your tent,
    uproot you from the land of the
    living.[r]
                                    Selah
8 The righteous will see and they will fear;
    but they will laugh at him:[s]
9 "Behold the man! He did not take God as
    his refuge,
    but he trusted in the abundance of
    his wealth,
    and grew powerful through his
    wickedness."[t]
III
10 But I, like an olive tree§ flourishing in the
    house of God,[u]
    I trust in God's mercy forever and
    ever.
11 I will thank you forever
    for what you have done.
    I will put my hope in your name—for it
    is good,[v]
    —in the presence of those devoted
    to you.

PSALM 53¶
A Lament over Widespread Corruption

1For the leader; according to *Mahalath*. A *maskil*
of David.

I
2 The fool says in his heart,[w]
    "There is no God."[x]
    They act corruptly and practice injustice;
    there is none that does good.
3 God looks out from the heavens
    upon the children of Adam,[y]
    To see if there is a discerning person[z]
    who is seeking God.

---

*[51:18] For you do not desire sacrifice: the mere offer-
ing of the ritual sacrifice apart from good dispositions is not
acceptable to God, cf. Ps 50.

†[51:20–21] Most scholars think that these verses were
added to the Psalm some time after the destruction of the
Temple in 587 B.C. The verses assume that the rebuilt Temple
will be an ideal site for national reconciliation.

‡[Psalm 52] A condemnation of the powerful and arrogant (Ps 52:3–6), who bring down upon themselves God's
judgment (Ps 52:7). The just, those who trust in God alone,
are gladdened and strengthened by the downfall of their traditional enemies (Ps 52:8–9).

§[52:10] Like an olive tree: the righteous will flourish in
the house of God like a well-watered olive tree, cf. Ps 92:14;
128:3.

¶[Psalm 53] A lament of an individual, duplicated in Ps
14, except that "God" is used for "the LORD," and Ps 53:6 is
different, cf. Ps 14.

---

i. [51:12] Ez 11:19. j. [51:13] Wis 1:5; 9:17; Is 63:11; Hg 2:5;
Rom 8:9. k. [51:16] Ps 30:10. l. [51:18] Ps 40:7; 50:8; Am
5:21–22; Hos 6:6; Is 1:11–15; Heb 10:5–7. m. [51:20] Jer 31:4; Ez
36:33. n. [52:2] 1 Sm 21:8; 22:6ff.

o. [52:4] Ps 12:3; 59:8; 120:2–3; Sir 51:3. p. [52:5] Jer 4:22; Jn
3:19–20. q. [52:6] Jer 9:4. r. [52:7] Ps 27:13; 28:5; 56:14; Jb 18:14;
Prv 2:22; Is 38:11. s. [52:8] Ps 44:14; 64:9. t. [52:9] Jb 31:24; Prv
11:28. u. [52:10] Ps 1:3; 92:12–14; Jer 11:16; 17:8. v. [52:11] Ps
22:23; 26:12; 35:18; 149:1. w. [53:2–6a] Ps 14:1–5a. x. [53:2] Ps
10:4; 36:2; Is 32:6; Jer 5:12. y. [53:2b–3] Rom 3:11–12. z. [53:3]
Ps 11:4; 102:20.

4 All have gone astray;
    each one is altogether perverse.
    There is not one who does what is
      good, not even one.*a*
      II
5 *b*Do they not know better, those who do
      evil,
    who feed upon my people as they
      feed upon bread?*c*
    Have they not called upon God?
6 They are going to fear his name with great
      fear,
    though they had not feared it before.
    For God will scatter the bones
      of those encamped against you.
    They will surely be put to shame,
      for God has rejected them.
      III
7 Who will bring forth from Zion
      the salvation of Israel?
    When God reverses the captivity of his
      people
    Jacob will rejoice and Israel will be
      glad.*d*

PSALM 54*
Confident Prayer in Great Peril

1For the leader. On stringed instruments. A
maskil of David, 2when the Ziphites came and
said to Saul, "David is hiding among us."*e*
      I
3 O God, by your name† save me.
    By your strength defend my cause.
4 O God, hear my prayer.
    Listen to the words of my mouth.
5 Strangers have risen against me;
    the ruthless seek my life;
    they do not keep God before them.*f*
              Selah
      II
6 God is present as my helper;*g*
    the Lord sustains my life.
7 Turn back the evil upon my foes;
    in your faithfulness, destroy them.*h*
8 Then I will offer you generous sacrifice
    and give thanks to your name,
    LORD, for it is good.
9 Because it has rescued me from every
      trouble,
    and my eyes look down on my foes.*i*

PSALM 55‡
A Lament over Betrayal

1For the leader. On stringed instruments. A
maskil of David.
      I
2 Listen, God, to my prayer;*j*
    do not hide from my pleading;
3   hear me and give answer.
    I rock with grief; I groan
4   at the uproar of the enemy,
    the clamor of the wicked.
    They heap trouble upon me,
    savagely accuse me.
5 My heart pounds within me;
    death's terrors fall upon me.
6 Fear and trembling overwhelm me;
    shuddering sweeps over me.
7 I say, "If only I had wings like a dove
    that I might fly away and find rest.*k*
8 Far away I would flee;
    I would stay in the desert.*l*
              Selah
9   "I would soon find a shelter from
    the raging wind and storm."
      II
10 Lord, check and confuse their tongues.
    For I see violence and strife in the
      city
11   making rounds on its walls day and
      night.
    Within are mischief and trouble;
12   treachery is in its midst;
    oppression and fraud never leave its
      streets.*m*
13 For it is not an enemy that reviled me—
    that I could bear–
    Not a foe who viewed me with contempt,
    from that I could hide.
14 But it was you, my other self,
    my comrade and friend,*n*
15 You, whose company I enjoyed,
    at whose side I walked
    in the house of God.
      III
16 Let death take them;
    let them go down alive to Sheol,*o*
    for evil is in their homes and bellies.

---

‡[Psalm 55] The psalmist, betrayed by intimate friends (Ps
55:14–15, 20–21), prays that God punish those oath breakers
and thus be acknowledged as the protector of the wronged.
The sufferings of the psalmist include both ostracism (Ps 55:4)
and mental turmoil (Ps 55:5–6), culminating in the wish to
flee society (Ps 55:7–9). The wish for a sudden death for one's
enemies (Ps 55:16) occurs elsewhere in the Psalms; an example
of such a death is the earth opening under the wicked Dathan
and Abiram (Nm 16:31–32). The psalmist, confident of vindication, exhorts others to a like trust in the God of justice (Ps
55:23). The Psalm is not so much for personal vengeance as for
a public vindication of God's righteousness now. There was no
belief in an afterlife where such vindication could take place.

---

*[Psalm 54] A lament in which the person under attack
calls directly upon God for help (Ps 54:3–5). Refusing to
despair, the psalmist hopes in God, who is active in history
and just (Ps 54:6–7). The Psalm ends with a serene promise to
return thanks (Ps 54:8–9).
†[54:3] **By your name:** one is present in one's name, hence
God as revealed to human beings.

---

a. [53:4] Ps 12:2. b. [53:5] Ps 79:6. c. [53:5] Ps 27:2; Is 9:11.
d. [53:7] Ps 85:2. e. [54:2] 1 Sm 23:19; 26:1. f. [54:5] Ps 86:14.
g. [54:6] Ps 118:7. h. [54:7] Ps 143:12. i. [54:9] Ps 59:11; 91:8;
92:12.

j. [55:2–3] Ps 5:2–3; 86:6; 130:1–2; Lam 3:56; Jon 2:3. k. [55:7]
Ps 11:1. l. [55:8] Jer 9:1; Rev 12:6. m. [55:12] Jer 5:1; 6:6; Ez
22:2; Heb 1:3; Zep 3:1. n. [55:14] Ps 41:10; Jer 9:3; Mt 26:21–24
par. o. [55:16] Ps 49:15; Nm 16:33; Prv 1:2; Is 5:14.

¹⁷ But I will call upon God,
    and the L<small>ORD</small> will save me.
¹⁸ At dusk, dawn, and noon
    I will grieve and complain,
    and my prayer will be heard.^p
¹⁹ He will redeem my soul in peace
    from those who war against me,
    though there are many who oppose
    me.
²⁰ God, who sits enthroned forever,^q
    will hear me and afflict them.

                        Selah

    For they will not mend their ways;
    they have no fear of God.
²¹ He stretched out his hand at his friends
    and broke his covenant.
²² Softer than butter is his speech,
    but war is in his heart.
    Smoother than oil are his words,
    but they are unsheathed swords.^r
²³ Cast your care upon the L<small>ORD</small>,
    who will give you support.
    He will never allow
    the righteous to stumble.^s
²⁴ But you, God, will bring them down
    to the pit of destruction.^t
    These bloodthirsty liars
    will not live half their days,
    but I put my trust in you.^u

PSALM 56[*]
Trust in God

¹For the director. According to *Yonath elem rehoqim.*[†] A *miktam* of David, when the Philistines seized him at Gath.^v

              I

² Have mercy on me, God,
    for I am treated harshly;
    attackers press me all the day.
³ My foes treat me harshly all the day;
    yes, many are my attackers.
    O Most High, ⁴when I am afraid,
    in you I place my trust.
⁵ I praise the word of God;
    I trust in God, I do not fear.^w
    What can mere flesh do to me?^x

             II

⁶ All the day they foil my plans;
    their every thought is of evil against
    me.

⁷ They hide together in ambush;
    they watch my every step;
    they lie in wait for my life.^y
⁸ They are evil; watch them, God!
    Cast the nations down in your anger!
⁹ My wanderings you have noted;
    are my tears not stored in your flask,[‡]
    recorded in your book?^z
¹⁰ My foes turn back when I call on you.
    This I know: God is on my side.
¹¹ I praise the word of God,
    I praise the word of the L<small>ORD</small>.
¹² In God I trust, I do not fear.
    What can man do to me?

             III

¹³ I have made vows to you, God;
    with offerings I will fulfill them,^a
¹⁴ For you have snatched me from death,
    kept my feet from stumbling,
    That I may walk before God
    in the light of the living.

PSALM 57[§]
Confident Prayer for Deliverance

¹For the director. Do not destroy.[¶] A *miktam* of David, when he fled from Saul into a cave.^b

             I

² Have mercy on me, God,
    have mercy on me.
    In you I seek refuge.
    In the shadow of your wings^{**} I seek refuge
    till harm pass by.^c
³ I call to God Most High,
    to God who provides for me.
⁴ May God send help from heaven to save me,
    shame those who trample upon me.
    May God send fidelity and mercy.

                        Selah

⁵ I must lie down in the midst of lions
    hungry for human prey.^d
    Their teeth are spears and arrows;
    their tongue, a sharpened sword.^e
⁶ Be exalted over the heavens, God;
    may your glory appear above all the
    earth.^f

---

‡[56:9] **Are my tears not stored in your flask:** a unique saying in the Old Testament. The context suggests that the tears are saved because they are precious; God puts a high value on each of the psalmist's troubles.

§[Psalm 57] Each of the two equal strophes contains a prayer for rescue from enemies, accompanied by joyful trust in God (Ps 57:2–5, 7–11). The refrain prays that God be manifested as saving (Ps 57:6, 12). Ps 108 is nearly identical to part of this Psalm (cf. Ps 57:8–11, Ps 108:2–6).

¶[57:1] **Do not destroy:** probably the title of the melody to which the Psalm was to be sung.

[57:2] **The shadow of your wings: probably refers to the wings of the cherubim (powerful winged animals) whose wings spread over the ark in the inner chamber of the Temple (1 Kgs 6:23–28).

---

*[Psalm 56] Beset physically (Ps 56:2–3) and psychologically (Ps 56:6–7), the psalmist maintains a firm confidence in God (Ps 56:5, 9–10). Nothing will prevent the psalmist from keeping the vow to give thanks for God's gift of life (Ps 56:13). A refrain (Ps 56:5, 11–12) divides the Psalm in two equal parts.

†[56:1] **Yonath elem rehoqim:** Hebrew words probably designating the melody to which the Psalm was to be sung.

p. [55:18] Dn 6:11.   q. [55:20] Ps 29:10; 93:2; Bar 3:3.   r. [55:22] Ps 12:3; 28:3; 57:5; 62:5; 64:4; Prv 26:24–28; Jer 9:7.   s. [55:23] Ps 37:5; Prv 3:5; 16:3; 1 Pt 5:7.   t. [55:24] Ps 28:1; 30:4; 40:3; 88:5; 143:7; Prv 1:12; Jon 2:7.   u. [55:24] Ps 25:2; 56:4; 130:5.   v. [56:1] 1 Sm 21:10.   w. [56:5] Ps 130:5.   x. [56:5] Ps 118:6; Heb 13:6.

y. [56:7] Ps 140:5–6.   z. [56:9] Ps 10:14; 2 Kgs 20:5; Is 25:8; Rev 7:17.   a. [56:13] Nm 30:3.   b. [57:1] 1 Sm 22:1.   c. [57:2] Ps 17:8; 36:8.   d. [57:5] Ps 17:11–12; 22:22; 58:7.   e. [57:5] Ps 11:2; 64:4.   f. [57:6] Ps 72:19; Nm 14:21.

II

7 They have set a trap for my feet;
  my soul is bowed down;
  They have dug a pit before me.
  May they fall into it themselves!^g
                                      Selah
8 My heart is steadfast, God,
  my heart is steadfast.
  I will sing and chant praise.^h
9 Awake, my soul;
  awake, lyre and harp!
  I will wake the dawn.*ⁱ
10 I will praise you among the peoples, Lord;
   I will chant your praise among the
   nations.^j
11 For your mercy towers to the heavens;
   your faithfulness reaches to the
   skies.^k
12 Exalt yourself over the heavens, God;
   may your glory appear above all the
   earth.

PSALM 58†
The Dethroning of Unjust Rulers

¹For the leader. Do not destroy.‡ A *miktam* of
David.

I

2 Do you indeed pronounce justice, O gods;§
  do you judge fairly you children of
  Adam?^l
3 No, you freely engage in crime;
  your hands dispense violence to the
  earth.

II

4 The wicked have been corrupt since birth;
  liars from the womb, they have gone
  astray.
5 'Their venom is like the venom of a snake,
  like that of a serpent stopping its
  ears,^m

6 So as not to hear the voice of the charmer
  or the enchanter with cunning
  spells.

III

7 O God, smash the teeth in their mouths;
  break the fangs of these lions,
  LORD!ⁿ
8 Make them vanish like water flowing
  away;^o
  trodden down, let them wither like
  grass.^p
9 Let them dissolve like a snail that oozes
  away,**
  like an untimely birth that never
  sees the sun.^q
10 Suddenly, like brambles or thistles,
   have the whirlwind snatch them
   away.^r
11 Then the just shall rejoice to see the
   vengeance
   and bathe their feet in the blood of
   the wicked.^s
12 Then people will say:
   "Truly there is a reward for the just;
   there is a God who is judge on
   earth!"

PSALM 59††
Complaint Against Bloodthirsty Enemies

¹For the director. Do not destroy.‡‡ A *miktam* of
David, when Saul sent people to watch his house
and kill him.^t

I

2 Rescue me from my enemies, my God;
  lift me out of reach of my foes.
3 Deliver me from evildoers;
  from the bloodthirsty save me.
4 They have set an ambush for my life;
  the powerful conspire against me.
  For no offense or misdeed of mine, LORD,
5 for no fault they hurry to take up
  arms.
  Come near and see my plight!
6 You, LORD God of hosts, are the
  God of Israel!
  Awake! Punish all the nations.
  Have no mercy on these worthless
  traitors.
                                      Selah

---

*[57:9] **I will wake the dawn**: by a bold figure the psalmist
imagines the sound of music and singing will waken a new
day.

†[Psalm 58] A lament expressing trust in God's power to
dethrone all powers obstructing divine rule of the world. First
condemned are "the gods," the powers that were popularly
imagined to control human destinies (Ps 58:2–3), then "the
wicked," the human instruments of these forces (Ps 58:4–6).
The psalmist prays God to prevent them from harming the
just (Ps 58:7–10). The manifestation of justice will gladden the
just; they will see that their God is with them (Ps 58:11). The
Psalm is less concerned with personal vengeance than with
public vindication of God's justice now.

‡[58:1] **Do not destroy**: probably the title of the melody to
which the Psalm was to be sung.

§[58:2] **Gods**: the Bible sometimes understands pagan
gods to be lesser divine beings who are assigned by Israel's
God to rule the foreign nations. Here they are accused of
injustice, permitting the human judges under their patronage
to abuse the righteous, cf. Ps 82.

¶[58:5–6] The image is that of a poisonous snake that is
controlled by the voice or piping of its trainer.

[58:9] **A snail that oozes away: empty shells suggested
to ancients that snails melted away as they left a slimy trail.

††[Psalm 59] A lament in two parts (Ps 59:2–9, 11b–17),
each ending in a refrain (Ps 59:10, 18). Both parts alternate
prayer for vindication (Ps 59:2–3, 4b–5, 11b–14) with vivid
depictions of the psalmist's enemies (Ps 59:4–5a, 7–8, 15–16).
The near curse in Ps 59:12–13 is not a crude desire for revenge
but a wish that God's just rule over human affairs be recognized now.

‡‡[59:1] **Do not destroy**: probably the title of the melody to
which the Psalm was to be sung.

---

g. [57:7] Ps 7:15; 9:16–17; 140:5–6.   h. [57:8] Ps 108:2.   i. [57:9] Jb
38:12.   j. [57:10] Ps 9:12; 18:50.   k. [57:11] Ps 36:6; 71:19.   l. [58:2]
Ps 82:2; Dt 16:19.   m. [58:5] Ps 64:4; 140:3; Rom 3:13.

n. [58:7] Ps 3:7.   o. [58:8] Wis 16:29.   p. [58:8] Ps 37:2.   q. [58:9]
Jb 3:16.   r. [58:10] Jb 21:18; Hos 13:3; Na 1:10.   s. [58:11] Ps 68:24;
Is 63:1–6.   t. [59:1] 1 Sm 19:11.

7 Each evening they return,
   growling like dogs, prowling the city.[u]
8 Their mouths pour out insult;
   sharp words are on their lips.
   They say: "Who is there to hear?"[v]
9 But you, LORD, laugh at them;
   you deride all the nations.[v]
10 My strength, for you I watch;
   you, God, are my fortress,
11   my loving God.

II

May God go before me,
   and show me my fallen foes.
12 Slay them, God,
   lest they deceive my people.
   Shake them by your power;
   Lord, our shield, bring them down.
13 For the sinful words of their mouths and
   lips
   let them be caught in their pride.
   For the lies they have told under oath[w]
14   destroy them in anger,
   destroy till they are no more.
   Then people will know God rules over
   Jacob,
   yes, even to the ends of the earth.[x]
                                          Selah
15 Each evening they return,
   growling like dogs, prowling the city.
16 They roam about as scavengers;
   if they are not filled, they howl.

III

17 But I shall sing of your strength,
   extol your mercy at dawn,
   For you are my fortress,
   my refuge in time of trouble.
18 My strength, your praise I will sing;
   you, God, are my fortress, my loving
   God.

PSALM 60[†]
Lament After Defeat in Battle

1 For the leader; according to "The Lily of. . . ."
A *miktam* of David (for teaching), 2 when he
fought against Aram-Naharaim and Aram-
Zobah; and Joab, coming back, killed twelve
thousand Edomites in the Valley of Salt.[y]

I

3 O God, you rejected us, broke our defenses;
   you were angry but now revive us.

4 You rocked the earth, split it open;[z]
   repair the cracks for it totters.
5 You made your people go through
   hardship,
   made us stagger from the wine you
   gave us.[a]
6 Raise up a banner for those who revere
   you,
   a refuge for them out of bow shot.
                                          Selah
7 ‡Help with your right hand and answer
   us
   that your loved ones may escape.

II

8 §In the sanctuary God promised:
   "I will exult, will apportion
   Shechem;
   the valley of Succoth§ I will measure
   out.
9 Gilead is mine, mine is Manasseh;
   Ephraim is the helmet for my head,
   Judah, my own scepter.¶
10 "Moab is my washbowl;
   upon Edom I cast my sandal."[b]
   I will triumph over Philistia."

III

11 Who will bring me to the fortified
   city?††
   Who will lead me into Edom?
12 Was it not you who rejected us, God?
   Do you no longer march with our
   armies?[c]
13 Give us aid against the foe;
   worthless is human help.
14 We will triumph with the help of God,
   who will trample down our foes.

PSALM 61‡‡
Prayer of the King in Time of Danger

1 For the leader; with stringed instruments. Of
David.

I

2 Hear my cry, O God,
   listen to my prayer!

---

‡[60:7–12] These verses occur again as the second half of
Ps 108.
§[60:8] **I will . . . apportion . . . measure out:** God lays
claim to these places. **The valley of Succoth:** probably the
lower stretch of the Jabbok valley.
¶[60:9] **Judah, my own scepter:** an allusion to the Testament of Jacob, Gn 49:10.
[60:10] **Moab is my washbowl: Moab borders the Dead
Sea, hence a metaphor for the country. **Upon Edom I cast my
sandal:** an ancient legal gesture of taking possession of land.
††[60:11] **The fortified city:** perhaps Bozrah, the fortified
capital of Edom, cf. Is 34:6; 63:1; Am 1:12.
‡‡[Psalm 61] A lament of the king who feels himself at the
brink of death (Ps 61:3) and cries out for the strong and saving presence of God (Ps 61:3b–5). The king cites the prayer
being made for him (Ps 61:7–8), and promises to give thanks
to God.

---

*[59:8] **Who is there to hear?:** a sample of the enemies' godless reflection. The answer is that God hears their blasphemies.
†[Psalm 60] The community complains that God has let
the enemy win the battle (Ps 60:3–5) and asks for an assurance
of victory (Ps 60:6–7). In the oracle God affirms ownership of
the land; the invasion of other nations is not permanent and
will be reversed ultimately (Ps 60:8–10). With renewed confidence, the community resolves to fight again (Ps 60:11). The
opening lament is picked up again (Ps 60:12), but this time
with new awareness of God's power and human limitation.

---

u. [59:7] Ps 55:11.   v. [59:9] Ps 2:4; 37:13; Wis 4:18.   w. [59:13] Prv
12:13; 18:7.   x. [59:14] Ps 83:18–19; Ez 5:13.   y. [60:2] 2 Sm 8:2, 3,
13; 1 Chr 18:2, 3, 12.

z. [60:4] Ps 75:4; Is 24:19.   a. [60:5] Ps 75:9; Is 51:17, 21–22; Jer
25:15.   b. [60:10] Ru 4:7–8.   c. [60:12] Ps 44:10.

³ From the ends of the earth˙ I call;
  my heart grows faint.
  Raise me up, set me on a rock,
⁴   for you are my refuge,
    a tower of strength against the foe.ᵈ
⁵ Let me dwell in your tent forever,
    take refuge in the shelter of your
      wings.ᵉ
                                    Selah

                    II
⁶ For you, O God, have heard my
      vows,
  you have granted me the heritage of
      those who revere your name.
⁷ Add days to the life of the king;
    may his years be as from generation
      to generation;ᶠ
⁸ ᵍMay he reign before God forever;
    send your love and fidelity† to
      preserve him—ʰ
⁹ I will duly sing to your name forever,
    fulfill my vows day after day.

PSALM 62‡
Trust in God Alone

¹For the leader; ʹal Jeduthun.§ A psalm of David.
                    I
² My soul rests in God alone,ⁱ
    from whom comes my salvation.
³ God alone is my rock and salvation,
    my fortress; I shall never fall.
⁴ How long will you set yourself against a
      man?
    You shall all be destroyed,
  Like a sagging wall
    or a tumbled down fence!
⁵ Even highly placed people
    plot to overthrow him.
  They delight in lies;
    they bless with their mouths,
    but inwardly they curse.ʲ
                                    Selah
                    II
⁶ My soul, be at rest in God alone,
    from whom comes my hope.
⁷ God alone is my rock and my salvation,
    my fortress; I shall not fall.

⁸ My deliverance and honor are with God,ᵏ
    my strong rock;
    my refuge is with God.
⁹ Trust God at all times, my people!
  Pour out your hearts to God our
      refuge!
                                    Selah
                    III
¹⁰ Mortals are a mere breath,
    the sons of man but an illusion;ˡ
  On a balance they rise;⁵
    together they weigh nothing.
¹¹ Do not trust in extortion;
    in plunder put no empty hope.
  On wealth that increases,
    do not set your heart.ᵐ
¹² ˮOne thing God has said;
    two things I have heard:ⁿ
  Strength belongs to God;
¹³   so too, my Lord, does mercy,
  For you repay each man
    according to his deeds.ᵒ

PSALM 63††
Ardent Longing for God

¹A psalm of David, when he was in the wilderness of Judah.ᵖ
                    I
² O God, you are my God—
    it is you I seek!
  For you my body yearns;
    for you my soul thirsts,
  In a land parched, lifeless,
    and without water.ᵍ
³ I look to you in the sanctuary
    to see your power and glory.
⁴ For your love is better than life;‡‡
    my lips shall ever praise you!
                    II
⁵ I will bless you as long as I live;
    I will lift up my hands, calling on
      your name.
⁶ My soul shall be sated as with choice food,

---

⁵[62:10] **On a balance they rise**: precious objects were weighed by balancing two pans suspended from a beam. The lighter pan rises.
[62:12] **One thing . . . two things: parallelism of numbers for the sake of variation, a common device in Semitic poetry. One should not literally add up the numbers, cf. Am 1:3; Prv 6:16–19; 30:15, 18, 21.
††[Psalm 63] A Psalm expressing the intimate relationship between God and the worshiper. Separated from God (Ps 63:2), the psalmist longs for the divine life given in the Temple (Ps 63:3–6), which is based on a close relationship with God (Ps 63:7–9). May all my enemies be destroyed and God's true worshipers continue in giving praise (Ps 63:10–11)!
‡‡[63:4] **For your love is better than life**: only here in the Old Testament is anything prized above life—in this case God's love.

---

*[61:3] **Ends of the earth**: "earth" being taken in its occasional meaning "the underworld," cf. Jon 2:3.
†[61:8] **Send your love and fidelity**: as in Ps 43:3 the psalmist asks God to send these two divine attributes like angels to protect the king.
‡[Psalm 62] A song of trust displaying serenity from experiencing God's power (the refrains of Ps 62:2–3 and Ps 62:6–7) and anger toward unjust enemies (Ps 62:4–5). From the experience of being rescued, the psalmist can teach others to trust in God (Ps 62:9–12).
§[62:1] **ʹAl Jeduthun**: apparently the Hebrew name for the melody.

---

d. [61:4] Ps 46:2. e. [61:5] Ps 17:8; 36:8; 57:2. f. [61:7] Ps 21:5.
g. [61:8] Ps 72:5; 89:5, 30, 37. h. [61:8] Ps 85:11; 89:15, 25; Prv
20:28. i. [62:2–3, 6–7] Ps 18:3; 31:3–4; 42:10; 118:8; 146:3. j. [62:5]
Ps 12:3; 28:3; 55:22; Prv 26:24–25.

k. [62:8] Ps 3:3; Is 26:4; 60:19. l. [62:10] Ps 39:6–7; 144:4; Jb 7:16;
Wis 2:5. m. [62:11] Jb 31:25; Eccl 5:9; Jer 17:11; Mt 6:19–21,
24. n. [62:12] Jb 40:5. o. [62:13] Ps 28:4; 31:24; 2 Sm 3:39; Jb
34:11; Jer 17:10; Mt 16:27; Rom 2:6; 2 Tm 4:14. p. [63:1] 1 Sm
24. q. [63:2] Ps 42:2; 143:6; Is 26:9.

with joyous lips my mouth shall
    praise you!
7 I think of you upon my bed,
    I remember you through the
      watches of the night
8 You indeed are my savior,
    and in the shadow of your wings I
      shout for joy.*r*
9 My soul clings fast to you;
    your right hand upholds me.

III

10 But those who seek my life will come to
    ruin;
    they shall go down to the depths of
      the netherworld!
11 Those who would hand over my life
    to the sword shall
    become the prey of jackals!
12 But the king shall rejoice in God;
    all who swear by the Lord* shall exult,
    but the mouths of liars will be shut!*s*

PSALM 64†
Treacherous Conspirators Punished by God

1For the leader. A psalm of David.

I

2 O God, hear my anguished voice;
    from a dreadful foe protect my life.
3 Hide me from the malicious crowd,
    the mob of evildoers.
4 They sharpen their tongues like swords,
    bend their bows of poison words.*t*
5 They shoot at the innocent from ambush,
    they shoot him in a moment and do
      not fear.
6 They resolve on their wicked plan;
    they conspire to set snares;
    they say: "Who will see us?"
7 They devise wicked schemes,
    conceal the schemes they devise;
    the designs of their hearts are hidden.*u*

II

8 God shoots an arrow at them;
    in a moment they are struck down.*v*
9 They are brought down by their own
    tongues;
    all who see them flee.*w*
10 Every person fears and proclaims God's
    actions,
    they ponder his deeds.

11 The righteous rejoices and takes refuge in
    the LORD;
    all the upright give praise.*x*

PSALM 65‡
Thanksgiving for God's Blessings

1For the leader. A psalm of David. A song.

I

2 To you we owe our hymn of praise,
    O God on Zion;
    To you our vows§ must be fulfilled,
3   ¶you who hear our prayers.
    To you all flesh must come*y*
4   with its burden of wicked deeds.
    We are overcome by our sins;
    only you can pardon them.*z*
5 Blessed the one whom you will choose
    and bring
    to dwell in your courts.
    May we be filled with the good things of
      your house,
    your holy temple!

II

6 You answer us with awesome deeds** of
    justice,
    O God our savior,
    The hope of all the ends of the earth
    and of those far off across the sea.*a*
7 You are robed in power,
    you set up the mountains by your
      might.
8 You still the roaring of the seas,*b*
    the roaring of their waves,
    the tumult of the peoples.*c*
9 Distant peoples stand in awe of your
    marvels;
    the places of morning and evening
    you make resound with joy.
10 ††You visit the earth and water it,
    make it abundantly fertile.*d*
    God's stream‡‡ is filled with water;
    you supply their grain.
    Thus do you prepare it:
11   you drench its plowed furrows,
    and level its ridges.

---

‡[Psalm 65] The community, aware of its unworthiness (Ps 65:3–4), gives thanks for divine bounty (Ps 65:5), a bounty resulting from God's creation victory (Ps 65:6–9). At God's touch the earth comes alive with vegetation and flocks (Ps 65:10–13).
§[65:2] **Vows:** the Israelites were accustomed to promising sacrifices in the Temple if their prayers were heard.
¶[65:3] **To you all flesh must come:** all must have recourse to God's mercy.
[65:6] **Awesome deeds: the acts of creating—installing mountains, taming seas, restraining nations (Ps 65:7–8)—that are visible worldwide (Ps 65:6, 9).
††[65:10–14] Apparently a description of the agricultural year, beginning with the first fall rains that soften the hard sun-baked soil (Ps 65:9–10).
‡‡[65:10] **God's stream:** the fertile waters of the earth derive from God's fertile waters in the heavenly world.

---

*[63:12] **All who swear by the Lord:** to swear by a particular god meant that one was a worshiper of that god (Is 45:23; 48:1; Zep 1:5).
†[Psalm 64] A lament of a person overwhelmed by the malice of the wicked who are depicted in the Psalms as the enemies of the righteous (Ps 64:2–7). When people see God bringing upon the wicked the evil they intended against others, they will know who is the true ruler of the world (Ps 64:8–10). The final verse is a vow of praise (Ps 64:11).

---

r. [63:8] Ps 17:8; 36:8. s. [63:12] Ps 107:42. t. [64:4] Ps 11:2; 37:14; 55:22; 57:5. u. [64:7] Ps 140:3; Prv 6:14. v. [64:8] Ps 7:13–14; 38:3; Dt 32:42. w. [64:9] Ps 5:11; 44:14; 52:6.

x. [64:11] Ps 36:8; 57:2. y. [65:3] Is 66:23. z. [65:4] Ps 32:1–2; 78:38; Is 1:18. a. [65:6] Is 66:19. b. [65:8] Ps 89:10; 107:29; Jb 38:11; Mt 8:26. c. [65:8] Is 17:12. d. [65:10] Lv 26:4; Is 30:23, 25; Jl 2:22–23.

With showers you keep it soft,
   blessing its young sprouts.
[12] You adorn the year with your bounty;
   your paths* drip with fruitful rain.
[13] The meadows of the wilderness also drip;
   the hills are robed with joy.
[14] The pastures are clothed with flocks,
   the valleys blanketed with grain;
   they cheer and sing for joy.[e]

PSALM 66[†]
Praise of God, Israel's Deliverer

[1]For the leader. A song; a psalm.

I

[2] Shout joyfully to God, all the earth;
   sing of his glorious name;
   give him glorious praise.[f]
[3] Say to God: "How awesome your deeds!
   Before your great strength your
     enemies cringe.
[4] All the earth falls in worship before you;[g]
   they sing of you, sing of your name!"
               Selah

II

[5] ‡Come and see the works of God,
   awesome in deeds before the
     children of Adam.
[6] He changed the sea to dry land;
   through the river they passed on
     foot.[h]
   There we rejoiced in him,
[7]   who rules by his might forever,
   His eyes are fixed upon the nations.
   Let no rebel rise to challenge!
               Selah

[8] Bless our God, you peoples;
   loudly sound his praise,
[9] Who has kept us alive
   and not allowed our feet to slip.[i]
[10] You tested us, O God,
   tried us as silver tried by fire.[j]
[11] You led us into a snare;
   you bound us at the waist as
     captives.
[12] §You let captors set foot on our neck;

we went through fire and water;
   then you led us out to freedom.[k]

III

[13] I will bring burnt offerings[ʃ] to your house;
   to you I will fulfill my vows,
[14] Which my lips pronounced
   and my mouth spoke in my distress.
[15] Burnt offerings of fatlings I will offer you
   and sacrificial smoke of rams;
   I will sacrifice oxen and goats.
               Selah
[16] Come and hear, all you who fear God,
   while I recount what has been done
     for me.
[17] I called to him with my mouth;
   praise was upon my tongue.
[18] Had I cherished evil in my heart,
   the Lord would not have heard.
[19] But God did hear
   and listened to my voice in prayer.
[20] Blessed be God, who did not reject my
     prayer
   and refuse his mercy.

PSALM 67**
Harvest Thanks and Petition

[1]For the leader; with stringed instruments. A
psalm; a song.

I

[2] May God be gracious to us†† and bless us;
   may his face shine upon us.[l]
               Selah
[3] So shall your way be known upon the earth,
   your victory among all the nations.[m]
[4] May the peoples praise you, God;
   may all the peoples praise you!

II

[5] May the nations be glad and rejoice;
   for you judge the peoples with
     fairness,
   you guide the nations upon the earth.[n]
               Selah
[6] May the peoples praise you, God;
   may all the peoples praise you!

III

[7] The earth has yielded its harvest;
   God, our God, blesses us.[o]

---

*[65:12] **Paths**: probably the tracks of God's storm chariot
dropping rain upon earth.

†[Psalm 66] In the first part (Ps 66:1–12), the community
praises God for powerful acts for Israel, both in the past (the
exodus from Egypt and the entry into the land [Ps 66:6]) and
in the present (deliverance from a recent but unspecified
calamity [Ps 66:8–12]). In the second part (Ps 66:13–20), an
individual from the rescued community fulfills a vow to offer
a sacrifice of thanksgiving. As often in thanksgivings, the rescued person steps forward to teach the community what God
has done (Ps 66:16–20).

‡[66:5–6] cf. the events described in Ex 14:1–15, 21; Jos
3:11–4:24 and Ps 114.

§[66:12] **You let captors set foot on our neck**: lit., "you
let men mount our heads." Conquerors placed their feet on

the neck of their enemies as a sign of complete defeat, cf. Jos
10:24. A ceremonial footstool of the Egyptian king Tutankhamen portrays bound and prostrate bodies of enemies ready
for the king's feet on their heads, and one of Tutankhamen's
ceremonial chariots depicts the king as a sphinx standing with
paw atop the neck of an enemy.

¶[66:13] **Burnt offerings**: cf. Lv 1:3–13; 6:1–4; 22:17–20.

**[Psalm 67] A petition for a bountiful harvest (Ps 67:7),
made in the awareness that Israel's prosperity will persuade
the nations to worship its God.

††[67:2] **May God be gracious to us**: the people's petition
echoes the blessing pronounced upon them by the priests, cf.
Nm 6:22–27.

---

e. [65:14] Is 44:23.   f. [66:2] Ps 65:14; Is 44:23.   g. [66:3–4] Ps
18:45; Mi 7:17.   h. [66:6] Ps 74:15; 114:3; Ex 14:21f; Jos 3:14ff; Is
44:27; 50:2.   i. [66:9] Ps 91:12; 121:3; 1 Sm 2:9; Prv 3:23.   j. [66:10]
Is 48:10.

k. [66:12] Is 43:2.   l. [67:2] Ps 4:7; 31:17; 44:4; 80:4; Dn 9:17.
m. [67:3] Jer 33:9.   n. [67:5] Ps 98:9.   o. [67:7] Ps 85:13; Lv 26:4;
Ez 34:27; Hos 2:23–24.

⁸ May God bless us still;
   that the ends of the earth may revere
     him.

PSALM 68*
The Exodus and Conquest, Pledge of Future Help

¹For the leader. A psalm of David; a song.

I

² †May God arise;
   may his enemies be scattered;
   may those who hate him flee before
     him.ᵖ
³ As the smoke is dispersed, disperse them;
   as wax is melted by fire,
   so may the wicked perish before God.�q
⁴ Then the just will be glad;
   they will rejoice before God;
   they will celebrate with great joy.

II

⁵ Sing to God, praise his name;
   exalt the rider of the clouds.‡
   Rejoice before him
     whose name is the LORD.ʳ
⁶ Father of the fatherless, defender of
     widowsˢ—
   God in his holy abode,
⁷ God gives a home to the forsaken,
   who leads prisoners out to
     prosperity,
   while rebels live in the desert.§

---

*[Psalm 68] The Psalm is extremely difficult because the Hebrew text is badly preserved and the ceremony that it describes is uncertain. The translation assumes the Psalm accompanied the early autumn Feast of Tabernacles (Sukkoth), which included a procession of the tribes (Ps 68:25–28). Israel was being oppressed by a foreign power, perhaps Egypt (Ps 68:31–32)—unless Egypt stands for any oppressor. The Psalm may have been composed from segments of ancient poems, which would explain why the transitions are implied rather than explicitly stated. At any rate, Ps 68:2 is based on Nm 10:35–36, and Ps 68:8–9 are derived from Jgs 5:4–5. The argument develops in nine stanzas (each of three to five poetic lines): 1. confidence that God will destroy Israel's enemies (Ps 68:2–4); 2. call to praise God as savior (Ps 68:5–7); 3. God's initial rescue of Israel from Egypt (Ps 68:8), the Sinai encounter (Ps 68:9), and the settlement in Canaan (Ps 68:10–11); 4. the defeat of the Canaanite kings (Ps 68:12–15); 5. the taking of Jerusalem, where Israel's God will rule the world (Ps 68:16–19); 6. praise for God's past help and for the future interventions that will be modeled on the ancient exodus-conquest (Ps 68:20–24); 7. procession at the Feast of Tabernacles (Ps 68:25–28); 8. prayer that the defeated enemies bring tribute to the Temple (Ps 68:29–32); 9. invitation for all kingdoms to praise Israel's God (Ps 68:33–35).

†[68:2] The opening line alluding to Nm 10:35 makes clear that God's assistance in the period of the exodus and conquest is the model and assurance of all future divine help.

‡[68:5] **Exalt the rider of the clouds**: God's intervention is in the imagery of Canaanite myth in which the storm-god mounted the storm clouds to ride to battle. Such theophanies occur throughout the Psalm: Ps 68:2–3, 8–10, 12–15, 18–19, 22–24, 29–32, 34–35. See Dt 33:26; Is 19:1.

§[68:7] **While rebels live in the desert**: rebels must live in the arid desert, whereas God's people will live in the well-watered land (Ps 68:8–11).

p. [68:2] Nm 10:35. q. [68:3] Ps 97:5; Jdt 16:15; Wis 5:14; Mi 1:4. r. [68:5] Ps 18:10; 104:3; Dt 33:26; Is 19:1. s. [68:6–7] Ps 103:6; 146:7, 9; Ex 22:20–22; Bar 6:37.

III

⁸ God, when you went forth before your
     people,ᵗ
   when you marched through the
     desert,
               Selah
⁹ The earth quaked, the heavens poured,
   before God, the One of Sinai,
   before God, the God of Israel.
¹⁰ You poured abundant rains, God,
   your inheritance was weak and you
     repaired it.
¹¹ Your creatures dwelt in it;
   you will establish it in your
     goodness for the poor, O God.

IV

¹² The Lord announced:
   "Those bringing news are a great
     Army.
¹³ The kings of the armies are in
     desperate flight.ᵘ
   Every household will share the spoil,
¹⁴ though you lie down among the
     sheepfolds,ᵛ
   you shall be covered with silver as
     the wings of a dove,
   her feathers bright as fine gold."
¹⁵ When the Almighty routs the kings there,
   it will be as when snow fell on
     Zalmon.¶

V

¹⁶ You mountain of God, mountain of
     Bashan,
   you rugged mountain, mountain of
     Bashan,
¹⁷ You rugged mountains, why look with
     envy
   at the mountain** where God has
     chosen to dwell,
   where the LORD resides forever?ʷ
¹⁸ God's chariots were myriad, thousands
     upon thousands;
   from Sinai the Lord entered the holy
     place.
¹⁹ You went up to its lofty height;
   you took captives, received slaves as
     tribute,ˣ
   even rebels, for the LORD God to
     dwell.

VI

²⁰ Blessed be the Lord day by day,
   God, our salvation, who carries us.ʸ
               Selah

¶[68:15] **Zalmon**: generally taken as the name of a mountain where snow is visible in winter, perhaps to be located in the Golan Heights or in the mountains of Bashan or Hauran east of the Sea of Galilee.

[68:17] **The mountain: Mount Zion, the site of the Temple.

t. [68:8–9] Ps 44:10; 114:4, 7; Jgs 5:4–5; Heb 12:26. u. [68:13] Jgs 5:19, 22. v. [68:14] Jgs 5:16. w. [68:17] Ps 132:13–14; Ez 43:7. x. [68:19] Ps 47:8; Eph 4:8–10. y. [68:20] Ps 34:2; 145:2; Is 46:3–4; 63:9.

²¹ Our God is a God who saves;
  escape from death is the LORD
  God's.
²² God will crush the heads of his enemies,
  the hairy scalp of the one who walks
  in sin.ᶻ
²³ The Lord has said:
  "Even from Bashan I will fetch
  them,
  fetch them even from the depths of
  the sea.˙
²⁴ You will wash your feet in your enemy's
  blood;
  the tongues of your dogs will lap
  it up."ᵃ

VII

²⁵ †Your procession comes into view, O God,
  your procession into the holy place,
  my God and king.
²⁶ The singers go first, the harpists follow;
  in their midst girls sound the
  timbrels.ᵇ
²⁷ In your choirs, bless God;
  LORD, Israel's fountain.
²⁸ In the lead is Benjamin, few in number;
  there the princes of Judah, a large
  throng,
  the princes of Zebulun, the princes
  of Naphtali, too.ᶜ

VIII

²⁹ Summon again, O God, your power,
  the divine power you once showed
  for us,
³⁰ From your temple on behalf of Jerusalem,
  that kings may bring you tribute.
³¹ Roar at the wild beast of the reeds,‡
  the herd of mighty bulls, the calves
  of the peoples;
  trampling those who lust after silver
  scatter the peoples that delight in
  war.
³² Let bronze be brought from Egypt,ᵈ
  Ethiopia hurry its hands to God.ᵉ

IX

³³ You kingdoms of the earth, sing to God;ᶠ
  chant the praises of the Lord,
                                    Selah˙
³⁴ Who rides the heights of the ancient
  heavens,
  Who sends forth his voice as a
  mighty voice?

³⁵ Confess the power of God,
  whose majesty protects Israel,
  whose power is in the sky.
³⁶ Awesome is God in his holy place,
  the God of Israel,
  who gives power and strength to his
  people.ᵍ
Blessed be God!

PSALM 69§
A Cry of Anguish in Great Distress

¹For the leader; according to "Lilies."¶ Of David.

I

² Save me, God,
  for the waters** have reached my
  neck.ʰ
³ I have sunk into the mire of the deep,
  where there is no foothold.
  I have gone down to the watery depths;
  the flood overwhelms me.ⁱ
⁴ I am weary with crying out;
  my throat is parched.
  My eyes fail,
  from looking for my God.ʲ
⁵ More numerous than the hairs of my head
  are those who hate me without
  cause.ᵏ
  Those who would destroy me are mighty,
  my enemies without reason.
  Must I now restore
  what I did not steal?††

II

⁶ God, you know my folly;
  my faults are not hidden from you.
⁷ Let those who wait in hope for you, LORD
  of hosts,
  not be shamed because of me.
  Let those who seek you, God of Israel,ˡ
  not be disgraced because of me.
⁸ For it is on your account I bear insult,
  that disgrace covers my face.ᵐ

§[Psalm 69] A lament complaining of suffering in language both metaphorical (Ps 69:2–3, 15–16, the waters of chaos) and literal (Ps 69:4, 5, 9, 11–13, exhaustion, alienation from family and community, false accusation). In the second part the psalmist prays with special emphasis that the enemies be punished for all to see (Ps 69:23–29). Despite the pain, the psalmist does not lose hope that all be set right, and promises public praise (Ps 69:30–36). The Psalm, which depicts the suffering of the innocent just person vividly, is cited often by the New Testament especially in the passion accounts, e.g., Ps 69:5 in Jn 15:25; Ps 69:22 in Mk 15:23, 36 and parallels and in Jn 19:29. The Psalm prays not so much for personal vengeance as for public vindication of God's justice. There was, at this time, no belief in an afterlife where such vindication could take place. Redress had to take place now, in the sight of all.

¶[69:1] "Lilies": apparently the name of the melody.

**[69:2] Waters: the waters of chaos from which God created the world are a common metaphor for extreme distress, cf. Ps 18:5; 42:8; 88:8; Jon 2:3–6.

††[69:5] What I did not steal: the psalmist, falsely accused of theft, is being forced to make restitution.

---

*[68:23] Even from Bashan . . . from the depths of the sea: the heights and the depths, the farthest places where enemies might flee.

†[68:25–28] Your procession: the procession renews God's original taking up of residence on Zion, described in Ps 68:16–19.

‡[68:31] The wild beast of the reeds: probably the Nile crocodile, a symbol for Egypt; see Ps 68:32 and Ez 29:2–5.

---

z. [68:22] Dt 32:42. a. [68:24] Ps 58:11; 1 Kgs 21:19; 22:38; Is 63:1–6. b. [68:26] Ps 81:2–3; 87:7; 149:3; 150:3–5; 2 Sm 6:5. c. [68:28] Is 8:23. d. [68:32] Ez 29:2ff. e. [68:32] Is 18:7; 45:14. f. [68:33] Ps 138:4.

g. [68:36] Ps 28:8; 29:11. h. [69:2] Ps 18:5; 93:3–4; Jb 22:11. i. [69:3] Ps 40:2; 124:4–5. j. [69:4] Ps 25:15; 119:82; 123:2; 141:8; Is 38:14. k. [69:5] Ps 40:13; Lam 3:52; Jn 15:25. l. [69:7] Ps 40:17. m. [69:8] Jer 15:15.

9 I have become an outcast to my kindred,
a stranger to my mother's children.[n]
10 Because zeal for your house has
consumed me,[*]
I am scorned by those who scorn
you.[o]
11 When I humbled my spirit with fasting,[p]
this led only to scorn.
12 When I clothed myself in sackcloth;
I became a byword for them.
13 Those who sit in the gate gossip about
me;
drunkards make me the butt of
songs.

III

14 But I will pray to you, LORD,
at a favorable time.
God, in your abundant kindness, answer
me
with your sure deliverance.[q]
15 Rescue me from the mire,[r]
and do not let me sink.
Rescue me from those who hate me
and from the watery depths.
16 Do not let the flood waters overwhelm
me,
nor the deep swallow me,
nor the pit close its mouth over me.
17 Answer me, LORD, in your generous love;
in your great mercy turn to me.
18 Do not hide your face from your servant;
hasten to answer me, for I am in
distress.[s]
19 Come and redeem my life;
because of my enemies ransom me.
20 You know my reproach, my shame, my
disgrace;
before you stand all my foes.
21 Insult has broken my heart, and I
despair;
I looked for compassion, but there
was none,[t]
for comforters, but found none.
22 Instead they gave me poison for my food;
and for my thirst they gave me
vinegar.[u]

IV

23 May their own table be a snare for them,
and their communion offerings a
trap.[v]
24 Make their eyes so dim they cannot see;
keep their backs ever feeble.
25 Pour out your wrath upon them;

let the fury of your anger overtake
them.
26 Make their camp desolate,
with none to dwell in their tents.[w]
27 For they pursued the one you struck,
added to the pain of the one you
wounded.
28 Heap punishment upon their
punishment;
let them gain from you no
vindication.
29 May they be blotted from the book of life;
not registered among the just![x]

V

30 But here I am miserable and in pain;
let your saving help protect me,
God,
31 [†]That I may praise God's name in song
and glorify it with thanksgiving.
32 That will please the LORD more than oxen,
more than bulls with horns and
hooves:[y]
33 "See, you lowly ones, and be glad;
you who seek God, take heart![z]
34 For the LORD hears the poor,
and does not spurn those in
bondage.
35 Let the heaven and the earth praise him,
the seas and whatever moves in
them!"

VI

36 For God will rescue Zion,
and rebuild the cities of Judah.[a]
They will dwell there and possess it;
37 the descendants of God's servants will
inherit it;
those who love God's name will
dwell in it.[b]

PSALM 70[‡]
Prayer for Divine Help

1 For the leader; of David. For remembrance.
2 Graciously rescue me, God![c]
Come quickly to help me, LORD![d]
3 Let those who seek my life
be confused and put to shame.[e]
Let those who desire my ruin
turn back in disgrace.
4 Let those who say "Aha!"[f]
turn back in their shame.

---

*[69:10] **Zeal for your house has consumed me**: the psalmist's commitment to God's cause brings only opposition, cf. Jn 2:17. **I am scorned by those who scorn you**: Rom 15:3 uses the verse as an example of Jesus' unselfishness.

n. [69:9] Jb 19:13–15. o. [69:10] Ps 119:139; Jn 2:17; Rom 15:3. p. [69:11–13] Ps 109:24–25; Jb 30:9; Lam 3:14. q. [69:14] Is 49:8. r. [69:15–16] Ps 28:1; 30:4; 32:6; 40:3; 88:5; Prv 1:12. s. [69:18] Ps 102:3; 143:7. t. [69:21] Lam 1:2. u. [69:22] Lam 3:15; Mt 27:34, 48; Mk 15:23. v. [69:23] Rom 11:9–10.

---

†[69:31] **That I may praise God's name in song**: the actual song is cited in Ps 69:33–35, the word "praise" in Ps 69:35 referring back to "praise" in Ps 69:31.
‡[Psalm 70] A lament of a poor and afflicted person (Ps 70:6) who has no resource except God, and who cries out to be saved from the enemy. The Psalm is almost identical to Ps 40:14–17.

---

w. [69:26] Acts 1:20. x. [69:29] Ps 139:16; Ex 32:32; Is 4:3; Dn 12:1; Mal 3:16; Rev 3:5. y. [69:32] Ps 40:7; 50:8–9, 14; 51:18; Is 1:11–15; Hos 6:6; Am 5:21–22; Heb 10:5–8. z. [69:33] Ps 22:27; 35:27; 70:5. a. [69:36] Is 44:26; Ez 36:10. b. [69:37] Ps 102:29; Is 65:9. c. [70:2–6] Ps 40:14–18. d. [70:2] Ps 71:12. e. [70:3] Ps 35:4, 26. f. [70:4] Ps 35:21, 25.

5 But may all who seek you
     rejoice and be glad in you,
     Those who long for your help
       always say, "God be glorified!"ᵍ
6 I am miserable and poor.
     God, come to me quickly!
     You are my help and deliverer.
     LORD, do not delay!

PSALM 71*
Prayer in Time of Old Age

I

1 In you, LORD, I take refuge;ʰ
     let me never be put to shame.ⁱ
2 In your justice rescue and deliver me;
     listen to me and save me!
3 Be my rock of refuge,
     my stronghold to give me safety;
     for you are my rock and fortress.ʲ
4 My God, rescue me from the hand of the
       wicked,
     from the clutches of the evil and
       violent.ᵏ
5 You are my hope, Lord;
     my trust, GOD, from my youth.
6 On you I have depended since birth;
     from my mother's womb you are my
       strength;ˡ
     my hope in you never wavers.
7 †I have become a portent to many,
     but you are my strong refuge!
8 My mouth shall be filled with your praise,
     shall sing your glory every day.

II

9 Do not cast me aside in my old age;
     as my strength fails, do not forsake
       me.
10 For my enemies speak against me;
     they watch and plot against me.ᵐ
11 They say, "God has abandoned him.
     Pursue, and seize him!
     No one will come to the rescue!"
12 God, be not far from me;
     my God, hasten to help me.ⁿ
13 Bring to a shameful end
     those who attack me;
     Cover with contempt and scorn
       those who seek my ruin.ᵒ
14 I will always hope in you
     and add to all your praise.

15 My mouth shall proclaim your just deeds,
     day after day your acts of
       deliverance,
     though I cannot number them all.ᵖ
16 I will speak of the mighty works of the
       Lord;
     O GOD, I will tell of your singular
       justice.

III

17 God, you have taught me from my youth;
     to this day I proclaim your
       wondrous deeds.
18 Now that I am old and gray,�q
     do not forsake me, God,
     That I may proclaim your might
       to all generations yet to come,ʳ
     Your power ¹⁹and justice, God,
       to the highest heaven.
     You have done great things;ˢ
       O God, who is your equal?ᵗ
20 Whatever bitter afflictions you sent me,
     you would turn and revive me.
     From the watery depths of the earth
       once more raise me up.
21 Restore my honor;
     turn and comfort me,
22 That I may praise you with the lyre
     for your faithfulness, my God,
     And sing to you with the harp,
       O Holy One of Israel!
23 My lips will shout for joy as I sing your
       praise;
     my soul, too, which you have
       redeemed.
24 Yes, my tongue shall recount
     your justice day by day.
     For those who sought my ruin
       have been shamed and disgraced.

PSALM 72‡
A Prayer for the King

¹Of Solomon.

I

2 O God, give your judgment to the king;
     your justice to the king's son;§ᵘ
     That he may govern your people with
       justice,
     your oppressed with right judgment,ᵛ
3 That the mountains may yield their
       bounty for the people,
     and the hills great abundance,ʷ

---

*[Psalm 71] A lament of an old person (Ps 71:9, 18) whose afflictions are interpreted by enemies as a divine judgment (Ps 71:11). The first part of the Psalm pleads for help (Ps 71:1–4) on the basis of a hope learned from a lifetime's experience of God; the second part describes the menace (Ps 71:9–13) yet remains buoyant (Ps 71:14–16); the third develops the theme of hope and praise.

†[71:7] A portent to many: the afflictions of the sufferer are taken as a manifestation of God's anger, cf. Dt 28:46; Ps 31:12.

g. [70:5] Ps 35:27. h. [71:1–3] Ps 31:2–4. i. [71:1] Ps 25:2. j. [71:3] Ps 18:3. k. [71:4] Ps 140:2. l. [71:6] Ps 22:11. m. [71:10] Ps 3:2; 22:8. n. [71:12] Ps 22:20. o. [71:13] Ps 35:4; 40:15; 70:3.

‡[Psalm 72] A royal Psalm in which the Israelite king, as the representative of God, is the instrument of divine justice (Ps 72:1–4, 12–14) and blessing (Ps 72:5–7, 15–17) for the whole world. The king is human, giving only what he has received from God. Hence intercession must be made for him. The extravagant language is typical of oriental royal courts.

§[72:2] The king . . . the king's son: the crown prince is the king's son; the prayer envisages the dynasty.

p. [71:15] Ps 35:28. q. [71:18] Is 46:3–4. r. [71:18] Ps 22:31–32; 48:14–15; 145:4. s. [71:19] Ps 72:18. t. [71:19] Ps 86:8. u. [72:2] Ps 99:4; Jer 23:5. v. [72:2] Prv 31:8–9. w. [72:3] Is 52:7; 55:12.

4 That he may defend the oppressed among
the people,
save the children of the poor and
crush the oppressor.

II

5 May they fear you with the sun,
and before the moon, through all
generations.*

6 May he be like rain coming down upon
the fields,
like showers watering the earth,*

7 That abundance may flourish in his days,
great bounty, till the moon be no
more.

III

8 *May he rule from sea to sea,
from the river to the ends of the
earth.*

9 May his foes kneel before him,
his enemies lick the dust.*

10 May the kings of Tarshish and the islands†
bring tribute,
the kings of Sheba and Seba offer
gifts.*

11 May all kings bow before him,
all nations serve him.*

12 For he rescues the poor when they cry out,
the oppressed who have no one to
help.

13 He shows pity to the needy and the poor*
and saves the lives of the poor.

14 From extortion and violence he redeems
them,
for precious is their blood‡ in his
sight.

IV

15 Long may he live, receiving gold from
Sheba,
prayed for without cease, blessed
day by day.

16 §May wheat abound in the land,
flourish even on the mountain
heights.
May his fruit be like that of Lebanon,
and flourish in the city like the
grasses of the land.*

17 May his name be forever;
as long as the sun, may his name
endure.*

May the tribes of the earth give blessings
with his name;§
may all the nations regard him as
favored.*

18 "Blessed be the LORD God, the God of
Israel,
who alone does wonderful deeds.*

19 Blessed be his glorious name forever;
may he fill all the earth with his glory.*
Amen and amen.

20The end of the psalms of David, son of
Jesse.

Third Book—Psalms 73–89

PSALM 73††
The Trial of the Just

1A psalm of Asaph.

How good God is to the upright,
to those who are pure of heart!

I

2 But, as for me, my feet had almost stumbled;
my steps had nearly slipped,

3 Because I was envious of the arrogant
when I saw the prosperity of the
wicked.*

4 For they suffer no pain;
their bodies are healthy and sleek.

5 They are free of the burdens of life;
they are not afflicted like others.

6 Thus pride adorns them as a necklace;
violence clothes them as a robe.

7 Out of such blindness comes sin;
evil thoughts flood their hearts.*

8 They scoff and spout their malice;
from on high they utter threats.*

9 ‡‡They set their mouths against the
heavens,
their tongues roam the earth.

§[72:17] **May the tribes of the earth give blessings with
his name:** an echo of the promise to the ancestors (Gn 12:3;
26:4; 28:14), suggesting that the monarchy in Israel fulfilled
the promise to Abraham, Isaac, and Jacob.
**[72:18–19] A doxology marking the end of Book II of the
Psalter.
††[Psalm 73] The opening verse of this probing poem
(cf. Ps 37; 49) is actually the psalmist's hard-won conclusion
from personal experience: God is just and good! The psalmist
describes near loss of faith (Ps 73:2–3), occasioned by observing
the wicked who blasphemed God with seeming impunity (Ps
73:4–12). Feeling abandoned despite personal righteousness,
the psalmist could not bear the injustice until an experience
of God's nearness in the Temple made clear how deluded the
wicked were. Their sudden destruction shows their imperma-
nence (Ps 73:13–20). The just can thus be confident, for, as the
psalmist now knows, their security is from God (Ps 73:1, 23–28).
‡‡[73:9] **They set their mouths against the heavens:** in an
image probably derived from mythic stories of half-divine
giants, the monstrous speech of the wicked is likened to enormous jaws gaping wide, devouring everything in sight.

---

*[72:8] **From sea to sea . . . the ends of the earth:** the
boundaries of the civilized world known at the time: from the
Mediterranean Sea (the western sea) to the Persian Gulf (the
eastern sea), and from the Euphrates (the river) to the islands
and lands of southwestern Europe, "the ends of the earth." The
words may also have a mythic nuance—the earth surrounded
by cosmic waters, hence everywhere.
†[72:10] **Tarshish and the islands:** the far west (Ps 48:6);
Arabia and Seba: the far south (1 Kgs 10:1).
‡[72:14] **Their blood:** cf. Ps 116:15.
§[72:16] The translation of the difficult Hebrew is tentative.

x. [72:5] Ps 89:37–38; Jer 31:35.   y. [72:6] Dt 32:2; Is 45:8;
Hos 6:3.   z. [72:8] Dt 11:24; Zec 9:10.   a. [72:9] Is 49:23; Mi
7:17.   b. [72:10] Ps 68:30; Is 60:5–6; 1 Kgs 10:1ff.   c. [72:11] Ps 47:8.
d. [72:13] Prv 31:9.   e. [72:16] Is 27:6; Hos 14:6–8; Am 9:13.
f. [72:17] Ps 21:7.

g. [72:17] Gn 12:3; 22:18; 26:4; Zec 8:13.   h. [72:18] Ps 41:14; 89:53;
106:48; 136:4.   i. [72:19] Ps 57:5; Nm 14:21.   j. [73:3] Ps 37:1; Jb
21:13.   k. [73:7] Jb 15:27.   l. [73:8] Ps 17:10.

¹⁰ ˙So my people turn to them
    and drink deeply of their words.
¹¹ They say, "Does God really know?"
    "Does the Most High have any
       knowledge?"ᵐ
¹² Such, then, are the wicked,
    always carefree, increasing their
       wealth.

              II
¹³ Is it in vain that I have kept my heart pure,
    washed my hands in innocence?ⁿ
¹⁴ For I am afflicted day after day,
    · chastised every morning.
¹⁵ Had I thought, "I will speak as they do,"
    I would have betrayed this
       generation of your children.
¹⁶ Though I tried to understand all this,
    it was too difficult for me,
¹⁷ Till I entered the sanctuary of God
    and came to understand their end.†

              III
¹⁸ You set them, indeed, on a slippery road;
    you hurl them down to ruin.
¹⁹ How suddenly they are devastated;
    utterly undone by disaster!
²⁰ They are like a dream after waking, Lord,
    dismissed like shadows when you
       arise.ᵒ

              IV
²¹ Since my heart was embittered
    and my soul deeply wounded,
²² I was stupid and could not understand;
    I was like a brute beast in your
       presence.
²³ Yet I am always with you;
    you take hold of my right hand.ᵖ
²⁴ With your counsel you guide me,
    and at the end receive me with
       honor.‡
²⁵ Whom else have I in the heavens?
    None beside you delights me on
       earth.
²⁶ Though my flesh and my heart fail,
    God is the rock of my heart, my
       portion forever.
²⁷ But those who are far from you perish;
    you destroy those unfaithful to you.
²⁸ As for me, to be near God is my good,
    to make the Lord GOD my refuge.

I shall declare all your works
    in the gates of daughter Zion.§

              PSALM 74⁵
Prayer at the Destruction of the Temple

¹A *maskil* of Asaph.

              I
Why, God, have you cast us off forever?˙˙�q
    Why does your anger burn against
       the sheep of your pasture?ʳ
² Remember your people, whom you
       acquired of old,
    the tribe you redeemed as your own
       heritage,
    Mount Zion where you dwell.ˢ
³ Direct your steps toward the utter
       destruction,
    everything the enemy laid waste in
       the sanctuary.
⁴ Your foes roared triumphantly in the
       place of your assembly;
    they set up their own tokens of
       victory.
⁵ They hacked away like a forester gathering
       boughs,
    swinging his ax in a thicket of trees.
⁶ They smashed all its engraved work,
    struck it with ax and pick.
⁷ They set your sanctuary on fire,
    profaned your name's abode by
       razing it to the ground.ᵗ
⁸ They said in their hearts, "We will destroy
       them all!
    Burn all the assembly-places of God
       in the land!"
⁹ ††Even so we have seen no signs for us,
    there is no prophet any more,ᵘ
    no one among us who knows for
       how long.
¹⁰ How long, O God, will the enemy jeer?ᵛ
    Will the enemy revile your name
       forever?

---

*[73:10] The Hebrew is obscure.

†[73:17] **And came to understand their end**: the psalmist
receives a double revelation in the Temple: 1) the end of the
wicked comes unexpectedly (Ps 73:18–20); 2) God is with me.

‡[73:24] **And at the end receive me with honor**: a perhaps deliberately enigmatic verse. It is understood by some
commentators as reception into heavenly glory, hence the
traditional translation, "receive me into glory." The Hebrew
verb can indeed refer to mysterious divine elevation of a righteous person into God's domain: Enoch in Gn 5:24; Elijah in
2 Kgs 2:11–12; the righteous psalmist in Ps 49:16. Personal
resurrection in the Old Testament, however, is clearly attested
only in the second century B.C. The verse is perhaps best left
unspecified as a reference to God's nearness and protection.

m. [73:11] Ps 10:11; Jb 22:13.   n. [73:13] Ps 26:6; Mal 3:14.
o. [73:20] Jb 20:8.   p. [73:23] Ps 121:5.

§[73:28] **In the gates of daughter Zion**: this reading follows the tradition of the Septuagint and Vulgate.

¶[Psalm 74] A communal lament sung when the enemy
invaded the Temple; it would be especially appropriate at the
destruction of Jerusalem in 587 B.C. Israel's God is urged to
look upon the ruined sanctuary and remember the congregation who worshiped there (Ps 74:1–11). People and sanctuary
are bound together; an attack on Zion is an attack on Israel.
In the second half of the poem, the community brings before
God the story of their origins—their creation (Ps 74:12–17)—
in order to move God to reenact that deed of creation now.
Will God allow a lesser power to destroy the divine project
(Ps 74:18–23)?

[74:1] **Forever: the word implies that the disaster is
already of long duration, cf. Ps 74:9 and note.

††[74:9] **Even so we have seen no signs . . .**: ancients often
asked prophets to say for how long a divine punishment was
to last, cf. 2 Sm 24:13. Here no prophet has arisen to indicate
the duration.

q. [74:1] Ps 10:1; 44:24; 77:8.   r. [74:1] Ps 80:5.   s. [74:2] Ps
68:17; 132:13; Ex 15:17; Jer 10:16; 51:19.   t. [74:7] Ps 79:1; Is
64:10.   u. [74:9] Lam 2:9.   v. [74:10] Ps 89:47.

11 Why draw back your hand,
    why hold back your right hand
        within your bosom?*
        II
12 †Yet you, God, are my king from of old,
    winning victories throughout the
        earth.
13 You stirred up the sea by your might;ʷ
    you smashed the heads of the
        dragons on the waters.ˣ
14 You crushed the heads of Leviathan,ʸ
    gave him as food to the sharks.
15 You opened up springs and torrents,
    brought dry land out of the primeval
        waters.‡
16 Yours the day and yours the night too;
    you set the moon and sun in place.
17 You fixed all the limits of the earth;
    summer and winter you made.ᶻ
18 Remember how the enemy has jeered,
    LORD,
    how a foolish people has reviled
        your name.
19 Do not surrender to wild animals those
        who praise you;
    do not forget forever the life of your
        afflicted.
20 Look to your covenant,
    for the recesses of the land
    are full of the haunts of violence.
21 Let not the oppressed turn back in shame;
    may the poor and needy praise your
        name.
22 Arise, God, defend your cause;
    remember the constant jeering of
        the fools.
23 Do not forget the clamor of your foes,
    the unceasing uproar of your
        enemies.

PSALM 75§
God the Judge of the World

¹For the leader. Do not destroy! A psalm of
Asaph; a song.

I
² We thank you, God, we give thanks;
    we call upon your name,
    we declare your wonderful deeds.
    [You said:]¶
³ "I will choose the time;
    I will judge fairly.
⁴ Though the earth and all its inhabitants
        quake,
    I make steady its pillars."ᵃ
                                    Selah
        II
⁵ So I say to the boastful: "Do not boast!"ᵇ
    to the wicked: "Do not raise your
        horns!"**
⁶ Do not raise your horns against heaven!
    Do not speak with a stiff neck!"ᶜ
⁷ For judgment comes not from east or
        from west,
    not from the wilderness or the
        mountains,ᵈ
⁸ But from God who decides,
    who brings some low and raises
        others high.ᵉ
⁹ Yes, a cup†† is in the LORD's hand,
    foaming wine, fully spiced.††
    When God pours it out,
        they will drain it even to the dregs;
        all the wicked of the earth will
            drink.ᶠ
¹⁰ But I will rejoice forever;
    I will sing praise to the God of
        Jacob,
¹¹ ᵍ[Who has said:]
    "I will cut off all the horns of the wicked,
        but the horns of the righteous will
            be exalted."

PSALM 76‡‡
God Defends Zion

¹For the leader; a psalm with stringed instruments. A song of Asaph.
        I
² Renowned in Judah is God,ʰ

---

*[74:11] **Why hold back . . . within your bosom**: i.e., idle beneath your cloak.

†[74:12–17] Comparable Canaanite literature describes the storm-god's victory over all-encompassing Sea and its allies (dragons and Leviathan) and the subsequent peaceful arrangement of the universe, sometimes through the placement of paired cosmic elements (day and night, sun and moon), cf. Ps 89:12–13. The Psalm apparently equates the enemies attacking the Temple with the destructive cosmic forces already tamed by God. Why then are those forces now raging untamed against your own people?

‡[74:15] **Waters**: lit., "rivers" (cf. Ps 24:7; Isa 50:2) upon which, or from which, in primordial times the earth is created.

§[Psalm 75] The psalmist gives thanks and rejoices (Ps 75:2, 10) for the direct intervention of God, which is promised in two oracles (Ps 75:3–4, 11). Expecting that divine intervention, the psalmist warns evildoers to repent (Ps 75:5–9).

¶[75:2] **You said**: supplied for clarity here and in Ps 75:11. The translation assumes in both places that the psalmist is citing an oracle of God.

[75:5] **Do not raise your horns!: the horn is the symbol of strength; to raise one's horn is to exalt one's own power as Ps 75:5 explains.

††[75:9] **A cup**: "the cup of God's wrath" is the punishment inflicted on the wicked, cf. Is 51:17; Jer 25:15–29; 49:12; Eze 23:31–33. **Spiced**: lit., "a mixed drink"; spices or drugs were added to wine, cf. Prv 9:2, 5.

‡‡[Psalm 76] A song glorifying Zion, the mountain of Jerusalem where God destroyed Israel's enemies. Zion is thus the appropriate site to celebrate the victory (Ps 76:3–4), a victory described in parallel scenes (Ps 76:5–7, 8–11). Israel is invited to worship its powerful patron deity (Ps 76:12).

---

w. [74:13] Ps 89:10.   x. [74:13] Is 51:9–10.   y. [74:14] Jb 3:8; 40:25; Is 27:1.   z. [74:16–17] Gn 1.

a. [75:4] Ps 46:3; 60:4; 93:1; 96:10; 104:5; 1 Sm 2:8; Is 24:19.   b. [75:5] 1 Sm 2:3; Zec 2:1–4.   c. [75:6] Jb 15:25.   d. [75:7] Mt 24:23–27.   e. [75:8] Jb 5:11; 1 Sm 2:7.   f. [75:9] Ps 60:5; Jb 21:20; Is 51:17, 21–22; Jer 25:15ff; Hab 2:16.   g. [75:11] Ps 92:11.

whose name is great in Israel.
3 On Salem* is God's tent, his shelter on
      Zion.
4   There the flashing arrows were
      shattered,
      shield, sword, and weapons of war.*

Selah

II

5 Terrible and awesome are you,
      stronger than the ancient
      mountains.†
6 Despoiled are the stouthearted;
      they sank into sleep;
      the hands of all the men of valor
      have failed.*
7 At your roar, O God of Jacob,
      chariot and steed lay still.
8 You, terrible are you;
      who can stand before you and your
      great anger?*
9 From the heavens you pronounced
      sentence;
      the earth was terrified and reduced
      to silence,
10 When you arose, O God, for judgment
      to save the afflicted of the land.

Selah

11 Surely the wrath of man will give you
      thanks;
      the remnant of your furor will keep
      your feast.

III

12 Make and keep vows to the LORD your
      God.*
      May all around him bring gifts to
      the one to be feared,
13 Who checks the spirit of princes,
      who is fearful to the kings of earth.

PSALM 77‡
Confidence in God During National Distress

1 For the leader; According to *Jeduthun*. A psalm
of Asaph.

I

2 I cry aloud to God,
      I cry to God to hear me.
3 On the day of my distress I seek the
      Lord;

by night my hands are stretched out
      unceasingly;*
      I refuse to be consoled.
4 When I think of God, I groan;
      as I meditate, my spirit grows faint.*

Selah

5 You have kept me from closing my eyes in
      sleep;
      I am troubled and cannot speak.
6 I consider the days of old;
      the years long past I remember.*
      At night I ponder in my heart;
      and as I meditate, my spirit probes:
8 "Will the Lord reject us forever,*
      never again show favor?
9 Has God's mercy ceased forever?
      The promise to go unfulfilled for
      future ages?
10 Has God forgotten how to show mercy,
      in anger withheld his compassion?"

Selah

11 § I conclude: "My sorrow is this,
      the right hand of the Most High has
      abandoned us."*

II

12 ¶ I will recall the deeds of the LORD;
      yes, recall your wonders of old.*
13 I will ponder all your works;
      on your exploits I will meditate.
14 Your way, God, is holy;
      what god is as great as our God?*
15 You are the God who does wonders;
      among the peoples you have
      revealed your might.*
16 With your mighty arm you redeemed
      your people,
      the children of Jacob and Joseph.*

Selah

17 The waters saw you, God;
      the waters saw you and lashed
      about,
      even the deeps of the sea** trembled.*
18 The clouds poured down their rains;
      the thunderheads rumbled;
      your arrows flashed back and forth.*
19 The thunder of your chariot wheels
      resounded;

---

*[76:3] **Salem**: an ancient name for Jerusalem, used here perhaps on account of its allusion to the Hebrew word for peace, *shalom*, cf. Gn 14:18; Heb 7:1–3.

†[76:5] **Ancient mountains**: conjectural translation of a difficult Hebrew phrase on the basis of Gn 49:26. The mountains are part of the structure of the universe (Ps 89:12–13).

‡[Psalm 77] A community lament in which the speaker ("I") describes the anguish of Israel at God's silence when its very existence is at stake (Ps 77:2–11). In response the speaker recites the story of how God brought the people into existence (Ps 77:12–20). The question is thus posed to God: Will you allow the people you created to be destroyed?

§[77:11] **I conclude**: lit., "I said." The psalmist, after pondering the present distress and God's promises to Israel, has decided that God has forgotten the people.

¶[77:12] **I will recall**: the verb sometimes means to make present the great deeds of Israel's past by reciting them, cf. Ps 78:42; 105:5; 106:7.

[77:17] **The deeps of the sea: Heb. *tehom*; the same word is used in Gn 1:2, where it alludes to the primeval seas which in ancient Semitic cosmography are tamed by God in creation, cf. Ps 74:12–17; 89:12–13 and notes.

m. [77:3] Ps 50:15; 88:2. n. [77:4] Jon 2:8. o. [77:7] Ps 143:5;
Dt 32:7. p. [77:8–10] Ps 13:2; 44:24; 74:1; 80:5; 89:47; Lam 3:31.
q. [77:11] Ps 17:7; 18:36; Ex 15:6, 12. r. [77:12] Ps 143:5. s. [77:14]
Ps 18:31; Ex 15:11. t. [77:15] Ps 86:10; 89:6. u. [77:16] Gn
46:26–27; Neh 1:10. v. [77:17] Ps 18:16; 114:3; Na 1:4. w. [77:18]
Ps 18:14–15; 29; 144:6; Jb 37:3–4; Wis 5:21; Hab 3:10–11; Zec 9:14.

---

h. [76:2] Heb 3:2. i. [76:4] Ps 46:10; 122:6–9. j. [76:6] 2 Kgs
19:35; Jer 51:39; Na 3:18. k. [76:8] Dt 7:21; 1 Sm 6:20; Na 1:6; Mal
3:2. l. [76:12] Nm 30:3.

your lightning lit up the world;
the earth trembled and quaked.[x]
20 Through the sea was your way;
your path, through the mighty waters,
though your footsteps were unseen.[y]
21 You led your people like a flock
by the hand of Moses and Aaron.[z]

PSALM 78*
A New Beginning in Zion and David

[1] A *maskil* of Asaph.

I

Attend, my people, to my teaching;
listen to the words of my mouth.
2 I will open my mouth in a parable,[†]
unfold the puzzling events of the
past.[a]
3 What we have heard and know;
things our ancestors have recounted
to us.[b]
4 We do not keep them from our children;
we recount them to the next
generation,
The praiseworthy deeds of the LORD and
his strength,
the wonders that he performed.[c]
5 God made a decree in Jacob,
established a law in Israel:[d]
Which he commanded our ancestors,
they were to teach their children;
6 That the next generation might come to
know,
children yet to be born.[e]
In turn they were to recount them to their
children,
7 that they too might put their
confidence in God,

*[Psalm 78] A recital of history to show that past gen-
erations did not respond to God's gracious deeds and were
punished by God making the gift into a punishment. Will
Israel fail to appreciate God's act—the choosing of Zion and
of David? The tripartite introduction invites Israel to learn the
lessons hidden in its traditions (Ps 78:1–4, 5–7, 8–11); each
section ends with the mention of God's acts. There are two
distinct narratives of approximately equal length: the wilderness events (Ps 78:12–39) and the movement from Egypt
to Canaan (Ps 78:40–72). The structure of both is parallel:
gracious act (Ps 78:12–16, 40–55), rebellion (Ps 78:17–20,
56–58), divine punishment (Ps 78:21–31, 59–64), God's readiness to forgive and begin anew (Ps 78:32–39, 65–72). While
the Psalm has been thought to reflect the reunification program of either King Hezekiah (late eighth century) or King
Josiah (late seventh century) in that the Northern Kingdom
(Ephraim, Joseph) is especially invited to accept Zion and the
Davidic king, a postexilic setting is also possible. Notable is
the inclusion of the David-Zion tradition into the history of
Israel recounted in the sources of the Pentateuch.
†[78:2] **Parable:** Hebrew *mashal* literally refers to some
sort of relationship of comparison and can signify a story
whose didactic potential becomes clear in the telling, as here
in the retrospective examination of the history of Israel. Mt
13:35 cites the verse to explain Jesus' use of parables.

x. [77:19] Ps 18:8; 97:4; 99:1; Ex 19:16; Jgs 5:4–5.   y. [77:20] Neh
9:11; Wis 14:3; Is 51:10; Hab 3:15.   z. [77:21] Ps 78:52; Is 63:11–
14; Hos 12:14; Mi 6:4.   a. [78:2] Ps 49:5; Mt 13:35.   b. [78:3] Ps
44:2.   c. [78:4] Ex 10:2; Dt 4:9; Jb 8:8.   d. [78:5] Ps 147:19; Dt
33:4.   e. [78:6] Ps 22:31–32; Dt 4:9; 6:7.

And not forget God's deeds,
but keep his commandments.
8 They were not to be like their ancestors,
a rebellious and defiant generation,[f]
A generation whose heart was not
constant,[g]
and whose spirit was not faithful
to God.
9 The ranks of Ephraimite archers,[‡]
retreated on the day of battle.
10 They did not keep God's covenant;
they refused to walk according to
his law.
11 They forgot his deeds,
the wonders that he had shown
them.

II
A

12 In the sight of their ancestors God did
wonders,
in the land of Egypt, the plain of
Zoan.[§h]
13 He split the sea and led them across,[i]
making the waters stand like walls.[j]
14 He led them with a cloud by day,
all night with the light of fire.[k]
15 He split rocks in the desert,
gave water to drink, abundant as the
deeps of the sea.[l]
16 He made streams flow from crags,
caused rivers of water to flow down.
B
17 But they went on sinning against him,
rebelling against the Most High in
the desert.[m]
18 They tested God in their hearts,
demanding the food they craved.[n]
19 They spoke against God, and said,
"Can God spread a table in the
wilderness?[o]
20 True, when he struck the rock,
water gushed forth,
the wadies flooded.
But can he also give bread,
or provide meat to his people?"
C
21 The LORD heard and grew angry;[p]
fire blazed up against Jacob;
anger flared up against Israel.
22 For they did not believe in God,
did not trust in his saving power.

‡[78:9] **Ephraimite archers:** Ephraim was the most
important tribe of the Northern Kingdom. Its military defeat
(here unspecified) demonstrates its infidelity to God, who
otherwise would have protected it.
§[78:12, 43] **Zoan:** a city on the arm of the Nile, a former
capital of Egypt.

f. [78:8] Dt 31:27; 32:5.   g. [78:8] Ps 95:10.   h. [78:12] Ps
106:7.   i. [78:13–14] Ps 136:13; Ex 14–15.   j. [78:13] Ex 14:22;
15:8.   k. [78:14] Ps 105:39; Ex 13:21; Wis 18:3.   l. [78:15] Ps
105:41; 114:8; Ex 17:1–7; Nm 20:2–13; Dt 8:15; Wis 11:4; Is
48:21.   m. [78:17] Dt 9:7; Ez 20:13.   n. [78:18] Ps 106:14; Ex 16:2–
36.   o. [78:19] Ps 23:5.   p. [78:21f] Nm 11; Dt 32:22.

²³ `So he commanded the clouds above;
and opened the doors of heaven.
²⁴ God rained manna upon them for food;
grain from heaven he gave them.*q*
²⁵ Man ate the bread of the angels;*†*
food he sent in abundance.
²⁶ He stirred up the east wind in the skies;
by his might God brought on the
south wind.
²⁷ He rained meat upon them like dust,
winged fowl like the sands of the
sea,
²⁸ They fell down in the midst of their camp,
all round their dwellings.
²⁹ They ate and were well filled;
he gave them what they had craved.
³⁰ But while they still wanted more,
and the food was still in their
mouths,
³¹ God's anger flared up against them,
and he made a slaughter of their
strongest,
laying low the youth of Israel.*r*
³² In spite of all this they went on sinning,
they did not believe in his wonders.

D
³³ God ended their days abruptly,
their years in sudden death.
³⁴ When he slew them, they began to seek
him;
they again looked for God.*s*
³⁵ They remembered*‡* that God was their
rock,
God Most High, their redeemer.
³⁶ But they deceived him with their mouths,
lied to him with their tongues.
³⁷ Their hearts were not constant toward
him;
they were not faithful to his
covenant.*t*
³⁸ §But God being compassionate forgave
their sin;
he did not utterly destroy them.
Time and again he turned back his anger,
unwilling to unleash all his rage.*u*
³⁹ He remembered that they were flesh,
a breath that passes on and does not
return.

III
A
⁴⁰ How often they rebelled against God in
the wilderness,
grieved him in the wasteland.
⁴¹ Again and again they tested God,
provoked the Holy One of Israel.
⁴² They did not remember his power,
the day he redeemed them from
the foe,*v*
⁴³ `When he performed his signs in Egypt,
his wonders in the plain of Zoan.*w*
⁴⁴ God turned their rivers to blood;
their streams they could not drink.
⁴⁵ He sent swarms of insects that devoured
them,*x*
frogs that destroyed them.
⁴⁶ He gave their harvest to the caterpillar,
the fruits of their labor to the locust.
⁴⁷ He killed their vines with hail,*y*
their sycamores with frost.
⁴⁸ He exposed their cattle to plague,
their flocks to pestilence.*z*
⁴⁹ He let loose against them the heat of his
anger,
wrath, fury, and distress,
a band of deadly messengers.
⁵⁰ He cleared a path for his anger;
he did not spare them from death,
but delivered their animals to the
plague.
⁵¹ He struck all the firstborn of Egypt,*a*
the first fruits of their vigor in the
tents of Ham.
⁵² Then God led forth his people like sheep,
guided them like a flock through the
wilderness.*b*
⁵³ He led them on secure and unafraid,
while the sea enveloped their
enemies.*c*
⁵⁴ And he brought them to his holy
mountain,
the hill his right hand had won.*d*
⁵⁵ He drove out the nations before them,
allotted them as their inherited
portion,
and settled in their tents the tribes
of Israel.

B
⁵⁶ But they tested and rebelled against God
Most High,
his decrees they did not observe.
⁵⁷ They turned disloyal, faithless like their
ancestors;
they proved false like a slack bow.

---

*[78:23–31] On the manna and the quail, see Ex 16 and Nm 11. Unlike Ex 16, here both manna and quail are instruments of punishment, showing that a divine gift can become deadly because of Israel's apostasy.

†[78:25] **Bread of the angels**: the translation "angels" comports with the supernatural origin of the manna, though the Hebrew *lechem 'abbirim* is more literally translated as "bread of the strong ones" or "bread of the mighty." In the context of the manna event, this phrase cannot possibly mean the Israelites or any human being.

‡[78:35] **Remembered**: invoked God publicly in worship. Their words were insincere (Ps 78:36).

§[78:38] God is always ready to forgive and begin anew, as in choosing Zion and David (Ps 78:65–72).

¶[78:43–55] Ex 7–12 records ten plagues. Here there are six divine attacks upon Egypt; the seventh climactic act is God's bringing Israel to the holy land.

---

q. [78:24] Ps 105:40; Ex 16:4, 14; Dt 8:3; Wis 16:20; Jn 6:31. r. [78:31] Nm 14:29. s. [78:34] Dt 32:15, 18; Is 26:16. t. [78:37] Ps 95:10; Is 29:13. u. [78:38] Ps 85:4; Ex 32:14; Is 48:9; Ez 20:22.

v. [78:42] Ps 106:21. w. [78:43f] Ps 105:27–36; 135:9; Ex 7:14–11:10; 12:29–36; Wis 16–18. x. [78:45] Ex 8:17. y. [78:47] Wis 16:16. z. [78:48] Ex 9:3. a. [78:51] Ps 105:36; 136:10; Ex 12:29. b. [78:52] Ps 77:21. c. [78:53] Ex 14:26–28. d. [78:54] Ex 15:17.

58 They enraged him with their high places,
　　and with their idols provoked him˙
　　　to jealous anger.ᵉ
　　　　　　C
59 God heard and grew angry;
　　he rejected Israel completely.
60 He forsook the shrine at Shiloh,ᵗᶠ
　　the tent he set up among human
　　　beings.
61 He gave up his might into captivity,
　　his glorious ark into the hands of
　　　the foe.ᵍ
62 God delivered his people to the sword;
　　he was enraged against his heritage.
63 Fire consumed their young men;
　　their young women heard no
　　　wedding songs.ʰ
64 Their priests fell by the sword;
　　their widows made no lamentation.
　　　　　　D
65 Then the Lord awoke as from sleep,
　　like a warrior shouting from the
　　　effects of wine.
66 He put his foes to flight;
　　everlasting shame he dealt them.
67 He rejected the tent of Joseph,
　　chose not the tribe of Ephraim.
68 ‡God chose the tribe of Judah,
　　Mount Zion which he loved.ⁱ
69 He built his shrine like the heavens,
　　like the earth which he founded
　　　forever.
70 He chose David his servant,
　　took him from the sheepfolds.ʲ
71 From tending ewes God brought him,
　　to shepherd Jacob, his people,
　　Israel, his heritage.ᵏ
72 He shepherded them with a pure heart;
　　with skilled hands he guided them.

PSALM 79§
A Prayer for Jerusalem

¹A psalm of Asaph.

---

*[78:58] **Provoked him**: lit., "made him jealous."
†[78:60] **Shiloh**: an important shrine in the north prior to Jerusalem. Despite its holy status, it was destroyed (Ps 78:60–64; cf. Jer 7:12, 14).
‡[78:68, 70] God's ultimate offer of mercy to the sinful, helpless people is Zion and the Davidic king.
§[Psalm 79] A communal lament complaining that the nations have defiled the Temple and murdered the holy people, leaving their corpses unburied (Ps 79:1–4). The occasion is probably the destruction of Jerusalem by the Babylonian army in 587 B.C. The people ask how long the withdrawal of divine favor will last (Ps 79:5), pray for action now (Ps 79:6–7), and admit that their own sins have brought about the catastrophe (Ps 79:8–9). They seek to persuade God to act for reasons of honor: the nations who do not call upon the Name are running amok (Ps 79:6); the divine honor is compromised (Ps 79:1, 10, 12); God's own servants suffer (Ps 79:2–4, 11).

e. [78:58] Dt 32:16, 21.　f. [78:60] Jos 18:1; 1 Sm 1:3; Jer 7:12; 26:6.　g. [78:61] 1 Sm 4:11, 22.　h. [78:63] Dt 32:25; Jer 7:34.　i. [78:68] Ps 48:2; 50:2; Lam 2:15.　j. [78:70] Ps 89:21; Ez 34:23; 37:24; 2 Chr 6:6.　k. [78:71] 1 Sm 16:11–13; 2 Sm 7:8.

　　　　　　I
O God, the nations have invaded your
　　inheritance;
　　they have defiled your holy temple;
　　they have laid Jerusalem in ruins.ˡ
2 They have left the corpses of your servants
　　as food for the birds of the sky,
　　the flesh of those devoted to you for
　　　the beasts of the earth.ᵐ
3 They have poured out their blood like
　　water
　　all around Jerusalem,
　　and no one is left to do the burying.ⁿ
4 We have become the reproach of our
　　neighbors,
　　the scorn and derision of those
　　　around us.ᵒ
　　　　　　II
5 How long, LORD? Will you be angry
　　forever?
　　Will your jealous anger keep
　　　burning like fire?ᵖ
6 Pour out your wrath on nations that do
　　not recognize you,
　　on kingdoms that do not call on
　　　your name,�q
7 For they have devoured Jacob,
　　laid waste his dwelling place.
8 Do not remember against us the iniquities
　　of our forefathers;
　　let your compassion move quickly
　　　ahead of us,
　　for we have been brought very low.ʳ
　　　　　　III
9 Help us, God our savior,
　　on account of the glory of your name.
　　Deliver us, pardon our sins
　　　for your name's sake.ˢ
10 Why should the nations say,
　　"Where is their God?"ᵗ
　　Before our eyes make known to the
　　　nations
　　that you avenge the blood of your
　　　servants which has been
　　　poured out.ᵘ
　　　　　　IV
11 Let the groaning of the imprisoned come
　　in before you;
　　in accord with the greatness of your
　　　arm
　　preserve those doomed to die.ᵛ
12 Turn back sevenfold into the bosom of
　　our neighbors
　　the insult with which they insulted
　　　you, Lord.ʷ
13 Then we, your people, the sheep of your
　　pasture,

l. [79:1] 2 Kgs 25:9–10; Lam 1:10.　m. [79:2] Jer 7:33.　n. [79:3] 1 Mc 7:17; Jer 14:16.　o. [79:4] Ps 44:14; 80:7; 123:3–4; Jb 12:4; Dn 9:16; Zep 2:8.　p. [79:5] Ps 13:2; 44:24; 89:47; Dt 4:24.　q. [79:6] Ps 14:4; Jer 10:25.　r. [79:8] Ps 142:7.　s. [79:9] Ez 20:44; 36:22.　t. [79:10] Ps 42:4; 115:2; Jl 2:17.　u. [79:10] Jl 4:21.　v. [79:11] Ps 102:21.　w. [79:12] Ps 89:51–52.

will give thanks to you forever;
　　from generation to generation
　　we will recount your praise.

PSALM 80*
Prayer to Restore God's Vineyard

¹For the leader; according to "Lilies." *Eduth.*† A
psalm of Asaph.

I

² O Shepherd of Israel, lend an ear,
　　you who guide Joseph like a flock!
　Seated upon the cherubim, shine forth˟
³　　upon Ephraim, Benjamin, and
　　　Manasseh.
　Stir up your power, and come to save us.
⁴　　ʸO God, restore us;
　　light up your face and we shall be
　　　saved.

II

⁵ LORD of hosts,
　　how long will you smolder in anger
　　while your people pray?ᶻ
⁶ You have fed them the bread of tears,
　　made them drink tears in great
　　　measure.‡ᵃ
⁷ You have left us to be fought over by our
　　　neighbors;
　　our enemies deride us.ᵇ
⁸ O God of hosts, restore us;
　　light up your face and we shall be
　　　saved.

III

⁹ You brought a vine§ out of Egypt;
　　you drove out nations and planted
　　　it.
¹⁰ You cleared out what was before it;
　　it took deep root and filled the land.
¹¹ The mountains were covered by its
　　　shadow,
　　the cedars of God by its branches.
¹² It sent out its boughs as far as the sea,¶
　　its shoots as far as the river.¶

¹³ Why have you broken down its walls,
　　so that all who pass along the way
　　　pluck its fruit?ᶜ
¹⁴ The boar from the forest strips the vine;
　　the beast of the field feeds upon it.ᵈ
¹⁵ Turn back again, God of hosts;
　　look down from heaven and see;
　Visit this vine,
¹⁶　　the stock your right hand has
　　　planted,
　　and the son** whom you made strong
　　　for yourself.
¹⁷ Those who would burn or cut it down—
　　may they perish at your rebuke.
¹⁸ May your hand be with the man on your
　　　right,††
　　with the son of man whom you
　　　made strong for yourself.
¹⁹ Then we will not withdraw from you;
　　revive us, and we will call on your
　　　name.
²⁰ LORD God of hosts, restore us;
　　light up your face and we shall be
　　　saved.

PSALM 81‡‡
An Admonition to Fidelity

¹For the leader; "upon the *gittith*."§§ Of Asaph.

I

² Sing joyfully to God our strength;ᵉ
　　raise loud shouts to the God of
　　　Jacob!
³ Take up a melody, sound the timbrel,
　　the pleasant lyre with a harp.
⁴ ¶¶Blow the shofar at the new moon,
　　at the full moon, on our solemn
　　　feast.ᶠ
⁵ For this is a law for Israel,
　　an edict of the God of Jacob,ᵍ
⁶ He made it a decree for Joseph
　　when he came out of the land of
　　　Egypt.

*[Psalm 80] A community lament in time of military defeat. Using the familiar image of Israel as a vineyard, the people complain that God has broken down the wall protecting the once splendid vine brought from Egypt (Ps 80:9–14). They pray that God will again turn to them and use the Davidic king to lead them to victory (Ps 80:15–19).

†[80:1] Lilies. . . . Eduth: the first term is probably the title of the melody to which the Psalm was to be sung; the second is unexplained.

‡[80:6] Both the Septuagint and the Vulgate translate this verse in the first person, i.e., "You have fed us the bread of tears."

§[80:9] A vine: a frequent metaphor for Israel, cf. Is 5:1–7; 27:2–5; Jer 2:21; Hos 10:1; Mt 21:33.

¶[80:12] The sea: the Mediterranean. The river: the Euphrates, cf. Gn 15:18; 1 Kgs 5:1. The terms may also have a mythic nuance—the seas that surround the earth; sea and river are sometimes paralleled in poetry.

**[80:16] The Vulgate and Septuagint use "son of man."

††[80:18] The man on your right: the Davidic king who will lead the army in battle.

‡‡[Psalm 81] At a pilgrimage feast, probably harvest in the fall, the people assemble in the Temple in accord with the Sinai ordinances (Ps 81:2–6). They hear a divine word (mediated by a Temple speaker) telling how God rescued them from slavery in Egypt (Ps 81:7–9), gave them the fundamental commandment of fidelity (Ps 81:9–11), which would bring punishment if they refused to obey (Ps 81:12–13). But if Israel repents, God will be with them once again, bestowing protection and fertility (Ps 81:14–16).

§§[81:1] Upon the gittith: probably the title of the melody to which the Psalm was to be sung or a musical instrument.

¶¶[81:4] New moon . . . full moon: the pilgrimage feast of harvest began with a great assembly (Lv 23:24; Nm 29:1), used the new moon as a sign (Nm 29:6), and included trumpets (Lv 23:24).

x. [80:2] Ps 23:1–3; 95:7; 100:3; Gn 48:15; Ex 25:22; 1 Sm 4:4; 2 Sm 6:2; Mi 7:14.　y. [80:4, 8, 20] Ps 4:7; 31:17; 67:2; 85:5; Nm 6:25; Dn 9:17.　z. [80:5] Ps 13:2; 44:24; 74:1; 79:5; 89:47; Dt 4:24.　a. [80:6] Ps 42:4; 102:10.　b. [80:7] Ps 44:14; 79:4; 123:3–4; Jb 12:4; Dn 9:16; Zep 2:8.

c. [80:13] Ps 89:41.　d. [80:14] Hos 2:14.　e. [81:2] Ps 43:4; 68:26; 149:3; 150:3–4; Jdt 16:1.　f. [81:4] Lv 23:24; Nm 29:1.　g. [81:5] Ex 23:14ff.

II

7 'I heard a tongue I did not know:
   "I removed his shoulder from the
      burden;[†]
   his hands moved away from the
      basket.[†h]
8 In distress you called and I rescued you;
   I answered you in secret with thunder;
   At the waters of Meribah[‡] I tested you:[i]
9 'Listen, my people, I will testify against you
                                          Selah
   If only you will listen to me, Israel![j]
10 There shall be no foreign god among you;[§k]
   you shall not bow down to an alien
      god.
11 'I am the Lord your God,
   who brought you up from the land
      of Egypt.
   Open wide your mouth that I may
      fill it.'
12 But my people did not listen to my words;
   Israel would not submit to me.
13 So I thrust them away to the hardness of
      their heart;
   'Let them walk in their own
      machinations.'[l]
14 O that my people would listen to me,
   that Israel would walk in my ways,[m]
15 In a moment I would humble their foes,
   and turn back my hand against their
      oppressors.[n]
16 Those who hate the Lord will try
      flattering him,
   but their fate is fixed forever.
17 But Israel I will feed with the finest wheat,
   I will satisfy them with honey from
      the rock."[o]

PSALM 82[¶]
The Downfall of Unjust Gods

1 A psalm of Asaph.

---

*[81:7] **I heard a tongue I did not know**: a Temple official speaks the word of God (Ps 81:5b–16), which is authoritative and unlike merely human words (cf. Nm 24:4, 16).

†[81:7] **I removed his shoulder from the burden**: A reference to the liberation of Israel from slavery in Egypt. The **basket**: for carrying clay to make bricks, cf. Ex 1:14.

‡[81:8] **Meribah**: place of rebellion in the wilderness; cf. Ex 17:7; Nm 20:13.

§[81:10] **There shall be no foreign god among you**: as in Ps 50 and 95, Israel is challenged to obey the first commandment of fidelity to God after the proclamation of the exodus.

¶[Psalm 82] As in Ps 58, the pagan gods are seen as subordinate divine beings to whom Israel's God had delegated oversight of the foreign countries in the beginning (Dt 32:8–9). Now God arises in the heavenly assembly (Ps 82:1) to rebuke the unjust "gods" (Ps 82:2–4), who are stripped of divine status and reduced in rank to mortals (Ps 82:5–7). They are accused of misruling the earth by not upholding the poor. A short prayer for universal justice concludes the Psalm (Ps 82:8).

h. [81:7] Ex 1:14; 6:6.   i. [81:8] Ps 95:8; Ex 2:23ff; 17:7; 19:16; Nm 20:13; 27:14.   j. [81:9] Ex 1:14; 6:6.   k. [81:10–11] Ex 20:2–6; Dt 5:6–10.   l. [81:13] Jer 3:17; 7:24.   m. [81:14] Is 48:18.   n. [81:15] Lv 26:7–8.   o. [81:17] Ps 147:14; Dt 32:13–14.

I

God takes a stand in the divine council,
   gives judgment in the midst of the
      gods.[p]
2 "How long will you judge unjustly
   and favor the cause of the wicked?[q]
                                          Selah
3 "Defend the lowly and fatherless;
   render justice to the afflicted and
      needy.
4 Rescue the lowly and poor;
   deliver them from the hand of the
      wicked."[r]

II

5 "'The gods neither know nor understand,
   wandering about in darkness,
   and all the world's foundations
      shake.
6 I declare: "Gods though you be,[††s]
   offspring of the Most High all of
      you,
7 Yet like any mortal you shall die;
   like any prince you shall fall."
8 Arise, O God, judge the earth,[‡‡]
   for yours are all the nations.

PSALM 83[§§]
Prayer Against a Hostile Alliance

1 A song; a psalm of Asaph.

I

2 God, do not be silent;
   God, do not be deaf or remain
      unmoved![t]
3 See how your enemies rage;
   your foes proudly raise their heads.
4 They conspire against your people,
   plot against those you protect.[u]
5 They say, "Come, let us wipe them out as a
      nation;
   let Israel's name be remembered no
      more!"
6 They scheme with one mind,
   they have entered into a covenant
      against you:[v]

**[82:5] The gods are blind and unable to declare what is right. Their misrule shakes earth's foundations (cf. Ps 11:3; 75:4), which God made firm in creation (Ps 96:10).

††[82:6] **I declare: "Gods though you be"**: in Jn 10:34 Jesus uses the verse to prove that those to whom the word of God is addressed can fittingly be called "gods."

‡‡[82:8] **Judge the earth**: according to Dt 32:8–9, Israel's God had originally assigned jurisdiction over the foreign nations to the subordinate deities, keeping Israel as a personal possession. Now God will directly take over the rulership of the whole world.

§§[Psalm 83] The community lament complains to God of the nations' attempts to wipe out the name of Israel (Ps 83:1–8). The psalmist sees all Israel's enemies throughout its history united in a conspiracy (Ps 83:2–8). May God destroy the current crop of enemies as the enemies of old were destroyed (Ps 83:9–12), and may they be pursued until they acknowledge the name of Israel's God (Ps 83:13–18).

p. [82:1] Is 3:13–14.   q. [82:2] Ps 58:2.   r. [82:4] Dt 1:17.   s. [82:6] 2 Pt 1:4.   t. [83:2] Ps 10:1; 44:24; 109:1.   u. [83:4] Jer 11:9. v. [83:6] Ps 2:2.

7 "The tents of Edom and the Ishmaelites,
   of Moab and the Hagrites,ʷ
8 Gebal, Ammon, and Amalek,ˣ
   Philistia and the inhabitants of
   Tyre.ʸ
9 Assyria, too, in league with them,
   backs the descendants of Lot.

                                        Selah

            II
10 ᵗDeal with them as with Midian;
   as with Sisera and Jabin at the wadi
   Kishon,ᶻ
11 Those destroyed at Endor,
   who became dung for the ground.ᵃ
12 Make their nobles like Oreb and Zeeb,
   all their princes like Zebah and
   Zalmunna,
13 Who made a plan together,
   "Let us take for ourselves the
   pastures of God."
14 My God, make them like tumbleweed,
   into chaff flying before the wind.ᵇ
15 As a fire raging through a forest,
   a flame setting mountains ablaze,ᶜ
16 Pursue them with your tempest;
   terrify them with your storm-wind.
17 Cover their faces with shame,
   till they seek your name,ᵗ LORD.
18 Let them be ashamed and terrified forever;
   let them perish in disgrace.
19 Let them know that your name is LORD,
   you alone are the Most High over all
   the earth.ᵈ

PSALM 84§
Prayer of a Pilgrim to Jerusalem

1 For the leader; "upon the *gittith*." A psalm of the
Korahites.

            I
2 How lovely your dwelling,
   O LORD of hosts!ᵉ

3 My soul yearns and pines
   for the courts of the LORD.ᶠ
   My heart and flesh cry out
   for the living God.
4 ˢAs the sparrow finds a home
   and the swallow a nest to settle her
   young,
   My home is by your altars,
   LORD of hosts, my king and my God!ᵍ
5 Blessed are those who dwell in your house!
   They never cease to praise you.

                                        Selah
            II
6 Blessed the man who finds refuge in you,
   in their hearts are pilgrim roads.
7 As they pass through the Baca valley,⁎⁎
   they find spring water to drink.
   The early rain covers it with blessings.
8 They will go from strength to strength††
   and see the God of gods on Zion.
            III
9 LORD God of hosts, hear my prayer;
   listen, God of Jacob.

                                        Selah
10 ‡‡O God, watch over our shield;
   look upon the face of your anointed.ʰ
            IV
11 Better one day in your courts
   than a thousand elsewhere.
   Better the threshold of the house of my
   God
   than a home in the tents of the
   wicked.
12 For a sun and shield is the LORD God,
   bestowing all grace and glory.
   The LORD withholds no good thing
   from those who walk without
   reproach.
13 O LORD of hosts,
   blessed the man who trusts in you!

PSALM 85§§
Prayer for Divine Favor

1 For the leader. A psalm of the Korahites.

⁎[83:7–9] Apart from the Assyrians, all the nations listed
here were neighbors of Israel. The Hagrites are a tribe of the
desert regions east of Ammon and Moab (1 Chr 5:10, 19–22).
Gebal is the Phoenician city of Byblos or perhaps a mountain region south of the Dead Sea. The descendants of Lot are
Moab and Edom (Gn 19:36–38 and Dt 2:9). These nations
were never united against Israel in the same period; the Psalm
has lumped them all together.
†[83:10–13] For the historical events, see Jgs 4–8.
‡[83:17] **Seek your name**: a variant of the more typical
phrase "to seek the face of God" (Ps 24:6; 27:8; 105:4). Seeking the face of God refers to the worshiper having recourse to
a temple or sanctuary where in non-Jewish contexts a statue
embodies the physical presence of the Deity. In Israel's ani-
conic tradition no visible image or statue can represent God.
This understanding is conveyed here concretely by use of the
term "your name" rather than the more typical "your face."
§[Psalm 84] Israelites celebrated three pilgrimage feasts in
Jerusalem annually. The Psalm expresses the sentiments of the
pilgrims eager to enjoy the divine presence.

¶[84:4] The desire of a restless bird for a secure home is an
image of the desire of a pilgrim for the secure house of God,
cf. Ps 42:2–3, where the image for the desire of the pilgrim is
the thirst of the deer for water.
⁎⁎[84:7] **Baca valley**: Hebrew obscure; probably a valley on
the way to Jerusalem.
††[84:8] **Strength to strength**: pass through outer and
inner wall.
‡‡[84:10] **Our shield . . . your anointed**: the king had a role
in the liturgical celebration. For the king as shield, cf. Ps 89:19.
§§[Psalm 85] A national lament reminding God of past
favors and forgiveness (Ps 85:2–4) and begging for forgiveness
and grace now (Ps 85:5–8). A speaker represents the people
who wait humbly with open hearts (Ps 85:9–10): God will be
active on their behalf (Ps 85:11–13). The situation suggests the
conditions of Judea during the early postexilic period, the fifth
century B.C.; the thoughts are similar to those of postexilic
prophets (Hg 1:5–11; 2:6–9).

w. [83:7] Nm 20:23; 1 Chr 5:10, 19.   x. [83:8] Ex 17:8.   y. [83:8]
Jos 13:2.   z. [83:10] Ex 2:15; Is 9:3; 10:26.   a. [83:11] Jer
8:2.   b. [83:14] Ps 1:4; 35:5; 58:10; Is 5:24; 10:17; 17:13; 29:5;
Ez 21:3.   c. [83:15] Ps 50:3.   d. [83:19] Ps 97:9; Dt 4:39; Dn
3:45.   e. [84:2] Ps 43:3–4; 122:1.

f. [84:3] Ps 42:2–3; 63:2–3; 143:6; Is 26:9.   g. [84:4] Ps 5:3.
h. [84:10] Ps 89:19.

I

2 You once favored, Lord, your land,
    restored the captives of Jacob.[i]
3 You forgave the guilt of your people,
    pardoned all their sins.

                      Selah

4 You withdrew all your wrath,
    turned back from your burning
        anger.[j]

II

5 Restore us, God of our salvation;
    let go of your displeasure with us.[k]
6 Will you be angry with us forever,
    prolong your anger for all
        generations?[l]
7 Certainly you will again restore our life,
    that your people may rejoice in you.
8 Show us, Lord, your mercy;
    grant us your salvation.

III

9 ʹI will listen for what God, the Lord, has
        to say;
    surely he will speak of peace
To his people and to his faithful.
    May they not turn to foolishness!
10 Near indeed is his salvation for those who
        fear him;
    glory will dwell in our land.
11 †Love and truth will meet;
    justice and peace will kiss.[m]
12 Truth will spring from the earth;
    justice will look down from heaven.[n]
13 Yes, the Lord will grant his bounty;
    our land will yield its produce.[o]
14 Justice will march before him,
    and make a way for his footsteps.

PSALM 86[‡]
Prayer in Time of Distress

1 A prayer of David.

I

Incline your ear, Lord, and answer me,
    for I am poor and oppressed.
2 Preserve my life, for I am devoted;
    save your servant who trusts in you.
You are my God; 3 be gracious to me, Lord;
    to you I call all the day.
4 Gladden the soul of your servant;
    to you, Lord, I lift up my soul.[p]
5 Lord, you are good and forgiving,

---

*[85:9] The prophet listens to God's revelation, cf. Heb 2:1.
†[85:11–13] Divine activity is personified as pairs of virtues.
‡[Psalm 86] An individual lament. The psalmist, "poor and oppressed" (Ps 86:1), "devoted" (Ps 86:2), "your servant" (Ps 86:2, 4, 16), "rescued . . . from the depths of Sheol" (Ps 86:13), attacked by the ruthless (Ps 86:14), desires only God's protection (Ps 86:1–7, 11–17).

i. [85:2] Ps 14:7; 126:4.   j. [85:4] Ps 78:38; Ex 32:14; Is 48:9.
k. [85:5] Ps 80:4.   l. [85:6] Ps 79:5; 89:47.   m. [85:11] Ps 89:15; 97:2.   n. [85:12] Is 45:8.   o. [85:13] Ps 67:7; Lv 26:4; Ez 34:27; Hos 2:23–24; Zec 8:12.   p. [86:4] Ps 25:1; 143:8.

---

    most merciful to all who call on
        you.[q]
6 Lord, hear my prayer;
    listen to my cry for help.[r]
7 On the day of my distress I call to you,
    for you will answer me.

II

8 None among the gods can equal you,
    O Lord;
    nor can their deeds compare to
        yours.[s]
9 All the nations you have made shall come
    to bow before you, Lord,
    and give honor to your name.[t]
10 For you are great and do wondrous deeds;
    and you alone are God.

III

11 Teach me, Lord, your way
    that I may walk in your truth,[u]
    single-hearted and revering your
        name.
12 I will praise you with all my heart,
    glorify your name forever, Lord my
        God.
13 Your mercy to me is great;
    you have rescued me from the
        depths of Sheol.[v]
14 O God, the arrogant have risen against
        me;
    a ruthless band has sought my life;
    to you they pay no heed.
15 But you, Lord, are a compassionate and
        gracious God,
    slow to anger, abounding in mercy
        and truth.[w]
16 Turn to me, be gracious to me;
    give your strength to your servant;
    save the son of your handmaid.[x]
17 Give me a sign of your favor:
    make my enemies see, to their
        confusion,
    that you, Lord, help and comfort me.

PSALM 87[§]
Zion the True Birthplace

1 ʸA psalm of the Korahites. A song.

I

His foundation is on holy
    mountains,
2 The Lord loves the gates[¶] of Zion
    more than any dwelling in Jacob.
3 Glorious things are said of you,
    O city of God!

                      Selah

---

§[Psalm 87] A song of Zion, like Ps 46; 48; 76; 132.
¶[87:2] The gates: the city itself, a common Hebrew idiom.

q. [86:5] Jl 2:13.   r. [86:6] Ps 5:2; 130:1–2.   s. [86:8] Ps 35:10; 89:9; Ex 15:11; Dt 3:24; Jer 10:6.   t. [86:9] Ps 22:28; Zec 14:16; Rev 15:4.
u. [86:11] Ps 25:4; 26:3; 27:11; 119:12, 35; 143:8, 10.   v. [86:13] Ps 30:4; 40:3; Jon 2:7.   w. [86:15] Ps 103:8; 130:7; 145:8; Ex 34:6.   x. [86:16] Ps 25:16; 116:16; Wis 9:5.   y. [87:1–2] Ps 76:2–3; 78:68–69.

II
4 Rahab and Babylon I count
      among those who know me.
   See, Philistia and Tyre, with Ethiopia,
      "This one was born there."
5 ˙And of Zion it will be said:
      "Each one was born in it."ᶻ
   The Most High will establish it;ᵃ
6   the LORD notes in the register of the
      peoples:
      "This one was born there."ᵇ

                                         Selah
7 So singers and dancers:
      "All my springs are in you."ᶜ

PSALM 88†
A Despairing Lament

¹A song; a psalm of the Korahites. For the leader;
according to *Mahalath*. For singing; a *maskil* of
Heman the Ezrahite.

I
2 LORD, the God of my salvation, I call out
      by day;
      at night I cry aloud in your presence.ᵈ
3 Let my prayer come before you;
      incline your ear to my cry.ᵉ
4 ‡For my soul is filled with troubles;ᶠ
      my life draws near to Sheol.
5 I am reckoned with those who go down to
      the pit;
      I am like a warrior without strength.
6 My couch is among the dead,
      like the slain who lie in the grave.
   You remember them no more;
      they are cut off from your influence.
7 You plunge me into the bottom of the pit,
      into the darkness of the abyss.
8 Your wrath lies heavy upon me;
      all your waves crash over me.ᵍ

                                         Selah
II
9 Because of you my acquaintances shun
      me;
      you make me loathsome to them;ʰ
   Caged in, I cannot escape;
10   my eyes grow dim from trouble.

   All day I call on you, LORD;
      I stretch out my hands to you.

11 §Do you work wonders for the dead?
      Do the shades arise and praise you?ⁱ
                                         Selah
III
12 Is your mercy proclaimed in the grave,
      your faithfulness among those who
      have perished?¶
13 Are your marvels declared in the darkness,
      your righteous deeds in the land of
      oblivion?
IV
14 But I cry out to you, LORD;
      in the morning my prayer comes
      before you.
15 Why do you reject my soul, LORD,
      and hide your face from me?
16 I have been mortally afflicted since youth;
      I have borne your terrors and I am
      made numb.
17 Your wrath has swept over me;
      your terrors have destroyed me.ʲ
18 All day they surge round like a flood;
      from every side they encircle me.
19 Because of you friend and neighbor shun
      me;ᵏ
      my only friend is darkness.

PSALM 89**
A Lament over God's Promise to David

¹A *maskil* of Ethan the Ezrahite.
A
I
2 I will sing of your mercy forever, LORDˡ
      proclaim your faithfulness through
      all ages.
3 ††For I said, "My mercy is established
      forever;
      my faithfulness will stand as long as
      the heavens.
4 I have made a covenant with my chosen one;
      I have sworn to David my servant:
5 I will make your dynasty stand forever
      and establish your throne through
      all ages."ᵐ
                                         Selah

§[88:11–13] The psalmist seeks to persuade God to act out
of concern for divine honor: the shades give you no worship,
so keep me alive to offer you praise.
¶[88:12] **Perished:** lit., "Abaddon," the deepest part of Sheol.
**[Psalm 89] The community laments the defeat of the
Davidic king, to whom God promised kingship as enduring as
the heavens (Ps 89:2–5). The Psalm narrates how God became
king of the divine beings (Ps 89:6–9) and how the Davidic
king became king of earthly kings (Ps 89:20–38). Since the
defeat of the king calls into question God's promise, the community ardently prays God to be faithful to the original promise to David (Ps 89:39–52).
††[89:3–5] David's dynasty is to be as long-lasting as the
heavens, a statement reinforced by using the same verbs
(establish, stand) both of the divine love and loyalty and of the
Davidic dynasty and throne, cf. Ps 89:29–30.

---

*[87:5–6] The bond between the exile and the holy city was
so strong as to override the exile's citizenship of lesser cities.
†[Psalm 88] A lament in which the psalmist prays for
rescue from the alienation of approaching death. Each of the
three stanzas begins with a call to God (Ps 88:2, 10, 14) and
complains of the death that separates one from God. The tone
is persistently grim.
‡[88:4–8] In imagination the psalmist already experiences
the alienation of Sheol.

z. [87:5] Gal 4:26.   a. [87:5] Ps 48:9.   b. [87:6] Is 4:3.   c. [87:7] Ps
68:26; 149:3.   d. [88:2] Ps 77:3.   e. [88:3] Ps 119:170.   f. [88:4–7]
Ps 28:1; 30:4; 40:3; 86:13; 143:7; Nm 16:33; Jb 17:1; Jon 2:7.   g. [88:8]
Ps 18:5; 32:6; 42:8; 69:2; Jon 2:4.   h. [88:9] Ps 38:12; 79:4; 80:7;
123:3–4; 142:8; Jb 12:4; 19:13; Lam 3:7; Dn 9:16.

i. [88:11] Ps 6:6; 30:10; 38:18; 115:17.   j. [88:17] Jb 6:4; 20:25.
k. [88:19] Jb 19:13.   l. [89:2] Is 63:7.   m. [89:5] Ps 61:7–8; 132:11;
2 Sm 7:8–16.

II

6 The heavens praise your marvels, LORD,
    your loyalty in the assembly of the
        holy ones.[n]
7 Who in the skies ranks with the LORD?
    Who is like the LORD among the
        sons of the gods?[*o]
8 A God dreaded in the council of the holy
        ones,
    greater and more awesome than all
        those around him!
9 LORD, God of hosts, who is like you?
    Mighty LORD, your faithfulness
        surrounds you.
10 You rule the raging sea;[p]
    you still its swelling waves.
11 You crush Rahab[†] with a mortal blow;
    with your strong arm you scatter
        your foes.
12 Yours are the heavens, yours the earth;
    you founded the world and
        everything in it.[q]
13 [‡]Zaphon and Amanus you created;
    Tabor and Hermon rejoice in your
        name.
14 You have a mighty arm.
    Your hand is strong; your right hand
        is ever exalted.
15 Justice and judgment are the foundation
        of your throne;
    mercy and faithfulness march before
        you.[r]
16 Blessed the people who know the war cry,
    who walk in the radiance of your
        face, LORD.
17 In your name they sing joyfully all the
        day;
    they rejoice in your righteousness.[s]
18 You are their majestic strength;
    by your favor our horn[§] is exalted.[t]
19 Truly the LORD is our shield,
    the Holy One of Israel, our king![u]

III

20 Then you spoke in vision;[v]
    to your faithful ones you said:

"I have set a leader over the warriors;
    I have raised up a chosen one from
        the people.
21 I have chosen David, my servant;
    with my holy oil I have anointed
        him.
22 My hand will be with him;[w]
    my arm will make him strong.
23 No enemy shall outwit him,
    nor shall the wicked defeat him.
24 I will crush his foes before him,
    strike down those who hate him.
25 My faithfulness and mercy will be with
        him;
    through my name his horn will be
        exalted.
26 ¶I will set his hand upon the sea,
    his right hand upon the rivers.
27 He shall cry to me, 'You are my father,[x]
    my God, the Rock of my salvation!'
28 I myself make him the firstborn,
    Most High[**] over the kings of the
        earth.
29 Forever I will maintain my mercy for
        him;[y]
    my covenant with him stands firm.
30 I will establish his dynasty forever,
    his throne as the days of the
        heavens.
31 If his descendants forsake my teaching,[z]
    do not follow my decrees,
32 If they fail to observe my statutes,
    do not keep my commandments,
33 I will punish their crime with a rod
    and their guilt with blows.
34 But I will not take my mercy from him,
    nor will I betray my bond of
        faithfulness.[a]
35 I will not violate my covenant;
    the promise of my lips I will not
        alter.[b]
36 By my holiness I swore once for all:[c]
    I will never be false to David.
37 ††His dynasty will continue forever,[d]
    his throne, like the sun before me.
38 Like the moon it will stand eternal,
    forever firm like the sky!"

Selah

---

*[89:7] **The sons of the gods**: "the holy ones" and "courtiers" of Ps 89:6, 8. These heavenly spirits are members of God's court.

†[89:11] **Rahab**: a mythological sea monster whose name is used in the Bible mainly as a personification of primeval chaos, cf. Jb 9:13; 26:12; Ps 74:13–14; Is 51:9.

‡[89:13] **Zaphon and Amanus**: two sacred mountains in northern Syria which came to designate the directions of north and south. **Tabor**: a high hill in the valley of Jezreel in northern Israel. **Hermon**: a mountain in Lebanon, forming the southern spur of the Anti-Lebanon range.

§[89:18, 25] **Horn**: a concrete noun for an abstract quality; horn is a symbol of strength.

¶[89:26] **The sea . . . the rivers**: geographically the limits of the Davidic empire (the Mediterranean and the Euphrates); mythologically, the traditional forces of chaos. See note on Ps 89:11.

[89:28] **Most High: a divine title, which is here extended to David as God's own king, cf. Ps 2:7–9; Is 9:5. As God rules over the members of the heavenly council (Ps 89:6–9), so David, God's surrogate, rules over earthly kings.

††[89:37–38] **Like the sun before me . . . like the sky**: as enduring as the heavenly lights, cf. Ps 89:2–5 and Ps 72:5, 17.

---

n. [89:6] Ps 29:1; 82:1; Jb 1:6; 5:1. o. [89:7–9] Ps 35:10; 86:8; 113:5; Ex 15:11; Jer 10:6. p. [89:10–11] Ps 65:8; 74:13–15; 107:29; Jb 7:12; Is 51:9–10. q. [89:12] Ps 24:1–2; 50:12; Dt 10:14; 1 Cor 10:26. r. [89:15] Ps 85:11–12; 97:2. s. [89:17] Ps 47:2; Zep 3:14. t. [89:18] Ps 112:9; 148:14. u. [89:19] Ps 47:9; 96:10; 97:1; 99:1; Is 6:3. v. [89:20–21] Ps 78:70; 132:11–12; 2 Sm 7:4, 8–16; 1 Chr 17:3, 7–14; Is 42:1; Acts 13:22.

w. [89:22–25] 1 Sm 2:9–10. x. [89:27–28] Ps 2:7; 110:2–3; 2 Sm 7:9, 14; Col 1:15, 18; Rev 1:5. y. [89:29–30] Ps 18:51; 61:8; 144:10; 2 Sm 7:11; Is 55:3. z. [89:31–33] Lv 26:14–33. a. [89:34] Ps 40:12; Sir 47:22. b. [89:35] Jer 33:20–21. c. [89:36] Am 4:2. d. [89:37–38] Ps 61:8; 72:5; Sir 43:6.

B

IV

39 But now you have rejected and spurned,*e*
    been enraged at your anointed.
40 You renounced the covenant with your
    servant,
    defiled his crown in the dust.
41 You broke down all city walls,*f*
    left his strongholds in ruins.
42 All who pass through seize plunder;
    his neighbors deride him.
43 You have exalted the right hand of his foes,
    have gladdened all his enemies.*g*
44 You turned back his sharp sword,
    did not support him in battle.
45 You brought to an end his splendor,
    hurled his throne to the ground.
46 You cut short the days of his youth,
    covered him with shame.

                    Selah

V

47 How long, LORD? Will you hide forever?
    Must your wrath smolder like fire?*h*
48 Remember how brief life is,
    how frail the sons of man you have
    created!*i*
49 What is man, that he should live and not
    see death?
    Who can deliver his soul from the
    power of Sheol?*j*

                    Selah

VI

50 Where are your former mercies, Lord,
    that you swore to David in your
    faithfulness?
51 Remember, Lord, the insults to your
    servants,
    how I have borne in my bosom the
    slander of the nations.*k*
52 Your enemies, LORD, insult;
    they insult each step of your anointed.
53 ˈBlessed be the LORD forever! Amen and
    amen!*l*

Fourth Book—Psalms 90–106

PSALM 90†
God's Eternity and Human Frailty

1A prayer of Moses, the man of God.

I

Lord, you have been our refuge
    through all generations.
2 Before the mountains were born,
    the earth and the world brought
    forth,
    from eternity to eternity you are
    God.*m*
3 You turn humanity back into dust,‡
    saying, "Return, you children of
    Adam!"*n*
4 A thousand years in your eyes
    are merely a day gone by,*o*
    Before a watch passes in the night,
5   §you wash them away;*p*
    They sleep,
    and in the morning they sprout
    again like an herb.
6 In the morning it blooms only to pass
    away;
    in the evening it is wilted and
    withered.¶*q*

II

7 Truly we are consumed by your anger,
    filled with terror by your wrath.
8 You have kept our faults before you,
    our hidden sins in the light of your
    face.*r*
9 Our life ebbs away under your wrath;*s*
    our years end like a sigh.
10 Seventy is the sum of our years,
    or eighty, if we are strong;
    Most of them are toil and sorrow;
    they pass quickly, and we are gone.
11 Who comprehends the strength of your
    anger?
    Your wrath matches the fear it
    inspires.
12 Teach us to count our days aright,
    that we may gain wisdom of heart.

III

13 Relent, O LORD! How long?
    Have pity on your servants!
14 Fill us at daybreak with your mercy,*t*
    that all our days we may sing for joy.
15 Make us glad as many days as you
    humbled us,
    for as many years as we have seen
    trouble.*u*

---

*[89:53] The doxology at the end of the third book of the Psalms; it is not part of Ps 89.

†[Psalm 90] A communal lament that describes only in general terms the cause of the community's distress. After confidently invoking God (Ps 90:1), the Psalm turns to a complaint contrasting God's eternity with the brevity of human life (Ps 90:2–6) and sees in human suffering the punishment for sin (Ps 90:7–12). The Psalm concludes with a plea for God's intervention (Ps 90:13–17).

‡[90:3] **Dust:** one word of God is enough to return mortals to the dust from which they were created. Human beings were created from earth in Gn 2:7; 3:19.

§[90:5] **You wash them away:** the Hebrew of Ps 90:4–5 is unclear.

¶[90:6] **It is wilted and withered:** the transitory nature of the grass under the scorching sun was proverbial, cf. Ps 129:6; Is 40:6–8.

e. [89:39–47] Ps 44:10–25. f. [89:41–42] Ps 80:13–14. g. [89:43] Lam 1:5. h. [89:47] Ps 13:2; 44:25; 74:10; 79:5; Dt 4:24. i. [89:48] Ps 39:5–6; 62:10; 90:9–10; 144:4; Jb 7:6, 16; 14:1, 5; Eccl 6:12; Wis 2:5. j. [89:49] Ps 90:3. k. [89:51] Ps 79:12. l. [89:53] Ps 41:14; 72:18; 106:48.

m. [90:2] Ps 48:15; 55:20; 93:2; 102:13; Heb 1:12. n. [90:3] Ps 103:14; 104:29; 146:4; Gn 3:19; 1 Mc 2:63; Jb 34:14–15; Eccl 3:20; 12:7; Sir 40:11. o. [90:4] 2 Pt 3:8. p. [90:5] Ps 89:48. q. [90:6] Ps 37:2; 102:11; 103:15–16; Jb 14:1–2; Is 40:6–8. r. [90:8] Ps 109:14–15; Hos 7:2. s. [90:9–10] Ps 39:5–7; 62:10; 102:24–25; 144:4; Gn 6:3; Jb 7:6, 16; 14:5; Prv 10:27; Eccl 6:12; Wis 2:5; Sir 18:8; Is 65:20. t. [90:14] Ps 17:15. u. [90:15] Nm 14:34; Jer 31:13.

16 Show your deeds to your servants,
　　your glory to their children.
17 May the favor of the Lord our God be
　　ours.[v]
　　Prosper the work of our hands!
　　Prosper the work of our hands!

PSALM 91[*]
Security Under God's Protection

I

1 You who dwell in the shelter of the Most
　　High,[†]
　　who abide in the shade of the
　　　Almighty,[†]
2 Say to the LORD, "My refuge and fortress,
　　my God in whom I trust."[w]
3 He will rescue you from the fowler's
　　snare,
　　from the destroying plague,
4 He will shelter you with his pinions,
　　and under his wings you may take
　　　refuge;[x]
　　his faithfulness is a protecting
　　　shield.
5 You shall not fear the terror of the night
　　nor the arrow that flies by day,[y]
6 Nor the pestilence that roams in
　　darkness,
　　nor the plague that ravages at
　　　noon.[z]
7 Though a thousand fall at your side,
　　ten thousand at your right hand,
　　near you it shall not come.
8 You need simply watch;
　　the punishment of the wicked you
　　　will see.[a]
9 Because you have the LORD for your
　　refuge
　　and have made the Most High your
　　　stronghold,
10 No evil shall befall you,
　　no affliction come near your tent.[b]
11 ‡For he commands his angels with regard
　　to you,[c]

to guard you wherever you go.[d]
12 With their hands they shall support you,
　　lest you strike your foot against a
　　　stone.[e]
13 You can tread upon the asp and the viper,
　　trample the lion and the dragon.[f]

II

14 Because he clings to me I will deliver him;
　　because he knows my name I will set
　　　him on high.[g]
15 He will call upon me and I will answer;[h]
　　I will be with him in distress;[i]
　　I will deliver him and give him honor.
16 With length of days I will satisfy him,
　　and fill him with my saving power.[j]

PSALM 92[§]
A Hymn of Thanksgiving for God's Fidelity

1 A psalm. A sabbath song.

I

2 It is good to give thanks to the LORD,
　　to sing praise to your name, Most
　　　High,[k]
3 To proclaim your love at daybreak,
　　your faithfulness in the night,
4 With the ten-stringed harp,
　　with melody upon the lyre.[l]
5 For you make me jubilant, LORD, by your
　　deeds;
　　at the works of your hands I shout
　　　for joy.

II

6 How great are your works, LORD![m]
　　How profound your designs!
7 A senseless person cannot know this;
　　a fool cannot comprehend.
8 Though the wicked flourish like grass[n]
　　and all sinners thrive,
　　They are destined for eternal destruction;
9 　　but you, LORD, are forever on high.
10 Indeed your enemies, LORD,
　　indeed your enemies shall perish;
　　all sinners shall be scattered.[o]

III

11 You have given me the strength of a wild
　　ox;[p]
　　you have poured rich oil upon me.[q]
12 My eyes look with glee on my wicked
　　enemies;
　　my ears shall hear what happens to
　　　my wicked foes.[r]

---

*[Psalm 91] A prayer of someone who has taken refuge in the Lord, possibly within the Temple (Ps 91:1–2). The psalmist is confident that God's presence will protect the people in every dangerous situation (Ps 91:3–13). The final verses are an oracle of salvation promising salvation to those who trust in God (Ps 91:14–16).

†[91:1] The shelter of the Most High: basically "hiding place" but in the Psalms a designation for the protected Temple precincts, cf. Ps 27:5; 31:21; 61:5. The shade of the Almighty: lit., "the shadow of the wings of the Almighty," cf. Ps 17:8; 36:8; 57:2; 63:8. Ps 91:4 makes clear that the shadow is an image of the safety afforded by the outstretched wings of the cherubim in the holy of holies.

‡[91:11–12] The words are cited in Lk 4:10–11; Mt 4:6, as Satan tempts Jesus in the desert.

v. [90:17] Ps 33:22.　w. [91:2] Ps 18:3; 31:3–4; 42:10; 142:6; 2 Sm 22:3.　x. [91:4] Ps 17:8; 36:8; 57:2; 63:8; Dt 32:11; Ru 2:12; Mt 23:37.　y. [91:5] Prv 3:25; Sg 3:8.　z. [91:6] Dt 32:24.　a. [91:8] Ps 92:12.　b. [91:10] Prv 12:21; Dt 7:15.　c. [91:11–12] Mt 4:6; Lk 4:10f.

§[Psalm 92] A hymn of praise and thanks for God's faithful deeds (Ps 92:2–5). The wicked, deluded by their prosperity (Ps 92:6–9), are punished (Ps 92:10), whereas the psalmist has already experienced God's protection (Ps 92:11–15).

d. [91:11] Heb 1:14.　e. [91:12] Ps 121:3; Prv 3:23.　f. [91:13] Is 11:8; Lk 10:19.　g. [91:14] Ps 9:11; 119:132.　h. [91:15] Jer 33:3; Zec 13:9.　i. [91:15] Is 43:2.　j. [91:16] Prv 3:2.　k. [92:2] Ps 33:1; 147:1.　l. [92:4] Ps 33:2; 144:9.　m. [92:6–7] Ps 131:1; 139:6, 17; Wis 13:1; 17:1.　n. [92:8] Ps 37:35.　o. [92:10] Ps 68:1–2; 125:5.　p. [92:11] Ps 75:11; Dt 33:17.　q. [92:11] Ps 23:5.　r. [92:12] Ps 91:8.

¹³ The just shall flourish like the palm tree,
  shall grow like a cedar of Lebanon.^s
¹⁴ ˚Planted in the house of the LORD,
  they shall flourish in the courts of
  our God.
¹⁵ They shall bear fruit even in old age,
  they will stay fresh and green,
¹⁶ To proclaim: "The LORD is just;
  my rock, in whom there is no wrong."^t

PSALM 93[†]
God Is a Mighty King

¹ The LORD is king,[‡] robed with majesty;
  the LORD is robed, girded with might.^u
  The world will surely stand in place,
  never to be moved.^v
² Your throne stands firm from of old;
  you are from everlasting.^w
³ [§]The flood has raised up, LORD;
  the flood has raised up its roar;
  the flood has raised its pounding
  waves.
⁴ More powerful than the roar of many
  waters,
  more powerful than the breakers of
  the sea,
  powerful in the heavens is the LORD.
⁵ Your decrees are firmly established;
  holiness befits your house, LORD,
  for all the length of days.

PSALM 94[¶]
A Prayer for Deliverance from the Wicked

I
¹ LORD, avenging God,
  avenging God, shine forth!^x

---

*[92:14] **Planted**: the just are likened to trees growing in the sacred precincts of the Temple, which is often seen as the source of life and fertility because of God's presence, cf. Ps 36:9, 10; Ez 47:1–12.

†[Psalm 93] A hymn celebrating the kingship of God, who created the world (Ps 93:1–2) by defeating the sea (Ps 93:3–4). In the ancient myth that is alluded to here, Sea completely covered the land, making it impossible for the human community to live. Sea, or Flood, roars in anger against God, who is personified in the storm. God's utterances or decrees are given authority by the victory over Sea (Ps 93:5).

‡[93:1] **The LORD is king**: lit., "the LORD reigns." This Psalm, and Ps 47; 96–99, are sometimes called enthronement Psalms. They may have been used in a special liturgy during which God's ascent to the throne was ritually reenacted. They have also been interpreted eschatologically, pointing to the coming of God as king at the end-time.

§[93:3] **The flood**: the primordial sea was tamed by God in the act of creation. It is a figure of chaos and rebellion, cf. Ps 46:4.

¶[Psalm 94] A lament of an individual who is threatened by wicked people. The danger affects the whole community. Calling upon God as judge (Ps 94:1–2), the Psalm complains about oppression of the holy community by people within (Ps 94:3–7). Bold declarations of faith follow: denunciation of evildoers (Ps 94:8–11) and assurance to the just (Ps 94:12–15). The Psalm continues with further lament (Ps 94:16–19) and ends with strong confidence in God's response (Ps 94:20–23).

---

s. [92:13] Ps 1:3; 52:10; Jer 17:8. t. [92:16] Dt 32:4. u. [93:1] Ps 47:8; 96:10; 97:1; 99:1. v. [93:1] Ps 75:2–3; 104:5. w. [93:2] Ps 55:20; 90:2; 102:13; Heb 1:12. x. [94:1] Na 1:2.

² Rise up, O judge of the earth;
  give the proud what they deserve!^y
II
³ How long, LORD, shall the wicked,
  how long shall the wicked glory?^z
⁴ How long will they mouth haughty
  speeches,
  go on boasting, all these evildoers?^a
⁵ They crush your people, LORD,
  torment your very own.
⁶ They kill the widow and alien;
  the orphan they murder.^b
⁷ They say, "The LORD does not see;
  the God of Jacob takes no notice."^c
III
⁸ Understand, you stupid people!
  You fools, when will you be wise?^d
⁹ Does the one who shaped the ear not
  hear?
  The one who formed the eye not see?^e
¹⁰ Does the one who guides nations not
  rebuke?
  The one who teaches man not have
  knowledge?
¹¹ The LORD knows the plans of man;
  they are like a fleeting breath.^f
IV
¹² Blessed the one whom you guide, LORD,^g
  whom you teach by your
  instruction,
¹³ To give rest from evil days,
  while a pit is being dug for the
  wicked.
¹⁴ For the LORD will not forsake his people,
  nor abandon his inheritance.^h
¹⁵ Judgment shall again be just,
  and all the upright of heart will
  follow it.
V
¹⁶ Who will rise up for me against the
  wicked?
  Who will stand up for me against
  evildoers?
¹⁷ If the LORD were not my help,
  I would long have been silent in the
  grave.ⁱ
¹⁸ When I say, "My foot is slipping,"
  your mercy, LORD, holds me up.^j
¹⁹ When cares increase within me,
  your comfort gives me joy.
VI
²⁰ Can unjust judges be your allies,
  those who create burdens by decree,
²¹ Those who conspire against the just
  and condemn the innocent to death?
²² No, the LORD is my secure height,
  my God, my rock of refuge,

---

y. [94:2] Jer 51:56; Lam 3:64. z. [94:3] Ps 13:2; 75:5; Jer 12:1. a. [94:4] Ps 73; Mal 2:17; 3:14. b. [94:6] Ex 22:21–22; Dt 24:17–22. c. [94:7] Ps 10:11; 64:6; 73:11; Jb 22:13–14; Ez 9:9. d. [94:8] Prv 1:22; 8:5. e. [94:9] Ex 4:11; Prv 20:12. f. [94:11] Ps 33:15; 1 Cor 3:20. g. [94:12] Ps 119:71; Jb 5:17. h. [94:14] 1 Sm 12:22; Sir 47:22. i. [94:17] Ps 6:6; 115:17. j. [94:18] Ps 145:14.

²³ ᵏWho will turn back their evil upon them¹
and destroy them for their
    wickedness.
Surely the LORD our God will
    destroy them!

PSALM 95*
A Call to Praise and Obedience

I

¹ Come, let us sing joyfully to the LORD;
cry out to the rock of our salvation.ᵐ
² Let us come before him with a song of
    praise,
joyfully sing out our psalms.
³ For the LORD is the great God,
the great king over all gods,ⁿ
⁴ Whose hand holds the depths of the
    earth;
who owns the tops of the
    mountains.
⁵ The sea and dry land belong to God,
who made them, formed them by
    hand.ᵒ

II

⁶ Enter, let us bow down in worship;
let us kneel before the LORD who
    made us.
⁷ For he is our God,
we are the people he shepherds,
the sheep in his hands.ᵖ

III

Oh, that today you would hear his voice:�q
⁸ Do not harden your hearts as at
    Meribah,
as on the day of Massah in the
    desert.†
⁹ There your ancestors tested me;
they tried me though they had seen
    my works.ʳ
¹⁰ Forty years I loathed that generation;
I said: "This people's heart goes
    astray;
they do not know my ways."ˢ
¹¹ Therefore I swore in my anger:
"They shall never enter my rest."‡

---

*[Psalm 95] Twice the Psalm calls the people to praise and
worship God (Ps 95:1–2, 6), the king of all creatures (Ps 95:3–
5) and shepherd of the flock (Ps 95:7a, 7b). The last strophe
warns the people to be more faithful than were their ancestors
in the journey to the promised land (Ps 95:7c–11). This invitation to praise God regularly opens the Church's official prayer,
the Liturgy of the Hours.

†[95:8] **Meribah**: lit., "contention"; the place where the
Israelites quarreled with God. **Massah**: "testing," the place
where they put God to the trial, cf. Ex 17:7; Nm 20:13.

‡[95:11] **My rest**: the promised land as in Dt 12:9. Heb 4
applies the verse to the eternal rest of heaven.

---

k. [94:23] Ps 7:16; 9:16; 35:8; 57:7; Prv 26:27; Eccl 10:8; Sir
27:26. l. [94:23] Ps 107:42. m. [95:1] Dt 32:15. n. [95:3] Ps
47:2; 135:5. o. [95:5] Ps 24:1–2. p. [95:7–11] Ps 81:8; 106:32; Heb
3:7–11, 15; 4:3, 5, 7. q. [95:7] Ps 23:1–3; 100:3; Mi 7:14. r. [95:9]
Nm 14:22; 20:2–13; Dt 6:16; 33:8. s. [95:10] Ps 78:8; Nm 14:34;
Dt 32:5.

PSALM 96§
God of the Universe

I

¹ Sing to the LORD a new song;ᵗ
sing to the LORD, all the earth.
² Sing to the LORD, bless his name;
proclaim his salvation day after day.
³ Tell his glory among the nations;
among all peoples, his marvelous
    deeds.ᵘ

II

⁴ 'For great is the LORD and highly to be
    praised,
to be feared above all gods.ᵛ
⁵ For the gods of the nations are idols,
but the LORD made the heavens.ʷ
⁶ Splendor and power go before him;
power and grandeur are in his holy
    place.

III

⁷ Give to the LORD, you families of nations,
give to the LORD glory and might;
⁸ give to the LORD the glory due his
    name!ˣ
Bring gifts and enter his courts;
⁹ bow down to the LORD, splendid in
    holiness.
Tremble before him, all the earth;
¹⁰ ʸdeclare among the nations: The
    LORD is king.
The world will surely stand fast, never to
    be shaken.
He rules the peoples with fairness.

IV

¹¹ Let the heavens be glad and the earth rejoice;
let the sea and what fills it resound;ᶻ
¹² let the plains be joyful and all that is
    in them.
Then let all the trees of the forest rejoice
¹³ before the LORD who comes,
who comes to govern the earth,ᵃ
To govern the world with justice
and the peoples with faithfulness.

PSALM 97**
The Divine Ruler of All

I

¹ The LORD is king; let the earth rejoice;
let the many islands be glad.ᵇ

---

§[Psalm 96] A hymn inviting all humanity to praise the glories of Israel's God (Ps 96:1–3), who is the sole God (Ps 96:4–6).
To the just ruler of all belongs worship (Ps 96:7–10); even inanimate creation is to offer praise (Ps 96:11–13). This Psalm has
numerous verbal and thematic contacts with Is 40–55, as does
Ps 98. Another version of the Psalm is in 1 Chr 16:23–33.

¶[96:4] For references to other gods, see comments on Ps
58 and 82.

**[Psalm 97] The hymn begins with God appearing in
a storm, a traditional picture of some ancient Near Eastern

---

t. [96:1] Ps 98:1; Is 42:10. u. [96:3] Ps 98:4; 105:1. v. [96:4]
Ps 48:2; 95:3; 145:3. w. [96:5] Ps 97:7; 115:4–8; Is 40:17; 1 Cor
8:4. x. [96:8] Ps 29:2. y. [96:10] Ps 75:4; 93:1. z. [96:11] Ps
98:7. a. [96:13] Ps 98:9. b. [97:1] Ps 75:4; 93:1; 96:10.

2 Cloud and darkness surround him;
    justice and right are the foundation
      of his throne.*c*
3 Fire goes before him,
    consuming his foes on every side.
4 His lightening illumines the world;
    the earth sees and trembles.*d*
5 The mountains melt like wax before the
    LORD,
    before the Lord of all the earth.*e*
6 The heavens proclaim his justice;
    all peoples see his glory.*f*

II

7 All who serve idols are put to shame,
    who glory in worthless things;
    all gods' bow down before him.*g*
8 Zion hears and is glad,
    and the daughters of Judah rejoice
    because of your judgments,
    O LORD.*h*
9 For you, LORD, are the Most High over all
    the earth,*i*
    exalted far above all gods.
10 You who love the LORD, hate evil,
    he protects the souls of the faithful,*j*
    rescues them from the hand of the
    wicked.
11 Light dawns for the just,
    and gladness for the honest of
    heart.*k*
12 Rejoice in the LORD, you just,
    and give thanks at the remembrance
    of his holiness.*l*

PSALM 98[†]
The Coming of God

1 A psalm.

I

Sing a new song to the LORD,
    for he has done marvelous deeds.*m*
His right hand and holy arm
    have won the victory.[‡]*n*

2 The LORD has made his victory known;
    has revealed his triumph in the sight
      of the nations,
3 He has remembered his mercy and
    faithfulness
    toward the house of Israel.
All the ends of the earth have seen
    the victory of our God.

II

4 Shout with joy to the LORD, all the earth;
    break into song; sing praise.
5 Sing praise to the LORD with the lyre,
    with the lyre and melodious song.
6 With trumpets and the sound of the horn
    shout with joy to the King, the LORD.*o*

III

7 Let the sea and what fills it resound,*p*
    the world and those who dwell
    there.
8 Let the rivers clap their hands,
    the mountains shout with them for
    joy,*q*
9 'Before the LORD who comes,
    who comes to govern the earth,*s*
To govern the world with justice
    and the peoples with fairness.

PSALM 99[§]
The Holy King

I

1 The LORD is king, the peoples tremble;
    he is enthroned on the cherubim,[¶]
    the earth quakes.*t*
2 Great is the LORD in Zion,
    exalted above all the peoples.
3 Let them praise your great and awesome
    name:
    Holy is he!*u*

II

4 O mighty king, lover of justice,
    you have established fairness;
    you have created just rule in Jacob.*v*
5 Exalt the LORD, our God;
    bow down before his footstool;[**]*w*
    holy is he!

---

gods (Ps 97:1–6); cf. Ps 18:8–16; Mi 1:3–4; Heb 3:3–15. Israel rejoices in the overthrowing of idol worshipers and their gods (Ps 97:7–9) and the rewarding of the faithful righteous (Ps 97:10–12).

*[97:7] **All gods**: divine beings thoroughly subordinate to Israel's God. The Greek translates "angels," an interpretation adopted by Heb 1:6.

†[Psalm 98] A hymn, similar to Ps 96, extolling God for Israel's victory (Ps 98:1–3). All nations (Ps 98:4–6) and even inanimate nature (Ps 98:7–8) are summoned to welcome God's coming to rule over the world (Ps 98:9).

‡[98:1] **Marvelous deeds . . . victory**: the conquest of all threats to the peaceful existence of Israel, depicted in the Psalms variously as a cosmic force such as sea, or nations bent on Israel's destruction, or evildoers seemingly triumphant. **His right hand and holy arm**: God is pictured as a powerful warrior.

---

c. [97:2] Ps 85:11; 89:15; Ex 19:6; Dt 4:11; 5:22; 1 Kgs 8:12. d. [97:4] Ps 18:8; 50:3; 77:18; 99:1; Jgs 5:4–5. e. [97:5] Jdt 16:15; Mi 1:4. f. [97:6] Ps 50:6. g. [97:7] Ps 96:5. h. [97:8] Ps 48:12. i. [97:9] Ps 83:19. j. [97:10] Ps 121:7. k. [97:11] Ps 112:4. l. [97:12] Ps 30:5. m. [98:1] Ps 96:1; Is 42:10. n. [98:1] Is 59:16; 63:5.

---

§[Psalm 99] A hymn to God as the king whose grandeur is most clearly seen on Mount Zion (Ps 99:2) and in the laws given to Israel (Ps 99:4). Israel is special because of God's word of justice, which was mediated by the revered speakers, Moses, Aaron, and Samuel (Ps 99:6–8). The poem is structured by the threefold statement that God is holy (Ps 99:3, 5, 9) and by the twice-repeated command to praise (Ps 99:5, 9).

¶[99:1] **Enthroned on the cherubim**: cherubim were composite beings with animal and human features, common in ancient Near Eastern art. Two cherubim were placed on the ark (or box) of the covenant in the holy of holies. Upon them God was believed to dwell invisibly, cf. Ex 25:20–22; 1 Sm 4:4; 2 Sm 6:2; Ps 80:2.

[99:5] **Footstool: a reference to the ark, cf. 1 Chr 28:2; Ps 132:7.

---

o. [98:6] Ps 47:6–7. p. [98:7] Ps 96:11. q. [98:8] Is 44:23; 55:12. r. [98:9] Ps 96:13. s. [98:9] Ps 67:5. t. [99:1] Ps 18:8–11; 80:2; 93:1; Ex 25:22; 1 Sm 4:4; 2 Sm 6:2. u. [99:3] Is 6:3. v. [99:4] Ps 72:1; Jer 23:5. w. [99:5] Ps 132:7.

III

⁶ Moses and Aaron were among his priests,
   Samuel among those who called on
      his name;
   they called on the LORD, and he
      answered them.ˣ
⁷ From the pillar of cloud he spoke to them;
   they kept his decrees, the law he had
      given them.ʸ
⁸ O LORD, our God, you answered them;
   you were a forgiving God to them,
   though you punished their offenses.ᶻ
⁹ Exalt the LORD, our God;
   bow down before his holy mountain;
   holy is the LORD, our God.

PSALM 100*
Processional Hymn

¹A psalm of thanksgiving.

   Shout joyfully to the LORD, all you lands;
²   serve the LORD with gladness;
   come before him with joyful song.
³ †Know that the LORD is God,
   he made us, we belong to him,
   we are his people, the flock he
      shepherds.ᵃ
⁴ Enter his gates with thanksgiving,
   his courts with praise.
   Give thanks to him, bless his name;ᵇ
⁵   good indeed is the LORD,
   His mercy endures forever,
   his faithfulness lasts through every
      generation.

PSALM 101‡
Norm of Life for Rulers

¹A psalm of David.

I

   I sing of mercy and justice;
   to you, LORD, I sing praise.
² I study the way of integrity;ᶜ
   when will you come to me?
   I act with integrity of heart
      within my household.§ᵈ
³ I do not allow into my presence anything
      base.

I hate wrongdoing;
   I will have no part of it.ᵉ
⁴ May the devious heart keep far from me;
   the wicked I will not acknowledge.
⁵ Whoever slanders a neighbor in secret
   I will reduce to silence.ᶠ
Haughty eyes and arrogant heartsᵍ
   I cannot endure.

II

⁶ I look to the faithful of the land¶
   to sit at my side.
Whoever follows the way of integrityʰ
   is the one to enter my service.
⁷ No one who practices deceit
   can remain within my house.
No one who speaks falsely
   can last in my presence.ⁱ
⁸ **Morning after morning I clear all the
   wicked from the land,
   to rid the city of the LORD of all
      doers of evil.

PSALM 102††
Prayer in Time of Distress

¹The prayer of one afflicted and wasting away
whose anguish is poured out before the LORD.

I

² LORD, hear my prayer;
   let my cry come to you.
³ Do not hide your face from me
   in the day of my distress.ʲ
Turn your ear to me;
   when I call, answer me quickly.
⁴ For my days vanish like smoke;ᵏ
   my bones burn away as in a furnace.
⁵. My heart is withered, dried up like grass,
   too wasted to eat my food.
⁶ From my loud groaning
   I become just skin and bones.
⁷ I am like a desert owl,
   like an owl among the ruins.
⁸ I lie awake and moan,
   like a lone sparrow on the roof.
⁹ All day long my enemies taunt me;

---

*[Psalm 100] A hymn inviting the people to enter the Temple courts with thank offerings for the God who created them.
†[100:3] Although the people call on all the nations of the world to join in their hymn, they are conscious of being the chosen people of God.
‡[Psalm 101] The king, grateful at being God's chosen (Ps 101:1), promises to be a ruler after God's own heart (Ps 101:2–3), allowing into the royal service only the God-fearing (Ps 101:3–8).
§[101:2] **Within my household**: the king promises to make his own household, i.e., the royal court, a model for Israel, banning all officials who abuse their power.

¶[101:6] **I look to the faithful of the land**: the king seeks companions only among those faithful to God.
[101:8] **Morning after morning: the morning is the normal time for the administration of justice (2 Sm 15:2; Jer 21:12) and for the arrival of divine aid (Ps 59:17; 143:8; Is 33:2). **I clear all the wicked from the land**: the king, as God's servant, is responsible for seeing that divine justice is carried out.
††[Psalm 102] A lament, one of the Penitential Psalms. The psalmist, experiencing psychological and bodily disintegration (Ps 102:4–12), cries out to God (Ps 102:1–3). In the Temple precincts where God has promised to be present, the psalmist recalls God's venerable promises to save the poor (Ps 102:13–23). The final part (Ps 102:24–28) restates the original complaint and prayer, and emphasizes God's eternity.

x. [99:6] Jer 15:1.   y. [99:7] Ex 33:9; Nm 12:5.   z. [99:8] Ex 32:11; Nm 20:12.   a. [100:3] Ps 23:1; 95:7; Mi 7:14; Is 64:7.   b. [100:4–5] Ps 106:1; 107:1; 118:1; 136:1; 138:8; Jer 33:11.   c. [101:2] Ps 26:11; Is 33:15.   d. [101:2] 1 Kgs 9:4.

e. [101:3] Prv 11:20.   f. [101:5] Prv 17:20; 30:10.   g. [101:5] Prv 21:4.   h. [101:6] Ps 26:11; Prv 20:7.   i. [101:7] Ps 5:5; Prv 25:5.   j. [102:3] Ps 69:18; 143:7.   k. [102:4–6] Ps 38:7–9.

in their rage, they make my name
    a curse.*
10 I eat ashes like bread,
    mingle my drink with tears.[l]
11 Because of your furious wrath,
    you lifted me up just to cast me
    down.
12 [m]My days are like a lengthening shadow;[n]
    I wither like the grass.

II

13 But you, LORD, are enthroned forever;
    your renown is for all generations.[o]
14 You will again show mercy to Zion;
    now is the time for pity;
    the appointed time has come.
15 Its stones are dear to your servants;
    its dust moves them to pity.
16 The nations shall fear your name, LORD,
    all the kings of the earth, your
    glory,[p]
17 Once the LORD has rebuilt Zion
    and appeared in glory,
18 Heeding the plea of the lowly,
    not scorning their prayer.
19 Let this be written for the next generation,
    for a people not yet born,
    that they may praise the LORD:[q]
20 †"The LORD looked down from the holy
    heights,
    viewed the earth from heaven,[r]
21 To attend to the groaning of the prisoners,
    to release those doomed to die."[s]
22 Then the LORD's name will be declared on
    Zion,
    his praise in Jerusalem,
23 When peoples and kingdoms gather
    to serve the LORD.[t]

III

24 He has shattered my strength in
    mid-course,
    has cut short my days.
25 I plead, O my God,
    do not take me in the midst of my
    days.‡[u]
    Your years last through all
    generations.
26 Of old you laid the earth's foundations;[v]
    the heavens are the work of your
    hands.
27 They perish, but you remain;
    they all wear out like a garment;

Like clothing you change them and they
    are changed,
28 but you are the same, your years
    have no end.
29 May the children of your servants live on;
    may their descendants live in your
    presence.[w]

PSALM 103[§]
Praise of Divine Goodness

1 Of David.

I

Bless the LORD, my soul;
    all my being, bless his holy name!
2 Bless the LORD, my soul;
    and do not forget all his gifts,
3 Who pardons all your sins,
    and heals all your ills,
4 Who redeems your life from the pit,[x]
    and crowns you with mercy and
    compassion,
5 Who fills your days with good things,
    so your youth is renewed like the
    eagle's.¶

II

6 The LORD does righteous deeds,
    brings justice to all the oppressed.[y]
7 He made known his ways to Moses,
    to the Israelites his deeds.
8 Merciful and gracious is the LORD,
    slow to anger, abounding in mercy.[z]
9 He will not always accuse,
    and nurses no lasting anger;
10 He has not dealt with us as our sins merit,
    nor requited us as our wrongs
    deserve.

III

11 For as the heavens tower over the earth,
    so his mercy towers over those who
    fear him.[a]
12 As far as the east is from the west,
    so far has he removed our sins from
    us.
13 As a father has compassion on his
    children,
    so the LORD has compassion on
    those who fear him.
14 For he knows how we are formed,
    remembers that we are dust.[b]

---

*[102:9] **They make my name a curse:** enemies use the psalmist's name in phrases such as, "May you be as wretched as this person!"

†[102:20–23] Both Ps 102:20–21 and Ps 102:22–23 depend on Ps 102:19.

‡[102:25] **In the midst of my days:** when the normal span of life is but half completed, cf. Is 38:10; Jer 17:11.

l. [102:10] Ps 42:4; 80:6.　m. [102:12] Ps 109:23; 144:4; Jb 8:9; 14:2; Eccl 6:12; Wis 2:5.　n. [102:12] Ps 90:5–6.　o. [102:13] Ps 55:20; 90:2; 93:2; 135:13; 145:13; Lam 5:19; Heb 1:12.　p. [102:16] Is 59:19; 66:18.　q. [102:19] Ps 22:31–32.　r. [102:20] Ps 11:4; 14:2.　s. [102:21] Ps 79:11.　t. [102:23] Is 60:3–4; Zec 2:15; 8:22.　u. [102:25] Ps 39:5; 90:10; Jb 14:5.　v. [102:26–28] Heb 1:10–12.

§[Psalm 103] The speaker in this hymn begins by praising God for personal benefits (Ps 103:1–5), then moves on to God's mercy toward all the people (Ps 103:6–18). Even sin cannot destroy that mercy (Ps 103:11–13), for the eternal God is well aware of the people's human fragility (Ps 103:14–18). The psalmist invites the heavenly beings to join in praise (Ps 103:19–22).

¶[103:5] **Your youth is renewed like the eagle's:** because of the eagle's long life it was a symbol of perennial youth and vigor, cf. Is 40:31.

w. [102:29] Ps 69:36–37.　x. [103:4] Ps 28:1; 30:4; 40:3; 69:16; 88:5; 143:7; Prv 1:12; Jon 2:7.　y. [103:6] Ps 146:6–7.　z. [103:8] Ps 86:15; 145:8; Ex 34:6–7; Nm 14:18; Jer 3:12; Jl 2:13; Jon 4:2.　a. [103:11] Is 55:9.　b. [103:14] Ps 90:3.

15 As for man, his days are like the grass;
　　he blossoms like a flower in the
　　　field.*c*
16 A wind sweeps over it and it is gone;
　　its place knows it no more.
17 But the LORD's mercy is from age to age,
　　toward those who fear him.
　　His salvation is for the children's children
18 of those who keep his covenant,
　　and remember to carry out his
　　　precepts.

IV

19 The LORD has set his throne in heaven;
　　his dominion extends over all.
20 Bless the LORD, all you his angels,*d*
　　mighty in strength, acting at his
　　　behest,
　　obedient to his command.
21 Bless the LORD, all you his hosts,
　　his ministers who carry out his will.
22 Bless the LORD, all his creatures,
　　everywhere in his domain.
　　Bless the LORD, my soul!

PSALM 104*
Praise of God the Creator

I

1 Bless the LORD, my soul!
　　LORD, my God, you are great
　　　indeed!
　　You are clothed with majesty and
　　　splendor,
2 robed in light as with a cloak.
　　You spread out the heavens like a tent;*e*
3 setting the beams of your chambers
　　upon the waters.†
　　You make the clouds your chariot;
　　traveling on the wings of the wind.
4 You make the winds your messengers;
　　flaming fire, your ministers.*f*

II

5 ‡You fixed the earth on its foundation,
　　so it can never be shaken.
6 The deeps covered it like a garment;

above the mountains stood the
　　waters.
7 At your rebuke they took flight;
　　at the sound of your thunder they
　　　fled.*g*
8 They rushed up the mountains, down the
　　valleys
　　to the place you had fixed for them.
9 You set a limit they cannot pass;
　　never again will they cover the
　　　earth.*h*

III

10 You made springs flow in wadies
　　that wind among the mountains.
11 They give drink to every beast of the field;*i*
　　here wild asses quench their thirst.
12 Beside them the birds of heaven nest;
　　among the branches they sing.
13 You water the mountains from your
　　chambers;
　　from the fruit of your labor the
　　　earth abounds.
14 You make the grass grow for the cattle
　　and plants for people's work
　　to bring forth food from the earth,
15 wine to gladden their hearts,
　　oil to make their faces shine,
　　and bread to sustain the human
　　　heart.
16 §The trees of the LORD drink their fill,
　　the cedars of Lebanon, which you
　　　planted.
17 There the birds build their nests;
　　the stork in the junipers, its home.*j*
18 The high mountains are for wild goats;
　　the rocky cliffs, a refuge for badgers.

IV

19 You made the moon to mark the seasons,*k*
　　the sun that knows the hour of its
　　　setting.
20 You bring darkness and night falls,
　　then all the animals of the forest
　　　wander about.
21 Young lions roar for prey;
　　they seek their food from God.*l*
22 When the sun rises, they steal away
　　and settle down in their dens.
23 People go out to their work,
　　to their labor till evening falls.

V

24 How varied are your works, LORD!
　　In wisdom you have made them all;
　　the earth is full of your creatures.*m*
25 There is the sea, great and wide!
　　It teems with countless beings,
　　living things both large and small.*n*

---

*[Psalm 104] A hymn praising God who easily and skill-
fully made rampaging waters and primordial night into a
world vibrant with life. The psalmist describes God's splendor in the heavens (Ps 104:1–4), how the chaotic waters were
tamed to fertilize and feed the world (Ps 104:5–18), and how
primordial night was made into a gentle time of refreshment
(Ps 104:19–23). The picture is like Gn 1:1–2: a dark and watery
chaos is made dry and lighted so that creatures might live. The
psalmist reacts to the beauty of creation with awe (Ps 104:24–
34). May sin not deface God's work (Ps 104:35)!

†[104:3] **Your chambers upon the waters**: God's heavenly
dwelling above the upper waters of the sky, cf. Gn 1:6–7; Ps
29:10.

‡[104:5–9] God places the gigantic disk of the earth
securely on its foundation and then, as a warrior, chases away
the enveloping waters and confines them under, above, and
around the earth.

§[104:16–18] Even the exotic flora and fauna of the high
mountains of the Lebanon range receive adequate water.

---

c. [103:15] Ps 37:2; 90:5–6; Is 40:7. d. [103:20] Ps 148:2; Dn
3:58. e. [104:2] Prv 8:27–28; Jb 9:8; Is 40:22; Gn 1:6–7; Am
9:6. f. [104:4] Heb 1:7.

g. [104:7] Ps 29:3. h. [104:9] Jer 5:22; Gn 9:11–15. i. [104:11–14]
Ps 147:8–9. j. [104:17] Ez 31:6. k. [104:19] Sir 43:6. l. [104:21]
Jb 38:39. m. [104:24] Ps 92:6; Sir 39:16. n. [104:25] Sir 43:26.

26 There ships ply their course
    and Leviathan,* whom you formed
        to play with.°
                    VI
27 All of these look to you
    to give them food in due time.ᵖ
28 When you give it to them, they gather;
    when you open your hand, they are
        well filled.
29 †When you hide your face, they panic.
    Take away their breath, they perish
    and return to the dust.�q
30 Send forth your spirit, they are created
    and you renew the face of the earth.
                    VII
31 May the glory of the LORD endure forever;
    may the LORD be glad in his works!
32 Who looks at the earth and it trembles,
    touches the mountains and they
        smoke!ʳ
33 I will sing to the LORD all my life;
    I will sing praise to my God while
        I live.ˢ
34 May my meditation be pleasing to him;
    I will rejoice in the LORD.
35 May sinners vanish from the earth,
    and the wicked be no more.
    Bless the LORD, my soul! Hallelujah!‡

PSALM 105§
God's Fidelity to the Promise

                    I
1 Give thanks to the LORD, invoke his
        name;ᵗ
    make known among the peoples his
        deeds!ᵘ
2 Sing praise to him, play music;
    proclaim all his wondrous deeds!
3 Glory in his holy name;
    let hearts that seek the LORD rejoice!
4 Seek out the LORD and his might;
    constantly seek his face.ᵛ

5 Recall the wondrous deeds he has done,
    his wonders and words of judgment,
6 You descendants of Abraham his servant,
    offspring of Jacob the chosen one!
                    II
7 He the LORD, is our God
    whose judgments reach through all
        the earth.
8 He remembers forever his covenant,
    the word he commanded for a
        thousand generations,
9 Which he made with Abraham,
    and swore to Isaac,ʷ
10 And ratified in a statute for Jacob,
    an everlasting covenant for Israel:
11 "To you I give the land of Canaan,
    your own allotted inheritance."ˣ
                    III
12 When they were few in number,ʸ
    a handful, and strangers there,
13 Wandering from nation to nation,
    from one kingdom to another people,
14 He let no one oppress them;
    for their sake he rebuked kings:¶
15 "'Do not touch my anointed ones,
    to my prophets do no harm.'"
                    IV
16 Then he called down a famine on the
        land,
    destroyed the grain that sustained
        them.††ᶻ
17 He had sent a man ahead of them,
    Joseph, sold as a slave.ᵃ
18 They shackled his feet with chains;
    collared his neck in iron,ᵇ
19 Till his prediction came to pass,
    and the word of the LORD proved
        him true.ᶜ
20 The king sent and released him;
    the ruler of peoples set him free.ᵈ
21 He made him lord over his household,
    ruler over all his possessions,ᵉ
22 To instruct his princes as he desired,
    to teach his elders wisdom.
                    V
23 Then Israel entered Egypt;ᶠ
    Jacob sojourned in the land of Ham.‡‡
24 God greatly increased his people,
    made them more numerous than
        their foes.ᵍ

*[104:26] **Leviathan**: a sea monster symbolizing primeval chaos, cf. Ps 74:14; Is 27:1; Jb 40:25. God does not destroy chaos but makes it part of the created order.

†[104:29–30] On one level, the spirit (or wind) of God is the fall and winter rains that provide food for all creatures. On another, it is the breath (or spirit) of God that makes beings live.

‡[104:35] **Hallelujah**: a frequent word in the last third of the Psalter. The word combines the plural imperative of praise (*hallelu*) with an abbreviated form of the divine name Yah(weh).

§[Psalm 105] A hymn to God who promised the land of Canaan to the holy people, cf. Ps 78; 106; 136. Israel is invited to praise and seek the presence of God (Ps 105:1–6), who is faithful to the promise of land to the ancestors (Ps 105:7–11). In every phase of the national story—the ancestors in the land of Canaan (Ps 105:12–15), Joseph in Egypt (Ps 105:16–22), Israel in Egypt (Ps 105:23–38), Israel in the desert on the way to Canaan (Ps 105:39–45)—God remained faithful, reiterating the promise of the land to successive servants.

¶[105:14] **Kings**: Pharaoh and Abimelech of Gerar, cf. Gn 12:17; 20:6–7.

[105:15] **My anointed ones . . . my prophets: the patriarchs Abraham, Isaac, and Jacob, who were "anointed" in the sense of being consecrated and recipients of God's revelation.

††[105:16] **The grain that sustained them**: lit., every "staff of bread."

‡‡[105:23, 27] **The land of Ham**: a synonym for Egypt, cf. Gn 10:6.

o. [104:26] Jb 3:8; 40:25, 29.   p. [104:27] Ps 136:25; 145:15–16.
q. [104:29] Ps 90:3; Jb 34:14–15; Eccl 3:20.   r. [104:32] Ps 144:5.
s. [104:33] Ps 146:2.   t. [105:1–15] 1 Chr 16:8–22.   u. [105:1] Ps 18:50; 96:3; 145:5; Is 12:4–5.   v. [105:4] Ps 24:6; 27:8.

w. [105:9] Gn 15:1ff; 26:3.   x. [105:11] Gn 12:7; 15:18.   y. [105:12–13] Dt 4:27; 26:5.   z. [105:16] Gn 41:54, 57.   a. [105:17] Gn 37:28, 36; 45:5.   b. [105:18] Gn 39:20.   c. [105:19] Gn 40–41.   d. [105:20] Gn 41:14.   e. [105:21] Gn 41:41–44.   f. [105:23] Gn 46:1–47:12; Acts 7:15.   g. [105:24] Ex 1:7; Acts 7:17.

²⁵ He turned their hearts to hate his people,
  to treat his servants deceitfully.ʰ
²⁶ He sent his servant Moses,
  and Aaron whom he had chosen.ⁱ
²⁷ They worked his signs in Egyptʲ
  and wonders in the land of Ham.
²⁸ He sent darkness and it grew dark,
  but they rebelled against his word.
²⁹ He turned their waters into blood
  and killed their fish.
³⁰ Their land swarmed with frogs,
  even the chambers of their kings.
³¹ He spoke and there came swarms of flies,
  gnats through all their country.
³² For rain he gave them hail,
  flashes of lightning throughout their
  land.
³³ He struck down their vines and fig trees,
  shattered the trees of their country.
³⁴ He spoke and the locusts came,
  grasshoppers without number.ᵏ
³⁵ They devoured every plant in the land;
  they devoured the crops of their
  fields.
³⁶ He struck down every firstborn in the
  land,
  the first fruits of all their vigor.
³⁷ He brought his people out,
  laden with silver and gold;ˡ
  no one among the tribes stumbled.
³⁸ Egypt rejoiced when they left,
  for fear had seized them.

VI

³⁹ He spread a cloud out as a cover,
  and made a fire to light up the
  night.ᵐ
⁴⁰ They asked and he brought them quail;
  with bread from heaven he filled
  them.ⁿ
⁴¹ He split the rock and water gushed forth;
  it flowed through the desert like a
  river.ᵒ
⁴² For he remembered his sacred promise
  to Abraham his servant.
⁴³ He brought his people out with joy,
  his chosen ones with shouts of
  triumph.
⁴⁴ He gave them the lands of the nations,
  they took possession of the wealth of
  the peoples,ᵖ
⁴⁵ That they might keep his statutes
  and observe his teachings.�q
  Hallelujah!

---

*[105:27–38] This Psalm and Ps 78:43–51 have an account of the plagues differing in number or in order from Ex 7:14–12:30. Several versions of the exodus story were current.

h. [105:25] Ex 1:8–14.   i. [105:26] Ex 3:10; 4:27.   j. [105:27–36] Ps 78:43–51; Ex 7–12.   k. [105:34] Jl 1:4.   l. [105:37] Ex 12:33–36.   m. [105:39] Ps 78:14; Ex 13:21–22; Wis 18:3.   n. [105:40] Ps 78:24–28; Ex 16:13–15; Nm 11:31ff; Wis 16:20.   o. [105:41] Ps 78:15–16; Ex 17:1–7; Nm 20:11.   p. [105:44] Dt 4:37–40.   q. [105:45] Dt 6:20–25; 7:8–11.

PSALM 106†
Israel's Confession of Sin

¹Hallelujah!

A

Give thanks to the LORD, who is good,
  whose mercy endures forever.ʳ
² Who can recount the mighty deeds of the
  LORD,
  proclaim in full God's praise?
³ Blessed those who do what is right,
  whose deeds are always just.ˢ
⁴ Remember me, LORD, as you favor your
  people;
  come to me with your saving help,ᵗ
⁵ That I may see the prosperity of your
  chosen ones,
  rejoice in the joy of your people,
  and glory with your heritage.

B

⁶ We have sinned like our ancestors;ᵘ
  we have done wrong and are guilty.

I

⁷ Our ancestors in Egypt
  did not attend to your wonders.
  They did not remember your manifold
  mercy;
  they defied the Most High at the
  Red Sea.
⁸ Yet he saved them for his name's sake
  to make his power known.ᵛ
⁹ He roared at the Red Sea and it dried up.
  He led them through the deep as
  through a desert.ʷ
¹⁰ He rescued them from hostile hands,
  freed them from the power of the
  enemy.
¹¹ The waters covered their oppressors;
  not one of them survived.
¹² Then they believed his words
  and sang his praise.ˣ

---

†[Psalm 106] Israel is invited to praise the God whose mercy has always tempered judgment of Israel (Ps 106:1–3). The speaker, on behalf of all, seeks solidarity with the people, who can always count on God's fidelity despite their sin (Ps 106:4–5). Confident of God's mercy, the speaker invites national repentance (Ps 106:6) by reciting from Israel's history eight instances of sin, judgment, and forgiveness. The sins are the rebellion at the Red Sea (Ps 106:6–12; see Ex 14–15), the craving for meat in the desert (Ps 106:13–15; see Nm 11), the challenge to Moses' authority (Ps 106:16–18; see Nm 16), the golden calf episode (Ps 106:19–23; see Ex 32–34), the refusal to take Canaan by the southern route (Ps 106:24–27; see Nm 13–14 and Dt 1–2), the rebellion at Baal-Peor (Ps 106:28–31; see Nm 25:1–10), the anger of Moses (Ps 106:32–33; see Nm 20:1–13), and mingling with the nations (Ps 106:34–47). The last, as suggested by its length and generalized language, may be the sin that invites the repentance of the present generation. The text gives the site of each sin: Egypt (Ps 106:7), the desert (Ps 106:14), the camp (Ps 106:16), Horeb (Ps 106:19), in their tents (Ps 106:25), Baal-Peor (Ps 106:28), the waters of Meribah (Ps 106:32), Canaan (Ps 106:38).

r. [106:1] Ps 100:5; 107:1; 1 Chr 16:34; Jer 33:11; Dn 3:89.   s. [106:3] Is 56:1–2.   t. [106:4] Ps 25:7; Neh 5:19.   u. [106:6–7] Ps 78:11–17; Ex 14:11; Lv 26:40; 1 Kgs 8:47; Bar 2:12; Dn 9:5.   v. [106:8] Ez 36:20–22.   w. [106:9] Ex 14:21–31; Is 50:2; 63:11–14; Na 1:4.   x. [106:12] Ex 15:1–21.

II

13 But they soon forgot all he had done;
   they had no patience for his plan.
14 In the desert they gave in to their
   cravings,
   tempted God in the wasteland.*y*
15 So he gave them what they asked
   and sent a wasting disease against
   them.*z*

III

16 In the camp they challenged Moses*a*
   and Aaron, the holy one of the Lord.
17 The earth opened and swallowed Dathan,
   it closed on the followers of Abiram.
18 Against their company the fire blazed;
   flames consumed the wicked.

IV

19 At Horeb they fashioned a calf,*b*
   worshiped a metal statue.
20 They exchanged their glory*
   for the image of a grass-eating bull.
21 They forgot the God who had saved them,
   who had done great deeds in Egypt,*c*
22 Amazing deeds in the land of Ham,
   fearsome deeds at the Red Sea.
23 He would have decreed their destruction,
   had not Moses, his chosen one,
   Withstood him in the breach†
   to turn back his destroying anger.*d*

V

24 Next they despised the beautiful land;*e*
   they did not believe the promise.
25 In their tents they complained;
   they did not heed the voice of the
   Lord.
26 So with raised hand he swore
   he would destroy them in the desert,
27 And scatter their descendants among the
   nations,
   disperse them in foreign lands.

VI

28 They joined in the rites of Baal of Peor,*f*
   ate food sacrificed to the dead.
29 They provoked him by their actions,
   and a plague broke out among them.
30 Then Phinehas rose to intervene,
   and the plague was brought to a halt.
31 This was counted for him as a righteous
   deed
   for all generations to come.

VII

32 At the waters of Meribah they angered
   God,*g*

and Moses suffered because of them.‡
33 They so embittered his spirit
   that rash words crossed his lips.

VIII

34 They did not destroy the peoples
   as the Lord had commanded them,*h*
35 But mingled with the nations
   and imitated their ways.*i*
36 They served their idols
   and were ensnared by them.*j*
37 They sacrificed to demons§
   their own sons and daughters,
38 Shedding innocent blood,
   the blood of their own sons and
   daughters,
   Whom they sacrificed to the idols of
   Canaan,
   desecrating the land with bloodshed.
39 They defiled themselves by their actions,
   became adulterers by their conduct.
40 So the Lord grew angry with his people,
   abhorred his own heritage.
41 He handed them over to the nations,
   and their adversaries ruled over
   them.*k*
42 Their enemies oppressed them,
   kept them under subjection.
43 Many times did he rescue them,
   but they kept rebelling and
   scheming
   and were brought low by their own
   guilt.*l*
44 Still God had regard for their affliction
   when he heard their wailing.
45 For their sake he remembered his
   covenant
   and relented in his abundant mercy,*m*
46 Winning for them compassion
   from all who held them captive.

C

47 Save us, Lord, our God;
   gather us from among the nations
   That we may give thanks to your holy
   name
   and glory in praising you.*n*
48 'Blessed be the Lord, the God of Israel,
   from everlasting to everlasting!
   Let all the people say, Amen!*o*
   Hallelujah!

---

‡[106:32] **Moses suffered because of them**: Moses was not allowed to enter the promised land because of his rash words (Nm 20:12). According to Dt 1:37, Moses was not allowed to cross because of the people's sin, not his own.

§[106:37] **Demons**: Hebrew *shedim* occurs in parallelism with "gods" in an important inscription from Transjordan and hence can also be translated "the gods."

¶[106:48] A doxology ending Book IV of the Psalter. It is not part of the Psalm.

---

*[106:20] **Their glory**: meant as a reference to God.
†[106:23] **Withstood him in the breach**: the image is that of Moses standing in a narrow break made in the wall to keep anyone from entering.

---

y. [106:14] Ps 78:18; Ex 15:24; 16:3; Nm 11:1–6. z. [106:15] Ps 78:26–31; Nm 11:33. a. [106:16–18] Nm 16; Dt 11:6; Is 26:11. b. [106:19–20] Ex 32; Dt 9:8–21; Jer 2:11; Acts 7:41; Rom 1:23. c. [106:21] Ps 78:42–58; Dt 32:18; Jer 2:32. d. [106:23] Ex 32:11; Dt 9:25; Ez 22:30. e. [106:24–27] Lv 26:33; Nm 14; Dt 1:25–36; Ez 20:15, 23. f. [106:28–31] Nm 25; Dt 26:14; Sir 45:23–24.

g. [106:32–33] Ps 95:8–9; Ex 17:1–7; Nm 20:2–13; Dt 6:16; 33:8. h. [106:34] Dt 7:1; Jgs 2:1–5. i. [106:35] Lv 18:3; Jgs 1:27–35; 3:5. j. [106:36–38] Lv 18:21; Nm 35:33; Dt 32:17; Jgs 2:11–13, 17, 19; 2 Kgs 16:3; Bar 4:7; 1 Cor 10:20. k. [106:41] Jgs 2:14–23. l. [106:43] Is 63:7–9. m. [106:45] Lv 26:42. n. [106:47] 1 Chr 16:35. o. [106:48] Ps 41:14; 72:18; 89:53; 1 Chr 16:36; Neh 9:5.

Fifth Book—Psalms 107–150

PSALM 107*
God the Savior of Those in Distress

1 "Give thanks to the LORD for he is good,
    his mercy endures forever!"[p]
2 Let that be the prayer of the LORD's
    redeemed,
    those redeemed from the hand of
    the foe,[q]
3 Those gathered from foreign lands,
    from east and west, from north and
    south.[r]

I

4 Some had lost their way in a barren
    desert;
    found no path toward a city to live in.
5 They were hungry and thirsty;
    their life was ebbing away.[s]
6 In their distress they cried to the LORD,
    who rescued them in their peril,
7 'Guided them by a direct path
    so they reached a city to live in.[u]
8 Let them thank the LORD for his mercy,
    such wondrous deeds for the
    children of Adam.
9 For he satisfied the thirsty,
    filled the hungry with good things.[v]

II

10 Some lived in darkness and gloom,
    imprisoned in misery and chains.
11 Because they rebelled against God's word,
    and scorned the counsel of the Most
    High,[w]
12 He humbled their hearts through
    hardship;
    they stumbled with no one to help.[x]
13 In their distress they cried to the LORD,
    who saved them in their peril;
14 He brought them forth from darkness and
    the shadow of death
    and broke their chains asunder.[y]
15 Let them thank the LORD for his mercy,
    such wondrous deeds for the
    children of Adam.
16 For he broke down the gates of bronze
    and snapped the bars of iron.

III

17 Some fell sick from their wicked ways,
    afflicted because of their sins.
18 They loathed all manner of food;[z]
    they were at the gates of death.
19 In their distress they cried to the LORD,
    who saved them in their peril,
20 Sent forth his word to heal them,[a]
    and snatched them from the grave.
21 Let them thank the LORD for his mercy,
    such wondrous deeds for the
    children of Adam.
22 Let them offer a sacrifice in thanks,
    recount his works with shouts of joy.

IV

23 Some went off to sea in ships,
    plied their trade on the deep waters.[b]
24 They saw the works of the LORD,
    the wonders of God in the deep.
25 He commanded and roused a storm wind;
    it tossed the waves on high.[c]
26 They rose up to the heavens, sank to the
    depths;
    their hearts trembled at the danger.
27 They reeled, staggered like drunkards;
    their skill was of no avail.[d]
28 In their distress they cried to the LORD,
    who brought them out of their peril;
29 He hushed the storm to silence,
    the waves of the sea were stilled.[e]
30 They rejoiced that the sea grew calm,
    that God brought them to the
    harbor they longed for.
31 Let them thank the LORD for his mercy,
    such wondrous deeds for the
    children of Adam.
32 Let them extol him in the assembly of the
    people,
    and praise him in the council of the
    elders.

V

33 †God changed rivers into desert,
    springs of water into thirsty ground;[f]
34 Fruitful land into a salty waste,
    because of the wickedness of its
    people.[g]
35 He changed the desert into pools of water,
    arid land into springs of water,[h]
36 And settled the hungry there;
    they built a city to live in.[i]
37 They sowed fields and planted vineyards,
    brought in an abundant harvest.[j]

---

*[Psalm 107] A hymn inviting those who have been res-cued by God to give praise (Ps 107:1–3). Four archetypal divine rescues are described, each ending in thanksgiving: from the sterile desert (Ps 107:4–9), from imprisonment in gloom (Ps 107:10–16), from mortal illness (Ps 107:17–22), and from the angry sea (Ps 107:23–32). The number four connotes totality, all the possible varieties of rescue. The same saving activity of God is shown in Israel's history (Ps 107:33–41); whenever the people were endangered God rescued them. The last verses invite people to ponder the persistent saving acts of God (Ps 107:42–43).

p. [107:1] Ps 100:4–5; 106:1; Jer 33:11. q. [107:2] Is 63:12.
r. [107:3] Is 43:5–6; 49:12; Zec 8:7. s. [107:5] Dt 8:15; 32:10;
Is 49:10. t. [107:7] Is 35:8; 40:3; 43:19. u. [107:7] Dt 6:10.
v. [107:9] Lk 1:53. w. [107:11] Is 42:7, 22; Jb 36:8–9; Prv 1:25.
x. [107:12] Ps 106:43. y. [107:14] Is 42:7; 49:9; 51:14.

---

†[107:33–41] God destroyed Sodom and Gomorrah in Gn 18–19, which the Psalm sees as the destruction of the wicked inhabitants of Canaan to prepare the way for Israel (Ps 107:33–34). God then led Israel through the desert to give them a fertile land (Ps 107:35–38) and protected them from every danger (Ps 107:39–41).

z. [107:18] Jb 6:6–7; 33:20. a. [107:20] Ps 147:15; Wis 16:12;
Is 55:11; Mt 8:8. b. [107:23] Sir 43:25. c. [107:25] Jon
1:4. d. [107:27] Is 29:9. e. [107:29] Ps 65:8; 89:10; Mt 8:26
par. f. [107:33] Is 35:7; 42:15; 50:2. g. [107:34] Gn 19:23–28;
Dt 29:22; Sir 39:23. h. [107:35] Ps 114:8; Is 41:8. i. [107:36] Ez
36:35. j. [107:37] Is 65:21; Jer 31:5.

38 *God blessed them, and they increased
greatly,
and their livestock did not decrease.¹
39 But he poured out contempt on princes,
made them wander trackless wastes,
40 Where they were diminished and brought
low
through misery and cruel
oppression.
41 While he released the poor man from
affliction,
and increased their families like
flocks.ᵐ
42 The upright saw this and rejoiced;ⁿ
all wickedness shut its mouth.
43 Whoever is wise will take note of these
things,ᵒ
and ponder the merciful deeds of
the Lᴏʀᴅ.

PSALM 108*
Prayer for Victory

¹A song; a psalm of David.

I

2 My heart is steadfast, God;ᵖ
my heart is steadfast.
Let me sing and chant praise.
3 Awake, lyre and harp!
I will wake the dawn. q
4 I will praise you among the peoples,
Lᴏʀᴅ;
I will chant your praise among the
nations.ʳ
5 For your mercy is greater than the
heavens;
your faithfulness, to the skies.ˢ

II

6 Appear on high over the heavens, God;
your glory above all the earth.
7 Help with your right hand and answer us
that your loved ones may escape.

8 God speaks in his holiness:†ᵗ
"I will exult, I will apportion
Shechem;
the valley of Succoth I will measure
out.
9 Gilead is mine, mine is Manasseh;
Ephraim is the helmet for my head,
Judah, my scepter.

10 Moab is my washbowl;
upon Edom I cast my sandal;ᵘ
I will shout in triumph over
Philistia."

11 Who will bring me to the fortified city?
Who will lead me into Edom?
12 Was it not you who rejected us, God?
Do you no longer march with our
armies?ᵛ
13 Give us aid against the foe;
worthless is human help.
14 We will triumph with the help of God,
who will trample down our foes.

PSALM 109‡
Prayer of a Person Falsely Accused

¹For the leader. A psalm of David.

I

2 O God, whom I praise, do not be silent,ʷ
for wicked and treacherous mouths
attack me.
They speak against me with lying tongues;
3 with hateful words they surround
me,
attacking me without cause.
4 In return for my love they slander me,
even though I prayed for them.
5 They repay me evil for good,
hatred for my love.ˣ

II

6 Appoint an evil one over him,
an accuser§ to stand at his right
hand,
7 That he may be judged and found guilty,
that his plea may be in vain.
8 May his days be few;
may another take his office.ʸ
9 May his children be fatherless,
his wife, a widow.ᶻ
10 May his children wander and beg,
driven from their hovels.
11 May the usurer snare all he owns,
strangers plunder all he earns.
12 May no one treat him with mercy
or pity his fatherless children.

‡[Psalm 109] A lament notable for the length and vehe-
mence of its prayer against evildoers (Ps 109:6–20); the cry to
God (Ps 109:1) and the complaint (Ps 109:22–25) are brief in
comparison. The psalmist is apparently the victim of a slander
campaign, potentially devastating in a society where reputation and honor are paramount. In the emotional perspective
of the Psalm, there are only two types of people: the wicked
and their poor victims. The psalmist is a poor victim (Ps
109:22, 31) and by that fact a friend of God and enemy of the
wicked. The psalmist seeks vindication not on the basis of personal virtue but because of God's promise to protect the poor.
§[109:6] An accuser: Hebrew satan, a word occurring in
Job 1–2 and Zec 3:1–2. In the latter passage Satan stands at the
right hand of the high priest to bring false accusations against
him before God. Here the accuser is human.

*[Psalm 108] A prayer compiled from two other Psalms:
Ps 108:2–6 are virtually the same as Ps 57:8–12; Ps 108:7–14
are the same as Ps 60:7–14. An old promise of salvation (Ps
108:8–10) is combined with a confident assurance (Ps 108:2–
6, 13) and petition (Ps 108:7, 12–13).
†[108:8] Holiness: may also be translated as "sanctuary" or
as referring to God's heavenly abode.

k. [107:38] Jb 12:23–25. l. [107:38] Dt 7:13–14. m. [107:41]
Ps 113:7. n. [107:42] Ps 58:11; 63:12. o. [107:43] Hos 14:10.
p. [108:2–6] Ps 57:8–12. q. [108:3] Jb 38:12. r. [108:4] Ps 9:12;
18:50; 148:13. s. [108:5] Ps 36:6; 71:19. t. [108:8–14] Ps 60:8–14.

u. [108:10] Ru 4:7–8. v. [108:12] Ps 44:10. w. [109:2] Ps 35:22;
83:1. x. [109:5] Ps 35:12; 38:21; Prv 17:13; Jer 18:20. y. [109:8]
Acts 1:20. z. [109:9] Ex 22:23; Jer 18:21.

¹³ May his posterity be destroyed,^a
       their name rooted out in the next
       generation.
¹⁴ May his fathers' guilt be mentioned to the
       Lord;
       his mother's sin not rooted out.^b
¹⁵ May their guilt be always before the
       Lord,^c
       till their memory is banished from
       the earth,^d
¹⁶ For he did not remember to show mercy,
       but hounded the wretched poor
       and brought death to the
       brokenhearted.
¹⁷ He loved cursing; may it come upon him;
       he hated blessing; may none come
       to him.
¹⁸ May cursing clothe him like a robe;
       may it enter his belly like water,
       his bones like oil.
¹⁹ May it be near as the clothes he wears,
       as the belt always around him.

²⁰ *May this be the reward for my accusers
       from the Lord,
       for those speaking evil against me.

                    III
²¹ But you, Lord, are my Lord,
       deal kindly with me for your name's
       sake;
       in your great mercy rescue me.
²² For I am poor and needy;
       my heart is pierced within me.
²³ Like a lengthening shadow I am gone,
       I am shaken off like the locust.
²⁴ My knees totter from fasting;^e
       my flesh has wasted away.
²⁵ I have become a mockery to them;
       when they see me, they shake their
       heads.
²⁶ Help me, Lord, my God;
       save me in your mercy.
²⁷ Make them know this is your hand,
       that you, Lord, have done this.
²⁸ Though they curse, may you bless;
       arise, shame them, that your servant
       may rejoice.
²⁹ Clothe my accusers with disgrace;
       make them wear their shame like a
       mantle.
³⁰ I will give fervent thanks to the Lord;
       before a crowd I will praise him.^f
³¹ For he stands at the right hand of the
       poor
       to save him from those who pass
       judgment on him.

*[109:20] **May this be the reward . . . from the Lord:** the
psalmist prays that God ratify the curses of Ps 109:6–19 and
bring them upon the wicked.

a. [109:13] Ps 21:11; Prv 10:7.   b. [109:14] Ex 20:5.   c. [109:15]
Ps 90:8.   d. [109:15] Ps 34:16.   e. [109:24–25] Ps 69:11–13.
f. [109:30] Ps 111:1.

PSALM 110[†]
God Appoints the King Both King and Priest

¹A psalm of David.

The Lord says to my lord:[‡]
   "Sit at my right hand,
   while I make your enemies your
   footstool."^{‡g}
² The scepter of your might:
   the Lord extends your strong
   scepter from Zion.
   Have dominion over your enemies!
³ Yours is princely power from the day of
   your birth.
   In holy splendor before the daystar,
   like dew I begot you.^h
⁴ The Lord has sworn and will not waver:
   "You are a priest forever in the
   manner of Melchizedek."^{§i}
⁵ At your right hand is the Lord,
   who crushes kings on the day of his
   wrath,^j
⁶ Who judges nations, heaps up corpses,
   crushes heads across the wide earth,
⁷ *Who drinks from the brook by the
   wayside
   and thus holds high his head.^k

PSALM 111**
Praise of God for Goodness to Israel

¹Hallelujah!

I will praise the Lord with all my heart^l

†[Psalm 110] A royal Psalm in which a court singer recites
three oracles in which God assures the king that his enemies
are conquered (Ps 110:1–2), makes the king "son" in traditional adoption language (Ps 110:3), gives priestly status to the
king and promises to be with him in future military ventures
(Ps 110:4–7).
‡[110:1] **The Lord says to my lord:** a polite form of
address of an inferior to a superior, cf. 1 Sm 25:25; 2 Sm 1:10.
The court singer refers to the king. Jesus in the synoptic gospels
(Mt 22:41–46 and parallels) takes the psalmist to be David and
hence "my lord" refers to the messiah, who must be someone
greater than David. **Your footstool:** in ancient times victorious
kings put their feet on the prostrate bodies of their enemies.
§[110:4] **Melchizedek:** Melchizedek was the ancient king of
Salem (Jerusalem) who blessed Abraham (Gn 14:18–20); like
other kings of the time he performed priestly functions. Heb 7
sees in Melchizedek a type of Christ.
¶[110:7] **Who drinks from the brook by the wayside:** the
meaning is uncertain. Some see an allusion to a rite of royal
consecration at the Gihon spring (cf. 1 Kgs 1:33, 38). Others
find here an image of the divine warrior (or king) pursuing
enemies so relentlessly that he does not stop long enough to
eat and drink.
**[Psalm 111] A Temple singer (Ps 111:1) tells how God is
revealed in Israel's history (Ps 111:2–10). The deeds reveal God's
very self, powerful, merciful, faithful. The poem is an acrostic,
each verse beginning with a successive letter of the Hebrew
alphabet.

g. [110:1] Mt 22:44; Acts 2:34–35; 1 Cor 15:25; Heb 1:13; 8:1; 10:12–
13; 1 Pt 3:22.   h. [110:3] Ps 2:7; 89:27; Is 49:1.   i. [110:4] Ps 89:35;
132:11; Gn 14:18; Heb 5:6; 7:21.   j. [110:5] Ps 2:9; Rev 2:27; 12:5;
19:15.   k. [110:7] Ps 3:4.   l. [111:1] Ps 138:1.

in the assembled congregation of the upright.*

2 Great are the works of the LORD,
  studied by all who delight in them.
3 Majestic and glorious is his work,
  his righteousness endures forever.
4 He won renown for his wondrous deeds;
  gracious and merciful is the LORD.ᵐ
5 He gives food to those who fear him,†
  he remembers his covenant forever.
6 He showed his powerful deeds to his people,
  giving them the inheritance of the nations.
7 The works of his hands are true and just,
  reliable all his decrees,
8 Established forever and ever,
  to be observed with truth and equity.
9 He sent release to his people,
  decreed his covenant forever;
  holy and fearsome is his name.
10 ‡The fear of the LORD is the beginning of wisdom;ⁿ
  prudent are all who practice it.
  His praise endures forever.

PSALM 112§
The Blessings of the Just

1Hallelujah!

Blessed the man who fears the LORD,
  who greatly delights in his commands.ᵒ
2 His descendants shall be mighty in the land,
  a generation of the upright will be blessed.
3 Wealth and riches shall be in his house;
  his righteousness⁵ shall endure forever.
4 Light shines through the darkness for the upright;ᵖ
  gracious, compassionate, and righteous.

5 It is good for the man gracious in lending,
  who conducts his affairs with justice.
6 For he shall never be shaken;
  the righteous shall be remembered forever.�q
7 He shall not fear an ill report;
  his heart is steadfast, trusting the LORD.
8 His heart is tranquil, without fear,
  till at last he looks down on his foes.
9 Lavishly he gives to the poor;
  his righteousness shall endure forever;ʳ
  his horn** shall be exalted in honor.
10 The wicked sees and is angry;
  gnashes his teeth and wastes away;
  the desire of the wicked come to nothing.

PSALM 113††
Praise of God's Care for the Poor

1Hallelujah!

I
Praise, you servants of the LORD,
  praise the name of the LORD.ˢ
2 Blessed be the name of the LORD
  both now and forever.
3 From the rising of the sun to its settingᵗ
  let the name of the LORD be praised.
II
4 High above all nations is the LORD;
  above the heavens his glory.ᵘ
5 Who is like the LORD our God,
  enthroned on high,
6   ᵛlooking down on heaven and earth?
7 He raises the needy from the dust,
  lifts the poor from the ash heap,ʷ
8 Seats them with princes,
  the princes of the people,
9 Gives the childless wife a home,
  the joyful mother of children.ˣ
Hallelujah!

PSALM 114‡‡
The Lord's Wonders at the Exodus

1 When Israel came forth from Egypt,
  the house of Jacob from an alien people,

---

*[111:1] **In the assembled congregation of the upright**: in the Temple, cf. Ps 149:1.
†[111:5] **Food to those who fear him**: probably a reference to the manna in the desert, which elsewhere is seen as a type of the Eucharist, cf. Jn 6:31–33, 49–51.
‡[111:10] **The fear of the LORD**: reverence for God.
§[Psalm 112] An acrostic poem detailing the blessings received by those who remain close to God by obedience to the commandments. Among their blessings are children (Ps 112:2), wealth that enables them to be magnanimous (Ps 112:3, 5, 9), and virtue by which they encourage others (Ps 112:4). The just person is an affront to the wicked, whose hopes remain unfulfilled (Ps 112:10). The logic resembles Ps 1; 111.
¶[112:3] **Righteousness**: in the Second Temple period the word acquired the nuance of liberality and almsgiving, cf. Sir 3:30; 7:10; Mt 6:1–4.

---

m. [111:4] Ps 103:8; 112:4.   n. [111:10] Prv 1:7; 9:10; Sir 1:16.
o. [112:1] Ps 1:1–2; 119:1–2; 128:1.   p. [112:4] Ps 37:6; 97:11; Prv 13:9; Is 58:10.

[112:9] **His horn: the symbol for vitality and honor.
††[Psalm 113] A hymn exhorting the congregation to praise God's name, i.e., the way in which God is present in the world; the name is mentioned three times in Ps 113:1–3. The divine name is especially honored in the Temple (Ps 113:1) but its recognition is not limited by time (Ps 113:2) and space (Ps 113:3), for God is everywhere active (Ps 113:4–5) especially in rescuing the lowly faithful (Ps 113:7–9).
‡‡[Psalm 114] A hymn celebrating Israel's escape from Egypt, journey through the wilderness, and entry into the

---

q. [112:6] Prv 10:7; Wis 8:13.   r. [112:9] Prv 22:9; 2 Cor 9:9.
s. [113:1] Ps 135:1.   t. [113:3] Mal 1:11.   u. [113:4] Ps 148:13.
v. [113:6] Ps 89:7–9.   w. [113:7] Ps 107:41; 1 Sm 2:7–8.   x. [113:9] 1 Sm 2:5; Is 54:1.

2 Judah became God's sanctuary,
   Israel, God's domain.^{y}
3 'The sea saw and fled;
   the Jordan turned back.^{z}
4 The mountains skipped like rams;
   the hills, like lambs.^{a}
5 Why was it, sea, that you fled?
   Jordan, that you turned back?
6 Mountains, that you skipped like rams?
   You hills, like lambs?
7 Tremble, earth, before the Lord,^{b}
   before the God of Jacob,
8 †Who turned the rock into pools of water,
   flint into a flowing spring.^{c}

PSALM 115‡
The Greatness of the True God

I

1 Not to us, Lord, not to us
   but to your name give glory
   because of your mercy and
   faithfulness.^{d}
2 Why should the nations say,
   "Where is their God?"^{§e}
3 Our God is in heaven
   and does whatever he wills.^{f}

II

4 Their idols are silver and gold,^{g}
   the work of human hands.^{h}
5 They have mouths but do not speak,
   eyes but do not see.
6 They have ears but do not hear,
   noses but do not smell.
7 They have hands but do not feel,
   feet but do not walk;

they produce no sound from their
   throats.
8 Their makers will be like them,
   and anyone who trusts in them.

III

9 'The house of Israel trusts in the Lord,^{i}
   who is their help and shield.^{j}
10 The house of Aaron trusts in the Lord,
   who is their help and shield.
11 Those who fear the Lord trust in the
   Lord,
   who is their help and shield.
12 The Lord remembers us and will bless us,
   will bless the house of Israel,
   will bless the house of Aaron,
13 Will bless those who fear the Lord,
   small and great alike.
14 May the Lord increase your number,
   yours and your descendants.
15 May you be blessed by the Lord,
   maker of heaven and earth.
16 "The heavens belong to the Lord,
   but he has given the earth to the
   children of Adam.^{k}
17 ††The dead do not praise the Lord,
   not all those go down into silence.^{l}
18 It is we who bless the Lord,
   both now and forever.
Hallelujah!

PSALM 116‡‡
Thanksgiving to God Who Saves from Death

I

1 I love the Lord, who listened
   to my voice in supplication,
2 Who turned an ear to me
   on the day I called.
3 I was caught by the cords of death;^{§§m}
   the snares of Sheol had seized me;
   I felt agony and dread.
4 Then I called on the name of the Lord,
   "O Lord, save my life!"

---

promised land, and the miracles of nature that bore witness to God's presence in their midst. In the perspective of the Psalm, the people proceed directly from Egypt into the promised land (Ps 114:1–2). Sea and Jordan, which stood like soldiers barring the people from their land, flee before the mighty God as the earth recoils from the battle (Ps 114:3–4). The poet taunts the natural elements as one taunts defeated enemies (Ps 114:5–6).

*[114:3–4] Pairs of cosmic elements such as sea and rivers, mountains and hills, are sometimes mentioned in creation accounts. Personified here as warriors, the pairs tremble in fear before the Divine Warrior. The quaking also recalls the divine appearance in the storm at Sinai (Ex 19:16–19) and elsewhere (Jgs 5:4–5; Ps 18:7–15).

†[114:8] The miracles of giving drink to the people in the arid desert, cf. Ex 17:1–7; Is 41:17–18.

‡[Psalm 115] A response to the enemy taunt, "Where is your God?" This hymn to the glory of Israel's God (Ps 115:1–3) ridicules the lifeless idols of the nations (Ps 115:4–8), expresses in a litany the trust of the various classes of the people in God (Ps 115:9–11), invokes God's blessing on them as they invoke the divine name (Ps 115:12–15), and concludes as it began with praise of God. Ps 135:15–18 similarly mocks the Gentile gods and has a similar litany and hymn (Ps 135:19–21).

§[115:2] Where is their God?: implies that God cannot help them.

¶[115:9–11] The house of Israel . . . the house of Aaron . . . those who fear the Lord: the laity of Israelite birth, the priests, and the converts to Judaism, cf. Ps 118:2–4; 135:19–21. In the New Testament likewise "those who fear the Lord" means converts to Judaism (cf. Acts 10:2, 22, 35; 13:16, 26).

**[115:16] The heavens: the Septuagint reads here "the heaven of heavens" or "the highest heavens," i.e., above the firmament. See note on Ps 148:4.

††[115:17] See note on Ps 6:5.

‡‡[Psalm 116] A thanksgiving in which the psalmist responds to divine rescue from mortal danger (Ps 116:3–4) and from near despair (Ps 116:10–11) with vows and Temple sacrifices (Ps 116:13–14, 17–19). The Greek and Latin versions divide the Psalm into two parts: Ps 116:1–9 and Ps 116:10–19, corresponding to its two major divisions.

§§[116:3] The cords of death: death is personified here; it attempts to capture the psalmist with snares and nets, cf. Ps 18:6.

y. [114:2] Ex 19:6. z. [114:3] Ps 66:6; 74:15; Ex 14:21f; Jos 3:14ff. a. [114:4] Ps 29:6; Wis 19:9. b. [114:7] Ps 68:9. c. [114:8] Ex 17:6; Nm 20:11. d. [115:1] Ez 36:22–23. e. [115:2] Ps 79:10. f. [115:3] Ps 135:6. g. [115:4–10] Ps 135:15–19; Wis 15:15–16; Is 44:9f; Jer 10:1–5. h. [115:4] Is 40:19.

i. [115:9] Ps 118:2–4. j. [115:9] Ps 33:20. k. [115:16] Gn 1:28. l. [115:17] Ps 6:6; 88:11ff; Sir 17:22f; Is 38:18. m. [116:3] Ps 18:5; Jon 2:3.

II

5 Gracious is the LORD and righteous;
   yes, our God is merciful.ⁿ
6 The LORD protects the simple;
   I was helpless, but he saved me.
7 Return, my soul, to your rest;
   the LORD has been very good to
   you.ᵒ
8 For my soul has been freed from death,
   my eyes from tears, my feet from
   stumbling.ᵖ
9 I shall walk before the LORD
   in the land of the living.*�q

III

10 †I kept faith, even when I said,
   "I am greatly afflicted!"ʳ
11 I said in my alarm,
   "All men are liars!"ˢ
12 How can I repay the LORD
   for all the great good done for me?
13 I will raise the cup of salvation‡
   and call on the name of the LORD.
14 I will pay my vows to the LORD
   in the presence of all his people.
15 §Dear in the eyes of the LORD
   is the death of his devoted.ᵗ
16 LORD, I am your servant,
   your servant, the child of your
   maidservant;ᵘ
   you have loosed my bonds.
17 I will offer a sacrifice of praise
   and call on the name of the LORD.ᵛ
18 I will pay my vows to the LORDʷ
   in the presence of all his people,
19 In the courts of the house of the LORD,
   in your midst, O Jerusalem.
Hallelujah!

PSALM 117⁵
The Nations Called to Praise

1 Praise the LORD, all you nations!
   Extol him, all you peoples!ˣ

---

*[116:9] **The land of the living**: the phrase elsewhere is an epithet of the Jerusalem Temple (cf. Ps 27:13; 52:5; Is 38:11). Hence the psalmist probably refers to being present to God in the Temple.
†[116:10] **I kept faith, even when I said**: even in the days of despair, the psalmist did not lose all hope.
‡[116:13] **The cup of salvation**: probably the libation of wine poured out in gratitude for rescue, cf. Ex 25:29; Nm 15:5, 7, 10.
§[116:15] **Dear in the eyes of the LORD**: the meaning is that the death of God's faithful is grievous to God, not that God is pleased with the death, cf. Ps 72:14. In Wis 3:5–6, God accepts the death of the righteous as a sacrificial burnt offering.
¶[Psalm 117] This shortest of hymns calls on the nations to acknowledge God's supremacy. The supremacy of Israel's God has been demonstrated to them by the people's secure existence, which is owed entirely to God's gracious fidelity.

n. [116:5] Ex 34:6. o. [116:7] Ps 13:6. p. [116:8] Ps 56:14; Is 25:8; Rev 21:4. q. [116:9] Ps 27:13; 56:14; Is 38:11. r. [116:10] 2 Cor 4:13. s. [116:11] Ps 12:2. t. [116:15] Ps 72:14; Is 43:4. u. [116:16] Ps 86:16; 143:12; Wis 9:5. v. [116:17] Lv 7:12ff. w. [116:18] Jon 2:10. x. [117:1] Rom 15:11.

---

2 His mercy for us is strong;
   the faithfulness of the LORD is
   forever.
Hallelujah!

PSALM 118**
Hymn of Thanksgiving

I

1 Give thanks to the LORD, for he is good,ʸ
   his mercy endures forever.
2 Let Israel say:
   his mercy endures forever.
3 Let the house of Aaron say,
   his mercy endures forever.
4 Let those who fear the LORD say,ᶻ
   his mercy endures forever.

II

5 In danger I called on the LORD;
   the LORD answered me and set me
   free.
6 The LORD is with me; I am not afraid;
   what can mortals do against me?ᵃ
7 The LORD is with me as my helper;
   I shall look in triumph on my foes.
8 Better to take refuge in the LORDᵇ
   than to put one's trust in mortals.
9 Better to take refuge in the LORD
   than to put one's trust in princes.

III

10 All the nations surrounded me;
   in the LORD's name I cut them off.
11 They surrounded me on every side;
   in the LORD's name I cut them off.
12 They surrounded me like bees;ᶜ
   they burned up like fire among
   thorns;
   in the LORD's name I cut them off.
13 I was hard pressed and falling,
   but the LORD came to my help.ᵈ
14 The LORD, my strength and might,
   has become my savior.ᵉ

IV

15 The joyful shout of deliverance
   is heard in the tents of the righteous:
   "The LORD's right hand works valiantly;
16   the LORD's right hand is raised;
   the LORD's right hand works
   valiantly."

**[Psalm 118] A thanksgiving liturgy accompanying a procession of the king and the people into the Temple precincts. After an invocation in the form of a litany (Ps 118:1–4), the psalmist (very likely speaking in the name of the community) describes how the people confidently implored God's help (Ps 118:5–9) when hostile peoples threatened its life (Ps 118:10–14); vividly God's rescue is recounted (Ps 118:15–18). Then follows a possible dialogue at the Temple gates between the priests and the psalmist as the latter enters to offer the thanksgiving sacrifice (Ps 118:19–25). Finally, the priests impart their blessing (Ps 118:26–27), and the psalmist sings in gratitude (Ps 118:28–29).

y. [118:1] Ps 100:5; 136:1f. z. [118:4] Ps 115:9–11. a. [118:6] Ps 27:1; Heb 13:6. b. [118:8f] Ps 146:3. c. [118:12] Dt 1:44. d. [118:13] Ps 129:1–2. e. [118:14] Ex 15:2; Is 12:2.

17 I shall not die but live
     and declare the deeds of the LORD.
18 The LORD chastised me harshly,
     but did not hand me over to death.

V

19 Open the gates of righteousness;
     I will enter and thank the LORD.*f*
20 This is the LORD's own gate,
     through it the righteous enter.
21 I thank you for you answered me;
     you have been my savior.
22 The stone the builders rejected
     has become the cornerstone.*g*
23 By the LORD has this been done;
     it is wonderful in our eyes.
24 This is the day the LORD has made;
     let us rejoice in it and be glad.
25 LORD, grant salvation!†
     LORD, grant good fortune!

VI

26 Blessed is he
     who comes in the name of the LORD.*h*
     We bless you from the house of the LORD.
27   The LORD is God and has
     enlightened us.
     Join in procession with leafy branches
     up to the horns of the altar.

VII

28 You are my God, I give you thanks;
     my God, I offer you praise.
29 Give thanks to the LORD, for he is good,
     his mercy endures forever.

PSALM 119‡
A Prayer to God, the Lawgiver

ALEPH
1 Blessed those whose way is blameless,
     who walk by the law of the LORD.*i*

---

*[118:22] **The stone the builders rejected**: a proverb: what is insignificant to human beings has become great through divine election. The "stone" may originally have meant the foundation stone or capstone of the Temple. The New Testament interpreted the verse as referring to the death and resurrection of Christ (Mt 21:42; Acts 4:11; cf. Is 28:16 and Rom 9:33; 1 Pt 2:7).

†[118:25] **Grant salvation**: the Hebrew for this cry has come into English as "Hosanna." This cry and the words in Ps 118:26 were used in the gospels to welcome Jesus entering the Temple on Palm Sunday (Mk 11:9–10).

‡[Psalm 119] This Psalm, the longest by far in the Psalter, praises God for giving such splendid laws and instruction for people to live by. The author glorifies and thanks God for the Torah, prays for protection from sinners enraged by others' fidelity to the law, laments the cost of obedience, delights in the law's consolations, begs for wisdom to understand the precepts, and asks for the rewards of keeping them. Several expected elements do not appear in the Psalm: Mount Sinai with its story of God's revelation and gift to Israel of instruction and commandments, the Temple and other institutions related to revelation and laws (frequent in other Psalms). The Psalm is fascinated with God's word directing and guiding human life. The poem is an acrostic; its twenty-two stanzas (of eight verses each) are in the order of the Hebrew alphabet.

f. [118:19] Is 26:2.   g. [118:22] Mt 21:42; Lk 20:17; Acts 4:11; Rom 9:33; 1 Pt 2:7.   h. [118:26] Mt 21:9; 23:39.   i. [119:1] Ps 1:1–2; 15:2; 112:1.

---

2 Blessed those who keep his testimonies,
     who seek him with all their heart.*j*
3 They do no wrong;
     they walk in his ways.
4 You have given them the command
     to observe your precepts with care.
5 May my ways be firm
     in the observance of your statutes!
6 Then I will not be ashamed
     to ponder all your commandments.
7 I will praise you with sincere heart
     as I study your righteous judgments.
8 I will observe your statutes;
     do not leave me all alone.

BETH
9 How can the young keep his way without fault?
     Only by observing your words.
10 With all my heart I seek you;
     do not let me stray from your commandments.
11 In my heart I treasure your promise,
     that I may not sin against you.
12 Blessed are you, O LORD;
     teach me your statutes.*k*
13 With my lips I recite
     all the judgments you have spoken.
14 I find joy in the way of your testimonies
     more than in all riches.
15 I will ponder your precepts
     and consider your paths.
16 In your statutes I take delight;
     I will never forget your word.

GIMEL
17 Be kind to your servant that I may live,
     that I may keep your word.
18 Open my eyes to see clearly
     the wonders of your law.
19 I am a sojourner in the land;§*l*
     do not hide your commandments from me.
20 At all times my soul is stirred
     with longing for your judgments.
21 With a curse you rebuke the proud
     who stray from your commandments.
22 Free me from disgrace and contempt,
     for I keep your testimonies.
23 Though princes meet and talk against me,
     your servant meditates on your statutes.

Each of the eight verses within a stanza begins with the same letter. Each verse contains one word for "instruction." The translation here given attempts to translate each Hebrew word for "instruction" with the same English word. There are, however, nine words for "instruction," not eight, so the principle of a different word for "instruction" in each verse cannot be maintained with perfect consistency. The nine words for "instruction" in the translation are: law, statute, commandment, precept, testimony, word, judgment, way, and promise.

§[119:19] **A sojourner in the land**: like someone without the legal protection of a native inhabitant, the psalmist has a special need for the guidance of God's teaching.

j. [119:2] Dt 4:29.   k. [119:12] Ps 25:4; 27:11; 86:11; 143:8, 10.   l. [119:19] Ps 39:13.

²⁴ Your testimonies are my delight;
   they are my counselors.
                DALETH
²⁵ My soul clings to the dust;ᵐ
   give me life in accord with your
      word.
²⁶ I disclosed my ways and you answered
      me;
   teach me your statutes.
²⁷ Make me understand the way of your
      precepts;
   I will ponder your wondrous deeds.
²⁸ My soul is depressed;
   lift me up acccording to your word.
²⁹ Lead me from the way of deceit;
   favor me with your law.
³⁰ The way of loyalty I have chosen;
   I have kept your judgments.
³¹ I cling to your testimonies, LORD;
   do not let me come to shame.
³² I will run the way of your
      commandments,
   for you will broaden my heart.
                HE
³³ LORD, teach me the way of your statutes;
   I shall keep them with care.ⁿ
³⁴ Give me understanding to keep your law,
   to observe it with all my heart.
³⁵ Lead me in the path of your
      commandments,ᵒ
   for that is my delight.
³⁶ Direct my heart toward your testimonies
   and away from gain.
³⁷ Avert my eyes from what is worthless;
   by your way give me life.
³⁸ For your servant, fulfill your promise
   made to those who fear you.
³⁹ Turn away from me the taunts I dread,
   for your judgments are good.
⁴⁰ See how I long for your precepts;
   in your righteousness give me life.
                WAW
⁴¹ Let your mercy come to me, LORD,
   salvation in accord with your
      promise.
⁴² Let me answer my taunters with a word,
   for I trust in your word.
⁴³ Do not take the word of truth from my
      mouth,
   for in your judgments is my hope.
⁴⁴ I will keep your law always,
   for all time and forever.
⁴⁵ I will walk freely in an open space
   because I cherish your precepts.
⁴⁶ I will speak openly of your testimonies
   without fear even before kings.
⁴⁷ I delight in your commandments,
   which I dearly love.

⁴⁸ *I lift up my hands to your
      commandments;
   I study your statutes, which I love.
                ZAYIN
⁴⁹ Remember your word to your servant
   by which you give me hope.
⁵⁰ This is my comfort in affliction,
   your promise that gives me life.
⁵¹ Though the arrogant utterly scorn me,
   I do not turn from your law.
⁵² When I recite your judgments of old
   I am comforted, LORD.
⁵³ Rage seizes me because of the wicked;
   they forsake your law.
⁵⁴ Your statutes become my songs
   wherever I make my home.
⁵⁵ Even at night I remember your name
   in observance of your law, LORD.
⁵⁶ This is my good fortune,
   for I have kept your precepts.
                HETH
⁵⁷ My portion is the LORD;
   I promise to observe your words.
⁵⁸ I entreat you with all my heart:
   have mercy on me in accord with
      your promise.
⁵⁹ I have examined my ways
   and turned my steps to your
      testimonies.
⁶⁰ I am prompt, I do not hesitate
   in observing your commandments.
⁶¹ Though the snares of the wicked surround
      me,
   your law I do not forget.
⁶² At midnight I rise to praise you
   because of your righteous
      judgments.
⁶³ I am the friend of all who fear you,
   of all who observe your precepts.
⁶⁴ The earth, LORD, is filled with your
      mercy;ᵖ
   teach me your statutes.
                TETH
⁶⁵ You have treated your servant well,
   according to your word, O LORD.
⁶⁶ Teach me wisdom and knowledge,
   for in your commandments I trust.
⁶⁷ Before I was afflicted I went astray,
   but now I hold to your promise.
⁶⁸ You are good and do what is good;
   teach me your statutes.
⁶⁹ The arrogant smear me with lies,
   but I keep your precepts with all my
      heart.
⁷⁰ Their hearts are gross and fat;�q
   as for me, your law is my delight.
⁷¹ It was good for me to be afflicted,
   in order to learn your statutes.

---

*[119:48] **I lift up my hands to your commandments**: to
lift up the hands was an ancient gesture of reverence to God.
Here the picture is applied to God's law.

---

m. [119:25] Ps 44:26.   n. [119:33] Ps 19:12.   o. [119:35] Ps 25:4;
27:11; 86:11; 143:8, 10.

p. [119:64] Ps 33:5.   q. [119:70] Ps 17:10; 73:7; Jb 15:27.

72 The law of your mouth is more precious
to me
than heaps of silver and gold.
YODH
73 Your hands made me and fashioned me;
give me understanding to learn your
commandments.
74 Those who fear you rejoice to see me,
because I hope in your word.
75 I know, LORD, that your judgments are
righteous;
though you afflict me, you are
faithful.
76 May your mercy comfort me
in accord with your promise to your
servant.
77 Show me compassion that I may live,
for your law is my delight.
78 Shame the proud for leading me astray
with falsehood,
that I may study your testimonies.
79 Let those who fear you turn to me,
those who acknowledge your
testimonies.
80 May I be wholehearted toward your
statutes,
that I may not be put to shame.
KAPH
81 My soul longs for your salvation;
I put my hope in your word.ʳ
82 My eyes long to see your promise.ˢ
When will you comfort me?
83 I am like a wineskin shriveled by smoke,ᵗ
but I have not forgotten your
statutes.
84 How long can your servant survive?
When will your judgment doom
my foes?
85 The arrogant have dug pits for me;
defying your law.
86 All your commandments are steadfast.
Help me! I am pursued without
cause.
87 They have almost put an end to me on
earth,
but I do not forsake your precepts.
88 In your mercy give me life,
to observe the testimonies of your
mouth.
LAMEDH
89 *Your word, LORD, stands forever;ᵘ
it is firm as the heavens.
90 Through all generations your truth
endures;
fixed to stand firm like the earth.
91 By your judgments they stand firm to this
day,
for all things are your servants.

92 Had your law not been my delight,
I would have perished in my
affliction.
93 I will never forget your precepts;
through them you give me life.
94 I am yours; save me,
for I cherish your precepts.
95 The wicked hope to destroy me,
but I seek to understand your
testimonies.
96 I have seen the limits of all perfection,
but your commandment is without
bounds.
MEM
97 How I love your law, Lord!†
I study it all day long.
98 Your commandment makes me wiser
than my foes,
as it is forever with me.
99 I have more insight than all my teachers,
because I ponder your testimonies.
100 I have more understanding than my
elders,
because I keep your precepts.ᵛ
101 I keep my steps from every evil path,
that I may observe your word.
102 From your judgments I do not turn,
for you have instructed me.
103 How sweet to my tongue is your promise,
sweeter than honey to my mouth!ʷ
104 Through your precepts I gain
understanding;
therefore I hate all false ways.
NUN
105 Your word is a lamp for my feet,
a light for my path.ˣ
106 I make a solemn vow
to observe your righteous
judgments.
107 I am very much afflicted, LORD;
give me life in accord with your
word.
108 Accept my freely offered praise;ʸ
LORD, teach me your judgments.
109 My life is always at risk,
but I do not forget your law.
110 The wicked have set snares for me,
but from your precepts I do not
stray.
111 Your testimonies are my heritage forever;
they are the joy of my heart.
112 My heart is set on fulfilling your statutes;
they are my reward forever.
SAMEKH
113 I hate every hypocrite;
your law I love.
114 You are my refuge and shield;
in your word I hope.

---

*[119:89–91] God's word creates the world, which manifests that word by its permanence and reliability.

r. [119:81] Ps 130:6.   s. [119:82] Ps 25:15; 123:1–2; 141:8.
t. [119:83] Jb 30:30.   u. [119:89] Is 40:8.

†[119:97] **Lord:** the inclusion of "Lord" follows the tradition of the Septuagint and the Vulgate.

v. [119:100] Jb 32:6; Wis 4:8–9.   w. [119:103] Ps 19:11.   x. [119:105]
Ps 18:29; Prv 6:23.   y. [119:108] Ps 50:14, 23; Heb 13:15.

¹¹⁵ Depart from me, you wicked,ᶻ
    that I may keep the commandments
        of my God.
¹¹⁶ Sustain me by your promise that I may live;
    do not disappoint me in my hope.
¹¹⁷ Strengthen me that I may be safe,
    ever to contemplate your statutes.
¹¹⁸ You reject all who stray from your
        statutes,
    for vain is their deceit.
¹¹⁹ Like dross you regard all the wicked on
        earth;
    therefore I love your testimonies.
¹²⁰ My flesh shudders with dread of you;
    I fear your judgments.

AYIN

¹²¹ I have fulfilled your righteous judgment;
    do not abandon me to my
        oppressors.
¹²² Guarantee your servant's welfare;
    do not let the arrogant oppress me.
¹²³ My eyes long to see your salvation
    and the promise of your
        righteousness.
¹²⁴ Act with mercy toward your servant;
    teach me your statutes.
¹²⁵ I am your servant; give me discernment
    that I may know your testimonies.
¹²⁶ It is time for the LORD to act;
    they have disobeyed your law.
¹²⁷ Truly I love your commandments
    more than gold, more than the finest
        gold.
¹²⁸ Thus, I follow all your precepts;
    every wrong way I hate.

PE

¹²⁹ Wonderful are your testimonies;
    therefore I keep them.
¹³⁰ The revelation of your words sheds light,
    gives understanding to the simple.
¹³¹ I sigh with open mouth,
    yearning for your commandments.
¹³² Turn to me and be gracious,ᵃ
    according to your judgment for
        those who love your name.
¹³³ Steady my feet in accord with your
        promise;
    do not let iniquity lead me.
¹³⁴ Free me from human oppression,
    that I may observe your precepts.
¹³⁵ Let your face shine upon your servant;
    teach me your statutes.
¹³⁶ My eyes shed streams of tears
    because your law is not observed.

SADHE

¹³⁷ You are righteous, LORD,
    and just are your judgments.ᵇ
¹³⁸ You have given your testimonies in
        righteousness
    and in surpassing faithfulness.

¹³⁹ I am consumed with rage,
    because my foes forget your words.
¹⁴⁰ Your servant loves your promise;
    it has been proved by fire.
¹⁴¹ Though belittled and despised,
    I do not forget your precepts.
¹⁴² Your justice is forever right,
    your law true.
¹⁴³ Though distress and anguish come upon
        me,
    your commandments are my
        delight.
¹⁴⁴ Your testimonies are forever righteous;
    give me understanding that I may
        live.

¹⁴⁵ I call with all my heart, O LORD;
    answer me that I may keep your
        statutes.
¹⁴⁶ I call to you to save me
    that I may observe your testimonies.
¹⁴⁷ I rise before dawn and cry out;
    I put my hope in your words.
¹⁴⁸ My eyes greet the night watches
    as I meditate on your promise.ᶜ
¹⁴⁹ Hear my voice in your mercy, O LORD;
    by your judgment give me life.
¹⁵⁰ Malicious persecutors draw near me;
    they are far from your law.
¹⁵¹ You are near, O LORD;
    reliable are all your commandments.
¹⁵² Long have I known from your testimonies
    that you have established them
        forever.

RESH

¹⁵³ Look at my affliction and rescue me,
    for I have not forgotten your law.
¹⁵⁴ Take up my cause and redeem me;ᵈ
    for the sake of your promise give
        me life.
¹⁵⁵ Salvation is far from sinners
    because they do not cherish your
        statutes.
¹⁵⁶ Your compassion is great, O LORD;
    in accord with your judgments, give
        me life.
¹⁵⁷ Though my persecutors and foes are
        many,
    I do not turn from your testimonies.
¹⁵⁸ I view the faithless with loathingᵉ
    because they do not heed your
        promise.
¹⁵⁹ See how I love your precepts, LORD;
    in your mercy give me life.
¹⁶⁰ Your every word is enduring;
    all your righteous judgments are
        forever.

SHIN

¹⁶¹ Princes persecute me without reason,
    but my heart reveres only your
        word.

---

z. [119:115] Ps 6:9; 139:19; Jb 21:14.   a. [119:132] Ps 25:16; 86:16.
b. [119:137] Tb 3:2.

c. [119:148] Ps 63:7; 77:7.   d. [119:154] Ps 43:1.   e. [119:158] Ps
139:22.

¹⁶² I rejoice at your promise,
as one who has found rich spoil.
¹⁶³ Falsehood I hate and abhor;
your law I love.
¹⁶⁴ Seven times a day I praise you
because your judgments are
righteous.
¹⁶⁵ Lovers of your law have much peace;ᶠ
for them there is no stumbling
block.
¹⁶⁶ I look for your salvation, LORD,
and I fulfill your commandments.
¹⁶⁷ I observe your testimonies;
I love them very much.
¹⁶⁸ I observe your precepts and testimonies;
all my ways are before you.

TAW
¹⁶⁹ Let my cry come before you, LORD;ᵍ
in keeping with your word, give me
understanding.
¹⁷⁰ Let my prayer come before you;
rescue me according to your
promise.
¹⁷¹ May my lips pour forth your praise,
because you teach me your statutes.
¹⁷² May my tongue sing of your promise,
for all your commandments are
righteous.
¹⁷³ Keep your hand ready to help me,
for I have chosen your precepts.
¹⁷⁴ I long for your salvation, LORD;
your law is my delight.
¹⁷⁵ Let my soul live to praise you;
may your judgments give me help.
¹⁷⁶ I have wandered like a lost sheep;
seek out your servant,
for I do not forget your
commandments.ʰ

PSALM 120*
Prayer of a Returned Exile

¹A song of ascents.†

The LORD answered me
when I called in my distress:ⁱ

² LORD, deliver my soul from lying lips,
from a treacherous tongue.ʲ

³ What will he inflict on you,
O treacherous tongue,
and what more besides?‡
⁴ A warrior's arrows
sharpened with coals of brush
wood!§ᵏ

⁵ 'Alas, I am a foreigner in Meshech,
I live among the tents of Kedar!
⁶ Too long do I live
among those who hate peace.
⁷ When I speak of peace,
they are for war.ˡ

PSALM 121**
The Lord My Guardian

¹A song of ascents.

I raise my eyes toward the mountains.††
From whence shall come my help?ᵐ
² My help comes from the LORD,
the maker of heaven and earth.ⁿ

³ He will not allow your foot to slip;ᵒ
or your guardian to sleep.
⁴ Behold, the guardian of Israel
never slumbers nor sleeps.
⁵ ‡‡The LORD is your guardian;
the LORD is your shade
at your right hand.ᵖ
⁶ By day the sun will not strike you,
nor the moon by night.�q
⁷ The LORD will guard you from all evil;
he will guard your soul.ʳ

---

‡[120:3] **More besides**: a common curse formula in Hebrew was "May the Lord do such and such evils to you [the evils being specified], and add still more to them," cf. 1 Sm 3:17; 14:44; 25:22. Here the psalmist is at a loss for a suitable malediction.
§[120:4] **Coals of brush wood**: coals made from the stalk of the broom plant burn with intense heat. The psalmist thinks of lighted coals cast at his enemies.
¶[120:5] Meshech was in the far north (Gn 10:2) and Kedar was a tribe of the north Arabian desert (Gn 25:13). The psalmist may be thinking generally of all aliens living among inhospitable peoples.
**[Psalm 121] A blessing given to someone embarking on a dangerous journey whether a soldier going on a campaign or a pilgrim returning home from the Temple. People look anxiously at the wooded hills. Will God protect them on their journey (Ps 121:1)? The speaker declares that God is not confined to a place or a time (Ps 121:2), that every step is guarded (Ps 121:3–4); night and day (Ps 121:5–6) God watches over their every movement (Ps 121:7–8).
††[121:1] **The mountains**: possibly Mount Zion, the site of the Temple and hence of safety, but more probably mountains as a place of dangers, causing anxiety to the psalmist.
‡‡[121:5–6] The image of shade, a symbol of protection, is apt: God as shade protects from the harmful effects that ancients believed were caused by the sun and moon.

---

*[Psalm 120] A thanksgiving, reporting divine rescue (Ps 120:1) yet with fervent prayer for further protection against lying attackers (Ps 120:2–4). The psalmist is acutely conscious of living away from God's own land where divine peace prevails (Ps 120:5–7).
†[120:1] **A song of ascents**: Ps 120–134 all begin with this superscription. Most probably these fifteen Psalms once formed a collection of Psalms sung when pilgrims went to Jerusalem, since one "ascended" to Jerusalem (1 Kgs 12:28; Ps 24:3; 122:4; Lk 2:42) or to the house of God or to an altar (1 Kgs 12:33; 2 Kgs 23:2; Ps 24:3). Less probable is the explanation that these Psalms were sung by the exiles when they "ascended" to Jerusalem from Babylonia (cf. Ezr 7:9). The idea, found in the Mishnah, that the fifteen steps on which the Levites sang corresponded to these fifteen Psalms (Middot 2:5) must underlie the Vulgate translation *canticum graduum*, "song of the steps" or "gradual song."

f. [119:165] Ps 72:7.   g. [119:169] Ps 88:3.   h. [119:176] Is 53:6; Jer 50:6; Lk 15:1–7.   i. [120:1] Jon 2:3.

j. [120:2] Ps 12:3–5; Sir 51:3.   k. [120:4] Ps 11:6; 140:11; Prv 16:27.
l. [120:7] Ps 35:20; 140:3–4.   m. [121:1] Jer 3:23.   n. [121:2] Ps 124:8;
146:6.   o. [121:3] Ps 66:9; 91:12; 1 Sm 2:9; Prv 3:23.   p. [121:5] Ps
16:8; 73:23.   q. [121:6] Wis 18:3; Is 25:4; 49:10.   r. [121:7] Ps 97:10.

⁸ The LORD will guard your coming and
going
both now and forever.ˢ

PSALM 122*
A Pilgrim's Prayer for Jerusalem

¹A song of ascents. Of David.

I

I rejoiced when they said to me,
"Let us go to the house of the
LORD."ᵗ
² And now our feet are standing
within your gates, Jerusalem.
³ Jerusalem, built as a city,
walled round about.†ᵘ
⁴ There the tribes go up,
the tribes of the LORD,
As it was decreed for Israel,
to give thanks to the name of the
LORD.ᵛ
⁵ There are the thrones of justice,
the thrones of the house of David.

II

⁶ For the peace of Jerusalem pray:
"May those who love you prosper!
⁷ May peace be within your ramparts,
prosperity within your towers."ʷ
⁸ For the sake of my brothers and friends I
say,
"Peace be with you."ˣ
⁹ For the sake of the house of the LORD, our
God,
I pray for your good.

PSALM 123‡
Reliance on the Lord

¹A song of ascents.

To you I raise my eyes,
to you enthroned in heaven.ʸ
² Yes, like the eyes of servants
on the hand of their masters,
Like the eyes of a maid
on the hand of her mistress,

So our eyes are on the LORD our God,
till we are shown favor.
³ Show us favor, LORD, show us favor,
for we have our fill of contempt.ᶻ
⁴ Our souls are more than sated
with mockery from the insolent,
with contempt from the
arrogant.

PSALM 124§
God, the Rescuer of the People

¹A song of ascents. Of David.

Had not the LORD been with us,
let Israel say,ᵃ
² Had not the LORD been with us,
when people rose against us,
³ Then they would have swallowed us alive,ᵇ
for their fury blazed against us.
⁴ Then the waters would have engulfed us,
the torrent overwhelmed us;ᶜ
⁵ then seething water would have
drowned us.
⁶ Blessed is the LORD, who did not leave us
to be torn by their teeth.
⁷ We escaped with our lives like a bird
from the fowler's snare;
the snare was broken,
and we escaped.
⁸ 'Our help is in the name of the LORD,
the maker of heaven and earth.ᵈ

PSALM 125**
Israel's Protector

¹A song of ascents.

Those trusting in the LORD are like Mount
Zion,
unshakable, forever enduring.ᵉ
² As mountains surround Jerusalem,
the LORD surrounds his people
both now and forever.ᶠ

---

*[Psalm 122] A song of Zion, sung by pilgrims obeying
the law to visit Jerusalem three times on a journey. The singer
anticipates joining the procession into the city (Ps 122:1–3).
Jerusalem is a place of encounter, where the people praise God
(Ps 122:4) and hear the divine justice mediated by the king
(Ps 122:5). The very buildings bespeak God's power (cf. Ps
48:13–15). May the grace of this place transform the people's
lives (Ps 122:6–9)!

†[122:3] **Walled round about**: lit., "which is joined to it,"
probably referring both to the density of the buildings and to
the dense population.

‡[Psalm 123] A lament that begins as a prayer of an individual (Ps 123:1), who expresses by a touching comparison
exemplary confidence in God (Ps 123:2). The Psalm ends in
prayer that God relieve the people's humiliation at the hands
of the arrogant (Ps 123:3–4).

§[Psalm 124] A thanksgiving which teaches that Israel's
very existence is owed to God who rescues them. In the first
part Israel's enemies are compared to the mythic sea dragon
(Ps 124:2b–3a; cf. Jer 51:34) and Flood (Ps 124:3b–5; cf. Is
51:9–10). The Psalm heightens the malice of human enemies
by linking them to the primordial enemies of God's creation.
Israel is a bird freed from the trapper's snare (Ps 124:6–8)—
freed originally from Pharaoh and now from the current
danger.

¶[124:8] **Our help is in the name**: for the idiom, see Ex
18:4.

**[Psalm 125] In response to exilic anxieties about the
ancient promises of restoration, the Psalm expresses confidence that God will surround the people as the mountains
surround Zion (Ps 125:1–2). The just will not be contami-
nated by the wicked (Ps 125:3). May God judge between the
two groups (Ps 125:4–5).

---

s. [121:8] Dt 28:6. t. [122:1] Ps 43:3–4; 84:2–5. u. [122:3] Ps
48:13–14. v. [122:4] Dt 16:16. w. [122:7] Ps 128:5. x. [122:8] Jn
20:19ff. y. [123:1] Ps 25:15; 119:82; 141:8.

z. [123:3] Ps 44:13–14; Jb 12:4. a. [124:1] Ps 129:1. b. [124:3]
Prv 1:12. c. [124:4] Ps 18:5; 69:2. d. [124:8] Ps 121:2; 146:6.
e. [125:1] Prv 10:25. f. [125:2] Dt 32:11.

³ The scepter of the wicked will not prevail
  in the land allotted to the just,*
Lest the just themselves
  turn their hands to evil.

⁴ Do good, LORD, to the good,
  to those who are upright of heart.*
⁵ But those who turn aside to crooked ways
  may the LORD send down with the
  evildoers.*
Peace upon Israel!*

PSALM 126†
The Reversal of Zion's Fortunes

¹A song of ascents.

I

When the LORD restored the captives of
  Zion,*
  we thought we were dreaming.
² Then our mouths were filled with
  laughter;
  our tongues sang for joy.*
Then it was said among the nations,
  "The LORD had done great things
  for them."
³ The LORD has done great things for us;
  Oh, how happy we were!
⁴ Restore our captives, LORD,
  like the dry stream beds of the Negeb.‡

II

⁵ Those who sow in tears
  will reap with cries of joy.*
⁶ Those who go forth weeping,
  carrying sacks of seed,
Will return with cries of joy,
  carrying their bundled sheaves.

PSALM 127§
The Need of God's Blessing

¹A song of ascents. Of Solomon.

I

Unless the LORD build the house,
  they labor in vain who build.

Unless the LORD guard the city,
  in vain does the guard keep watch.
² It is vain for you to rise early
  and put off your rest at night,
To eat bread earned by hard toil—
  all this God gives to his beloved in
  sleep.*

II

³ Certainly sons are a gift from the LORD,
  the fruit of the womb, a reward.*
⁴ Like arrows in the hand of a warrior
  are the sons born in one's youth.
⁵ Blessed is the man who has filled his
  quiver with them.
He will never be shamed
  for he will destroy his foes at the
  gate.¶

PSALM 128**
The Blessed Home of the Just

¹A song of ascents.

I

Blessed are all who fear the LORD,
  and who walk in his ways.*
² What your hands provide you will enjoy;
  you will be blessed and prosper:*
³ Your wife will be like a fruitful vine
  within your home,
Your children like young olive plants
  around your table.*
⁴ Just so will the man be blessed
  who fears the LORD.

II

⁵ May the LORD bless you from Zion;
  may you see Jerusalem's prosperity
  all the days of your life,*
⁶ and live to see your children's
  children.*
Peace upon Israel!*

PSALM 129††
Against Israel's Enemies

¹A song of ascents.

---

*[125:3] **The land allotted to the just**: lit., "the lot of the righteous." The promised land was divided among the tribes of Israel by lot (Nm 26:55; Jos 18). The righteous are the members of the people who are obedient to God. If the domination of the wicked were to continue in the land, even the just would be infected by their evil attitudes.

†[Psalm 126] A lament probably sung shortly after Israel's return from exile. The people rejoice that they are in Zion (Ps 126:1–3) but mere presence in the holy city is not enough; they must pray for the prosperity and the fertility of the land (Ps 126:4). The last verses are probably an oracle of promise: the painful work of sowing will be crowned with life (Ps 126:5–6).

‡[126:4] **Like the dry stream beds of the Negeb**: the psalmist prays for rain in such abundance that the dry riverbeds will run.

§[Psalm 127] The Psalm puts together two proverbs (Ps 127:1–2, 3–5) on God establishing "houses" or families. The prosperity of human groups is not the work of human beings but the gift of God.

¶[127:5] **At the gate**: the reference is not to enemies besieging the walls of a city but to adversaries in litigation. Law courts functioned in the open area near the main city gate. The more adult sons a man had, the more forceful he would appear in disputes, cf. Prv 31:23.

**[Psalm 128] A statement that the ever-reliable God will bless the reverent (Ps 128:1). God's blessing is concrete: satisfaction and prosperity, a fertile spouse and abundant children (Ps 128:2–4). The perspective is that of the adult male, ordinarily the ruler and representative of the household to the community. The last verses extend the blessing to all the people for generations to come (Ps 128:5–6).

††[Psalm 129] A Psalm giving thanks for God's many rescues of Israel over the long course of their history (Ps 129:1–4); the people pray that their oppressors never know the joy of harvest (Ps 129:5–8).

---

g. [125:4] Ps 18:25ff.   h. [125:5] Prv 3:32.   i. [125:5] Ps 128:6.
j. [126:1] Ps 14:7.   k. [126:2] Jb 8:21.   l. [126:5] Bar 4:23; Is 65:19.

m. [127:2] Eccl 2:24.   n. [127:3] Ps 115:14; 128:3; Dt 28:11; Prv 17:6.   o. [128:1] Ps 112:1.   p. [128:2] Ps 112:3.   q. [128:3] Ps 144:12; Jb 29:5.   r. [128:5] Ps 20:3; 134:3.   s. [128:6] Jb 42:16; Prv 17:6.   t. [128:6] Ps 125:5.

I

Viciously have they attacked me from my
youth,
let Israel say now.*

2 Viciously have they attacked me from my
youth,*
yet they have not prevailed against
me.

3 Upon my back the plowers plowed,
as they traced their long furrows.*

4 But the just LORD cut me free
from the ropes of the wicked.*

II

5 May they recoil in disgrace,
all who hate Zion.

6 May they be like grass on the rooftops†
withered in early growth,*

7 Never to fill the reaper's hands,
nor the arms of the binders of sheaves,

8 And with none passing by to call out:
"The blessing of the LORD be upon
you!‡
We bless you in the name of the
LORD!"*

PSALM 130§
Prayer for Pardon and Mercy

¹A song of ascents.

I

Out of the depths¶ I call to you, LORD;
2 Lord, hear my cry!
May your ears be attentive
to my cry for mercy.*

3 If you, LORD, keep account of sins,
Lord, who can stand?*

4 But with you is forgiveness
and so you are revered.**

II

5 I wait for the LORD,
my soul waits
and I hope for his word.*

6 My soul looks for the Lord
more than sentinels for daybreak.*
More than sentinels for daybreak,
7 let Israel hope in the LORD,
For with the LORD is mercy,
with him is plenteous redemption,*

8 And he will redeem Israel
from all its sins.*

PSALM 131††
Humble Trust in God

¹A song of ascents. Of David.

LORD, my heart is not proud;
nor are my eyes haughty.
I do not busy myself with great matters,
with things too sublime for me.*

2 Rather, I have stilled my soul,
Like a weaned child to its mother,
weaned is my soul.*

3 Israel, hope in the LORD,
now and forever.

PSALM 132‡‡
The Covenant Between David and God

¹A song of ascents.

I

Remember, O LORD, for David
all his hardships;

2 How he swore an oath to the LORD,
vowed to the Mighty One of Jacob:§§

3 "I will not enter the house where I live,*
nor lie on the couch where I sleep;

4 I will give my eyes no sleep,
my eyelids no rest,

5 Till I find a place for the LORD,
a dwelling for the Mighty One of
Jacob."

6 "We have heard of it in Ephrathah;¶¶
we have found it in the fields of
Jaar.¶¶

---

*[129:4] **The ropes of the wicked**: usually understood as
the rope for yoking animals to the plow. If it is severed, the
plowing (cf. Ps 129:3) comes to a halt.

†[129:6] **Like grass on the rooftops**: after the spring rains,
grass would sprout from the coat of mud with which the flat
roofs of simple houses were covered, but when the dry summer began there was no moisture in the thin roof-covering to
sustain the grass.

‡[129:8] **The blessing of the LORD be upon you**: harvesters greeted one another with such blessings, cf. Ru 2:4.

§[Psalm 130] This lament, a Penitential Psalm, is the *De
profundis* used in liturgical prayers for the faithful departed.
In deep sorrow the psalmist cries to God (Ps 130:1–2), asking for mercy (Ps 130:3–4). The psalmist's trust (Ps 130:5–6)
becomes a model for the people (Ps 130:7–8).

¶[130:1] **The depths**: Sheol here is a metaphor of total
misery. Deep anguish makes the psalmist feel "like those
descending to the pit" (Ps 143:7).

[130:4] **And so you are revered: the experience of God's
mercy leads one to a greater sense of God.

††[Psalm 131] A song of trust, in which the psalmist gives
up self-sufficiency (Ps 131:1), like a babe enjoying the comfort of its mother's lap (Ps 131:2), thus providing a model for
Israel's faith (Ps 131:3).

‡‡[Psalm 132] A song for a liturgical ceremony in which the
ark, the throne of Israel's God, was carried in procession to the
Temple. The singer asks that David's care for the proper hous-
ing of the ark be regarded with favor (Ps 132:1–5), and tells
how it was brought to Jerusalem (Ps 132:6–10). There follows
God's promise of favor to the Davidic dynasty (Ps 132:11–12)
and to Zion (Ps 132:13–17). The transfer of the ark to the tent
in Jerusalem is described in 2 Sm 6.

§§[132:2, 132:5] **Mighty One of Jacob**: one of the titles of
Israel's God, cf. Gn 49:24; Is 49:26; 60:16.

¶¶[132:6] **Ephrathah**: the homeland of David, cf. Ru 4:11.
The fields of Jaar: poetic for Kiriath-jearim, a town west of
Jerusalem, where the ark remained for several generations, cf.
1 Sm 7:1–2; 2 Sm 6:2; 1 Chr 13:5–6.

---

u. [129:1] Ps 124:1.   v. [129:2] Ps 118:13.   w. [129:3] Is 51:23.
x. [129:6] Is 37:27.   y. [129:8] Ps 118:26.   z. [130:2] Ps 5:2–3;
55:2–3; 86:6; Lam 3:55–56; Jon 2:3.   a. [130:3] Na 1:6.   b. [130:5]
Ps 119:81.

c. [130:6] Is 21:11; 26:9.   d. [130:7] Ps 86:15; 100:5; 103:8.
e. [130:8] Ps 25:22; Mt 1:21.   f. [131:1] Ps 139:6.   g. [131:2] Is
66:12–13.   h. [132:3] 2 Sm 7; 1 Chr 28:2.

7 Let us enter his dwelling;
   let us worship at his footstool."*

8 "Arise, LORD, come to your resting place,*
   you and your mighty ark.

9 Your priests will be clothed with justice;
   your devout will shout for joy."

10 For the sake of David your servant,
   do not reject your anointed.

II

11 The LORD swore an oath to David in
   truth,
   he will never turn back from it:*
   "Your own offspring* I will set upon your
   throne.

12 If your sons observe my covenant,
   and my decrees I shall teach them,
   Their sons, in turn,
   shall sit forever on your throne."

13 Yes, the LORD has chosen Zion,
   desired it for a dwelling:

14 "This is my resting place forever;
   here I will dwell, for I desire it.

15 I will bless Zion with provisions;
   its poor I will fill with bread.

16 I will clothe its priests with salvation;
   its devout shall shout for joy.*

17 There I will make a horn sprout for
   David;*"
   I will set a lamp for my anointed.

18 His foes I will clothe with shame,
   but on him his crown shall shine."

PSALM 133†
A Vision of a Blessed Community

¹A song of ascents. Of David.

How good and how pleasant it is,
   when brothers‡ dwell together as one!

2 Like fine oil on the head,§*
   running down upon the beard,

Upon the beard of Aaron,
   upon the collar of his robe.

3 Like dew* of Hermon* coming down
   upon the mountains of Zion.*
   There the LORD has decreed a blessing,
   life for evermore!*

PSALM 134**
Exhortation to the Night Watch to Bless God

¹A song of ascents.

O come, bless the LORD,
   all you servants of the LORD††
You who stand in the house of the LORD
   throughout the nights.*

2 Lift up your hands toward the sanctuary,*
   and bless the LORD.

3 May the LORD bless you from Zion,
   the Maker of heaven and earth.*

PSALM 135‡‡
Praise of God, the Ruler
and Benefactor of Israel

¹Hallelujah!

I

Praise the name of the LORD!
   Praise, you servants of the LORD,*

2 Who stand in the house of the LORD,
   in the courts of the house of our
   God!*

3 Praise the LORD, for the LORD is good!
   Sing to his name, for it brings joy!

4 §§For the LORD has chosen Jacob for
   himself,
   Israel as his treasured possession.*

II

5 For I know that the LORD is great,
   that our Lord is greater than all
   gods.*

---

*[132:17] **A horn sprout for David**: the image of the horn, a symbol of strength, is combined with that of a "sprout," a term used for the Davidic descendant (cf. Jer 23:5; 33:15; Zec 3:8; 6:12). Early Christians referred the latter designation to Christ as son of David (Lk 1:69).

†[Psalm 133] A benediction over a peaceful community, most probably the people Israel, but appropriate too for Israelite families (Ps 133:1). The history of Israel, whether of its ancestors in the Book of Genesis or of later periods, was a history of distinct groups struggling to live in unity. Here that unity is declared blessed, like the holy oils upon the priest Aaron or the dew of the rainless summer that waters the crops (Ps 133:2–3).

‡[133:1] **Brothers**: in biblical Hebrew this word includes both the male and female members of a group united by blood relationships or by shared experiences and values. In this Psalm, the term could be applied most appropriately to the people of Israel, those privileged by God to be his chosen children.

§[133:2] **Oil on the head**: oil was used at the consecration of the high priest (Ex 30:22–33).

¶[133:3] **Dew**: dew was an important source of moisture in the dry climate (Gn 27:28; Hos 14:6). **Hermon**: the majestic snow-capped mountain visible in the north of Palestine.

**[Psalm 134] A brief liturgy exhorting all those who serve in the Jerusalem Temple during the night (cf. Is 30:29) to praise God with words and gestures. Although he is the Creator of the whole universe, God's blessings emanate in a unique way from Zion, the city of Jerusalem.

††[134:1] **Servants of the LORD**: priests and Levites, cf. Dt 10:8; Ps 113:1; 135:1; Dn 3:85.

‡‡[Psalm 135] The hymn begins and ends with an invitation to praise God (Ps 135:1–3, 19–20) for the great act of choosing Israel (Ps 135:4). The story of Israel's emergence as a people is told in Ps 135:5–14; God created and redeemed the people, easily conquering all opposition. God's defeat of hostile powers means that the powers themselves and their images are useless (Ps 135:15–18). The last three verses appear also in Ps 115:4–8.

§§[135:4] Though all nations are God's, Israel has a special status as God's "treasured" people: Ex 19:5; Dt 7:6; 14:2; 26:18; Mal 3:17.

---

i. [132:7] Ps 99:5.   j. [132:8–10] Ps 2:2; 89:21; 95:11; Nm 10:35; 2 Chr 6:41–42; Sir 24:7.   k. [132:11–14] Ps 68:17; 1 Kgs 8:13; Sir 24:7.   l. [132:11] Ps 110:4; 2 Sm 7:12.   m. [132:16] 2 Chr 6:41; Is 61:10.   n. [132:17] Is 11:1; Jer 33:15; Ez 29:21; Zec 3:8; Lk 1:69.   o. [133:2] Ex 30:25, 30.

p. [133:3] Hos 14:6.   q. [133:3] Dt 28:8; 30:20.   r. [134:1] Ps 135:1–2; 1 Chr 9:33.   s. [135:2] Ps 28:2; 141:2.   t. [134:3] Ps 20:3; 128:5; Nm 6:24.   u. [135:1] Ps 113:1.   v. [135:2] Ps 134:1.   w. [135:4] Ps 33:12; 144:15; Ex 19:6; Dt 7:6.   x. [135:5] Ps 95:3; Ex 18:11.

6 Whatever the LORD desires
    he does in heaven and on earth,
    in the seas and all the depths.*y*
7 It is he who raises storm clouds from the
        end of the earth,
    makes lightning for the rain,
    and brings forth wind from his
        storehouse.*z*

III

8 He struck down Egypt's firstborn,*a*
    of human being and beast alike,
9 And sent signs and wonders against you,
        Egypt,
    against Pharaoh and all his servants.
10 It is he who struck down many nations,*b*
    and slew mighty kings—
11 Sihon, king of the Amorites,
    and Og, king of Bashan,
    all the kings of Canaan—
12 And made their land a heritage,
    a heritage for Israel his people.
13 O LORD, your name is forever,
    your renown, from generation to
        generation!*c*
14 For the LORD defends his people,
    shows mercy to his servants.*d*

IV

15 The idols of the nations are silver and
        gold,*e*
    the work of human hands.
16 They have mouths but do not speak;
    they have eyes but do not see;
17 They have ears but do not hear;
    nor is there breath in their mouths.
18 Their makers will become like them,
    and anyone who trusts in them.

V

19 House of Israel, bless the LORD!*f*
    House of Aaron, bless the LORD!
20 House of Levi, bless the LORD!
    You who fear the LORD, bless the
        LORD!
21 Blessed be the LORD from Zion,
    who dwells in Jerusalem!
    Hallelujah!

PSALM 136*
Hymn of Thanksgiving for
God's Everlasting Mercy

I

1 Praise the LORD, for he is good;*g*
    for his mercy endures forever;

2 Praise the God of gods;
    for his mercy endures forever;
3 Praise the Lord of lords;
    for his mercy endures forever;

II

4 Who alone has done great wonders,*h*
    for his mercy endures forever;
5 Who skillfully made the heavens,*i*
    for his mercy endures forever;
6 Who spread the earth upon the waters,*j*
    for his mercy endures forever;
7 Who made the great lights,
    for his mercy endures forever;
8 The sun to rule the day,
    for his mercy endures forever;
9 The moon and stars to rule the night,*k*
    for his mercy endures forever;

III

10 Who struck down the firstborn of Egypt,*l*
    for his mercy endures forever;
11 And led Israel from their midst,
    for his mercy endures forever;
12 With mighty hand and outstretched arm,*m*
    for his mercy endures forever;
13 Who split in two the Red Sea,
    for his mercy endures forever;
14 And led Israel through its midst,
    for his mercy endures forever;
15 But swept Pharaoh and his army into the
        Red Sea,*n*
    for his mercy endures forever;
16 Who led the people through the desert,*o*
    for his mercy endures forever;

IV

17 Who struck down great kings,*p*
    for his mercy endures forever;
18 Slew powerful kings,
    for his mercy endures forever;
19 Sihon, king of the Amorites,
    for his mercy endures forever;
20 Og, king of Bashan,
    for his mercy endures forever;
21 And made their lands a heritage,
    for his mercy endures forever;
22 †A heritage for Israel, his servant,
    for his mercy endures forever.

V

23 The Lord remembered us in our low
        estate,
    for his mercy endures forever;
24 Freed us from our foes,
    for his mercy endures forever;

---

*[Psalm 136] The hymn praises Israel's God ("the God of gods," Ps 136:2), who has created the world in which Israel lives. The refrain occurring after every line suggests that a speaker and chorus sang the Psalm in antiphonal fashion. A single act of God is described in Ps 136:4–25. God arranges

the heavens and the earth as the environment for human community, and then creates the community by freeing them and giving them land. In the final section (Ps 136:23–25) God, who created the people and gave them land, continues to protect and nurture them.

†[136:22] **A heritage for Israel:** the land was given to Israel by God to be handed on to future generations.

---

y. [135:6] Ps 115:3.   z. [135:7] Ps 148:8; Jer 10:13; 51:16; Jb 37:9.   a. [135:8–9] Ps 78:51; 105:27, 36; 136:10; Ex 12:29.   b. [135:10–12] Ps 136:17–22; Nm 21:21–35; Dt 2:24–3:17.   c. [135:13] Ps 102:13; Ex 3:15.   d. [135:14] Dt 32:36.   e. [135:15–18] Ps 115:4–6, 8.   f. [135:19–20] Ps 118:2–4.   g. [136:1] Ps 100:5; 118:1.

h. [136:4] Ps 72:18.   i. [136:5] Gn 1:9–19.   j. [136:6] Ps 24:2.   k. [136:9] Jer 31:35.   l. [136:10] Ex 12:29, 51; 14:22, 27; 15:22; Ps 78:51–52; 135:8.   m. [136:12] Dt 4:34.   n. [136:15] Ex 14:21f.   o. [136:16] Dt 8:2, 15.   p. [136:17–22] Ps 135:10–12.

²⁵ And gives bread to all flesh,
    for his mercy endures forever.
VI
²⁶ Praise the God of heaven,
    for his mercy endures forever.

PSALM 137*
Sorrow and Hope in Exile

I
¹ By the rivers of Babylon
    there we sat weeping
    when we remembered Zion.^q
² On the poplars in its midst
    we hung up our harps.^r
³ For there our captors asked us
    for the words of a song;
Our tormentors, for joy:
    "Sing for us a song of Zion!"
⁴ But how could we sing a song of the LORD
    in a foreign land?
II
⁵ If I forget you, Jerusalem,
    may my right hand forget.^s
⁶ May my tongue stick to my palate
    if I do not remember you,
If I do not exalt Jerusalem
    beyond all my delights.
III
⁷ Remember, LORD, against Edom
    that day at Jerusalem.
They said: "Level it, level it
    down to its foundations!"^t
⁸ Desolate Daughter Babylon, you shall be
    destroyed,
    blessed the one who pays you back
    what you have done us!^u
⁹ †Blessed the one who seizes your children
    and smashes them against the rock.^v

PSALM 138‡
Hymn of a Grateful Heart

¹Of David.

---

*[Psalm 137] A singer refuses to sing the people's sacred songs in an alien land despite demands from Babylonian captors (Ps 137:1–4). The singer swears an oath by what is most dear to a musician—hands and tongue—to exalt Jerusalem always (Ps 137:5–6). The Psalm ends with a prayer that the old enemies of Jerusalem, Edom and Babylon, be destroyed (Ps 137:7–9).

†[137:9] **Blessed the one who seizes your children and smashes them against the rock:** the children represent the future generations, and so must be destroyed if the enemy is truly to be eradicated.

‡[Psalm 138] A thanksgiving to God, who came to the rescue of the psalmist. Divine rescue was not the result of the psalmist's virtues but of God's loving fidelity (Ps 138:1–3). The act is not a private transaction but a public act that stirs the surrounding nations to praise God's greatness and care for the people (Ps 138:4–6). The psalmist, having experienced salvation, trusts that God will always be there in moments of danger (Ps 138:7–8).

q. [137:1] Ez 3:15; Lam 3:48.   r. [137:2] Is 24:8; Lam 5:14.
s. [137:5] Jer 51:50.   t. [137:7] Jer 49:7; Lam 4:21–22; Ez 25:12–14.
u. [137:8] Is 47:1–3; Jer 50–51.   v. [137:9] Hos 14:1.

I
I thank you, Lord, with all my heart;^w
    in the presence of the angels[§] to you
    I sing.
² I bow low toward your holy temple;
    I praise your name for your mercy
    and faithfulness.
For you have exalted over all
    your name and your promise.
³ On the day I cried out, you answered;
    you strengthened my spirit.
II
⁴ All the kings of earth will praise you,
    LORD,
    when they hear the words of your
    mouth.
⁵ They will sing of the ways of the LORD:
    "How great is the glory of the
    LORD!"
⁶ The LORD is on high, but cares for the
    lowly^x
    and knows the proud from afar.
⁷ Though I walk in the midst of dangers,
    you guard my life when my enemies
    rage.
You stretch out your hand;
    your right hand saves me.
⁸ The LORD is with me to the end.
    LORD, your mercy endures forever.
    Never forsake the work of your
    hands!

PSALM 139¶
The All-knowing and Ever-present God

¹For the leader. A psalm of David.
I
    LORD, you have probed me, you know me:
²   you know when I sit and stand;**^y
    you understand my thoughts from
    afar.
³ You sift through my travels and my rest;
    with all my ways you are familiar.
⁴ Even before a word is on my tongue,
    LORD, you know it all.
⁵ Behind and before you encircle me
    and rest your hand upon me.
⁶ Such knowledge is too wonderful for me,
    far too lofty for me to reach.^z

---

§[138:1] **In the presence of the angels:** heavenly beings who were completely subordinate to Israel's God. The earthly Temple represents the heavenly palace of God.

¶[Psalm 139] A hymnic meditation on God's omnipresence and omniscience. The psalmist is keenly aware of God's all-knowing gaze (Ps 139:1–6), of God's presence in every part of the universe (Ps 139:7–12), and of God's control over the psalmist's very self (Ps 139:13–16). Summing up Ps 139:1–16, 17–18 express wonder. There is only one place hostile to God's rule—wicked people. The psalmist prays to be removed from their company (Ps 139:19–24).

[139:2] **When I sit and stand: in all my physical movement.

w. [138:1] Ps 9:1.   x. [138:6] Lk 1:51–52.   y. [139:2] 2 Kgs 19:27; Jb 12:3.   z. [139:6] Ps 131:1.

7 Where can I go from your spirit?
  From your presence, where can I
     flee?
8 If I ascend to the heavens, you are there;
  if I lie down in Sheol, there you are.ᵃ
9 If I take the wings of dawn*
  and dwell beyond the sea,*
10 Even there your hand guides me,
  your right hand holds me fast.
11 If I say, "Surely darkness shall hide me,
  and night shall be my light"†—
12 Darkness is not dark for you,
  and night shines as the day.
  Darkness and light are but one.ᵇ

II

13 You formed my inmost being;
  you knit me in my mother's womb.ᶜ
14 I praise you, because I am wonderfully
     made;
  wonderful are your works!
  My very self you know.
15 My bones are not hidden from you,
  When I was being made in secret,
  fashioned in the depths of the earth.‡
16 Your eyes saw me unformed;
  in your book all are written down;ᵈ
  my days were shaped, before one
     came to be.

III

17 How precious to me are your designs,
     O God;
  how vast the sum of them!
18 Were I to count them, they would
     outnumber the sands;
  when I complete them, still you are
     with me.ᵉ
19 When you would destroy the wicked,
     O God,
  the bloodthirsty depart from me!ᶠ
20 Your foes who conspire a plot against
     you
  are exalted in vain.

IV

21 Do I not hate, LORD, those who hate you?
  Those who rise against you, do I not
     loathe?ᵍ
22 With fierce hatred I hate them,
  enemies I count as my own.

23 Probe me, God, know my heart;
  try me, know my thoughts.ʰ

*[139:9] Take the wings of dawn: go to the extremities of the east. Beyond the sea: uttermost bounds of the west; the sea is the Mediterranean.
†[139:11] Night shall be my light: night to me is what day is to others.
‡[139:15] The depths of the earth: figurative language for the womb, stressing the hidden and mysterious operations that occur there.

a. [139:8] Jb 23:8–9; Jer 23:23–24.   b. [139:12] Jb 12:22.   c. [139:13] Wis 7:1; Eccl 11:5; Jb 1:21.   d. [139:16] Mal 3:16.   e. [139:18] Jb 11:7.   f. [139:19] Jb 21:14.   g. [139:21] Ps 119:158.   h. [139:23] Ps 17:3; 26:2.

24 See if there is a wicked path in me;
  lead me along an ancient path.§

PSALM 140§
Prayer for Deliverance from the Wicked

¹For the leader. A psalm of David.

I

2 Deliver me, LORD, from the wicked;
  preserve me from the violent,ⁱ
3 From those who plan evil in their hearts,
  who stir up conflicts every day,
4 **Who sharpen their tongue like a serpent,
  venom of asps upon their lips.ʲ
                                   Selah

II

5 Keep me, LORD, from the clutches of the
     wicked;
  preserve me from the violent,
  who plot to trip me up.ᵏ
6 ††The arrogant have set a trap for me;
  they have spread out ropes for a net,
  laid snares for me by the wayside.
                                   Selah
7 I say to the LORD: You are my God;ˡ
  listen, LORD, to the words of my pleas.
8 LORD, my master, my strong deliverer,
  you cover my head on the day of
     armed conflict.
9 LORD, do not grant the desires of the
     wicked one;
  do not let his plot succeed.
                                   Selah

III

10 Those who surround me raise their heads;
  may the mischief they threaten
     overwhelm them
11 Drop burning coals upon them;ᵐ
  cast them into the watery pit never
     more to rise.

12 Slanderers will not survive on earth;
  evil will hunt down the man of
     violence to overthrow him.
13 For I know the LORD will take up the
     cause of the needy,
  justice for the poor.

§[139:24] Lead me along an ancient path: the manner of living of our ancestors, who were faithful to God's will, cf. Jer 6:16.
¶[Psalm 140] A lament seeking rescue from violent and treacherous foes (Ps 140:2–6). The psalmist remains trusting (Ps 140:7–8), vigorously praying that the plans of the wicked recoil upon themselves (Ps 140:9–12). A serene statement of praise ends the Psalm (Ps 140:13). The psalmist is content to be known as one of "the needy," "the poor," "the just," "the upright" (Ps 140:13), a class of people expecting divine protection.
**[140:4] Similar metaphors for a wicked tongue are used in Ps 52:2; 55:20; 58:3.
††[140:6] Have set a trap . . . have spread out ropes for a net: the same figure, of hunters setting traps, occurs in Ps 9:16; 31:5; 35:7; 64:6, cf. Mt 22:15; Lk 11:54.

i. [140:2] Ps 71:4.   j. [140:4] Ps 64:4; Rom 3:13.   k. [140:5] Jer 18:22; Ps 56:7; 57:7.   l. [140:7] Ps 31:15.   m. [140:11] Ps 11:6; 120:4; Gn 19:24.

¹⁴ Then the righteous will give thanks to
your name;
the upright will dwell in your
presence.ⁿ

PSALM 141*
Prayer for Deliverance from the Wicked

¹A psalm of David.

LORD, I call to you; hasten to me;
listen to my plea when I call.
² Let my prayer be incense† before you;
my uplifted hands† an evening
offering.ᵒ
³ Set a guard, LORD, before my mouth,
keep watch over the door of my
lips.ᵖ
⁴ Do not let my heart incline to evil,
to perform deeds in
wickedness.
On the delicacies of evildoers
let me not feast.
⁵ ‡Let a righteous person strike me; it is
mercy if he reproves me.
Do not withhold oil from my
head�q
while my prayer opposes their evil
deeds.
⁶ May their leaders be cast over the cliff,
so that they hear that my speeches
are pleasing.
⁷ Like the plowing and breaking up of the
earth,
our bones are strewn at the mouth
of Sheol.
⁸ For my eyes are upon you, O LORD, my
Lord;ʳ
in you I take refuge; do not take
away my soul.
⁹ Guard me from the trap they have set for
me,
from the snares of evildoers.ˢ
¹⁰ Let the wicked fall into their own nets,
while only I pass over them
safely.

---

*[Psalm 141] A lament of an individual (Ps 141:1–2) who
is keenly aware that only the righteous can worship God properly and who therefore prays to be protected from the doomed
wicked (Ps 141:3–10).
†[141:2] Incense: lit., "smoke," i.e., the fragrant fumes arising from the altar at the burning of sacrificial animals or of
aromatic spices; also used in Rev 5:8 as a symbol of prayer. My
uplifted hands: the gesture of supplication, cf. Ps 28:2; 63:5;
88:10; 119:48; 134:2; 143:6.
‡[141:5–7] The Hebrew text is obscure.

n. [140:14] Ps 11:7; 16:11; 17:15. o. [141:2] Ps 134:2; Ex
30:8. p. [141:3] Sir 22:27. q. [141:5] Prv 9:8; 25:12. r. [141:8]
Ps 25:15; 123:1–2. s. [141:9] Ps 142:4.

PSALM 142§
A Prayer in Time of Trouble

¹A maskil of David, when he was in the cave.ᵀ
A prayer.

² With my own voice I cry to the LORD;
with my own voice I beseech the LORD.
³ Before him I pour out my complaint,
tell of my distress in front of him.
⁴ When my spirit is faint within me,ᵗ
you know my path.ᵘ
As I go along this path,
they have hidden a trap for me.ᵛ
⁵ I look to my right hand to seeʷ
that there is no one willing to
acknowledge me.
My escape has perished;
no one cares for me.
⁶ I cry out to you, LORD,
I say, You are my refuge,ˣ
my portion in the land of the living.ʸ
⁷ Listen to my cry for help,
for I am brought very low.ᶻ
Rescue me from my pursuers,
for they are too strong for me.
⁸ Lead my soul from prison,
that I may give thanks to your name.
Then the righteous shall gather around me**
because you have been good to me.

PSALM 143††
A Prayer in Distress

¹A psalm of David.

LORD, hear my prayer;
in your faithfulness listen to my
pleading;
answer me in your righteousness.
² Do not enter into judgment with your
servant;
before you no one can be just.ᵃ
³ The enemy has pursued my soul;

---

§[Psalm 142] In this lament imploring God for help (Ps
142:2–4), the psalmist tells how enemies have set a trap (Ps
142:4–5), and prays for rescue (Ps 142:6–8). The speaker feels
utterly alone (Ps 142:5), exhausted (Ps 142:7), and may even
be imprisoned (Ps 142:7). Prison is possibly a metaphor for
general distress. The last two verses are the vow of praise,
made after receiving an assurance of divine help (Ps 142:7).
¶[142:1] In the cave: cf. 1 Sm 22:1; 24:1–3; Ps 57:1.
**[142:8] Then the righteous shall gather around me: in
the Temple, when the psalmist offers a thanksgiving sacrifice.
††[Psalm 143] One of the Church's seven Penitential Psalms,
this lament is a prayer to be freed from death-dealing enemies.
The psalmist addresses God, aware that there is no equality
between God and human beings; salvation is a gift (Ps 143:1–
2). Victimized by evil people (Ps 143:3–4), the psalmist recites
("remembers") God's past actions on behalf of the innocent (Ps
143:5–6). The Psalm continues with fervent prayer (Ps 143:7–9)
and a strong desire for guidance and protection (Ps 143:10–12).

t. [142:4] Ps 143:4. u. [142:4] Ps 139:24. v. [142:4] Ps 141:9.
w. [142:5] Ps 16:8; 73:23; 121:5. x. [142:6] Ps 91:2, 9. y. [142:6]
Ps 16:5; 27:13; 116:9; Is 38:11. z. [142:7] Ps 79:8. a. [143:2] Eccl
7:20; Jb 4:17; Rom 3:20.

he has crushed my life to the ground.[b]
He has made me dwell in darkness
    like those long dead.[c]
4 My spirit is faint within me;
    my heart despairs.[d]
5 I remember the days of old;
    I ponder all your deeds;
    the works of your hands I recall.[e]
6 I stretch out my hands toward you,
    my soul to you like a parched land.[f]
                              Selah
7 Hasten to answer me, LORD;
    for my spirit fails me.
Do not hide your face from me,
    lest I become like those descending
      to the pit.[g]
8 In the morning let me hear of your mercy,
    for in you I trust.
Show me the path I should walk,
    for I entrust my life to you.[h]
9 Rescue me, LORD, from my foes,
    for I seek refuge in you.
10 Teach me to do your will,
    for you are my God.
May your kind spirit guide me
    on ground that is level.
11 For your name's sake, LORD, give me life;
    in your righteousness lead my soul
      out of distress.
12 In your mercy put an end to my foes;
    all those who are oppressing my soul,
    for I am your servant.[i]

PSALM 144[*]
A Prayer for Victory and Prosperity

1 Of David.

I

†Blessed be the LORD, my rock,
    who trains my hands for battle,
    my fingers for war;
2 My safeguard and my fortress,
    my stronghold, my deliverer,
My shield, in whom I take refuge,
    who subdues peoples under me.

II

3 ‡LORD, what is man that you take notice of
    him;
    the son of man, that you think of him?[j]
4 §Man is but a breath,
    his days are like a passing shadow.[k]
5 ¶LORD, incline your heavens and come down;
    touch the mountains and make
      them smoke.[l]
6 Flash forth lightning and scatter my foes;
    shoot your arrows and rout them.
7 Reach out your hand from on high;
    deliver me from the many waters;
    rescue me from the hands of foreign
      foes.
8 Their mouths speak untruth;
    their right hands are raised in lying
      oaths.**
9 O God, a new song I will sing to you;
    on a ten-stringed lyre I will play for
      you.[m]
10 You give victory to kings;
    you delivered David your servant.[n]
From the menacing sword 11deliver me;
    rescue me from the hands of foreign
      foes.
Their mouths speak untruth;
    their right hands are raised in lying
      oaths.

III

12 May our sons be like plants[o]
    well nurtured from their youth,
Our daughters, like carved columns,
    shapely as those of the temple.
13 May our barns be full
    with every kind of store.
May our sheep increase by thousands,
    by tens of thousands in our fields;
    may our oxen be well fattened.
14 May there be no breach in the walls,
    no exile, no outcry in our streets.[p]
15 Blessed the people so fortunate;
    blessed the people whose God is the
      LORD.[q]

PSALM 145[††]
The Greatness and Goodness of God

1 Praise. Of David.

---

*[Psalm 144] The Psalm may reflect a ceremony in which the king, as leader of the army, asked God's help (Ps 144:1–8). In Ps 144:9 the poem shifts abruptly from pleading to thanksgiving, and (except for Ps 144:11) shifts again to prayer for the people. The first section (Ps 144:1–2) is a prayer of thanks for victory; the second (Ps 144:3–7a), a humble acknowledgment of human nothingness and a supplication that God show forth saving power; the third (Ps 144:9–11), a promise of future thanksgiving; the fourth (Ps 144:12–15), a wish for prosperity and peace. A prayer for deliverance from treacherous foes serves as a refrain after the second and third sections (Ps 144:7b–8, 11). Except for its final section, the Psalm is made up almost entirely of verses from other Psalms.
†[144:1–2] Composed of phrases from Ps 18:3, 35, 47–48.

b. [143:3] Ps 7:6. c. [143:3] Lam 3:6. d. [143:4] Ps 142:4; Jb 17:1. e. [143:5] Ps 77:6, 12. f. [143:6] Ps 42:2; 63:2. g. [143:7] Ps 28:1; 30:4; 88:5; Prv 1:12. h. [143:8] Ps 25:4; 27:11; 86:11; 119:12, 35. i. [143:12] Ps 116:16.

‡[144:3] Similar to Ps 8:4.
§[144:4] Composed of phrases from Ps 39:6; 102:12.
¶[144:5–7] Adapted in large part from Ps 18:10, 15, 17; 104:32.
[144:8b, 11b] **Their right hands are raised in lying oaths: the psalmist's enemies give false testimony.
††[Psalm 145] A hymn in acrostic form; every verse begins with a successive letter of the Hebrew alphabet. Acrostic poems usually do not develop ideas but consist rather of loosely connected statements. The singer invites all to praise God (Ps 145:1–3, 21). The "works of God" make God present and invite human praise (Ps 145:4–7); they climax in a confession (Ps 145:8–9). God's mighty acts show forth divine kingship (Ps 145:10–20), a major theme in the literature of early Judaism and in Christianity.

j. [144:3] Jb 7:17. k. [144:4] Ps 62:10; 90:9–10; Jb 7:16; Eccl 6:12; Wis 2:5. l. [144:5] Is 63:19. m. [144:9] Ps 33:2–3. n. [144:10] Ps 18:51. o. [144:12] Ps 128:3. p. [144:14] Is 65:19. q. [144:15] Ps 33:12.

I will extol you, my God and king;
  I will bless your name forever and
    ever.
2 Every day I will bless you;
  I will praise your name forever and
    ever.*r*
3 Great is the LORD and worthy of much
    praise,*s*
  whose grandeur is beyond
    understanding.
4 One generation praises your deeds to the
    next
  and proclaims your mighty works.*t*
5 They speak of the splendor of your
    majestic glory,
  tell of your wonderful deeds.*u*
6 They speak of the power of your awesome
    acts
  and recount your great deeds.*v*
7 They celebrate your abounding goodness
  and joyfully sing of your justice.
8 The LORD is gracious and merciful,
  slow to anger and abounding in
    mercy.*w*
9 The LORD is good to all,
  compassionate toward all your
    works.*x*
10 All your works give you thanks, LORD
  and your faithful bless you.*y*
11 They speak of the glory of your reign
  and tell of your mighty works,
12 Making known to the sons of men your
    mighty acts,
  the majestic glory of your rule.
13 Your reign is a reign for all ages,
  your dominion for all generations.*z*
  The LORD is trustworthy in all his words,
  and loving in all his works.
14 The LORD supports all who are falling
  and raises up all who are bowed
    down.*a*
15 The eyes of all look hopefully to you;
  you give them their food in due
    season.*b*
16 You open wide your hand
  and satisfy the desire of every living
    thing.
17 The LORD is just in all his ways,
  merciful in all his works.*c*
18 The LORD is near to all who call upon
    him,
  to all who call upon him in truth.*d*
19 He fulfills the desire of those who fear
    him;
  he hears their cry and saves them.*e*

20 The LORD watches over all who love him,
  but all the wicked he destroys.*f*
21 My mouth will speak the praises of the LORD;
  all flesh will bless his holy name
    forever and ever.

PSALM 146*

Trust in God the Creator and Redeemer

1 Hallelujah!
2 Praise the LORD, my soul;
  I will praise the LORD all my life,
  sing praise to my God while I live.*g*

I

3 Put no trust in princes,
  in children of Adam powerless to
    save.*h*
4 Who breathing his last, returns to
    the earth;
  that day all his planning comes to
    nothing.*i*

II

5 Blessed the one whose help is the God of
    Jacob,
  whose hope is in the LORD, his God,
6 The maker of heaven and earth,
  the seas and all that is in them,*j*
  Who keeps faith forever,
7 secures justice for the oppressed,*k*
  who gives bread to the hungry.
  The LORD sets prisoners free;*l*
8 the LORD gives sight to the blind.
  The LORD raises up those who are bowed
    down;*m*
  the LORD loves the righteous.
9 The LORD protects the resident alien,
  comes to the aid of the orphan and
    the widow,*n*
  but thwarts the way of the wicked.
10 The LORD shall reign forever,
  your God, Zion, through all
    generations!*o*
  Hallelujah!

PSALM 147†

God's Word Restores Jerusalem

1 Hallelujah!

---

*[Psalm 146] A hymn of someone who has learned there
is no other source of strength except the merciful God. Only
God, not mortal human beings (Ps 146:3–4), can help vulnerable and oppressed people (Ps 146:5–9). The first of the five
hymns that conclude the Psalter.
†[Psalm 147] The hymn is divided into three sections by
the calls to praise in Ps 147:1, 7, 12. The first section praises the
powerful creator who restores exiled Judah (Ps 147:1–6); the
second section, the creator who provides food to animals and
human beings; the third and climactic section exhorts the holy
city to recognize it has been re-created and made the place of
disclosure for God's word, a word as life-giving as water.

---

r. [145:2] Ps 34:2.   s. [145:3] Ps 48:2; 95:3; 96:4; Jb 36:26.   t. [145:4]
Ps 22:31–32; 48:14–15; 71:18; 78:4; Ex 10:2; Dt 4:9.   u. [145:5] Ps
96:3; 105:2.   v. [145:6] Ps 66:3.   w. [145:8] Ps 86:5, 15; 103:8; Ex
34:6; Sir 2:11.   x. [145:9] Ps 103:13; Wis 11:24.   y. [145:10] Dn
3:57.   z. [145:13] Ps 10:16; 102:13; 146:10; Lam 5:19; Dn 3:33;
Rev 11:15.   a. [145:14] Ps 94:18; 146:8.   b. [145:15] Ps 136:25;
104:27–28; Mt 6:25–26.   c. [145:17] Dt 32:4.   d. [145:18] Dt 4:7;
Is 55:6; 58:9.

e. [145:19] Ps 34:18.   f. [145:20] Jgs 5:31.   g. [146:2] Ps 103:1;
104:33.   h. [146:3] Ps 118:8–9.   i. [146:4] Ps 90:3; 104:29; 1 Mc 2:63;
Jb 34:14–15; Eccl 3:20; 12:7; Sir 40:11; Is 2:22.   j. [146:6] Ps 121:2;
124:8; Ex 20:11; Acts 14:15; Rev 14:7.   k. [146:7] Ps 103:6.   l. [146:7]
Ps 68:7; Is 49:9; 61:1.   m. [146:8] Ps 145:14.   n. [146:9] Ps 68:6; Dt
10:18.   o. [146:10] Ps 145:13; Lam 5:19.

I

How good to sing praise to our God;
   how pleasant to give fitting praise.[p]
2 The LORD rebuilds Jerusalem,
   and gathers the dispersed of Israel,[q]
3 Healing the brokenhearted,
   and binding up their wounds.[r]
4 He numbers the stars,
   and gives to all of them their names.[s]
5 Great is our Lord, vast in power,
   with wisdom beyond measure.[t]
6 The LORD gives aid to the poor,
   but casts the wicked to the ground.[u]

II

7 Sing to the LORD with thanksgiving;
   with the lyre make music to our
   God,[v]
8 *Who covers the heavens with clouds,
   provides rain for the earth,
   makes grass sprout on the
   mountains,[w]
9 Who gives animals their food
   and young ravens what they cry for.[x]
10 †He takes no delight in the strength of
   horses,
   no pleasure in the runner's stride.[y]
11 Rather the LORD takes pleasure in those
   who fear him,
   those who put their hope in his
   mercy.

III

12 Glorify the LORD, Jerusalem;
   Zion, offer praise to your God,
13 For he has strengthened the bars of your
   gates,
   blessed your children within you.[z]
14 He brings peace to your borders,
   and satisfies you with finest wheat.[a]
15 ‡He sends his command to earth;
   his word runs swiftly![b]
16 Thus he makes the snow like wool,
   and spreads the frost like ash;[c]
17 He disperses hail like crumbs.
   Who can withstand his cold?
18 Yet when again he issues his command, it
   melts them;
   he raises his winds and the waters
   flow.

19 He proclaims his word to Jacob,
   his statutes and laws to Israel.[d]
20 He has not done this for any other nation;
   of such laws they know nothing.
Hallelujah!

PSALM 148[§]
All Creation Summoned to Praise

1 Hallelujah!

I

Praise the LORD from the heavens;
   praise him in the heights.
2 Praise him, all you his angels;
   give praise, all you his hosts.[e]
3 Praise him, sun and moon;
   praise him, all shining stars.
4 Praise him, highest heavens,[¶]
   you waters above the heavens.
5 Let them all praise the LORD's name;
   for he commanded and they were
   created,[f]
6 Assigned them their station forever,
   set an order that will never change.

II

7 Praise the LORD from the earth,
   you sea monsters and all the deeps
   of the sea;[g]
8 Lightning and hail, snow and thick
   clouds,
   storm wind that fulfills his
   command;
9 Mountains and all hills,
   fruit trees and all cedars;[h]
10 Animals wild and tame,
   creatures that crawl and birds that
   fly;[i]
11 Kings of the earth and all peoples,
   princes and all who govern on earth;
12 Young men and women too,
   old and young alike.
13 Let them all praise the LORD's name,
   for his name alone is exalted,
   His majesty above earth and heaven.[j]
14 **He has lifted high the horn of his people;
   to the praise of all his faithful,
   the Israelites, the people near to
   him.
Hallelujah!

---

*[147:8–9] God clothes the fields and feeds the birds, cf. Mt 6:26, 30.

†[147:10–11] Acknowledging one's dependence upon God rather than claiming self-sufficiency pleases God, cf. Ps 20:8; 33:16–19.

‡[147:15–19] God speaks through the thunder of nature and the word of revealed law, cf. Is 55:10–11. The weather phenomena are well known in Jerusalem: a blizzard of snow and hail followed by a thunderstorm that melts the ice.

§[Psalm 148] A hymn inviting the beings of heaven (Ps 148:1–6) and of earth (Ps 148:7–14) to praise God. The hymn does not distinguish between inanimate and animate (and rational) nature.

¶[148:4] **Highest heavens**: lit., "the heavens of the heavens," i.e., the space above the firmament, where the "upper waters" are stored, cf. Gn 1:6–7; Dt 10:14; 1 Kgs 8:27; Ps 104:3, 13.

[148:14] **Has lifted high the horn of his people: the horn symbolizes strength, the concrete noun for the abstract. Of all peoples, God has chosen Israel to return praise and thanks in a special way.

p. [147:1] Ps 33:1; 92:2.   q. [147:2] Is 11:12; 56:8; Jer 31:10.   r. [147:3] Jb 5:18; Is 30:26; 61:1; Jer 33:6.   s. [147:4] Is 40:26.   t. [147:5] Jdt 16:13; Jer 51:15.   u. [147:6] Ps 146:9; 1 Sm 2:7–8.   v. [147:7] Ps 71:22.   w. [147:8] Ps 104:13f; Jb 5:10; Jer 14:22; Jl 2:23.   x. [147:9] Jb 38:41; Mt 6:26.   y. [147:10] Ps 20:8; 33:16–18.   z. [147:13] Ps 48:14.   a. [147:14] Ps 81:17.   b. [147:15] Ps 33:9.   c. [147:16] Jb 6:16; 37:10; 38:22.

d. [147:19] Ps 78:5; Bar 3:37; Dt 4:7–8.   e. [148:2] Ps 103:20f; Dn 3:58–63.   f. [148:5] Ps 33:9; Gn 1:3f; Jdt 16:14.   g. [148:7] Ps 135:6; Gn 1:21.   h. [148:9] Is 44:23.   i. [148:10] Ps 30:5; Gn 1:21, 24f; Dt 4:7.   j. [148:13] Ps 30:5; Dt 4:7.

PSALM 149*
Praise God with Song and Sword

¹Hallelujah!

Sing to the LORD a new song,
  his praise in the assembly of the
    faithful.ᵏ
² Let Israel be glad in its maker,
  the people of Zion rejoice in their
    king.
³ Let them praise his name in dance,
  make music with tambourine and
    lyre.†ˡ
⁴ For the LORD takes delight in his people,
  honors the poor with victory.
⁵ Let the faithful rejoice in their glory,
  cry out for joy on their couches,‡
⁶ With the praise of God in their mouths,
  and a two-edged sword in their
    hands,ᵐ
⁷ To bring retribution on the nations,
  punishment on the peoples,ⁿ
⁸ To bind their kings in shackles,
  their nobles in chains of iron,
⁹ To execute the judgments decreed for
    them—

such is the gloryˢ of all God's
    faithful.
Hallelujah!

PSALM 150ˢ
Final Doxology

¹Hallelujah!

Praise God in his holy sanctuary;**ᵒ
  give praise in the mighty dome of
    heaven.
² Give praise for his mighty deeds,ᵖ
  praise him for his great majesty.
³ Give praise with blasts upon the horn,�q
  praise him with harp and lyre.
⁴ Give praise with tambourines and dance,
  praise him with strings and pipes.ʳ
⁵ Give praise with crashing cymbals,
  praise him with sounding cymbals.
⁶ Let everything that has breath
  give praise to the LORD!ˢ
Hallelujah!

---

§[149:9] **The glory:** what brings honor to the people is their readiness to carry out the divine will, here conceived as punishing injustice done by the nations.

¶[Psalm 150] The Psalm is a closing doxology both for the fifth book of the Psalms (Ps 107–149) and for the Psalter as a whole. Temple musicians and dancers are called to lead all beings on earth and in heaven in praise of God. The Psalm proclaims to whom praise shall be given, and where (Ps 150:1); what praise shall be given, and why (Ps 150:2); how praise shall be given (Ps 150:3–5), and by whom (Ps 150:6).

[150:1] **His holy sanctuary: God's Temple on earth. The **mighty dome of heaven:** lit., "[God's] strong vault"; heaven is here imagined as a giant plate separating the inhabited world from the waters of the heavens.

---

*[Psalm 149] A hymn inviting the people of Israel to celebrate their God in song and festive dance (Ps 149:1–3, 5) because God has chosen them and given them victory (Ps 149:4). The exodus and conquest are the defining acts of Israel; the people must be ready to do again those acts in the future at the divine command (Ps 149:6–9).

†[149:3] **Make music with tambourine and lyre:** the verse recalls the great exodus hymn of Ex 15:20.

‡[149:5] **On their couches:** the people reclined to banquet.

---

k. [149:1] Ps 22:23; 26:12; 35:18; 40:10; Jdt 16:1. l. [149:3] Ps 68:26; 81:2–3; 87:7; 150:3–4. m. [149:6] Neh 4:10–12; 2 Mc 15:27. n. [149:7] Wis 3:8.

o. [150:1] Dn 3:53. p. [150:2] Dt 3:24. q. [150:3ff] Ps 81:3–4; 149:3; 2 Sm 6:5; 1 Chr 13:8; 16:5, 42; 2 Chr 5:12–13; 7:6. r. [150:4] Ps 68:26; Ex 15:20. s. [150:6] Rev 5:13.

THE BOOK OF
PROVERBS

THE BOOK OF
PROVERBS

Proverbs is an anthology of collections of sayings and instructions. Many of the sayings and perhaps some instructions were composed in the monarchic period (late eleventh to the early sixth centuries). Editing of the whole book was done in the early postexilic period, in the view of most scholars; at that time chaps. 1–9 would have been added as the introduction. Whether the material originated among royal scribes (as 25:1 seems to suggest) imitating common literary genres, or whether it arose among tribal elders inculcating traditional ways, is disputed. The origin of the material, however, need not be imagined in an either/or scenario. Folk wisdom and observations could surely have been elaborated and re-expressed by learned scribes: "What oft was thought but ne'er so well expressed" (Alexander Pope). There can be no doubt, however, that Proverbs is sophisticated literature by talented writers, winning readers with its compelling portrait of wisdom and inviting them to see life afresh, "wisely," through its wit, originality, and shrewd observation.

The primary purpose of the book is to teach wisdom, not only to the young and inexperienced (1:2–4) but also to the advanced (1:5–6). Wisdom in the ancient Near East was not theoretical knowledge but practical expertise. Jewelers who cut precious stones were wise; kings who made their dominion peaceful and prosperous were wise. One could be wise in daily life, too, in knowing how to live successfully (having a prosperous household and living a long and healthy life) and without trouble in God's universe. Ultimately wisdom, or "sound guidance" (1:5), aims at the formation of character.

In the ancient Near East, people assumed that wisdom belonged to the gods, who were wise by reason of their divinity; human beings needed to have wisdom *granted* them by the gods. Creation accounts of neighboring cultures depict creation in two stages. In the first stage, human beings lived an animal-like existence, without clothes, writing, or kingship (proper governance). Over time, the gods came to realize that such a low grade of existence made the human race inadequate as their servants, so they endowed the race with "wisdom," which consisted of culture (e.g., kingship) and crafts (e.g., knowledge of farming, ability to weave). Such wisdom elevated the race to a "human" level and made them effective servants of the gods. Furthermore, divine wisdom was *mediated* to human beings through earthly institutions—the king, scribes (who produced wise writings), and heads of families (fathers, sometimes mothers). These traditional mediators appear in Proverbs: the book is credited to King Solomon, and kings are respectfully mentioned as pillars of society (e.g., 16:12–15); *writings* are a source of wisdom (1:1–7); the father instructing his son is the major paradigm of teaching. Proverbs differs, however, from other wisdom books in concentrating on wisdom itself, treating it as a virtually independent entity and personifying it as an attractive woman. Other books urge readers to perform wise acts, but Proverbs urges them to seek wisdom itself and portrays wisdom as a woman seeking human beings as disciples and companions.

Chapters 1–9 introduce the book, drawing attention to wisdom itself and its inherent value rather than exhorting to particular wise actions. The chapters personify wisdom as a woman and draw an extended analogy between finding a wife, or founding and maintaining a house(hold), and finding wisdom. The collections following chap. 9 consist largely of independent, two-line sayings, yielding their often indirect or paradoxical meaning only to readers willing to ponder them. To reflect on the sayings is perhaps what chaps. 1–9 mean by living with Wisdom and dwelling in her house.

The Book of Proverbs can make an important contribution to Christians and Jews today. First, it places the pursuit of wisdom over the performance of individual wise acts. To seek wisdom above all things is a fundamental option and a way of life. Second, it portrays the quest as filled with obstacles. There are men and women who offer a substitute for the real thing; discernment is required. Third, the book teaches that acquiring wisdom is both a human task and a divine gift. One can make oneself ready to receive by discipline, but one cannot take so divine a gift. Fourth, wisdom is in the world but it is not obvious to people entirely caught up with daily activities. The instructions and the aphorisms of the book can free the mind to see new things. Christians will see in personified Wisdom aspects of Jesus Christ, who they believe is divine wisdom sent to give human beings true and full life. Yet there is a universal dimension to Proverbs, for in its attention to human experience it creates a link to all people of good will.

The genres and themes of Proverbs continued on in Sirach, Wisdom of Solomon, and the later *Pirqe Abot* (The Sayings of the Fathers), a treatise in the Mishnah, which became the object of commentary in *Abot de Rabbi Nathan*. The New Testament saw Jesus as a wisdom teacher and employed the tradition of personified wisdom of chaps. 2 and 8 to express his incarnation. The Letter of James is an instruction resembling those in Proverbs. Wisdom traditions influenced the Gospels of Matthew and Luke through a common source (see, e.g., Mt 11:25-27 and Lk 10:21-22, which seem to derive their father-son language, at least in part, from the parental language of Proverbs). The Gospel of John regards Jesus as incarnate wisdom descended from on high to offer human beings life and truth and make disciples of them, a view largely reflected in Proverbs 1-9. In later Judaism, Hebrew ethical wills, in which parents hand on to their children their wisdom, borrowed from the genre of instruction.

The original audience of the instructions and sayings seems to have been male. The father addresses his son, marriage is finding a wife, success often is serving the king or farming effectively. The book itself, however, expands the traditional audience of youths (1:4) to include older, more experienced, people (1:5). It broadens the father-son language by mentioning the mother, and incorporates sayings on human experience generally. The father teaching his son becomes a model for anyone teaching a way of life to another person. The canonical process furthered such inclusiveness, for Proverbs was made part of the Bible that addresses *all* Israel.

The Book of Proverbs has nine sections:

    I. Title and Introduction (1:1-7)
    II. Instructions of Parents and of Woman Wisdom (1:8-9:18)
    III. First Solomonic Collection of Sayings (10:1-22:16)
    IV. Sayings of the Wise (22:17-24:22)
    V. Further Sayings of the Wise (24:23-34)
    VI. Second Solomonic Collection, Collected Under King Hezekiah (25:1-29:27)
    VII. Sayings of Agur and Others (30:1-33)
VIII. Sayings of King Lemuel (31:1-9)
    IX. Poem on the Woman of Worth (31:10-31)

Part II is judged by many scholars to contain ten instructions (1:8-19; chap. 2; 3:1-12, 21-35; 4:1-9, 10-19, 20-27; chap. 5; 6:20-35; chap. 7), three wisdom poems (1:20-33; chap. 8; 9:1-6 + 11, 13-18), and two interludes (3:13-20; 6:1-19).

I. TITLE AND INTRODUCTION

CHAPTER 1

Purpose of the Proverbs of Solomon*

1 The proverbs† of Solomon,ᵃ the son of
David,
king of Israel:
2 That people may know wisdom and
discipline,‡
may understand intelligent sayings;
3 May receive instruction in wise conduct,
in what is right, just and fair;
4 That resourcefulness may be imparted to
the naive,§
knowledge and discretion to the
young.
5 The wise by hearing them will advance in
learning,
the intelligent will gain sound
guidance,
6 To comprehend proverb and byword,
the words of the wise and their
riddles.
7 Fear of the LORD¶ is the beginning of
knowledge;ᵇ
fools despise wisdom and discipline.

II. INSTRUCTIONS OF PARENTS AND OF WOMAN WISDOM

The Path of the Wicked: Greed and Violence**

8 Hear, my son, your father's instruction,
and reject not your mother's teaching;
9 A graceful diadem will they be for your
head;

a pendant for your neck.
10 My son, should sinners entice you,
11 do not go if they say, "Come along
with us!
Let us lie in wait for blood,
unprovoked, let us trap the
innocent;
12 Let us swallow them alive, like Sheol,
whole, like those who go down to
the pit!
13 All kinds of precious wealth shall we
gain,
we shall fill our houses with booty;
14 Cast in your lot with us,
we shall all have one purse!"
15 My son, do not walk in the way with
them,
hold back your foot from their path!
16 [For their feet run to evil,
they hasten to shed blood.ᶜ]
17 In vain a net is spread††
right under the eyes of any bird—
18 They lie in wait for their own blood,
they set a trap for their own lives.
19 This is the way of everyone greedy for
loot:
it takes away their lives.

Wisdom in Person Gives a Warning‡‡

20 Wisdom cries aloud in the street,
in the open squares she raises her
voice;ᵈ
21 Down the crowded ways she calls out,
at the city gates she utters her words:
22 §§"How long, you naive ones, will you

---

*[1:1–7] The prologue explains the purpose of the book.
The book has a sapiential, ethical, and religious dimension:
to bring the inexperienced to knowledge and right conduct,
to increase the facility of those already wise for interpreting
proverbs, parables and riddles, and to encourage the fulfillment of one's duties to God.

†[1:1] **Proverbs**: the Hebrew word *mashal* is broader than
English "proverb," embracing the instructions of chaps. 1–9 and
the sayings, observations, and comparisons of chaps. 10–31.

‡[1:2] **Discipline**: education or formation which dispels
ignorance and corrects vice. Note the reprise of v. 2a in v. 7b.

§[1:4] **Naive**: immature, inexperienced, sometimes the
young, hence easily influenced for good or evil.

¶[1:7] **Fear of the LORD**: primarily a disposition rather
than the emotion of fear; reverential awe and respect toward
God combined with obedience to God's will.

**[1:8–19] A parental warning to a young person leaving
home, for them to avoid the company of the greedy and violent. Two ways lie before the hearer, a way that leads to death
and a way that leads to life. The trap which the wicked set
for the innocent (v. 11) in the end takes away the lives of the
wicked themselves (v. 19). This theme will recur especially in
chaps. 1–9. A second theme introduced here is that of founding (or managing) a household and choosing a spouse. A third
theme is the human obstacles to attaining wisdom. Here (and
in 2:12–15 and 4:10–19), the obstacle is men (always in the
plural); in 2:16–19; 5:1–6; 6:20–35; chap. 7; 9:13–18, the obstacle to the quest is the "foreign" woman (always in the singular).

a. [1:1] Prv 10:1; 25:1; 1 Kgs 4:32.   b. [1:7] Prv 9:10; Jb 28:28; Ps
111:10; Sir 1:16.

††[1:17] A difficult verse. The most probable interpretation
is that no fowler lifts up the net so the bird can see it. The verse
might be paraphrased: God does not let those who walk on evil
paths see the net that will entrap them. The passive construction ("a net is spread") is sometimes used to express divine
activity. Verse 16 is a later attempt to add clarity. It is a quotation from Is 59:7 and is not in the best Greek manuscripts.

‡‡[1:20–33] Wisdom is personified as in chaps. 8 and 9:1–6.
With divine authority she proclaims the moral order, threatening to leave to their own devices those who disregard her
invitation. All three speeches of Woman Wisdom have common features: a setting in city streets; an audience of simple
or naive people; a competing appeal (chap. 7 is the competing
appeal for chap. 8); an invitation to a relationship that brings
long life, riches, repute.

The structure of the speeches is: A: setting (vv. 20–21); B:
Wisdom's withdrawal, rebuke and announcement (vv. 22–23);
reason and rejection I (vv. 24–27); reason and rejection II
(vv. 28–31); summary (v. 32); C: the effects of Wisdom's presence (v. 33). Wisdom's opening speech is an extended threat
ending with a brief invitation (v. 33). Her second speech is
an extended invitation ending with a brief threat (8:36). The
surprisingly abrupt and harsh tone of her speech is perhaps to
be explained as a response to the arrogant words of the men
in the previous scene (1:8–19).

§§[1:22–23] There is textual confusion. Verse 22bc (in the
third person) is an addition, interrupting vv. 22a and 23a (in
the second person). The addition has been put in brackets, to
separate it from the original poem. The original verses do not
ask for a change of heart but begin to detail the consequences
of disobedience to Wisdom.

c. [1:16] Is 59:7.   d. [1:20] Prv 8:1–3; 9:3.

love naivete,
²³ How long will you turn away at my
reproof?
[The arrogant delight in their arrogance,
and fools hate knowledge.]
Lo! I will pour out to you my spirit,
I will acquaint you with my words:
²⁴ 'Because I called and you refused,
extended my hand and no one took
notice;ᵉ
²⁵ Because you disdained all my counsel,
and my reproof you ignored—
²⁶ I, in my turn, will laugh at your doom;
will mock when terror overtakes you;
²⁷ When terror comes upon you like a storm,
and your doom approaches like a
whirlwind;
when distress and anguish befall you.'
²⁸ Then they will call me, but I will not
answer;
they will seek me, but will not find me,
²⁹ Because they hated knowledge,
and the fear of the LORD they did
not choose.
³⁰ They ignored my counsel,
they spurned all my reproof;
³¹ Well, then, they shall eat the fruit* of their
own way,
and with their own devices be glutted.
³² For the straying of the naive kills them,
the smugness of fools destroys them.
³³ But whoever obeys me dwells in security,
in peace, without fear of harm."ᶠ

CHAPTER 2

The Blessings of Wisdom†

¹ My son, if you receive my words
and treasure my commands,
² Turning your ear to wisdom,‡
inclining your heart to
understanding;
³ Yes, if you call for intelligence,
and to understanding raise your voice;
⁴ If you seek her like silver,
and like hidden treasures search
her out,
⁵ Then will you understand the fear of the
LORD;

the knowledge of God you will find;
⁶ For the LORD gives wisdom,
from his mouth come knowledge
and understanding;ᵍ
⁷ He has success in store for the upright,
is the shield of those who walk
honestly,
⁸ Guarding the paths of justice,
protecting the way of his faithful ones,
⁹ Then you will understand what is right
and just,
what is fair, every good path;
¹⁰ For wisdom will enter your heart,
knowledge will be at home in your
soul,
¹¹ Discretion will watch over you,
understanding will guard you;
¹² §Saving you from the way of the wicked,
from those whose speech is perverse.
¹³ From those who have left the straight
paths
to walk in the ways of darkness,
¹⁴ Who delight in doing evil
and celebrate perversity;
¹⁵ Whose ways are crooked,
whose paths are devious;
¹⁶ ¶Saving you from a stranger,
from a foreign woman with her
smooth words,ʰ
¹⁷ One who forsakes the companion of her
youth
and forgets the covenant of her God;
¹⁸ For her path sinks down to death,
and her footsteps lead to the shades."ⁱ
¹⁹ None who enter there come back,
or gain the paths of life.
²⁰ Thus you may walk in the way of the good,
and keep to the paths of the just.
²¹ ††For the upright will dwell in the land,ʲ
people of integrity will remain in it;
²² But the wicked will be cut off from the
land,
the faithless will be rooted out of it.

---

§[2:12–15] As in 1:8–19, there is an obstacle to the quest
for wisdom—deceitful and violent men. Cf. also 4:10–19.
They offer a way of life that is opposed to the way of wisdom.
¶[2:16–19] A second obstacle and counter-figure to Wisdom, personified as an attractive woman, is the "stranger," or
"foreigner," from outside the territory or kinship group, hence
inappropriate as a marriage partner. In Proverbs she comes to
be identified with Woman Folly, whose deceitful words promise life but lead to death. Woman Folly appears also in chap.
5, 6:20–35, chap. 7 and 9:13–18. **Covenant:** refers to the vow
uttered with divine sanction at the woman's previous marriage, as the parallel verse suggests. She is already married and
relations with her would be adulterous.
[2:18] Shades: the inhabitants of Sheol.
††[2:21–22] Verses 21–22 echo the ending of Wisdom's
speech in 1:32–33, in which refusing Wisdom's invitation
meant death and obedience to her meant life. The same set of
ideas is found in Ps 37 (especially vv. 3, 9, 11, 22, 29, 34, and
38): to live on (or inherit) the land and to be uprooted from
the land are expressions of divine recompense.

---

*[1:31] **Eat the fruit:** sinners are punished by the consequences of their sins. Wisdom's voice echoes that of the parents in vv. 8–19. The parents mediate wisdom in vv. 8–19, but
here Wisdom herself speaks.
†[2:1–22] Chapter 2 is a single poem, an acrostic of twenty-
two lines, the number of consonants in the Hebrew alphabet.
In vv. 1–11, the letter *aleph,* the first letter of the alphabet, predominates, and in vv. 12–22, the letter *lamed,* the first letter of
the second half of the alphabet. A single structure runs through
the whole: if (*aleph*) you search . . . then (*aleph*) the Lord/
Wisdom will grant . . . saving (*lamed*) you from the wicked
man/woman . . . thus (*lamed*) you can walk in the safe way. . . .
‡[2:2–3] **Wisdom . . . understanding . . . intelligence:**
various names or aspects of the same gift.

e. [1:24] Is 65:2, 12; 66:4; Jer 7:13.   f. [1:33] Prv 8:33–34.

g. [2:6] Jb 32:8; Wis 7:25; Sir 1:1; Jas 1:5.   h. [2:16] Prv 5:3, 20; 6:24;
7:5; 22:14.   i. [2:18] Prv 5:5; 7:27.   j. [2:21] Prv 10:7, 30; Jb 18:17;
Ps 21:9–13; 37:22, 28.

CHAPTER 3

Confidence in God Leads to Prosperity*

1 My son, do not forget† my teaching,
　take to heart my commands;
2 For many days, and years of life,ᵏ
　and peace, will they bring you.
3 Do not let love and fidelity forsake you;
　bind them around your neck;
　write them on the tablet of your
　　heart.
4 Then will you win favor and esteem
　before God and human beings.
5 Trust in the Lᴏʀᴅ with all your heart,
　on your own intelligence do not
　　rely;
6 In all your ways be mindful of him,
　and he will make straight your
　　paths.
7 Do not be wise in your own eyes,ˡ
　fear the Lᴏʀᴅ and turn away from
　　evil;
8 This will mean health for your flesh
　and vigor for your bones.
9 Honor the Lᴏʀᴅ with your wealth,
　with first fruits of all your produce;ᵐ
10 Then will your barns be filled with
　　plenty,
　with new wine your vats will
　　overflow.
11 The discipline of the Lᴏʀᴅ, my son, do
　　not spurn;ⁿ
　do not disdain his reproof;
12 ‡For whom the Lᴏʀᴅ loves he reproves,
　as a father, the son he favors.ᵒ

The Benefits of Finding Wisdom§

13 Happy the one who finds wisdom,
　the one who gains understanding!ᵖ
14 Her profit is better than profit in silver,
　and better than gold is her revenue;
15 She is more precious than corals,
　and no treasure of yours can
　　compare with her.ᑫ
16 Long life is in her right hand,
　in her left are riches and honor;
17 Her ways are pleasant ways,
　and all her paths are peace;
18 She is a tree of lifeˢ to those who grasp her,
　and those who hold her fast are
　　happy.ʳ
19 The Lᴏʀᴅ by wisdom founded the earth,
　established the heavens by
　　understanding;
20 By his knowledge the depths** are split,
　and the clouds drop down dew.

Justice Toward One's Neighbor Brings Blessing††

21 My son, do not let these slip from your
　　sight:
　hold to deliberation and planning;

§[3:13–20] An encomium of Wisdom through the listing of her benefits to the human race and the depiction of her role in creation. Wisdom, or understanding, is more valuable than silver and gold. Its fruit is long life, riches, honor and happiness (vv. 13–18). Even the creation of the universe and its adornment (Gn 1) were not done without wisdom (vv. 19–20). The praise of Wisdom foreshadows the praise of a noble wife in the final poem (31:10–31), even to the singling out of the hands extended in a helpful way toward human beings.

¶[3:18] A tree of life: in the Old Testament this phrase occurs only in Proverbs (11:30; 13:12; 15:4) and Genesis (2:9; 3:22, 24). The origins of the concept are obscure; there is no explicit mention of it in ancient Near Eastern literature, though on ancient seals trees are sometimes identified as trees of life. When the man and the woman were expelled from the garden, the tree of life was put off limits to them, lest they "eat of it and live forever" (Gn 3:22). The quest for wisdom gives access to the previously sequestered tree of life. The tree of life is mentioned also in the apocryphal work 1 Enoch 25:4–5. Rev 2 and 22 mention the tree of life as a source of eternal life.

**[3:20] Depths: for the Hebrews, the depths enclosed the great subterranean waters; the rain and dew descended from the waters above the firmament; cf. Gn 1:6–10; Jb 26:8, 12; Ps 18:15; 24:2. The cosmogony provides the reason why Wisdom offers such benefits to human beings: the world was created in wisdom so that all who live in accord with wisdom live in tune with the universe.

††[3:21–35] As in other instructions, the father in vv. 21–26 urges the son to seek wisdom, which in this case means practicing the virtues of "deliberation and planning," a specification of wisdom. Practicing these virtues brings protection from violence (vv. 22–26) and friendship with God (vv. 32–35). The language is like Ps 91.
　Verses 27–35 are arranged according to a clear order. Serving God requires serving one's neighbor through kindness (vv. 27–28), maintaining peace with the good (vv. 29–31), having no envy of the wicked (v. 31), because the Lord's friendship and kindness are with the just, not with the wicked. Matching the six exhortations of vv. 1–12, vv. 27–34 contain six prohibitions. The righteous/wicked contrast is progressively developed: in contrast to the wicked, the righteous are in God's inner circle, their houses are blessed, they deal with a merciful God, and obtain honor.

*[3:1–12] The instruction consists of a series of six four-line exhortations in which the second line of each exhortation mentions a reward or benefit. In the first five exhortations, the teacher promises a reward: long life, a good name, divine protection, health, abundant crops. The last exhortation, vv. 11–12, departs from the command-reward scheme, implying that being a disciple of the Lord does not guarantee unalloyed bliss: one must allow God freedom to "reprove" or educate. The process of education is like that described in chap. 2: the father first invites his son (or disciple) to memorize his teaching (v. 1), then to enter upon a relationship of trust with him (v. 3), and finally to place his trust in God, who takes up the parental task of education (v. 5). Education begun by the parent is brought to full completion by God.
　†[3:1] Do not forget: this word and several others in the section such as "teaching," "commands," "years of life," and the custom of affixing written teaching to one's body, occur also in Deuteronomy. This vocabulary suggests that Proverbs and Deuteronomy had a common origin in the scribal class of Jerusalem. This section (and vv. 21–34) subtly elaborates Dt 6:5–9, "You shall love the Lord with all your heart (v. 5) . . . Take to heart these words (v. 1) . . . Recite them when you are at home and when you are away (v. 23) . . . when you lie down (v. 24) . . . Bind them (v. 3) on your arm as a sign and let them be a pendant on your forehead" (v. 21).
　‡[3:12] One might be tempted to judge the quality of one's relationship to God by one's prosperity. It is an inadequate criterion, for God as a teacher might go counter to student expectations. The discipline of God can involve suffering.

k. [3:2] Prv 4:10; 9:11; 10:27.　l. [3:7] Rom 11:25; 12:16.　m. [3:9] Ex 34:26; Lv 27:30; Dt 26:2; Sir 7:31; 35:7.　n. [3:11] Heb 12:5–6.　o. [3:12] Jdt 8:27; Rev 3:19.

p. [3:13] Prv 8:34–35.　q. [3:15] Prv 8:11, 19; Wis 7:8–11.　r. [3:18] Prv 4:13; 8:35; 11:30; Gn 2:9; 3:22.

²² So will they be life to your soul,[*]
  and an adornment for your neck.
²³ Then you may go your way securely;
  your foot will never stumble;
²⁴ When you lie down, you will not be
  afraid,
  when you rest, your sleep will be
  sweet.
²⁵ Do not be afraid of sudden terror,
  of the ruin of the wicked when it
  comes;
²⁶ For the LORD will be your confidence,
  and will keep your foot from the
  snare.
²⁷ Do not withhold any goods from the
  owner
  when it is in your power to act.
²⁸ Say not to your neighbor, "Go, come back
  tomorrow,
  and I will give it to you," when all
  the while you have it.
²⁹ Do not plot evil against your neighbors,
  when they live at peace with you.
³⁰ Do not contend with someone without
  cause,
  with one who has done you no harm.
³¹ Do not envy the violent
  and choose none of their ways:^s
³² To the LORD the devious are an
  abomination,
  but the upright are close to him.
³³ The curse of the LORD is on the house of
  the wicked,
  but the dwelling of the just he
  blesses;
³⁴ Those who scoff, he scoffs at,^t
  but the lowly he favors.
³⁵ The wise will possess glory,
  but fools will bear shame.

CHAPTER 4

The Teacher as Model Disciple[†]

¹ Hear, O children, a father's instruction,
  be attentive, that you may gain
  understanding!

² Yes, excellent advice I give you;
  my teaching do not forsake.
³ When I was my father's child,
  tender, the darling of my mother,
⁴ He taught me and said to me:
  "Let your heart hold fast my words:^u
  keep my commands, and live!
⁵ Get wisdom,[‡] get understanding!
  Do not forget or turn aside from the
  words of my mouth.
⁶ Do not forsake her, and she will preserve
  you;
  love her, and she will safeguard you;
⁷ The beginning of wisdom is: get wisdom;
  whatever else you get, get
  understanding.
⁸ Extol her, and she will exalt you;
  she will bring you honors if you
  embrace her;
⁹ She will put on your head a graceful
  diadem;
  a glorious crown will she bestow
  on you."

The Two Ways[§]

¹⁰ Hear, my son, and receive my words,
  and the years of your life shall be
  many.^v
¹¹ On the way of wisdom I direct you,
  I lead you on straight paths.
¹² When you walk, your step will not be
  impeded,
  and should you run, you will not
  stumble.
¹³ Hold fast to instruction, never let it go;
  keep it, for it is your life.
¹⁴ ¶The path of the wicked do not enter,
  nor walk in the way of the evil;

---

*[3:22] **Your soul:** Heb. *nephesh* means "throat, esophagus; life; soul." The meanings are connected. The throat area is the moist, breathing center of the body, which stands for life and for self. The figure of speech is called metonymy, in which one word is substituted for another on the basis of a causal relation, e.g., eye for sight, arm for power, or, as here, "throat area" for life. Proverbs sometimes plays on this concrete meaning of life (e.g., 21:23).

†[4:1–9] The teacher draws a parallel between his teaching the disciples now and his father's teaching him in his youth (vv. 3–4): what my father taught me about wisdom is what I am teaching you. The poem implies that the teacher has acquired wisdom and has in fact been protected and honored as his father promised long ago. Thus the teacher has the authority of someone who has been under wisdom's sway since earliest youth.

There are two sections, a call for attention and introduction of the speaker (vv. 1–3) and the father's quoting of his own

father's teaching (vv. 4–9). Beginning with v. 5, the father's words are no longer quoted, wisdom herself becoming the active agent; she becomes the subject, not the object, of the verbs. Three Hebrew verbs are repeated in the two parts, "to forsake" in vv. 2 and 6, "to keep/guard" in vv. 4 and 6, and "to give/bestow" in vv. 2 and 9. Each verb in its first appearance has the father's words as its object; in its second appearance each verb has wisdom as its subject or object. The teaching process is like that in 2:1–22 and 3:1–12: heeding the words of one's parent puts one in touch with wisdom, who completes the process and bestows her gifts.

‡[4:5, 7] **Get wisdom:** the same Hebrew word "to get" can mean to acquire merchandise and to acquire a wife (18:22; 31:10); both meanings are in keeping with Proverbs' metaphors of acquiring wisdom over gold and silver and of acquiring wisdom as a personified woman, a wife.

§[4:10–19] A central metaphor of the poem is "the way." The way of wisdom leads directly to life (vv. 10–13); it is a light that grows brighter (v. 18). The wise are bound to shun (vv. 14–17) the dark and violent path of the wicked (v. 19). Singleness of purpose and right conduct proceed from the heart of the wise as from the source of life (vv. 23–26), saving them from destruction on evil paths (4:27; 5:21–23). As in 1:8–19 and 2:12–15, the obstacles to the quest are men and their way. Elsewhere in chaps. 1–9, the obstacle is the foreign woman (2:16–19; chap. 5; 6:20–35; chap. 7; 9:13–18).

¶[4:14–15] One is always free to choose. The righteous may choose to leave their path to walk on the wicked path and the wicked may choose the righteous path.

---

s. [3:31] Prv 23:17; 24:1, 19; Ps 37:1. t. [3:34] Prv 1:26. u. [4:4] Dt 6:1–6. v. [4:10] Prv 3:2.

¹⁵ Shun it, do not cross it,
turn aside from it, pass on.
¹⁶ For they cannot rest unless they have
done evil;
if they do not trip anyone they lose
sleep.
¹⁷ For they eat the bread of wickedness
and drink the wine of violence.
¹⁸ But the path of the just is like shining
light,
that grows in brilliance till perfect
day.˙
¹⁹ The way of the wicked is like darkness;
they do not know on what they
stumble.

With Your Whole Being
Heed My Words and Live†

²⁰ My son, to my words be attentive,
to my sayings incline your ear;
²¹ Let them not slip from your sight,
keep them within your heart;
²² For they are life to those who find them,ʷ
bringing health to one's whole being.
²³ With all vigilance guard your heart,
for in it are the sources of life.
²⁴ ‡Dishonest mouth put away from you,
deceitful lips put far from you.
²⁵ Let your eyes look straight ahead
and your gaze be focused forward.
²⁶ Survey the path for your feet,
and all your ways will be sure.
²⁷ Turn neither to right nor to left,
keep your foot far from evil.

CHAPTER 5

Warning Against Adultery§

¹ My son, to my wisdom be attentive,
to understanding incline your ear,
² That you may act discreetly,

and your lips guard what you know.
³ Indeed, the lips of the stranger drip
honey,¶
and her mouth is smoother than oil;ˣ
⁴ But in the end she is as bitter as
wormwood,
as sharp as a two-edged sword.
⁵ Her feet go down to death,
her steps reach Sheol;ʸ
⁶ Her paths ramble, you know not where,
lest you see before you the road to
life.
⁷ So now, children, listen to me,
do not stray from the words of my
mouth.
⁸ Keep your way far from her,ᶻ
do not go near the door of her
house,
⁹ Lest you give your honor˙˙ to others,ᵃ
and your years to a merciless one;
¹⁰ Lest outsiders take their fill of your
wealth,
and your hard-won earnings go to
another's house;
¹¹ And you groan in the end,
when your flesh and your body are
consumed;
¹² And you say, "Oh, why did I hate
instruction,
and my heart spurn reproof!
¹³ Why did I not listen to the voice of my
teachers,
incline my ear to my instructors!
¹⁴ I am all but ruined,
in the midst of the public assembly!"
¹⁵ Drink water†† from your own cistern,
running water from your own well.
¹⁶ Should your water sources be dispersed
abroad,
streams of water in the streets?

---

*[4:18] **Till perfect day:** lit., "till the day is established"; this may refer to full daylight or to noonday.

†[4:20–27] Acquiring wisdom brings life and health. The learning process involves two stages: (1) hearing the teacher's words and treasuring them in the heart; (2) speaking and acting in accord with the wisdom that one has stored in one's heart. Seven organs of the body are mentioned: ear, eyes, heart, mouth, lips, eyelids ("gaze," v. 25), feet. Each of the organs is to be strained to its limit as the disciple puts wisdom into practice. The physical organ stands for the faculty, e.g., the eye for sight, the foot for movement. The figure of speech is called metonymy; one word is substituted for another on the basis of a causal relation.

‡[4:24–27] In vv. 20–21 the faculties of hearing (ear) and seeing (eye) take in the teaching and the heart stores and ponders it, so in the second half of the poem, vv. 24–27, the faculties of speech, sight, and walking enable the disciple to put the teaching into practice.

§[5:1–23] This is the first of three poems on the forbidden woman, the "stranger" outside the social boundaries (cf. 2:16–19); the other two are 6:20–35 and chap. 7. Understanding and discretion are necessary to avoid adultery, which leads

astray and begets bitterness, bloodshed, and death (vv. 1–6). It destroys honor, wastes the years of life, despoils hard-earned wealth, and brings remorse in the end (vv. 7–14). Conjugal fidelity and love bring happiness and security (vv. 15–20). Cf. 6:20–7:27. The structure of the poem consists of a two-line introduction; part one consists of three stanzas of four lines each warning of the forbidden woman's effect on her lovers (vv. 3–14); part two consists of a stanza of twelve lines exhorting the disciple to marital fidelity (vv. 15–20); and a final stanza of six lines on the perils of the woman (vv. 21–23).

¶[5:3] A metaphorical level is established in the opening description of the forbidden woman: her lips drip honey and her feet lead to death. By her lies, she leads people away from the wisdom that gives life.

[5:9] **Honor: the words "life" and "wealth" have also been read in this place. **A merciless one:** the offended husband; cf. 6:34–35.

††[5:15–16] **Water:** water may have an erotic meaning as in Sg 4:15, "[You are] a garden fountain, a well of living water." Eating and drinking can be metaphors expressing the mutuality of love. The wife is the opposite of the adulterous woman; she is not an outsider, not unfeeling, not a destroyer of her husband's self and goods. The best defense against adultery is appreciating and loving one's spouse. The best defense against folly is to appreciate and love wisdom.

---

w. [4:22] Prv 8:35.

x. [5:3] Prv 7:5.   y. [5:5] Prv 2:18; 7:27.   z. [5:8] Prv 7:25.   a. [5:9] Sir 9:6.

¹⁷ Let them be yours alone,
  not shared with outsiders;
¹⁸ Let your fountain be blessed and have joy
  of the wife of your youth,
¹⁹ your lovely hind, your graceful doe.[*]
  Of whose love you will ever have your fill,
  and by her ardor always be
  intoxicated.
²⁰ Why then, my son, should you be
  intoxicated with a stranger,
  and embrace another woman?
²¹ Indeed, the ways of each person are plain
  to the LORD's sight;
  all their paths he surveys;^b
²² By their own iniquities the wicked will be
  caught,
  in the meshes of their own sin they
  will be held fast;
²³ They will die from lack of discipline,
  lost because of their great folly.

CHAPTER 6

Miscellaneous Proverbs[†]

Against Going Surety for One's Neighbor

¹ [‡]My son, if you have become surety to
  your neighbor,^c
  given your hand in pledge to another,
² You have been snared by the utterance of
  your lips,
  caught by the words of your mouth;
³ So do this, my son, to free yourself,
  since you have fallen into your
  neighbor's power:

---

*[5:19] **Lovely hind . . . graceful doe**: ancient Near Eastern symbols of feminine beauty and charm; cf. Sg 2:7, 9, 17.

†[6:1–19] Four independent pieces akin to those in 30:1–5, 6–11, 12–15, and 16–19. Some judge the verses to be an ancient addition, but the fact that the pieces differ from the other material in chaps. 1–9 is not a strong argument against their originality. Ancient anthologies did not always have the symmetry of modern collections. An editor may have placed the four pieces in the midst of the three poems on the forbidden woman to shed light on some of their themes. Verses 1–5 warn against getting trapped by one's words to another person (the Hebrew word for "another" is the same used for the forbidden woman); vv. 6–11 proposes the ant as a model of forethought and diligence; vv. 12–15 describes the reprobate who bears some similarity to the seductive woman, especially as portrayed in chap. 7; vv. 16–19 depicts the typical enemy of God, underscoring the person's destructive words.

‡[6:1–5] Unlike other instructions that begin with "my son," this instruction does not urge the hearer to store up the father's words as a means to wisdom, but only to avoid one practice—going surety for one's neighbor. The warning is intensified by repetition of "neighbor" and "free yourself," the mention of bodily organs, and the imagery of hunting. **Given your hand in pledge**: lit., "struck your hands"; this was probably the legal method for closing a contract. To become surety meant intervening in favor of the insolvent debtor and assuming responsibility for the payment of the debt, either by obtaining it from the debtor or substituting oneself. Proverbs is strongly opposed to the practice (11:15; 17:18; 20:16; 22:26–27; 27:13) apparently because of the danger it poses to the freedom of the one providing surety.

b. [5:21] Jb 14:16; 31:4; 34:21. c. [6:1] Prv 11:15; 22:26; Sir 8:13; 29:19.

Go, hurry, rouse your neighbor!
⁴ Give no sleep to your eyes,
  nor slumber to your eyelids;
⁵ Free yourself like a gazelle from the
  hunter,
  or like a bird from the hand of the
  fowler.

The Ant and the Sluggard at Harvest

⁶ [§]Go to the ant,^d O sluggard,
  study her ways and learn wisdom;
⁷ For though she has no chief,
  no commander or ruler,
⁸ She procures her food in the summer,
  stores up her provisions in the
  harvest.
⁹ How long, O sluggard, will you lie there?
  when will you rise from your sleep?
¹⁰ A little sleep, a little slumber,
  a little folding of the arms to rest—[¶]
¹¹ Then poverty will come upon you like a
  robber,
  and want like a brigand.

The Scoundrel

¹² ^{**}Scoundrels, villains, are they
  who deal in crooked talk.
¹³ Shifty of eye,
  feet ever moving,
  pointing with fingers,
¹⁴ They have perversity in their hearts,
  always plotting evil,
  sowing discord.
¹⁵ Therefore their doom comes suddenly;
  in an instant they are crushed
  beyond cure.

What the Lord Rejects

¹⁶ There are six things the LORD hates,
  yes, seven^{††} are an abomination to him;

---

§[6:6–11] The sluggard or lazybones is a type in Proverbs, like the righteous and the wicked. Sometimes the opposite type to the sluggard is the diligent person. Other extended passages on the sluggard are 24:30–34 and 26:13–16. The malice of the type is not low physical energy but the refusal to act. To describe human types, Proverbs often uses comparisons from the animal world, e.g., 27:8 (bird); 28:1, 15 (lion); 30:18–19 (eagle, snake); 30:24–28 (ant, badger, locust, lizard).

¶[6:10] This verse may be regarded as the sluggard's reply or as a continuation of the remonstrance.

**[6:12–15] Proverbs uses types to make the point that certain ways of acting have inherent consequences. The typifying intensifies the picture. All the physical organs—mouth, eyes, feet, fingers—are at the service of evil. Cf. Rom 6:12–13: "Therefore, sin must not reign over your mortal bodies so that you obey their desires. And do not present the parts of your bodies to sin as weapons for wickedness, but present yourselves to God as raised from the dead to life and the parts of your bodies to God as weapons of righteousness."

††[6:16] **Six . . . seven**: this literary pattern (n, n + 1) occurs frequently; cf., e.g., Am 1–2; Prv 30:18–19.

d. [6:6] Prv 30:25.

17 ʾHaughty eyes, a lying tongue,
    hands that shed innocent blood,
18 A heart that plots wicked schemes,
    feet that are quick to run to evil,
19 The false witness who utters lies,
    and the one who sows discord
      among kindred.

Warning Against Adultery†

20 Observe, my son, your father's
    command,
    and do not reject your mother's
      teaching;
21 Keep them fastened over your heart
    always,
    tie them around your neck.
22 When you lie down they‡ will watch over
    you,
    when you wake, they will share your
      concerns;
    wherever you turn, they will guide
      you.
23 For the command is a lamp, and the
    teaching a light,
    and a way to life are the reproofs
      that discipline,
24 Keeping you from another's wife,
    from the smooth tongue of the
      foreign woman.ᵉ
25 Do not lust in your heart after her
    beauty,
    do not let her captivate you with her
      glance!ᶠ
26 For the price of a harlot
    may be scarcely a loaf of bread,
    But a married woman
    is a trap for your precious life.

27 ˢCan a man take embers into his bosom,
    and his garments not be burned?
28 Or can a man walk on live coals,
    and his feet not be scorched?
29 So with him who sleeps with another's
    wife—
    none who touches her shall go
      unpunished.ᵍ
30 Thieves are not despised
    if out of hunger they steal to satisfy
      their appetite.
31 Yet if caught they must pay back sevenfold,
    yield up all the wealth of their house.
32 But those who commit adultery have no
    sense;
    those who do it destroy themselves.
33 ⁵They will be beaten and disgraced,
    and their shame will not be wiped
      away;
34 For passion enrages the husband,
    he will have no pity on the day of
      vengeance;
35 He will not consider any restitution,
    nor be satisfied by your many bribes.

CHAPTER 7

The Seduction**

1 ††My son, keep my words,
    and treasure my commands.

§[6:27–29] There is a play on three words of similar sound, *ʾîsh*, "man," *ʾishshâ*, "woman," and *ʾēsh*, "fire, embers." The question, "Can a man (*ʾîsh*) take embers (*ʾēsh*) into his bosom / and his garments not be burned?", has a double meaning. "Into his bosom" has an erotic meaning as in the phrase "wife of one's bosom" (Dt 13:6; 28:54; Sir 9:1). Hence one will destroy one's garments, which symbolize one's public position, by taking fire/another's wife into one's bosom.

¶[6:33–35] The nature of the husband's vengeance is disputed, some believing it is simply a physical beating whereas others hold it is public and involves the death penalty because Lv 20:20 and Dt 22:22 demand the death penalty.

**[7:1–27] The third and climactic instruction on adultery and seduction is an example story, of the same type as the example story in 24:30–34. By its negative portrayal of the deceitful woman, who speaks in the night to a lone youth, it serves as a foil to trustworthy Wisdom in chap. 8, who speaks in broad daylight to all who pass in the street.

As in 6:20–24, the father warns his son to keep his teaching to protect him from the dangerous forbidden woman. The father's language in 7:4 ("Say to Wisdom, 'You are my sister,' and call Understanding 'Friend'") sets this admonition apart, however; it is the language of courtship and love. If the son makes Woman Wisdom his companion and lover, she will protect him from the other woman. As in chap. 5, loving the right woman protects the man from the wrong woman.

As motivation, the father in vv. 6–23 tells his son of an incident he once observed while looking out his window—a young man went to the bed of an adulterous woman and wound up dead. As in chap. 5, the realistic details—the purposeful woman, the silent youth, the vow, the perfumed bed—have a metaphorical level. Ultimately the story is about two different kinds of love.

††[7:1–3] Verses 1–3 are artistically constructed. "Keep" in v. 1a recurs in v. 2a; "commands" in v. 1b recurs in v. 2a; the imperative verb "live" occurs in the very center of the three lines; v. 3, on preserving the teaching upon one's very person, matches vv. 1–2, on preserving the teaching internally by memorizing it.

*[6:17–19] The seven vices, symbolized for the most part by bodily organs, are pride, lying, murder, intrigue, readiness to do evil, false witness, and the stirring up of discord.

†[6:20–35] The second of three instructions on adultery (5:1–23; 6:20–35; and chap. 7). The instructions assume that wisdom will protect one from adultery and its consequences: loss of property and danger to one's person. In this poem, the father and the mother urge their son to keep their teaching constantly before his eyes. The teaching will light his way and make it a path to life (v. 23). The teaching will preserve him from the adulterous woman who is far more dangerous than a prostitute. Prostitutes may cost one money, but having an affair with someone else's wife puts one in grave danger. The poem bluntly urges self-interest as a motive to refrain from adultery. The poem has three parts. I (vv. 20–24, ten lines), in which v. 23 repeats "command" and "teaching" of v. 20 and "keeping" in v. 24 completes the fixed pair initiated by "observe" in v. 20; II (vv. 25–29, ten lines) is a self-contained argument comparing the costs of a liaison with a prostitute and a married woman; III (vv. 30–35, twelve lines) draws conclusions from the comparison of adultery with theft: the latter involves property only but adultery destroys one's name and very self. The best protection against such a woman is heeding parental instruction, which is to be kept vividly before one's eyes like a written tablet.

‡[6:22] **They**: Heb. has "she." If this verse is not out of place, then the antecedent of "she" is command (v. 20), or perhaps wisdom.

e. [6:24] Prv 2:16; 7:5.   f. [6:25] Ex 20:17; Dt 5:21; Sir 9:8; 25:20; Mt 5:28.

g. [6:29] Sir 9:9.

² Keep my commands and live,*
 and my teaching as the apple of
 your eye;
³ Bind them on your fingers,
 write them on the tablet of your
 heart.ʰ
⁴ Say to Wisdom, "You are my sister!"†
 Call Understanding, "Friend!"
⁵ That they may keep you from a stranger,
 from the foreign woman with her
 smooth words.ⁱ
⁶ For at the window of my house,
 through my lattice I looked out‡
⁷ And I saw among the naive,
 I observed among the young men,
 a youth with no sense,
⁸ Crossing the street near the corner,
 then walking toward her house,
⁹ In the twilight, at dusk of day,
 in the very dark of night.
¹⁰ Then the woman comes to meet him,
 dressed like a harlot, with secret
 designs.
¹¹ She is raucous and unruly,
 her feet cannot stay at home;
¹² Now she is in the streets, now in the open
 squares,
 lurking in ambush at every corner.
¹³ Then she grabs him, kisses him,
 and with an impudent look says to
 him:
¹⁴ "I owed peace offerings,
 and today I have fulfilled my vows;
¹⁵ So I came out to meet you,
 to look for you, and I have found you!
¹⁶ With coverlets I have spread my couch,
 with brocaded cloths of Egyptian
 linen;
¹⁷ I have sprinkled my bed§ with myrrh,
 with aloes, and with cinnamon.
¹⁸ Come, let us drink our fill of love,
 until morning, let us feast on love!
¹⁹ For my husband is not at home,¶
 he has gone on a long journey;

²⁰ A bag of money he took with him,
 he will not return home till the full
 moon."
²¹ She wins him over by repeated urging,
 with her smooth lips she leads him
 astray."ʲ
²² He follows her impulsively,
 like an ox that goes to slaughter;
 Like a stag that bounds toward the net,
²³ till an arrow pierces its liver;
 Like a bird that rushes into a snare,
 unaware that his life is at stake.
²⁴ So now, children, listen to me,††
 be attentive to the words of my
 mouth!
²⁵ Do not let your heart turn to her ways,
 do not go astray in her paths;
²⁶ For many are those she has struck down
 dead,
 numerous, those she has slain.
²⁷ Her house is a highway to Sheol,
 leading down into the chambers of
 death.ᵏ

CHAPTER 8

The Discourse of Wisdom‡‡

¹ Does not Wisdom call,
 and Understanding raise her voice?ˡ

---

*[7:2] Live: here as elsewhere (Gn 20:7; 42:18; 2 Kgs 18:32; Jer 27:12, 17; Ez 18:32), the imperative ("Live!") is uttered against the danger of death, e.g., "Do such and such and you will live (= survive the danger); why should you die?"

†[7:4] You are my sister: "sister" and "brother" are examples of love language in the ancient Near East, occurring in Egyptian love poetry and Mesopotamian marriage songs. In Sg 4:9, 10, 12; 5:1, the man calls the woman, "my sister, my bride." Intimate friendship with Woman Wisdom saves one from false and dangerous relationships.

‡[7:6–7] I looked out . . . I saw . . . : the perspective is unusual. The narrator looks through a window upon the drama in the street.

§[7:17] Bed: a bed can designate a place of burial in Is 57:2; Ez 32:25; 2 Chr 16:14. Myrrh . . . aloes: the spices could be used for funerals as for weddings (Jn 19:39). It is possible that the language is ambivalent, speaking of death as it seems to speak of life. As the woman offers the youth a nuptial feast, she is in reality describing his funerary feast.

¶[7:19–20] For my husband is not at home: the woman is calculating. She knows exactly how long her husband will be gone.

h. [7:3] Dt 6:8. i. [7:5] Prv 2:16; 6:24.

**[7:21] The verbs "to win over" (lit., "to lead astray") and "to lead off" can be used of leading animals such as a donkey (Nm 22:23) or sheep (Jer 23:2 and 50:17). The animal imagery continues as the youth is compared to an ox, a fallow deer, and a bird in the moment they are slaughtered. None of the animals are aware of their impending death.

††[7:24–27] The father addresses "children," a larger audience than his own son; the story is typical, intended for others as an example. The story is a foil to the speech of the other woman in chap. 8.

‡‡[8:1–36] Chapter 8 is Wisdom's longest speech in the book. Wisdom is here personified as in 1:20–33. She exalts her grandeur and origin, and invites all (vv. 1–11) to be attentive to her salutary influence in human society (vv. 12–21), for she was privileged to be present at the creation of the world (vv. 22–31). Finally, she promises life and the favor of God to those who are devoted to her, death to those who reject her.

The poem has four sections, each (except the fourth) with two parts of five lines each:

I.	A. vv. 1–5	B. vv. 6–10
II.	A. vv. 12–16	B. vv. 17–21
III.	A. vv. 22–26	B. vv. 27–31
IV.	vv. 32–36	

Within chaps. 1–9, chap. 8 is the companion piece to Wisdom's first speech in 1:20–33. There she spoke harshly, giving a promise only in the last line; here she speaks invitingly, giving a threat only in the last line.

Chapter 8 is the best-known chapter in Proverbs and has profoundly influenced Jewish and Christian thought. The most explicit and lengthy biblical comment is in Sir 24; it too has thirty-five lines in seven five-line stanzas and develops the theme of Wisdom's intimacy with God and desire to be with human beings. The Gospel of John portrays Jesus in the language of wisdom in Proverbs: Jesus, like Wisdom, calls out to people to listen to him, promises to tell them the truth, seeks disciples, invites them to a banquet, and gives them life. Writers in the patristic period used the language of pre-existent wisdom to express the idea of the pre-existent Word with God.

j. [7:21] Prv 5:3; 6:24. k. [7:27] Prv 2:18–19; 5:5. l. [8:1] Prv 1:20–21; 9:3.

² On the top of the heights along the road,
  at the crossroads she takes her stand;
³ By the gates at the approaches of the city,
  in the entryways she cries aloud:
⁴ "To you, O people, I call;
  my appeal is to you mortals.
⁵ You naive ones, gain prudence,
  you fools,* gain sense.
⁶ Listen! for noble things I speak;
  my lips proclaim honest words.
⁷ †Indeed, my mouth utters truth,
  and my lips abhor wickedness.
⁸ All the words of my mouth are sincere,
  none of them wily or crooked;
⁹ All of them are straightforward to the
    intelligent,
  and right to those who attain
    knowledge.
¹⁰ Take my instruction instead of silver,
  and knowledge rather than choice
    gold.
¹¹ [For Wisdom is better than corals,
  and no treasures can compare with
    her.ᵐ]
¹² I, Wisdom, dwell with prudence,
  and useful knowledge I have.
¹³ [The fear of the LORD is hatred of evil;]
  Pride, arrogance, the evil way,
  and the perverse mouth I hate.ⁿ
¹⁴ Mine are counsel and advice;
  Mine is strength; I am understanding.‡
¹⁵ By me kings reign,
  and rulers enact justice;
¹⁶ By me princes govern,
  and nobles, all the judges of the earth.
¹⁷ Those who love me I also love,
  and those who seek me find me.
¹⁸ With me are riches and honor,ᵒ
  wealth that endures, and
    righteousness.
¹⁹ My fruit is better than gold, even pure
    gold,
  and my yield than choice silver.ᵖ
²⁰ On the way of righteousness I walk,
  along the paths of justice,
²¹ Granting wealth to those who love me,
  and filling their treasuries.

²² §"The LORD begot me, the beginning of
    his works,
  the forerunner of his deeds of long
    ago;�q

²³ From of old I was formed,⁵
  at the first, before the earth.ʳ
²⁴ "When there were no deeps I was brought
    forth,
  when there were no fountains or
    springs of water;
²⁵ Before the mountains were settled into
    place,
  before the hills, I was brought forth;
²⁶ When the earth and the fields were not
    yet made,
  nor the first clods of the world.
²⁷ When he established the heavens, there
    was I,ˢ
  when he marked out the vault over
    the face of the deep;
²⁸ When he made firm the skies above,
  when he fixed fast the springs of the
    deep;
²⁹ When he set for the sea its limit,
  so that the waters should not
    transgress his command;
  When he fixed the foundations of earth,
³⁰ then was I beside him as artisan;††
  I was his delight day by day,
  playing before him all the while,
³¹ Playing over the whole of his earth,
  having my delight with human
    beings.
³² ‡‡Now, children, listen to me;
  happy are they who keep my ways.
³³ Listen to instruction and grow wise,
  do not reject it!
³⁴ Happy the one who listens to me,
  attending daily at my gates,
  keeping watch at my doorposts;
³⁵ For whoever finds me finds life,ᵘ
  and wins favor from the LORD;

and created the universe, adorning it with beauty and variety, and establishing its wonderful order (vv. 27–30). The purpose of the two cosmogonies (vv. 22–26 and 27–31) is to ground Wisdom's claims. The first cosmogony emphasizes that she was born before all else (and so deserving of honor) and the second underscores that she was with the Lord during the creation of the universe. The pre-existence of Woman Wisdom with God is developed in Sir 24 and in New Testament hymns to Christ, especially in Jn 1 and Col 1:15–20.

¶[8:23] **Formed**: since the other verbs of the origin of Wisdom in these verses describe birth, it is likely that the somewhat uncertain verb is to be understood of birth as in Ps 139:13.

**[8:24–26] Perhaps the formless mass from which God created the heavens and the earth; cf. Gn 1:1–2; 2:4–6.

††[8:30] **Artisan**: the translation of the Hebrew word *'āmôn* has been controverted since antiquity. There have been three main opinions: (1) artisan; (2) trustworthy (friend); (3) ward, nursling. The most likely explanation is that *'āmôn* is artisan, related to Akkadian *ummānu*, legendary sages and heroes who brought divine gifts and culture to the human race. **I was his delight**: the chiastic or ABBA structure of vv. 30–31 unifies the four lines and underscores the analogy between Woman Wisdom's intimate relation to the Lord and her intimate relation to human beings, i.e., "delight" + "playing" parallels "playing" + "delight." She is God's friend and intimate and invites human beings to a similar relationship to God through her.

‡‡[8:32–36] The final appeal of Woman Wisdom to her disciples is similar to the appeal of the father in 7:24–27.

*[8:5] **Naive ones ... fools**: see note on 1:4.

†[8:7–8] The truth and sincerity of wisdom are absolute because they are of divine origin. They can neither deceive nor tolerate deception. The intelligent understand and accept this. "Straight" and "crooked" in Hebrew and English are metaphors for true, trustworthy and false, deceitful.

‡[8:14] What is here predicated of Wisdom is elsewhere attributed to God (Jb 12:13–16).

§[8:22–31] Wisdom is of divine origin. She is represented as existing before all things (vv. 22–26), when God planned

m. [8:11] Prv 3:15; Wis 7:8.   n. [8:13] Prv 6:16–17; 16:5.   o. [8:18] Prv 3:16.   p. [8:19] Prv 3:14.   q. [8:22] Wis 9:9; Sir 1:1; 24:9.

r. [8:23] Sir 1:4.   s. [8:27] Prv 3:19; Sir 24:4–5.   t. [8:30] Wis 9:9.   u. [8:35] Prv 3:13–18; 4:22.

³⁶ But those who pass me by do violence to
    themselves;
    all who hate me love death."

CHAPTER 9

The Two Women Invite
Passersby to Their Banquets*

Woman Wisdom Issues Her Invitation

¹ Wisdom has built her house,†
    she has set up her seven columns;
² She has prepared her meat, mixed her
    wine,
    yes, she has spread her table.
³ She has sent out her maidservants; she
    calls‡
    from the heights out over the city:ᵛ
⁴ "Let whoever is naive turn in here;
    to any who lack sense I say,
⁵ Come, eat of my food,
    and drink of the wine I have mixed!
⁶ Forsake foolishness that you may live;§
    advance in the way of
    understanding."

---

*[9:1–6, 13–18] Wisdom and folly are represented as
women, each inviting people to her banquet. Wisdom's banquet symbolizes joy and closeness to God. Unstable and senseless Folly furnishes stolen bread and water of deceit and vice
that bring death to her guests. The opposition between wisdom
and folly was stated at the beginning of chaps. 1–9 (folly in
1:8–19 and wisdom in 1:20–33) and is maintained throughout,
down to this last chapter.

In comparable literature, gods might celebrate their sovereign by building a palace and inviting the other gods to come
to a banquet and celebrate with them. Presumably, Woman
Wisdom is celebrating her grandeur (just described in chap. 8);
her grand house is a symbol of her status as the Lord's friend.
In order to enter the sacred building and take part in the banquet ("eat of my food"), guests must leave aside their old ways
("forsake foolishness").

Verses 7–12 are unrelated to the two invitations to the banquet. They appear to be based on chap. 1, especially on 1:1–7,
22. The Greek version has added a number of verses after v. 12
and v. 18. In the confusion, 9:11 seems to have been displaced
from its original position after 9:6. It has been restored to its
original place in the text.

†[9:1] House: house has a symbolic meaning. Woman Wisdom encourages marital fidelity (2:16–19; 5; 6:20–35; 7), which
builds up a household (cf. chap. 5). Some scholars propose that
an actual seven-pillared house is referred to, but so far none
have been unearthed by archaeologists. Seven may simply connote completeness—a great house.

Some scholars see a connection between the woman's house
here and the woman's house in the final poem (31:10–31). In
chap. 9, she invites the young man to enter her house and feast,
i.e., to marry her. Chapter 31 shows what happens to the man
who marries her; he has a house and enjoys "life" understood
as consisting of a suitable wife, children, wealth, and honor.

‡[9:3] She calls: i.e., invites; this is done indirectly through
her maidservants, but the text could also mean that Wisdom
herself publicly proclaims her invitation.

§[9:6] That you may live: life in Proverbs is this-worldly,
consisting in fearing God or doing one's duty toward God,
enjoying health and long life, possessing wealth, good reputation, and a family. Such a life cannot be attained without God's
help. Hence Wisdom speaks not of life simply but of life with
her; the guest is to live in Wisdom's house.

---

v. [9:3] Prv 8:1–2.

Miscellaneous Aphorisms

⁷ Whoever corrects the arrogant earns
    insults;
    and whoever reproves the wicked
    incurs opprobrium.
⁸ Do not reprove the arrogant, lest they
    hate you;
    reprove the wise, and they will love
    you.ʷ
⁹ Instruct the wise, and they become still
    wiser;
    teach the just, and they advance in
    learning.
¹⁰ The beginning of wisdom is fear of the
    LORD,
    and knowledge of the Holy One is
    understanding.ˣ
¹¹ For by me your days will be multiplied
    and the years of your life
    increased.ʸ
¹² If you are wise, wisdom is to your
    advantage;
    if you are arrogant, you alone shall
    bear it.

Woman Folly Issues Her Invitation

¹³ ⸤Woman Folly is raucous,ᶻ
    utterly foolish; she knows
    nothing.
¹⁴ She sits at the door of her house
    upon a seat on the city heights,
¹⁵ Calling to passersby
    as they go on their way straight
    ahead:
¹⁶ "Let those who are naive turn in here,
    to those who lack sense I say,
¹⁷ Stolen water is sweet,
    and bread taken secretly is
    pleasing!"**
¹⁸ Little do they know that the shades are
    there,
    that her guests are in the depths of
    Sheol!††

¶[9:13–18] Woman Folly is the mirror image of Woman
Wisdom. Both make identical invitations but only one of the
offers is trustworthy. Their hearers must discern which is the
true offer. She is depicted with traits of the adulterous woman
in 2:16–19; chap. 5; 6:20–35; chap. 7. Woman Folly is restless
(cf. 7:11), her path leads to the underworld (2:18; 5:5; 7:27),
and she is ignorant (5:6). In this final scene, she appears in single combat with her great nemesis, Woman Wisdom. Though
the invitations of the two women appear at first hearing to be
the same, they differ profoundly. Wisdom demands that her
guests reject their ignorance, whereas Woman Folly trades on
their ignorance.

**[9:17] "Stolen water" seems to refer to adultery, for "water"
in 5:15–17 refers to the wife's sexuality; "stolen" refers to stealing the sexuality belonging to another's household. "Secret"
evokes the furtive meeting of the wife and the youth in chap. 7.

††[9:18] The banquet chamber of Folly is a tomb from
which no one who enters it is released; cf. 7:27. Shades: the
Rephaim, the inhabitants of the underworld.

---

w. [9:8] Sir 10:27. x. [9:10] Prv 1:7; Jb 28:28; Ps 111:10; Sir
1:16. y. [9:11] Prv 3:2; 16:4, 10; 10:27. z. [9:13–18] Prv 7:7–27.

III. FIRST SOLOMONIC
COLLECTION OF SAYINGS*

CHAPTER 10

1 The Proverbs of Solomon:
   A wise son gives his father joy,
      but a foolish son is a grief to his
         mother.†a

2 Ill-gotten treasures profit nothing,
      but justice saves from death.‡b

3 The LORD does not let the just go hungry,
      but the craving of the wicked he
         thwarts.§

4 The slack hand impoverishes,
      but the busy hand brings riches.c

5 A son who gathers in summer is a credit;
      a son who slumbers during harvest,
         a disgrace.

6 Blessings are for the head of the just;
      but the mouth of the wicked
         conceals violence.¶

7 The memory of the just serves as
         blessing,
      but the name of the wicked will rot.**

8 A wise heart accepts commands,
      but a babbling fool will be
         overthrown.††

9 Whoever walks honestly walks securely,
      but one whose ways are crooked will
         fare badly.

10 One who winks at a fault causes trouble,
      but one who frankly reproves
         promotes peace.

11 The mouth of the just is a fountain of
         life,
      but the mouth of the wicked
         conceals violence.

12 Hatred stirs up disputes,
      d but love covers all offenses.‡‡

13 On the lips of the intelligent is found
         wisdom,
      but a rod for the back of one without
         sense.§§

14 The wise store up knowledge,
      but the mouth of a fool is imminent
         ruin.

15 The wealth of the rich is their strong
         city;
      the ruin of the poor is their poverty.¶¶

16 The labor of the just leads to life,
      the gains of the wicked, to futility.***e

17 Whoever follows instruction is in the path
         to life,
      but whoever disregards reproof goes
         astray.f

18 Whoever conceals hatred has lying lips,
      and whoever spreads slander is a fool.

19 Where words are many, sin is not
         wanting;
      but those who restrain their lips do
         well.g

20 Choice silver is the tongue of the just;
      the heart of the wicked is of little
         worth.

21 The lips of the just nourish many,
      but fools die for want of sense.†††

22 It is the LORD's blessing that brings
         wealth,h

---

*[10:1–22:16] The Proverbs of Solomon are a collection of three hundred and seventy-five proverbs on a wide variety of subjects. No overall arrangement is discernible, but there are many clusters of sayings related by vocabulary and theme. One thread running through the whole is the relationship of the "son," the disciple, to the parents, and its effect upon the house(hold). In chaps. 10–14 almost all the proverbs are antithetical; "the righteous" and "the wicked" (ethical), "the wise" and "the foolish" (sapiential), and "the devout, the pious" and "the irreverent" (religious). Chapters 15–22 have fewer sharp antitheses. The sayings are generally witty, often indirect, and are rich in irony and paradox.

†[10:1] The opening saying ties the whole collection to the first section, for "son," "father," and "mother" evoke the opening line of the first instruction, "Hear, my son, your father's instruction, and reject not your mother's teaching." The son is the subject of parental exhortation throughout chaps. 1–9. This is the first of many sayings on domestic happiness or unhappiness, between parents and children (e.g., 15:20; 17:21) and between husband and wife (e.g., 12:4; 14:1). Founding or maintaining a household is an important metaphor in the book.

Adult children represented the family (headed by the oldest married male) to the outside world. Foolishness, i.e., malicious ignorance, brought dishonor to the parents and the family.

‡[10:2] **Death:** untimely, premature, or sorrowful. The word "death" can have other overtones (see Wis 1:15).

§[10:3] The last of the three introductory sayings in the collection, which emphasize, respectively, the sapiential (v. 1), ethical (v. 2), and religious (v. 3) dimensions of wisdom. In this saying, God will not allow the appetite of the righteous to go unfulfilled. The appetite of hunger is singled out; it stands for all the appetites.

¶[10:6] This saying, like several others in the chapter, plays on the different senses of the verb "to cover." As in English, "to cover" can mean to fill (as in Is 60:2) and to conceal (as in Jb 16:18). Colon B can be read either "violence *fills* the mouth (= head) of the wicked" or "the mouth of the wicked *conceals* violence." The ambiguity is intentional; the proverb is meant to be read both ways.

**[10:7] The name of the righteous continues to be used after their death in blessings such as "May you be as blessed as Abraham," but the wicked, being enemies of God, do not live on in anyone's memory. Their names rot with their bodies.

††[10:8] The wise take in instruction from their teachers but those who expel or pour out folly through their words will themselves be expelled.

‡‡[10:12] **Love covers all offenses:** a favorite maxim in the New Testament; cf. 1 Cor 13:7; Jas 5:20; 1 Pt 4:8. Cf. also Prv 17:9.

§§[10:13] An unusual juxtaposition of "lips" and "back." Those who have no wisdom on their lips (words) are fated to feel a punishing rod on their back.

¶¶[10:15] An observation rather than a moral evaluation of wealth and poverty; but cf. 18:10–11.

***[10:16] Wages are a metaphor for reward and punishment. The Hebrew word does not mean "sin" here but falling short, a meaning that is frequent in Proverbs. Cf. Rom 6:1: "But what profit did you get then from the things of which you are now ashamed? For the end of those things is death."

†††[10:21] The wise by their words maintain others in life whereas the foolish cannot keep themselves from sin that leads to premature death.

---

a. [10:1] Prv 1:1; 15:20; 17:25; 19:13; 25:1; 29:15.   b. [10:2] Prv 11:4, 6.   c. [10:4] Prv 6:11; 12:24; 13:4; 20:13; 28:19.

d. [10:12] 1 Cor 13:4–7; 1 Pt 4:8.   e. [10:16] Prv 11:18–19.   f. [10:17] Prv 15:10.   g. [10:19] Prv 17:27; Sir 20:17; Jas 1:19.   h. [10:22] Sir 11:22.

and no effort can substitute for it.*
²³ Crime is the entertainment of the fool;
    but wisdom is for the person of
    understanding.
²⁴ What the wicked fear will befall them,
    but the desire of the just will be
    granted.
²⁵ When the tempest passes, the wicked are
    no more;
    but the just are established forever.
²⁶ As vinegar to the teeth, and smoke to the
    eyes,
    are sluggards to those who send
    them.
²⁷ Fear of the LORD prolongs life,
    but the years of the wicked are cut
    short.ⁱ
²⁸ The hope of the just brings joy,
    but the expectation of the wicked
    perishes.†
²⁹ The LORD is a stronghold to those who
    walk honestly,
    downfall for evildoers.
³⁰ The just will never be disturbed,
    but the wicked will not abide in the
    land.
³¹ The mouth of the just yields wisdom,
    but the perverse tongue will be cut
    off.
³² The lips of the just know favor,
    but the mouth of the wicked,
    perversion.‡

CHAPTER 11

¹ False scales are an abomination to the
    LORD,
    but an honest weight, his delight.§ʲ
² When pride comes, disgrace comes;
    but with the humble is wisdom.¶
³ The honesty of the upright guides them;
    the faithless are ruined by their
    duplicity.

⁴ Wealth is useless on a day of wrath,**ᵏ
    but justice saves from death.
⁵ The justice of the honest makes their way
    straight,
    but by their wickedness the wicked
    fall.††ˡ
⁶ The justice of the upright saves them,
    but the faithless are caught in their
    own intrigue.
⁷ When a person dies, hope is destroyed;ᵐ
    expectation pinned on wealth is
    destroyed.‡‡
⁸ The just are rescued from a tight spot,
    but the wicked fall into it instead.
⁹ By a word the impious ruin their neighbors,ⁿ
    but through their knowledge the just
    are rescued.§§
¹⁰ When the just prosper, the city rejoices;ᵒ
    when the wicked perish, there is
    jubilation.
¹¹ Through the blessing of the upright the
    city is exalted,
    but through the mouth of the
    wicked it is overthrown.
¹² Whoever reviles a neighbor lacks sense,
    but the intelligent keep silent.
¹³ One who slanders reveals secrets,ᵖ
    but a trustworthy person keeps a
    confidence.
¹⁴ For lack of guidance a people falls;
    security lies in many counselors.�q
¹⁵ Harm will come to anyone going surety
    for another,ʳ
    but whoever hates giving pledges is
    secure.¶¶
¹⁶ A gracious woman gains esteem,
    and ruthless men gain wealth.***
¹⁷ Kindly people benefit themselves,
    but the merciless harm themselves.

---

*[10:22] Human industry is futile without divine approval;
cf. Ps 127:1–2; Mt 6:25–34.
†[10:28] The thought is elliptical. Joy comes from fulfillment of one's plans, which the righteous can count on.
The opposite of joy thus is not sadness but unfulfillment
("perishes").
‡[10:32] The word used for "favor" is favor shown by an
authority (God or the king), not favor shown by a peer. A
righteous person's words create a climate of favor and acceptance, whereas crooked words will not gain acceptance. In
Hebrew as in English, straight and crooked are metaphors for
good and wicked.
§[11:1] The word pair "abomination" and "delight" (=
acceptable) to God is common in Proverbs. Originally the
language of ritual, the words came to be applied to whatever
pleases or displeases God (cf. also 11:20). False weights were a
constant problem even though weights were standardized. Cf.
20:23; Hos 12:8; Am 8:5.
¶[11:2] Disgrace is the very opposite of what the proud so
ardently want. Those who do not demand their due receive
wisdom.

i. [10:27] Prv 3:2; 4:10; 9:11; 14:27.   j. [11:1] Prv 16:11; 20:10; Lv
19:35–36.

**[11:4] Cf. note on 10:2. A day of wrath is an unforeseen
disaster (even death). Only one's relationship to God, which
makes one righteous, is of any help on such a day.
††[11:5] In Hebrew as in English, "way" means the course
of one's life; similarly, "straight" and "crooked" are metaphors
for morally straightforward and for bad, deviant, perverted.
‡‡[11:7] An ancient scribe added "wicked" to person in
colon A, for the statement that hope ends at death seemed to
deny life after death. The saying, however, is not concerned
with life after death but with the fact that in the face of death
all hopes based on one's own resources are vain. The aphorism
is the climax of the preceding six verses; human resources
cannot overcome mortality (cf. Ps 49:13).
§§[11:9] What the wicked express harms others; what the
righteous leave unsaid protects. Verses 9–14 are related in
theme: the effect of good and bad people, especially their words,
on their community.
¶¶[11:15] Proverbs is opposed to providing surety for
another's loan (see note on 6:1–5) and expresses this view
throughout the book.
***[11:16] Wealth and esteem are good things in Proverbs,
but the means for acquiring them are flawed. As precious gifts,
they must be granted, not taken. The esteem of others that
depends on beauty is as fleeting as beauty itself (cf. 31:30) and
the wealth acquired by aggressive behavior lasts only as long
as one has physical strength.

k. [11:4] Prv 10:2. l. [11:5] Prv 28:18. m. [11:7] Prv 10:28; Wis
3:18. n. [11:9] Prv 29:5. o. [11:10] Prv 28:12; 29:2. p. [11:13]
Prv 20:19. q. [11:14] Prv 15:22; 20:18; 24:6. r. [11:15] Prv 6:1–2.

¹⁸ The wicked make empty profits,
  but those who sow justice have a
    sure reward.^s
¹⁹ Justice leads toward life,
  but pursuit of evil, toward death.
²⁰ The crooked in heart are an abomination
    to the LORD,
  but those who walk blamelessly are
    his delight.[*]
²¹ Be assured, the wicked shall not go
    unpunished,
  but the offspring of the just shall
    escape.
²² Like a golden ring in a swine's snout
  is a beautiful woman without
    judgment.[†]
²³ The desire of the just ends only in good;
  the expectation of the wicked is wrath.
²⁴ One person is lavish yet grows still richer;
  another is too sparing, yet is the
    poorer.[‡]
²⁵ Whoever confers benefits will be amply
    enriched,
  and whoever refreshes others will be
    refreshed.
²⁶ Whoever hoards grain, the people curse,
  but blessings are on the head of one
    who distributes it!
²⁷ Those who seek the good seek favor,
  but those who pursue evil will have
    evil come upon them.[§]
²⁸ Those who trust in their riches will fall,
  but like green leaves the just will
    flourish.^t
²⁹ Those who trouble their household
    inherit the wind,
  and fools become slaves to the wise
    of heart.
³⁰ The fruit of justice is a tree of life,
  and one who takes lives is a sage.[¶]
³¹ If the just are recompensed on the earth,
  how much more the wicked and the
    sinner!^{**u}

CHAPTER 12

¹ Whoever loves discipline loves
    knowledge,
  but whoever hates reproof is stupid.^{††v}
² A good person wins favor from the LORD,
  but the schemer he condemns.^{‡‡}
³ No one is made secure by wickedness,
  but the root of the just will never be
    disturbed.^{§§}
⁴ A woman of worth is the crown of her
    husband,^w
  but a disgraceful one is like rot in his
    bones.^{¶¶}
⁵ The plans of the just are right;
  the designs of the wicked are deceit.^{***}
⁶ The words of the wicked are a deadly
    ambush,
  but the speech of the upright saves
    them.^{†††}
⁷ Overthrow the wicked and they are no
    more,
  but the house of the just stands firm.
⁸ For their good sense people are praised,
  but the perverse of heart are
    despised.^{‡‡‡}
⁹ Better to be slighted and have a servant
  than put on airs and lack bread.^x
¹⁰ The just take care of their livestock,
  but the compassion of the wicked
    is cruel.^{§§§}
¹¹ Those who till their own land have food
    in plenty,
  but those who engage in idle
    pursuits lack sense.^{¶¶¶y}

---

divine judgment is exercised on all human action, even the best. The thought should strike terror into the hearts of habitual wrongdoers.

††[12:1] Discipline in Proverbs is both doctrine and training. The path to wisdom includes obedience to teachers and parents, acceptance of the community's traditions.

‡‡[12:2] The antithesis is between the good person who, by reason of that goodness, already has divine acceptance, and the wicked person who, despite great effort, gains only condemnation.

§§[12:3] Human beings are described as "made secure" in Jb 21:8; Ps 101:7; 102:29. "Root" in the context means enduring to succeeding generations, as in Mal 3:19 and Jh 8:17.

¶¶[12:4] In Proverbs a crown is the result and sign of wise conduct. A good wife is a public sign of the husband's shrewd judgment and divine blessing (crown), whereas a bad wife brings him inner pain (rot in the bones).

***[12:5] The opposite of "just" is not injustice but "deceit." The wicked will be deceived in their plans in the sense that their planning will not succeed.

†††[12:6] Words are a favorite theme of Proverbs. The words of the wicked effect harm to others whereas the words of the righteous protect themselves.

‡‡‡[12:8] The heart, the seat of intelligence, will eventually be revealed in the actions that people do, either for praise or for blame.

§§§[12:10] The righteous are sympathetically aware of the needs of their livestock and prosper from their herd's good health. The wicked will pay the price for their self-centeredness and cruelty.

¶¶¶[12:11] The second line clarifies the first: idleness will give one plenty of nothing. "Lacking sense" is a common phrase for fools.

---

*[11:20] The terminology of ritual (acceptable and unacceptable sacrifice, "abomination" and "delight") is applied to human conduct as in v. 1. The whole of human life is under divine scrutiny, not just ritual.

†[11:22] Ear and nose rings were common jewelry for women. A humorous saying on the priority of wisdom over beauty in choosing a wife.

‡[11:24] A paradox: spending leads to more wealth.

§[11:27] The saying is about seeking one thing and finding another. Striving for good leads to acceptance by God; seeking evil means only that trouble will come. The same Hebrew word means evil and trouble.

¶[11:30] Most translations emend Hebrew "wise person" in colon B on the basis of the Greek and Syriac translations to "violence" (similar in spelling), because the verb "to take a life" is a Hebrew idiom for "to kill" (as also in English). The emendation is unnecessary, however, for the saying deliberately plays on the odd meaning: the one who takes lives is not the violent but the wise person, for the wise have a profound influence upon life. There is a similar wordplay in 29:10.

**[11:31] The saying is not about life after death; "on the earth" means life in the present world. The meaning is that

---

s. [11:18] Prv 10:16.   t. [11:28] Ps 52:9–10.   u. [11:31] 1 Pt 4:18.

v. [12:1] Prv 15:5, 10; Sir 21:6.   w. [12:4] Prv 31:10; Sir 21:1, 16.
x. [12:9] Sir 10:26.   y. [12:11] Prv 28:19; Sir 20:27.

¹² A wicked person desires the catch of evil
people,
but the root of the righteous will
bear fruit.*
¹³ By the sin of their lips the wicked are
ensnared,
but the just escape from a tight spot.
¹⁴ From the fruit of their mouths people
have their fill of good,^z
and the works of their hands come
back upon them.†
¹⁵ The way of fools is right in their own
eyes,
but those who listen to advice are
the wise.
¹⁶ Fools immediately show their anger,
but the shrewd conceal contempt.
¹⁷ Whoever speaks honestly testifies truly,
but the deceitful make lying
witnesses.‡^a
¹⁸ The babble of some people is like sword
thrusts,
but the tongue of the wise is healing.
¹⁹ Truthful lips endure forever,
the lying tongue, for only a
moment.§
²⁰ Deceit is in the heart of those who plot
evil,
but those who counsel peace have
joy.
²¹ No harm befalls the just,
but the wicked are overwhelmed
with misfortune.
²² Lying lips are an abomination to the
LORD,^b
but those who are truthful, his
delight.
²³ The shrewd conceal knowledge,
but the hearts of fools proclaim
folly.¶
²⁴ The diligent hand will govern,
but sloth makes for forced labor.^c

²⁵ Worry weighs down the heart,
but a kind word gives it joy.^d
²⁶ The just act as guides to their neighbors,
but the way of the wicked leads
them astray.
²⁷ Sloth does not catch its prey,
but the wealth of the diligent is
splendid.
²⁸ In the path of justice is life,
but the way of abomination leads
to death.

CHAPTER 13

¹ A wise son loves correction,
but the scoffer heeds no rebuke.**
² From the fruit of the mouth one enjoys
good things,^e
but from the throat of the
treacherous comes violence.††
³ Those who guard their mouths preserve
themselves;‡‡
those who open wide their lips bring
ruin.^f
⁴ The appetite of the sluggard craves but has
nothing,
but the appetite of the diligent is
amply satisfied.
⁵ The just hate deceitful words,
but the wicked are odious and
disgraceful.
⁶ Justice guards one who walks
honestly,
but sin leads the wicked astray.^g
⁷ One acts rich but has nothing;
another acts poor but has great
wealth.§§
⁸ People's riches serve as ransom for their
lives,
but the poor do not even hear a
threat.¶¶

---

*[12:12] A difficult, possibly corrupt saying, but there is no good alternative to the Hebrew text. The wicked desire what the malevolent have captured or killed, but their actions will go for naught because they invite punishment. The righteous, on the other hand, will bear fruit.

†[12:14] The saying contrasts words and deeds. "Fruit" here is not what one normally eats, as in 1:31; 8:19; 31:16, 31, but the consequences of one's actions. In the second line the things that issue from one's hands (one's deeds) come back to one in recompense or punishment. Prv 13:2a and 18:20 are variants. Cf. Mt 7:17; Gal 6:8.

‡[12:17] What is the rule of thumb for judging legal testimony? Look to the ordinary conduct and daily speech of a witness.

§[12:19] The saying has a double meaning: lies are quickly found out whereas truthful statements endure; truth-tellers, being favored by God, live long lives, whereas liars invite punishment.

¶[12:23] "Knowledge" here is "what one knows, has in one's heart," not knowledge in general. Fools reveal all they have stored in their heart and it naturally turns out to be folly. Revealing and concealing are constant themes in Proverbs.

**[13:1] Another in the series on the household, this one on the relation of parents and children. See under 10:1. The scoffer in Proverbs condemns discipline and thus can never become wise. Wise adult children advertise to the community what they received from their parents, for children become wise through a dialectical process involving the parents. A foolish adult child witnesses to foolish parents.

††[13:2] One's mouth normally eats food from outside, but in the moral life, things are reversed: one eats from the fruit of one's mouth, i.e., one experiences the consequences of one's own actions. Since the mouth of the treacherous is filled with violence, one must assume that they will some day endure violence.

‡‡[13:3] **Preserve themselves**: in Hebrew, literally to preserve the throat area, the moist breathing center of one's body, thus "life," "soul," or "self." There is wordplay: if you guard your mouth (= words) you guard your "soul." Fools, on the other hand, do not guard but open their lips and disaster strikes. A near duplicate is 21:23.

§§[13:7] Appearances can be deceiving; possessions do not always reveal the true state of a person.

¶¶[13:8] Related to v. 7. Possessions enable the wealthy to pay ransom but the poor are "protected" by lack of possessions: they never hear the threat of the pursuer. Cf. the use of the word "threat" in Is 30:17.

---

z. [12:14] Prv 13:2; 18:20.   a. [12:17] Prv 14:5.   b. [12:22] Prv 6:17.   c. [12:24] Prv 10:4; 13:4.

d. [12:25] Prv 15:13; 17:22.   e. [13:2] Prv 12:14; 18:20.   f. [13:3] Prv 18:7; 21:23.   g. [13:6] Prv 11:3, 5–6.

⁹ The light of the just gives joy,
   but the lamp* of the wicked goes out.^h
¹⁰ The stupid sow discord by their
      insolence,
   but wisdom is with those who take
      counsel.
¹¹ Wealth won quickly dwindles away,
   but gathered little by little, it grows.ⁱ
¹² Hope deferred makes the heart sick,
   but a wish fulfilled is a tree of life.[†]
¹³ Whoever despises the word must pay for
      it,[‡]
   but whoever reveres the command
      will be rewarded.
¹⁴ The teaching of the wise is a fountain of
      life,
   turning one from the snares of
      death.
¹⁵ Good sense brings favor,
   but the way of the faithless is their
      ruin.[§]
¹⁶ The shrewd always act prudently
   but the foolish parade folly.[¶]
¹⁷ A wicked messenger brings on disaster,
   but a trustworthy envoy is a healing
      remedy.
¹⁸ Poverty and shame befall those who let go
      of discipline,
   but those who hold on to reproof
      receive honor.^{**}
¹⁹ Desire fulfilled delights the soul,
   but turning from evil is an
      abomination to fools.
²⁰ Walk with the wise and you become
      wise,
   but the companion of fools fares
      badly.^j
²¹ Misfortune pursues sinners,
   but the just shall be recompensed
      with good.
²² The good leave an inheritance to their
      children's children,
   but the wealth of the sinner is stored
      up for the just.

²³ The tillage of the poor yields abundant
      food,
   but possessions are swept away for
      lack of justice.^{††}
²⁴ Whoever spares the rod hates the child,
   but whoever loves will apply
      discipline.^k
²⁵ When the just eat, their hunger is
      appeased;
   but the belly of the wicked suffers
      want.

CHAPTER 14

¹ Wisdom builds her house,
   but Folly tears hers down with her
      own hands.^{‡‡}
² Those who walk uprightly fear the Lord,
   but those who are devious in their
      ways spurn him.
³ In the mouth of the fool is a rod for
      pride,
   but the lips of the wise preserve
      them.
⁴ Where there are no oxen, the crib is
      clean;
   but abundant crops come through
      the strength of the bull.^{§§}
⁵ A trustworthy witness does not lie,
   but one who spouts lies makes a
      lying witness.^{¶¶l}
⁶ The scoffer seeks wisdom in vain,
   but knowledge is easy for the
      intelligent.
⁷ Go from the face of the fool;
   you get no knowledge from such
      lips.
⁸ The wisdom of the shrewd enlightens
      their way,
   but the folly of fools is deceit.^{***}
⁹ The wicked scorn a guilt offering,
   but the upright find acceptance.
¹⁰ The heart knows its own bitterness,
   and its joy no stranger shares.^{†††}

---

*[13:9] **Light . . . lamp**: symbols of life and prosperity;
cf. 4:18–19.

†[13:12] "Tree of life" occurs in Gn 2–3, Prv 3:18; 11:30;
13:12; 15:4, and Rev 2:7; 22:2, 14, 19. It provides food and
healing.

‡[13:13] **Must pay for it**: lit., "is pledge to it," i.e., just as
one who has pledged or provided surety for another's loan is
obligated to that pledge, so one is not free of a command until
one performs it.

§[13:15] As the behavior of the wise wins them favor that
increases their prosperity, like Abigail with David in 1 Sm 25,
so the way (= conduct) of the faithless ruins their lives.

¶[13:16] Like 12:23 and 15:2, 3, the saying is about revealing and concealing. The wise reveal their wisdom in their
actions whereas fools "parade," spread out their folly for all to
see. The verb is used of vendors spreading their wares and of
birds spreading their wings.

**[13:18] The saying plays on letting go and holding on.
Wisdom consists in not rejecting discipline and being open to
the comments of others, even if they are reproving comments.

††[13:23] An observation on the poor. The lands of the
poor are as fertile as anyone's, for nature does not discriminate
against them. Their problem is lack of justice, which puts their
harvest at risk from unscrupulous human beings.

‡‡[14:1] The relationship between Wisdom, personified as
a woman, and building a house is a constant theme. As elsewhere, the book here warns against the wrong woman and
praises the right woman.

§§[14:4] If one has no animals, one does not have the burden
of keeping the crib full, but without them one will have no crops
to fill the barn. Colon B reverses the sense of colon A and also
reverses the consonants of *bar* ("clean") to *rab* ("abundant").

¶¶[14:5] On discerning the truthfulness of witnesses; see
12:17.

***[14:8] Wisdom enables the shrewd to know their path is
right but folly leads fools on the wrong path ("deceit"), which
calls down retribution.

†††[14:10] The heart in Proverbs is where a person's sense
impressions are stored and reflected upon. It is thus one's most
personal and individual part. One's sorrows and joys (= the full

---

h. [13:9] Prv 24:20.   i. [13:11] Prv 28:20, 22.   j. [13:20] Sir 6:34;
8:8, 17.

k. [13:24] Prv 19:18; 22:15; 23:13–14; 29:15; Sir 30:1, 8–13.   l. [14:5]
Prv 12:17.

¹¹ The house of the wicked will be
destroyed,
but the tent of the upright will
flourish.*^m
¹² Sometimes a way seems right,
but the end of it leads to death!ⁿ
¹³ Even in laughter the heart may be sad,
and the end of joy may be sorrow.
¹⁴ From their own ways turncoats are
sated,
from their own actions, the loyal.
¹⁵ The naive believe everything,
but the shrewd watch their steps.[†]
¹⁶ The wise person is cautious and turns
from evil;
the fool is reckless and gets
embroiled.
¹⁷ The quick-tempered make fools of
themselves,
and schemers are hated.
¹⁸ The simple have folly as an adornment,
but the shrewd wear knowledge as
a crown.[‡]
¹⁹ The malicious bow down before the good,
and the wicked, at the gates of the
just.
²⁰ Even by their neighbors the poor are
despised,
but a rich person's friends are many.^o
²¹ Whoever despises the hungry comes up
short,
but happy the one who is kind to
the poor![§]
²² Do not those who plan evil go astray?
But those who plan good win
steadfast loyalty.
²³ In all labor there is profit,
but mere talk tends only to loss.
²⁴ The crown of the wise is wealth;
the diadem of fools is folly.
²⁵ The truthful witness saves lives,
but whoever utters lies is a betrayer.
²⁶ The fear of the Lord is a strong defense,
a refuge even for one's children.
²⁷ The fear of the Lord is a fountain of life,
turning one from the snares of death.
²⁸ A multitude of subjects is the glory of the
king;
but if his people are few, a prince is
ruined.

²⁹ Long-suffering results in great wisdom;
a short temper raises folly high.^{¶p}
³⁰ A tranquil mind gives life to the body,
but jealousy rots the bones.
³¹ Those who oppress the poor revile their
Maker,
but those who are kind to the needy
honor him.^q
³² The wicked are overthrown by their
wickedness,
but the just find a refuge in their
integrity.
³³ Wisdom can remain silent in the
discerning heart,
but among fools she must make
herself known.**^r
³⁴ Justice exalts a nation,
but sin is a people's disgrace.^{††}
³⁵ The king favors the skillful servant,
but the shameless one incurs his
wrath.

CHAPTER 15

¹ ^{‡‡}A mild answer turns back wrath,^s
but a harsh word stirs up anger.^{§§}
² The tongue of the wise pours out
knowledge,
but the mouth of fools spews folly.
³ The eyes of the Lord are in every place,
keeping watch on the evil and the
good.
⁴ A soothing tongue is a tree of life,
but a perverse one breaks the spirit.
⁵ The fool spurns a father's instruction,
but whoever heeds reproof is
prudent.^{¶¶t}
⁶ In the house of the just there are ample
resources,
but the harvest of the wicked is in peril.
⁷ The lips of the wise spread knowledge,
but the heart of fools is not steadfast.***
⁸ The sacrifice of the wicked is an
abomination to the Lord,^u

¶[14:29] A series of puns on short and long; lit., "long of nostrils (idiom for "patient"), large in wisdom, / short in breath (idiom for "impatient"), makes folly tall."

**[14:33] Wisdom can remain silent in a wise person as a welcome friend. But it must speak out among fools, for the dissonance is so strong.

††[14:34] The rare noun "disgrace" occurs elsewhere only in Lv 20:17. In measuring the greatness of a nation, one is tempted to consider territory, wealth, history, but the most important criterion is its relationship to God ("justice").

‡‡[15:1–7] These verses form a section beginning and ending with the topic of words.

§§[15:1] Paradoxically, where words are concerned soft is powerful and hard is ineffective.

¶¶[15:5] One becomes wise by keeping and foolish by rejecting. One must accept the tradition of the community.

***[15:7] "Lips" and "heart" are a fixed pair, in Proverbs signifying, respectively, expression and source. The wise disseminate what they have in their heart, but the wicked are unsound even in the source of their words, their hearts.

---

range of emotions) cannot be shared fully with another. Verse 13 expresses the same individuality of the human person.

*[14:11] The traditional fixed pair "house" and "tent" is used to express the paradox that a house can be less secure than a tent if there is no justice.

†[14:15] The naive gullibly rely on others' words whereas the shrewd watch their own steps.

‡[14:18] The inner quality of a person, simple or wise, will eventually be revealed.

§[14:21] The paradox is that anyone who spurns the hungry will lack something, but anyone who shows mercy (presumably by giving to the poor) will gain prosperity.

---

m. [14:11] Prv 3:33; 12:7; 15:25.   n. [14:12] Prv 16:25.   o. [14:20] Prv 19:4, 7; Sir 6:8, 12.

p. [14:29] Prv 16:32; 19:11; Jas 1:19.   q. [14:31] Prv 17:5.   r. [14:33] Prv 1:22; 8:1.   s. [15:1] Prv 25:15; Sir 6:5.   t. [15:5] Prv 12:1; 13:18.   u. [15:8] Prv 21:27; Eccl 4:17; Is 1:11–15.

but the prayer of the upright is his
delight.
9 The way of the wicked is an abomination
to the Lord,
but he loves one who pursues
justice.ᵛ
10 Discipline seems bad to those going
astray;
one who hates reproof will die.*
11 Sheol and Abaddon† lie open before the
Lord;
how much more the hearts of
mortals!
12 Scoffers do not love reproof;
to the wise they will not go.
13 A glad heart lights up the face,
but an anguished heart breaks the
spirit.ʷ
14 The discerning heart seeks knowledge,
but the mouth of fools feeds on
folly.‡
15 All the days of the poor are evil,
but a good heart is a continual
feast.§
16 ⁵Better a little with fear of the Lord
than a great fortune with anxiety.
17 Better a dish of herbs where love is
than a fatted ox and hatred with it.
18 The ill-tempered stir up strife,ˣ
but the patient settle disputes.
19 The way of the sluggard is like a thorn
hedge,
but the path of the diligent is a
highway.
20 A wise son gives his father joy,
but a fool despises his mother.ʸ
21 Folly is joy** to the senseless,
but the person of understanding
goes the straight way.
22 Plans fail when there is no counsel,
but they succeed when advisers are
many.††ᶻ

23 One has joy from an apt response;
a word in season, how good it is!‡‡ᵃ
24 The path of life leads upward for the
prudent,
turning them from Sheol below.§§
25 The Lord pulls down the house of the
proud,
but preserves intact the widow's
landmark.
26 The schemes of the wicked are an
abomination to the Lord,ᵇ
but gracious words are pure.⁵⁵
27 The greedy tear down their own house,
but those who hate bribes will live.***
28 The heart of the just ponders a response,
but the mouth of the wicked spews
evil.
29 The Lord is far from the wicked,
but hears the prayer of the just.
30 A cheerful glance brings joy to the heart;
good news invigorates the bones.
31 The ear that listens to salutary reproofᶜ
is at home among the wise.†††
32 Those who disregard discipline hate
themselves,
but those who heed reproof acquire
understanding.
33 The fear of the Lord is training for wisdom,
and humility goes before honors.ᵈ

CHAPTER 16

1 Plans are made in human hearts,
but from the Lord comes the
tongue's response.‡‡‡
2 All one's ways are pure§§§ in one's own eyes,
but the measurer of motives is the
Lord.ᵉ
3 Entrust your works to the Lord,
and your plans will succeed.
4 The Lord has made everything for a
purpose,
even the wicked for the evil day.⁵⁵⁵

---

*[15:10] Discipline, always a good thing in Proverbs,
seems bad to those deliberately wandering from justice.
†[15:11] **Sheol and Abaddon**: terms for the abode of the
dead, signifying the profound obscurity which is open nevertheless to the sight and power of God; cf. 27:20.
‡[15:14] The contrasts include heart (organ of reflection)
and mouth (organ of expression), and the wise and fools. One
type feeds its mind with wisdom and the other feeds its face
with folly.
§[15:15] Good heart does not refer to good intentions but
to an instructed mind. Wisdom makes poverty not only bear-
able but even joyful like the joy of feast days.
⁵[15:16–17] The sages favor wealth over poverty—but not
at any price; cf. Ps 37:16.
**[15:21] The word "joy" occurs in the first line of vv. 20,
21, and 23. The state of folly is joy to a fool but the wise person
is totally absorbed in keeping on the right or straight road.
††[15:22] Failure to consult makes it likely a plan will not
succeed. The point is nicely made by contrasting the singular
number in the first line ("no counsel") with the plural number
in the second line ("many advisors").

‡‡[15:23] Conversation is the art of saying the right thing
at the right time. It gives pleasure to speaker and hearer alike.
§§[15:24] Death is personified as Sheol, the underworld.
"Up" and "down" in Hebrew as in English are metaphors for
success and failure (see Dt 28:43). One who stays on the path
of life need not fear the punishment that stalks sinners.
⁵⁵[15:26] "Pure" here means acceptable. The language of ritual (acceptable or pure) is applied to ordinary human actions.
"Gracious words" are words that bring peace to the neighbor.
***[15:27] The same lesson as the opening scene of Proverbs
(1:8–19): one cannot build a house by unjust gain. Injustice
will come back upon a house so built.
†††[15:31] To become wise, one must hear and integrate
perspectives contrary to one's own, which means accepting
"reproof." Wisdom does not isolate one but places one in the
company of the wise.
‡‡‡[16:1] Words, like actions, often produce results different from those which were planned, and this comes under the
agency of God.
§§§[16:2] "Pure" in a moral sense for human action is found
only in Job and Proverbs. As in v. 1, the contrast is between
human intent and divine assessment.
⁵⁵⁵[16:4] Even the wicked do not lie outside God's plan.

---

v. [15:9] Prv 11:20; 21:21. w. [15:13] Prv 12:25; 17:22; Sir 30:22.
x. [15:18] Prv 6:21; 29:22; Sir 28:11. y. [15:20] Prv 10:1; 29:3.
z. [15:22] Prv 11:14.

a. [15:23] Prv 25:11; Sir 20:6. b. [15:26] Prv 6:18. c. [15:31] Prv
25:12. d. [15:33] Prv 1:7; 19:12; Sir 1:24. e. [16:2] Prv 21:2.

⁵ Every proud heart* is an abomination to
       the LORD;ᶠ
   be assured that none will go
       unpunished.
⁶ By steadfast loyalty guilt is expiated,
   and by the fear of the LORD evil is
       avoided.†
⁷ When the LORD is pleased with someone's
       ways,
   he makes even enemies be at peace
       with them.
⁸ Better a little with justice,
   than a large income with injustice.
⁹ The human heart plans the way,
   but the LORD directs the steps.‡ᵍ
¹⁰ An oracle is upon the king's lips,
   no judgment of his mouth is false.§
¹¹ Balance and scales belong to the LORD;
   every weight in the sack is his
       concern.ʰ
¹² Wrongdoing is an abomination to kings,
   for by justice the throne endures.ⁱ
¹³ The king takes delight in honest lips,
   and whoever speaks what is right
       he loves.ʲ
¹⁴ The king's wrath is a messenger of death,ᵏ
   but a wise person can pacify it.
¹⁵ A king's smile means life,
   and his favor is like a rain cloud in
       spring.¶
¹⁶ How much better to get wisdom than
       gold!
   To get understanding is preferable
       to silver.**ˡ
¹⁷ The path of the upright leads away from
       misfortune;
   those who attend to their way guard
       their lives.††

¹⁸ Pride goes before disaster,
   and a haughty spirit before a fall.
¹⁹ It is better to be humble with the poor
   than to share plunder with the
       proud.ᵐ
²⁰ Whoever ponders a matter will be
       successful;
   happy the one who trusts in the
       LORD!
²¹ The wise of heart is esteemed for
       discernment,
   and pleasing speech gains a
       reputation for learning.
²² Good sense is a fountain of life to those
       who have it,
   but folly is the training of fools.
²³ The heart of the wise makes for eloquent
       speech,
   and increases the learning on their
       lips.
²⁴ Pleasing words are a honeycomb,
   sweet to the taste and invigorating to
       the bones.
²⁵ Sometimes a way seems right,
   but the end of it leads to death!ⁿ
²⁶ The appetite of workers works for them,
   for their mouths urge them on.‡‡ᵒ
²⁷ Scoundrels are a furnace of evil,
   and their lips are like a scorching fire.
²⁸ Perverse speech sows discord,
   and talebearing separates bosom
       friends.ᵖ
²⁹ The violent deceive their neighbors,
   and lead them into a way that is not
       good.
³⁰ Whoever winks an eye plans perversity;
   whoever purses the lips does evil.§§
³¹ Gray hair is a crown of glory;�q
   it is gained by a life that is just.
³² The patient are better than warriors,
   and those who rule their temper,
       better than the conqueror of
       a city.ʳ
³³ Into the bag the lot is cast,
   but from the LORD comes every
       decision.¶¶

CHAPTER 17
¹ Better a dry crust with quiet

---

*[16:5] **Proud heart**: lit., "high of heart." To forget one is
a fallible human being is so basic an error that one cannot
escape exposure and punishment.

†[16:6] As v. 5 used the language of worship to express
what is acceptable or not to God, so this saying uses similar
language to declare that lovingly loyal conduct undoes the
effects of sin.

‡[16:9] As in vv. 1–3, the antithesis is between human
plans and divine disposal. The saying uses the familiar metaphor of path for the course of life.

§[16:10] Six sayings on the king and his divine authority
begin here, following the series of sayings about the Lord's
governance in 15:33–16:9, in which "LORD" was mentioned
nine times.

¶[16:15] The last of six sayings about the king. In the previous verse, royal wrath means death; in this verse royal favor
means life. It is significant that royal favor is compared to
something not under human control—the clouds preceding
the spring rains.

**[16:16] The point of comparison is the superiority of the
pursuit of wisdom and gold, not the relative merits of wealth
and wisdom.

††[16:17] In the metaphor of the two ways, the way of the
righteous is protected and the way of the wicked is unprotected. Since the path of the righteous leads therefore away
from trouble, one's task is to stay on it, to "attend to" it.

‡‡[16:26] The adage puzzled ancient and modern commentators. The meaning seems to state the paradox that a person
does not toil to feed the gullet but that the gullet itself "toils" in
the sense that it forces the person to work. As often in Proverbs,
the sense organ stands for the faculty by metonymy. Cf. Eccl 6:7.

§§[16:30] A restless or twitching eye or lip betrays the condition of the heart (cf. 6:13).

¶¶[16:33] Dice were given meanings of "yes" or "no" and
then cast for their answer. What came out was the decision.
Here the saying interprets the sequence of actions: a human
being puts the dice in the bag but what emerges from the bag
is the Lord's decision.

---

f. [16:5] Prv 6:16–17; 8:13.   g. [16:9] Prv 19:21; 20:24; Jer
10:23.   h. [16:11] Prv 11:1.   i. [16:12] Prv 25:5.   j. [16:13] Prv
14:35; 22:11.   k. [16:14] Prv 19:12; 20:2.   l. [16:16] Prv 8:10–11.

m. [16:19] Prv 11:2.   n. [16:25] Prv 14:12.   o. [16:26] Prv 10:4.
p. [16:28] Prv 6:14, 19; 17:9; 26:22; Sir 28:15.   q. [16:31] Prv 20:29.
r. [16:32] Prv 14:29.

than a house full of feasting with
strife.*

2 A wise servant will rule over an unworthy
son,
and will share the inheritance of the
children.†

3 The crucible for silver, and the furnace for
gold,
but the tester of hearts is the Lord.

4 The evildoer gives heed to wicked lips,
the liar, to a mischievous tongue.

5 Whoever mocks the poor reviles their
Maker;
whoever rejoices in their misfortune
will not go unpunished.ˢ

6 Children's children are the crown of the
elderly,
and the glory of children is their
parentage.

7 Fine words ill fit a fool;
how much more lying lips, a noble!

8 A bribe seems a charm to its user;
at every turn it brings success.‡

9 Whoever overlooks an offense fosters
friendship,
but whoever gossips about it
separates friends.§

10 A single reprimand does more for a
discerning person
than a hundred lashes for a fool.¶

11 The wicked pursue only rebellion,
and a merciless messenger is sent
against them.**

12 Face a bear robbed of her cubs,
but never fools in their folly!††

13 If you return evil for good,
evil will not depart from your house.†t'

14 The start of strife is like the opening of a
dam;
check a quarrel before it bursts forth!

15 Whoever acquits the wicked,ᵘ whoever
condemns the just—
both are an abomination to the Lord.

16 Of what use is money in the hands of
fools
when they have no heart to acquire
wisdom?§§

17 A friend is a friend at all times,
and a brother is born for the time of
adversity.ᵛ

18 Those without sense give their hands in
pledge,
becoming surety for their neighbors.ʷ

19 Those who love an offense love a fight;ˣ
those who build their gate high¶¶
court disaster.

20 The perverse in heart come to no good,
and the double-tongued fall into
trouble.***

21 Whoever conceives a fool has grief;
the father of a numskull has no joy.

22 A joyful heart is the health of the body,
but a depressed spirit dries up the
bones.ʸ

23 A guilty person takes out a bribe from the
pocket,
thus perverting the course of
justice.†††

24 On the countenance of a discerning
person is wisdom,ᶻ
but the eyes of a fool are on the ends
of the earth.‡‡‡

25 A foolish son is vexation to his father,
and bitter sorrow to her who bore
him.ᵃ

26 It is wrong to fine an innocent person,
but beyond reason to scourge
nobles.

27 Those who spare their words are truly
knowledgeable,
and those who are discreet are
intelligent.ᵇ

28 Even fools, keeping silent, are considered
wise;
if they keep their lips closed,
intelligent.§§§

---

*[17:1] A "better than" saying, stating the circumstances when a dry crust is better than a banquet. Peace and fellowship give joy to a meal, not the richness of the food. For a similar thought, see 15:16 and 16:8.

†[17:2] Ability is esteemed more highly than ties of blood.

‡[17:8] An observation on the effect of the bribe upon the bribe-giver: it gives an intoxicating feeling of power ("seems"). In v. 23 the evil effects of a bribe are noted.

§[17:9] A paradox. One finds (love, friend) by concealing (an offense), one loses (a friend) by revealing (a secret). In 10:12 love also covers over a multitude of offenses.

¶[17:10] A wonderful comment on the openness and sensitivity of the wise and the foolish. One type learns from a single word and for the other one hundred blows are not enough.

**[17:11] The irony is that such people will meet up with what they so energetically pursue—in the form of an unrelenting emissary sent to them.

††[17:12] Humorous hyperbole. An outraged dangerous beast poses less danger than a fool.

‡‡[17:13] The paradox is that to pay out evil for good means that the evil will never leave one's own house.

s. [17:5] Prv 14:31. t. [17:13] Mt 5:39; Rom 12:17; 1 Thes 5:15; 1 Pt 3:9. u. [17:15] Prv 24:24; Is 5:23.

§§[17:16] The exhortation to acquire or purchase wisdom is common in Proverbs. Fools misunderstand the metaphor, assuming they can buy it with money. Their very misunderstanding shows they have no "heart" = mind, understanding. Money in the hand is no good without such a "heart" to store it in.

¶¶[17:19] **Build their gate high**: a symbol of arrogance.

***[17:20] The saying employs the familiar metaphors of walking = conducting oneself ("fall into trouble"), and of straight and crooked = right and wrong ("perverse," "double-tongued").

†††[17:23] A sharp look at the sly withdrawing of a bribe from the pocket and a blunt judgment on its significance.

‡‡‡[17:24] Wisdom is visible on the countenance (i.e., mouth, lips, tongue) of the wise person; its ultimate source is the heart. Fools have no such source of wisdom within them, a point that is nicely made by referring to the eye of the fool, roving over the landscape.

§§§[17:28] Related to v. 27. Words provide a glimpse into the heart. In the unlikely event that fools, who usually pour out words (15:2), were to say nothing, people would not be

v. [17:17] Prv 18:24. w. [17:18] Prv 6:1–2; 11:15. x. [17:19] Prv 15:18. y. [17:22] Prv 12:25; 15:13. z. [17:24] Eccl 8:1. a. [17:25] Prv 10:1; 29:15. b. [17:27] Prv 10:19; Sir 1:21; Jas 1:19.

CHAPTER 18

1 One who is alienated seeks a pretext,
   with all persistence picks a quarrel.
2 Fools take no delight in understanding,
   but only in displaying what they
   think.*
3 With wickedness comes contempt,
   and with disgrace, scorn.
4 The words of one's mouth are deep waters,
   the spring of wisdom, a running
   brook.†c
5 It is not good to favor the guilty,
   nor to reject the claim of the just.d
6 The lips of fools walk into a fight,
   and their mouths are asking for a
   beating.‡
7 The mouths of fools are their ruin;
   their lips are a deadly snare.e
8 The words of a talebearer are like dainty
   morsels:
   they sink into one's inmost being.f
9 Those slack in their work
   are kin to the destroyer.
10 ⁵The name of the LORD is a strong tower;
   the just run to it and are safe.
11 The wealth of the rich is their strong
   city;g
   they fancy it a high wall.
12 Before disaster the heart is haughty,h
   but before honor is humility.
13 Whoever answers before listening,i
   theirs is folly and shame.⁵
14 One's spirit supports one when ill,
   but a broken spirit who can bear?**
15 The heart of the intelligent acquires
   knowledge,
   and the ear of the wise seeks
   knowledge.††
16 Gifts clear the way for people,
   winning access to the great.j
17 Those who plead the case first seem to be
   in the right;

then the opponent comes and
   cross-examines them.‡‡
18 The lot puts an end to disputes,
   and decides a controversy between
   the mighty.§§
19 A brother offended is more unyielding
   than a stronghold;
   such strife is more daunting than
   castle gates.⁵⁵
20 With the fruit of one's mouth one's belly is
   filled,
   with the produce of one's lips one is
   sated.***k
21 Death and life are in the power of the
   tongue;l
   those who choose one shall eat its
   fruit.†††
22 To find a wife is to find happiness,
   a favor granted by the LORD.m
23 The poor implore,
   but the rich answer harshly.
24 There are friends who bring ruin,
   but there are true friends more loyal
   than a brother.n

CHAPTER 19

1 Better to be poor and walk in integrity
   than rich and crooked in one's ways.o
2 Desire without knowledge is not good;
   and whoever acts hastily, blunders.‡‡‡
3 Their own folly leads people astray;
   in their hearts they rage against the
   LORD.§§§
4 Wealth adds many friends,
   but the poor are left friendless.p

---

‡‡[18:17] A persuasive speech in court can easily make one forget there is another side to the question. When the other party speaks, people realize they made a premature judgment. The experience at court is a lesson for daily life: there are two sides to every question.
§§[18:18] See note on 16:33.
⁵⁵[18:19] The Greek version, followed by several ancient versions, has the opposite meaning: "A brother helped by a brother is like a strong and lofty city; it is strong like a well-founded palace." The Greek is secondary as is shown by the need to supply the phrase "by a brother"; further, the parallelism is inadequate. The Hebrew is to be preferred.
***[18:20] Fruit from the earth is our ordinary sustenance, but "the fruit of one's lips," i.e., our words, also affect our well-being. If our words and our deeds are right, then we are blessed, our "belly is filled."
†††[18:21] This enigmatic saying has provoked many interpretations, e.g., judicious speech brings a reward; those who love the tongue in the sense of rattling on must face the consequences of their loquacity. This translation interprets the verb "love" in colon B in its occasional sense of "choose" (e.g., 12:1; 20:13; Dt 4:37) and interprets its pronominal object as referring to both death and life in colon A. Death and life are set before every person (cf. Dt 30:15–20) and we have the power to choose either one by the quality of our deeds. Words (= "the tongue") are regarded here as the defining actions of human beings.
‡‡‡[19:2] When not guided by wisdom, appetite—or desire—is not good. "Running feet" (so the Hebrew) miss the mark, i.e., do not reach their destination.
§§§[19:3] One's own folly destroys one's life. It is an indication of that folly that one blames God rather than oneself.

---

able to see their folly and would presume them intelligent. Alas, the saying is contrary to fact.
*[18:2] One grows in wisdom by listening to others, but fools take delight in expounding the contents of their minds.
†[18:4] Words express a person's thoughts ("deep waters"), which in turn become accessible to others. Cf. 20:5a.
‡[18:6] The bold personification of lips and mouth is similar to Ps 73:9, "They set their mouths against the heavens, their tongues roam the earth." Careless words can lead one into serious trouble.
§[18:10–11] Contrast this judgment with the observation in 10:15.
⁵[18:13] To speak without first listening is characteristic of a fool; cf. 10:14; Sir 11:8.
**[18:14] The paradox is that something as slight as a column of air offers protection against the encroachment of death. If it is stilled, nothing, no matter how powerful, can substitute for it.
††[18:15] "Knowledge" here refers to what one knows, not knowledge in itself. The mind acquires and stores it, the ear strains toward it.

c. [18:4] Prv 20:5; Jn 7:38. d. [18:5] Prv 24:23; 28:21. e. [18:7] Prv 10:14; 12:13; 13:3; Eccl 10:12. f. [18:8] Prv 26:22. g. [18:11] Prv 10:15. h. [18:12] Prv 11:2; 16:18; Sir 10:15. i. [18:13] Sir 11:8. j. [18:16] Prv 21:14.

k. [18:20] Prv 12:14; 13:2. l. [18:21] Sir 37:18. m. [18:22] Prv 12:4; 19:14; Sir 7:26. n. [18:24] Prv 17:17. o. [19:1] Prv 28:6. p. [19:4] Prv 14:20; Sir 13:20–23.

5 The false witness will not go unpunished,
  and whoever utters lies will not
  escape.*q
6 Many curry favor with a noble;
  everybody is a friend of a gift giver.
7 All the kin of the poor despise them;
  how much more do their friends
  shun them!†
8 Those who gain sense truly love
  themselves;
  those who preserve understanding
  will find success.‡
9 The false witness will not go unpunished,
  and whoever utters lies will perish.
10 Luxury is not befitting a fool;
   much less should a slave rule over
   princes.
11 It is good sense to be slow to anger,
   and an honor to overlook an
   offense.§
12 The king's wrath is like the roar of a lion,
   but his favor, like dew on the grass.¶r
13 The foolish son is ruin to his father,s
   and a quarrelsome wife is water
   constantly dripping.**
14 Home and possessions are an inheritance
   from parents,
   but a prudent wife is from the LORD.t
15 Laziness brings on deep sleep,
   and the sluggard goes hungry.u
16 Those who keep commands keep their
   lives,
   but those who despise these ways
   will die.v
17 Whoever cares for the poor lends to the
   LORD,w
   who will pay back the sum in full.
18 Discipline your son, for there is hope;
   but do not be intent on his death.††x
19 A wrathful person bears the penalty;
   after one rescue, you will have it to
   do again.

20 Listen to counsel and receive
   instruction,
   that you may eventually become
   wise.
21 Many are the plans of the human heart,
   but it is the decision of the LORD
   that endures.y
22 What is desired of a person is fidelity;
   rather be poor than a liar.‡‡
23 The fear of the LORD leads to life;
   one eats and sleeps free from any
   harm.
24 The sluggard buries a hand in the dish;
   not even lifting it to the mouth.z
25 Beat a scoffer and the naive learn a
   lesson;
   rebuke the intelligent and they gain
   knowledge.a
26 Whoever mistreats a father or drives away
   a mother,
   is a shameless and disgraceful
   child.§§b
27 My son, stop attending to correction;
   start straying from words of
   knowledge.¶¶
28 An unprincipled witness scoffs at justice,
   and the mouth of the wicked pours
   out iniquity.
29 Rods are prepared for scoffers,
   and blows for the backs of fools.c

CHAPTER 20

1 Wine is arrogant, strong drink is riotous;
  none who are intoxicated by them
  are wise.***d
2 The terror of a king is like the roar of a
  lion;e
  those who incur his anger forfeit
  their lives.
3 A person gains honor by avoiding strife,
  while every fool starts a quarrel.†††
4 In seedtime sluggards do not plow;
  when they look for the harvest, it is
  not there.

---

*[19.5] The punishment fits the crime; those who abuse
the legal system will be punished by the same system. They
will not be acquitted.
†[19:7] Closely related to vv. 4 and 6. An observation, not
without sympathy, on the social isolation of poor people.
‡[19:8] Wisdom benefits the one who practices it.
§[19:11] The paradox is that one obtains one thing by giving up another.
¶[19:12] An observation on the exercise of royal power.
Both images suggest royal attitudes are beyond human control. Colon A is a variant of 20:2a and colon B of 16:15b.
**[19:13] One of many sayings about domestic happiness.
The perspective is male; the two greatest pains to a father is a
malicious son and an unsuitable wife. The immediately following saying is on the noble wife, perhaps to make a positive
statement about women.
††[19:18] The pain of disciplining the young cannot be
compared with the danger no discipline may bring. The chief
reason for disciplining the young is their capacity to change;
excluded thereby are revenge and punishment.

‡‡[19:22] The proverb has been read in two ways: (1) "Desire
(greed) is a shame to a person," which assumes the rare Hebrew
word for "shame" is being used; (2) "What is desired in a person
is fidelity." The second interpretation is preferable. The context
may be the court: better to forego money (a bribe) than perjure
oneself.
§§[19:26] Children who disgrace the family equivalently
plunder their father's wealth and expel their mother from the
home.
¶¶[19:27] The meaning was disputed even in antiquity. The
interpretation that most respects the syntax is to take it as ironic
advice as in 22:6: to stop (listening) is to go (wandering).
***[20:1] The cause stands for its effect (wine, drunken
behavior). In Proverbs wine is a sign of prosperity and a symbol of feasting (3:10; 4:17; 9:2, 5) but also a potential threat to
wisdom as in 20:1; 21:17; 23:29–35.
†††[20:3] The honor that one might seek to gain from fighting comes of itself to the person who refrains from fighting.

---

q. [19:5] Dt 19:16–20; Dn 13:61. r. [19:12] Prv 20:2. s. [19:13]
Prv 10:1; 17:25. t. [19:14] Prv 18:22. u. [19:15] Prv 6:9–
10. v. [19:16] Prv 13:13; 16:17. w. [19:17] Prv 14:21; 22:9;
28:27. x. [19:18] Prv 13:24; 23:13–14.

y. [19:21] Prv 16:9. z. [19:24] Prv 26:15. a. [19:25] Prv 17:10;
21:11. b. [19:26] Sir 3:16. c. [19:29] Prv 26:3. d. [20:1] Prv
23:29–35. e. [20:2] Prv 19:12.

⁵ The intention of the human heart is deep
    water,
    but the intelligent draw it forth.ᵉᶠ
⁶ Many say, "My loyal friend,"
    but who can find someone worthy
    of trust?
⁷ The just walk in integrity;
    happy are their children after them!
⁸ A king seated on the throne of judgment
    dispels all evil with his glance.†
⁹ Who can say, "I have made my heart
    clean,ᵍ
    I am cleansed of my sin"?‡
¹⁰ Varying weights, varying measures,
    are both an abomination to the
    LORD.ʰ
¹¹ In their actions even children can
    playact
    though their deeds be blameless and
    right.§
¹² The ear that hears, the eye that sees—
    the LORD has made them both.ᶜ
¹³ Do not love sleep lest you be reduced to
    poverty;
    keep your eyes open, have your fill
    of food.
¹⁴ "Bad, bad!" says the buyer,
    then goes away only to boast.**
¹⁵ One can put on gold and abundant
    jewels,
    but wise lips are the most precious
    ornament.††
¹⁶ Take the garment of the one who became
    surety for a stranger;ⁱ
    if for foreigners, exact the pledge!‡‡
¹⁷ Bread earned by deceit is sweet,
    but afterward the mouth is filled
    with gravel.
¹⁸ Plans made with advice succeed;
    with wise direction wage your war.

¹⁹ A slanderer reveals secrets;
    so have nothing to do with a
    babbler!
²⁰ Those who curse father or mother—
    their lamp will go out§§ in the dead
    of night.ʲ
²¹ Possessions greedily guarded at the
    outset
    will not be blessed in the end.¶¶
²² Do not say, "I will repay evil!"
    Wait for the LORD, who will help
    you.***ᵏ
²³ Varying weights are an abomination to
    the LORD,
    and false scales are not good.ˡ
²⁴ Our steps are from the LORD;ᵐ
    how, then, can mortals understand
    their way?†††
²⁵ It is a trap to pledge rashly a sacred gift,
    and after a vow, then to reflect.‡‡‡
²⁶ A wise king winnows the wicked,
    and threshes them under the
    cartwheel.§§§
²⁷ A lamp from the LORD is human
    life-breath;
    it searches through the inmost
    being.¶¶¶
²⁸ His steadfast loyalty safeguards the king,
    and he upholds his throne by
    justice.ⁿ
²⁹ The glory of the young is their strength,
    and the dignity of the old is gray hair.ᵒ
³⁰ Evil is cleansed away by bloody lashes,
    and a scourging to the inmost being.

CHAPTER 21

¹ A king's heart is channeled water in the
    hand of the LORD;

---

*[20:5] The heart is where human plans are made and stored; they remain "deep water" until words reveal them to others. The wise know how to draw up those waters, i.e., express them. Cf. 18:4.

†[20:8] The royal throne is established in justice and the king is the agent of that justice.

‡[20:9] A claim to sinlessness can be merely self-deception; see 16:2; cf. also 15:11.

§[20:11] The verb in colon A can mean either "to make oneself known" or "to play another person" (as in Gn 42:7 and 1 Kgs 14:5, 6). The second meaning makes a better parallel to colon B. The meaning is that if a child can playact, an adult can do so even more. Actions do not always reveal character.

¶[20:12] Human judgments are not ultimate; the Lord expects proper use of these faculties.

**[20:14] Bartering invites playacting and masking one's true intent. The truth of words depends on their context.

††[20:15] Wisdom is said to be preferable to gold in 3:14; 8:10, 19; 16:16. Colon B suggests that the gold and jewelry here are ornaments for the face (cf. Gn 24:53; Ex 3:22; Is 61:10). Wise lips are the most beautiful adornment, for they display the wisdom of the heart.

‡‡[20:16] The text is not clear. See 27:13. Caution in becoming surety is always advised (cf. 6:1–3), and it is especially advisable with strangers.

§§[20:20] **Their lamp will go out:** misfortune, even death, awaits them; cf. 13:9; Ex 21:17.

¶¶[20:21] By definition, an inheritance is not gained by one's own efforts but is received as a gift. If, when one first receives the inheritance, one drives everyone away, one treats it as if one acquired it by one's own efforts. In an agricultural society, an inheritance would often be a field that would require God's blessing to be fertile.

***[20:22] Appointing oneself an agent of divine retribution is dangerous. Better to wait for God to effect justice. Cf. 24:17–18.

†††[20:24] An indication of the Lord's inscrutable providence; cf. Jer 10:23; see Prv 21:2; cf. also 14:12.

‡‡‡[20:25] This verse cautions against making vows without proper reflection; cf. Dt 23:22–25; Eccl 5:4–5.

§§§[20:26] The king is responsible for effecting justice. Judgment is portrayed in agricultural imagery—exposing grain to a current of air so that the chaff is blown away, and passing a wheel over the cereal to break the husk. Winnowing as image for judgment is found throughout the Bible.

¶¶¶[20:27] A parallel is drawn between the life-breath that is God's gift (Jb 32:8; 33:2) coursing through the human body (Is 2:22) and the lamp of God, which can be a symbol of divine scrutiny. In Zep 1:12, God declares, "And in that day I will search through Jerusalem with lamps."

---

f. [20:5] Prv 18:4. g. [20:9] 1 Kgs 8:46; 2 Chr 6:36; Eccl 7:20; 1 Jn 1:8. h. [20:10] Prv 11:1; 20:23. i. [20:16] Prv 27:13.

j. [20:20] Prv 30:11, 17; Ex 21:17; Lv 20:9; Mt 15:4. k. [20:22] Prv 24:29; Sir 28:1; Mt 5:39; Rom 12:17, 19; 1 Thes 5:15; 1 Pt 3:9. l. [20:23] Prv 11:1; 20:10. m. [20:24] Prv 16:9. n. [20:28] Prv 16:12. o. [20:29] Prv 16:31.

God directs it where he pleases.*

2 All your ways may be straight in your
own eyes,
but it is the Lord who weighs
hearts.ᵖ

3 To do what is right and just�q
is more acceptable to the Lord than
sacrifice.†

4 Haughty eyes and a proud heart—
the lamp of the wicked will fail.‡

5 The plans of the diligent end in profit,
but those of the hasty end in loss.§

6 Trying to get rich by lying
is chasing a bubble over deadly
snares.

7 The violence of the wicked will sweep
them away,
because they refuse to do what is
right.

8 One's path may be winding and
unfamiliar,
but one's conduct is blameless and
right.⁵

9 It is better to dwell in a corner of the
housetop
than in a mansion with a
quarrelsome woman.**ʳ

10 The soul of the wicked desires evil;
their neighbor finds no pity in their
eyes.

11 When scoffers are punished the naive
become wise;
when the wise succeed, they gain
knowledge.ˢ

12 The Righteous One appraises the house of
the wicked,
bringing down the wicked to ruin.¹¹

13 Those who shut their ears to the cry of the
poor
will themselves call out and not be
answered.

14 A secret gift allays anger,
and a present concealed, violent
wrath.‡‡

15 When justice is done it is a joy for the
just,
downfall for evildoers.§§ᵗ

16 Whoever strays from the way of good
sense
will abide in the assembly of the
shades.¶¶

17 The lover of pleasure will suffer want;
the lover of wine and perfume will
never be rich.

18 The wicked serve as ransom for the just,
and the faithless for the upright.***ᵘ

19 It is better to dwell in a wilderness
than with a quarrelsome wife and
trouble.

20 Precious treasure and oil are in the house
of the wise,
but the fool consumes them.

21 Whoever pursues justice and kindness
will find life and honor.†††

22 The wise person storms the city of the
mighty,
and overthrows the stronghold in
which they trust.

23 Those who guard mouth and tongue
guard themselves‡‡‡ from trouble.ᵛ

24 Proud, boastful—scoffer is the name:
those who act with overbearing
pride.

25 The desire of sluggards will slay them,
for their hands refuse to work.§§§

---

*[21:1] "Channeled water" in Is 32:2 and Prv 5:16 is water
that fertilizes arid land. It takes great skill to direct water,
whether it be water to fertilize fields or cosmic floods har-
nessed at creation, for water is powerful and seems to have a
mind of its own. It also requires great skill to direct the heart
of a king, for it is inscrutable and beyond ordinary human
control.

†[21:3] External rites or sacrifices do not please God
unless accompanied by internal worship and right moral conduct; cf. 15:8; 21:27; Is 1:11–15; Am 5:22; Mal 1:12.

‡[21:4] Heart and eyes depict, respectively, the inner and
the outer person. "Haughty eyes" peering out from a "proud
heart" show a thoroughly arrogant person. How can such a
person flourish! Their lamp, which signifies life, will go out.

§[21:5] The antitheses are diligent and impetuous. The
metaphor characterizing each type is taken from the world of
commerce. Planning is important; bustle leads to waste.

¶[21:8] One cannot always read others' hearts from their
behavior. Unconventional conduct need not indicate evil
motives.

**[21:9] In Proverbs, two great obstacles to a happy house-
hold are foolish children and quarrelsome spouses. The nag-
ging wife is also mentioned in 19:13 and 27:15; 25:24 is a
duplicate.

††[21:12] It is difficult to ascertain the subject of the saying. Some hold it is the Lord, the "Righteous One," who is
normally the executor of justice in Proverbs. Others believe
it is the just person who is the agent of divine justice. "Righteous One" is a title for God in Is 24:16. The best argument

for making God the subject of the verb is that elsewhere in
Proverbs righteous human beings never do anything to the
wicked; only God does.

‡‡[21:14] Proverbs offers several remedies for anger—a soft
word (15:1), patience, and a bribe. The last remedy implies a
certain disdain for the disordered passion of anger, for it can
be so easily assuaged by a discreetly offered "gift."

§§[21:15] The second line is a duplicate of 10:29b.

¶¶[21:16] **Assembly of the shades**: those who dwell in
Sheol.

***[21:18] In this bold paradox, the ransom that protects
the righteous is the wicked person who attracts, like a lightning rod, the divine wrath that might have been directed at
the righteous.

†††[21:21] The paradox is that one comes upon something
other than what one pursued. The way to (long and healthy)
life and honor is the vigorous pursuit of virtue.

‡‡‡[21:23] **Themselves**: see note on 13:3. To guard your
"self" (lit., "throat," the moist and breathing center of the
body, by metonymy, "life"), you must guard your tongue.
Speech in Proverbs is the quintessential human activity and
often has a meaning broader than speech alone; it can stand
for all human activity. Acting rightly is the best way to protect
yourself from evil.

§§§[21:25] Desire, or appetite, is the impulse toward food
and drink (see Ps 42:3) which spurs animals and human
beings into action. But sluggards cannot lift hand to mouth;
they bury their hand in the dish (19:24), and so their appetite
is thwarted.

---

p. [21:2] Prv 16:2.   q. [21:3] 1 Sm 15:22; Hos 6:6.   r. [21:9] Prv
21:19; 25:24; 27:15; Sir 25:23.   s. [21:11] Prv 19:25.

t. [21:15] Prv 10:29.   u. [21:18] Prv 11:8.   v. [21:23] Prv 13:3.

26 Some are consumed with avarice all the
    day,
    but the just give unsparingly.
27 The sacrifice of the wicked is an
    abomination,
    the more so when they offer it with
    bad intent.ʷ
28 The false witness will perish,ˣ
    but one who listens will give lasting
    testimony.
29 The face of the wicked hardens,
    but the upright maintains a straight
    course.*
30 No wisdom, no understanding,
    no counsel prevail against the
    LORD.
31 The horse is equipped for the day of
    battle,
    but victory is the LORD's.

CHAPTER 22

1 A good name is more desirable than great
    riches,
    and high esteem, than gold and
    silver.†ʸ
2 Rich and poor have a common bond:
    the LORD is the maker of them all.ᶻ
3 The astute see an evil and hide,
    while the naive continue on and pay
    the penalty.‡ᵃ
4 The result of humility and fear of the
    LORD
    is riches, honor and life.§
5 Thorns and snares are on the path of the
    crooked;
    those who would safeguard their
    lives will avoid them.
6 Train the young in the way they should
    go;
    even when old, they will not swerve
    from it.¶

7 The rich rule over the poor,
    and the borrower is the slave of the
    lender.**
8 Those who sow iniquity reap calamity,ᵇ
    and the rod used in anger will fail.††
9 The generous will be blessed,
    for they share their food with the
    poor.
10 Expel the arrogant and discord goes too;
    strife and insult cease.
11 The LORD loves the pure of heart;ᶜ
    the person of winning speech has a
    king for a friend.
12 The eyes of the LORD watch over the
    knowledgeable,
    but he defeats the projects of the
    faithless.
13 The sluggard says, "A lion is outside;ᵈ
    I might be slain in the street."‡‡
14 The mouth of the foreign woman is a deep
    pit;ᵉ
    whoever incurs the LORD's anger
    will fall into it.
15 Folly is bound to the heart of a youth,
    but the rod of discipline will drive
    it out.§§
16 Oppressing the poor for enrichment,
    giving to the rich: both are sheer
    loss.¶¶

IV. SAYINGS OF THE WISE***

pronoun in the Hebrew phrase, lit., "his own way." The most
natural solution is to take the whole as ironic advice (like
19:27): yes, go ahead and let the young do exactly what they
want; they will become self-willed adults.
    **[22:7] An observation on money and power. One who bor-
rows becomes poor in the sense of indebted, a slave to the lender.
    ††[22:8] Agricultural metaphors express the failure of mali-
cious actions. In the first line, bad actions are seeds yielding
trouble. In the second line, "the rod" is a flail used to beat
grains as in Is 28:27.
    ‡‡[22:13] To avoid the effort required for action, the slug-
gard exaggerates the difficulties that must be overcome.
    §§[22:15] Folly is attached to children as the husk is
attached to the grain. "Rod" here, as in v. 8, seems to be the
flail. Discipline is the process of winnowing away the folly.
    ¶¶[22:16] A difficult saying. One possibility is to take it as a
seemingly neutral observation on the plight of the poor: taking money from the poor is relatively easy for the powerful
but it is dangerous as the poor have the Lord as their defender
(24:22–23), who will punish their oppressors. Giving to the
rich, perhaps to win their favor by presents and bribes, is
equally a waste of money, for the rich will always do what they
please in any case.
    ***[22:17–24:22] This collection consists of an introduction
(22:17–21) urging openness and stating the purpose of the
Words and diverse admonitions, aphorisms, and counsels. It
is written with faith in the Lord, shrewdness, and a satirical
eye. The first part seems aimed at young people intent on a
career (22:22–23:11); the second is taken up with the concerns
of youth (23:12–35); the third part is interested in the ultimate
fate of the good and the wicked (24:1–22). The whole can be
described as a guidebook of professional ethics. The aim is to
inculcate trust in the Lord and to help readers avoid trouble
and advance their careers by living according to wisdom. Its
outlook is very practical: avoid bad companions because in
time you will take on some of their qualities; do not post bond
for others because you yourself will be encumbered; do not

---

*[21:29] The wicked cannot deter the righteous from
walking the straight path, i.e., from practicing virtue.
    †[22:1] "Good name" (Heb. shem) and "high esteem"
(Heb. chen) are declared to be of more value than great riches.
Human beings belong to a community and without the acceptance of that community, which is built on esteem and trust,
human life is grievously damaged. Riches are less essential to
the human spirit.
    ‡[22:3] The wise see dangers before they are engulfed by
them whereas fools, through dullness or boldness, march
right on.
    §[22:4] Humiliation can be an occasion for knowing one's
place in God's world. Such knowledge is part of fear (or revering) of the Lord. Revering the Lord brings the blessings of
wealth, honor, and long life. The saying is perhaps meant to
counter the view that humiliation is an unmixed evil; something good can come of it.
    ¶[22:6] One of the few exhortations in the collection (cf.
14:7; 16:3; 19:18, 20). "Way" in the first colon has been taken
in two different senses: (1) the morally right way, "according
to the way one ought to go"; (2) personal aptitude, i.e., the
manner of life for which one is destined, as "the way of Egypt"
(Is 10:24). Neither interpretation, however, accounts for the

---

w. [21:27] Prv 15:8; Sir 34:21–23.   x. [21:28] Prv 19:5, 9.   y. [22:1]
Eccl 7:1.   z. [22:2] Prv 29:13.   a. [22:3] Prv 27:12.

b. [22:8] Jb 4:8; Sir 7:3; Hos 8:7.   c. [22:11] Mt 5:8.   d. [22:13] Prv
26:13.   e. [22:14] Prv 23:27.

¹⁷   The Words of the Wise:[*]
Incline your ear, and hear my words,^f
and let your mind attend to my
teaching;
¹⁸ For it will be well if you hold them within
you,
if they all are ready on your lips.
¹⁹ That your trust may be in the LORD,
I make them known to you today—
yes, to you.
²⁰ Have I not written for you thirty sayings,
containing counsels and knowledge,
²¹ To teach you truly
how to give a dependable report to
one who sends you?
²² Do not rob the poor because they are poor,
nor crush the needy at the gate;[†]
²³ For the LORD will defend their cause,^g
and will plunder those who plunder
them.
²⁴ Do not be friendly with hotheads,
nor associate with the wrathful,
²⁵ Lest you learn their ways,
and become ensnared.
²⁶ Do not be one of those who give their
hand in pledge,
those who become surety for debts;^h

²⁷ For if you are unable to pay,
your bed will be taken from under
you.[‡]
²⁸ Do not remove the ancient landmark[§]
that your ancestors set up.ⁱ
²⁹ Do you see those skilled at their work?
They will stand in the presence of
kings,
but not in the presence of the obscure.

CHAPTER 23

¹ ¶When you sit down to dine with a ruler,
mark well the one who is before you;
² Stick the knife in your gullet^{**}
if you have a ravenous appetite.
³ Do not desire his delicacies;
it is food that deceives.
⁴ Do not wear yourself out to gain wealth,
cease to be worried about it;
⁵ When your glance flits to it, it is gone!
For assuredly it grows wings,
like the eagle that flies toward
heaven.^{††}
⁶ ‡‡Do not take food with unwilling hosts,
and do not desire their delicacies;
⁷ For like something stuck in the throat is
that food.
"Eat and drink," they say to you,
but their hearts are not with you;
⁸ The little you have eaten you will vomit
up,

---

promote yourself too aggressively because such promotion is self-defeating; do not abuse sex or alcohol because they will harm you; do not emulate your peers if they are wicked (23:14; 24:1, 19) because such people have no future. Rather, trust the vocation of a sage (22:29–23:9).

The Egyptian *Instructions of Amenemope* (written ca. 1100 B.C.) was discovered in 1923. Scholars immediately recognized it as a source of Prv 22:17–23:11. The Egyptian work has thirty chapters (cf. Prv 22:20); its preface resembled Prv 22:17–21; its first two admonitions matched the first two in Proverbs (Prv 22:22 25). There are many other resemblances as well, some of which are pointed out in the notes. The instruction of a father to his son (or an administrator to his successor) was a well-known genre in Egypt; seventeen works are extant, spanning the period from 2500 B.C. to the first century A.D. The instructions aimed to help a young person live a happy and prosperous life and avoid mistakes that cause difficulties. They make concrete and pragmatic suggestions rather than hold up abstract ideals. Pragmatic though they were, the instructions were religious; they assumed that the gods implanted an order in the world (Egyptian *maat*), which is found both in nature and in the human world. *Amenemope* represents a stage in the development of the Egyptian genre, displaying a new inwardness and quest for serenity while still assuming that the practice of virtue brings worldly success. Proverbs borrows from the Egyptian work with great freedom: it does not, for example, import as such the Egyptian concept of order; it engages the reader with its characteristic wit, irony, and paradox (e.g., 22:26–27; 23:1–3).

*[22:17–23:35] The maxims warn against: robbing the poor and defenseless (22:22–23), anger (22:24–25), giving surety for debts (22:26–27), advancing oneself by socializing with rulers (23:1–2), anxiety for riches (23:4–5), forcing oneself on a grudging host (23:6–8), intemperance in food and drink (23:19–21, 29–35), and adultery (23:26–28). They exhort to: careful workmanship (22:29), respect for the rights of orphans (23:10–11), correction of the young (23:13–14), filial piety (23:15–16, 22–25), and fear of the Lord (23:17–18).

†[22:22] **At the gate**: of the city, where justice was administered and public affairs discussed; cf. Ru 4:1. Cf. also Ps 69:13; 127:5; Prv 24:7; 31:23, 31. The Lord will personally avenge those who have no one to defend them.

‡[22:27] Providing surety for a debtor puts one in danger of having the very basics of one's life suddenly seized.

§[22:28] **Landmark**: marks the boundary of property. To remove it is the equivalent of stealing land. A similar warning is contained in 23:10.

¶[23:1–9] Four admonitions for someone aspiring to be a sage: be careful about advancing your career by socializing with the great (vv. 1–3); avoid greed (vv. 4–5); do not force yourself on an unwilling host (vv. 6–8); do not waste your wisdom on those who cannot profit from it (v. 9).

[23:2] Stick the knife in your gullet: a metaphor for self-restraint. The usual translation, "Put a knife to your throat," is misleading, for in English it is a death threat. The exhortation is humorously exaggerated: stick the table-knife in your own gullet rather than take too much food. It assumes that the young courtier is unused to opulent banquets and will be tempted to overindulgence.

††[23:5] The frustration of covetous intent and elusiveness of wealth are portrayed by the sudden flight of an eagle. *Amenemope*, chap. 7, has a similar statement: "Do not set your heart on wealth. There is no ignoring Fate and Destiny; / Do not let your heart go straying." Proverbs imagines covetous intent as a flight of the eyes, whereas *Amenemope* imagines it as a straying of the heart.

‡‡[23:6–8] Some humorous advice on not trading on the courtesy of unwilling hosts who, for convention's sake, use the language of welcome. *Amenemope*, chap. 11, gives similar advice: "Do not intrude on a man in his house, / Enter when you have been called; / He may say 'Welcome' with his mouth, / Yet deride you in his thoughts." "Unwilling," lit., "evil of eye," is usually translated "stingy," but the context suggests unwilling. In v. 8, the unwanted guest vomits up the food, thus destroying the desired good impression. Proverbs regards the uninvited banqueters as thieves who will suffer the consequences of their theft. *Amenemope*, chap. 11, is relevant: "Do not covet a poor man's goods, . . . A poor man's goods are a block in the throat, / It makes the gullet vomit."

---

f. [22:17] Prv 5:1.   g. [22:23] Prv 23:11.   h. [22:26] Prv 6:1–2; 11:15; 17:18.

i. [22:28] Prv 23:10; Dt 19:14; 27:17.

and you will have wasted your
    agreeable words.
9 Do not speak in the hearing of fools;
    they will despise the wisdom of your
    words.ʲ
10 Do not remove the ancient landmark,ᵏ
    nor invade the fields of the
    fatherless;*
11 For their redeemer is strong;
    he will defend their cause against
    you.ˡ
12 Apply your heart to instruction,
    and your ear to words of knowledge.
13 †Do not withhold discipline from youths;
    if you beat them with the rod, they
    will not die.ᵐ
14 Beat them with the rod,ⁿ
    and you will save them from Sheol.
15 My son, if your heart is wise,
    my heart also will rejoice;
16 And my inmost being will exult,
    when your lips speak what is right.
17 Do not let your heart envy sinners,ᵒ
    but only those who always fear the
    Lᴏʀᴅ;‡
18 For you will surely have a future,
    and your hope will not be cut off.ᵖ
19 Hear, my son, and be wise,
    and guide your heart in the right
    way.
20 Do not join with wine bibbers,
    nor with those who glut themselves
    on meat.
21 For drunkards and gluttons come to
    poverty,
    and lazing about clothes one in rags.
22 §Listen to your father who begot you,
    do not despise your mother when
    she is old.
23 Buy truth and do not sell:
    wisdom, instruction, understanding!
24 The father of a just person will exult
    greatly;
    whoever begets a wise son will
    rejoice in him.�q

25 Let your father and mother rejoice;
    let her who bore you exult.
26 ¶My son, give me your heart,
    and let your eyes keep to my ways,
27 For the harlot is a deep pit,
    and the foreign woman a narrow
    well;
28 Yes, she lies in wait like a robber,ʳ
    and increases the number of the
    faithless.
29 **Who scream? Who shout?
    Who have strife? Who have anxiety?
    Who have wounds for nothing?
    Who have bleary eyes?
30 Whoever linger long over wine,
    whoever go around quaffing wine.ˢ
31 Do not look on the wine when it is red,
    when it sparkles in the cup.
    It goes down smoothly,
32   but in the end it bites like a serpent,
    and stings like an adder.
33 Your eyes behold strange sights,
    and your heart utters incoherent
    things;
34 You are like one sleeping on the high
    seas,
    sprawled at the top of the mast.
35 "They struck me, but it did not pain me;
    they beat me, but I did not feel it.
    When can I get up,
    when can I go out and get more?"††

CHAPTER 24

1 ‡‡Do not envy the wicked,
    nor desire to be with them;ᵗ
2 For their hearts plot violence,
    and their lips speak of foul play.
3 By wisdom a house is built,
    by understanding it is established;
4 And by knowledge its rooms are filled
    with every precious and pleasing
    possession.
5 The wise are more powerful than the
    strong,
    and the learned, than the mighty,ᵘ

---

*[23:10] In Israel ownership of property and other legal rights were vested mainly in the father as head of the family; thus the widow and fatherless child were vulnerable, left prey to those who would exploit them.

†[23:13–14] The young will not die from instructional blows but from their absence, for (premature) death results from uncorrected folly. The sardonic humor means the exhortation is not to be taken literally, as an argument for corporal punishment. The next verses (vv. 15–16) are exceedingly tender toward the young.

‡[23:17] Those whom one admires or associates with exercise enormous influence. Do not join the wicked, who are a doomed group. The warning is repeated in 24:1–2, 19–20.

§[23:22–23] Father and mother are associated with truth and wisdom. One should no more rid oneself of truth and wisdom than rid oneself of one's parents, who are their source.

¶[23:26–28] The exhortation is a condensed version of chap. 7 with its emotional appeal to "my son" to avoid the forbidden woman (7:1–5), her traps (7:21–23), and her intent to add the youth to her list of victims (7:24–27). As in 23:15, 19, 22, a trustful and affectionate relationship between student and teacher is the basis of teaching. The danger of the woman is expressed in imagery that has sexual overtones (cf. 22:14).

**[23:29–35] A vivid description of the evil effects, physical and psychological, of drunkenness. The emphasis is on the unwise behavior, the folly, caused by alcohol. Cf. 20:1.

††[23:35] Drunkards become insensible to bodily and moral harm. Their one desire is to indulge again.

‡‡[24:1–22] A new section (24:1–14)—on the fates of the wicked and foolish—begins with a warning not to take the foolish as role models. The same admonition is repeated in 23:17–18 and 24:19–20. In 24:1, the verb means "to be jealous, zealous; to emulate." The motive stated in the other passages—the wicked have no future—is indirectly stated here.

j. [23:9] Prv 9:7. k. [23:10] Prv 22:28. l. [23:11] Prv 22:23.
m. [23:13] Prv 13:24; 19:18; Sir 30:1. n. [23:14] Prv 29:15, 17.
o. [23:17] Prv 3:31; 24:1, 19. p. [23:18] Prv 24:14. q. [23:24] Prv
10:1.

r. [23:28] Prv 7:10–27. s. [23:30] Prv 20:1; Sir 19:2; Hos 4:11.
t. [24:1] Prv 3:31; 23:17; Ps 37:1. u. [24:5] Prv 21:22.

⁶ For by strategy war is waged,
    and victory depends on many
        counselors.ᵛ
⁷ ˙Wise words are beyond fools' reach,ʷ
    in the assembly they do not open
        their mouth;
⁸ As they calculate how to do evil,
    people brand them troublemakers.
⁹ The scheme of a fool gains no acceptance,
    the scoffer is an abomination to the
        community.
¹⁰ †Did you fail in a day of adversity,
    did your strength fall short?
¹¹ Did you fail to rescue those who were
        being dragged off to death,‡
    those tottering, those near death,
¹²   because you said, "We didn't know
        about it"?
    Surely, the Searcher of hearts knows
        and will repay all according to their
        deeds.ˣ
¹³ §If you eat honey, my son, because it is
        good,
    if pure honey is sweet to your taste,
¹⁴ Such, you must know, is wisdom to your
        soul.
    If you find it, you will have a future,
        and your hope will not be cut off.ʸ
¹⁵ ⁋Do not lie in wait at the abode of the just,
    do not ravage their dwelling places;
¹⁶ Though the just fall seven times, they rise
        again,
    but the wicked stumble from only
        one mishap.
¹⁷ ˙˙Do not rejoice when your enemies fall,
    and when they stumble, do not let
        your heart exult,
¹⁸ Lest the Lᴏʀᴅ see it, be displeased with
        you,
    and withdraw his wrath from your
        enemies.
¹⁹ Do not be provoked at evildoers,
    do not envy the wicked;

²⁰ For the evil have no future,
    the lamp of the wicked will be put
        out.ᶻ
²¹ My son, fear the Lᴏʀᴅ and the king;
    have nothing to do with those who
        hate them;
²² For disaster will issue suddenly,
    and calamity from them both, who
        knows when?

V. FURTHER SAYINGS OF THE WISE††

²³ These also are Words of the Wise:
    To show partiality in judgment is not
        good.ᵃ
²⁴ Whoever says to the guilty party, "You are
        innocent,"
    will be cursed by nations, scorned
        by peoples;
²⁵ But those who render just verdicts will
        fare well,
    and on them will come the blessing
        of prosperity.
²⁶ An honest reply—
    a kiss on the lips.‡‡
²⁷ Complete your outdoor tasks,
    and arrange your work in the field;
    afterward you can build your house.§§
²⁸ Do not testify falsely against your
        neighborᵇ
    and so deceive with your lips.
²⁹ Do not say, "As they did to me, so will I
        do to them;ᶜ
    I will repay them according to their
        deeds."⁋⁋

---

††[24:23–34] A little collection between the thirty sayings
of 22:17–24:22 and the Hezekiah collection in chaps. 25–29.
Its title (v. 23) suggests that editors took it as an appendix. At
this point, the Greek edition of Proverbs begins to arrange the
later sections of the book in a different order than the Hebrew
edition.
    An editor has arranged originally separate sayings into
two parallel groups.

	I.	II.
Conduct in court:	Judges (vv. 24–25)	Witnesses (v. 28)
Speaking, thinking:	Good speech (v. 26)	Bad speech (v. 29)
Wisdom in work:	Positive (v. 27)	Negative (vv. 30–34)

‡‡[24:26] The kiss is a gesture of respect and affection. The
greatest sign of affection and respect for another is to tell that
person the truth.
    §§[24:27] **House**: can refer to both the building and the
family (cf. 2 Sm 7). In the context established by the placement
noted above under 24:23, the saying means that neglect of
one's field is a sign that one is not building the house properly.
In an agricultural society especially, the concept of household
includes fields for animals and crops. On the metaphorical
level, one may lay a careful preparation before embarking on
a great project. This verse is sometimes interpreted as advocating careful and practical preparation for marriage.
    ⁋⁋[24:29] Retribution is a long and complex process that
belongs to the Lord, not to individuals. Cf. vv. 12d, 17–18.

---

*[24:7–9] The verses are unclear; most scholars take them
as two or even three single sayings, but, taken singly, the
verses are banal. They are best taken as a single statement.
Just as vv. 3–6 described the advantages of wisdom, so vv. 7–9
describe the disadvantages of its opposite, folly: it alienates
one from the community (v. 7), for fools become notorious (v.
8), dooming their plans and ostracizing themselves.
    †[24:10–12] Excuses for not coming to the aid of one's
neighbor in serious trouble do not suffice before God, who
sees through self-serving excuses.
    ‡[24:11] **Rescue . . . death**: perhaps refers to the legal res-
cue of those unjustly condemned to death.
    §[24:13–14] God's word is sometimes said to be sweeter
than honey, e.g., Ps 119:101–103. Cf. also Ps 19:11; Prv 16:24;
Ez 3:3; Sir 24:19–22.
    ⁋[24:15–16] The just will overcome every misfortune that
oppresses them. *Seven times* is an indefinite number.
    **[24:17–18] The admonition is linked to the previous by
the words "fall" and "stumble." Premature public celebration of the downfall of enemies equivalently preempts the retribution that belongs to God.

---

v. [24:6] Prv 20:18.   w. [24:7] Sir 6:21.   x. [24:12] Ps 62:13; Sir
16:12; Mt 16:27; Rom 2:6.   y. [24:14] Prv 23:18.

z. [24:20] Prv 13:9.   a. [24:23] Prv 18:5; 28:21; Lv 19:15; Dt 1:17;
16:19.   b. [24:28] Prv 19:5; 25:18.   c. [24:29] Prv 20:22.

³⁰ ʼI passed by the field of a sluggard,
   by the vineyard of one with no sense;
³¹ It was all overgrown with thistles;
   its surface was covered with nettles,
   and its stone wall broken down.
³² As I gazed at it, I reflected;
   I saw and learned a lesson:
³³ A little sleep, a little slumber,ᵈ
   a little folding of the arms to rest—
³⁴ Then poverty will come upon you like a
   robber,
   and want like a brigand.

VI. SECOND SOLOMONIC COLLECTION, COLLECTED UNDER KING HEZEKIAH†

CHAPTER 25

¹These also are proverbs of Solomon.ᵉ The servants of Hezekiah,‡ king of Judah, transmitted them.

² §It is the glory of God to conceal a matter,
   and the glory of kings to fathom a
   matter.¶
³ Like the heavens in height, and the earth
   in depth,
   the heart of kings is unfathomable.
⁴ ¨Remove the dross from silver,
   and it comes forth perfectly purified;
⁵ Remove the wicked from the presence of
   the king,
   and his throne is made firm through
   justice.
⁶ ††Claim no honor in the king's presence,
   nor occupy the place of superiors;

⁷ For it is better to be told, "Come up
   closer!"
   than to be humbled before the
   prince.ᶠ
⁸ What your eyes have seen
   do not bring forth too quickly
   against an opponent;
   For what will you do later on
   when your neighbor puts you to
   shame?
⁹ ‡‡Argue your own case with your
   neighbor,
   but the secrets of others do not
   disclose;
¹⁰ Lest, hearing it, they reproach you,
   and your ill repute never ceases.
¹¹ Golden apples in silver settings
   are words spoken at the proper time.
¹² A golden earring or a necklace of fine
   gold—
   one who gives wise reproof to a
   listening ear.
¹³ Like the coolness of snow in the heat of
   the harvest
   are faithful messengers for those
   who send them,
   lifting the spirits of their masters.
¹⁴ Clouds and wind but no rain—
   the one who boasts of a gift not
   given.
¹⁵ By patience is a ruler persuaded,ᵍ
   and a soft tongue can break a bone.
¹⁶ §§If you find honey, eat only what you
   need,
   lest you have your fill and vomit
   it up.
¹⁷ Let your foot be seldom in your
   neighbors' house,
   lest they have their fill of you—and
   hate you.
¹⁸ A club, sword, or sharp arrow—
   the one who bears false witness
   against a neighbor.ʰ
¹⁹ A bad tooth or an unsteady foot—
   a trust betrayed in time of trouble.¶¶
²⁰ Like the removal of clothes on a cold day,
   or vinegar on soda,
   is the one who sings to a troubled
   heart.

---

*[24:30–34] Neglect of one's fields through laziness ruins all plans to build a house (v. 27). This vignette is a teaching story, like those in 7:1–27; Ps 37:35–36.

†[25:1–29:27] Chaps. 25–29 make up the fifth collection in the book, and the third longest. King Hezekiah reigned in Judah in 715–687 B.C. According to 2 Kgs 18–20 and 2 Chr 29–32, he initiated political and religious reforms after the destruction of the Northern Kingdom in 722 B.C. Such reforms probably included copying and editing sacred literature such as Proverbs. Prv 25:1 is an important piece of evidence about the composition of the book, suggesting this collection was added to an already-existing collection also attributed to Solomon. The older collection is probably 10:1–22:16 (or part of it). By the end of the eighth century B.C., therefore, there existed in Israel two large collections of aphorisms.
   Chap. 25 has two general themes: (1) social hierarchy, rank, or position; (2) social conflict and its resolution.
‡[25:1] The servants of Hezekiah: presumably scribes at the court of Hezekiah. Transmitted: lit., "to move, transfer from," hence "to collect," and perhaps also to arrange and compose.
§[25:2–7] The topic is the king—who he is (vv. 2–3) and how one is to behave in his presence (vv. 4–7).
¶[25:2] God and king were closely related in the ancient world and in the Bible. The king had a special responsibility for divine justice. Hence, God would give him special wisdom to search it out.
**[25:4–5] Wisdom involves virtue as well as knowledge. As in Ps 101 the king cannot tolerate any wickedness in the royal service.
††[25:6–7] An admonition with a practical motive for putting the teaching into practice. Pragmatic shrewdness suggests

that we not promote ourselves but let others do it for us. See Lk 14:7–11.
‡‡[25:9–10] Another admonition on the use of law courts to settle personal disputes. Speak privately with your opponent lest others' personal business become public and they resent you.
§§[25:16–17] The two admonitions are complementary, expressing nicely the need to restrain the inclination for delightful things, whether for honey or friendship.
¶¶[25:19] "A time of trouble" defeats all plans (cf. 10:2; 11:4). At such times human resources alone are like a tooth that falls out as one bites or a foot that goes suddenly lame.

---

d. [24:33] Prv 6:10–11.   e. [25:1] Prv 1:1.

f. [25:7] Lk 14:8–10.   g. [25:15] Prv 15:1, 4.   h. [25:18] Ex 20:16.

²¹ 'If your enemies are hungry, give them
　　food to eat,
　　if thirsty, give something to drink;ⁱ
²² For live coals you will heap on their
　　heads,
　　and the Lᴏʀᴅ will vindicate you.
²³ The north wind brings rain,
　　and a backbiting tongue, angry looks.
²⁴ It is better to dwell in a corner of the
　　housetop
　　than in a mansion with a
　　quarrelsome wife.†ʲ
²⁵ Cool water to one faint from thirst
　　is good news from a far country.
²⁶ A trampled fountain or a polluted
　　spring—‡
　　a just person fallen before the wicked.
²⁷ To eat too much honey is not good;
　　nor to seek honor after honor.§
²⁸ A city breached and left defenseless
　　are those who do not control their
　　temper.

CHAPTER 26¶

¹ Like snow in summer, like rain in harvest,
　　honor for a fool is out of place.**
² Like the sparrow in its flitting, like the
　　swallow in its flight,
　　a curse uncalled-for never lands.††
³ The whip for the horse, the bridle for the
　　ass,
　　and the rod for the back of fools.ᵏ

⁴ ‡‡Do not answer fools according to their
　　folly,
　　lest you too become like them.
⁵ Answer fools according to their folly,
　　lest they become wise in their own
　　eyes.
⁶ Those who send messages by a fool
　　cut off their feet; they drink down
　　violence.
⁷ §§A proverb in the mouth of a fool
　　hangs limp, like crippled legs.
⁸ Giving honor to a fool
　　is like entangling a stone in the sling.
⁹ A thorn stuck in the hand of a drunkard
　　is a proverb in the mouth of fools.
¹⁰ An archer wounding all who pass by
　　is anyone who hires a drunken fool.
¹¹ As dogs return to their vomit,
　　so fools repeat their folly.ˡ
¹² You see those who are wise in their own
　　eyes?
　　There is more hope for fools than
　　for them.
¹³ ¶¶The sluggard says, "There is a lion in the
　　street,
　　a lion in the middle of the square!"ᵐ
¹⁴ The door turns on its hinges
　　and sluggards, on their beds.
¹⁵ The sluggard buries a hand in the dish,
　　too weary to lift it to the mouth.ⁿ
¹⁶ In their own eyes sluggards are wiser
　　than seven who answer with good
　　judgment.
¹⁷ Whoever meddles in the quarrel of
　　another
　　is one who grabs a passing dog by
　　the ears.
¹⁸ Like a crazed archer
　　scattering firebrands and deadly
　　arrows,
¹⁹ Such are those who deceive their
　　neighbor,
　　and then say, "I was only joking."
²⁰ ***Without wood the fire dies out;
　　without a talebearer strife subsides.
²¹ Charcoal for coals, wood for fire—

---

*[25:21–22] A memorable statement of humanity and moderation; such sentiments could be occasionally found even outside the Bible, e.g., "It is better to bless someone than to do harm to one who has insulted you" (Egyptian *Papyrus Insinger*). Cf. Ex 23:4 and Lv 19:17–18. Human beings should not take it upon themselves to exact vengeance, leaving it rather in God's hands. This saying has in view an enemy's vulnerability in time of need, in this case extreme hunger and thirst; such a need should not be an occasion for revenge. The motive for restraining oneself is to allow God's justice to take its own course, as in 20:22 and 24:17–19. **Live coals**: either remorse and embarrassment for the harm done, or increased punishment for refusing reconciliation. Cf. Mt 5:44. Rom 12:20 cites the Greek version and interprets it, "Do not be overcome by evil but overcome evil with good."

†[25:24] A humorous saying about domestic unhappiness: better to live alone outdoors than indoors with an angry spouse. Prv 21:9 is identical and 21:19 is similar in thought.

‡[25:26] "Spring" is a common metaphor for source. The righteous should be a source of life for others. When they fail, it is as if a spring became foul and its water undrinkable. It is not clear whether the righteous person yielded to a scoundrel out of cowardice or was simply defeated by evil. The latter seems more likely, for other proverbs say the just person will never "fall" (lit., "be moved," 10:30; 12:3). The fall, even temporary, of a righteous person is a loss of life for others.

§[25:27] **Nor . . . honor**: the text is uncertain.

¶[26:1–28] Concrete images describe the vices of fools (vv. 1–12), of sluggards (vv. 13–16), of meddlers (vv. 17–19), of talebearers (vv. 20–22), and of flatterers (vv. 23–28).

**[26:1] There is no fit ("out of place") between weather and agricultural season.

††[26:2] The point is the similarity of actions: a hovering bird that never lands, a groundless curse that never "lands." It hangs in the air posing no threat to anyone.

‡‡[26:4–5] There is no contradiction between these two proverbs. In their answers, the wise must protect their own interests against fools. Or perhaps the juxtaposition of the two proverbs suggests that no single proverb can resolve every problem in life.

§§[26:7–9] Fools either abuse or are unable to use whatever knowledge they have. **A thorn**: a proverb is "words spoken at the proper time" (25:11). Fools have no sense of the right time; their statements are like thorns that fasten on clothing randomly.

¶¶[26:13–16] Each verse mentions the sluggard, whom Proverbs regards with derision. The criticism is not against low energy but failure to act and take responsibility. Proverbs' ideal is the active person who uses heart, lips, hands, feet to keep to the good path. The verses are examples of the sardonic humor of the book.

***[26:20–22] The three proverbs have a common theme—the destructive power of slanderous words. Certain words are repeated: wood and fire, talebearer.

---

i. [25:21] Rom 12:20.　j. [25:24] Prv 21:9.　k. [26:3] Prv 19:29; Sir 33:25.

l. [26:11] 2 Pt 2:22.　m. [26:13] Prv 22:13.　n. [26:15] Prv 19:24.

such are the quarrelsome,
    enkindling strife.[o]
22 The words of a talebearer are like dainty
    morsels:
    they sink into one's inmost being.[*p]
23 Like a glazed finish on earthenware
    are smooth lips and a wicked heart.[†]
24 With their lips enemies pretend,
    but inwardly they maintain deceit;
25 When they speak graciously, do not trust
    them,[q]
    for seven abominations[‡] are in their
    hearts.
26 Hatred can be concealed by pretense,
    but malice will be revealed in the
    assembly.[§]
27 Whoever digs a pit falls into it;
    and a stone comes back upon the
    one who rolls it.[r]
28 The lying tongue is its owner's enemy,
    and the flattering mouth works ruin.

CHAPTER 27

1 Do not boast about tomorrow,
    for you do not know what any day
    may bring forth.
2 Let another praise you, not your own
    mouth;
    a stranger, not your own lips.
3 Stone is heavy, and sand a burden,
    but a fool's provocation is heavier
    than both.[s]
4 Anger is cruel, and wrath overwhelming,
    but before jealousy who can stand?[¶]
5 **Better is an open rebuke
    than a love that remains hidden.
6 Trustworthy are the blows of a friend,
    dangerous, the kisses of an enemy.[††]
7 One who is full spurns honey;
    but to the hungry, any bitter thing
    is sweet.

8 Like a bird far from the nest
    so is anyone far from home.[‡‡]
9 Perfume and incense bring joy to the heart,
    but by grief the soul is torn asunder.
10 Do not give up your own friend and your
    father's friend;
    do not resort to the house of your
    kindred when trouble strikes.
    Better a neighbor near than kin far away.[§§]
11 Be wise, my son, and bring joy to my heart,
    so that I can answer whoever taunts
    me.[¶¶]
12 The astute see an evil and hide;
    the naive continue on and pay the
    penalty.[t]
13 Take the garment of the one who became
    surety for a stranger;[u]
    if for a foreign woman, exact the
    pledge![***]
14 Those who greet their neighbor with
    a loud voice[†††] in the early
    morning,
    a curse can be laid to their charge.
15 For a persistent leak on a rainy day
    the match is a quarrelsome wife;[v]
16 Whoever would hide her hides a
    stormwind
    and cannot tell north from south.
17 Iron is sharpened by iron;
    one person sharpens another.[‡‡‡]
18 Those who tend a fig tree eat its fruit;
    so those attentive to their master
    will be honored.
19 As face mirrors face in water,
    so the heart reflects the person.
20 Sheol and Abaddon can never be
    satisfied;[w]
    so the eyes of mortals can never be
    satisfied.[§§§]

---

*[26:22] Malicious gossip is compared to delicious food that is swallowed and lodges in the deepest recesses of one's body. Negative comments are seldom forgotten. Prv 18:8 is a duplicate.

†[26:23] Heart = what is within, and lips (words) = what is expressed, are compared to an earthenware jar covered with glaze.

‡[26:25] **Seven abominations**: many evil intentions.

§[26:26] Hate may be concealed for a time, but it will eventually issue in a deed and become known in the public assembly. There is a play on words: the consonants of the word "hatred" (śn) are literally concealed in the word "pretense" (mśn).

¶[27:4] Anger generally subsides with time but jealousy coolly calculates and plots revenge.

**[27:5–6] Verses 5 and 6 are concerned with true friendship. "Better than" sayings often declare one thing superior to another in view of some value, e.g., 15:17, vegetables are better than meat in view of a milieu of love. In v. 5, a rebuke is better than an act of affection in view of discipline that imparts wisdom.

††[27:6] The present translation is conjectural. The meaning seems to be that a friend's rebuke can be life-giving and an enemy's kiss can be deadly (like the kiss of Judas in Mt 26:48).

o. [26:21] Prv 15:18; 29:22. p. [26:22] Prv 18:8. q. [26:25] Sir 12:10; 27:33. r. [26:27] Eccl 10:8; Sir 27:25–26. s. [27:3] Sir 22:14–15.

‡‡[27:8] The bird symbolizes vulnerability as it flees before danger as in Is 10:14; 16:2; and Ps 11:1. For the importance of place in human life, see Jb 20:8–9. People are defined by their place, but, tragically, war, poverty, or illness can force them from it.

§§[27:10] The adage is about the difference between friends and kin in a crisis. Two admonitions are grounded in one maxim (colon C). The same Hebrew word means both "one who is near" and "friend." The whole proverb urges the reader to cultivate old family friends and neighbors and not to rely exclusively on kin in times of trouble, for kin may not be there for us.

¶¶[27:11] A father's command to a son to be wise, another way of saying that sons or daughters bring joy or shame to their parents.

***[27:13] See note on 20:16.

†††[27:14] One interpretation takes the proverb as humorous and the other takes it as serious: (1) an overly loud and ill-timed greeting (lit., "blessing") invites the response of a curse rather than a "blessing" (greeting); (2) the loud voice suggests hypocrisy in the greeting.

‡‡‡[27:17] Iron sharpens the "face" (*panim* = surface, edge) of iron, and a human being sharpens the "face" (*panim* = face, words) of another. Human beings learn from each other and grow in wisdom by conversing.

§§§[27:20] Sheol, the underworld abode of the dead, is personified as a force that is never satisfied and always desires

t. [27:12] Prv 22:3. u. [27:13] Prv 20:16. v. [27:15] Prv 21:9; 25:24. w. [27:20] Prv 30:16; Eccl 4:8.

21 The crucible for silver, the furnace for
        gold,
    so you must assay the praise you
        receive.
22 Though you pound fools with a pestle,
    their folly never leaves them.
23 *Take good care of your flocks,
    give careful attention to your herds;
24 For wealth does not last forever,
    nor even a crown from age to age.
25 When the grass comes up and the new
        growth appears,
    and the mountain greens are
        gathered in,
26 The lambs will provide you with clothing,
    and the goats, the price of a field,
27 And there will be ample goat's milk for
        your food,
    food for your house, sustenance for
        your maidens.

CHAPTER 28

1 The wicked flee though none pursue;
    but the just, like a lion, are
        confident.
2 If a land is rebellious, its princes will be
        many;
    but with an intelligent and wise
        ruler there is stability.†
3 One who is poor and extorts from the
        lowly
    is a devastating rain that leaves no
        food.‡
4 Those who abandon instruction§ praise
        the wicked,
    but those who keep instruction
        oppose them.
5 The evil understand nothing of justice,¶
    but those who seek the LORD
        understand everything.
6 Better to be poor and walk in integrity
    than rich and crooked in one's ways.ˣ

7 Whoever heeds instruction is a wise son,
    but whoever joins with wastrels
        disgraces his father.
8 Whoever amasses wealth by interest and
        overcharge**
    gathers it for the one who is kind to
        the poor.
9 Those who turn their ears from hearing
        instruction,ʸ
    even their prayer is an abomination.
10 Those who mislead the upright into an
        evil way
    will themselves fall into their own pit,
    but the blameless will attain
        prosperity.
11 The rich are wise in their own eyes,
    but the poor who are intelligent see
        through them.
12 When the just triumph, there is great
        glory;
    but when the wicked prevail, people
        hide.††
13 Those who conceal their sins do not
        prosper,
    but those who confess and forsake
        them obtain mercy.‡‡
14 Happy those who always fear;§§
    but those who harden their hearts
        fall into evil.
15 A roaring lion or a ravenous bear
    is a wicked ruler over a poor people.
16 The less prudent the rulers, the more
        oppressive their deeds.
    Those who hate ill-gotten gain
        prolong their days.
17 Though a person burdened with blood
        guilt is in flight even to the
        grave,
    let no one offer support.
18 Whoever walks blamelessly is safe,
    but one whose ways are crooked
        falls into a pit.
19 Those who cultivate their land will have
        plenty of food,
    but those who engage in idle pursuits
        will have plenty of want.ᶻ

---

more. Cf. Is 5:14 and Hos 13:14. The saying is applicable to modern consumerism.

*[27:23–27] A little treatise on farming in the form of admonitions. It proposes the advantages of field and flock over other forms of wealth. Herds are the most productive wealth, for their value does not diminish; they are a source of money, clothing, and food. The thought is conservative and traditional but the development is vivid and concrete.

†[28:2] The first line expresses the paradox that rebellion, far from doing away with rulers, actually multiplies them. The second line is corrupt.

‡[28:3] The reference may be to tax farmers who collected taxes and took a commission. The collectors' lack of wealth was the cause of their oppression of poor farmers. They are like a rain too violent to allow crops to grow.

§[28:4] **Instruction**: *torah*; the word is used both for the teaching of the wise and the law of Moses.

¶[28:5] **Understanding nothing of justice** plays on the twofold sense of justice as righteousness and as punishment that comes on the wicked. On the other hand, **those who seek the LORD understand everything**, i.e., that the Lord punishes the wicked and rewards the righteous (themselves).

**[28:8] Interest and overcharge were strictly forbidden in the old law among Israelites because it was presumed that the borrower was in distress; cf. Ex 22:25; Lv 25:35–37; Dt 23:20; Ps 15:5; Ez 18:8. Divine providence will take the offender's wealth; cf. Eccl 2:26.

††[28:12] People react in opposite ways to the triumph of good and evil. To the triumph of good, they react by public display, public celebration, and to the triumph of evil, by hiding.

‡‡[28:13] Concealing the faults of another is a good thing in Proverbs (17:9), but concealing one's own sins is not. Ps 32:1–5 expresses the anguish caused by concealing one's sins rather than bringing them to light so they can be healed by God.

§§[28:14] **Fear** is a different verb than in the phrase "to fear (or revere) the Lord." In its only other biblical occurrence (Is 51:13), the verb means to dread an oppressor. The saying states a paradox: those who fear in the sense of being cautious are declared happy, whereas those who are fearless will fall into traps they did not "fear." In short, there is good fear and bad fear.

---

x. [28:6] Prv 19:1.

y. [28:9] Prv 15:8; 21:27.   z. [28:19] Prv 12:11.

²⁰ The trustworthy will be richly blessed;
　　but whoever hastens to be rich will
　　not go unpunished.^{*a*}
²¹ To show partiality is never good:^{*b*}
　　for even a morsel of bread one may
　　do wrong.[*]
²² Misers hurry toward wealth,
　　not knowing that want is coming
　　toward them.[†]
²³ Whoever rebukes another wins more
　　favor
　　than one who flatters with the
　　tongue.
²⁴ Whoever defrauds father or mother and
　　says, "It is no sin,"^{*c*}
　　is a partner to a brigand.
²⁵ The greedy person stirs up strife,
　　but the one who trusts in the Lord
　　will prosper.
²⁶ Those who trust in themselves are fools,
　　but those who walk in wisdom are
　　safe.
²⁷ Those who give to the poor have no lack,^{*d*}
　　but those who avert their eyes, many
　　curses.
²⁸ When the wicked prevail, people
　　hide;
　　but at their fall the just abound.^{*e*}

CHAPTER 29

¹ Those stiff-necked in the face of reproof
　　in an instant will be shattered
　　beyond cure.[‡]
² When the just flourish, the people
　　rejoice;
　　but when the wicked rule, the
　　people groan.^{§f}
³ Whoever loves wisdom gives joy to his
　　father,
　　but whoever consorts with harlots
　　squanders his wealth.
⁴ By justice a king builds up the land;
　　but one who raises taxes tears it
　　down.[¶]

⁵ Those who speak flattery to their neighbor
　　cast a net at their feet.^{**}
⁶ The sin of the wicked is a trap,
　　but the just run along joyfully.^{*g*}
⁷ The just care for the cause of the poor;
　　the wicked do not understand such
　　care.^{††}
⁸ Scoffers enflame the city,
　　but the wise calm the fury.^{*h*}
⁹ If a wise person disputes with a fool,
　　there is railing and ridicule but no
　　resolution.
¹⁰ The bloodthirsty hate the blameless,
　　but the upright seek his life.^{‡‡}
¹¹ Fools give vent to all their anger;
　　but the wise, biding their time,
　　control it.^{*i*}
¹² If rulers listen to lying words,
　　their servants all become
　　wicked.
¹³ The poor and the oppressor meet:^{*j*}
　　the Lord gives light to the eyes of
　　both.
¹⁴ If a king is honestly for the rights of the
　　poor,
　　his throne stands firm forever.^{*k*}
¹⁵ The rod of correction gives wisdom,
　　but uncontrolled youths disgrace
　　their mothers.^{*l*}
¹⁶ When the wicked increase, crime
　　increases;
　　but the just will behold their
　　downfall.^{§§}
¹⁷ Discipline your children, and they will
　　bring you comfort,
　　and give delight to your soul.
¹⁸ Without a vision the people lose
　　restraint;
　　but happy is the one who follows
　　instruction.^{¶¶}
¹⁹ Not by words alone can servants be
　　trained;^{*m*}

---

*[28:21] Cf. 24:23. Verse 21b warns that even in a light matter one must remain impartial.

†[28:22] "Bad of eye" is the Hebrew idiom for miserly. Misers fail to see that poverty is hurrying toward them because of their wrong attitude toward wealth. Because misers are "bad of eye," they do not see the danger.

‡[29:1] The idiom "to stiffen one's neck" occurs in a context of not heeding a message in Dt 10:16 and 2 Kgs 17:14. To stiffen one's neck in this sense risks having it broken, as in 1 Sm 4:18.

§[29:2] Popular response to a just or unjust ruler is expressed in sound—shouts of joy or groans of anguish. "Rejoice" can mean to express one's joy, i.e., joyous shouts.

¶[29:4] In Hebrew as in English high and low are metaphors for prosperity and depression. A king who is just "causes the land to stand up," i.e., to be prosperous, and one who makes taxes high brings a country low.

**[29:5] When one addresses deceptive words to someone's face, one equivalently throws a net at their feet to snare them.

††[29:7] As in 12:10 (on care for animals), the righteous care for those who are without a voice and often treated like animals. Colon B has a double meaning: the wicked have no such knowledge (care for the poor) and they have no knowledge (wisdom), for they are fools.

‡‡[29:10] An enigmatic saying in that "seek one's life" is a common idiom for killing. The saying probably plays on the idiom, interpreting "to seek the life of another" not as killing but as caring for another (as in 11:30).

§§[29:16] When the wicked grow numerous they sow the seeds of their own destruction, for there is a corresponding increase in offenses calling down divine retribution.

¶¶[29:18] This much-cited proverb has been interpreted in several different ways. "Vision" and "instruction" mean authoritative guidance for the community. People are demoralized without credible leadership, but any individual heeding traditional instruction can still find happiness. As in 15:15 wisdom enables an individual to surmount days of trouble.

---

a. [28:20] Prv 13:11.　b. [28:21] Prv 24:23.　c. [28:24] Mk 7:11–13. d. [28:27] Prv 19:17; Sir 4:3–8.　e. [28:28] Prv 28:12.　f. [29:2] Prv 11:10; 28:12, 28.

g. [29:6] Prv 12:13.　h. [29:8] Prv 11:11.　i. [29:11] Prv 12:16; 25:28; Sir 21:26.　j. [29:13] Prv 22:2.　k. [29:14] Prv 16:12; 20:28; 25:5. l. [29:15] Prv 13:24; 22:15; 23:13–14; Sir 22:6; 30:1.　m. [29:19] Sir 33:25–30.

for they understand but do not
respond.*

20 Do you see someone hasty in speech?[n]
There is more hope for a fool!

21 If servants are pampered from
childhood
they will turn out to be stubborn.

22 The ill-tempered stir up strife,
and the hotheaded cause many sins.[o]

23 Haughtiness brings humiliation,
but the humble of spirit acquire
honor.[†p]

24 Partners of a thief hate themselves;[‡]
they hear the imprecation but do
not testify.

25 Fear of others becomes a snare,
but the one who trusts in the LORD
is safe.

26 Many curry favor with a ruler,
but it is from the LORD that one
receives justice.

27 An abomination to the just, the evildoer;
an abomination to the wicked, one
whose way is straight.

VII. SAYINGS OF AGUR AND OTHERS

CHAPTER 30

1§The words of Agur, son of Jakeh the Massaite:

The pronouncement of mortal man: "I am
weary, O God;
I am weary, O God, and I am
exhausted.

2 I am more brute than human being,
without even human intelligence;

3 ‖Neither have I learned wisdom,

nor have I the knowledge of the
Holy One.

4 Who has gone up to heaven and come
down again—
who has cupped the wind in the
hollow of the hand?
Who has bound up the waters in a cloak—
who has established all the ends of
the earth?
What is that person's name, or the name
of his son?"**

5 ††Every word of God is tested;[q]
he is a shield to those who take
refuge in him.

6 Add nothing to his words,[r]
lest he reprimand you, and you be
proved a liar.

7 ‡‡Two things I ask of you,
do not deny them to me before I die:

8 Put falsehood and lying far from me,
give me neither poverty nor riches;
provide me only with the food I need;

9 Lest, being full, I deny you,
saying, "Who is the LORD?"
Or, being in want, I steal,
and profane the name of my God.

10 Do not criticize servants to their master,
lest they curse you, and you have to
pay the penalty.

11 §§There are some who curse their fathers,
and do not bless their mothers.[s]

12 There are some pure in their own eyes,
yet not cleansed of their filth.

13 There are some—how haughty their eyes!
how overbearing their glance!

14 There are some—their teeth are swords,
their teeth are knives,
Devouring the needy from the earth,
and the poor from the human race.

15 ‖‖The leech has two daughters:

---

*[29:19] The give and take of reproving is not possible for servants or slaves. Ancient custom dictated silent acquiescence for them. There is no open and free dialogue, which is part of ancient discipline.

†[29:23] One's prideful height brings one down and one's lowly state brings glory.

‡[29:24] Hate themselves: because they not only incur guilt as accomplices but, by their silence, bring down on themselves the curse invoked on the unknown guilty partner. Such a case is envisioned in Lv 5:1. After a theft, a public proclamation was made, enforced by a curse. No one in a town or city could avoid hearing it. The curse hung over the accomplice. By doing nothing, neither directly stealing nor confessing, accomplices put themselves in serious danger.

§[30:1–6] Scholars are divided on the original literary unit. Is it vv. 1–3, 1–4, 1–5, or 1–6? The unit is probably vv. 1–6, for a single contrast dominates: human fragility (and ignorance) and divine power (and knowledge). A similar contrast is found in Jb 28; Ps 73; Is 49:1–4. The language of self-abasement is hyperbolic; cf. 2 Sm 9:8; Ps 73:21–22; Jb 25:4–6. Agur: an unknown person. Massaite: from Massa in northern Arabia, elsewhere referred to as an encampment of the Ishmaelites (Gn 25:14). But Heb. massa may not be intended as a place name; it might signify "an oracle," "a prophecy," as in Is 15:1; 17:1; etc.

‖[30:3–4] Agur denies he has secret heavenly knowledge. The purpose of the denial is to underline that God directly gives wisdom to those whose conduct pleases him.

n. [29:20] Sir 9:18; Prv 26:12.   o. [29:22] Prv 15:18; 22:24.
p. [29:23] Prv 11:2; 16:18; 18:12.

**[30:4] The Hebrew text has the phrase "do you know?" at the end of v. 4, which is supported by the versions. The phrase, however, does not appear in the important Greek manuscripts Vaticanus and Sinaiticus and spoils the sense, for Agur, not God, is the questioner. The phrase seems to be an addition to the Hebrew text, borrowed from Job 38:5, where it also follows a cosmic question.

††[30:5–6] Verse 5, like the confession of the king in Ps 18:31 (and its parallel, 2 Sm 22:31), expresses total confidence in the one who rescues from death. Agur has refused a word from any other except God and makes an act of trust in God.

‡‡[30:7–9] A prayer against lying words and for sufficiency of goods, lest reaction to riches or destitution lead to offenses against God.

§§[30:11–14] Perverted people are here classified as unfilial (v. 11), self-righteous (v. 12), proud (v. 13) and rapacious (v. 14).

‖‖[30:15–16] Here begins a series of numerical sayings; the pattern is n, n + 1. The slight variation in number (two and three, three and four) is an example of parallelism applied to numbers. The poetic technique is attested even outside the Bible. Two daughters: "Give," and "Give": the text is obscure; as the leech (a bloodsucking worm) is insatiable in its desire for blood (v. 15), so are the nether world for victims, the barren womb for offspring, the earth for water,

q. [30:5] Ps 12:7; 18:31.   r. [30:6] Dt 4:2; 13:1.   s. [30:11] Prv 20:20.

"Give," and "Give."
Three things never get their fill,
    four never say, "Enough!"
16 Sheol, a barren womb,*
    land that never gets its fill of water,
    and fire, which never says, "Enough!"
17 The eye that mocks a father,
    or scorns the homage due a mother,
Will be plucked out by brook ravens;
    devoured by a brood of vultures.
18 *Three things are too wonderful for me,
    yes, four I cannot understand:
19 The way of an eagle in the sky,
    the way of a serpent upon a rock,
The way of a ship on the high seas,
    and the way of a man with a woman.
20 This is the way of an adulterous woman:
    she eats, wipes her mouth,
    and says, "I have done no wrong."†
21 ‡Under three things the earth trembles,
    yes, under four it cannot bear up:
22 Under a slave who becomes king,
    and a fool who is glutted with food;*
23 Under an unloved woman who is wed,
    and a maidservant who displaces
      her mistress.
24 §Four things are among the smallest on
      the earth,
    and yet are exceedingly wise:
25 Ants—a species not strong,
    yet they store up their food in the
      summer;
26 Badgers—a species not mighty,
    yet they make their home in the
      crags;
27 Locusts—they have no king,
    yet they march forth in formation;
28 Lizards—you can catch them with your
      hands,
    yet they find their way into kings'
      palaces.

29 *Three things are stately in their stride,
    yes, four are stately in their carriage:
30 The lion, mightiest of beasts,
    retreats before nothing;
31 The strutting cock, and the he-goat,
    and the king at the head of his
      people.
32 **If you have foolishly been proud
    or presumptuous—put your hand
      on your mouth;
33 For as the churning of milk produces
      curds,
    and the pressing of the nose
      produces blood,
    the churning of anger produces
      strife.

VIII. SAYINGS OF KING LEMUEL††

CHAPTER 31
1The words of Lemuel, king of Massa,‡‡ the instruction his mother taught him:

2   What are you doing, my son!§§
    what are you doing, son of my
      womb;
    what are you doing, son of my vows!
3   Do not give your vigor to women,
    or your strength¶¶ to those who ruin
      kings.
4   It is not for kings, Lemuel,
    not for kings to drink wine;
    strong drink is not for princes,
5   Lest in drinking they forget what has been
      decreed,
    and violate the rights of any who are
      in need.
6   Give strong drink to anyone who is
      perishing,
    and wine to the embittered;

---

and fire for fuel (v. 16). **Sheol:** here not so much the place of the dead as a force (death) that eventually draws all the living into it; cf. 27:20; Is 5:14; Hb 2:5. **Land . . . fire:** land (especially the dry land of Palestine) always absorbs more water; fire always requires more fuel.

*[30:18–19] The soaring flight of the eagle, the mysterious movement upon a rock of the serpent which has no feet, the path of the ship through the trackless deep, and the marvelous attraction between the sexes; there is a mysterious way common to them all.

†[30:20] This verse portrays the indifference of an adulterous woman who casually dismisses her guilt because it cannot be traced.

‡[30:21–23] Shaking heavens are part of general cosmic upheaval in Is 14:16; Jl 2:10; Am 8:8; Jb 9:6. Disturbances in nature mirror the disturbance of unworthy people attaining what they do not deserve. **Glutted with food:** someone unworthy ends up with the fulfillment that befits a wise person. **Unloved woman:** an older woman who, contrary to expectation, finds a husband.

§[30:24–28] The creatures may be small, but they are wise in knowing how to govern themselves—the definition of wisdom. **Badgers:** the rock badger is able to live on rocky heights that provide security from its enemies. **Locusts:** though vulnerable individually their huge swarms are impossible to deflect.

t. [30:16] Prv 27:20.   u. [30:22] Prv 19:10; Eccl 10:6–7.

¶[30:29–31] Four beings with an imperiousness visible in their walk. Only the lion is described in detail; the reader is expected to transpose its qualities to the others.

**[30:32–33] The same Hebrew verb, "to churn, shake," is applied to milk, the nose (sometimes a symbol of anger), and wrath. In each case something is eventually produced by the constant agitation. The wise make peace and avoid strife, for strife eventually harms those who provoke it.

††[31:1–9] Though mothers are sources of wisdom in Proverbs (1:8; 6:20), the mother of Lemuel is special in being queen mother, which was an important position in the palace. Queen mothers played an important role in ancient palace life because of their longevity, knowledge of palace politics, and loyalty to their sons; they were in a good position to offer him sound counsel. The language of the poem contains Aramaisms, a sign of its non-Israelite origin.

The first section, vv. 3–5, warns against abuse of sex and alcohol (wine, strong drink) lest the king *forget the poor.* The second section, vv. 6–9, urges the use of alcohol (strong drink, wine) so that the downtrodden *poor* can *forget* their poverty. The real subject of the poem is justice for the poor.

‡‡[31:1] **Massa:** see note on 30:1–6.

§§[31:2] **My son:** in the Septuagint, "my son, my firstborn."

¶¶[31:3] The Hebrew word here translated "strength" normally means "ways," but the context and a cognate language support "authority" or "strength" here.

⁷ When they drink, they will forget their
misery,
and think no more of their troubles.
⁸ Open your mouth in behalf of the mute,
and for the rights of the destitute;
⁹ Open your mouth, judge justly,
defend the needy and the poor!

IX. POEM ON THE WOMAN OF WORTH*

¹⁰ Who can find† a woman of worth?ᵛ
Far beyond jewels is her value.
¹¹ Her husband trusts her judgment;
he does not lack income.
¹² She brings him profit, not loss,‡
all the days of her life.
¹³ She seeks out wool and flax
and weaves with skillful hands.
¹⁴ Like a merchant fleet,§
she secures her provisions from afar.
¹⁵ She rises while it is still night,
and distributes food to her
household,
a portion to her maidservants.
¹⁶ She picks out a field and acquires it;
from her earnings she plants a
vineyard.
¹⁷ She girds herself with strength;

she exerts her arms with vigor.¶
¹⁸ She enjoys the profit from her dealings;
her lamp is never extinguished at
night.**
¹⁹ She puts her hands to the distaff,
and her fingers ply the spindle.††
²⁰ She reaches out her hands to the poor,
and extends her arms to the needy.
²¹ She is not concerned for her household
when it snows—
all her charges are doubly clothed.
²² She makes her own coverlets;
fine linen and purple are her clothing.
²³ Her husband is prominent at the city gates
as he sits with the elders of the land.‡‡
²⁴ She makes garments and sells them,
and stocks the merchants with belts.
²⁵ She is clothed with strength and dignity,
and laughs at the days to come.§§
²⁶ She opens her mouth in wisdom;
kindly instruction is on her tongue.
²⁷ She watches over¶¶ the affairs of her
household,
and does not eat the bread of idleness.
²⁸ Her children rise up and call her blessed;
her husband, too, praises her:
²⁹ "Many are the women of proven worth,
but you have excelled them all."
³⁰ Charm is deceptive and beauty fleeting;
the woman who fears the Lord is to
be praised.***
³¹ Acclaim her for the work of her hands,
and let her deeds praise her at the
city gates.

---

*[31:10–31] An acrostic poem of twenty-two lines; each line begins with a successive letter of the Hebrew alphabet. As with many other acrostic poems in the Bible, the unity of the poem is largely extrinsic, coming not from the narrative logic but from the familiar sequence of letters. The topic is the ideal woman described through her activity as a wife. Some have suggested that the traditional hymn extolling the great deeds of a warrior has been transposed to extol a heroic wife; the focus is on her exploits. She runs a household distinguished by abundant food and clothing for all within, by its trade (import of raw materials and export of finished products), and by the renown of its head, her husband, in the community. At v. 28, the voice is no longer that of the narrator but of her children and husband as they praise her. The purpose of the poem has been interpreted variously: an encomium to offset the sometimes negative portrayal of women in the book, or, more symbolically (and more likely), a portrait of a household ruled by Woman Wisdom and a disciple of Woman Wisdom, i.e., he now has a worthy wife and children, a great household, renown in the community.

†[31:10] **Who can find . . . ?**: in 20:6 and Eccl 8:1 the question implies that finding such a person is well-nigh impossible.

‡[31:12] **Profit, not loss**: a commercial metaphor.

§[31:14] **Like a merchant fleet**: she has her eye on the far horizon, like the ship of a merchant ready to bring supplies into her larder. It is the only simile ("like") in the poem.

v. [31:10] Prv 12:4; Sir 26:1–4, 13–18.

¶[31:17] The metaphor of clothing oneself is used to show the woman's readiness. One can gird on weapons of war and might and splendor (Ps 69:7; Is 52:9).

[31:18] **Her lamp is never extinguished at night: indicates abundance of productive work and its accompanying prosperity; cf. 20:20; Jb 18:6.

††[31:19] The wife weaves linen cloth from flax and wool from fleece, which she cultivated according to v. 13. **Distaff**: staff for holding the flax, tow, or wool, which in spinning was drawn out and twisted into yarn or thread by the spindle or round stick.

‡‡[31:23] The husband is mentioned for the first time since vv. 10–12 but as "her husband." He will not be mentioned again until v. 28, where he praises her.

§§[31:25] **Laughs at the days to come**: anticipates the future with joy, free of anxiety.

¶¶[31:27] **Watches over**: Hebrew ṣopiyyâ, perhaps a pun on the Greek sophia (= wisdom). **Bread of idleness**: she does not eat from the table of others but from her own labors.

***[31:30] The true charm of this woman is her religious spirit, for she fears the Lord; cf. note on 1:7.

MAPS

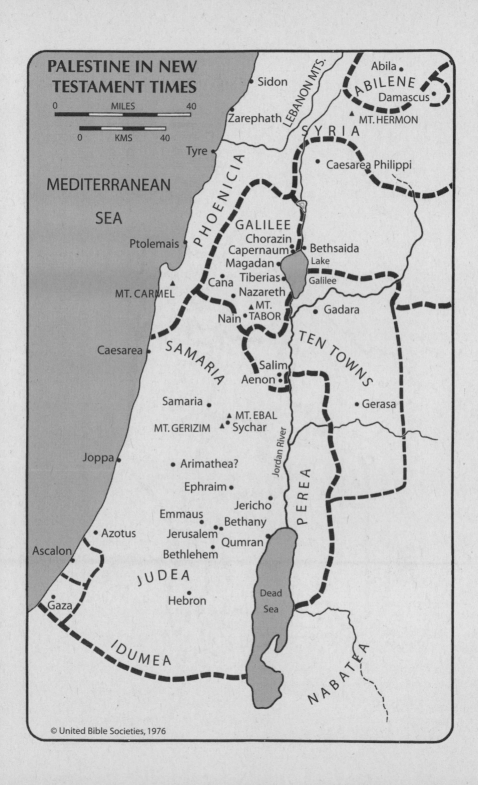

PALESTINE IN NEW TESTAMENT TIMES

MILES 0 — 40

KMS 0 — 40

MEDITERRANEAN

SEA

Sidon

Abila

ABILENE

Damascus

Zarephath

LEBANON MTS.

SYRIA

MT. HERMON

Tyre

PHOENICIA

Caesarea Philippi

Ptolemais

GALILEE

Chorazin

Capernaum • Bethsaida

Magadan

Lake

Cana

Tiberias

Galilee

MT. CARMEL

Nazareth

MT. TABOR

Gadara

Nain

Caesarea

SAMARIA

TEN TOWNS

Salim

Aenon

Samaria

MT. EBAL

Gerasa

MT. GERIZIM

Sychar

Jordan River

Joppa

Arimathea?

Ephraim

PEREA

Jericho

Emmaus

Bethany

Azotus

Jerusalem

Qumran

Ascalon

Bethlehem

Gaza

JUDEA

Hebron

Dead Sea

IDUMEA

NABATEA

© United Bible Societies, 1976

JERUSALEM IN NEW TESTAMENT TIMES

| 0 | YARDS | 400 |
| 0 | METERS | 400 |

Walls in the time of Jesus
Later walls built by Agrippa I
Present-day wall

Road to Caesarea

Early wall of unknown origin and date

Road to Joppa

Road to Jericho

Pool of Bethzatha

Antonia Fortress (Praetorium?)

Golgotha

Portico

Sheep Gate

Solomon's Porch

Gethsemane

TEMPLE

Bridge

Pool

To Mount of Olives

Tombs

Hasmonean Palace

Stairs

Street

Royal Portico

Herod's Palace

Hippodrome

Road to Bethany

Theater?

Herodian Street

Gihon Spring

Tunnel

Pool

Aqueoluct

?

Pool of Siloam

K i d r o n   V a l l e y

H i n n o m   V a l l e y

Enrogel Spring

Road to Bethlehem

Road to the Dead Sea

© United Bible Societies, 1976

PAUL'S 1st AND
2nd JOURNEYS

----- First Journey
——— Second Journey

© United Bible Societies, 1978

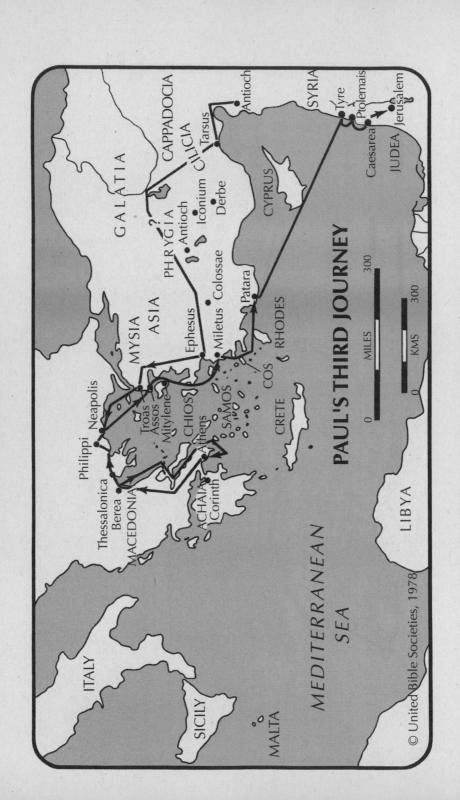

PAUL'S THIRD JOURNEY

ITALY

SICILY

MALTA

MEDITERRANEAN SEA

LIBYA

CRETE

MACEDONIA

Thessalonica
Berea
Philippi
Neapolis

ACHAIA
Corinth
Athens

SAMOS
CHIOS
Mitylene
Assos
Troas

MYSIA
ASIA

Ephesus

Miletus   Colossae

Patara

COS

RHODES

GALATIA

PHRYGIA

Antioch
Iconium
Derbe

CAPPADOCIA

CILICIA
Tarsus

Antioch

SYRIA

CYPRUS

Tyre
Ptolemais
Caesarea
Jerusalem

JUDEA

MILES
0   300

KMS
0   300

© United Bible Societies, 1978

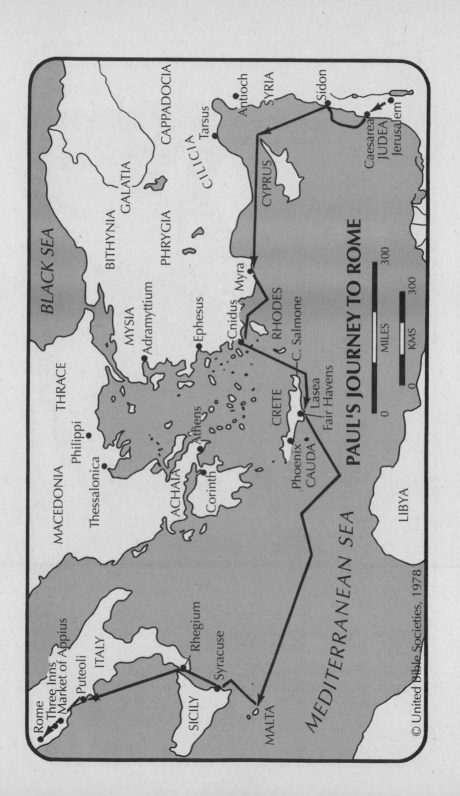

PAUL'S JOURNEY TO ROME

© United Bible Societies, 1978

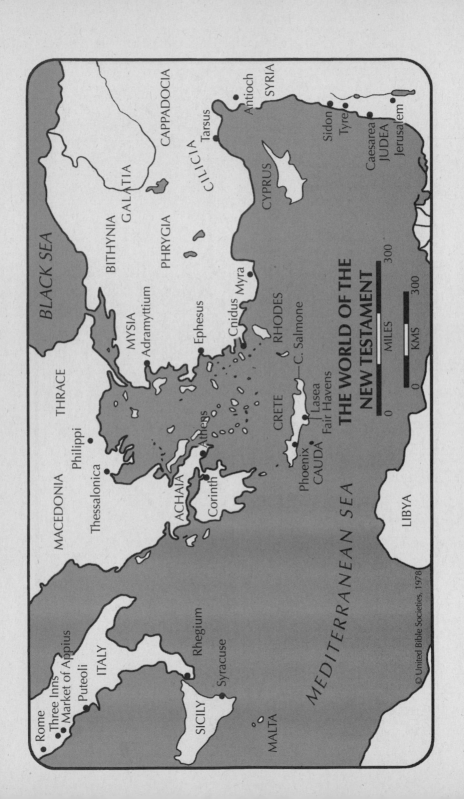

THE WORLD OF THE
NEW TESTAMENT

© United Bible Societies, 1978